Psychology suggests pathways that invite us to discover. These pathways offer some clear guideposts, many intriguing choices, and even a sense of mystery. A few pathways are relatively orderly and well disciplined; others are rich with sensory experience. Some pathways may look well traveled and familiar, but others offer doors that open into areas never visited before. Please join me in exploring the diverse pathways that characterize psychology.

Margaret W. Matlin

PSYCHOLOGY

SECOND EDITION

44.75

MARGARET W. MATLIN

SUNY Geneseo

HARCOURT BRACE COLLEGE PUBLISHERS

Fort Worth   Philadelphia   San Diego   New York   Orlando   Austin   San Antonio
Toronto   Montreal   London   Sydney   Tokyo

Publisher   Ted Buchholz
Acquisitions Editor   Eve Howard
Developmental Editor   Karl Yambert
Senior Project Editor   Margaret Allyson
Senior Production Manager   Kathleen Ferguson
Art Director   Garry Harman
Picture Development Editor   Greg Meadors
Literary Permissions Editor   Julia C. Stewart

ISBN: 0-15-501028-X

Library of Congress Catalog Card Number: 93-80816

Address for Editorial Correspondence:
Harcourt Brace College Publishers
301 Commerce Street, Suite 3700
Fort Worth, Texas 76102

Address for Orders:
Harcourt Brace & Company
6277 Sea Harbor Drive
Orlando, Florida 32887
1-800-782-4479 or 1-800-433-0001 (in Florida)

Cover Photograph by Peter Paige.
Other photo credits and copyright acknowledgments begin on page 725 and
constitute a continuation of this page.

Printed in the United States of America

4 5 6 7 8 9 0 1 2 3   032   1 2 3 4 5 6 7 8 9 0

To Beth and Sally Matlin

and all college students who care about people
and want to learn more about them.

Margaret W. Matlin received her BA in psychology from Stanford University and her MA and PhD in experimental psychology from the University of Michigan. She holds the title of Distinguished Teaching Professor at State University of New York at Geneseo, where she has taught courses since 1971 in introductory psychology, experimental psychology, statistics, sensation and perception, cognitive psychology, human memory, human development, conflict resolution, issues in feminism, and psychology of women. In 1977, she received the State University of New York Chancellor's Award for Excellence in Teaching, and in 1985 she was awarded the American Psychological Association Teaching of Psychology Award in the 4-year college and university division. Her previous books include *The Pollyanna Principle: Selectivity in Language, Memory and Thought; Human Experimental Psychology; Sensation and Perception* (fourth edition in preparation); *Cognition* (currently in its third edition), and *Psychology of Women* (currently in its second edition). Her husband Arnie is a pediatrician in Geneseo, New York. Her daughter Beth teaches elementary school in the Boston public schools. Her daughter Sally is a student at Stanford University, where she is majoring in anthropology with a focus on Latin America.

PREFACE

Psychology is a supremely fascinating discipline, spanning topics as diverse as a single cortical neuron and international conflict resolution. Its research methods range from highly controlled laboratory experiments to lengthy, unstructured interviews. Some psychological phenomena are well understood, yet many remain mysterious or paradoxical. (For example, why do some people risk their lives for the welfare of complete strangers, while others murder their own family members?) Even our theoretical approaches emphasize diversity in how psychologists view human beings.

The challenge for an author of an introductory psychology textbook is to synthesize this variety. The author must also present the material in a clear, interesting fashion that is guided by the principles of human memory. In addition, the author must encourage students to appreciate scientific research methods. Finally, the author must convey the diversity of human experience in the 1990s.

GOALS

In preparing to write both the first and second edition of this textbook, I was guided by several important goals. In teaching introductory psychology to several thousand students, I had used five different textbooks prior to writing my own. Each book had its strengths, but no book fulfilled all the essential requirements for an ideal textbook for the 1990s. Accordingly, four major objectives helped focus both the original and the revised editions of *Psychology*.

1. *To synthesize the broad range of knowledge about psychology.* I have written four other textbooks: *Human Experimental Psychology, Sensation and Perception, Cognition,* and *Psychology of Women.* This background in such disparate areas provides an unusually broad perspective about the discipline of psychology. This perspective enables me to point out relationships between topics that might initially seem unrelated. Students can benefit from a textbook that clarifies how certain phenomena covered within a chapter are interrelated.

   In addition, *Psychology* emphasizes consistent patterns in psychological processes. For example, in the social psychology of stereotypes, people are guided by heuristics similar to those used in visual perception and in cognitive tasks. The text also synthesizes both classic and extremely current resources. Finally, three important themes are woven through the 19 chapters of the book, providing even further cohesiveness.

2. *To present complex topics in an interesting, clear, and well-organized fashion.* Research in human memory demonstrates that material is more memorable when it is high in imagery, so the book includes numerous examples supplied by my students and from my own experience. (Students responded especially enthusiastically to the emphasis on examples.) Both professors and students have praised the clarity of my textbooks, and I have made every effort to maintain that standard.

   In addition, research in human memory emphasizes the importance of organization. Accordingly, every chapter is organized into two to five sections, each followed by a section summary to encourage integration before beginning the next section. Within each section, I often review what we have discussed and preview what we will cover next. The textbook also features numerous pedagogical aids (see pages 16 and 17). Some authors assume that student-oriented features are important only for lower-level students. I strongly argue that *all* students profit when these features are thoughtfully conceived. The clear majority of students in my introductory psychology classes at SUNY Geneseo ranked in the top 10% of their high-school classes. Nevertheless, they have told me that they appreciate such features as section summaries, mnemonic tips, and pronunciation guides.

Finally, research on the self-reference effect in memory has demonstrated that people retain material better if they relate it to their own experience. An important objective in writing *Psychology* was to encourage students to think about their own psychological processes—from saccadic eye movements to the fundamental attribution error. Typically, they have taken these processes for granted prior to a course in psychology. In many cases, I include a demonstration to make the phenomenon more memorable; other times, I urge students to recall relevant experiences.

3. *To emphasize research methodology.* The excitement of psychological research lured me away from a biology major when I was a college freshman, and I later received my PhD in experimental psychology. Furthermore, I wrote my first textbook in experimental psychology. A separate chapter on research methods is especially important in the 1990s. Chapter 2 discusses methodological issues, which are also emphasized throughout the book. The specific facts of psychology may be substantially different 20 years from now. However, students who have developed the ability to analyze a study critically will be able to evaluate new research and to question studies that were not appropriately conducted. Furthermore, this textbook should encourage students to apply the principles of research methods to their own experiences. Students need to learn that critical thinking skills need not be confined to formal research.

4. *To convey the variety and diversity of human experience.* My expertise in the psychology of women has sensitized me to the invisibility of many groups of people in current textbooks. In contrast, the biological drawings in this textbook do not depict only white male skulls, issues of gender are integrated throughout, elderly people are described in substantial detail, and the experiences of people of color are frequently addressed. In the 1990s, a psychology textbook especially benefits from a multicultural approach that admires and respects diversity.

FEATURES

Consistent with these goals, I have developed some important features that both students and instructors have appreciated.

1. Three important themes are emphasized throughout the book:
   - Humans are extremely competent; their performance is generally rapid and accurate, and most errors can be traced to strategies that are typically adaptive.
   - Humans differ widely from one another; as a consequence, people often respond differently to the same stimulus situation.
   - Psychological processes are complex; most psychological phenomena are caused by multiple factors.

2. Section summaries appear at frequent intervals throughout the chapters, so that students can integrate material before they proceed to a new topic.

3. Demonstrations or informal experiments encourage students to illustrate a well-known study or important principle, making the material more memorable.

4. New terms are shown in boldface type, with a definition included in the same sentence. These terms also appear at the end of each chapter so that students can test themselves, and they also are listed with definitions in the glossary at the end of the book.

5. Chapters 2 through 19 each include an in-depth section that examines recent research on a selected topic. This feature is an important mechanism for achieving depth as well as breadth in an introductory psychology textbook. In addition, these sections provide an opportunity to emphasize research methodology.

6. A set of review questions encourages students to consolidate their knowledge, apply the information to real-life situations, and test the adequacy of their learning.

7. A list of recommended readings, appropriate for introductory psychology students, provides resources for students who want additional information on topics related to the chapter material.

WHAT'S NEW IN THE SECOND EDITION?

The first edition of *Psychology* received strong praise for its writing style, pedagogical features, and chapter organization. I retained these strengths in the second edition.

Readers will notice that the second edition is most dramatically different in the addition of new research. Our discipline has made tremendous advances in just a few years! In preparing this edition, I integrated 1476 new references, or 52% of the total. Furthermore, 1056 of the 2820 references in the bibliography are from the 1990s—37% of the total. I made a special effort to integrate the recent research on biological bases of behavior; new developments in cognitive approaches are also emphasized. Although every section of this textbook has been rewritten and updated, some of the more noteworthy changes are the following:

- Chapter 1 has added a sixth perspective—the sociocultural approach—to the discussion of contemporary approaches in psychology.

- Chapter 2 includes many new examples, along with a reorganized section on the correlation method.

- Chapter 3 was restructured, and a new introduction focuses students' attention on several general principles of the nervous system. A new in-depth section has been added, describing how neuroscience research techniques have been used to shed light on object recognition.

- Chapter 4 features a new in-depth section on illusory contours.

- Chapter 5 now includes discussion of attention, as well as a new in-depth section on the subtle effects of sleep deprivation.

- Chapter 6 contains new sections on the biological components of classical and instrumental conditioning.

- Chapter 7 has added new coverage on the connectionist (PDP) approach to memory and on the biological basis of long-term memory, as well as a new in-depth section on explicit and implicit measures of retrieval.

- Chapter 8 has been reorganized, adding new material on the analogy approach to problem solving, mindlessness, and the availability heuristic.

- Chapter 9 now contains new material on metacomprehension and the chimp-language controversy, as well as a new in-depth section on bilingualism.

- Chapter 10 includes the new research on children's cognitive development, as well as expanded coverage of relationships with siblings and friends.

- Chapter 11 has added new material on married couples, ethnicity, and successful aging.

- Chapter 12 includes new material on the biological factors related to hunger, on achievement motivation, and on subjective well-being.

- Chapter 13 has added new information on the psychodynamic approach, on the biological basis of personality, and on the social cognitive approach.

- Chapter 14 has been reorganized and now contains an in-depth section on gender comparisons in intelligence and new coverage of ethnic-group comparisons.
- Chapter 15 includes new information on cognitive issues in phobias and schizophrenia; coverage of personality disorders has also been expanded.
- Chapter 16 now discusses interpersonal psychotherapy and stress inoculation training, as well as updated material on therapy and ethnic groups.
- Chapter 17 contains new coverage of environmental psychology, the cognitive basis of stereotypes, and reducing biases.
- Chapter 18 contains a new in-depth section on explanations for altruism, as well as material on social loafing and reactive devaluation.
- Chapter 19 has updated the coverage on social support and health, on psychological reactions to AIDS, and on smoking-prevention programs.

SUPPLEMENTARY MATERIALS

My editors and I agreed that ancillary material developed for many introductory psychology textbooks often appears to have been hastily written, with little or no attempt to coordinate the separate books. All three of the primary ancillary authors had worked with me on the first edition of this textbook, and we began planning the revisions of these ancillaries soon after the first edition had been published. The authors have exchanged material with one another so that, for example, the questions in the Study Guide could be similar in format, style, and difficulty to the questions in the Test Bank. This coordination also ensured that the same learning objectives could be emphasized in the Instructor's Manual and the Study Guide. The Chapter Summaries are also coordinated for the Instructor's Manual and the Study Guide. I thoroughly admire the talents of the three ancillary authors who worked on these projects!

Study Guide (by Drew C. Appleby and Margaret W. Matlin)

Drew Appleby is an award-winning professor at Marian College in Indiana and is well known for numerous activities focusing on the teaching of psychology. Dr. Appleby's sensitivity to students and his mastery of the subject matter are clear in all parts of the Study Guide. We decided to organize the exercises in the Study Guide so that the first task in each section is the easiest (matching). Students next attempt a related task (fill-in-the-blank), and then they try the task most similar to the one on typical in-class examinations (multiple choice). Each section ends with thought projects that encourage students to contemplate and answer more comprehensive questions. The Study Guide emphasizes an organization by sections so that students can read a section in the textbook and then immediately work on that same material in the Study Guide.

Test Bank (by Susan D. Lonborg and Margaret W. Matlin)

Susan Lonborg, the West Coast member of our writing team, teaches courses such as counseling psychology and human sexuality at Central Washington University. Dr. Lonborg had provided such exceptionally thoughtful critiques when she served as a reviewer on the first edition that we knew we wanted her to write one of the ancillaries. The new Test Bank includes approximately 200 items for each chapter, and it emphasizes conceptual questions and applied questions that require synthesis and application. It also includes factual questions that test the acquisition of basic information. In response to professors' requests, we have added several dozen new questions to each chapter, making a special effort to construct many new difficult questions.

Instructor's Manual with Video Instructor's Guide (by Lori R. Van Wallendael and Margaret W. Matlin)

Lori Van Wallendael is an enthusiastic and well-read faculty member at the University of North Carolina at Charlotte. Dr. Van Wallendael drew from her experience in teaching both classic and highly current topics in introductory psychology to produce an exceptional set of lecture ideas. She developed many wonderful classroom demonstrations (many new to this edition) that she found helpful in her own introductory psychology classes. Together, Dr. Van Wallendael and I previewed dozens of psychology films and videos, because we are convinced that instructors will find our evaluative summaries in the Instructor's Manual more helpful than the capsule summaries supplied by film distributors. In addition, Dr. Van Wallendael provided the Video Instructor's Guide (new to this edition) to integrate both the teaching modules of the *Discovering Psychology* video series and the images of the *Dynamic Concepts in Psychology* laserdisc with the textbook.

Other Teaching Aids

Video and Laserdisc Materials

- The *Dynamic Concepts in Psychology* laserdisc, developed by John Mitterer, covers every major concept of introductory psychology. Media include animated sequences, video footage, still images, and demonstrations of well-known experimental paradigms. Adhesive bar codes facilitate quick access to images during lectures. Level III software (Macintosh or DOS) permits preprogramming of classroom presentations.

- The *Infinite Voyage* laserdisc series incorporates on-location, interview, laboratory, and candid footage produced by WQED of Pittsburgh to provide compelling coverage of high-interest topics in psychology.

- The *Discovering Psychology* video series is an introductory psychology television course hosted by Philip Zimbardo. It includes 26 half-hour programs on 13 one-hour tapes.

- The *Discovering Psychology Teaching Modules* condense the telecourse into approximately four hours of viewing time. The Video Instructor's Guide provides descriptions and teaching suggestions for the 15 modules (84 total segments), which are available on videotape or laserdisc.

- *Harcourt Brace Quarterly: A Video News Magazine,* produced in conjunction with CBS Television, brings current psychological applications from today's headlines into your classroom. Segments are compiled from the CBS Nightly News, CBS This Morning, 48 Hours, and Street Stories with Ed Bradley to provide over an hour of contemporary video applications to the study of psychology. Instructor's Notes synopsize each segment, which typically run 2-5 minutes (and longer for 48 Hours and Street Stories segments).

- *The Brain* teaching modules compile key segments of the PBS television series, *The Brain,* into 30 video modules of about 6 minutes each.

- *The Mind* video modules, developed by Frank Vattano in cooperation with WNET of New York, offer selections from the PBS series *The Mind* to illustrate important concepts in introductory psychology.

Testing Materials

- *ExaMaster* computerized Test Banks for Matlin's *Psychology*, Second Edition, are available in DOS, Macintosh, and Windows formats. The nearly 4000 test items are classified by difficulty level (easy, moderate, difficult) and question type (factual, application, conceptual).

- *EasyTest* lets you create a test from a single screen. It will construct a test using the questions you have chosen from the database, or it will randomly select questions according to your specifications.

- *FullTest* allows you to select questions as you preview them on screen; edit existing questions; add your own questions; add or edit graphics (DOS version only); link related questions, instructions, and graphics; randomly select questions from a wide range of criteria; create your own criteria on two open keys; block specific questions from random selection; and print up to 99 different versions of the same test and answer sheet.

- *RequesTest* lets you order tests that conform to your criteria. Call 1-800-447-9457, and Harcourt Brace will compile the tests and either mail or fax them to you within 48 hours.

- *ExamRecord*, our gradebook program, is free with ExaMaster software. ExamRecord lets you record, curve, graph, and print your students' grades.

Software

- *Personal Discovery* by Eric Sandberg allows students to learn to apply psychological principles to everyday life through a series of self-description, self-exploration, and extended personal planning activities. DOS and Macintosh formats.

- *Supershrink* by Joseph Lowman introduces students to clinical interviewing techniques by allowing them to take the role of a HELPLINE crisis volunteer with clients Victor (Supershrink I) or Jennifer (Supershrink II). DOS format.

- *The Psychology Experimenter* performs actual experiments singly or in groups, and allows you to create and modify experiments of your own design. Data can be stored, displayed, and printed out. DOS format.

- *Brainstack* provides an interactive self-guided tour of the human cerebral cortex. Includes self-study quiz and on-line index. Macintosh format.

- *Psychlearn* by David Glanzer consists of five experiments in which the student participates as subject. DOS and Apple formats.

Overhead Transparencies

A number of overhead transparencies pertinent to introductory psychology, many of them specific to particular textbooks, are available. Contact your local Harcourt Brace representative for more information.

ACKNOWLEDGMENTS

One of the pleasures of writing a preface is the opportunity to praise and thank the dozens of people who have helped to create and develop a textbook. Harcourt Brace has published three of my textbooks, and I continue to be impressed with the many highly competent people associated with this company. My gratitude goes to Eve Howard, psychology editor, for her superb help in clarifying the purpose of this second edition and for providing feedback throughout the many months of writing; I admire her expertise and good judgment.

Once again, Margaret Allyson proved to be an ideal project editor! Her intelligence, organizational skills, and attention to detail were superbly helpful throughout the production of this textbook, and her sense of humor made even the most tedious tasks more pleasurable. Elizabeth Alvarez and J. R. Peacock were exceptional in their careful proofreading, editing, and reference checking. Julia Stewart was especially conscientious in tracking down permissions. Finally, Kathleen Ferguson deserves my sincere gratitude for her careful attention to important details and time constraints.

Garry Harman deserves special appreciation for his outstanding work on the textbook's design; he managed to create a clear and attractive layout that enhanced my pedagogical objectives. Brenda Chambers achieved an arrangement of text, photos, tables, and demonstrations that is both pedagogically sound and esthetically pleasing. Greg Meadors performed heroically as my photo researcher, tracking down photos of desserts in college cafeterias, Hungarian chess players, and hundreds of other challenging scenes. Once more, Linda Webster performed a superbly efficient and professional job on the glossary and the indexes. Karl Yambert was especially helpful in locating an unusually strong group of reviewers for this textbook. Finally, Craig Johnson and Leigh Tedford deserve my compliments for their hard work on the brochures and numerous other components of marketing.

Numerous psychologists deserve praise for their suggestions, comments on style and content, and lists of additional references. These reviewers and consultants helped me write a much more accurate and lucid textbook than I could have managed on my own.

I would like to thank the individuals who reviewed the first edition:

Lauren Alloy, *Temple University*

Donna Alexander-Redmayne, *Antelope Valley College*

Anne Anastasi, *Fordham University*

Joel Aronoff, *Michigan State University*

Frank Bagrash, *California State University at Fullerton*

Johnston Beach, *United States Military Academy*

Kayla Bernheim, *Livingston County Mental Health Center*

Galen Bodenhausen, *Michigan State University*

John Bonvillian, *University of Virginia*

Scott Borelli, *Boston University*

Robert Bornstein, *Miami University (Ohio)*

Charles Brewer, *Furman University*

William Calhoun, *University of Tennessee at Knoxville*

John Caruso, *Southeast Massachusetts University*

Patricia Chavez y Marquez, *Antelope Valley College*

Eva Clark, *Stanford University*

Francis Coletti, *United States Military Academy*

Kim Dolgin, *Ohio Wesleyan University*

Michael Domjan, *University of Texas at Austin*

Claire Etaugh, *Bradley University*

Leslie Fisher, *Cleveland State University*

Morton Friedman, *University of California at Los Angeles*

Laurel Furumoto, *Wellesley College*

Betty Gaines, *Midland College*

Richard Gibbons, *Iowa State University*

Jean Giebenhain, *College of St. Thomas*

Margaret Gittis, *Youngstown State University*

Robert Guttentag, *University of North Carolina at Greensboro*

Richard Griggs, *University of Florida*

Maury Haraway, *Northeast Louisiana University*

Lewis Harvey, *University of Colorado at Boulder*

Douglas Herrmann, *National Institute of Mental Health*

Winfred Hill, *Northwestern University*

Lyllian Hix, *Houston Community College System*

Margaret Intons-Peterson, *Indiana University at Bloomington*

Alice M. Isen, *Cornell University*

W. Jake Jacobs, *University of Arizona*

Valerie James-Aldridge, *University of Texas, Pan American*

James Jones, *University of Delaware*

Rick Kasschau, *University of Houston*

Daniel Kimble, *University of Oregon*

Alfred Kornfeld, *Eastern Connecticut State University*

John Kounias, *Tufts University*

Terry Knapp, *University of Nevada at Las Vegas*

James Knight, *Humboldt State University*

Michael Knight, *Central State University*

Robert Levy, *Indiana State University*

Susan Lonborg, *Central Washington University*

Kurt Mahoney, *Mesa Community College*

Barton Mann, *University of North Carolina at Chapel Hill*

Deborah McDonald, *New Mexico State University*

Elizabeth McDonel, *University of Alabama*

Linda Musun-Miller, *University of Central Arkansas*

Tibor Palfai, *Syracuse University*

Harold Pashler, *University of California at San Diego*

David Payne, *State University of New York at Binghamton*

James Pennebaker, *Southern Methodist University*

E. Jerry Phares, *Kansas State University*

Edward Rinalducci, *University of Central Florida*

Laurie Rotando, *Westchester County Community College*

Kenneth Rusiniak, *Eastern Michigan University*

James Ryan, *University of Wisconsin at La Crosse*

Edward Sadalla, *Arizona State University*

David Sanders, *Oregon State University*

Warren Street, *Central Washington University*

Ross Thompson, *University of Nebraska at Lincoln*

Lori Van Wallendael, *University of North Carolina at Charlotte*

Michael Vitiello, *University of Washington*

Mary Roth Walsh, *University of Lowell*

Wilse Webb, *University of Florida*

Susan Krauss Whitbourne, *University of Massachusetts at Amherst*

Thanks also to the careful and insightful reviewers for this second edition:

James Ackil *(Western Illinois University)*

Debora R. Baldwin *(University of Tennessee at Knoxville)*

Nathan Bernstein *(East Stroudsburg University)*

William Davidson *(Angelo State University)*

John M. Davis *(Southwest Texas State University)*

Wendy Domjan *(University of Texas at Austin)*

Robert Engbretson *(Southern Illinois University at Edwardsville)*

Stephen Franzoi (Marquette University)

Michael Gayle *(SUNY-New Paltz)*

Robert Gehring *(University of Southern Indiana)*

Kenneth Graham *(Muhlenberg College)*

Mary Louise Kean *(University of California at Irvine)*

Philipp J. Kraemer *(University of Kentucky at Lexington)*

Peter Leppmann *(University Guelph)*

Donald F. McCoy *(University of Kentucky at Lexington)*

David McDonald *(University of Missouri at Columbia)*

Deborah McDonald *(New Mexico State University)*

Carolyn Mangelsdorf *(University of Washington at Seattle)*

Sandra S. Moe *(Capilano College)*

Debra Ann Poole *(Central Michigan University)*

Margaret L. Potter *(Moorhead State University)*

Janet D. Proctor *(Purdue University)*

Lillian Range *(University of Southern Mississippi)*

Jayne Rose *(Augustana College)*

Julia Rux *(DeKalb Community College)*

Susan Schenk *(Texas A & M University)*

Philip Smith *(University of Prince Edward Island)*

Michael Sobocinski *(Valparaiso University)*

Donna J. Tyler Thompson *(Midland College)*

Frank J. Vattano *(Colorado State University at Fort Collins)*

Tova Vitiello *(Kirkwood Community College)*

Sharlene Walbaum *(Quinnipiac College)*

Linda J. Weldon *(Essex Community College)*

Paul J. Wellman *(Texas A & M University)*

My thanks also go to my superb student reviewers, who conscientiously read either the manuscript for the first edition or made suggestions for the second edition. I was truly impressed with their expertise, diligence, and honesty. My appreciation goes to Rachel Andrews, Amy Bolger, Jonathan Blumenthal, Sheryl Mileo,

Claudia Militello, Matthew Prichard, Heather Wallach, Joseph Wesley, and Martin Williams.

In addition, many colleagues, students, and friends supplied examples, ideas, information, and references. I thank Charles Brewer, Ganie DeHart, Karen Duffy, Lisa Elliot, Frederick Fidura, Hugh Foley, Tina Folmsbee, John Fox, Lori Gardinier, Becky Glass, Walter Harding, Amy Holm, Eve Howard, Patricia Keith-Spiegel, Maria Kountz, Mary Kroll, James McNally, Peter Muzzonigro, Barbara Nodine, Lynn Offerman, Paul Olczak, Robert Owens, Catherine Perna, Cathleen Quinn, George Rebok, Ramon Rocha, Lanna Ruddy, Donna Shapiro, M. Shelton Smith, John Sparrow, Maura Thompson, Leonore Tiefer, Gail Walker, Helen S. White, Edward Whitson, Rodney Williams, and Melvyn Yessenow. A special note of appreciation goes to Susan K. Whitbourne for her helpful comments in reading Chapters 15 and 16 with an eye toward DSM-IV revisions.

I would also like to thank many of my undergraduate students at SUNY Geneseo who located errors or unclear sections in the first edition of *Psychology*. Their careful suggestions were helpful in revising the textbook. Thanks are due to Rachel Andrews, Shannon Basher, Christopher Brown, Jennifer Clarke, Kevin Donsbach, Lisa Dunham, Jenny Eng, Katherine Eng, Margaret Gee, Jennifer Halleran, Helen Hanwit, Kimberley Kittle, Erika Mack, Kelli Meyer, Kathleen Quinn, Jeanette Rosenbaum, Amy Samartino, Patricia Seith, Gretchen Teal, Noël J. Thomas, Rosanne Vallone, Thomas A. P. van Geel, Joseph Wesley, and Lotus Yung.

However, no acknowledgment section would be complete without emphasizing contributions from my professors. They inspired me to pursue psychology and inspired me to view our field as an evolving discipline—in which every answer provokes a still greater number of questions. I would like to thank Leonard Horowitz—my undergraduate mentor, Gordon Bower, Albert Hastorf, Douglas Lawrence, Eleanor Maccoby, Walter Mischel, and Karl Pribram of Stanford University. Thanks, also, to Bob Zajonc—my dissertation advisor, John Atkinson, David Birch, Robyn Dawes, Edwin Martin, Arthur Melton, Richard Pew, Irving Pollack, W. P. Tanner, and Daniel Weintraub at the University of Michigan. Thanks also to Drew Appleby for all the useful suggestions he offered on both editions of the textbook. Mary Roth Walsh deserves my deep gratitude for providing references, suggestions, and interesting points of view on numerous issues throughout the textbook.

Many other people have helped in various phases of the preparation of this book. Mary Lou Perry, Shirley Thompson, and Constance Ellis provided countless services that allowed me to devote more time to writing. Several students—Christine Lauer, Rebecca Sitler, and Dawn DiAngelo—were exemplary in tracking down references, photocopying material, sending for reprints, and checking the accuracy of my bibliography. In addition, five members of the Milne Library staff at SUNY Geneseo provided superb expertise and assistance: Judith Bushnell, Paula Henry, Diane Johnson, Harriet Sleggs, and Paul MacLean. Ron Pretzer, Louise Wadsworth, and Drew Appleby all deserve high praise for their wonderful photos of students, children, and a variety of unlikely objects.

My last, most enthusiastic acknowledgment goes to the members of my family. Thanks to my daughters, Beth and Sally, for providing helpful examples, posing for photographs, helping to develop some of the demonstrations . . . and also for being wonderful human beings who inspire me to write for people like them. To my husband, Arnie, I give my deepest thanks for his technical expertise and suggestions, and also for helpfully locating dozens of articles in his medical journals. More importantly, I appreciate his love, his committed encouragement, and his spectacular sense of humor. My parents deserve the final note of appreciation: Thanks to Helen White for encouraging my enthusiasm for learning and my love of language, and to Donald White for encouraging my enjoyment of science and for providing a model of a professional who is truly excited about his work.

Margaret W. Matlin

CONTENTS IN BRIEF

T ABLE OF CONTENTS

CHAPTER 3   THE BIOLOGICAL BASIS OF BEHAVIOR   59

| CHAPTER 4 | SENSATION AND PERCEPTION 95 |

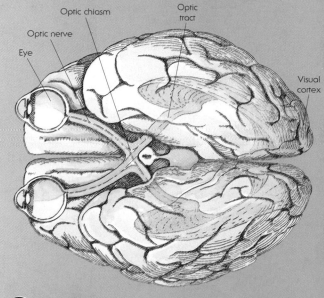

Optic chiasm
Optic tract
Optic nerve
Eye
Visual cortex

CHAPTER 8   THINKING   245

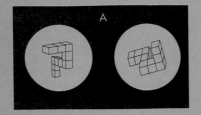

CHAPTER 9 | LANGUAGE AND CONVERSATION **271**

CHAPTER 12   MOTIVATION AND EMOTION   371

| CHAPTER 13 | PERSONALITY 407 |

CHAPTER 14 ASSESSING INTELLIGENCE AND PERSONALITY **445**

CHAPTER 19 HEALTH PSYCHOLOGY **625**

PSYCHOLOGY

C H A P T E R   1
INTRODUCING PSYCHOLOGY

One recent semester, I asked the students in my introductory psychology class about their impressions of psychology and psychologists. On the first day of class—even before the course syllabus was distributed—I asked them to imagine what a typical psychologist would do in a typical day. A representative student wrote, "The psychologist meets with people of all ages and talks with them about their lives, thoughts, problems, etc. Then the psychologist analyzes and provides feedback to the people to help them." Fully 80% of the students described a psychologist helping people with their personal problems.

It is true that many psychologists counsel people; this textbook will examine psychological disorders and the treatment of these disorders. However, the scope of psychology is much broader than many students anticipate. In fact, most of the book explores how "normal" people perceive, think, experience emotions, and interact socially. Typical questions we will consider include the following: Why do you forget someone's name just 14 seconds after you were introduced? Why does your heart beat faster when you just missed being hit by a car? Why do you blame your tardiness on the traffic, rather than on a basic tendency toward being late, yet you listen suspiciously when a friend offers the same explanation? This textbook emphasizes the broad scope of psychology, including topics that range from biological research on neurons to social-psychology studies on large crowds of people.

Psychology can be defined as the scientific study of behavior and mental processes. Let us examine the components of that definition. *Scientific study* means that psychologists use systematic, well-organized methods to learn about psychological processes. As we emphasize later in this chapter and in more detail in Chapter 2, psychologists do not gather their data by casual speculation. Instead, they use a variety of more careful methods that include experiments as well as objective observation. *Behavior* means physical actions that can be seen or heard, such as touching or speaking aloud. However, psychology also includes *mental processes,* which cannot be seen or heard—for instance, perceiving, dreaming, remembering, and making decisions.

Psychologists differ with respect to the goals they emphasize. Among these goals are the following:

1. *describing* behaviors and mental processes, based on careful, systematic observation;

2. *explaining* why these behaviors and mental processes occurred;

3. *predicting* future events on the basis of past events; and

4. *changing* behaviors and mental processes so that they are more appropriate.

In general, research psychologists focus on the first three goals. In contrast, **applied psychologists** have received training in these three areas, but they are more concerned with *changing* both actions and thoughts.

Let us clarify these different goals with examples of psychologists who study children's aggression. Some psychologists *describe* children's aggressive behavior in a classroom. Others *explain* why children are more aggressive after watching a violent movie. Still others might try to *predict* how aggressive each child will be in first grade, based on his or her aggressiveness as a kindergartener. Finally, applied psychologists would attempt to *change* the children's behavior, reducing their level of aggression. In summary, a single psychology topic can be explored from a wide diversity of perspectives.

This diversity of perspectives also characterizes the history of psychology. This chapter begins with an overview of the different theoretical approaches that psychologists have adopted in their scientific study of behavior and mental processes. After this survey of psychology's past, a section on psychology's present looks at the current theoretical approaches, as well as occupations in psychology. Next we consider three important themes that recur throughout this book and can help you appreciate some underlying consistencies in psychology. The final section includes suggestions about using this textbook effectively.

Do opposites attract? A person who favors the armchair approach might speculate about the answer. However, when psychologists use the empirical approach, they might conduct research to determine whether couples resemble each other in characteristics such as attractiveness, background, leisure activities, and personality.

PSYCHOLOGY'S PAST

Psychology is simultaneously very old and very new. Greek philosophers such as Plato and Aristotle speculated about human nature more than 2,000 years ago. In the seventeenth century, European philosophers such as John Locke and René Descartes debated whether we are born with certain abilities or whether we acquire them through experience. So, psychology is very old when we consider that people have contemplated psychological ideas for 20 centuries.

These early philosophers used an "armchair approach," reasoning and speculating about the nature of psychology—without scientific study. Suppose you were to sit in your own chair and ponder a psychological question, for example, whether you were born with the ability to hear the difference between two similar speech sounds. You *might* reach the correct answer, but the armchair approach often produces misleading answers. For instance, try Demonstration 1.1, which asks you to evaluate some popular sayings based on the armchair approach and casual observation.

In contrast to the armchair approach, psychologists in recent years have depended upon **empirical evidence,** the kind of scientific evidence obtained by careful observation or experimentation. Demonstration 1.1 shows that our intuitions are often contradicted by empirical evidence that is gathered by research psychologists.

The history of speculations about psychology is very old. However, if we consider the history of *empirical psychology,* then the discipline is very new, particularly in comparison with other sciences. For example, the Italian physicist Galileo (1564–1642) used the telescope to discover the changing phases of Venus and the moons of Jupiter more than three centuries ago (Haugeland, 1985). Interestingly, scientists developed effective methods to explore distant planets long before they began to investigate human behavior and thought.

DEMONSTRATION 1.1 Evaluating Popular Sayings

Below are 10 popular sayings. Each of these sayings has been examined by psychologists. Read each one and decide whether you think the psychological evidence supports or does not support the saying. Write *true* or *false* in front of the saying. Turn to the end of the chapter to find what current researchers have concluded.

_____ 1. Misery loves company.

_____ 2. Spare the rod and spoil the child.

_____ 3. The squeaky wheel gets the grease.

_____ 4. Actions speak louder than words.

_____ 5. Beauty is only skin deep.

_____ 6. Cry and you cry alone.

_____ 7. Marry in haste, repent at leisure.

_____ 8. Familiarity breeds contempt.

_____ 9. He who lives by the sword dies by the sword.

_____ 10. Opposites attract.

Any attempt to name a date for the beginning of empirical psychology would be somewhat arbitrary (Danziger, 1990). However, the birthdate is usually considered to be 1879, when the German psychologist Wilhelm Wundt founded his laboratory. Let us begin our history at this point.

Wilhelm Wundt

Wilhelm Wundt (pronounced "*Vill*-helm Voont," 1832–1920) is typically said to be the founder of empirical psychology. In 1879, Wundt created the first institute for research in experimental psychology at the University of Leipzig, Germany. For the first time in history, students in this new discipline could conduct psychological research. In the 1990s, we are accustomed to psychology as an academic subject; we need to remind ourselves that psychology courses were not available prior to Wundt's era (Schlesinger, 1985).

Wundt argued that psychology had been progressing slowly because it relied on casual armchair speculation (Blumenthal, 1975). Wundt preferred more formal, careful methodology. For example, some of his research involved **introspection,** that is, observing one's own conscious psychological reactions. Wundt insisted that introspection should be conducted in a rigorous fashion, following careful training in standardized techniques for introspection. Wundt's approach, developed more fully by his students, was called **structuralism,** because it examined the structure of the mind and the organization of the basic elements of sensations, feelings, and images. Structuralists argued that every experience could be broken down into its primitive components.

One reason Wundt is so important in the history of psychology is that he was impressively productive as a researcher. In roughly 50 years of work, he published about 500 research papers and books, writing about 60,000 printed pages (Gardner, 1985; Schlesinger, 1985). His interests ranged widely and included memory, language, emotion, abnormal psychology, religion, history, and art (Blumenthal, 1975).

Consider a typical Wundt study, one on memory. For a fraction of a second, Wundt presented to trained observers a set of letters such as this:

r v n e
w o z g
m b t u

Wundt found that most observers could report no more than six letters, yet they claimed they *saw* more (Wundt, 1912/1973). The additional letters seemed to slip away from memory in the process of recalling them. As you will see in Chapter 7, this fragile, fleeting characteristic of memory was explored again half a century later in an important study. This topic is now called sensory memory (Sperling, 1960). Impressively, the basic phenomenon was initially described by psychology's first systematic researcher.

Wundt deserves credit not only for his findings, but also for his methods. For example, he emphasized the importance of **replications,** or studies in which a phenomenon is tested several times, often under different conditions. For instance, the study with the letters could be repeated several times, each time with a different group of participants and a different arrangement of letters. When a study has been replicated, we can be more confident that its conclusions are accurate.

William James

American psychologists at the end of the nineteenth century were more influenced by William James (1842–1910) than by Wilhelm Wundt. James's less formal approach emphasized the kinds of questions we encounter in daily life. He wrote extensively about **consciousness,** which we now define as our awareness of the environment and of ourselves (Chapter 5). James also developed a theory explaining that our emotional reactions arise from the way we perceive our physiological re-

Wilhelm Wundt, the founder of academic psychology.

William James, the first major American psychologist.

sponses (Chapter 12). His views on numerous other areas, such as perception and reasoning, are still considered relevant (Dember, 1990; Nickerson, 1990).

James was particularly interested in how consciousness and other psychological processes help human beings. This emphasis on the functions of psychological activities inspired the name for James's approach to psychology, called functionalism. **Functionalism** argues that psychological processes are adaptive; they allow humans to survive and to adapt successfully to their surroundings.

Whereas Wundt was known for his laboratory, James was admired for his textbooks. For several decades, American psychology students read either the two-volume *Principles of Psychology* (1890) or the shorter version, *Psychology, Briefer Course* (1892). Professors referred to the longer version as "James," and they nicknamed the shorter version "Jimmy" (Hilgard, 1987). A century later, the two-volume work has been called "probably the most significant psychological treatise ever written in America" (Evans, 1990, p. 11).

Many of James's ideas seem remarkably modern. For example, he emphasized that the human mind is active and inquiring, a view still current today (Matlin, 1994). James also suggested that humans have two different kinds of memory. As Chapter 7 will note, this proposal was reemphasized nearly 80 years later (Atkinson & Shiffrin, 1968).

American Psychology in the Early Twentieth Century

Many of Wundt's students left Germany for the United States (Benjamin et al., 1992). Some of them, such as Edward Titchener, continued in Wundt's tradition. Titchener founded a psychology laboratory at Cornell University and expanded the introspection technique to areas such as thinking and complex feelings (Danziger, 1990). However, other students developed different agendas. G. Stanley Hall, at Johns Hopkins University, founded the American Psychological Association and promoted research on child development. Figure 1.1 describes eight men and women who made important early contributions to psychology in the United States.

One of these psychologists, John B. Watson (1878–1958), initiated a new approach to psychology known as behaviorism. **Behaviorism** stresses the study of observable behavior, instead of hidden mental processes. Watson had originally conducted research with animals, because he admired the objective research that could be conducted on their observable behaviors. In contrast, he found little value in studying consciousness or using introspective techniques (Buckley, 1989; Watson, 1913).

Behaviorism appealed to American psychologists because it offered some practical applications (O'Donnell, 1985; Schnaitter, 1987). Wundt's introspection technique and James's ideas about the nature of consciousness and emotions were both important in developing theories about psychology, but neither suggested how these theories could be applied in everyday life.

The behaviorists' emphasis on observable behavior led them to reject any terms referring to mental events, such as *idea, thought,* or *mental image.* In fact, early behaviorists classified thinking as simply a form of speech. They thought that they should be able to detect tiny movements of the tongue (an observable behavior) if they could develop the appropriate equipment. Behaviorists argued that vague, invisible constructs such as *thought* were simply unnecessary.

Behaviorism dominated psychology in North America from the 1920s through the 1950s (Innis, 1992). As one author wrote, "If you were to knock on the door of an academic psychologist's office in the 1930s, the chances were better than nine out of ten that you would be answered by a behaviorist" (Schlesinger, 1985, p. 13). Thus, American research psychology in the early twentieth century rejected unobservable mental processes, consciousness, and introspection. Instead, psychologists embraced the behaviorist approach, which emphasized observable behavior.

G. Stanley Hall (1844–1924). Student of Wundt; founder of American Psychological Association.

Christine Ladd-Franklin (1847–1930). Taught at Johns Hopkins and Columbia; formulated a theory of color vision.

Mary Whiton Calkins (1863–1930). Student of William James; pioneer in memory research; first woman president of American Psychological Association.

Edward Bradford Titchener (1867–1927). Student of Wundt; developed introspection techniques in the United States; taught at Cornell.

Margaret Floy Washburn (1871–1939). First woman to receive a PhD in psychology; wrote a book on animal behavior that foreshadowed behaviorism.

Edward Lee Thorndike (1874–1949). Student of William James; investigated trial-and-error animal learning.

John B. Watson (1878–1958). Founder of behaviorism, which influenced U.S. psychology for over 50 years.

Leta Stetter Hollingworth (1886–1939). Pioneer in the psychology of women; she discredited the view that menstruation was debilitating to women.

Figure 1.1
Some early U.S. psychologists.

European Psychology in the Early Twentieth Century

Behaviorism may have captivated Americans, but it had no loyal following in Europe. Instead, European psychology in the early part of this century was influenced by three new psychological approaches: Gestalt psychology, the psychoanalytic approach of Sigmund Freud, and the early cognitive psychology approach.

The Gestalt (pronounced "Geh-*shtahlt*") approach originated in Germany at the beginning of the twentieth century. According to the **Gestalt approach,** we perceive objects as well-organized, whole structures, instead of separated, isolated parts. Gestalt psychologists stressed that our ability to see shapes and patterns is determined by subtle relationships among the parts. For instance, consider the square shown in Figure 1.2. This object looks well organized; it seems to be a complete figure, a cohesive square, rather than four isolated lines. The Gestalt psychologists had an important impact on research in visual perception (Chapter 4), and they also conducted influential research in problem solving (Chapter 8).

Europe's most important contribution to psychology came from Sigmund Freud (1856–1939), an Austrian physician. Freud was specifically interested in neurology and psychological problems. He argued that people are driven by sexual urges, a view that was not warmly greeted when it was introduced during the straitlaced Victorian period. In addition, Freud emphasized that human behavior is motivated by the unconscious—by thoughts and desires far below the level of conscious awareness. Psychologists trained in Wundt's laboratory did not welcome this focus on unconscious experiences.

Freud's emphasis on sexuality and unconscious processes meant that he entered the game with two strikes against him. Nevertheless, Freud's theories eventually gained widespread popularity among therapists. However, psychoanalytic theory did not have a major impact on *research* psychology. Instead, early researchers in North America supported behaviorism. Researchers in Europe were likely to favor Wundt's approach, the Gestalt approach, or else a new orientation called the cognitive psychology approach.

The cognitive psychology approach emphasizes mental processes, and its best known European advocate was Jean Piaget (pronounced "Zhohn Pe-ah-*zhay*"). Piaget, who lived from 1896 to 1980, was a Swiss theorist whose ideas about children helped shape our knowledge about the development of thought. Piaget proposed that even young babies think, though their thoughts are connected with their senses and their body movements. He argued that their thinking changes during childhood, becoming more abstract and complex. Chapter 10 explores Piaget's theories about children's cognitive development in some detail.

From psychology's early beginnings in Wundt's laboratory in Germany, the discipline developed and diversified. By the 1930s, the field included behaviorists in North America, many Europeans continuing in Wundt's tradition, therapists practicing Freudian psychoanalysis, Gestalt psychologists investigating organizational principles, and cognitive psychologists exploring human thought processes.

Figure 1.2
According to Gestalt psychologists, this square forms a well-organized, complete figure.

SECTION SUMMARY

PSYCHOLOGY'S PAST

- Psychology, the scientific study of behavior and mental processes, was first studied systematically by Wundt, who emphasized careful research techniques.
- William James examined human consciousness and wrote influential textbooks.
- Behaviorism, which emphasized research on observable behaviors, dominated American psychology from the 1920s through the 1950s.
- Important European trends in the early twentieth century included the Gestalt approach, Freud's psychoanalytic approach, and the cognitive approach.

PSYCHOLOGY TODAY

As we complete the second half of this century, some of the earlier approaches have lost their strong support, though they have influenced contemporary approaches. For instance, Wundt's emphasis on careful research is still current. Modern cognitive psychology is clearly inspired by ideas about mental processes proposed by Wundt, James, and Gestalt psychologists (Simon, 1992). Let us now shift our attention to contemporary psychology.

Six Contemporary Approaches in Psychology

The first page of this chapter emphasized the broad scope of psychology, from microscopic neurons to large crowds of people. In fact, psychology spans the enormous distance between **biology,** which examines the structure and function of living things, and **sociology,** which studies how groups and institutions function in society. It would be impossible for a single approach to be endorsed by researchers as diverse

Jean Piaget, whose theory of children's thinking helped shape current ideas about developmental psychology.

TABLE 1.1 Chapters in the Textbook Emphasizing the Six Major Current Approaches in Psychology

	THE CURRENT APPROACHES					
	Biological	Behaviorist	Cognitive	Sociocultural	Psychodynamic	Humanistic
Ch. 3: The Biological Basis of Behavior	●					
Ch. 4: Sensation and Perception	●					
Ch. 5: States of Consciousness	●					
Ch. 6: Learning	●	●				
Ch. 7: Memory	●		●			
Ch. 8: Thinking			●			
Ch. 9: Language and Conversation			●	●		
Ch. 10: Development in Infancy and Childhood			●	●		
Ch. 11: Development From Adolescence Through Old Age			●	●	●	
Ch. 12: Motivation and Emotion	●		●			
Ch. 13: Personality	●	●	●	●	●	●
Ch. 14: Assessing Intelligence and Personality			●	●		
Ch. 15: Psychological Disorders	●	●	●	●	●	
Ch. 16: Treating Psychological Disorders	●	●	●	●	●	●
Ch. 17: Social Cognition			●	●		
Ch. 18: Social Influence				●		
Ch. 19: Health Psychology	●	●	●	●		

as a psychologist investigating the neurons in the visual system and a social psychologist interested in stereotypes about gender.

Six general approaches dominate contemporary psychology. Let's summarize them in the same order as they will be covered in more detail in the later chapters of this textbook. As Table 1.1 shows, the biological approach is introduced in the chapter on the biological basis of behavior, behaviorism dominates the learning chapter, and the cognitive approach is first discussed in detail in the memory chapter. The sociocultural perspective is prominent in the last half of the book. Finally, the psychodynamic and humanistic approaches are more concerned with personality and psychotherapy, so they take leading roles toward the end of the book.

The Biological Approach In recent decades, an increasing number of psychologists have favored the biological approach to behavior and mental processes (Boneau, 1992). This **biological approach** or **neuroscience approach** proposes that each behavior, emotion, and thought is caused by a physical event in the brain or other part of the nervous system. People who favor this approach are likely to examine how various regions of the brain and various brain chemicals are related to psychological processes.

The psychologists we discussed in the previous section could not use the biological approach because the early techniques were not sophisticated enough to reveal useful information about psychology. Chapter 3 introduces you to some research techniques that psychologists and neuroscientists use in the 1990s. These techniques include electrically stimulating a region of the brain and recording signals from the brain. Researchers can also examine a person who has an unusual disorder. For instance, neuroscientists interested in memory examined a young man who was accidentally stabbed through his nostril—into his brain (Squire, 1987). He now has a very specific problem; he cannot learn any new material. Researchers also use the biological approach to study topics such as drug abuse and medication for psychological disorders.

The Behaviorist Approach We already introduced the behaviorist approach, with its emphasis on observable behavior. Chapter 6 will examine how this approach was further developed by B. F. Skinner (1904–1990), a behaviorist who had an especially strong impact on the psychology of learning (Lattal, 1992). Chapter 16 will also describe how behavioral approaches are used in treating many psychological disorders.

One of behaviorism's most enduring contributions involves research methods. Behaviorists insisted that psychological concepts must be precisely defined and that responses must be objectively measured. These research methods are central in the cognitive approach, one of the most popular contemporary approaches (Simon, 1992).

The Cognitive Approach Earlier, we noted that Wilhelm Wundt, William James, and Jean Piaget all provided important contributions to the cognitive approach. However, the behaviorist influence was so strong from about 1920 to 1960 that researchers in North America paid little attention to hidden mental processes.

The **cognitive approach** focuses on unobservable mental processes such as perceiving, remembering, thinking, and understanding. For instance, as your eyes race across this page, you can perceive meaningful letters, rather than a clutter of random squiggles. You can also remember the meaning of words. You also think about many topics while you read; for example, right now you might be thinking about whether you understand the definition for the *cognitive approach*. And you can understand ideas (for instance, why the behaviorists' emphasis on objective measurement is important). Researchers in cognitive psychology find a challenge in creating precise definitions for invisible mental processes and devising methods for measuring these processes objectively. For example, Chapter 8 shows how cognitive psychologists have conducted careful research on mental images, an especially challenging topic to examine objectively.

The cognitive approach certainly differs from the earlier behaviorist tradition with respect to its emphasis on unobservable mental activities. Cognitive psychologists also view humans differently. The early behaviorists held that humans were relatively passive organisms, who waited for an appropriate stimulus from the environment before they responded. In contrast, the cognitive approach argues that people eagerly acquire information. They combine information from several sources, and their cognitive processes often transform this information. For example, you can probably think of an occasion when two friends told you two different stories about an important event. Think of the cognitive efforts you made to reconcile the discrepancies, and how you reinterpreted some portions of each story.

Beginning in the 1960s, many North American psychologists shifted their loyalty away from behaviorism (Hilgard et al., 1991). Some reasons they began endorsing the cognitive view include the following:

1. Psychologists discovered that complex human processes could not be explained using only the terms from behavioral learning theory. For example, behaviorist approaches cannot account for the complexity of language structure or the organization of memory.

2. Jean Piaget's theories of human development had won the respect of child psychologists and educators.

3. Perhaps most important, the information-processing approach was developed. According to the information-processing approach, incoming information is selected, combined with previous information, and rearranged in various ways. The information-processing approach emphasizes that this processing is accomplished through a series of stages (Massaro & Cowan, 1993).

B. F. Skinner promoted the behaviorist approach during the 60-year span of his career.

This student has just formed a mental image of an elephant; yet how can such unobservable processes be examined empirically? Chapter 8 explores how cognitive psychologists have tackled challenging questions like this.

Excitement about the cognitive approach grew rapidly. By about 1970, most researchers interested in memory, thinking, and language had adopted this new approach. In fact, the period between the late 1960s and the early 1970s is often called the "cognitive revolution" (Baars, 1986). The cognitive approach was soon applied to other areas, such as motivation, personality, and psychotherapy. In each case, theorists emphasized the importance of people's thoughts and how the human mind could manipulate, transform, and even distort these thoughts. As Table 1.1 illustrated, the cognitive approach now has an important influence on most topics in this textbook. In these chapters, we will also examine new theoretical developments in cognitive psychology.

Sigmund Freud (1856–1939), the founder of the psychoanalytic theory.

The Sociocultural Approach According to the **sociocultural approach,** our behavior and mental processes are strongly influenced by social context, which includes factors such as culture, ethnic group, and gender. In the 1990s, many psychologists appreciate how these sociocultural factors have a major impact on our behaviors and thoughts. Some of the relevant topics we consider later in the book include the following: (1) How are bilinguals different from people who know only one language? (2) How is a person's parenting style influenced by his or her ethnic group? (3) Why do women have higher rates of depression than men? (4) What impact does social class have on the kind of help a person receives for a psychological disorder?

The Psychodynamic Approach Although the cognitive approach and the sociocultural approach are both extremely popular among psychologists, most students in introductory psychology courses are more likely to recognize the name of Sigmund Freud. The **psychodynamic approach** emphasizes three central points: (1) childhood experiences determine adult personality, (2) unconscious mental processes influence everyday behavior, and (3) conflict underlines most human behavior. A narrower term, the **psychoanalytic approach,** refers specifically to Freud's original theory. Compared with Freud, more recent psychodynamic theorists place more emphasis on social roles and less emphasis on sexual forces.

The psychodynamic approach is an extremely influential theory of personality disorders. Even therapists who favor other approaches have received substantial training in psychodynamic theory. Terms such as *unconscious, ego,* and *repression* are so common in our everyday vocabulary that we may forget their origins in psychoanalytic theory.

We discussed earlier how Sigmund Freud developed his theory at the beginning of the twentieth century. Chapter 13 (Personality) describes the theory in more detail, as it applies to personality development. Chapter 16 (Treating Psychological Disorders) examines the psychodynamic approach to treating psychological disorders. In addition, Chapter 11 (Development From Adolescence Through Old Age) explores a theory of identity development proposed by Erik Erikson, one of the most prominent psychodynamic theorists.

The Humanistic Approach We have seen that behaviorism developed out of a dissatisfaction with Wundt's and James's approaches, and the cognitive approach arose from dissatisfaction with the behaviorist approach. Similarly, the humanistic approach developed out of a dissatisfaction with the two major theories that dominated the first half of the twentieth century, the psychoanalytic and behaviorist approaches. American psychologists, such as Carl Rogers and Abraham Maslow, argued that the psychoanalytic approach to personality and psychological disorders focused on the "sick" side of human beings. Furthermore, they pointed out that behaviorism only examined simple behaviors. They preferred a theory that emphasized the more positive human qualities as well as more complex and noble human goals.

The **humanistic approach** stresses that humans have enormous potential for personal growth. They have the ability to care deeply for other people and to establish meaningful, productive lives for themselves. Chapter 13 (Personality) examines Carl Rogers's person-centered approach to personality and psychotherapy, as well as Abra-

Carl Rogers (1902–1987), a major humanistic theorist.

ham Maslow's theory that people seek self-actualization, or fulfillment of their true potential.

Psychology in the 1990s This chapter has traced the origins of psychology. We began with Wundt's efforts to transform the discipline into an empirical science and James's views of human consciousness. We continued through the founding of behaviorism in the United States and the development of Gestalt, psychoanalytic, and cognitive approaches in Europe. Then we examined six current perspectives: the biological, behaviorist, cognitive, sociocultural, psychodynamic, and humanistic approaches. This overview emphasizes that psychologists have not been inspired throughout their history by one all-encompassing theory, one single truth.

When Wilhelm Wundt decided to conduct research on human behavior and mental processes, no one handed him a proclamation about the best way to proceed. He began at a logical starting point, by asking people to report on their own psychological processes and by conducting some basic experiments. Behaviorists advanced the discipline by stressing that concepts should be precisely defined and that responses must be measured objectively. Cognitive psychologists then adopted this emphasis on precision and objectivity, and they applied these techniques to mental processes. Viewpoints in research psychology continue to change, each new approach attempting to improve upon the previous approaches or to address other issues. The history of psychology is not smoothly continuous. Instead, it is fragmented, and different approaches emphasize different aspects of behavior and mental processes (Hilgard et al., 1991; Smith, 1988).

Similarly, the viewpoints on treating psychological disorders have continued to change. We can safely say that few current therapists uphold every word that Sigmund Freud ever wrote. Furthermore, most therapists acknowledge that some psychological disorders can be partly linked to a biological problem, so that drug therapy may be helpful. Most therapists also see the value of some behaviorist techniques based on learning theory and cognitive techniques designed to change inappropriate behaviors and thought patterns. Furthermore, they may practice humanistic listening principles and be aware of the importance of sociocultural influences. Thus, a therapist may strongly prefer one of the six approaches, but borrow techniques from the other five. The complexity of human psychology requires a complex approach in treating disorders, rather than strict loyalty to just one approach.

Professions in Psychology

We have emphasized the diversity in the goals of psychology as well as in the historical and current approaches to psychology. This diversity also applies to the

Abraham Maslow (1908–1970), a major humanistic theorist.

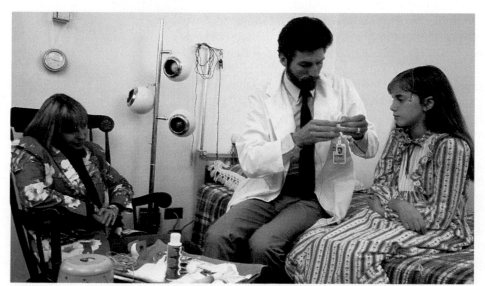

A biological psychologist at a sleep clinic fastens on electrodes to learn more about this young girl's sleep disorders.

occupational specialties within psychology. Let us first discuss four representative specialties that emphasize basic research and then consider three applied specialties that stress practical applications of psychological knowledge.

Biological psychologists, also called physiological psychologists, examine how behavior is influenced by genetic factors, the brain, the nervous system, and other biological factors.

Experimental psychologists conduct research on topics such as perception, learning, cognition (which includes memory, thinking, and language), motivation, and emotion.

Developmental psychologists examine how humans mature and change throughout the life span. Most developmental psychologists specialize in one part of the life span, such as childhood or old age.

Personality psychologists investigate how people are influenced by relatively stable inner factors. A typical research question would be whether people who have high scores on a particular personality characteristic behave differently from those with low scores.

Two important applied specialties in psychology are concerned with helping people who have psychological problems. **Clinical psychologists** assess and treat people with psychological disorders. On the basis of interviews and psychological tests, they suggest a diagnosis of the problem. Then they provide either individual or group psychotherapy. Counseling psychologists represent a profession that is growing in importance. Like clinical psychologists, **counseling psychologists** assess and treat people, but their clients are likely to have less severe problems. Some counseling psychologists provide marriage or career counseling; others work in college mental health clinics.

Incidentally, many people confuse clinical and counseling psychologists with a group of medical professionals known as psychiatrists. **Psychiatrists** receive training in medicine, rather than psychology, and their medical orientation emphasizes treating certain disorders with medication. Thus, psychiatrists are *not* psychologists.

The other major profession in applied psychology—besides clinical and counseling psychology—is industrial/organizational psychology. **Industrial/organizational psychologists** focus on human behavior in business and industry. Some may help organizations hire and train employees; others study the work setting, with the goal of improving work productivity, morale, and job satisfaction. Still others measure consumer attitudes toward a company's products.

We have looked at a variety of research and applied specializations within psychology. You may be curious, however, about some of the characteristics of psychologists. According to current U.S. statistics, 71% of all bachelor's degrees and 58% of all PhD degrees in psychology are currently awarded to women (U.S. Department of Education, 1992). Thus, the status of women in psychology has changed considerably since the beginning of the century, when Harvard University refused to grant a PhD to Mary Whiton Calkins—even though William James described her as his brightest student (Russo, 1983; Scarborough & Furumoto, 1987).

Table 1.2 lists bachelor's degree and PhD recipients in the United States, according to ethnic group. The history of Black and Hispanic psychologists has been traced by Guthrie (1976). A prominent early Black psychologist was Gilbert Haven Jones, who received his PhD degree in Germany in 1901. J. Henry Alston, shown in Figure 1.3, was the first African American to publish research in a major psychology journal. His 1920 paper examined the perception of heat and cold, a topic mentioned in Chapter 4. Many Black and Hispanic psychologists have been active researchers in the area of minority children's scores on psychological tests, a topic examined in Chapter 14. For instance, George Sanchez, shown in Figure 1.4, was one of the first psychologists to discuss how the tests produced biased scores for Mexican-American children (Guthrie, 1976). Sanchez is sometimes called the father of Chicano psychology (Padilla, 1988). Stanley Sue's (1992) article on Asian-American psychology

Developmental psychologists examine infants to study cognitive processes such as attention.

Dr. Maria Kountz is a clinical psychologist who teaches at Beaver College in Glenside, Pennsylvania, and counsels clients who have personal problems.

TABLE 1.2 Ethnic Group Representation Among U.S. Recipients of Bachelor's and PhD Degrees in psychology for 1989–1990		
ETHNIC GROUP	**NUMBER OF BACHELOR'S DEGREES IN PSYCHOLOGY**	**NUMBER OF PhD DEGREES IN PSYCHOLOGY**
White (non-Hispanic)	45,822	2,909
Black (non-Hispanic)	3,267	117
Hispanic	2,068	124
Asian	1,678	62
Native American	218	17

[*Source:* U.S. Department of Education, 1992]

describes how Asian students in previous decades were not encouraged to enter psychology. In 1971, for example, Dr. Sue was the only full-fledged clinical psychologist from a Chinese background in a U.S. university.

In the 1990s, several programs have been developed to encourage people of color to pursue graduate degrees. For example, the Ethnic Minority Fellowship Program, sponsored by the American Psychological Association, offers financial assistance for training in research, the neurosciences, and clinical psychology.

The variety of theoretical approaches and professions examined in this section illustrates the diversity of psychology. However, underlying this diversity is a unified concern. All psychologists—no matter what specialty they pursue—are concerned with the scientific study of behavior and mental processes. The next section explores three themes that can be traced throughout many diverse topics within psychology.

Figure 1.3
J. Henry Alston, the first Black psychologist to publish a paper in a major psychology journal.

SECTION SUMMARY

PSYCHOLOGY TODAY

- The biological approach to psychology proposes that all behaviors and mental processes correspond to physical events in the brain and other parts of the nervous system.

- The behaviorist approach emphasizes observable behavior and contributes to learning theory and psychotherapy.

- The cognitive approach focuses on unobservable mental processes and emphasizes how people actively acquire, combine, and transform information.

- The sociocultural approach stresses that psychological processes are influenced by factors such as culture, ethnic group, and gender.

- The psychodynamic approach points out the importance of childhood experiences, unconscious mental processes, and conflict.

- The humanistic approach emphasizes humans' enormous potential for personal growth.

- Viewpoints in both research psychology and therapy continue to change in the 1990s.

- Some occupations in psychology emphasize research (e.g., biological, experimental, developmental, and personality psychologists), whereas others emphasize applications (e.g., clinical, counseling, and industrial/organizational psychologists).

- The majority of bachelor's and PhD degrees are currently awarded to women; people of color still receive a relatively small fraction of psychology degrees.

Figure 1.4
George Sanchez, an early critic of intelligence tests that were biased against Hispanics and other people of color.

THREE IMPORTANT THEMES IN PSYCHOLOGY

In writing this textbook, I asked myself the following question: Suppose that students who had read this textbook were asked—10 years later—to list several main points they recalled from the book. What points would I want them to remember? Three themes that recur throughout psychology seem most important. These themes are neither difficult nor surprising; instead, they are straightforward. I'll frequently point out these themes in future chapters. Keep the themes in mind as you read the textbook, and try to identify additional examples—even when they are not specifically noted.

Theme 1: Humans Are Extremely Competent

You have had many years of experience as a human being. However, you probably do not fully appreciate the talents that you and other humans share. For instance, suppose you answer your telephone and the speaker says, "Is this Max's Pizza Parlor?" You manage to decode the stream of sounds effortlessly, understand the speaker's question, and answer—equally effortlessly—"No, I'm sorry, but you have the wrong number." This accomplishment may not sound particularly dazzling unless you realize that no computer can analyze language and respond appropriately with even a fraction of your own degree of competence.

The theme that humans are competent is especially prominent in the first half of the textbook. The theme is first introduced in Chapter 3 when we discuss the biological components of behavior. Here we see that the human nervous system permits information to travel quickly; the brain also has numerous specialized parts that perform specific functions. Our miraculous talents can be traced to our miraculous nervous system.

The competence theme also occurs frequently throughout the chapter on sensation and perception, particularly in the discussion of vision and hearing. However, the theme is most prominent in the three chapters on human cognition—memory, thinking, and language. Our cognitive processes are fast, accurate, and flexible. Naturally, humans occasionally make errors. However, in many cases, these errors can be traced to a general strategy that usually produces correct responses, in a minimum length of time. Thus, even our errors tend to be "smart mistakes." By the time you have completed this textbook, you should be much more impressed with your mental abilities.

Theme 2: Humans Differ Widely From One Another

We noted earlier that one goal of psychologists is to predict behavior. However, humans differ so impressively from one another that prediction is often difficult. Consider, in contrast, how easily we can make predictions in some other disciplines. For example, if I take a tablespoon of vinegar and add it to a tablespoon of baking soda, I can predict that the mixture will foam and produce a fizzing noise. In fact, I tried that three times, each with a different kind of vinegar, and the results were boringly predictable. Each time, the mixture foamed and fizzed. In psychology, however, predictions cannot be made with the same accuracy. I can take one student, add a lecture on visual perception, and that student will foam and fizz with excitement. Another student, similar from all outward appearances, may fall asleep and begin to snore loudly. The individual differences among students—or any other humans— mean that they often respond in different ways to the same identical stimulus.

Individual differences are not especially prominent when we consider the processes that are largely biological, as in Chapter 3 (The Biological Basis of Behavior) and Chapter 4 (Sensation and Perception). However, beginning with Chapter 5 (States of Consciousness), we will often focus on this human variation.

Individual differences make clear-cut results more difficult to obtain in psychological research. For instance, suppose that a group of researchers wants to test a new method of improving memory. Students first perform one memory task. Next

Students in any classroom—like any group of humans—display individual differences.

they are told how to use the new memory-improvement method, and then they perform a second memory task. Compared to the first task, some students' scores improve, some decline, and some remain the same—demonstrating impressive individual differences. The researchers must determine whether the two sets of scores are substantially different from each other, compared to the individual differences.

Researchers in some areas of psychology consider individual differences to be a nuisance, a factor that decreases their chances of obtaining significant experimental results. However, researchers in other areas—particularly in the psychology of personality—concentrate specifically on studying these individual differences. In fact, personality researchers examine the factors that produce these individual differences. One psychologist's garbage is another psychologist's favorite dish.

Throughout this textbook, we will often compare various groups of humans when we focus on people who differ in characteristics such as gender, ethnic group, and sexual preference. In general, we will conclude that differences *between* groups are smaller than differences *within* groups. For example, in Chapter 14 we will note that males occasionally score higher than females on some mathematics tests. However, the difference between males and females is small compared to the differences within males or the differences within females. Just consider the variation within males, for example. You probably know males who are extremely skilled in math, but you also know males who find the subject extremely difficult. The variation within any human group is an important example of the general theme that humans differ widely from one another.

Theme 3: Psychological Processes Are Complex

When we examine the factors that influence human behavior, we seldom identify just one important factor. For example, suppose that researchers want to determine why 10-year-olds perform better on a memory test than 6-year-olds. They are likely to find that the explanation is complex and involves many factors. One factor may be that the older children are more familiar with the vocabulary. Another factor may be that the older children are more likely to figure out relationships between words on the list and remember the words in clusters. Still another factor may be that the older children realize that they need to figure out a memory strategy, whereas the younger children do not believe they need to make a special effort to coax the words into memory. In short, most behavior is caused by multiple factors.

Furthermore, this complexity theme also operates when we try to figure out why two kinds of behavior are related to each other. For instance, in Chapter 6, we see that the amount of violent television a child watches is related to that child's aggressive behavior. Three different factors probably account for this relationship: (1) Watching violent television encourages children to act aggressively; (2) Aggressive children like to watch violent television programs; and (3) The kind of family that allows children to watch violent television also tends to allow children to act aggressively. A single explanation is not sufficient.

The complexity theme is found throughout the textbook. For example, in Chapter 4 you will learn that our ability to hear depends upon an elaborate arrangement of auditory receptors, neurons, and tiny bones. At the end of the book, in Chapter 18, you will see that your tendency to be altruistic and helpful depends upon a complex set of factors, such as your ability to empathize with another person, your mood, and whether you are in a hurry.

The theme that human behavior is complex should encourage you to be suspicious of simple, one-factor explanations. For example, suppose you read in the newspaper that fathers who are emotionally cold and unresponsive are likely to have daughters who develop eating disorders. Remember that many factors, other than the father's emotions, are likely to be responsible. (Furthermore, the individual differences theme should encourage you to speculate that emotional unresponsiveness may promote an eating disorder in some young women, but have no effect on some other young women.)

If humans were less competent, if individual differences were smaller, and if explanations could be simple, this textbook would be very short. We would have all the answers, researchers would be unemployed, and we would not need therapists or other applied psychologists. However, the reality is that humans are amazingly competent, so we need to explain all their different talents. Humans also differ enormously, so we need to realize that people may respond differently to the same stimulus, and we need to explain these individual differences. Finally, psychological processes are complex, and the explanations for behavior are difficult to unravel. Psychologists have probably learned more about behavior and mental processes in the last 30 years than in the previous 3,000. Still, we do not yet have all the answers, and in fact we have not even asked all the interesting questions.

Your ability to hear the tones produced by this violinist depends upon a complicated arrangement of structures in your auditory system. This is an example of Theme 2.

SECTION SUMMARY

THREE IMPORTANT THEMES IN PSYCHOLOGY

● Theme 1 states that humans are extremely competent.

● Theme 2 states that humans differ widely from one another.

● Theme 3 states that psychological processes are complex.

HOW TO USE THIS BOOK

Psychology includes several features to help you understand, learn, and remember the material. This section tells you how to use these features most effectively.

Notice that each chapter begins with an outline. Before reading a new chapter, inspect the outline and try to understand the structure of the topic. For instance, on page 21, notice that Chapter 2 is divided into three sections: The Major Research Methods, Research Issues, and Analyzing the Data.

An important feature of this textbook is a summary at the end of each major section in a chapter. These "Section Summaries" allow you to review the material frequently and to master relatively short topics before moving on to new areas. When you reach the end of a section, test yourself to see whether you can remember the important points. Then read the section summary and notice which items you forgot or remembered incorrectly. Finally, test yourself again and recheck your accuracy. Some students have told me that they like to read only one section at at time, check themselves on the section summary, and then take a break. Then when they return to the textbook, they find it helpful to review previous section summaries before beginning the new material.

I have tried to apply many psychological principles in writing this textbook. Research on memory has demonstrated that people remember material better when it is illustrated with examples. Therefore I include many examples from my experience as well as examples my students have provided. You will also remember more effectively if you think of examples from your own experience. For instance, the section on short-term memory in Chapter 7 points out that memory is often fragile; an item you just heard can disappear from memory if your attention is distracted. When you read a statement like this, try to determine whether it matches your own experiences. Pause, try to recall some specific examples, and write them in the margins. Psychologists have found that one of the most effective methods of enhancing recall is to ask people to relate the material to themselves (e.g., Rogers et al., 1977). You have lived with yourself for many years now, so take advantage of your experience.

This textbook also includes informal experiments labeled "demonstrations." You have already tried a demonstration on page 3. Each demonstration can be done quickly and usually requires no special equipment. In most cases, you can perform the demonstrations by yourself. These demonstrations should also help to make the material more concrete and easy to remember. More tips on improving memory are discussed throughout Chapter 7.

Notice, also, that new terms appear in boldface type (for example, **psychology**). A definition is included in the same sentence as the term so that you do not need to search an entire paragraph to discover the term's meaning. Each term also appears in the glossary at the end of the book and in the index. If your professor uses a psychology term during a lecture, and you cannot recall its meaning, check the glossary for a brief definition, or look in the index to find where the topic is discussed in more detail. A phonetic pronunciation is provided where a new term or a person's name (like Wilhelm Wundt) does not have an obvious pronunciation. (The accented syllable will appear in italics.)

Chapters 2 through 19 each contain an "In Depth" section, which examines recent research on a selected topic relevant to the chapter. These sections look closely at the research methods and the results of studies on a topic that currently intrigues psychologists.

A set of review questions can be found at the end of each chapter. Many review questions ask you to apply your knowledge to a practical problem. Other review questions encourage you to integrate information from several parts of a chapter. Prior to an exam, you may find it helpful to review all the section summaries in a chapter, then try to answer the review questions.

A list of new terms is included at the end of each chapter. You can study these new terms by trying to supply a definition and—where relevant—an example for each new term. You can monitor your accuracy by checking either the glossary or the pages of the textbook.

The final feature of each chapter is a list of recommended readings. This list supplies you with resources if you want to write a paper on a particular topic or if an area interests you. In general, I included books, chapters, and articles that provide more than a general overview of a topic but are not overly technical.

The major point of this section is that psychological principles can be used to help you master psychology. By actively thinking about the material and reviewing it systematically, you will find that you can remember more of the important concepts of psychology.

SECTION SUMMARY

HOW TO USE THIS BOOK

- This section contains many tips to help you learn the material more effectively.
- Recall can be enhanced by reviewing the material frequently, thinking of examples of psychological principles from your own life, and testing your knowledge.

R E V I E W   Q U E S T I O N S

1. Suppose you are describing your college courses to a high-school acquaintance. Based on this chapter, how would you define psychology? Describe the four goals of psychology to this student. Describe an example of research or an applied project that psychologists could conduct for each of these four goals.

2. What is the armchair approach to psychology? How does it differ from the empirical approach? Which approach would the behaviorists be likely to favor?

3. Wilhelm Wundt is often considered the founder of contemporary psychology. What did he study, and how rigorous were his methods?

4. Three important facets of American research psychology have been the psychology of William James, the behaviorist movement, and the cognitive revolution. Describe each of these approaches, and contrast them with respect to factors you consider to be important.

5. Before you began this chapter, what had you heard about Sigmund Freud's theory? Does that information match what you read here? Why or why not?

6. What does the cognitive psychology approach emphasize? What are its origins in European psychology, and what does it borrow from American psychology? Why did its popularity rise later in this century? What is the humanistic approach, and how did it come about?

7. Describe the six current psychology approaches: biological, behaviorist, cognitive, sociocultural, psychodynamic, and humanistic. If you were to pursue a career in psychology or some related area, which of these approaches would you be likely to find most useful? Which approach(es) would be most relevant for a physician? A classroom teacher? A businessperson? A social worker?

8. Contrast the view of human beings that is provided by those who favor the behaviorist, cognitive, psychodynamic, and humanistic approaches. Which approach(es) do you find most consistent with your own view of humans?

9. Imagine that a number of psychologists from a variety of specialty areas in psychology have gathered together for a conference on aggression. Each of the following will present a paper on his or her work related to aggression: a biological psychologist, an experimental psychologist, a developmental psychologist, a personality psychologist, a clinical psychologist, and an industrial/organizational psychologist. Suggest a sample paper topic for each of the six psychologists.

10. What are the three themes presented near the end of the chapter? Explain each theme, and provide your own example for each one, based on some observations from the last few days.

N E W   T E R M S

psychology
applied psychologists
empirical evidence
introspection
structuralism
replications
consciousness
functionalism
behaviorism
Gestalt approach
biology
sociology
biological approach
neuroscience approach

cognitive approach
sociocultural approach
psychodynamic approach
psychoanalytic approach
humanistic approach
biological psychologists
experimental psychologists
developmental psychologists
personality psychologists
clinical psychologists
counseling psychologists
psychiatrists
industrial/organizational psychologists

ANSWERS TO DEMONSTRATIONS

DEMONSTRATION 1.1.

1. True—Depressed people are more likely to seek emotional support from others than are people who are not depressed.

2. False—Children who are severely punished when young are more likely to develop psychological problems in adulthood than are those whose parents "spared the rod."

3. True—When management students were asked to decide the salary levels of various job candidates, they awarded higher salaries to the applicants who had requested higher salaries.

4. True—When students watched videotapes of people whose self-descriptions conflicted with their actual behavior on characteristics such as "shy" and "friendly," their judgments were influenced much more strongly by what the people did than what they said.

5. False—Attractive people turn out to have higher self-esteem and to be better treated than less attractive people. (We discuss the issue of physical attractiveness in detail in Chapter 2.)

6. True—Students who had talked on the phone to depressed people are not interested in spending time with these people, compared to students who had talked to nondepressed people.

7. True—People who marry young or after just a short courtship are more likely to seek a divorce later on, in comparison to those who marry after age 20 or after a long courtship.

8. False—In a variety of studies, people have indicated their preference for items (such as words, symbols, and photos) that they have seen frequently.

9. True—If we transform the ancient sword into the modern handgun, the saying has clear support; gunshot deaths are much more likely to occur in homes where a gun is kept, and guns are more likely to kill a resident than an intruder, by a ratio of about 350 to 1.

10. False—Numerous studies on both friendships and romantic relationships show that people tend to be attracted to individuals who are similar to themselves, not different.

Sources: Jordan, 1989; Kohn, 1988

RECOMMENDED READINGS

Guthrie, R. V. (1976). *Even the rat was white: A historical view of psychology.* New York: Harper & Row. The title of the book refers to psychology's early neglect of racial and ethnic minorities; this book helps to correct this neglect, especially by presenting biographies of pioneering Black psychologists.

Hilgard, E. R. (1987). *Psychology in America: A historical survey.* San Diego, CA: Harcourt Brace Jovanovich. Written by a researcher who contributed to many areas of psychology, this textbook provides an in-depth history of American psychology and includes biographies of dozens of important psychologists.

Scarborough, E., & Furumoto, L. (1987). *Untold lives: The first generation of American women psychologists.* New York: Columbia University Press. This fascinating book includes chapter-long biographies of several early women psychologists, including Calkins, Washburn, and Ladd-Franklin, shorter portraits of other women, and an analysis of the forces that limited women's academic achievements at the beginning of this century.

Schultz, D. P., & Schultz, S. E. (1982). *A history of modern psychology* (5th ed.). Fort Worth, TX: Harcourt Brace Jovanovich. This textbook provides a readable, mid-level overview of psychology's history, with special emphasis on behaviorism and the psychodynamic perspective.

Woods, P. J. (1987). *Is psychology the major for you? Planning for your undergraduate years.* Washington, DC: American Psychological Association. Students interested in psychology should consider buying their own copies of this book, because it contains useful information on deciding whether to major in psychology, preparing for careers, applying for jobs, and applying for graduate school. To order a copy, send a check for $11.95 (which includes postage and handling) to: Order Department, American Psychological Association, 1400 North Uhle Street, Arlington, VA 22201.

CHAPTER 2

RESEARCH METHODS IN PSYCHOLOGY

A student I know named Heidi told me about a recent unpleasant experience. A medical problem had been bothering her for several months, so she went to our college health center. The physician who saw her asked several superficial questions and then told her not to worry; the problem was not significant. As Heidi described this encounter to me, she speculated that perhaps the physician might have treated the problem more seriously if she had been a male, rather than a female.

In other words, Heidi made an informal speculation about the relationship between a person's gender and medical judgments about that person. As it happened, Heidi was able to examine this speculation more formally, because she was required to conduct a research project for a psychology course in which she was enrolled. She created two sample paragraphs, each describing a student with a hypothetical medical problem. She presented each paragraph to undergraduate students, half the time using a male name in the scenario, half the time a female name. (Of course, ideally she would have given the scenarios to physicians, but a large sample of physicians was not available in our rural county.) The participants were asked to judge whether or not the student in the scenario should go to the health center.

When Heidi analyzed the results, she found that the participants gave similar responses to the scenario with the male student and the scenario with the female student. Although this study does not allow Heidi to make any statements about how *physicians* might treat males and females differently, she can conclude that her data provide no evidence for students showing bias on the basis of gender (Lang, 1992). Other researchers could go beyond these preliminary results, for example by using a wider variety of scenarios.

Heidi had speculated that a patient's gender would influence medical judgments. Similarly, you've probably speculated often about human thoughts and behavior. Does weather influence our mood? What is the best way to help a friend stop smoking? Do couples who live together before marriage have a different divorce rate from those who do not? Questions like these have also intrigued psychologists.

Psychological research and everyday speculation address similar kinds of questions. However, they differ in their approach to the problem. Everyday speculation typically uses a single test of a question, as well as informal observation—such as Heidi's observations in the health center. In contrast, psychological research uses repeated tests and formal, systematic observation. As a consequence, the conclusions reached in everyday life are necessarily tentative and ambiguous, whereas the conclusions reached in psychological research can be much firmer.

A background in psychology research methods can help you understand why psychologists take certain precautions in conducting a study. This chapter therefore provides background information to help you analyze more critically the material in the remainder of this book.

An understanding of research methods can also help you become a more effective critical thinker. When you use **critical thinking,** you decide what to believe and how to act after you carefully evaluate the evidence and the reasoning in a situation. Several years from now, you probably will not recall much of the specific information in this textbook, but if you have improved your critical thinking, you will still be able to use the basic principles of methodology to help you evaluate psychological claims (Bell, 1991; Stanovich, 1992).

Through research, we can test informal speculations, for example, whether the patient's gender influences people's medical judgments.

An understanding of research methods can also help you apply your critical thinking skills when you read advertisements and summaries of psychology studies, often found in the popular media. For example, a newspaper article summarized a study in which 92% of adolescent women with eating disorders described their relationships with their fathers as "distant." After reading this chapter, you should be able to ask critical questions about such a study. For instance, what percentage of adolescent women *without* eating disorders would report distant relationships with their fathers? Maybe the relationships are not really distant, but the young women perceive them inaccurately. Furthermore, the article implies that distant fathers cause their daughters to develop eating disorders, but could it also be possible that the daughters' unusual behavior alienates the fathers?

Finally, an appreciation of research methods can help you think more clearly about your own behavior and make more rational decisions (Wood, 1984). For example, suppose you study conscientiously for a biology exam, arranging for eight hours of sleep the night before, and you receive a C+. For the next exam, you study less and sleep less, receiving a B. Can you conclude that you will receive an even higher score on the third exam by studying and sleeping even less? After reading this chapter, you should be on the lookout for alternative explanations of relationships. (For instance, the second exam might have been easier, or you may have become more accustomed to the instructor's exams.)

This chapter begins by exploring several major research methods. The second section includes some important research issues, such as the problem of measuring behavioral responses, the issue of avoiding biases in psychological studies, and social and ethical aspects of psychological research. The final section provides a brief overview of data analysis, which considers how psychologists summarize the data they collect from their studies and how they draw conclusions based on these data.

THE MAJOR RESEARCH METHODS

Psychological research is based on the scientific method. The **scientific method** includes four basic steps:

1. Identify the research problem.
2. Design and conduct a study, gathering appropriate data.
3. Examine the data.
4. Communicate the results.

Psychologists use six major methods to explore behavior. Each method approaches the steps of the scientific method from a different perspective, and each has strengths and weaknesses. By combining several different approaches, researchers can achieve a much more complete picture of psychological processes. For instance, the experimental method is especially useful when you want to determine the cause of a particular behavior. In contrast, naturalistic observation tells little about causes, but it helps us understand how people and animals behave in their normal lives.

The six methods also differ in the amount of control the researchers can exercise when they conduct their studies. In experimental studies, researchers can control what the participants see, hear, and do. In naturalistic observation, those who are being studied control their own behavior; the researchers observe but do nothing to control or change the participants' behavior.

The Experimental Method

The experimental method is the most effective way to identify a cause-and-effect relationship. In an **experiment,** researchers systematically manipulate a variable under controlled conditions and observe how the participants respond. For example, suppose you want to study the effects of music on students' accuracy in solving mathematical problems. In an experiment, you could systematically manipulate the music students hear while they solve problems. Perhaps half of the students work in a quiet room, and the other half work in a room with a tape recorder playing moderately loud popular music.

In an experiment, researchers manipulate one variable (e.g., presence or absence of music), and they observe how the participants respond (e.g., number of mathematics problems correctly solved). They try to hold constant the other variables that are not being tested (e.g., lighting in the room and type of math problems being solved). If the behavior changes when only that manipulated variable is changed, then the researchers can conclude that they have discovered a cause-and-effect relationship (e.g., between the presence of music and problem solving).

Independent and Dependent Variables When you design an experiment, the first step is to state a hypothesis. A **hypothesis** is a tentative set of beliefs about the nature of the world, a statement about what you expect to happen if certain conditions are true (Halpern, 1989). A hypothesis can be stated in an "if . . . then" format: *If* certain conditions are true, *then* certain things will happen. For example:

A hypothesis tells what relationship a researcher expects to find between an independent variable and a dependent variable. The **independent variable** is the variable that the experimenters manipulate. They decide how much of that variable to present to the participant. The independent variable is described in the *if* part of the "if . . . then" statement of the hypothesis. In the previous example, the independent variable is whether or not the music is presented to the participants.

The **dependent variable** concerns the responses that the participants make; it is a measure of their behavior. The dependent variable is described in the *then* part of the "if . . . then" statement of hypothesis. In our example, the dependent variable is the problem solving of the students, which we could measure in terms of the number of problems correctly solved in a specified number of minutes.

You can remember the two kinds of variables by noting that the dependent variable *depends* upon the value of the independent variable. For example, the problem solving (dependent variable) *depends* upon the presence or absence of music (the independent variable). Students often have difficulty identifying terms such as independent and dependent variable in an example, even when they can define these terms perfectly (McKelvie, 1992). Therefore, try Demonstration 2.1 to help you clarify these important terms.

Experimental and Control Conditions In an experiment, the researcher must arrange to test at least two conditions that are specified by the independent variable. In the simple example of the music experiment, we could test one group of students in a "no-music" condition and a second group in a "music" condition. In other words, one group, the **control condition,** is left unchanged; the students receive no special treatment. The second group, the **experimental condition,** is changed in some way. A particular variable is present in the experimental condition that is absent in the control condition. (In this study, music is either present or absent.)

Most of the experiments described in this book involve more than just two conditions. The music study could compare four conditions: a no-music control and three experimental conditions (soft, medium, and loud music). However, all experiments require some kind of comparison between conditions. If you have only one condition, you do not have an experiment, and you cannot draw conclusions about cause and effect.

Let's consider why causal conclusions cannot be drawn from just a single condition. You have probably read advertisements for so-called subliminal tapes. Each

DEMONSTRATION 2.1   Identifying the Independent and the Dependent Variables

To help you understand independent and dependent variables, read the first three examples. Then, for the next three examples, list what you believe to be the independent and the dependent variables. You can check the answers at the end of this chapter.

HYPOTHESIS	INDEPENDENT VARIABLE	DEPENDENT VARIABLE
1. If prison guards treat inmates courteously, then inmates will comply better with prison rules.	Nature of guards' interactions (courteous vs. rude)	Extent of compliance with rules (e.g., proper mealtime conduct)
2. If residents in a nursing home can control aspects of their lives, then they will be healthier.	Personal control (e.g., allowed to decide about bedroom decorations vs. no input in decision)	Health measures (e.g., number of days with medical complaints)
3. If students learn Spanish vocabulary words by creating vivid mental images, then they will learn the words better.	Learning method (mental images vs. no special instruction)	Score on a vocabulary test
4. If people consume caffeine prior to bedtime, then they will take longer to fall asleep.	?	?
5. If another person is present in the room, then an individual will take longer to respond to an emergency.	?	?
6. If people are praised for helping another person, then they are more likely to help others in the future.	?	?

Note: Hypotheses are often stated in formats that do not use the specific words *if* and *then*. For example, Hypothesis 1 might appear as *Inmates comply better with prison rules when prison guards treat them courteously.* To identify the independent and dependent variables, simply reword the hypothesis in an *if . . . then* format.

---

tape recording presumably contains positive messages, spoken so quietly that they cannot be consciously heard. Instead, the listener hears only soothing music or natural sounds, such as gentle winds or ocean waves. The ads claim, however, that the subconscious mind responds to the hidden messages and that these messages will transform your life. Each ad features testimonials from people about their weight loss, improved self-image, increased memory, better sex life, and other life transformations. One testimonial on weight loss reads,

> *I have lost 15 pounds without too much effort using your [weight control] tape. To say I'm extremely pleased is putting it mildly. Thank you so much for making this help available.*

Intrigued by these ads, I wrote to seven companies that offered subliminal tapes. In each case, I requested information on experimental studies that contrasted the performance of experimental and control groups. So far, no company has replied. The companies probably never tested the tapes experimentally. As a result, we hear testimonials, and their enthusiasm might convince an uncritical thinker that the tapes work miracles.

However, suppose that one company decides to test the weight-loss tape using a single condition. In this single condition, everyone listens to the tape, complete with the subliminal message. Suppose, as well, that 80% of the people report at least some weight loss. The problem is that we do not know what percentage of people in a control condition—who never listened to subliminal tapes—would have reported at least some weight loss. Without a comparison condition, we cannot draw conclusions.

Let us sketch the basic design for an experiment to test the effects of the tape. People could be assigned to either the control condition (tape with no "subliminal" message) or the experimental condition (tape with "subliminal" message). The participants would be weighed, given the necessary instructions, and then weighed again several weeks later. If the people in the experimental group lost substantially more

This student is listening to a subliminal tape while he studies. However, we do not have research evidence that these tapes are effective.

weight than those in the control group, we could conclude—tentatively—that the tapes might have caused the effect. Proper controls allow researchers to draw cause-and-effect conclusions that are inappropriate when the control groups are absent.

The companies may not have tested the tapes scientifically, but several psychologists have. Moore (1991, 1992a, 1992b) and Greenwald and his colleagues (1991) have tested tapes that—if you believe the companies' claims—help you lose weight, stop smoking, read faster, improve your memory, and enhance your self-esteem. None of these studies demonstrated that the tapes objectively fulfilled their claims.

Confounding Variables A **confounding variable** is any variable—other than the independent variable—that is not equivalent in all conditions. Confounding variables can lead researchers to draw incorrect conclusions. Suppose that at the beginning of the weight loss study, the people in the "subliminal" condition were, on the average, 45 pounds overweight, whereas people in the other condition were an average of 25 pounds overweight. Original weight would be a confounding variable. If people in the "subliminal" condition showed greater loss, this advantage might really be traceable to the fact that it is easier for someone who is 45 pounds overweight to lose a large number of pounds than it is for someone who is only 25 pounds overweight. That is, the "subliminal" messages may have been irrelevant.

How can researchers guard against confounding variables? One common method uses random assignment. As the name implies, **random assignment** means that people are assigned to experimental groups using a system—such as a coin toss—which ensures that everybody has an equal chance of being assigned to any one group. If the number of participants in the study is sufficiently large, then random assignment usually guarantees that the various groups will be reasonably similar with respects to important characteristics.

If researchers use precautions such as random assignment to reduce confounding variables, then they have a **well-controlled study.** With a well-controlled study, we can feel more confident about drawing cause-and-effect conclusions in an experiment.

An Example of an Experiment Consider an experiment by James Pennebaker, Janice Kiecolt-Glaser, and Ronald Glaser (1988). Their study—in which students talked about personal problems—has important implications for both psychotherapy and health psychology. These researchers begin their article by acknowledging the research showing that psychotherapy clearly benefits people's mental health. However, can the discussion of personal problems also benefit people's *physical* health?

To answer this question, the researchers randomly assigned 50 healthy undergraduates to one of two conditions. The control-group students wrote about trivial experiences, and the experimental-group students wrote about traumatic personal events. Students in both groups wrote for 20 minutes on each of four consecutive days. Those in the control group were instructed to write each day about a trivial topic, such as the shoes they were currently wearing or their plans for the remainder of the day. Those in the experimental group were instructed to write about their deepest thoughts and feelings concerned with the most traumatic experiences of their lives; they could choose a different topic each day or the same topic for all four days. Thus, the independent variable was the nature of the writing task, trivial or traumatic.

Pennebaker and his colleagues were interested in several dependent variables: immune-system measures, blood pressure, and number of visits to the health center. The first two variables were measured on the fourth day of the study and again six weeks later. Compared to control-group students, the students in the experimental group showed improved immune-system responses and lower blood pressure in the six-week measures.

Let's look at the third dependent measure, visits to the health center. The researchers consulted records from the student health center and calculated the aver-

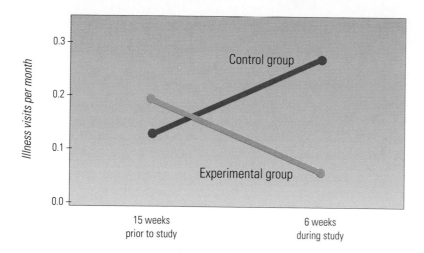

Figure 2.1

Average number of health center visits for students in an experimental group, who discussed a traumatic event, and for students in a control group, who discussed a trivial event. (Pennebaker et al., 1988)

age number of health-center visits per month, both for the 15 weeks prior to the study and for the 6 weeks following the writing task. Figure 2.1 shows these results. As you can see, the control group showed an increase in visits, probably reflecting the normal increase in illness during the month of February. During the same period, however, the experimental group showed an impressive drop, rather than an increase. Apparently, physical health can sometimes be influenced by examining important personal problems. We will examine this issue again in Chapter 19.

Conclusions About Experiments We have discussed the experimental method, in which researchers manipulate a variable and observe how the participants respond. If the conditions in an experiment are carefully controlled and confounding variables are avoided, the researchers can conclude that a change in the independent variable actually *caused* a change in the dependent variable. (For instance, Pennebaker and his colleagues (1988) could conclude that writing about personal traumas caused students to visit the health center less often.)

The experimental method has one clear advantage over the other approaches: It is the only method that allows us to infer firm cause-and-effect relationships. In some other methods that are less well controlled, alternative explanations for the results prevent the researchers from concluding that the independent variable is causally related to the dependent variable. In still other methods, the researchers' goal is to observe, rather than to interpret the cause of behavior.

The strength of the experimental method—its control over the important variables—is also its weakness. That is, a situation in which all the variables are carefully controlled is not a normal, natural situation. As a result, we may have difficulty generalizing from observations in an experiment to the real world (Christensen, 1991). For example, we may not be able to generalize from a study that examines memory for nonsense words presented on a computer screen in a psychology laboratory and draw conclusions about students learning about introductory psychology in a college classroom. Similarly, the research by Pennebaker and his colleagues may not be generalizable to a real-life therapy setting.

Let us turn now to the studies in which the experimenter has less control. These studies are particularly useful in explaining how people and animals behave in their normal lives. In addition, we often need to use one of these other methods when it is impossible to assign people randomly to groups or to manipulate the independent variable.

The Quasi-Experiment

The prefix *quasi-* means "resembling" or "sort of," as in the word *quasi-official.* Similarly, a **quasi-experiment** resembles an experiment, but it does not meet all the criteria of a full-fledged experiment. The most important criterion missing from quasi-experiments is random assignment to groups. In an experiment, a coin toss or some other random system can be used to decide which person belongs in which group (for instance, which students are assigned to the experimental group and which to the control group).

However, ethical or practical reasons often prevent random assignment. Consider a study about whether sibling jealousy was influenced by an older child's presence at the birth of a younger sibling (DelGiudice, 1986). The researcher certainly could not randomly assign these families to the present-at-birth or absent-at-birth conditions. Instead, the family and the older sibling needed to make that decision. Thus, the participants assigned themselves to one of the two conditions. (Incidentally, the results showed no difference between the two conditions in sibling jealousy.)

An excellent example of a quasi-experiment is one by Langer and Rodin (1976) with people in nursing homes. These researchers noted that an important negative characteristic of nursing homes is that the staff takes control over the residents' lives, seldom allowing them any responsibility or choices. Typically, an elderly person must wake up at a specified time, watch the movies that he or she is told to watch, and hold to the routine that someone else has established. Langer and Rodin hypothesized that residents who were given more control over their lives would have better psychological adjustment.

These researchers selected a nursing home in which they could test their hypothesis. From the perspective of experimental design, it would have been ideal to use random assignment in placing people in either the control group (with the standard treatment and no decision-making power) or the experimental group (with decision-making power). However, it would be impractical to have half of the residents on each floor of the home assigned to one treatment group and half to another. And it would be unethical to move the residents so that they could live in the randomly assigned location. Instead, one floor in the home was selected as the control condition, and the other was selected as the experimental condition. The nursing home staff filled out questionnaires about the personal characteristics of the residents before the study began, and the researchers found that the two groups were roughly equivalent before the experimental manipulation. However, because the researchers could not use random assignment, the two groups may have differed on some important confounding variable not examined in the questionnaire (e.g., intelligence or susceptibility to disease).

The independent variable in Langer and Rodin's study was the type of communication given to the residents in a group meeting. The residents of one floor (experimental condition) were told that the residents themselves should be responsible for decisions about movie selections, room arrangement, visiting, and so forth. They were also given a small plant as a gift, which they were told to care for as they wished. The residents of the other floor (control condition) were told that the staff should be responsible for all decisions. They, too, were given a small plant, but they were told that a staff member would take care of it for them. The experimental group therefore had substantially more control over their lives and possessions.

After three weeks, the staff members were asked to complete questionnaires about all the residents. Compared to people in the control group, the residents in the experimental group showed much greater improvement in their activity level, alertness, and general happiness. The members of the experimental group were also much more likely to participate in nursing home social activities. Moreover, in a follow-up 18 months later, only 15% of the experimental members had died, in contrast to 30% of the control group (Rodin & Langer, 1977). Thus, the study has important theoretical implications about the importance of personal responsibility, as well as practical implications for the management of nursing homes.

Quasi-experiments are also ideal when researchers want to determine whether a new program works in a school, or whether a new policy would be helpful in a factory. In these real-life situations (unlike the psychology laboratory), we typically can-

A quasi-experimental study has shown that residents of a nursing home are more active, alert, and happy—and they live longer—when they are encouraged to be responsible for themselves. Here a nursing-home resident arranges his clothes in his closet.

not assign people at random to conditions; they already belong to a preformed group. However, by obtaining the appropriate measures before the study begins, we can determine whether the groups are somewhat similar. Then we can manipulate the independent variable and draw tentative conclusions. Clearly, however, when researchers report the findings of a quasi-experiment, they need to discuss potential confounding variables.

The Correlational Method

In **correlational research,** psychologists try to determine whether two variables or measures are related. They obtain two measures on each person (or situation) and try to establish whether the data reveal a systematic pattern. Correlational research involves neither random assignment to groups nor the manipulation of variables. Researchers do not intentionally *change* anything, though they may administer a test or a questionnaire to gather necessary data.

After obtaining measures on the group that is being studied, the researchers calculate a statistic called the correlation coefficient. A **correlation coefficient** is a number that indicates the direction and the strength of a relationship between two variables; it can range between –1.00 and +1.00. The correlation coefficient is often symbolized as r (e.g., $r = +.28$).

Correlations allow researchers to make predictions about future behavior, based on past behavior. (You may recall that one goal of psychology, mentioned in Chapter 1, is to predict behavior.) When two variables concerned with behavior are strongly correlated, we can predict future behavior quite accurately on the basis of past behavior. In contrast, when the correlation is weak, predictions are not accurate. For example, we know that there is a moderately strong correlation between grades in high school (Variable 1) and grades in college (Variable 2). Therefore, if administrators know a student's high-school grades, they can predict this student's college grades with a moderate degree of accuracy.

Kinds of Correlations Correlational research can produce a positive correlation, a zero correlation, or a negative correlation. In a **positive correlation,** people who receive a *high* score on Variable 1 are likely to receive a *high* score on Variable 2. Furthermore, people who receive a *low* score on Variable 1 are likely to receive a *low* score on Variable 2.

Consider this example of a positive correlation. Shaver and Brennan (1992) wanted to determine whether various personality characteristics were correlated with the way people feel about their romantic partners. One correlation they calculated concerned the relationship between warmth and a secure style in romantic relationships. Shaver and Brennan reported a positive correlation between these two measures. In other words, those who considered themselves to be warm people tended to report that they could easily get close to others (secure style); those who considered themselves not to be very warm tended to report that they had difficulty achieving close relationships. Figure 2.2 shows data consistent with these results.

Correlations whose values are close to zero (e.g., +.09, .00, and –.09) are called zero correlations. A **zero correlation** indicates no substantial relationship between the two variables. Consider an example of a zero correlation—one that might surprise you. Some people believe that the full moon brings forth peculiar behavior. For instance, a lawyer friend of mine claims that whenever she receives numerous phone calls about robberies and murders—rather than more ordinary legal cases—her calendar consistently indicates that the moon has been full. (In fact, the word *lunacy* is based on the Latin word for moon, *luna.*) I am sorry to disappoint you, but a comprehensive study by Rotton and Kelly (1985) indicated a zero correlation between phases of the moon and several different measures of "lunacy," such as murders, other criminal offenses, and admissions to mental hospitals. Figure 2.3 shows a typical example of no relationship between two variables.

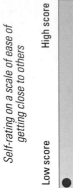

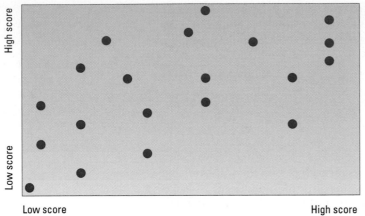

Figure 2.2

An example of a positive correlation between people's ratings of whether they are a warm person and whether they easily get close to other people in a romantic relationship. Note: Each dot represents the values on the two variables measured for one student. (Hypothetical data, consistent with Shaver & Brennan, 1992)

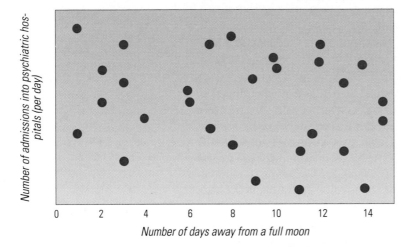

Figure 2.3

An example of a zero correlation; phase of the moon is not correlated with the number of admissions to psychiatric hospitals. (Hypothetical data, consistent with findings of Rotton & Kelly, 1985)

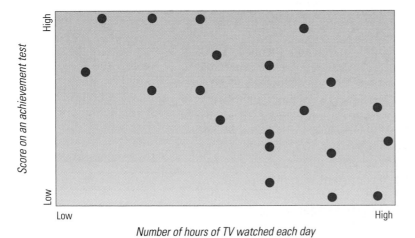

Figure 2.4

An example of a negative correlation between the number of hours of television a student watches each day and his or her score on an achievement test. Note: Each dot represents the values on the two variables measured for one student. (Hypothetical data, consistent with Keith et al., 1986)

A **negative correlation** means that people who receive a *high* score on Variable 1 usually receive a *low* score on Variable 2. Also, people with a *low* score on Variable 1 usually receive a *high* score on Variable 2. Consider an example of a negative correlation in Figure 2.4. According to research by Keith and his colleagues (1986), high-school seniors who spend a large number of hours watching television each day (i.e., high scores on that variable) are likely to receive low scores on an academic achievement test. Also, students who seldom watch television are likely to receive high scores on an achievement test.

So far, we have emphasized the direction of the correlation, that is, whether the correlation is positive or negative. We also need to discuss the *strength* of the correlation. A correlation is strong if the absolute value of the correlation coefficient is close to 1.00. Thus, when $r = +.93$, we have a strong positive correlation. Similarly, when $r = -.93$, we have a strong negative correlation. In fact, those correlations are equally strong, because $-.93$ is just as close to -1.00 as $+.93$ is to $+1.00$. Students often mistakenly believe that strength depends upon direction, so that any positive correlation would be stronger than any negative correlation. However, strength is independent of direction; to assess strength, just ignore the $+$ or $-$ sign in front of the number. (Incidentally, in this textbook and elsewhere, you will see many examples of correlations unadorned by $+$ and $-$ signs; these are all positive correlations. In other words, assume that .47 is positive *unless* it is preceded by a $-$ sign.)

A correlation is weak if the absolute value of the correlation coefficient is close to zero (e.g., $+.23$ or $-.27$). In psychology, we are more likely to find weak correlations than strong correlations. As emphasized by one of our themes, behavior is complex; many other variables can contaminate a relationship between our two target variables, reducing the strength of the correlation. We will see many examples of weak positive correlations throughout the book.

Figure 2.5 provides some guidelines for interpreting correlation coefficients. As you can see, a relationship can range from a strong negative correlation, through a zero correlation, and on to a strong positive correlation.

Interpreting Correlations Correlational research is useful when psychologists want to determine whether two variables are related to each other and when random assignment and manipulation of variables are not possible. For example, a study by Taylor and Brown (1988) examined the relationship between psychological adjustment and awareness of one's faults. They could not possibly assign people at random to the well-adjusted and maladjusted groups. ("O.K., Sam, you're in the well-adjusted group. Tough luck, Joe, get over here in the maladjusted group.") Nor could they actively manipulate variables. ("O.K., Sam, here's what we're going to do to improve your life. And Joe, here's how we'll make you miserable.") Instead, researchers using correlational methods must study the characteristics that people bring with them to the study.

A correlational study tells us whether or not two variables are related. However, when we only have correlational information, we often cannot determine which variable is the cause and which is the effect, or whether another explanation may be possible.

For example, let's consider another finding in Shaver and Brennan's (1992) study on personality characteristics and relationships with romantic partners. They also reported a positive correlation ($r = +.32$) between depression and an avoidant style in romantic relationships. (An avoidant person reports feeling uncomfortable being close to other people.) Here are two possible explanations for the correlation:

1. A person who is depressed will avoid becoming close to other people, including potential romantic partners.

2. A person who has difficulty developing close relationships with other people, including romantic partners, will become depressed.

Figure 2.5

Interpreting the strengths of various correlation coefficients.

Strong negative correlation	Moderate negative correlation	Weak negative correlation	Zero correlation	Weak positive correlation	Moderate positive correlation	Strong positive correlation

-1.00 -.90 -.80 -.70 -.60 -.50 -.40 -.30 -.20 -.10   0 +.10 +.20 +.30 +.40 +.50 +.60 +.70 +.80 +.90 +1.00

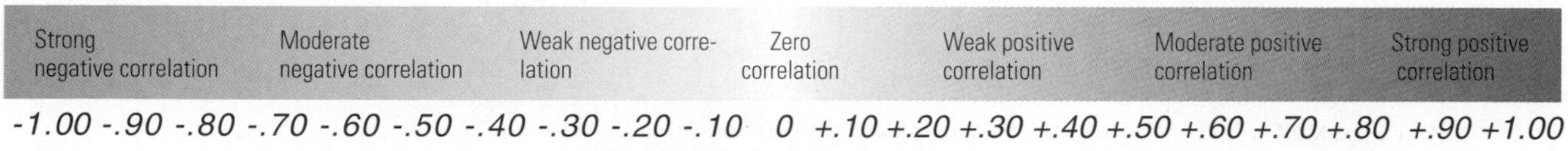

Depression → Avoidant style in romantic relationship

Figure 2.6

Depression and an avoidant style in romantic relationships are correlated; both of these causal relationships probably contribute to the correlation.

In reality, both options are probably correct. In many situations involving correlations, psychological relationships are complicated; Variable 1 causes Variable 2 to some extent, but Variable 2 also causes Variable 1. We can indicate these two causal relationships in Figure 2.6 by showing arrows going in both directions.

The phrase "correlation is not necessarily causation" is important when we try to interpret correlations. Just because two variables are related, we cannot conclude that one actually causes the other. It *may* be that Variable 1 causes Variable 2. However, Variable 2 may really cause Variable 1.

Furthermore, a third variable (perhaps not yet identified) can be responsible for both Variable 1 and Variable 2. For example, a recent study reported that people's vitamin C intake is correlated with various measures of health (Cowley & Church, 1992). Specifically, people who consumed large amounts of vitamin C (either from fruits and vegetables or from vitamin supplements) tended to have a low incidence of heart disease. Can you see why these results are difficult to interpret? Yes, perhaps vitamin C actively improves your health. However, another variable may really be responsible: conscientiousness about health. Maybe people who are very conscientious about their health make certain that they consume the right amount of vitamin C. In addition, they also make sure that they eat low-cholesterol diets and that they exercise frequently; both of these precautions would produce a lower incidence of heart disease. Perhaps most of the correlation between vitamin C intake and health can really be explained by the fact that each variable is correlated with conscientiousness about health, as Figure 2.7 suggests. (Incidentally, can you think of a third variable that could explain the positive correlation that Shaver and Brennan discovered, as we discussed on the previous page?)

Consider this example in which a correlation can be completely explained by a third variable. Some years ago, research on motorcycle accidents revealed that the number of accidents was highly correlated with the number of tattoos the riders had (Martin, 1990). How can we interpret this correlation? Do people cheer themselves up after an accident by hustling over to the nearest tattoo parlor? (A → B) On the other hand, do motorcycle riders gaze at their tattoos—rather than the road—so that they crash their motorcycles? (A ← B) Wouldn't it be more reasonable to propose that some factor such as risk-taking—which encourages people to drive dangerously—would also encourage them to get a tattoo?

In summary, then, the correlational method allows us to discover whether variables are related to each other. This advantage is particularly helpful in real-life settings where an experiment would be impossible. However, a major disadvantage of correlational research is that we cannot draw the firm cause-and-effect conclusions

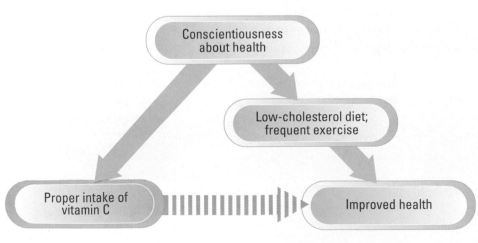

Figure 2.7

Taking vitamin C may not directly cause improved health. Instead, the kind of people who consume enough vitamin C may also be the kind who take other health precautions.

that an experiment permits. Correlational research does generate cause-and-effect *hypotheses* that can be tested later, using the experimental method. For example, the study on vitamin C suggests that an experiment should be conducted in which people are randomly assigned to either an experimental condition where they receive vitamin C or to a control condition.

The Survey Method

According to a survey, 20% of Americans eat their corn on the cob from side to side, whereas 80% rotate the corn, eating it in a spiraled pattern. Furthermore, 68% lick the flap of an envelope from left to right, rather than right to left. These and other earth-shaking statistics are included in a book called *The First Really Important Survey of American Habits* (Poretz & Sinrod, 1989). As anyone can testify who read a newspaper during the recent elections in either the United States or Canada, people thrive on surveys!

In the **survey method,** researchers select a large group of people and ask them questions about their behaviors or thoughts. Typically, the researchers also collect **demographic information** about the characteristics often used to classify people, such as gender, age, marital status, race, education, income, and so forth.

When survey results have been collected for many years, we can determine whether the responses have changed systematically across the years. For instance, Figure 2.8 shows the trend since 1976 in the percentage of college students who selected "to gain a general education" and "to make more money" in answering a question about important reasons for attending college (Dey et al., 1992; McNally, 1993).

We discussed earlier that this chapter should encourage you to adopt a more critical attitude toward the psychological research reported in the media. Some common problems in surveys include the following:

1. The sample studied in a survey may not be typical of the entire population, a point we will discuss more thoroughly in a later section on sampling.

2. People may distort their answers to make themselves appear more positive (Mishler, 1986).

3. People may not recall information accurately (Loftus et al., 1985; Pearson et al., 1992). For instance, in a survey assessing whether Americans have been the victims of crime, respondents may forget to report some minor incidents.

The survey produces valuable descriptive information. The results may also be useful in a correlational study. For instance, researchers could determine whether the relationship between a student's family income and the endorsement of the goal "to make more money" involves a positive, zero, or negative correlation. (What would you guess?) Keep in mind, however, that the survey method typically cannot be used to determine the causes of human behavior.

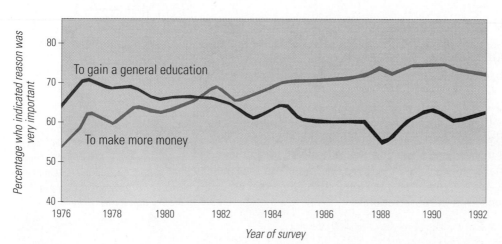

Figure 2.8

Reasons noted as very important in deciding to go to college. (Based on Dey et al., 1992; McNally, 1993)

In-Depth Interviews and Case Studies

So far, we have discussed methods in which the ideal researcher remains distant, uninvolved, and neutral. Researchers meet the participants briefly (if at all) and interact with them minimally. Some theorists argue, however, that these methods have their limitations (e.g., Gergen, 1988; Jack, 1988; McHugh et al., 1986). They point out that qualitative methods, such as interviews and case studies, provide essential information about human behavior, thought, and emotion.

An **in-depth interview** requires the interviewer to gather answers to open-ended questions, often over a period of many hours or days. For example, Belenky and her colleagues (1986) questioned 135 women, one at a time, for two to five hours each. The interview focused on these women's thoughts about knowledge. Some women thought that all information from "experts" was trustworthy; others relied more on their own knowledge and sense of what was correct.

In-depth interviews often require the interviewer to achieve warmth and rapport with participants (Benmayor, 1987). For instance, Alvarez (1987) would have learned relatively little about the Black Puerto Rican woman she interviewed if she had not been fluent in Spanish and if she had not grown close to the woman during previous meetings. In this excerpt from the interview, the woman shared her thoughts about child rearing:

> *I brought my children up in the twentieth century. I wasn't too free with them but neither was I too strict. . . . I raised them without having to fight, without having to hit them . . . and with my daughters little by little I went on explaining to them about sex because, you know, it's not good to live in ignorance. (p. 60, translated from Spanish)*

A **case study** is an in-depth description and analysis of a single person (Shaughnessy & Zechmeister, 1990). The data in a case study typically include an interview, observation, and test scores. Most often, the individual selected for a case study is highly unusual (Bromley, 1986). For instance, Curtiss (1977) reports a case study on Genie, whose parents kept her locked in a small bedroom, most often harnessed to a potty chair. For almost 14 years, Genie never heard any language except her father's swearing. Curtiss's study specifically focused on Genie's language development, which evolved slowly after Genie's "release" and never achieved the richness of normal language. For example, here is an interchange between Genie and her foster mother, when Genie was 18 (Curtiss, 1977, p. 28):

Genie: *At school is washing car.*

Mother: *Whose car did you wash?*

Genie: *People car.*

Mother: *How many cars did you wash?*

Genie: *Two car.*

Students in my classes often ask what eventually happened to Genie. Rymer (1992a; 1992b) describes how Genie was moved through a series of foster homes, eventually ending up in an institution where she apparently has not been given appropriate care. Her current language skills are minimal. This particular case study does not have a happy ending.

Both the in-depth interview and the case study provide a much fuller appreciation of an individual than any other methods. A skillfully conducted study helps us understand what it is like to live inside someone else's skin. In addition, interviews and case studies are also useful in providing ideas that can be explored further using other research methods. Naturally, however, the researchers do not claim that their findings hold true for all people—or even many people. Nor do they claim that we can draw cause-and-effect conclusions from the observations.

Genie drew this figure when she was about 16 years old. She drew the figure of the mother and labeled it, "I miss Mama." She then drew the baby and indicated that it was "Baby Genie."

Naturalistic Observation

One of the goals of psychology discussed in Chapter 1 is to describe behavior. Naturalistic observation is especially appropriate for this goal. As the name implies, **naturalistic observation** involves systematic observing and recording in a natural setting (Shaughnessy & Zechmeister, 1990; Weick, 1985). Researchers often use naturalistic observation as a first step in a research project to identify variables that would be worthwhile studying with one of the other research techniques.

A second function of naturalistic observation is to gather descriptive information about the typical behavior of people or animals. For instance, one hardworking researcher in the late 1800s decided to determine what bees did in their daily lives and whether the complimentary phrase "busy bee" was truly appropriate. He systematically tagged a series of bees and observed them carefully. No single bee ever worked more than 3 1/2 hours a day. Instead the lazy little slouches spent most of their time doing nothing (Hubbell, 1988). An intriguing recent example of naturalistic observation is Jane Goodall's (1990) report of her 30 years of naturalistic observation on chimpanzees in Tanzania, a country in eastern Africa. Goodall's book examines such topics as social interactions, sexual relationships, and power struggles in a small group of chimps that she has observed in detail.

A third function of naturalistic observation is to provide data for use with another technique, such as the experimental method, the quasi-experiment, or the correlational method. For example, Dunn and Shatz (1989) observed young children at home with their mothers and older siblings, for two hours each. They recorded each child's conversations, focusing on the number of times the child intruded upon a remark made to someone else. The researchers than used the correlational method and discovered that the age of a child was positively correlated with the number of intrusions he or she made.

We have noted that naturalistic observation is used in generating research ideas, gathering descriptive information, and providing data for other studies. In all cases, however, a hallmark of this method is that behavior is observed (and not manipulated) in natural settings.

Suppose that you wanted to conduct naturalistic observation in this college classroom. Some behaviors you might choose to explore include where students sit in relation to the front of the classroom, whether people tend to sit near others of their own ethnic group, demographic characteristics of students who ask questions, and how long before the end of the lecture the students begin to pack up their books. Can you think of other possible topics?

Comparing the Methods

Table 2.1 lists the six research methods we have discussed, together with each method's advantages and disadvantages. Clearly, some questions can be more readily answered with one method than with others. However, in the 1990s, psychologists are increasingly likely to favor a multimethod approach, with several studies using different research techniques to examine a psychological issue. Furthermore, as we will see in the in-depth section, a single study can combine several methods.

S E C T I O N   S U M M A R Y

THE MAJOR RESEARCH METHODS

- Critical thinking requires the careful evaluation of evidence and reasoning in a situation; the scientific method involves identifying the research problem, conducting a study, examining the data, and communicating the results.

- In the experimental method, researchers manipulate variables and observe how the participants respond; conditions are carefully controlled, and participants are randomly assigned to conditions.

- Quasi-experiments are used when random assignment is impossible; however, variables can still be manipulated with this method.

- Correlational research establishes whether two variables are related; this method uses neither random assignment nor manipulation of variables. Correlations do not typically allows us to know which variable is the cause and which is the effect, or whether a third variable is responsible for the relationship.

- The survey method is used to collect information about the behaviors and thoughts of a relatively large group of people.

- An in-depth interview requires extensive questioning of participants; a case study also typically includes an interview, observation, and psychological testing.

- In naturalistic observation, the researcher observes people or animals in their natural setting.

- Each research method has its strengths and weaknesses, and many questions can be most effectively answered by combining several research methods.

RESEARCH ISSUES

We have examined six research methods commonly used in psychology, and we noted some problems associated with each one. However, some potential problems are more general; they are not limited to just one of the six methods. In this section, we consider these more general research issues, which include sampling, measuring responses, assessing age differences, and avoiding biases. We also discuss social and ethical aspects of research. This section on research issues concludes with an in-depth discussion of research on physical attractiveness, in which we consider how several different research methods have approached the important topic of personal appearance.

Sampling

When researchers want to test a hypothesis, they must select participants for the study. We seldom have the resources to study an entire population (for instance, all humans living in the Western Hemisphere). Instead, we gather a **sample** by selecting individuals who are representative of the population from which they are drawn. Our goal is to discover something about the population from which the sample was drawn (Kidder & Judd, 1986). For instance, the American Council on Education's

TABLE 2.1 Comparing Psychological Research Methods

METHOD	ADVANTAGES	DISADVANTAGES
Experiment	1. Can control potentially confounding variables. 2. Can draw cause-and-effect conclusions.	1. May be difficult to generalize to real-world settings.
Quasi-experiment	1. Can study behavior in real-world settings. 2. Can draw tentative cause-and-effect conclusions.	1. Cannot control confounding variables as well as in an experiment. 2. Cause-and-effect conclusions are not as firm as with experimental method.
Correlation	1. Can study behavior in real-world settings. 2. Can determine whether two variables are related.	1. Cannot draw cause-and-effect conclusions.
Surveys	1. Can obtain descriptive information about large groups of people. 2. Provides data for use in studies using other methods.	1. Results may be biased because of atypical sample, overly positive answers, and inaccurate recall. 2. Cannot draw cause-and-effect conclusions.
Case study and in-depth interview	1. Provides in-depth information on individuals. 2. Provides ideas for further research.	1. Cannot generalize the results to other individuals. 2. Cannot draw cause-and-effect conclusions.
Naturalistic observation	1. Provides information about people and animals in real-world settings. 2. Provides ideas for further research and data for use in studies using other methods.	1. Cannot draw cause-and-effect conclusions.

study on college students' reasons for attending college (Figure 2.8) examined a sample of 213,630 people, rather than all U.S. college students (Dey et al., 1992).

When you read articles about psychology research, either in psychology journals and textbooks or in the popular media, be sure to note the sample size. You can trust an experiment conducted on 100 people more than an experiment conducted on 8. Furthermore, you can trust the study on reasons for college attendance more than if the sample had been smaller. Sample size is therefore an important criterion in judging a study.

A second important factor relevant to sampling is that the participants should be randomly chosen. In a **random sample,** every member of the population has an equal chance of being selected. When a sample is random, we are more likely to have a **representative sample,** in which the characteristics of the sample are similar to the characteristics of the population. In contrast, in a **biased sample,** some members of the population are more likely to be chosen than others.

The sample must be similar to the population because eventually we want to be able to generalize our findings to the population from which the sample was selected. For example, from the data gathered by the American Council on Education, we want to say something more general about all U.S. college students. Fortunately, the sample in this survey *is* similar to all U.S. college students, so we can generalize the results.

One of the most famous cases of a biased sample—where the sample was not similar to the general population—occurred during the presidential campaign of 1936 (Snodgrass et al., 1985). A magazine called *Literary Digest* conducted a poll, based on more than 2 million responses, and predicted that the Republican candidate Alf Landon would win. Do you remember President Landon? In actuality, Franklin D. Roosevelt won that election, receiving close to two-thirds of the popular vote.

The problem was that the *Digest* had a biased sample, because the sample was selected from telephone directories and lists of *Digest* subscribers. The sample had overrepresented wealthy people, who could afford telephones and magazine subscriptions during the Depression era . . . and who tended to vote Republican. The sample was not representative of the population of Americans who actually cast votes in that election.

Whenever you read about the results of a survey, ask yourself whether some factor might produce a biased sample. For example, whenever a survey depends upon people voluntarily choosing to respond, those more motivated people may constitute a biased sample. For example, in 1992, CBS tried a TV program called "America on the Line," in which viewers were invited to phone about their responses to various survey questions. Whereas 53% of respondents to that program said that they were worse off now than a year ago, only 32% of a carefully chosen, random survey provided that response (Fishkin, 1992). Even the best mail surveys achieve only a 50% to 70% return rate from the general public (Dillman, 1991). Again we need to ask whether people who manage to complete and mail back a survey differ in any relevant characteristics from the general population.

Unbiased samples are important in surveys when we want to assess the views of a large population. However, sampling is also important in other research methods when we want to make general statements about the results. We can only generalize the results to people similar to our sample. For example, the experiment by Pennebaker and his colleagues (1988) was conducted with college students; most were presumably White and middle-class. Perhaps the benefits of remembering a traumatic event cannot be generalized to newly arrived immigrants who barely managed to escape a war in their homeland.

Measuring Responses

Psychologists are typically concerned with hidden mental processes such as memory, anxiety, and attitudes. For each psychological concept they study, psychologists construct an operational definition. An **operational definition** is a precise definition that specifies exactly what operations will be performed and how the concept is to be measured. For example, suppose that researchers studying pain perception want to assess people's tolerance for pain. Their operational definition for pain tolerance might be, "number of seconds that an individual keeps both hands submerged in ice water at 33°F before withdrawing them."

One advantage of operational definitions is that they allow us to understand exactly how a variable was measured. Research can therefore be more objective than if the criteria are ambiguous. For example, Nobel Prize winner Linus Pauling is a longtime advocate of vitamin C as a cold preventer. He was once asked whether it was true that he and his wife (both of whom consume large amounts of vitamin C) no longer suffer from colds. He apparently responded that it was true; they do not get colds at all, just sniffles (Gilovich, 1991). Wouldn't you feel more reassured if you were convinced that the operational definition for "sniffles" was substantially different from the operational definition for a cold?

A second advantage of operational definitions is that they permit other researchers to replicate a study using the same system of measurement. Similarly, if two researchers are examining the same topic and their results differ, the discrepancy can often be traced to a difference in their operational definitions.

Let us consider three representative approaches to measuring responses, in other words, three different classes of operational definitions. These include self-report, behavioral measures, and physiological measures. As you will see, the conclusions that researchers draw from their study often depend on the operational

Suppose that a cafeteria or dining hall on your campus wanted to assess the popularity of this new dessert, which is relatively nutritious and low in fat. What of kind of operational definitions could they use to assess student reactions?

definitions they choose. This point will be illustrated with examples from the research on gender comparisons in empathy. (Empathy involves feeling the same emotion as another person is feeling. Thus, a person who is empathic can hear a friend tell about the death of a favorite relative and experience the same feelings of sadness, loneliness, and loss that the friend experiences.)

Self-Report When researchers use **self-report** to assess psychological processes, they ask participants to report their own thoughts, emotions, behaviors, or intentions. Commonly, self-reports are measured with a rating scale, such as the one shown in Demonstration 2.2. The rating scale allows us to capture a hidden process such as empathy or anger or happiness and represent it with a concrete number. The numbers can then be analyzed statistically, as the last section of this chapter illustrates. In many cases, self-report is the most useful measure of people's subjective experience.

An important drawback to self-reports is that people are likely to give biased answers, reporting that they are much more noble, normal, and nice than they truly are. Psychologists would like the response measure to reflect reality. However, when we try to measure reality, the measurement process often intrudes on people's normal responses, giving us a distorted, rose-colored view of reality.

One kind of bias in self-reports is that people often tend to respond the way they believe they are *supposed* to respond. According to a common stereotype, women are supposed to show empathy, whereas men are supposed to remain cool and objective. The research on empathy indeed shows a substantial gender difference in self-reported empathy. In a review of the research. Eisenberg and Lennon (1983) found that women consistently rated themselves higher than did men on self-report statements such as the one in Demonstration 2.2, "I tend to get emotionally involved in a friend's problems." One semester, I asked students in my introductory psychology class to rate themselves on this item on a slip of paper, indicating their gender but omitting their name. The average man rated himself 4.0, whereas the average woman rated herself 5.0. (The maximum score was 7.0.)

Do these self-reports reflect reality, or are they biased, drifting in the direction of the popular stereotypes about "appropriate" behavior for women and men? Unfortunately, we cannot peel away a person's scalp, look at a little dial on the brain, and discover that the *true* empathy rating (unbiased by stereotypes) is really a 3. However, two other methods for measuring responses may seem more appealing: behavioral and physiological measures.

Behavioral Measures **Behavioral measures** objectively record people's observable behavior. For instance, as we see in the part of Chapter 14 on personality assessment, psychologists who want to measure a person's aggressive tendencies might use naturalistic observation, recording the number of aggressive acts performed in a

---

DEMONSTRATION 2.2 Gender Comparisons

Assemble 10 index cards and one blank envelope, and go to a location with a large number of males and females. (If you live in a coed dorm, you are all set.) Approach five females and five males individually and ask if they have a spare moment. Explain that you are conducting an informal survey. Hand everybody an index card, and ask them to rate themselves on a scale where 1 = "not at all" and 7 = "very much." Then explain that the item you would like them to rate themselves on is "I tend to get emotionally involved in a friend's problems." Everyone should simply supply a number from 1 to 7, and then indicate F for female and M for male. Stress that they should not write their name on the card but should place it face down in the envelope. When you have collected all 10 responses, figure out an average score for females by adding up the scores for the five female respondents and dividing by 5. Repeat the process for the male respondents. Are the two averages substantially different from each other?

specified time. They might argue that these measures would be more objective and less biased than the person's self-report about aggressive tendencies.

Of course, if individuals know they are being observed, their behavior could be just as biased a reflection of reality as any self-report. Furthermore, behavioral measures cannot be used in research on some invisible mental processes. How would you obtain behavioral measures on something entirely invisible and private, such as the content of people's daydreams?

One kind of behavioral measure assesses nonverbal behavior, such as facial expressions. In a study of children's empathy, boys and girls listened to a tape recording of an infant crying. Measuring facial expression, the researchers found no gender differences in empathy (Eisenberg & Lennon, 1983).

Physiological Measures A third option in measuring psychological processes is to obtain **physiological measures,** which are objective recordings of physiological states such as heart rate, breathing rate, perspiration, and brain activity. We will examine some of these physiological measures in Chapter 3 on the biological basis of behavior, in Chapter 5 on sleep patterns, and in Chapter 12 on emotions.

One physiological measure of psychological processes is called the electrodermal response. When you perspire more, your skin changes its electrical conductivity, as registered by this machine.

Physiological measures provide objective numbers that are unlikely to be distorted by the desire to look good. The problem, however, is that the body only has a limited number of ways of responding, and many different emotions can produce the same response. Suppose, for instance, that a man's palms start to sweat (as measured by an index called the electrodermal response). That physiological response could reflect increased excitement, anxiety, or sexual arousal. Which one should we choose? A physiological measure simply tells us we have more sweat—the sweat droplets do not appear with little labels identifying which emotion generated them.

Let us return to the question of gender comparisons in empathy. According to Eisenberg and Lennon (1983), researchers have obtained a variety of physiological measures on people watching an adult being shocked or an infant crying. Physiological measures such as heart rate, pulse, and blood pressure show no gender differences in empathy.

Conclusions About Response Measurement Approaches You have learned that self-reports may be biased, that behavioral measures cannot be gathered for some psychological processes, and that we often cannot interpret the origin of physiological measures. Should psychology researchers just pack up and go home? Obviously not. It is true that no flawless response measure exists, just as no flawless research method exists. However, we can obtain a clearer picture of reality when research on a particular topic is conducted with a variety of response measures. In the case of empathy, for instance, the fact that gender differences appear in self-report—but evaporate when measured behaviorally or physiologically—should make you suspicious. Men and women are probably similar in their empathic reactions, and their self-reports are probably distorted to match the stereotype that women *should* be empathic and men *should* be emotionally uninvolved.

Assessing Age Differences

So far in this section on research issues, we have addressed the problems of sampling and response measurement, which are general concerns in most psychological research. Now consider a more specific problem, one that is critical in the two chapters on developmental psychology: How should we study age differences?

When we investigate how children, adolescents, and adults develop, we often want to compare people of different ages. For instance, a study on the development of children's attitudes toward politics might examine whether the attitudes of 10-year-olds, 12-year-olds, and 14-year-olds differ. The problem with the age variable, however, is that we cannot randomly assign people to different age categories. Most 30-year-olds would object to being transformed into 50-year-olds—even if we had the technology to do so.

Developmental psychologists typically use one of two methods of assessing age differences. In the **longitudinal method,** researchers select one group of individuals who are the same age and then retest them periodically as they grow older. For example, researchers who are interested in political attitudes might select a sample of 10-year-old children and retest this same group when they are 12 and 14 years old. (In other words, they would need at least four years to complete the study.) If you are especially interested in tracking individual differences across time, the longitudinal method is the logical choice (Berk, 1991).

In the longitudinal method, a researcher follows a group of people (all the same age) as they grow older. For example, these students could be tested again two and four years later.

In the second approach, the **cross-sectional method,** researchers test individuals of different ages at the same time. For instance, next Tuesday a researcher might select samples of children who are 10, 12, and 14 years old, questioning them about their political attitudes. The cross-sectional method has an obvious advantage: Researchers can complete a study in a single day, instead of several years.

Each of these two methods has advantages and disadvantages. Because neither method uses random assignment, both can be plagued by confounding variables—though the two methods differ in the kinds of confounding variables that infect them. The problem is that factors other than age can influence the differences among scores. For instance, the longitudinal method can be confounded by time of measurement. Suppose that researchers measured the political attitudes of 10-year-olds living in the United States in 1990 and returned to test these same children in 1992. They might find that the 12-year-olds were much more negative about politics and politicians than they were two years before. Should the researchers propose that children undergo a transformation in their thinking between the ages of 10 and 12? The researchers would be wise to look for alternative hypotheses. For instance, at the first time of measurement, in 1990, fewer members of Congress resigned because of unsavory financial matters than at the second time of measurement, in 1992. Another problem with the longitudinal approach is that some of the research participants may drop out or move away.

The cross-sectional method has a different set of confounding variables. For instance, suppose that researchers would like to determine whether 30-year-olds, 45-year-olds, and 60-year-olds differ in their intellectual functioning. They administer intelligence tests, using three groups of people of the appropriate age. The results indicate a distinct drop in the older groups. Is it all downhill after 30, with intelligence inevitably decreasing? The confounding variable in this case is that each group was born in a different era. The three groups differ in their educational experiences. Many more of the 30-year-olds would have attended college, in comparison to 45- and 60-year-olds. Their higher scores could perhaps be traced to having had greater intellectual stimulation. In fact, cross-sectional research frequently shows a decrease in intellectual performance after age 30. In contrast, longitudinal research, tracing the same group of individuals across time (and therefore controlling for factors such as college attendance) shows little change in intellectual performance up to the age of 60 (Baltes & Kliegl, 1989).

In the best of all worlds, researchers would use methods combining the cross-sectional and longitudinal approaches. In fact, formal techniques have been developed that combine the two approaches (e.g., Baltes, 1973; Berk, 1991; Schaie, 1965). Furthermore, when we can contrast the results of two approaches, we learn more than with either method alone. For instance, in the research on intellectual performance, we learned that lack of education—and not age-related decline—may explain why older people received lower test scores.

Avoiding Gender and Ethnic Biases

Many parts of this chapter discuss biases that can creep into psychological research and distort the results. For example, a biased sample will not provide an accurate picture of the population, and a biased self-report will not provide an accurate picture of an individual's true reactions. Confounding variables, such as amount of education, can lead to a biased picture of age-related changes in intelligence. One of psychology's goals is to discover how psychological processes operate, and these biases can lead us to incorrect conclusions.

Biased studies can be especially harmful when the results are used to discriminate against certain groups of people. For instance, at the beginning of this century, people from certain ethnic groups received low scores on intelligence tests, and these data were used to restrict the immigration of people from these groups. The confounding variable here was familiarity with the English language and American culture.

Biases can operate at any stage of the research process, from the formulation of the hypothesis, to designing and performing the study, to interpreting the data, to communicating the findings (Cannon et al., 1988; Halpern, 1992; Matlin, 1993a). For instance, researchers should avoid studying single-sex samples, unless they have a plausible reason for doing so—such as a study on emotional reactions to one's own pregnancy (Cotton, 1990; Gannon et al., 1992). Also, participants should be carefully selected to avoid confounding variables. If we want to study the mental health of men and women, we should compare men who are employed with women who are employed. Suppose we were to compare employed men with nonemployed women. Then employment status would be an important confounding variable, especially because nonemployed women are more likely than employed women to have psychological problems (McHugh et al., 1986; Warr & Parry, 1982). Any gender difference might therefore be traceable to the confounding variable of employment.

Researchers should also avoid ethnic biases. For example, a study on ethnic differences in child rearing should control for social class, an important potential confounding variable. Research that examines some ethnic groups must address additional problems, such as translating the instructions appropriately, as Marín and Marín (1991) point out in their book, *Research with Hispanic Populations*.

Biases can also enter when the researchers interpret their data and write summaries of their results. One common mistake, for example, is that researchers are likely to report any gender differences their study may have demonstrated. In contrast, if they find no gender differences, they yawn and fail to report this finding; they think gender similarities are boring. You can anticipate the problem that arises: Psychology journals will end up with many published articles noting gender differences, and the gender similarities will be underrepresented (Denmark et al., 1988; Matlin, 1993a).

A second mistake researchers make when they write their research summaries is to magnify group differences. For instance, an author might write, "Although only 35% of Blacks responded that . . ., fully 39% of Whites. . . ." The words "only" and "fully" seem so different that the reader may fail to appreciate that the groups differ by only 4%.

The previous examples on bias have focused on gender and ethnic group. However, researchers should guard against all kinds of biases and assumptions about social class, disability, age, and sexual orientation—as well as gender and ethnicity. Whenever biases favor one group, they may harm another group, limiting the group members' potential for achievement and life satisfaction.

Social Aspects of Research

Whenever people interact, they have the possibility of influencing one another. Chapters 17 and 18 examine these social interactions in some detail. However, we need to remember that psychological research often requires social interactions between the researchers and the participants. During these interactions, researchers may convey certain expectations, and participants may develop certain expectations. Both sets of expectations may influence the outcome of a study, leading the researchers astray in their search for accurate information about psychological processes.

Experimenter Expectations The term **experimenter bias** means that researchers' biases and expectations can influence the results of a study. The major researcher in this area is Robert Rosenthal. He found, for example, that research assistants who expected a group of laboratory rats to be exceptionally bright actually obtained exceptional performance from these animals, compared to assistants who expected their rats to be slow learners. Furthermore, elementary school teachers who expected certain students to be bright actually obtained better performance from these students, relative to other students of similar ability (Rosenthal, 1968, 1973).

Rosenthal's (1976) review of relevant studies showed that experimenter bias operated in about one-third of those studies. In other words, experimenter bias does not always influence people's responses. Still, it operates often enough for us to be concerned that significant results in a study may be due to the researchers' expectations.

Demand characteristics are the clues that the research participants discover about the nature of the study. In this case, an important source of demand characteristics is the piece of equipment being pointed out by the researcher.

Participants' Expectations The participants—as well as the experimenters—develop expectations about what is supposed to happen in a research study. Students who enter a psychology lab to participate in a study often wonder what the study is *really* about. "What is under the box?" "Are we being watched through that funny-looking mirror?" "The professor said it was about memory, but I wonder if it really is. . . . " Humans seldom sit passively, waiting to be studied by psychologists. Instead, they actively consider alternative hunches, searching for clues about the true purpose of the study.

The clues that the participants discover are called the **demand characteristics** (Orne, 1962). Demand characteristics include rumors they hear about the study, the description supplied when they signed up to participate, the activities of the researchers, and the laboratory setting itself. All of these clues are called demand characteristics because the participants believe that these clues *demand* certain responses. For instance, suppose that you have gathered information about a study that suggests the researchers want to see whether people will conform to the opinion of the majority. The clues *demand* that you conform. Now you might decide to cooperate, or you might decide not to—but the point is that you developed certain expectations. These expectations may influence how you respond and may therefore change the nature of the results. People may behave the way they *think* they should behave, instead of behaving naturally. In short, bias can intrude, based on the expectations of either the researchers or the participants.

Ethical Aspects of Research

Psychologists study living creatures. We need to make certain that we do not harm these creatures in the process of learning more about them. In recent decades, the American Psychological Association, the Canadian Psychological Association, and a variety of government agencies have developed ethical principles and regulations that specify how people and animals should be treated in psychological research (American Psychological Association, 1990, 1992; Canadian Psychological Association, 1991; Office for Protection from Research Risks, 1986). Table 2.2 lists some of the ethical principles concerning human participants. In most colleges and Universities where psychological research is conducted, committees must approve research on both humans and animals.

As you can see, ethical treatment begins with the very first contact. For example, the researchers must describe the study carefully (see Item 1); any dangers should be pointed out. Participants also have the right to say "No, thanks" at any point during the study (see Item 2). Let's examine the other three items in more detail and then consider the ethical treatment of animals in psychological research.

Avoiding Potential Harm Any experiment that is likely to cause permanent harm must be avoided. When researchers need to study physical pain in an experiment, they should participate in the experiment themselves before testing any participants.

TABLE 2.2 Some of the APA Ethical Principles for Research with Human Participants

1. The researcher must inform participants about all aspects of the research that are likely to influence their decision to participate in the study, including factors such as risks and discomfort.
2. Participants must have the freedom to say that they do not wish to participate in a research project; they may also withdraw from the research at any time.
3. The researcher must protect the participant from physical and mental discomfort, harm, and danger.
4. If deception is necessary, researchers must determine whether its use is justifiable; participants must be told about any deception after they have completed the study.
5. Information supplied by participants must be kept confidential, and researchers must be sensitive about invading the participants' privacy.

Source: American Psychological Association, 1990, 1992

Researchers must avoid mental harm as well as physical harm. They must keep in mind the important principle of respecting the dignity of other people (Canadian Psychological Association, 1991). Thus, a study that encourages low self-esteem would be ethically questionable. Fortunately, psychologists' current awareness of ethical principles, as well as governmental regulations, make it highly unlikely that you will ever participate in a study involving either physical or mental harm.

Avoiding Unnecessary Deception The relationship between the researcher and the participants should be based on openness and honesty. Whenever possible, the researcher must avoid deception. Unfortunately, this rule was sometimes violated in previous decades. In one of the most serious violations, a researcher recorded information about gay men by passing as gay at private gatherings. He recorded people's license plates and then traced the car owners through the police. Later, he went to the men's homes to interview them (Warwick, 1975). Note that this unethical study violated every one of the current-day principles listed in Table 2.2.

In some studies, however, modest deception may be necessary. If researchers describe precisely what will happen during a study, the demand characteristics will distort the results and make them meaningless. For example, consider a study on perceptual attention in which participants are told to pay attention to the sentences presented via earphone to their right ear. Later, they are tested on these sentences, as well as on other sentences presented to their left (unattended) ear. If they had been told initially that they would be tested on these other sentences, their attention certainly would have shifted, and the results would be useless.

An important part of any psychological research is debriefing. Proper **debriefing** requires telling the participants afterward about the purpose of the study, the nature of the anticipated results, and any deceptions used. The purpose of debriefing is partly educational; if people donate their time to a project, they deserve to learn something from the experience. If deception was used, the debriefing also identifies any false information. Researchers must also be certain that participants' questions have been answered and that all of their concerns have been addressed.

Ensuring Privacy Privacy means that people can decide for themselves whether they want to share their feelings, thoughts, and personal information with others. For example, participants must feel free to say that they do not choose to answer personal questions on a survey. Any personal information should also be kept confidential, rather than being shared with other people. Data must also be gathered anonymously, so that the researchers cannot identify which person supplied which data.

DEMONSTRATION 2.3 Ethical Issues in Psychological Research

Each of the following paragraphs describes a research study that was actually conducted. After reading them, rank all in terms of their compliance with ethical standards discussed in this section. Give a ranking of *1* to the most ethical study and a ranking of *6* to the one you consider least ethical. It should be stressed that the clear majority of psychological research complies with all ethical principles; most cases cited here are unusual ones presented to ethics review committees.

_____ A. A researcher wanted to create a realistic experiment, so he told participants that they were being hired for a semipermanent job. At the end of the day, they were told it was only an experiment. One person had turned down other jobs because of this job.

_____ B. A professor asked her students to do her a favor by staying after class to fill out a brief questionnaire. She added that the task was voluntary, but when one of the students began to leave, she said, "Well, I'm certainly glad the rest of you are willing to help me out."

_____ C. Students are given a list of paired words to memorize. Afterward, their recall is tested. The researcher then announces, "Now we'll go on to something else," and instructs them to solve simple jigsaw puzzles. Fifteen minutes later, the students are again asked to recall the pairs, even

though they had been led to believe they would not be tested further on this material.

_____ D. As part of a study, students completed a "life-goals inventory" and a "graduate school potential test." The researcher then informs some of them that the test results indicated that they are not graduate school material. One student decides to give up her goal of graduate work in English. The researcher later informed them that the purpose of the research was to see whether life goals would be clarified by discouraging or encouraging evaluations.

_____ E. An experimenter gave research participants an insoluble task to perform. He assured them that the task could be solved, intending to make them angry.

_____ F. Students participating in a survey about cheating are told that they should not write their names on the survey so that the results could be kept confidential. However, the questionnaire includes many demographic questions, asking students to supply their gender, major, year, and so forth. After turning in the questionnaire, several students worry that the information may allow them to be identified.

Check page 56 to see how a professional psychologist answered this demonstration.

Sources: American Psychological Association, 1973; Faden et al., 1986; Keith-Spiegel & Koocher, 1985.

We have seen that human subjects should be treated humanely in psychological research, avoiding physical harm, mental harm, unnecessary deception, and invasion of privacy. Try Demonstration 2.3 to discover your own ideas about ethical issues in psychology. Then we turn our attention from human participants to animals.

Ensuring the Ethical Treatment of Animals The ethical standards set by the American Psychological Association (1992), the Canadian Psychological Association (1991), and the Committee on the Use of Animals in Research (1991) all contain information about the high standards of care required for the humane treatment of animals. Federal regulations also specify strict guidelines when research involves surgery, pain, or potential harm.

There are now more than 200 animal rights groups in the United States and Canada (Plous, 1991). Often these activists and those who do research with animals seem to be talking across an abyss, with little success in communicating (Sperling, 1988). Animal rights activists have broken into research laboratories, releasing animals and creating damage that has been estimated to exceed $1 billion (Miller, 1991). Meanwhile, the researchers argue that the activists' claims about harm to animals have been greatly exaggerated (Coile & Miller, 1984; Greenough, 1992).

Research with animals has helped biologists and medical researchers to develop treatment for high blood pressure, diabetes, blood diseases, Parkinson's disease, and acquired immunodeficiency syndrome (AIDS). Psychologists have studied animals to establish the basic principles of learning (Chapter 6). They have also used animals in such research areas as the relationship between stress and disease, the treatment of eating disorders, the relief of pain, and the development of drugs used to treat mental illness (Committee on the Use of Animals in Research, 1991; Greenough, 1991; Miller, 1985). We often hear people say that scientists should try harder to find a cure for AIDS or cancer, or that they should conduct more research on drug addiction (Feeney, 1987). It is not clear how such research should progress without experiments on animals. Should a potentially helpful new cancer treatment be administered to humans without first testing animals?

Obviously, research animals should be well treated, and all unnecessary pain must be avoided. Ultimately, you need to decide for yourself whether you support animal research. You may truly believe that human lives should not have priority over animal lives, and you may conscientiously avoid eating meat or wearing leather products. Or you may agree with most psychologists, who maintain that no animals should suffer needlessly, but that animal research is justified in producing results that may ultimately promote human welfare.

The ethical standards for research on animals specify that all animals should be well treated, avoiding unnecessary pain.

IN DEPTH: Research on Physical Attractiveness

Be honest. Can you truthfully say that when you meet a person for the first time, you pay no attention to physical attractiveness? If your self-report is honest, you will probably admit that personal appearances do affect your judgment. You have probably heard about bias that is based on ethnicity or gender. This "In Depth" section examines another form of discrimination, specifically, bias on the basis of personal appearance (Freedman, 1986).

Numerous studies have demonstrated that physically attractive people are typically judged to have more socially desirable personalities than less attractive people. In other words, people seem to believe that "what is beautiful is good" (Dion, 1986). This effect extends to different ethnic groups and to different age groups. For instance, Black, White, and Mexican-American students think that cute babies from all three ethnic groups are more likely than less attractive babies to be happy, well behaved, and smart (Stephan & Langlois, 1984). This preference for attractive faces even holds true when infants are doing the judging! Langlois and her colleagues (1991) found that 6-month-old infants prefer to look at attractive faces.

In this "In Depth" discussion, we consider several studies that illustrate how different research methods approach a psychological question. We first discuss the experimental method, then a study that combines naturalistic observation and correlational research, and finally an in-depth interview.

Experimental Method Can our first impressions of a person's attractiveness influence that person's future behavior? Mark Snyder, Elizabeth Tanke, and Ellen Berscheid (1977) were interested in this question, but they faced a problem. To eliminate confounding variables, they would have to assign people randomly to either an "attractive" or an "unattractive" condition—ordinarily an impossible task. Let us see how Snyder and his colleagues solved this problem.

Female and male undergraduates at the University of Minnesota volunteered to participate in a study of "the processes by which people become acquainted with each other." They were scheduled in male-female pairs. The pairs were unacquainted and never actually met face to face during the study—they conversed only by telephone. Each member of the pair completed a background questionnaire about academic major, high school attended, and so forth, and the form was given to the conversational partner. In addition, each male student received a snapshot,

People judge that cute babies are more likely than less attractive babies to be happy, well behaved, and smart.

with the explanation that it was a photo of his partner. In reality, however, the photo showed either an attractive or unattractive female student from another college. (Attractiveness was operationally defined as the average rating supplied by 20 other college-age men, using a 10-point rating scale.) This procedure allowed each male-female pair to be randomly assigned to either an "attractive female" or an "unattractive female" condition.

Each pair then conversed for 10 minutes, using microphones and headphones; these conversations were tape-recorded. The dependent variable that most interested the researchers was the nature of the female's interactions. Would the women whose partners thought they were attractive actually start to talk in a more friendly, socially skilled manner?

Each of the tape recordings was rated by a different sample of student judges, who were not told about the perceived physical attractiveness of the women on the tapes. They heard only the tapes of the women's voices, and they judged each woman on the basis of adjectives such as friendliness and warmth, as well as questions such as "How much is she enjoying herself?" These student judges rated the conversations of the presumably attractive women as being more poised, sexually warm, and outgoing. As the authors point out, "What had initially been reality in the minds of the men had now become reality in the behavior of the women with whom they had interacted . . ." (p. 661). The independent variable (perceived attractiveness of a conversational partner) did indeed have a significant influence on the dependent variable (conversational behavior of the partner). To some extent, we become what people expect us to be.

Combining Naturalistic Observation and Correlational Research The experiment by Snyder and his colleagues demonstrated the importance of attractiveness, using an experiment in the laboratory. But what happens in real life? Are people really treated differently if they are attractive?

Research by Gregory Smith (1985) combines naturalistic observation with correlational methods to provide some interesting answers with young children. Smith studied middle-class White preschoolers between the ages of 2 years, 9 months, and 5 years, 7 months. Using naturalistic observation, he recorded the behavior of each child in the preschool classroom for a five-minute session on five separate days. In particular, he recorded how other children treated this child. Were the other children prosocial—helping, patting, and praising the target child? Were these other children physically aggressive—hitting, pushing, or kicking this child?

The next step was to establish whether these naturalistic observations about behavior toward a child were correlated with that child's attractiveness. As an operational definition of attractiveness, Smith asked college students to rate each child, based on a photograph of the child's face.

Interestingly, attractiveness was correlated with the way little girls were treated, but not little boys. Specifically, the more attractive little girls tended to receive more prosocial treatment; the correlation was +.73. Furthermore, the more attractive little girls also tended to receive less physical aggression; the correlation was −.41. In other words, cute little girls get helped more and they are hit less. How about the little boys? For them, physical attractiveness was not related to either prosocial behavior ($r = +.05$) or physical aggression ($r = +.03$). Smith's study is especially interesting because it illustrates one positive correlation, one negative correlation, and two zero correlations. Figure 2.9 shows Smith's actual data for these four correlations. Notice that attractiveness matters more for little girls than for little boys, consistent with the greater emphasis on attractiveness for females of all ages (Freedman, 1986; Leinbach & Fagot, 1991; Wolf, 1991).

In the discussion of the correlational method earlier in the chapter, we emphasized that we cannot typically identify the cause and the effect in a correlation. In the case of attractiveness and prosocial behavior toward little girls, for instance, the major part of the correlation can probably be traced to the fact that a pretty face elicits pleasant behavior from other people (A → B). However, another factor may also contribute to the correlation; pleasant behavior produces smiles and self-confidence in a little girl, and so she looks especially attractive in a photograph (A ← B).

In-Depth Interviews So far, beauty seems to bring benefits, at least to females. However, the interview approach suggests that the relationship is more complex. For instance,

According to the research by Snyder, Tanke, and Berscheid (1977), if this young man believes that his conversational partner is an attractive woman, she may actually start to talk in a more socially skilled and friendly manner.

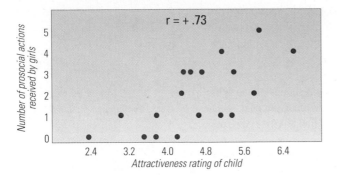

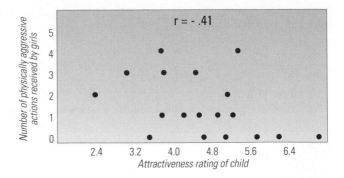

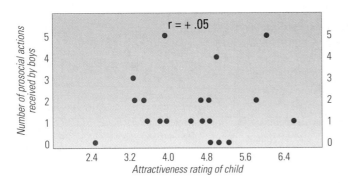

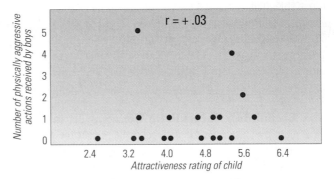

Hatfield and Sprecher (1986) interviewed several people who pointed out how good looks can backfire. Here is a short excerpt from one professional woman they interviewed:

> Here's something that happened to me recently: I was elected to be on an important state committee—a 30-member committee, all men. But I was nominated in a devastating way. An important committee member stood up and announced in front of everyone, "We have to have Audry on the committee—she's the prettiest thing here." I was stunned! Shocked! I couldn't say anything. I wasn't prepared for such a statement. . . . We were all there because we had professional credentials. After getting over my initial astonishment, my reaction was to get very, very angry. (pp. 66–67)

Conclusions About Attractiveness From the experiment by Snyder and his colleagues (1977), we learned how looks can influence how people behave—when confounding variables have been removed. Smith's (1985) study, which combined naturalistic observation with correlational research, showed how attractiveness is related to the way children are treated in a real-life situation. Finally, in-depth interviews help complete the picture, illustrating that good looks may sometimes distract other people from an individual's professional competence.

Alice Eagly and her colleagues (1991) have reviewed 76 different studies that focus on adolescents' and adults' reactions to attractiveness. As we might suspect, their analysis shows that the findings are complex, because attractiveness has different effects on different dependent variables. In general, people believe that attractive people are much more sociable and popular than less attractive people. The effect is weaker when people make judgments about adjustment and intelligence, and the effect is weaker still for judgments about personal integrity and concern for others. But physical attractiveness has a darker side as well; people believe that attractive people are more likely to be vain. In short, the nature of the relationship between physical attractiveness and personal characteristics depends upon our operational definition of those personal characteristics.

Figure 2.9

Smith's (1985) attractiveness study.

(upper left) The relationship between attractiveness and prosocial treatment for girls.

(upper right) The relationship between attractiveness and physically aggressive treatment for girls.

(lower left) The relationship between attractiveness and prosocial treatment for boys.

(lower right) The relationship between attractiveness and physically aggressive treatment for boys.

RESEARCH ISSUES

- A sample should be sufficiently large and also unbiased.

- An operational definition specifies exactly how a psychological concept is to be measured; the operational definition of participants' responses can be assessed by self-report, behavioral measures, and physiological measures.

- Age differences are typically assessed by either the cross-sectional or the longitudinal methods.

- Researchers must guard against gender, ethnic, and other biases at every step in the research process.

- Two social factors, experimenter expectations and participants' expectations, can distort research results.

- Important ethical considerations include recruiting participants honestly, avoiding potential harm and unnecessary deception, ensuring privacy, and treating animals properly.

- A research issue, such as physical attractiveness, is best investigated by combining several different research approaches.

ANALYZING THE DATA

After psychologists have gathered the data, they must summarize and interpret it. For example, suppose that you tried Demonstration 2.2, asking five women and five men to rate themselves using numbers between 1 and 7 on the statement "I tend to get emotionally involved in a friend's problems." Let's say that the ratings you gathered are the data shown in Table 2.3. Researchers who want to convey their findings to other psychologists would find it awkward to write, "The five women gave ratings of 4, 5, 5, 5, and 6, whereas the five men gave ratings of 2, 4, 4, 4, and 6." And the situation becomes preposterous if you tested dozens of people, rather than just 10.

Researchers have developed standardized, efficient methods for describing their data that avoid listing every individual person's score. They have also developed

---

TABLE 2.3 Calculating the Mean, Median, and Mode

Imagine that you tried Demonstration 2.2 and gathered the following data on men's and women's empathy:

Women: 4 5 5 5 6
Men: 2 4 4 4 6

1. Calculate the **mean** for each group:

$$\text{For the women} = \frac{4 + 5 + 5 + 5 + 6}{5} = \frac{25}{5} = 5.0$$

$$\text{For the men} = \frac{2 + 4 + 4 + 4 + 6}{5} = \frac{20}{5} = 4.0$$

2. Calculate the **median** for each group:

For the women = 4 5 ⑤ 5 6   5 is the score in the middle
For the men   = 2 4 ④ 4 6   4 is the score in the middle

3. Calculate the **mode** for each group:

For the women = 4 ⟨5 5 5⟩ 6   5 is the most frequent score
For the men   = 2 ⟨4 4 4⟩ 6   4 is the most frequent score

standardized methods for drawing conclusions about their data. These methods allow them to determine whether the differences between groups or the relationships between variables are significant. Let us first discuss how researchers describe data and then consider how they draw conclusions. Appendix A provides more detailed information about statistics, with an emphasis on statistical formulas and calculations.

Descriptive Statistics: Summarizing the Data

In any group of data, two of the most important features you would like to know are some measure of central tendency ("What is the typical score?") and a measure of variability ("Are the other scores clustered closely around the typical score, or are they more spread out?") These **descriptive statistics** allow us to summarize data in a brief, useful form that other researchers can easily interpret.

Central Tendency When we summarize the data, we need some measure of **central tendency,** or a measure of the most typical, characteristic score. For instance, with the men's scores in Table 2.3, what is the number that best captures their ratings? (The name *central tendency* makes sense if you realize that all the numbers have a *tendency* to cluster toward some *central* number.) We have three ways of measuring central tendency.

1. The **mean** is the simple average of all scores, obtained by adding all the scores together and dividing by the number of scores. For the women, we perform this calculation:

$$\frac{4+5+5+5+6}{5} \quad \longleftarrow \quad \textbf{\textit{Add together all scores}}$$
$$\longleftarrow \quad \textbf{\textit{Divide by 5 (the number of scores)}}$$

The mean for the women is 5.0, whereas a similar calculation for the men yields a mean of 4.0. The mean is usually the most valuable measure of central tendency, because it is used when we want to draw conclusions about the data (as shown in the discussion of inferential statistics and in Appendix A).

2. The **median** is the score that falls precisely in the middle of a distribution of scores. (The word *median* sounds like *middle*.) To calculate a median, arrange the scores in order from lowest to highest and identify the score in the middle, with half the scores below and half the scores above. For the data in Table 2.3, the median for the women is 5, and the median for the men is 4.

The median is an especially useful measure of central tendency when a small number of scores lie extremely far from the mean. For example, suppose that a psychology department collects data on the first-year salaries of students who have graduated from their bachelor's program, as shown in Table 2.4. Notice that the median income, $20,000, is close to the majority of scores. In contrast, the mean income is $28,833. The single high score, $100,000, produces an enormous distortion in the mean, but not in the median.

3. The **mode** is the score that occurs most often in a group of scores. The mode can be established by simply inspecting the data and noting which number appears most frequently. For the data in Table 2.3, the mode is 5 for the women and 4 for the men. (Incidentally, in Table 2.3, the mean, median, and mode are all the same within each distribution, an unusual occurrence in most studies. In Table 2.4, you can see that they are different.)

Variability Once we know a measure of central tendency such as the mean, we have some feeling for the data. However, these central-tendency measures can only tell us where the center of the data lies—not the extent to which the scores are spread out. Measures of **variability** give us a feeling for the extent to which the scores differ from one another.

TABLE 2.4 The Median Is Sometimes a More Representative Measure of Central Tendency Than Is the Mean

Annual income of 9 graduates of a hypothetical psychology bachelor's program:

$16,500 $17,000 $19,000 $20,000 $20,000 $21,000 $22,000 $24,000 $100,000

Mean income for the graduates = $28,833. (Note that the mean is greatly increased by the one extremely high income.)

Median income for the graduates = $20,000. (Note that the median is not greatly increased by the one extremely high income; the median is therefore an effective measure of central tendency for this distribution.)

An example can illustrate why we need information about variability—as well as central tendency—to convey an adequate statistical picture of the data. Suppose that Dr. Ted Schwartz teaches introductory psychology at two different colleges. Class A and Class B each have 40 students. He grades the first examination and calculates that the mean number of items correct is 35 (out of 50) for each of the two classes. In addition, he calculates that the median for each class is also 35, and the mode is 35 as well. For each class he constructs a **histogram,** a graph in which the data are arranged so that they show the frequency of each score (Figure 2.10).

The three measures of central tendency are identical for the two classes. However, you can see from the histograms that Class A shows great variability, with the scores widely scattered. In contrast, the scores in Class B are clustered close to the mean. Dr. Schwartz could make good use of this information about the variability of test scores. With Class A, he may need to give extra help to people with low scores, and he might contemplate special enrichment material for the outstanding students. In contrast, with Class B, he knows that if he aims the lectures at the average students, the level will be appropriate for everyone, because of the low variability.

Let us consider two ways of measuring variability.

1. The **range** is the difference between the highest and the lowest scores. Class A's scores are spread between 23 and 47, so the range is 24 (that is, 47 minus 23). Class B's scores, in contrast, have a range of only 8 (39 minus 31). The range gives us a very quick estimate of variability in the scores.

2. The **standard deviation** is the more commonly used measure, and it is based on how far each score deviates from the mean. Psychologists use the standard deviation when they want to draw conclusions about their data, for instance, to see whether they have an important difference between two groups. It takes much longer to calculate the standard deviation than to calculate the range. (The formula is shown in Appendix A.) However, the standard deviation gives a much more complete picture of the variability than does the range, because the standard deviation takes into account the specific value of *every* number in the distribution, not just the highest and the lowest. A calculation for the two distributions in Figure 2.10 lists the standard deviation as 5.7 for Class A, but only 2.2 for Class B. As you might imagine, larger standard deviations indicate greater variability.

Figure 2.10

Examples of variability.

(left) The histogram for Class A (hypothetical data).

(right) The histogram for Class B (hypothetical data).

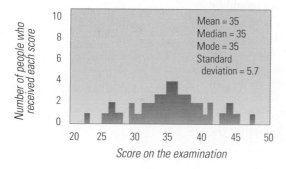

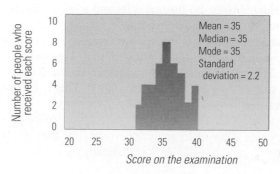

Inferential Statistics: Drawing Conclusions About the Data

So far, we have only discussed descriptive statistics, which describe a distribution's central tendency and variability. When psychologists conduct experiments, quasi-experiments, and correlational research, they want to draw conclusions. They use **inferential statistics** to draw these conclusions about their data. In everyday language, an inference is a conclusion based on evidence. For instance, from a toddler's tear-stained face, you might make the inference that the child had been crying. Our everyday inferences are very casual. In contrast, inferential statistics provide a formal procedure for using data to test for **statistical significance,** that is, whether the findings are likely to be due to chance alone, or whether the differences are major—that is, greater than expected by chance. Three important issues in inferential statistics include how inferential statistics can help us draw conclusions about two groups, statistical versus practical significance, and meta-analysis.

Drawing Conclusions About Two Groups with Inferential Statistics

Let us return to the example of men's and women's self-ratings on the statement, "I tend to get emotionally involved in a friend's problems." One semester, I asked students in my class to rate themselves on that statement, using a 7-point scale. The 41 men in the class supplied a mean rating of 4.05, whereas the 100 women supplied a mean rating of 5.03. Inferential statistics allowed me to decide if the difference between those two means—roughly 1 point on the rating scale—was statistically significant.

A single point on a rating scale might not seem to merit a statistical analysis. However, when comparing two groups statistically, we need to consider three factors:

1. the size of the difference between the two means (a large difference is more likely to produce a statistically significant difference);

2. the size of the standard deviations (small standard deviations are more likely to produce a statistically significant difference);

3. the number of people tested (large numbers are more likely to produce a statistically significant difference).

In the case of this comparison, the standard deviations were fairly small and the number of people tested was fairly large, so that a 1-point difference might indeed be important.

An analysis that uses inferential statistics tells us how likely it is that the results we obtained could have occurred by chance alone. Suppose, for instance, that the analysis told us that a difference of 1 point or larger would be likely to occur by chance about 50% of the time, that is, with a probability *(p)* of .50. We would respond with a yawn—that difference is certainly not worth any excitement. However, if a difference of that size occurred by chance only 10% of the time ($p = .10$), we might become somewhat more excited . . . but would we have reason to become *very* excited? By tradition, psychologists have agreed that they are willing to say that a finding is statistically significant if it is likely to occur by chance alone less than 5% of the time, which is symbolized as $p < .05$. In other words, this is the formal boundary between what are considered to be ho-hum results and a major difference that we would be likely to duplicate if we repeated the study.

In the case of men's and women's responses to the question about emotional involvement, a statistical analysis showed that a 1-point difference between the groups (with 141 participants and the specified standard deviations) would be likely to occur less than 1 time in 10,000 ($p < .0001$). This is far less than .05, so we can conclude that the difference is statistically significant.

Statistical analyses allow us to compare two or more groups, to see if they are different. They also allow us to analyze correlational data, to determine whether the relationship between two variables is statistically significant.

Statistical Versus Practical Significance Statistical significance means that the data were tested with a standard statistical test, and they met the established criterion for significance. In contrast, **practical significance** means that the results have some important, practical implications for the real world. A study may therefore demonstrate statistical significance but not practical significance. For instance, in one study examining gender differences in mathematics performance, 440,000 high-school students were tested. The results demonstrated a statistically significant gender difference, with male students performing better. However, an inspection of the means for the test scores indicated that the difference was $\frac{6}{10}$ of 1 point. It is hard to imagine how roughly half a point difference could have practical significance, that is, any important implications for the way people should treat male and female students in the real world (Fox et al., 1979).

Meta-Analysis Let us consider one final issue in inferential statistics. Suppose that several clinical psychologists are interested in the treatment of phobias, which are intense, irrational fears of particular objects (e.g., snakes). They have systematically examined all the articles published in psychology journals to determine whether Therapy A or Therapy B is most effective in treating phobias. In all, nine studies favor Therapy A, four favor Therapy B, and three show no difference. What should the researchers conclude? If they simply tally the outcomes, Therapy A seems preferable, but not consistently so.

A new technique called meta-analysis has revolutionized the way in which psychologists draw conclusions when the previously published psychology articles show conflicting results (Green & Hall, 1984). **Meta-analysis** is a systematic statistical method for synthesizing the results from numerous studies on a given topic (Hyde, 1986). This method statistically combines the results from all these studies, yielding a single number that tells us whether a particular factor has an overall effect on behavior. For example, in Eagly and her coauthors' (1991) review of the research on attractiveness, they conducted a meta-analysis on the studies. In 69 of the 76 studies, the more attractive people received higher ratings on personality characteristics than did the less attractive people. The meta-analysis yielded a measure called the effect size *(d)* which was 0.61. By customary standards, this effect size is considered to be in the moderate to large range. In short, the meta-analysis demonstrated that people do

On the standardized mathematics test these students are taking, the males may receive an average score that is less than a point higher than the average score for the females, indicating statistical significance. However, those results would have no practical significance for the way the teacher instructs males and females in the classroom.

associate physical attractiveness with favorable personality characteristics. Meta-analysis will be mentioned many times throughout this book, for example, in the discussion of intellectual abilities, psychological therapy, and social psychology.

Data analysis is important in all sciences. It is particularly critical in psychology because most psychological research yields numbers. Because humans vary so much from one another and because behavior is so complex, a casual inspection of these data seldom allows us to draw a clear-cut conclusion. Instead, psychologists must calculate descriptive statistics, which portray the data's central tendency and variability, and inferential statistics, which provide a systematic method for drawing conclusions about statistical significance.

SECTION SUMMARY
ANALYZING THE DATA

- The central tendency can be measured by the mean, median, and mode.
- The variability can be measured by the range and the standard deviation.
- Inferential statistics specify a formal procedure to be used in testing statistical significance and drawing conclusions; a study may show statistical significance without having substantial practical significance; meta-analysis is a technique that allows us to draw conclusions about a large number of individual studies.

REVIEW QUESTIONS

1. Name and briefly describe each of the six major research methods, listing their advantages and disadvantages. Then, concentrating on the topic of eating and body weight, describe an example of a study that could be conducted using each of the six methods.

2. Suppose that you are interested in the factors that influence college students' performance on examinations, and—with their consent—you would like to collect data on your classmates' performance on their first examination in introductory psychology; these scores therefore provide one variable for your study. Describe how you could use the experimental, the quasi-experimental, and the correlational methods to conduct three different studies on this topic.

3. Suppose that you are interested in the topic of abused children. Describe how you could use the correlational, survey, case study, and naturalistic observation methods to conduct four different studies on this topic.

4. Dr. Mayra Lopez is a clinical psychologist who would like to test a new method of helping clients overcome snake phobia. How might she assess the dependent variable—that is, people's responses to snakes both before and after therapy—using each of the three methods of measuring responses discussed in the second section of the chapter?

5. What does the phrase "correlation is not necessarily causation" mean? Suppose that you gather data on sixth-graders in gym class, and you discover that there is a positive correlation between the number of positive remarks the gym teacher makes to each child and the athletic performance of the child. What three explanations could you provide for this correlation? If you wanted to establish more firmly whether one of these explanations is true—that praise enhances athletic performance—how would you conduct this study?

6. Imagine that a new magazine is being published, aimed exclusively at college students and costing $5.00 an issue. In an early issue, they include a survey, inviting readers to respond. The survey concerns college students' attitudes toward scholarships, part-time work, and spare-time activities. How might the sample of students who respond be biased, and why should any summary of the study be cautious about its generalizations?

7. Dr. Ralph Bradburn is an applied psychologist who has been hired to determine attitudes toward the automatic-teller service at a large bank. The bank's executives speculate that as people grow older, they grow more skeptical about using machines, such as the automatic-teller service. Dr. Bradburn decides to assess attitudes toward machines, using a cross-sectional approach and asking for volunteers from various age groups. Describe at least two problems with this study.

8. Analyze the experiment on attractiveness by Snyder and his colleagues from the standpoint of social aspects of the experiment, specifically experimenter bias and demand characteristics.

9. In one of the most frequently quoted studies in psychology, local citizens volunteered for a "learning" experiment, in which they were told to shock another person, the "learner," whenever he made a mistake. This person actually received no shock, but pretaped screams from the other room conveyed the impression that he was being hurt. When the volunteers said they wanted to discontinue the study, they were told that they must continue (Milgram, 1963, 1965). What criticisms could you offer about ethical aspects of this study if it were to be proposed in the 1990s?

10. Psychologists try to discover accurate factual information about psychological processes. Name as many factors and biases as you can recall from this chapter that would interfere with the discovery of accurate results.

N E W   T E R M S

critical thinking	representative sample
scientific method	biased sample
experiment	operational definition
hypothesis	self-report
independent variable	behavioral measures
dependent variable	physiological measures
control condition	longitudinal method
experimental condition	cross-sectional method
confounding variable	experimenter bias
random assignment	demand characteristics
well-controlled study	debriefing
quasi-experiment	descriptive statistics
correlational research	central tendency
correlation coefficient	mean
positive correlation	median
zero correlation	mode
negative correlation	variability
survey method	histogram
demographic information	range
in-depth interview	standard deviation
case study	inferential statistics
naturalistic observation	statistical significance
sample	practical significance
random sample	meta-analysis

A N S W E R S   T O   D E M O N S T R A T I O N S

DEMONSTRATION 2.1 4. The independent variable is caffeine consumption (caffeine present versus caffeine absent), and the dependent variable is the amount of time taken to fall asleep; 5. the independent variable is the presence or absence of another person in the room, and the dependent variable is the amount of time taken to respond to an emergency; 6. the independent variable is the presence or absence of praise; the dependent variable is whether or not the person provides help in a specified situation.

DEMONSTRATION 2.3 Dr. Patricia Keith-Spiegel, an expert in psychological ethics, was invited to provide her assessment of the ethics of these six episodes. She responded,

> *Although I would want more information about each of these studies before making definitive ratings, I have ranked the studies on the basis of their potential for harms and wrongs as a consequence of participation. Studies C (rated first, or least objectionable) and E (rated third) may create momentary upsets among some participants, assuming that they will be "debriefed" promptly after the experimental trial. Study E is the more unsettling of the two because the attempt to elicit an uncomfortable emotion was purposeful and willful. Neither study appears, on the basis of the information given, to be a particularly significant piece of work, nor do we know if any attempt was made to study the phenomenon of interest in a way that did not involve deception. Two of the conditions that should pertain in order to justify the use of deception techniques are (1) the research should hold out the prospect for important findings, and (2) all other alternatives to deception should be carefully considered and ruled out as unfeasible.*
>
> *Study F (rated second) is judged as only somewhat objectionable as opposed to a serious violation of the participant's rights to confidentiality. (I am assuming that the researchers were simply insensitive to the possibility that participants might fret because of the delicate subject of the survey and that the researchers have no intention of identifying anyone.)*
>
> *Study B (rated fourth) illustrates the ethical infraction of coercion; that is, a professor places students over which she holds some power (i.e., the assignment of a grade) in a position where full voluntary consent is not possible. This concern is proven out when she ridicules a student for exercising the right to refuse participation.*
>
> *Studies A (rated fifth) and D (rated sixth) are of greatest concern because the potential for wrong and harm to participants is high. Study A illustrates a harm that actually materialized. The more typical participant in Study A probably lost a day of life that might have been spent in more meaningful and productive ways otherwise and endured some degree of disappointment. Study D is rated as the most reprehensible because trusting students, most of whom are struggling with their decisions about their futures and feeling vulnerable about them, are given bogus feedback that could deflate their self-confidence. Had the researchers "debriefed" within an hour after inflicting the deception, little harm would probably have been done (although one always wonders what happens to the trust of deceived participants toward psychologists!). The most unsettling element of Study D is that considerable time was purposely allowed to pass before the researchers "came clean" with the students. The students had the time to fret, to possibly begin to doubt themselves, to become confused. Here is also an instance where debriefing the participants does not necessarily "disabuse" them. That is, even when the students learn that it was all "just research," that does not necessarily restore them to their former senses of self. (Keith-Spiegel, 1990)*

In summary, Dr. Keith-Spiegel's rankings (where 1=most ethical) are as follows: A. 5; B. 4; C. 1; D. 6; E. 3; and F. 2.

RECOMMENDED READINGS

American Psychological Association. (1982). *Ethical principles in the conduct of research with human participants*. Washington, DC: Author. This handbook outlines the important ethical issues in research with humans, providing examples of unethical studies.

Canadian Psychological Association. (1992). *Companion manual to the Canadian Code of Ethics for Psychologists, 1991*. Chelsea, Quebec: Author. This recent publication provides interesting examples of ethically questionable research.

Christensen, L. B. (1991). *Experimental methodology* (5th ed.). Boston: Allyn & Bacon. Christensen's clearly written textbook emphasizes the experimental method, so it concentrates on important issues such as controlling variables and designing experiments. However, it also includes chapters on topics such as quasi-experimental methods, ethics, and writing research reports.

Eagly, A. H., Ashmore, R. D., Makhijani, M. G., & Longo, L. C. (1991). What is beautiful is good, but . . . : A meta-analytic review of research on the physical attractiveness stereotype. *Psychological Bulletin, 110,* 109–128. This article provides a superb review of the research concerned with this chapter's "In Depth" topic. It also shows you an excellent application of the meta-analysis technique, discussed at the end of the chapter.

Gilovich, T. (1991). *How we know what isn't so: The fallibility of human reason in everyday life*. New York: Free Press. Gilovich's book is a wonderful introduction to critical thinking; it examines how we reach inappropriate conclusions based on informal, unscientific observations.

Shaughnessy, J. J., & Zechmeister, E. B. (1990). *Research methods in psychology* (2nd ed.). New York: McGraw-Hill. Here is another well-written methodology textbook. Compared to Christensen's book, this one places more emphasis on naturalistic observation, surveys, and case studies.

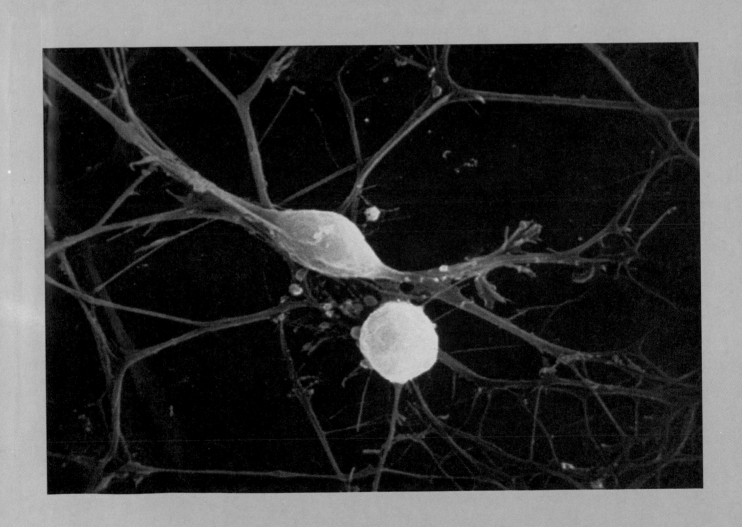

CHAPTER 3
THE BIOLOGICAL BASIS OF BEHAVIOR

I magine that you are an inventor, assigned the task of creating a human brain. This brain must control some very basic body functions, such as breathing and circulation. It must also control human movements, both simple ones like walking and the more astonishing leaps of basketball players and Olympic ice skaters. The brain you design must be able to perceive the odor of a skunk as well as the intricacies of a symphony. It must be able to learn the simplest response and to remember the details of an event from decades earlier. This brain must also account for human passions, from noble ones like love and helpfulness, to lamentable ones like hatred and prejudice. Furthermore, this invention must fit inside the human skull as neatly as your own brain does.

In this chapter, we will examine the human brain and the rest of the nervous system, providing even more testimony about the remarkable capabilities of these structures. This chapter will illustrate three important principles, which are related to the themes of human competence and human complexity:

1. The structure of the brain is impressively complex, as we would expect of any organ that must accomplish so many tasks.

2. Most psychologically interesting activities (even ones as simple as moving your eyes when you read this sentence) require the cooperation of many different regions of the brain.

3. Different regions of the nervous system have different, specialized functions (Broca, 1861; Churchland & Sejnowski, 1992). For example, cells in a region toward the back of your brain respond only to simple lines, whereas cells located on the top of your brain direct the movement of your left thumb.

We'll begin this chapter by examining the general organization of the nervous system, as well as the techniques that researchers use to investigate the nervous system. The second section looks more carefully at the human brain, discussing both the normal brain and brain disorders. The chapter concludes with a summary of genetics; we will see that 23 microscopic chromosome pairs carry the complete genetic formula for producing a new human being.

INTRODUCTION TO THE NERVOUS SYSTEM

The Neuron

The **neuron** is a specialized cell that processes, stores, and transmits information throughout your body. No one really knows how many neurons the human body contains. However, one well-educated guess is about 100 billion, that is, 100,000,000,000 neurons (Hubel, 1979; Soper & Rosenthal, 1988; Thompson, 1985). We should emphasize that even this basic unit in the nervous system is impressively complex, and this chapter can provide only a brief overview of the topic.

Neuron Structure Neurons come in many sizes and shapes, depending on their function in the nervous system. Figure 3.1 shows one representative neuron, drawn schematically to show the important parts: the dendrites, cell body, and axon. Figure 3.2 is a photograph of actual neurons, greatly magnified so that you can appreciate their structure. Let us discuss some of the features of a typical neuron.

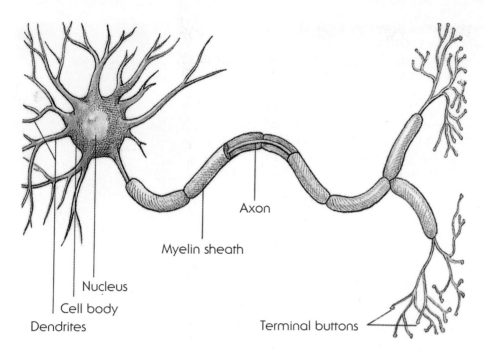

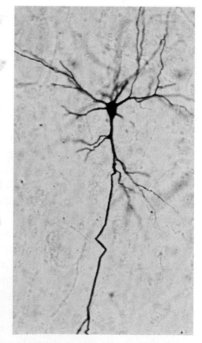

Figure 3.1

A schematic drawing of a representative neuron.

The **dendrites** of neurons are slender, branched fibers that carry impulses in the direction of the cell body in a neuron. The name *dendrite* comes from the Greek word for tree, and if you use your imagination, you can indeed see a tree-like structure in the dendrites. The greater the area of the dendrites, the more information they can receive from other neurons (Kalat, 1992).

The prominent central structure in Figure 3.1 is the **cell body,** the area of the neuron that contains the cell nucleus, as well as other structures that help the cell function properly. However, keep in mind that Figures 3.1 and 3.2 show greatly enlarged neurons. Even though the cell body looks relatively large in these illustrations, the cell bodies found in mammals are usually less than 0.1 mm in diameter, barely visible to the human eye (Kalat, 1992).

Finally, notice the long fiber in the middle of Figure 3.1, called the *axon.* The **axon** carries information away from the cell body, toward other neurons. Some axons are so short that they are not visible to the unaided eye; others are so long that they reach from the spinal cord to the toes. (You can remember that the neural impulses travel through the structures in the neuron in reverse alphabetical order: dendrite, cell body, axon.)

Neuron Function The neuron is not a simple biological device that passively relays signals (Trehub, 1992). Instead, it is part of an electrochemical system in which chemical substances and electrical signals interact in a complex fashion. Specifically, an inactive neuron has many negatively charged atoms and molecules inside its cell membrane. When the dendrite is stimulated, the cell membrane opens up its miniature passageways. The positively charged atoms and molecules rush inward. As a result, the neuron's charge becomes less negative (depolarized) for an instant. That depolarization spreads down the dendrite and into the cell body.

The neuron is somewhat finicky. If a neuron receives an electrical signal that is too weak, it will not pass on the message to a nearby neuron. A structure within the cell body combines all these weak signals. If there is enough of an excitatory signal to reach a certain threshold, then the axon membrane depolarizes. This brief change in an axon's electrical charge is called an **action potential.** This electrical signal then travels rapidly down to the far end of the axon, at a rate of about 100 meters per second.

Action potentials obey an all-or-none law. If the total input from all signals reaches the specified threshold, an action potential occurs, and the impulse is transmitted. If the total input falls short, no action potential occurs. In other words, the

Figure 3.2

A photograph of a neuron from a cat's cerebral cortex (greatly magnified).

nervous system does not allow any partial action potentials. Impressively, under ideal conditions a neuron can produce as many as 1,000 action potentials per second.

A feature that aids the transmission of neural messages is that the larger axons in the nervous system are coated with an insulating material called the **myelin sheath,** which is part fat and part protein. The myelin sheath helps the action potential travel faster along the axon. It also helps insulate the axon from other nearby axons. Without the myelin sheath, the messages in neighboring axons might become scrambled with each other. Obviously, a sophisticated message system must avoid scrambled communications. As you may know, **multiple sclerosis (MS)** is a disease that destroys the myelin sheath, causing numbness, weakness, visual disturbances, and motor problems.

All the fine qualities of the neuron would be wasted if there was no way for neurons to communicate with one another. Clearly, neurons must connect to other neurons. The location at which the axon of one neuron connects with the dendrite of a neighboring neuron is called the **synapse.** Turn back to Figure 3.1 and notice the knobs located at the far end of the axon; these knobs are called **terminal buttons.** Figure 3.3 shows a highly magnified view of several of these terminal buttons.

Early researchers thought that the terminal buttons from one axon rested directly on the dendrite of the adjoining axon. However, with more refined microscopic investigation of the synapse, researchers discovered that a narrow space separates the two adjacent neurons. The two neurons do not actually touch.

How does the electrical message from one neuron leap across the synapse to reach the neighboring neuron, that is, the postsynaptic neuron? Figure 3.4 shows a schematic diagram of one of the approximately 10 trillion synapses in the brain. As you can see, the electrical signal is conducted down the axon to the terminal button. The arrival of this electrical signal triggers the release of **neurotransmitters,** which are chemical substances stored in many tiny vesicles (containers) in the terminal buttons. Each vesicle dumps its entire contents into the synapse, and these chemicals spread across the channel to the postsynaptic neurons (Agnati et al., 1992). Let us examine these neurotransmitters and other chemical messengers in more detail.

Chemical Message Systems

We have seen that the neuron can transmit information from its cell body down its axon both quickly and efficiently; this information causes the release of neurotransmitters from the axon's ending. Your body releases not only neurotransmitters, but also two other chemical messengers, which are called neuromodulators and hormones.

Neurotransmitters As we discussed, the vesicles release neurotransmitters. Depending on both the nature of the neurotransmitter and the kind of receptor, the postsynaptic neuron can be either excited or inhibited. In an **excitatory potential,** the vesicles release a neurotransmitter that excites the postsynaptic neuron. As a consequence, that postsynaptic neuron is more likely to produce an action potential. In contrast, in an **inhibitory potential,** the vesicles release a neurotransmitter that inhibits the postsynaptic neuron. As a result, this second neuron is less likely to produce an action potential.

Any given neuron can have many excitatory and inhibitory synapses on it. The rate at which this neuron produces action potentials will depend largely on the combination of excitatory and inhibitory inputs at any point in time.

Table 3.1 lists several major neurotransmitters. One important neurotransmitter is **acetylcholine,** abbreviated **ACh.** ACh is found in synapses in the brain, where it is important in such functions as arousal, attention, memory, aggression, sexuality, and thirst (Panksepp, 1986). For example, research on memory suggests that ACh helps change the connection strengths among neurons, thereby affecting the formation of new patterns of associations (Kosslyn & Koenig, 1992).

ACh can also be found at the junction between neurons and muscle fibers, where it acts as an excitatory neurotransmitter, causing muscle fibers to contract.

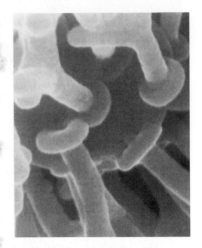

Figure 3.3

An electromicrograph of several terminal buttons (magnified 11,250 times their normal size). (Lewis, Everhart, & Zeevi, 1969)

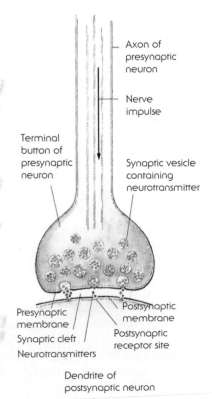

Figure 3.4

A schematic diagram of a synapse.

TABLE 3.1 Some Important Neurotransmitters and Their Functions

NEUROTRANSMITTER	FUNCTION
Acetylcholine (ACh)	Important in arousal, attention, memory, aggression, sexuality, thirst, muscle contraction.
Dopamine	Deficit of dopamine is associated with Parkinson's disease; dopamine is involved in muscle action, learning, and memory.
Gamma amino butyric acid (GABA)	GABA is the major inhibitory neurotransmitter in the central nervous system; also associated with anxiety and sleep.
Norepinephrine (also called noradrenaline)	Contributes to arousal; involved in memory, sleep, and mood.
Serotonin	Important to sleep, pain perception, and emotion.

Several deadly poisons influence ACh production. For example, the poisonous bite of a black widow spider is effective because it produces a flood of ACh from the vesicles into the synapses between the neurons and the muscle fibers. This extra release of ACh produces violent muscle contractions and—frequently—death. Our very survival therefore depends upon the vesicles releasing the right amount of ACh, neither too much nor too little.

A second neurotransmitter, **dopamine,** can act as an inhibitory neurotransmitter in the brain. You may know someone with **Parkinson's disease,** which involves symptoms such as tremors of the hands, altered body posture, and difficulty walking (Rao et al., 1992). Parkinson's disease has been traced to a deficit in dopamine production, caused by a deterioration in the neurons in the part of the brain that releases this neurotransmitter. One drug used to treat Parkinson's disease is L-DOPA, a substance that the body converts into dopamine, thereby replenishing its supply. There are several dozen other neurotransmitters, in addition to those mentioned in Table 3.1, and new neurotransmitters are discovered each year (Bridgeman, 1988).

What is the impact of these neurotransmitters on the postsynaptic neuron? It takes about 50 microseconds (one 20-thousandth of a second) for a neurotransmitter to reach the dendrite of the postsynaptic neuron. Once the neurotransmitter is on the other side, it interacts with specialized membranes. These membranes contain gates that are "guarded" by protein molecules. In much the same fashion as a key opens a lock, the neurotransmitter enters the membrane by moving the protein molecules aside and fitting neatly into the keyhole.

The neurotransmitter attaches itself in position onto the dendrite on the other side of the synaptic cleft, upsetting the electrical balance in the dendrite. In an excitatory potential, the nature of this imbalance makes an action potential more likely to occur in the axon of this second neuron. (Figure 3.5 summarizes the stages in excitatory synaptic transmission.) In an inhibitory potential, an action potential is *less* likely to occur in the postsynaptic neuron.

Neuromodulators Besides releasing neurotransmitters, neurons also release chemical substances called neuromodulators, which also act at the synapse. As the name suggests, **neuromodulators** modify the effects of neurotransmitters. As a consequence, neuronal activity is either increased or decreased. Neuromodulators are also likely to spread beyond the synapse and influence more distant neurons (Carlson, 1991).

One important category of neuromodulators is the endorphins. **Endorphins** are chemicals that occur naturally in the brain; when they are released, endorphins decrease a person's sensitivity to pain. These substances were discovered in the early 1970s, when researchers noticed that certain regions of the brain are particularly sensitive to drugs such as morphine (Pert & Snyder, 1973). This finding may not seem particularly significant until you consider an important point. Morphine does not occur naturally inside the human body. So why should our brains be so cleverly designed that morphine can fit in at the synapse in a lock-and-key fashion?

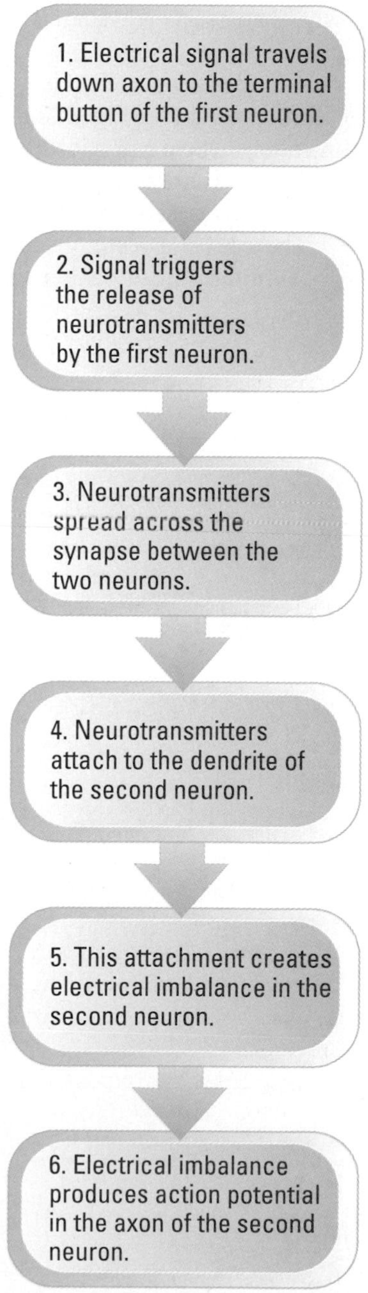

1. Electrical signal travels down axon to the terminal button of the first neuron.

2. Signal triggers the release of neurotransmitters by the first neuron.

3. Neurotransmitters spread across the synapse between the two neurons.

4. Neurotransmitters attach to the dendrite of the second neuron.

5. This attachment creates electrical imbalance in the second neuron.

6. Electrical imbalance produces action potential in the axon of the second neuron.

Figure 3.5

The stages in excitatory synaptic transmission.

Researchers realized that some similar substances must occur naturally inside our bodies; in other words, these substances are *endogenous*. In fact, some endogenous substances were discovered soon afterward (e.g., Goldstein, 1976; Snyder, 1977). They were called *endorphins,* as a shortened name for endogenous morphinelike substances.

Many of the drugs that are used to treat psychological disorders act like neuro-modulators. Almost every drug used in psychiatry acts by increasing or decreasing neuronal activity at the synapse (Snyder, 1985). We'll discuss neuromodulators again when we examine pain perception (Chapter 4) and medications used in treating psychological disorders (Chapter 16).

The Endocrine System The nervous system and neurotransmitters provide extremely rapid service for messages, and neuromodulators operate somewhat more slowly. The endocrine system is the slowest of the three systems in transmitting messages.

The **endocrine system** is a collection of glands that release their chemicals into the bloodstream. (See Figure 3.6.) The nervous system has its own independent communication network provided by the neurons. In contrast, the endocrine system is cleverly and economically designed to spread its messages through the bloodstream. The chemicals released by the endocrine system are called **hormones.**

The most important gland in the endocrine system is the pituitary gland. Part of the **pituitary gland** contains neurons, which receive neural messages via axons

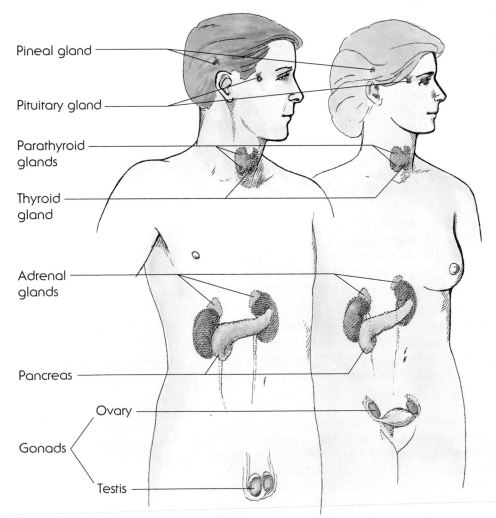

Pineal gland

Pituitary gland

Parathyroid glands

Thyroid gland

Adrenal glands

Pancreas

Ovary

Gonads

Testis

Figure 3.6

Some of the more important endocrine glands in the human body.

from the brain; a different part of the pituitary receives hormonal messages through the bloodstream. The pituitary receives these neural and hormonal messages and responds by releasing its own hormones. One substance it releases is growth hormone. If it releases too little growth hormone during childhood, the child will become a midget (Rieser & Underwood, 1990). If it releases too much, the child will become a giant.

Pituitary hormones also influence the hormone production of other endocrine glands. For example, one pituitary hormone influences the **thyroid gland,** a gland producing its own hormone that is important in regulating the body's metabolism.

A second pituitary hormone stimulates the adrenal glands, which are two lumpy structures perched on top of the kidneys. The **adrenal glands** produce several dozen hormones, which perform critical tasks such as regulating the concentration of minerals in the body. The adrenal glands also produce sex hormones, such as androgen hormones. **Androgen hormones** produce changes in males during early prenatal development, guiding the development of the male reproductive system. The adrenal glands also manufacture **epinephrine** (also known as *adrenaline*), which makes your heart pound vigorously if you are frightened.

A third pituitary hormone stimulates the **gonads,** or sex glands. As Figure 3.6 shows, the gonads include the testes in males and the ovaries in females. Like the adrenal glands, the gonads produce a variety of hormones that are crucial in sexual development and reproduction.

In summary, then, the endocrine system contains several glands that manufacture important hormones, which are transported via the bloodstream. The efficiency of using this circulatory system for both blood and hormones is another example of Theme 1. In fact, imagine the alternatives if hormones could not be conveyed through the bloodstream. Our bodies would need to be equipped with a different, special-function system, or else hormones would be circulated in a haphazard fashion—with dire consequences for our growth and metabolism.

So far, we have considered the body's elaborate communication systems. The neurons allow messages to be transmitted in a fraction of a second, using neurotransmitters as the chemical messengers. Two other chemical messengers, neuromodulators and hormones, allow more leisurely communication and regulation. Let's turn our attention to the research methods neuroscientists use to study the brain and the rest of the nervous system. Then we will examine what this research has revealed about the structure and function of the nervous system.

Neuroscience Research Methods

Researchers in the interdisciplinary field of neuroscience have developed techniques as diverse as observing the behavior of an individual with brain damage and recording messages from a single neuron. As we will see later in the "In Depth" section, researchers often obtain a more complete picture of brain functioning when several methods are used to attack the same problem. You may recall that we reached the same conclusion about psychology research methods in Chapter 2.

Case Study As Chapter 2 explained, a **case study** is a careful in-depth examination of one individual. Researchers have advocated using the case study method with brain-damaged people to help them understand the functioning of people with normal brains.

Consider the case of a man known by his initials, N.A., who had joined the Air Force after a year of junior college. His roommate was playing with a miniature fencing foil when N.A. turned suddenly toward him and was stabbed through the right nostril, a thrust that was deep enough to penetrate the brain. (Later research showed that the sword had damaged a portion of the thalamus—shown in Figure 3.14—that is associated with memory.) N.A. lost consciousness temporarily, and he also showed some temporary paralysis. Twenty years later, Squire (1987) reported that N.A. had a high intelligence quotient (IQ), and he carried on normal conversations. However,

N.A. has a very specific deficit: He forgets some kinds of new material. For example, he loses track of his belongings, forgets what he has done, and forgets the people he has visited. His mother, who lives nearby, prepares meals for him. However, he often forgets that the meals are in the refrigerator, and he goes out to a restaurant instead. He forgets to take his medication, and he forgets to refill his prescriptions. He stubbornly refuses to keep reminder notes, saying that these notes would operate like crutches that would prevent him from exercising his memory. The destruction of a small portion of N.A.'s brain has affected his entire life!

The case study technique provides some valuable clues to the mechanisms that might explain a deficit in behavior (Heilman & Valenstein, 1985). However, several current researchers argue that case studies have some important limitations (Churchland & Sejnowski, 1992; Hannay, 1986). For instance, we may not want to generalize to other people on the basis of just one case study. Also, a person is likely to have brain damage that affects several areas; although these areas are near each other, they may have different functions. Thus, researchers may have difficulty untangling the various symptoms and tracing them to the appropriate parts of the brain. Let us examine some other research techniques that help pinpoint the relationship between brain structures and behaviors.

Lesion Production A **lesion** is a wound or disruption of the brain. Lesions can be produced in laboratory animals to confirm some suspicions about the functions of brain structures. (In contrast, the previous section on case studies discussed brain lesions that occur by accident in humans.)

The reasoning behind the lesion technique is that researchers can figure out which kind of behavior is changed in an animal once an area of its brain has been destroyed; that part of the brain may be responsible for the altered behavior. For example, if an animal can no longer see after a region of the brain has been destroyed, we can conclude that this region plays some role in vision. However, Carlson (1991) notes that we often need to interpret the results very carefully. For example on what basis does the researcher conclude that the animal is blind? Perhaps it bumps into objects or fails to run toward a light signaling food. Maybe the researcher should conclude that the lesion produced a deficit in motor coordination, not a deficit in vision.

Brain Stimulation Researchers can also examine the brain by electrically stimulating a localized region. When **electrical stimulation** is used, the researcher places a small electrode in a specific location of the brain and delivers a weak electrical current. For example, a neurosurgeon may want to operate on a patient with severe epilepsy in order to remove the portion of the brain that causes the seizures. Prior to surgery, the neurosurgeon identifies the suspicious region of the brain (typically using EEG, which we discuss shortly). Then the patient receives a local anesthetic so that he or she can be conscious during surgery but experience no pain. A piece of the skull is then temporarily removed, and the neurosurgeon delivers electrical stimulation in the vicinity of the suspicious region. The purpose of this investigation is to identify the functions of the brain tissue in this region so that surgery can be conducted without disrupting areas that are important for normal functioning. For example, stimulation of one region might disrupt memory, whereas stimulation in another region might cause a tingling in the mouth. The neurosurgeon would leave the memory area intact, but would consider operating in the second region. Figure 3.7 shows a map that was constructed by using this procedure. Naturally, brain stimulation techniques help people with serious neurological disorders, but they also provide a useful map of the brain's functions (Carlson, 1991; Penfield & Jasper, 1954).

Brain Recording Neuroscientists use several methods to record signals from the brain. For example, in the **electroencephalography** or **EEG** method, they place electrodes on the scalp. The electrical messages from the thousands of neurons beneath the electrodes are then recorded on graph paper, as Figure 3.8 shows. The EEG

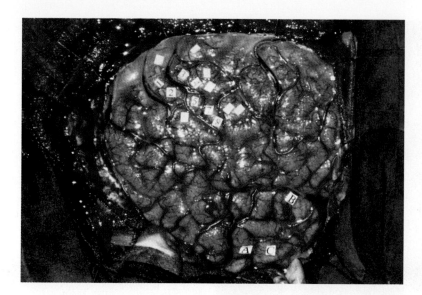

Figure 3.7

Mapping resulting from the brain stimulation technique. The numbered tags mark responses from stimulation of the sensory and motor cortex. The lettered tags indicate epileptic abnormality on the electrical recording of the cortex to guide surgical removal. (Reprinted with permission of neurosurgeon Dr. William Feindel, Montreal Neurological Institute)

is one of the older research methods, but it is still helpful in diagnosing brain disease (Churchland & Sejnowski, 1992). It has also provided useful information about brain activity when people are sleeping, as we will see in Chapter 5. Unfortunately, however, the EEG cannot provide precise information about brain activity. After all, an EEG "listens" to thousands of neurons at once.

A second brain-recording technique obtains more precise information. This method is used with animals, rather than humans, because it can cause neurological damage. In the **single-cell recording technique,** the researcher inserts a tiny electrode next to (or even into) a single neuron. For example, this technique has been used to help us understand how individual neurons function. We will also consider this technique again in Chapter 4. As we will discuss, researchers can insert an electrode into a neuron of an animal's visual cortex. By presenting a variety of stimuli, the researchers can determine the kind of visual pattern that produces the most vigorous electrical activity from the neuron.

Imaging Techniques Several new techniques provide a picture of the living human brain, typically using computers to combine a series of images of the brain. These techniques are invaluable in diagnosing the part of the brain that might be affected by head injury or a tumor, and they also provide useful information for researchers. The three most common imaging techniques are known by their initials: CT scan, PET scan, and MRI.

A **computed tomography,** or **CT scan,** passes X-ray beams through the head from a variety of angles, plotting a two-dimensional picture that resembles a horizontal "slice" through the brain. Then the patient's head is moved either up or down, and a second picture is plotted from this new position. Eventually, an entire series of computer-generated pictures is assembled.

A **positron emission tomography,** or **PET scan,** traces the chemical activity of various parts of the living brain (Resnick, 1992). A tiny amount of a radioactive chemical is injected into blood vessels that carry the chemical to the brain, and the active cells in the brain temporarily accumulate this chemical. A machine then passes X-ray beams through the head.

Figure 3.9 shows PET scans of normal people who were asked to perform various tasks while the PET scan was taken. Current journals are filled with reports about how the normal brain works, based on PET scans. For example, in a recent study, Haier and his colleagues (1992) asked young men to practice a computer game that required visual-motor coordination. As their performance improved, the brain activity in the relevant regions decreased. Apparently, practice makes perfect, and it also makes the brain more efficient!

Figure 3.8

An example of the EEG technique: The electrical message from the neurons beneath the electrodes on this person's scalp is being recorded on the graph paper.

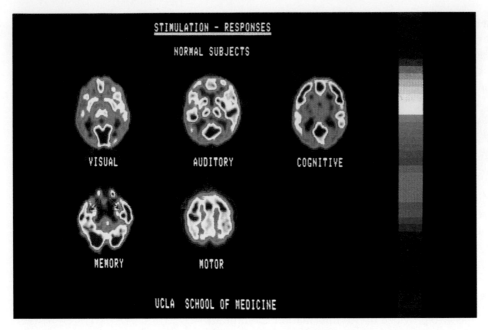

Figure 3.9
PET scans of normal people performing different types of tasks. Red indicates the highest level of cell activity; purple indicates the lowest level. Five tasks are illustrated.
Visual: Participants open their eyes and look at a visual screen. This activates the visual cortex (arrows).
Auditory: Participants listen to music and language, which activates the right and left auditory cortex (arrows).
Cognitive: Participants count backward from 100 by 7's. This activates the frontal cortex (arrows).
Memory: Participants are asked to recall previously learned facts. This activates small structures called the hippocampus (arrows).
Motor: Participants touch their fingers to the thumb of the right hand. This activates the left motor cortex (slanted arrow) and supplementary motor cortex (vertical arrow).

A third imaging technique is **magnetic resonance imaging,** or **MRI;** this technique is similar to a CT scan. However, instead of an X-ray beam, it passes a strong (but harmless) magnetic field through a patient's head. The MRI scanner picks up radiation from hydrogen molecules, which are present in different concentrations in different tissues. This technique provides a picture of a "slice" of the human brain, and it is particularly useful for detecting lesions (Regenbogen, 1988).

Researchers use all three imaging techniques to learn more about psychological disorders, such as autism, depression, and schizophrenia. For example, CT scans and MRIs have been conducted on people with schizophrenia (a disorder discussed in Chapter 15 that involves disorganized thoughts). The results show that the front part of the brain is often unusually small, compared with the brain structures of people who are not schizophrenic. PET scans confirm that the front part of the brain is less active in schizophrenics than in non-schizophrenics (e.g., Andreasen, 1989; Holcomb et al., 1989; Resnick, 1992; Suddath et al., 1990).

In short, neuroscientists have observed the nervous system at all levels, from the isolated neuron to the normal human brain. As we will see in later chapters, their research has clarified topics as diverse as a rabbit blinking when a tone is presented (Chapter 6), a person trying to recall an acquaintance's name (Chapter 7), and someone trying to cope with severe depression (Chapter 15).

The Divisions of the Nervous System

You've learned about the structure of the neuron, three kinds of chemical messengers, and the techniques used to probe the nervous system. Let's place the nervous system in context in the human body. Figure 3.10 shows the major divisions of the nervous system. As you can see, the major distinction is between the central and peripheral nervous systems. If you place a paper clip on this page, you can turn to it for reference. Most of this chapter examines the central nervous system, specifically the brain. However, we begin with the peripheral nervous system. Without this vitally important system, you could not stay alive long enough to finish reading this sentence.

The Peripheral Nervous System The word *peripheral* refers to things that are not central. Peripheral vision, for example, involves the edges of your visual field, rather than the central part. Similarly, the **peripheral nervous system** consists of everything in the nervous system except the brain and spinal cord. The peripheral nervous system transmits messages from the sensory receptors to the **central nervous system** (that is, the spinal cord and brain), and it also transmits messages back out from the central nervous system to the muscles and glands. This communication between the two nervous systems typically takes place via **nerves,** which are bundles of axons from neurons in the peripheral nervous system.

The peripheral nervous system is further divided into two parts, the somatic division and the autonomic division. The **somatic division** consists of sensory neurons that transmit sensory information into the central nervous system, as well as motor neurons that carry motor commands out of the central nervous system to the muscles. You use this somatic division when you scratch your nose, chew gum, or perform any other voluntary action.

In contrast, the **autonomic division** helps control the glands, blood vessels, the intestines, the heart, and other internal organs. The autonomic nervous system usually works automatically. Unlike the actions in the somatic division, you do not need to decide to make your heart beat for the next 60 seconds. (You can remember the name *autonomic* because it resembles the word *automatic.*)

The autonomic division is further divided into two parts, the sympathetic nervous system and the parasympathetic nervous system. These two systems provide neurons for each of the glands, blood vessels, and internal organs in the autonomic division.

The **sympathetic system** prepares the body for action. Its neurons' endings secrete epinephrine, (a substance we discussed on page 65), which increases your heart rate and dilates the pupils of your eye. It makes you sweat, and it makes you blush. The sympathetic neurons also connect with hair follicles and with tiny arteries in the skin. The next time you find yourself in a frightening situation, notice how your heart beats faster, your pupils grow wide, and you sweat and blush. Furthermore, people say that when they are frightened, their "hair stands on end." Humans cannot demonstrate this feature of the sympathetic system as dramatically as an alley cat does, but you might notice tiny goosebumps on your arm.

The **parasympathetic system** generally works in the opposite direction. It tends to slow down your body functions and conserves energy. For example, the parasympathetic system slows your heartbeat and constricts your pupils. Its neurons secrete the neurotransmitter ACh. (Incidentally, it may be helpful to remember that the sympathetic system spends energy; the parasympathetic system preserves it.) Working together, these two systems ensure that your body maintains its balance. Immediately after a frightening experience, the sympathetic system is dominant. Soon after, however, the body's alarm system alerts the parasympathetic system to relax the functions and bring the body back to normal.

Figure 3.10

The divisions of the nervous system.

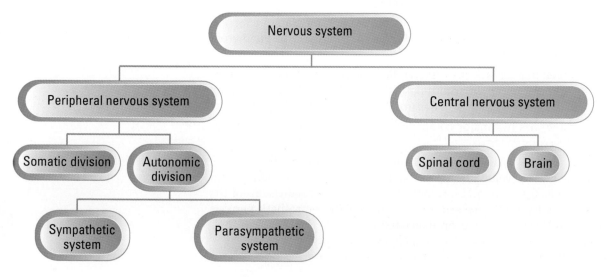

The sympathetic and the parasympathetic systems often work in an antagonistic fashion, with one increasing and the other decreasing an organ's activity. This is true for the heart, the pupils, the intestines, and the lungs. The two systems work together to achieve **homeostasis,** or a constant, ideal internal environment. However, they sometimes work in parallel. For example, during sexual activity, the parasympathetic system is responsible for a swelling of the sexual organs, and the sympathetic system is responsible for orgasm. The impressive coordination of the two systems is an important example of Theme 1, that humans are well designed to function in their environments.

The Central Nervous System The other major division of the nervous system is the central nervous system. As Figure 3.10 shows, the two components of the central nervous system are the spinal cord and the brain.

The **spinal cord** is a column of neurons that runs from the base of the brain, down the center of the back. A series of bones protects the spinal cord, just as the skull protects the brain. The spinal cord is the oldest part of the central nervous system, both in terms of evolution and in terms of the developing embryo prior to birth (Bridgeman, 1988). Its basic organization is similar for all vertebrates. For the more primitive vertebrates, the spinal cord forms the major part of the central nervous system. For humans, it performs more basic functions, providing a gateway for signals to and from the peripheral nervous system.

You could not function without the various parts of the peripheral nervous system, and damage to the spinal cord causes major disabilities. However, psychologists are much more interested in the one remaining structure in the nervous system—the brain. We consider the brain in the next section of this chapter.

SECTION SUMMARY

INTRODUCTION TO THE NERVOUS SYSTEM

- In general, the brain's structure is complex, most activities require the cooperation of many brain regions, and the brain regions have specialized functions.

- The neuron consists of dendrites, a cell body, and an axon; it transmits messages to nearby neurons via neurotransmitters.

- Neurotransmitters can be excitatory or inhibitory; too much or too little of a given neurotransmitter can produce disorders and even death.

- Neuromodulators modify neurotransmitter activity; endorphins are one kind of neuromodulator, and they modify pain perception.

- The endocrine system releases hormones; the most important gland in the endocrine system is the pituitary, which stimulates other glands such as the thyroid gland, the adrenal gland, and the gonads.

- Some methods used in neuroscience research include the case study, lesion production, brain stimulation, brain recording (EEG and the single-cell recording technique), and imaging techniques (CT scans, PET scans, and MRIs).

- The nervous system has two major components: the peripheral nervous system and the central nervous system

- The peripheral nervous system is divided into two components: the somatic division (which involves voluntary action) and the autonomic division (which controls glands, blood vessels, and internal organs). The two subdivisions of the autonomic nervous system are the sympathetic and the parasympathetic nervous system, which work together in a coordinated fashion.

- The central nervous system has two components, the spinal cord and the brain.

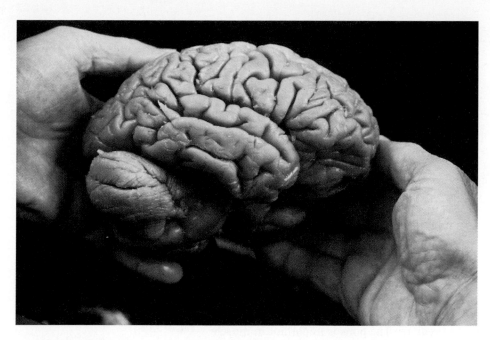

Figure 3.11
The human brain.

THE BRAIN

Your brain looks somewhat like a 3-pound lump of leftover lukewarm oatmeal. Its texture is very soft and jellylike. In fact, it is so fragile that researchers have difficulty handling a fresh brain from a recently deceased human without damaging it (Carlson, 1991). Figure 3.11 shows a specimen of a human brain. As you can see, the appearance of the brain is not particularly impressive.

However, the human brain is the most complicated object known (Coen, 1985). The brain never rests, even when we are asleep. The various chemical and electrical systems in the brain are changing constantly. Some writers claim that the brain resembles a computer, but the analogy is not entirely accurate. The brain is much more complex than the computers that have been developed so far, and computers cannot grow or change (Ornstein & Thompson, 1984). The complicated brain certainly intrigues contemporary researchers. One index of this interest is that the Society for Neuroscience has grown from 500 members in 1970 to 20,415 in 1992 (Wheeler, 1992).

In this section, we will first explore the regions of the human brain and then consider the two cerebral hemispheres and brain disorders. We'll conclude with an "In Depth" section on neuroscience research on visual object recognition.

Regions of the Human Brain

If you check back to Figure 3.10, you will notice the label, "brain." Now we will verbally dissect this astonishing brain to examine its structures. Figure 3.12 provides an overview of the brain's organization to help you appreciate how the components fit into the overall structure. Figure 3.13 shows a schematic diagram of important structures in the brain.

The Hindbrain The **hindbrain** is located in the bottom portion of the brain, and it includes several important structures. The **medulla** can be found just above the spinal cord. It can be considered a broader, fancier extension of the spinal cord. The medulla has several important functions, such as controlling breathing and heart rate. The *medulla* sounds rather *dull,* but you could not survive without it.

The **pons** is a bulging structure located above the medulla. The word *pons* means bridge, and this structure serves the function of a bridge by connecting the

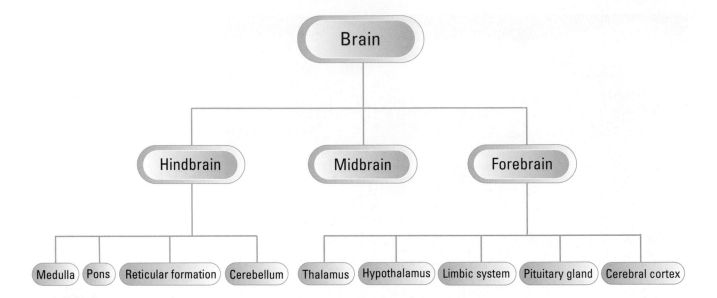

lower brain regions with the higher brain regions. The pons is important in muscle control, such as facial expression and the skillful use of our fingers (Glees, 1988).

As Figure 3.13 shows, the **cerebellum** looks like a miniature version of the entire brain, tacked on at the lower rear portion of the brain. The cerebellum is one of the oldest structures in the evolution of mammals' nervous systems (Thompson, 1985). It is well developed in fish, birds, and lower mammals. In fact, the cerebellum

Figure 3.12
The major parts of the brain.

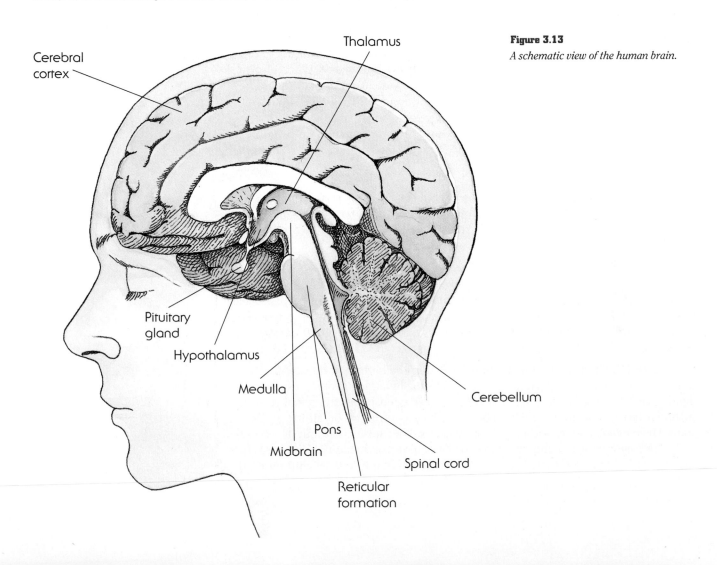

Figure 3.13
A schematic view of the human brain.

occupies a much larger percentage of total brain space in your pet cat's brain than in your own. The cerebellum plays an important role in learning, as we will see in Chapter 6. It is also important in maintaining posture and in controlling motor movements. For example, people with a lesion in the cerebellum have difficulty passing the finger-nose test with their eyes closed (Glees, 1988). Try Demonstration 3.1, which illustrates this simple test—one typically included in the standard neurological examination.

Also, notice the structure called the **reticular formation,** which runs up from the hindbrain, through to the midbrain. Axons from the reticular formation even reach upward into the cerebral cortex at the top of the brain. This structure is important in attention and in sleep (two topics covered in Chapter 5), as well as in simple learning tasks (McGinty & Szymusiak, 1988).

The Midbrain The **midbrain** continues upward from the pons portion of the hindbrain. All signals that pass between the spinal cord and the forebrain must pass through this structure. Furthermore, visual information passes through the midbrain on its route from the eyes to the forebrain. In the midbrain, visual information is also coordinated with motor movements, as Demonstration 3.2 illustrates. The midbrain also helps control other motor movements and plays a role in sleep.

Before we approach the more complex forebrain region, let's review where we have been. The hindbrain controls some basic functions such as breathing and heart rate (the medulla), and it connects the lower and the higher brain regions (the pons); it controls movement (the cerebellum), and it is important in attention, sleep, and learning (the reticular formation). The midbrain plays a role in vision, motor movement, and sleep. You could not survive without your hindbrain and your midbrain. However, the forebrain is most important in perception, memory, thought, and social behavior—those aspects of human life most relevant to psychology.

The Forebrain In humans, the **forebrain** is the largest part of the brain. It includes the cerebral cortex, the structure that interests us most, but several other parts of the forebrain are also critical in human behavior. Many structures discussed in this section come in pairs. For example, your cortex has both a right temporal lobe and a left temporal lobe. Later, we will discuss some consequences of this arrangement.

1. The **thalamus** plays an important role in perception; you can see the thalamus pictured in Figure 3.14. Nearly all the information from the senses is processed by the thalamus on its route from the sensory receptors to the cerebral cortex. (The one exception is smell, which travels a more direct route.) The thalamus does not simply send messages along in a passive fashion. Instead, it organizes and transforms

The cerebellum is important in the control of this dancer's motor movements.

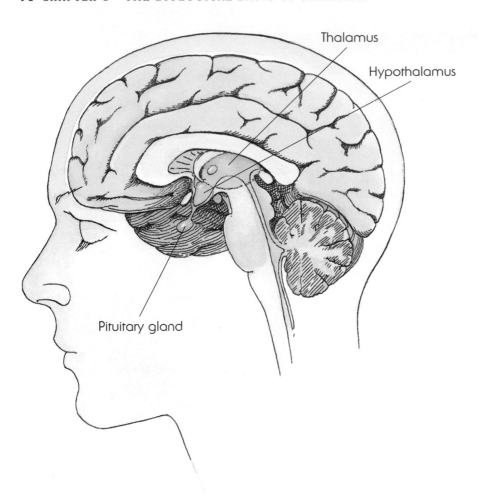

Figure 3.14

The thalamus, the hypothalamus, and the pituitary gland.

information. As we see in the next chapter, vision and the other senses are impressively complicated. As you read this sentence, the information registered by your visual sensory receptors must travel a complex route and be reorganized several times by structures such as the thalamus.

2. The **hypothalamus** lies just below the thalamus (the prefix *hypo* means *under*). This relatively small structure controls the autonomic nervous system, which you may recall is the part of the nervous system responsible for the glands, blood vessels, and internal organs. The hypothalamus features several distinct clusters of neurons that regulate different kinds of motivated behavior such as eating, drinking, sexual behavior, aggression, and activity level. This structure is no larger than a kidney bean, and yet each of its regions is critically important to normal functioning. For example, stimulation of one region of the hypothalamus causes an animal to gorge itself—even after a full meal. Stimulation of a nearby region causes it to stop eating entirely (McGinty & Szymusiak, 1988).

3. The pituitary gland is the hormone-producing gland that we discussed in connection with the endocrine system (p. 64). The pituitary gland is not technically part of the brain, but it is regulated by the nearby hypothalamus.

4. The **limbic system** consists of several related parts such as the hippocampus and the amygdala. Figure 3.15 shows some of the components included in the limbic system. The limbic system is classified as a system because the components are connected with one another and they work together in an integrated fashion.

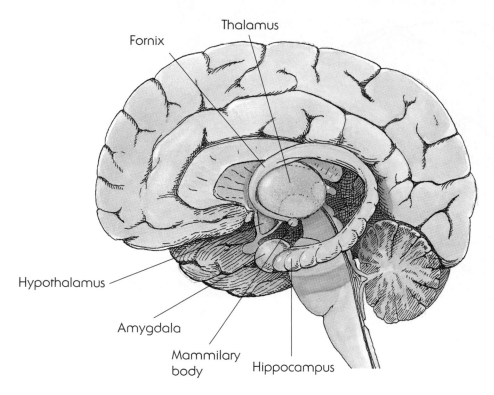

Thalamus

Fornix

Hypothalamus

Amygdala

Mammilary body

Hippocampus

Figure 3.15

The components of the limbic system.
Note: *This diagram shows only the left member of each pair.*

The limbic system helps regulate the emotions, and it also plays a critical role in motivation, learning, and memory (Aggleton, 1992; Squire, 1992). For example, one case study described a man with severe epilepsy. To try to control the disabling seizures, the surgeons removed his hippocampus and his amygdala. Following surgery, he was reasonably accurate in recalling old memories. However, he was unable to form and recall memories for events following his surgery (Gazzaniga, 1986; Milner et al., 1968). Chapter 7 discusses the case study of H.M. in more detail.

5. The **cerebral cortex** is the outer surface of the two cerebral hemispheres of the brain; it processes all perceptions and complex thoughts. The entire cerebral cortex is only as thick as the cover of this textbook, but it is essential in perception, memory, and higher mental processes.

Figure 3.16 shows another view of the brain, looking down from above. Once again, appreciate the wrinkled, walnutlike appearance. This view also highlights the fact that the brain has two cerebral hemispheres. Although these two half-brains look nearly identical, we will see that they perform somewhat different functions.

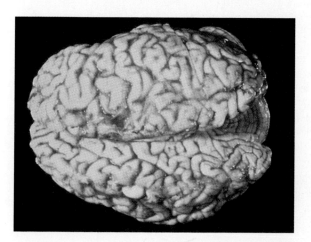

Figure 3.16

The cerebral cortex (as seen from overhead).

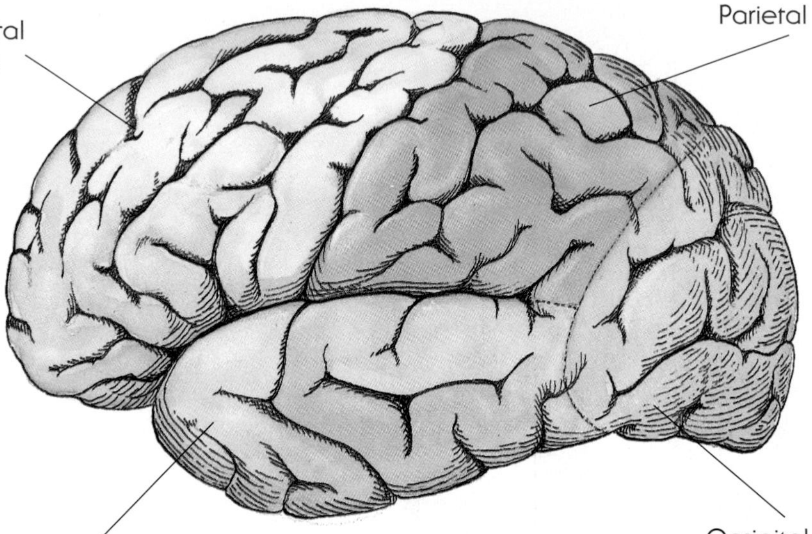

Frontal lobe

Parietal lobe

Temporal lobe

Occipital lobe

Figure 3.17

A schematic drawing of the cerebral cortex, as seen from the side.

Figure 3.17 is a schematic drawing of the left side of the brain. As you can see, the brain is divided into four lobes or regions, based on their structure and function. Let us start this overview of the cerebral cortex with the **occipital lobe** (pronounced "ox-*sip*-ih-tul"), located at the back of the head. An important part of this region of the brain is the visual cortex. As Chapter 4 explains, information travels from the receptors in the eyes, through the thalamus, to the visual cortex. If you place the palm of your hand just above the back of your neck, the visual cortex lies right in front of your hand.

One important feature of the visual cortex is its spatial arrangement. Specifically, the pattern of information on the retina (the sensory receptors inside the eye) corresponds fairly closely to the pattern of information on part of the visual cortex; this correspondence is called a **retinotopic arrangement.** Try Demonstration 3.3 to appreciate this retinotopic arrangement.

Moving upward and forward from the occipital lobe—which contains the visual cortex—we reach the parietal lobe (pronounced "puh-*rye*-ih-tull"). The **parietal lobe** registers information about body movement, the location of body parts, and touch. At the front of the parietal lobe is the somatosensory cortex, the part of the brain that handles the skin senses. Take a moment to appreciate these senses, though we dis-

---

DEMONSTRATION 3.3   The Spatial Arrangement in the Visual Cortex

Stand in front of a full-length mirror. An image of yourself is now being registered on the retina, at the back of each eye. We could make a map illustrating how each point on the retina is represented on the visual cortex. When you look at a road map, you see that Illinois is closer to Michigan than it is to California. This road map therefore corresponds to geographic reality. Similarly, when you look at yourself in this mirror, the map on your visual cortex represents your left eyebrow as being closer to your left eye than it is to your feet. This visual-cortex map is therefore similar to the pattern of stimulation on your retina.

However, do not take this retinotopic arrangement too literally because many factors make this representation less than perfect. For example, about half of the neurons in the visual cortex receive information from the very small portion in the central part of your retina. This is the part of the retina in which vision is crisp and clear. If you look in the mirror at your chin, for instance, you will see your chin very clearly. At this moment, your chin is taking up far more than its fair share of your visual cortex. If you maintain your gaze on your chin, note that the part of your body below your waist becomes increasingly blurry. Your knees and toes occupy only a small part of the visual cortex.

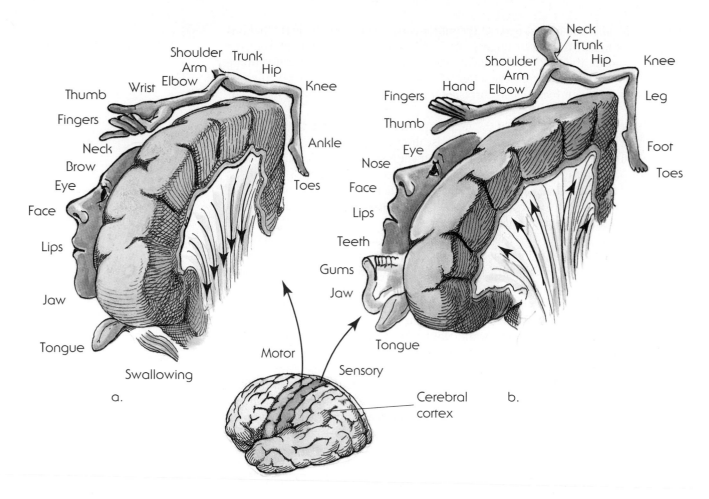

Figure 3.18

A portion of the left cortex: (a) A diagram of the regions of the motor cortex that control various body parts. The size of each body part corresponds to the amount of space on the cortex that controls each body part. (b) A diagram of the regions of the somatosensory cortex that receives signals from various body parts. The size of each body part corresponds to the amount of space on the cortex that receives signals from that body part. (After Penfield & Rasmussen, 1950)

cuss them more completely in the next chapter. Right now, your right hand may be touching a page of this textbook, you may feel a slight pressure from the watch on your wrist, and the room temperature may seem slightly cold. In addition to the sensations of touch and temperature, you may also feel pain in another part of your body, muscle tension somewhere else, and an itch in yet another region. Each of these skin senses will be registered on your somatosensory cortex.

Figure 3.18b shows how touch sensations are registered on the somatosensory cortex. As you can see, the skin on certain parts of your body (such as your lips) receives more than its fair share of the cortex. As Demonstration 3.4 illustrates, the body parts that are represented by large regions of the somatosensory cortex are relatively sensitive in discriminating between one index card and two index cards.

Moving farther forward to the **frontal lobe,** we find that an important area here is the motor cortex. The cells in this region control voluntary movement for different parts of the body. Figure 3.18a shows the motor cortex, with the parts of the body it controls. As you will notice, this figure resembles Figure 3.18b. The parts of the body

---

DEMONSTRATION 3.4   Sensitivity to Touch

Take two index cards and hold them so that they are just barely separated. Touch their corners to your lips, and you can easily feel the two distinct surfaces. Now hold the cards in the same position to touch your arm; does it seem like just one thick surface? How far apart do you need to hold the two cards to sense two distinct surfaces? Experiment with touching other parts of your body, and see whether the most sensitive parts correspond to the body parts that are represented as being larger on Figure 3.18b. In both vision and sensitivity to touch, greater space on the cortex allows for more precise perceptions.

that correspond to the largest parts of the motor cortex tend to be the parts that humans use the most. We use our fingers often, and we make very precise movements with them (notice the precise movements you make with your pen to differentiate the handwritten letter a from the letter σ). Without special training, you could never do this with your toes (which correspond to a relatively small part of the motor cortex).

As you can see, large parts of the motor cortex are also devoted to the lips and tongue, which humans use to make very precise discriminations when they talk. Notice how your tongue makes only a slight adjustment inside your mouth to turn *save* into *shave* or *tip* into *chip*. It is fortunate that you are blessed with a structure as agile as your tongue to make these important motor movements. Think how slurred your speech would be if your mouth contained a body part associated with less precise movements, such as your knee or elbow!

If you compare Figure 3.17 with the lower portion of Figure 3.18, you'll notice a large portion of the frontal lobe that is not assigned to the motor cortex; this region is called the **prefrontal cortex.** Some neuroscientists claim that the prefrontal cortex is the least understood and most complex region of the brain (Goldman-Rakic, 1988). One task that the prefrontal cortex handles is remembering which of two stimuli occurred more recently (Grafman, 1989). For example, if you had a lesion in a particular part of the prefrontal cortex, you would not be able to decide which term you saw more recently in this textbook, *endorphin* or *occipital lobe.* The prefrontal cortex is also responsible for complex cognitive tasks, such as making plans, forming concepts, and inhibiting actions that are inappropriate (Grafman, 1989). For example, I know a man with a lesion in the prefrontal cortex who often asks inappropriate questions at the wrong time during a group discussion. Earlier in this chapter, we noted that schizophrenics typically have underdeveloped frontal lobes; this anatomical deficit corresponds to their symptom of disordered thought.

The prefrontal cortex also helps regulate your mood. People with a lesion in this region are often depressed (Stuss et al., 1992). They may laugh or cry at inappropriate moments (Grafman, 1989; Haaland, 1992). Furthermore, they seem to be unaware of their deficits (Stuss, 1991). In summary, the prefrontal cortex is a critically important region of the brain that manages emotions and takes responsibility for the kinds of higher mental functions that make us into socially sensitive beings who have long-range goals.

The last part of the cerebral cortex is the **temporal lobes,** which are located on each side of your head. (You can remember that the temporal lobes are near the temples of your forehead.) The temporal lobes contain the auditory cortex, which processes information about sounds, speech, and music. A person with a lesion in the left temporal lobe may have difficulty understanding and producing language. However, the specific pattern of deficits is not related in a clear-cut fashion to the part of the temporal lobe that is damaged (De Bleser, 1988). Part of the temporal lobe also accomplishes complex visual tasks, including some you take for granted. A person with a lesion in this region might have difficulty recognizing that a particular arrangement of features is actually a face! Later in the chapter, our "In Depth" section will focus on people who have difficulty recognizing specific visual objects, due to lesions in their temporal lobe.

We have identified several important structures throughout the four lobes of the cerebral cortex. In many cases, a specific location on the cerebral cortex is associated with a specific function, as in the case of part of the visual cortex in the occipital lobe. However, many mysteries remain. For example, brain damage in some areas of the frontal lobe often produces no major deficits in behavior (Stuss & Benson, 1984). Furthermore, large regions of the cortex simply do not respond to electrical stimulation. Students in introductory psychology courses sometimes assume that psychologists have already answered all the interesting questions about the origins of behavior. However, the cerebral cortex probably has more uncharted regions than there are on the globe.

Furthermore, different parts of a structure may perform more than one function. For example, we discussed how the reticular formation handles processes as different from each other as sleep and learning.

In addition, most psychological processes require the participation of more than one portion of the brain. For example, Chapter 4 considers saccadic eye movements, which are used when you read or drive. They do not seem particularly complicated. However, researchers have determined that saccadic eye movements require the cooperation of many structures in the brain, including part of the midbrain, a region of the cerebral cortex, and probably additional structures that have not yet been identified (Goldberg & Bruce, 1986).

This discussion should remind you of the theme that most psychological processes have more than one explanation—more than one cause. Naturally, this complexity challenges introductory psychology students, who must try to make sense out of the information. Clearly, the human nervous system did not evolve into a neat, orderly set of organs, each with only a single, well-defined function. Evolution did not have the goal of developing a brain whose structures would be easy to memorize. Instead, evolution has produced a brain that is amazingly skillful in performing a wide variety of tasks both quickly and accurately. The speed and accuracy of human behavior, as you will recall, is itself another theme of this textbook.

Let us now turn to three additional issues related to the human brain. Do the two hemispheres of the brain function differently? What happens when part of the brain is destroyed, through a stroke or Alzheimer's disease? How have neuroscientists determined how visual objects are represented in the cortex?

When you drive, you make saccadic eye movements to keep track of the road, as well as objects on either side of your car. These eye movements are directed by many different structures in the brain.

The Two Cerebral Hemispheres

Turn back to Figure 3.16 to remind yourself that the cortex is divided into two distinct hemispheres. An important characteristic of the brain is that for the sensory and motor areas of the cortex, the right side of the cortex is more strongly connected with the left side of the body. Furthermore, the left side of the cortex is more strongly connected with the right side of the body. This crossover pattern is known as a **contralateral arrangement.** Because of this crossover arrangement, you may know someone who has had a stroke in the left cerebral cortex whose greatest difficulties involve the *right* side of the body. This person may have difficulty using the right hand (due to left motor cortex damage) and the right hand may also feel numb (due to left somatosensory cortex damage).

A second important characteristic of the brain is called **lateralization.** Lateralization means that the two hemispheres have somewhat different functions, though we should not exaggerate these differences. We can learn about hemispheric comparisons from people who have had a special operation called the split-brain procedure and also from more subtle observations on normal humans with intact brains.

Lateralization and the Split-Brain Procedure The normal brain features a bridge between the two hemispheres, called the **corpus callosum,** which is a thick bundle of about 800,000 axons (Trevarthen, 1987). The corpus callosum permits communication between the two hemispheres, so that a message received in one hemisphere can be quickly transmitted to the other hemisphere. Figure 3.19 shows where the corpus callosum is located.

During the 1960s, a group of researchers—which included psychologists Roger Sperry and Michael Gazzaniga—began to explore what happens when the corpus callosum is cut, literally producing a split brain. They examined people who had such disabling epilepsy that a seizure beginning in one hemisphere would spread across the corpus callosum to the other hemisphere. Encouraged by earlier research on cats and monkeys, these researchers hoped they could reduce the intensity of seizures by cutting the corpus callosum that linked the two hemispheres.

Operations on a small number of people with severe epilepsy have typically been very successful. The split-brain patients usually experience fewer, less severe epileptic seizures. Furthermore, they seem to behave normally in their daily lives

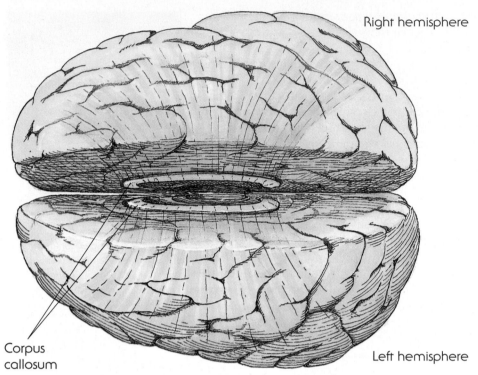

Right hemisphere

Corpus callosum

Left hemisphere

Figure 3.19

An overhead view of the corpus callosum, dissected to indicate how it joins the two hemispheres together.

(Bradshaw, 1989). However, research in the laboratory revealed subtle deficits—which we will consider shortly—and allowed researchers to see how each hemisphere functions when it is separated from the other hemisphere.

To understand this research, you need to keep in mind the contralateral arrangement of the brain. For example, everything that appears in your left visual field would be registered in the *right* side of your visual cortex. In contrast, everything that appears to the right would be registered in the *left* side of your visual cortex.

In the normal brain, information about an object in the left visual field (and therefore the right hemisphere) can be shared with the left hemisphere; the signal quickly travels across the corpus callosum. Imagine what would happen if this structure were cut, as in Figure 3.19. Information in the left visual field would still reach the right hemisphere. However, it could not travel across to the left hemisphere. (A person with a split brain could register this object in the left hemisphere only by turning his or her head until the object was included in the right visual field, something that can be done very easily in daily life.)

In the laboratory, researchers asked the split-brain patients to sit at a table and gaze straight ahead (Sperry, 1982; Gazzaniga & LeDoux, 1978). Then the researchers presented a photo of an object, perhaps a spoon, to the right visual field (i.e., the left hemisphere). The patients had no difficulty identifying the object (see Figure 3.20a). These results confirmed researchers' strong suspicions that the left hemisphere is primarily responsible for language.

Now let us consider what happens when the same photo of the spoon was presented to the left visual field (i.e., the right hemisphere). When asked what they had seen, patients typically replied "nothing" (Figure 3.20b). Here, the information about the spoon is sent to the right hemisphere, where it is "trapped." In a person with a normal brain, that information could travel across the corpus callosum to the "verbal" left hemisphere, and the person could easily say "spoon." However, in a person with a split brain, the right hemisphere apparently lacks the verbal skills to report that the object is a spoon.

The right hemisphere may be mute, but it is not helpless, as Figure 3.20c shows. In this second left-visual-field condition, patients were asked to reach behind

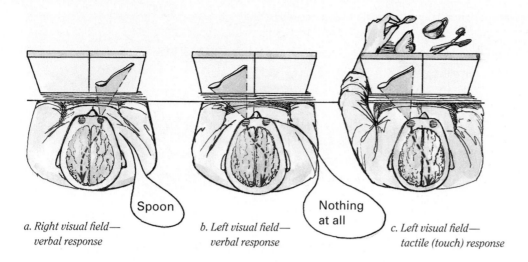

a. Right visual field—
verbal response

b. Left visual field—
verbal response

c. Left visual field—
tactile (touch) response

the screen with their left hand and identify by touch the object that had been presented on the screen. As you can see, the patient correctly grasps the spoon. These results confirmed researchers' strong suspicions that the right hemisphere is skilled in identifying spatial information, such as the shapes of objects. With the help of the left hand (also controlled by the right hemisphere), the patient could easily identify the spoon-shaped object. In his review of many studies, Gazzaniga (1983) concluded that the split-brain research illustrated a clear-cut difference between the two hemispheres.

Lateralization in People with Intact Brains Fewer than 100 people with split brains have been studied for lateralization effects. Unless you are one of those rare people, you may be wondering if lateralization is relevant to your brain. As it turns out, research on people with normal communication between the hemispheres reveals some important differences between the left and the right hemispheres. However, we should be careful not to exaggerate those differences.

Research on people with intact brains shows increased brain wave activity, metabolism, and blood flow in the left hemisphere when a person is speaking. In contrast, these same measures show that the right hemisphere is more active when a person performs certain perceptual tasks (Springer & Deutsch, 1989). However, the differences are not overwhelming. In most cases, the less active hemisphere is simply responding at a lower level.

Another way of studying lateralization involves dichotic (pronounced die-*kot*-ick) listening. In the **dichotic listening technique,** people wear earphones that present two different simultaneous messages, one to each ear. These dichotic listening studies have demonstrated that most listeners are more accurate in perceiving the right-ear message—the one that travels to the left hemisphere (Bryden & Steenhuis, 1991). Similarly, people perform visual language tasks more accurately and with greater speed when the words appear in the right visual field (left hemisphere), rather than the left visual field (Hardyck, 1991).

We have been singing the praises of the left hemisphere. What can the right hemisphere do? As one psychologist pointed out, the right hemisphere was once considered "swampland," but it now has the status of prime real estate (Searleman, 1988). The right hemisphere must be important because brains require large amounts of glucose and oxygen. Evolution would not produce such a large right hemisphere if its only function were to occupy space in the right half of the skull (Levy, 1983).

As mentioned earlier, the right hemisphere seems to specialize in spatial tasks. For example, people with damaged right hemispheres sometimes cannot discriminate between two visual stimuli. They also have trouble filling in the missing parts of a puzzle and—in extreme cases—they cannot discriminate between people's faces (Corballis, 1983).

Figure 3.20
Testing a split-brain patient in three different conditions.

When people are asked to construct this block design out of these blocks, the task primarily requires right-hemisphere activity.

TABLE 3.2 Some Tasks on Which One of the Hemispheres Shows Superiority

TASK	LEFT HEMISPHERE	RIGHT HEMISPHERE
Vision	Translation of letters into sounds	Recognition of faces
Hearing	Language sounds	Nonlanguage sounds; music
Memory	Verbal memory	Visual memory
Language	Grammar, relations among word concepts	Humor, emotional content, understanding beyond the level of the sentence
Mathematics	Arithmetic	Geometry
Problem solving	Problems to solved, analytically	Problems to solved, holistically
Complex tasks	Tasks to be performed, one part at a time	Tasks to be performed, all parts simultaneously

Sources: Joanette & Brownell, 1990; Kolb & Whishaw, 1985; Tucker & Williamson, 1984.

Table 3.2 shows some of the tasks for which the left and right hemisphere are at least somewhat specialized. Remember, however, that the two hemispheres do *not* function like two independent brains. For example, when you read a story, the left hemisphere translates the written words into their appropriate sounds, figures out grammatical relationship in the sentence, and notes the relations among word concepts. Your right hemisphere decodes the visual information, understands metaphors, figures out the story's structure, and appreciates the story's humorous and emotional aspects. Similarly, both hemispheres are important in tasks involving creativity or logic. Both hemispheres are also equally skilled in tasks such as comparing two cartoon faces (Bradshaw, 1989; Hellige, 1991; Joanette & Brownell, 1990; Levy, 1985).

We must conclude that both hemispheres can perform most tasks, but one hemisphere is usually faster and more accurate (Allen, 1983.) As Levy (1985) concludes, "Normal people have not half a brain nor two brains but one gloriously differentiated brain, with each hemisphere contributing its specialized abilities" (p. 44).

Brain Disorders

Brain Injury According to one estimate, 400,000 U.S. residents each year experience brain damage from accidents, sports injuries, and other traumatic events (Peterson, 1980). Many will be left with cognitive, motor, and personality problems. In addition, many lose interest in their environment and seem unaware that they have a problem (Prigatano, 1992).

Another common cause of brain damage is a **stroke,** a disorder in which a blood clot or some other obstruction reduces blood flow to a region of the brain (Zivin & Choi, 1991). Every year about 1% of all people in their 60s experience a stroke (Kalat, 1988). A stroke is a life-threatening event, because 30% to 40% of stroke victims die within one year, and 20% to 30% are left with a severe, permanent disability (Anderson, 1992; Zivin & Choi, 1991). These disabilities include paralysis, loss of vision, and **aphasia**—that is, a language difficulty (Anderson, 1992).

In the near future, stroke victims may be treated with a new compound called tissue plasminogen activator, a substance that rapidly removes blood clots and limits the extent of the brain damage (Zivin & Choi, 1991). At present, the new brain imaging techniques allow physicians to locate the exact site of the damage (Brown & Bornstein, 1991). Therapists also work with stroke victims, for example in helping people with aphasia learn to communicate once again (Sarno, 1991).

Occasionally, the brain demonstrates **plasticity** or flexibility. That is, when one part of the brain is injured, another part may take over some of those functions. Unfortunately, however, this flexibility is the exception, rather than the rule. Usually, recovery from a stroke is very slow, and a person may never regain his or her original level of functioning.

A dramatic but controversial new development in brain recovery is a treatment for Parkinson's disease. We mentioned this disorder in connection with dopamine; it

A hospital therapist working with a stroke victim.

Figure 3.21
Dr. William Langston, together with Juanita Lopez, who had been unable to feed or dress herself prior to surgery. After treatment, she could move easily, and she required only 30% of her previous medication dose.

involves problems such as tremors and difficulty walking. According to a recent report, researchers injected dopamine-rich brain tissue from aborted fetuses into the brains of 13 individuals suffering from Parkinson's disease. Ten of the 13 patients improved after the treatment, including Juanita Lopez, who is shown in Figure 3.21 (Widner et al., 1992). We'll have to await future research reports to know about long-term benefits. Now let us consider a particularly well-known brain disorder, Alzheimer's disease.

Alzheimer's Disease This year, several hundred thousand North Americans will begin to lose their ability to remember simple things. They will not recall whether they turned off the oven or whether they let the cat out. They will not remember the names of common objects, and they will no longer be able to balance a checkbook (Wurtman, 1984). They have a specific disorder called **Alzheimer's disease,** a condition that involves a severe decline in thinking skills and emotions, gradually growing worse over time (Kimble, 1992; Nebes, 1992).

According to a careful estimate, about 10% of people over the age of 65 have probable Alzheimer's disease (Evans et al., 1989). Because of the increasing life span, researchers believe that the number of U.S. citizens with Alzheimer's disease will increase from the current estimate of 4 million victims to about 14 million by the year 2040 (Myshko, 1991).

Unfortunately, no biochemical test can reliably identify Alzheimer's disease (Heston & White, 1991). Instead, physicians make a diagnosis on the basis of medical history, physical examination, appropriate psychological tests, and an image of the brain obtained by one of the techniques we discussed earlier. The accuracy of diagnosis may be as high as 90% if the examination includes both medical and psychological tests (U.S. Congress, 1987).

Here are some of the most prominent symptoms of Alzheimer's disease:

1. Decreased memory, especially for events that occurred recently (Van Hoesen & Damasio, 1987);

2. Deterioration of language skills, for example, finding the appropriate name for a common object (Nebes, 1989, 1992; Rebok et al., 1990) and writing a sentence (see Figure 3.22);

3. Decreased spatial ability, which includes poor performance on spatial tasks such as the one shown at the bottom of page 81 and getting lost in familiar environments (Hostetler, 1988; Rebok et al., 1990);

4. Slower responses on tasks requiring thought (Nebes & Brady, 1992; Nebes et al., 1992);

5. Mood problems, including depression and irritability, and other symptoms of psychological disorder, such as hallucinations.

A woman with Alzheimer's disease.

Figure 3.22
Sentences produced by Alzheimer's patients who were instructed to write a complete sentence.

The woman who wrote this sentence said she was trying to write, "I like the country."

The woman who wrote this sentence said she was trying to write "looking forward to a very good lunch."

As you can see, these are cognitive abilities we take for granted; *of course,* we can remember, speak, know where we are, and think quickly! However, people with Alzheimer's disease can survive as long as 25 years after the symptoms first develop. After all, their midbrain and hindbrain regions are fairly normal, and these structures keep them alive. During that extended period, they will often interact with a visitor in a competent fashion that seems quite normal. Poignantly, though, a few minutes later they may not recognize the visitor or know what year it is.

Alzheimer's disease causes profound changes in the human brain. One major change is a dramatic loss of neurons, especially in the cortex and the limbic system. Figure 3.23 compares the brain of a patient who had Alzheimer's disease with the brain of a person without the disease. As you can see, the cortex is much smaller. Even the neurons that remain may show degeneration. Another common abnormality is a large number of amyloid plaques, which are clumps of protein that form around the degenerated nerve cells in the cortex and the limbic system (Hardy & Higgins, 1992; Selkoe, 1991). Alzheimer's patients also have less of a substance that produces the neurotransmitter acetylcholine, which is important in functions such as attention and memory (Katzman, 1986).

In recent years, neuroscientists have developed several drugs designed to treat Alzheimer's disease, but many that once looked promising have been disappointing (e.g., Erickson, 1991; Thompson et al., 1990). Currently, researchers are optimistic about a new substance called tacrine. According to a large-scale study, patients who received tacrine showed smaller declines in cognitive scores during the six-week trial period than did the patients in the control group (Davis et al., 1992; Growdon, 1992). At present, we do not know whether the benefits are long lasting or whether tacrine will join the list of disappointing possibilities. Alzheimer's disease still remains one of the most serious threats to the health and well-being of people throughout North America.

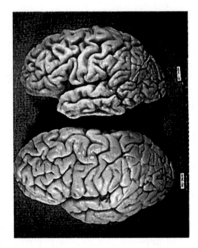

Figure 3.23
Examples of the brain of a person who had Alzheimer's disease (upper) and a normal brain (lower).

IN DEPTH: Neuroscience Research on Visual Object Recognition

Imagine your frustration if you awoke tomorrow and could not name the objects around you—even common objects such as a book, a chair, and a cup of coffee. This disorder is called visual agnosia (pronounced "ag-*know*-zhia"). In **visual agnosia,** a person has normal basic visual abilities and no evidence of a general disorder such as Alzheimer's disease; however, he or she cannot recognize objects by sight.

Visual agnosia is a relatively rare disorder that has been studied extensively by Martha Farah, who received the prestigious National Academy of Sciences Troland Award in 1992 for her work on vision. As Farah (1990) points out, people with visual agnosia have vision that appears to be normal on many tasks. For example, when two people with visual agnosia were asked to copy

Figure 3.24

Examples of drawings made by people who had experienced a head injury that produced damage in the temporal lobe; both were asked to copy a figure of a horse. (From Farah et al., 1991)

Figure produced by L.H., a 36-year-old man whose case is discussed on this page.

Figure produced by M.B., a 30-year-old woman who experienced a head injury the previous year; she also has difficulty identifying faces and recognizing many other living objects, though she can read normally.

a drawing of a horse, they produced the sketches in Figure 3.24 (Farah et al., 1991). As you can see, these drawings are adequate; people with visual agnosia can see angles, lines, and curves. However—amazingly—the two individuals could not name the object they had just drawn.

Let us examine visual agnosia in some detail, because this topic illustrates how neuroscience research can help us understand a normal human skill that we typically take for granted. Let's see why neuroscientists have identified the temporal lobe as the site for visual object recognition, and then we will examine some other issues in research on visual agnosia.

The Temporal Lobe and Visual Object Recognition Each of the research techniques we discussed at the beginning of this chapter provides a different perspective on a particular brain process. The study of visual object recognition has been advanced through the use of three techniques: the case study method, lesion production, and the single-cell recording technique.

Martha Farah (1990) has described how the case study method reveals information about people with a specific kind of visual agnosia, which involves difficulty recognizing faces. For example, one man could accurately perform a variety of visual tasks, such as identifying which of 20 photos of cats represented a Siamese cat. However, he could not identify relatives or close friends unless he heard them speak (DeRenzi, 1986). In a vivid case study, Pallis (1955) described a brain-injured man who saw a stranger staring at him in a restaurant. He then asked a nearby person to identify this stranger. As it turned out, he had been looking at himself in a mirror!

Let's consider in more detail the case of L.H., a 36-year-old man who had been in an accident at age 18 (Farah et al., 1991). The brain injury affected the occipital lobe, the right temporal lobe, and the right side of the frontal lobe. (Check Figure 3.17 to remind yourself where these structures are located.) Nevertheless, he recovered remarkably well from the accident and subsequent surgery, and he even completed college and graduate school. His conversational skills are normal, and he has no difficulty finding words. His basic visual skills are generally normal; his drawing of a horse is shown in Figure 3.24. However, he cannot recognize faces, and he has some difficulty identifying animals, plants, and food. In all, he correctly identified only 52% of all drawings of living things, compared with 84% of nonliving things.

In the section on research techniques, we mentioned some problems with the case study method. For example, when people are in an accident—unfortunately for both themselves and for science—the brain damage is not limited to a neat, well-defined region of the cortex. In the case of L.H., any of several regions of the brain might be linked with his visual agnosia. Researchers need to supplement the case histories with experimental research techniques, in which they have greater control over the region of the brain they examine.

David Plaut and Martha Farah (1990) describe how the lesion production technique has been used in animal research. For example, in the classic research, neuroscientists removed small portions of the temporal lobe of the cortex in monkeys in order to identify which brain regions were associated with which visual skills. Naturally, they could not use a verbal naming task with monkeys, so they needed to devise a dependent variable that could reveal the monkeys' visual deficits. They selected a visual discrimination task, in which monkeys saw two visually similar designs. If the monkeys pressed a button next to one design, they received a reward; if they pressed the button next to the unrewarded pattern, they received nothing. Monkeys in a control condition can easily learn which design will be rewarded. However, monkeys with lesions in the lower part of the temporal lobe (the inferotemporal cortex) performed very poorly on this task and other similar ones (e.g., Blum et al., 1950; Mishkin, 1966; Pribram, 1954). Object recognition was virtually impossible without this part of the cortex.

Research using the single-cell recording technique confirms that the inferotemporal cortex is involved in recognizing visual objects. As Chapter 4 describes, vision researchers were frustrated in their early attempts to understand how parts of the brain were involved in vision. They inserted a tiny electrode into many regions of an animal's cortex, presented a variety of simple stimuli, and found that the neurons refused to respond. Later, they discovered that cells in the inferotemporal cortex did not respond to simple lines and angles, but they did respond to more complex stimuli. For example, Robert Desimone and his colleagues (1984) located neurons in the inferotemporal cortex that showed only random production of action potentials when a stimulus such as a hand or a brush was displayed in the visual field. However, as Figure 3.25 shows, these neurons responded somewhat more enthusiastically to a picture of a monkey's face, seen at an angle. Furthermore, you can see that the neurons were even more responsive when either of two front-view pictures of monkey faces were presented.

As Plaut and Farah (1990) caution, we cannot generalize from this study and assume that the mechanisms of face recognition can explain how we recognize other objects. (For example, you do not have a cell in your inferotemporal cortex that allows you to recognize your psychology textbook!) However, research using case studies, the lesion production technique, and the single-cell recording technique all establish that the inferotemporal cortex is crucial in recognizing complex visual patterns.

Other Issues in Visual Agnosia Research The most recent studies in visual agnosia focus on people who have very specific recognition problems. For example, Farah and her colleagues (1991) describe two people who have great difficulty recognizing pictures of living things such as a rabbit or corn on the cob. However, they have little difficulty identifying nonliving stimuli, such as a piano or a windmill.

If you recall the discussion from Chapter 2 about well-controlled research, you might be suspicious that these peculiar results might be traceable to some confounding variable. Perhaps the researchers selected uncommon living objects (such as an ostrich or a mango), and the other items were more common (such as a house or a chair). Farah and her coauthors used a statistical

Figure 3.25

How a face-selective cell in a monkey's inferotemporal cortex responds to a variety of stimuli. (Based on Desimone et al., 1984)

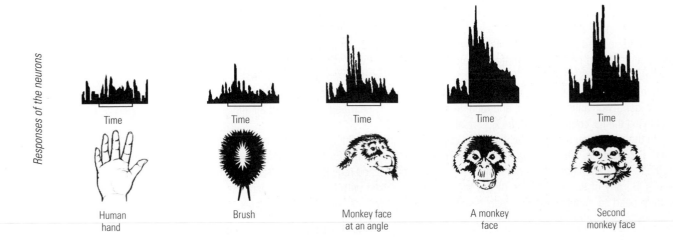

technique that took frequency, familiarity, and visual complexity into account. The important determinant of recognition accuracy was still whether the item was living rather than nonliving.

The results of Farah and her colleagues suggest that the ability to recognize objects from a special class (e.g., living objects) is represented in a relatively small portion of the brain. Like most interesting research, this study raises as many questions as it answers. For example, can children have such specific agnosias, and—if so—what would these findings imply about learning? Can we identify any other specific deficits that can help us understand agnosia? These findings also raise a more general question about research methods, specifically the case study: What if we find just one human with an even more specific deficit—perhaps a deficit in recognizing different vegetables? Is the evidence from this one individual sufficient for us to draw general conclusions about the organization of the human brain?

SECTION SUMMARY

THE BRAIN

- The hindbrain includes the medulla, the pons, the cerebellum, and the reticular formation; this region helps regulate basic functions such as breathing, body movement, and sleep. The midbrain is important in processes such as vision, motor movement, and sleep.

- The forebrain includes the thalamus, the hypothalamus, the pituitary gland, and the limbic system (all structures critical in relaying information, controlling hormone production, and regulating motivation and emotion). The forebrain also includes the cerebral cortex, which is responsible for vision, the skin senses, motor movements, hearing, and all complex thought processes.

- The two hemispheres of the brain have a contralateral arrangement; also, the hemispheres are somewhat different in their functions, but the differences should not be exaggerated.

- Brain disorders can arise from injury (e.g., a head injury or a stroke). Alzheimer's disease involves decreased memory, language skills, and spatial ability, as well as slower responses and mood problems; changes can be observed in the brain structure of people with Alzheimer's disease.

- Research on visual agnosia has employed the case study method, lesion production, and the single-cell recording technique to demonstrate that the inferotemporal cortex plays a role in visual object recognition; other research points out that agnosia for specific classes of objects is very specialized.

BEHAVIORAL GENETICS

So far, this chapter has emphasized two of the three themes of this textbook. We have seen that the biological determinants of behavior are complex; even simple behaviors require the cooperation of many regions of the brain. We have also seen that the nervous system allows humans to function quickly and efficiently. However, Chapter 3 has not yet even hinted at the third theme, individual differences. This section, which explores how genetics influences behavior, has important implications for the variation among humans.

Furthermore, genetics is important in this chapter because the information in your genes controlled your development from a single-celled creature into a fully functioning adult. Your genes are responsible for the fact that your cerebellum controls your balance, part of your temporal lobe recognizes complex patterns, and your adrenal glands secrete epinephrine in response to a fearful situation.

At several points throughout this textbook, we discuss how genetics influences behavior. For example, Chapter 10 examines how genetics is important in prenatal development and how genetics influences children's personality. In Chapter 14, we explore how genetic research helps psychologists determine hereditary factors related to intelligence. Chapter 15 points out that depression and schizophrenia are at least partly inherited. To provide a basis for these future topics, we need to discuss three topics: genes and chromosomes, methods for studying behavioral genetics, and the nature-nurture question.

Genes and Chromosomes

Genes are the basic units of heredity. In humans, the genes are located on 23 pairs of **chromosomes.** In virtually every cell in your body, you have 46 chromosomes carrying the genetic information that had a critical role in making you into yourself. One set of 23 chromosomes was contributed by your father; the other set came from your mother.

It is not clear why we humans have precisely 23 pairs of chromosomes. One primitive species of worm has only one pair of chromosomes, but a type of one-celled marine organism has about 800 pairs (Davis & Solomon, 1986). Figure 3.26 shows several chromosome pairs.

As you may know, one of the 23 pairs of chromosomes determined whether you would be male or female; this pair is called the **sex chromosomes.** Females have a pair of sex chromosomes called X chromosomes (symbolized XX). Males have one sex chromosome called X and one called Y (symbolized XY). That Y chromosome is much smaller than the X chromosome. Ironically, then, a single chromosome pair determines a characteristic that most humans consider to be vitally important—whether you are male or female. As we discuss issues related to gender comparisons and gender stereotypes in later chapters, keep in mind that all this controversy can be traced to a pair of chromosomes so tiny that they must be magnified hundreds of times before they are visible.

Methods for Studying Behavioral Genetics

Researchers interested in genetics have devised several methods for understanding more about the relationship between genetics and behavior. These techniques include the investigation of genetic abnormalities, twin studies, and adoption studies. These methods are most likely to be used in studying personality, cognitive abilities, and psychological disorders (Plomin & Neiderhiser, 1992).

Investigating Genetic Abnormalities Researchers are rapidly working on the genetic map for human beings. In fact, one researcher observed that scientists are literally discovering one gene each day (Wheeler, 1991). Many of their discoveries help us understand how genetic abnormalities are related to psychological characteristics. For example, **Down syndrome** usually results from having a third 21st chromosome, rather than the normal pair of two chromosomes. Individuals with Down syndrome are typically retarded and have smaller brain size. When interacting with other people, they are often friendly and cheerful. More than 300 abnormal characteristics have been identified for Down syndrome (Plomin et al., 1990). As Figure 3.27 shows, they often have distinctive round faces, with small folds of skin across the inner edge of the eyes.

Furthermore, some psychological disorders now appear to have a genetic origin. For example, a gene on the 21st chromosome is apparently involved in some cases of inherited Alzheimer's disease (Loehlin et al., 1988; Tanzi et al., 1987).

Twin Studies Jerry Levey and Mark Newman are identical twins who were separated at birth. When they were finally reunited, the two middle-aged bachelors discovered that they shared an uncanny number of peculiar characteristics. Both were compulsive flirts, and both were raucously good-humored. They both liked beer and drank the same brand. Both drank from the bottle, with the little finger extended underneath the bottom of the bottle. Both were volunteer fire fighters (Rosen, 1987).

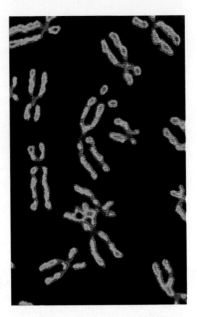

Figure 3.26
Human chromosomes (greatly magnified).

Figure 3.27
This young woman has Down syndrome, yet she can interact helpfully with children in a day-care setting.

The identical twins on the left probably behave quite similarly. In contrast, the fraternal twins on the right probably behave quite differently.

Anecdotes like this are certainly impressive, but we need to remain skeptical. For example, where is the control condition? Any pair of unrelated individuals who are the same age would probably be able to identify a number of amazing coincidences. Furthermore, researchers have been able to study only about 300 pairs of identical twins who were reared apart (Plomin et al., 1990).

Researchers are more likely to compare **identical twins** (who came from a single fertilized egg and are genetically identical) with **fraternal twins** (who came from two separate eggs and are thus no more genetically similar than two siblings). These comparisons of identical and fraternal twins are called **twin studies.** In most research, identical twins are more similar to each other than are fraternal twins (e.g., Plomin et al., 1990).

Adoption Studies A third approach in behavioral genetics is to study individuals who have been adopted. In **adoption studies,** researchers try to determine whether adopted children are more like their biological parents (who contribute genes) or their adoptive parents (who contribute a home environment). In some cases, adopted children are more likely to resemble their biological parents than their adoptive parents. For example, studies have been conducted on schizophrenia, which involves disordered thought—as we discussed earlier in the chapter. Adoption studies show that an adopted person who develops schizophrenia is more likely to have a biological parent with schizophrenia than to have an adoptive parent with schizophrenia (Plomin et al., 1990). In this case, genes are more important than home environment.

Both twin studies and adoption studies assess the relative contribution of genes and environment to human behavior. These studies provide important information for a long-standing controversy in psychology known as the nature-nurture question.

The Nature-Nurture Question

Stop reading for a moment and try to think about a particular skill you have or a specific characteristic that makes you unusual. How would you explain this particular attribute? Is it determined by the genes you inherited from your biological parents—in other words, is it traceable to **nature?** Alternatively, is this characteristic due to the way you were reared—in other words, is it traceable to **nurture?** You probably cannot draw a simple conclusion, because the issue is complex. For example, suppose you are musically gifted, and you know that one parent is also extremely musical. Perhaps that parent passed on the relevant genes to you. However, another explanation is that a musical parent is likely to encourage musical talent in a child.

We raise the nature-nurture question at several points throughout this book, because it is a major theme in psychological research. You will see that psychologists cannot provide a clear-cut "It's all nature" or "It's all nurture" response. However, psychologists now acknowledge that many characteristics have a genetic (or nature) component. These include intelligence, school achievement, reading disabilities, psychological disorders, criminal behavior, some personality characteristics, some attitudes, and career choice (Goldsmith, 1993; Plomin et al., 1990).

An important concept in the nature-nurture debate is heritability. **Heritability** estimates how much of the variation in some characteristic can be traced to differences in heredity, as opposed to differences in environment (Kalat, 1992). Heritability can vary between .00 and 1.00. A heritability figure near .00 indicates that little of the variation can be traced to heredity. In contrast, a heritability figure near 1.00 indicates that almost all the variation can be traced to heredity. For example, studies suggest that the heritability for intelligence is between .50 and .70 (DeFries et al., 1987; Loehlin et al., 1988; Plomin, 1990a). However, the heritability figure can vary substantially, depending on the populations that are studied, the environment in which the individuals were reared, and the way they are tested.

Our overview of the biological basis of behavior has introduced the structure and functions of the nervous system as well as behavioral genetics. The chapter described how electrical impulses travel throughout the nervous system; how structures in the brain regulate perception, thought, and behavior; and how tiny structures called genes carry information related to psychological characteristics. We must now move beyond the biological level to consider how people experience the world through sensation and perception.

SECTION SUMMARY

BEHAVIORAL GENETICS

- Humans have 23 chromosome pairs, each containing a number of pairs of genes.

- Techniques for studying behavioral genetics include the study of genetic abnormalities (e.g., Down syndrome), twin studies, and adoption studies.

- The nature-nurture question considers what portion of the differences in psychological characteristics can be traced to nature (genetics) and what portion can be traced to nurture (rearing); heritability is a measure of the relative contribution provided by genetics.

1. Draw a representative neuron, labeling the dendrites, cell body, axon, myelin, synapse, and terminal buttons. In the first section of this chapter, some of the described reactions are chemical, whereas others are electrical. List which reactions belong to each category.

2. What are the three kinds of chemical messengers discussed in this chapter? What function does each kind of messenger perform, and how do the three kinds differ from each other?

3. Figure 3.10 outlined the divisions of the nervous system. Try to reproduce this figure, being certain to include the following terms in your diagram: autonomic division, central nervous system, sympathetic system, brain, peripheral nervous system, spinal cord, somatic division, parasympathetic system, and (at the top of the diagram) the nervous system. Then try to recall some recent activity that required using each portion of the nervous system. Check your accuracy by consulting Figure 3.10 on page 69.

4. Suppose that neuroscientists wanted to know more about the way that auditory stimuli (sounds) are processed in the brain. List each neuroscience research method described in this chapter and speculate how each could be used to provide information about hearing.

5. You probably know someone whose physician requested one of the three imaging techniques described in this chapter after this person had a head injury, a stroke, or a serious disease; you may also know someone who had neurosurgery to remove a tumor in the brain. Describe in as much detail as possible the way these medical procedures are performed.

6. Figure 3.12 outlined the organization of the brain. Try to reproduce as many of the organs as you can recall, listing the structures under the heading of hindbrain, midbrain, and forebrain. Then consult Figure 3.12 (page 72) to complete your diagram. Using a pen of a different color, jot down notes about the functions performed by each structure. Try to notice which of these structures have similar functions, and try to identify overall differences among the functions of the three major regions of the brain.

7. Two characteristics of the brain were discussed in connection with the cerebral hemispheres. Define the term *contralateral arrangement* and explain how this term is relevant for a person who has a stroke that affects one hemisphere. Then explain how the research on the split-brain procedure and on dichotic listening provides information about lateralization.

8. Imagine that a friend has just discovered that an elderly relative has been diagnosed as having Alzheimer's disease. What kind of information could you supply about the general nature of the disease, its symptoms, and its neurological changes? Also, briefly summarize what this chapter has mentioned about several other problems: Parkinson's disease, multiple sclerosis, head injuries, strokes, and Down syndrome.

9. Imagine that a high-school student whom you know needs a quick overview of genetics. Summarize the information from the last part of the chapter. Be sure to include genes and chromosomes, genetic research methods, and the naturenurture issue. Illustrate the nature-nurture issue with your own example.

10. In preparation for Chapter 4, summarize what you know about the way the brain processes sight, sound, and touch. Your information is most complete for sight, because we discussed how both simple visual stimuli and complex visual stimuli are processed.

NEW TERMS

neuron
dendrites
cell body
axon
action potential
myelin sheath
multiple sclerosis
synapse
terminal buttons
neurotransmitters
excitatory potential
inhibitory potential
acetylcholine (ACh)
dopamine
Parkinson's disease
neuromodulators
endorphins
endocrine system
hormones
pituitary gland
thyroid gland
adrenal glands
androgen hormones
epinephrine
gonads
case study
lesion
electrical stimulation
electroencephalography (EEG)
single-cell recording technique
computed tomography (CT scan)
positron emission tomography (PET scan)
magnetic resonance imaging (MRI)
peripheral nervous system
central nervous system
nerves
somatic division
autonomic division
sympathetic system
parasympathetic system

homeostasis
spinal cord
hindbrain
medulla
pons
cerebellum
reticular formation
midbrain
forebrain
thalamus
hypothalamus
limbic system
cerebral cortex
occipital lobe
retinotopic arrangement
parietal lobe
frontal lobe
prefrontal cortex
temporal lobes
contralateral arrangement
lateralization
corpus callosum
dichotic listening technique
stroke
aphasia
plasticity
Alzheimer's disease
visual agnosia
genes
chromosomes
sex chromosomes
Down syndrome
identical twins
fraternal twins
twin studies
adoption studies
nature
nurture
heritability

RECOMMENDED READINGS

Carlson, N. R. (1991). *Physiology of behavior* (4th ed.). Boston: Allyn and Bacon. Carlson's textbook is somewhat more advanced than Kalat's textbook; the chapter on neuroscience research methods is particularly helpful.

Churchland, P. S., & Sejnowski, T. J. (1992). *The computational brain*. Cambridge, MA: MIT Press. Students who are interested in computer simulations of brain functions would enjoy this book, which also contains a useful appendix on neuroscience research methods.

Farah, M. J. (1990). *Visual agnosia: Disorders of object recognition and what they tell us about normal vision*. Cambridge, MA: MIT. Martha Farah's clear and interesting examination of a variety of visual agnosias will be useful for any students who were intrigued by the "In Depth" section in this chapter.

Kalat, J. W. (1992). *Biological psychology* (4th ed.). Belmont, CA: Wadsworth. Students who used this textbook in a course in physiological psychology at my college were especially enthusiastic about this straightforward, interesting textbook; you will admire the numerous color photos and diagrams.

Heston, L. L., & White, J. A. (1991). *The vanishing mind: A practical guide to Alzheimer's disease and other dementias*. New York: Freeman. This book will be valuable for anyone who wants current, scientific, and yet clearly written information about Alzheimer's disease and other related disorders.

Plomin, R. (1990b). *Nature and nurture*. Pacific Grove, CA: Brooks/Cole. Plomin is one of the foremost researchers in behavioral genetics, and this student-oriented book provides a good introduction to genes and heredity.

CHAPTER 4
SENSATION AND PERCEPTION

Right now, you are actively sensing and perceiving. Your eyes race across this page, registering lines, dots, and squiggles that will be transformed into meaningful words. Looking up from your book, you encounter a rich assortment of objects that vary in shape and color. You perceive that some objects are nearby, but the building you see from your window seems miles away. At the same time, your auditory system may be tracking the screeching brakes of an automobile or fragments of a conversation in the hallway. Your skin senses may detect the room temperature, the mild pain of too-tight shoes, or the pressure of your chair against your back. A trip to the dining room can activate an equally rich variety of taste and smell experiences. During every waking moment, you are constantly sensing and perceiving.

Sensation refers to the immediate, basic experiences that simple stimuli generate—such as the sensation of cold when rain strikes your cheek or the sensation of red from a blotch of color on a painter's canvas. In contrast, **perception** requires the interpretation of those basic sensations; perception involves organization and meaning. Suppose that a friend plays a note on the piano. The loudness and pitch of that note are *sensations*. However, if you hear the first five notes and realize that they form a melody, rather than random sounds, you experience a *perception*. In reality, the distinction between sensation and perception is not clear-cut. How complex can a stimulus become before it crosses the boundary into perception? How much interpretation is required before sensation wanders into the territory of perception? Psychologists concede that the boundary between these two terms is blurred.

People usually take sensation and perception for granted. After all, you manage without effort to see, hear, touch, smell, and taste. You open your eyes and see pencils, trucks, and petunias. You open your mouth, insert a spoonful of food, and taste chocolate ice cream, garlic bread, or a chicken enchilada. These processes seem so commonplace, yet they have intrigued psychologists and philosophers for centuries. The basic dilemma is this: How are the qualities of objects—for example, the frog in Figure 4.1—re-created inside your head? The picture lies an arm's length in front of you. Still, the frog's color, shape, and features are conveyed to your cortex so that you experience a reasonably accurate, well-organized representation of the frog.

This chapter explores how we achieve accurate, well-organized perceptions of sights, sounds, skin senses, smells, and tastes. An important prelude to that exploration is psychophysics, which focuses on measuring sensations.

PSYCHOPHYSICS

How can we measure how the world appears? Sensation is a private activity. A person who decides to watch your sensory processes at work soon grows bored, because so little activity is visible. **Psychophysics** is an area of psychology that examines the relationship between physical stimuli (such as sights or sounds) and people's psychological reactions to those stimuli. Suppose two trombone players play a C on their instruments, and Joe's C is slightly higher than Carlos's C. In other words, the two *physical* stimuli differ slightly. Will their conductor be able to discriminate between the two tones, indicating that they are *psychologically* different? Can this conductor perceive the physical difference?

Figure 4.1

In perception, the qualities of an object (for example, of this photograph of a frog) are re-created inside your head.

A typical study in psychophysics might assess people's psychological reactions to a faint tone. The intensity of the physical stimulus—that faint tone—can be measured precisely in units devised by physicists. Measuring people's psychological reactions is more challenging. For more than a century, researchers have been devising psychophysical methods for converting these private psychological reactions into objective numbers. These numbers inform us about human sensory ability, and they also provide objective measures for research in perception.

Basically, psychophysicists ask two kinds of questions: (1) Can people detect this low-intensity stimulus? (2) Can people discriminate between these two similar stimuli? Let us consider these questions separately.

Detection

Suppose that you are tasting a fruit punch at a party. Is that subtle flavor some kind of alcohol? Or suppose your neighbors have asked you to keep an eye on their house while they are away on vacation. Is that a faint light in their dining room? These two situations require detection. In **detection** studies, psychologists present low-intensity stimuli and record whether people report them. Psychologists can study detection using either of two major approaches to detection: the classical psychophysics approach or the signal detection theory approach.

The Classical Psychophysics Approach The goal of the classical psychophysics approach to detection is to establish a threshold. A **detection threshold** is the smallest amount of energy required for the observer to report the stimulus on half (50%) of the trials. For example, if researchers want to measure the detection threshold for light, they must establish how intense the light must be for the observers to say, "I see it" half the time and "I don't see it" half the time.

Just how sensitive are the senses? Table 4.1 shows examples of some very impressive detection thresholds. However, do not conclude that psychophysicists spend their work hours dropping bee wings on people's cheeks. They are more likely to use carefully calibrated hairlike fibers to assess detection thresholds for touch.

The Signal Detection Approach The more current approach to detection rejects the concept of an absolute threshold, in which a stimulus is consistently perceived if it is greater than the threshold and not perceived if it is less than the threshold (Gescheider, 1985; Luce & Krumhansl, 1988). According to this newer approach, your likelihood of hearing a faint noise depends on your expectations and motivation.

A student, Bruce Edington, provided a good example of how our responses depend on expectations. Bruce had applied for a job, and the manager had stressed that Bruce could expect a phone call between 3:30 and 4:00 on a particular afternoon. Within that 30-minute period, Bruce was convinced that he heard the phone start to ring two or three times. His "I hear it" responses were more common than in other circumstances because of (1) the high probability that the phone should actually ring during that period and (2) the important benefits of answering the phone if it did

Signal detection theory predicts that the expectations and motivations of this air traffic controller will influence the likelihood of his detecting an incoming plane on the horizon.

TABLE 4.1 Several Approximate Detection Threshold Values	
SENSORY PROCESS	**APPROXIMATE DETECTION THRESHOLD**
Vision	A candle flame seen at 30 miles on a dark clear night.
Hearing	The tick of a watch at 20 feet under quiet conditions.
Touch	The wing of a bee falling on your cheek from a distance of ½ inch.
Smell	One drop of perfume diffused into the entire volume of a three-room apartment.
Taste	One teaspoon of sugar in 2 gallons of water.

Source: Adapted from Galanter, 1962. Used with permission.

ring, in contrast to the major drawbacks of not answering the phone. In fact, Bruce's expectations were so strong that he probably would have run to the phone if the doorbell had rung! Bruce's story illustrates how our expectancies influence the probability of saying, "I detect this stimulus."

The classic psychophysics approach ignores factors such as a person's motivations for saying, "Yes, I detect the stimulus." That approach simply records the number of *yes* and *no* responses. In contrast, **signal detection theory** assesses both the observer's **sensitivity** (or ability to detect a weak stimulus) and the observer's **criterion** (or willingness to say, "I detect the stimulus," when it is not clear whether the stimulus has been presented). Thus, Bruce Edington's responses in this situation depended on the sensitivity of his hearing. Furthermore, Bruce's motivation and expectation about the phone call encouraged him to adopt a lenient criterion when he was waiting for the call. He was willing to believe that the phone had rung, even if there was only the *slightest* chance that it rang. Two common determinants of a person's criterion in signal detection theory are (1) the probability that the stimulus will occur and (2) the benefits and drawbacks associated with making the particular response. In Bruce's case, these two factors conspired to send him running to the phone—even when no stimulus had occurred.

The important contribution of signal detection theory to psychophysics is that it reminds us of the variability within each human. We are not rigid "detection machines" who consistently report "I perceive it" whenever a stimulus reaches a specific intensity. Instead, our knowledge of the situation determines whether or not we perceive a particular stimulus.

Discrimination

We have examined one major psychophysical skill, detecting a weak stimulus. Another psychophysical task we often perform is discriminating between two similar stimuli. In **discrimination** studies, experimenters present two stimuli; then they assess how different these stimuli must be in order for the observer to report, "These two are distinguishably different." Consider some discrimination tasks that people perform every day. Is the margin on my report the same size as on the model report the professor gave us, or is it slightly smaller? Does this chicken recipe have the same amount of lime as the one in the Afrilanka Restaurant, or is it more sour? When singing the national anthem before a ballgame, does your note match the one sung by the voice over the loudspeaker, or is it slightly lower?

The classical research on discrimination produced an important concept, the just-noticeable difference. As the name implies, the experimenter changes the physical stimulus until a **just-noticeable difference** (or **jnd**) is produced. For instance, researchers have determined that humans can just barely notice the difference between 60 candles burning in one room and 61 candles in the same room.

Suppose, however, that we start with 120 candles. Will observers be able to detect the difference between 120 and 121 burning candles? An early researcher, Ernst Weber (pronounced *Vay*-bur), noticed that two stimuli must differ by a constant proportion in order to create a just-noticeable difference. According to **Weber's law,** a weak or small stimulus does not require much change before we notice that it has changed; a strong or large stimulus requires a proportionately greater change before we notice that it has changed. In fact, researchers have discovered that observers cannot notice the difference between 120 and 121 candles. However, the difference between 120 and 122 candles is noticeable.

Research on Weber's law has determined that the exact value of the constant proportion will vary from task to task. For instance, we are very sensitive to changes in the pitch of a tone. If two tones differ by less that 1% (0.33%, to be exact), we can detect the difference between them. However, we are not very sensitive to changes in the intensity of smell. Two smells must differ by about 25% for us to detect the difference between them. Therefore, you should be able to tell the difference between four and five sprays of air-freshener spread throughout a room.

Is Weber's law accurate? Researchers know that judgments are influenced by the context in which the stimuli appear (Poulton, 1989). Still, a wide variety of studies on vision, hearing, and the other senses have demonstrated that Weber's law is reasonably accurate in predicting sensory discrimination.

Try noticing some applications of Weber's law. For example, you may notice a 5-pound weight loss on a slender friend, but a plumper friend may need to lose 10 pounds to produce a just-noticeable difference. Similarly, people complain about a 4-cent raise in the price of a postage stamp, but they may not notice a 4-cent increase in the cost of a gallon of gas.

Psychophysics is a useful tool for assessing people's private sensory responses and for converting those private responses into numbers. These numbers are valuable in research about sensation and perception. Furthermore, the detection thresholds and some of the discrimination thresholds also illustrate the theme that humans are endowed with extremely impressive equipment, which allows them to perform both accurately and efficiently.

S E C T I O N   S U M M A R Y

PSYCHOPHYSICS

- Sensation refers to the immediate experiences generated by simple stimuli; perception involves additional organization and meaning. In reality, the distinction between the two terms is blurred.

- Psychophysics investigates the relationship between physical stimuli and psychological reactions to those stimuli.

- Two approaches to detection are the classical psychophysical approach, involving detection thresholds, and signal detection theory, which points out that expectations and motivations influence an observer's criterion.

- In research on discrimination, Weber's law says that small changes can be readily noticed when the stimulus is weak or small; strong or large stimuli require proportionately greater changes before these changes are noticeable.

VISION

Take a minute to notice your perceptual experiences at this very moment. You may be aware of sound, touch, smell, and taste, but sight is probably most prominent. This extraordinarily rich visual sense supplies us with knowledge (e.g., about Weber's law), social information (e.g., a friend's scowling face), entertainment (e.g., a movie), and survival information (e.g., a traffic light). Vision often dominates our perceptual experiences, and it also dominates the research in sensation and perception. As a result, our knowledge about the visual system, sensory processing, and complex visual phenomena is much more complete than the knowledge about the other senses. Let us begin by considering the structure of the eye and the rest of the visual system.

The Visual System

The human eye is about the size of a large olive, yet it performs an impressive variety of tasks with remarkable accuracy and efficiency. The eye processes information about color, shape, motion, and distance—even though it is less than two inches wide.

The visual stimulus that initiates this impressive variety of tasks is light. Light is one form of electromagnetic radiation. Electromagnetic radiation includes all forms of waves produced by electrically charged particles. For example, a star in the Big Dipper, which is 90 light-years away, generates electrically charged particles.

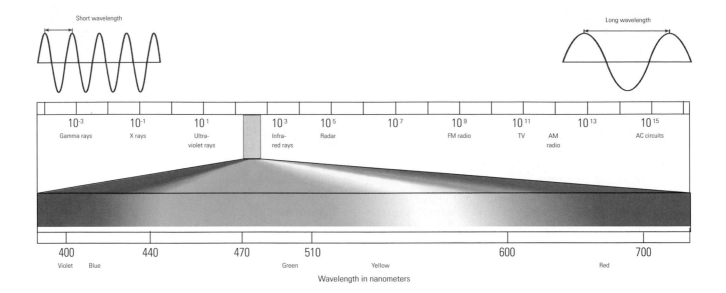

Short wavelength

Long wavelength

| 10^{-3} | 10^{-1} | 10^1 | | 10^3 | 10^5 | 10^7 | 10^9 | 10^{11} | 10^{13} | 10^{15} |
| Gamma rays | X rays | Ultra-violet rays | | Infra-red rays | Radar | | FM radio | TV   AM radio | | AC circuits |

| 400 | 440 | 470 | 510 | 600 | 700 |
| Violet   Blue | | | Green   Yellow | | Red |

Wavelength in nanometers

Ultimately, that stimulus produces physiological changes in the light receptors in your eyes, enabling you to see a distinct pinpoint of light in the clear night sky.

Figure 4.2 shows that humans see only a small part of the electromagnetic radiation spectrum. We cannot see the shorter ultraviolet rays that tan our skin or the longer infrared rays or radio waves.

Light travels in waves, and **wavelength** is the distance between two peaks in these waves. This distance is measured in nanometers (abbreviated nm), which equal 1 billionth of a meter. We see light in the wavelength range between about 400nm and 700nm.

Wavelength is a characteristic of light that helps to determine the **hue** or color of a visual stimulus. The height of the light wave, or **amplitude,** is the characteristic that determines the **brightness** of a visual stimulus. Thus, the wavelengths in a bright sky-blue color are relatively close together and tall, whereas the wavelengths in a dark shade of red are relatively far apart and short.

The Anatomy of the Eye Figure 4.3 shows the major structures of the eye. The **cornea** is a clear membrane with a curved surface that helps to bend light rays when they enter the eye. Just behind the cornea is the **iris,** a ring of muscles that contracts and dilates to change the amount of light that enters the eye. The color of the iris can range from pale blue to dark brown. The **pupil** is the opening in the center of that colored iris.

Directly behind the iris and the pupil is the **lens,** a structure which changes shape to focus on objects that are nearby or far away. The lens completes the process begun by the cornea of bending the light rays so that they gather in focus at the back of the eye, at a point on or near the retina.

The **retina** absorbs light rays and converts them into patterns of action potentials that can be transmitted to the brain by the neurons; this process is called **transduction.** The retina is a critically important part of the eye, even though it is only as thick as a page of this book. A tiny region in the center of the retina is called the **fovea** (pronounced *foe*-vee-uh), the area in which vision is the most precise.

Cells in the Retina Figure 4.4 illustrates four different kinds of retinal cells that play a critical role in converting light into sight. The two kinds of cells that respond to light are called **receptor cells,** or cones and rods. **Cones** are responsible for color vision, and they operate best when the lighting is good. **Rods** do not code color; regardless of the wavelength of the stimulus, they lead to the perception of blacks, grays, and whites. When the lighting is poor, rods function better than cones. If you

*Figure 4.2

The electromagnetic spectrum (upper portion). The lower portion represents an expanded version of the visible spectrum.

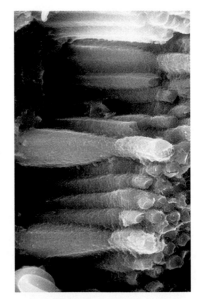

An enlarged photograph of rods and cones on the retina, as shown by an electron microscope. Note that the cylinder-shaped structures are rods and the tapered structures are cones. (The receptors are shown in a left-right orientation, the same as in Figure 4.4, and are magnified roughly 1000 times normal size.)

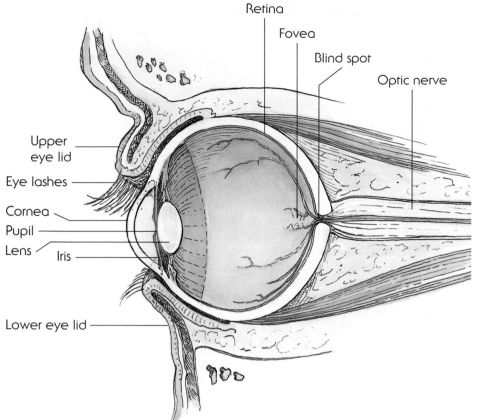

Retina
Fovea
Blind spot
Optic nerve

Upper
eye lid

Eye lashes

Cornea
Pupil
Lens
Iris

Lower eye lid

Figure 4.3
Inside the human eye (side view).

Figure 4.4
*A diagram of the kinds of cells in the
retina.*

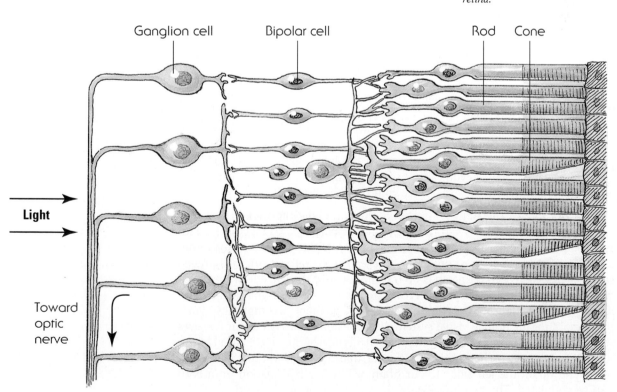

Ganglion cell
Bipolar cell
Rod
Cone

Light

Toward
optic
nerve

are outside at night, you cannot see an object's customary color, but the rods allow you to see various shades of gray.

These two kinds of receptors also differ in their distribution throughout the retina. Cones are concentrated primarily in the fovea; rods are located mostly outside the fovea. Each retina contains only about 6 million cones, in contrast to about 125 million rods (Pugh, 1988).

A poorly designed visual system might feature only one kind of light receptor, which would need to perform a variety of tasks in a variety of different conditions. Instead, humans have two specialized kinds of receptors, each excelling in its own area—another illustration of the theme that we are remarkably well equipped to function in our environment. Your cones excel in transmitting color information in a well-lit situation, for example when you inspected the photograph of the frog in Figure 4.1. In contrast, rods are active when you stargaze at night. Rods are highly sensitive in detecting faint spots of light when the illumination is poor (Schnapf & Baylor, 1987). Because we have two specialized receptor systems, we can see under a much broader range of lighting conditions than if we had only cones or only rods.

The cones and rods use transduction to convert light into electrical activity at the cell membrane. This electrical message is received by the **bipolar cells** and passed on to the ganglion cells, the next level of visual processing. The **ganglion cells** collect synaptic messages from the bipolar cells and send this information (in the form of action potentials) out of the eye, in the direction of the brain.

The entire retina contains more than 130 million cones and rods, but only about 1 million ganglion cells. As a result, many receptor cells must share synaptic connections with each ganglion cell. On the retina—as in life itself—the sharing is far from equal. The cones receive more than their share. In the foveal region of the retina, which is rich with cones, a typical ganglion cell might receive information from fewer than 10 cones. When a cone-rich area of the retina examines an intricate picture, most of the tiny details will be passed on to the ganglion cells. In contrast, in the rod-rich edges of the retina, a ganglion cell might receive information from 100 rods. Suppose that this region of the retina was exposed to a pattern of narrow black-and-white stripes. The rods might accurately pick up that detailed information about the stripes. However, all of this information is fed into a single ganglion, which does not have the ability to transmit all that detail. Instead of precise stripes, the ganglion would simply code a blurry gray. An important implication of this unequal sharing of ganglion cells is that vision is sharper in the cone-rich fovea than in the rod-rich edges.

Figure 4.4 also shows how the axons of the ganglion cells gather together. This collection of ganglion-cell axons is called the optic nerve. The **optic nerve,** which is nearly the same diameter as your little finger, travels out of the eye and onward to higher levels of visual processing. Turn back to Figure 4.3 to notice that the location where the optic nerve leaves the retina is called the **blind spot.** Neither rods nor cones inhabit the blind spot, so you cannot see anything that reaches this part of the retina. Try Demonstration 4.1 to experience your own blind spot.

From the Eye to the Brain Figure 4.5 illustrates how information travels in its route to the visual cortex. As you can see, the optic nerves come together at a location called the **optic chiasm** (pronounced *kye*-as-em). At this point, the axons from the ganglion cells regroup. As a consequence, everything that was originally registered on the left half of each retina ends up traveling toward the left side of the brain; everything from the right half of each retina travels toward the right side. As you might guess, this complicated partial crossover arrangement accomplishes something important for the human visual system. We have **binocular vision;** our two eyes work together, and we have partially overlapping fields of view. An object ahead of you on your left is registered on both retinas. However, information about that object will eventually end up on the left side of your brain, where the information from both eyes can be compared. The two images are slightly different; in the section on distance perception, we'll see why this binocular disparity is important.

Close your right eye and look at the X with your left eye. Gradually move this page toward your eye and then away. Keep the distance in the range of 8–24 inches, and do not let your focus drift away from the X. At some point, the tree will fall on your blind spot, and it will seem to disappear.

In daily life, you are usually unaware of the blind spot for two reasons. First, each eye usually picks up an object that the other eye misses. Secondly, the human visual system spontaneously completes an object in which a part is missing (Ramachandran, 1992; Ramachandran & Gregory, 1991). The "In Depth" section in this chapter examines illusory contours, a similar tendency in which the visual system actively fills in the missing information.

                                                                                    X

Those ganglion cells that originated in the retina and traveled through the optic chiasm transfer their messages to new sets of neurons in the thalamus and in the midbrain. These new neurons then travel to the visual cortex. As you may recall from Chapter 3, the **visual cortex** is the part of the brain that is concerned with vision. It is located at the back of your brain, just above your neck, and it is about the size of a credit card (Livingstone, 1987).

Cortical Neurons How do the cells in the visual cortex operate? Researchers in neuroscience have uncovered important information about the structure and function of the visual cortex. Much of this research has used the single-cell recording technique. As Chapter 3 described, the **single-cell recording technique** involves inserting a microelectrode into an animal's cortex in order to record action potentials from individual cells.

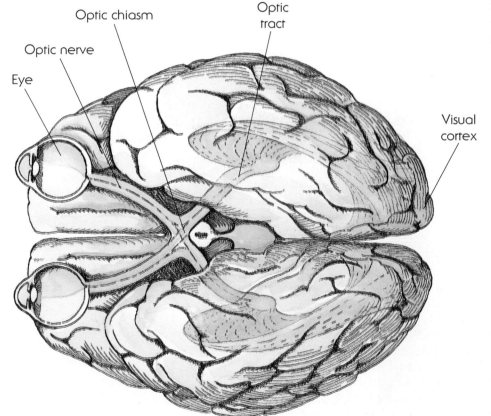

Figure 4.5

The visual pathway from the eye to the cortex.

Two prominent researchers, David Hubel and Torsten Wiesel (1965, 1979), examined the region of the visual cortex where the messages from the retina first arrive. First they inserted the microelectrode into a specific cortical neuron. Then they systematically presented a series of visual stimuli to the specific region of the retina that was thought to be monitored by that cortical neuron. For each stimulus, Hubel and Wiesel recorded the response rate. Then they moved on to another cell to test its sensitivity to the visual stimuli.

Hubel and Wiesel discovered that the cells in that part of the visual cortex were specialized with respect to the kind of visual stimulus that provoked the highest response rate. For example, some cells have been called **feature detectors** because they respond to very specific features located in a more complex stimulus. For example, one particular neuron might produce a sudden burst of activity only when a vertical line is presented. Another neuron may require a horizontal line, and yet another "prefers" a line tilted 15 degrees. Other neurons in different parts of the visual cortex respond most to moving objects, rather than to objects that remain stationary. Still other neurons are so picky that they might respond energetically only if a right angle containing lines of certain lengths moved diagonally upward and toward the right (Lennie, 1980). We will examine some important consequences of these feature detectors in the section on shape perception.

Researchers have now identified 32 areas in the primate brain that are concerned with vision (Kosslyn & Koenig, 1992; Van Essen et al., 1992). The region that Hubel and Wiesel originally explored is just one of these areas. In an examination of other areas, Zeki (1992) used the PET scan technique. As Chapter 3 noted, the **PET scan**, or **positron emission tomography,** traces the chemical activity within the brain when people perform specific tasks. Zeki found that a boldly colored abstract painting produced the greatest activity in an area close to the center of the visual cortex. In contrast, a pattern of moving black-and-white squares produced the greatest activity in a different area, close to the ear. Interestingly, vision is such an important activity that roughly half of our cerebral cortex plays some role in processing visual images (Glickstein, 1988).

Neurons in several other areas of the cortex respond only to complex visual patterns. Thompson (1985) describes how Charles Gross and his colleagues at Harvard University stumbled upon the ideal stimulus for one region of the cortex. Gross and his colleagues were using the single-cell recording technique in a monkey. They had presented the customary variety of visual stimuli, such as simple lines and bars of

If a PET scan were to be performed while you are looking at this picture, an area close to the center of your visual cortex would show the greatest neural activity.

light. The neuron being monitored by the electrode failed to respond to these stimuli, and so the researchers decided to move on to another cell. One experimenter bid that cell a symbolic farewell by waving his hand in front of the monkey's eye. The cell immediately began to fire rapidly to the moving hand! The excited researchers then cut out a variety of hand-shaped stimuli and waved them in front of the monkey's eye. This cell proved to respond most excitedly to a hand that was shaped like a monkey's paw. You may recall that the "In Depth" section in Chapter 3 examined more recent research on this region of the brain, called the inferotemporal cortex. Neuroscientists now know that this region is crucial in recognizing complex stimuli in both monkeys and humans.

As we have toured the visual system, we have seen that the cells involved in the first step of visual processing—the rods and the cones—require only a small amount of light to respond. Within the visual cortex, however, the cells become increasingly finicky, until they respond only to selected stimuli containing certain contours and movement patterns. Later in this chapter, we will examine the distinctive-features approach to shape perception, which argues that the cortical cells' specific sensitivities to lines, angles, and contours are essential in helping us recognize shapes such as letters of the alphabet.

Basic Visual Functions

We have seen that the visual system can extract information about the lines and angles in an object's shape. In addition, the visual system can appreciate fine details, and it can adapt to a wide variety of lighting conditions. To perform other tasks, the eyes can also move in ways you may not have previously appreciated.

Acuity Suppose that you are walking in an isolated area, and you spot a shape in the distance—is it a person or a bush? Does the dot on the horizon represent one tree or two trees close together? Is that a yellow spot—perhaps a yellow flower—next to the birch tree? These all represent acuity tasks. **Visual acuity** is the ability to see precise details in a scene. Because visual acuity tests are easy to administer, they represent the standard method of measuring visual ability (Olzak & Thomas, 1986). People differ somewhat from one another on numerous perceptual tasks. However, we are most aware of differences in visual acuity, because people with poor acuity need corrective lenses. Table 4.2 describes three common kinds of focusing disorders that influence acuity—nearsightedness, farsightedness, and astigmatism—as well as some other visual problems.

What does it mean to have 20/40 vision on an acuity test? Usually this kind of score is obtained by asking an observer to read an eye chart that has rows of letters ranging from large to small, while standing 20 feet away from the chart. If you can read the letters that a person with normal vision can read at 20 feet, then you have 20/20 vision. Suppose that you can read letters at 20 feet that a person with normal vision can read at 40 feet; your acuity would therefore be called 20/40 vision. A person whose vision with corrective lenses is poorer than 20/200 is considered legally blind (Landers, 1988).

Dark Adaptation You have probably had an experience like this: In the middle of a sunny afternoon, you enter a movie theater. The movie has already started, and you grope your way through the theater, reaching for what you hope is the back of an empty seat, rather than someone's shoulder. (My grandfather was once asked whether he had known the woman who had sat on him in a dark theater. Thinking fast, he replied that he did not know her name, but he could identify her nationality: She was a Laplander.) After several minutes in the dark, however, you can easily see which seats are empty.

The darkened theater experience is one example of **dark adaptation;** your eyes adjust and become more sensitive as you remain in the dark. As you have discovered, your sensitivity increases tremendously after just 10 minutes. Dark adaptation allows

TABLE 4.2 Some Common Visual Disorders

FOCUSING DISORDERS

Nearsightedness. If the eyeball is too long or the lens of the eye is too thick, the images of objects are focused in front of the retina. Nearsighted people can see only *nearby* objects clearly.

Farsightedness. If the eyeball is too short or the lens of the eye is too thin, the images of objects are focused at a point behind the retina. Farsighted people can see only *distant* objects clearly.

Astigmatism. People with astigmatism have a cornea that is irregularly curved, with some areas having more curvature than others. As a result, some regions will appear blurry.

DISORDERS INVOLVING EYE COORDINATION

Strabismus. This disorder occurs when the muscles of the two eyes do not work together. Thus, an object that is registered on the fovea of one eye will not be registered on the other fovea. This disorder should be corrected in early childhood to allow the development of proper binocular vision. The disorder occurs in about 2% of all children (Vaughan et al., 1989).

Stereoblindness. If strabismus is not corrected, stereoblindness develops. People with this disorder cannot use the depth information from binocular vision to aid distance perception (discussed on pp. 113–114).

DISORDERS OF THE LENS AND RETINA

Cataracts. Cataracts occur when the lens loses its transparency and becomes too cloudy; light cannot pass through to the retina. Some loss of lens transparency is normal in people over the age of 70 (Vaughan et al., 1989). If vision is seriously impaired, the lens of the eye can be surgically removed and a substitute lens implanted, or special corrective lenses can be worn.

Diabetic retinopathy. This disorder occurs when people have had severe diabetes for many years, causing fluid to leak out from the thickened blood vessels that supply the retina. Diabetic retinopathy is one of the leading causes of blindness in North America (Vaughan et al., 1989).

OTHER VISUAL DISORDERS

Corneal damage. An object can scratch the cornea or become lodged in the cornea. The outer layer of the cornea protects the eye from disease germs. Consequently, anyone with corneal damage should immediately receive medical care.

Glaucoma. Normally, the fluids inside the eyeball maintain the eye's characteristic shape. However, in glaucoma, extra fluid within the eye causes too much pressure and can lead to deterioration of the ganglion cells in the retina and optic nerve. In the United States, 1.5% of people over the age of 40 have glaucoma. People over 40 should be tested periodically for glaucoma in order to prevent blindness.

us to extend the range of light levels in which the visual system can function. The illumination from the bright noon sun is about 100 million times as intense as the illumination from the moon (Hood & Finkelstein, 1986). Nonetheless, the visual system is so superbly designed that we can function in both kinds of illumination, as well as in the vast intermediate region.

How can we explain dark adaptation? Consistent with the theme that humans are complicated, most psychological processes have more than one explanation. Three mechanisms help account for dark adaptation: (1) The pupils dilate to let more light pass through. (2) In comparison to rods exposed to light, our dark-adapted rods contain a greater amount of the special chemical that determines sensitivity (Pugh, 1988). (3) Neurons beyond the level of the rods must also play an important role, though the details of their action are unclear (Green & Powers, 1982).

Eye Movements One function of the visual system is so obvious that we seldom appreciate what it accomplishes for us: Our eyes move, rather than remaining in a fixed position. One kind of eye movement is called **pursuit movement,** which is the eye movement we use to track a moving object.

Your eyes use smooth pursuit movements to follow the flight of a bird.

DEMONSTRATION 4.2 Saccadic Eye Movements

Glance over at the opposite page and select a word in the middle of the column. Focus on that specific word, and notice how the letters are increasingly fuzzy in the words that are farther from your target word. (If you cannot explain why, check the discussion of rods and cones in the retina.)

Now start to read the entire sentence. Are you aware that your eye is advancing across the page in small, jerky leaps? Try to read the next sentences by letting your eyes roll smoothly across the page. You will probably find that your eyes can indeed move smoothly, but you do not seem to be perceiving the words.

Demonstration 4.2 illustrates a second important kind of eye movement, known as saccadic movement (pronounced suh-*kaad*-dick). **Saccadic movement** refers to the rapid, jumpy movement we use to advance the eye from one location to the next. Turn back to Figure 4.3 and notice the fovea, the region of the retina with the best acuity. Saccadic movements are necessary to bring the fovea into position in line with the object you want to see most clearly (Rayner & Pollatsek, 1987).

When we read, the size of the average saccadic movement is between 5 and 10 letters (McConkie & Zola, 1984). The eye tends to skip past blank regions and words that offer little information, such as *the* and *an* (Balota et al., 1985; Rayner & Pollatsek, 1987). Psychologists have also examined the **perceptual span,** which is the region you see when your eyes pause after a saccadic movement. If you are reading English, your perceptual span is lopsided; it is likely to include a region 3–4 letters to the left of the focus point and 6–10 letters to the right (Rayner & Pollatsek, 1987). After all, you read English from left to right, and you need to know what to expect in the material you will soon be reading, rather than what you have already seen. Interestingly, readers of Hebrew (which is a right-to-left language) have perceptual spans that are lopsided in the opposite direction (Pollatsek et al., 1981).

The information about saccadic movements provides clear evidence for the theme that humans are well equipped to function in their environment. The eye is designed so that a small region of the retina has excellent visual acuity. Furthermore, the visual system allows our eyes to jump across the page, exposing new words to the fovea. Finally, our eye movements allow us to skip over the useless regions of the text, and the perceptual span allows us to see where we are going more clearly than where we have been.

Color Vision

I know an artist who had just finished preparing the family meal when she noticed that everything she was about to serve was yellow. To add visual interest to the dinner, she stirred several drops of blue food coloring into the creamed corn. Her father refused to eat the corn; his expectations about customary food color had been entirely disrupted. Color is such a critical part of an object's identity that we may protest when its color is altered.

Most of the early research on color vision was inspired by a debate about two different color-vision theories, called trichromatic theory and opponent-process theory (Haber, 1985). Some creative theorizing and more recent research on the physiology of color vision have resolved the conflict peacefully (Boynton, 1988). We now know that both color-vision theories are correct, but they apply to different parts of the visual processing system. Let us see how the two theories have been integrated.

The **trichromatic theory** of color vision points out that the retina contains three kinds of cones, each sensitive to light from a different portion of the spectrum. This theory was originally proposed in the 1800s by an English physician named Thomas Young and a German physiologist named Hermann von Helmholtz. About a century later, researchers began to uncover physiological evidence that the visual system indeed does contain three kinds of cones (Dartnall et al., 1983; Rushton, 1958). According to Davidoff (1991), one kind of cone is most sensitive to short wavelengths (in the 430-nm range), another to medium wavelengths (in the 530-nm range), and a third to long wavelengths (in the 560-nm range). By combining different stimulation levels from each of these three kinds of cones, the visual system can produce the wide variety of perceptions we experience in our daily lives.

Trichromatic theory explains how we can discriminate the various colors of the spectrum, but it leaves some questions unanswered. For example, why is it that we can perceive a greenish blue but not a yellowish blue? And how can we explain **chromatic adaptation,** a phenomenon shown in Demonstration 4.3, in which prolonged exposure to yellow produces blue, and prolonged exposure to green produces red?

Ewald Hering, a German physician, developed the opponent-process theory in the late 1800s to account for color phenomena such as impossible color combinations and chromatic adaptation. According to the current interpretation of color vision, trichromatic theory explains how the cones gather color information. This information is then passed on to the ganglion cells and other cells, which operate in an opponent-process fashion.

According to current explanations, **opponent-process theory** describes the mechanisms of ganglion cells and other cells closer to the cortex; specifically, these cells respond by increasing their activity when one color is present and decreasing their activity when another color is present. For example, one cell will increase activity when yellow is present and decrease it when blue is present. A different cell will increase activity when blue is present and decrease it when yellow is present. Thus, this set of cells works in an opposing, or mirror-image, fashion. A second opponent system works the same way for red and green. A third opponent system responds to light and dark. These three opponent processes occur at the ganglion level and also in the thalamus, another location on the route to the visual cortex.

Let us see how opponent-process theory explains the two color phenomena discussed earlier. You cannot see a yellowish blue because the cell that increases its activity to yellow will decrease its activity to blue and vice versa. (Similarly, you cannot see a greenish red.) You saw a blue background for the stars in Demonstration 4.3 because prolonged viewing of yellow produced chromatic adaptation, weakening the yellow response and leaving its opponent color—blue—relatively strong and activated. (Similarly, prolonged staring at the green stripes will leave the opponent color—red—relatively strong and activated.)

DEMONSTRATION 4.3 Chromatic Adaptation

Set a sheet of plain white paper to the side of the picture below. Stare at the picture for 30 to 40 seconds, focusing on the star in the lower right corner and being certain not to move your eyes. Quickly transfer your gaze to the white paper and notice the afterimage. You can blink several times to preserve the afterimage.

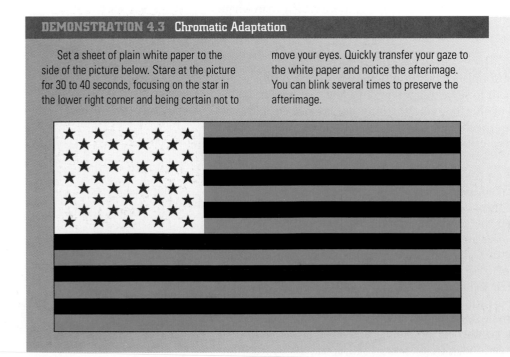

DEMONSTRATION 4.4 An Example of an Item from a Color-Deficiency Test

Find a location in which the lighting is a little less bright than you normally would use for reading. Examine the test item below. What numbers do you see? The answers appear at the end of the chapter. This item tests for sensitivity to deep reds. A complete test of color deficiencies would include a large number of items in each of many colors.

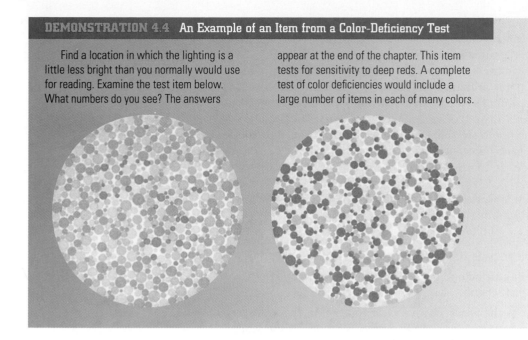

For some of you reading this section, the discussion about color phenomena may not match your personal experience. You may have a **color deficiency,** or difficulty in discriminating between different colors. Although color deficiencies are relatively rare in females, about 5% of males have a color deficiency. Try Demonstration 4.4, which is a typical item in a much more extensive test for color deficiencies.

Incidentally, note that the appropriate term is *color deficiency*. The term *color blindness* is inaccurate because most of the people affected do see some colors. Only a very small number of people see no color at all. The perceptual world of these truly color-blind people is similar to your world on a dark night—everything is simply a different shade of gray (Hurvich, 1981).

Shape Perception

We have seen how the visual system can see fine details in a scene (acuity). It can function in both bright sunlight and pale moonlight, and it can execute several different kinds of specialized movements. The visual system can also process information about color. However, this list is only a small sample of the visual system's talents. Now let us consider the topics more commonly associated with perception than with sensation. These topics include the perception of shape, motion, distance, constancy, and illusion.

Without shape perception, our visual world would consist of random patches of light and dark, a disorderly mass of colored and uncolored fragments. However, our perception is quite orderly. For example, look up from your book and notice that your visual world contains objects with distinct borders and clear-cut shapes. Even the messiest room reveals pattern and organization, and we can recognize objects—a lamp, a psychology professor, and a letter of the alphabet. Our shape perception is usually a highly accurate mirror of reality. Two important aspects of shape perception are organization and pattern recognition.

Organization If you look out a nearby window, you will appreciate that the visual world is organized. An automobile seems to form a distinct shape against the background of the parking lot, and the lamppost does not blend into the grass beneath it. One important component of the organization in our perceptual worlds is called the **figure-ground relationship.** When two areas share a common boundary (e.g., the contour of the automobile and the parking lot that surrounds it), the figure is the distinct shape with clearly defined edges. The ground is simply the part that is left over, forming the background in the scene. Take a moment to glance through some of the pictures in this textbook, noting the relationship between the figure and the ground.

In the section on history in the first chapter of this book, you were introduced to the Gestalt approach, which was prominent in Europe in the first decades of this century (Hochberg, 1988). According to the **Gestalt approach,** we perceive objects as well-organized, whole structures, instead of separate, isolated parts. The Gestalt psychologists stressed that our ability to see shape and pattern is determined by subtle interrelationships among the parts (Greene, 1985). One area in which the Gestalt influence is still very prominent is in research on the figure-ground relationship (Banks & Krajicek, 1991).

Edgar Rubin (1915/1958), a Gestalt psychologist from Denmark, reached several conclusions about the figure-ground relationship:

1. The figure has a definite shape, whereas the ground seems shapeless. Notice the clear shape of the seagull on page 106 in contrast to the shapeless sky.

2. The ground seems to continue behind the figure. For example, you *know* that the sky extends behind that seagull.

3. The figure seems closer to the viewer, with a clear location in space. In contrast, the ground seems farther away; it lacks a clear location. In the seagull picture, for example, the sky is clearly farther away from you.

In almost all cases, the figure-ground relationship is clear-cut. Occasionally, however, the relationship is ambiguous, often because an artist has created it that way. Perhaps you have seen examples of ambiguous figure-ground relationships, such as those created by the American artist Bev Doolittle. As Doolittle says, "I want to change the experience of seeing" (Maclay, 1990, p. 15). Indeed, you will need to see figure and ground differently in Figure 4.6 in order to force the faces in the background to become figures.

We discriminate figure from ground, imposing one important kind of organization on our visual experience. We also organize visual stimuli into patterns and groups. The Gestalt psychologists developed several laws of grouping to describe why certain objects seem to go together, instead of remaining isolated and independent:

Figure 4.6

"The Forest Has Eyes" by Bev Doolittle, 1984. © The Greenwich Workshop, Inc.

1. The **law of proximity** (or law of nearness) states that objects near each other tend to be perceived as a unit.
2. The **law of similarity** states that objects similar to each other tend to be seen as a unit.
3. The **law of good continuation** states that we tend to perceive smooth, continuous lines, rather than discontinuous fragments.
4. The **law of closure** states that a figure with a gap will be perceived as a closed, intact figure.

Each of these laws is illustrated in Figure 4.7. The figure-ground relationship and these laws of grouping help organize our visual world and encourage pattern recognition.

Pattern Recognition How do we recognize patterns? The process seems so simple. As you read, you recognize the letters in a word. A tall, slender person approaches—wearing a moustache, plaid shirt, and ragged jeans—and you recognize Henry from your political science class. You can recognize familiar people in countless situations, whether they are near or far, standing or sitting, laughing or crying, in sunshine or in shadow (Corballis, 1988).

Psychologists acknowledge that it is a major challenge to explain how we can recognize objects so readily. One early theory explains how we can recognize simple, two-dimensional patterns such as letters of the alphabet. A more recent theory examines how we can recognize more complex, three-dimensional objects.

The distinctive-features approach is an early theory of pattern recognition developed by Eleanor Gibson; it focuses on how we identify simple patterns such as letters of the alphabet. Gibson (1969) argues that we differentiate between letters on the basis of **distinctive features,** which are characteristics such as straight versus curved

Figure 4.7

The Gestalt laws of grouping.

(upper left) The law of proximity. You perceive the stamps in the foreground as a unit, because you group items together that are near each other.

(upper right) The law of similarity. You group this arrangement in terms of horizontal rows, grouping together the cats on this wrapping paper because they are facing the same direction.

(lower left) The law of good continuation. You see the design on this plaid shirt in terms of straight, continuous lines rather than lines that form right-angle zigzags.

(lower right) The law of closure. You see the left-hand border of this greeting card as a closed, intact edge, even though it is interrupted by the leaf that the dove is carrying.

lines. Thus, the letter *E* has four straight lines, whereas the letter *O* has none. We recognize the letter *C* because it is the only curved letter with an opening at the side that is also symmetrical. The distinctive-features approach to pattern perception is based on feature detectors, those neurons in the visual cortex that are sensitive to lines, angles, and contours (discussed on page 104).

According to the more recent theory of Irving Biederman (1987, 1990), we recognize more complex patterns in terms of their parts, or components. The basic assumption of **recognition-by-components theory** is that an object can be represented as an arrangement of simple three-dimensional shapes. These basic shapes, which Biederman calls **geons,** can be combined like letters of the alphabet to create something meaningful. Figure 4.8 shows five of the proposed 24 geons, together with several objects that can be constructed from the geons. Although the recognition-by-components model has not yet been extensively tested, the early reports for normal humans and for people with specific visual deficits are compatible with the model (Banks & Krajicek, 1991; Biederman et al., 1991).

Both the distinctive-feature approach and the recognition-by-components theory emphasize how the senses process the basic stimuli. However, shape perception also involves cognitive factors. In the section on signal detection theory, we saw that expectations and prior knowledge influence the probability of saying, "Yes, I perceive the stimulus." Similarly, pattern recognition also depends upon expectations and prior knowledge, as well as sensory activity. Psychologists acknowledge that pattern recognition depends upon both bottom-up and top-down processing.

Bottom-up processing depends on the information from the senses at the bottom (or most basic) level of perception. The stimulus is registered on the retina, and the rods, the cones, and other neurons begin to produce bursts of electrical activity, which ultimately reach the visual cortex. However, bottom-up processing may not be sufficient for you to recognize a classmate you know slightly, especially when viewing him under less-than-ideal circumstances. Top-down processing is also necessary.

Top-down processing emphasizes the importance of the observers' concepts, expectations, and prior knowledge—the kind of information stored at the top (or highest level) of perception. Part of the reason you recognize your classmate when you see him is that you expect to see him in certain places. Out of context—in your hometown hardware store—he would be more difficult to recognize.

Bottom-up and top-down processing work together in the nonvisual senses, too. For example, consider a typical question that a friend might ask, "Whuh djuh do yesterday?" The syllable *djuh* cannot be decoded merely by the action of bottom-up processing; this sound pattern does not correspond to any known word. Instead, top-down processing assists perception, because the context of the surrounding words informs us that the mystery syllable must be a slurred variation of *did you.*

Some of the most convincing evidence for top-down processing comes from research on letter recognition. According to the word-superiority effect, we perceive letters better when they appear in words than when they appear in strings of unrelated letters (Krueger, 1992; Taylor & Taylor, 1983). For example, suppose you are looking at a sequence of blurry letters. You can recognize the letter *A* more easily when you see it in the word *THAT* than when you see it in the unpronounceable, meaningless nonword *TTAH* (Chastain, 1986; Reicher, 1969). The surrounding letters in the word *THAT* provide a context that facilitates the recognition of each of the letters. If the word-superiority effect (and, more generally, top-down processing) did not operate, you would not be able to read so quickly and so accurately. In fact, you would probably still be reading the first chapter of this book!

Motion Perception

Our discussion of perception has emphasized shapes that are static—a letter frozen on a textbook page or a horse immobilized in a painting. But you glance up from your textbook to a world rich with motion. Consider a basketball game, for ex-

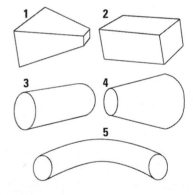

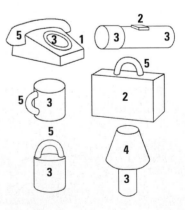

Figure 4.8

Examples of geons (above) and representative objects that can be constructed from the geons (below). (Source: Biederman, 1990)

ample. You perceive players running and jumping, balls soaring and bouncing, and spectators waving their arms and leaping to their feet.

Motion perception is a basic skill. Even primitive animals and insects such as the fly have excellent motion perception (Johansson, 1985; Ullman, 1983). In recent years, some of the most interesting discoveries about motion perception involve **biological motion,** which is the pattern of movement exhibited by people and other living things. Gunnar Johansson, a Swedish psychologist, attached small flashlight bulbs to the major joints of a male colleague, as shown in Figure 4.9. Johansson made a movie of this man as he moved around the darkened room. Johansson then showed the movie to groups of observers who were asked to interpret the pattern of lights. Even though the movie showed only 12 tiny lights, the observers could readily tell the difference between walking and jogging movements. When the man pretended to limp, the observers spotted the change in body movement (Johansson, 1975; Johannson et al., 1980). Other researchers have discovered that observers watching a pattern of lights can distinguish a female walker from a male walker (Cutting, 1983). Observers can also tell whether a person is preparing to throw an object 6 feet or 30 feet (Runeson & Frykholm, 1983).

Biological motion is complicated to describe mathematically, yet it is easy for our visual system to process (Johansson, 1985). Because we are so quick and so accurate in identifying various kinds of biological motion, researchers have proposed that some neurons may be specially organized to decode and interpret the motion of other living organisms (Johansson, 1985).

Distance Perception

Except for reading, most of our visual activity requires looking at objects that are solid rather than flat, or examining pictures or television screens, which try to capture depth and distance. Let us move into the third dimension to consider distance perception.

A major challenge for psychologists interested in perception is to explain how we are able to know that an object has depth, as well as height and width, and how we can appreciate that an eraser is closer to us than the chalkboard. After all, the retina can only register height and width; the chalkboard is not represented as being *deeper* into the surface of the retina in comparison with the eraser.

Numerous factors contribute to depth perception. In fact, most perception textbooks list at least a dozen (e.g., Coren et al., 1994; Goldstein, 1989; Matlin & Foley, 1992). As you can probably guess by reading this far in the textbook, any process that occurs so automatically and so accurately is likely to be facilitated by a variety of factors.

Some of these sources of information about distance are **monocular**—they can be seen with just one eye and can also be represented in a painting or a photograph.

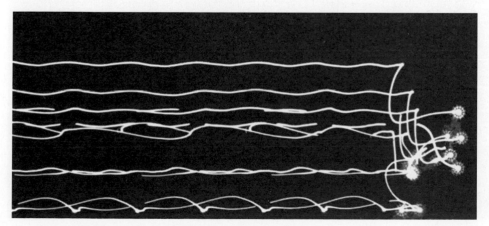

Figure 4.9

To illustrate biological motion, a man wears flashlight bulbs at his joints, and a film is made of his movements. In this particular photo, the camera shutter was kept open for several seconds and the lights trace paths in the picture. He was initially sitting in a chair at the right of the photo with one leg swung over the other. Then he stood up and walked across the floor to the left.

These monocular factors, which are illustrated in Figures 4.10 and 4.11, include the following:

1. *Relative size:* If two similar objects appear together, we judge the one that occupies more space on the retina to be closer to us. (Notice the relative size of the arches in Figure 4.10.)

2. *Overlap:* When one object overlaps another, we judge the completely visible object to be closer than the partly covered object.

3. *Texture gradient:* The texture of surfaces becomes denser as the distance increases. Although this is an important factor in distance perception, its value has only recently been acknowledged (Gibson, 1979; Hagen, 1985). Notice, for example, how the texture of the wheat in Figure 4.11 is much more tightly packed and dense toward the horizon. (To appreciate texture gradient, turn the picture upside down and notice how the texture looks bizarre.)

4. *Linear perspective:* Parallel lines appear to meet in the distance, as you probably learned in art class. We now take perspective for granted when we look at art, but paintings prior to the fifteenth century look flat because artists did not include linear perspective cues (Wade & Swanston, 1991).

5. *Atmospheric perspective:* Distant objects often look blurry and bluish. Notice in Figure 4.11 that the distant mountains look grayish blue.

Other information about depth is **binocular,** requiring two eyes. The most important binocular factor can be traced to the fact that your eyes are about 3 inches apart. This distance guarantees that any object closer than about 20 feet will present a slightly different view to each eye. The difference between the two retinal images of an object is known as **binocular disparity.** Your visual system is so sensitive to binocular disparity that it can detect different views that correspond to one thousandth of a millimeter when registered on the retina (Yellott, 1981). To give you a feeling for this degree of precision, the wire on a paperclip is about one millimeter thick; imagine splitting this slender wire into one thousand parts to create a detectable difference. The visual cortex contains cells that are sensitive to these tiny discrepancies and fire at a high rate when they detect binocular disparity (Ohzawa et al., 1990).

Binocular information is clearly helpful in depth perception, and people are substantially more accurate when they receive information from both eyes, rather than just one eye (Foley, 1980, 1985). Take a moment to review the disorders involving eye coordination, listed earlier on page 106, to appreciate why these disorders should not be treated casually.

Figure 4.10

Distance is obvious in this photo because it provides information about relative size, overlap, texture gradient, and linear perspective.

Figure 4.11

In this photo, distance is conveyed by relative size (the hills), texture gradient (the wheat), and atmospheric perspective (the gray mountains in the distance).

Constancy

When you move around in the world, you approach objects and then move away. However, the telephone does not seem to grow in size as you run to answer it. The image of a bus on your retina grows larger as it approaches you, yet you do not perceive a size change. As Figure 4.12 shows, a book assumes a different shape on your retina when you view it from a different angle; it projects a trapezoid shape, rather than a rectangle. Still, you know it did not *really* change its shape. The phenomenon described in these examples is constancy. **Constancy** means that we perceive objects as having constant characteristics (such as size and shape), even when there are changes in the information about them that reaches your eyes (Wade & Swanston, 1991). Perception therefore allows us to go beyond the information registered on our retinas.

Size constancy means that an object's perceived size stays the same, even though the distance changes between the viewer and the object. Demonstration 4.5 illustrates size constancy. One factor that contributes to size constancy is that we are familiar with an object's customary size. You know a bus's customary size, so even when it is two blocks away, you know that it has not shrunk. Another explanation for size constancy is that we unconsciously take distance into account when we see an object (Rock, 1983). Without being consciously aware of the process, we can figure out an object's true size. The process cannot involve complicated, conscious calculations, however, because even animals seem to use this principle (Gogel, 1977).

An important American theorist, James J. Gibson (1959), argued that perception is much more direct. We do not need to perform any calculations—conscious or unconscious—because the environment is rich with information. For example, you know the size of an object by comparing it to the texture of the surrounding area. If this textbook were placed on a tile floor, it would just about cover one linoleum tile, whether you viewed it from a distance of 3 feet or 30 feet. Tile, grass, strands of yarn in a carpet, and other kinds of background textures all provide a kind of yardstick against which we can preserve size constancy.

The visual system also demonstrates other kinds of constancy. **Shape constancy** means that an object's perceived shape stays the same, despite changes in its orientation toward the viewer. A compact disc does not distort itself into an oval when we view it from an angle; we know it remains round. Shape constancy is even stronger when shapes appear in the context of meaningful clutter—such as a messy office desk—rather than when the shapes are shown against a clean background (Lappin & Preble, 1975).

In addition, our visual system demonstrates **lightness constancy;** that is, an object's perceived lightness stays the same, in spite of changes in the amount of light falling on it. A pair of black shoes continues to look black in the bright sun, although these shoes may reflect more light than the white pages of this textbook if you were reading the book in a dimly lit corner. The visual system acknowledges that black shoes are dark, relative to other lighter objects in the scene.

One last important constancy is **color constancy;** in general, an object's perceived hue tends to stay the same, despite changes in the wavelength of the light it reflects. Thus, a blue shirt seems to stay about the same color, whether we view it in

Figure 4.12

This textbook seems to maintain its rectangular shape, even though it would project a trapezoidal shape onto your retina if you were to view it from the angle shown in the lower photo.

DEMONSTRATION 4.5 Size Constancy

Hold up your right hand, with your palm facing you, about 10 inches in front of your face. At the same time, hold up your left hand, also with your palm facing you, but stretch out your left arm as far as possible. Your hands create images of two different sizes on your retina. However, do your hands appear to differ in size? Most people report that they do not; instead, they report size constancy. (Based on Wade & Swanston, 1991)

the bright sunlight, in artificial light, or even under a faintly colored light bulb. However, researchers have noted that the human visual system shows only approximate color constancy. For example, some colors in a painting may appear slightly different if you view them by daylight and then under incandescent illumination at night (Jameson & Hurvich, 1989; Thompson et al., 1992).

Notice how the constancies simplify our perceptual world. We can rely upon objects to remain the same, even when we change the way in which we view those objects. Imagine the nightmare we would face otherwise! Objects would expand and shrink, stretch into uncharacteristic shapes, grow light and dark, and assume unexpected colors. Perhaps a major movie producer will adopt this nightmarish idea. Coming soon to a theater near you . . . the new film, *A World Without Constancies!*

IN DEPTH: Illusions and Illusory Contours

Try Demonstration 4.6, the Poggendorff illusion, before you read further. An **illusion** is an incorrect perception that does not correspond to the actual physical stimulus. Illusions lead us to make errors in the orientations of lines (as in Demonstration 4.6), in the lengths of lines, and in the perception of contours.

Why do psychologists study visual illusions? One reason is that they are intriguing and fun. Our perception is typically so accurate that we are puzzled when we make a mistake. A second reason—as you will see in this section—is that the study of illusions helps us understand the underlying perceptual processes (Westheimer, 1988). If the visual system makes consistent mistakes, we can draw conclusions about how visual information is altered as it passes from the retina to the cortex. We will also see in the chapters on memory and cognition that our occasional errors help psychologists identify some general principles about how people think.

A final reason for studying illusions is that they have practical applications. For example, in the Poggendorff illusion that you just saw, a line disappears at an angle behind a solid figure. Then it appears on the other side of the figure in a position that seems inappropriate. In 1965, the Poggendorff illusion was responsible for a tragic plane crash (Coren & Girgus, 1978). Two airplanes were about to land in the New York City area. A cloud formation was between them, and the Poggendorff illusion created the perception that they were heading directly toward each other (similar to the line on the left and the bottom line on the right in Demonstration 4.6). Quickly, the two pilots changed their paths to correct what seemed to be an error. The planes collided. Four people died and 49 others were injured . . . and only an illusion was to blame.

One of the major categories of illusions is the line-length illusions. Let us examine these illusions and then turn our attention to a second category that has inspired dozens of studies in the last decade, illusory contours.

Line-Length Illusions Figure 4.13 shows two versions of the most famous visual illusion—the Müller-Lyer illusion. In each case, the two lines are really the same length. However,

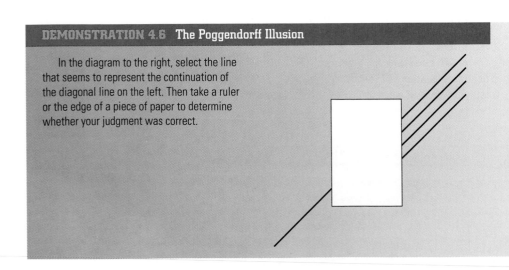

DEMONSTRATION 4.6 The Poggendorff Illusion

In the diagram to the right, select the line that seems to represent the continuation of the diagonal line on the left. Then take a ruler or the edge of a piece of paper to determine whether your judgment was correct.

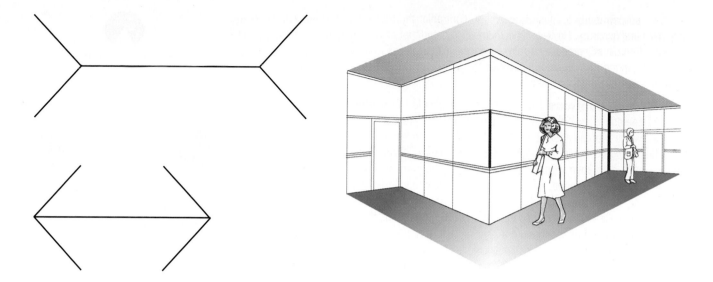

the "wings outward" version of the classic illusion looks about 25% longer than the "wings inward" version. One of several factors contributing to this illusion is that people judge the wings outward version to be longer because the eyes move a longer distance to perceive the entire figure. When our eyes move a longer distance, we tend to perceive the figure to be longer (Coren, 1981).

One theme in this textbook concerns individual differences. In the case of visual illusions, some people perceive a large difference between the two versions of the Müller-Lyer, whereas others perceive them to be reasonably similar. Coren and Porac (1987) found a negative correlation between a person's spatial ability and his or her susceptibility to the Müller-Lyer illusion. Specifically, people who were skilled at detecting a hidden figure, which was concealed among irrelevant lines, tended to judge the two versions of the Müller-Lyer illusion to be fairly similar. Spatially skilled people can ignore the irrelevant "wings" and focus purely on line length in the Müller-Lyer illusion. In general, we tend to be somewhat similar to one another in our perceptions—certainly our perceptions are more similar than our personalities. However, we do show some individual differences in areas such as the perception of illusions.

Figure 4.14 shows the Ponzo illusion, a second line-length illusion. The bar on top looks longer in this illusion, and perhaps you can figure out why. We interpret the converging set of 11 lines as conveying linear perspective: The top of the figure definitely seems farther away. Therefore, the horizontal bar that appears in the "distant" part of the figure must also be farther away. The rules of constancy tell us that we must take distance into account in judging the size of an object, so we judge that "distant" bar to be larger. This explanation for the Ponzo illusion and others that contain strong depth cues is called the **theory of misapplied constancy** (Gillam, 1980).

Figure 4.13
Müller-Lyer illusion.

(left) The classic Müller-Lyer illusion.

(right) In this variant of the classic Müller-Lyer illusion, compare the length of the two dark vertical lines. The additional distance cues make the illusion even stronger.

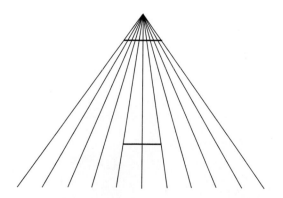

Figure 4.14
The Ponzo illusion.

Our susceptibility to illusions seems to contradict the theme that humans are extremely competent and accurate. However, this theme also noted that many of our errors can be traced to strategies that usually produce correct responses. In most cases, cues suggesting linear perspective *do* correspond to a real world in which the point of convergence is more distant. It is therefore a "smart mistake" to see depth in Figure 4.14.

Illusory Contours Figure 4.15 is an example of an **illusory contour,** a figure in which we see edges even though they are not physically present. For example, this figure seems to show a white triangle against a background of three circles and an outlined triangle.

Illusory figures have two important characteristics (Meyer & Petry, 1987). First, a distinct surface—such as a solid white triangle—seems to be present. The surface often seems to be brighter than the background, even though the intensity registered on the retina is actually identical (Kanizsa, 1976). Second, a distinct edge or contour appears to surround the illusory figure. This edge even continues in regions that lack a true contour (e.g., the white regions between the black circles and the outlined triangle).

Psychologists have enthusiastically created hundreds of illusory contours, many with geometric figures (e.g., Petry & Meyer, 1987) and some with human figures (e.g., Bonaiuto et al., 1991). Several of these are shown in Figure 4.16.

Why do we see illusory contours? Stanley Coren and Clare Porac (1983) argue that we create illusory contours because we see simple, familiar figures in preference to meaningless, disorganized parts. As the Gestalt approach argues, our perceptions tend to be well organized. In Figure 4.15, for example, we could see circles with wedges sliced out, alternating with three V-shaped lines. Instead of this unnecessarily complicated interpretation, we prefer to use distance cues, such as overlap, to sort out the picture. Therefore, we see a white triangle placed in front of the background.

As some authors suggest, illusory contours arise because the visual system essentially tries to solve a mystery or a problem when it attempts to sort out figure and ground (e.g., Parks, 1986; Rock, 1987). Notice that this distance-cue explanation involves top-down processing. Our expectations and prior knowledge—about the way one object blocks the objects behind it—make sense of an otherwise puzzling and disorderly jumble.

Coren and Porac supported their distance-cue explanation with an experiment in which observers were asked to judge the distance of various parts of illusory-contour figures. They used

Figure 4.15
An example of an illusory contour. Note that the white upright triangle appears to be bordered by a clear-cut contour, even in the regions where no physical contour actually appears. (Source: Kanisza, 1976)

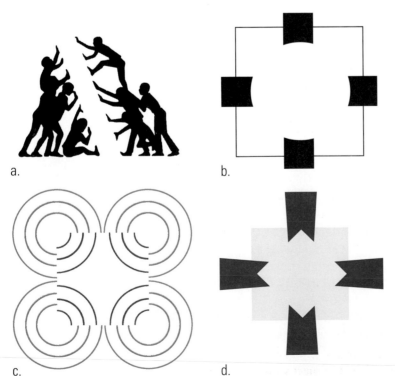

a.

b.

c.

d.

Figure 4.16
Several examples of illusory contour. Note that illusory contours can be obtained with colored figures, as well as black and white.

a special piece of equipment to present a spot that appeared to vary in distance from the observer. This spot could be located on any portion of the illusory-contour figure (e.g., within the white triangle in Figure 4.15, or in the area just above one of the partial circles, outside the illusory triangle). Observers were instructed to adjust the apparent distance of this spot until it seemed to be the same distance away from them as the part of the stimulus on which the spot was superimposed. The results showed that the observers selected a setting for the figure that was about 25% closer than the selected setting for the background. Indeed, observers interpret the figure to be significantly closer than the background.

Research by Hans Wallach and Virginia Slaughter (1988) emphasizes the importance of top-down processing. They examined subjective contours that involved six irregular shapes, such as the shape shown in Figure 4.17. The students in their experiment examined three such figures; three similar figures were not presented during this first phase. (The experiment was well controlled; half the students saw shapes A, B, and C, but not D, E, and F. The other half saw shapes D, E, and F, but not A, B, and C.) Then everyone saw all six illusory-contour figures, like Figure 4.18. In each case, the students were instucted to report whether or not they saw an illusory contour.

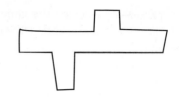

Figure 4.17
In Wallach and Slaughter's (1988) research, a participant might first examine this shape.

Figure 4.18
After seeing the irregular shape above, a participant in Wallach and Slaughter's (1988) research would be asked whether he or she saw an illusory contour in this figure.

The results showed that people reported seeing an illusory contour for 71% of the cases in which the irregular shape had been previously exposed. In contrast, they reported an illusory contour for only 41% of the cases in which the shape had not been exposed. Our memory for an unusual pattern apparently encourages top-down processing. As a result, we see a distinct contour in a design, even when no real contour can be registered on our retina. Thus, we can learn about normal perception by examining illusions; specifically, our visual system organizes stimuli, makes sense out of them, and encourages the formation of contours.

This discussion of illusory contours has emphasized top-down processing, consistent with an emphasis in this field. However, some researchers are beginning to examine physiological explanations for the phenomenon. Specifically, some cells in the visual cortex seem to respond to illusory contours (e.g., Ramachandran, 1987; Winckelgren, 1992). The complete theory of illusory contours has not yet been developed. As Diane Halpern and her coauthors (1983) remarked, "The search for the best theory to explain the perception of contours that do not physically exist has proven as illusory as the nature of the contours themselves" (p. 293).

SECTION SUMMARY

VISION

- The cones and the rods in the retina absorb light rays. During transduction, light is converted to action potentials, which are passed onto other neurons and eventually reach the visual cortex.

- At least 32 regions in the cortex process visual information.

- Two important features of vision are visual acuity and dark adaptation. In addition, the eye can make pursuit movement and saccadic movement.

- We perceive color because of two processes: (1) The three kinds of cones are sensitive to different portions of the spectrum, as trichromatic theory points out, and (2) pairs of cells at the ganglion level and beyond work in an opponent-process fashion.

- Shape perception is aided by the figure-ground relationship and the Gestalt laws of grouping.

- Two important theories of pattern recognition are distinctive-features theory (Gibson) and recognition-by-components theory (Biederman); top-down processing also facilitates pattern recognition.

- Humans can readily recognize biological motion and can accurately identify subtle differences in motion.

- We perceive distance and depth because of a variety of monocular factors (e.g., overlap and texture gradient) and also because of binocular disparity.

- The visual system demonstrates constancy. Size constancy, shape constancy, lightness constancy, and color constancy ensure that an object's qualities are perceived as staying the same, even when we view that object from different distances and angles and in different lighting conditions.

- Illusions are incorrect perceptions that help psychologists to identify important consistencies in visual processing. For example, the Ponzo illusion shows that we may rely too strongly on constancy, and illusory contours illustrate the importance of top-down processing.

HEARING

Vision is certainly our most prominent perceptual ability. However, people who are both deaf and blind often miss their hearing more than their vision. For example, Helen Keller once wrote in a letter:

> *I am just as deaf as I am blind. The problems of deafness are deeper and more complex, if not more important, than those of blindness. Deafness is a much worse misfortune. For it means the loss of the most vital stimulus—the sound of the voice that brings language, sets thoughts astir and keeps us in the intellectual company of [other people] . . . If I could live again I should do much more than I have for the deaf. I have found deafness to be a much greater handicap than blindness. (Cited in Ackerman, 1990, pp. 191–192)*

To examine this important component of perception, we must first examine the nature of sound and the characteristics of the auditory system. Then we will consider two theories of pitch perception as well as several qualities of sound perception. Chapter 9, on language and communication, explores the important topic of speech perception. Also, Chapter 10 considers the recent research on infants' astonishing speech-perception skills.

The Nature of Sound

I live in a house in the woods, a location that might seem to be nearly soundless. However, when I close my eyes and concentrate on hearing, the variety of sounds is astonishing. I can hear the light rain on the roof and the windowpanes, the humming of the heating system, and the ice-cube maker noisily depositing a dozen cubes in the refrigerator. Each of these widely different sounds is caused by tiny disturbances in air pressure called **sound waves.** The air pressure rapidly compresses and expands as the sound waves travel to your eardrum, causing it to move slightly. The perception of these successive pressure changes is called **sound.** Amazingly, the movement of invisible air molecules is strong enough to produce hearing.

One important attribute of sound is **frequency,** which is the number of cycles a sound wave completes in 1 second. If you strike middle C on the piano, you produce a sound wave that vibrates up and down 262 times each second. Another important attribute of sound is **amplitude,** or the size of the change in pressure created by the sound wave. As we discuss in more detail later, the physical quality of frequency is roughly equivalent to the psychological experience of *pitch,* whereas amplitude is roughly equivalent to *loudness.*

The Auditory System

The sound waves need to be transformed into neural messages, and the auditory system is neatly designed to accomplish this. As Ackerman (1990) writes, the auditory system looks like a contraption that an ingenious plumber has put together with spare parts! Still, each structure accomplishes some function. Figure 4.19 shows how sound enters the **auditory canal,** the tube running inward from the outer ear. The sound waves bounce against the **eardrum,** which is a thin membrane that vibrates in sequence with the sound waves.

Resting on the other side of the eardrum are three small bones in the middle ear, which an imaginative early anatomist named the hammer, the anvil, and the stirrup. These bones are the smallest ones in the human body, but they have an impor-

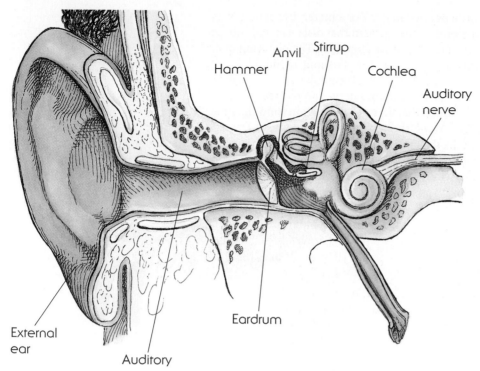

Hammer Anvil Stirrup Cochlea Auditory nerve

External ear

Auditory

Eardrum

Figure 4.19
The anatomy of the ear.

tant function. Sound waves travel through air to the middle ear, but liquid is on the other side of the middle ear. Sound waves cannot travel easily from the air into the liquid. Fortunately, the auditory system is superbly constructed so that these three bones partly compensate for this problem by magnifying the pressure on the inner ear.

The most important structure in the inner ear is the cochlea (pronounced *coke*-lee-uh). The **cochlea** is a bony, fluid-filled coil that contains the auditory receptors, which are called **hair cells.** The hair cells are therefore equivalent to the cones and the rods in vision. These hair cells are embedded in a part of the cochlea called the **basilar membrane** and are illustrated in greatly magnified form in Figure 4.20.

Pressure from the stirrup on the cochlea causes waves in the fluid within the cochlea. These waves produce a vibration in the membrane on which the hair cells

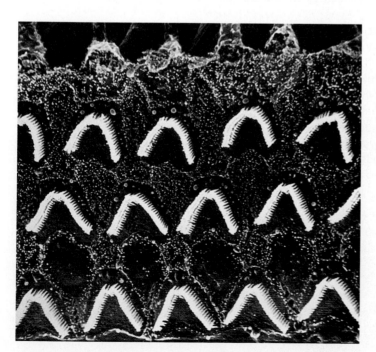

Figure 4.20

Overhead view of hair cells embedded in the basilar membrane of the cochlea. Each little fiber in the V-shaped patterns represents one hair cell. This photograph is greatly magnified. Each hair cell is about 35μ in length (Pickles, 1988), which is about 1/20 of the thickness of one textbook page.

sit. When those hair cells move as little as one-*billionth* of a meter, transduction occurs (Hudspeth, 1989). The hair cell converts energy from that displacement into action potentials, and the auditory nerve picks up these impulses. The vibrating of air molecules, the pounding of a miniature hammer, the sloshing of liquid in the cochlea, and the stimulation of microscopic hairs are all complex actions that are necessary to convert sound into a form that the auditory nerve can receive.

The **auditory nerve** is a bundle of axons that carries information from the inner ear toward higher levels of processing. Along the way, information passes through several structures, including a part of the thalamus near the location where visual information also passes. The information eventually travels to the **auditory cortex,** whch is primarily located in a deep groove on each side of the surface of the brain and codes both simple and complex auditory stimuli. Because this location is so inaccessible, studying the auditory cortex is difficult (Gulick et al., 1989). As a result, we know less about the auditory cortex than we do about the visual cortex (Brugge & Reale, 1985). The auditory cortex is relatively large in humans, probably because language is more developed in humans than in other animals (Kiang & Peake, 1988).

How the Auditory System Registers Frequency

When we discussed color vision, we examined two theories of color vision that were once considered incompatible. We now know that both theories are correct. Similarly, the history of research on hearing once featured a battle between two theories about the mechanism used by the auditory system to register frequency. If you play the lowest note on the piano, you perceive a different pitch than if you played that highest note. But how does the complex auditory system manage to record these differences? Researchers now conclude that the two important theories are both correct; together they explain how the auditory system processes the frequency of a sound wave.

According to **place theory,** each frequency of vibration produces a vibration in a particular *place* on the basilar membrane. (Remember that the basilar membrane contains the hair cells, which are the receptors in the auditory system.) A very low tone causes the greatest vibration in the part of the basilar membrane that is farthest away from the stirrup; a very high tone causes the greatest vibration closer to the stirrup. Imagine yourself running your finger along the keys of the piano, from the lowest notes to the highest notes. Initially, the ripple would be largest at the far end of the basilar membrane, and the hair cells resting on that part of the membrane would produce rapid electrical discharges. By the end of your demonstration, the hair cells closer to the stirrup would be most active.

Place theory emphasizes the location of the vibration, whereas frequency theory emphasizes how often the membrane vibrates. More specifically, **frequency theory** states that the entire basilar membrane vibrates at the same frequency as the tone that is sounded. Thus, if the frequency of the stimulus is 400 cycles per second, the basilar membrane responds by vibrating at a rate of 400 cycles per second.

Figure 4.21 shows how the two theories are actually compatible. As you can see, frequency theory accounts mostly for low- and middle-frequency ranges. Place theory accounts mostly for middle- and upper-frequency ranges. Notice that the middle range is particularly well cared for. The speech sounds, which are so important in our social interactions, fall in this middle range. This arrangement does not seem to be a coincidence. As Kiang and Peake (1988) remark:

> *Each organism responds to sounds in ways appropriate for survival in its ecological niche. Humans use hearing to monitor the environment, to locate sound sources, to identify sound generators, and, most importantly for a social animal, to communicate with others. . . . (p. 277)*

In addition, note the similarity with the two kinds of receptors in the visual system, rods and cones. We have two ways of registering visual stimuli and two ways of

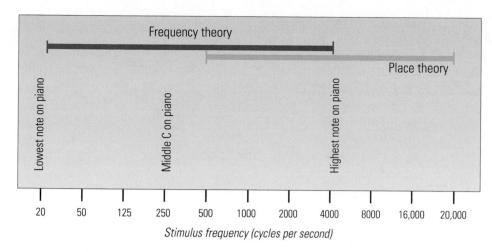

Figure 4.21
Frequency theory and place theory operate in partly overlapping ranges.

registering auditory stimuli. As a consequence, we can perceive an impressive range of sights and sounds.

Hearing Disabilities

About 28 million people in the United States have hearing disabilities (National Institute on Deafness and Other Communication Disorders, 1989). One kind of impairment is called **conduction deafness;** it involves problems in either the outer or the middle ear. These disabilities always involve a problem with the mechanical aspects of the auditory system, so that sound cannot be conducted appropriately from the eardrum to the receptors (Gulick et al., 1989). A hearing aid is typically useful for a person with conduction deafness.

The other kind of impairment is called **nerve deafness;** it involves problems in the inner ear, specifically in the cochlea or auditory nerve. For example, the hair cells illustrated in Figure 4.20 can be destroyed by repeated exposure to extremely loud noises (Gulick et al., 1989). People who work with very noisy equipment or listen to loud music for an extended period of time—without protection—may experience nerve deafness. A person with complete nerve deafness cannot be helped by a simple hearing aid. The hearing aid can *conduct* the sound waves, but the receptors or the auditory nerve are too damaged to transmit the message.

Characteristics of Sound

When you hear a sound, you can distinguish its pitch, loudness, timbre, and localization. Let us consider these features.

1. **Pitch** is the psychological reaction that corresponds to the physical characteristic of frequency. The highest note on a piccolo has a frequency of about 3,700 cycles per second. The pitch of that note is much higher than the pitch of the lowest note on the bass tuba, which has a frequency of only 39 cycles per second. Intriguingly, our experience with specific language sounds can influence our pitch perception. For example, people living in the south of England perceive some musical illusions differently than people living in Southern California (Deutsch, 1992).

2. **Loudness** is the psychological reaction that corresponds to the physical characteristic of amplitude; loudness is measured in decibels, abbreviated dB. Table 4.3 shows some representative sounds of different amplitudes. At present, government regulations specify that workers cannot be exposed to more than a 90-dB sound level for 8 hours a day (Kryter, 1985). However, people expose themselves to much louder sounds as a form of entertainment. For example, Hartman (1982) found that the sound level at two bars near his college averaged about 125 dB. One-third of the college students who regularly visited these places showed substantial hearing loss.

Young Alexa Ray Joel wears ear protectors to reduce the danger of hearing loss when she attends concerts featuring her father, Billy Joel.

TABLE 4.3 Some Representative Amplitudes of Everyday Noises, as Measured by the Decibel Scale of Loudness

LEVEL	LOUDNESS (DECIBELS)	EXAMPLE
Substantial hearing loss	180	Rocket launching pad
	160	Loudest rock band
Intolerable	140	Jet airplane taking off
	120	Very loud thunder
Very noisy	100	Heavy automobile traffic
Loud	80	Loud music from radio
Moderate	60	Normal conversation
Faint	40	Quiet neighborhood
	20	Soft whisper
Very faint	0	Softest sound detectable by human ear

3. **Timbre** (pronounced *tam*-burr) refers to sound quality. You are certainly familiar with the two previous characteristics, pitch and loudness, but the term *timbre* may be unfamiliar. The squeaky brakes on your friend's car may produce a sound that exactly matches the pitch and loudness of a tone produced by the finest soprano in the Metropolitan Opera Company. However, these two sounds differ in timbre. You can immediately recognize voices on the telephone that are identical in pitch and loudness, again because they differ in timbre.

If pitch is related to frequency, and loudness is related to amplitude, what physical feature of sound corresponds to timbre? The answer is tone complexity. Some sounds are composed of a small number of sound waves; the timbre of these sounds is pure and clean. (Consider the timbre of a tone played by a professional flutist, for example.) Other sounds consist of many sound waves combined; the timbre of these is richer and less crisp-sounding. (Consider the timbre of a violin or a guitar.) Timbre involves qualities such as richness, mellowness, and brightness (Evans, 1982).

4. **Localization** refers to our ability to determine the direction from which a sound is coming. When you hear water dripping, you can locate the appropriate faucet. When your alarm rings in the early morning hours, your arm reaches out in (approximately) the correct direction. How do we manage to localize sound? The hair cells in the ear can register the physical characteristics of sound such as frequency, amplitude, and complexity. However, hair cells cannot code that the alarm is ringing near your left arm rather than near your right knee (Oldfield & Parker, 1986).

In the section on vision, we saw the usefulness of binocular vision. We can figure out where objects are located because we have two eyes. Similarly, we can figure out where a sound comes from because we have two ears. We can localize sounds to some extent by using just one ear (Middlebrooks & Green, 1991). However, the major factor in explaining sound localization is that your ears are about six inches apart. As a consequence, they receive somewhat different stimuli. For example, when the alarm clock rings near your left arm, the noise reaches your left ear slightly before it reaches your right ear. In addition, your head creates a barrier, so the amplitude of the sound is somewhat fainter when it reaches your right ear. These two factors and other sources of information about a sound's location enable us to locate a sound within one degree of its true location (Matlin & Foley, 1992; Phillips & Brugge, 1985).

Now try Demonstration 4.7 to illustrate your accuracy in localizing sounds. Then pause for a moment to appreciate the variety of sounds around you. Your auditory system manages to process the sound of someone talking on the phone next door, a car horn honking out in the street, or your yellow highlighter squeaking as it marks passages in this book.

The tones produced by the members of this Cajun band differ not only in pitch and loudness, but also in timbre. Furthermore, your auditory system provides localization information; you can report that the fiddle appears at the left of the band, whereas the guitar appears at the right.

DEMONSTRATION 4.7   Sound Localization

Locate an object that makes a distinctive above-threshold noise (e.g., a dripping faucet, a ticking clock, or a distant radio). This object should be located in a room that is uniformly lit. If one part of the room is brighter than other parts, you may rely on visual cues to locate the object. Once you have selected the object, stand several feet away, plug your ears with your fingers, close your eyes, and turn around several times until you are not certain which direction you are facing. Then stop and point to the source of the sound as quickly as possible. How accurate were you?

SECTION SUMMARY

HEARING

- In hearing, the auditory system tranduces sound waves into neural messages in the form of action potentials. The hair-cell receptors in the cochlea transmit information through the auditory nerve to the auditory cortex.

- A sound's frequency is registered by means of both the place on the basilar membrane that vibrates and the frequency with which the membrane vibrates.

- Two different hearing disabilities are conduction deafness and nerve deafness.

- Four characteristics of sound that humans can appreciate are pitch, loudness, timbre, and localization.

THE OTHER PERCEPTUAL SYSTEMS

Vision and hearing clearly dominate the other perceptual abilities. However, think what you would experience if all your other perceptual systems were absent, with vision and hearing as your only sources of information about the outside world. Without touch and the other skin senses, you would expose yourself to objects that are harmfully heavy, sharp, and hot—objects that your warning systems typically help you avoid. Without the sense of smell, you would walk into rooms filled with smoke or poisonous gases. Without taste, you might not be motivated to eat. Let us begin with the skin senses and then consider two related sensory processes, smell and taste.

Touch and the Other Skin Senses

Your skin is the largest sensory system you possess. It features more than two square yards of skin receptors located across your entire body surface, dwarfing the relatively small receptive surfaces of the retina and the basilar membrane. However, we appreciate the skin senses much less than vision or hearing. The skin senses warn you that you must go around a large object, rather than through it, that another object could cause tissue damage, and that the outdoor temperature is dangerously cold. Thus, the skin senses include touch, pain, and temperature perception. Let us consider the first two of these in more detail.

Touch   We experience both passive and active touch. In **passive touch,** an object is placed on the skin. For example, researchers may measure detection thresholds for different parts of the body. You are more sensitive to a light touch on your lip than on the bottom of your toe (Weinstein, 1968).

A common phenomenon of all sensory systems is adaptation. In **adaptation,** the perceived intensity of a repeated stimulus decreases over time. All your skin surfaces—whether on your lip or on your toe—show adaptation. For example, are you aware right now of the pressure of your watch against your wrist? The wristband is depressing your skin's surface just as much as when you slipped the watch on this morning. However, touch adaptation guarantees that you will stop noticing touch after a few minutes of mild constant pressure. Our sensory systems are designed to signal *change,* rather than constant stimulation, and adaptation is an excellent example of this tendency.

In passive touch, people wait to be prodded or poked by objects. In contrast, we use **active touch** when we actively explore objects. In everyday life, we use active touch much more frequently than passive touch (Heller, 1991). At this moment, for example, you may be rubbing your finger along the edge of a desk. In 5 to 10 minutes, you will be actively running your finger along the right margin of this book, preparing to turn the page. Unaided by vision, you can fasten a zipper, determine whether fruit is ripe, or thread a nut onto a bolt in some hidden part of your automobile (Heller & Schiff, 1991a).

We also use active touch to identify objects, as Demonstration 4.8 illustrates. In general, we are much more accurate in identifying objects when we use our fingers to explore them, rather than relying simply on passive touch (Appelle, 1991; Gibson, 1962; Heller, 1984).

This person is using active touch to read Braille.

Pain You do not need to be persuaded why we need vision, hearing, and touch. However, you may wonder why we need pain. Some people cannot feel pain, and you might initially envy them. However, children who are born with pain insensitivity have bitten off their tongue and fingers by mistake. Adults may not detect a ruptured appendix or cancer in time to seek adequate treatment. One woman died from damage to her spine; she had not made the usual kinds of posture adjustments we routinely make when our muscles begin to ache (Sternbach, 1968, 1978).

Pain is a complex experience, involving both sensory and emotional components (Fernandez & Turk, 1992). Those emotional components can be so intense that pain may drive a person to suicide (Melzack, 1990). Pain is also mystifying. Consider the following observations:

1. About 70% of people who have had an arm or a leg amputated continue to report pain in the missing limb, even though pain receptors cannot be stimulated; this phenomenon is called **phantom limb pain** (Melzack, 1992).

2. A soldier in World War II reported intense pain when a bullet nicked his forehead, yet he felt nothing some time later when his leg was torn off (Wallis, 1984).

3. A patient who believed her leg pain was caused by a minor problem could control the pain with small doses of codeine; when she discovered it was due to cancer, she needed much greater amounts of medication (Cassell, 1990).

These examples illustrate that pain perception involves more than merely the stimulation of pain receptors. Pain requires not only a physiological explanation, but also a psychological explanation (Melzack, 1986).

The most widely accepted explanation of pain is Ronald Melzack and Patrick Wall's **gate-control theory,** which proposes that you experience pain only if the pain messages pass through a gate in the spinal cord on their route to the brain. When the gate is open, we feel pain. However, the brain can send messages to the spinal cord, indicating that the gate should be closed. If the gate is closed, pain messages are blocked from reaching the brain. As a consequence, we do not feel pain (Melzack, 1986; Melzack & Wall, 1965; Whitehead & Kuhn, 1990). For example, the brain's

---

DEMONSTRATION 4.8 Active Touch

Assemble about a dozen miscellaneous objects of similar sizes that you find in your room, such as a small paper clip, a safety pin, a rubber band, a coin, a ring, and so forth. Place them on a clean surface, such as a desk, and close your eyes. Touch an object and identify it by exploring with your active touch. Do you have difficulty on any of these items, or is the task an easy one?

messages probably helped to block pain perception when the soldier's leg was torn off. Gate-control theory shows how top-down processing, discussed in connection with visual pattern perception, can also influence pain perception.

Chapter 3 discussed **endorphins,** which are neuromodulators that occur naturally in the brain and decrease a person's sensitivity to pain. Endorphins probably play an important role in the gate-control mechanism, though the specifics of endorphins and the representation of pain in the cortex are not well understood (Talbot et al., 1991). However, researchers have discovered a phenomenon called **stress-induced analgesia;** psychological stress triggers the release of endorphins, making painful stimuli seem less intense (Coren et al., 1994; Lewis et al., 1984; Wiertelak et al., 1992).

We also know that cognitive processes can alter pain perception, for example during childbirth. In a review of 150 relevant studies, Fernandez and Turk (1989) found that people reported less pain when they used strategies such as thinking about pleasant images. Once again, top-down processes influence perception.

In this section on the skin senses, we have seen that our perceptual processes provide us with the ability to *stop* noticing a stimulus. They also allow us to recognize objects by their shape, especially when we use active touch. These perceptual processes cause us to feel pain in some circumstances, but to stop feeling pain in other situations. Once again, we see that humans are well equipped to interact with their environment.

One of the paradoxes of pain is that this football player may experience tissue damage, yet he may feel little pain.

Smell

Smell is a mysterious sense; of all the research in perception, only 2% of journal articles examine smell (Almagor, 1990; Teghtsoonian, 1983). One reason for this neglect is that smell is simply less important to humans, compared with the other senses. Another reason is the difficulty of classifying the stimuli for smell. We can describe visual and auditory stimuli in terms of characteristics such as wave frequency and amplitude. But how can we transform the stench of an ancient tuna sandwich or the fragrance of chocolate chip cookies into wavelengths? With odorous stimuli, we must settle for qualitative descriptors such as spicy, minty, and citruslike.

Furthermore, we know less about odor receptors than about visual receptors. However, researchers have discovered a large family of genes that seem to be associated with proteins located in the nasal passages. Surprisingly, these proteins appear to be chemically related to light-sensitive molecules in the retina and therefore may provide information about odor receptors and the perception of smell (Barinaga, 1991a; Buck & Axel, 1991).

In the previous section, you learned about adaptation to touch. Similarly, we often experience adaptation to odors. Have you ever walked into a locker room, permeated with the odor of dozens of sweaty bodies? The odor was initially strong, yet after a few minutes you no longer noticed it. Indeed, the perceived intensity of an odor decreases substantially during adaptation (Cain, 1988; Engen, 1991). Within one minute, the perceived intensity drops to about 30% of its original level.

We humans are reasonably competent at detecting odors, but we are not especially accurate in identifying a particular odor (Engen, 1991; Richardson & Zucco, 1989). In my classes, I sometimes ask students to sniff and identify the contents of several opaque jars. Some odors consistently produce a pained expression on the students' faces as they struggle to identify the mysteriously familiar substance. Pencil shavings and crayons are particularly likely to elicit this annoyed reaction. The ability to recognize that an odor is familiar, combined with the inability to identify its name, is called the **tip-of-the-nose phenomenon** (Engen, 1987; Lawless & Engen, 1977). This experience is similar to the more common tip-of-the-tongue phenomenon, in which a word for which you are searching refuses to leap forth from memory.

Research on odor identification has demonstrated that some odors can be recognized easily; coffee, paint, and chocolate pose no challenge. In contrast, fewer than

After about a minute near this cookie store, the fragrance of these cookies will be only about one-third of its original intensity.

20% of the participants in one study were able to identify correctly odors such as cigar, cat feces, ham, and sawdust (Desor & Beauchamp, 1974).

People are reasonably accurate in recognizing other humans by their odors. In this research, people are asked to wear a T-shirt for one day. Then participants in the experiment sniff these dirty T-shirts and try to identify the wearer. College students can recognize their own odors fairly well (Russell, 1976). Furthermore, mothers can recognize which T-shirts were worn by their children, even when these children are 2-day-old newborns (Porter et al., 1983; Porter & Moore, 1981).

Another group of researchers in smell perception are concerned with practical applications. One profitable application of smell perception is the development of perfumes (Brady, 1982; Moskowitz, 1978). Each year Americans spend billions of dollars on perfume. The scent strips inserted in magazine advertisements cost $35,000 more to produce than standard advertisements, but they boost perfume sales substantially (Gibbs, 1988).

Let us now consider the last of the perceptual systems—taste. As we will see, smell and taste help create the experience of flavor.

Scent strips are often inserted in magazines in order to increase perfume sales.

Taste

Taste refers to the perceptions created when a substance makes contact with the special receptors in the mouth (Bartoshuk, 1971, 1991a). When psychologists use the word *taste* correctly, they are referring only to perceptions such as sweetness. Thus, *taste* refers to only a narrow range of sensory experiences, namely, sweet, sour, bitter, and salty.

Flavor, a much broader term, includes smell, touch, temperature, and pain—in addition to taste (Bartoshuk, 1991b). For example, the flavor of spicy chili includes impressions such as the pungent smell of onion and cumin, the creamy smooth texture of an exploded bean on your tongue, the piping-hot temperature, and the distinct pain from the chili pepper.

One of the most important taste phenomena is taste adaptation. A first sip of lemonade is so sour that your lips instantly pucker. After a few sips, though, the drink is more tolerable; the sourness has apparently decreased. Taste adaptation is similar to the adaptation of touch and odor that we have already discussed. As Figure 4.22 shows, the perceived intensity of a taste decreases quickly. After about half a minute of sipping, the lemonade does not taste nearly as sour as the first mouthful. However, people recover rapidly from adaptation. If you stop drinking the lemonade for just half a minute and then take a sip, your lips will pucker once more.

The most important application of taste is in the area of food technology. Before it reaches the consumers, a new breakfast cereal must be judged on qualities such as

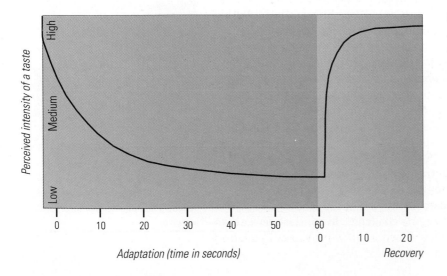

Figure 4.22

Adaptation to a specific taste, and subsequent recovery.

sweetness, crispiness, and aroma. Flavor enhancement is a new branch of food technology that contributes to medical therapy. For example, a man who was recovering from surgery had a craving for mashed potatoes that clearly could not be satisfied by the intravenous feeding required during the postoperative period. Dr. Susan Schiffman, a prominent researcher in the area of flavor and taste, was able to supply him with a powder that smelled and tasted exactly like mashed potatoes yet dissolved completely on the tongue (Blackburn, 1988). Schiffman has also helped to develop powders and sprays with flavors such as peanut butter and jelly, pizza, and—one surgical patient's request—southern boiled fatback and green beans.

These flavor enhancers can also help treat obesity and encourage elderly people to eat. Some elderly people have decreased taste sensitivity. They eat less, because the food seems so boringly bland. In contrast, Schiffman found that elderly individuals at a retirement home ate more beef when its flavor had been boosted by a beef flavor enhancer. If fashion magazines are filled with scent strips from luxury perfumes, what can we expect in the future from the gourmet food magazines? Will *Bon Appétit* include flavor strips for well-aged Camembert cheese? Will *Gourmet* reek with Peking duck flavor enhancer? Clearly, the research on sensation and perception can produce practical applications as well as theoretical advances.

A. K. Das is a professional tea taster in Assam, India. However, he does not simply judge the taste of a tea. He also assesses the color and texture of the dry tea leaves, as well as the color and fragrance of the tea liquid.

SECTION SUMMARY

THE OTHER PERCEPTUAL SYSTEMS

- Research on touch shows that different parts of the body differ in their sensitivity to touch and that we show adaptation to touch after continued stimulation. Furthermore, active touch is more useful than passive touch in identifying objects.

- Pain requires a psychological explanation in addition to a physiological explanation, because higher level, top-down factors influence pain perception.

- Other factors important in pain perception include gate-control theory, endorphins, stress-induced analgesia, and the influence of cognitive processes on pain.

- People show adaptation to odors. Some odors are difficult to identify, but people are reasonably accurate in recognizing other humans by their odors.

- Taste is a more limited term than flavor. People show adaptation to tastes. Flavor enhancers are helpful in medical therapy.

REVIEW QUESTIONS

1. Describe a recent experience that involved detection. How could you measure a detection threshold in this situation, using the classical psychophysical approach? If the signal detection approach were used instead, what factors would have determined your criterion? Now describe a recent situation involving discrimination; discuss how the concept of just-noticeable differences applies here.

2. Imagine that you are witnessing a car crash. Simultaneously, you register both visual and auditory stimuli. Trace how these two kinds of stimuli would be processed, beginning with the receptors and ending at the cortex.

3. Vision and hearing share several similarities. For example, color perception and pitch perception each have two theoretical explanations. Describe as many other similarities as you can recall.

4. What factors provide visual information about an object's distance? What factors provide information about the distance of an auditory stimulus?

5. The section on shape perception described how the figure-ground relationship and the Gestalt laws of grouping help organize visual stimuli. Discuss these two topics, listing the Gestalt laws. Now apply each of these principles to auditory stimuli: How is our hearing organized?

6. In the section on shape perception, we discussed how perception involves both bottom-up and top-down processes. Describe these two approaches and then discuss how they could be applied to signal detection theory, shape perception, illusory contour, and pain perception.

7. One theme of this book is that humans are extremely competent and accurate. How can you reconcile this theme with the information about illusions and illusory contour?

8. The concept of adaptation was discussed in connection with vision, touch, smell, and taste. Describe these four topics, providing an example of each that is based on your recent experience.

9. Throughout this chapter, we discussed perceptual disorders and individual differences. Describe as many as you can recall.

10. This chapter emphasized vision and hearing more than the other senses. However, some of the same principles apply to touch, smell, and taste. Based on your knowledge, predict the following: (a) applying signal detection theory to odor detection; (b) figure-ground perception in taste; (c) odor constancy when you take a deep breath of an odor; (d) the law of nearness applied to touch.

N E W   T E R M S

sensation
perception
psychophysics
detection
detection threshold
signal detection theory
sensitivity
criterion
discrimination
just-noticeable difference (jnd)
Weber's law
wavelength
hue
amplitude (vision)
brightness
cornea
iris
pupil
lens
retina
transduction
fovea
receptor cells
cones
rods
bipolar cells
ganglion cells
optic nerve
blind spot
optic chiasm
binocular vision
visual cortex
single-cell recording technique
feature detectors
PET scan (positron emission tomography)
visual acuity

dark adaptation
pursuit movement
saccadic movement
perceptual span
trichromatic theory
chromatic adaptation
opponent-process theory
color deficiency
figure-ground relationship
Gestalt approach
law of proximity
law of similarity
law of good continuation
law of closure
distinctive features
recognition-by-components theory
geons
bottom-up processing
top-down processing
biological motion
monocular
binocular
binocular disparity
constancy
size constancy
shape constancy
lightness constancy
color constancy
illusion
theory of misapplied constancy
illusory contour
sound waves
sound
frequency
amplitude (hearing)
auditory canal

eardrum

cochlea

hair cells

basilar membrane

auditory nerve

auditory cortex

place theory

frequency theory

conduction deafness

nerve deafness

pitch

loudness

timbre

localization

passive touch

adaptation

active touch

phantom limb pain

gate-control theory

endorphins

stress-induced analgesia

tip-of-the-nose phenomenon

taste

flavor

A N S W E R S   T O   D E M O N S T R A T I O N

DEMONSTRATION 4.4   57, 15

R E C O M M E N D E D   R E A D I N G S

Coren, S., Ward L. M., & Enns, J. T. (1994). *Sensation & perception* (4th ed.). Fort Worth: Harcourt Brace & Company. This upper-level book provides a complete overview of sensation and perception, including chapters on individual differences in perception as well as the role of experience in perception.

Engen, T. (1991). *Odor sensation and memory.* Westport, CT: Praeger. This book is written by a very prominent researcher in the discipline of smell; it includes readable discussions of topics such as odor memory, odor pollution, and loss of odor sensitivity.

Heller, M. A., & Schiff, W. (Eds.). (1991b). *The psychology of touch.* Hillsdale, NJ: Erlbaum. Although this book focuses primarily on active touch, it also contains chapters on the physiology of touch, temperature perception, and the development of touch perception.

Matlin, M. W., & Foley, H. J. (1992). *Sensation and perception* (3rd ed.). Boston: Allyn & Bacon. This mid-level textbook emphasizes cognitive processes in perception, and it contains many applications for everyday experiences and for professionals.

Shepherd, R. N. (1990). *Mind sights.* New York: Freeman. This book contains numerous illusions and ambiguous figures, which were created by Roger Shepard, a prominent researcher in the area of visual imagery.

CHAPTER 5

STATES OF CONSCIOUSNESS

The philosopher Daniel Dennett (1991) muses about consciousness, the topic of his recent book *Consciousness Explained:*

> *The mystery of consciousness has many ways of introducing itself, and it struck me anew with particular force one recent morning as I sat in my rocking chair reading a book. I had apparently just looked up from my book, and at first had been gazing blindly out the window, lost in thought, when the beauty of my surroundings distracted me from my theoretical musings. Green-golden sunlight was streaming in the window that early spring day, and the thousands of branches and twigs of the maple tree in the yard were still clearly visible through a mist of green buds, forming an elegant pattern of wonderful intricacy. The windowpane is made of old glass, and has a scarcely detectable wrinkle line in it, and as I rocked back and forth, this imperfection in the glass caused a wave of synchronized wiggles to march back and forth across the delta of branches, a regular motion superimposed with remarkable vividness on the more chaotic shimmer of the twigs and branches in the breeze. (p. 26).*

Consciousness is your awareness of external and internal stimuli. This awareness may include thoughts about the external world, including sunlight, maple trees, and window panes. The awareness may also concern internal stimuli, such as Dennett's thoughts about the book he had been reading, and your own thoughts about the topic of consciousness.

Scientific psychology began with the study of consciousness in the laboratory of Wilhelm Wundt, whose introspection technique we examined in Chapter 1 (Kihlstrom, 1987). During the last century, the popularity of consciousness has fluctuated dramatically. William James included a chapter on consciousness in his important psychology textbook (James, 1890). Several decades later, the behaviorists rejected consciousness. It was considered an inappropriate topic for scientific study because it was difficult to observe or measure with a clear-cut operational definition. As a result, consciousness had essentially vanished from the psychological scene by the middle of this century (Hearnshaw, 1987; Hilgard, 1986).

Consciousness re-emerged during the 1960s, however, as the cognitive psychology approach gained popularity. In fact, an influential cognitive psychologist named Howard Gardner has proposed that consciousness is likely to become one of the most important topics of the future (Gardner, 1988).

Let us begin our exploration of consciousness by considering waking consciousness and attention, which occupy the major part of our lives. Then we will examine two altered states of consciousness, sleeping and drug-induced states. Our final topic, hypnosis and meditation, is more controversial; psychologists disagree whether hypnosis and meditation can induce truly altered states of consciousness.

WAKING CONSCIOUSNESS AND ATTENTION

Most of this textbook focuses on our normal waking state. When you remember, think, and speak, you are awake and conscious. Your social interactions also involve normal waking consciousness. Two questions about consciousness have recently intrigued psychologists: (1) To what extent are we aware of our thought processes? and (2) What happens when we try to eliminate a thought from consciousness? Another important area that is often intertwined with consciousness—attention—is our final topic in this section.

Consciousness About Higher Mental Processes

Are you aware of your thought processes? Can you accurately assess how you remembered something? Do you know why you came up with the solution to a particular problem? This issue of consciousness about our own cognitions has stimulated a controversy among psychologists. For example, consider this question: "What is your mother's maiden name?" Now answer a second question, "How did you arrive at the answer to the first question?" The name probably leapt swiftly into your consciousness, yet you probably found that you could not explain your thought processes. The name simply seemed to "pop" into memory (Miller, 1962).

As Nisbett and Wilson (1977) argued, we often have little direct access to our thought processes. We may be completely conscious of the *products* of our higher mental activities (for instance, your mother's maiden name), but we are usually not conscious of the *process* that created the product (for example, how you retrieved that information from memory). "The sorting, sifting, and shuffling that preceded the recollection seem to be hidden from us" (Lyons, 1986, p. 101).

However, we can be conscious of other, more leisurely thought processes (Nelson, 1992). If you are searching for somebody's name that is on the tip of your tongue, you can trace your process as you coax that name out of hiding. Perhaps you first realized the first letter of the name, then another name it resembled, and then its number of syllables. In addition, people seem to have access to consciousness when they report their thought processes about creative projects, such as writing poetry (Perkins, 1981). Finally, access to consciousness is more likely under conditions that encourage us to pay attention to important stimuli at the time they occur (Farthing, 1992). In summary, some mental processes are available to consciousness, whereas others remain hidden and relatively mysterious.

Thought Suppression

When the Russian novelist Dostoevsky was young, he apparently tormented his young brother by telling him *not* to think of a white bear (Wegner et al., 1987). Similarly, if you have ever tried to avoid thinking about food while dieting, you know the difficulty of trying to chase these undesired thoughts out of consciousness. Smokers trying to give up cigarettes and depressed people trying to cheer themselves can also verify the difficulty of thought suppression. **Thought suppression** is the intentional, conscious removal of a thought from consciousness (Wegner, 1992).

To test the difficulty of thought suppression, Wegner and his coauthors (1987) instructed a group of students *not* to think about a white bear during a five-minute period. When they *did* think about a white bear, they were told to ring a bell. They rang the bell an average of more than three times during the first minute, and one time during each subsequent minute. They clearly had difficulty suppressing white-bear thoughts! After this five-minute period, they were told that they could now think freely about a white bear. Now they showed a rebound effect, with about 60% more white-bear thoughts than a control group. In other words, when we try to eliminate an unwanted thought, that thought may come back even stronger at a later time. This topic has important implications for eating (Chapter 12), psychologically troubling thoughts (Chapters 15 and 16), and smoking (Chapter 19).

Notice an interesting contrast between the two topics we have discussed in connection with consciousness. We first saw that people have difficulty bringing into consciousness their thoughts about their higher mental processes. Then we saw in the section on thought suppression that people also have difficulty eliminating from consciousness the thoughts they consider undesirable.

When people are instructed not *to think about a white bear, they have difficulty suppressing these thoughts. Can you think of situations in which you had trouble eliminating unwanted thoughts from consciousness?*

Attention

Consciousness and attention are closely related. Consciousness is your aware-ness of stimuli; **attention** means a concentration of mental activity. Right now, you may be conscious of many stimuli surrounding you as you read this paragraph. How-ever, your attention may be focused on the material you are reading. This section ex-amines three components of attention: divided attention, selective attention, and search.

Divided Attention In **divided attention,** people try to distribute their atten-tion among two or more competing tasks. One example of divided attention is trying to listen simultaneously to your professor and to a nearby conversation. Another ex-ample, with even more competing tasks, occurred when you first learned to drive. Re-member what it was like to pull out of a parking space for the first time? You had to simultaneously watch the traffic, determine that you had the correct gear, notice how close your fenders were to the cars on each side, and regulate the accelerator. If your driving instructor was talking at the same time, the divided-attention task probably seemed overwhelming!

Consider a laboratory version of a divided-attention situation. Neisser and Becklen (1975) asked participants to watch a television screen. As Figure 5.1 shows, the screen displayed two different kinds of games taking place simultaneously. One was a hand-slapping game that you may have played when you were younger. The participants were instructed to press a switch with their right hand whenever one player successfully slapped the other's hand. In the other game shown on the televi-sion screen, three men moved around a room, passing the ball to one another. The participants were told to press a switch with their left hand whenever the ball was passed from one player to another. Neisser and Becklen found that the participants had no trouble following one game at a time. However, when the participants were required to monitor both games simultaneously, their performance deteriorated. In fact, they made eight times as many errors in the divided-attention task in contrast to the error rate when monitoring only one game.

Your early driving experiences may have resembled the divided-attention situa-tion of the participants in Neisser and Becklen's study. You could easily watch the traffic, just as you could easily monitor a hand-slapping game. The challenge comes when you must perform another perceptual task simultaneously. After several years of driving experience, however, you can easily drive through heavy traffic while lis-tening to the radio and talking to a friend.

Divided attention is difficult when we first begin learning a task. However, prac-tice makes perfect. For example, college students in one experiment successfully learned to read stories to themselves while simultaneously categorizing words that were read to them, such as writing down the category ANIMAL when they heard the word DOG (Spelke et al., 1976). In another study, an experienced typist managed to recite nursery rhymes while typing an unrelated passage at high speed (Shaffer, 1975). Try reciting "Mary Had a Little Lamb" while typing a paragraph from this text-book. Unless you are an experienced typist, either your speed or your accuracy will suffer on this divided-attention task. However, practice can alter the limits of atten-tional capacity. We do not seem to have a built-in, fixed limit to the number of tasks we can perform simultaneously (Allport, 1989; Hirst, 1986).

Selective Attention In **selective attention,** two or more messages are pre-sented simultaneously; people are instructed to focus attention on one message and ignore everything else. Notice that divided attention and selective attention both in-volve two or more simultaneous tasks. However, divided attention requires you to pay attention to everything. In contrast, selective attention requires you to focus on only one task.

Think about a selective-attention task you recently faced. Maybe you tried to listen to the news while a conversation elsewhere in the room threatened to distract

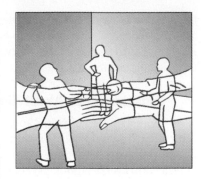

Figure 5.1

Outline tracings of the divided-attention task studied by Neisser and Becklen (1975).

Because of selective attention, these students can focus their attention on the conversation in their own group and ignore the other conversation.

you. You have probably found that if you conscientiously attend to one message, you notice little about other messages presented at the same time.

In the laboratory, auditory selective attention is often studied in a **dichotic listening task;** listeners are instructed to repeat a message presented to one ear while ignoring a different message presented to the other ear. The research generally shows that people seldom notice important features of the unattended message. For example, if the message in the attended ear is spoken quickly, people may not even notice whether the message in the unattended ear is in English or German (Cherry, 1953). However, in some circumstances, people do notice characteristics of the unattended message (Johnston & Dark, 1986). For example, when sexually explicit words are presented to the unattended ear, college students notice these words and are not as accurate in monitoring the primary message (Nielsen & Sarason, 1981).

Try Demonstration 5.1, which illustrates the difficulty of *visual* selective attention; this task is called the Stroop effect. According to the **Stroop effect,** people take much longer to say the color of a stimulus when it is used to print an inappropriate color name, rather than appearing as a simple solid color. For example, in Demonstration 5.1, you probably took much longer to say the color "yellow" when that color was used to print the inappropriate color name *red* than when it appeared as a solid yellow rectangle. Notice how the Stroop effect illustrates selective attention: People take longer to name a color when they are distracted by another very prominent feature of the stimulus—that is, the meaning of the word itself. As adult readers, we automatically attend to word meaning and find it difficult to attend to a less salient feature, the color of the stimulus.

The effect was first demonstrated by J. R. Stroop (1935), who found that people took roughly twice as long on the selective attention task as on the task of naming the colors of solid rectangles. Since the original experiment, more than 400 additional studies have examined variations of the Stroop effect (MacLeod, 1991).

Try noticing your own attention patterns. Which selective-attention tasks seem most difficult? When do you notice the characteristics of the message that you are supposed to be ignoring? Does a selective-attention task suddenly become a divided-attention task when you try to monitor *two* interesting conversations?

Search Searching requires you to focus your attention on locating specific targets. Try Demonstration 5.2 and decide which search task is easier. From the research of Anne Treisman and her colleagues, we know that search involves either of

---

DEMONSTRATION 5.1 The Stroop Effect

For this demonstration, you will need a watch with a second hand. First, measure how long it takes to name the colors listed immediately below. Your task is to say out loud the names of the ink colors, ignoring the meaning of the words. Measure the amount of time it takes to go through this list *five* times. (Keep a tally of the number of repetitions.) Record that time.

RED BLUE GREEN YELLOW GREEN RED BLUE YELLOW BLUE RED
YELLOW GREEN YELLOW GREEN BLUE RED RED GREEN YELLOW BLUE

Now you will try a second color-naming task. Measure how long it takes to name the colors listed below. Your task is to say out loud the names of these ink colors. Measure the amount of time it takes to go through this list five times. (Again, keep a tally of the number of repetitions.) Record that time.

RED BLUE GREEN YELLOW GREEN RED BLUE YELLOW BLUE RED
YELLOW GREEN YELLOW GREEN BLUE RED RED GREEN YELLOW BLUE

DEMONSTRATION 5.2 Preattentive Processing Versus Focused Attention

Cover the two designs below before you read further.

A. In this part of the demonstration, see how long it takes you to locate the blue figure. Remove the cover from the left-hand design and find the blue figure.

B. Now see how long it takes you to locate the blue X in the other design. Remove the cover and find the blue X.

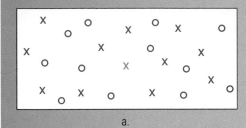

a.

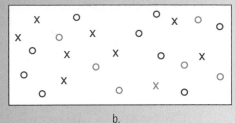

b.

two kinds of attention (Treisman, 1986, 1991; Treisman & Gelade, 1980). In one kind of search, called **preattentive processing,** you automatically register the features in a display of objects. For example, in Part A of Demonstration 5.2, you used preattentive processing because the blue figure seemed to "pop out" almost effortlessly. In this low-level kind of attention, you attend only to isolated features, such as "blue."

The second, more complicated kind of search is called focused attention. **Focused attention** requires processing objects one at a time. In Part B, you used focused attention to examine each object in the box. The blue X did not simply "pop out" from the display. As you can imagine, focused attention is more time consuming than preattentive processing. Notice how you use focused attention when searching a telephone directory for a friend's name, because you must skim through each name on the list. In contrast, you use preattentive processing to locate the one blue shirt when all the other shirts on the rack are white.

S E C T I O N   S U M M A R Y

WAKING CONSCIOUSNESS AND ATTENTION

- The topic of consciousness has fluctuated greatly in popularity throughout the history of psychology.

- We seem to have only limited access to some thought processes, yet we are apparently conscious of other more leisurely mental activities.

- Thought suppression is difficult, and it often produces a rebound effect in which the unwanted thoughts are especially prominent.

- In divided-attention situations, people have difficulty performing two tasks simultaneously; however, practice improves their accuracy.

- In selective-attention situations, people pay complete attention to one auditory task and typically notice little about the unattended message; the Stroop effect is a visual selective-attention task in which a word's meaning interferes with naming the color of the ink.

- Two kinds of search are the relatively automatic preattentive processing and the more time-consuming focused attention.

SLEEPING AND DREAMING

If you are typical of most people, you will spend close to 25 years asleep during your lifetime. During **sleep,** your body is less active and you are less responsive to the environment (Oswald, 1987a). When you are asleep, you may be relatively unresponsive, but your brain is very active. In fact, recordings from the brains of sleeping animals demonstrate that the overall level of neuron activity is just as great during sleep as when they are awake (Kimble, 1988).

Let's begin by looking at the sleeping-and-waking cycle. Then we will consider the stages of sleep, sleep deprivation, the reasons why we sleep, and sleep disorders. The final part of this section examines dreams, providing further evidence for the active nature of sleep.

Circadian Rhythms

Each day of your life, you experience a cycle that includes both a sleeping and a waking period. These cycles are called circadian (pronounced "sur-*kay*-dee-un") rhythms, based on the Latin *circa dies,* meaning "about a day." Therefore, a **circadian rhythm** has a cycle that lasts approximately 24 hours.

Part of the reason you maintain a 24-hour cycle is that your world is filled with reminders about time. Clocks and watches remind you of the precise time of day. The position of the sun and the outdoor temperature give approximate time clues. Mealtimes offer still further clues that help you maintain that 24-hour schedule. All of these clues that encourage you to adopt a 24-hour cycle are know as **zeitgebers** (pronounced "*tsite*-gay-burs"), a German word for "time givers."

Free-Running What would happen if we were deprived of zeitgebers? Would we still obey an internal biological clock, or would our circadian rhythms run haywire? To answer this question, researchers have asked volunteers to live for several weeks in isolation from zeitgebers. They give up their watches, radios, televisions, and telephones and live for several weeks in a place where sunlight cannot penetrate. Typical locations include underground caves in the United States and in the Swiss Alps, as well as specially constructed apartments. The research staff who work with these volunteers are instructed not to wear watches and to avoid time-related greetings such as "good morning" and "good night."

In a typical study, the volunteers initially keep to a rigid, predetermined schedule. They go to sleep at midnight and are wakened by the staff at 8 a.m. (Coleman, 1986). After 20 days of this routine, the rules change. The volunteers are free to decide when to go to sleep and when to awake.

If humans were perfectly circadian, they would continue to maintain that midnight-to-8 a.m. schedule, a 24-hour cycle, even without zeitgebers. However, nearly all people show the same pattern: On the first night, they go to sleep at 1 a.m. and sleep until 9 a.m. On each subsequent night, they fall asleep about one hour later; they also arise about one hour later each subsequent morning. This natural tendency to adopt a 25-hour cycle, one hour later each day, is known as **free-running.** Because of this free-running tendency, volunteers request their scrambled eggs for breakfast at 8 in the evening after about 12 days without zeitgebers.

Some individuals have deprived themselves of zeitgebers for extended periods of time. For example, a Parisian woman named Véronique Le Guen lived for several months in a cave, deprived of time cues. During 105 real days, she experienced only 43 sleep-wake cycles. In a typical "day," she spent 40 hours awake and 34 hours asleep. Apparently, our cycles can even expand to three days in length, when our zeitgebers are absent (Hall, 1991).

Disrupted Circadian Rhythms In the twentieth century, North Americans are likely to experience two reasons for disrupted circadian rhythms: shift schedules and jet lag. In both cases, sleep patterns become irregular, and people make more errors during waking hours (Anch et al., 1988).

About 20% of workers in the United States are on **shift schedules,** in which they must work during the normal sleeping hours (Moorcroft, 1987). As a consequence, they sleep fewer hours, and they wake up more often during sleep. In fact, a review of all the studies conducted on shift work concluded that 62% of shift workers complained about sleep disturbances, in contrast to 20% of day workers (Coleman, 1986). It makes sense that they have difficulty sleeping during the day, because the rest of the world is scheduled to be particularly active then . . . telephones ring, automobiles honk, and children squabble. Furthermore, shift workers often fall asleep on the job. In one survey, more than half of the shift workers admitted to falling asleep at work on a regular basis (Coleman, 1986). In many cases, these brief naps may be harmless. However, an unannounced late-night inspection of a nuclear plant found 5 of the 13 employees asleep—a report that did not amuse nearby residents.

Consider also the train crash described by Coleman (1986). At 4:45 in the morning, the engineer and the head brakeman had both fallen asleep. Their 115-car train was speeding down a hill on the same track as another freight train; they had slept through the flashing yellow signals 20 miles earlier. They awoke too late to stop the train, and two people on the other train were killed. Just nine days earlier, five crew members were killed in a train accident at 3:55 a.m. As it turns out, 3 a.m. is the lowest point in the body's cycle of alertness. The workers on these trains had been obeying their biological clocks, rather than the more fragile clocks imposed by their work schedules.

Jet travel is another very effective way to disrupt circadian rhythms. One summer, I traveled to Sydney, Australia. When I arrived, it was 2 p.m. on a Sunday in Australia, but it was 11 p.m. on *Saturday* in New York. It took several days for me to adjust my internal clock. **Jet lag** is the term for the disturbances in body rhythm caused by lengthy journeys involving time-zone changes. In contrast, travelers do not experience jet lag when they fly in a north-south direction, without changing any time zones (Gregory, 1987).

The research of Charles Czeisler and his colleagues suggests that shift workers and jet travelers can both be helped by systematic exposure to bright light and darkness (e.g., Czeisler et al., 1990; Jewett et al., 1991). For example, Czeisler and his coworkers (1989) found that they could shift people's sleep-wake schedules by six hours by exposing them to bright light, ordinary indoor light, and darkness. Ordinarily, a jet traveler would require at least nine days to adjust to this new schedule; systematic exposure to lighting could accomplish the shift within three days.

Variations in Sleep Patterns Our theme of individual differences is prominent when we look at the variations in the amount of sleep people require. For example, in one case study, a 70-year-old woman averaged 67 minutes of sleep each night (Meddis et al., 1973). She showed no signs of fatigue, and she was puzzled that other people wasted so much time sleeping. Even a population of normal undergraduate students shows tremendous variation in sleep durations, as Figure 5.2 shows (Hicks et al., 1990).

Where do you and your friends fit in that distribution? In general, researchers have not found many systematic differences between habitual short sleepers and long sleepers (Mendelson, 1987; Webb, 1982). However, contrary to what we might expect, people who require little sleep actually seem to be somewhat more energetic and alert during the day than those who require more sleep (Hicks & Guista, 1982).

Age has a significant influence on sleep. Newborns sleep about 15 hours a day (Kimble, 1988). Elderly people sleep about six hours a day and are more likely to report difficulty falling asleep and staying asleep (Friedman et al., 1991; Monk et al., 1991). Rediehs and her colleagues (1990) conducted a meta-analysis of 27 studies on sleep patterns in old age. (As Chapter 2 described, a **meta-analysis** systematically synthesizes results from numerous studies.) Rediehs and her coauthors found that males were somewhat more likely than females to show changes in their sleep patterns as they grew older.

We have seen that people differ in the amount of sleep they require. However, another way in which they differ is in the timing of their sleep. Some people function best in the early morning, and their efficiency falls off as evening approaches; they have great difficulty adjusting to shift work, jet lag, and any other change in schedule. In contrast, those who work best at night have relatively little difficulty adjusting

It is daytime in this airport, but these jet passengers are still operating according to biological clocks established in their own countries.

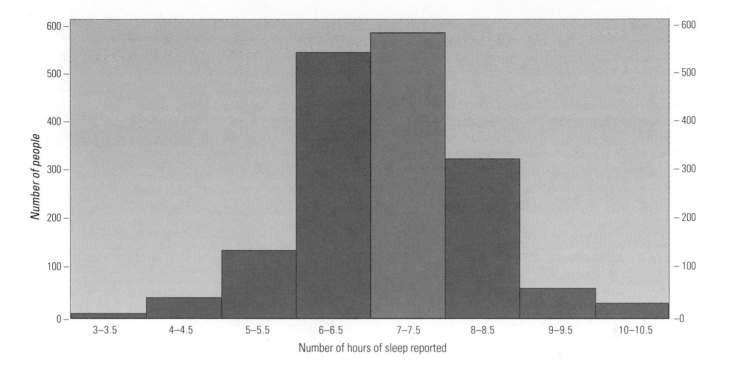

to new schedules (Coleman, 1986). Intriguingly, married couples are likely to have more marital problems if they are mismatched (Larson et al., 1991). So if you are a morning person, choose a partner who also is a morning person!

Morning people and night people also differ in the time of day when they are most likely to make stereotyped kinds of judgments, according to research by Bodenhausen (1990). Morning people, who function best before noon, were likely to fall back on stereotyped judgments if they were tested in the afternoon or evening. (For example, they were more likely to say that athletes are cheaters and Hispanics are physically aggressive.) In contrast, night people were likely to make stereotyped judgments in the morning. At their "peak time," both groups of people were more rational and systematic in their thinking. In short, individual differences in circadian rhythms have important implications for social interactions.

Stages of Sleep

We have examined the pattern of the sleep-wake cycle. Now let us look at the cyclic patterns that occur during sleep. Sleep consists of five different stages, each with a different kind of brain activity.

Conducting Sleep Research To study sleep, researchers cannot casually stroll into volunteers' houses, perch on a chair near the bed, and watch these somewhat self-conscious folks begin to snooze. Instead, research must be conducted in a sleep laboratory, usually located in a sleep clinic. A sleep lab consists of several bedrooms next to an observation room.

Imagine that you have volunteered to participate in a sleep experiment. You have just arrived at the lab and have introduced yourself to the researchers—and because you have just finished reading about circadian rhythms, you realize that these people certainly qualify as shift workers. You get ready for bed, and then the researchers tape the electrodes of an electroencephalogram onto your scalp (and, fortunately, you remember reading in Chapter 3 how the EEG painlessly measures electrical activity in the brain). In addition, the researchers fasten on additional electrodes to measure your eye movements and your muscle tension (see Figure 5.3). They may also measure your breathing rate, your heart rate, and your level of genital arousal (Anch et al., 1988).

Figure 5.2

Self-reported sleep durations for college students. (Based on data from Hicks et al., 1990)

Do you think these young men would be likely to cheat on an examination? Your response to this question may depend upon whether you are a morning or a night person, and what time of day it is.

How well do you suspect you would sleep in this strange setting, attached to all these wires? Researchers generally ignore any data collected the first night because sleep patterns are likely to be distorted by the unfamiliarity of the situation (Moorcroft, 1989). The following night, though, the sleep project begins in earnest, and the researchers start to collect various measures. When you first climb into bed, you will probably remain awake and alert for a few minutes. Your EEG will show mostly **beta waves,** which are rapid brain waves that have a frequency of at least 14 per second. Then you close your eyes and relax. Your EEG begins to show a pattern of **alpha waves,** which occur at the slower frequency of 8 to 12 per second. Figure 5.4 shows the difference between these two brain-wave patterns. Soon afterwards, you begin to drift from a pleasant drowsiness into the stages of sleep.

Figure 5.3

A person prepared for a night's sleep in a sleep laboratory.

The Five Stages Throughout the night, you will drift back and forth among five sleep stages.

In **Stage 1 sleep,** the EEG records small, irregular brain waves. You are drifting into a light sleep. You can be readily awakened from Stage 1 sleep.

In **Stage 2 sleep,** the EEG shows very rapid bursts of activity known as sleep spindles. If a sleep researcher sneezed next door, you probably would not hear it.

In **Stage 3 sleep,** your EEG begins to show a few delta waves, at the very slow frequency of about 2 per second. Your breathing slows substantially, and your muscles are completely relaxed.

In **Stage 4 sleep,** the EEG now shows almost exclusively delta waves. You are now in deep sleep. The researchers could probably wander into your room without waking you.

These four stages of sleep do not tell the complete story, however. You do not simply drift downward into deep sleep after you crawl into bed, and drift upward into light sleep as morning approaches. Instead, you spend the first 30 to 45 minutes progressing from Stage 1 to Stage 4, and the next 30 to 45 minutes reversing the direction, back up to Stage 1.

At this point you enter the fifth stage of sleep called rapid eye movement, or REM sleep. During **REM sleep,** your eyes move rapidly beneath your closed eyelids, giving this stage its name. Your body movements stop and your peripheral muscles relax (Chase & Morales, 1990). During REM sleep, the EEG shows long sections in which the brain waves resemble the waves in Stage 1. Your heart beats rapidly, and

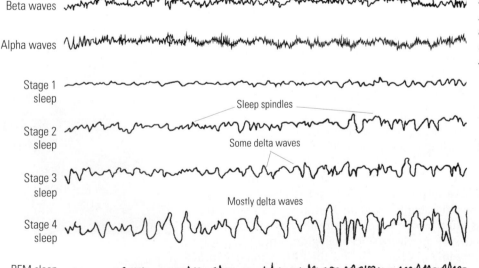

Figure 5.4

EEG patterns (measured by changes in voltage) of the two stages prior to sleep, the four non-REM stages, and REM sleep.

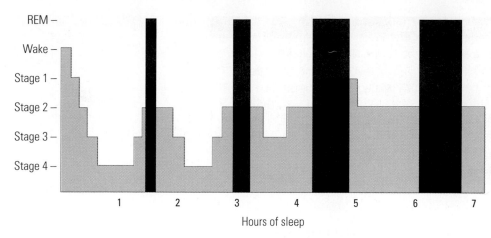

Figure 5.5
A typical sleeper's pattern of normal sleep. Note that there are four stages of sleep and that the black bars represent REM sleep.

you breathe quickly and irregularly. Your genitals are likely to show arousal—with moisture and swelling in the vaginal area for females and erections for males.

REM sleep is also associated with dreaming. When people are awakened during REM sleep, about 90% report that they have just had a vivid dream (Coleman, 1986). We will discuss dreams more extensively later in this chapter.

A healthy adult has between four and six sleep cycles each night, with each cycle lasting about 90 minutes (Anch et al., 1988). Figure 5.5 illustrates a typical night's sleep patterns.

The brain's activity, as revealed by the EEG, is related to the stages of sleep. Several structures in the brain are responsible for sleep. As Chapter 3 mentioned, the reticular formation in the hindbrain seems to play an important role, for example, in REM sleep. Also, when the reticular formation receives electrical stimulation, a sleeping person wakes up. Furthermore, damage to the reticular formation will produce prolonged sleep (Kalat, 1992; Pinel, 1993). Part of the hypothalamus also appears to control circadian rhythms, and a part of the forebrain located in front of the hypothalamus seems to regulate the amount of time we spend sleeping (Pinel, 1990). Consistent with the complexity that is a theme of this book, several different brain structures must work in cooperation to regulate our sleep activities.

IN DEPTH: The Effects of Sleep Deprivation

In 1965, a California high-school student named Randy Gardner decided to stay awake for 264 hours as part of a science fair project. During his last night of the project, Randy went to an arcade with a sleep researcher, where they played about a hundred games on a baseball machine. Despite his sleep deprivation, Randy won every game. After 11 days without sleep, Randy went to sleep. You might guess that he would sleep for several days, to compensate for the deprivation, but he slept only 14 hours and 40 minutes. Surprisingly, he experienced no major problems during his sleep-deprived period, and no difficulties afterwards (Anch et al., 1988).

Some more recent work by a group of Israeli researchers demonstrates the complex effects of sleep deprivation, a finding that certainly supports Theme 3 of this textbook. They argue that a variety of factors determine whether sleep deprivation affects behavior. (Babkoff et al., 1991; Mikulincer et al., 1989). In other words, we cannot simply say, "Yes, sleep deprivation affects behavior" or "No, sleep deprivation does not affect behavior." Instead, we need to know several characteristics of the task (e.g., whether it is interesting or dull) before we can predict whether sleep deprivation will influence performance.

In a review of the literature, for example, Harvey Babkoff and his colleagues (1991) illustrate how the interest level of the task has an influence on conclusions about sleep deprivation. Suppose that you have gone without sleep for 36 hours, and then you are instructed to work on an interesting task, such as the baseball game that Randy Gardner played. Performance on an interesting task often shows no decline for sleep deprivation periods of up to 42 hours. However, suppose that you are deprived of sleep for 36 hours, and then you are instructed to work on an

DEMONSTRATION 5.3 Performing a Boring Task

For each of the following statements, look at the pair of letters and say whether the statement is true or false.

A B   1. The A is to the left of the B.
B A   2. The B is to the right of the A.
B A   3. The A is not to the left of the B.
A B   4. The B is to the right of the A.
A B   5. The B is not to the right of the A.

B A   6. The A is to the left of the B.
Λ B   7. The A is not to the right of the B.
B A   8. The B is not to the left of the A.

If you are currently sleep deprived, you will not be able to complete as many problems during a 20-second period as if you were well rested.

extremely boring task. For instance, a researcher might tell you to watch a blank screen and press a button whenever a dim red light appears. Performance on a boring task often shows a decline after just a few hours of sleep deprivation.

Consider these typical results reported by Babkoff and his coauthors (1991) for a boring task. They presented Hebrew letters that were the equivalent of our letters A and B. Research participants in a sleep-deprivation study were instructed to look at a pair of letters and answer whether statements about the position of the letters were true or false. The researchers then measured the number of problems attempted in a one-minute period. Demonstration 5.3 shows some representative items.

Figure 5.6 shows how participants performed on this boring task, as a function of sleep deprivation. As you can see, performance shows a clear decline as a function of the number of hours of sleep deprivation.

However, do you notice another characteristic of Figure 5.6, aside from the general decline over time? Specifically, the performance does not show a smooth, linear (straight line) decrease during those 72 hours of sleep deprivation. Instead, the figure shows systematic peaks in the performance at 18:00 (6 p.m.) on Day 1, Day 2, and Day 3. Can you also see the troughs, where performance is poorest, at the beginning of each day at a bit before 6 a.m.? People show a systematic cyclical pattern in their performance, consistent with the circadian rhythms we discussed

Figure 5.6

Average number of problems attempted, as a function of sleep deprivation. (Source: Babkoff et al., 1991)

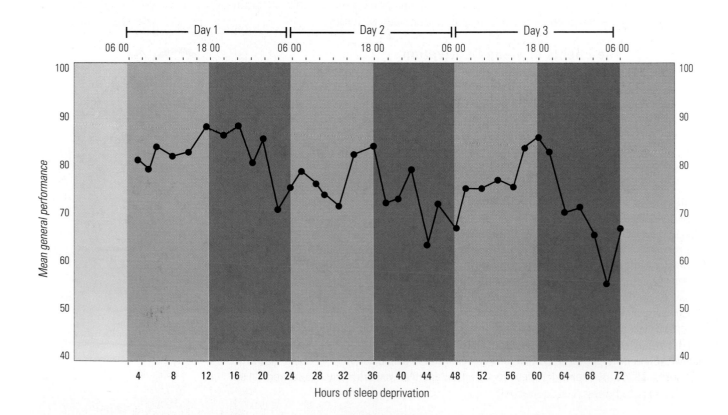

← Start here

If you are currently sleep-deprived, you would make many errors in tracing this star if you were instructed to use your nondominant hand (e.g., your left hand if you are right-handed) and if you could only see that hand in a mirror.

earlier. They perform best about dinner time and worst sometime before breakfast. Finally, notice that as sleep deprivation progresses, people do even worse during the 6 a.m. session than they did on the previous day.

So far we have seen that we cannot predict how sleep deprivation influences performance unless we know two factors: (1) the interest level of the task, and (2) the time of day when the task is performed. Babkoff and his colleagues (1991) also identified a third factor: (3) the difficulty of the task.

In a representative study on task difficulty, Babkoff and his colleagues asked people to trace over a star design. In the easy task condition, people were instructed to use their dominant hand, and they were allowed to see their hand as it traced the star pattern. In this easy task condition, people showed no performance decrement, even after 72 hours of sleep deprivation. However, in the most difficult condition, participants were instructed to use their nondominant hand. In addition, they could not watch their hand directly. Instead, they watched their hand in a mirror, which made all their hand movements appear upside down. In this very difficult task condition, people made many more errors as the hours of sleep deprivation increased.

In summary, then, sleep deprivation affects performance in a complex way, consistent with Theme 3. If you are working on an interesting, easy task at an optimal time of day, sleep deprivation will probably have little effect on performance. However, if you are working on a boring, difficult task early in the morning, you can expect an abysmal performance!

Why Do We Sleep?

We have seen throughout this book that a particular human behavior is likely to have more than one explanation. Because sleep is a behavior that we perform for 7 or 8 hours each day, we probably have more than one reason for sleeping. Two of the most likely reasons are that sleep is restorative and that sleep is adaptive.

The Restorative Function Sleep as a restorative process is an idea that is literally thousands of years old. The Greek philosopher Aristotle, for instance, proposed that some substances build up during the day, and the nightly sleep rids our body of these poisons. However, researchers have not identified specific "negative" substances eliminated during sleep.

In contrast, researchers have found that the body does manufacture useful substances when we are asleep. Specifically, growth hormone secretions are at their maximum during slow-wave sleep (Stages 3 and 4). Furthermore, brain-protein synthesis is at its maximum during REM sleep (Anch et al., 1988).

Researchers have also found that people who have performed vigorous physical activities—such as running a marathon—sleep longer afterward. They are particularly likely to have more of the delta-wave sleep associated with sleep Stages 3 and 4 (Shapiro, 1982). This relationship implies that greater exertion requires more time for the body to be restored to normal.

The Adaptive Function Another possibility emphasizes the evolutionary purpose of sleep (Moorcroft, 1989; Webb, 1988). The specific pattern of sleep developed by each species may have increased the likelihood of that species' survival. "Nonresponding" during the dark hours may have been useful for humans. Those humans who slept in caves at night were more likely to pass on their genes to future generations. In contrast, those humans who spent their nights wandering around in the dark were less likely to find food to eat and more likely to have accidents or be eaten by wild beasts. After all, the human visual system has much lower acuity at night than during the day. The mechanisms for sleep may persist in modern human brains, even though we no longer need sleep for the same reasons as our prehistoric ancestors.

So, why do we sleep? Clearly, all the answers have not yet been gathered. However, two important reasons are that we sleep to restore our bodies and to keep us (or, more accurately, our distant ancestors) out of trouble.

Sleep Disorders

So far, we have emphasized normal sleep patterns. However, millions of North Americans do not enjoy a normal night's sleep, followed by sleep-free daytime activities. One resource, for example, lists more than 60 sleep disorders (Williams & Karacan, 1985). We will consider two general classes, insomnia and excessive daytime sleepiness.

Insomnia **Insomnia** refers to difficulty in falling asleep and/or remaining asleep. The more formal term for these sleeping problems is **Disorders of Initiating and Maintaining Sleep,** or **DIMS.** However, we will join most sleep researchers in using the more familiar name, insomnia (Hobson, 1988).

About 35% of adults complain about insomnia in any given year, and it is a persistent problem for about 15% to 30% of the population (Fredrickson, 1987). In the words of one of the most famous sleep researchers, "If we include all of its forms, insomnia is probably the most common medical complaint in the world" (Dement, 1986, p. 43).

Who is most likely to suffer from insomnia? As we noted earlier, older people have more problems than younger people. When we consider all age groups, women

---

TABLE 5.1 Treating Insomnia

Here are some general precautions recommended by some resources on insomnia (Buchholz, 1988; Coleman, 1986; Empson, 1989; Hoch & Reynolds, 1986; Moorcroft, 1989; Reynolds, 1986):

1. Do not read or do work in bed; keep the bed as a powerful stimulus to sleep.

2. Go to bed only when you are sleepy, and get up at a regular time.

3. Do not lie in bed thinking or worrying. Get up and do something boring until you are sleepy. Some people find it helpful to describe their worries briefly on a sheet of paper.

4. Once you are in bed, relax your muscles and imagine yourself in a soothing setting, perhaps lying on the beach with a warm sun, gentle breezes, and the restful sound of waves.

5. Omit caffeine and alcohol for several hours prior to bedtime.

6. Schedule any exercise at least 2 hours before bedtime.

7. Avoid long-term use of sleeping pills. Some pills are useless; others produce pill dependency, and some may have dangerous side effects (Cowley, 1991; "Sleeping Pills and Anti-Anxiety Drugs," 1988).

8. Improve your sleeping environment; make sure that the room is quiet, dark, and the correct temperature.

9. If all else fails, contact one of the hundreds of sleep centers throughout the United States. A list of centers, as well as brochures on various sleep disorders, is available from the National Sleep Disorders Foundation, 122 South Robertson Boulevard, Suite 201, Los Angeles, CA 90048.

have more problems than men. Insomnia is also about three times more common for psychiatric patients as for people in the general population (Fredrickson, 1987; Williams & Karacan, 1985).

Researchers have identified several kinds of insomnia. For example, most people have experienced transient insomnia at some time in their lives, perhaps just before a major exam or after a fight with the boss. Transient insomnia does not need any special attention. In learned insomnia, people are extremely anxious about whether they will sleep well. Ironically, the harder they try to fall asleep, the worse their insomnia becomes. People with learned insomnia can usually be treated in about five weeks by encouraging them to worry less and to substitute a more positive approach to sleep. Other insomnias arise from psychiatric or physiological factors, or are caused by poor sleep habits. Finally, subjective insomnia occurs when a person complains of insomnia, even when he or she has normal sleep patterns. Table 5.1 lists some suggestions for correcting insomnia.

A person with narcolepsy may fall asleep at inappropriate times, even in the middle of a meal.

Disorders of Excessive Sleepiness People who sleep too much during the day after a full night's sleep have **Disorders of Excessive Sleepiness,** or **DOES.** Obviously, their learning, performance, and social interactions are likely to suffer (Spielman & Herrera, 1991).

Sleep apnea involves frequent lapses of breathing during sleep. A person with sleep apnea may experience interrupted breathing more than 300 times each night. Each time, the individual wakes up briefly and then begins to breathe normally again. Sleep apnea can usually be traced to physical explanations, such as narrow respiratory passages (Dement, 1986; Kwentus et al., 1985). As you might imagine, people who awake dozens of times each night will be sleepy during the day.

A second disorder of excessive sleepiness is called narcolepsy. People with **narcolepsy** have uncontrollable bouts of disabling sleep during the day (Martinez-Arizala & McCarthy, 1987). Even though they may sleep 12 hours each night, they still find themselves falling asleep, for example during lectures and movies. Paradoxically, they also fall asleep when they are *over*stimulated. For example, Coleman (1986) describes a moose hunter who frequently fell asleep, collapsing in his tracks, whenever he started to pull the trigger when aiming at a moose. Narcolepsy appears to be caused by an abnormality in the neurotransmitters in the part of the brain that controls REM sleep. Often, it can be treated with stimulant drugs such as amphetamines. In short, then, sleep disorders can be based on biological processes, as well as on inappropriate learning.

Dreaming

In our dreams, we depart from the constraints of our conscious daytime thoughts. Some dreams are so different from ordinary awareness that they were once thought to be caused by the visits of alien beings (Oswald, 1987b). Figures 5.7 and 5.8 show two representations of these night visitors.

As mentioned earlier, most dreaming is associated with REM sleep. The non-REM sleep associated with Stages 1 through 4 seems to involve a different kind of mental activity (Koulack, 1991). In a classic study, Foulkes (1962) asked people who had just awakened, "What was passing through your mind?" People who had been in one of the non-REM stages of sleep usually reported that they were thinking. In contrast, those who had been in REM sleep usually reported a more vivid, emotional, storylike episode.

The chapter on the biological basis of behavior discussed how the two hemispheres of the brain performed somewhat different kinds of mental activity. The kind of thinking involved in our dreams seems to be produced primarily by our more verbal left hemisphere. Perhaps the right hemisphere helps construct some of the visual features of the images in our dreams. However, it is primarily the left hemisphere that creates the plots of our dreams (Antrobus, 1987). Let us consider some

Figure 5.7

"A Maiden's Dream" by Lorenzo Lotto.

Figure 5.8

"Nightmare" by Henry Fuseli.

information about the content of dreams and then we will discuss several explanations for why we dream.

The Content of Dreams What do people dream about? In your dreams, you may fly above the rooftops or walk through solid brick walls, though dreams are often duller than might be supposed.

The content of your dreams appears to be related to the thoughts you had just before falling asleep (Botman & Crovitz, 1989/1990; Rados & Cartwright, 1982). However, the stimuli from the outside world that figure so prominently during waking consciousness have minimal influences on our dream experiences. Sometimes a telephone ringing while a person is dreaming can encourage someone to dream of a phone call. However, external stimuli are not incorporated into dreams in any consistent fashion (Lavie & Hobson, 1986).

When we are dreaming, we are usually not really aware that we are dreaming. However, about 20% of people experience lucid dreaming at least once a month (Snyder & Gackenbach, 1988). In **lucid dreaming,** a person experiences a dream world that seems vividly real, and yet he or she can think clearly and remember information about waking life (LaBerge, 1990). Lucid dreaming is paradoxical, because a person seems to maintain consciousness during dreaming, even though sleep is considered an altered state of consciousness.

Sometimes, lucid dreamers can modify the content of their dreams. For example, a British woman reported that she had recurrent dreams about a disastrous telegram. Every time this dream occurred, she would merely remind herself that she was dreaming and shift the plot of her dream (Galvin, 1982).

Research on lucid dreaming is beginning to blossom (Foulkes, 1990). Laboratory research has established, for example, that lucid dreaming is not simply an intrusion of wakefulness during sleep (Gackenbach & LaBerge, 1988). However, the research depends upon subjective reports about dreams, and self-reports are difficult to verify (LaBerge, 1990). As noted in Chapter 2 and in this chapter's discussion of awareness about higher mental processes, self-reports about consciousness may create special problems (Foulkes, 1990).

A lucid dream can be either pleasant or unpleasant, but a nightmare is inherently unpleasant. A **nightmare** is an intense dream that occurs during REM sleep and causes anxiety or fearfulness (Oswald, 1987b). If sleepers awake quickly from their nightmares, they may be aware that they were unable to move. Our muscles are somewhat paralyzed during REM sleep, yet we are unaware of this paralysis during normal dreaming.

Why Do We Dream? Sigmund Freud's influential theory is examined more thoroughly in later chapters. Freud provided the first major theory of dreams, although his book *The Interpretation of Dreams* sold very few copies when it was published in 1900 (Coleman, 1986).

For Freud, as well as current psychoanalytic theorists, dreams provide access to the unconscious (Miller, 1989). According to this approach, all sexual and aggressive impulses are disguised in our dreams. Thus, dreams can be decoded into their true meaning. For example, a dream about a tunnel might represent a vagina, whereas a dream about shaving might represent masturbation. An analyst could presumably uncover these hidden messages and provide awareness to the dreamer. As you can imagine, hypotheses about symbolism in dreams cannot be readily tested.

Freud argued that we can satisfy some of our sexual wishes and other forbidden desires through our dreams. Thus, dreams provide a "safety valve." Without them, energy from these desires would reach unacceptable levels and threaten our psychological well-being.

A different view of the function of dreams is based on current neurophysiology and cognitive psychology; it is called the **neurocognitive model.** This approach has been developed primarily by J. Allan Hobson and John Antrobus. A core concept is the **activation-synthesis hypothesis,** which proposes that the hindbrain transmits a

Sleep researchers have not determined whether our dreams are symbolic or whether they represent the brain's attempt to interpret random signals.

haphazard pattern of signals to the cerebral cortex *(activation),* and then the cerebral cortex tries to make sense out of all these random signals *(synthesis)* (Hobson, 1988, 1990; Hobson & McCarley, 1977).

Antrobus (1990, 1991) has updated this activation-synthesis model. He describes it in terms of the connectionist approach, which we introduced in Chapter 1 and will discuss in more detail in Chapter 7. According to the **connectionist approach,** the activation of one cue leads to the activation of other, related concepts. When you are awake, and you see your friend Chris, the visual stimulus of Chris activates in your cerebral cortex some other concepts that you have associated with Chris (perhaps the name of Chris's hometown, her major, when you first met her, and so forth). When you are asleep, the outside world does not provide any signals to your cerebral cortex. However, the hindbrain provides signals, and your cortex treats those signals as if they came from the outside world. Specifically, each signal still leads to the activation of other, related concepts.

Sometimes the signals from the hindbrain reach the portions of the central cortex that are concerned with vision. Activation of this part of the cortex will produce a visual image that is bright, clearly focused, and colorful. This activation will spread to other, connected concepts. Meanwhile, another signal from the hindbrain may reach a different part of the visual cortex, producing a visual image that is unrelated to the first image. This activation also spreads to other connected concepts. Other signals activate still other parts of the cortex (including nonvisual areas).

Our cognitive processes are as active when we dream as when we are awake. These processes work to find a satisfactory solution to this complicated pattern of information—some segments of which may be in conflict with each other. Basically, they attempt to "dream up" a story line that weaves together these unrelated items. To some extent, the top-down processes described in Chapter 4 will employ our expectations and concepts to make sense out of this assorted miscellany. Also, our motivations (e.g., for food, sex, or achievement) may guide these attempts to construct a sensible solution. However, Antrobus (1991) argues that the primary flow of information during sleep is bottom-up, involving stimulation from the hindbrain to the cortex. Also, as you've certainly noticed, our dreams do *not* make as much sense as the events in our waking lives, though most are reasonably well organized (Weinstein et al., 1991).

To help you understand the neurocognitive approach to dreams, try Demonstration 5.4.

SECTION SUMMARY

SLEEPING AND DREAMING

- We maintain circadian rhythms partly because of zeitgebers and partly because of our internal clocks; without zeitgebers, we would run on a 25-hour clock.

- Shift schedules and jet lag disrupt the normal circadian rhythms, producing disrupted sleep and poorer work performance; exposure to cycles of light and dark may be helpful.

- People vary widely in the amount of sleep they obtain, as well as the time of day when they function best.

- When people go to sleep, they drift from light sleep (Stage 1) through deep sleep (Stage 4) and then back again to light sleep; at this point, they enter REM sleep, when most dreaming occurs; this cycle is repeated four to six times each night.

- Structures in the brain that regulate sleep include the reticular formation, the hypothalamus, and the forebrain.

- We cannot predict whether sleep deprivation will impair performance unless we know the interest level and difficulty of the task, as well as the time of day when it is performed.

DEMONSTRATION 5.4 Relating the Neurocognitive Model to Your Own Dream

To try this demonstration, you need to remember the major themes of one dream. You may find it easier to recall a dream if you arrange to lie in bed for a few minutes after awakening one morning; try to lie quietly, letting your mind flow freely. Write down a few key words, and fill in any gaps when you review the dream a few minutes later.

Try to identify those elements of your dream that seem vividly visual; Hobson and Antrobus would suggest that these were produced by stimulation from the hindbrain to the visual cortex. Can you identify any fragments that would suggest stimulation of other senses (e.g., motor or auditory)? Now figure out how the connectionist approach would explain how each basic clue (e.g., a visual image) was enriched by related concepts. How did the story line of your dream manage to connect the elements of your dream? Did any elements remain unconnected?

We need to keep in mind, however, the earlier point that we often lack insight about the way our higher mental processes operate. Our after-the-fact speculations may not match what really happened!

- Two theories explaining our need for sleep are that sleep is restorative and that it is adaptive.

- Insomnia is a common sleep disorder; two disorders of excessive sleepiness are sleep apnea and narcolepsy.

- The left hemisphere of the brain is important in dreaming, and dream content is often related to thoughts that precede sleep; lucid dreamers can think clearly while dreaming.

- One theory of dreams is the Freudian theory that dreams are symbolic. Another theory is the neurocognitive model, which proposes that the hindbrain sends random signals, and the cerebral cortex makes sense of these signals by relying on connections with related concepts (connectionism), with some assistance from top-down processing and motivational factors.

DRUGS THAT INFLUENCE CONSCIOUSNESS

We began this chapter by examining normal waking consciousness. Then we explored sleep, an altered state of consciousness that involves reduced body activity, different patterns in the brain's electrical activity, and less coherent thoughts. Both of these states of consciousness occur quite naturally as part of everyday life. Now we consider how consciousness can be altered when people use drugs. The United States spent $6.5 billion on drug law enforcement and criminal justice in 1990 (Holloway, 1991), suggesting that drug-altered consciousness is an important issue. In this section, we will define some basic terms, then consider three categories of drugs, and finally examine patterns of drug use. In Chapter 10, we will discuss how drug use during pregnancy can harm the developing baby.

Basic Terminology

Psychoactive drugs are chemical substances that influence the brain, altering consciousness and producing psychological changes. Psychoactive drugs usually work via the neurotransmitters. As we noted in Chapter 3, **neurotransmitters** are chemical substances stored in the neurons that alter the electrical activity of the postsynaptic neuron. Psychoactive drugs typically increase or decrease the availability of neurotransmitters, or they may even compete with these neurotransmitters.

In many cases, frequent use of a psychoactive drug can produce **tolerance,** which is currently defined as the ability to withstand higher doses than could be tolerated earlier (Leccese, 1991). Tolerance seems to involve physiological adaptation to a particular drug (Poulos & Cappell, 1991). People who stop taking the psychoactive drug may experience **withdrawal symptoms,** which are undesirable effects of discontinued drug use. These symptoms vary, depending upon the psychoactive drug, but may include nausea, vomiting, abdominal cramps, and muscle spasms.

A related term, **dependence,** means that continued use of a psychoactive drug is necessary to prevent withdrawal symptoms. Dependence involves two components: (1) avoiding the negative symptoms of withdrawal, and (2) experiencing the positive, reinforcing qualities associated with the drug (Wise, 1988). People who are dependent on a psychoactive drug often take increasing amounts of the drug and may try unsuccessfully to control substance use. They spend many hours each day obtaining the substance, taking it, and recovering from it. They may become *psychologically* dependent on the drug—as well as *physically* dependent—as it becomes an important part of their life. Furthermore, intoxication or withdrawal symptoms may interfere with work, school, and social responsibilities (Marlatt, 1992). For example, an alcoholic student I know missed more than 80% of his classes one semester, failed several courses, and will not graduate with his classmates.

Psychoactive drugs include illegal drugs such as LSD and cocaine. Psychoactive drugs also include the nicotine in a package of cigarettes, the caffeine in a cup of coffee, and the alcohol in the holiday eggnog. Still, these legal drugs alter consciousness and can cause as much harm as those illegal substances. In this chapter, we will consider three categories of psychoactive drugs: depressants, stimulants, and hallucinogens. Table 5.2 lists some of these drugs.

Depressants

Depressants are drugs that depress central nervous system functioning. These substances reduce pain and tension, and they slow down a person's thinking and action. The depressants include tranquilizers such as Valium and barbiturates such as Seconal. These depressants are prescription drugs used to treat psychological disorders; we discuss them in Chapter 16.

Another important class of depressants is the **opiates,** which include drugs such as morphine and heroin. These drugs suppress pain at the level of the spinal cord and within the brain (Jaffe, 1991). Opiates imitate the action of **endorphins,** the substances discussed in Chapters 3 and 4 that occur naturally in the brain and, when released, decrease a person's sensitivity to pain. Addicts who inject opiates report a blissful feeling and a decrease in anxiety. When they stop taking an opiate, they often experience severe withdrawal symptoms. Non-addict patients who receive opiates for pain relief often report only a sense of tranquility, rather than a major alteration in mood (Jaffe, 1991).

TABLE 5.2 Some Important Psychoactive Drugs

DEPRESSANTS	
1. Tranquilizers (e.g., Valium)	3. Opiates (e.g., morphine, heroin)
2. Barbiturates (e.g., Seconal)	4. Alcohol

STIMULANTS	
1. Caffeine	3. Amphetamines (e.g., Dexedrine)
2. Nicotine	4. Cocaine and crack

HALLUCINOGENS	
1. Lysergic acid diethylamide (LSD)	3. Marijuana
2. Phencyclidine piperidine (PCP, or angel dust)	

Alcohol is the most familiar of the depressants. Alcohol is often misunderstood, because many people assume that is a stimulant. They claim that alcohol makes a person more "stimulated" and outgoing. However, it is actually a depressant because it slows down the rate of impulses throughout the central nervous system. Alcohol also depresses (or slows the functioning of) parts of the cortex that keep people from performing actions that they know are inappropriate. In other words, alcohol is a disinhibitor, which explains why shy people may seem to lose some inhibitions after a few drinks. With additional alcohol, the brain's activity becomes even more depressed. People talk with slurred speech, they lose their coordination, and they fall asleep. Let us consider the magnitude of the alcohol problem and then examine in more detail how alcohol affects psychological processes.

Drunk-driving accidents kill about 22,000 people each year.

The Alcohol Problem The week I began to revise this chapter, the local newspaper carried a grim story. A 20-year-old man had consumed about 10 drinks of whiskey and soda. The police stopped his car, escorted him home because he had clearly been drinking, and impounded his car. Once home, he drove off in his father's company truck, at a speed of more than 90 miles per hour. The speeding truck eventually crashed into a small car, killing its driver—a fitness buff who had risen early to drive to her exercise club before going to work.

Alcohol also kills people on college campuses. In October 1991, for example, some representative deaths included a student who passed out and choked to death on his own vomit, a student who died of cardiac arrest after drinking at a fraternity party, a student who fell four stories from a rooftop, and a student who drowned accidently in a river ("Take a Look at College Drinking," 1992).

Nationwide, nearly half of the violent deaths from accidents, suicide, and homicide are alcohol related. About 22,000 people are killed each year just from drunk driving. By one estimate, the risk of a fatal car crash is more than eight times higher for a drunk driver than for a sober one (Blum, 1991). The cost of alcoholism—in terms of treatment, loss of productivity, and property damage—is more than $128 billion each year (Blum, 1991).

Before you read further, try Demonstration 5.5, which is based on a questionnaire distributed to students at 14 colleges in Massachusetts (Wechsler & Isaac, 1992). If these results are representative of institutions throughout North America, we must conclude that alcohol abuse is a common problem at college.

The results of the survey showed that only 9% of the men and 14% of the women reported that they had consumed no alcohol in the past year. A major concern was the incidence of **binge drinking,** defined as having consumed five or more drinks in a row at least once in the past two weeks. In this sample, 56% of the men and 36% of the women would be considered binge drinkers. Furthermore, roughly half of the binge drinkers (47% of men, 48% of women) had been drunk twice or more in the past month, in comparison with less than 5% of the nonbinge drinkers. Binge drinking has other important health consequences. Binge drinkers are three times as likely as nonbinge drinkers to engage in unplanned sexual activity after

---

DEMONSTRATION 5.5 A Questionnaire About Drinking Habits

Answer each of the following questions as honestly and accurately as possible.

1. Have you had an alcoholic drink at any point in the last year?
2. Have you consumed five or more drinks in a row in the past 2 weeks? (The definition of a "drink" is a 12-ounce container of beer, a 4-ounce glass of wine, one mixed drink, or a shot of liquor.)
3. How many times in the past month have you been drunk? (The definition of "being drunk" is losing control of your physical coordination, becoming very unsteady, dizzy, or sick to your stomach.)

(Based on Wechsler & Isaac, 1992)

drinking. Furthermore, binge-drinking men are four times more likely to be involved in fights (Wechsler & Isaac, 1992).

We have looked at the dimensions of the alcohol problem, especially on college campuses. Now let's consider the more general issue of how alcohol influences psychological processes.

The Effects of Alcohol Let's examine in more detail how alcohol impairs thought, raises levels of violence, and influences expectations about its consequences.

As Steele and Josephs (1990) conclude, alcohol intoxication impairs almost every aspect of thinking. For instance, a person who is drunk will have difficulty processing several cues at the same time, encoding meaning from incoming information, and forming abstract concepts. As a result, a drunk person may pick up some important cues that encourage action, but this same person may miss other cues that suggest he or she should definitely *not* act.

Steele and Josephs propose that the impaired thinking has an important consequence for a person who is drunk: He or she will not respond normally to important cues. Imagine this situation. You are living off campus and have just had a fierce argument with your landlord. You're now at a party at the house next door, and you turn your head to face this despised landlord. If you are sober, you will experience response conflict. On the one hand, you want to scream at him, but you also realize an instant later that a terrible scene would be embarrassing—and you might even be evicted. So you grit your teeth and suppress your rage. However, suppose that you encounter your landlord after several drinks. His face is a cue that provokes anger, but alcohol has suppressed your awareness of the unfortunate consequences of telling him off. So your anger erupts . . . and the next morning you're searching for a new apartment.

We can see how this restricted attention—and failure to consider negative consequences—can lead to violence in social situations. For example, alcohol is involved in about 65% of murders, 88% of knifings, 65% of spouse batterings, and 55% of physical child abuse cases (Kent, 1990; Steele & Josephs, 1990). Moreover, as Pernanen's (1991) survey of a Canadian community illustrated, many incidents of alcohol-related violence are not reported to the police. A review of the research conducted in laboratory settings confirms that alcohol increases aggression (Bushman & Cooper, 1990).

As you have been reading about the effects of alcohol, perhaps you've thought about a potential problem with this research. In Chapter 2 you learned that people's expectations can influence the dependent variable. Perhaps people who have had too much to drink have confused thoughts and act violently because they *expect* alcohol to make them this way. Psychologists have become increasingly interested in the importance of people's expectations (Goldman et al., 1991; Leigh, 1989; McKim, 1991). To what extent does a drinker's expectations about the effects of alcohol actually influence his or her behavior?

A special research design can be used to sort out the effects of the drug itself, as opposed to the effects of people's expectations about how they *should* behave. This design, called the **balanced-placebo design,** consists of four groups of participants, half of whom expect that they will be drinking alcohol and half of whom do not. Furthermore, half of the participants actually do receive alcohol and half do not (see Table 5.3). This kind of design allows researchers to discover the situations in which behavior is influenced either by alcohol or by expectations about alcohol. For example, it is possible that alcohol makes people uncoordinated only when they think that they are drinking alcohol (Condition 1), but it has no effect when they think their beverage contains no alcohol (Condition 2).

Jay Hull and Charles Bond (1986) located a total of 36 experiments that used the balanced-placebo design. They then conducted a meta-analysis. These researchers concluded that alcohol *consumption* had a significant effect on nonsocial

TABLE 5.3 The Balanced-Placebo Design to Test the Effects of Alcohol

		EXPECTED BEVERAGE CONTENT	
		Alcohol	**No Alcohol**
TRUE BEVERAGE CONTENT	**Alcohol**	Condition 1	Condition 2
	No Alcohol	Condition 3	Condition 4

behavior. Specifically, it impaired memory and motor behavior, and it improved mood. These three effects occurred whether or not people thought they were drinking alcohol. (In other words, Condition 1 and Condition 2 in Table 5.3 were similar.) Surprisingly, however, alcohol consumption did not make people feel more sexually aroused. In contrast, the current conclusion is that alcohol consumption does significantly increase aggression (Bushman & Cooper, 1990; Hull & Bond, 1986).

How did alcohol *expectation* affect behavior? That is, do people who think that the orange juice contains vodka actually behave differently from those who think they are drinking straight orange juice? People who thought they were drinking alcohol were no more likely to experience impaired memory or motor behavior or improved mood. In contrast, those who thought they were drinking alcohol were more likely to report an increase in sexual arousal. Expectation did not influence the fifth variable, aggression. Table 5.4 provides an overview of these results.

Let us apply these conclusions. Suppose that a young man has opened a bottle of vodka and consumed several ounces of it. The physiological effects of the alcohol cause him to forget, to act uncoordinated, to feel happy, and to become more aggressive. Because he knows he has consumed alcohol, he also reports feeling more sexually aroused; expectancy rather than alcohol itself causes this increase in sexual arousal.

Americans have mixed feelings about alcohol; they acknowledge its dangers, yet they associate alcohol with good times. A congressman was once asked to explain his attitude toward whiskey. His reply captures this ambivalence:

If you mean the demon drink that poisons the mind, pollutes the body, desecrates family life and inflames sinners, then I'm against it. But if you mean the elixir of Christmas cheer, the shield against winter chill, the taxable potion that puts needed funds into public coffers to comfort little crippled children, then I'm for it. This is my position, and I will not compromise. (Lender & Martin, 1982, p. 169)

TABLE 5.4 The Effects of Alcohol Consumption and Alcohol Expectation on Nonsocial and Social Behavior

	ALCOHOL CONSUMPTION	ALCOHOL EXPECTATION
	NONSOCIAL BEHAVIOR	
Memory	Significant effect	No effect
Motor behavior	Significant effect	No effect
Mood	Significant effect	No effect
	SOCIAL BEHAVIOR	
Sexual arousal	No effect	Significant effect
Aggression	Significant effect	No effect

Sources: Bushman & Cooper, 1990; Hull & Bond, 1986

Unfortunately, however, too many people seem to feel invulnerable to the harmful consequences of this drug. Business executives, government officials, family members, classmates, and regrettably even some of you reading this book will have your lives altered by the effects of alcohol.

Stimulants

Stimulants, as the name implies, are chemicals that increase central nervous system functioning. In general, they work by increasing the release of neurotransmitters such as dopamine in the cortex and the reticular activating system (Dusek & Girdano, 1987). Stimulants include caffeine, nicotine, the amphetamines, and cocaine.

Caffeine is the stimulant found in coffee, tea, and some soft drinks. This particular stimulant increases your metabolism, creating a highly awake state. Your heart will probably start to pound faster, and your blood pressure may increase. Caffeine may seem innocent, yet the caffeine in 20 cups of coffee could be lethal if consumed all at once (Dusek & Girdano, 1987).

Next to caffeine, nicotine is the stimulant that is most widely used in the United States. As you know, nicotine is found in cigarettes and other tobacco products. Nicotine clearly causes dependence. A heavy smoker will try to maintain a high level of nicotine by reaching for a cigarette first thing in the morning and continuing to smoke regularly throughout the day (Orford, 1985).

Cigarette smoking is the largest single preventable cause of early death and disability in North America. Smoking has such harmful health consequences that we discuss these consequences—as well as smoking cessation and smoking prevention programs—in the health psychology chapter (Chapter 19).

Amphetamines, such as Dexedrine, stimulate both the central nervous system and the sympathetic branch in the autonomic nervous system. These highly addicting drugs increase the concentration of dopamine and norepinephrine at the synapses. Specifically, amphetamines enhance the release of neurotransmitters and they also block the reuptake (Fischman & Foltin, 1991). As a consequence, neurotransmitters continue to bombard the receptors.

Amphetamines increase both heart rate and blood pressure. Amphetamine users report a feeling of happiness, and other people are likely to notice that users are more talkative and jumpy. Amphetamines can produce irritability and anxiety, and they also interfere with sleep. Some students, disregarding the harmful effects of amphetamines, take these drugs to help them resist sleep for an all-night study session prior to an examination. However, when they actually take the exam, they are likely to discover that they have difficulty paying attention. In addition, their judgment, problem-solving ability, and accuracy are likely to be impaired (Dusek & Girdano, 1987).

Cocaine is an even more potent stimulant. Cocaine blocks the reuptake of dopamine and norepinephrine, producing feelings of excitement and pleasure in the drug user (Holloway, 1991). Large doses and repeated use can produce anxiety, hallucinations, insomnia, and aggressive behavior. In some cases, even a relatively small dose can lead to cardiac arrest and death.

Cocaine is potentially the most addictive drug known to humans (Wallace, 1991). However, individual differences in addictive tendencies are large. Apparently some cocaine users seem to be able to control its use; most, however, increase their use and become addicted (Dusek & Girdano, 1987; Fisher et al., 1987; Washton & Gold, 1987).

In the mid-1970s, a powerful, extremely addictive form of cocaine—called crack—appeared on the market. When smoked, the active ingredients travel swiftly to the brain, providing an even more potent "rush" than cocaine (Wallace, 1991). Crack also produces more medical complications and more psychological disorders than cocaine. For example, crack users are more likely to attempt suicide, their thinking is more disordered, and they are more likely to be violently aggressive (Honer et al., 1987).

Hallucinogens

Hallucinogens are chemical substances that alter people's perceptions of reality and may cause vivid **hallucinations** (strong mental images that seem as if they truly occurred, in the absence of physical stimuli). Hallucinogens include several synthetic drugs, such as LSD and PCP, as well as substances extracted from plants, such as marijuana.

LSD, or lysergic acid diethylamide, is an extremely powerful hallucinogen. A tiny speck can alter consciousness within 15 minutes and last up to 12 hours (Strange & Shapiro, 1991). Shortly after taking LSD, a person typically becomes extremely emotional, with intense laughing or crying. The shapes and colors of objects in the room soon look altered. The LSD user may experience synesthesia, a crossing of the sensory responses in which people seem to hear colors and see sounds. Less often, users experience hallucinations. They may report that they see religious figures or enchanted places. LSD clearly impairs cognitive processes, because a person who has taken LSD has difficulty concentrating, appears confused, and refuses to perform simple intellectual tasks. Some report that it promotes insight about oneself (Baumeister, 1991). Other LSD users may experience intense panic, which can require medical attention.

PCP, or phencyclidine piperidine, is often known by its street name, angel dust. PCP has complex properties: It can be a stimulant, a depressant, a hallucinogen, and a painkiller—all at the same time. The most common effect is that PCP users feel depersonalized, as if they are separated from the people and objects around them. Time seems to slow down, motor coordination decreases, speech becomes senseless, and users may experience hallucinations. PCP users may also feel invulnerable, leading them to take risks and to commit violent acts (Dusek & Girdano, 1987).

Marijuana is considered to be a minor hallucinogen. It is derived from the flowers and leaves of a weed called *Cannabis sativa*. Like other hallucinogens, marijuana alters the perception of sights, sounds, and touch. People who use marijuana every day claim that it encourages them to contemplate and increase their self-understanding. However, a study of regular marijuana users showed that they often avoided thinking about the pain they had experienced in their childhood, and they failed to see how they were partially responsible for their current failures in interpersonal relationships (Hendin et al., 1987).

According to a recent statement by the American Academy of Pediatrics (1991), "Marijuana should not be considered a benign [harmless] drug. Marijuana use has been associated with cardiovascular, pulmonary, reproductive, and possible immunologic consequences" (p. 1070). Specifically, marijuana use can produce faster heart rate, constriction in the lungs, reduced fertility, and possible changes in the immune system.

Marijuana also affects thought processes. It appears to influence the hippocampus region of the limbic system (see Figure 3.15), which may explain how marijuana affects concentration and attention (Johnson, 1991). It also impairs cognitive activities such as reading comprehension, memory, arithmetic, and problem solving (American Academy of Pediatrics, 1991; Dusek & Girdano, 1987).

People who regularly use marijuana tend to have poor academic performance, and they are more likely to commit theft and vandalism. In general, heavy marijuana users are less likely to be concerned about goal-directed behavior (American Academy of Pediatrics, 1991; Dusek & Girdano, 1987). In short, recent information suggests that marijuana is not an innocent substance, because it can produce medical problems, cognitive deficits, and a change in life goals.

The Huicholes, an indigenous community in Mexico, often use a hallucinogen named peyote. The vivid, unusual figures in this yarn painting are characteristic of the hallucinations produced by peyote.

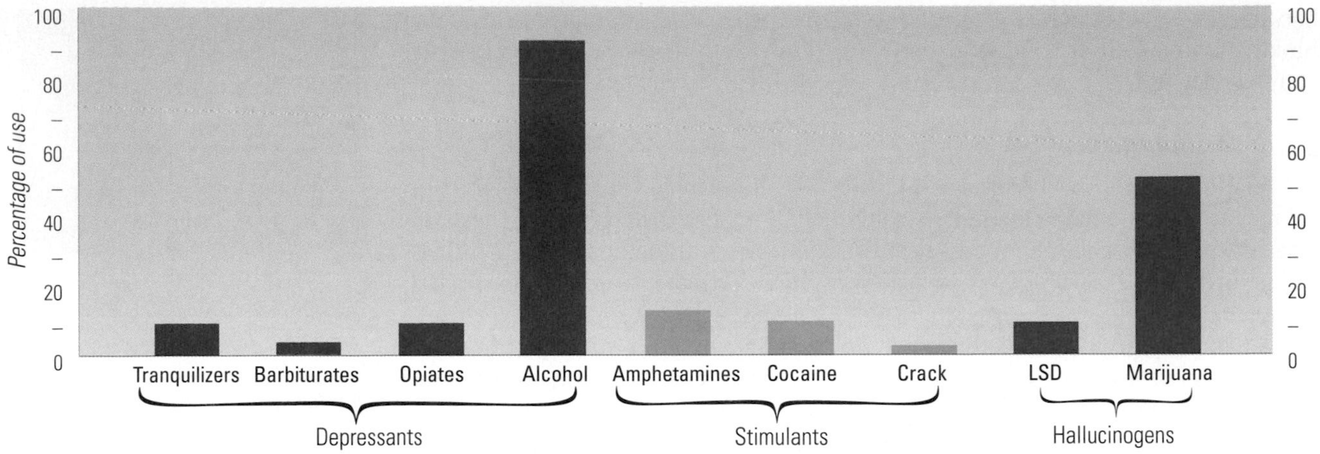

Percentage of use

Tranquilizers | Barbiturates | Opiates | Alcohol | Amphetamines | Cocaine | Crack | LSD | Marijuana

Depressants | Stimulants | Hallucinogens

Psychoactive Drug Use

During a typical month in the United States, at least 14 million people consumed some type of illicit drug (Lipsitt & VandenBos, 1992). According to current estimates, the United States has about 2.4 million crack and cocaine addicts and about 1 million heroin addicts (Holloway, 1991).

Some demographic factors are related to drug use. For example, in the United States, males are somewhat more likely than females to report using an illicit drug during the previous year (32% vs. 26%). Probably the only psychoactive, nonprescription drug that males and females use equally is cigarettes (Johnston et al., 1991). Racial differences have also been reported. Alcohol problems and alcohol-related deaths are especially high among Native Americans (Oetting et al., 1989; Gibbons, 1992). But sometimes the race differences are more complex. For instance, alcohol problems are greater for Mexican-American and Puerto Rican men than for Anglo men. However, alcohol problems are *less* for Mexican-American and Puerto Rican women than for Anglo women (Gilbert, 1989). In other words, cultural norms often depend upon a person's gender.

Still, almost every group in North America experiences some drug problems. For instance, when you think of an alcoholic, don't you think of a middle-aged person? Unfortunately, about 1 million alcoholics in the United States are elderly (Finn, 1991).

Let's look at the drug use of college students. Figure 5.9 shows the percentage of full-time college students in the United States who report ever using the specified drug (Johnston et al., 1991). Figure 5.10 illustrates drug use in Canada for people between the ages of 15 and 24 (Eliany et al., 1992). Figure 5.10 is based on both college

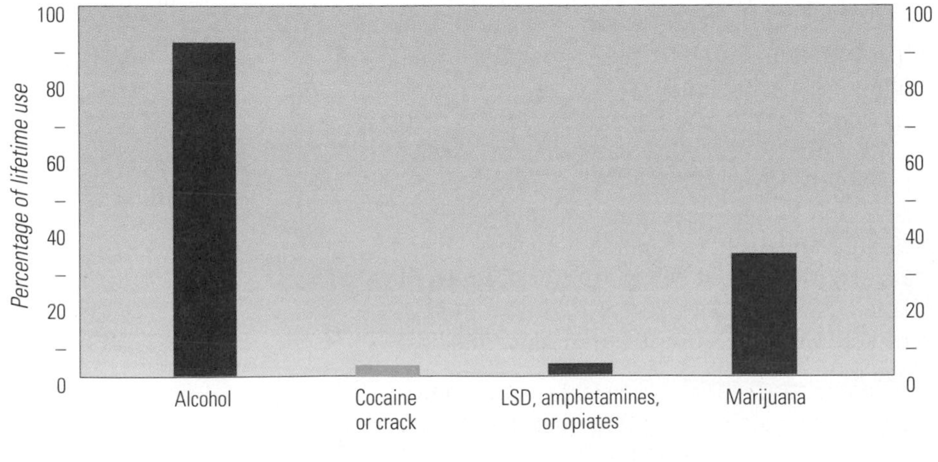

Figure 5.9

Drug use among full-time college students in the United States, illustrating the percentage who report using the drug in their lifetime. (Based on Johnston et al., 1991)

Percentage of lifetime use

Alcohol | Cocaine or crack | LSD, amphetamines, or opiates | Marijuana

Figure 5.10

Drug use among Canadians between the ages of 15 and 24, both college and noncollege. (Based on Eliany et al., 1992)

and noncollege individuals, and the drugs included in the survey overlap only partially with those in the U.S. survey. Still, both surveys show that nearly everyone tries alcohol, and a much smaller proportion try marijuana and other drugs.

We saw at the beginning of this section that alcohol use and abuse is still widespread. However, the use of other drugs might be declining gradually in both the United States and Canada (Adlaf & Smart, 1991; Johnston et al., 1991; Smart & Adlaf, 1992). For example, a 1990 survey of U.S. high-school seniors found that 48% had used an illicit drug at least once. This figure is significantly less than the 66% reporting illicit drug use in 1982 (Freiberg, 1991). At present, however, we have not discovered a way to publicize the dangerous side effects of these psychoactive drugs so that North Americans will stop being casual about altering their states of consciousness.

S E C T I O N   S U M M A R Y

DRUGS THAT INFLUENCE CONSCIOUSNESS

- Tolerance means the ability to withstand higher drug doses than earlier; withdrawal symptoms are the undesirable effects of discontinued drug use; and dependence means that continued drug use is required to avoid withdrawal.

- The depressants include tranquilizers, barbiturates, opiates, and alcohol.

- Binge drinking is common on college campuses; alcohol suppresses awareness of negative consequences. It also influences memory, motor behavior, mood, and aggression; when people believe they have consumed alcohol—even if they have not—they report being more sexually aroused.

- Stimulants include caffeine, nicotine, the amphetamines, cocaine, and crack; they increase central nervous system functioning, and they also produce dangerous side effects.

- Hallucinogens such as LSD, PCP, and marijuana alter people's perception, memory, and other cognitive abilities; marijuana can produce medical problems, cognitive deficits, and changes in life goals.

- Gender and race influence drug use; although most young people have tried alcohol and many have tried marijuana, drug use has shown some decline in North America.

HYPNOSIS AND MEDITATION

Sections 2 and 3 in this chapter examined two ways in which consciousness can be altered from its normal waking state. Psychologists agree that both sleep and drug-induced states are very different from normal waking consciousness. Now we will consider hypnosis and meditation, which were once thought to be distinctly different from being awake. However, most current psychologists believe that both hypnosis and meditation are simply at the more relaxed end of normal waking consciousness.

Hypnosis

Hypnosis is a social interaction in which one person (the subject) responds to suggestions offered by another person (the hypnotist); these responses may focus on perception, memory, and action (Kihlstrom, 1985). We should stress that hypnosis is *not* sleep. In fact, EEG records and other brain measures have not demonstrated significant differences between the hypnotic state and normal waking consciousness (Brown, 1991; "Hypnosis," 1991; Wester, 1986).

To induce a hypnotic trance, hypnotists encourage subjects to relax. They may repeat suggestions such as "Your eyelids are getting heavy" in a rhythmic, monotonous voice, or they may encourage subjects to watch a swinging pocket watch. A competent hypnotist can induce a trance within about 15 minutes, although individuals differ widely in their susceptibility to hypnosis (Hilgard, 1991; "Hypnosis," 1991).

Deeply hypnotized people report very unusual sensations. They say that they feel very relaxed; however, some say that their bodies feel light, yet others report they feel heavy. Some report floating, some sinking (Bowers, 1976). In response to suggestions from the hypnotist, people may report that their arms rise up involuntarily, that a mosquito is buzzing around their legs, and that ammonia smells like an expensive perfume (Balthazard & Woody, 1985). Many psychotherapists argue that hypnosis helps resolve clinical problems. However, they often do not conduct carefully controlled experiments to provide empirical evidence for their success (Baker, 1987). Furthermore, we should note that "stage hypnotists" count on their subjects to cooperate and fake some of the suggestions. Thus, the volunteer who apparently believes he is Frank Sinatra crooning "Strangers in the Night" is probably an extravert who does not want to disappoint the audience (Barber, 1986).

Let us begin by looking at several hypnotic phenomena. Then we will consider the two major theories of hypnosis. Before reading further, however, try Demonstration 5.6.

Specific Hypnotic Phenomena Part of the reason that hypnosis is so intriguing is that hypnotized people seem to behave quite differently from people in the normal waking state. Let's examine five kinds of behavior produced by hypnotized people.

1. *Suggestibility.* Hypnotized people are likely to respond to suggestions from the hypnotist. For example, the hypnotist may suggest that the subjects' hands are slowly being drawn closer together. The subjects often report afterwards that they felt their hands drawing together automatically and involuntarily (Bowers, 1984). However, Lynn and his colleagues (1990) argue that these impressions are incorrect; hypnotized people actively and voluntarily try to fulfill the hypnotic suggestions.

The hypnotist may give the subject instructions under hypnosis that are to be carried out after returning to the conscious waking state; this phenomenon is called **posthypnotic suggestion.** The hypnotist typically also instructs the subject not to recall anything about the hypnosis session after leaving the hypnotic state; this phenomenon is called **posthypnotic amnesia.** Suppose, for example, that the hypnotist instructs a hypnotized man that he must scratch his head when he hears a whistle, soon after returning to the waking state. The hypnotist also tells this man that he will

The hypnotist has encouraged this woman to relax. A susceptible person may be hypnotized within 15 minutes.

DEMONSTRATION 5.6 Beliefs About Hypnosis

Take a moment to consider how you have been exposed to the topic of hypnosis before reading about it in this chapter. Have you read about it in newspapers, magazines, novels, or other textbooks? Has hypnosis been shown on television programs, or have you heard it mentioned in movies? Have you discussed hypnotism with your friends, or has it been a topic in any previous course? Finally, have you seen a stage hypnotist perform?

Based on the information from all these sources, complete the following questionnaire by answering "true" or "false".

1. When a hypnotist tells subjects that their hands will draw together, they may report that their hands do seem to come together automatically.

2. When the hypnotist instructs subjects that they will be unable to see a visual stimulus, that stimulus becomes truly invisible.

3. If a woman is hypnotized during childbirth, her labor pains can be reduced.

4. Hypnosis increases the accuracy of a person's memory about forgotten events.

5. Under hypnosis, people are more likely to "recall" events that never really occurred.

6. Under hypnosis, people can be "regressed" so they act exactly the way they did when they were younger.

The answers can be found at the end of the chapter.

recall nothing about these instructions. After leaving the hypnotic state, the man hears a whistle and immediately begins to scratch himself. When asked why he is scratching, the man simply replies, "I had a sudden itch."

2. *Pain perception.* People who have been hypnotized respond differently than unhypnotized people to a painful stimulus (Spiegel et al., 1989). In childbirth, for instance, women who have been hypnotized report less pain during labor, and the actual duration of labor is shorter. Hypnosis has also been used effectively for people suffering from severe burns. When the hypnotist suggests that the patient feels cool and comfortable, people report less pain, and they also request less narcotic medication (Ewin, 1986; Kihlstrom, 1985; Venn, 1986). A well-controlled experiment has confirmed that hypnotized burn patients are more likely than control-group patients to report a reduction in pain (Patterson et al., 1992).

In Chapter 4, we noted that pain is influenced by psychological factors as well as physiological factors. The research on hypnosis provides additional evidence that thoughts and suggestions influence our perception of pain, although the explanations for its effectiveness are not yet clear.

3. *Other perceptual effects.* Hypnotists can encourage people to perceive objects that are not present (**positive hallucinations**). For example, a hypnotized woman may be encouraged to "see" a mosquito buzzing around her head. People can also be encouraged *not* to see objects that are present (**negative hallucinations**). A hypnotized person may be encouraged to believe that a nearby chair is invisible.

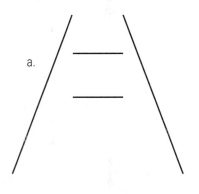

a.

Several studies, however, suggest that the sensory information is still processed by the brain in the case of negative hallucinations. For example, one group of researchers studied the Ponzo illusion (Figure 5.11a) and induced the negative hallucination that the slanted lines on each side would disappear. Subjects were then instructed to judge the relative length of the two horizontal lines. If the two slanted lines were truly invisible, subjects should report that the horizontal lines are equally long, because they should see only the two lines in Figure 5.11b. In fact, they reported that the top line was longer, indicating that their visual systems were still processing the slanted lines. Thus, those mysterious slanted lines were registered in the subjects' visual systems, even though people were not conscious of them (Miller et al., 1973).

4. *Memory.* You have probably seen a Grade-B movie plot that goes something like this . . . the Sweet Young Thing has been a witness to a blood-curdling murder, yet she cannot remember what the murderer looked like. Enter the hypnotist, typically with flashing stars and pinwheels shooting out from his eyes. "Look deep into my eyes," he chants. The S. Y. T. looks deep into his eyes, and her eyes go blank and dreamy. Then she suddenly shouts, "I now remember it as clear as day! He had black oily hair, slicked back behind his ears, piercing black eyes, and a wart on his left nostril, just above a drooping mustache." The hero tracks down the villain, who is promptly brought to justice.

b.

Unfortunately, the research on hypnotically improved memory is not as convincing as the late-night movie plot. In fact, research typically demonstrates that hypnosis is no more effective than control-group instructions in retrieving "lost" memories (Geiselman et al., 1985; Register & Kihlstrom, 1987; Smith, 1983). For example, in a representative study, Sheehan (1988) reported,

> *Results from the program failed to demonstrate any increment in accurate memory due to hypnosis, and the accuracy of memory reports in hypnosis was at times significantly reduced. (p. 296)*

A major problem with "hypnotically refreshed" memory is **confabulation;** hypnotized subjects may simply make up an item to replace one that they cannot retrieve. In one study, for instance, Dwyan and Bowers (1983) presented 60 pictures of common objects. Then the participants in the study were encouraged to remember as

Figure 5.11

The Ponzo illusion (above) and same horizontal lines without the slanted framing lines (below).

many pictures as they could, over a period of seven days. By this time, the typical subject had recalled 38 of the 60 items. Then came the critical test: Would hypnosis bring forth more memories than standard instructions? Half of the participants were then hypnotized and told to relax, focusing all their attention on the pictures they had seen a week ago. The other half were simply told to relax and focus attention on the pictures; they were not hypnotized.

As Figure 5.12 shows, the hypnotized people recalled more than twice as many items that had not previously been mentioned, in contrast to the control group. However, if you look closely, you will see that most of these items were incorrect. That is, they were not on the original list. In fact, the ratio of correct to incorrect items is similar for the hypnotized and the control groups. Hypnotized people may simply be less cautious about reporting items as true memories. Sometimes they will report something they actually saw, but they are more likely to simply manufacture a memory.

Occasionally, newspapers report the successful use of hypnosis to solve a criminal case. In one impressive case, schoolchildren on a bus had been kidnapped, and the driver recalled very little of this stressful event. Under hypnosis, the driver recalled the license plate numbers of the kidnappers. Admittedly, this is a convincing story, yet Smith (1983) reminds us of a rule we stressed in Chapter 2: Where was the control group? How do we know it was the hypnosis that was effective, rather than a relaxing atmosphere and the encouragement for the bus driver to try to reinstate the context at the time of the kidnapping? We really have no evidence that hypnosis per se encouraged the additional recall.

The research on hypnosis and the discovery of the confabulation effect have had an important impact on the use of hypnosis in the courtroom. Specifically, the American Medical Association has recommended that witnesses who have been previously hypnotized should not give courtroom testimony (Orne, 1986). In short, hypnosis is not a magical key that unlocks the unconscious and reveals buried memories.

5. *Age regression.* In **age regression,** a hypnotized person is given suggestions to reexperience an event that occurred at an earlier age and to act like and feel like a child of that particular age. Like the concept of hypnotically refreshed memory, the concept of age regression seems very dramatic. It is impressive, for example, to watch a 40-year-old begin to print like a kindergartener. However, careful examination almost always shows that people may *report* that the experience of being a child is convincingly realistic but that the actions are not really childlike. Furthermore, the memories are likely to be inaccurate.

Consider the hypnotized subject who was regressed to age 6. He wrote with childlike printing—but perfect spelling—"I am conducting a psychological experiment which will assess my psychological capacity" (Orne, 1951). Reviewing 60 years

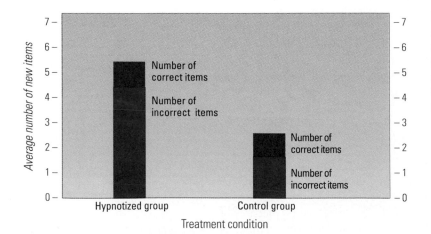

Figure 5.12
New items "recalled" by hypnotized and control groups. Note that the hypnotized group recalls a slightly greater number of correct items, but also many more incorrect items. (Based on Dwyan & Bowers, 1983)

of research on age regression, Nash (1987) concludes, "There is no evidence for a literal reinstatement of childhood functioning during hypnotic-age-regression procedures" (p. 42).

Theories of Hypnosis We have seen that hypnotized people often behave differently from people in the normal waking state, though the differences are not as dramatic as the media suggest. People report that they obey the hypnotist's instructions involuntarily (though the actions are really voluntary). They report no longer seeing objects (though visual-illusion studies demonstrate that they do). Hypnosis does not enhance memory substantially, and hypnosis does not produce realistic age regression. People do report less pain; measures of labor duration during childbirth and requests for pain medication confirm that pain perception *is* altered during hypnosis. How can we explain these results? Two theories are particularly popular: neodissociation theory and social role theory.

Neodissociation theory, proposed by Ernest Hilgard (1986), stresses that hypnosis produces a dissociation or division in consciousness, so that behaviors, thoughts, and feelings operate independently, as if there are two separate channels. Evidence for this theory comes from the **hidden-observer phenomenon,** in which a hypnotized person seems to have two separate selves. One part is apparently hypnotized and the other part is more rational (Hilgard et al., 1975). For example, imagine that a hypnotized woman reports that she feels no pain when her hand is plunged into icy water. However, she has been told that her other hand has access to a part of her consciousness that is hidden from her hypnotized self. This other "hidden observer" hand makes a response to indicate that the freezing water is indeed excruciatingly painful. Notice that this phenomenon resembles lucid dreaming, though lucid dreaming is much less common (Kihlstrom, 1985; Zamansky & Bartis, 1985).

Social role theory stresses that the hypnotized person simply acts out a social role consistent with the social situation. This explanation was first proposed by William James more than a century ago (Kihlstrom & McConkey, 1990), but it was developed more fully by Theodore Barber (1979). Social role theory argues that people bring certain expectations with them to a hypnosis experiment, consistent with our discussion of demand characteristics in Chapter 2. Hypnotized people act the way they believe they are supposed to act by bringing their arms together as instructed by the hypnotist, by printing like 6-year-old children, and by reporting that the ice bath is not painful.

Social role theory points out that the hidden-observer instructions merely let the hypnotized subjects know that they have permission to report the pain that they have felt all along (Kihlstrom, 1985). In fact, when people are told that their "hidden observer" is *insensitive* to pain, then the pain ratings are low for the hidden observer. In other words, people's expectations about how they are supposed to act have an important influence on their hypnotic responses.

Does social role theory explain all hypnotic effects, or just many of them? Alternatively, does hypnosis produce an altered state of consciousness, as Hilgard suggests, with one part of the mind transformed and the other part cool and rational? Unfortunately, the answer is not clear-cut because the research is still inconclusive.

Meditation

Meditation uses a variety of techniques to focus attention and to avoid rambling or worried thoughts (Shapiro, 1984). Some meditation techniques focus on body movement, like the Sufi whirling dervishes shown in Figure 5.13. Other techniques, such as the one shown in Figure 5.14, emphasize that the meditator should be motionless and passive. Another common technique focuses attention on a specific repeated sound, excluding other thoughts from consciousness (West, 1987).

Some meditation techniques encourage people to focus their concentration on an external object. For instance, Deikman (1966) encouraged people to focus upon a blue vase. They each reported that their perception of the vase shifted, often to a

Figure 5.13
The Sufi whirling dervishes claim that they enter an altered state of consciousness through an energetic, twirling dance.

Figure 5.14
A different kind of meditative technique is said to produce an altered state of consciousness through quiet meditation.

deeper, more intense blue. Others said that the vase seemed to change shape or size. One person reported feelings of merging with the vase, "as though it were almost part of me." It may be useful at this point to recall the social roles explanation of hypnosis and apply it to meditation. Imagine yourself seated in front of a vase, after receiving instructions about meditation techniques. Would you really feel comfortable reporting to the meditation instructor—after many minutes of staring at that vase—"No, it was blue when I started and blue when I finished"?

People who are enthusiastic about meditation claim that it can be helpful in reducing arousal. However, comprehensive reviews by David Holmes (1984a, 1987) are not very optimistic about these effects. Holmes argues that most of the research on meditation has serious flaws. For example, many researchers report case studies, which offer intriguing accounts. However, we cannot draw conclusions about the effectiveness of meditation unless we have a control group. Other appropriate research compares people instructed to meditate with people instructed to rest and relax. Unfortunately for meditation enthusiasts, meditation is no more likely than relaxation to reduce physiological arousal. For example, breathing rate, blood pressure, and heart rate do not show any consistent differences (Holmes, 1984a, 1987).

According to Holmes, meditation does not change objective measures of arousal. People may *feel* as if they have entered a different state of consciousness, just as they subjectively report that their hands are automatically pulled together in a hypnosis experiment. Some supporters accept subjective reports as sufficient proof that people have entered an altered state. However, most psychologists require some change in an observable measure—not simply a self-report—before they acknowledge that meditation differs from normal waking consciousness.

SECTION SUMMARY
HYPNOSIS AND MEDITATION

● People who have been hypnotized respond to the hypnotist's suggestions (though their actions are probably voluntary); they show altered pain perception; visual perception and memory do not appear substantially altered; and people do not show convincing age regression.

● Two major theories of hypnosis are neodissociation theory and social role theory.

● People who meditate claim that it reduces arousal, but experimental research shows that meditation is no more effective than relaxation in reducing physiological arousal.

R E V I E W   Q U E S T I O N S

1. What is consciousness? Briefly describe the major topics in this chapter, noting those that seem to involve major changes from the active mode of consciousness and those that may not differ substantially from normal waking consciousness.

2. Several parts of this chapter examine people's insights into their mental processes. Discuss this issue with respect to these topics: (a) consciousness about higher mental processes, (b) lucid dreaming, and (c) the hidden-observer phenomenon.

3. The section on waking attention emphasized three related phenomena: (a) we often have difficulty removing an idea from consciousness; (b) we often have difficulty dividing our attention between two tasks; and (c) when we pay attention to one task, we often fail to notice characteristics of another task. Discuss the research in these three areas and think of an example of each area that you recently encountered.

4. One of the main points in the second section is that sleep is an active process. Discuss this concept, being sure to mention (a) EEGs, (b) body movement, and (c) dreams.

5. How do zeitgebers help us maintain circadian rhythms? How are the concepts of free-running, shift schedules, jet lag, and exposure to variations in light all relevant to circadian rhythms? Where relevant, think of an example of each.

6. Imagine that you have had no sleep for the last two nights. Select six tasks that you must perform at some point today, and predict on the basis of Babkoff's research in the "In Depth" section how well you will perform each task, compared to your performance when well rested.

7. Imagine that a high-school student you know is intrigued with the topic of sleep and asks you, "Why do we sleep?" Summarize the major reasons as clearly as possible. Then suppose that the student asks, "Why do we dream?" Again, summarize the major explanations.

8. What are the three major kinds of psychoactive drugs described in this chapter? For each category, make a list of some general physical and psychological effects. We discussed expectancy effects in connection with alcohol. How could expectancy effects be relevant for some of the other drugs?

9. Explain Steele and Josephs' (1990) proposal that alcohol alters attention to cues, creating your own example to clarify their proposal. How is their approach related to the material at the beginning of the chapter on divided and selective attention?

10. From what you read and heard prior to reading this chapter, would you have concluded that hypnosis and meditation were substantially different from the normal waking state? What would you conclude now, based on the research discussed in this chapter?

N E W   T E R M S

consciousness
thought suppression
attention
divided attention
selective attention
dichotic listening task
the Stroop effect
preattentive processing
focused attention
sleep
circadian rhythm
zeitgebers
free-running
shift schedules
jet lag
meta-analysis
beta waves
alpha waves
Stage 1 sleep
Stage 2 sleep
Stage 3 sleep
Stage 4 sleep
REM sleep
insomnia
Disorders of Initiating and Maintaining Sleep
    (DIMS)
Disorders of Excessive Sleepiness (DOES)
sleep apnea
narcolepsy

lucid dreaming
nightmare
neurocognitive model
activation-synthesis hypothesis
connectionist approach
psychoactive drugs
neurotransmitters
tolerance
withdrawal symptoms
dependence
depressants
opiates
endorphins
binge drinking
balanced-placebo design
stimulants
hallucinogens
hallucinations
hypnosis
posthypnotic suggestion
posthypnotic amnesia
positive hallucinations
negative hallucinations
confabulation
age regression
neodissociation theory
hidden-observer phenomenon
social role theory
meditation

A N S W E R S   T O   D E M O N S T R A T I O N

DEMONSTRATION 5.6   1. T; 2. F; 3. T; 4. F; 5. T; 6. F

R E C O M M E N D E D   R E A D I N G S

Anch, A. M., Browman, C. P., Mitler, M. M., & Walsh, J. K. (1988). *Sleep: A scientific perspective*. Englewood Cliffs, NJ: Prentice Hall. This clearly written undergraduate textbook examines topics such as normal sleep, circadian rhythms, dreaming, and sleep disorders.

Babkoff, H., Caspy, T., Mikulincer, M., & Sing, H. C. (1991). Monotonic and rhythmic influences: A challenge for sleep deprivation research. *Psychological Bulletin, 109,* 411–428. This is an ideal article to introduce you to research on sleep; it offers more detail on sleep deprivation, the subject of the "In Depth" section.

Farthing, G. W. (1992). *The psychology of consciousness*. Englewood Cliffs, NJ: Prentice Hall. Farthing's textbook offers a mid-level overview of every topic in this chapter, as well as discussion of related topics such as introspection and daydreaming.

Glass, I. B. (Ed.). (1991). *The international handbook of addiction behaviour.* London: Tavistock/Routledge. This useful handbook contains 52 short chapters on specific topics such as the genetic basis of alcoholism, the opiates, the adolescent addict, and family therapy for alcohol problems.

McKim, W. A. (1991). *Drugs and behavior: An introduction to behavioral pharmacology* (2nd ed.). Englewood Cliffs, NJ: Prentice Hall. McKim's textbook is well-organized and clearly written; the chapter on research design provides an excellent background on the problems of conducting experiments on drugs.

Steele, C. M., & Josephs, R. A. (1990). Alcohol myopia: Its prized and dangerous effects. *American Psychologist, 45* 921–933. This article reviews the literature and presents Steele and Josephs' theory about alcohol's effects on responding to cues.

CHAPTER 6

LEARNING

In Chapter 4, we examined how your sensory systems allow you to perceive sights, sounds, tactile and painful stimuli, smells, and tastes. Chapter 5 discussed how you sometimes pay attention to these perceptions and sometimes ignore them. However, these perceptions do not simply lie trapped and useless in your cerebral cortex. As the next four chapters emphasize, you use this perceptual information when you learn, remember, think, and use language.

Our current chapter focuses on three kinds of learning. Consider the following examples:

1. *Classical conditioning:* A young man and his girlfriend live 200 miles apart, and they can visit only about twice a month. She owns a distinctive winter coat, which is white with broad red, yellow, and green stripes. One day this fellow spots a bearded man wearing a similar coat. His heart starts pounding rapidly, and his hands grow moist—even though he knows the person wearing the coat cannot *possibly* be his girlfriend (Mazur, 1990).

2. *Operant conditioning:* Rick is a 4-year-old child who talks constantly and disrupts activities at his day-care center. His parents decide to award him a star sticker every time his day-care teacher gives a positive report. The stickers can be exchanged for enjoyable activities, such as going to the movies or having a friend over to play. After several months of this program, Rick's behavior is much less disruptive (Basher, 1991).

3. *Observational learning:* I can vividly recall a spring concert at our local high school. Because the event was the seniors' final performance, the teacher had asked individual juniors to reminisce briefly about each graduating senior. The first junior began, "I don't know what I can say about Judy, but . . . ." Then the second junior began his farewell, "I don't know what I can say about Bill, but . . . ." In all, two-thirds of the students began their farewells with the same identical phrase—to the amusement of half the audience and the dismay of the rest.

What characteristics do these three examples share? They all illustrate different kinds of **learning,** which we will define as a relatively permanent change in behavior or knowledge due to experience. Let us consider the elements of this definition in more detail. First, notice that the definition uses the word *change*, rather than *improvement*. Learning can involve misconduct and undesirable behavior (for example, learning to steal or to harm other people), as well as socially appropriate behavior. This change involves not only our outward behavior, but also our knowledge. For example, you may know how to bandage a sprained ankle after watching a first-aid video, even if you have not actually performed this activity. Finally, we need the phrase "due to experience" because we want to eliminate many other kinds of changed behavior that are not considered learning. For example, drugs, injury, disease, genetics, and maturation all produce changes in behavior; however, none of these changes involves learning (Chance, 1988).

Learning is essential to humans because it allows us to change and acquire a complex set of sophisticated skills. To appreciate the importance of learning, imagine that you had an identical twin who was raised since birth with no opportunities to learn. Reared in a barren room, your twin never learned to speak, to read, to form emotional relationships, or to explore the world. Imagine this twin in your shoes right now and visualize this person trying to live your life for the next 24 hours. We often fail to acknowledge the importance of learning unless we consciously make an effort to imagine life without it.

This chapter explores three basic and important kinds of learning, each illustrating a relatively permanent change in behavior or knowledge that can be traced to experience. The first topic is classical conditioning, a topic that is more complex than it initially appears. In the section on operant conditioning, we consider how rewards and punishments influence behavior. Finally, we discuss how people learn by watching others, in the section on observational learning.

CLASSICAL CONDITIONING

In **classical conditioning,** we learn that certain environmental stimuli can predict certain events. Consider this example. Eight-month-old Billy and his family have just moved to a new home. Billy is quietly playing in the bedroom when a gust of wind makes the wind chimes jingle. An instant later, the wind blows Billy's bedroom door shut with a resounding bang. Startled, little Billy flinches and then screams vigorously. This startled reaction is a natural, unlearned response.

The next morning, Billy is lying in his crib when the wind once again jingles the chimes, followed by another loud bang from the bedroom door. Billy is likely to learn that there is a predictive relationship in his environment. That is, the jingling of the wind chimes predicts that the door will slam loudly. After several similar experiences, Billy may begin to flinch and scream as soon as the wind chimes jingle.

In classical conditioning—prior to any learning—an unconditioned stimulus elicits an unconditioned response. The **unconditioned stimulus** is defined as the stimulus in classical conditioning that elicits an unlearned response. The **unconditioned response** is defined as an unlearned response to a stimulus—a response that occurs naturally.

In our previous example, the loud noise from the slamming door can be labeled as an unconditioned stimulus, and the startled reaction can be labeled as an unconditioned response (Figure 6.1). The wind chimes initially produce no reaction. However, they become a reliable predictor for the loud noise. The chimes soon produce a response of flinching and screaming, even before the door actually slams.

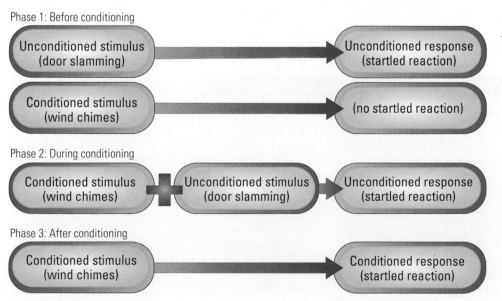

Phase 1: Before conditioning

Unconditioned stimulus (door slamming) → Unconditioned response (startled reaction)

Conditioned stimulus (wind chimes) → (no startled reaction)

Phase 2: During conditioning

Conditioned stimulus (wind chimes) + Unconditioned stimulus (door slamming) → Unconditioned response (startled reaction)

Phase 3: After conditioning

Conditioned stimulus (wind chimes) → Conditioned response (startled reaction)

Figure 6.1

An example of classical conditioning.

During learning, the organism learns that there is a reliable, predictable relationship between the conditioned stimulus (for instance, the wind chimes) and the unconditioned stimulus (for instance, the door slamming). When classical conditioning has taken place, the conditioned stimulus now elicits a conditioned response. The **conditioned stimulus** is defined as the stimulus that is predictive of the unconditioned stimulus. (That is, the jingling of wind chimes is predictive of a slamming door.) The **conditioned response** is defined as the response that is elicited by the conditioned stimulus.

Take a few minutes to review these four terms and learn them, because they are used throughout this section. Students often find it helpful to keep in mind that *unconditioned* refers to stimuli and responses that do not require learning; this reaction occurs spontaneously. The other two terms, *conditioned* stimuli and responses, require conditioning; learning produces this conditioning.

Try applying these terms to a different example. Let us assume that you enjoy eating meat and that the taste of steak makes your mouth water. One summer day, you smell the smoke from a neighbor's charcoal fire. Your mouth immediately begins to water, even though you never get an opportunity to taste the meat. Identify the unconditioned stimulus, the unconditioned response, the conditioned stimulus, and the conditioned response. Then try an example of classical conditioning in Demonstration 6.1, which also contains the answer to the barbecued steak question.

Classical conditioning can produce extremely powerful reactions. For example, Leo (1985) describes how a Latin American refugee who had fled to Canada froze in terror when a well-wisher presented him with a gift basket. The basket contained two pineapples, a welcome gift for most people. However, before fleeing his native country, this refugee had been forced to watch as a military guard hacked several prisoners to death with a machete, then calmly carved up a ripe pineapple—without wiping the blade— and ate the bloodstained slices.

Classical conditioning was traditionally considered to be a low-level, automatic kind of learning. In fact, critics typically claimed that classical conditioning was "all spit and twitches" because researchers usually examined salivary responses and reflexes involving muscle movement. In the last 30 years, that view has changed. Classical conditioning may indeed be simpler than many other kinds of learning. However, it often requires remembering stimuli for hours or even days. Furthermore, conditioning involves more than the simple pairing of the conditioned stimulus with the unconditioned stimulus. As this chapter will demonstrate, even classical conditioning provides an example of our theme about complexity. Finally, learning theorists have developed explanations for how classical conditioning can account for a wide range of behaviors, including responses in the immune system, reactions to substance abuse, eating behavior, and even sexual behavior (Turkkan, 1989a).

DEMONSTRATION 6.1   An Example of Classical Conditioning

Take a balloon and blow it up until it is as inflated as possible. Ask a friend to participate in a brief demonstration, and stand with the balloon about 2 feet from the friend. Take a sharp pair of scissors and move the point toward the inflated balloon, watching your friend's facial expression and body movements. People usually shut their eyes and contract the muscles in the upper part of their bodies during this demonstration. In this case, the loud noise of a balloon popping is the unconditioned stimulus, and the changes in facial expression and body movements represent the unconditioned response. The sight of a balloon about to be popped is the conditioned stimulus (often predictive of a popping noise), which through classical conditioning comes to produce the change in facial expression and body movements, or the conditioned response.

Incidentally, in the earlier example, the unconditioned stimulus is the flavor of meat on the tongue, the unconditioned response is mouth-watering, the conditioned stimulus is the aroma of barbecued steak, and the conditioned response is mouth-watering.

To understand classical conditioning more fully, let's first discuss two well-known early studies and then examine important components of classical conditioning, such as acquisition and stimulus generalization. Then we will explore some important new theoretical developments, which have changed the way psychologists view classical conditioning. Our final two topics are the biological basis of classical conditioning and some practical applications of this kind of learning.

Influential Research in Classical Conditioning

Pavlov's Conditioned Salivation Experiment The history of many disciplines might have been completely different if a particular early researcher had been somewhat less curious or less persistent. For example, what might have happened if the Russian physiologist Ivan Pavlov had continued to study the digestive systems of dogs, rather than making a detour when he observed an interesting psychological phenomenon?

In 1904, Pavlov had received a Nobel prize for his research on physiology. Some of his work used a procedure that measured the production of saliva. Not surprisingly, when meat powder was placed in a dog's mouth, its saliva production increased. However, Pavlov observed that the mere *sight* of food caused an increase in saliva production. More intriguing still, saliva production increased at the mere sight of the experimenter. Even the sound of the experimenter's footsteps elicited salivation.

Pavlov prided himself on being an objective scientist. In fact, the workers in his laboratory were fined if they used any subjective, nonphysiological language (Hergenhahn, 1988). His decision to pursue research on psychological determinants of salivation was therefore a difficult one.

Figure 6.2 shows the experimental equipment used in Pavlov's early research on classical conditioning. Notice that the tube running from the dog's cheek allowed the saliva to be collected and measured. Later equipment developed by both Pavlov and his associates permitted more precise recordings of saliva production (Goodwin, 1991).

The three critical phases of Pavlov's research are shown in Figure 6.3. Before conditioning had begun, the unconditioned stimulus (meat powder) produced an

Figure 6.2

Sketch of Pavlov's early apparatus.
(Based on Yerkes and Morgulis, 1909)

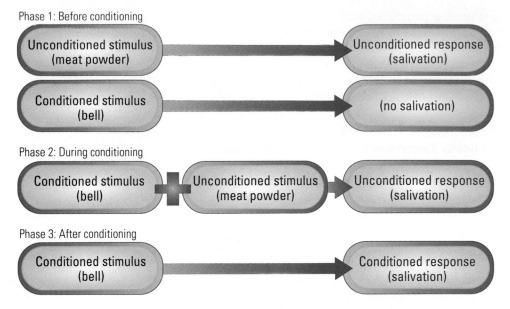

Phase 1: Before conditioning

Unconditioned stimulus (meat powder) → Unconditioned response (salivation)

Conditioned stimulus (bell) → (no salivation)

Phase 2: During conditioning

Conditioned stimulus (bell) + Unconditioned stimulus (meat powder) → Unconditioned response (salivation)

Phase 3: After conditioning

Conditioned stimulus (bell) → Conditioned response (salivation)

Figure 6.3

Classical conditioning in Pavlov's study.

unconditioned response (salivation). Pavlov had selected the sound of a bell to serve as the conditioned stimulus. Before conditioning, the bell produced no salivation. Instead, the dog simply looked in the direction of the sound.

During conditioning, the conditioned stimulus (the bell) was followed by the unconditioned stimulus (the meat powder), which continued to produce the unconditioned response (salivation). The conditioned stimulus and the unconditioned stimulus were paired together in this fashion for several trials.

After a number of conditioning trials, Pavlov discovered that the sound of the bell was sufficient to produce salivation. The meat powder did not need to be presented at all. Similarly, a baby may flinch and scream when the wind chimes jingle—the door does not need to slam—and your friends may tense their muscles when the balloon grows dangerously large, even though it has not yet popped.

Watson and Rayner's Conditioned Fear Study Another well-known study was conducted in the United States by John Watson and Rosalie Rayner (1920). These researchers tested an 11-month-old baby named Albert, who showed no fear of animals prior to testing. However, he showed a clear-cut fear reaction whenever a researcher made a loud noise by striking a hammer against a large steel bar located immediately behind Albert's back. (The noise therefore served as the unconditioned stimulus, and the fear reaction was the unconditioned response.)

Watson and Rayner used a white rat as a conditioned stimulus. Whenever Albert reached out to touch the rat, the hammer clanged loudly against the steel bar. After seven pairings of the rat and the noise, Albert cried and avoided the rat, even when the loud noise was no longer delivered. Watson and Rayner concluded that a fear could be learned through conditioning.

Although this study is one of the most famous in all psychology, it was not one of the best. For example, Turkkan (1989b) points out that the research design does not technically qualify as an example of classical conditioning, because the researchers waited until Albert reached for the rat, before striking the steel bar. (As you will learn shortly, this process involves operant conditioning.) Also, Harris (1979) points out a major ethical problem with the study. Watson knew a month in advance that Albert's mother planned to remove him from the research project. Nevertheless, Watson apparently did not decondition the child to make certain that he had no remaining fear of rats. Watson's study would be unacceptable by today's ethical standards. As you know, research participants should not experience unnecessary discomfort or harm. Albert certainly experienced discomfort from the loud noise, and he may have experienced harm if he continued to fear white objects resembling rats after the experiment had ended.

Components of Classical Conditioning

Now that we have discussed several examples, let us examine some components of classical conditioning more closely. You will see that once conditioning has been acquired, it can be applied in some new circumstances (stimulus generalization)—but not all (stimulus discrimination). Furthermore, a conditioned response can be eliminated (extinction), though it may return again (spontaneous recovery). This section therefore helps you appreciate some of the complexities of classical conditioning; this form of learning involves more than the acquisition of a single conditioned response that remains unchanged throughout a lifetime.

Acquisition **Acquisition** is the process of learning a new response. In classical conditioning, acquisition involves producing a conditioned response to a conditioned stimulus. Figure 6.4 shows a typical acquisition curve. As you can see, at the beginning of testing, the conditioned stimulus does not elicit the conditioned response. For example, Pavlov's dogs did not initially salivate when the bell rang. During the first few trials, however, the strength of the conditioned response grows rapidly. Later in the testing session, the increase in the strength of the conditioned response is more gradual.

Figure 6.4 shows a fairly leisurely acquisition rate, in which many trials are necessary for the conditioned response to reach its maximum strength. You can probably think of many exceptions to this pattern—cases that require only a single pairing of the conditioned stimulus and the unconditioned stimulus. The Latin American exile mentioned earlier in the chapter acquired his fear of pineapples from a single barbaric act. Another example of one-trial learning occurred several years ago, when my family and I were driving together and had stopped at an intersection, with our flasher indicating a left-hand turn. An inattentive driver rear-ended us, causing some injuries and demolishing our car. For weeks afterward, we all experienced anxiety whenever we were stopped at an intersection and a car approached quickly from the rear. No repeated pairings were necessary; we had learned this anxiety in a single trial. In classical conditioning, acquisition can be rapid—even immediate—when the unconditioned stimulus is intense.

Stimulus Generalization Both people and animals show **stimulus generalization,** which means that if they learn a response to one particular stimulus, similar stimuli will also tend to elicit that response (Houston, 1991). For example, the car that rear-ended my family's car was large, old, and beige. Nevertheless, our fear of

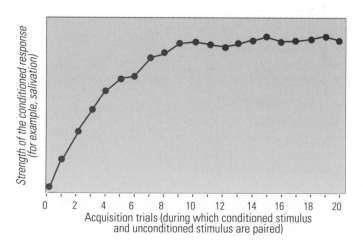

Figure 6.4

The acquisition of a conditioned response (typical data).

cars approaching from the rear was not limited to just this kind of car. I suspect that a large, old, *blue* car would have produced a substantial anxiety response during the month after the accident. My heart might have beat faster even if a brand-new red sports car had approached too quickly.

As you might expect, new stimuli that are highly similar to the conditioned stimulus are more likely than dissimilar stimuli to produce the conditioned response. For example, Figure 6.5 shows data from rabbits that had been conditioned to blink their eyes to a particular tone with a frequency of 1200 Hz (that is, a pitch slightly more than two octaves above middle C.) Conditioning was produced by presenting a brief puff of air to the eye, immediately after the tone had been sounded. When the rabbits were tested later, the largest number of conditioned responses was produced by the original tone, 1200 Hz. However, other tones produced some conditioned responses as well. For instance, a tone of 800 Hz (3 notes lower on the piano) produced a substantial response rate, and even a tone of 400 Hz (11 notes lower on the piano) produced some conditioned responses.

Stimulus generalization is useful, both for animals and for humans. After all, classical conditioning involves learning predictive relationships. Our learning would be limited indeed if we never generalized beyond the exact same conditioned stimulus that was originally presented. Instead, generalization allows us to predict what is likely to happen in new situations. Stimulus generalization is an example of the theme that organisms are well equipped to function in their environments.

Stimulus Discrimination Of course, stimulus generalization could be carried too far. If we generalized to every new stimulus that vaguely resembled the conditioned stimulus, we would often act inappropriately. Therefore, we need to differentiate between similar stimuli, through a process called **stimulus discrimination.** For example, a child who has been burned by a gas stove will learn that no harm comes from touching a photograph of a fire. Thus, stimulus generalization and stimulus discrimination work together. Stimulus generalization ensures that we expand our learning beyond the immediate conditioned stimulus. However, stimulus discrimination operates to guarantee that we do not generalize too broadly or inappropriately.

Extinction Suppose that a dog has learned to salivate to a bell, and then the bell is presented repeatedly *without* the meat powder. Would the dog continue to drool? Pavlov reported that after only five or six trials without meat powder, the dogs no longer produced saliva when the bell was sounded. This is an example of **extinction**, or a gradual disappearance of a conditioned response that happens when a conditioned stimulus is repeatedly presented without the unconditioned stimulus. Several months after our car accident, for example, my heart no longer pounded when a car approached from behind.

In general, then, extinction allows us to stop responding when a conditioned stimulus is no longer predictive of an unconditioned stimulus. For example, there is no strong predictive relationship between *car approaching from behind* and *car crashes*. I can probably live all my life with no other car approaching from behind and producing a car crash. Therefore, remembering this relationship is not useful.

The blinking red light on top of an ambulance is a conditioned stimulus for most people, because the unconditioned stimulus (the siren) with which it is associated produces an unconditioned response (your heart beats faster).

Most people show some stimulus generalization from the ambulance's red light to the blinking yellow light on the top of a tow truck.

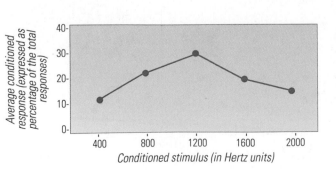

Figure 6.5

Stimulus generalization for a rabbit conditioned with a tone of 1200 Hz frequency. (Based on Liu, 1971).

Spontaneous Recovery When a period of time has passed following extinction, and the conditioned stimulus is presented once more, the conditioned response may temporarily reappear; this phenomenon is called **spontaneous recovery.** For example, Figure 6.6 shows data gathered by Pavlov (1927). When the unconditioned stimulus (meat powder) was no longer presented, salivation gradually dropped to zero. Then Pavlov waited two hours and presented the conditioned stimulus (the bell) once again. Notice that the conditioned stimulus elicited a noticeable amount of saliva. However, with further presentations of the conditioned stimulus—and no unconditioned stimulus—the response would quickly extinguish once more.

Recent Developments in Classical Conditioning

Several decades ago, the research on classical conditioning seemed to be dying out (Turkkan, 1989a). Psychologists thought that they understood this form of learning. After all, what could possibly be complicated about drooling dogs and blinking rabbits? The typical introductory psychology textbook defined classical conditioning as a process in which an unconditioned stimulus is repeatedly paired with a conditioned stimulus, until the conditioned stimulus comes to elicit a response, even when the unconditioned stimulus is not presented. Psychologists now realize that this definition is incorrect (Rescorla, 1988; Rescorla & Holland, 1982; Spear et al., 1990). Let us discuss four major problems with the earlier views of classical conditioning, as well as the current position on each issue.

Single-Trial Learning Classical conditioning does not necessarily require repeated pairings between the conditioned stimulus and the unconditioned stimulus, as the earlier definition had specified. As we discussed earlier in connection with the Latin American refugee and the pineapple, a single trial can be sufficient to develop a conditioned response.

Predictive Relationships The earlier view had stated that learning would occur whenever a neutral conditioned stimulus was followed by an unconditioned stimulus. That is, contiguity or simple pairing between the conditioned stimulus and the unconditioned stimulus was sufficient to produce learning. We now know that contiguity is *not* sufficient. Let us consider an experiment that demonstrates why simple contiguity is not enough.

People who have allergic reactions to shellfish can usually eat "finny" fish safely—and vice versa. Stimulus discrimination allows people to learn that it's fine to eat one category of fish, but not the other, even though both are called fish and live in similar habitats.

Figure 6.6

Extinction and spontaneous recovery of a conditioned response. (Based on Pavlov, 1927)

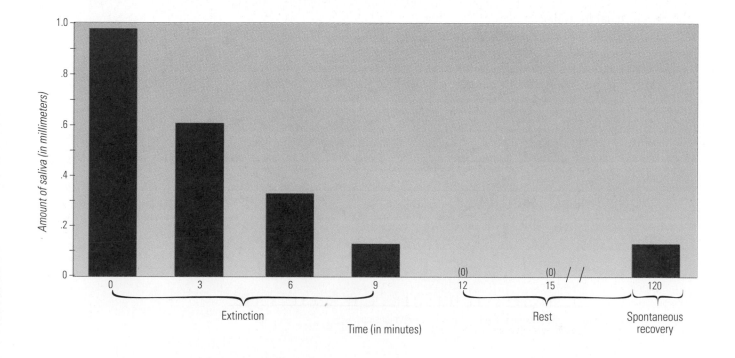

Amount of saliva (in millimeters) — Time (in minutes)

Extinction · Rest · Spontaneous recovery

Robert Rescorla (1968) studied classical conditioning in rats, using a tone as the conditioned stimulus and a shock as the unconditioned stimulus. He suspected that learning would not occur unless the tone consistently predicted the shock. Situation 1 in Figure 6.7 shows a predictive relationship between the tone and the shock. That is, the shock never occurred except when the tone had been sounded.

In Situation 2, however, Rescorla added some extra unconditioned stimuli. That is, rats received additional shocks when the tone was *not* presented. In both cases, there is contiguity between the conditioned stimulus and the unconditioned stimulus; the tone is always presented with shock. Both situations also have an identical number of pairings. However, only Situation 1 has a *predictive relationship* between the tone and the shock. Try placing yourself in the position of the rat and figure out whether you would learn to fear the tone in Situation 2. The tone is always followed by shocks, but extra shocks are thrown in without the forewarning of the tone. Or imagine Billy and the wind chimes example from the beginning of this section; would Billy react to the chimes if the door often slammed when the chimes did not jingle?

In fact, Rescorla found that the two situations produced different learning patterns. As he had suspected, conditioning occurred in Situation 1 but not in Situation 2. Simple contiguity is *not* enough. The tone must also provide information about whether the shock will occur. Experiments such as Rescorla's encouraged psychologists to revise their definition of classical conditioning (Rescorla, 1988). If you check the definition for classical conditioning at the beginning of the chapter, you'll see that it emphasized predictive relationships.

Biological Preparedness The earlier view stressed that any perceivable stimulus could function as a conditioned stimulus. However, research by John Garcia and his colleagues showed that some associations are much more readily learned than others (Garcia, 1984; Garcia et al., 1972; Garcia & Koelling, 1966). These studies examined the effects of radiation on laboratory rats. Radiation (an unconditioned stimulus) produces nausea (an unconditioned response). The research examined **taste aversion,** the development of intense dislike for a food through conditioning.

Garcia and Koelling (1966) found that classical conditioning could be established when sweet-tasting water was paired with radiation. After a single trial in which they experienced nausea, rats learned to avoid the sweet-tasting water. In a second condition, bright, noisy water (that is, water accompanied by flashing lights and loud noises) was paired with radiation. No conditioning occurred; the rats did not learn to avoid the water.

The startling observation in these studies is that *taste* could be readily conditioned to nausea, whereas *sight* and *sound* could not. Apparently, the nervous system of mammals has developed through evolution so that certain associations are learned more easily than others. In the case of rats, the nervous system is "biased" to remem-

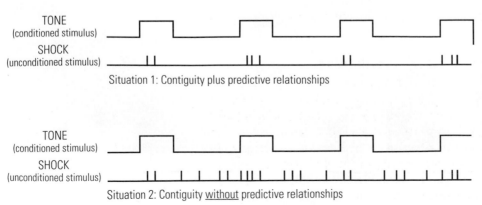

Situation 1: Contiguity plus predictive relationships

Situation 2: Contiguity <u>without</u> predictive relationships

Figure 6.7

Two situations similar to those used in Rescorla's (1968) experiment. Note: An elevation for tone *indicates that the tone is being presented; a hatch-mark for* shock *indicates that a shock is being presented at that time.*

ber the taste of foods that are associated with nausea. Because sight and sound are typically not related to nausea, they cannot serve as effective conditioned stimuli for nausea.

This built-in bias, which ensures that some relationships between stimuli and responses will be learned more readily than others, is called **biological preparedness.** The concept of biological preparedness altered the traditional view of classical conditioning by demonstrating that all stimuli are *not* created equal. Depending upon the kind of conditioning to be acquired, some stimuli are easier to learn than others.

Biological preparedness explains why coyotes can easily acquire taste aversion. In one program, ranchers placed a nausea-producing substance on lamb carcasses. Coyotes that ate this meat often avoided killing lambs in the future.

Delay Between Conditioned Stimulus and Unconditioned Stimulus

The earlier view emphasized that classical conditioning could only occur when the conditioned stimulus came *immediately* before the unconditioned stimulus. In Pavlov's classic study, for example, the sound of the buzzer was immediately followed by the meat powder. In many cases, conditioning requires this split-second timing. However, more recent research points out that conditioning can occur even when there is a delay between the conditioned stimulus and the unconditioned stimulus.

Once again, the most convincing research involves taste aversion, but this time with humans. When cancer patients eat food that has a distinctive flavor—followed by X rays or medication that causes nausea and vomiting—the patients show taste aversion. That is, they avoid the distinctively flavored food in the future (Flaherty, 1985).

Taste aversion studies have demonstrated, though, that associations can be formed between the distinctive flavor and the X rays or drugs, even though they may be separated in time by several hours (Revusky, 1971). Thus, split-second timing between the conditioned stimulus and unconditioned stimulus is *not* an absolute requirement for conditioning.

We mentioned that the earlier view of classical conditioning would not predict taste-aversion learning when the conditioned stimulus and the unconditioned stimulus are separated by a long delay. However, it does make sense from a biological standpoint, and it also provides further testimony for the theme that organisms are well adapted to their environments. In their natural habitats, animals learn to avoid poisonous foods, and most poisons produce delayed symptoms. The conditioned stimulus (the food) must somehow be represented in memory throughout that long delay period (Rescorla & Holland, 1982).

In summary, we have seen that classical conditioning can occur without repeated pairings. Furthermore, predictability is the essential feature, rather than simple pairing. In addition, some stimuli produce better conditioning than others. Finally, the conditioned stimulus and the unconditioned stimulus can be separated by several hours.

Classical conditioning may be one of the most basic kinds of learning that any organism can demonstrate. However, the more recent research illustrates that even this relatively simple learning is much more sophisticated than psychologists had originally suspected. Consistent with an important theme of this book, psychological processes are complicated. The essence of classical conditioning is not simple pairing, but predictive relationships.

Biological Components of Classical Conditioning

Research on the biological basis of classical conditioning offers additional support for our theme of complexity. Whether the research is conducted on humans or on other animals, different neural structures seem to be involved for different kinds of learning (Ivry, 1992). For example, when a lesion is made in a rabbit's cerebellum, the rabbit will not be able to learn a specific kind of eyeblink response. However, that lesion will have no effect on heart-rate conditioning (Lavond et al., 1984).

Let us examine this eyeblink response in more detail, because the biological explanation for this response has been extensively studied in recent decades. As it happens, rabbits have an unusual inner eyelid called the nictitating membrane, which slides over a rabbit's eye to protect it when a puff of air is presented; this response is called the **nictitating-membrane reflex.** A rabbit can be conditioned by presenting a tone (the conditioned stimulus) just before the puff of air. Initially, the rabbit does not respond to the tone. However, with repeated trials, the nictitating membrane slides over the eye in response to the tone, even when the puff of air is not presented. Classical conditioning has occurred.

One brain structure that is involved in nictitating-membrane conditioning is the cerebellum. (See Figure 3.13 for the location of the cerebellum in humans.) For example, when a lesion is made in the rabbit's cerebellum, the animal no longer shows evidence of conditioning; when the tone is presented, the nictitating membrane does not move. However, the unlearned reflex is not harmed; when the puff of air is presented, the normal nictitating-membrane reflex occurs (McCormick et al., 1982).

Another brain structure involved in some memory tasks is the hippocampus; Figure 3.15 shows the location of the hippocampus in humans. The hippocampus *is not* involved when the conditioning task is simple and the tone stays on while the puff of air is presented. However, the hippocampus *is* involved when the tone is turned off half a second before the puff of air is presented (Solomon et al., 1983). A rabbit with a lesion in the hippocampus cannot acquire this more complicated conditioned response. Additional research has confirmed that specific cells within the hippocampus increase their frequency of firing during acquisition, and they decrease their frequency of firing during extinction (Berger et al., 1983; Berger & Thompson, 1982). Current researchers are trying to establish how the hippocampus is involved in remembering the tone for the short period of time before the puff of air is presented, and also how the hippocampus and the cerebellum interact (Schmajuk & DiCarlo, 1991; 1992).

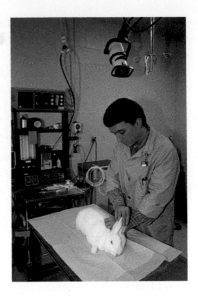

Researchers interested in the biological basis of classical conditioning have often studied the nictitating-membrane reflex in rabbits.

Applications of Classical Conditioning

One of the most important applications of classical conditioning focuses on the taste aversion problem in cancer patients. Classical conditioning has also been used to explain some unexpected reactions among drug addicts. A third major application will be considered in Chapter 16, when we examine how classical conditioning can be applied in psychotherapy.

Taste Aversion Conditioned taste aversion may be one of the best documented learned responses (Bernstein & Meachum, 1990). According to one account, more than 1,300 articles on the subject were published between 1977 and 1989 (Locurto, 1989).

For a number of years, Ilene Bernstein and her colleagues have been examining how taste aversion develops in young cancer patients. Children who receive chemotherapy often acquire an intense dislike for the particular food they ate prior to chemotherapy. In an important early study, Bernstein (1978) tested whether children would develop conditioned taste aversion to a new flavor of ice cream, which she labeled "Mapletoff." Half of the children, who were between the ages of 2 and 16, were given a serving of Mapletoff ice cream prior to chemotherapy with a drug that causes nausea and vomiting. The other half of the children served as a control group. The control group received similar drug treatment, but no Mapletoff beforehand.

Two to 4 weeks later, the children in both groups were given a choice: They could either eat Mapletoff ice cream or play with a game. Only 21% of the children who had eaten Mapletoff prior to chemotherapy chose to eat the ice cream, in contrast to 67% of the children who had no previous experience with the Mapletoff (Bernstein, 1978). Clearly, most children in the experimental group had been conditioned to dislike the Mapletoff flavor.

Conditioned taste aversion creates nutritional problems, especially because taste aversion is typically strongest for meat and other sources of protein (Midkiff &

TABLE 6.1 Setup for Broberg and Bernstein's (1987) Study on Conditioned Taste Aversion			
	SEQUENCE OF EVENTS		
	1	**2**	**3**
EXPERIMENTAL GROUP:	Meal	LifeSavers	Chemotherapy
CONTROL GROUP:	Meal	(nothing)	Chemotherapy

Bernstein, 1985). Cancer patients need to eat, and they also need their chemotherapy. How can the dilemma be solved? We saw in an earlier section that the problem is not solved by waiting several hours after eating before giving the drug.

Broberg and Bernstein (1987) devised a clever answer. Conditioned taste aversion is especially likely to develop for unfamiliar tastes. (After all, a familiar food such as a pancake is likely to have a long history of positive associations.) Therefore, these researchers gave children in the experimental condition an unusual flavor of Life-Savers candy to eat immediately after the meal. The researchers selected two uncommon flavors, root beer and coconut, so that an intense dislike for these flavors would not have an effect on later nutrition. Children in the control group received no Life-Savers. All were then given chemotherapy (see Table 6.1).

Later testing showed that the children who had received the LifeSavers were more positive about eating the kinds of food that had been included in the earlier meal. In contrast, the control-group children were more likely to have developed taste aversions. It seems that the LifeSavers had served as a scapegoat for the first group, protecting the more nutritious food from acquiring taste aversions.

More recent research has demonstrated that aversions are more likely to be associated with the *smell* of the food, rather than its taste (Bartoshuk, 1991a). Perhaps further research will focus more on modifying the classical conditioning of odors.

Conditioning and the Effects of Psychoactive Drugs In Chapter 4 we discussed psychoactive drugs such as heroin. Some psychologists argue that an important reaction to a variety of these psychoactive drugs can be traced to classical conditioning (Poulos & Cappell, 1991). Specifically, research has addressed why drug addicts tend to respond more strongly to the substance when they take their customary dose in an unfamiliar environment.

A key point in this mysterious response is that when some drugs are used, a conditioned response is produced that is the *opposite* of the unconditioned response. For example, the unconditioned response to morphine is a reduction in sensitivity to pain. However, if that morphine is consistently taken in a distinctive-looking setting, then the setting itself will produce a conditioned response of *greater* sensitivity to pain (Hinson et al., 1986; Krank, 1989; Siegel, 1988). Also, the unconditioned response to heroin is a decrease in breathing rate. However, if heroin is always injected in a certain room, then certain features of the room will act as conditioned stimuli, producing an increase in breathing rate. When a drug user injects heroin in a familiar setting, these two effects counteract each other, an adaptive response that results in a normal breathing rate.

Can you anticipate what would happen when a drug addict uses heroin in an unfamiliar setting where the customary cues are missing? These new surroundings will not elicit the conditioned response that normally counteracts some of the effects of heroin. The heroin is therefore more powerful than normal and more likely to produce a strong reaction. For example, breathing rate will decrease but not be balanced by the typical increase in breathing rate caused by conditioning. In fact, researchers have discovered that heroin addicts receiving emergency treatment for an overdose usually report that they had injected only a normal dose. However, 70% had injected the drug in an unfamiliar setting (Siegel, 1984). Classical conditioning may possibly account for a large proportion of deaths from heroin overdoses.

The needle, the table, and other objects in this room may become conditioned stimuli for this heroin user.

S E C T I O N   S U M M A R Y
CLASSICAL CONDITIONING

- Learning is a relatively permanent change in behavior or knowledge due to experience.

- Classical conditioning involves learning in which certain environmental stimuli can predict certain events.

- In an influential study, Pavlov paired a bell (conditioned stimulus) with meat powder (unconditioned stimulus) until the sound of the bell produced salivation (conditioned response), even when the meat powder was no longer presented. Similarly, Watson and Rayner conditioned a fear of rats in a baby by pairing a rat with a loud noise.

- Five important components of classical conditioning are acquisition, stimulus generalization, stimulus discrimination, extinction, and spontaneous recovery.

- Current theory about classical conditioning includes the following points: (a) conditioning can be accomplished in a single trial; (b) predictive relationships between the conditioned stimulus and the unconditioned stimulus are essential; (c) biological preparedness ensures that some relationships between stimuli and responses will be learned more readily than others; and (d) the conditioned stimulus and the unconditioned stimulus can be separated by several hours.

- Different kinds of classical conditioning involve different brain structures; the nictitating-membrane reflex in rabbits involves the cerebellum and—if a delay separates the tone and the puff of air—the hippocampus.

- Two applications of classical conditioning are conditioned taste aversion and drug-overdose problems.

OPERANT CONDITIONING

We have seen that classical conditioning can explain why your mouth waters at the smell of burning charcoal and why your heart pounds harder when you see a flashing signal on a tow truck. Classical conditioning can also account for some emotional reactions. However, it cannot explain how a child learns to put away her toys or why you are reading this textbook right now—rather than watching television or socializing with your friends. We need to turn to a second kind of conditioning to explain these behaviors.

In **operant conditioning,** or **instrumental conditioning,** we learn to make a response because it produces a reinforcing effect. That reinforcing effect may be praise from a parent (in the case of a child who has put away her toys) or a good test grade (in the case of reading a textbook). Operant conditioning also involves learning when *not* to make a response because it produces a punishing effect. You will not repeat a joke that produced only an embarrassed silence from your friends, and after one nearly fatal experience with chewing on an electric cord, a dog will not repeat that behavior (Wellman, 1993). In operant conditioning, the important association is between the response and whatever happens afterward (Rescorla, 1987).

Before describing operant conditioning in more detail, we should clarify the distinction between classical conditioning and operant conditioning. Classical conditioning involves responding to events (specifically, conditioned and unconditioned stimuli) over which we have no control. In contrast, operant conditioning involves responding voluntarily to situations in which our actions determine what happens to us (Domjan, 1989). As you'll recall, the unconditioned responses in classical conditioning are typically involuntary and reflexlike. A loud noise elicits a fear response, and meat powder elicits salivation. In contrast, the responses in operant conditioning

Figure 6.8

Experimental setup for Thorndike's research on operant conditioning.

are spontaneous. You can choose whether to read a textbook, and children can choose whether or not to pick up their toys.

Let us begin by examining two well-known studies that demonstrate operant conditioning. Then we will consider the important components of operant conditioning, new developments in this area, and biological explanations for operant conditioning. Our final section explores some applications.

Influential Research in Operant Conditioning

Thorndike's Puzzle Box Even before Pavlov investigated salivating dogs, the American psychologist Edward L. Thorndike (1898) examined puzzle-solving cats. As Figure 6.8 shows, a hungry cat was placed inside a special cage. When the cat stepped on a special lever, the door would open. The cat could then escape from the box and receive a food reward.

The cats did not show any systematic strategies in trying to escape from the puzzle box. Instead, they would scramble around the cage until they accidentally stepped on the lever. Over time, they reached the goal more quickly, but a typical cat might require 40 trials before it mastered the art of quickly pressing the lever, then escaping through the door. Thorndike explained the acquisition of this behavior by proposing the law of effect. The **law of effect** says that responses resulting in rewarding consequences are learned, whereas responses with punishing consequences are weakened and not learned (Schunk, 1991; Thorndike, 1913). In Thorndike's research, the cats learned to repeat the behavior of pressing the lever because of its rewarding consequences.

Skinner's Conditioning Research B. F. Skinner (1904–1990) was a prolific writer whose first book, *The Behavior of Organisms: An Experimental Analysis*, was published in 1938. His final article was completed the night before he died of leukemia on August 18, 1990 (Skinner, 1990).

Skinner designed a learning chamber to study animal behavior more effectively than Thorndike's puzzle box. The chamber contained either a lever that could be pressed or a disk that could be pecked to receive a food reward. Figure 6.9 shows a pigeon pecking a disk, which allows a food pellet to drop into the tray below. The apparatus also records the number of times the pigeon pecks the disk. This record provides a clear picture of the rate of learning, and it allows researchers to examine how a particular variable affects behavior. For example, they could examine how the rate at which the pigeon receives food (for example, every trial versus every tenth trial) can influence the pecking rate.

Figure 6.9

The experimental setup for Skinner's research on operant conditioning.

Components of Operant Conditioning

Let's explore some important components of operant conditioning. We will begin with an overview of reinforcement and punishment, and then consider other features such as shaping, the discriminative stimulus, and extinction.

Reinforcement and Punishment In an effort to make academic advising more effective, West Chester University has faculty advisers write letters to students to congratulate them on their academic achievements. However, if a student misses a scheduled appointment with an adviser, the adviser posts a "wanted" poster—complete with the student's picture—near the dormitory cafeterias (Dodge, 1992). The advisers hope that the reinforcement will encourage further achievements, and that the punishment will discourage missed appointments.

We have two ways of offering reinforcement and two ways of providing punishment, as illustrated in Table 6.2. As you can see, **positive reinforcement** involves adding something positive to the situation after the correct response has been made. For example, one of my students baby-sat for a 7-year-old named Melissa while her parents went on a two-week business trip. The student praised Melissa warmly for her high math scores, and Melissa ended the semester with her first A in math (Ianazzi, 1992).

In **negative reinforcement,** something negative is taken away or avoided. For example, when you sit down to drive a car and you fasten your seat belt, the unpleasant sound of the seat-belt buzzer is removed. (Think how stunningly ineffective that signal would be if it played a selection by your favorite musician, rather than making that obnoxious noise!) Unfortunately, the term *negative reinforcement* confuses more students than virtually any other phrase in psychology (Kimble, 1992). One problem is that the word *negative* usually implies something bad or punishing, yet negative reinforcement actually ends up being pleasant. It may be helpful to emphasize the upbeat word *reinforcement* in the phrase "negative *reinforcement.*"

Positive and negative reinforcement have similar consequences; they both strengthen or reinforce the behavior they follow and increase the chances that the behavior will be repeated. Thus, positive reinforcement from a baby-sitter should increase the probability of good math performance, and negative reinforcement from the cessation of the seat-belt buzzer should increase the probability of fastening the seat belt.

Now let's consider the two kinds of punishment. **Punishment** can involve adding something negative or taking away something positive (Skinner, 1953). One student recalls a high-school coach who routinely used the "adding something negative" kind of punishment; any baseball player who made an error during practice would be required to stay after and run an extra lap (Bilyk, 1992). Another student vividly remembers how her parents encouraged them with the "taking away something positive" form of punishment: "If you kids aren't ready for bed by 7:30, you can't watch *The Muppet Show!*" (Seith, 1992).

Punishment tends to decrease the probability of the response that it follows, making that response less likely in the future. Thus, the baseball team may end up

An example of negative reinforcement would be if this child were told by a parent, "If you eat all your salad, you won't have to eat your lima beans"—thereby taking away something unpleasant.

TABLE 6.2 Two Kinds of Reinforcement and Two Kinds of Punishment.

	TWO KINDS OF STIMULI	
	Positive	**Negative**
ADD SOMETHING	Positive reinforcement	Punishment
TAKE AWAY SOMETHING	Punishment	Negative reinforcement

Note: A stimulus can be positive or negative, and it can be added or taken away.

making fewer errors, and young children may procrastinate less. Now try Demonstration 6.2 to make certain that you understand the concepts of reinforcement and punishment.

The Punishment Dilemma Let us discuss punishment in more detail. Few aspects of learning theory or child rearing inspire as much controversy as the use of punishment (Axelrod, 1983; Schwartz, 1989). Nevertheless, punishment is frequently used in one form or another. For example, naturalistic observation of elementary and junior-high school teachers has revealed that they yell at students at the rate of one scolding every two minutes (Schwartz, 1984; Van Houten & Doleys, 1983). Here are some of the problems with punishment:

1. Punishment may decrease the frequency of an inappropriate behavior, but it does not automatically increase the frequency of the behavior we want. A father may swat his daughter for saying something rude to the neighbor, and she may utter fewer rude remarks in the future. However, she does not learn what remarks *are* appropriate.

2. Through classical conditioning, fear and anxiety may become associated with the punisher or the environment in which punishment is given. For example, if a teacher yells loudly at a young boy for poor performance, then the teacher, the classroom, and even studying may arouse anxiety (Lieberman, 1990).

3. In order to deliver punishment, the punisher must pay attention to the offender. This attention may in fact be reinforcing—precisely the opposite of the desired effect. A teacher who spends a full two minutes lecturing Spike, the class bully, may find that attention reinforces him for his previous aggressive behavior. In the future, Spike may be even more likely to brutalize his classmates (Serbin & O'Leary, 1975).

4. Punishment provides a model of aggressive behavior, via observational learning (to be discussed in the next section). The person who is being punished learns that aggression is a way to solve problems. The research on child abuse provides a tragic example of how people learn to imitate an aggressive model. This research has noted that many people who were abused as children—though certainly not all—will grow up to be abusing parents ("How Often," 1991; Strauss & Gelles, 1980; Widom, 1989).

DEMONSTRATION 6.2 *Understanding* **Reinforcement and Punishment**

The following quiz tests your mastery of the concepts of reinforcement and punishment.

1. Is negative reinforcement used to increase or decrease behavior?

2. Do people usually look forward to negative reinforcement?

3. Do you think teachers should avoid using negative reinforcement?

4. Which of the following is an example of negative reinforcement? (You can select more than one.) Also, categorize each of the other examples.
   a. Because you talked back, you will have to stay after school.
   b. You will have to stay after school until you clean your desk.

   c. If you do all of your reading assignments without bothering other students, I will not have to call your parents.
   d. Because you scored lower than 80% on this test, you will be required to submit a final paper.
   e. If you submit all of your remaining weekly assignments on time, you may toss out your lowest quiz grade.

5. In terms of its effects on students' behavior, is negative reinforcement more similar to punishment or positive reinforcement?

(The answers are at the end of the chapter.)

Source: Based on Tauber, 1988.

Realistically, however, we are not likely to eliminate punishment. Every parent, teacher, or pet owner occasionally feels that some sort of punishment is necessary. Learning theorist Barry Schwartz (1989) suggests that if you must punish, the delay between response and punishment should be as short as possible. It is not effective to threaten, "You just wait until your father gets home!" Furthermore, punishment should be consistent. It is not effective to punish cheating today but allow the child to cheat without punishment tomorrow.

A better alternative to punishment is to reinforce a response that is incompatible with the undesired response. If you want children to be less aggressive, praise them when they are interacting in a friendly fashion. This technique requires more thought than does punishment, but it is more likely to produce long-term behavior change (Skinner, 1971, 1988a).

I recall learning as an undergraduate student about the virtues of reinforcing incompatible responses, but I was never fully convinced until about 10 years later. We had invited a family from a nearby city to join us for brunch. We had not met the two sons, Roy and Reginald, but we expected a pleasant morning because they were about the same age as our preschool daughters. The doorbell rang, we opened the door, and the older boy greeted us, "I am a lion and I'm going to tear your house apart." Apparently he was speaking for his younger brother as well, because the two proceeded to rip apart books, scatter toys everywhere, and intimidate our daughters. Every few minutes, a parent would mutter, "Stop that, Roy" or "Don't do that, Reginald." The parents may have intended these remarks as punishment, but they were ineffective.

At one point, though, we looked over to see that Roy, Reginald, and our daughters were quietly talking and playing tea party. My husband commented, "My goodness, you are all playing so nicely together now! That's wonderful!" Roy and Reginald looked up and their jaws dropped with astonishment. Their mother remarked, "They're not used to praise." Now I am not going to claim that their behavior during the rest of the morning qualified them for the Children of the Month Award, but they were noticeably nicer for the rest of the visit. They had been reinforced for pleasant social interactions, and these responses are incompatible with antisocial behavior.

Shaping Imagine a 6-year-old boy learning to swim. His teacher has asked him to try the basic crawl for the first time. The boy's legs are bent, his arms are awkward, and his head protrudes too far out of the water. Still, the teacher shouts an encouraging, "Good, keep it up." By the end of the lesson, the teacher would require a more refined technique before praising the swimmer. If the boy later trains for the swim team, he would have to be much better before earning reinforcement. Teachers, parents, and other people who want to encourage a particular behavior are likely to use shaping. **Shaping** is the systematic reinforcement of gradual improvements toward the desired behavior.

Shaping relies on the fact that both humans and animals show a great deal of variability in their behavior (Epstein, 1991). During shaping, the teacher or the experimenter reinforces only the responses that are closer and closer to the desired goal.

Shaping is a valuable tool because it encourages the learner to acquire a new behavior relatively quickly. A rat in a learning chamber does not spontaneously stroll over to the lever, rise up on its hind paws, and deftly press the lever . . . on the first try. Instead, the experimenter first delivers a food reinforcement when the rat is in the general vicinity of the lever. Then the criterion is made more strict—to earn the food, the rat must lift its paw in the vicinity of the lever. Ultimately, the experimenter reinforces only those responses in which the rat completely depresses the lever (see Figure 6.10). Thus, both the swimmer and the lever-pressing rat are reinforced for gradual improvements in performance.

Schedules of Reinforcement Think about how operant learning applies to your own life. How often do you receive reinforcement for good behavior or correct responses? Unless you are a very fortunate person, your answer is, "Not very often."

Figure 6.10

At the end of shaping, the rat must completely depress the lever with its paw in order to receive the pellet of food.

TABLE 6.3	Four Common Partial Reinforcement Schedules		
		REINFORCEMENT DEPENDS UPON	
		Number of Responses	**Passage of Time**
REINFORCEMENT IS	**Regular**	Fixed Ratio	Fixed Interval
	Irregular	Variable Ratio	Variable Interval

In operant learning, the term **continuous reinforcement schedule** applies to situations in which the subject is reinforced on every correct trial. Candy and beverage machines usually reinforce the user according to a continuous reinforcement schedule. Every time you insert the appropriate coins, you should be rewarded by receiving food or drink. However, in our daily lives, other humans rarely provide continuous reinforcement for appropriate behavior.

We are much more likely in our daily lives to receive a **partial reinforcement schedule** (or intermittent reinforcement schedule), in which reinforcement is provided only part of the time. Let's examine four kinds of partial reinforcement, which are listed in Table 6.3. In each case, the person or the animal needs to make the appropriate response before reinforcement can be delivered.

1. In a **fixed-ratio schedule,** reinforcement is given after a fixed number of responses have been made. For example, Dee's Doughnut Shop in Canandaigua, New York, keeps a tally of its patrons' doughnut purchases. After I accumulate 12 tally marks, I will be rewarded with a dozen free doughnuts.

2. In a **fixed-interval schedule,** reinforcement is given for the first correct response made after the specified period of time has passed. For example, many people receive a paycheck every two weeks when they arrive at work.

3. In a **variable-ratio schedule,** reinforcement is given after a varying number of responses have been made. For example, consider a rat pressing a bar for a food pellet, which it receives—on the average—every 5 bar presses. The first pellet may come after 2 presses, the next after 7 presses, and the next after 6, averaging out to 1 pellet for each 5 responses:

$$\left(\frac{2 + 7 + 6}{3} = 5 \right)$$

However, unlike in the fixed-ratio schedule, the rat never knows exactly when the pellet is coming. Similarly, gamblers who play the slot machines are placed on a variable-ratio schedule, though they usually are not reinforced at the average rate of every fifth trial!

4. In a **variable-interval schedule,** reinforcement is given for the first response you make after a varying period of time has passed. For example, suppose you have a friend whose telephone is often busy. When you want to reach him, you typically dial the number every few minutes until you are successful. Sometimes you have a 20-minute wait, but sometimes you are successful after just 2 minutes.

The different schedules of reinforcement produce different response patterns. For instance, your response rate will be higher with ratio schedules, because reinforcement is linked to the number of responses. Furthermore, variable schedules produce a steadier rate of responding. Wouldn't you study more regularly if you did not know which day your professor would give a weekly quiz than if you could expect a quiz every Friday?

Secondary Reinforcers   When researchers reinforce a hungry rat with a pellet of food for pressing a lever, they are delivering a primary reinforcer. A **primary reinforcer** is a reinforcer that can satisfy a basic biological need, most likely food or

Gambling is a good example of a variable-ratio schedule of reinforcement. Research has shown that many compulsive gamblers experienced one big win at some point in their early gambling.

water. Most human behavior, however, is controlled by **secondary reinforcers,** which are reinforcers that do not satisfy a basic biological need but acquire their rewarding power by association with another established reinforcer.

For example, many learning chambers are designed so that they make a clicking noise as they release a pellet of food. The animal associates that click with the primary reinforcer, food. Soon, the clicking sound serves as a secondary reinforcer. Try to think of the things that are most reinforcing to you—perhaps money, praise from someone you admire, or a good grade. It is hard to argue that a good grade satisfies a basic biological need. Instead, it is a secondary reinforcer.

For this child, winning an award serves as a secondary reinforcer.

The Discriminative Stimulus We have been discussing how and when reinforcement can be delivered in an operant conditioning study. During learning, the stimuli associated with the learning environment become associated with the relationship between the stimulus and that reinforcement. For example, a pigeon in a learning chamber may learn that only when a yellow button is lit up (the stimulus) will its pecking (response) lead to food (reinforcement). If the button is not lit up, the pigeon could peck incessantly without producing a morsel of food. In this example, the yellow button is serving as a discriminative stimulus. A **discriminative stimulus** is a stimulus signaling that a response will be reinforced.

Ellen Reese (1986) provides an example from human behavior. In our culture, the behavior of dishwashing leads to social reinforcement. If you wash dishes at a friend's house, you usually receive praise. However, you would not be praised if you removed *clean* dishes from the cabinet and washed them. Your dishwashing behavior—no matter how magnificent—would not be reinforced. Dishwashing leads to reinforcement only in the presence of *dirty* dishes, because dirty dishes in this example serve as the discriminative stimulus. Similarly, you learn that shouting at the top of your lungs is reinforced when the discriminative stimulus is a political rally, but not a funeral or an elegant restaurant.

Extinction You know the term *extinction* from classical conditioning. When the conditioned stimulus is presented repeatedly without the unconditioned stimulus, the conditioned response gradually weakens and disappears, producing extinction. In operant conditioning, extinction occurs when an organism repeatedly makes a response without reinforcement. You are certainly familiar with extinction if you have ever inserted coins into a pay phone and received no dial tone. After two or three unsuccessful attempts, any sane person *should* show extinction!

An important principle of learning is that both people and animals show rapid extinction if they have previously received continuous reinforcement, rather than partial reinforcement. Suppose you have a car that has always started reliably. For two years now, you have turned the key in the ignition, and 100% of the time you have been reinforced by the comforting purr of the motor. With this continuous reinforcement schedule, you will extinguish very quickly if you turn the key several times one morning and discover no reinforcing purr. In contrast, suppose you have a car that occasionally starts on the first turn of the key, but it often does not start until two, three, or even six attempts. With this partial reinforcement schedule, you will resist extinction. You are likely to keep turning that key, praying for reinforcement, and you are likely to wear out the battery before you extinguish. Figure 6.11 compares the extinction patterns under continuous reinforcement versus partial reinforcement.

The principle of slow extinction with partial reinforcement helps us understand the extraordinary persistence of some individuals. Maybe an uncle of yours keeps trying out for a part in the local theater productions because once—seven years ago—he was rewarded with a small part. Musicians, athletes, and painters all keep working, lured by the hope that the next attempt may bring them reinforcement. Or consider a toddler in her crib whose parents sometimes (but not always) let her out of bed at night when she has cried for a long time. She is likely to keep crying, lured by the hope that the next heart-wrenching sob may win her freedom.

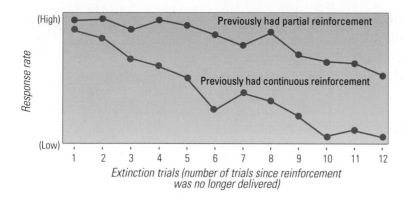

Figure 6.11

During extinction, the response rate drops much more rapidly when animals have previously had continuous reinforcement than when they have had partial reinforcement (typical results).

A Detailed Example of Operant Conditioning Let us review these components of operant conditioning by applying them to an example. Imagine that you are a fourth-grade student who has decided to play the clarinet in the school band. Your band teacher may give you positive reinforcement for producing a particular note on your instrument ("That's very good!") or negative reinforcement ("You've done your scales right this time, so you won't have to do any more scales this morning."). If you do not practice at home, your parents may deliver punishment of the "adding something negative" variety ("Why don't you ever practice? Do you think we have money to throw away on a clarinet?"). Alternatively, they may use punishment of the "taking away something positive" variety ("You won't get your allowance this week.").

Skilled music teachers (and skilled parents) emphasize reinforcement more than punishment. A good teacher would praise you for improvement in tone, rhythm, and accuracy. Punishment for improper techniques or wrong notes should be used sparingly and should be delivered soon after the mistake has been made.

This teacher would also use shaping. A beginning student would receive praise for producing even the most primitive squawk, but a few days later would be required to produce a more decent tone. By high school, however, this same student would have to play a passable rendition of a Mozart clarinet concerto to win reinforcement.

Music teachers cannot use continuous reinforcement, praising their students for every correct note or every correct passage. Instead, they use some kind of partial reinforcement, most likely variable ratio. However, some teachers may reinforce half of the responses, on the average, whereas others might reinforce an average of only once every 12th lesson.

The notes and the notations in the student's music book would serve as discriminative stimuli. The student receives praise for playing a perfect B flat, only when a B flat is written on the page. A spectacular loud fortissimo wins no smiles if the passage is marked pianissimo.

It is hard to imagine how primary reinforcers could be associated with clarinet playing. Would a parent withhold food when a child does not practice? In contrast, the secondary reinforcers are numerous: receiving praise from the teacher, parents, and Uncle Len; receiving a high rating in solo competitions; being selected as first chair of the first clarinet section; and earning the "Outstanding Music Student" award at the end of the year. However, the critical secondary reinforcement comes from the student listening and hearing that the playing sounds appropriate. In fact, the major task of a music teacher is to encourage students to identify how the music should sound. Indeed, the teacher must turn good sound into a powerful secondary reinforcer (Domjan, 1989).

Unfortunately, however, many students experience extinction. An incompetent teacher may not provide reinforcement, parents may not deliver praise, or the student may no longer experience reinforcement in the form of self-satisfaction. Other, different behaviors—perhaps playing football or being a cheerleader—may win more social reinforcement from other students. Without any reinforcement, the student is not likely to continue playing the instrument.

How would you use the principles of learning theory to explain the performance of this young violin player?

Recent Developments in Operant Conditioning

In the first part of the chapter, we saw that major new developments in classical conditioning focus on the relationship between the conditioned stimulus and the unconditioned stimulus. In operant conditioning, the major new developments concern the role of the discriminative stimulus, the nature of reinforcement, and the learning abilities of animals.

The Role of the Discriminative Stimulus Early theories of operant conditioning argued that during learning, an association forms between the discriminative stimulus and the response. Later theories suggested that the critical association is between the stimulus and the reinforcement. However, consistent with our theme of complexity, the current view is that the discriminative stimulus becomes associated with the relationship between the response and the reinforcement—rather than with either of them individually (Colwill & Rescorla, 1990; Rescorla, 1991; Roitblat & von Fersen, 1992). According to this view, the discriminative stimulus sets the occasion upon which the response produces the reinforcement. For example, a pile of dirty dishes sets the occasion for which dishwashing will produce praise.

The Nature of Reinforcement Early theories of operant conditioning argued that reinforcement worked for physiological reasons. A rat, deprived of food, pressed a lever to deliver pellets of food. The food reduced its hunger drive, "stamping in" the behavior of pressing the lever (Domjan, 1993).

In recent decades, however, ideas about reinforcement have changed. Many theorists now propose that reinforcement's major function is to reorganize behavior. In an important experiment, Staddon and Simmelhag (1971) delivered a food reinforcer to pigeons every 15 seconds, regardless of their behavior. Early in the training sessions, these researchers observed a wide variety of behaviors; the pigeons bobbed their heads and flapped their wings, apparently connecting these behaviors with the reinforcement. However, after 20 sessions, the pigeons were most often seen pecking at the wall near the food dispenser at the time the reinforcement was to be delivered. Thus, organisms initially show variability, but reinforcement limits this variability. With further experience, both animals and people select behaviors that seem to increase their chances for success (Domjan, 1987).

Let us return to the example of the hard-to-start car to see how reinforcement reorganizes behavior. Suppose that you slide into the car seat, cross your fingers, sit up straight, and jiggle the key in the ignition before turning the key, and it starts. On future trials, you are most likely to repeat the behavior associated with the ignition—jiggling the key—rather than crossing your fingers or sitting up straight, even if none of the behaviors actually help start the car (Domjan & Burkhard, 1986). In summary, current theorists propose that reinforcement reorganizes behavior, changing the actions we choose to do.

Operant Conditioning Abilities of Animals Even before Charles Darwin proposed his theory of evolution, scientists wondered about the limits of animal intelligence. Darwin's theory prompted them to study animal learning as a way of tracing the roots of human intelligence (Domjan, 1987). Many researchers have tried to determine the upper limits of animals' intelligence. For example, in Chapter 9 we discuss the moderate success of researchers who have taught chimpanzees to communicate using sign language and other symbolic languages. Some have also reported the impressive abilities of insects, birds, and other animals to appreciate time, number, spatial relationships, and the use of tools (e.g., Gallistel, 1990; Griffin, 1991).

Still other researchers have demonstrated that animals can acquire subtle concepts (Herrnstein, 1984; Roitblat, 1987). Consider a study in which pigeons acquired the concept of *tree* by watching a series of slides (Herrnstein et al., 1976). About half of the slides were pictures of trees—sometimes a part of a tree, sometimes one tree, and sometimes a forest. When a picture of a tree was presented, the pigeon could peck at a key and receive a food pellet. Pecking when the other pictures were present

earned no pellet. After a number of training sessions, a new set of pictures was presented as a test. The pigeons were highly accurate in discriminating trees from non-trees (see Figure 6.12). This kind of achievement makes us wonder whether the term "birdbrain" is really more a compliment than an insult!

Other researchers, however, have emphasized the limits of animal learning. That is, animals may seem smart in learning some tasks that are compatible with their natural abilities and slow-witted on other tasks that do not match these natural abilities (Gould & Marler, 1987). Furthermore, according to the **instinctive drift principle,** when an animal is engaged in operant conditioning, its behavior will drift in the direction of instinctive behaviors related to the task it is learning (Breland & Breland, 1961; Gardner & Gardner, 1988).

For example, Keller and Marian Breland trained about 6,000 animals belonging to 38 species, including animals as exotic as reindeer, porpoises, and whales. In one case, they began to train a raccoon to pick up a single coin and to deposit that coin in a piggy bank. This kind of animal act might be interesting at a zoo or other tourist attraction. However, the Brelands found that the raccoon refused to let go of the coin. Instead, it would clutch it firmly or rub coins together for several minutes in a miserly fashion that resembled Mr. Scrooge, rather than a thrifty piggy-bank user. Pigs also refused to learn how to "save money." Instead, they would drop the money on the way to the "bank," then root around for it, toss it up in the air, and drop it again. Both species showed instinctive drift, because raccoons instinctively manipulate objects, as Figure 6.13 illustrates, and pigs instinctively root around for food. Current learning theorists acknowledge that these behaviors must be incorporated into any contemporary theory:

> Perhaps the most important discovery has been that species-specific, obligatory behaviors are not annoying artifacts, to be eliminated from experiments and forgotten in theories: they are instead the foundation of the learning process. (Gardner & Gardner, 1988, p. 447)

Biological Components of Operant Conditioning

Researchers who examine the biological components of learning acknowledge that classical conditioning is easier to study than operant conditioning (Thompson & Donegan, 1986). However, both kinds of learning are similar in that different neural structures seem to be involved for different kinds of learning. For example, when the operant task requires mastering a spatial map such as a maze, the parietal cortex is involved. (See Figure 3.17 for the location of the parietal lobe in humans.) However, when the operant task emphasizes a sequence of events (e.g., the components must be performed in a certain order), then part of the frontal region of the cortex is involved.

Both classical conditioning and operant conditioning involve some part of the limbic system. However, classical conditioning involves the hippocampus—at least on some tasks—and operant conditioning makes more use of the amygdala (White & Milner, 1992). (See Figure 3.15 for the location of the amygdala in humans.) Consider this research by Gaffan and Harrison (1987). Monkeys had been trained to discriminate

Figure 6.12

The research of R. J. Herrnstein shows that pigeons can distinguish a variety of tree photos from pictures of irrelevant items.

Figure 6.13

Because raccoons instinctively handle objects, it is difficult to teach them to perform a trick in which they must release the objects; this is an example of instinctive drift.

between visual stimuli, receiving a tone as secondary reinforcement. (The tone had previously been associated with a food reward.) After lesions were made in the amygdala, the animals could no longer perform accurately.

Additional research has provided extensive evidence that epinephrine is the relevant neurotransmitter in the amygdala (McGaugh, 1989). Other research demonstrating the importance of epinephrine shows that memory for an operant response is enhanced by low to moderate doses of epinephrine and impaired by higher doses (McGaugh & Gold, 1988). In summary, then, the region of the cortex that is involved in operant conditioning depends upon the specific nature of the task. Within the limbic system, however, the amygdala is a "key player," most likely involving the actions of epinephrine.

Applications of Operant Conditioning

Operant conditioning has produced some important practical applications. Two of these are computer-assisted instruction and behavior modification.

Computer-Assisted Instruction In **computer-assisted instruction (CAI),** students learn at their own rate, using computers that are programmed to deliver individualized instruction. Information is presented in small chunks, and students master a relatively easy chunk before proceeding to a somewhat more difficult topic. Students answer questions and receive immediate feedback about whether each response is correct. Furthermore, fast learners can complete the lessons at a more rapid rate, rather than experiencing boredom as they wait for the rest of the class to master a concept. Programs can also be designed to be interactive, presenting information and review if a student's answers indicate weakness in a particular area. Computers can also personalize instruction. For example, the math performance of elementary school children soared when each child's own name was mentioned in a problem (Anand & Ross, 1987).

B. F. Skinner enthusiastically supported the way CAI could apply operant learning principles, and many studies have suggested that CAI is more successful than traditional classroom methods (Skinner, 1987, 1988b). However, some of the research is not carefully controlled. As you know from Chapter 2, a group of children using CAI must be compared with an equivalent group using traditional methods. Also, the experiment (or quasi-experiment) must provide some additional experience for the control group to balance the novelty of CAI instruction (Schunk, 1991). In fact, one review of the research concluded that CAI is *not* consistently more effective than traditional classroom teaching—when the studies were appropriately controlled (Clark & Salomon, 1986).

Behavior Modification The most popular application of operant learning is **behavior modification,** which is the systematic use of techniques from learning theory to change human behavior. Behavior modification can be used in treating problems as diverse as drug addictions, depression, child abuse, and pain management (Bellack et al., 1990). Behavior modification has also been used to help mentally retarded individuals, especially with language and social skills (Matson, 1990; Whitman et al., 1990).

Behavior modification programs include several important steps (Martin & Pear, 1992; Michael, 1985):

1. Define the problems in behavioral terms that are concrete. For example, a teacher who wants to decrease a child's aggressiveness may focus on his hitting, kicking, and biting. The definition emphasizes actions rather than thoughts or wishes. Do you want to increase a certain behavior or decrease it?

2. Decide how to measure the relevant behavior in a consistent manner. For example, if you have decided that you want to increase the amount of time you spend studying, you might measure that behavior in terms of hours per day.

3. Take a **baseline measure,** or the response rate before you begin the behavior modification program.

Computer-assisted instruction can use cartoons and other visual aids to help children learn spelling, arithmetic, and other academic subjects.

4. Figure out reinforcers or punishers for the target behavior, and carry out the program, still measuring the response rate.

5. If the program is going well, continue. If it is not, try changing the reinforcer or punisher. You may find, for example, that you initially chose an inappropriate reinforcer. Martin and Pear (1992) describe how a retarded child rejected the candy they had originally selected as a reinforcer, but she responded well when the reinforcer consisted of playing briefly with a toy purse.

In a behavior modification program in an industrial setting, praise can act as a reinforcer.

An important concept in behavior modification is called a token economy. In a **token economy,** good behavior is quickly reinforced by a symbol or token, and these tokens can be accumulated and exchanged for a reinforcer (Sulzer-Azaroff & Mayer, 1991). For example, a sixth-grade teacher applied a token economy by handing out tokens every time a student finished an assignment. Students wrote their names on the tokens, which served as lottery tickets for prizes such as a small pocket radio. Her students showed a dramatic improvement in the number of assignments they completed (Skinner, 1988b).

Behavior modification has been used in business as well as in education. Programs have been implemented to improve productivity, worker safety, and management-employee relations, as well as to reduce shoplifting, tardiness, and absenteeism (Martin & Pear, 1992). Chapter 16 also examines how behavior therapy can be used for psychological disorders.

Now that you have been introduced to the basic principles of operant conditioning and behavior modification, try Demonstration 6.3.

SECTION SUMMARY

OPERANT CONDITIONING

- Operant conditioning involves learning to make a response because it produces a rewarding effect and learning not to make a response because it produces a punishing effect.

- Two important areas of operant conditioning research involved cats learning how to escape from a puzzle box (Thorndike) and animals pressing a lever or a disk to receive a food reward (Skinner).

- Psychologists distinguish among positive reinforcement, negative reinforcement, and punishment; in general, reinforcing a response that is incompatible with an undesired response is more effective than administering punishment.

DEMONSTRATION 6.3 Applying the Principles of Behavior Modification

Identify one specific behavior of yours that you would like to change. Perhaps you would like to spend more time studying a particular course, or you wish you snacked less between meals, or you think you should make fewer sarcastic comments. Select a behavior that occurs (or should occur) several times each day. Following Michael's (1985) outline of behavior modification,

1. Define the problem in terms of concrete behavioral terms that are specific, rather than general.

2. Determine how you will measure this behavior consistently. Construct a tally sheet that you can carry with you to record the number of responses made each day.

3. For 1 week, take a baseline measure before you begin with rewards.

4. Identify an appealing reward. (We will avoid punishment and negative reinforcement for the purposes of this demonstration.) The reward might be something small you can enjoy often, or something large, for which you will accumulate tokens (e.g., check marks) over a period of time. Begin the program and record your behavior for 2 weeks.

5. If the program is going well, continue. (You may wish to alter the schedule of reinforcement, however.) If it is not going well, reassess and try to find a more attractive reward.

- Other important components of operant conditioning are shaping, schedules of reinforcement, the discriminative stimulus, secondary reinforcers, and extinction.

- New developments in operant conditioning include the view that the discriminative stimulus is associated with the relationship between the response and the reinforcement, that reinforcement reorganizes behavior, and that animals have impressive learning capacity—though it may be limited by instinctive drift.

- Operant conditioning has been applied in computer-assisted instruction and in behavior modification.

OBSERVATIONAL LEARNING

So far we have seen how classical and operant conditioning can explain how we acquire fears, salivary responses, eyeblinks, motor responses, better performance in school and at work, and a wide variety of other skills. However, many of your daily actions cannot be explained by even the broadest interpretation of conditioning approaches. Classical and operant conditioning are especially limited in accounting for the rapid acquisition of *new* behaviors (Schunk, 1991).

Consider, for example, your very first attempt at driving. You knew exactly where to insert the key and exactly where to place your hands on the steering wheel. Or consider how someone learns to split firewood with an ax; how can this fairly complex sequence of actions be explained by a trial-and-error approach? Of course, operant conditioning is helpful in explaining how you perfect your skills and how you maintain them. However, neither classical conditioning nor operant conditioning can account for the speed and accuracy with which you acquire a behavior that you have never previously attempted.

To account for numerous human accomplishments—especially those a person performs for the first time—we need to consider the third major kind of learning: observational learning. In **observational learning,** we acquire new behaviors by watching and imitating the behavior of others. Observational learning is also known as **modeling,** because the learner imitates a model. It is also called **social learning,** because learning occurs in a social situation by watching other people.

Let us begin our discussion of observational learning by considering some of the important early research. Next, the "In Depth" section discusses media violence and aggression. We end with a brief overview of applications of observational learning.

Influential Research in Observational Learning

Bandura's Research In the most widely cited research in observational learning, children watched adults as they behaved aggressively with a large inflated toy doll. Throughout a series of studies, Albert Bandura and his colleagues examined whether the children would imitate the adult models (Bandura et al., 1961, 1963). In a typical session, a nursery school child works busily on a picture. Then an adult in a different part of the room approaches a Bobo doll, an inflatable clownlike toy that is weighted on the bottom so that it pops back up whenever it is knocked down. For about 10 minutes, this adult brutalizes Bobo, hitting it with a hammer, knocking it down, and sitting on it. The adult accompanies these aggressive actions with remarks such as, "Kick him" and "Sock him in the nose."

The child is then led into a second room, filled with numerous enticing toys. However, the child is told that the toys are being saved for other children, a comment guaranteed to arouse frustration. Finally, the child is brought to a third room, containing several toys and—you guessed it—a Bobo doll. Bandura and his colleagues watched through hidden windows and noted the children's behavior.

The children who had been exposed to the violent model were likely to beat up on Bobo, even repeating the same phrases and mimicking the identical aggressive actions. In contrast, other children who had not observed a violent adult model were much less likely to treat Bobo aggressively. Children showed this observational learning, whether they directly observed the aggressive adult or viewed the aggression in a film. Notice that observational learning is involved because these particular aggressive behaviors were performed for the first time.

Later Research Bandura's original studies demonstrated that children would show observational learning, even when neither the adult nor the child received reinforcement. Later research, often using the same kind of Bobo doll, showed that the likelihood of imitation is influenced by whether the adult model is rewarded or punished for being aggressive.

In a representative study, Mary Rosekrans and Willard Hartup (1967) had preschool children watch an adult female model playing with toys. She sometimes beat the Bobo doll with a hammer, and she also poked a fork into handmade clay figures. As in earlier research, she made hostile comments such as, "Wham, bam, I'll knock your head off" and "Punch him, punch him, punch his legs full of holes." These aggressive actions were followed by one of two reactions from another adult: (1) In the reinforcement condition, the adult praised the aggressive model with remarks such as "Good for you! I guess you really fixed him that time." (2) In the punishment condition, the adult scolded the model with remarks such as, "Now look what you've done, you've ruined it." After watching the model's aggressive actions and seeing her behavior either reinforced or punished, the children in the two conditions were then allowed to play with the same toys. A third group of children, who had not seen an aggressive model, also played with the toys.

As Figure 6.14 shows, those who had watched an aggressive model being reinforced were much more aggressive than children in the other two groups. Notice, then, that children do not blindly imitate a model's actions. Instead, they are likely to mimic these actions most carefully only when the model receives praise and approval from others.

Components of Observational Learning

We have seen that people can acquire certain behaviors even without reinforcement. However, we have also seen that reinforcement of the model influences the likelihood that an observer will perform a certain behavior. Let us now discuss some additional useful terminology in observational learning.

An important concept in observational learning is **vicarious reinforcement,** which occurs when the model receives reinforcement. (You may be familiar with the concept of vicarious pleasure, which occurs when a person derives pleasure from someone else's happiness.) Thus, when the children saw the adult receive praise for poking the clay figure, they themselves experienced vicarious reinforcement. Similarly, **vicarious punishment** occurs when the model receives punishment (Bandura, 1986).

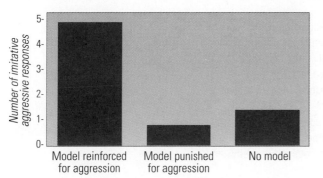

Figure 6.14

Imitative aggressive responses, as a function of whether observers had seen the model being reinforced or punished or had seen no model. (Based on data from Rosekrans & Hartup, 1967)

Bandura also stresses that people can experience **intrinsic reinforcement,** an internalized sense of satisfaction at performing well. You may be singing in the shower, knowing that your voice cannot be heard, and feel proud of your mellow tone on a high note. Alternatively, **intrinsic punishment** occurs when you scold yourself for poor performance. If you receive a low score on a section of the study guide for this chapter, you are likely to experience intrinsic punishment, even though no one else will see your score.

Bandura's recent additions to observational learning theory reflect the current emphasis on cognitive psychology (Bandura, 1986). In particular, he stresses that a learner observing a model does *not* acquire a perfectly accurate, exact replica of the model's behavior. Instead, a child who watches an adult attacking a Bobo doll acquires a **schema** (pronounced "*skee*-muh") or generalized idea that captures the important components, but not every exact detail. The child's performance will contain many important components but will not be an exact duplicate of every gesture or comment made by the adult. In the next chapter, we discuss further implications of schemas in memory.

Figure 6.15
This young boy and girl are likely to have acquired their body language by observational learning.

Psychologists believe that observational learning theory is particularly effective in explaining social behavior. For example, children may learn many gender stereotyped behaviors by imitating models, either people they know or characters from television programs or movies (Matlin, 1993a; Mischel, 1966). For example, a young girl may learn that she is supposed to act helpless in an emergency. I recall watching a Saturday morning cartoon in which the only female was a mother who fainted during an interplanetary crisis. (Her preteen son came to the rescue and saved the universe.)

Vicarious reinforcement is also useful in explaining social behavior. For instance, a young boy may watch a male high-school student receiving admiring smiles and cheers for hitting another student who seemed to be taunting him. A junior-high girl may experience intrinsic reinforcement as she practices a demure, stereotypical "feminine" smile in the mirror. Observational learning helps account for the difference in body language shown by the girl and the boy in Figure 6.15. However, one of the most important examples of observational learning involves the media.

IN DEPTH: Media Violence and Observational Learning

The early research on observational learning showed that children become more aggressive after watching a violent model. In a popular magazine, Bandura (1963) pointed out that parents were unwittingly exposing their children to violent models on television.

Media violence remains a major problem in the 1990s. According to some estimates, in an average year the American child typically sees about 1,000 murders, rapes, or assaults on television. This child also sees nearly 20,000 commercials each year, often featuring toys that encourage further aggression (Strasburger, 1991). Even preschoolers watch more than 27 hours of television per week (Centerwall, 1992). Television is likely to be the major educational tool for most American children. By the time they graduate from high school, teenagers have usually spent 15,000 to 18,000 hours in front of the TV set, in contrast to 12,000 hours in classroom instruction (Strasburger, 1991).

For the last three decades, researchers have examined how television violence influences viewers' behavior. Consistent with a theme of our book, the picture that emerges is complicated. As this section illustrates, exposure to violent media does not inevitably cause viewers to become aggressive, but it does make aggression more likely in certain situations. Furthermore, observational learning is not the only mechanism that encourages a relationship between television violence and aggressive behavior.

Our examination of the relationship between media violence and aggression is especially useful because we can compare several research methods: the experiment, the quasi-experiment, and the correlational technique. We introduced these research methods in Chapter 2, and now we will review them.

The Experimental Method In the **experimental method,** the researchers manipulate the independent variable to determine its effects on the dependent variable, that is, the behavior of the participants in the experiment. In research on television violence, the independent variable is typically the kind of television show that people watch or the amount of violent television they watch. The dependent variable is some measure of their aggressive behavior or aggressive tendencies.

Let's consider a representative study by Wendy Josephson (1987), who examined not only the effects of violent television, but also the effects of a cue reminding children about the violent program they had viewed. She studied second- and third-grade boys, who were placed in groups of six children; the groups were randomly assigned to conditions. Children in the nonviolence control group saw a 14-minute segment of a television program about a boys' bike-racing team. Children in the violence condition saw a 14-minute segment of a television program that began with the brutal killing of a police officer by a group of snipers and ended with all the snipers either dead or unconscious. (These two segments differed in violence, but not in excitement or interest level, as established by rating scales and physiological measures.) Finally, children in the violence-plus-cue condition saw this same violent show, but they were also shown a reminder-cue (a walkie-talkie, similar to one in the violent show) just before the dependent variable was measured.

The dependent variable in Josephson's study was the number of aggressive behaviors each group of six made during a subsequent game of floor hockey. These behaviors included hitting another boy with a hockey stick, pulling his hair, and calling him names.

Figure 6.16 shows the average number of aggressive behaviors for each of the three conditions during the nine minutes of the floor hockey game. As you can see, aggression was relatively low for the boys who had seen the nonviolent TV segment, and it was significantly higher for those who had seen the violent TV segment. However, aggression was even higher for those who had seen the violent TV segment and then were reminded about it because they were shown a walkie-talkie just before the game began.

Naturally, many of the experiments on media violence do not show such dramatic effects. Wendy Wood and her colleagues (1991) conducted a meta-analysis on the experiments that had examined this question. (As Chapter 2 described, a **meta-analysis** is a systematic statistical method for synthesizing the results from numerous studies on a given topic.) Combining the results of 28 experiments, Wood and her coauthors found that exposure to media violence does increase aggression in children and adolescents. The strength of the effect is in the small to moderate range.

The advantage of the experimental method, which was used in Josephson's (1987) study as well as in the 27 other experiments included in the meta-analysis, is that it allows the

Children watch violent programs on television, and they also see ads for toys that encourage even more violence, such as this toy in which the dummies' body parts fly off when the car crashes.

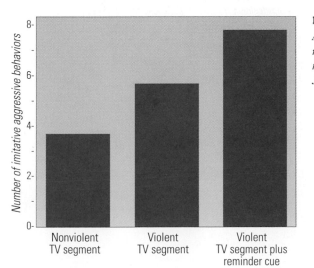

Figure 6.16

Average number of aggressive behaviors made by each group of 6 boys, as a function of condition. (Based on Josephson, 1987)

experimenter to control the study rigorously. For example, Josephson was able to assign the children to the three groups on a random basis. She was also able to control the nature of the TV programs. Finally, the children's aggression could be operationally defined and measured in a well-controlled setting, free from the kinds of distractions and complications that abound in a more naturalistic setting.

However, the disadvantage of the experimental method is that we do not know whether we can generalize from the clean results obtained in a well-controlled setting to the messiness of real-life settings. For this reason, researchers also need to conduct quasi-experiments and correlational research.

The Quasi-Experimental Method In a **quasi-experiment,** the researchers cannot randomly assign participants to different groups. Instead, they locate a situation in which groups already exist that differ substantially from each other. For example, Joy, Kimball, and Zabrack (1986) located a town in a remote part of Canada that had no television prior to 1974, when one station was made available. This town therefore experienced a *change* in television-viewing patterns. In contrast, a second town had one station available both before and after 1974. A third town had four stations available both before and after 1974. Notice that these last two towns did not experience a change in television-viewing patterns.

Figure 6.17 shows the increase in the number of physically aggressive responses, between 1973 and 1974, made by children in the three towns. When television was introduced to children in the first town, they showed a large increase in aggression. In contrast, children in the other two towns experienced no change in television availability during that same time period, and they did not dramatically change their aggressive behavior.

This quasi-experiment shows us that introducing television to a community might have a real-life impact on the children's aggressive tendencies. However, keep in mind that the experimenters did not randomly assign the children to the three community groups, and therefore the three groups may have differed substantially to begin with. These researchers discovered from census figures that the towns were identical in population size and income level, but they might have differed in some characteristics not measurable in a census. For instance, children in the remote community may have been more likely to have a "frontier attitude." They may have welcomed adventures and aggressive confrontations. It is possible (though we cannot know for sure) that they were more responsive to aggression than children in the less rural communities. We do not know whether children in these other, more typical communities would have responded to increased availability of television by becoming more aggressive.

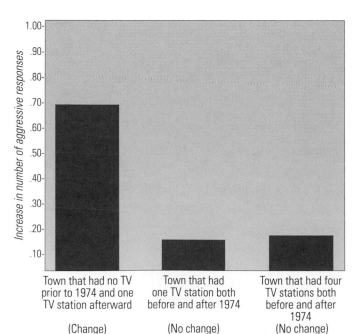

Figure 6.17

The increase in the number of aggressive responses, as a function of change in television availability. (Based on Joy et al., 1986)

Correlational Research **Correlational research** attempts to determine whether two variables are related. As in a quasi-experiment, researchers gather data in real-life settings. In correlational research, they do not actively manipulate any variable. Many studies have shown that television-viewing patterns and aggressive behavior are significantly correlated (e.g., Greenberg, 1975; Huesmann, 1986; Singer & Singer, 1981). In general, these correlations are moderate, rather than strong (Condry, 1989; Eron & Huesmann, 1987; Friedrich-Cofer & Huston, 1986). We would not expect the correlations to be strong, because so many factors other than media viewing could influence aggressive behavior (Wood et al., 1991).

Correlational research presents several major problems. One problem is that the researchers cannot control the independent variable. In the case of research on media violence, researchers cannot control what programs viewers watch and the conditions under which they watch these programs (Condry, 1989).

A second problem was discussed in Chapter 2: Some "third variable" may be responsible for the apparent relationship between two variables. In the example we are considering, the amount of violent television a child watches is correlated with his or her aggressive behavior. However, that relationship may really be traceable to a third variable, the characteristics of the child's parents. Specifically, the kind of parents who prohibit their children from watching violent TV shows are also likely to discourage aggressive behavior in their children. Fortunately, statistical techniques can be used to determine whether a correlation between television-viewing patterns and aggressive behavior still exists when we have taken some of these possible "third variables" into account. In general, the studies show that the correlation does remain significant (e.g., Liebert & Sprafkin, 1988; McLeod et al., 1972; Singer et al., 1984).

A third major problem with correlational studies is known as the "directionality problem." As Chapter 2 discussed, in a correlation we do not know whether Variable A caused Variable B or whether Variable B caused Variable A. In fact, *both* explanations could apply to the media violence issue:

1. Television violence causes aggressive behavior.
2. Aggressive behavior causes viewing of television violence. (For example, children who are already aggressive may like to watch violent programs, whereas less aggressive children prefer nonviolent programs.)

Extensive research on television violence and aggression in five different countries suggests that both of these explanations of the correlation are correct. Once again, psychological processes require complex explanations. L. Rowell Huesmann and Leonard Eron (1986) arranged for children between the ages of 6 and 11 to be studied over a two-year period in Australia, Finland, Poland, Israel, and the United States. Their analysis of the results led them to conclude that children who frequently watch violent TV programs are more likely to learn how to behave aggressively. Furthermore, children who have learned how to behave aggressively are more likely to be unpopular with their classmates and to perform poorly in school, two factors that make them likely to watch even more of these violent TV programs. A vicious circle begins, encouraging even more aggressive behavior.

Conclusions About Media Violence The studies we have examined are representative of hundreds of studies on media violence that have been summarized in other resources (e.g., Comstock & Paik, 1991; Condry, 1989; Eron & Huesmann, 1987; Liebert & Sprafkin, 1988; Wood et al., 1991). Most studies conclude that exposure to violent media does increase viewers' aggression, though some researchers disagree (Freedman, 1986; Potts et al., 1986; Sprafkin et al., 1987).

Furthermore, some children are clearly more affected by media violence than others. For instance, Heath and her colleagues (1986) concluded that television violence is particularly dangerous for children who have been abused. These children see aggression modeled in their daily lives, as well as on the television set. In contrast, children with little real contact with violence may not be as likely to learn aggressive behavior from the media. These conclusions are clearly consistent with our theme of individual differences.

Psychologists also acknowledge that several different mechanisms account for the relationship between television violence and aggressive behavior. We have focused on observational

This child may have learned his aggressive behavior from watching violent television, but he also may have been more likely to watch violent television because he was more aggressive than other children.

learning in this section. Consistent with the theme of complexity, we need to consider additional influential factors such as vicarious reinforcement, the excitatory effects of television, and the activation of other related aggressive thoughts[*] (Berkowitz, 1984; Huesmann et al., 1983).

Applications of Observational Learning

In Chapter 13, we will discuss how Bandura has applied observational learning to personality development. Two other areas in which observational learning has been applied are in educational psychology and clinical psychology.

Educational Psychology In the section on operant conditioning, we discussed how computer-assisted instruction and behavior modification (specifically a token economy) have been used in education. Clearly, observational learning also has numerous applications in teaching. For example, students learn how to pronounce French vocabulary and how to play football, mostly by observational learning. Also, observational learning plays an important role when their teachers learn how to teach.

Cognitive psychologists have developed additional techniques based on observational learning. For example, in **cognitive modeling,** a teacher performs actions while verbalizing reasons for those actions (Schunk, 1991). For instance, suppose that a teacher wants to use cognitive modeling to show students how to solve the arithmetic problem, 245 divided by 5. The teacher could write on the board, while commenting:

> *First I need to decide what number to divide the 5 into. I start on the left and move to the right until I find a number that is large enough. Is 2 large enough to be divided by 5? No, but 24 is. O.K., so my first division will be 5 into 24. Now I want a number that I can multiply by 5 that will give me an answer that's the same as or slightly smaller than 24. How about 5? Well, 5 times 5 is 25, so that's too large. But 4 times 5 is 20, so that will work . . .*

Notice that the teacher models not only correct procedures, but also how to cope with errors. Research on cognitive modeling shows that children learn division more effectively using this technique than with more traditional teaching methods (Schunk, 1991).

Clinical Psychology Observational learning is also important in the origins and treatment of **phobic disorders,** which are intense fears that have no rational basis (Domjan & Burkhard, 1986). At one point, many theorists believed that phobic disorders were caused by classical conditioning. For example, someone might develop a snake phobia following a snake bite, producing an extreme fear of the sight of snakes. However, most people with phobias cannot recall a traumatic conditioning event to account for their fears (Barlow, 1988).

Instead, a major component of phobia acquisition seems to come from observational learning. In a series of studies, laboratory-reared monkeys learned to fear snakes. Prior to learning, these young monkeys showed no fear of snakes. Then they were introduced to their parents, who had been reared in the wild. The young monkeys watched as their parents reacted fearfully to real and toy snakes. After brief observation periods, the offspring avoided and appeared afraid of snakes in much the same fashion that their parents had demonstrated (Cook et al., 1985; Mineka et al., 1984). Phobias seem to arise when we watch someone being afraid, rather than when we experience pain directly. Many therapists now help people overcome their phobias by encouraging them to watch movies of a person dealing with the feared animal and showing no apparent signs of anxiety. Thus, observational learning can help people eliminate phobias.

---

[*] *Additional information about media violence is available from the following organization: Stop War Toys Campaign, 339 Lafayette Street, New York, NY 10012.*

In this chapter, we have examined three kinds of learning: classical conditioning, operant conditioning, and observational learning. Each approach provides an important mechanism for changing behavior and acquiring new skills. However, you have learned many concepts and changed many behaviors since you began to read this chapter, and only a portion of these changes can be traced to the kinds of learning we examined. As a human, you also have the capacity to change because of your memory capacity, your thinking skills, and your language ability. The next three chapters examine these topics.

SECTION SUMMARY

OBSERVATIONAL LEARNING

- Observational learning involves acquiring new behaviors by watching and imitating the behavior of others.

- Bandura's research involved children imitating an adult's aggressive behavior toward a Bobo doll; later research showed that imitation is influenced by whether the adult model was reinforced or punished for being aggressive.

- Important components of observational learning include vicarious reinforcement and punishment, intrinsic reinforcement and punishment, and the acquisition of schemas.

- Research on the relationship between television violence and children's aggression has used the experimental, quasi-experimental, and correlational methods. Most research shows that TV violence is moderately related to aggression. However, the relationship is complex and many mechanisms other than observational learning also play an important role.

- Observational learning has applications in educational psychology and clinical psychology.

REVIEW QUESTIONS

1. Suppose that you are driving along the road and you spot a pothole right in front of you. As soon as you see it, your body automatically tightens and you flinch, in preparation for the jolt. Explain how classical conditioning accounts for your reaction. Be sure to use the appropriate terms from this chapter.

2. Try to recall Pavlov's experiment. Make diagrams of the unconditioned stimulus, the conditioned stimulus, and the responses in three phases: (a) before conditioning, (b) during conditioning, and (c) after conditioning. First check Figure 6.3 to see if your diagrams are correct. Then do the same exercise for the Watson and Rayner experiment with Albert and the white rat. Finally, describe how the terms *stimulus generalization, stimulus discrimination, extinction,* and *spontaneous recovery* could apply to Albert and the rat.

3. Suppose that you know a high-school student whose notes from a beginning psychology class include this definition of classical conditioning: "Classical conditioning involves the repeated pairing of any conditioned stimulus and any unconditioned stimulus. The unconditioned stimulus must follow immediately after the conditioned stimulus for learning to occur." Describe several problems with this definition. Be sure to provide evidence that pairing (contiguity) is not sufficient.

4. How do classical and operant conditioning differ? Describe how Thorndike's and Skinner's classic research differs from the situations studied by Pavlov and Watson and Rayner.

5. Imagine that you are baby-sitting for a child who makes Bart Simpson look angelic. Describe how you could use positive reinforcement, negative

reinforcement, and both kinds of punishment to improve the child's behavior. Discuss some of the problems with punishment. Also describe how you could apply these additional tools: shaping, secondary reinforcer, and token economy.

6. Think of examples that you have encountered in college of each of the four schedules of reinforcement you learned about in this chapter. Also identify several examples of shaping. Finally, think of examples of discriminative stimuli and secondary reinforcers in your college education.

7. Turn to Figures 3.13, 3.15, and 3.17 in Chapter 3 and identify the brain structures on those figures that are comparable to the animal brain structures that researchers have pinpointed as being associated with classical and operant conditioning.

8. Describe how observational learning helped you master a particular sport or hobby you enjoy. Mention whether reinforcement was important in your acquisition of this skill. If so, what kind of reinforcement operated?

9. Describe the three research methods that were discussed in the "In Depth" section on media violence and aggression. Did the information in this section match or disagree with your previous thoughts on the issue of media violence?

10. Imagine that you are teaching elementary school mathematics. You have decided to begin a behavior modification program to encourage students to perform more accurately on their in-class arithmetic assignments. Describe how you would design this program. At some point, mention each of these terms: reinforcement, schedule of reinforcement, shaping, and token economy. Then select some concept in arithmetic and explain how you would use cognitive modeling, as described in the section on observational learning, to teach that concept.

N E W   T E R M S

learning
classical conditioning
unconditioned stimulus
unconditioned response
conditioned stimulus
conditioned response
acquisition
stimulus generalization
stimulus discrimination
extinction
spontaneous recovery
taste aversion
biological preparedness
nictitating-membrane reflex
operant conditioning
instrumental conditioning
law of effect
positive reinforcement
negative reinforcement
punishment
shaping
continuous reinforcement schedule
partial reinforcement schedule
fixed-ratio schedule
fixed-interval schedule

variable-ratio schedule
variable-interval schedule
primary reinforcer
secondary reinforcer
discriminative stimulus
instinctive drift principle
computer-assisted instruction (CAI)
behavior modification
baseline measure
token economy
observational learning
modeling
social learning
vicarious reinforcement
vicarious punishment
intrinsic reinforcement
intrinsic punishment
schema
experimental method
meta-analysis
quasi-experiment
correlational research
cognitive modeling
phobic disorder

A N S W E R S   T O   D E M O N S T R A T I O N

DEMONSTRATION 6.2 1. increase; 2. yes; 3. no; 4. b, c, and e. Furthermore, a and d are punishment; 5. positive reinforcement.

R E C O M M E N D E D   R E A D I N G S

Domjan, M. (1993). *The principles of learning and behavior* (3rd ed.) Pacific Grove, CA: Brooks/Cole. This mid-level textbook offers a clear, up-to-date overview of learning theory, with an emphasis on classical and instrumental conditioning.

Lattal, K. A. (Ed.). (1992). Special issue: Reflections on B. F. Skinner and psychology. *American Psychologist, 47*(11). This special issue contains 19 articles that summarize the contributions of B. F. Skinner to psychology. They provide insights on operant conditioning and behaviorism, as well as his ideas on topics such as human development, social behavior, and applied psychology.

Martin, G., & Pear, J. (1992). *Behavior modification: What it is and how to do it* (4th ed.). Englewood Cliffs, NJ: Prentice Hall. If you would like to apply behavior modification, this clearly written and well-organized book provides specific details as well as practice exercises.

Schwartz, B., & Reisberg, D. (1991). *Learning and memory.* New York: Norton. Schwartz and Reisberg's textbook provides a sophisticated discussion of learning theory, connecting some of these concepts to topics in cognitive psychology that we will examine in Chapters 7 and 8.

Wood, W., Wong, F. Y., & Chachere, J. G. (1991). Effects of media violence on viewers' aggression in unconstrained social interaction. *Psychological Bulletin, 109,* 371–383. This article by Wendy Wood and her colleagues provides an example of how a good literature review ought to be written. It clearly reviews the experimental research on media violence, discusses a meta-analysis of the research, and compares media violence with other factors that influence human aggression.

C H A P T E R 7

MEMORY

magine what would happen if your memory suddenly disappeared, right in the middle of this sentence. You would not be able to remember your own name. You would look in the mirror and see a stranger staring back. In fact, you would not even remember that mirrors are supposed to reflect the viewer! Furthermore, you could not even read this far in the paragraph, because you would be unable to recognize any letters or understand any words.

Memory involves storing information over time. This information can be stored for less than a second or as long as your lifetime. For example, you use memory when you must store the beginning of a word (perhaps *mem-*) until you hear the end of the word (*-ory*). You also use memory when you recall the name of your favorite childhood toy. Memory requires three stages: encoding, storage, and retrieval. During **encoding**, the first stage, we transform sensory stimuli into a form that can be placed in memory. During **storage**, the second stage, we hold the information in memory for later use—perhaps less than 1 second, perhaps 50 years. During **retrieval**, the third stage, we successfully locate the item and use it.

Throughout this chapter, we will emphasize three general characteristics of human memory:

1. Human memory is active, rather than passive. Your memory does not record an event as accurately as a video recorder; instead, memory actively blends that event with other relevant information. For example, a memory of an event that happened when you were 10 may be influenced by stories you have heard from other family members.

2. Memory accuracy depends upon how we encode material. For example, you will remember the definition for *encoding* if you think about its meaning; you will forget that definition if you simply glance at it.

3. Memory accuracy depends upon how we measure retrieval. You may have noticed that your score is higher on a multiple-choice test than on a fill-in-the-blank test.

This chapter is organized in terms of an extremely influential model of memory that was proposed by Atkinson and Shiffrin in 1968. Figure 7.1 presents a simplified version of this model. As you can see, this model has three components. Information first enters **sensory memory,** which is a storage system that records information from the senses with reasonable accuracy. Sensory memory can hold a large number

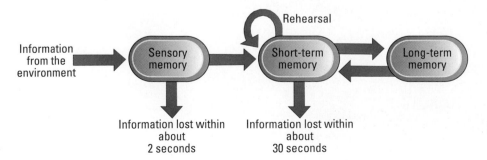

Figure 7.1

A simplified version of Atkinson and Shiffrin's model of memory.

of items, but each item fades extremely quickly—in less than 2 seconds. Some of the material from sensory memory then passes on to short-term memory. **Short-term memory (STM)**—which is also known as **working memory**—contains only the small amount of material we are currently using. Memories in STM are reasonably fragile, and they can be lost from memory within about 30 seconds unless they are somehow repeated or rehearsed. According to the Atkinson and Shiffrin model, some information passes from short-term memory to long-term memory. **Long-term memory (LTM)** has an unlimited capacity. It stores memories that are decades old, as well as memories that arrived a few minutes ago. These memories are also much more permanent than those in sensory memory and short-term memory.

Many psychologists now believe that the distinction between short-term memory and long-term memory is more blurry than Atkinson and Shiffrin originally envisioned (e.g., Ellis, 1987). However, current memory theories typically include this basic distinction (Estes, 1991). Let us discuss sensory memory, short-term memory, and long-term memory. Then, in the last portion of the chapter, we will discuss methods for improving your memory.

SENSORY MEMORY

Sensory memory holds information for a brief period after the physical stimulus is no longer available. It holds information in a relatively unprocessed form, rather than making it more meaningful. Demonstration 7.1 shows several examples of sensory memory.

Why do we need sensory memory? Sensory memory has two major purposes. First, we need to keep an accurate record of the physical stimulus for a brief time while we select the most important stimuli for further processing. In Chapter 5 (States of Consciousness), you learned that humans cannot pay attention to all stimuli at the same time. Consider the rich variety of stimuli that are entertaining your senses at this very moment. You can see the words on the page in front of you as well as other details surrounding your book—your hands, perhaps a desk, a notebook, and a lamp. Maybe you hear the squeak of your marker as you underline an important point. You also may hear faint music in the background. Perhaps your other senses are rapidly accumulating information about the room temperature, the scratchiness of your sweater, the aroma from the cafeteria, and the stale taste of cinnamon gum. Of course, the environment in which you are studying is probably simple compared to the overwhelming stimulation of a busy city scene. In any setting, your sensory memory briefly records this rich stimulation. Then you pay attention to only a fraction of the information in this recording.

A second reason we need sensory memory is because the stimuli that are bombarding your senses are constantly and rapidly changing. Consider what happens when your professor asks the question, "Why do we need sensory memory?" The *wh* sound has completely disappeared by the time you hear the word *memory*. Still, you need to retain information about the pitch of the voice at the beginning of the

On a busy street, an amazing variety of stimuli enter sensory memory.

DEMONSTRATION 7.1 Examples of Sensory Memory

Iconic (visual) memory. Take a flashlight into a dark room and turn it on. Swing your wrist around in a circular motion, shining the flashlight onto a distant wall. If your motion is quick enough, you will see a complete circle. Your visual sensory memory stores the beginning of the circle while you examine the end.

Echoic (auditory) memory. With your hand, beat a quick rhythm on the desk. Can you still hear the echo after the beating is finished?

Sensory memory for touch. Rub the palm of your hand quickly along the horizontal edge of your desk. Can you still feel the sharp edge, even after your hand is off the desk?

sentence to compare it with the pitch information at the end of the sentence. The rising pitch in the professor's voice allows you to conclude that this sentence was a question.

Atkinson and Shiffrin (1968) suggested that we could have sensory memory for all the senses discussed in Chapter 4—vision, hearing, smell, taste, and the skin senses. However, researchers have primarily concentrated on vision (iconic memory) and hearing (echoic memory).

Iconic Memory

Visual sensory memory is called **iconic memory** (pronounced eye-*conn*-ick). The investigation of iconic memory is challenging, because it is so fragile that it usually fades before we finish measuring it. For example, glance as quickly as possible at the chart of letters in Figure 7.2, and then immediately try to recall as many letters as possible. You are likely to recall only four or five letters from that chart. However, does it seem that you actually registered more items than you were able to report—perhaps as many as 10 letters? Did those additional letters fade during the brief time in which you reported the first 4 or 5 letters?

Unfortunately, we cannot rely upon people's introspections. To measure the true capacity of iconic memory, a young graduate student named George Sperling (1960) figured out a new method. Previous researchers had used the whole-report technique; participants were asked to list all the letters they had seen (as you just did). In contrast, Sperling devised a **partial-report technique,** which requires participants to report only a specified portion of the display. Just after the chart of letters disappeared, Sperling presented a tone that indicated which line of the chart should be reported. Specifically, a high tone indicated that the top row should be reported, a middle tone indicated the middle row, and a low tone indicated the bottom row.

Imagine that you are participating in Sperling's experiment. As Figure 7.2 shows, the chart flashes on for just a fraction of a second. Then a high tone sounds, indicating that you should report as much as possible from the top line. Notice that when you were actually seeing the chart, you had no clue as to which line you would later be asked to recall. Therefore, we can assume that if you had reported three letters from the top line (perhaps S Q H), you also could have reported letters from either the middle row or the bottom row—if those had been requested instead of the top row. To estimate the total number of items in iconic memory, we can therefore take the number of correct items on any one line and multiply by 3.

Sperling discovered that people recalled an average of slightly more than 3 items for one line when the partial-report technique was used. Therefore, he estimated that iconic memory holds between 9 and 10 items. However, these items fade so rapidly that a person using the whole-report technique could report only 4 or 5 of them before the remaining items disappeared from iconic memory.

Iconic memory allows you to see a trace of a visual stimulus for a brief moment after it has disappeared. If someone quickly swings a sparkler, you may briefly see a complete circle.

Task 1. Chart flashes for ½₀ second

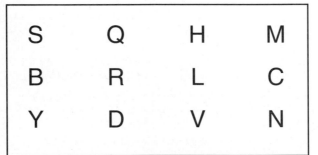

S	Q	H	M
B	R	L	C
Y	D	V	N

Task 2. A tone indicates which line must be reported (e.g., a high tone)

Task 3. The observer reports letters from the indicated row (e.g., S Q H)

Figure 7.2
Order of events in Sperling's (1960) study.

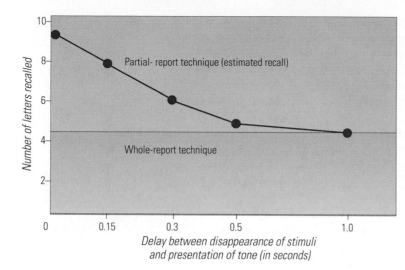

Figure 7.3

Number of letters reported, as a function of method (partial-report vs. whole-report) and delay since exposure of chart.

In other conditions, Sperling delayed the signal tone. With just a half-second delay between the disappearance of the stimulus and the presentation of the tone, people reported only 1 or 2 items in each row, making an estimated total of only 4 or 5 items. In other words, iconic memory fades so rapidly that it vanishes in less than a second. In fact, recall deteriorates to the same unspectacular level as in the whole-report technique. Figure 7.3 shows the results for both the immediate and delayed recall, in comparison to the recall when the whole-report technique is used.

Cognitive psychologists were extremely interested in Sperling's results. Following Sperling's research, hundreds of experiments have been conducted on iconic memory, using a wide variety of research procedures. They typically demonstrate that items remain in iconic memory for less than half a second after the physical stimulus has disappeared (Long, 1980; van der Heijden, 1981).

More recent research on iconic memory suggests that we may have two or more different kinds of brief visual memory (Cowan, 1988; Irwin & Yeomans, 1986). The first kind may briefly prolong the visual stimulus, whereas the second kind may involve some slight processing of the visual information. Consistent with a theme of this book, psychological processes are complicated—often more complicated than researchers initially propose. Recent research also suggests that iconic memory helps to keep your visual world stable, to counteract constant eye movement (Banks & Kracijek, 1991; Irwin et al., 1990). Chapter 4 described how your eyes make saccadic movements as they jump across a page of a book. Iconic memory may help you preserve one image long enough so that it can be compared with the image registered after your eyes have moved ahead. Without iconic memory, you might not be able to read this sentence!

Echoic Memory

Auditory sensory memory is called **echoic memory**. The name *echoic memory* is particularly appropriate, because at times it seems that a sound echoes briefly inside your head. Have you ever noticed that your professor's words seem to reverberate inside your head for a few moments after they have been spoken? Fortunately, this internal echoing allows you to hold the sounds in sensory memory, process them, and write them down a second or two later.

An important demonstration of echoic memory was modeled after Sperling's (1960) partial-report technique. We have discussed Sperling's use of an auditory signal to indicate which part of the visual stimulus was to be reported. Darwin, Turvey, and Crowder (1972) neatly reversed Sperling's study by using a visual signal to indicate which part of the auditory stimulus was to be reported from echoic memory.

Echoic memory guarantees that students will be able to hear this professor's words echoing in their heads, so that they can take notes after the auditory stimulus has disappeared.

Darwin and his colleagues used headphones to present three different auditory messages to the participants. Figure 7.4 shows how this was done. One series of items (*J 4 T*) was presented to a person's right ear. A second series of items (*A 5 2*) was presented to the left ear. A third series of items (*3 M Z*) was presented in such a way that it appeared to come from the middle. All three series were presented at the same time. After hearing all three, people were shown a visual cue on a screen that indicated which of the three series they should report.

These researchers found that the partial-report technique allowed people to report a larger estimated number of items than with the whole-report technique, in which people tried to report all 9 items. These results are similar to Sperling's results for iconic memory. Thus, sensory memory stores items for a brief time—so brief that this memory disappears before people can list all its items.

This study also pointed out some differences between the two kinds of sensory memory. Specifically, the capacity of echoic memory seems to be about 5 items, which is considerably fewer than the 9 to 10 items in iconic memory. However, echoic memory lasts about 2 seconds (Crowder, 1982; Darwin et al., 1972; Lu et al., 1992)—about four times as long as iconic memory. This information matches our daily experience. Finding everyday examples of iconic memory is difficult because it fades before we are aware it is operating. In contrast, we can easily think of examples of echoic memory. After the clock in a bell tower has struck, does it still seem to reverberate in your head? When a friend has spoken and you were not really paying attention, can you reconstruct his words if you immediately "listen" to the echo?

In the section on iconic memory, we noted that researchers are now suggesting at least two different kinds of iconic memory. Similarly, Cowan (1984, 1988) summarizes evidence for two kinds of echoic memory. Cowan suggests that one kind of echoic memory simply stores sounds and decays in less than 1 second, whereas a second kind of echoic memory may partly analyze the information and last several seconds. In any event, echoic memory may be more complicated than the simple storehouse that was originally proposed.

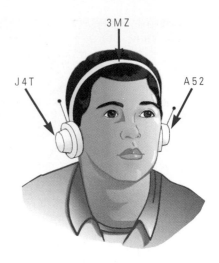

Figure 7.4

A person participating in an echoic memory study.

S E C T I O N   S U M M A R Y

SENSORY MEMORY

- Memory is active, rather than passive; memory accuracy depends upon the method of encoding and on the measure of retrieval.
- Atkinson and Shiffrin's model of memory includes sensory memory, short-term memory, and long-term memory.
- Iconic memory, originally assessed by Sperling's partial-report technique, holds 9 to 10 visual items for about half a second.
- Echoic memory, also measured by techniques such as partial report, holds about 5 auditory items for about 2 seconds.

SHORT-TERM MEMORY (WORKING MEMORY)

You have probably had an experience like this. You are standing at a pay telephone, looking up a phone number. You find the number, repeat it to yourself, and close the phone book. You take out the coins, insert them, and raise your finger to dial. Amazingly, you cannot remember it. The first digits were 243, and there was a 5 somewhere, but you have no idea what the other numbers were! They deserted your short-term memory in about half a minute.

As mentioned earlier, only a handful of items will make their way from sensory memory into short-term memory. In fact, only the material to which we pay attention will be transferred to STM. For example, you probably did not pay attention to the street sounds when you were locating the phone number, so they vanished from echoic memory without being transferred to STM. Furthermore, memories stored in STM can be lost within about 30 seconds unless they are somehow repeated. While you were locating the coins, inserting them, and beginning to dial, your attention was directed away from the phone number. As Chapter 5 explains, we remember very little when we do not pay attention to an item. Less than a minute later, those unattended numbers have departed from your consciousness.

At this point, you might be wondering how our occasionally poor performance in short-term memory can be reconciled with the theme that humans are extraordinarily competent in adapting to their environment. Strange as it might seem, there are some advantages to forgetting. Would you really want your memory to be cluttered with a phone number you dialed in fifth grade or the cost of a pack of gum you bought last year? In general, short-term memory retains information long enough for us to deal with it. However, short-term memory also allows us to forget material that is no longer useful.

As we noted earlier, short-term memory is sometimes called working memory. The name is appropriate because it handles the material we are currently working with, rather than the items that were unattended in sensory memory or the items stored away in long-term memory (Baddeley, 1986, 1992). Let us now consider some characteristics of short-term memory, including encoding, duration, and capacity, as well as some details on the working-memory view of this brief form of memory.

Encoding in Short-Term Memory

How do we transform the stimuli from sensory memory into a form that can be stored in short-term memory? We can use two different kinds of processing and store the material in several different forms.

Type of Processing You can encode sensory stimuli using either effortful or automatic processing. When using **effortful processing**, you make a deliberate attempt to place something in memory. You use effortful processing when you meet someone new and repeat this person's name to yourself or try to remember it by thinking of others with the same first name.

In contrast, **automatic processing** involves no direct effort to place something into memory. For example, can you recall *where* on the page the diagram of the Atkinson-Shiffrin model appeared (Figure 7.1)? You may have encoded the diagram's location, even though you made no effort to memorize this information. We are especially likely to use automatic processing to record information about spatial location, time, and number of occurrences (Hasher & Zacks, 1979, 1984).

In general, we are more aware of items we acquire with effortful processing than with automatic processing (Cowan, 1988). For example, you may *know* that you committed the Atkinson-Shiffrin model to memory. However, you probably did not realize that you often know a diagram's location.

Storage Form Just as information can be encoded using either effortful or automatic processing, it can also be stored in several different forms. Suppose, for example, that you have just looked up a term in the index of a textbook, and you have learned that it is mentioned on pages 20, 42, and 68. How do you keep these page numbers in your short-term memory until you can locate them? Do you encode them in terms of the way they sound, the way they look, or some aspect of their meaning?

It probably seems that you encoded the page numbers in terms of their sound. Perhaps you can even "hear" yourself repeating "twenty, forty-two, sixty-eight." The experimental evidence strongly supports an acoustic code—that is, storage in terms of an item's sound (Wickelgren, 1965; Yu et al., 1985).

In one representative study, Wickelgren presented people with a tape recording of an eight-item list consisting of four letters and four digits in random order. A typical item might be 4NF92GV8. As soon as the list was presented, people tried to recall it. Wickelgren was particularly interested in the kinds of substitutions people made. For example, if they did not recall the *V*, what did they substitute in its place? He found that they tended to insert an item that was acoustically similar. For example, instead of *V* they might substitute a *B, C, D, E, G, P,* or *T*—all letters with the "ee" sound. Furthermore, if they substituted a number for *V*, it would most likely be the similar-sounding number *3*.

Acoustic encoding in STM is so strong that we are even likely to encode acoustically when the material is presented visually, for example, when we look at page numbers in an index (Salamé & Baddeley, 1982). However, we sometimes encode items visually, in terms of the way the stimulus looks (e.g., Frick, 1988; Brandimonte et al., 1992). You probably encoded the boxes and arrows in the Atkinson-Shiffrin diagram visually, rather than acoustically. Short-term memories can also be encoded in terms of meaning (e.g., Wickens et al., 1976). In summary, then, encoding in short-term memory primarily focuses on sound. However, consistent with Theme 1, humans can be flexible and adaptive; they can also store information in STM in terms of the way it looks or what it means.

The Duration of Short-Term Memory

How long does material last in short-term memory before it is forgotten? An approach that answered this question can be called the Brown/Peterson & Peterson technique, after a British psychologist, John Brown (1958), and two American psychologists, Lloyd Peterson and Margaret Peterson (1959), who independently devised similar methods of assessing short-term memory.

Peterson and Peterson asked people to study a series of stimuli, each stimulus consisting of just three unrelated letters of the alphabet. The participant saw a single stimulus, then counted backward by threes for a short period, and then tried to recall those three letters. For the first few trials, performance was reasonably accurate. Figure 7.5 shows typical results after a large number of trials, each time with a different triad of letters. Notice that recall was only 80% accurate for these three letters a mere 3 seconds after they had been presented. However, with just an 18-second delay, recall had plummeted to close to zero. Keep in mind that people were counting backward during the delay period, and this task apparently prevented them from rehearsing or repeating the items silently to themselves. Unless information can somehow be repeated in short-term memory, it can be lost in less than 20 seconds.

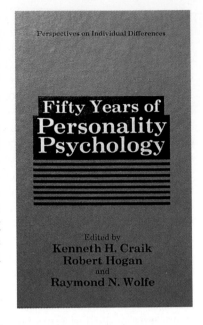

If you glanced at the cover of this book in the library, would you encode the title in STM in terms of sound, visual appearance, or meaning?

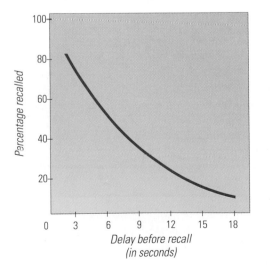

Figure 7.5

Percentage of letters recalled with the Brown/Peterson & Peterson technique (typical results after a large number of previous recall trials with different stimuli).

The Size of Short-Term Memory

You have little trouble remembering a 4-digit street address, such as 2614, for a short period. However, a standard 7-digit phone number (346-3421) is more challenging. If you add on an area code to make the phone number 10 digits (617-346-3421), you probably will not remember the entire number correctly.

In 1956, George Miller wrote a very influential article called "The Magical Number Seven, Plus or Minus Two: Some Limits on Our Capacity for Processing Information." Miller proposed that we cannot keep many items in short-term memory at one time. In particular, he suggested that people can remember about seven items (give or take two), or between five and nine items.

Miller used the term **chunk** to describe the basic unit in short-term memory. Thus, we can say that short-term memory holds about seven chunks. A chunk can be a single number or a single letter, because people can remember roughly seven numbers or letters if they are in random order.

However, numbers and letters can often be organized into larger units. For example, you may know that the Boston area code is 617 and that all the phone numbers at a particular college begin with the same numbers—346. If 617 forms one chunk and 346 forms another chunk, then the entire phone number, 617-346-3421, really has only six chunks. It may be within your memory span.

Suppose that you need to remember a list of items, perhaps some things to bring upstairs from the basement. How long does that list need to be before it is worthwhile to organize it into chunks? MacGregor (1987) has estimated that when you must recall about four items, both organized and unorganized memory are equally efficient. However, when the number of items in short-term memory reaches five or more, people who know how to use their memory efficiently will perform better if they group some of the information into chunks.

Miller's original article argued that the memory span was about the same size, whether the items to be stored were numbers or words, and whether these items were encoded acoustically, visually, or in terms of meaning. More recent research concludes that the nature of the material really does have an influence on the size of the memory span. Specifically, the size of the memory span is largest for numbers, intermediate for letters, and smallest for words. Also, we remember more items if they can be encoded acoustically than if they can only be encoded visually or in terms of meaning (Frick, 1988; Zhang & Simon, 1985). As we noted at the beginning of the chapter, memory accuracy is influenced by the method of encoding.

Working Memory: A New View of Short-Term Memory

So far, you have learned that material can be encoded in short-term memory in several ways, that items in STM fade rapidly, and that only a limited number of items can fit in STM. In the past decade, however, researchers have paid more attention to the active nature of short-term memory. Alan Baddeley (1986, 1992) created a new name for short-term memory to emphasize its active nature: *working memory.* Baddeley's working memory is not simply a passive storehouse with a number of shelves to hold chunks of information. Instead, he emphasizes that working memory actively manipulates information. Therefore, working memory is more like a workbench where material is constantly being handled, combined, and transformed.

Furthermore, this "workbench" has three different parts. Baddeley proposes three components because of some puzzling earlier research. Some years earlier, Baddeley and Hitch (1974) found that people were able to rehearse a series of random numbers while accurately performing a reasoning task. Thus, working memory is not just a single storage bin. Instead, working memory seems to have several components, which can operate partially independently of each other.

One component of Baddeley's model is called the **phonological loop;** this proposed component stores a limited number of sounds. Memories in the phonological

This student can perform accurately on a spatial reasoning task, even though she is simultaneously using her articulatory loop to say a series of numbers.

loop decay within 2 seconds unless the material is rehearsed. A second component in this theoretical model is the **visuospatial sketch pad;** it stores visual and spatial information. Baddeley suggests that this component operates like a pad of paper you might use to work on a geometry problem. The capacity of the visuospatial sketch pad is also limited. However, the limits of these two components are independent. If several items are cycling through your phonological loop, you can still handle many items in your visuospatial sketch pad.

The final component of Baddeley's model is the most important. Baddeley suggests that the **central executive** integrates information from the phonological loop and the visuospatial sketch pad, as well as material retrieved from long-term memory. The central executive also plays a major role in planning and controlling behavior (Baddeley, 1988; Morris & Jones, 1990). For example, if you are now trying to decide whether to take a break after reading the summary on short-term memory, your central executive is playing a major role in that decision!

At present, we know about the coding, duration, size, and components of short-term or working memory. Researchers know less about the biological explanations for this brief form of memory. However, neuroscientists have conducted some research with monkeys performing various working-memory tasks that require a brief delay before responding (e.g., Friedman & Goldman-Rakic, 1988). According to Goldman-Rakic (1990), the preliminary results suggest that working memory is handled by a network of interconnected regions in the cortex (specifically in the prefrontal cortex discussed on page 78) and in the limbic system (specifically in the amygdala and the mammillary bodies, as shown in the diagram on page 75).

Now we need to turn our attention from the very fragile sensory memory and the somewhat fragile working memory to long-term memory. Here we move beyond echoes and workbenches and examine a storehouse that more closely resembles a well-stocked library.

SECTION SUMMARY

SHORT-TERM MEMORY (WORKING MEMORY)

- Material stored in short-term memory can be lost within about 30 seconds unless it is somehow repeated.

- Material can be encoded into short-term memory using effortful or automatic processing; it is most often encoded acoustically, though other forms are possible.

- Research using the Brown/Peterson & Peterson technique has demonstrated that material in short-term memory can be easily forgotten.

- In general, short-term memory holds about seven items, though its capacity depends on the nature of the items and the type of encoding.

- According to Baddeley's model, working memory consists of a phonological loop, a visuospatial sketch pad, and a central executive, all comprising a memory that is active rather than passive.

LONG-TERM MEMORY

Take a moment to contemplate the information stored in your long-term memory. For instance, think how you learned that you had been accepted into the college you now attend. Can you remember what you were wearing when you opened the letter? Which people first heard the good news? Although you may recall trivial details like these, your long-term memory sometimes disappoints you. For example, see how well you do on Demonstration 7.2 and Demonstration 7.3.

In this section, we see how long-term memories are encoded, stored, retrieved, and forgotten. We end by discussing two more general issues, the connectionist

DEMONSTRATION 7.2 Acquisition and Memory

Which of the U.S. coins below is the real one? The correct answer is supplied later in the text.

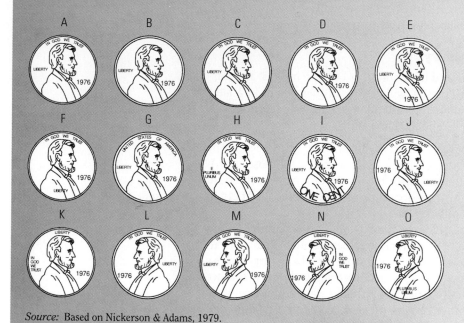

Source: Based on Nickerson & Adams, 1979.

DEMONSTRATION 7.3 Depth of Processing

Read each of the following questions and answer "yes" or "no" with respect to the word that follows. As soon as you are done, cover the words.

1. Is the word in capital letters?   BOOK
2. Would the word fit the sentence:
   "I saw a _____ in a pond"?   duck
3. Does the word rhyme with BLUE?   safe
4. Would the word fit the sentence:
   "The girl walked down the _____"?   house
5. Does the word rhyme with FREIGHT?   WEIGHT
6. Is the word in small letters?   snow
7. Would the word fit the sentence:
   "The _____ was reading a book"?   STUDENT
8. Does the word rhyme with TYPE?   color
9. Is the word in capital letters?   flower
10. Would the word fit the sentence:
    "Last spring we saw a _____"?   robin
11. Does the word rhyme with SMALL?   HALL
12. Is the word in small letters?   TREE
13. Would the word fit the sentence:
    "My _____ is six feet tall"?   TEXTBOOK
14. Does the word rhyme with BOOK?   look
15. Is the word in capital letters?   FOX

Now, without looking back over the words, try to remember as many of them as possible. Count the number correct for each of the three kinds of tasks: physical appearance (letter size), sound (rhyming), or meaning ("Would the word fit the sentence?"). On which task was your memory most accurate?

approach to long-term memory and the biological basis of memory. Throughout this section, we see that our long-term memory usually serves us well. We typically remember general, important ideas quite accurately. However, the active nature of memory and other factors lead us to forget some details. In addition, our accuracy is influenced by the way we encode material and the way retrieval is measured.

Encoding in Long-Term Memory

In the next 24 hours, you will see and hear hundreds of facts, images, and miscellaneous bits of information. How accurately will you recall these items at a later time? Three factors associated with encoding—attention, depth of processing, and encoding specificity—all influence the likelihood of recall.

Attention Did you select the correct coin in Demonstration 7.2? In a study by Nickerson and Adams (1979), less than half of the participants correctly chose coin A. Furthermore, people perform abysmally when asked to draw from memory the head and tail of coins. For example, only a third of people correctly draw Lincoln facing to the right on a U.S. penny (Rubin & Kontis, 1983).

Why do we fail to encode this kind of information in long-term memory? As you may have figured out, you do not need to pay attention to details other than color in order to spend that penny. We need to consider why memory works the way it does (Bruce, 1985). One reason we fail to remember the details of many objects is that we do not need to bother paying attention to trivia. Why should we cram our cerebral cortex with details about coins and other objects when we could be encoding and storing more interesting, important information?

Depth of Processing When you tried Demonstration 7.3, was your memory performance influenced by the way you had processed the words while you were encoding them? In 1972, Craik and Lockhart proposed that psychologists should not focus on the distinction between short-term memory and long-term memory that Atkinson and Shiffrin (1968) had emphasized. Craik and Lockhart argued that we should stress, instead, **depth of processing,** or the method people use to mentally process stimuli. When you see a list of words, you can use a shallow kind of processing that involves judgments about the appearance of the letters in the words or the sound of the words. Alternatively, you can use a deeper, more complex kind of processing, involving judgments about whether a word's meaning is appropriate for a particular sentence.

In Demonstration 7.3, you were probably more accurate in recalling the words that you had processed at a deep level, in terms of their meaning. When Craik (1977) tried a longer, more elaborate version of this demonstration, he found the results shown in Figure 7.6. As you see, words that had been processed in terms of meaning were recalled much more accurately than words processed in terms of sound, and about four times as accurately as words processed in terms of physical appearance.

Why do deep levels of processing promote recall? One reason is that an item processed at a deep level is distinctive, very different from the other items in memory. A second reason is that you use elaboration when you process at a deep level. Elaboration requires rich processing in terms of meaning, so that a word like *duck* will be connected with the fact that a duck is a bird, that it has feathers, that you have seen ducks on ponds, and many other possible associations (Anderson & Reder, 1979; Cohen et al., 1986; Craik & Lockhart, 1986).

The deepest, most effective way of processing stimuli is in terms of your own experience—a phenomenon called the **self-reference effect.** Suppose that you are asked to look at a list of adjectives and decide whether each word could be applied to yourself. When people study words using these self-reference instructions, they recall about twice as many items as when they process words in terms of meaning (Klein & Kihlstrom, 1986; Rogers et al., 1977). This self-reference effect operates not only for college students but also for young children and elderly adults (Halpin et al., 1984; Rogers, 1983).

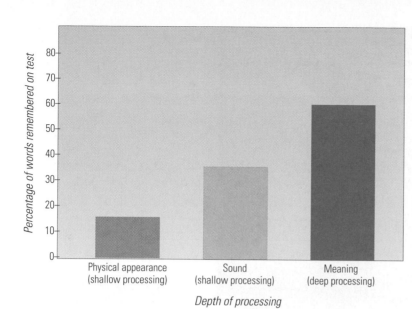

Figure 7.6

Effects of depth of processing on memory. (Based on Craik, 1977)

Consider this representative study on the self-reference effect. College students read a story about a fictional character's senior year in high school. Students in the self-reference condition were instructed to note the similarities and dissimilarities between their own experiences as high-school seniors and those of the fictional student. In contrast, students in the control condition were instructed to note the major ideas in the story. The results showed that students in the self-reference condition later recalled a significantly greater number of items (Reeder et al., 1987).

Think about how you can apply this research on depth of processing. When you read a textbook or review your class notes, try to process the material as deeply as possible. Think about what you are reading, and try to give it meaning by rephrasing a section in your own words. Also, take advantage of the self-reference effect. For instance, when you read about encoding specificity in the next section, try to think of relevant examples of the way your memory is enhanced by contextual cues. At the end of this chapter, we discuss memory improvement techniques. As you will see, many of these are effective because they promote deeper, more distinctive, and more elaborate processing. In contrast, consider the kind of shallow processing in which your eyes drift across the words, with no real awareness of what you have read. This superficial processing is nearly useless.

Encoding Specificity You have certainly had an experience like this. You are in the bedroom and realize that you need something from the kitchen. Once you are in the kitchen, however, you have no idea why you went there. Without the context in which you encoded the item you wanted, you cannot retrieve this memory. You return to the bedroom, filled with context cues, and you immediately remember what you wanted.

This example illustrates the **encoding specificity principle,** which states that recall is better if the retrieval context is like the encoding context (Begg & White, 1985; Eich, 1985; Tulving, 1983). In contrast, forgetting is more likely when the two contexts do not match (for example, the bedroom and the kitchen).

The encoding specificity principle predicts that recall will be greatest when testing conditions match the learning conditions. Smith and his coworkers (1978) showed that environmental factors are an important part of the testing conditions. In one experiment, they asked people to learn material in two very different settings. On one day they learned words in a windowless room with a large blackboard and no cabinets, and the experimenter was formally dressed in a coat and tie. On another day they learned a different set of words in a smaller room with two windows, located in a different section of the campus, with the experimenter dressed in a flannel shirt and

If this student is using a deep level of processing, her recall will be much better than if she is only using superficial processing.

jeans. On the third day, people were tested on both word lists. Half of the participants took the test in the windowless room with the formal experimenter, and half took it in the room with windows and the informal experimenter.

The results showed that performance was much better for material that had originally been learned in the same setting. People tested in the same context recalled an average of 14 words, whereas people tested in a different context recalled an average of only 9 words. Thus, if the word *swan* had been learned in the windowless room, it was recalled better in that room than in the room with windows.

However, we should not overemphasize the influence of context. Although the clear majority of research shows at least some modest evidence of context effects, other carefully conducted studies show no influence (Bjork & Richardson-Klavehn, 1987). Theme 3 states that psychological processes are complex, and these contrasting results clearly illustrate this complexity.

One explanation for some inconsistencies is called the outshining hypothesis. Imagine that you look at the sky on a moonless night, and you can just barely see a particular star. However, if the moon were full, the star would be outshone. Similarly, the **outshining hypothesis** proposes that context can trigger memory when better memory cues are absent; however, context can be completely outshone when other, better cues are present. In general, when you know the material well, then the memory cues from that material are strong enough to outshine the relatively weak context cues. However, when you have not learned the material completely, context cues can help trigger memory (Smith, 1988).

Encoding specificity operates often enough that you should try to take advantage of this principle when you are taking a test. Obviously, the effect is not powerful enough to compensate for not studying. However, if you cannot recall an answer, try to re-create the context in which you originally learned the material. If the question concerns textbook material, try to visualize where you were sitting when you read that section, as well as the part of the textbook in which it appeared. If the question asks about lecture material, can you visualize your professor discussing the topic?

This section has emphasized the importance of encoding; you cannot possibly recall something that was never encoded in the first place! Thus, you will recall material more accurately if you pay attention to it, process it deeply, and match the encoding context with the retrieval context.

Autobiographical Memory

Autobiographical memory is memory for events from one's own life (Neisser, 1989). The original research on human memory examined recall for meaningless nonsense syllables (Ebbinghaus, 1885). However, researchers in the 1990s have changed their focus. Autobiographical memory has become an increasingly popular topic because psychologists currently emphasize ecological validity (e.g., Loftus, 1991). **Ecological validity** means that results obtained in research should be generalizable to real-life settings (Cohen, 1989). Research conducted in a laboratory setting sometimes produces findings that are useful for everyday memory. Also, the laboratory certainly provides more control over irrelevant variables (Banaji & Crowder, 1989). However, it is easier to generalize research in which people recall real-life events than when they learn lists of meaningless nonsense words. In this section on autobiographical memory, we discuss two topics, eyewitness testimony and flashbulb memory.

Eyewitness Testimony In 1979, a Catholic priest awaited trial for several armed robberies. Seven witnesses had identified him as the "gentleman bandit," referring to the polite manners and elegant clothes that the robber had worn. During the trial, many witnesses identified the priest as the one who had committed the robberies. Suddenly, however, the trial was halted: Another man had confessed to the robberies (Rodgers, 1982). Figure 7.7 shows the innocent priest and the real criminal, Ronald Clouser, who certainly do not look like identical twins!

Reports like this one have led psychologists to question the reliability of eyewitness testimony. By one estimate, more than 2,000 people are wrongfully convicted each year in the United States on the basis of a faulty eyewitness testimony (Loftus & Ketcham, 1991). Although our long-term memory serves us very well in most aspects of daily life, the research on eyewitness testimony demonstrates that we are not very accurate in remembering details about an event that lasted a few seconds and occurred some time ago. Our memory is good, but it cannot be expected to be as accurate as a videotape recorder.

Elizabeth Loftus and her colleagues have identified another important source of inaccuracy in eyewitness testimony. After people witness an event, someone may

Figure 7.7

Father Bernard Pagano (left), who was almost convicted of armed robbery, and the real criminal, Ronald Clouser (right).

supply misleading information. This misleading post-event information may bias their recall.

In an important experiment, Loftus, Miller, and Burns (1978) showed a series of slides to participants in their study. In this sequence, a sports car stopped at an intersection, and then it turned and hit a pedestrian. Half of the participants saw a slide with a yield sign at the intersection; the other half saw a stop sign. Twenty minutes to 1 week after the slides had been shown, the participants answered questions about the details of the accident. A critical question contained information that was either consistent with a detail in the original slide series or else did not mention the detail. For example, some people who had originally seen the yield sign were asked, "Did another car pass the red Datsun while it was stopped at the yield sign?" (consistent). Other people were asked the same question with the word *stop* substituted for *yield* (inconsistent). For still other people, the sign was not mentioned (neutral).

After a delay of 20 minutes to 1 week, participants were shown two slides, one with a stop sign and one with a yield sign. They were asked to identify which slide they had originally seen. As Figure 7.8 shows, people who had received inconsistent information were substantially less accurate than people in the other two conditions.

Several studies have replicated the harmful effects of misleading post-event information (e. g., Shaughnessy & Mand, 1982). In related studies, researchers introduce misleading information so that the research participants are encouraged to hold new, incorrect memories. Nevertheless, the participants are just as confident about the accuracy of these new memories as they are about their genuine memories (Loftus et al., 1989; Loftus & Hoffman, 1989).

The research on eyewitness testimony confirms a point we made at the beginning of this chapter. We do not store a memory of an event in a passive fashion, isolated from all other information. Instead, post-event information may be incorporated into that memory, changing it or altering it substantially (Loftus, 1992). Memory is an active process, not a passive one.

Flashbulb Memory Can you remember details about what you were wearing or doing when you heard about an important happy or tragic event? People often have very vivid memories of a situation in which they first learned of a surprising and emotionally arousing event, a phenomenon called **flashbulb memory.**

My clearest flashbulb memory, like most of my generation, is of learning that President John Kennedy had been shot. I was a sophomore at Stanford University, just ready for a midday class in German. I had entered the classroom from the right, and I was just about to sit down at a long table on the right-hand side of the classroom. The sun was streaming in from the left. There was only one other person seated in the classroom, a blond fellow named Dewey. He turned around and said, "Did you hear that President Kennedy has been shot?" I also recall my reaction and the reactions of others as they entered the classroom. Kennedy was shot about 30 years ago, yet trivial details about the news of it are stunningly clear to many people today. You can probably think of personal events in your own life that triggered flashbulb memories—the death of a relative, a piece of important good news, or an amazing surprise.

People are most likely to recall certain characteristics in their flashbulb memory such as where they were, what ongoing event was interrupted by the news, and the person who told them the news (Brown & Kulik, 1977).

A person with a vivid flashbulb memory may claim that the memory is highly accurate. However, people often forget some of the details of the event (Christianson, 1989). For example, Neisser and Harsch (1992) found that some people were almost totally incorrect in recalling their activities when they learned about the Challenger disaster. To study flashbulb memory properly, we need to ask whether these memories are any more accurate than our memories for less exciting events. We need a control group for comparison (Brewer, 1992; Rubin, 1992). In fact, these memories

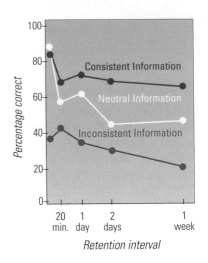

Figure 7.8

The effect of type of information and delay on proportion of correct answers. (Source: Loftus et al., 1978)

that seem so vivid can probably be explained by ordinary memory mechanisms such as deep processing and frequent repetition (McCloskey et al., 1988).

Schemas and Memory

Take a moment to recall the sequence of events during the last time you went to a fast-food restaurant. You entered the restaurant, stood in line while inspecting the list of options above the counter, told the cashier what you wanted, paid, and received your food. Then you took your tray to a table, ate the food, discarded the waste, and left the restaurant. You have probably visited fast-food restaurants often enough to develop a general idea for the events that will happen and the order in which they will occur. In other words, you have developed a **schema** (pronounced *skee*–muh), or a generalized idea about objects, people, and events that are encountered frequently. You have also developed a schema for "first day of a college course," "attending a concert," and "making a telephone call."

We notice the common features of each of these events through repeated experience with similar kinds of activities (Barclay, 1986). We do not need to remember precise details about much of our daily life (did the ticket taker at the concert stand

---

DEMONSTRATION 7.4 Schemas and Memory

After reading these instructions, cover them and the rest of the text in this demonstration so that only the picture shows. Present the picture to a friend, with the instructions, "Look at this picture of a psychologist's office for a brief time." Half a minute later, close the book and ask your friend to list everything that is in the room.

Source: Based on Brewer & Treyens, 1981.

on the right or the left?). Instead, we take advantage of schemas. They allow us to process large amounts of material and summarize the many regularities in our lives. Schemas provide structure for memory. Try Demonstration 7.5 before you read further.

DEMONSTRATION 7.5 Schemas and Memory for Stories

Part 1

Read each sentence below, count to five, answer the question, and go on to the next sentence.

SENTENCE	QUESTION
The girl broke the window on the porch.	Broke what?
The tree in the front yard shaded the man who was smoking his pipe.	Where?
The cat, running from the barking dog, jumped on the table.	From what?
The tree was tall.	Was what?
The cat running from the dog jumped on the table.	Where?
The girl who lives next door broke the window on the porch.	Lives where?
The scared cat was running from the barking dog.	What was?
The girl lives next door.	Who does?
The tree shaded the man who was smoking his pipe.	What did?
The scared cat jumped on the table.	What did?
The girl who lives next door broke the large window.	Broke what?
The man was smoking his pipe.	Who was?
The large window was on the porch.	Where?
The tall tree was in the front yard.	What was?
The cat jumped on the table.	Where?
The tall tree in the front yard shaded the man.	Did what?
The dog was barking.	Was what?
The window was large.	What was?

Part 2

Cover the preceding sentences. Now read each of the following sentences and decide whether it is a sentence from the list in Part 1. The answers will be discussed later.

1. The girl who lives next door broke the window. (old _____, new _____)
2. The tree was in the front yard. (old _____, new _____)
3. The scared cat, running from the barking dog, jumped on the table. (old _____, new _____)
4. The window was on the porch. (old _____, new _____)
5. The tree in the front yard shaded the man. (old _____, new _____)
6. The cat was running from the dog. (old _____, new _____)
7. The tall tree shaded the man who was smoking his pipe. (old _____, new _____)
8. The scared cat was running from the dog. (old _____, new _____)
9. The girl who lives next door broke the large window on the porch. (old _____, new _____)
10. The tall tree shaded the girl who broke the window. (old _____, new _____)
11. The cat was running from the barking dog. (old _____, new _____)
12. The girl broke the large window. (old _____, new _____)
13. The scared cat ran from the barking dog that jumped on the table. (old _____, new _____)
14. The girl broke the large window on the porch. (old _____, new _____)
15. The scared cat which broke the window on the porch climbed the tree. (old _____, new _____)
16. The tall tree in the front yard shaded the man who was smoking his pipe. (old _____, new _____)

Source: Based on Jenkins, 1974.

Schemas operate at several stages of the memory process. For example, schemas help to determine what items are acquired in memory. Consider a study by Brewer and Treyens (1981). Participants in this study waited, one at a time, in the room pictured in Demonstration 7.4. The experimenter explained that this was his office, and he needed to check the laboratory to see if the previous person had completed the experiment. After 35 seconds, the experimenter asked the participant to move to a nearby room. Here, each person was given a surprise test: Recall everything in the room in which he or she had waited.

The results showed that people were likely to recall objects consistent with the "office schema." Nearly everyone remembered the desk, the chair next to the desk, and the wall. However, few recalled the wine bottle, the coffeepot, and the picnic basket. These items were not consistent with the office schema, so they were not acquired in memory.

In addition, some people remembered items that were *not* in the room. Many remembered books, though none had been in sight. (Check your friend's list from Demonstration 7.4–did he or she mention books?) When we try to reconstruct a memory, schemas also operate to ensure that we supply educated guesses that are consistent with these schemas. In contrast, your friend probably did not invent items that were *inconsistent* with the office schema, such as a hair dryer, a tree, or a hot-air balloon.

Schemas also operate when we hear a story and store its meaning. Try Demonstration 7.5, a simplified version of a study by Bransford and Franks (1971). How many sentences did you think you recognized in the second half?

Bransford and Franks asked the participants in their study to listen to sentences that belonged to several different stories. Then they took a recognition test that contained only new sentences, many of which were combinations of the earlier sentences. Nonetheless, people were convinced that they had seen these exact sentences before. A sentence such as "The tall tree in the front yard shaded the man who was smoking his pipe" was consistent with the schema they had developed for this particular story. It seems that people gather information together from individual sentences to construct a schema. People think that they have previously seen a sentence that combines all these ideas. Once the sentences have been fused in memory in the form of a schema, they cannot untangle them into their original components and recall those components word for word.

However, people are not likely to say that they recognize a sentence that is inconsistent with the schema. You probably did not check "old" for test item 10, "The tall tree shaded the girl who broke the window."

We are especially likely to use schemas when we must retain information for many hours or days. For instance, Harris and his colleagues (1989) asked college students in Kansas to read a story that was consistent with either American culture or traditional Mexican culture. In a typical Mexican-style story about two people on a date, the young man's older sister accompanied the couple as a chaperone. The American version had no chaperone. When story recall was tested 30 minutes after reading the material, recall of both versions was accurate. After a two-day delay, however, a significant number of the Mexican-schema stories had shifted in the direction consistent with American schemas. Specific details such as the chaperone were no longer mentioned.

Notice how this information on schemas reveals the active nature of memory. Schemas help shape what we encode into memory—for example, from an office scene. Schemas also mold and integrate isolated sentences into cohesive stories. Schemas even determine what information will be retained in long-term memory, because concepts incompatible with schemas are often forgotten.

The concept of schemas is closely related to an important principle we will emphasize in the chapter on thinking (Chapter 8). Specifically, many thought processes are governed by heuristics. **Heuristics** are rules-of-thumb that are generally accurate. The use of schemas is one example of a heuristic. That is, an effective rule-of-thumb is to use a schema to organize your memory of an object or an event. In general, schemas will help you to acquire the important memories, reconstruct the appropriate missing items, and organize isolated sentences into a story. Consistent with one of our themes, our memory usually functions well. However, if we depend too heavily on a heuristic, we can make mistakes. We make mistakes, for example, when we depend too heavily on the office schema and fail to notice what is unique about this particular office. Now let us consider in more detail how we retrieve items from memory.

The Retrieval Process

Take a moment to think about all the information stored in your long-term memory. You store memories of people you have not seen in years, information about songs that left the Top 40 list long ago, ideas about events that occurred when you were in first grade, and a wealth of general information about vocabulary. With this incredibly large storehouse of memories, it is amazing that you can manage to retrieve any specific piece of information—such as the name of your second-grade teacher. Let's consider how long material can be stored prior to retrieval and what happens when retrieval fails.

Permastore Several years ago, my family and I traveled to Spain. It had been close to 30 years since my high-school Spanish courses, but I was amazed at how much I could recall. Admittedly, my verbs were flawed in the past tense, and I startled a Spanish child with my question about the fairy tale "Goldilocks and the Three Eyes (*Ojos*)" rather than "Goldilocks and the Three Bears (*Osos*)." Still, it was comforting to know that long-term memory was so durable.

Harry Bahrick (1984) examined very long term memory with nearly 800 participants who had studied Spanish in high-school or college courses. The interval between acquisition and retrieval ranged from 0 to 50 years. Even 50 years later, people recalled about 40% of the vocabulary, idioms, and grammar they had originally learned. Bahrick proposed the name **permastore** to refer to this relatively permanent, very long term form of memory. The astonishing durability of permastore contrasts markedly with the fragility of material in both sensory and short-term memory.

Tip-of-the-Tongue Experience You have certainly had an experience like this. You are trying to remember the name of a sporting goods store, because you want to call to see how late it is open. You are squirming with impatience because you cannot quite recall it . . . it is somebody's last name, it is three syllables long, and the first letter is in the middle of the alphabet, maybe a *J*. This is an example of the **tip-of-the-tongue experience,** the sensation you have when you are confident that you know the word for which you are searching, yet you cannot recall it.

A classic study on the tip-of-the-tongue experience was conducted by Brown and McNeill (1966). These researchers challenged people by giving them the definition for an uncommon English word, such as "The green-colored matter found in plants" or "The art of speaking in such a way that the voice seems to come from another place." Sometimes people immediately supplied the appropriate word, and other times they were confident that they did not know it. However, in some cases, the definition produced a tip-of-the-tongue state. Brown and McNeill wrote that this state felt like being on the brink of a sneeze—an accurate description.

People who were in the midst of a tip-of-the-tongue experience were asked to provide words that resembled the target word in terms of sound. When the target word was *sampan,* for example, people provided these similar-sounding words: *Saipan, Siam, Cheyenne, sarong, sanching,* and *symphoon.* In general, research on the tip-of-the-tongue experience shows that people are reasonably accurate in guessing the characteristics of the target word. For example, they guess the first letter of the target word correctly between 50% and 70% of the time. They also guess the appropriate number of syllables between 47% and 83% of the time (Brown, 1991).

Can you recall the name of this category of cartoon character, which was popular in the early 1980s? If so, its name is in your permastore. If not, check the answer at the end of this chapter.

DEMONSTRATION 7.6 Explicit Memory

List the names of the Seven Dwarfs from the fairy tale "Snow White and the Seven Dwarfs." You may list them in any order you wish. Then check the answers at the end of the chapter to determine how many you recalled correctly. The results will be discussed later in this section.

Source: Based on Miserandino, 1991

The tip-of-the-tongue phenomenon demonstrates that, even when we cannot recall the target word for which we are searching, we do have some knowledge about the way the word sounds. The phenomenon also demonstrates how memory is structured. The word *chlorophyll* is not simply thrown into memory along with *banana* and *jinx*. Instead, it is encoded so that it is closely linked with other similar-sounding words (maybe *chlorine* and *cholesterol*), and *ventriloquist* is associated with similar-sounding words such as *ventilate.* From other research, we know that retrieval is related not only to memory structure, but also to the way this retrieval is assessed.

IN DEPTH: **Explicit and Implicit Measures of Retrieval**

Before you read further, try Demonstration 7.6 and Demonstration 7.7, which illustrate two ways of measuring retrieval. This section highlights an important point made at the beginning of the chapter; memory accuracy depends on how we measure retrieval.

Try to imagine this scene. A young woman is walking aimlessly down the street, and she is eventually picked up by the police. She seems to be suffering from an extreme form of amnesia, because she has lost all memory of who she is. Unfortunately, she is carrying no identification. Then the police have a breakthrough idea; they ask her to begin dialing phone numbers. Amazingly, she dials her mother's number—though she is not aware whose number she is dialing (Adler, 1991).

This true story illustrates the difference between explicit and implicit measures of memory. **Explicit memory** involves the conscious recollection of your previous experiences (Schacter, 1992). The most common measure of explicit memory is **recall,** in which you must reproduce items that had been learned earlier. Demonstration 7.6 measured recall. Another explicit memory measure is **recognition,** in which you must identify which items on a list had been learned

---

DEMONSTRATION 7.7 Implicit Memory

For each of these items, look at the first letters and supply a complete English word. (Incidentally, some may have more than one possible answer; just give the first one that comes to mind.)

GRU_____

DAN_____

SNE_____

COM_____

VIX_____

DOP_____

CUP_____

SLE_____

The answers will be supplied and discussed later in this section.

Source: Based on Miserandino, 1991

earlier. (For example, a recognition test for the Seven Dwarfs would require you to identify which of the following are the correct names: Sleepy, Drippy, Snoozy, Grumpy, Dopey . . . .) Explicit memory requires *intentional* retrieval of information.

In contrast, **implicit memory** involves performing a task, that is, actually *doing* something. A researcher who is testing implicit memory typically avoids using words such as *memory* or *remember.* In the anecdote about the woman with amnesia, dialing a phone number was a test of implicit memory. We typically do not consciously recollect information when we perform skills that require implicit memory. For example, a skilled typist does not need to be conscious of where each letter is located on the keyboard. Similarly, a trained pole vaulter will not need to pause a moment before jumping, to remember the purpose for holding the pole (Nelson, 1993).

Demonstration 7.7 showed one example of an implicit memory test, in which you are instructed to form complete words by filling in the blanks. Another implicit memory test involves **free associations;** people are instructed to supply the first word that comes to mind in response to a stimulus word. (For example, what is your free association to the word *strawberry?*) Implicit memory is demonstrated if a person supplies a word from a list of items that had been exposed earlier. For example, some of the items in Demonstration 7.7 could be completed with names of the Seven Dwarfs (Grumpy, Sneezy, Dopey, and Sleepy), which you saw earlier on the answers to Demonstration 7.6, listed at the end of the chapter. In contrast, the control-group items referred to the names of the reindeer in "The Night Before Christmas" (Dancer, Comet, Vixen, and Cupid). Your performance on these control-group items was probably quite poor. Let's now examine the research, concentrating on two principal studies.

Your college courses in academic areas such as psychology almost always use explicit memory tests, such as an essay or fill-in-the-blank test (recall) or a multiple-choice test (recognition).

Research on Amnesic People Some of the pioneering work on implicit memory examined people with **amnesia,** or loss of memory. In a classic study, Elizabeth Warrington and Lawrence Weiskrantz (1970) presented some English words to four amnesics. Then they gave the amnesics two explicit memory tasks, one testing recall and one testing recognition. Compared to normal people in a control group, the amnesics performed poorly.

So far, the results are not surprising. However, everyone also completed two implicit memory tasks. These were presented as word-guessing games rather than recall tasks—though they actually measured memory for words shown earlier. In one game, English words such as *METAL* were presented in a mutilated form, with sections of each letter missing. Participants were told to guess which word was represented. In the second implicit memory task, people saw the first few letters, and they were instructed to produce the first word that came to mind. Amazingly, the implicit memory scores of the amnesics and the people in the control group were virtually identical. Both groups correctly identified about 45% of the mutilated words, and both groups correctly completed about 65% of the word stems. These results have been replicated many times since the original research (MacLeod & Bassili, 1989; Roediger, 1990). Apparently, then, amnesia seems to affect explicit memory but not implicit memory.

Research on Normal People Following Anesthesia Suppose you were to be anesthetized in preparation for major surgery. Under surgery, you would feel no pain; after surgery, you would not be able to recall anything that occurred during the operation. However, John Kihlstrom and his colleagues (1990) wondered whether general anesthesia affects implicit memory as completely as it seems to affect explicit memory (that is, recall and recognition).

Kihlstrom and his coauthors studied 30 surgical patients who were scheduled for routine procedures such as abdominal surgery. The researchers prepared two tape recordings, each consisting of two words that are often associated with each other (for example, *ocean-water* or *butter-bread*). For each patient, one randomly selected tape was presented during surgery; let's call these the experimental items. The other tape was never presented; we will call these the control items.

This skilled secretary can type accurately and rapidly, relying on her implicit memory for the location of the letters on the keyboard. However, if she were given an explicit test, she might not be able to recall the letters' positions. If you are a reasonably good typist, you might try recalling the location of letters on a standard keyboard. Then check your accuracy.

The tape of experimental items was played continuously as soon as the patient was appropriately anesthetized, and the tape was stopped when the operation was complete, typically about an hour later. The patients were then allowed to recover from the anesthetic prior to testing, a delay that typically lasted 1½ hours. Then the researchers tested their memory for the material that had been presented when they were anesthetized. In one explicit memory task, the experimenter read the first word of each pair (e. g., *ocean* and *butter*) and asked what word had

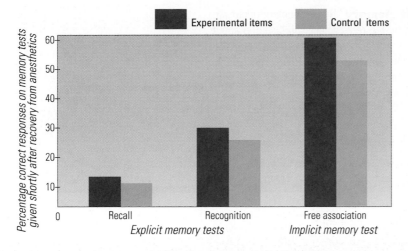

Figure 7.9

Percentage of correct responses for experimental and control items, as assessed by two explicit memory tests (recall and recognition) and one implicit memory test (free association). Note that performance on the two kinds of items differs significantly only on the implicit memory test.

been paired with that stimulus during the earlier presentation. In a second explicit memory task, the experimenter asked the patients to recognize which words had been presented and which had not. Figure 7.9 shows that explicit performance on the experimental items was no better than on the control items, which had never been presented.

Kihlstrom and his colleagues also included one implicit memory test. This was a free-association test, in which the patients were given the first word of each pair and asked to say the first word that came to mind. Like all implicit memory tests, the task involved *doing* something, rather than an emphasis on *remembering* something. On this implicit memory test, their performance was significantly better on the experimental items than on the control items. Furthermore, a delayed test roughly two weeks later showed similar results: The patients remembered no better than chance on the explicit memory tasks, but the implicit memory test showed that they remembered a substantial amount.

These findings have important practical implications for surgical procedures; members of hospital staffs should know that the patients are likely to remember something about the conversations they hear when they are unconscious! They will not be able to recall or recognize those items, but those implicit memories may influence what they actually do.

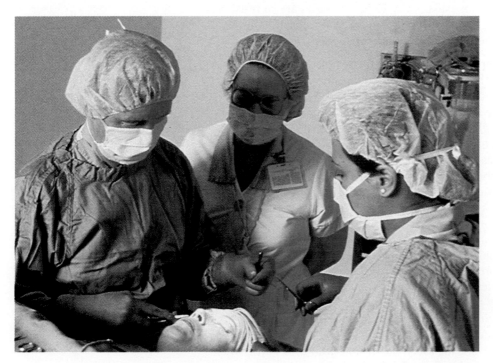

This surgical patient will not be able to recall or recognize any information that this hospital team is discussing while she was anesthetized. However, implicit memory tests might reveal some memory of that information.

Explanations for Explicit and Implicit Memory The excitement about implicit memory is growing even stronger in the 1990s. However, researchers still disagree about why these explicit and implicit measures often produce such different results (Nelson, 1993). Some argue that the two kinds of tests measure different processes. Specifically, explicit tests involve top-down processing, which emphasizes a person's concepts, expectations, and prior knowledge. In contrast, implicit tests involve bottom-up processing, which emphasizes information at the sensory level (Roediger, 1990). Other researchers believe that implicit memory involves a different part of the brain than the part that handles explicit memory (Schacter, 1992). This argument is far from being resolved, and the future is likely to include many explicit arguments about implicit memory.

Theories of Forgetting

So far, this section on long-term memory has emphasized how information is encoded in memory, and also how it is retrieved. Now let us consider how this information may be forgotten. What is the name of the early psychologist who tested cats in puzzle boxes, as described in Chapter 6? Who is the psychologist whose research team studied implicit memory in anesthetized patients? Did one or both of these names escape your memory, not even approaching the tip of your tongue? How would you explain their disappearance? Let us consider several theories that psychologists have proposed for forgetting in long-term memory.

Decay Psychologists who support the **decay** position say that each item in memory decays spontaneously as time passes. Several days after you originally saw Thorndike's name, that memory faded and perhaps even disappeared completely—unless you somehow reviewed it. Decay theory matches many personal experiences. When you are trying to recall something you had meant to tell a friend, does it sometimes seem that this particular memory has faded entirely?

A basic problem with decay theory involves the physical explanation for that decay. Although the theory seems consistent with information from neuroscience, no precise biochemical or structural changes have yet been identified (Solso, 1991). Decay theory is also overly simple. The process of forgetting does not resemble a giant eraser, methodically making all memories uniformly less visible. If decay were the only factor operating, we could not explain why some memories are so resistant to forgetting, why you so easily forget how to program your VCR, and why you won't forget how to ride a bike, even if you haven't ridden one since your 12th birthday.

Interference A second approach, **interference** theory, states that forgetting occurs because other items get in the way of the information you want to remember. That is, other items cause interference.

Two kinds of interference are illustrated in Figure 7.10. Suppose that you studied Spanish for several years in high school, and then you began to learn French in college. In **proactive interference,** old memories work in a forward direction to interfere with new memories. Specifically, you would have difficulty remembering the new French word *chien,* because the old Spanish word *perro* would get in the way.

In **retroactive interference,** new memories work in a backward direction to interfere with old memories. You would have difficulty recalling the old Spanish word *perro,* because the new French word *chien* would get in the way. (Incidentally, one way to remember these two kinds of interference is to note that *pro*gress means moving forward, whereas *retro*spect means looking backward.)

Try to think of examples of proactive and retroactive interference. For instance, when you are familiar with a particular car, have you ever driven a different car and experienced proactive interference as you try to remember where the light switch is on this new car? If you become accustomed to the new car, however, you will find that retroactive interference will operate. You will forget details about the car you drove originally. Interference is also relevant for every North American driver who must learn to drive on the left side of the road in Great Britain. Both decay and interference are important sources of forgetting (Mensink & Raaijmakers, 1988; Reitman, 1974).

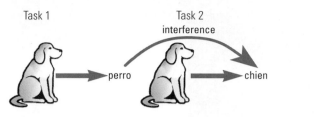
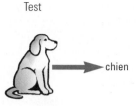

Task 1   Task 2   Test
interference

perro   chien   chien

A. In proactive interference, words that are learned in Task 1
interfere when you try to recall words learned in Task 2

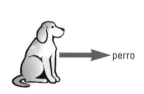

Task 1   Task 2   Test
interference

perro   chien   perro

B. In retroactive interference, words that are learned in Task 2
interfere when you try to recall words learned in Task 1

Figure 7.10
Examples of proactive and retroactive interference.

Retrieval Failure I once told a friend that one of the best movies I had ever seen was *The Official Story*. He replied that he had never seen it. "I'm sure you've seen it," I urged. "There's this incredible scene when Norma Aleandro is listening to her friend's description of how she had been tortured." Again, my friend returned a blank look. "OK, it's the film where this schoolteacher slowly realizes that her adopted daughter was probably the child of a woman murdered by the Argentinian military. . . ." The light dawned· "Oh, the film from Argentina! Why didn't you say so?"

You have probably experienced similar frustrations in which an item remains stubbornly buried until the right cue coaxes it forth. This third explanation of forgetting is called **retrieval failure**; it specifies that memory failures occur when the proper retrieval cues are not available. For my friend, the title of a movie, the name of the actress, and a memorable scene could not function as proper retrieval cues, though the name of the country in which it took place immediately prompted recall.

Earlier in the chapter we discussed two topics related to retrieval failure. In the section on encoding, we discussed the encoding specificity principle. (In case you are currently experiencing retrieval failure, this section discussed how people recalled a greater number of words if they learned these words in the same room in which they were tested.) Furthermore, the tip-of-the-tongue phenomenon occurs when the retrieval process breaks down.

Research on retrieval failure has demonstrated that if the sound of a word is emphasized during encoding, retrieval failure is likely to occur when meaning—rather than sound—is emphasized during retrieval. For example, as part of a study, people learned words by focusing on their sound: A word such as *hail* was preceded by the question, "Does it rhyme with *pail?*" Later, retrieval was poor when the hint emphasized meaning (e.g., "It's associated with snow") but excellent when the hint emphasized sound (e.g., "It rhymes with *bail*"). However, if meaning was emphasized during encoding, meaning provided the best retrieval cues (Fisher & Craik, 1977). As we emphasized at the beginning of the chapter, memory performance is strongly influenced by the way material is encoded and the way retrieval is measured.

Motivated Forgetting A friend of mine who is a financial consultant told me that he sometimes forgets to return phone calls—especially phone calls to unpleasant people. In **motivated forgetting,** people forget unpleasant memories, such as a poor exam score or a rude remark to an old friend (Davis & Schwartz, 1987). Memory researchers since the early 1900s have demonstrated that we do indeed remember

If these children forget the events that occurred during this Halloween party, the forgetting may be traced to decay, interference, retrieval failure, or motivated forgetting.

pleasant events better than unpleasant ones (Matlin & Stang, 1978). However, the explanation for these findings is not clear. Sigmund Freud, whose theory of personality is examined in Chapter 13, proposed that we forget unpleasant events because of **repression,** or pushing back unacceptable thoughts into the unconscious. Research does not consistently support this active blocking of unpleasant memories (e. g., Baddeley, 1990).

In summary, then, we forget because of decay, interference, retrieval failure, and motivated forgetting. Chapter 3 also discussed how head trauma, strokes, and Alzheimer's disease can produce additional forgetting. Consistent with a theme of the book, forgetting is so complex that it requires a variety of different explanations. Now let us consider an important, general model of long-term memory.

The Connectionist Approach to Long-Term Memory

I am thinking of an object that is orange, it grows below the ground, and it is a vegetable that rabbits like. What is it? Human memory has a remarkable characteristic that we usually take for granted: One thing reminds us of another (Johnson-Laird, 1988). Each of those clues reminded you of several possible candidates, and all the clues converged on *carrot*.

According to an extremely influential model, the **connectionist approach,** the activation of one cue leads to the activation of other, related concepts. As we noted in Chapters 1 and 5, connectionism is a model of the nervous system based on networks that link together individual units. Connectionism is also known as the **parallel distributed processing approach** or the **PDP approach.** Let's examine some of the important characteristics of this complex model.

1. *The processes are parallel, not serial.* When you thought about the answer to the carrot question, you did not conduct a **serial search,** handling the characteristics one at a time. That is, you did not conduct a complete search of all orange objects before beginning a second search of all below-ground objects, and then all rabbit-endorsed vegetables. Instead, you conducted a **parallel search,** handling all the characteristics at the same time. Because the processes are parallel, we can accomplish cognitive tasks very quickly—as Theme 1 emphasizes.

2. *Knowledge is distributed throughout the connections between units, rather than being stored in a specific location in the brain.* James McClelland, one of the

TABLE 7.1	Attributes of Representative Individuals Whom a College Student Might Know		
NAME	**MAJOR**	**YEAR**	**POLITICAL ORIENTATION**
Joe	Art	Junior	Liberal
Marti	Psychology	Sophomore	Liberal
Sam	Engineering	Senior	Conservative
Liz	Engineering	Sophomore	Conservative
Roberto	Psychology	Senior	Liberal

major creators of the connectionist model, described how our knowledge about a group of individuals might be stored in terms of connections that link these people together with their personal characteristics. His original example portrayed members of two gangs of small-time criminals (McClelland, 1981). We will use a simpler and presumably more familiar example featuring five college students. Table 7.1 lists these students, together with their college majors, year in school, and political orientation. Figure 7.11 shows how this information could be represented in network form. Naturally, this figure represents only a fraction of the number of people a college student is likely to know, and only a fraction of the characteristics associated with each student.

If the connections are well-established, then an appropriate clue allows you to locate the characteristics of a specified individual (McClelland et al., 1986; Rumelhart et al., 1986). For example, if you enter the system with the name *Roberto*, you discover that he is a psychology major, a senior, and politically liberal.

3. *We can draw conclusions, even when we lack appropriate information.* Specifically, the connectionist approach allows us to fill in missing information about an item, based on information about similar items; this process is referred to as making a **default assignment**. Suppose, for example, that you meet Christina, who is an engineering student. Someone asks you about Christina's political preferences, and you have never discussed politics with her. This question activates information about the political leanings of other engineering students. Based on a default assignment, you reply that she is probably conservative. Notice how the default assignment

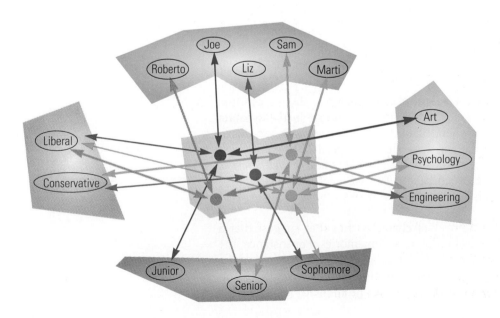

Figure 7.11

A figure illustrating the units and connections for the individuals shown in Table 7.1.

concept meshes nicely with our discussion on schemas and memory; when we see a photo of an office, we "remember" characteristics of typical offices.

4. *We can still carry out most cognitive processes, even if the information is incomplete or faulty*. If your car's battery is dead, that one faulty part will prevent the car from moving forward. In contrast, your cognitive processes are much more flexible (Churchland & Churchland, 1990). For example, suppose someone describes a student as a tall male in your introductory psychology class from Los Angeles. You may be able to identify the appropriate student—even though you know that he is from Pasadena.

5. *Sometimes we have partial recall for some information, rather than complete, perfect memory*. The brain's ability to provide partial memory is called **graceful degradation.** An example of graceful degradation is the tip-of-the-tongue experience that we discussed on page 224. You can often describe exactly what target you are seeking, and you may even know the target's first letter and number of syllables. However, the word itself refuses to leap into memory.

6. *Every new event changes the strength of connections between relevant units*. For example, while you have been reading about the PDP approach, you have been changing the strength of connections between the word *connectionism* and terms such as *default assignment* and *graceful degradation*. The next time you see the term *connectionism*, the links with these related terms are likely to be strong and therefore easily activated.

Many psychologists argue that the connectionist approach represents the most important theoretical shift in recent decades (Schneider, 1987). Some supporters are especially enthusiastic that the approach was designed to be consistent with the neurological structure of the brain (McNaughton & Morris, 1987). Clearly, connectionism figures prominently in theories about memory in the 1990s, and it may be the standard approach in the future.

The Biological Basis of Long-Term Memory

You have just read the definition for *graceful degradation*. If you processed that information at a deep level, the definition is now stored in your long-term memory. What changes took place at the level of the neuron to ensure its successful storage? What brain structures were involved in learning and storing that definition? Unfortunately, as Cotman and Lynch (1990) explain, learning and memory are among the most challenging topics for neuroscientists to explain. Even though researchers have been pursuing intriguing possibilities for many decades, they do not agree upon a single explanation. This difficulty can be traced partly to the impressively vast storage capacity of long-term memory. Let us look at some tentative explanations focusing on the neuron and chemical messengers, and then we will examine the structures in the brain that are most involved in long-term memory.

Changes in the Neuron and Chemical Messengers For about a century, neuroscientists have assumed that memory must involve changes in the synaptic connections between cells (Cotman & Lynch, 1990). More recent research has identified a process that might be responsible for these changes. Specifically, researchers present brief electrical stimulation to neurons in the brains of anesthetized animals (e.g., Bliss & Lømo, 1973; Cotman & Lynch, 1990). This electrical stimulation produces an increase in synaptic transmission that lasts for weeks afterwards, a phenomenon called **long-term potentiation.**

Long-term potentiation has a number of characteristics that suggest that a similar process occurs during the formation of normal memories. For instance, the long-term potentiation is limited to the synapses that are active at the time of the electrical stimulation; the inactive synapses are not changed. Long-term potentiation also occurs in many locations in the brain, though most prominently in the limbic system and the cortex—which we will see are regions closely identified with long-term memory. Finally, like memory, long-term potentiation can last for many weeks (and perhaps longer), even though the actual stimulation lasts just a fraction of a second (Abraham et al., 1991).

Incidentally, long-term potentiation may remind you of the sixth characteristic we listed for connectionism—that every new event changes the strength of connections. As we noted, connectionism was designed to be consistent with characteristics of the nervous system.

Long-term potentiation seems like a wonderful explanation for the formation of memories. The creation and decay of long-term potentiation is even correlated with the learning and forgetting of behavioral tasks (Abraham et al., 1991). However, we cannot yet be certain. Our legal system tries to prevent us from saying that a suspect is a criminal, based only on evidence that this person was present at the time of the crime and acts the way the criminal did. Similarly, we cannot firmly identify long-term potentiation as a perpetrator of memories, based only on circumstantial evidence.

Other researchers have pointed out that the neurotransmitters you read about in Chapter 3 are vitally important in memory. For example, people with Alzheimer's disease have decreased amounts of the neurotransmitter called acetylcholine. Other research shows that young adults show severe memory impairment when injected with a drug that blocks acetylcholine synapses (Beatty et al., 1986). Furthermore, when monkeys are given a drug that increases the action of acetylcholine, they perform worse than normal (Mishkin & Appenzeller, 1987). Obviously, neurotransmitters play an important role in memory. However, the specific mechanisms need to be more fully clarified.

Brain Structures Involved in Memory Two parts of the brain that are important in long-term memory are the hippocampus and the cerebral cortex.

The hippocampus appears to be necessary for explicit memories, but not for implicit memories (Squire et al., 1993). Consider the case of a man known by the initials H.M., who underwent neurosurgery when he was 27 years old. H.M. had been suffering from life-threatening epilepsy, and the surgeon removed selected parts of both temporal lobes of the cortex (see Figure 3.17) and portions of the hippocampus, a structure in the limbic system (see Figure 3.15). The surgery was successful in controlling H.M.'s epileptic seizures. However, the operation had an unexpected and tragic side effect that made him the most famous neurology patient of all time. Mysteriously, H.M. could accurately recall events that happened in his childhood, long before his surgery, but he could not remember what had happened after the surgery (Milner, 1970; Scoville & Milner, 1957).

For example, H.M.'s family moved several months after the surgery. When he was questioned one year after the move, he had not yet learned his new address. He could not recall the names of people he saw every day. He might read a magazine article on one day and not recognize that he had read the same article on the three previous days.

H.M. could retain some items in his short-term memory for several minutes, as Milner (1970) describes:

This man has anterograde amnesia. In a conversation he appears reasonably normal in many respects. However, he cannot form long-term memories and would be unable to recall your name after several minutes.

> *Thus he was able to retain the number 584 for at least 15 minutes, by continuously working out elaborate mnemonic schemes. When asked how he had been able to retain the number for so long, he replied: "It's easy. You just remember 8, subtract it from 17, and it leaves 9. Divide 9 in half and you get 5 and 4, and there you are: 584. Easy." (p. 37)*

However, a minute later, H.M. could not recall either the number or the elaborate memory device. In fact, he could not even recall that the examiner had given him a number to remember! H.M. is one of a few humans who truly has a memory like a sieve; his long-term memory seems to retain no new information. Surprisingly, though, his speech and his intelligence remain normal. You might talk with H.M. for several minutes before noticing that anything is wrong with his memory.

H.M. suffers from **anterograde amnesia,** an impaired ability to form long-term memory for new information. Formal testing reveals many clear-cut deficits. For example, he cannot recognize the names of people who became famous after his operation, and he cannot recall information about current events (Gabrieli et al., 1988; Ogden & Corkin, 1991). He has great difficulty remembering the spatial location of small toys arranged on a testing board (Smith, 1988). In other words, his explicit memory is defective, and he cannot transfer information from short-term memory to long-term memory. However, his implicit memory is reasonably good. For example, his performance improves each day he works on a challenging problem like the one in Demonstration 8.1. He may not remember having worked on it the previous day, but his ability to improve shows that implicit memory is functioning (Ogden & Corkin, 1991).

Research on other people with amnesia supports the suspicion that the hippocampus is important in forming long-term memories. For example, one group of researchers conducted magnetic resonance imaging studies on amnesic and control-group individuals (Press et al., 1989). As Chapter 3 described, **magnetic resonance imaging** involves passing a strong magnetic field through a person's head. The results showed that the hippocampus in the amnesics was roughly half as large as the hippocampus in the control-group individuals; some neuroscientists argue that a structure's size is modestly correlated with its ability to function. Figure 7.12 shows representative magnetic resonance images for an amnesic and a normal person.

As Squire (1992) explains, amnesia involves damage to the hippocampus or related structures, presumably impairing the capacity for long-term potentiation. Without a functioning hippocampus, you could not learn about amnesia. Without a functioning hippocampus, you would have no chance of remembering that we discussed the hippocampus in connection with classical conditioning. (The hippocampus is involved in a conditioned eyeblink response when there is a delay between the conditioned stimulus and the unconditioned stimulus.)

The hippocampus may be essential for forming long-term memories, but those memories are ultimately stored in the cerebral cortex (Mishkin & Appenzeller, 1987; Squire, 1992). As Killackey (1990) points out, the cortex is much more developed in humans than in other animals. This expanded cortex provides storage area for the impressive amount of information that humans are able to hold in their long-term

Figure 7.12

Magnetic resonance images for an amnesic person and a control-group person. The arrows point to the hippocampus, which is significantly smaller in the person with amnesia. (Source: Squire et al., 1990)

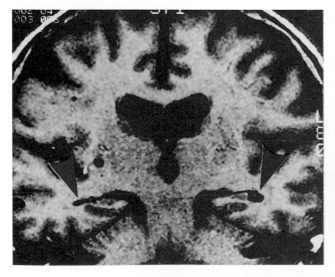
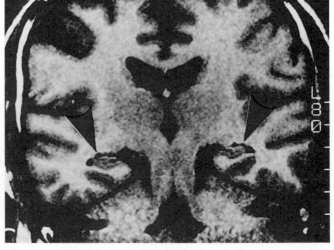

MRI for Amnesic Person

MRI for Control-Group Person

memory. The importance of the cortex is confirmed by animal research showing memory loss following lesions in the cortex. We also know that people with Alzheimer's disease have a substantially smaller cortex region than people with normal memory capacities. However, in general, neuroscientists have not explored the cortex as extensively as the hippocampus. In the words of two prominent researchers, the present work on the biology of memory has only mapped a rough landscape for future exploration (Mishkin & Appenzeller, 1987).

SECTION SUMMARY:
LONG-TERM MEMORY

- In general, we are more likely to encode an item in long-term memory if we paid attention to it, if it has been deeply processed, and if the retrieval context matches the encoding context.

- Eyewitnesses may recall events incorrectly if they heard other information prior to recall; flashbulb memories seem vivid, but they can be explained by ordinary memory mechanisms.

- Schemas generally improve our memory for events that happen frequently; however, we make mistakes if we rely on them too heavily.

- Research on retrieval shows that we can recall information stored in memory for decades (permastore) and that we have some knowledge of a word for which we are searching, even if we cannot recall the exact target (tip-of-the-tongue experience).

- Explicit memory involves the conscious recollection of previous experiences (e.g., recall or recognition); implicit memory involves performing a task (e.g., completing a word or supplying a free association). Research on amnesics and people who have been anesthetized shows poor performance on explicit memory tests and relatively good performance on implicit memory tests.

- We forget because of decay, interference, retrieval failure, and motivated forgetting.

- The connectionist approach is an influential new model based on networks, in which processes are parallel and knowledge is distributed throughout a network; other features include default assignment, processing with faulty input, graceful degradation, and strengthening of connections by new events.

- Research on the neuronal basis of long-term memory suggests that long-term potentiation may be responsible for the growth of memory; neurotransmitters such as acetylcholine may also be responsible.

- Research on people with amnesia demonstrates that the hippocampus is important in forming new memories; additional research demonstrates that those memories are stored in the cortex.

MEMORY IMPROVEMENT

Our investigation of memory has emphasized the fragility of sensory memory, the limited capacity of short-term memory, and the complexity of long-term memory. Now we shift from description to application. Your memory has excellent potential; how can you improve it?

We have mentioned several points already. First, you cannot remember something if it never enters memory. If you want to remember something—whether it is the details on a penny or someone's name—pay attention to it. Then be certain that you use a deep level of processing when you attempt to learn the material. You have probably had the occasional experience of discovering that your eyes have moved across several pages of text, yet you have no idea what you have read. That extremely shallow kind of processing will not trap any information in long-term memory. Instead try to think about the meaning of what you read, and rephrase a passage in your own words. Better still, remember the self-reference effect and see if you can relate the material to your own experiences.

Another suggestion for memory improvement comes from the encoding specificity principle. At the time of recall, try to re-create the context in which you originally learned the material.

Let us look at some other general principles of memory improvement, as well as some specific mnemonics (pronounced ni-*mon*-icks, with a silent *m*). **Mnemonics** is the use of a strategy to help memory. First we will examine four categories of memory improvement techniques. Our final topic is the most important of all. When you develop your metamemory, you become more aware that memory strategies should be used flexibly and that you need to regulate your study strategies effectively.

Practice

As simpleminded as it sounds, one way to improve memory is to increase your practice time—merely spend longer learning the material, no matter what technique you prefer. Each semester some of my introductory psychology students come in to ask for help after receiving a low grade on an exam. One of my first questions is, "How long did you spend studying?" An amazing number will provide an answer such as, "Well, I read every chapter and I looked over my notes." Except for a few lucky people, most students cannot master the material with only one exposure to the textbook and one review of lecture notes. Instead, they must read through the material two or three times, each time practicing the retrieval of information. (For example, what is the definition of *mnemonics?*)

The **total time hypothesis** states that the amount you learn depends on the total amount of time you practice (Baddeley, 1982). However, it would not be very effective to spend three extra hours studying for an exam if you spent those three hours letting your eyes simply drift across the pages of your textbook and notebook. It also would not be very effective simply to rehearse the material, repeating it over word for word. If you have resolved to improve your test performance, spend more time studying; however, study wisely and use the memory strategies discussed in this section. (Incidentally, try Demonstration 7.8 before you read further.)

Another important rule about practice is called the **spacing effect;** you will recall more material if you distribute your practice throughout several study sessions. In contrast, you will remember less material if you mass your learning into a single, uninterrupted session (Baddeley, 1982). Research consistently supports the spacing effect, and it is one of the most dependable findings in experiments on human memory (Dempster, 1988). I intentionally divided each chapter in this textbook into two to five sections to encourage you to take advantage of the spacing effect. An ideal way to study is to read one section of a chapter, complete the relevant section in the Study Guide, and then take a break. After the break, check the section summary for the part you just read. Then continue with the next section. Also, when you review material before a test, spread your study sessions across several days. Do not try to master it all on one day.

The spacing effect also applies to material you want to remember years from now. For example, Bahrick and Hall (1991) found that people recalled most of the material from high-school mathematics courses if they had an opportunity to rehearse it in college math courses (e.g. calculus). In contrast, students with similar grades in high-school mathematics courses—but no opportunities to practice the material in college—recalled very little.

If this student wants to remember the names of the people she is meeting on a job interview, she should try the expanding-retrieval-practice technique.

Suppose you have a relatively small number of items to remember, such as a list of four names of important people you have just met on a job interview. You will be much more likely to remember the names if you use a related technique called **expanding retrieval practice;** each time you practice retrieving the names, increase the delay period (Bjork, 1988). Imagine that you have just been introduced to several important people on a job interview. Repeat their names as soon as you have been introduced. Then rehearse them after 2 minutes, then 5 minutes, then 10 minutes. Incidentally, this technique even works well for people with Alzheimer's disease (Camp & McKitrick, 1992; McKitrick et al., 1992).

DEMONSTRATION 7.8 **Instructions and Memory**

Learn the following list of pairs by repeating the members of each pair several times. For example, if the pair is CAT-WINDOW, say over and over to yourself, "CAT-WINDOW, CAT-WINDOW, CAT-WINDOW." Just repeat the words, and do not use any other study method. Allow yourself one minute for this list.

CUSTARD-LUMBER	IVY-MOTHER
JAIL-CLOWN	LIZARD-PAPER
ENVELOPE-SLIPPER	SCISSORS-BEAR
SHEEPSKIN-CANDLE	CANDY-MOUNTAIN
FRECKLES-APPLE	BOOK-PAINT
HAMMER-STAR	TREE-OCEAN

Now, try to recall as many responses as possible. Cover up the pairs above.

ENVELOPE	_____	JAIL	_____
FRECKLES	_____	IVY	_____
TREE	_____	SHEEPSKIN	_____
CANDY	_____	BOOK	_____
SCISSORS	_____	LIZARD	_____
CUSTARD	_____	HAMMER	_____

Learn the following list of pairs by visualizing a mental picture in which the two objects in each pair are in some kind of vivid interaction. For example, if the pair is CAT-WINDOW, you might make up a picture of a cat jumping through a closed window, with the glass shattering all about. Just make up a picture and do not use any other study method. Allow yourself one minute for this list.

SOAP-MERMAID	MIRROR-RABBIT
FOOTBALL-LAKE	HOUSE-DIAMOND
PENCIL-LETTUCE	LAMB-MOON
CAR-HONEY	BREAD-GLASS
CANDLE-DANCER	LIPS-MONKEY
DANDELION-FLEA	DOLLAR-ELEPHANT

Now, try to recall as many responses as possible. Cover up the pairs above.

CANDLE	_____	DOLLAR	_____
DANDELION	_____	CAR	_____
BREAD	_____	LIPS	_____
MIRROR	_____	PENCIL	_____
LAMB	_____	SOAP	_____
FOOTBALL	_____	HOUSE	_____

Now, count the number of correct responses on each list. Did you recall a greater number of words with the imagery instructions?

Mental Imagery

Mental imagery refers to mental representations of things that are not physically present. The characteristics of these mental images are discussed in the next chapter, but now we focus on the ways imagery can help your memory. For example, in Demonstration 7.8, were you more accurate when you constructed a visual image in Part 2 than when you simply rehearsed the pairs in Part 1?

This demonstration is a simplified version of a study by Bower and Winzenz (1970). Participants in one of their conditions repeated the pairs silently to themselves, whereas participants in the imagery condition tried to construct a mental image linking the two words in vivid interaction. Each group saw 15 pairs. When they were tested, people in the repetition condition recalled an average of 5.2 items. In contrast, people in the imagery condition recalled 12.7 items—more than twice as many.

The key-word method is one of several mnemonics that relies on imagery. It is particularly useful when you want to link two items together and one of those items is not an English word. Let us say that you are learning Italian, and you want to remember that *roccia* means *cliff*. From the Italian word, *roccia*, you could derive a similar-sounding English key word, *roach*. Then picture a cockroach about to fall off a cliff, as in Figure 7.13. Thus, the **key-word method** uses visual imagery to link a key-word with another word. When Scruggs and his colleagues (1986) told fourth- and fifth-graders how to use this technique, they found that students improved their learning of Italian vocabulary by about 50%.

The key-word method can also be used to learn people's names, although it requires some effort. However, the time investment is worthwhile, because undergraduates complain that they forget people's names more than anything else (Crovitz & Daniel, 1984). The key-word method has been successfully used to help schoolchildren remember material in spelling, science, and social studies (Mastropieri & Scruggs, 1991) and to help those with Alzheimer's disease learn people's names (Hill et al., 1987).

Another useful mnemonic based on imagery is the method of loci (pronounced *low*-sigh). The **method of loci** instructs people to associate items to be learned with a series of physical locations. For instance, in your home you might identify several noticeable places, or loci, such as the driveway, inside the garage, the front door, the coat closet, and the kitchen sink. Let us say you need to remember a shopping list that includes hot dogs, cat food, tomatoes, bananas, and orange juice. You could make up an image for each of these items and imagine each in one of those home locations. For instance, picture giant *hot dogs* rolling down the *driveway*, a monstrous *cat eating food* in the *garage*, ripe *tomatoes* splattering all over the *front door*, bunches of *bananas* swinging in the *closet*, and a huge vat of *orange juice* gurgling down the kitchen sink (Bower, 1970). Then when you enter the supermarket, mentally walk the route from driveway to kitchen sink, recalling the items in order.

The method sounds unlikely, but does it work? In one study, people who had used the method-of-loci technique recalled about twice as many items as people in a control group when both groups were tested five weeks after the original learning (Groninger, 1971). Anschutz and her coauthors (1985) found that the method of loci was also helpful for elderly adults when they actually went shopping in a grocery store.

This section has emphasized that visual imagery is a powerful mnemonic. It is valuable when you simply want to link two English words together. Furthermore, the key-word method can help you learn foreign language vocabulary as well as people's names. Finally, you can use the method of loci to learn a list of items.

Organization

In the book *Your Memory: A User's Guide*, Alan Baddeley (1982) points out that long-term memory is like a huge library. Unless the information is stored in it in an

Figure 7.13
Key-word representation of roccia = cliff.

organized fashion, you will not be able to retrieve an item when you need it. Organization can help in two ways. First, it structures the material you are learning, so that when you recall a fragment, the rest of the material is also accessible. Second, organization relates the newly learned material to your previous knowledge, providing a structured body of information.

One of the most effective ways to organize material is to construct a hierarchy. A **hierarchy** is a system in which items are arranged in a series of classes, from the most general to the most specific. For instance, earlier in the book, Figure 3.10 showed how the divisions of the nervous system can be arranged in a hierarchy. Hierarchies encourage learners to arrange items into an orderly system that can boost recall more than 200% (Bower et al., 1969).

A popular mnemonic that makes use of organization is the first-letter technique (Herrmann, 1991). Maybe a piano teacher taught you that the notes falling on the lines in a musical selection can be remembered by taking the first letters of the sentence, "<u>E</u>very <u>G</u>ood <u>B</u>oy <u>D</u>oes <u>F</u>ine," and the notes that fall between the lines spell FACE. (See Figure 7.14.) Perhaps you even constructed your own mnemonics when faced with memorizing trigonometry formulas, chemical symbols, or lists of countries and their capital cities.

Finally, rhymes can provide a useful organizational structure, and people use them frequently in real-world memory tasks (Kelly & Rubin, 1988; Rubin & Wallace, 1989). If you're trying to recall the number of days in November, you probably will begin to recite the helpful rhyme, "Thirty days has September . . . ."

External Mnemonics

What would you do if you wanted to remember 10 things you needed to do before leaving on a trip? Unless they suddenly outlawed paper, you would probably write down a list. In other words, you would be likely to use an external mnemonic rather than one of the internal mnemonics we have been discussing.

When students are asked how often they actually use various memory aids, they report that they frequently rely on reminder notes, shopping lists, and calendars. Many times, they ask someone else to remind them, although they suspect this method is not very reliable (Harris, 1980; Intons-Peterson & Fournier, 1986). In general, students report that they tend to use external memory aids more often than internal aids when trying to remember to do something (for example, remembering to bring a pencil for a test) and for spatial rather than verbal tasks (for example, remembering information from a map).

Metamemory

Perhaps the most important advice about memory improvement is to develop your **metamemory,** or your knowledge and awareness about your own memory (Matlin, 1993b). When you try out a mnemonic strategy, ask yourself whether this device seems to be working. As we have stressed repeatedly, people differ tremendously from one another. Imagery may work for a classmate, but not for you.

You should also monitor your memory. If you think you know a particular list of items, test yourself and see whether your performance matches your expectations.

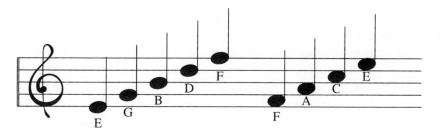

Figure 7.14

The first-letter mnemonics "<u>E</u>very <u>G</u>ood <u>B</u>oy <u>D</u>oes <u>F</u>ine" and FACE help beginning music students learn to read music.

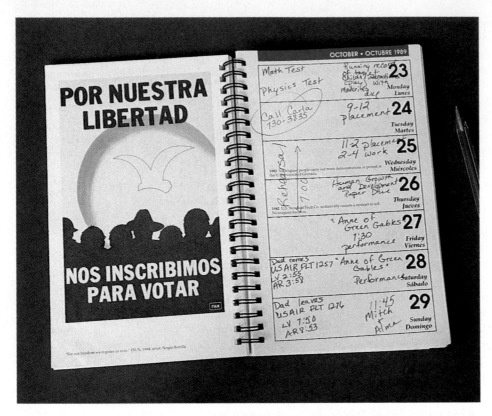

A calendar is an example of an external mnemonic.

Suzuki-Slakter (1988) found that students are not very accurate in predicting the effectiveness of various memory strategies. Specifically, they were overconfident about the effectiveness of simple rote memorization. They were underconfident about the effectiveness of more helpful memory strategies, such as imagery; when they used imagery, their performance was much better than they had expected.

Research on metamemory also tells us that students need to regulate their study strategies more effectively. Specifically, you should spend most of your time on the difficult material that you have not yet mastered, rather than dwelling on the material that is comfortably familiar (Nelson & Leonesio, 1988). For example, when you review this chapter for an exam, spend more time mastering the difficult material (perhaps the sections on the connectionist approach and biological aspects of memory) rather than the topics you already know. Plan which strategies you will use for which areas, so that you develop a flexible repertoire of techniques (Herrmann, 1991). Your memory has a tremendous potential to store information, and if you focus on metamemory, you can maximize that potential.

SECTION SUMMARY

MEMORY IMPROVEMENT

- The chapter has already discussed several memory hints: paying attention, deep levels of processing, and the encoding specificity principle.
- Memory also improves with increased practice time, when repetitions are spaced, and when the delay period increases between subsequent repetitions.
- Mental imagery is a useful mnemonic; the key-word method and the method of loci are two mnemonics that use imagery.
- Organization facilitates retrieval; organizational strategies include hierarchies, first-letter mnemonics, and rhymes.

- In real-world settings, external mnemonics are popular.
- Metamemory development is central in memory improvement; this includes checking to see if performance matches expectations and spending more study time on difficult items.

REVIEW QUESTIONS

1. Explain why sensory memory is necessary in both vision and hearing. Give some examples from everyday activities. Why is it so difficult to measure, and how have these difficulties been overcome with creative research methods?

2. Compare sensory memory, short-term memory, and long-term memory with respect to their capacity and duration. How is each of them measured?

3. What is the major form of encoding in short-term memory? What other kinds of encoding can be used? Give examples of each kind, together with evidence from research. From what you know about long-term memory, what kinds of encoding take place for items stored in long-term memory?

4. Organization was mentioned in connection with both short-term memory and the improvement of memory. Why is organization effective in each case? Think of recent examples when you used organization in a memory task. Why wasn't organization mentioned in connection with sensory memory?

5. What principle does each of these examples illustrate? (a) You cannot remember the words to a song you learned in high school, but they come flooding back when you find your old radio. (b) You were searching a friend's term paper for typographical errors, and you cannot recall much of the paper's contents. (c) A friend tells you that her car's windshield-wiper switch is on the left of her steering wheel; you cannot recall where it is located on your car, but when you sit in the driver's seat, you reach in exactly the right direction.

6. What does the material on amnesia tell us about implicit and explicit retrieval, and what does it tell us about the importance of the hippocampus?

7. Long-term memory is relatively permanent, yet we still forget. What are the four theories of forgetting, and what does the research on flashbulb memories and on eyewitness testimony suggest about the permanence of long-term memory?

8. What proof does this chapter offer about the active nature of memory? List as many examples as you can. What evidence does this chapter offer about the importance of encoding and retrieval measurement?

9. Describe the important characteristics of the connectionist approach to long-term memory. What other memory phenomena do these characteristics explain?

10. Think of as many memory strategies as you can, and select at least one portion of this chapter to learn using each strategy. Why would you need to consider metamemory as you study for an examination on this chapter?

NEW TERMS

memory
encoding
storage
retrieval
sensory memory
short-term memory (STM)
working memory
long-term memory (LTM)
iconic memory
partial-report technique
echoic memory
effortful processing
automatic processing
chunk
phonological loop
visuospatial sketch pad
central executive
depth of processing
self-reference effect
encoding specificity principle
outshining hypothesis
autobiographical memory
ecological validity
flashbulb memory
schema
heuristics
permastore
tip-of-the-tongue experience
explicit memory
recall

recognition
implicit memory
free associations
amnesia
decay
interference
proactive interference
retroactive interference
retrieval failure
motivated forgetting
repression
connectionist approach
parallel distributed processing approach
    (PDP approach)
serial search
parallel search
default assignment
graceful degradation
long-term potentiation
anterograde amnesia
magnetic resonance imaging
mnemonics
total time hypothesis
spacing effect
expanding retrieval practice
mental imagery
key-word method
method of loci
hierarchy
metamemory

RECOMMENDED READINGS

Baddeley, A. (1990). *Human memory: Theory and practice*. Boston: Allyn and Bacon. Baddeley's textbook is especially strong in its description of working memory, autobiographical memory, and connectionism.

Johnson, G. (1991). *In the palaces of memory: How we build the worlds inside our heads*. New York: Knopf. Johnson's enthusiastic book profiles three neuroscientists who have conducted research on the biological basis of memory.

Loftus, E. F., & Ketcham, K. (1991) *Witness for the defense*. New York: St. Martin's Press. In this book, memory-researcher Elizabeth Loftus shows how eyewitness testimony is used and misused in the courtroom.

Schacter, D. L. (1992). Understanding implicit memory: A cognitive neuroscience approach. *American Psychologist, 47*, 559–569. Schacter's review article briefly summarizes the important information about implicit memory and explicit memory, from the perspective of a researcher who believes that these memories involve different regions of the brain.

Searleman, A., & Herrman, D. J. (1994). *Memory from a broader perspective*. New York: McGraw-Hill. Consistent with the title of their textbook, these authors place memory within the larger context of internal (biological) factors as well as external (environmental) factors; their chapter on memory for social interactions is especially interesting.

Winograd, E., & Neisser, U. (Eds.). (1992) *Affect and accuracy in recall: Studies of "flashbulb" memories*. New York: Cambridge University Press. This volume contains chapters highlighting the research on flashbulb memory; these research summaries are both readable and interesting, and they emphasize ecologically valid research.

A N S W E R S   T O   D E M O N S T R A T I O N

DEMONSTRATION 7.6   The names of the seven dwarfs are Sleepy, Dopey, Grumpy, Sneezy, Happy, Doc, and Bashful.

Incidentally, the cartoon character shown on page 224 is a Smurf.

CHAPTER 8

THINKING

Consider the following examples of thinking:

1. You are visiting a college campus for the first time, and someone explained how to reach the student union from the admissions office. Now you are standing in the student union and need to return to the admissions office. You use *mental imagery* to reconstruct your original route and landmarks, which will help you retrace your steps.

2. You are scheduled to make a presentation in your communications class in 10 minutes, and you have discovered that the hem of your pants has come unraveled. You use *problem solving* and borrow a stapler from a nearby office, which provides a satisfactory temporary fastener.

3. You are standing on a street corner in New York City when a well-dressed gentleman apologizes for bothering you, but his pocket has been picked, including his train ticket back to Connecticut. Could you give him enough money to buy another ticket? You use *decision making* to conclude that he is probably one of those small-time con artists you have read about, rather than a person who deserves your compassion.

These three examples illustrate three different kinds of tasks that require thinking—namely, mental imagery, problem solving, and decision making. In **thinking**, we manipulate our mental representations to reach a conclusion.

Thinking is included in the larger category of mental activities called cognition. **Cognition** involves the acquisition, storage, retrieval, and use of knowledge. Chapter 4 focused on how our perceptual systems acquire knowledge, and Chapter 7 emphasized how our memory stores and retrieves that knowledge. The current chapter emphasizes how we *use* knowledge; we will explore how humans combine, manipulate, and transform knowledge when we think. For example, when we form a mental image of a geographic area, we transform statements into images. When we solve problems, we combine isolated facts to help us reach a goal. When we make deci-

DEMONSTRATION 8.1 Mental Rotations

Which of these pairs of objects are the same, and which are different?

Source: From Shepard & Metzler, 1971.

sions, we combine information from different sources to help us make a choice or a judgment. In each case, then, we demonstrate our impressive ability to synthesize and use information.

Throughout this chapter, we emphasize top-down processing. As discussed in the chapter on sensation and perception, **top-down processing** stresses the importance of our concepts, expectations, and prior knowledge. Naturally, thinking also requires **bottom-up processing**, which depends upon the information from our senses. For example, when we solve a math problem, we perceive numbers or geometric shapes (bottom-up processing). However, we also depend upon prior knowledge and strategies (top-down processing). When we think, we often use a special kind of top-down processing called heuristics. **Heuristics** are rules-of-thumb that are generally accurate. We will see how heuristics typically help us think quickly and accurately when we form mental images, solve problems, and make decisions. This speed and accuracy are consistent with Theme 1. However, we will see how people occasionally overuse these generally useful rules-of-thumb; we will see how heuristics can sometimes produce "smart mistakes."

MENTAL IMAGERY

Imagine a large pink pig wearing a tuxedo jacket and a top hat, fastening ice skates around its two rear legs, and skating gracefully across a frozen pond. Suddenly the pig reaches a crack in the ice where it falls through dramatically, plunging deep into a tub of chocolate fudge ice cream, concealed below the surface. Presumably, you have never witnessed this event. However, you can easily construct this sequence using mental imagery. **Mental imagery** refers to mental representations of things that are not physically present. A mental image resembles a perceptual image in many respects. Unlike a perceptual image, however, a mental image is not produced by the stimulation of sensory receptors, such as the rods and the cones of the eye (Finke, 1989). Instead, we generate the mental image via our cognitive processes.

How often do we use imagery? Stephen Kosslyn and his colleagues (1990) asked students to keep a diary of the mental images that occurred in their daily lives. The students reported that about two-thirds of their images were visual. The remaining one-third of the images involved the other senses—hearing, touch, taste, and smell. Psychologists' research preferences are also dominated by vision. Researchers occasionally study topics such as imagery for sound and touch (for example, Klatzky et al., 1991; Reisberg, 1992). However, most of the research focuses on visual imagery.

The first part of this section on mental imagery explores the characteristics of mental images. The second part investigates cognitive maps, which are mental representations that we use to find our way from one location to another.

Characteristics of Mental Images

Take a moment to construct a mental image of the cover of this textbook. Now contemplate how that particular image could be stored. Is it stored in a picturelike form, so that it resembles the experience you have when you actually look at the textbook cover and stimulate the receptors in your retina? This is the view of theorists who claim that information is stored in analog codes. An **analog code** is a representation that closely resembles the physical object (Kosslyn, 1980; Shepard, 1978). Psychologists who favor analog codes argue that mental imagery resembles perceptual experience.

However, psychologists who favor the **propositional viewpoint** argue that we store information in terms of abstract description. These descriptions can then be used to generate a mental image (Pylyshyn, 1978, 1984). For example, these theorists would argue that you store an abstract description of your textbook cover and could use that description to create an image. In other words, those who favor the propositional viewpoint suggest that we store images in memory the same way we store facts—no picturelike analog code is necessary (Klatzky, 1992). The controversy between the analog and the propositional approaches has not been resolved. However, we will see that some important evidence supports the analog approach.

How can we find out whether a mental image is stored in analog form or in propositional form? In fact, how can we discover anything about the characteristics of mental images, because they cannot be readily observed? After all, you can watch a rat pressing a bar, but what could you hope to learn by watching someone construct a mental image? We could ask people to introspect about their images. However, as noted in Chapter 5, people often do not have conscious access to their mental processes. Your description of how you constructed a mental image may not accurately capture what you did (Nisbett & Wilson, 1977; Pinker, 1985).

The research on mental imagery took a giant step forward when Roger Shepard had an unusual half-dream on November 16, 1968. He was just emerging from sleep on that morning when he visualized a three-dimensional structure magically rotating in space. This vivid image inspired a carefully controlled study on mental imagery (Cooper & Shepard, 1984; Shepard, 1978). Let us examine this research on the rotation of mental images. Then we discuss the size of mental images as well as some of their other important characteristics.

Rotating Mental Images Try Demonstration 8.1, which is based on the study inspired by Shepard's dream. Notice that in the first pair of designs (A), the left-hand figure can be converted into the right-hand figure by keeping the figure flat on the page like a picture and rotating it clockwise. Suddenly, the two figures match up, and you reply "same." The middle pair (B), however, requires a rotation in the third dimension. You may, for example, take the two-block "arm" that is jutting out toward you and push it over to the left and away from you. Suddenly, again, figures match up, and you reply "same." In the case of the pair on the right (C), all attempts to match the figures fail, and you conclude "different."

Roger Shepard and his colleague Jacqueline Metzler (1971) asked eight observers to judge 1,600 pairs of line drawings like these and to indicate whether the figures were the same or different. In each case, the experimenters measured the amount of time required for a decision.

As Figure 8.1 shows, the reaction time was strongly influenced by the amount of rotation required to line a figure up with its mate. It takes much longer to rotate a figure 160° than to rotate it a mere 20°. However—surprisingly—reaction times were similar for picture-plane rotations (as in pair A) and for third-dimension rotations (as in pair B).

The Shepard and Metzler study provides support for the analog view of mental imagery. Consistent with that approach, the operations we perform on mental images are similar to the operations we would perform on the actual physical objects. If you

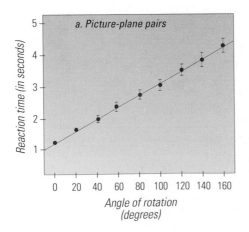

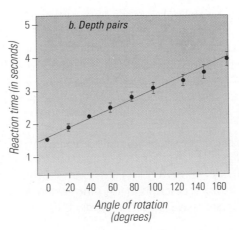

Figure 8.1

Reaction time for deciding that pairs of figures are the same, as a function of the angle of rotation and the nature of the rotation. Note: The center of each circle indicates the mean, and the bars on either side provide an index of the variability. (Source: Shepard & Metzler, 1971)

were holding two objects in your hands, trying to decide whether they were the same, it would take longer to rotate an object 160° than to rotate it 20°. However, rotating an object clockwise or counterclockwise in a picture plane would take the same amount of time as rotation in the third dimension.

The theme of individual differences reveals itself once more in the research on mental images. For instance, people who receive low scores on tests of spatial ability take about twice as long to rotate an object mentally, in comparison with people with high scores (Just & Carpenter, 1985).

In recent years, neuroscientists have investigated mental rotation. They examine humans who are brain damaged and use various brain-imaging methods such as PET scans to study normal humans (Farah, 1989; Kosslyn, 1988; Pellizzer & Georgopoulos, 1993). They have discovered that the parietal region of the cortex is involved when we rotate objects mentally. Furthermore, the right hemisphere is more active than the left hemisphere.

Imagery and Size Imagine a rabbit standing next to a fly. Now answer this question: Does a rabbit have an eyebrow? Next imagine a rabbit standing next to an elephant. Now answer this question: Does a rabbit have a beak?

Questions like these were part of a carefully planned series of experiments by Stephen Kosslyn, who has been a major researcher in imagery. Kosslyn (1975) wanted to discover whether people would judge large images more quickly than small images. A major problem, however, is the difficulty of controlling the size of someone's mental images. Kosslyn figured that a mental image of a rabbit next to a fly would force people to imagine a relatively large rabbit. In contrast, a mental image of a rabbit next to an elephant would produce a relatively small rabbit.

When you look at real-life pictures of animals, you can see all the details quite clearly on a large picture. On the other hand, details are squeezed so close together on a small picture that you will take longer to make judgments about them. If this same rule for real-life pictures also holds true for the pictures in our head, then people should make judgments more quickly with a large mental image (as in a rabbit next to a fly) than with a small mental image (as in a rabbit next to an elephant). Kosslyn's results support his prediction. People made judgments that were 0.21 of a second faster with a large mental image than with a small mental image. Because people made all these judgments, relatively quickly, that difference of about one-fifth of a second was substantial. Once again, we make judgments about mental images the same way we make judgments about actual pictures. Thus, this research supports the analog approach.

Other Characteristics of Mental Images We have seen that our mental images resemble physical objects with respect to the way they can be rotated and with respect to their size. Other investigations have shown similarities between mental images and physical objects in the way we make judgments about distance (e.g., Intons-Peterson et al., 1992) and about angles and shapes (e.g., Paivio, 1978; Shepard & Chipman, 1970). In addition, a mental image interferes with your perception of a physical stimulus, just as two physical stimuli interfere with each other (Segal & Fusela, 1970). Furthermore, neuroscience research shows that the visual cortex is especially active when people are instructed to create visual images (Farah, 1988; Goldenberg et al., 1988; Kosslyn & Koenig, 1992).

a. A large mental image of a rabbit

b. A small mental image of a rabbit

As Stephen Kosslyn demonstrated, you can make judgments about a large image (for example, a rabbit next to a fly) more quickly than judgments about a small image (for example, a rabbit next to an elephant).

DEMONSTRATION 8.2 Cognitive Maps

Answer the following questions about pairs of cities:

1. Is Reno, Nevada, to the east or west of San Diego, California?

2. Is Rome, Italy, to the north or south of Philadelphia?

In short, a variety of studies demonstrates that our thought processes typically treat mental images much like the perceptions of the physical objects they represent. As a consequence, most theorists favor a variation of the analog approach to mental imagery (e.g., Finke, 1989; Intons-Peterson, 1993). Now let us consider how we use visual imagery to form cognitive maps.

Cognitive Maps

A **cognitive map** is the internal representation of the way our spatial environment is arranged (Ormrod et al., 1988). We construct these cognitive maps when we try to imagine how a room might look if we rearranged the furniture or how to saw various pieces of wood from a sheet of lumber. We even construct cognitive maps when we read a description of a scene in a novel (Franklin & Tversky, 1990).

Researchers have discovered that people use several important heuristics when they construct cognitive maps. These rules-of-thumb usually help us think quickly and accurately. However, if we depend too heavily on these heuristics, we can make mistakes. Specifically, our cognitive maps may show geographic regions as being more regular than they really are (Tversky, 1990). Try Demonstration 8.2 before you read about the three heuristics we frequently use when we create cognitive maps.

The 90°-Angle Heuristic Moar and Bower (1983) studied people who had lived in Cambridge, England, for at least five years. Specifically, these researchers asked residents to draw sketches of several intersecting streets. The people showed a clear tendency to "regularize" the angles so that they were closer to 90° angles. Figure 8.2 shows some typical results. Three streets in Cambridge formed a triangle that contained actual angles of 63°, 50°, and 67°. As you can see, people estimated these same angles to be 78°, 88°, and 84°.

This systematic distortion can be explained by the **90°-angle heuristic**; when two roads meet, they typically form a 90° angle. As a result, we are likely to represent and remember angles in a mental map as being closer to 90° than they really are. Heuristics allow us to simplify, but sometimes simplification produces errors. You may recall from the discussion of schemas and memory that we tend to store a schema, rather than a precise version that accurately represents all the little details. A schema for an office, as we saw in Demonstration 7.4, is a simplification that produces errors. Similarly, the simplification "all street angles are close to 90°" also leads to errors.

The Rotation Heuristic According to the **rotation heuristic**, figures that are slightly tilted will be remembered as being either more vertical or more horizontal than they really are. For example, you are likely to remember the coastline of California as being more vertical than it really is. If your mental map suffers from this distortion, Reno, Nevada, would indeed be east of San Diego, California. (Figure 8.3 shows the true location of these two cities.) When Tversky (1981) questioned students at a California university, 69% showed evidence of the rotation heuristic. In their mental maps, the coastline was rotated in a more north-south direction than is true on a geographically correct map.

The Alignment Heuristic According to the **alignment heuristic**, we remember figures as being more lined up than they really are. To test the alignment heuristic, Tversky (1981) presented pairs of cities to students, who were asked to select which member of each pair was north (or east) of the other city. For example, one of those pairs was Rome-Philadelphia. As Figure 8.4 shows, Rome is actually north of Philadelphia. However, because of the alignment heuristic, people tend to line up the United States and Europe so that they are in the same latitude. Because people know that Rome is in southern Europe and Philadelphia is at the north end of the United States, they often conclude—incorrectly—that Philadelphia is north of Rome.

The results indicated that the students showed a consistent tendency to use the alignment heuristic. For example, 78% judged Philadelphia to be north of Rome, and 12% judged they were the same latitude. Only 10% correctly answered that Rome

If you were a participant in research on mental imagery and interference, you would have difficulty perceiving a small blue arrow on a screen if you had been instructed to make a mental image of a tree.

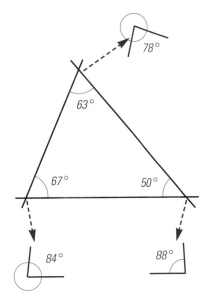

Figure 8.2

A triangle formed by three streets in Cambridge (shown in black). The mental maps for those angles are shown in red. Note that on the mental maps, the angles are closer to 90 degrees.

Figure 8.3

The actual location of two cities whose locations are likely to be distorted by the rotation heuristic.

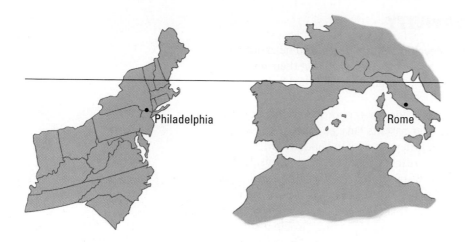

Figure 8.4

The actual location of two cities whose locations are likely to be distorted by the alignment heuristic.

was north of Philadelphia. On all eight pairs of cities that Tversky tested, an average of 66% supplied the incorrect answer.

The rotation and alignment heuristics may initially sound similar. However, the rotation heuristic involves rotating a single building, country, or other figure in a clockwise or counterclockwise fashion so that its border is oriented in a nearly north-south or east-west direction. In contrast, alignment involves lining up a number of buildings, countries, or figures in a straight row. Both heuristics are similar, however, because they encourage us to construct cognitive maps that are more orderly than they should be. (See Figure 8.5.)

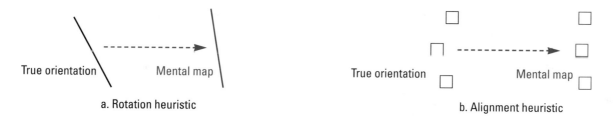

The three heuristics we have examined—regularization of angles, rotation, and alignment—all encourage us to simplify our environment and represent it as more regular than it really is. In general, these heuristics make sense, because our cities tend to have right angles, pictures are generally hung on walls in a vertical orientation rather than at a slant, and houses are typically lined up evenly along the streets. However, when we rely too strongly on these heuristics, we miss the important details that makes each region unique. That angle at the intersection is really 70°, not 90°; that coastline does not run exactly north-south; and those continents are not really arranged in a straight line.

Figure 8.5

The rotation and alignment heuristics.

SECTION SUMMARY

MENTAL IMAGERY

- People take longer to mentally rotate a figure 160° rather 20°, just as they take longer to rotate a physical object a greater number of degrees.

- People take longer to make judgments about small mental images than large ones, just as they take longer to make judgments about small physical objects.

- In general, the data on imagery support the analog-code approach, rather than the propositional viewpoint.

- Our cognitive maps are more regular than the actual geographic environment, because we use the 90°-angle heuristic, the rotation heuristic, and the alignment heuristic.

PROBLEM SOLVING AND CREATIVITY

Bob has a problem. Someone stole his child development textbook, and he cannot afford to buy a new one. All the other students in the class will be using their books to study for this Thursday's exam, and the library's copy has been checked out already. How can he manage to obtain a book?

Julia has a problem. She finished her paper for her economics course but she left it in the family car when she went home. Her parents have parked the car in the airport—400 miles from Julia's university—and they are now in Vancouver.

We use **problem solving** when we want to reach a certain goal, and this goal is not readily available. In these two examples, for instance, the book and the economics paper are not available. Problem solving is a major human activity in our interpersonal relationships as well as our occupations in this high-technology society (Lesgold, 1988). In this section, we will discuss problem understanding, problem-solving strategies, expertise, and barriers to problem solving. Our last topic is creativity, a special kind of problem solving.

Understanding the Problem

Some years ago, the companies housed in a New York City skyscraper faced a major problem. People in the building continually complained that the elevators moved too slowly. After some of the companies threatened to move out, plans were made to add an extremely expensive set of new elevators. Before the new construction began, however, someone decided to add mirrors in the lobbies near the elevators. The complaints stopped. Apparently, the original problem-solvers had not properly understood the problem. In fact, the real problem was the boredom of waiting for the elevators to arrive, rather than their slow speed (Thomas, 1989).

When you understand a problem, you construct a mental representation of its important parts (Greeno, 1977). You pay attention to the important information and ignore the irrelevant clutter that could distract you from the goal. For example, if you pay attention, the following problem proposed by Halpern (1989) is an easy one:

> *Suppose you are a bus driver. On the first stop you pick up 6 men and 2 women. At the second stop 2 men leave and 1 woman boards the bus. At the third stop 2 men leave and 1 woman boards the bus. At the third stop 1 man leaves and 2 women enter the bus. At the fourth stop 3 men get on and 3 women get off. At the fifth stop 2 men get off, 3 men get on, 1 woman gets off, and 2 women get on. What is the bus driver's name? (p. 392)*

Many complicated problems become much simpler if you first devise some kind of external representation—for example, some method of representing the problem on paper. (Mayer, 1988; Sternberg, 1986a). Let us consider several kinds of external representations. (Incidentally, if you still do not understand the bus problem, read the first sentence more carefully.) Try Demonstration 8.3 before reading further.

DEMONSTRATION 8.3 Representing Problems

Read the information and answer the final question. (The answer is at the end of the chapter.)

Five people are in a hospital. Each one has only one disease, and each has a different disease. Each one occupies a separate room; the room numbers are 101–105.

1. The person with asthma is in Room 101.
2. Ms. Jones has heart disease.
3. Ms. Green is in Room 105.
4. Ms. Smith has tuberculosis.
5. The woman with mononucleosis is in Room 104.
6. Ms. Thomas is in Room 101.
7. Ms. Smith is in Room 102.
8. One of the patients, other than Ms. Anderson, has gall bladder disease.

What disease does Ms. Anderson have and in what room is she?

Symbols Sometimes the most effective way to represent a problem is to use symbols, as you learned to do in high-school algebra. The major problem is learning to translate words into symbols. During this translation process, students may over-simplify the problem statements. For instance, if the problem reads "the rate in still water is 12 miles per hour more than the rate of the current," college students frequently represent the statement in a simpler form, such as "the rate in still water is 12 miles per hour" (Mayer, 1982, 1985). Obviously, a problem cannot be correctly solved if the words were not correctly translated into symbols.

Matrices The **matrix** is a chart that represents all possible combinations, and it is an excellent way to keep track of items, particularly when the problem is complex. Schwartz (1971) found that people solving "whodunit" problems such as the one in Demonstration 8.3 were more likely to reach a correct solution if they used a matrix like the one in the answer to the demonstration, at the end of the chapter.

Other Methods The method of representation that works best quite naturally depends upon the nature of the problem. Symbols and matrices are not always useful. Sometimes a simple list is best. A graph or a diagram can be used to solve a problem that is largely spatial. A visual image is often helpful, as my plumber once discovered when she was trying to fix my humidifier and needed a round metallic part. She represented the problem by trying to visualize this part and then determined where else she had seen an object like this—on an old lamp in her basement.

Problem-Solving Strategies

Once you have represented the problem, you can pursue a variety of strategies in solving it. Some methods are very time consuming, but they always produce an answer—maybe immediately and maybe several years later. Other methods require less time, but they may not produce a solution.

Algorithms An **algorithm** is a method that always produces a solution to a problem sooner or later. An income tax form is one example of an algorithm; following the steps precisely always produces a solution. An algorithm that is useful for other problems is a systematic random search, in which you try out all possible answers. Suppose that your watch is missing and you know that it must be somewhere in your room. You could start with the back left-hand corner and systematically search every cubic inch of the room, moving from left to right and up and down. You will find your watch, but this strategy is inefficient and unsophisticated because it considers all possibilities, even the unlikely ones (Newell & Simon, 1972).

Algorithms are useful, but we are more likely to use heuristics—those rules-of-thumb mentioned in connection with memory and cognitive maps. In problem solving, heuristics are selective searches that examine only the options most likely to produce a solution. For example, there is no point in searching the empty air for your watch, and it is unlikely that your watch is on the top shelf of the bookcase. Heuristics, unlike algorithms, do not guarantee a solution, but they do make a solution very likely. In your search for your watch, you might adopt a two-step heuristic, "First I'll look where I usually put it, and then I'll search all the flat surfaces." Let us consider two problem-solving strategies that use heuristics.

Means-Ends Analysis In a **means-ends analysis**, the problem solver divides the problem into a number of subproblems, or smaller problems. Each of these sub-problems is solved by figuring out the difference between your present situation and your goal, and then reducing that difference, for example by removing barriers (Mayer, 1991). In other words, you figure out which "ends" you want and then determine what "means" you will use to reach those ends. For example, the student with the stolen textbook, mentioned at the beginning of this section, might decide to borrow a textbook from a student who took the course last semester. "Borrowing a textbook" then becomes the "ends" that he wants to achieve. The problem can then be

DEMONSTRATION 8.4 The Hobbits-and-Orcs Problem

Try solving this problem. (The answer is at the end of the chapter.)

Three Hobbits and three Orcs arrive at a riverbank, and they all wish to cross onto the other side. Fortunately, there is a boat, but unfortunately, the boat can only hold two creatures at one time. Also, there is another problem. Orcs are vicious creatures, and whenever there are more Orcs than Hobbits on one side of the river, the Orcs will immediately attack the Hobbits and eat them up. Consequently, you should be certain that you never leave more Orcs than Hobbits on any riverbank. How should the problem be solved? (It must be added that the Orcs, though vicious, can be trusted to bring the boat back!)

divided into several subproblems: (1) make a list of friends and friends of friends who took the course last semester, (2) contact these people, and (3) pick up the book.

Try the Hobbits-and-Orcs problem in Demonstration 8.4. This demonstration illustrates a difficulty with the means-ends approach. Sometimes the correct solution to a problem depends upon temporarily increasing—rather than reducing—the difference between the original situation and the goal. It is painful to move anybody *backward* across the river to where they originally began (Gilhooly, 1982; Thomas, 1974).

In real life, as in Hobbits-and-Orcs problems, the best way to move forward is sometimes to move backward temporarily. Suppose that you are writing a paper and you thought you had successfully solved one subproblem, locating the relevant resources. You are now working on the second subproblem, reading the resources, and you realize that the topic is too narrow. You have to move backward to an earlier stage and locate additional resources before you move forward again.

Means-ends analysis has been examined with a computer simulation approach. In **computer simulation**, a researcher writes a computer program that will perform the task using the same strategies that a human would. For example, a researcher might try to write a program for the Hobbits-and-Orcs problem. This program would make some false starts, just as you did on Demonstration 8.4. This program should be no better at solving the problem than a human would be, but it also should be no worse.

The researcher tests the program by having it solve a problem and noting whether the steps it takes match the steps that humans typically take in solving the problem. The computer simulation approach forces the theorist to be clear and unambiguous about the components of the theory (Gilhooly, 1982).

Allen Newell and Nobel prize winner Herbert Simon developed a computer program called **General Problem Solver**, or **GPS**, a program whose basic strategy is means-ends analysis (Newell & Simon, 1972). The goal of the General Problem Solver is not simply to solve problems in the most efficient way, but to mimic the processes that normal humans use when they tackle these problems (Gardner, 1985). The GPS was based on information that was gathered from sessions in which people tried to solve a variety of problems and described their thoughts out loud as they worked on the problems.

The General Problem Solver used several different methods that people typically try. For example, it was programmed to compare the situation at the beginning of the problem with the final goal of the problem, and to try to reduce this difference by pursuing a secondary goal that was similar to the final goal. The GPS could solve transport problems like the Hobbits-and-Orcs problem, letter-number codes, and some trigonometry problems. However, the generality of the GPS was not as great as psychologists had originally hoped, so more sophisticated and flexible computer programs have been devised (Gardner, 1985; Waldrop, 1988). For example, a new program has been devised to play chess. This sophisticated program can beat all but a few chess masters (Hsu et al., 1990).

The Analogy Approach When we use the **analogy approach**, we use a solution to an earlier problem to help solve a new one. For example, did you ever consider why the windshield wiper on your car sweeps quickly across the glass and then pauses before taking another sweep? Inventor Bob Kearns was driving in the rain one day and realized that he—like many drivers with the old-fashioned wipers—was mesmerized by the leisurely back-and-forth rhythm of the wipers. He suddenly realized that a windshield wiper should work more like an eyelid. After all, we are rarely distracted when our eyelids sweep rapidly across the surface of our eyes! By creating an analogy between a windshield and the human eye, Kearns invented the intermittent windshield wiper (Seabrook, 1993).

Like the means-ends approach, the analogy heuristic usually—but not always—produces a correct solution. Analogies are useful in mathematics. For example, in geometry you probably learned to appreciate the similarity between a problem in a homework assignment and a geometry proof in your textbook. Educators know about the power of analogies. According to a survey, most college-level courses in critical thinking emphasize the use of analogies (Halpern, 1987).

Unfortunately, people often fail to apply the analogy heuristic correctly. For example, people often hesitate to transfer what they learned previously when they solve new problems (Mayer, 1988). For example, after solving one algebra problem that involves boats in a river, they often fail to use the same strategies on a similar problem 15 minutes later. In other cases, people form the incorrect analogy because they pay more attention to the specific objects and terms in the question than to the underlying, important meaning of the question (Novick, 1988). They may also fail to appreciate the relationships between the terms in the problem. Finally, even when people do understand the true analogy, they often make a mistake. Students tend to be more accurate if teachers encourage them to construct a table that clearly lists the important variables in both the previous and the new problem (Reed et al., 1985).

In summary, the analogy strategy is often useful. However, problem solvers may fail to notice the correct analogy, and they also make errors in interpreting the analogy.

How Expertise Helps Problem Solving

So far we have discussed how a generic human solves problems; we have not focused on the individual differences of Theme 2. As you might imagine, however,

The intermittent windshield wiper was invented by someone who created an analogy between the windshield and the human eye.

individual differences in problem solving can be impressive. How do experts differ from novices? Experts are not simply "smarter" than other people in all fields of knowledge. Instead, experts excel primarily in their own domains of expertise (Bédard & Chi, 1992; Glaser & Chi, 1988). You wouldn't expect a racetrack expert to excel at making French pastries! Here are some of the important areas where experts are more skilled than novices:

1. Experts store more information about their discipline in long-term memory (Anderson, 1993). For example, expert chess players are far better than novices at remembering various chess positions, even though the two groups are similar in remembering random arrangements of the chess pieces (de Groot, 1966). In many cases, experts may be more skilled than novices at transforming the stimuli into meaningful "chunks." Memory for relevant information is an important part of problem solving (Anderson, 1987).

2. Experts are likely to use more sophisticated models to represent abstract problems. They are also more likely to use appropriate mental images (Clement, 1991; Larkin, 1985; Larkin & Simon, 1987). For example, a neuroscientist has a more sophisticated and elaborate mental image of a neuron than does a beginning biology student.

3. Experts are more likely to apply analogies appropriately in their area of expertise. They are more likely to focus on the underlying meaning of the original problem, rather than on its surface structure (Novick, 1988). When they study the original problem, they are also more likely to try to explain why each step in that problem was required (Chi et al., 1989). Because they understand the original problem so well, they are more skilled at transferring that knowledge to a new, analogous problem.

4. Experts are faster and more efficient than novices. For example, some people are expert anagram-solvers. They seem to consider several alternate solutions at the same time (Novick & Coté, 1992). When experts see anagrams such as DNSUO, RCWDO, and PPRAE, the solution occurs to them in less than 2 seconds. In contrast, novices consider the alternative solutions one at a time. (Incidentally, are you a novice or an expert anagram solver?)

5. Experts have superior metacognitive skills related to problem solving in their area. **Metacognition** means your knowledge and awareness about your own thought processes. (We investigated one component of metacognition—called metamemory—in Chapter 7.) Experts are more aware when they are making an error, and they are more skilled at distributing their time appropriately when they solve problems (Glaser & Chi, 1988). In short, experts are more skilled than novices at numerous phases of problem solving. They are even more skilled at assessing their progress as they continue to work on a problem.

How Mindlessness Blocks Problem Solving

Before you read this section, try Demonstration 8.5, which illustrates one of the barriers to successful problem solving.

Have you ever found yourself solving a problem in the same old familiar way you have handled previous problems—and then discovered that another approach would have been much better? We saw in the section on analogies that we often solve problems successfully if we use a method that has proven useful in the past. However, we may rely too rigidly on our previous information and overuse our top-down processes, falling victim to mindlessness.

According to Ellen Langer, **mindlessness** means that we use information too rigidly, without becoming aware of the potentially novel characteristics of the current situation (Langer, 1989a, 1989b; Langer & Piper, 1987). In other words, we behave mindlessly when we rely too rigidly on previous categories. We fail to attend to the specific details of the current stimulus; we underuse our bottom-up processes.

Judit Polgar, a 15-year-old, plays 20 opponents simultaneously. Compared with a novice chess player, she probably stores more information about chess in her memory, uses more appropriate mental images, makes analogies with previous successful problem solutions, works faster, and shows superior metacognitive skills regarding the solution of chess problems.

DEMONSTRATION 8.5 Duncker's Candle Problem

Imagine you are in a room that contains only the material shown in this picture. You must find a way to attach the candle to the wall of this room so that it burns properly and wax does not drip on the floor. The solution appears at the end of the chapter.

One example of mindlessness is **functional fixedness**, which means that the function we assign to an object tends to remain fixed or stable. Successful problem solving often requires overcoming functional fixedness. For example, my sister described a creative solution to a problem she faced on a business trip. She had bought a take-out dinner from a wonderful Indian restaurant. Back in her hotel, she discovered that the bag contained no plastic spoons or forks, and the hotel dining room had closed several hours earlier. What to do? She searched the hotel room, discovered a plastic shoehorn in the "complimentary packet," washed it thoroughly, and enjoyed her chicken biriyani. To overcome functional fixedness, she had to realize that an object designed for one function (putting on shoes) could also serve another function (conveying food to the mouth).

The Duncker candle problem is the classic example in which the problem solver must overcome functional fixedness (Duncker, 1945). People typically think of the matchbox as simply a container for matches. Because its function seems fixed, they mindlessly ignore another possible function, as a "candle holder" (Weisberg & Suls, 1973).

Functional fixedness applies to the objects in problem solving. Another kind of mindlessness, *mental set*, applies to people when they solve problems. With a **mental set**, problem solvers keep using the same solution they have used in previous problems, even though there may be easier ways of approaching the problem. For instance, you are familiar with the kind of number puzzles in which you try to figure out the pattern that explains why a sequence of numbers has a particular order. Try figuring out why these numbers are arranged in the following order: 8, 5, 4, 9, 1, 7, 6, 3, 2, 0.

Functional fixedness and mental sets both demonstrate that mistakes in cognitive processing are usually rational. In general, objects in our world have fixed functions. We typically use a shoe horn to help a foot slip into a shoe, and we typically use a spoon to help food slip into our mouths. The strategy of using one tool for one task and another tool for another task is generally wise because each was specifically designed for its own task. Functional fixedness occurs, however, when we apply that strategy too rigidly and fail to realize that a clean shoehorn can make a suitable spoon.

Similarly, you are wise to apply the knowledge you learned in earlier problems when solving the present problem. (After all, that is the basis of the analogy strategy.) However, in the case of mental sets, we mindlessly apply the past-experience strategy too rigidly and fail to notice more effective solutions. For example, you might solve a number-series problem by trying to determine whether two adjacent numbers differ by a constant amount. Instead, you could solve the problem by thinking of other ways of arranging the items, such as in alphabetical order (eight, five, four, nine . . .).

Creativity

Creativity means the ability to produce unusual, high-quality solutions when solving problems (Eysenck, 1991). According to this definition, a solution can be unusual—even one of a kind—and still not qualify as being creative. For example, the nineteenth-century essayist Charles Lamb noted that one way to roast a pig would be to put it into a house and then burn down the house. Yes, it is an unusual solution, but it does not meet the criterion of being high quality. Similarly, a friend of mine who knew I liked both chocolate and garlic brought a plate of chocolate-covered garlic cloves to a dessert potluck. The dish was certainly unique, but since only two people had the courage to try this dessert—and they did not take second helpings—it probably would not be considered high quality.

Think of a person you know whom you consider to be creative. Most people—experts included—associate creativity with creative solutions to problems, responses on creativity tests, scientific explanations, and music or the visual arts (Tardif & Sternberg, 1988). However, people also can be creative in making up a pun, having a dream, or designing a new building (Perkins, 1981).

Measuring Creativity Creativity is extremely difficult to study, especially because the measurement of creativity is so challenging (Eysenck, 1991). Psychologists and educators have designed numerous creativity tests (Mansfield & Busse, 1981). Two of the most popular are illustrated in Demonstration 8.6.

The Divergent Production Tests and the Remote Associates Test, like other measures of creativity, have some potential to predict which people will be creative outside of laboratory testing situations, in school and in work settings. However, the correlations with real-life creativity are not particularly strong (Mumford & Gustafson, 1988; Nickerson et al., 1985). Take a moment to think about a work setting with which you are familiar, and consider several reasons why these creativity tests are not strongly correlated with on-the-job creativity.

Do you think that creativity is related to intelligence? In general, the research suggests that these two characteristics are related, but not identical (Baron, 1988; Haensly & Reynolds, 1989; Sternberg, 1990a). If we look at a broad sample of people, intelligence is somewhat correlated with creativity. One explanation for this correlation is that a person must be at least moderately intelligent to work in an occupation that encourages creative projects (Hayes, 1989). Intelligence seems to be necessary but not sufficient to produce creativity. In order for a person to be creative, he or she

People usually associate creativity with music, painting, and science, but the striking design of the Opera House in Sydney, Australia, is another example of creativity.

DEMONSTRATION 8.6 Two Tests of Creativity

1. The Divergent Production Test measures people's ability to think of a wide variety of responses to a question. Try some representative items.

   a. To the right are four shapes. Combine them to make each of the following objects: a face, a lamp, a piece of playground equipment, a tree. Each shape may be used once, many times, or not at all in forming each object. Each shape may be expanded or shrunk to any size.

   b. Suppose that people reached their final height at age 2, and so normal adult height was less than 3 feet. In a 1-minute period, list as many consequences as possible that would result from this change.

   c. Many words begin with an L and end with an N. List as many words as possible, in a 1-minute period, that

   have the form L_____N. (You can insert as many letters as you wish between the L and the N.)

2. The Remote Associates Test measures people's ability to see the relationships between ideas that are remote from each other. For each set of three words, try to think of a fourth word that is related to all three words. For example, the words ROUGH, RESISTANCE, and BEER suggest the word DRAFT, because of the phrases ROUGH DRAFT, DRAFT RESISTANCE, and DRAFT BEER. (The answers are at the end of the chapter.)

   a. FOOD   CATCHER   HOT
   b. TUG   GRAVY   SPEED
   c. ARM   COAL   PEACH
   d. TYPE   GHOST   STORY
   e. COUNTRY   GOLF   SANDWICH

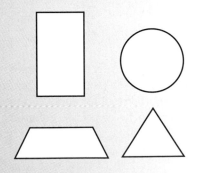

also needs to have other favorable factors, such as knowledge, the right kind of personality (for instance, a tolerance of uncertainty), and the motivation to work on creative tasks (Sternberg & Lubart, 1991). As we will see in the next section, creativity also requires the right kind of social setting.

Creativity and Evaluation One of the most important discoveries about creativity in recent decades is that it can be inhibited if people know they are going to be evaluated (Amabile, 1983; Hennessey & Amabile, 1984). In a typical experiment, college students were told to compose a poem. Half were told that the experimenter was simply interested in their handwriting, rather than the content of the poem. These students therefore did not expect to be evaluated on their creativity. The other half of the students were told that the experimenter was interested in the poem's content, and they would receive a copy of the judges' evaluations. In other words, these students knew they would be evaluated.

Each of the poems was judged by people who were poets. As you can see from Figure 8.6, the creativity scores were much higher for students who had no expectation that their poetry would be judged. In contrast, creativity was reduced when students thought that someone would be judging their poetry. Figure 8.6 shows that creativity was consistently inhibited by concern about evaluation—whether people worked in a group or by themselves.

Amabile's research suggests some significant recommendations. For instance, our educational system evaluates children. Even elementary school students know that their teachers will be judging their artwork, poems, stories, and other creative efforts. This expectation of evaluation is likely to reduce children's creativity (Ryan, 1984). Amabile's studies pose an interesting challenge for educators: How can we design education, so that children's creativity can blossom, in a system where teachers are expected to provide evaluations?

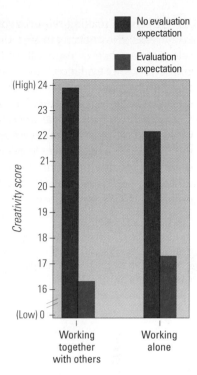

Figure 8.6
The influence of evaluation expectation and working condition on creativity. (Based on Amabile, 1983)

SECTION SUMMARY

PROBLEM SOLVING AND CREATIVITY

- Problem solving requires identifying the real problem and paying attention.
- A problem is often easier to understand if you can construct an external representation, for instance by using symbols or matrices.
- When you use an algorithm to solve a problem, you will reach a solution, but this strategy is inefficient; heuristics such as a means-ends analysis or the analogy approach are typically more useful.
- Expert problem-solvers differ from novices with respect to the amount of information stored in long-term memory, the problem representation, analogy use, speed, and metacognitive skills.
- Problem solving can be blocked by mindlessness, such as functional fixedness and mental set; in both cases, old ideas inhibit new solutions.
- Creativity is difficult to measure; intelligence is necessary but not sufficient to produce creativity.
- When people expect to be evaluated, their creativity can be inhibited.

DECISION MAKING

Every day you make dozens of decisions. Which line in the post office will move the fastest? Would the course in human development be more interesting if you signed up for Dr. Lopez's class or Dr. Hastings's? Can you finish reading the rest of this chapter before you have to leave for your chemistry lab?

Decision making requires you to make a choice about the likelihood of uncertain events. It can occur in situations when you make predictions about the future, select among two or more alternatives, and make estimates about frequency when you have scanty evidence. In decision making, we often lack clear-cut rules that outline how to make the best decision. Decision making, like other thinking tasks, requires us to combine, manipulate, and transform our stored knowledge.

When we have no rules or step-by-step procedures to use in decision making, we tend to rely on heuristics. As you know, heuristics are rules-of-thumb, or strategies that are likely to produce a correct solution. Heuristics are typically very useful, especially because they help us to simplify the overwhelming amount of information we could potentially consider when we need to make a decision (Hogarth, 1987). The problem arises, however, because we fail to appreciate that heuristics have their limitations. Even good rules-of-thumb should be applied with caution.

Throughout this section, we discuss studies that point out errors in decision making. However, these errors should not lead you to conclude that humans are limited, foolish creatures (Crandall, 1984). Instead, consider the similarity between errors in decision making and errors in perception, that is, illusions (Nisbett & Ross, 1980). Turn back to Figure 4.14 on page 117, and re-examine the Ponzo illusion. The major explanation for this illusion is the theory of misapplied constancy, which states that we take the constancy rule (one that we *should* use in most circumstances) and apply it inappropriately. Similarly, we make errors in decision making when we take these normally useful heuristics and apply them inappropriately. As Baron (1991, p. 487) says, we are "sometimes systematically irrational," and we make "smart mistakes."

In this section on decision making, we will look at three important heuristics: availability, representativeness, and anchoring and adjustment. Then we examine how decision making is influenced by the way a question is asked or framed. We conclude by examining people's confidence in their decisions. Now try this demonstration.

This woman is trying to decide which shampoo to buy. One has a more familiar name, but the other is less expensive. Heuristics will probably guide her decision.

DEMONSTRATION 8.7 **Familiarity and Availability**

Read the following list of words. Then turn to Demonstration 8.8 on page .263. for further instructions.

Louisa May Alcott
Alice Walker
John Dickson Carr
Laura Ingalls Wilder
Thomas Hughes
Jack Lindsay
Edward George Lytton
Margaret Mitchell

Michael Drayton
Henry Vaughan
Edith Wharton
Richard Watson Gilder
Judith Krantz
Agatha Christie
Robert Lovett
Maya Angelou
Virginia Woolf
Judy Blume
George Nathan

Allan Nevins
Henry Crabb Robinson
Jane Austen
Joseph Lincoln
Charlotte Brontë
Arthur Hutchinson
James Hunt
Toni Morrison
Brian Hooker
Harriet Beecher Stowe

IN DEPTH: The Availability Heuristic

We will examine the availability heuristic in detail because it has inspired several recent studies. Let's first consider an example.

Suppose that someone asks you whether your college has more biology majors or geology majors. Presumably, you have not memorized the enrollment statistics. Therefore, you would be likely to answer the question in terms of the relative number of people in these two majors whose names come to mind. You can easily retrieve the names of biology majors ("Sara, Lucia,

Chi-Ming...") because your memory has stored the names of dozens of people in this major. However, you can think of only one person's name in geology. Because examples of biology majors were easy to retrieve, you conclude that your college has more of them. In this case, making a decision based on the number of examples that come to mind could be a fairly reliable way to answer the question.

We use the **availability heuristic** whenever we estimate frequency or probability in terms of how easy it is to think of examples of something (Tversky & Kahneman, 1973). When deciding which major is more popular, for instance, it is easier to think of examples of biology majors than geology majors. The availability heuristic is useful, insofar as the availability (or ease with which examples are remembered) is correlated with true, objective frequency. However, as you will see, there are other factors that influence memory retrieval but are *not* correlated with objective frequency. Any factor that distorts the ease with which we think of examples will produce systematic inaccuracies in our frequency judgments (MacLeod & Campbell, 1992).

One factor that influences memory retrieval is recency. In general we can recall an event better if it happened yesterday, rather than a year ago. For example, you can probably recall the details about the latest world crisis more clearly than the details of the 1991 war with Iraq.

Familiarity is a second factor that influences memory retrieval. Familiarity distorts frequency judgments in the same way that recency distorts these judgments. Specifically, we are likely to recall items better if they are familiar, rather than unfamiliar. For instance, Demonstration 8.7 shows 14 names of well-known women authors and 15 names of not very familiar men authors. You probably remembered the familiar women's names more readily, and so you estimated that the list contained more women's names than men's names. In other words, availability was more influenced by familiarity than by true, objective frequency.

This demonstration is a modification of a study by Tversky and Kahneman (1973), who presented people with lists of 39 names. A typical list might contain 19 names of famous women and 20 names of less famous men. After hearing the list, they were asked to judge whether the list contained more men's names or more women's names. About 80% of the participants mistakenly guessed that the group with the most famous, familiar names was the more frequent, even though that group was objectively less frequent.

The Availability Heuristic and Judgments About Oneself Some of the recent research has examined how the availability heuristic influences people's judgments about themselves. For example, Schwarz and his colleagues (1991) asked participants to recall 6 examples of their own assertive behavior. Even shy people can manage to recall 6 examples; these examples come readily to mind. Participants in another condition were asked to recall 12 examples of their own assertive behavior. This task is more challenging; these examples require more effort to recall. When everyone was asked to rate his or her own assertiveness, those in the easy-task condition (high availability) rated themselves as more assertive than those in the difficult-task condition (low availability).

Similarly, MacLeod and Campbell (1992) manipulated the ease with which people recalled pleasant and unpleasant events (by encouraging them into either a good or a bad mood). Later, people who had recalled pleasant events estimated that their future would contain more pleasant events than unpleasant events. In contrast, people who had recalled more unpleasant events estimated a larger number of unpleasant events in their future. Once again, availability influences people's frequency judgments.

A third area in which the availability heuristic influences people's decisions about themselves concerns self-efficacy. As you will learn in more detail in Chapter 13, **self-efficacy** is the feeling individuals have that they are competent and effective. Daniel Cervone (1989) examined how people's self-efficacy could be influenced by the availability of thoughts about themselves. Cervone specifically examined how envisioning future activities could influence people's feelings of self-efficacy for solving problems that involve maze-like graphs.

Prior to the task, Cervone asked undergraduates to think about factors that could influence their performance on the task. Some were instructed to imagine positive factors (for example, "What do you think are some personal characteristics that may make it easy for you to find solutions to the graphs?"). Others were instructed to imagine negative factors (for example, "What do you think are some personal characteristics that may make it difficult for you to find solutions to the graphs?"). Still others received no instructions about imagining.

Cervone assessed the influence of these imagination instructions on two dependent variables. One variable was people's self-efficacy, which was measured in terms of the number of graph problems they expected to solve. As you can see from Figure 8.7, people who had thought of factors that would make the task difficult did indeed have low levels of self-efficacy. In contrast, people who imagined factors that would make the task easy and people in the control condition had relatively high self-efficacy.

The imagination instructions even influenced the students' behavior. Cervone's second dependent variable involved task persistence; how many trials would an individual persist on the graph problems before switching to a different task? As you can see from Figure 8.8, the task persistence mirrored the self-efficacy results. Specifically, those people who had thought of factors that would make the task difficult were likely to give up. In contrast, people in the other two groups were more likely to persist on this task.

Cervone's study suggests some practical implications. If you want to boost your confidence and persistence on a task, think about the factors that could help you persist. In other words, make these factors more available. In contrast, avoid thinking about factors that could make you fail!

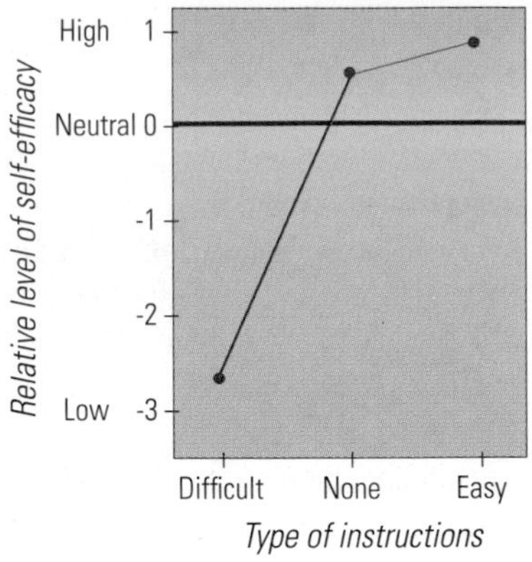

The Availability Heuristic and Medical Decisions Another practical implication of the availability heuristic involves people's decisions about medical procedures and disease. For example, Pauker and Kopelman (1992) point out in a prestigious medical journal how availability can be biased by recency. The article described a physician who was reluctant to recommend a particular medical procedure for a patient. Another of his patients had recently undergone this procedure and had developed a serious neurological disorder. Pauker and Kopelman point out that physicians should be unbiased decision makers. They should carefully weigh all costs and benefits, and they should not be overly influenced by the most recent events.

Availability also influences the public's opinion of diseases and other causes of death. For example, newspapers do not tend to report deaths due to diabetes or emphysema, even though these diseases cause 16 times as many deaths as do accidents (Slovic et al., 1982). Because we cannot easily think of examples of people dying from these two diseases, we do not judge them to be very serious. As Yates (1990) points out, the evening television news is not likely to announce, "Asthma kills 25 in Kansas! Details at 11!"

A serious consequence of these misjudgments is that people are not likely to take preventive measures against a disease they believe to be rare (Kristiansen, 1983). Plous (1993) creatively suggests that organizations such as the American Cancer Society should launch public information campaigns that raise the availability of the names of these diseases that receive less publicity. For example, a billboard might say, "THIS YEAR, MORE PEOPLE WILL DIE FROM STOMACH CANCER THAN FROM CAR ACCIDENTS." If thoughts about the dangers of this disease are readily available, people would be more likely to seek medical advice when they detect any early signs of the disease.

In summary, the availability heuristic is used when we estimate frequency in terms of how easily we can think of examples. However, this generally useful rule-of-thumb can be distorted by recency and familiarity. The availability heuristic can influence judgments about ourselves on characteristics such as assertiveness, the pleasantness of our future lives, and our sense of self-efficacy. Finally, availability can also influence doctors' decisions and the public's ideas about the danger of various diseases.

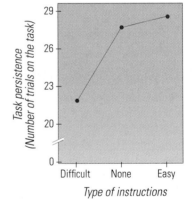

Figure 8.7
The effect of instructions (imagining factors that would make a task difficult, no instructions, imagining factors that would make a task easy) on self-efficacy. Note: People rated their self-efficacy on graphs relative to their self-efficacy on anagrams. (Based on Cervone, 1989)

Figure 8.8
The effect of instructions (imagining factors that would make a task difficult, no instructions, imagining factors that would make a task easy) on task persistence. (Bases on Cervone, 1989)

The Representativeness Heuristic

Suppose that you have a normal penny with both a head (H) and a tail (T). You toss it six times. Which seems like the more typical outcome: (a) H H H H H H; (b) H H H T T T; or (c) H T T H H T? Most people select the last option. After all, you know that a coin tossed six times is likely to come up heads three times and tails three times. It would be much less likely to come up heads all six times in your sample. Furthermore, you know that coin tossing should produce heads and tails in random order. Option *b,* H H H T T T, has the right number of heads and tails, but it does not look very random. The last option, H T T H H T, looks like the most typical, representative outcome.

When you use the **representativeness heuristic,** you decide whether the sample you are judging looks typical and appropriate. For instance, a sample of coin tosses should have 50% heads and no systematic order in the pattern of heads and tails.

When people make decisions about the relative frequency of different samples, such as coin tosses, they often seem to be unaware of the true probabilities (Kahneman & Tversky, 1972). For example, the *specific* sequence H T T H H T is no more likely to occur than the *specific* sequence H H H H H H. However, we do not consider the true probabilities. Instead, we base our decision on representativeness.

We should stress that representativeness usually leads to the correct choice in everyday decisions. For example, suppose you were asked which of the following samples of IQs would be more likely: (1) 100, 100, 100, 100, 100, or (2) 140, 140, 140, 140, 140. You would appropriately select the first option because the sample mean of 100 matches the mean of 100 in the population, and more people have IQs of 100 than IQs of 140. Representativeness is generally a useful heuristic that produces wise decision making. However, when we overuse it, we can make incorrect decisions.

Base Rate and Representativeness Representativeness is so compelling that people tend to ignore the **base rate,** or how often the item occurs in the population. For example, Kahneman and Tversky (1973) gave people this description:

> *Jack is a 45-year-old man. He is married and has four children. He is generally conservative, careful, and ambitious. He shows no interest in political and social issues and spends most of his free time on his many hobbies which include home carpentry, sailing and mathematical puzzles. (p. 241)*

People were told that this paragraph described one person selected from a group of 30 engineers and 70 lawyers; what was the probability that he was one of the 30 engineers?

The participants in this study typically ignored the base rate (that is, the fact that 70% of the sample consisted of lawyers). Instead, they focused on the fact that Jack's characteristics were representative of an engineer. As Gilovich (1991) points out, we expect examples to look like the categories of which they are members. That

Advertisements such as this one should make the names of some serious diseases much more available to the general public.

description of Jack looks most like an engineer. We fail to note that—with more than twice as many lawyers as engineers in the sample—the description probably fits a larger number of lawyers.

The Conjunction Fallacy and Representativeness   Be sure to try Demonstration 8.8 before you read further. Now look at your answers, specifically numbers 4 and 7. Which did you think was more likely, "Linda is a bank teller" or "Linda is a bank teller and is active in the feminist movement"?

When Tversky and Kahneman (1983) presented problems like these, students answered that Linda was much more likely to be a bank teller who is active in the feminist movement. Students studying for their PhDs in decision making—who had several advanced courses in probability—were just as likely to make this mistake as undergraduates who had little mathematical background.

Let us see why this decision was incorrect. Which is more likely, that someone is a psychology major or that this person is a psychology major at a college in New York? Whenever we add a restriction such as "at a college in New York," we decrease the probability because we are eliminating some people. There are more bank tellers in this country than there are bank tellers active in the feminist movement—because we have eliminated the group of bank tellers who are not active in the feminist movement (see Figure 8.9). Statistically, the probability of any two events (such as "bank teller and feminist") occurring together cannot be greater than the probability of either one of those events occurring alone (such as "bank teller"). However, people commit the **conjunction fallacy:** They judge the probability of the conjunction (two events occurring together) to be greater than the probability of one event.

The conjunction fallacy can be traced to the representativeness heuristic. The characteristic "feminist" is very representative of someone who is single, outspoken, a philosophy major, concerned about social justice, and an antinuclear activist. A person with these characteristics does not seem likely to become a bank teller, but she seems highly likely to be a feminist. By adding the extra detail of "feminist" to "bank teller," we have actually decreased the number of people in the group. However, we have increased the believability of the description. The description is now more representative, so we decide that it is more likely.

When used appropriately, the representativeness heuristic can help us make good decisions. However, the frequent misuse of this heuristic suggests that we should pause when trying to decide which of two options is more likely. One option may sound much more attractive because the description is so very representative—so very typical. However, before selecting this option, be sure to pay sufficient attention to the base rate, and make certain that you are not committing the conjunction fallacy.

The Anchoring and Adjustment Heuristic

Recently I saw an advertisement for boots in a catalog. The chatty description included this passage, written from the perspective of the company president:

The truth is, I like boots very much. I just don't like most of the boots that I see for sale. I am offended by boots costing $875. I am deeply offended by boots costing $1,200.

The price of this company's boots? A mere $247. I found myself momentarily agreeing that the price seemed reasonable. And then it occurred to me: I had fallen victim to the anchoring and adjustment heuristic. My anchor for a price of boots had been momentarily (and very inappropriately) set at $1,200. Even knocking off a few hundred dollars, $247 seemed justifiable . . . until I regained a better perspective.

In the **anchoring and adjustment heuristic,** we make an estimate by guessing a first approximation (an anchor) and then making adjustments to that number on the

Would you guess that this man is a poet or a successful businessman? If you focus on representativeness, rather than base rate, you would respond "poet." However, he is the successful owner of a music store in Geneseo, New York.

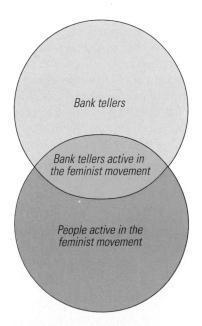

Bank tellers

Bank tellers active in the feminist movement

People active in the feminist movement

Figure 8.9

A diagram showing the relationship between the sets described in Demonstration 8.8. As this diagram shows, the number of bank tellers must be larger than the number of bank tellers who are active in the feminist movement. (See Demonstration 8.8.)

basis of additional information. Like the other two heuristics we have examined, this heuristic often leads to a reasonable answer. However, people typically rely too heavily on the anchor, and their adjustments are usually too small (Slovic et al., 1974; Tversky & Kahneman, 1982).

Consider a study in which people were asked to estimate various quantities (Tversky & Kahneman, 1974). A typical question asked participants to estimate the percentage of African countries that belong to the United Nations. Before requesting the reply, the experimenters spun a wheel while the participants watched. At random, the wheel selected a number between 0 and 100. The participants were asked to indicate whether their answer to the question was higher or lower than the selected number, and to supply an estimate.

Even though the selected number had been chosen completely at random, it still acted as an anchor for people's estimates. For example, if the wheel had stopped on 10, people estimated that 25% of the African countries were in the United Nations. If the wheel had stopped on 65, people estimated 45%. In other words, a number that had no real relationship to the question had served as an anchor for the response. People did make adjustments from this number, in the direction of the correct answer. However, these adjustments were typically far too small.

Keep the anchoring and adjustment heuristic in mind when you next need to estimate a quantity. Provide an educated guess as a first anchor. Then make adjustments from that anchor, based on other information. However, urge yourself to make appropriately large adjustments. Suppose, for instance, that you are trying to figure out how many bottles of soda pop to order for a party, to which about 12 people will come. You bought 12 bottles for 6 people last February, so twice that, or 24, would be a first approximation, or anchor. But now it is July, and people are likely to be thirstier. You are serving spicy Buffalo-style chicken wings, so people need to soothe their tongues, and the party is likely to last longer. If you rely too strongly on the anchor, you are sure to run short. Keep in mind that each of those new pieces of information requires a substantial adjustment upward from that original anchor. You really should double your original estimate!

Decision Frames

We have seen that decision-makers use three heuristics that are generally helpful. They make estimates on the basis of the ease with which they can recall examples (availability). They decide which option is more likely on the basis of whether it looks typical (representativeness). They estimate quantity by making a first guess and then making modest adjustments (anchoring and adjustment). In each case, however, people may use a heuristic inappropriately, and they underestimate the importance of other relevant information. In the case of a **decision frame,** people are influenced by the wording of a question, and they again underestimate the importance of other relevant information.

Imagine that you have decided to see a play, and you have paid $10 for the ticket. As you enter the theater, you discover that you have lost the ticket. The office did not record ticket purchases, so you cannot recover the ticket. Would you pay $10 for another ticket for the play? Now change the scenario somewhat. Imagine, instead, that you have decided to see a play, and you plan to pay $10 for the ticket. As you enter the theater, you discover that you have lost a $10 bill. Would you still pay $10 for the ticket for the play?

In both cases, the amount of money involved is $10, yet the decision frame is different for these two problems. We seem to organize our expenses into separate mental accounts. In the first example, buying a second ticket to the play seems to raise the ticket price to $20—perhaps more than we want to spend. When Kahneman and Tversky (1984) asked participants in their study, only 46% said that they would pay $10 for another ticket. In contrast, in the second example, we do not tally the lost $10 in the same account. We view this loss as being generally irrelevant to the ticket.

In fact, 88% of the participants in Kahneman and Tversky's study said that they would purchase the ticket in this second condition.

If we consider only mathematics when we make the decision, we would see that the two examples are identical. However, we are distracted by the wording of the question, or the context in which it appears. The framing effect is just as persistent as the famous Müller-Lyer illusion you saw in Figure 4.13. You know that the lines are supposed to be the same length, just as you know that the $10 ticket loss equals the $10 bill loss. In both cases, however, the frame (either geometric or verbal) influences the interpretation.

This information on framing should encourage you to analyze whether a decision you are making is inappropriately influenced by the question's wording. Researchers have discovered many applications of decision frames. For instance, credit card companies have found that customers prefer the phrase *cash discount,* rather than *credit card surcharge*—even though the same money is involved (Thaler, 1980). Furthermore, when people are asked to narrrow down the pool of applicants for a job, they eliminate more applicants when they are told to accept the most suitable applicants than when they are told to reject the least suitable applicants (Huber et al., 1987). In addition, conflicts arise over environmental issues because policy officials usually frame the decision in economic terms, whereas community residents frame the decision in terms of personal health risks (Vaughan & Seifert, 1992).

The framing of a decision is also important in medical decisions. In one study, people were told about two options for treating someone's lung cancer. The surgical option was described as having a lower survival rate over the short term but a higher survival rate over the long term—in contrast to the nonsurgical option. When the options were presented in terms of *living,* 84% of the participants said they preferred surgery. When the options were presented in terms of *dying,* 56% preferred surgery. Clearly, physicians who offer options to patients can influence patients' choices by the language frame in which the question is presented (McNeil et al., 1982; Payne, 1985).

Research on decision frames shows that people are influenced by the way information is worded. Would shoppers be as likely to purchase this ground beef if the label said, "20% fat"?

Overconfidence About Decisions

In July 1988, the USS Vincennes was in the Persian Gulf. Its radar system detected an airplane taking off from an Iranian airport, flying directly toward the ship. Captain Will Rogers was faced with a decision: Was the unknown aircraft attacking his ship, or was it simply a civilian airplane? Captain Rogers decided to launch two missiles at the aircraft. As both Rogers and the rest of the world soon learned, the plane was only a civilian airline, and all 290 passengers aboard the plane died when the plane was shot down. As a panel of decision-making theorists pointed out, Captain Rogers had been overconfident about his original judgment (Bales, 1988). He failed to verify the characteristics of the plane and whether it was ascending or descending.

We saw earlier in this chapter that people often make less than ideal decisions. They use the availability, representativeness, and anchoring and adjustment heuristics too frequently, and they are influenced by the framing of the question. Given these sources of error, people should not be very confident about their decision-making skills. However, instead of being underconfident, people are typically *overconfident.* We are especially likely to be overconfident when the judgment is difficult and when we are novices in a discipline, rather than experts (Keren, 1987; Plous, 1993).

What are the reasons for this overconfidence? One factor is that people are often unaware that their knowledge is based on very questionable assumptions (Slovic et al., 1982). Also, we notice evidence that supports our decision, and we neglect evidence that supports the options we rejected (Dawes, 1988). In fact, we may have difficulty even recalling those rejected options! If we cannot even recall the other options, we are likely to be overly confident that our decisions are correct (Gettys et al., 1986). The next time you need to make an important decision, keep in mind this information about overconfidence!

In 1988, Captain Will Rogers of the USS Vincennes decided to launch missiles at an airplane taking off from Iran, and 290 passengers were killed. Decision theorists have concluded that this error is an example of overconfidence in decision making.

This chapter has focused on the way top-down processing and heuristics influence our cognitive processes. When we create mental images, solve problems, and make decisions, we rely upon our previous experiences and some important rules-of-thumb. These factors generally help us think quickly and accurately. When we overuse previous experience and heuristics, however, we make unwelcome errors. In Chapter 17 will discuss how these same factors operate in social cognition, when we make decisions about other people and when we try to explain their actions.

S E C T I O N   S U M M A R Y

DECISION MAKING

- When we use the availability heuristic, we estimate frequency in terms of how easily examples come to mind. This heuristic is usually accurate, but it can be distorted by recency and familiarity.

- The availability heuristic can influence judgments about our own assertiveness, the pleasantness of our futures, and our sense of self-efficacy, as well as decisions about medical issues.

- When we use the representativeness heuristic, we make decisions on the basis of whether the sample we are judging looks typical. This heuristic is generally accurate, but people often pay too little attention to the base rate or they fall victim to the conjunction fallacy.

- When we use the anchoring and adjustment heuristic, we rely too heavily on the anchor and make inadequate adjustments when considering additional information.

- When we make decisions, we are often influenced by the decision frame, or wording of a question.

- We are likely to be overconfident that our decisions are correct.

R E V I E W   Q U E S T I O N S

1. An important theme running through this chapter is that people tend to use a small number of general rules when they work on a cognitive task. Explain how people use heuristics in cognitive maps, problem solving, and decision making.

2. In what ways do people treat mental images the same as they treat the perceptions of physical objects? Discuss the research evidence on this issue that supports the analog code approach to mental images.

3. With respect to mental imagery, predict what will happen in each of these situations: (a) You are trying to remember whether your friend parts his hair on the left or on the right, and you have constructed a small mental image, rather than a large one. (b) You are trying to reconstruct a traffic accident at a corner where two roads meet at a 75° angle. (c) You are drawing a map for a friend, based on your recall of a route; one town is not quite north of the other, and the road connecting them is tilted about 20° from the vertical.

4. At the beginning of the chapter, we noted that thinking involves the manipulation and use of knowledge. Describe how each of the three topics in this chapter uses knowledge, and illustrate each topic with an example from your recent experience.

5. The section on problem solving discussed methods of representing a problem. Think of a problem that could be effectively represented by each of the following methods: symbols, matrices, graphs, and visual images.

6. Think about the last time you lost something. Describe how you might have used each of the following problem-solving strategies to search for the missing

object: the algorithm of a systematic random search, means-ends analysis, and analogy.

7. The analogy method of problem solving suggests that we should look for similar situations in our past experiences. Why do the problem-solving barriers suggest that we should not rely too heavily on our past experiences? Why does the research on expertise suggest that past experience is useful?

8. Which decision-making heuristic does each of the following examples illustrate? (a) You try to estimate how long it will take to read a chapter in another textbook, based on the fastest rate at which you can read a chapter in this textbook. (b) You see a bearded professor wearing a hand-woven jacket, and you decide that he is a member of the art department (which has 5 members), rather than a member of one of the science departments (which have a total of 40 members). (c) Someone asks you how common amnesia is, and you reply that it is quite common, based on your recall of recent soap-opera plots.

9. According to an old saying, you can view a cup as being either half full or half empty. Why is this saying relevant to decision frames? Summarize some of the information about decision frames.

10. This chapter contains some practical advice about your thought processes. List 8 to 10 practical tips that you could use to make your thinking processes more effective.

NEW TERMS

thinking	computer simulation
cognition	General Problem Solver (GPS)
top-down processing	analogy approach
bottom-up processing	metacognition
heuristics	mindlessness
mental imagery	functional fixedness
analog code	mental set
propositional viewpoint	creativity
cognitive map	decision making
90°-angle heuristic	availability heuristic
rotation heuristic	self-efficacy
alignment heuristic	representativeness heuristic
problem solving	base rate
matrix	conjunction fallacy
algorithm	anchoring and adjustment heuristic
means-ends analysis	decision frame

ANSWERS TO DEMONSTRATIONS

DEMONSTRATION 8.3   Ms. Anderson has mononucleosis, and she is in Room 104. To solve this problem you can set up a matrix with the names of the patients and the room numbers listed. Then read through the list of statements. In three cases, we find out which patient is in which room; this information allows us to place the word *yes* (indicated in red on the chart on page 269) in three locations in the matrix, and to eliminate these rooms and these people from the "still uncertain" list. (A blue check on the chart on page 269 indicates we have taken care of these rooms and people.) We can also note the disease (in green) where appropriate.

Because Ms. Jones has heart disease, she cannot be the patient with mononucleosis in Room 104; she must be in Room 103. Therefore, Ms. Anderson must be the patient with mononucleosis in Room 104.

	(asthma)			(mono-nucleosis)	
	101	102	103	104	105
Anderson	✓	✓			✓
(heart disease) Jones	✓	✓			✓
(gall bladder?) Green	✓	✓	✓	✓	yes
(tuberculosis) Smith	✓	yes	✓	✓	✓
(gall bladder?) Thomas	yes	✓	✓	✓	✓

DEMONSTRATION 8.4   In the Hobbits-and-Orcs problem, let us let R represent the right bank and L represent the left bank. Here are the steps in the solution:

1. Move 2 Orcs, R to L.
2. Move 1 Orc, L to R.
3. Move 2 Orcs, R to L.
4. Move 1 Orc, L to R.
5. Move 2 Hobbits, R to L.
6. Move 1 Orc, 1 Hobbit, L to R.
7. Move 2 Hobbits, R to L.
8. Move 1 Orc, L to R.
9. Move 2 Orcs, R to L.
10. Move 1 Orc, L to R.
11. Move 2 Orcs, R to L.

DEMONSTRATION 8.5   The solution involves attaching part of the matchbox to the wall, then melting some wax to attach the candle to the platform.

DEMONSTRATION 8.6   a. DOG; b. BOAT; c. PIT; d. WRITER; e. CLUB.

RECOMMENDED READINGS

Finke, R. A. (1989). *Principles of mental imagery.* Cambridge, MA: MIT Press. Finke is well known for his research on mental imagery; this book is a clear, well-organized overview of the characteristics of mental images.

Matlin, M. W. (1994). *Cognition* (3rd ed.). Fort Worth, TX: Harcourt Brace & Company. This textbook includes chapters on imagery, problem solving, and decision making, as well as related topics such as logical reasoning.

Plous, S. (1993). *The psychology of judgment and decision making.* New York: McGraw Hill. This interesting textbook includes chapters on each of the decision-making heuristics discussed in the present chapter. It also examines other perspectives on decision making, as well as related topics from social psychology.

Solso, R. L. (1991). *Cognitive psychology* (3rd ed.). Boston: Allyn and Bacon. Solso's textbook includes chapters on imagery, problem solving, and decision making. Students may also be interested in the separate chapters on expertise and on artificial intelligence.

Weisberg, R. W. (1993). *Creativity: Beyond the myth of genius* (2nd ed.). New York: Freeman. Weisberg's book examines creative problem solving, as well as scientific and artistic creativity. He also examines some of the myths that have arisen about creativity.

CHAPTER 9
LANGUAGE AND CONVERSATION

Imagine how your life would be transformed if you were forbidden to use language during the next 24 hours. You could not read any books or attend any lectures. Television, radio, and most forms of entertainment would be eliminated. And what would your life be like without conversation? A colleague who was drafted and sent to Vietnam recalls discussing possible war injuries with his Army friends. Which human ability seemed most precious—sight or mobility, for example? In fact, he concluded that the ability to sit and have a conversation with someone—to enjoy language—seemed most important (Beach, 1989).

Our ability to speak and listen has made human culture possible. Language enables this big-brained, loudmouthed, featherless species to create artistic and scientific innovations and to interact with each other in extremely complex ways (Miller, 1981). In fact, language is central to our understanding of human psychological processes (Miller, 1990).

Language is an astonishing accomplishment. When we want to understand and produce speech, we must activate our perceptual skills ("Did the speaker say *bear* or *pear*?" "Is that scrawled signature *Tim* or *Tom*?") In fact, we need all our cognitive skills, because language depends upon memory, imagery, problem solving, and decision making—the topics of our last two chapters. However, language is also the most social of our cognitive activities. We typically use language with other people, and our knowledge of the social world helps us interpret the language we hear and select the words we speak. Therefore, this chapter foreshadows the social interactions that we will examine more closely in the last chapters of the book.

This chapter is divided into three sections: understanding language, producing language, and language and thinking. The important topic of language development is examined in Chapter 10.

UNDERSTANDING LANGUAGE

When we understand language, we hear a set of noises or look at an arrangement of scribbles. Somehow we manage to make sense of them, using our knowledge about sounds, letters, words, language rules, and information about the world. An important part of understanding spoken language is speech perception. Other topics in this section include how we understand meaning and how we manage to read written passages.

Speech Perception

You turn on the television, and the soap opera hero says, "But I really love you, Felicia . . . " That wiggling of the tongue, contortion of the lips, and throbbing of the larynx produce sound vibrations that eventually reach the receptors in your ears (and presumably Felicia's as well). Your auditory system manages to translate these vibrations into a series of sounds that you perceive to be speech.

Speech perception is an extremely complex process (Coren et al., 1994; Matlin & Foley, 1992). However, we usually pay little conscious attention to this process. We tend to concentrate on the message, rather than the language used to deliver this message.

Bottom-Up and Top-Down Processing In Chapter 4, we discussed how visual shape perception depends on both bottom-up and top-down processing. **Bottom-up processing** begins with information from the sensory receptors, in other words, at the bottom (or lowest level) of perception. **Top-down processing** emphasizes how perception is shaped by observers' concepts, expectations, and prior knowledge—in other words, the kind of information stored at the top (or highest level) of perception. Thus, you recognize yourself in the mirror partly because the rods and cones in your retina are gathering information about hair color, facial shape, and skin complexion (bottom-up). But your prior knowledge informs you that you are the most likely person to appear in that mirror (top-down).

Speech perception, like visual shape perception, is guided by both bottom-up and top-down perception. You recognize each **phoneme** (or basic sound unit of speech, such as the sounds *th*, *a*, and *t* in the word *that*) partly because the receptors in your cochlea gather precise information about pitch and other characteristics of the sound (bottom-up). However, your concepts, expectations, and prior knowledge are also critically important. If someone says, "The dentist told the girl to brush her tee__," your top-down processing skills are scarcely challenged. The context of the sentence as well as the context of the word fragment *tee-* assure you that the missing phoneme is *th* rather than *b*, *m*, or *z* (Massaro, 1987).

Humans are so skilled at top-down perception that they sometimes believe they hear a phoneme that is truly missing, an effect known as **phoneme restoration**. In a classic experiment, Warren and Warren (1970) played three sentences for the listeners in their study. These sentences were identical with one exception: A different word was spliced onto the end of each sentence. In each case, a coughing sound was inserted in the location indicated by the asterisk:

1. It was found that the *eel was on the axle.
2. It was found that the *eel was on the shoe.
3. It was found that the *eel was on the orange.

These researchers found that the listeners reported hearing different words, as a function of the context. The "word" *eel* was heard as *wheel* in the first sentence, *heel* in the second, and *peel* in the third.

Phonemic restoration is a kind of illusion. People think that they hear a phoneme, even though the correct sound vibrations never reach their ears (Warren 1984). Additional experiments have confirmed that top-down processing encourages us to "hear" a phoneme or even a word that is not there (Cooper et al., 1985; Huttenlocher & Goodman, 1987; Samuel & Ressler, 1986).

We are so tolerant of missing sounds and mispronunciations in sentences that we often fail to notice children's highly inaccurate pronunciations. For instance, one of my students recalled singing a Christmas carol in which the shepherds "washed their socks by night" instead of "watched their flocks by night." Another remembered a carol that began "O come all ye hateful: Joy, Phil, and their trumpet." Adults typically tolerate children's mispronunciations because their top-down processing encourages them to hear what their expectations predict.

DEMONSTRATION 9.1   Resolving Ambiguous Boundaries Between Words

When we try to determine where the boundaries lie that separate the words in spoken language, we face a task that resembles this one. The string of letters below lacks the white spaces that typically separate the words in written language. Where would you place the boundaries? Two answers appear at the end of the chapter, but you may be able to think of others.

THEREDONATEAKETTLEOFTENCHIPS.

Source: Based on Jusczyk, 1986.

Word Boundaries Have you ever overheard a conversation in a language that you do not know? The words seem to run together in a continuous stream, with few boundaries between them. However, when you hear your native language, you hear distinct words. When you read, you see white spaces clearly identifying the boundaries between words. When you listen, the "white spaces" seem almost as distinct.

In most cases, however, the actual spoken language does not have clear-cut pauses to mark the boundaries. In fact, researchers have discovered that English speakers use a pause or other physical marker for less than 40% of the word boundaries (Cole & Jakimik, 1980; Flores d'Arcais, 1988). Demonstration 9.1 shows a task that is the visual equivalent of identifying boundaries in spoken language.

Listeners are quite remarkable in using the rhythms of speech and their own stored knowledge to figure out which sounds should be grouped together (Cutler, 1987). Fortunately, most of the time, top-down processing helps us interpret those unclear boundaries correctly. However, as the previous chapter on thinking emphasized, heuristics that usually work correctly can sometimes produce an error. Consider the grandmother who heard a line from a Beatles song. She was more familiar with illness than with hallucinogenic experiences, and so she heard "the girl with colitis goes by," rather than "the girl with kaleidoscope eyes" (Safire, 1979). Similarly, a student first heard a Creedence Clearwater Revival song entitled "Bad Moon on the Rise" when she was in a bar. She interpreted a key line as "bathroom on the right." (Wellman, 1993). We can make errors when we rely too heavily on expectations, rather than on the information in the auditory stimulus.

Understanding and Meaning

When we understand language, we do much more than perceive phonemes and identify the boundaries between words. We also decode the meaning of the language we hear. We identify meaning in word fragments, in concepts, and in larger units.

Morphemes A **morpheme** is the smallest language unit that has meaning. A morpheme can be a fragment of a word, as long as it conveys meaning. Thus, the fragments *un-*, *-est*, *-s*, and *-ly* are all morphemes because each of these suggests meaning (e.g., *un*easy, tall*est*, textbook*s*, and slow*ly*). A morpheme can also be an entire word, such as *the*, *small*, and *language*. Notice, then, that the word *unfriendly* contains three morphemes, or meaning units.

Conceptual Meaning Psychologists and others interested in language find it challenging to describe how humans store conceptual meaning in memory. For example, think about the meaning of the concept *apple*. In your many years of experience with apples, you know the characteristics of apples, you know several varieties of apples, and you know that *apple* belongs to the larger category of *fruit*.

One theory of meaning, the **network model**, proposes that concepts are organized in memory in a netlike pattern, with many interconnections. The meaning of a particular concept, such as *apple*, depends upon the concepts with which it is connected (Collins & Loftus, 1975). As you can guess, this theory resembles the more elaborate connectionist approach we examined in the chapter on memory.

Figure 9.1 shows what one person's network structure might look like for the word *apple*. Keep in mind that each of these concepts in this figure has its own individual network structure. Try imagining a network of associations surrounding each of the other items in the network, such as *nutritious*, *red*, and *fruit*. Clearly, the representation of meaning in memory is both rich and complex.

According to the network model, when you perceive the name of a concept, that particular location becomes activated. In addition, the activation spreads to the nearby terms, much like dropping a rock into a pool of water (Wessells, 1982). So when you perceive the word *apple*, all its important characteristics are activated in your memory.

According to the network model of conceptual meaning, a photo of this rose will activate related concepts such as flower, fragrant, thorns, *and perhaps* Valentine's Day.

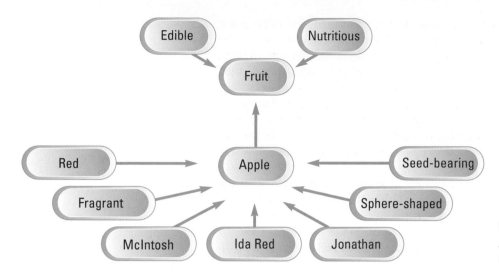

Figure 9.1

An example of a network structure for the concept apple.

A second theory of meaning argues that we organize each concept according to a **prototype**, or best example of a concept. This approach emphasizes how we establish meaning by placing items in categories; its focus is different from the network model's emphasis on a concept's important attributes. The **prototype approach** points out that people decide whether an item belongs to a category by comparing that item with a prototype. For example, your prototype for a bird is probably a feathered creature with wings, shaped like a robin or a sparrow. If an unfamiliar creature outside your window resembles this prototype, you categorize it as a bird.

An important assumption of the prototype approach is that all members of a category are *not* created equal. Instead, a category has a **graded structure**, in which the most representative or prototypical members have priority and the category's nonprototypical members have lower status (Barsalou, 1987; Neisser, 1987; Rosch, 1973). For example, consider the category, *vehicle*. Prototypical vehicles, such as *car* and *truck* have priority in this category. Somewhere further down the line are less prototypical vehicles, such as *tractor* and *raft*. At the bottom of the pile lie those non-prototypical vehicles, such as *wheelbarrow* and *elevator* (Rosch & Mervis, 1975).

Prototypes have unusual prominence, as research by Eleanor Rosch and her colleagues has demonstrated. For instance, when people are asked to provide examples of particular categories, they supply prototypes more often than nonprototypes (Mervis, Catlin, & Rosch, 1976). If you ask some friends to name a vegetable, they are likely to supply prototypes such as *carrots* or *peas*, rather than nonprototypes such as *pumpkin* or *mushrooms*.

Furthermore, prototypes can substitute for a category name in a sentence; non-prototypes cannot (Rosch, 1977). Try substituting a prototypical fruit name (e.g., *apple*) in the sentence, "One of my favorite desserts is fruit pie." Now notice the bizarre results when you substitute a nonprototypical fruit name (e.g., *olive*). People also learn concepts more readily when they are organized around a prototype, rather than a nonprototype (Rosch, 1973). Everything considered, prototypes have a special, privileged status (Smith, 1989).

The network model and the prototype approach both help resolve the mystery of how we understand conceptual meaning. The network model emphasizes that our thoughts about one concept will automatically activate thoughts about related concepts. The prototype approach explains the organization of categories, so that *vehicle* makes us think of *car*, rather than *wheelbarrow*. Now let us consider larger units of meaning, beyond these individual concepts.

Interpreting Strings of Words Suppose that you turn on the radio, and the weather forecaster says, "It will be colder on Tuesday, with possible snow flurries

According to the prototype approach to conceptual meaning, a robin is a prototypical bird, whereas a peacock is nonprototypical.

developing Tuesday night." According to the most widely accepted view of language comprehension, you divide that sentence into constituents, instead of analyzing the sentence one word at a time. A **constituent** is a group of words that seems to belong together as a unit. Typically, a constituent contains more than one word but less than an entire sentence (Clark & Clark, 1977). In the case of the weather forecaster's message, you would probably divide that sentence into two major parts, with the comma as the dividing line. Each of those major parts could be divided into smaller constituents (for example, "It will be colder"). Listeners seem to extract the gist (or general meaning) from each constituent group of words; they do not analyze a sentence on a word-by-word basis.

Listeners develop a variety of heuristics for identifying constituents (Clark & Clark, 1977; Kimball, 1973). For example, when you hear the word *with* in the forecaster's report, you know that a noun must eventually come. Listeners also rely on word parts, such as *-er*, *-y*, and *-ly* to indicate the part of speech of a word. Thus, *-er* words are often nouns, whereas *-y* words are usually adjectives and *-ly* words are usually adverbs.

As adult speakers, you are so skilled at identifying constituent structure that you can perform this operation on sentences that are close to nonsense. Consider these lines from Lewis Carroll's poem "Jabberwocky":

> *Twas brillig, and the slithy toves*
> *did gyre and gimble in the wabe:*

In the final constituent, for example, the words *in* and *the* help us to divide the sentence and identify *wabe* as a noun. Earlier, the word part *-s* suggests that *toves* is either a noun or a verb. Once again, we use heuristics, or rules-of-thumb, to help us solve the language puzzle.

Surface Structure and Deep Structure At the age of 27, the linguist Noam Chomsky described a new approach to language, sometimes referred to as the Chomskyan revolution (Miller, 1991; Rosenberg, 1993). Chomsky (1957, 1965) proposed that people listening to their native language have the ability to understand the abstract relationships underlying the strings of words they actually hear. His model distinguished between a sentence's surface structure and its deep structure. **Surface structure** is represented by the words that are actually spoken or written. In contrast, **deep structure** is the underlying, more abstract representation of the sentence.

Two sentences may have different surface structures but similar deep structures, as in the following sentences:

> *The student read the book.*
> *The book was read by the student.*

Two sentences can also have identical surface structure but different deep structures, as in the ambiguous sentence,

> *The police must stop drinking after midnight.*

The meaning of this sentence seems to flip back and forth between its two different deep structures. We have difficulty keeping both meanings in mind simultaneously (Miller, 1981).

Chomsky devised rules to describe how listeners transform surface structure into deep structure, and how speakers transform the deep structure they wish to express into the specific words they utter. Currently, most psychologists support Chomsky's notion of the distinction between surface and deep structure, though they are less likely to support some of his more specific predictions (Garnham, 1985; Prideaux, 1985; Tartter, 1986).

DEMONSTRATION 9.2   Figuring Out the Meaning of a Word From Context

Read the paragraph below. Then define, as precisely as possible, the two words that are italicized. (The answers are shown at the end of the chapter.)

Two ill-dressed people—the one a tired woman of middle years and the other a tense young man—sat around a fire where the common meal was almost ready. The mother, Tanith, peered at her son through the *oam* of the bubbling stew. It had been a long time since his last *ceilidh* and Tobar had changed greatly; where once he had seemed all legs and clumsy joints, he now was well-formed and in control of his hard, young body. As they ate, Tobar told of his past year, re-creating for Tanith how he had wandered long and far in his quest to gain the skills he would need to be permitted to rejoin the company. Then all too soon, their brief *ceilidh* over, Tobar walked over to touch his mother's arm and quickly left.

Source: Based on Sternberg & Powell, 1983.

Reading

You probably spend several hours a day reading. You read textbooks, notes scribbled on blackboards, notices on bulletin boards, newspapers, and the list of in- gredients on cereal boxes. By now, reading is typically automatic, something you can take for granted.

However, reading skills are actually very impressive and complex. Skilled read- ing requires that numerous component processes work in harmony with each other (Perfetti, 1993). For example, your eyes must move forward in saccadic movements, and you must use shape perception to identify the individual letters. (Both of these processes were examined in Chapter 4.) You must also recognize the words you are reading and figure out the meaning of unfamiliar words. Furthermore, you can ac- complish all these tasks at the rate of about 300 words per minute (Carver, 1990). Reading is another example of our theme that humans are extremely competent creatures.

Word Recognition   As you read this sentence to yourself, how do you actually recognize the words? This page is decorated with some little squiggles, interrupted by white spaces. How do those squiggles lead you to a word's meaning? According to the most influential model of reading, called the **dual-encoding model**, we can reach a word's meaning through either of two routes (Crowder & Wagner, 1992; Van Orden et al., 1990). The dual-encoding model argues that we can recognize common words di- rectly from the printed symbols. For example, you look at the word *ball*, and that visual pattern leads you directly to information in your memory about that word's meaning.

What happens when you see a difficult or unfamiliar word, such as *nonphono- logically* or *pseudoword?* According to the dual-encoding model, you first translate these unusual words from the ink marks on the page to a sound code, and then locate the word's meaning. (Think about it. Doesn't it seem that you pronounced these two words silently as you read them?) This dual-encoding arrangement helps us read the common words quickly and the uncommon words carefully.

Using Context to Decode the Meaning of an Unknown Word   Suppose that you had never previously seen the word *squiggles,* as it was used at the begin- ning of the section on word recognition. How could you find out the meaning of this new word? Sternberg and Powell (1983) emphasize that people exploit a rich variety of context cues. Be sure to try Demonstration 9.2 before you read further.

Sternberg and Powell argue that we use helpful context cues to discover the meaning of a new word. For example, consider the sentence:

At dawn, the blen arose on the horizon and shone brightly.

The phrase *at dawn* is a context cue telling us when the *blen* arose. The words *arose* and *shone* describe its actions, and *on the horizon* provides an important cue about where it occurs. With all these different cues, an experienced reader can easily understand that the nonsense word *blen* stands for *sun*.

To test their theory about context cues, Sternberg and Powell (1983) asked high-school students to read passages such as the one in Demonstration 9.2. The students then provided a definition for each italicized word in the passage (for instance, *oam* and *ceilidh*). The results showed a strong positive correlation between the number of context cues available for each word and the accuracy with which readers defined that word. Thus, top-down processing, aided by context cues, helps us understand unfamiliar words, just as it facilitates the perception of speech sounds.

Metacomprehension When you were reading about the Sternberg and Powell study, did you pause for a moment to think about whether you understood this research? If so, you engaged in metacomprehension. **Metacomprehension** refers to our thoughts about reading comprehension, and it is related to the concept of metamemory discussed in Chapter 7.

Unfortunately, most college students are not very accurate in their metacomprehension skills. For example, they often believe that they understand a paragraph they have just read. However, when they are then given a multiple-choice test on the material, they choose the wrong answer (Maki & Berry, 1984; Pressley & Ghatala, 1988). College students often think they understand a passage they have read because they are familiar with the general topic. They may not realize that they do not know the specific information well enough to recall it on an examination. One way to improve metacomprehension is to take a pretest, such as those found in a textbook's study guide. The feedback from this pretest can help students assess the accuracy of their metacomprehension (Glenberg et al., 1987; Matlin, 1993b).

If these college students are typical, their metacomprehension is not highly accurate. They are likely to believe that they understood a passage in their textbook, yet they will miss the relevant question on their examination.

SECTION SUMMARY

UNDERSTANDING LANGUAGE

- Speech perception requires both bottom-up and top-down processing; the phonemic restoration effect demonstrates the importance of top-down processing.

- Listeners easily perceive word boundaries, even though no clear-cut pause appears in the spoken language.

- According to the network model, concepts are organized in memory in an interconnecting netlike pattern; according to the prototype approach to concepts, people decide whether an item belongs to a category by comparison with a prototype.

- People seem to extract meaning from language by analyzing constituents, rather than isolated words; they use a variety of heuristics to identify those constituents.

- Language can be viewed in terms of both surface structure and deep structure.

- According to the dual-encoding model of reading, people access the meaning of a common word directly from the printed page, but an uncommon word must first be translated into sound.

- Readers depend on many context cues to determine the meaning of an unknown word.

- College students may overestimate how much they understand in a written passage; metacomprehension can be improved via pretests.

PRODUCING LANGUAGE

It is amazing that we manage to understand speech, but it is even more astonishing that we can produce it. After all, language is constantly innovative. We continually produce sentences that no one has ever uttered previously in the history of the English language (Chomsky, 1988). For instance, as I was writing the last sentence, my daughter phoned, and her first sentence had certainly never been produced before: "Mom, I need to know the name of the director and the date of the movie *The Return of Martin Guerre* for my History of the Family paper, and I figured you'd be able to find that out faster than any library."

In order to produce language, we must first construct a thought, a general idea that must be conveyed. That thought must then be arranged into constituents. Then, the tongue, lips, and other vocal apparatus need to move appropriately (Yeni-Komshian, 1993). This section on language production begins with an overview of the way we plan our speech. We spend more time, however, on the social aspects of language production. We will also discuss nonverbal communication and the ape-language controversy.

Speech Planning

When we plan a sentence, we usually know the subject of our statement and we have a general idea of the verb we want to use. However, we often wait to select the exact verb until we have begun speaking (Lindsley, 1975). Two problems that may occur when we construct a sentence are linearization and speech errors.

The Linearization Problem When you speak, you may have a general thought you want to express, or a mental image that needs to be conveyed verbally. These rather shapeless ideas need to be translated into a statement that is linear, with one word following after another in a line. This dilemma is called the **linearization problem** (Bock, 1987; Foss, 1988). Try noticing how linearization usually occurs without effort. Occasionally, however, it may be a struggle. Have you ever wanted to convey an idea, and everything needs to be said at the very beginning?

Psychologists and other researchers interested in language have begun to tackle the linearization problem. For instance, we know that when people need to list two or more items, they generally place short words before long ones, pleasant words before unpleasant, and prototypes before nonprototypes (Kelly et al., 1986; Matlin & Stang, 1978; Pinker & Birdsong, 1979).

Speech Errors The speech we produce is usually well formed (Bock, 1987). However, our everyday conversation often differs from perfect English. Notice how people often pause in the middle of a sentence. They may start a new sentence before finishing the previous one, because the statement had been poorly planned. They also use a **filled pause**, which is an interruption in the flow of speech, such as "um" and "er." Incidentally, you may notice that your English literature or philosophy professor uses more of these filled pauses than professors in the social sciences or natural sciences. The reason may be that factual, structured disciplines—like economics or biology—do not require the speaker to choose among many options for completing a sentence. A more loosely structured discipline allows many choices. While your English professor pauses to decide what to say, he or she may insert an "um" or some other filled pause (Schachter et al., 1991).

Another kind of speech error is a **slip of the tongue**, an error in which sounds are rearranged between two or more different words. Slips of the tongue fall into three basic categories (Dell, 1986):

1. Sound errors occur when sounds in nearby words are exchanged (e.g., *Snow flurries → flow snurries*)

According to Stanley Schachter and his colleagues, this mathematics professor would be less likely than a humanities professor to use filled pauses in her lecture.

2. Morpheme errors occur when morphemes (those small, meaningful units in language, such as *-ly* or *in-*) are exchanged in nearby words (e.g., *Self-destruct instruction → self-instruct destruction*).

3. Word errors occur when words are exchanged (e.g., *Writing a letter to my mother → writing a mother to my letter*).

According to a recent theory of slips of the tongue, a speaker who is planning a sentence will construct a representation of that sentence at the word level (Dell, 1986, 1988). As we noted earlier, the speaker selects many words in a sentence before beginning to pronounce the initial word. According to Dell's connectionist explanation, once a word has been selected, it will activate the component sounds that are linked with it. We usually speak the most highly activated sound. In most cases, the sound is correct. However, a single component sound may be activated by several different words, producing an unusually high activation level for that sound. As a result, the highly activated sound might burst forth at the wrong time in the sentence. For example, consider the familiar tongue twister:

She sells seashells.

You are likely to say *sheashells* as the third word, because the *sh* sound is so highly activated by the *sh* in *she* and *shells*. Table 9.1 shows some of the slips of the tongue that my students produced when they were asked to keep records of their errors.

This section has explored how speakers plan their sentences. Speakers mold ideas into a linear sequence, though they make occasional errors. However, speech is typically used to communicate with other humans. Let us consider these social components of language.

TABLE 9.1 Some Typical Slips of the Tongue

SPEECH ERROR	WHAT WAS INTENDED
"Porking at Yark Landing."	"Parking at York Landing."
"I was gabberflasted."	"I was flabbergasted."
"I wish there was a refrigerator in this light."	"I wish there was a light in this refrigerator."
"Go lump in a jake."	"Go jump in a lake."
"I need to send an aunt to my card."	"I need to send a card to my aunt."
"The shun comes shining through."	"The sun comes shining through."
"My daughter was a real sumbthucker."	"My daughter was a real thumbsucker."
"I got my tang tongueled."	"I got my tongue tangled."

Social Aspects of Language

You may occasionally talk to yourself or write yourself a reminder note. However, the major reason you talk is to share information with other people. Think about what you have said so far today. You may have requested, informed, persuaded, and complimented. We direct our words to other people, and our goal is to affect the people with whom we are talking (Burgoon, 1990; Dell & Brown, 1991).

Herbert Clark (1985, 1991) proposes that conversation is like a complicated dance, a collective activity that requires two people to coordinate their efforts. Speakers do not simply utter words aloud and expect to be understood. Instead, they consider their conversational partners. They make numerous assumptions about those partners and design their language appropriately.

When we speak, this complicated dance requires precise coordination. The partners need to coordinate turn-taking and their understanding of ambiguous terms. Just as dancers need to know whether their partners are familiar with certain dance steps, speakers need to know whether their conversational partners have the appropriate background knowledge (Harris et al., 1980). Dancers make adjustments if they find that their partners do not know a particular step. Similarly, conversational partners make adjustments if their attempts to communicate have not been successful (McCann & Higgins, 1990).

The social aspect of language is known as **pragmatics**. Pragmatics involves how we use language to communicate and to accomplish our social goals (Nofsinger, 1991). Let's first discuss how speakers attend to their listeners' background knowledge. We will also consider conversational interactions and politeness. All these topics emphasize that language is our most social cognitive activity.

Listeners' Background Knowledge Speakers are typically concerned about their listeners' familiarity with a topic. You are likely to use simplified language in speaking with children or with people who do not speak your language proficiently. When the listener does not seem to understand, you typically replace difficult words and phrases with easier ones (Cutler, 1987; Dell & Brown, 1991).

Speakers usually assume that listeners have appropriate knowledge about a conversational topic. For example, we noted in Chapter 7 that people develop a **schema**, or a generalized idea about objects, people, and events that are encountered frequently. For instance, a typical schema would be the sequence of events that occur when someone attends a concert. Speakers count on their listeners' schemas to "fill in the blanks." Suppose that you say to a friend, *I went to the concert last night but someone else was sitting in my seat*. You are counting on your friend to know schematic background information, such as the fact that your ticket indicated a seat number and that two people cannot sit in the same seat simultaneously.

We also count on our listeners to share background knowledge about people and objects in our culture. For example, if you say, *Lisa skipped all the way home from school*, you can count on your listener to conclude that Lisa is a female child. In terms of the network model discussed in connection with word meaning, your listener's network surrounding the name *Lisa* includes the concept *female*. The networks surrounding *skipping* and *school* both include the concept *child*. Thus, speakers and listeners have an easier time engaging in a conversational dance because they have similar background knowledge and—equally important—because they *know* that they both share this knowledge.

Two people participating in a conversation assume that they share similar schemas and background knowledge.

We are most likely to appreciate the importance of background information when we discover that our knowledge base does not match that of our conversational partner. For example, a colleague remembers travelling to London as a young adult. She asked a new acquaintance whether she could use her bathroom—and was surprised to be led into a room with only a sink and a bathtub (Walbaum, 1993).

Conversational Interactions Imagine that Cindy is calling a hair salon to make an appointment with the woman who last cut her hair, though she cannot remember the woman's name. Cindy and the receptionist will perform a short dance as they try to make certain that they are speaking about the same person:

Cindy: *She's short, about five feet two inches.*
Receptionist: *Oh, maybe you mean Marilyn. She has short brown wavy hair.*
Cindy: *Yes, that's right, and glasses? And she went to Puerto Rico last summer?*
Receptionist: *Yes, that's Marilyn Peters.*
Cindy: *Yes, that name sounds right.*

Notice what happens in this conversational interaction. Both partners put in extra effort together to make certain that they agree they are referring to the same person. Even total strangers collaborate. An important feature of conversational interaction is that the participants check, question, and confirm (Clark & Brennan, 1991). That part of the conversation is ended only when both are certain that they are talking about the same person and have established common ground.

DEMONSTRATION 9.3   Collaborating to Establish Common Ground

For this demonstration, you need to make two photocopies of these figures. Then locate two volunteers and a watch that can measure time in seconds. Cut the figures apart, keeping each sheet's figures in a separate pile and making certain the dot is at the top of each figure. Appoint one person to be the "director"; this person should arrange the figures in random order in two rows of six figures each. This person's task is to describe the first figure in enough detail so that the "matcher" is able to identify that figure and place it in position 1 in front of him or her. (Neither person should be able to see the other's figures.) The goal is for the matcher to place all 12 figures in the same order as the director's figures. They may use any kind of verbal descriptions they choose, but no gestures or imitation of body position. Record how long it takes them to reach their goal, and then make sure that the figures do match up. Ask them to try the game two more times, with the same person serving as director. Record the times again, and note whether the time decreases on the second and third trials; are they increasingly efficient in establishing common ground? Do they tend to develop a standard vocabulary (e.g., "the ice skater") to refer to a given figure?

Researchers have examined how this collaboration process operates when people work together to arrange complex figures. Demonstration 9.3 is a modification of this study by Clark and Wilkes-Gibbs (1986).

The participants in the study played this game for six trials. (Each trial consisted of arranging all 12 figures in order.) On the first trial, the director required nearly four turns to describe a figure and make certain that the matcher understood the reference. However, as Figure 9.2 shows, the director and the matcher soon developed a mutual shorthand. Just as two dancers become more skilled at coordinating their motor movements as they practice together, conversational partners become more skilled in communicating efficiently.

Interestingly, other studies by Clark and his colleagues have shown that bystanders cannot truly appreciate a conversation in which they do not participate. In this research, a bystander merely watched and listened while two participants worked together on the figures task in Demonstration 9.2. When the bystander was later substituted for one of the conversational partners, the established names for the figures were no longer useful (Schober & Clark, 1989; Wilkes-Gibbs & Clark, 1992). Apparently, the common ground only works for the two people who collaborated to establish this common ground. In other words, it may take two to tango, and a bystander cannot step in without disrupting the dance.

We have examined how conversational partners coordinate the content of their conversation. They also coordinate the conversational format by obeying certain established rules. One rule is that the speakers are supposed to take turns (Nofsinger, 1991; Stasser & Taylor, 1991). Speakers do not talk at the same time, and they do not typically pause leisurely in the middle of the conversation.

Notice how telephone conversations also have a specified format, including alternation. The answerer must speak first, but only briefly. The caller must then provide identification and expect a brief acknowledgment before proceeding. We also follow a specified etiquette when we close a conversation (Jacobs, 1985). We gradually "wind down" the interaction and require a number of alternations before we hang up. Typically, the leave-taking portion of the conversation also involves plans for an interaction in the future (Clark, 1985).

Politeness When I was about 10 years old, I accompanied my younger sister to the home of her best friend, Carol, where we planned to have lunch. After we had finished our sandwiches, Carol's mother served thick slices of cake to my sister and Carol, unintentionally forgetting me. I struggled to formulate a request that was as polite as possible. I adopted a mournful expression and said, "Does the cake taste good, Carol?" From the perspective of a 10-year-old, my request had reached the heights of diplomacy. From my perspective as an adult, decades later, the choice of words was comical.

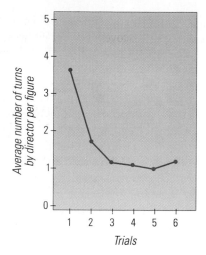

Figure 9.2

Average number of turns that directors took on each figure, as a function of trial number. (Source: Clark and Wilkes-Gibbs, 1986)

DEMONSTRATION 9.4 Politeness

Read the following requests:

1. Could you possibly by any chance lend me your car for just a few minutes?

2. May I borrow your car please?

3. Would you have any objections to my borrowing your car for a while?

4. There wouldn't, I suppose, be any chance of your being able to lend me your car for just a few minutes, would there?

5. Lend me your car.

6. I'd like to borrow your car, if you wouldn't mind.

Now rank these requests from most polite (putting that item's number in the first blank) to least polite:

____ ____ ____ ____ ____ ____

Finally, decide which of those items you would *never* use because they are either too polite or too rude.

Language researchers believe that "politeness means putting things in such a way as to take account of the feelings of the other person" (R. Brown, 1988, p. 749). Try Demonstration 9.4, which focuses on different degrees of politeness, before you read further.

Did your answers to Demonstration 9.4 reveal that more polite requests are almost always longer? In a book on politeness, Penelope Brown and Stephen Levinson (1987) order those statements (from most to least polite): 4, 1, 3, 6, 2, 5. They argue that when people want to be polite, their statements are more complicated and indirect. When they want to make a polite request, they typically begin with small talk, irrelevant to the request, and then they word their question in a fashion that leaves an escape option. Consider, how you might approach a professor for a letter of recommendation. After some preliminary small talk, you might ask, "I wonder if you know me well enough to write a letter of recommendation?" You reason that any professor who would not write a positive letter could simply claim that he or she does not know you well.

Until now, you may not have spent much time worrying about precisely how you attempt to convey politeness in your requests. As we noted in the chapter on consciousness, people are often unaware of their higher mental processes. In most cases, we do not consciously plot how we will be polite in our conversational interactions (Brown & Levinson, 1987). We may be aware that various phrases vary in politeness only when we need to make a major request (such as a letter of recommendation) or when the rules of politeness have been seriously violated. Politeness usually comes as easily to our lips as phonemes do. Otherwise, we would still be lost in thought at the breakfast table, wondering whether to say "Would you mind passing the salt?" or "Please pass the salt."

Nonverbal Communication

So far, we have only considered verbal language. However, people communicate with each other in many different ways. They can transmit messages by words, by tone of voice, by body movement, and by facial expression. The term **nonverbal communication** refers to all human communications that do not involve words (Dittmann, 1987; Webbink, 1986). In other words, there is more to conversation than a written transcript captures.

Try saying the sentence "I'm really happy you got the job" with great enthusiasm and positive emotion, consistent with the verbal message. Now try saying those same words with sarcasm and bitterness. Notice how your tone of voice, hand movements, posture, rate of speaking, and facial expressions all change dramatically, As it turns out, nonverbal behavior is often as important as actual words in conveying meaning in a social setting. According to some estimates, between 60% and 70% of meaning is conveyed nonverbally (Burgoon, 1985).

Nonverbal communication includes a large number of varied behaviors, such as the following (Burgoon, 1985; Patterson, 1983; Webbink, 1986):

1. **Paralanguage**, or the use of vocal cues other than the words themselves, such as voice tone, pitch, pauses, and inflection of the voice;
2. **Gestures**, or hand movements that accompany speech;
3. Body orientation or posture;
4. Body movement, such as squirming or playing with a watchband;
5. Interpersonal distance;
6. Touch;
7. Eye behavior, such as the direction of gaze;
8. Facial expression.

In Chapter 12, we will discuss some of these nonverbal behaviors, especially facial expression, when we examine how people convey and interpret emotion. Right now, however, let us consider gestures and the nonverbal regulation of conversation.

A major part of meaning is conveyed by nonverbal communication, rather than by words.

Gestures One kind of gesture is called an emblem. An **emblem** is a nonverbal action that is clearly understood by most members of a culture. Each emblem can be translated into a verbal phrase (Deaux & Wrightsman, 1988; McNeill, 1985). Two examples are a wave of the hand in greeting, and the first finger pointing to the side of the head, moving in small circles, indicating that a person is crazy. Try thinking of the emblems for the following phrases: "It stinks," "stop," "be quiet," "I don't want to hear it." and "come here." Even though you can readily think of a dozen other emblems, middle-class Americans have a smaller number of emblems than most other groups, probably fewer than 100 (Ekman, 1976). At this point, try Demonstration 9.5 to see how many emblems you can identify.

One other common kind of gesture is an illustrator. An **illustrator** is a nonverbal action that accompanies speech and quite literally provides an illustration. For example, as you say the sentence, "He was a *very* tall man," you might raise one arm high over your head and bend your fingers forward. A surgeon describing an operation may also use illustrators to indicate making incisions and sutures. Incidentally, illustrators are helpful, but they are no substitute for the words. When people try to guess a speaker's message from illustrators—unaccompanied by speech—their accuracy is better than chance, but far from perfect (Krauss et al., 1991).

Nonverbal Regulation of Conversation The format of a conversation often depends as much on paralanguage and other nonverbal cues as on the actual words that are spoken (Deaux & Wrightsman, 1988; Duncan & Fiske, 1977). For example, a person who wants to interrupt may shift posture and use sounds such as

---

DEMONSTRATION 9.5 **Recognizing Emblems**

Make a list of as many emblems as you can recall. (For the sake of decency, eliminate the R-rated and the X-rated ones.) Keep working on this list, adding to it whenever you think of a new one, until you have a list of 20 items. Then ask a friend to try to decode your emblems. In each case, do not provide any context or circumstances in which the emblem is likely to be used. Also, do not use any accompanying words. Simply perform one gesture at a time and see whether your friend can guess the appropriate meaning. You may wish to compare your list with others in the class. Working together, can you all identify close to 100 emblems?

Which of these two people would encourage you to end a conversation quickly, by the use of nonverbal communication?

"ah" and "er." If you are speaking and decide to stop talking, you are likely to reduce your pitch and loudness, relax your hand position, glance at your partner, and slow your speech (Cappella, 1985).

You also use characteristic nonverbal behaviors to begin and end a conversation. Suppose that you and a friend are approaching each other on your college campus. Your eyes meet, and you nod or wave from a distance. However, you do not continue your gaze as you approach. (In fact, if you have some distance to walk before meeting, you'll find that it is nearly impossible to keep gazing continuously for the entire distance!) During the last seconds of your approach, you renew eye contact, smile, and maybe touch each other. Later, when you want to end the interaction, you will interrupt eye contact, lean in the direction you were going, and perhaps nod your head. You will wait for your conversational partner to match some of these actions before saying goodbye (Webbink, 1986).

In this section, we have seen how nonverbal communication conveys meaning and regulates our conversations. These actions add to our spoken language, providing richness and an extra dimension (Cassell & McNeill, 1991).

The Chimp-Language Controversy

Few research questions have produced as much controversy as the chimp-language debate (Savage-Rumbaugh, 1986). Can chimpanzees communicate the way we humans do?

The first reports were clearly pessimistic. For example, Hayes (1951) tried to teach a chimpanzee to pronounce English words. After six years of continuous training, the chimp could say only *cup, mama,* and *papa.* However, chimps are physically unable to pronounce many of the sounds in human speech, so it is not really fair to measure language skill in terms of pronunciation (Roitblat, 1987).

Several subsequent research groups worked with concrete symbols and sign language, rather than the production of speech sounds. For example, Beatrix and Allen Gardner (1975, 1989) taught chimpanzees to use American Sign Language. Their first subject, Washoe, learned more than 100 signs, and she also combined signs into simple sentences. For example, when she saw a small rubber doll in her drinking cup, she signed "Baby in my drink." More recently, Washoe and three other chimps taught Washoe's adopted chimpanzee son 55 different signs without the aid of human teachers (Fouts, 1987; Fouts et al., 1989).

A more pessimistic account of chimpanzee's language skills came from Terrace and his colleagues (Terrace, 1979, 1981; Terrace et al., 1979). Terrace had tried to teach sign language to a chimp called Nim Chimpsky (named after Noam Chomsky, the linguist who examined surface and deep structure). Nim had learned about 125 symbols by the age of 4. Still, Terrace argued that Nim's language was substantially

Washoe makes the sign for "doll."

inferior to children's language, which might include 3,000 words by age 4. Also, Nim produced shorter sentences than children do, he produced less spontaneous language, and he interrupted more.

Within the last decade, however, researchers have been examining the language capacities of a species of apes that is more like humans. Whereas the earlier research had tested the common chimpanzee, Sue Savage-Rumbaugh and her colleagues are studying the "pygmy chimpanzee." This much rarer chimp is known as the bonobo. The language skills of one of these bonobos, named Kanzi, surpasses the abilities of all other chimps (e.g., Greenfield & Savage-Rumbaugh, 1990, 1991; Savage-Rumbaugh, 1991a; Savage-Rumbaugh et al., 1990). For example, Kanzi can touch lighted symbols on a board to answer questions presented through his earphones, as Figure 9.3 shows.

Unlike the common chimps, Kanzi produces spontaneous statements and also uses symbols to ask about objects that are not physically present. For example, at one point, Kanzi touched the symbol "hide" and then tugged at the researcher's hand, indicating that the researcher should help him search for a tool that had been hidden in the woods. Kanzi also understands spoken English to some extent, even when he is given novel instructions. For example, when the experimenter told Kanzi, "Put the water on the carrot," Kanzi responded by tossing the carrot outside into the rain (Savage-Rumbaugh, 1991b).

Kanzi can understand spoken English sentences involving simple requests. However, he has trouble with more challenging requests. If you tell a 2-year-old child to give a ball and a cup to a researcher, the child will gather both objects before heading across the room. Kanzi rarely manages this task; he cannot concentrate on that many things at once (Savage-Rumbaugh, 1991b).

What can we conclude about chimp language? Under the right conditions, the brightest chimps can acquire a vocabulary that is dwarfed by a young child's word mastery. Even these smartest chimps cannot understand commands we take for granted. Furthermore, chimps primarily communicate about their physical needs, not about signal detection theory, religion, or Jane Austen's novels. Even a bright chimp like Kanzi cannot discuss whether chimps can master language. It seems safe to conclude that chimps can learn a basic vocabulary and simple sentence structure. Chimp language is more sophisticated than we would have guessed in the 1950s when the first chimp struggled to pronounce *cup*. However, ape language clearly cannot match the fluency, flexibility, and complexity of human language.

Figure 9.3

In this picture, a bonobo chimpanzee named Kanzi hears questions through earphones and points to the appropriate answer on a board. The experimenter cannot hear the questions and does not know the answers, so she cannot transmit cues to Kanzi.

S E C T I O N   S U M M A R Y

PRODUCING LANGUAGE

- When we begin to say a sentence, we usually know the subject of the sentence, but not the verb; we often face the linearization problem when formulating a sentence.
- Two kinds of speech errors are filled pauses and slips of the tongue.
- Conversations require coordination; speakers must take their listeners' background knowledge into account and work to establish common ground.
- Conversations have specified formats, such as alternating turn taking and characteristic beginnings and endings to conversations.
- Polite statements are generally long and indirect, compared with less polite statements; they also offer the listener an opportunity to escape from the request.
- Nonverbal behavior enriches verbal communication, as in the case of emblems and illustrators, as well as in the regulation of conversational format.
- Chimps can acquire basic vocabulary and sentence structure, but not more complicated commands or abstract concepts.

LANGUAGE AND THINKING

The topics of language and thinking are intertwined throughout this chapter. You look at an ambiguous sentence and think about its two underlying meanings. When you construct a sentence, you think about how to arrange the concepts in a linear order. You try to describe an event to your aunt, and you think about the background knowledge she needs to understand the story.

In this final section, we will directly address the relationship between language and thinking by examining two important topics. The section on the Whorfian hypothesis asks whether our thought processes are influenced by the language we use. The "In Depth" section on bilingualism focuses on the thought processes of people who have mastered two or more languages.

The Whorfian Hypothesis

Classical Chinese features a dozen different characters for varieties of cattle. For example, a separate character is used for a cow with a very long back. Could people make more refined distinctions between different kinds of cows because of their enriched terminology? In contrast, the Chinese language has no word for *privacy* (Hoosain, 1991). Does the absence of this word mean that Chinese speakers cannot appreciate the concept of privacy?

Benjamin Lee Whorf was a fire-prevention inspector who was also an amateur linguist. He raised one of the most intriguing questions about language when he asked whether the language we speak influences our thought processes (Whorf, 1956). The **Whorfian hypothesis**, or **linguistic determinism**, states that the structure of language influences the structure of thought. Furthermore, the Whorfian hypothesis argues that a person speaking one language might subdivide the conceptual world differently from a person speaking another language. For instance, a speaker of classical Chinese should divide the concept *cow* into a greater number of pieces than does a speaker of contemporary English. Because speakers of different languages have different ways of carving up their concepts, Whorf argued that these speakers would actually view the world differently.

At present, most language researchers would not argue that the worldview of a German, Japanese, or Spanish speaker is vastly different from the worldview of an English speaker. These researchers might propose, however, that language influences the content of particular thoughts (Hunt & Agnoli, 1991; Matlin, 1985). Two areas

Could people who spoke classical Chinese make more careful distinctions between types of cows, because their language has 12 different characters to refer to cattle?

that have been investigated are (1) whether color terms influence thoughts about color and (2) whether gender-biased language produces gender-biased thought.

Color Terms Can we remember a color more accurately if we have a readily available name for the color in English? For instance, you would probably call the color at the top of Figure 9.4 "red." English speakers would show substantial agreement about this name. In contrast, we would probably not agree about a name for the color at the bottom of Figure 9.4. I would describe it as "sort of brownish green, like the inside of an avocado that has been exposed to the air for a day." You would probably choose some other phrase. In fact, a dozen of us looking at this color would create a dozen different descriptions.

In a classic study, Brown and Lenneberg (1954) examined whether language is related to thinking. For example, would the language used to describe a color (for instance, the extent to which people could agree on a color's name) be related to some measure of thinking (for instance, how easily the color could be recognized)? Their results confirmed this relationship. The colors that produced a description with high agreement, such as the red in Figure 9.4, were easier to recognize than colors for which people could not agree on a name, such as old-avocado-insides green. This research seemed to provide firm evidence that language influences the structure of thought. That is, if we have a good, available name for something, we can remember it better and recognize it when we see it again.

However, some colors—such as a pure, true red—might be recognized more easily because they are prototypes, or the best examples of a color. Heider (1972) conducted research with the Dani people of New Guinea, who have only two color names, roughly equivalent to "dark" and "light." In the Dani language, both colors in Figure 9.4 would be called "dark." In a memory test, Heider showed that the Dani recognized prototypical colors such as true red better than nonprototypical colors such as brownish green. Prototypical colors are simply "better," even to people who do not call these prototypical colors by special names. In fact, Heider argues that people recognized the red color in Brown and Lenneberg's (1954) study because that color was prototypical—not because it was called a special name.

Other research by Kay and Kempton (1984) confirms Heider's (1972) general conclusion: The names we assign to colors do not influence our cognitive reactions to those colors. In other words, the research on color fails to support the Whorfian hypothesis; language has no overwhelming influence on thought. Let us now consider an area in which language does seem to influence thought.

Figure 9.4

People show substantial agreement in labeling the red color on the top; they show little agreement for the green color on the bottom.

Gender-Biased Language Several years ago, I opened the newspaper and read an article about a home-school counselor at a local elementary school. The (male) counselor was quoted as saying, "When a child sees that he has something in common with me, it's like a miracle the way he opens up." I visualized a troubled boy, feeling relaxed and comfortable with the counselor, sharing his concerns and discussing possible alternatives. But then I wondered what happened to the troubled girls. Had the counselor's choice of the pronoun "he" reflected a greater interest in the problems of male students? Were their problems more conspicuous? Did the troubled girls who visited the counselor rarely have anything in common with the counselor, and therefore they rarely opened up? Most important to the Whorfian hypothesis, did the counselor's use of the word "he" tend to limit his thinking so that he directed his services to more boys than girls? Does the language we use tend to bias us toward thinking about males more than females?

The problem illustrated in this example is called the **generic masculine**, the use of masculine pronouns and nouns to refer to all human beings—both males and females—instead of males alone. A teacher may have told you that the word "he" really includes women as well as men. Similarly, for many years, the biology department at my college offered a course called "Biology of Man," and they argued that "man" referred to both females and males. (The course title was later changed to a gender-neutral name, Human Biology.)

In the dictionary, "he" may refer to "he and she," and "man" may refer to "men and women." Are these generic-masculine terms *truly* gender neutral? Alternatively, are generic-masculine terms more likely than gender-neutral terms to produce thoughts about males? Researchers have needed to design creative experiments to answer these question. After all, how can you measure something as internal and private as "thoughts about gender," when measurement of the dependent variable requires overt responses? Researchers have used a variety of devices for translating these internal thoughts into measurable responses. The research overwhelmingly shows that generic-masculine terms (such as "he") are more likely than gender-neutral terms (such as "he or she" and "they") to produce thoughts oriented toward males (Henley, 1989; Matlin, 1985).

One study, for example, used picture selection as the dependent variable. Students were asked to search for potential illustrations for a textbook. The results showed that when the chapter titles were "Social Man" or "Industrial Man"—rather than "Society," "Industrial Life," or other gender-neutral terms—students were more likely to choose all-male photographs (Scheider & Hacker, 1973).

Another study selected word usage as the dependent variable. Students were instructed to write stories based on a topic sentence, such as, "In a large coeducational institution, the average student will feel isolated in his introductory courses" (Moulton et all., 1978, p. 1034). Other students were given a similar topic sentence, except that the word "his" was replaced by gender-neutral terms such as "his or her." In each case, the students wrote a paragraph based on the topic sentence. The results showed that the students were significantly more likely to write about males when the topic sentence featured a generic masculine pronoun. In contrast, gender-neutral terms produced more stories about females. The language we use does influence thought. Specifically, the "he" calls forth mental images in which males predominate and females are relatively invisible.

Other studies about the generic masculine have used different dependent variables to assess the kinds of thoughts produced by generic masculine terms. For instance, Martyna (1980) constructed a number of sentences such as, "When someone prepares for an exam, he must do some studying." Other variations of that sentence used either "they" or "he or she" instead of the generic masculine, "he." Students were shown a sentence, accompanied by a picture of someone performing the appropriate activity, such as the photo in Figure 9.5. In each case, the students were asked to decide whether the sentence did or did not apply to the picture. The results showed

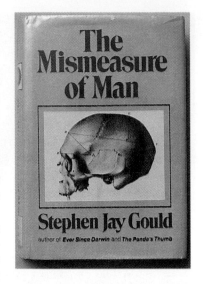

Students reading this book title would be likely to think more often about males than females.

Figure 9.5

Many students judge that the sentence "When someone prepares for an exam, he must do some studying" does not apply to this picture.

TABLE 9.2 Suggestions for Nonsexist Language

1. Use the plural form. "Students can monitor their progress" can replace "A student can monitor his progress."
2. Use "his or her" or "her or his," as in the sentence, "A student can monitor her or his progress."
3. Use "you." The sentence "Suppose that you have difficulty recalling your social security number" involves the reader or the listener more than "Suppose that a person has difficulty recalling his social security number"—and it is also less sexist.
4. Reword the sentence to eliminate the pronoun. "The best judge of the value of counseling is usually the client" can replace "The client is usually the best judge of the value of his counseling."

Source: Based on American Psychological Association, 1983, p. 45.

that the sentence with the "he" form (the generic masculine) was judged not to apply to the picture of the female in 40% of the trials. When people saw the word "he," they found it disconcerting to see a picture of a woman. Once again, generic masculine terms like "he" suggest thoughts about men, rather than women.

Other research demonstrates that the generic masculine may have important implications for career choices. In one study, students saw a generic masculine version of a paragraph describing psychologists. They later rated psychology as an unattractive profession for women. In contrast, students who had seen a gender-neutral version gave more favorable ratings (Briere & Lanktree, 1983). Language could therefore influence thought so forcefully that a woman might not think about a career that had been described in generic masculine terms.

After examining the research on gender-biased language, the American Psychological Association adopted a policy that favors gender-neutral language. Some of their suggestions are included in Table 9.2. We will examine some of the biases against females in North American culture later in this textbook. Gender bias is extremely complex, and many different factors contribute to the problem. Furthermore, gender bias created gender-biased language in the first place. Still, psychologists acknowledge that generic masculine terms create problems (e.g., American Psychological Association, 1983; Association for Women in Psychology, 1975). With reference to the Whorfian hypothesis, when we use language that focuses on males, we tend to eliminate females from our thinking.

IN DEPTH: Bilingualism

This chapter on language has considered some impressively challenging cognitive tasks, such as language comprehension, reading, and speaking. These tasks require the simultaneous coordination of cognitive skills, social knowledge, and physical gestures. We can marvel that humans can manage all these tasks in one language . . . and then we remind ourselves that many people master at least two languages.

A **bilingual** speaker is a person who uses two languages that differ in speech sounds, vocabulary, and syntax. A **multilingual** speaker uses three or more languages. However. psychologists typically use the term bilingual to include multilinguals as well (Taylor & Taylor, 1990). The bilingual's native language is referred to as the **first language**, and the non-native language is the **second language**.

If we consider the entire world, most people are at least somewhat bilingual (Snow, 1993). Some people live in officially bilingual regions, such as Quebec, Belgium, and Switzerland. Some become bilingual because their first language is not used for school and business. For example, Zulu speakers in South Africa must learn English. Immigrants frequently need to master the language of their new country. Figure 9.6 shows a message sent to Boston residents; people who learn a second language often need to master new written characters, as well as words and grammar.

What You Should Know About Automatic Dialing Services.

This is an important notice. Please have it translated.

Este é um aviso importante. Queira mandá-lo traduzir.

Este es un aviso importante. Sírvase mandarlo traducir.

ĐÂY LÀ MỘT BẢN THÔNG CÁO QUAN TRỌNG
XIN VUI LÒNG CHO DỊCH LẠI THÔNG CÁO ẤY

Ceci est important. Veuillez faire traduire.

本 通 知 很 重 要．请 将 之 译 成 中文．

នេះគឺជាដំណឹងល្អ សូមមេត្តាបកប្រែជូនផង

Figure 9.6

A notice sent to Boston residents by a telephone company. The languages on the notice are English, Portuguese, Spanish, Vietnamese, French, Chinese, and Cambodian.

Wallace Lambert, a pioneer in research on bilingualism, received the Distinguished Scientific Award for the Applications of Psychology, given by the American Psychological Association. Lambert introduced an important distinction between additive and subtractive bilingualism. In **additive bilingualism**, an individual acquires proficiency in a second language with no loss in the first language. Both languages are respected and considered prestigious. For example, English speakers in Quebec usually learn French if they run a business. In **subtractive bilingualism**, the new language replaces the first language. Unfortunately, most linguistic minority groups in the United States and Canada are pressured to develop high-level skills in English at the expense of their first language, producing subtractive bilingualism (Lambert, 1990). The North American educational system does not worry about keeping an immigrant child fluent in a first language such as Spanish, Vietnamese, or Arabic. As a result, these children usually experience subtractive bilingualism.

In this chapter, we have emphasized that language is social as well as cognitive. Social factors are also important in bilingualism, because one of the most important predictors of a person's skill in acquiring a second language is his or her attitude toward the people who speak that language. In a representative study, researchers tried to predict the ability of English Canadian high-school students in learning French (Gardner & Lambert, 1959; Lambert, 1992). The students' *attitude* toward French Canadians was just as important as their cognitive *aptitude* for learning languages.

The topic of bilingualism is so interesting and complex that some colleges offer an entire course in the subject. Because we are considering bilingualism within the context of language and thinking, we will focus on two topics: (1) How do bilinguals and monolinguals compare on a variety of cognitive tasks? and (2) How do bilinguals and monolinguals compare on their awareness of language?

General Cognitive Comparisons The early theorists proclaimed that bilingualism is harmful. For example, Jespersen (1922) said, "The brain effort required to master the two languages instead of one certainly diminishes the child's power of learning other things which might and ought to be learnt" (p. 148). According to that view, your cognitive capacity is limited; if part of that space is occupied by a second language, your other thought processes will suffer (Lambert, 1990).

The early research on bilingualism seemed to support that position. However, this research was seriously flawed by confounding variables. Lower-class bilinguals were compared with middle-class monolinguals. Furthermore, all of the achievement and IQ testing was conducted in the monolingual child's language—most often English (Reynolds, 1991a).

In 1962, Peal and Lambert conducted the first well-controlled study comparing monolinguals with bilinguals. You can imagine the impact of their findings: Bilinguals were more advanced in school, they scored better on tests of first-language skills, and they showed greater mental flexibility (Peal & Lambert, 1962). The original research was conducted in Montreal, and

For this student who is learning Spanish, her attitude toward Latin Americans is as important as her aptitude in terms of linguistic skills.

the results have been confirmed by carefully conducted research in Singapore, Switzerland, South Africa, Israel, and New York (Lambert, 1990).

In addition to gaining fluency in a second language, bilinguals seem to have a number of advantages over monolinguals:

1. Bilinguals actually acquire more expertise in their native (first) language. For example, English-speaking Canadian children whose classes are taught in French gain greater understanding of English language structure (Diaz, 1985; Lambert et al., 1991).

2. Bilingual children are more sensitive to some pragmatic aspects of language. For example, English-speaking children whose classes are taught in French are more aware that when you speak to a blindfolded child, you need to supply additional information (Genesee et al., 1975).

3. Bilingual children are more likely to show cognitive flexibility on tests of creativity, such as thinking of a wide variety of different uses for a paper clip (Hamers & Blanc, 1989; Scott, 1973).

4. Bilingual children are better at following complicated instructions (Hamers & Blanc, 1989; Powers & López, 1985).

5. Bilinguals perform better on tests of nonverbal intelligence that require reorganization of visual patterns, and on concept formation tasks that require mental flexibility (Peal & Lambert, 1962).

Are there any *disadvantages* to being bilingual? In general, these are minor. People who use two languages extensively may subtly change their pronunciation of some speech sounds in both languages (Caramazza et al., 1973). Bilinguals are also slightly slower in making some decisions about language, though these are unlikely to interfere with communication. For example, an English-French bilingual may pause longer before deciding whether a passage is written in English or in French (Taylor & Taylor, 1990). Bilinguals may take somewhat longer to decide whether a string of letters (either a nonsense word or an English word) is actually an English word (Ransdell & Fischler, 1987)

The research on bilingualism has been summarized by Insup Taylor, a multilingual who speaks Korean, Japanese, and English. As she concludes, "Bilinguals may experience a slight disadvantage in language-processing speed over monolinguals, but this disadvantage is far outweighed by the advantages of being able to function in two languages" (Taylor & Taylor, 1990, p. 340).

Awareness of Language   Now that we have considered how bilinguals perform on a variety of cognitive tasks, let us turn to a more specific question: How do monolinguals and bilinguals compare with respect to **metalinguistics**, or knowledge about the form and structure of language? We have already considered two concepts related to metalinguistics. In Chapter 7, we considered metamemory, or knowledge and awareness about memory. Also, when we examined reading earlier in this chapter, we considered metacomprehension, or our thoughts about reading comprehension. Metalinguistics does not focus upon the meaning of language; instead, it emphasizes people's awareness about the structure or form of language.

As Ellen Bialystok (1991, 1992) emphasizes, the research on bilingualism and metalinguistics is complicated. Consistent with the complexity theme of this textbook, bilinguals do not consistently score higher than monolinguals on tests of metalinguistic awareness (e.g., Galambos & Goldin-Meadow, 1990; Galambos & Hakuta, 1988). However, we can identify many areas in which bilinguals clearly know more about the way language operates.

Let us focus on a study by Bialystok (1988), in which she tested linguistic awareness in three groups of Canadian children who were between the ages of 6½ and 7. One group spoke only English. A second group was partially bilingual; they had been raised speaking English, but they were enrolled in a school where they had been taught entirely in French for about two years. A third group was fully bilingual; they had spoken both French and English throughout childhood, and they now attended a French school.

Bialystok gave the children five metalinguistic tasks, which are illustrated in Demonstration 9.6. As you can see, the first two tasks focused on the arbitrariness of language—the fact

DEMONSTRATION 9.6 Linguistic Awareness

Try each of the tasks described below. They should not be challenging, because they were designed for children. However, by trying them you can develop your own appreciation of metalinguistics. If you know a child between the ages of 5 and 8, try asking the child these questions.

1 The Arbitrariness of Language
   a. Suppose you were making up names for things, and you decided to call the sun "the moon" and the moon "the sun." What would you call the thing in the sky when you go to bed at night? What would the sky look like when you're going to bed?
   b. Imagine that the names of cats and dogs were changed around. What would this animal's name be? What sound would it make?

2. Concept of Word
   a. Which of the following is a word? (1) happy; (2) will be coming; (3) three; (4) chair
   b. What is a word? How can you tell if something is a word?

3. Correcting Grammatical Errors
   For each of these two sentences, say the grammatically correct version of the sentence:
   a. There isn't no snow today.
   b. Where they are going?

Source: Based on Bialystok, 1988

that the sun is arbitrarily called *sun* in English, but it could just as easily have been called a *glonk* or a *moon*. The children were also tested for their knowledge of the characteristics of words and for their understanding of grammatical rules.

The results of Bialystok's study showed that the fully bilingual children scored significantly higher than the monolingual children on three of the tasks: the sun/moon task, the definition of *word*, and correcting grammatical errors. (The partially bilingual group obtained scores in between the two other groups.) For example, on the task where children were instructed to define *word*, the monolingual children most often answered "don't know." The partially bilingual children usually responded by naming different words or supplying a partially correct definition such as "a word is something you can say." The fully bilingual children supplied definitions such as "words are combinations of letters that mean something"—amazingly sophisticated for a first-grader!

The three groups did not differ significantly on the two other tasks. Most were very resistant to changing the names of familiar pets. Also, the three groups did not differ in their judgments about what constituted a word (even though they differed in their skill in defining a word.)

According to Bialystok (1992), the awareness of language requires different kinds of cognitive skills. However, the cognitive skill where bilinguals have the most significant advantage over monolinguals involves control of processing. To solve a task that requires **control of processing**, you must pay attention to some aspect of language that is fairly subtle and typically ignored. For example, to solve the sun/moon problem, you need to separate the word from its usual meaning and pay attention to a more subtle alternative, in which the moon has a new name. This control of processing should be familiar to you from Demonstration 5.1 (p. 137); on this Stroop task, you needed to suppress your tendency to say the name of the ink's color and pay attention to a more subtle alternative, the meaning of the word itself. Both the metalinguistic tasks and the Stroop task require **selective attention**; you must focus your attention on one aspect of the task and ignore everything else.

But why are bilinguals better on these challenging selective-attention tasks? They are simply more sensitive to their linguistic input (Bialystok, 1992). They are accustomed to hearing things referred to in two different forms. They also know that they must pay attention to the language itself, as well as its meaning. Furthermore, they realize that they sometimes need to address different people in different languages, which draws attention to the alternative forms of language. In short, bilinguals are fully aware that language conveys meaning. However, they also have an enriched perspective because they are more aware of the structure of language.

Jim Good, known as Jaime Bueno to his friends in Nicaragua, acquired fluency in Spanish through his many years of humanitarian work in that country. His metalinguistic skills are likely to be more sophisticated than if he had remained monolingual.

S E C T I O N   S U M M A R Y

LANGUAGE AND THINKING

- According to the Whorfian hypothesis, the structure of language influences the structure of thought, and speakers of different languages should view the world differently.

- Some research on color terms suggests that color labels do not have a strong influence on the way we think about colors.

- Many studies, using a variety of different approaches, have demonstrated that the use of the generic masculine is more likely to produce thoughts about males, whereas gender-neutral terms are more likely to produce thoughts about both genders.

- Bilinguals excel on some general cognitive tasks, such as expertise in their first language, sensitivity to pragmatics, cognitive flexibility, following complex instructions, and nonverbal intelligence.

- Bilinguals also excel at the kind of metalinguistic tasks that require control of processing, or paying attention to the less obvious features of language.

R E V I E W   Q U E S T I O N S

1. How do bottom-up and top-down processes operate when you listen to someone talking? How is speech perception similar to the perception of written words? (You may need to review pages 111–112 in Chapter 4 to answer this second question.) Why does the phonemic restoration effect demonstrate top-down processing?

2. Several parts of this chapter focused on meaning. Describe the network theory and the prototype theory of meaning. Then point out how we determine the meaning of an unfamiliar word, for instance during reading. How does this last process resemble top-down processing?

3. A person listening to a sentence can figure out much more information than the physical stimulus registered by the receptors in the cochlea. Provide support for this statement by discussing the word-boundary issue, the surface structure-deep structure issue, and any other relevant topics.

4. How would the dual-encoding model explain how you are able to ascertain the meaning of the words you are reading in this question?

5. What are some of the processes involved in planning a sentence? Think about the sentence you produced when you answered that question; how was the linearization problem relevant?

6. In order to carry on a conversation, two people must work together and be finely attuned to each other. Explain how the following factors are important in a conversation: background knowledge, collaboration to establish common ground, turn taking, and politeness. Include information on both verbal and nonverbal communication.

7. From your background on the chimp-language controversy, describe the ways in which chimp language resembles human language and the ways in which it differs. Comment also on the relative skills of the two species of chimpanzees.

8. Suppose that you know a person who always uses generic masculine terms such as "he" and "man." What information could you tell him or her about the way people interpret these terms?

9. Discuss the cognitive and language skills of bilinguals. If the Whorfian hypothesis were correct, and speakers of different languages did carve up the world differently, what are the implications for bilinguals?

10. Some psychologists argue that language is our most impressive cognitive skill. Describe why language requires us to use a wide variety of other cognitive skills, such as perception, attention, memory, imagery, problem solving, decision making, and so forth. Also point out why language requires the skillful use of knowledge about other people.

N E W   T E R M S

bottom-up processing
top-down processing
phoneme
phoneme restoration
morpheme
network model
prototype
prototype approach
graded structure
constituent
surface structure
deep structure
dual-encoding model
metacomprehension
linearization problem
filled pause
slip of the tongue
pragmatics

schema
nonverbal communication
paralanguage
gestures
emblem
illustrator
Whorfian hypothesis
linguistic determinism
generic masculine
bilingual
multilingual
first language
second language
additive bilingualism
subtractive bilingualism
metalinguistics
control of processing
selective attention

R E C O M M E N D E D   R E A D I N G

Gardner, R. A., Gardner, B. T., & Van Cantfort, T. E. (Eds.). (1989). *Teaching sign language to chimpanzees*. Albany, NY: State University of New York Press. This fascinating book contains chapters written by people who taught sign language to Washoe, her adopted son, and other chimps.

Nofsinger, R. E. (1991). *Everyday conversation*. Newbury Park, CA: Sage. Here is a clearly written book that summarizes the social aspects of language and conversation.

Reynolds, A. G. (Ed.). (1991b). *Bilingualism, multiculturism, and second language learning: The McGill Conference in Honour of Wallace E. Lambert*. Hillsdale, NJ: Erlbaum. In this book, many researchers who have been associated with Wallace Lambert summarize the research on the linguistic and social consequences of bilingualism.

Taylor, I., & Taylor, M. M. (1990). *Psycholinguistics: Learning and using language*. Englewood Cliffs, NJ: Prentice Hall. This undergraduate textbook contains material on language comprehension and production, the social aspects of conversation, and bilingualism.

ANSWERS TO DEMONSTRATIONS

DEMONSTRATION 9.1   Two possibilities are: (1) "There, Don ate a kettle of ten chips" and (2) "The red on a tea kettle often chips."

DEMONSTRATION 9.2   *Oam* means steam, and a *ceilidh* is a visit.

CHAPTER 10

DEVELOPMENT IN INFANCY AND CHILDHOOD

When my daughter Sally was 4 years old, she brought a music box to me and asked how it worked. I pried open the lid and pointed out the rotating cylinder, with its carefully spaced, protruding knobs. Then I showed her how those knobs struck the little prongs on the other side, producing a melody. She gazed intently at the various structures, prodding them with her finger. I felt a warm glow of pleasure at Sally's growing understanding of objects and the way they worked. And then she asked, "But where does the little man sit to play the piano?" For an adult, music-box melodies require a mechanical explanation. For a 4-year-old, melodies must be produced by a human, even—in the case of a music box—a very tiny human.

When we interact with young children, we are often convinced that a wide gulf separates children's beliefs from those of adults. We will see evidence of this gulf throughout the chapter. However we will also see that infants and children are remarkably competent in many areas. They have many abilities that a casual observer may not notice. In these areas, infants and adults are somewhat similar.

In this chapter and Chapter 11, we focus on human development. **Development** refers to the changes in physical, cognitive, and social abilities that occur throughout the life span.

Three important questions are often asked in connection with human development. We note them now and raise each of them again later in the chapters:

1. The **nature-nurture question:** Can development be primarily explained by nature, inborn factors, and genetics? Alternatively, is development primarily determined by nurture, that is, by learning and experience? For example, does little Rigoberto start to walk at about 12 months because his genes have specified that his muscles, bones, and coordination will be appropriately mature at this age (nature)? On the other hand, does he walk only after he has had enough experience and training (nurture)? The appropriate answer is that development is determined by both nature and nurture, just as the area of a rectangle is determined not simply by its width or its length, but by both in combination (Maccoby, 1990a).

2. The **continuity-stages question:** Is development a gradual process, with adults simply having a greater *quantity* of some particular skill? Alternatively, do children and adults differ in the *quality* of their psychological processes? For example, children and adults differ in the amount of material they remember. But do adults simply have *more* memory skills (continuity), or do they have a *different kind* of memory skills (stages)? Although many skills show continuity throughout development, we see evidence for stages in several areas of development. For example, we will see in the research on memory that older children and adults employ memory strategies that younger children never use. Their approach to memory is qualitatively different, suggesting that memory is characterized by stages, rather than continuity.

3. The **stability-change question:** Do people maintain their personal characteristics as they mature from infants into adults (stability)? Alternatively, do these characteristics shift (change)? The stability-change question asks whether the individuals in a group maintain the same relative ranks on a particular characteristic as they grow older (Bornstein, 1989). For example, did the shy boy who sat next to you

This toddler is just beginning to walk. Should we explain this behavior in terms of nature or nurture?

in second grade remain shy, or did he become a relatively outgoing, friendly young man? We see in our discussion of infant temperament that there is some stability as infants mature into children, but the stability is far from complete.

We consider how infants and children develop in four areas: (1) physical and perceptual skills, (2) cognitive knowledge, (3) gender awareness, and (4) personality and social characteristics. As you can see, the topics in this chapter follow the same order as those in the textbook itself, beginning with more biological areas and ending with more social areas.

At conception, a sperm cell from the father fertilizes an egg cell from the mother.

PHYSICAL AND PERCEPTUAL DEVELOPMENT

In just 9 months, a barely visible human egg matures into a baby ready to be born. The newborn has remarkably well-developed perceptual abilities, though his or her motor abilities are limited. Compared to a colt that manages to walk shortly after birth, a newborn has little reason to brag. Just a few years later, however, this same baby may run fast enough to escape from parents at a crowded airport and may be able to pry loose the tops from "childproof bottles." Let us begin at the beginning.

Prenatal Development

Conception occurs when a sperm cell from the father fertilizes an egg cell (or ovum) from the mother. The fertilized egg begins to divide rapidly and attaches itself to the wall of the uterus.

Before the second month of the **prenatal** (or prebirth) **period,** the developing human is called an **embryo.** At this stage, the cells continue to divide rapidly and begin to develop specialized functions. For instance, cells that are part of the primitive visual system develop about 3 weeks after conception. At 4 weeks, other cells start to develop into arms and legs. Around 6 weeks, the face starts to form. The embryo begins to look and function like a human.

The **fetal period** begins 2 months after conception and lasts until the baby is born about 7 months later. As you can see from Figure 10.1, the 4-month-old fetus already looks remarkably human, even though it weighs less than half a pound and is only about 6 inches long. Around this time, the mother begins to feel her baby's movements for the first time.

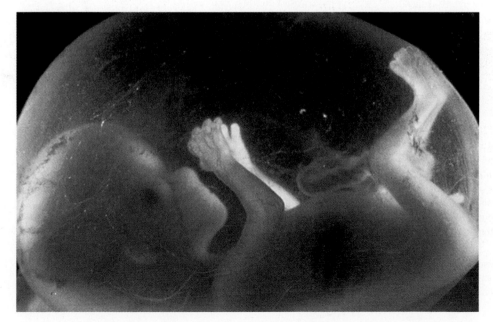

Figure 10.1
A fetus 4 months after conception.

The brain, heart, lungs, and other important organs develop further during the next few months of pregnancy. If the mother gives birth prematurely, seven months after conception, these organs are sufficiently well developed, and the baby is likely to survive (Snow, 1989). During the last 2 months, the fetus's appearance changes little, though it does grow larger.

Hazards of Prenatal Development

Unfortunately, the developing embryo and fetus can be harmed by numerous substances and diseases, as shown in Table 10.1. In addition, brain development and physical health can also be impaired if the mother's nutrition is inadequate. Let us discuss in more detail two of the most common harmful substances—alcohol and tobacco.

Pregnant women who drink alcohol may harm their babies significantly. Heavy drinking can produce **fetal alcohol syndrome,** as shown in Figure 10.2. As you can

TABLE 10.1 Harmful Substances and Diseases that Can Affect the Developing Fetus

HARMFUL AGENT	POSSIBLE DANGER
Substances	
Alcohol	Heavy drinking can produce fetal alcohol syndrome, including facial deformity, growth defects, malformed heart and urinary tract, mental retardation, and irritability.
Cigarettes	Heavy smoking can lead to premature birth, low birth weight, defective attention span, and school problems.
Cocaine	Use may lead to premature birth and low birth weight; behavioral effects are controversial (e.g., Mayes et al., 1992), but babies may be less alert and less responsive to stimulation.
Marijuana	Heavy use can lead to premature birth and abnormal reaction to stimulation.
Caffeine	High consumption may be linked with premature birth and miscarriages.
Aspirin	Heavy use can produce prenatal bleeding and low birth weight.
Tranquilizers	Regular use can produce respiratory problems in newborns.
Barbiturates	Large doses can produce respiratory problems in newborns.
Diseases	
Rubella (German measles)	Before the 11th week of pregnancy, likely to cause heart defects, deafness, and blindness in babies.
Genital herpes	Can cause infant death, blindness, and retardation.
Acquired Immunodeficiency Syndrome (AIDS)	Can be transmitted to the fetus; symptoms usually appear when the infant is about 6 months old, and infants rarely survive more than 8 months after the symptoms appear.

Sources: Berk, 1991; "Fetal Alcohol Syndrome," 1990; Iosub et al., 1987; Mayes et al., 1992; Miller et al., 1982; Shaffer, 1989; Snow, 1989; Streissguth et al., 1984; Sullivan-Bolyai et al., 1983; Vorhees & Mollnow, 1987.

a. A 3-year-old girl from Sweden.   *b. A 10-year-old girl from Chicago.*   *c. A 6-year-old boy from Seattle.*

see from these photographs, the characteristic facial features may include widely spaced eyes and a flattened nose.

A mechanism known as the **blood-brain barrier** keeps many chemicals from entering the brain. Unfortunately, alcohol can cross that barrier, causing damage to the brain. In fact, fetal alcohol syndrome is one of the most common known causes of mental retardation in the United States ("Fetal Alcohol Syndrome," 1990). Some studies suggest that even small doses of alcohol are potentially harmful to the fetus. Therefore, many experts suggest that pregnant women should not consume *any* alcohol (Steinmetz, 1992).

About 30% of pregnant women smoke cigarettes (Brooke et al., 1989). Their babies are more likely than the babies of nonsmokers to be born prematurely. If they carry their babies to full term, these babies are more likely to have a low birth weight (Sexton & Hebel, 1984). In fact, women who smoke five or more cigarettes a day are likely to produce babies with retarded growth (Nieburg et al., 1985). As these babies grow older, they are likely to have attention problems and difficulty in reading and arithmetic (Vorhees & Mollnow, 1987).

Sadly, the developing fetus can also be harmed if someone else in the house smokes, providing passive exposure to the harmful substances in cigarettes. A newborn whose father smokes at home faces about two-thirds the risk of reduced birth weight compared with a newborn whose *mother* smoked (Rubin et al., 1986; Schwartz-Bickenbach et al., 1987). Advertisements like the one in Figure 10.3 should also mention the hazards that passive smoking can create for the developing fetus.

Birth and the Newborn

Researchers are not sure exactly what factors trigger childbirth in humans. However, one relevant structure seems to be the hypothalamus of the fetus, which signals the pituitary and adrenal glands to produce hormones. These hormones travel to the mother's uterus, leading to the start of labor contractions (Palca, 1991).

The newborn who emerges during childbirth does not look much like the infants in magazine advertisements. The strenuous trip through the birth canal often leaves babies with a squashed nose and a lopsided head. They are probably red and wrinkled, and more scrawny than the advertisements show. During the **neonatal period,** or first 4 weeks after birth, babies' features resume their normal shape, and their bodies start to fill out. A major task for the newborns is to master circulation, respiration, digestion, and temperature control. In addition, newborns develop rapidly in both motor and perceptual skills, as we see in the next two sections.

Figure 10.2
Three children who have fetal alcohol syndrome.

Figure 10.3
A stop smoking ad from the American Cancer Society.

Motor Development

General Trends   Motor development usually follows certain patterns as newborns mature into children. For instance, the **cephalocaudal principle** states that parts of the body near the head (*cephalo* in Greek) develop before the parts near the feet (*caudal* literally means *tail* in Greek). Even prior to birth, the upper part of the fetus becomes active before the bottom part (Hall & Oppenheim, 1987). Newborn babies also have much better head control than leg control.

Furthermore, the **proximodistal principle** states that the parts near the center of the infant's body (*proximo* means *near* in Latin) develop before the more distant parts. For example, babies can control their arm movements earlier than the movements of their more distant wrists or fingers (Snow, 1989).

Motor Milestones   Figure 10.4 shows some important milestones or accomplishments during **infancy,** a period that extends from birth through the first 12–18 months of life. Notice that the chart shows an average age, just below each sketch. The range, listed after each milestone, indicates the 25th to 90th percentiles. For example, most babies begin to walk just after their first birthday. However, the range tells you that 25% begin walking before 11 ½ months, and 10% after 14 ½ months. Leg strength is the major determinant of walking, and babies vary greatly in the ability to support body weight on a single leg (Thelen, 1992). In infancy, as in all human development, individual differences are strong.

In some cultures, parents value children who are late walkers. The Zinacantecos in Chiapas, Mexico, keep a fire burning in the middle of their living areas as a source of heat. However, the fire creates a hazard for children who are not yet cognitively sophisticated enough to appreciate the danger (Greenfield & Childs, 1991). As a consequence, the Zinacantecos express concern about children who begin to walk at an early age.

On the other hand, walking enriches an infant's world because it allows independent exploration (Gibson, 1988). Toddlers can expand their cognitive and social horizons. They can explore new places in the park, and they can wander over to people they would not otherwise meet. Most important, they can decide for themselves what parts of the world merit further investigation.

Figure 10.4

Average age and variation for major motor milestones in infancy. (After Frankenburg & Dodds, 1967; Shirley, 1931) Note: The variation is expressed as a range that includes the 25th to 90th percentiles.

2 months
Raise head to
45 degrees
(1.5 – 4)

2.8 months
Roll over front
to back
(2.5 – 5)

4 months
Sit with support
(1.5 – 4.5)

5.5 months
Sit without
support
(4.5 – 8)

5.8 months
Stand holding on
(5 – 10)

7.6 months
Pull self to standing position
(6 – 10)

9.2 months
Walk holding on
to furniture
(7.5 – 13)

10 months
Crawl and creep
(7 – 12)

11.5 months
Stand alone
(9.5 – 14)

12.1 months
Walk without
assistance
(11.5 – 14.5)

DEMONSTRATION 10.1 The Development of Fine Motor Skills

Take a pen or pencil in the hand that you normally use for writing. Hold it in your fist, with the point facing down. Write your name on a piece of paper, keeping your wrist and fist rigid and using only upper-arm muscles to make movements. Experiment with letters of varying sizes. Next hold your pen or pencil with your thumb and first two fingers, again forcing your shoulder muscles to do as much of the work as possible. Once more, try letters of varying sizes. Finally, for comparison, print your name as you would normally. Notice how you obtain more motor control and produce neater printing with the motor movements used in later development.

Fine Motor Skills Try Demonstration 10.1 to illustrate another important area of motor development. Your large muscles allow you to sit and walk, but your fine motor skills allow you to write and draw. When you first held a crayon as a toddler, you grabbed it in your fist and moved it primarily by using the muscles in your upper arm (as specified by the proximodistal principle). Then you learned to hold it with your thumb and first two fingers, though most movement was still directed by the upper-arm muscles. Just before you entered kindergarten, you gained fine motor control and could master more precise crayon movements. At this point, too, you had acquired the fine motor skills that would allow you to print letters of the alphabet, an ability that would develop even further throughout elementary school.

Perceptual Development

When babies emerge from 9 months of gestation, they open their eyes for their first view of the world that has become so familiar to us. What do they see? Is it the disorganized "blooming, buzzing confusion," as claimed by America's first psychologist, William James (1890, p. 488)? And what do these newborns experience in the world of sound, touch, smell, and taste?

Forty years ago, we knew very little about infants' perceptual abilities. After all, infants are too young to talk, so how can they communicate their impressions of their perceptual worlds? Fortunately, in recent decades, researchers have become increasingly skilled at figuring out innovative techniques for learning about infant perception (Aslin, 1988). Furthermore, the more researchers investigate infant perception, the more competent young infants seem to be (Bower, 1989).

Vision As recently as the 1960s, textbooks claimed that newborns were blind at birth (Aslin, 1988). The landmark work of Robert Fantz (1961) showed otherwise. He placed infants inside a special chamber and attached pairs of test objects (e.g., a patch of narrow stripes and a patch of gray) onto the ceiling above them. Researchers recorded the amount of time the infant spent looking at each of the two objects. If little Janie looks significantly longer at the stripes than at the gray patch, then she must be able to tell the difference between the two stimuli. Figure 10.5 shows narrow stripes that a 1-month-old can just barely differentiate from the gray patch below the stripes. Notice that Fantz designed a method for measuring infants' **acuity,** that is, their ability to see precise details.

Babies are also more skilled in recognizing human faces than was once suspected. Between 1 and 3 months of age, babies develop the ability to distinguish between parents and strangers (Barrera & Maurer, 1981; Bushnell, 1982). At about 3 months, they also prefer looking at face-like patterns rather than other designs (Dannemiller & Stephens, 1988; Morton & Johnson, 1991). Furthermore, by 7 months of age, infants can distinguish between happy and surprised facial expressions (Caron et al., 1982).

Can infants perceive distance? Imagine a 7-month-old baby girl crawling rapidly from the upstairs bedroom toward the stairway. She pauses on the top step, looking down on the next step. Does that lower step look farther away to her? Figure

Figure 10.5
A 1-month-old baby can just discriminate the stripes on the top from the gray patch on the bottom, when both are presented at a distance of 10 inches from the baby's eyes.

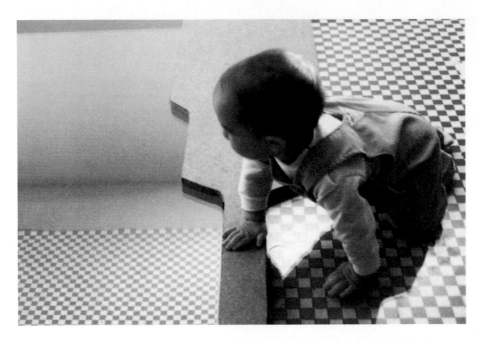

Figure 10.6

The visual cliff used by Gibson and Walk (1960) to test distance perception. Notice that the clear glass lies above a surface that appears to be shallow on the right and deep on the left.

10.6 shows an example of a visual cliff, an apparatus in which the infant is placed between a side that looks shallow and a side that looks deep. Gibson and Walk (1960) found that 6- to 14-month-old babies systematically crawled to the shallow side of the apparatus, avoiding the side that looked deeper and farther away. Using other techniques that involve physiological measures—rather than requiring infants to crawl—researchers discovered that infants as young as 2 months can distinguish between the deep and the shallow sides of a visual cliff (Campos et al., 1970; Hetherington & Parke, 1986). Distance perception receives an additional boost around 4 months of age, when babies begin to use binocular depth information (Aslin, 1988). In distance perception, two eyes are better than one.

Pause for a moment and consider why it is difficult to resolve the nature-nurture question with respect to the issue of distance perception. If a 2-month-old baby boy manages to distinguish between the deep and the shallow side of a visual cliff, this ability can possibly be traced to nature; he may have been born with this distance perception, or else his genes specified that distance perception should develop by his second month of life. But it is also possible that nurture plays an important role. By 2 months of age, he has had experience with objects moving closer and farther, so he has learned some of the visual cues that are associated with distance. We would feel more confident that distance perception could be traced to nature if it were demonstrated in a baby who was 5 minutes old, without any real experience in the visual world. However, even the most clever vision researcher has not yet discovered how babies can "tell" us what they know about distance perception at this tender age. And we cannot creep inside their heads to discover how the world actually looks to them.

In the chapter on sensation and perception, we considered **size constancy** which means that an object seems to stay the same size despite changes in the distance between the viewer and the object. Adults know that a teddy bear does not really grow larger as we approach it, but what does an infant perceive? The current belief is that newborns have some primitive form of size constancy, and it may be fairly well developed by about 4 months of age (Aslin & Smith, 1988; Day, 1987). Fortunately, then, young infants experience some stability in their visual world. Teddy bears, bottles, and grandparents do not seem to expand dramatically as infants are moved closer to them and shrink just as dramatically as the distance increases.

Hearing We have seen that young infants are reasonably precocious in their visual abilities. However, they are even more impressive in their hearing abilities, especially in the area of speech perception. For instance, infants as young as 1 month can hear the difference between sounds as similar as *bah* and *pah*. (Try saying these words out loud to appreciate how similar they are.) In fact, by 6 months of age, infants can discriminate between virtually any two **phonemes** (or basic sound units of speech) used in language (Aslin & Smith, 1988; Eimas et al., 1971). Also by 6 months, infants respond differently to a phoneme that is prototypical in their language, in comparison to a nonprototypical sound (Kuhl et al., 1992). In recent years, psychologists have developed many innovative techniques that allow infants to reveal their sophistication in responding to auditory stimuli (Schneider & Trehub, 1992).

In fact, 6-month-old infants can even hear distinctions between sounds that older infants and adults can no longer hear. For instance, babies raised in English-speaking households can tell the difference between two different kinds of *t* sounds that are important in the Hindi language spoken in India. By the ripe old age of 10 months, however, babies in English-speaking homes can no longer tell the difference between these two sounds (Werker & Tees, 1984).

By the age of 7 months, babies appreciate that when they hear a happy voice, it should be coming from a happy-looking face. Similarly, an angry voice should come from an angry-looking face (Walker-Andrews, 1986). In summary, then, babies are fairly sophisticated in appreciating the subtle properties of speech sounds. These abilities prepare them to be very receptive to the conversations that surround them and to be ready to speak by about 1 year of age—as we see in the section on language development.

Other Perceptual Skills Touch is important in the world of young infants because it provides contact with adults and other people with whom they will form loving relationships. Touch is also important in connection with several reflexes. For example, you can demonstrate the **rooting reflex** if you touch a baby's cheek on one side of the mouth; the baby's head will turn in the direction of the touch. This reflex makes sense, because it allows babies to find a nipple that has slipped to the side of their mouth.

Infants also have a fairly well-developed sense of smell. For example, they can smell the difference between their mother and a stranger by 6 weeks of age or even earlier (Cernoch & Porter, 1985; Russell, 1976).

Taste buds seem to be functional at birth. Even 1-day-old babies prefer sweet liquids to unflavored water (Desor et al., 1977; Mistretta, 1981). Unfortunately for our later health, we seem to be born with a sweet tooth—even before we really have teeth. This preference for sweet tastes can clearly be traced to a nature explanation, because a 1-day-old has not lived long enough for nurture to influence preferences (Crook, 1987). Because sweet tastes are characteristic of carbohydrates—a source of nutrition—this inborn preference makes sense from an evolutionary perspective.

In summary, the material on perception in young infants provides important support for the theme that humans are remarkably will equipped for experiencing the world. In appreciation of the remarkable capacities of the young infant, researchers often use the phrase, "the amazing newborn."

By the age of 6 weeks or earlier, the infant can distinguish between the smell of mother and the smell of a stranger.

S E C T I O N S U M M A R Y
PHYSICAL AND PERCEPTUAL DEVELOPMENT

- Three important issues in human development are the nature-nurture question, the continuity-stages question, and the stability-change question.

- During prenatal development, the fertilized egg becomes an embryo and then a fetus.

- Factors that can harm the fetus during prenatal development include poor nutrition, alcohol, cigarettes, cocaine, marijuana, caffeine, aspirin, tranquilizers, and barbiturates; harmful diseases include rubella, herpes, and AIDS.

- Two general trends in motor development are the cephalocaudal and proximodistal principles; also, motor milestones vary considerably, and other cultures may not value early walking.

- Infants have some degree of visual acuity by 1 month of age, depth perception by 2 months, face recognition by 3 months, and size constancy by 4 months.

- Infants' hearing is even more advanced, particularly in the area of speech perception. Touch sensitivity is evident in certain reflexes. Young infants can also smell the difference between their mother and a stranger, and they prefer sweet tastes as soon as they are born.

COGNITIVE DEVELOPMENT

We have seen that young infants possess some remarkable perceptual skills. They can take in stimuli from the outside world and make sense of them. Their perceptual world is not a "blooming, buzzing confusion." Instead, the world is reasonably orderly. What can they accomplish with these reasonably orderly perceptions? As we see in this section, they are able to remember, think, and use language.

Memory

Infancy We have already seen that infants can remember how their mothers look, sound, and smell—before these young babies are 3 months old. Infants can even remember some sounds they heard before they were born. In one study, newborns preferred a passage from a Dr. Seuss book that their mothers had read aloud each day during the last 3 months of pregnancy, rather than a similar passage they had never heard (DeCasper & Spence, 1986).

The most extensive research on infant memory has been conducted by Carolyn Rovee-Collier and her associates, using operant conditioning. As Chapter 6 explained, **operant conditioning** involves learning to make a response because it produces a reinforcing effect. Rovee-Collier applied operant conditioning in her research by connecting the infant's ankle to a mobile with a ribbon, so that his or her kicks would make the mobile move (see Figure 10.7). Young infants love this game, and they shriek with delight when their kicking activates the mobile. The infant learns the connection between kicking (the response) and mobile movement (the reinforcing effect). Then the researchers test memory by waiting several days and presenting the mobile once again. Will the baby remember to kick?

Using this technique, Rovee-Collier and other researchers have discovered that a 3-month-old typically remembers how to activate the mobile after a delay as long as 12 days (Rovee-Collier, 1987; Rovee-Collier & Hayne, 1987). Infants are also sensitive to context effects. Context can include something concrete, such as the lining on the crib, or something abstract, such as emotional response (Rovee-Collier et al., 1985; Shields & Rovee-Collier, 1992; Singer & Fagen, 1992). With infants, a moderate change in the context can lead to complete forgetting.

Childhood In some respects, children's and adults' memories are similar. For instance, consider **sensory memory,** the system that records information from the senses and lasts less than two seconds. Children and adults have sensory memories that are similar in capacity and duration (Engle et al., 1981; Hoving et al., 1978). Children's recognition memory is also reasonably accurate (Kail, 1984; Perry & Wrightsman, 1991). If you show children some magazine ads and later ask them to identify which ads look familiar, they will probably respond accurately.

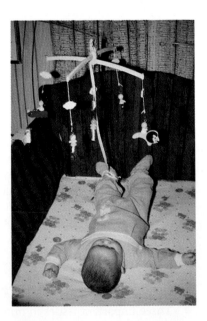

Figure 10.7
The operant conditioning technique, used to test infant memory.

Children have a clear disadvantage on other kinds of memory tasks, however. Their short-term memory is clearly limited (Kail, 1992). The average 2-year-old can remember only two items in a row, in contrast to about seven items for 12-year-olds and adults (Dempster, 1981). Young children also perform relatively poorly when we measure long-term memory in terms of recall, rather than recognition (Howe et al., 1992a, 1992b; Myers & Perlmutter, 1978).

Why should young children perform so poorly on these memory tasks? One reasonable explanation is that young children have poorly developed **metamemory,** or knowledge and awareness about their memory. Specifically, young children do not seem to realize that they need to make a special effort to remember and that they need to use special memory strategies (Schneider, 1984; Small, 1990; Swanson, 1987). They think that they will be able to remember a list of items by simply looking at it, without using deep processing.

As children grow older, however, they become more accurate in predicting their own memory abilities, and they are more aware that they need to *work* to improve their memory (Wellman, 1985; Yussen & Levy, 1975). Their improving metamemory skills make them aware they need to use strategies.

Two of the strategies that children learn to use are rehearsal and organization. **Rehearsal,** or merely repeating the items to be remembered, is not particularly effective, but it is better than nothing. Flavell and his colleagues (1966) watched children's spontaneous lip movements, indicating silent rehearsal, as they learned a list of items. The 10-year-olds in the group were much more likely to use rehearsal than the 5- and 7-year-olds.

In the memory chapter, you learned that organization is a valuable memory strategy because it allows you to group similar items together and provide a structure for encoding and recall. In a representative study, Moely and her colleagues (1969) presented children with pictures in a random order that belonged to several categories, perhaps including a hat and a shirt as examples of clothing, a desk and a sofa as examples of furniture, and so forth. Older children were much more likely than younger children to rearrange the pictures. However, young children who were specifically instructed to rearrange the pictures showed an improvement in their recall. Thus, these young children do not spontaneously realize that organization would be a useful strategy, though they do have the ability to organize items and to use organization as a memory aid. In summary, young children have inadequate metamemeory skills, so they do not tend to use strategies. Because they do not use strategies, their memory performance suffers.

This girl thinks that she can memorize these objects by merely looking at them. Without deep processing, however, she will remember very few items.

Thinking: Piaget's Approach and Other Viewpoints

Jean Piaget (pronounced "Zhohn Pea-ah-*zhay*") was a Swiss theoretician who lived from 1896 to 1980. His theory of cognitive development has had a profound impact on developmental psychology. However, we will also consider some contradictory evidence that suggests the theory has some important weaknesses (Beilin, 1992; Chapman, 1988).

Piaget argued that children are active learners, rather than passive "sponges" waiting around to soak up stimuli from the environment. In fact, Piaget's work was probably one of the principal factors that led to the decreased enthusiasm for the stimulus-response behaviorist approach (Gelman, 1983; Ginsburg & Koslowski, 1976).

An important central concept in Piaget's theory can be called meaning-making. **Meaning-making** refers to children's active attempts to make sense out of their world and their experiences (Kuhn, 1984). They try to construct general principles based on these experiences. For example, children are likely to have seen many examples of a glass filled with liquid, and they construct an idea that the level of liquid in a glass forms a line that is parallel with the bottom of the glass. If you ask a child to draw a line showing how the liquid would look in a tilted glass, he or she will probably draw a line parallel with the bottom of the glass. (See Figure 10.8.) No child has ever *seen* liquid defy the laws of gravity, forming a slanted surface. However, their drawings do not reflect their visual experiences. Instead, the drawings reflect their meaning-making, or their understanding of the relationship between liquids and containers.

Piaget proposed two related concepts to account for the way people use and modify stimuli they encounter. In **assimilation,** we deal with these stimuli in terms of our current thought structures. For example, a boy seeing a little pony for the first time might call it *doggie,* because *doggie* is a concept that is part of his current thought structure. (You might find it helpful to remember that in *assimilation,* the child treats the stimulus as if it is *similar* to a familiar concept.) Imagine, however, what might happen if children used only assimilation. How would their thought structures grow more complex?

Accommodation, the mirror image of assimilation, occurs when assimilation fails. In **accommodation,** our thought structures change to fit the stimuli we encounter. For example, the previous concept *doggie*—which had been used to refer to medium-sized, hairy, four-legged creatures—might now be divided into two categories, *doggie* and *horsie.*

Throughout this chapter, you have used both assimilation and accommodation. For example, when you were reading about size constancy in the perceptual development section, you could fit some of this information into your existing concepts about size constancy (assimilation). However, you also changed your concepts to include the new information that constancy is found in infants as young as 4 months of age (accommodation). Accommodation is the force that pushes development ahead.

Piaget described four major periods of human development. With respect to the continuity-stages question discussed at the beginning of this chapter, Piaget clearly voted for "stages." He argued that certain periods in cognitive development appear in a fixed order. Also, each period is necessary for the formation of the period that follows (Piaget, 1983). Furthermore, each period differs qualitatively (in terms of *kind* of thinking) from other periods, rather than simply differing quantitatively (in terms of *amount,* such as number of correct items). An outline of Piaget's four periods is

Figure 10.8

When children are shown a drawing of liquid in a glass and asked to draw a line indicating the level when the glass is tilted, they draw a line parallel with the bottom of the glass, as in the figure on the bottom.

TABLE 10.2	An Outline of Piaget's Four Periods of Cognitive Development	
PERIOD	**APPROXIMATE AGE**	**DESCRIPTION**
Sensorimotor	Birth–2 years	1. The infant interacts with the world through sensory and motor activities.
		2. The infant learns that objects exist even when they are not visible.
Preoperational	2–7 years	1. The child represents objects with words and mental images.
		2. The child still shows egocentrism.
Concrete operational	7–11 years	1. The child demonstrates conservation.
		2. The child shows more logical thinking.
Formal operational	11 years up to adulthood	1. The person can reason abstractly; concrete objects no longer need to be present.
		2. The person can form and test hypotheses.

Source: Ginsburg & Opper, 1988.

A young child who sees this pony for the first time can use assimilation and call it a doggie *or use accommodation, creating a new category called* horsie.

Figure 10.9

Piagetian theory states that the young infant lacks object permanence; for her, a favorite toy that is hidden beneath the blanket no longer seems to exist. However, recent research suggests that infants do have object permanence when it is tested with different measures.

shown in Table 10.2. Let us look at Piaget's description of these periods and then evaluate his theory in light of current research.

Sensorimotor Period Piaget used the term **sensorimotor period** because the infant's major cognitive tasks include sensory activities (such as seeing and hearing) and motor activities (such as kicking, sucking, and reaching). Piaget believed that babies have not yet developed language and symbols, but they can perform some actions. According to Piaget, these actions constitute the first forms of intelligence. In the first weeks of life, basic reflexes like the sucking reflex are most important.

Piagetian theory proposes that young infants do not have a sense of **object permanence,** which is the knowledge that an object exists even if it is temporarily out of sight (see Figure 10.9). Toward the end of the sensorimotor period, however, babies become experts at finding a missing object, even when it is moved several times. As we will discuss, however, recent experimental evidence demonstrates that Piaget underestimated infants' knowledge during the sensorimotor period.

Preoperational Period A critical characteristic of the **preoperational period** is the development of language. Piaget argued that children can now represent thought by using symbols and words, rather than simple physical actions. Language provides an enormous advantage to children because they can now refer to objects that are not physically present.

Another critical characteristic of the preoperational child is egocentrism. When adults use the word *egocentrism* in everyday speech, we imply selfishness. However, Piaget used **egocentrism** to mean that a child sees the world from only one point of view, his or her own. Little Tanya may annoy her parents by standing directly between them and the television set. *She* can see the program perfectly well; from her point of view, there is no problem. Egocentrism diminishes gradually throughout childhood.

Concrete Operational Period During the **concrete operational period,** children acquire important mental operations, that is, methods of manipulating information mentally. One of these operations is called conservation. Children who show **conservation** realize that a given quantity stays the same, no matter how its shape or physical arrangement may change. Figure 10.10 shows a preoperational child, who

Figure 10.10

A preoperational child fails to show conservation.

The child believes that two similar glasses contain the same amount of liquid

She watches the liquid being poured from one container to the other.

She indicates that the taller, thinner glass contains more liquid.

believes that a tall, thin glass contains more milk. She is so impressed by the height of the liquid in the new container that she fails to realize that the other glass is wider—or that the amounts must be equal because nothing was added or subtracted. Piaget argued that children in the concrete operational period acquire conservation, though current research suggests that younger children understand conservation. Try Demonstration 10.2 to test conservation in children.

Children also show more logical thinking during the concrete operational period. For instance, they no longer believe that inanimate objects are alive. One of my students asked several children what their stuffed animals did at night when everyone was asleep. Four-year-old Thomas, in the preoperational period, said, "They play, but then go back to sleep when they get tired." Ruth, much more logical and concrete operational at the age of 7, replied, "My dad says they get up and play, but I don't believe him. They can't do that."

Formal Operational Period In the concrete operational period, children can reason logically and maturely on many different problems—as long as the problem is physically present. However, they have trouble with more abstract reasoning.

Teenagers and adults who are in the **formal operational period** can think scientifically. They can use **hypothetico-deductive reasoning,** constructing possible solutions to a problem and then creating a systematic plan for selecting a correct solution. They can solve problems without the help of a concrete representation. They can also contemplate complex ideas and think flexibly about a variety of problems. In a typical problem, people are asked to determine which of several factors influences the speed of a swinging pendulum. Younger children construct hypotheses haphazardly and test them inadequately. People in the formal operational period, however, systematically vary factors such as the weight of the pendulum and the length of the string on which the pendulum dangles. After careful observation, they correctly conclude that the length of the string is the critical factor.

The Current Status of Piaget's Theory Clearly, Piaget created an extremely comprehensive and complex theory of cognitive development. No other theorist has proposed such a complete picture of children's thinking. He identified intriguing concepts—such as object permanence and conservation—that no one else

---

DEMONSTRATION 10.2 **The Development of Conservation**

In this demonstration, you will be examining conservation of number. First locate one or more children between the ages of 5 and 8. Form two rows of 10 pennies each, with both rows similarly spaced (see *a*). Ask the child whether both rows contain the same number of pennies or whether one contains more. Once the child has determined that the

rows contain the same number, push the pennies in the bottom row closer together (see *b*). Ask again whether the two rows have the same number or whether one row has more. Finally, ask the child to explain his or her answer.

You may also wish to test conservation of liquid, using Figure 10.10 as a guide.

a. Two horizontal rows, each with 10 pennies, lined up so that the two sets of edges are matching.

b. Two horizontal rows, each with 10 pennies, lined up so that the bottom row is denser.

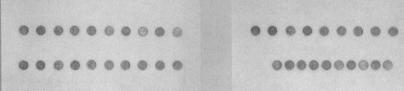

had ever investigated. In addition, his theory inspired thousands of studies, which is one indication that researchers have judged his work to be extremely interesting (Beilin, 1992; Case, 1987.)

Nevertheless, Piaget's theory can be criticized in several respects. For example, he did not pay much attention to individual differences (Case, 1987), a theme stressed throughout this textbook.

A large number of studies have also demonstrated that Piaget underestimated the capabilities of young infants (Flavell, 1992). Consider object permanence, for example. Piaget assessed object permanence by noting whether the infant manually searched for the missing object. However, infants might perform poorly on this dependent variable—not because of an underdeveloped concept of object permanence, but because infants are limited in their ability to plan their search strategies (Baillargeon, 1992). Earlier we saw that psychologists were able to discover remarkable perceptual skills in infants by designing creative research methods. Similarly, Renée Baillargeon and her colleagues have used a variety of creative techniques to demonstrate that infants as young as 3 months of age know a great deal about object permanence and other properties of objects (e.g., Baillargeon 1986; 1991; Baillargeon et al., 1985). These studies assess the amount of time an infant looks at an object or an event, rather than Piaget's measure, manual search.

Let's consider a study on object permanence by Baillargeon and DeVos (1991). In this research, 3½-month-old infants watched carrot-like cartoon figures as they traveled along a track, behind a screen. (See Figure 10.11.) The researchers first tested **habituation,** during which a stimulus is presented many times until the individual stops responding to it (in this case, looking at it). They included this condition to make sure that the infants considered the short carrot and the tall carrot to be equally interesting; indeed, the infants looked at both figures for equal amounts of time.

During the test phase, infants sometimes saw a possible event, during which the short carrot passed behind a screen without being visible through the opening in the screen. They also saw an impossible event, in which the tall carrot passed behind the same screen; it should have been visible in the opening, but it was not. The infants looked significantly longer at the impossible event than at the possible event.

Figure 10.11

Schematic representation of the habituation phase (which demonstrated that infants are equally interested in the short carrot and the tall carrot) and the test phase (which demonstrated that infants were surprised when the tall carrot was not visible through the opening in the screen). (Based on Baillargeon & Devos, 1991)

Habituation events

Short carrot event

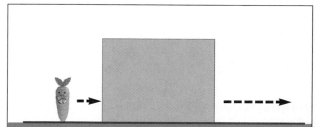

Tall carrot event

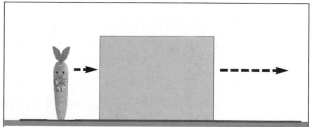

Test events

Possible event

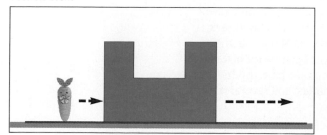

Impossible event

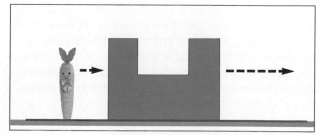

This suggests that they expected the tall carrot to maintain its existence, even though hidden; they were surprised when it failed to appear in the opening. Infants apparently know that objects should not disappear when they are hidden!

Another feature of Piaget's sensorimotor period that researchers now question is Piaget's claim that infants are not capable of symbolic thought. For example, Mandler (1988) argues that infants have the capacity to form concepts. Babies as young as 9 months of age can distinguish between the categories of airplanes and birds, even though both kinds of objects are similar in shape (Mandler, 1992a; Mandler & McDonough, 1993). Mandler (1992b) believes that this sophisticated cognitive development can be traced to infants' perceptual analysis—which we examined earlier—rather than their motor interactions with objects. Other research with children who have physical disabilities confirms that motor activity is not essential for children's cognitive development (Bebko et al., 1992). In other words, a better name for the sensorimotor period might really be the perceptual-analysis period.

In general, Piaget was correct about the order in which children master cognitive tasks (Flavell, 1985). However, children progress unevenly in their cognitive development, so that a child may be preoperational according to one measure and concrete operational according to a second measure. Most current developmental psychologists believe that Piaget overstated the "stages" part of his theory; they are more likely to see some continuities in cognitive development (Flavell, 1992). They are also likely to argue that conclusions about children's competence on a task depend upon how this skill is measured. We saw that infants' competence on object-permanence tasks depends upon research methods. Similarly, children show conservation at an earlier age than Piaget proposed when researchers use simpler, more interesting experimental setups (Gelman, 1969, 1983). Conservation is more complicated than Piaget described, because it depends upon task characteristics.

In summary, Piaget proposed a broad, complex theory of the development of thinking. However, even Piaget underestimated the rich, complicated nature of infants' and children's thoughts. The complexity of humans makes it difficult to explain their behavior in any general, sweeping statements. Very clearly, the complexity theme applies not only to adults, but also to infants and young children.

Jean Mandler's research suggests that infants can form concepts, contrary to Piaget's theory. For example, infants can distinguish between airplanes and birds, even though their shapes are similar.

Language Development

"Mama!" (8 months)

"Hi, Mom!" (1 year, 4 months)

"Don't cry, honey." (1 year, 5 months)

"My grandma gave me this dolly, Cara. My grandma is my mommy's mommy. I have another grandma, too. She's my daddy's mommy. And Aunt Elli is my daddy's sister." (2 years, 9 months)

These selections from the early language of my daughter are typical of the remarkable accomplishment involved in language acquisition. Within a period of 2 to 3 years, all normal children progress from one-word utterances to complex descriptions about relationships. In fact, language acquisition is the most impressive intellectual accomplishment many people ever perform (Miller & Gildea, 1987).

Consider, for instance, that the average 6-year-old has some mastery of about 14,000 words. To acquire a vocabulary this large, children must learn about nine new words each day from the time they start speaking until their sixth birthday (Clark, 1991). Perhaps even more impressive than the size of children's vocabulary is their expertise in combining these words into phrases that have never been heard before, such as "My dolly dreamed about toys" (2 years, 2 months). Let us see how children's language evolves as we explore early language, grammar, pragmatics, and several theoretical explanations of language acquisition.

Early language In the section on speech perception, we saw that young children have a head start on language. Infants are impressively accomplished at making distinctions among speech sounds.

Children's early vocalizations pass through a series of stages. Infants make cooing sounds around 2 months of age. Cooing includes a variety of sounds that are usually made with rounded lips and typically involve *oo* sounds. At 6 to 8 months, babies begin babbling, or making sounds that include both vowels and consonants, such as *dadada* (Bates et al., 1993). Their speech now sounds more similar to adult language. Interestingly, deaf infants who have been exposed to sign language also begin at about this time to "babble" with their hands, producing systematic but meaningless actions that are not found in hearing children (Petitto & Marentette, 1991).

Children say their first words around the time of their first birthday, though one study showed that the production vocabulary for 12-month-olds ranged between 0 and 52 words (Fenson et al., 1991). The sudden increase in vocabulary size between 12 and 28 months may be linked to rapid increases in synaptic connections in the cortex (Bates et al., 1993). The growth in comprehension is even more rapid than the growth in production during this period (Hirsh-Pasek & Golinkoff, 1991; Reznick & Goldfield, 1992).

Children's first words include many overextensions. An **overextension** is the use of a word to refer to other objects in addition to the appropriate object. Around the age of 2 years, children often show overextensions for common words such as *dog* and *ball*. For example, one child produced the name *dog* for nine species of dog and one toy dog—all appropriate labels. However, he also used *dog* to apply to a bear, a wolf, a fox, a doe, a rhinoceros, a hippopotamus, and a fish—all overextensions (Thomson & Chapman, 1977). Notice incidentally, that the linguistic term *overextension* corresponds to the Piagetian term *assimilation*.

Grammar One important aspect of grammar is **syntax,** or the organizational rules for determining word order, sentence organization, and relationships among words (Owens, 1992). Syntax becomes relevant as soon as young children begin combining two words into a single phrase. Children typically begin producing two-word phrases around the age of 20 months (Bohannon, 1993). Here are some representative first phrases (Clark & Clark, 1977; de Villiers & de Villiers, 1985):

"Push car"	*(action-object)*
"Daddy pants"	*(possessor-possessed)*
"Baby sleeping"	*(actor-action)*

Notice that these early phrases express a wide variety of relationships. Also, the word order in the phrases suggests an early awareness of English word order.

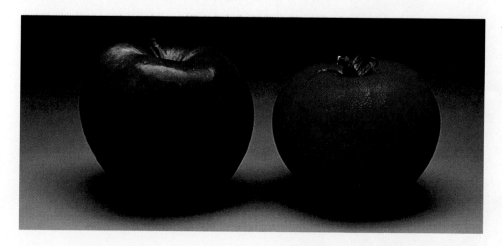

A young child may use an overextension and call a tomato an apple.

Another characteristic of these sentences is **telegraphic speech,** which includes nouns and verbs but leaves out the extra words such as prepositions, *a,* and *the,* which serve only a grammatical function. (The name is derived from a telegram, in which the nonessential words are omitted.) Notice in the three earlier examples that the child expresses only the essential meaning, omitting the extra, less important words.

Pragmatics As noted in Chapter 9, the term **pragmatics** refers to the social aspects of language. Children need to learn what should be said—and what should *not* be said. One of my students described his family's embarrassment when a younger brother shouted to an elderly gentleman on his way to the bathroom during a party, "Mommy says to make sure to aim straight so you don't get the seat wet!"

Children also learn to master courtesy words, such as *please* and *may I.* Naturalistic observation in nursery schools has shown that 3- and 4-year-olds frequently use these polite terms to obtain a toy (Garvey, 1984).

Children must also master another pragmatic skill, the art of taking turns in a conversation. Sophisticated turn-taking requires each speaker to anticipate when the other person will complete his or her remark, a skill that demands an impressive knowledge of language structure. Two-year-olds have conversational gaps of about 1.5 seconds, in contrast to about 0.8 seconds for adults (McTear, 1985).

We saw that Piaget believed young children have difficulty adopting another person's point of view. However, research on children's language shows that preschoolers can adapt their language to their listeners' level of understanding. For example, Shatz and Gelman (1973) found that 4-year-olds described a toy differently when speaking with a 2-year-old than when speaking to a peer or an adult. Specifically, their conversation to 2-year-olds used short, simple utterances, with more repetition. Once again, Piaget apparently underestimated the cognitive skill of young children.

Children learn language so they can accomplish social goals that are important to them (Rice, 1989). As Marilyn Shatz commented in an interview:

Children are very impatient to be members of the family, genuine members. They learn very early that speech is the way to realize and maintain contact with other family members and, at the same time, to be taken seriously. A 2-year-old already has the goal of being a person in the family instead of a baby, of being someone to interact linguistically with instead of an object of discussion. (Roşu & Natanson, 1987, p. 5)

The telegraphic language of young children omits the nonessential words. For example, this child might describe his pet with the phrase, "doggie ball."

In speaking to his younger brother, this preschooler would use simpler vocabulary and shorter sentences than when speaking with an adult.

This enthusiasm about learning language encourages children to master the words, grammar, and pragmatics of speech.

Theories of Language Acquisition Let us now turn to three important explanations that have been proposed for language acquisition: the learning view, the inborn view, and the cognitive view.

1. *Language is acquired by learning.* According to the behaviorist view, language acquisition can be explained by principles of learning such as the ones you read about in Chapter 6. Young children learn to associate certain objects with the sounds of words. They imitate the words and the grammar they hear around them. Adults provide reinforcement for correct language in the form of smiles, hugs, and the food or other objects requested by children (Kymissis & Poulson, 1990; Skinner, 1957). Just as a pigeon in an operant conditioning task learns to peck a button to receive a pellet of food, a young child learns to say "cookie" to receive a cookie.

Learning theory sounds logical, and learning is clearly an important part of language acquisition. However, it cannot account for all the characteristics of language. For instance, simple imitation cannot explain how children manage to produce grammatical forms and novel sentences they have never heard before. What child has heard his parent say, "I holded two mices"? I assure you my daughter never heard her parents say, "My dolly dreamed about toys." Furthermore, operant conditioning theory suggests that children learn grammar by being rewarded for proper grammatical constructions and punished, in the form of a correction, for improper constructions. However, researchers have found that parents are eager to correct children for factual errors, but not grammatical errors. Thus, a parent corrects a child for calling a tomato an apple. However, "I holded two mices" elicits no reaction (Bohannon, 1993; Brown et al., 1968).

2. *Language is inborn.* According to the inborn view, language development is genetically programmed. In the words of Noam Chomsky, the foremost supporter of this view,

> *Language learning is not really something that the child does; it is something that happens to the child placed in an appropriate environment, much as the child's body grows and matures in a predetermined way when provided with appropriate nutrition and environmental stimulation. (Chomsky, 1988, p. 134)*

Some evidence for this view comes from the fact that language tends to appear at roughly the same age in a wide variety of cultures, and the same kinds of meanings are encoded in children's early words and sentences (Rice, 1989; Slobin, 1985). If similar trends occur in widely different learning environments, then humans must be born with a language-making capacity. Naturally, however, this language-making capacity must be combined with learning the rules and specific vocabulary of the language in which the child is reared.

3. *Language depends upon cognition.* According to the **cognition-first view,** language depends upon achievements in cognitive development (Johnson, 1985; Rosenberg, 1993). Thus, children's first words are related to their sensorimotor actions with objects. Furthermore, toddlers begin to say "all gone" about the same time they can solve more complicated object-permanence tasks. Now that they appreciate what "all gone" means, they begin to talk about it (Rice, 1989).

The cognitive view also emphasizes that children are active language learners (Flavell, 1985; Moskowitz, 1978). They continually analyze what they hear, testing hypotheses and trying to fit together the pieces of the language jigsaw puzzle. The child is not simply a pigeon, pressing a button and awaiting a reward, as the learning view suggests. The child is not just a flower, unfolding according to a preordained genetic plan, as the inborn theory suggests. Instead, the child is a junior scientist, actively working to discover the explanations underlying language.

DEMONSTRATION 10.3 Speaking Motherese

Locate a doll that resembles an infant as closely as possible in features and size. Select a friend who has had experience with children, and ask him or her to imagine that the doll is a niece or nephew who has just arrived for a first visit. Encourage your friend to interact with the baby as he or she normally would. Observe your friend's language for qualities such as pitch, variation in pitch, vocabulary, sentence length, repetition, and intonation. Also observe nonverbal communication. What qualities are different from the language your friend typically uses with adults?

Source of idea: Ganie DeHart (1990)

We have stressed repeatedly that language is complicated. You will not be surprised, then, to read that the answer to the language-acquisition question also must be complicated. Children manage to master language because of learning principles, an inborn ability, and an active, problem-solving approach.

Another important factor that facilitates children's language acquisition is that adults who raise children tend to use language that is ideally suited for language-learners. The language spoken to children is called **motherese;** motherese language involves simple vocabulary, emphasis on important words, well-formed short sentences, long pauses, slow rate of speech, and high voice pitch (Fernald & Mazzie, 1991; Rice, 1989). (You'll notice the gender-bias in the name *motherese;* perhaps it should be called *parentese* instead.) Cross-cultural research in Europe, Asia, Latin America, and Africa has confirmed a widespread tendency for mothers to use different language when speaking to infants and young children than when speaking to adults (Bornstein et al., 1992; Fernald, 1991). Demonstration 10.3 illustrates motherese.

In summary, children acquire language because they are remarkably well equipped. In addition, they use learning to supplement their inborn abilities, and they are active in their approach to language. Adults also help to make language acquisition more manageable by adjusting their communication style to accommodate children's linguistic skills.

SECTION SUMMARY

COGNITIVE DEVELOPMENT

- Research using operant conditioning has shown that 3-month-olds can remember an activity up to 12 days later and that infants are sensitive to context.

- Children do not differ substantially from adults in their sensory memory or their recognition memory, but their short-term memory and long-term recall memory are clearly inferior in comparison with adults.

- Children have poorly developed metamemory and therefore do not realize that they must use memory strategies; as a consequence, their memory performance suffers.

- Piaget's theory stresses that children actively try to make meaning out of their world. He proposed four periods in cognitive development: sensorimotor, preoperational, concrete operational, and formal operational.

- Although Piaget's theory has been extremely influential, it has been criticized for its lack of attention to individual differences, its underestimation of infants' skills with object permanence and concepts, and its overemphasis on stages.

- Early language development includes cooing and babbling; overextensions are common among the early words.

- Children's first phrases express a wide variety of relationships, and they are telegraphic; language acquisition also requires mastery of pragmatic rules.

● An explanation of language acquisition needs to be complex, involving learning mechanisms, inborn language ability, a relationship between language and cognition, and parents' using language that encourages children's developing linguistic competence.

GENDER-ROLE DEVELOPMENT

Adults believe that gender is extremely important, even during infancy. For example, one pair of researchers asked parents of newborns to telephone friends and relatives to announce their baby's birth (Intons-Peterson & Reddel, 1984). In 80% of the cases, the first question asked was basically, "Is it a boy or a girl?" People eventually asked questions about the health of the mother or the baby, but only after they had established whether the baby was female or male.

We also know that people respond differently to baby girls than to baby boys. In a study by Condry and Condry (1976), people watched a series of videotapes of an infant, who was labeled female half the time and male half the time. At one point, the baby cried when a jack-in-the-box opened suddenly. When people thought they were watching a baby girl, they judged that the baby was afraid. When they thought they were watching a baby boy, they judged that the emotional reaction was much more active: the baby was angry. In reality, everyone saw exactly the same video. However, the labels "female" and "male" had biased the viewers' judgments. Gender clearly matters to adults.

In the previous sections, we have seen that young children possess impressive perceptual and cognitive talents. As we will see in this section, young children are also knowledgeable about **gender roles,** which are our expectations about appropriate activities for females and males (Katz & Boswell, 1986). Let us first discuss what children know about gender, then consider explanations for gender-role development.

IN DEPTH: Children's Concepts of Gender

We have just seen that adults hold different beliefs about male and female infants. At what point do infants make a distinction between males and females, and what do young children believe about the characteristics of males and females?

Distinguishing Between Males and Females In the previous sections, we have seen that infants are surprisingly competent. They can make perceptual discriminations, remember events, demonstrate object permanence, and form concepts—even before they are a year old. Thus, it should not surprise you that babies have also acquired information about gender. For example, Beverly Fagot and Mary Leinbach (1993) tested whether infants place males and females in different categories. In a typical session, infants between the ages of 5 and 12 months saw a series of slides of the heads and shoulders of different women. (The slides showed a variety of clothing, hair styles, facial expressions, and so forth.) After a number of trials, the infants lost interest in the slides; they had habituated. Then the researchers presented a test slide, showing either a male or a female. Those infants who were 9 months and older looked significantly longer at the slide of the male than at the slide of the female. This same pattern of increased looking-time for the contrasting category was demonstrated when the infants were habituated to slides of men and then saw a test slide of a woman.

Thus, by their patterns of looking, infants are "telling" us that they can discriminate between males and females. This interesting finding needs to be examined further in other replications, but some exploratory research suggests that hair length is one critical factor in infants' gender categories (Fagot & Leinbach, 1993).

Personality Characteristics Gloria Cowan and Charles Hoffman (1986) studied boys and girls who were either in the 2 ½- to 3-year-old range or in the 3 ½- to 4-year-old range. The researchers used the cross-sectional approach, as described in Chapter 2, so that these children represented different groups of children who were tested at the same time. (An alternative

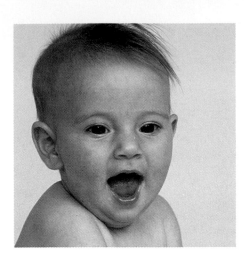

Figure 10.12

Photos of two infants, similar to those used in Cowan and Hoffman's (1986) study.

approach would have been to use the longitudinal approach, following those same 2 ½- to 3-year-old children one year later when they were 3 ½ to 4 years old.) The children represented a variety of ethnic, religious, and socioeconomic backgrounds.

The children were shown two pictures of infants, one a girl and one a boy. (However, in a pretest, another group of children the same age could not guess the infants' sexes accurately.) For example, the infants in Figure 10.12 might be introduced, "This baby is a boy named Tommy (pointing to the baby on the left), and this baby is a girl named Susie (pointing to the baby on the right)." Next the experimenters checked to make certain the children recalled which was the girl and which was the boy. Then the children were asked "One of these babies is big, and one is little; point to the baby which is big." (The experimenters were careful to reverse the photos on half the trials and also to vary the order of the adjectives.) They also asked children to make decisions about seven other adjective pairs, such as mad-scared, strong-weak, and soft-hard.

The results showed that the children chose a stereotyped response 64% of the time. That is, they tended to say that the boy baby was big, mad, strong, and hard, whereas the girl baby was small, scared, weak, and soft. The results were statistically significant, indicating that even preschoolers have stereotypes about gender. However, boys and girls were equally stereotyped. Furthermore, the younger and the older children were equally stereotyped.

In a second study, Cowan and Hoffman (1986) presented line drawings of a boy and a girl, who were also introduced by name. In this study, 5-year-olds showed stereotyping 77% of the time. By the age of 5, then, children are fairly knowledgeable about the stereotypical personality characteristics that boys and girls are supposed to have.

Other Characteristics Children also know that boys and girls have different clothing and different toys. For example, Carol Martin and Jane Little (1990) studied boys and girls who ranged in age from 3 to 5 ½. Three pictures were arranged in front of a child; one showed a boy, one showed a girl, and one showed a boy and a girl together. Then the researchers showed the child a picture of a child's clothing (for example, a boy's suit or a girl's fancy dress), with the instructions to place the clothing next to the person who would be most likely to wear it. As you can see in Figure 10.13, children's knowledge about "appropriate" clothing clearly increased with age. The researchers found a similar increase in children's knowledge about stereotypical toys, such as a tool kit and doll clothes.

Children also acquire strong beliefs about which occupations are suitable for men and for women (Fagot et al., 1992; Inton-Peterson, 1988; Trepanier & Romatowski, 1985). They also hold strong opinions about appropriate behavior for males and females, condemning a boy for wearing nail polish to nursery school or a girl for having a crew cut (Smetana, 1986). Under some circumstances, their ideas about gender are so strong that they will even choose to play with a boring toy that is considered appropriate for their own gender, rather than an exciting toy associated with the other gender (Frey & Ruble, 1992). For some children, knowledge about gender leads to inflexibility.

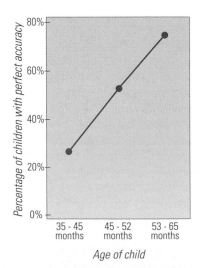

Figure 10.13

Percentage of children who correctly identified all six items of boys' and girls' clothing. (Based on Martin & Little, 1990)

Theories of Gender-Role Development

We have seen that males and females differ significantly. Furthermore, a small number of gender differences—such as play patterns—emerge during childhood (Maccoby, 1990b). Psychologists currently favor three leading theories about the development of gender. These include the social-learning theory, the cognitive-developmental theory, and the gender-schema theory.

Social-Learning Theory According to **social-learning theory,** two major mechanisms explain how girls learn to act "feminine" and boys learn to act "masculine": (1) they receive rewards and punishments for their own behavior, and (2) they watch and imitate the behavior of others (Jacklin, 1989; Mischel, 1966). As you can see, this theory resembles the theory that children acquire language by learning.

Social-learning theory sounds plausible. Little Bobby wins smiles for playing with the fire truck, but his parents look horrified when he emerges from the bedroom wearing his sister's ballet costume. Furthermore, the models provided by television feature dominant men, solving problems and giving orders, and submissive women, concerned primarily with family and romantic relationships (Gunter, 1986).

However, social-learning explanations cannot be completely responsible for gender typing. For instance, parents have been found to treat their own sons and daughters fairly similarly (Jacklin, 1989). In fact, Lytton and Romney (1991) conducted a meta-analysis, the systematic statistical method for synthesizing results from numerous studies, which we discussed in Chapter 2. The results of the meta-analysis on North American studies showed that parents treated boys and girls similarly on 18 different measures of gender-role socialization such as discouragement of aggression and encouragement of dependency. (The only significant effect concerned parents' encouragement of gender-typed activities.) Another problem for social-learning theory is that children do not consistently prefer to imitate models who are the same gender as they are (Matlin, 1993a; Raskin & Israel, 1981). We need to look for additional explanations to supplement the social-learning approach.

According to a meta-analysis by Lytton and Romney (1991), parents treat their sons and daughters similarly.

Cognitive-Developmental Theory According to **cognitive-developmental theory,** children's own thought processes are primarily responsible for the development of gender typing. Inspired by the work of Piaget, psychologist Lawrence Kohlberg argued that children learn about gender roles in the same way that they learn about other concepts, such as conservation and morality (Kohlberg, 1966; Kohlberg & Ullian, 1974). Like Piaget, Kohlberg emphasized that children actively work to make meaning out of the information they learn about gender.

By age 3, children identify themselves as male or female. About a year later, children can accurately classify other people as female or male. However, Kohlberg argued that many 4-year-olds fail to appreciate **gender constancy,** which is the concept that a person's gender stays the same in spite of changes in outward physical appearance. We saw earlier that young children think the quantity of milk changes when poured from a short, fat glass to a tall, thin glass. Similarly, they believe that a man can become a woman by wearing a dress or carrying a purse, and that a woman can transform herself into a man by cutting her hair very short. In both cases, children are misled by external appearances.

Once children have acquired gender concepts, they begin to show systematic preferences. A child who realizes she is a girl, for example, prefers feminine objects and activities. She may pat only "girl dogs," ignoring the "boy dogs." Research supports this concept of systematic preferences (e.g., Matlin, 1993a; Thompson, 1975).

However, cognitive-developmental theory predicts that a boy must know he is a boy before he begins to prefer trucks to dolls, yet little Bobby may prefer his fire truck to Raggedy Ann before he can say whether he is a boy or a girl. The stages do not consistently unfold according to the ages and the order Kohlberg specified (Jacklin, 1989). For example, Bem (1989) reports that Kohlberg underestimated children's awareness of gender constancy; as we have noted earlier, some research techniques do not capture children's true abilities. Furthermore, the theory does not explain why children select gender as the critical factor in classifying people, objects, and activities. Why not eye color or size?

Gender-Schema Theory According to Sandra Bem, **gender-schema theory** proposes that children use gender as an important schema to structure and guide their view of the world. As the memory chapter noted, a schema is a generalized idea that organizes one's perceptions and thoughts. In our culture, gender is extremely important, and children learn to emphasize gender in their own lives. As we saw earlier, the first question to new parents usually concerns gender. We also interpret a baby's crying differently, depending upon whether we think the baby is a boy or a girl. According to gender-schema theory, children develop gender schemas, and they learn that the world should be divided into two important categories that are the polar opposites of each other—male and female (Bem, 1981, 1985, 1993; Liben & Signorella, 1987).

Gender-schema theory combines social-learning theory and cognitive-developmental theory. It specifies that gender typing is a learned phenomenon. As children grow up, they learn society's definition of what it means to be female or male. Gender-schema theory also stresses, however, that children's own thought processes encourage gender development. Thus, little Jenny heads for the kitchen center in nursery school because she has been rewarded for domestic activities and because she has seen more women than men in the kitchen. However, she also prefers the baking set because she realizes that she is a girl, and girls should prefer kitchen activities.

At present, gender-schema theory is the dominant explanation for how children acquire gender-related thoughts and behaviors (Jacklin, 1989). A prime advantage of gender-schema theory is its acknowledgment that complex explanations are required to account for the complexity of the way we think about gender and the way in which our actions are influenced by gender. Table 10.3 summarizes the three theories of gender typing examined in this section.

Gender-schema theory suggests that this boy learns how to act masculine and this girl learns how to act feminine because they have learned society's definition of masculinity and femininity and because their own thoughts encourage the development of gender-stereotyped behavior.

TABLE 10.3 The Three Major Theories of Gender Development

SOCIAL-LEARNING THEORY

Rewards and punishments ⎫
Observation and imitation ⎭ → Gender-typed behavior

COGNITIVE-DEVELOPMENTAL THEORY

Child identifies self as female or male → Child prefers same-gender objects/activities → Gender-typed behavior

GENDER-SCHEMA THEORY

Culture emphasizes gender → Gender schema → Gender-typed behavior

SECTION SUMMARY

GENDER-ROLE DEVELOPMENT

- Adults stress the importance of gender in questions to parents of newborns and in their responses to infants, part of the general tendency to emphasize gender.

- Infants can distinguish between males and females; young children believe that males and females have different personalities and other characteristics.

- The three leading theories about gender typing include social-learning theory, cognitive-developmental theory, and gender-schema theory.

PERSONALITY AND SOCIAL DEVELOPMENT

The general organization of this textbook began with the biological aspects of behavior and then moved on to cognitive areas; the last part of the book will focus on individual differences and social relationships. Similarly, this chapter began by considering biological aspects of human development, such as motor and perceptual development. Then it moved on to cognitive areas: memory, thinking, and language. The third topic, gender, involved both cognitive development and social relationships. In this last section of the chapter, we consider personality and social development, foreshadowing the chapters in the last part of the book.

An important concept in this section is **socialization,** or the acquisition of motives, values, knowledge, and behavior needed to function adequately in adult society (Maccoby, 1984). In general, psychologists who study personality development and socialization tend to focus on individual differences, or the variation between individuals who are the *same* age. A typical study might examine the personality characteristics of 4-year-olds whose parents have different styles of child rearing. In contrast, psychologists who study cognitive development tend to focus on the performance of children who are *different* ages, as well as explanations for any differences. For instance, a study on children's memory might examine how long-term memory improves between the ages of 5 and 9 and how the increased use of memory strategies can explain this memory improvement. Thus, the research on personality and social development has a different flavor from the research on cognitive development.

It is also important to emphasize how personality and social development depend closely upon all of the processes we have discussed in this chapter. We began by discussing motor development; consider how children who have the ability to walk can increase their social interactions. Toddlers can rush in to see who has arrived at the front door, and they can wander in search of social excitement at the airport, the grocery store, and the playground. When infants perfect their perceptual skills, they can recognize how the important people in their lives look, sound, and smell. Clearly, these perceptual skills are necessary in forming social bonds with parents and siblings.

The development of memory allows children to recall past social events, to form schemas about social situations, and to predict how people will act toward them in the future. As children's thinking matures, their egocentrism declines. If they can take another person's point of view, they are less likely to act selfishly (Maccoby, 1984). As stressed earlier, language development enables children to become true members of a family group, able to share their own ideas and desires.

The development of gender roles also has important implications for personality and social behavior. Children's thoughts about whether they are male or female influence their social behavior. Perhaps more important, children develop gender schemas so that they begin to expect different behavior from the males and females in their lives. They acquire stereotypes, believing that men *should* be more aggressive, strong, and independent.

This section begins by considering early temperament—the origins of individual differences. We also discuss self-concept, another important component of personality. Our examination of children's social interactions includes relationships with other people, the day-care dilemma, the development of positive social interactions, and children's ethnic backgrounds. Our final topic provides an overview of the status of children in contemporary society.

Temperament

Temperament refers to individual differences in behavior that are present early in life and show stability as the individual matures (Bates, 1989; Eaton & Saudino, 1992). Figure 10.14 shows two sisters. According to their mother, the sister at right has always been relatively calm, whereas the sister at left has consistently been much more sensitive to stimuli. Temperament is typically assessed through home observations, laboratory observations, or—most common of all—questionnaires in which parents provide information about their children (Rothbart & Mauro, 1990).

Psychologists, physicians, and educators have become increasingly interested in the topic of temperament in recent years (Goldsmith & Rieser-Danner, 1990). Some of the dimensions of temperament they have studied include positive emotionality, negative emotionality, adaptability to change, attention span, and activity level (Bates, 1989; Rothbart & Mauro, 1990).

Jerome Kagan and his colleagues have concentrated their research on one temperament category, inhibited versus uninhibited behavior. **Inhibited children** are fearful of strangers and unfamiliar objects or events; about 15% to 20% of healthy 1- to 2-year-olds can be categorized as inhibited (Robinson et al., 1992). **Uninhibited children** approach strangers and unfamiliar objects or events without hesitation; about 25% to 30% of healthy 1- to 2-year-olds can be categorized as uninhibited. (The remaining children—about half of the population—fall somewhere between the two extremes.)

This research has addressed an important question, related to an issue we discussed earlier: Do children show stability or change with respect to the inhibited-uninhibited dimension? In general, children who are inhibited and afraid as infants tend to remain so, but there are many exceptions (Kagan et al., 1988). One study selected 4-month-old children who were classified as either inhibited or uninhibited, based on their reaction to unfamiliar people and objects (Kagan & Snidman, 1991). When these children were retested, 40% of the inhibited children were highly inhibited at both 14 and 21 months of age; not a single uninhibited child responded in a highly inhibited fashion. On the other hand 52% of the uninhibited children—but only 10% of the inhibited children—responded in a highly uninhibited fashion. So this research shows that many children remain in the same category; however, it also shows that many children become more moderate in their response patterns. Children clearly have the potential to change.

Researchers have also looked at biological factors that might be correlated with temperament (e.g., Gunnar et al., 1989); Kagan, 1992; Kagan & Snidman, 1991). This research shows that inhibited children tend to have higher levels of **cortisol,** a hor-

Figure 10.14
Two siblings in the same family can differ tremendously in their temperament.

mone that is related to stress. When inhibited children experience stress, their heart rates increase and their pupils dilate more, in contrast to uninhibited children. Inhibited children are also more likely than uninhibited children to have a low threshold of reactivity in their amygdala, hypothalamus, and sympathetic nervous system. That is, these structures are likely to become active when the situation is only mildly stressful. We will examine some other biological components of personality in Chapter 13 that provide additional support for the "nature" side of the nature-nurture controversy.

Self-Concept

The **self-concept** is a schema of thoughts and feelings about oneself as an individual. The self-concept begins to develop in infancy. As we see in the next chapter, self-concepts become much more elaborate during adulthood as people contemplate their abilities, priorities, and life goals.

Newborns do not have a sense of self, because they are not aware that they are separate from other people and objects (Snow, 1989). Infants between the ages of 2 to 6 months begin to sense that they are physically separated from mother or other caretakers and that they have different experiences from these other people (Stern, 1985).

An important component of self-concept is self-recognition, which is the ability to recognize your own image (Fogel, 1984). In one study, Lewis and Brooks (1978) unobtrusively placed a spot of rouge on babies' faces, so that they were unaware they had been marked. Then the babies were allowed to look in the mirror. Infants between the ages of 9 and 12 months simply looked in the mirror but showed no distinctive reactions. One-quarter of babies in the 15- to 18-month age range and three-quarters of babies in the 21- to 24-month age range stared in the mirror and touched the rouge spot on their own face. As if to say, "Hey, that's me!" they acknowledged that the babies with the silly red spots were indeed themselves (Figure 10.15).

The theory of Erik Erikson (1950, 1968) provides one of the most comprehensive descriptions of the development of self-concept. Erikson's theory proposed eight stages of development throughout the life cycle. We will consider the first four stages in this chapter. The adult development chapter considers the last four stages and also examines identity development in more detail.

Erikson suggested that an individual confronts a specific task or dilemma during each of the eight stages. Healthy development is more likely if the individual resolves the tasks successfully. As Table 10.4 shows, a child in Stage 1 can develop trust

Figure 10.15

This little girl shows self-recognition; she is touching the spot on her face that corresponds to the red spot on the mirror.

TABLE 10.4	Erikson's Theory of Psychosocial Development (Birth Through Childhood)		
STAGE	**AGE**	**PSYCHOSOCIAL TASK**	**DESCRIPTION OF TASK**
1	0–1	Trust versus mistrust	The infant whose needs are met by caretakers develops a sense of trust in others.
2	1–3	Autonomy versus doubt	The toddler tries to learn independence and self-confidence.
3	3–6	Initiative versus guilt	The young child learns to initiate his or her own activities.
4	6–12	Competence versus inferiority	The child tries to develop skill in physical, cognitive, and social areas.

Source: Erikson, 1950, 1968.
Note: A complete list of Erikson's eight psychosocial stages appears in Table 11.2 on page 356.

if caretakers provide food, warmth, and affection. During Stage 2, the toddler learns to walk and act independently, without feeling ashamed. In Stage 3, the child begins to explore with newly developed cognitive and motor skills; he or she can now plan activities without adults' help. Stage 4 applies to the school-age child, who can become competent in sports, academics, and social interactions.

Social Relationships

So far, we have looked at children's early personality characteristics and their growing sense of self. Of course a child does not grow up in a vacuum. Let's see how children interact with parents, siblings, and peers. We will begin with two aspects of relationships with parents: infants' attachment to their parents and the parents' styles of interacting with their children.

Infants' Attachment to Their Parents The close emotional bond of affection between an infant and his or her caregivers is called **attachment**. Infants reveal their attachment in different ways as they mature (Goldberg, 1993). When infants are 8 or 9 months old, they have the perceptual and cognitive abilities to discriminate between people. They may raise their arms toward a parent, but not a stranger (Bretherton, 1985). They may also cry or whine when a parent leaves the room, a behavior called separation protest. Interestingly, Gunnar and her colleagues (1992) have found that infants' levels of cortisol are significantly elevated during separation protest. At about 10 months of age, babies develop the ability to crawl. This motor skill allows them to become more effective in staying near the people to whom they feel attachment (Ainsworth, 1989).

As you might expect, some babies have a more positive attachment experience than others. According to the major classification system, a baby who shows **secure attachment** tends to use the caretaker as a secure base for exploration. A baby may wander away from the caregiver for a while to explore the surroundings, returning frequently; after separation from a caregiver, the baby actively seeks interaction. A baby who shows **anxious resistant attachment** displays a mixture of seeking and resisting contact with the caregiver. Finally, a baby who shows **anxious avoidant attachment** enjoys exploration; after separation, the baby actively avoids the caretaker (Ainsworth, 1979, 1989; Sroufe et al., 1992).

In general, patterns of attachment show high stability during infancy and childhood (Ainsworth, 1990; Collins & Gunnar, 1990). Also, infant-mother and infant-father attachments are fairly similar. However, one difference is that positive interactions with mothers are most likely to occur in caretaking situations, whereas positive interactions with fathers usually occur during play (Collins & Gunnar, 1990; Cox et al., 1992).

What causes these individual differences in attachment? Securely attached infants tend to have mothers who are sensitive to their needs and are affectionate (Isabella, 1993; Teti & Nakagawa, 1990; Teti et al., 1991). Babies who show the two kinds of anxious attachment have less responsive mothers. Those with an anxious resistant pattern sometimes (but not always) have experienced extreme poverty and physical neglect. Those with an anxious avoidant background sometimes (but, again, not always) have experienced physical abuse (Sroufe et al., 1992). Bretherton (1992) points out that in a society where many families experience poverty and stress, children are less likely to have the advantage of secure attachment. Consistent with the sociocultural approach introduced in Chapter 1, contextual factors such as socioeconomic class can have an impact on development.

Attachment patterns are also related to children's later adjustment. Securely attached infants are more likely to become competent, curious, and happy children (Collins & Gunnar, 1990; Santrock & Yussen, 1989).

Parenting Styles We have seen that responsive, caring parents are more likely to have securely attached infants. Another way in which parents differ involves the kind of control they use with their children. Diana Baumrind (1971) proposed

Positive interactions between infants and fathers are especially likely to occur during play.

that the most effective parents are affectionate, but they provide control when necessary. These **authoritative parents** respect each child's individuality, they are loving, and they allow children to express their own points of view. However, they have clear-cut standards, which they uphold in a consistent fashion (Maccoby, 1992). Baumrind's research examined 103 preschool children raised according to the three different parenting styles. Children with authoritative parents were more likely to be self-reliant, competent, content, and socially responsible.

In contrast, **authoritarian parents** demand unquestioning obedience from their children. They punish children forcefully when children do not meet their standards, and they are less likely to be affectionate. Children from authoritarian families tend to be unhappy, distrustful, and ineffective in social interactions. The terms *authoritative* and *authoritarian* sound similar. However, in *authoritative* homes, the parents are firm but caring sources of authority or expertise. The word *authoritarian* is typically associated with a dictatorial person who demands unquestioning obedience.

Finally, **permissive parents** make few demands on their children, allowing them to make their own decisions. Some permissive parents simply do not care what their children do. Other permissive parents are involved in their children's lives but believe that children should be allowed freedom and choice. In one extreme case, a 14-year-old son moved his parents out of their large bedroom suite and claimed it for himself, along with an expensive stereo system and television! You will not be surprised to hear that he has never learned to live according to established rules, and he has few friends (Santrock & Yussen, 1989). In Baumrind's research, the children from permissive families were immature, they had little self-control, and they explored less than children from authoritarian and authoritative families.

In later research, Baumrind (1975) used the longitudinal method to track the nursery school children into adolescence. In general, children from authoritative families still tended to be most socially competent and mature. Other research confirms that children are most likely to thrive when their parents are warm and affectionate, yet expect socially appropriate behavior from their offspring (Lamborn et al., 1991).

Interactions with Siblings So far, we have emphasized the importance of parents. However, 80% of children also have siblings (Dunn, 1991). If you grew up with sisters or brothers, you will agree with developmental psychologists that siblings can have an enormous impact on a child's social development. By interacting with siblings, a child learns how to negotiate conflict, cooperate, play with others—and argue (Collins & Gunnar, 1990; Dunn, 1988).

Sibling relationships differ tremendously. For some children, a sibling is an exciting, affectionate playmate. For others, a sibling is a bossy, aggressive person who can make your life miserable (Dunn, 1991; Teti, 1992). In general, a child will adjust well to the birth of a younger sibling if he or she is securely attached and is skilled at taking the perspective of other people, rather than being egocentric (Teti, 1992).

One of the most interesting recent findings about siblings is that two children growing up in the same household with the same parents are likely to be very different from each other. In fact, they often differ from one another nearly as much as two unrelated children growing up in different families (Dunn, 1991; Dunn & Plomin, 1990). Siblings differ because of **nonshared environmental experiences:** parents treat each child differently, siblings create different environments for each other, and each child has different experiences outside the family. Furthermore, during late childhood, children often deliberately try *not* to be like their siblings, a process called **sibling deidentification** (Teti, 1992). Ironically, then, genetically similar siblings try their best to be different from the people they have the greatest potential to resemble!

Interactions with Friends As children mature, they develop relationships with people outside the family, and these relationships become increasingly important. For instance, fourth-graders say that mothers and fathers are the most frequent source of support for them. By the seventh grade, friends are just as supportive as

Through interactions with their siblings, children learn how to play cooperatively.

parents, and by the tenth grade, friends are seen as being more supportive (Furman & Buhrmester, 1992). Children rely on their friends during stressful times, such as the transition to junior high school (Berndt, 1989).

The nature of friendship also changes as children mature. Young children base their friendships on rather superficial characteristics, such as living near each other and liking to play the same games. However, by the time children reach the age of 9 or 10, they emphasize more abstract qualities, such as loyalty, commitment to the other person, and trustworthiness (Rizzo, 1989). A friend is someone with whom you can share your intimate thoughts; two friends care about each other's emotional well-being, not just about whether you like the same activities. In fact, Rizzo argues that friendship is an important factor in encouraging children to develop positive, prosocial behavior toward other people—strangers, as well as family members and friends. Let us now turn our attention to this prosocial behavior.

Prosocial Behavior

A student in my human development class described her 3-year-old nephew's concern for other family members. When his 6-month-old sister cries, he pats her back until she falls asleep. On several occasions, when his mother was sleeping, he climbed into his sister's crib to play with her, so that her crying would not wake their mother. This young boy's compassion for his sister and mother conflicts with Piaget's view that children are egocentric. Even young children can sometimes view the world from the perspective of another person and realize that a sister needs comforting and a mother needs sleep.

Prosocial behavior or **altruism** is action that benefits another person. Prosocial behavior can include comforting, helping, sharing, rescuing, and cooperating (Zahn-Waxler & Smith, 1992). How does prosocial behavior develop during childhood, and what factors are related to this positive form of social interaction?

The Development of Prosocial Behavior Even very young children show evidence of prosocial behavior. Zahn-Waxler and her coauthors (1992a) asked mothers to simulate various emotions during their normal interactions with their young children. For example, a mother might pretend to bump her head, say "ouch," and rub herself. More than half of all 13- to 15-month-olds made at least one prosocial behavior, usually hugging or patting. By 2 years of age, 26 out of the 27 children showed prosocial behavior. Two-year-olds actively try to help someone who seems to be suffering. However, these helpful efforts may reveal some degree of egocentrism. If Jimmy sees that Janey is crying, he may run to bring *his* mother, even though Janey's mother is closer.

We might expect prosocial behavior to increase during childhood. However, researchers have *not* found consistent increases in sharing and helping between the ages of 3 and 9 (Grusec, 1991a; Marcus, 1986; Zahn-Waxler et al., 1986). Cognitive skills increase rapidly during this developmental period, so we might expect prosocial behavior to increase as well. It is possible that North American parents and schoolteachers place too little emphasis on cooperative, helpful behavior.

Factors Related to Prosocial Behavior In general, prosocial children are likely to have parents who are nurturant and supportive, often modeling prosocial behavior themselves (Eisenberg & Mussen, 1989; Zahn-Waxler & Smith, 1992). For instance, people who were active in the civil rights movement in the 1950s and 1960s were likely to have parents who had vigorously worked for social causes in previous decades (Mussen & Eisenberg-Berg, 1977).

Prosocial behavior may also be influenced by temperamental factors that are biologically based (Eisenberg & Mussen, 1989; Zahn-Waxler et al., 1992b). Earlier in this section, we discussed how certain temperamental characteristics are relatively stable throughout childhood. Individuals differ in responding to another person's distress. These styles of prosocial responding tend to remain stable into the early school years.

Even young children can be prosocial; in this photograph, a boy tries to console his brother.

In general, boys and girls are similar in their willingness to help other people (Doescher & Sugawara, 1990; Maccoby, 1986; Pelletier-Stiefel et al., 1986). This finding is consistent with the general conclusion that gender differences in behavior are relatively small (Matlin, 1993a). Now that you are familiar with some of the dimensions of prosocial behavior, try Demonstration 10.4. We will examine prosocial behavior again in Chapter 18, with a special focus on explanations for altruism.

The Day-Care Dilemma

In 1990, 54% of all women with children under age 6 were working outside the home (Hofferth & Phillips, 1991a). Statistics such as this raise a vitally important question: How do child-care arrangements influence children?

Unfortunately, this question cannot be answered easily. In fact, the day-care dilemma highlights the theme that humans are extremely complex. The effects of day care on children probably depend upon a wide variety of such variables as the age and gender of the child, the temperament of the child, the quality of the child-care center, the economic background of the family, and the number of hours each week that the child attends day care (Fox & Fein, 1990; Hofferth & Phillips, 1991b; Lande et al., 1989; Lerner & Galambos, 1991).

Furthermore, the answer to the day-care dilemma depends upon the dependent variable we choose. Day care seems to have different kinds of influence on children's cognitive development, their social behavior, and their attachment to parents. Finally, we should emphasize the difficulty of drawing firm conclusions in circumstances where carefully controlled experiments cannot be conducted.

In other words, we are not likely to conclude either that "day care is good" or that "day care is bad" for all children in all conditions for all dependent variables. Let us consider some of the findings, concentrating on cognitive development, social relationships, and attachment during infancy.

In general, children who have been in day care are likely to be somewhat advanced in intellectual development, compared with children cared for at home. Although there are exceptions, day-care children between the ages of 1½ and 5 tend to receive higher scores on tests of reading, mathematics, and general intelligence (Baydar & Brooks-Gunn, 1991; Clarke-Stewart, 1991; Dunham & Dunham, 1992; Vandell & Ramanan, 1992). However, home-care children typically catch up once they enter school. We can conclude that day care does not seem to harm the cognitive development of young children; it may even be helpful.

The picture is more complex when we consider social development. Children who have participated in day care tend to be more socially skilled in some areas. They show more cooperative behavior and confidence in social interactions, and they are more skilled at taking another person's point of view (Howes & Olenick, 1986; Phillips et al., 1987; Scarr & Eisenberg, 1993). However, some studies have reported higher levels of aggression for children in day care (Haskins, 1985; Phillips et al., 1987). One explanation for these contradictions may be that day-care children are more likely to think for themselves and want their own way—not that they are maladjusted (Clarke-Stewart, 1989).

The most controversial issue, however, concerns infants' attachment with their mothers—that close emotional bond we discussed earlier in this section. Reviews of

DEMONSTRATION 10.4 Observing Prosocial Behavior

Save this demonstration for the next time you eat at a fast-food restaurant or other setting that has many children. Try to note any examples of prosocial behavior in these children, such as helping, comforting, complimenting, and sharing. Also note examples of antisocial behavior, such as aggression, negative comments, and selfishness. How do the two numbers compare? If you find a particularly prosocial or antisocial family group, can you identify any characteristics of the parents that might contribute to the children's behavior?

The quality of care is a critical factor in the day-care dilemma. Development is optimal when children can interact often with nurturant adults.

the research suggest that day care has a small effect. For instance, Clarke-Stewart (1989) reviewed 17 studies on attachment. Overall, 29% of infants whose mothers were not employed or worked part time could be classified as insecurely attached. In contrast, 36% of infants whose mothers worked full time could be classified as insecurely attached. In summary, this analysis revealed a difference of 7% between the two conditions, a difference that was statistically significant. A series of meta-analyses by McCartney and Phillips (1988) confirmed that day care had only a small effect on attachment patterns. These two reviews suggest that infants with day-care experience are fairly similar to infants with home-care experience.

Many psychologists are beginning to approach the day-care dilemma from a different perspective. They suggest that the more important issue is to document the negative consequences of not providing high-quality child care (Fine & Gordon, 1989; Silverstein, 1991). Research has demonstrated that children are much more likely to thrive in high-quality child-care centers (Field, 1993; Howes et al., 1992). Unfortunately, however, teachers and other staff members in child-care centers are notoriously underpaid, and their turnover rate is high (Scarr & Eisenberg, 1993; Whitebook et al., 1989). In the 1990s, people concerned about children need to work together to develop quality child-care centers where the caregivers are warm and nurturing and where children can develop cognitively, socially, and emotionally.

Children and Their Ethnic Backgrounds

The theme of individual difference has been prominent throughout this textbook. When we consider children from different ethnic backgrounds, we can appreciate even more clearly that children's life experiences may differ widely. Table 10.5 shows the number of U.S. residents in several major ethnic groups. Table 10.6 provides a sense of the ethnic diversity in Canada by showing the number of immigrants during a 10-year period. In Canada, immigrants constitute 16% of the population (Badets, 1993; Dumas, 1990). Let us first consider four ethnic groups, and then we will look at the more general issue of ethnic bias.

Four Ethnic Groups As Table 10.5 shows, 11% of the U.S. population is African American, or Black. We should not exaggerate the differences between Black and White children, or ignore the variation within each group. However, some evidence shows that Black families are more likely than White families to emphasize emotions and feelings. They also stress social connectedness, or responsibilities to a

TABLE 10.5 Estimated Number of U.S. Residents in Major Ethnic Groups in 1990

ETHNIC GROUP	NUMBER OF PEOPLE	PERCENT OF THE POPULATION
White (non-Hispanic)	199,686,000	76%
Black	29,986,000	11%
Hispanic	22,354,000	9%
Asian	7,274,000	3%
Native American	1,959,000	1%

Source: Based on U.S. Bureau of the Census, 1992

family or group, rather than the "rugged individualism" associated with White families. Black families also value high levels of stimulation, preferring action that is lively and energetic (Boykin, 1986; Boykin & Toms, 1985).

Many Black children grow up in extended families, where grandmothers, sisters, aunts, and cousins take care of each other's children (Collins, 1987). The extended family provides a stabilizing influence, especially among economically poor mothers. Black families see more relatives in an average week than do White families, and they are more likely to consider their relatives' advice to be important (Wilson, 1986).

White Americans often assume that prejudice against Black people ended decades ago and that Black workers may even have an advantage in the job market. However, Blacks still earn lower wages than Whites, even when education and occupation are equivalent. In fact, the average Black college graduate earns less than the average White male high-school dropout (Hess et al., 1988). As a consequence of their parents' lower incomes, Black children are more likely to be economically disadvantaged. One-half of minority children are raised in poverty, in contrast to one-quarter of all children in the United States (Horowitz & O'Brien, 1989).

Children seem to be aware of such Black-White differences as skin color, hair texture, and facial features by the time they reach the age of 3 (Aboud, 1988). Black children apparently acquire this knowledge before White children do (Milner, 1983). In one study, kindergartners who were just entering an integrated school already preferred children from their own ethnic group (Finkelstein & Haskins, 1983). Because attitudes about race and ethnicity are formed before children attend school, children tend to stay with members of their own ethnic group, without interacting much with classmates from other groups. Even at a school with both Blacks and Whites, children may not have many opportunities for interracial interactions (Shaffer, 1989). White children who are prejudiced before entering school may not have the chance

TABLE 10.6 Number of People Immigrating to Canada Between 1980 and 1989, According to Place of Birth

PLACE OF BIRTH	NUMBER OF IMMIGRANTS
Asia	629,231
Europe	341,041
Latin America	116,135
Caribbean	91,344
Africa	64,431

Source: Based on J. Dumas, 1990, Table 16

to learn that they can be friends with Black children—especially if the two groups live in different neighborhoods. As children continue through the kindergarten year, they show even stronger preferences for friends from the same ethnic background. These trends become stronger still during grade school (Finkelstein & Haskins, 1983; Hartup, 1983).

Hispanic Americans or Latinos are currently 9% of the U.S. population, and this ethnic group is expected to outnumber African Americans by the year 2000 (Vasquez & Barón, 1988). *Hispanic* refers to all people of Spanish, Portuguese, or Latin American descent. They share language, values, and customs. However, a Mexican-American child growing up in a farming region in central California may have very different experiences from a Puerto Rican child growing up in Manhattan.

Mexican Americans are the largest Hispanic subgroup in the United States (Garbarino & Kostelny, 1992). They emphasize affiliation and the need for warm, supportive relationships (Vasquez & Barón, 1988). Some studies of children's social development show that Mexican-American children show more cooperative behavior at a younger age than White Anglo children (Martinez & Mendoza, 1984). Puerto Ricans, the second-largest subgroup, place a similar emphasis on prosocial behavior. In research on toddlers, White Anglo mothers valued children's ability to cope independently with the stress of being left alone. In contrast, Puerto Rican mothers valued children's ability to stay calm and good natured, with strong attachment to their mother (Harwood, 1992; Harwood & Miller, 1991).

Like Hispanics, Asian Americans come from many different countries. Asian Americans include, in order of population, Chinese, Filipinos, Japanese, Vietnamese, Koreans, Asian Indians, and more than 23 other ethnic-cultural groups (True, 1990).

Asian Americans are often labeled the "model minority" because of their high education and income levels. For instance, adult Asian Americans are twice as likely as White Americans to hold a college degree (Tsai & Uemura, 1988). Many cultural values of Asian Americans resemble those of middle-class White Americans. For example, both groups emphasize education and achievement for their children. However, Asian Americans typically emphasize family, duty, and interpersonal harmony, whereas White Americans stress individuality and independence (Nagata, 1989; Tsai & Uemura, 1988). Asian Americans tend to be reluctant to reveal personal problems to people outside the family (Garbarino & Kostelny, 1992); we will consider the implications of this tendency when we discuss psychotherapy in Chapter 16.

Native Americans probably represent the most diverse ethnic group in the United States, with 200 tribal languages and 517 different native backgrounds. Native Americans may share a common geographic origin and a common history of being invaded and dispossessed by White Americans. However, their languages, values, and current life-styles may have little in common (Garbarino & Kostelny, 1992; LaFromboise et al., 1993).

Native Americans are likely to value independence in their children (Garbarino & Kostelny, 1992; LaFromboise & Lowe, 1989). For example, parents encourage children to make their own decisions and develop independence at an early age. However, school officials and social-service agencies may consider this encouragement to be overly permissive and even negligent (Gray & Cosgrove, 1985).

Although we have mentioned some general characteristics of the parents and children of each ethnic group, we need to reemphasize the diversity within each group. Even if we focus on one specific subgroup—perhaps Chinese Americans—the variability *within* that subgroup is always greater than the variability *between* groups (Bronstein & Quina, 1988).

Biases Against Children of Color John Diamond, an African American, recalls his pain when a White boy told him that he wouldn't be allowed to join the other neighborhood children at the Elk's Club swimming pool in Detroit during the 1970s

Another example of our theme of individual differences is represented in the diversity of ethnic groups in North America. These photos represent children from White, Black, Hispanic, Asian, and Native-American backgrounds.

(Diamond, 1991). Carlos Manjarréz, a Mexican American, remembers how the real-estate agent tried to discourage his family from buying a home in the Anglo suburbs (Manjarréz, 1991). It's no wonder that Anglo children learn prejudice from their parents, or that children of color learn to be prejudiced against their own ethnic group (Aboud, 1988). Parents, educators, and therapists face a difficult task when they work to develop ethnic pride in children of color in a prejudiced society (Edelman, 1993; Hopson & Hopson, 1990).

In Chapter 17, we will examine in more detail the general nature of prejudice, discrimination, and stereotyping. When we consider how these biases develop in young children, we need to examine how television provides children with a distorted view of ethnic diversity. For example, Blacks are underrepresented on many TV shows. In 82% of children's programs, people of different ethnic backgrounds never appear together (Barcus, 1983; Liebert & Sprafkin, 1988).

Treatment of Blacks on television has improved somewhat in recent years, but the treatment of other minorities has not changed substantially. For instance, Hispanic Americans fill less than 2% of all the roles, although they constitute 9% of the population. Furthermore, almost all Hispanic TV characters are men; Hispanic women scarcely exist on television. Finally, Asians and Hispanics are typically portrayed either as villains or as victims of violence (Gerbner et al., 1986; Liebert & Sprafkin, 1988).

When we think about children, we must consider their diversity. They represent a wide variety of ethnic groups whose cultural values and aspirations may differ substantially. Try to visualize a children's television show that could capture this diversity and portray these children playing with each other, as in Figure 10.16, and providing viewers with models of prosocial behavior.

The Status of Children in Today's Society

Most of us want to believe that children receive top priority in the United States. However, in an international survey of child health for 1990, 19 countries ranked better than the United States in infant mortality rate (Children's Defense Fund, 1992). Countries such as Spain, Italy, and Singapore reported fewer infants dying before the age of 1 year. Canada fared much better, ranking fourth among the countries in the survey.

Figure 10.16
Children in this New York neighborhood represent a variety of ethnic groups.

Let us consider some of the threats that North American children face as we approach the twenty-first century. Some of these threats were unheard of when you were an infant. Consider acquired immunodeficiency syndrome (AIDS), for example. By September, 1993, U.S. pediatric AIDS cases numbered 4,906 (HIV/AIDS Surveillance Report, 1993). Other infants will die or face serious problems because their mothers used cocaine or other narcotics during pregnancy, an issue discussed earlier in the chapter. Still other children—perhaps one million a year—are abused or severely neglected (Besharov, 1990).

In the section on ethnicity, we noted that one-quarter of all children and one-half of all children of color are raised in poverty. As emphasized by the sociocultural approach to psychology, poverty has crucial consequences for children's welfare. One-quarter of pregnant women in America receive no prenatal care (Children's Defense Fund, 1988). Only half of U.S. children living in families below the poverty level receive Medicaid coverage for medical care (Wise & Meyers, 1988). Thus, many children lack medical care both before and after birth. The Index of Social Health for Children and Youth considers factors such as infant mortality, child abuse, and poverty. This index for the United States has dropped from its highest point, with a value of 78 in 1976, to an all-time low of 44 in 1990 (Miringoff, 1992).

Although the poverty rate for Canada is lower than for the United States, the surveys still show that more than 1 million Canadian children live in poverty ("Campaign 2000," 1992). Some Canadian ethnic groups experience especially high poverty rates. For example, among aboriginal (Canadian-Indian) groups, 44% of families live in poverty (Ryerse, 1990).

Consider, also, the lives of homeless children. According to one estimate, children and their parents now comprise more than one-third of all the people in homeless shelters (Berck, 1992). Compared to other children, homeless children are more likely to experience health problems, hunger, poor nutrition, cognitive deficits, and psychological problems (Rafferty & Shinn, 1991).

Divorce is another potentially traumatic experience that can disrupt virtually all aspects of children's lives. Recent estimates show that between 40% and 50% of all children can expect to spend at least 5 years in a single-parent home. Many of these children will adjust successfully to their new life circumstances, but a substantial number may suffer long-term negative effects (Furstenberg & Cherlin, 1991; Weitzman & Adair, 1988).

In addition, children's sense of well-being is threatened by violence. We discussed the high incidence of television violence in Chapter 6, and many children also experience real-life violence. In one school in Brooklyn, three children were shot dead and one teacher was wounded within a three-month period (Feldman, 1992). Children can also kill themselves and others accidentally; more than 1.2 million latchkey children under the age of 12 have access to guns in their own homes ("Youths learn alternatives," 1992). As an editorial in a pediatric journal concludes, "The picture that emerges for some of our children is that they are awash in a sea of violence—at home, in the neighborhood, in school, and in the media" (Fulginiti, 1992, p. 671).

Children and their parents now constitute about one-third of all people in homeless shelters.

Others who are concerned about children's well-being point out that we are hurrying young people through childhood. They are worried that some regions are urging universal preschool education (Rescorla et al., 1991). Rushed into full-time school settings, 4-year-olds are deprived of playtime, which is valuable for children's overall development (Zigler, 1987). One pediatrician complained that the middle- and upper-class parents in her Manhattan practice enroll their children in a $1,000 cram course to prepare for entrance exams—for kindergarten (Rubenstein, 1986).

David Elkind (1981, 1987) is a psychologist well known for his work in Piagetian research. Elkind points out Piaget's warning that children should not be pushed; instead, they should develop at their own pace. Many American parents, however, want to rush their children through each stage of cognitive development as rapidly as

Figure 10.17
An example of a "hurried child."

possible. Americans buy designer jeans for their toddlers, equip them with miniature briefcases, and supply them with grown-up makeup and hairstyles (Figure 10.17). Elkind urges us not to hurry our children, but to allow them instead their right to be children.

In this chapter, we have seen that young children are miraculous human beings, capable of impressive perceptual, cognitive, and social skills. However these miraculous beings face obstacles such as disease, deprivation, and life-threatening violence. Horowitz and O'Brien (1989) provide an important caution about our responsibility to make life safer for children:

> *Children are ever the future of a society. Every child who does not function at a level commensurate with his or her possibilities, every child who is destined to make fewer contributions to society than society needs, and every child who does not take his or her place as a productive adult diminishes the power of that society's future. (p. 445)*

S E C T I O N   S U M M A R Y
PERSONALITY AND SOCIAL DEVELOPMENT

- Children's socialization is heavily influenced by the development of motor skills, cognitive skills, and gender roles.

- Temperament (e.g., inhibited versus uninhibited style) shows some stability as children mature.

- Erik Erikson's theory traces the development of self-concept through stages that emphasize trust, independence, planning, and competence during childhood.

- Securely attached infants are likely to have sensitive, affectionate mothers and to become relatively happy toddlers; authoritative parents are more likely than authoritarian or permissive parents to have competent, content, and socially responsible children.

- Sibling relationships differ tremendously; furthermore, siblings differ tremendously from each other.

- As children mature, friends become increasingly more important; also, friendships shift from being based on similar interests to an emphasis on loyalty and abstract qualities.

- Prosocial behavior can be seen in children as young as 1 year of age; however, prosocial behavior does not increase substantially between the ages of 3 and 9.

- Day care is a complex issue; it may enhance cognitive development, it has mixed effects on social development, and it may slightly increase insecure attachment.

- Ethnic groups differ somewhat in their emphasis on social connectedness rather than individualism and other child-rearing patterns, though within-group differences are substantial; television tends to encourage biases against children of color.

- Children do not receive top priority in contemporary society; some problems they face include AIDS, child abuse, drug-related disorders, poverty, homelessness, divorce, violence, and being pushed to grow up too fast.

REVIEW QUESTIONS

1. The introduction to this chapter presented three important issues in developmental psychology: the nature-nurture, continuity-stages, and stability-change questions. Discuss each issue and point out how one or more of these questions is important for each of the following topics: (a) early perceptual skills; (b) cognitive development; (c) infant temperament; and (d) self-concept (Erikson).

2. Briefly trace the course of prenatal development, and then describe the newborn. Suppose you have a pregnant friend; what kinds of precautions would you suggest during her pregnancy?

3. Suppose that your friend has now delivered a healthy baby. What kinds of abilities could you describe that she might expect during the early weeks of life? Mention perceptual skills, memory, thinking (especially stressing recent research here), and language?

4. Imagine that a family has a 12-year-old and a 5-year-old. Name some memory tasks on which these two children would differ, and some on which they would be similar. Why could metamemory and memory strategies partially explain some differences?

5. The term *egocentrism* was described in the section on the Piagetian approach to thinking. How is egocentrism important in children's thinking? To what extent are children egocentric with respect to language pragmatics and their prosocial skills?

6. What are the three major theories of language acquisition and the three theories of gender-role development? Do you see any similarities between the two sets of theories?

7. What do preschoolers know about gender? What evidence do we have that even infants know something about gender?

8. We discussed parents at several points throughout this chapter. How are parents relevant in language development, attachment, parenting style, ethnicity, and the current problems children face?

9. Describe some of the relationships that infants and children have with other people. How is prosocial behavior relevant in these relationships?

10. Imagine that you have been named the director of a newly created national organization, which will address the needs of children in the 1990s. If the funds were generous, what kinds of programs would you initiate to help children and provide support services for them?

NEW TERMS

development
nature-nurture question
continuity-stages question
stability-change question
prenatal period
embryo
fetal period
fetal alcohol syndrome
blood-brain barrier
neonatal period
cephalocaudal principle
proximodistal principle
infancy
acuity
size constancy
phonemes
rooting reflex
operant conditioning
sensory memory
metamemory
rehearsal
meaning-making
assimilation
accommodation
sensorimotor period
object permanence
preoperational period
egocentrism
concrete operational period
conservation
formal operational period

hypothetico-deductive reasoning
habituation
overextension
syntax
telegraphic speech
pragmatics
cognition-first view
motherese
gender roles
social-learning theory
cognitive-developmental theory
gender constancy
gender-schema theory
socialization
temperament
inhibited children
uninhibited children
cortisol
self-concept
attachment
secure attachment
anxious resistant attachment
anxious avoidant attachment
authoritative parents
authoritarian parents
permissive parents
nonshared environmental experience
sibling deidentification
prosocial behavior
altruism

RECOMMENDED READINGS

Children's Defense Fund. (1992). *The state of America's children 1992*. Washington, DC: Author. This book is issued yearly by the influential advocate group, Children's Defense Fund. It includes dozens of useful statistical tables about the status of children in the United States on issues such as health, child care, and education; it also contains recommendations for change.

Howe, M. L., Brainerd, C. J., & Reyna, V. F. (Eds.). (1992). *Development of long-term retention*. New York: Springer-Verlag. Many prominent researchers in the area of memory development contributed chapters to this volume.

Intons-Peterson, M. J. (1988). *Children's concepts of gender*. Norwood, NJ: Ablex. It is difficult to summarize the wealth of information on the development of gender roles; this book is currently the best available resource.

Owens, R. E., Jr. (1992). *Language development: An introduction* (3rd ed.). New York: Merrill. Owens's textbook offers a very readable, comprehensive overview of language development, including coverage of topics such as neurolinguistics, pragmatics, adult language development, bilingualism, and language disorders.

Sroufe, L. A., Cooper, R. G., & DeHart, G. B. (1992). *Child development: Its nature and course* (2nd ed.). New York: McGraw Hill. This mid-level textbook will be useful for students who want a clear and comprehensive overview of child development.

CHAPTER 11

DEVELOPMENT FROM ADOLESCENCE THROUGH OLD AGE

S everal years ago, six teenagers attacked a jogger in Central Park. They beat her with a metal pipe, raped her, and left her in a coma. Why would adolescents hurt a complete stranger? In contrast, other New York City teenagers spend their spare time working in soup kitchens, volunteering in hospitals, and tutoring younger children. Why would adolescents help complete strangers? And how could two groups of adolescents—so similar in many respects—respond so differently to other humans?

An elderly woman feels weary and depressed. Commenting on her life, she says, "I've been so disgusted and discouraged to wind up like this" (Day, 1991, p. 4). Another elderly woman, who runs an interracial community center, says in the film *Acting Our Age,* "I don't think I'll retire from seeking justice and equality as long as I live and I can get one foot in front of another and can raise my voice." Why do these two women differ so conspicuously from each other?

Throughout this chapter, we will see many examples of the theme of individual differences. Another common thread that weaves throughout this chapter is the discrepancy between myth and reality; in many cases, the common beliefs about adolescents and elderly people are very different from these individuals' actual experiences.

This is our second chapter on human development. As in the previous chapter, we discuss physical and perceptual development, cognitive development, gender issues, and personality and social development. Our age range includes adolescence (the period between about 12 and the late teens), adulthood (from about 20 to 65), and later adulthood or old age (from about 65 onward).

PHYSICAL AND PERCEPTUAL DEVELOPMENT

Physical Changes During Adolescence

Puberty is the period of development in which a young person becomes physically capable of sexual reproduction (Nielsen, 1991). Puberty begins when the hypothalamus signals the pituitary gland (Figure 3.14) to begin releasing special hormones. In turn, these hormones cause the adolescent female's ovaries greatly to increase their production of estrogen. The elevated estrogens are responsible for breast development, broadening of the hips, and the beginning of menstruation. Similarly, the hormones from the pituitary cause the adolescent male's testes greatly to increase their production of androgen. The elevated androgen levels are responsible for muscle development, increased body hair, and changes in the vocal cords.

Menarche and Menstruation Menarche (pronounced "*men*-are-kee") is the first menstrual period. The average age of menarche in North America is now about 13, but it can begin as early as 8 or as late as 16 (Caspi & Moffit, 1991; Golub, 1992). Thus, individual differences are obvious in the timing of menarche, and also in other puberty milestones.

Young women are likely to have mixed emotions when their first menstrual period occurs. They are likely to describe their feelings as "excited but scared" or "happy and embarrassed." In general, those who mature early are likely to have a more negative attitude about the experience (Golub, 1992).

Children vary impressively in the age at which they reach puberty, as illustrated in this group of elementary-school children.

Typical symptoms accompanying menstruation include cramps, backache, and swelling (due to water retention). Menstrual pain is also known as **dysmenorrhea;** pain during menstruation is likely, though not every woman experiences it.

The so-called premenstrual syndrome is more controversial than dysmenorrhea. **Premenstrual syndrome,** also called **PMS,** refers to a variety of symptoms that may occur during the week preceding menstruation; these symptoms may include headache, painful breasts, and a variety of psychological reactions such as depression, anxiety, and irritability. However, there is no generally accepted definition of premenstrual syndrome (Golub, 1992). Clearly, the popular media have created the impression that PMS is widespread and that scientists agree about the symptoms (Chrisler & Levy, 1989). In reality, however, some women may indeed experience PMS symptoms, but not everyone does. Furthermore, in a general sample of women, ratings of an individual's mood depended more on the day of the week—whether it was Monday or Friday—than whether she was premenstrual or postmenstrual (Englander-Golden et al., 1986; McFarlane et al., 1988).

Let's also dispel another myth. In 1914, Leta Hollingworth demonstrated that women performed as well on cognitive tests when they were menstruating as at other times of the month. Current researchers agree that cognitive skills do not change throughout the menstrual cycle (Asso, 1983; Golub, 1992; Sommer, 1983). In other words, a teenager should not panic if her period arrives the day before her SATs.

Puberty in Males We know relatively little about boys' reactions to body changes during puberty. In general, though, boys are more positive than negative about their first experience with **ejaculation** (release of semen). However, they are usually somewhat frightened about the event, and they seldom discuss its occurrence (Brooks-Gunn & Reiter, 1990).

A book entitled *Changing Bodies, Changing Lives* records two boys' impressions about puberty:

When I was 14 I went around for about two weeks with this dirty smudge on my upper lip. I kept trying to wash it off, but it wouldn't wash. Then I really looked at it and saw it was a mustache. So I shaved! For the first time.

All of a sudden I realized my voice was low. On the telephone people started thinking I was my father, not my mother. (Bell, 1980)

Compared with the dramatic body changes in adolescence, the physical changes in adulthood are somewhat less dramatic. However, changes such as balding and wrinkles can clearly influence a person's self-image.

Physical Changes in Adulthood

As adults grow older, their skin develops wrinkles, and height may decrease. Older adults may still "feel" young, however. They may be confused about their identity when seeing wrinkles and graying hair in the mirror or when others refer to them as that "old lady" or "old man" (Whitbourne, 1985).

Female hormone levels begin to decrease around age 30, and the average woman experiences menopause by age 50. **Menopause** occurs when menstrual periods have stopped for at least a year (Golub, 1992). Contrary to many myths, most women do not regret the loss of fertility that accompanies menopause (Datan et al., 1987). In fact, many women view menopause positively (Martin, 1987). Finally, let us dispel that major menopause myth: Researchers have repeatedly demonstrated that menopause is *not* linked with depression (Golub, 1992; Matthews et al., 1990; McKinlay et al., 1987). Middle age is a stressful time for many women. However, stressful factors—such as our culture's reactions to older women—are more important than menopause in determining the psychological well-being of a middle-aged woman.

Men may also experience a physical change during middle age. The **male climacteric** (pronounced "klie-*mack*-terr-ick") includes decreased fertility and decreased frequency of orgasm (Whitbourne, 1992). About 1 in 20 middle-aged men report symptoms such as fatigue, depression, and general physical complaints (Henker, 1981). However, mood is not related to male hormone levels. With both women and men, stressful factors—and not hormones—account for mood changes.

A different change in adulthood has more important consequences than either menopause or the male climacteric: A consistent finding is that adults who are middle-aged and older have slower reaction times than young adults (Hale et al., 1991; Salthouse, 1991). Perhaps these slower reaction times can be traced to brain changes that make the central nervous system less able to process many incoming stimuli. Sadly, slower reaction time is one of the causes of the high rate of traffic accidents in elderly people. According to statistics, accident rates are still relatively low for middle-aged drivers, between the ages of 45 and 74. However, drivers who are over 75 have an accident rate that is higher than all other groups except 16- to 24-year-olds (Carney, 1989).

How much longer can an elderly person expect to live? The average 65-year-old man can currently expect to live to the age of 80; the average 65-year-old woman will reach the age of 84 (Barinaga, 1991b). In Chapter 19, our discussion of health psychology will examine some of the factors related to longevity.

One reason that elderly drivers have a relatively high accident rate is that their reaction times are slower. Older drivers can compensate by taking precautions, such as not "tailgating" the driver ahead of them.

Changes in Perceptual Ability

Before examining perceptual changes during aging, let us discuss a potential methodological problem in studies using elderly people. Suppose that we test a group of college students, whose average age is 19, and a group of nursing-home residents, whose average age is 78. Let us suppose that we find much higher scores for the college students on a test of speech perception. We should not attribute the difference in their scores totally to age, because the two groups also differ with respect to several confounding variables.

As discussed in Chapter 2, a **confounding variable** is a factor—other than the factor being studied—that is not equivalent in all conditions. For instance, the confounding variables in this example could include health, amount of education, and medications. In unbiased research, the elderly population that is being compared with college students should be healthy, well educated, and not taking medicines that could alter performance. Both groups should also be equally familiar with the testing instruments (Carp, 1989).

Vision The most significant change in the structure of the eye during aging is the thickening of the lens (shown in Figure 4.3). One important consequence of the thickened lens is that the retina receives only one-third as much light as for a young adult. The lens also becomes less elastic, so that elderly people have difficulty seeing nearby objects. Older people often need special glasses for reading and other close-up work. A final important consequence is that elderly people are more sensitive to glare (Koretz & Handelman, 1988; Schieber, 1992; Stokes, 1992).

These visual changes, combined with decreased acuity in old age, produce distorted vision. Figure 11.1 shows how a grocery store might look to a young adult and an older adult (Pastalan, 1982). Fortunately, however, the most important contours and details are still retained. For most elderly people, vision is decreased but still adequate—especially with the help of corrective lenses. Some visual problems arise in driving, however. For example, elderly people are more likely than young adults to report problems such as reading signs, seeing through the windshield, and reading information on the instrument panel (Kline et al., 1992).

Figure 11.1
Scene at a store, as it would look to a young adult (above) and an older adult (below).

Hearing Elderly people frequently have difficulty in hearing high-pitched tones. Somewhere between 10% and 35% of people over the age of 65 have trouble perceiving speech sounds. Elderly people usually hear even less if they try to listen in a room that echoes or distorts the speech sounds (Schieber, 1992; Whitbourne, 1985). As you can imagine, telephone conversations are difficult when the connection is faulty. When speaking with an elderly person with hearing loss, try to lower the pitch of your voice and eliminate distracting background noises.

The Other Senses Researchers are not certain how the skin senses, smell, and taste change as we grow older. One problem is that elderly people vary even more than young adults in their sensitivities (Whitbourne, 1986a). Consider the skin senses, for example—specifically, sensitivity to touch, temperature, and pain. In all three areas, some studies report that elderly people are less sensitive than young adults, yet other studies report no age differences (Schieber, 1992; Whitbourne, 1985). Thus, one elderly person may be relatively insensitive to cold, which could cause a problem in cold climates. However, another elderly person may react the same as a younger adult.

Elderly people are typically less sensitive to odors than younger adults, though some studies show no age change (Schieber, 1992; Stevens & Cain, 1987; Whitbourne, 1985). As a consequence, some elderly people may be less likely than younger individuals to detect gas leaks or smoke from fires. The number of taste buds also decreases as we grow older. Although individual differences are large, taste sensitivity may sometimes decrease (Moore et al., 1982; Schieber, 1992; Whitbourne, 1985). Elderly people who are less sensitive to both smell and taste may complain that food is less flavorful. As a consequence, they may oversalt their food or avoid nutritious food because it seems bland. Obviously, both these eating habits can create nutritional problems.

Although perceptual processes can change as we grow older, we need to emphasize the theme of individual differences. You may know elderly people whose perceptual world has changed very little since they were teenagers.

Because sensitivity to odors and to taste tends to decrease with age, this dinner may not be as flavorful to this elderly man as it is to his younger relatives.

S E C T I O N   S U M M A R Y

PHYSICAL AND PERCEPTUAL DEVELOPMENT

- During puberty, girls develop breasts and begin to menstruate; boys develop muscles, body hair, and lower voices, and they experience their first ejaculation.

- During menopause, women's menstrual periods stop; during middle age, male fertility also decreases. However, mood changes in middle age are not linked to hormonal changes.

- Reaction times are slower for elderly people, contributing to an increased accident rate.

- Visual changes during aging include difficulty seeing nearby objects, sensitivity to glare, and reduced acuity.

- Although individual differences are large, some elderly people are less able to perceive speech sounds, skin senses (touch, temperature, and pain), odors, and tastes.

COGNITIVE DEVELOPMENT

Irene Hulicka (1982) shares an illustrative story about the way people judge cognitive errors made by elderly people. A competent 78-year-old woman served a meal to her guests, and the meal was excellent except that she had used Clorox instead of vinegar in the salad dressing. Her concerned relatives attributed the error to an impaired memory and general intellectual decline, and they discussed placing her in a nursing home. As it turned out someone else had placed the Clorox in the cupboard where the vinegar was kept. Understandably, she had reached for the wrong bottle, which was similar in size, shape, and color to the vinegar bottle.

Some time later, the same group of people were guests in another home. A young woman in search of hair spray reached into a bathroom cabinet and found a can of the right size and shape. She proceeded to drench her hair with Lysol. In this case, however, no one suggested that the younger woman be institutionalized; they merely teased her about her absentmindedness. Thus, a cognitive error can be interpreted differently, depending upon the age of the person who made the mistake.

In this section on cognitive development, we first consider memory in the elderly. Then we discuss thinking from both the Piagetian perspective and the perspective of intelligence measurement. Our final topic is moral development.

Memory in the Elderly

As you grow older, your performance on some memory tasks will decline, but you will not notice any change on some other tasks. For instance, researchers have found little developmental change in sensory memory (Birren et al., 1983; Kline & Schieber, 1981). In other words, if a teenager and her grandmother are listening to the radio, the speaker's message should persist equally long in their echoic memory.

Short-term memory is also roughly equivalent for young and elderly adults when the task is straightforward and there is no time pressure (Craik, 1992; Rebok, 1987). For example, the teenager and her grandmother should recall a phone number equally accurately several seconds after it was announced on the radio. However, age differences sometimes emerge on more complicated tasks. For example, in one study, people were given short lists of unrelated words, with the instructions to report the words in correct alphabetical order. In some conditions, the elderly participants reported only half as many correct items as the younger participants (Craik, 1990). Elderly people also perform relatively poorly when words are spoken rapidly and when words are in random order, rather than resembling English sentences (Stine et al., 1989).

When we consider long-term memory, the age differences are small on tasks involving recognition. Thus, a 70-year-old would be as likely as a 20-year-old to recognize a name as being familiar (Craik et al., 1987; Lavigne & Finley, 1990). Age differences are also small on **implicit memory** tasks—those that require performing a task. For instance, Light and Singh (1987) presented a number of words, such as PAPER, and later asked people to complete some word fragments, such as P_P_R. Elderly people performed as well as young adults on tasks like this (e.g., Light & Albertson, 1989; Lovelace & Coon, 1991).

How do elderly people perform on long-term memory tasks that require recall? (For example, can you *recall* the name of any researcher mentioned in the paragraph on short-term memory?) Zelinski and Gilewski (1988) conducted a **meta-analysis,** statistically synthesizing the results from numerous studies. This analysis of 36 studies showed that young adults recalled significantly more material than elderly adults. However, the age differences were relatively small when the material to be recalled was an essay (rather than a story) and when the participants were highly verbal (rather than low in verbal ability).

As you can see, the results of the research on memory are consistent with our theme of complexity. Do elderly people have memory difficulties? We cannot provide a simple answer. Instead, our response must depend upon the characteristics of the memory task and the participants' own ability level.

Elderly people often notice that their memory is not as accurate as it was in previous years (Hulicka, 1982; Lovelace & Twohig, 1984). Try Demonstration 11.1 to see whether your own memory failures match the kinds of problems that elderly people report. Fortunately, healthy, well-educated elderly people report that they use certain mnemonics more often than they did when they were younger. For instance, they are more likely to use calendars, shopping lists, and reminders (Lovelace & Twohig, 1984). In summary, many elderly people make efforts to compensate for their memory difficulties.

Will this elderly man remember what he has read as accurately as a younger person would? In some cases, his memory will be fine. However, the answer depends upon the nature of the material, how memory is tested, and his own verbal ability.

Thinking: Piaget's Approach

In Chapter 10, we noted that Jean Piaget's theory of cognitive development proposed a final stage called formal operations. Teenagers and adults who are in the **formal operational period** can think scientifically and systematically (see Table 10.2).

Psychologists have conducted research to test whether adults typically reach the formal operational stage. Using a variety of tasks that measure the ability to reason abstractly and test hypotheses, they have concluded that Piaget may have been too optimistic. In fact, only 40% to 80% of adults in these studies have moved beyond concrete operations to formal operations (Kuhn, 1992; Ward & Overton, 1990). Naturally, people trained in abstract thinking usually perform better than untrained people, and some tests of formal operations are easier than others. However, we must conclude that people do not automatically progress from concrete operations to formal operations (Flavell, 1992). Although Piaget seems to have underestimated the cognitive abilities of infants, he apparently overestimated the logical skills of adults.

However, we need to emphasize our theme of individual differences once more. Some theorists now suggest that a small number of adults are capable of thinking at a level even more sophisticated than formal operations. During this more advanced **problem-finding stage** of cognitive development, people can think creatively, solve complex problems that are not clear-cut, and ask intriguing new questions (Arlin, 1989; Labouvie-Vief, 1992; Simonton, 1990). They typically show this highly sophisticated level of thinking in their domain of expertise, rather than in all areas—consistent with our conclusions in Chapter 8 about expertise.

General Cognitive Performance

As we grow older, does our general cognitive ability tend to decline? Is your 80-year-old neighbor less intelligent than she was as a young adult? Some argue that intellectual functioning inevitably declines in old age. After all, elderly people have a reduced number of neurons as well as alterations in neuronal structure (Scheibel, 1992). However, even those gloomy theorists admit that good health, an active life, and intellectual stimulation can make the decline less noticeable (Schooler, 1987).

Several theorists argue that some kinds of intelligence decline more than other kinds (Horn & Cattell, 1967). Specifically, they propose that **fluid intelligence,** or the ability to solve new problems, reaches a peak in the late teens and then declines slowly but steadily throughout adulthood. Fluid intelligence is related to neuronal breakdown during aging, and it is also correlated with performance on a variety of memory tasks (Belsky, 1990; Cockburn & Smith, 1991). In contrast, theorists propose that **crystallized intelligence**—which involves specific acquired skills such as

The Indian film director Satyajit Ray made the brilliant film, "Home and the World," when he was 63 years old. Developmental theorists would argue that Ray excelled at problem finding and crystallized intelligence; these cognitive skills can continue to grow throughout adulthood.

DEMONSTRATION 11.2 Moral Judgment

Read the following paragraph and then answer the question.

In Europe a woman was near death from a special kind of cancer. There was one drug that the doctors thought might save her. It was a form of radium that a druggist in the same town had recently discovered. The drug was expensive to make, but the druggist was charging 10 times what the drug cost him to make. He paid $200 for the radium and charged $2,000 for a small dose of the drug. The sick woman's husband, Heinz, went to everyone he knew to borrow the money, but he could only get together $1,000, which is half of what it cost. He told the druggist that his wife was dying and asked him to sell it cheaper or let him pay later. But the druggist said, "No, I discovered the drug, and I am going to make money from it." So Heinz got desperate and broke into the man's store to steal the drug for his wife.

Question: Should Heinz have done this? Why or why not?

Source: Based on Kohlberg, 1969, p. 379.

verbal ability—continues to grow throughout adulthood. In general, research supports the distinction between these two kinds of intelligence and their different paths of development across the life course (Whitbourne, 1986a).

We should also emphasize that experience can compensate for some kinds of cognitive decline. For instance, a 65-year-old typist actually strikes the keys more slowly than a younger typist. However, the older typist's years of practice compensate for that deficit. In fact, Salthouse (1987) found that older and younger typists were similar in their typing speeds.

In our discussion of cognitive development, we have considered only healthy older adults. As we noted in Chapter 3, people with Alzheimer's disease experience severe cognitive and emotional impairment. Thus, several million North Americans with this disorder experience a decline in both fluid and crystallized intelligence.

Moral Development

Before you read further, try Demonstration 11.2. The moral dilemma in this story is one of 11 that Lawrence Kohlberg (1964, 1984) constructed to examine the development of moral thinking. Kohlberg analyzed the reasoning that people used with these moral dilemmas. He then created a stage theory of moral development, in the tradition of Piaget's theory of general cognitive development. In categorizing people's responses, Kohlberg ignored whether people said that Heinz should or should not steal the drug. Instead, Kohlberg focused on the reasons they provided.

Kohlberg identified three broad periods of moral development, each divided into two stages. As you can see, the stages parallel those Piaget proposed. In both theories, thinking becomes less concrete and more focused on abstract principles as individuals mature. Let us examine each of the six stages, together with a representative answer to the moral dilemma about Heinz.

Preconventional morality *(in which decisions are based on rules that are made by other people):*

Stage 1: Reasoning is based on avoiding punishment. For example, Heinz should not steal the drug because he might be sent to jail.
Stage 2: Reasoning is based on self-interest, with the hope that good deeds will be repaid. For example, Heinz should steal the drug because his wife will repay him after she recovers.

Conventional morality *(in which decisions are based on internalized standards derived from interactions with others):*

Stage 3: Reasoning is based on pleasing others and being a good person. For example, Heinz should steal the drug because his wife will admire him.
Stage 4: Reasoning is based on upholding the law. For example, Heinz should not steal because stealing breaks the law.

Postconventional morality *(in which decisions are based on one's own abstract principles about right and wrong):*

Stage 5:   Reasoning is based on personal standards and the fact that it is best for society if people obey the law. For example, Heinz should not steal the drug because it is bad for society if people steal whenever they become desperate.

Stage 6:   Reasoning is based on personal standards, even if the standards conflict with the law. For example, Heinz should steal the drug because human life should be more important than upholding the law.

In general, the results of research on Kohlberg-type moral dilemmas show that Stage 1 responses are rare beyond adolescence. Stage 2 responses are the most common category for 10- and 12-year-olds, but they drop gradually and then disappear by about 30 years of age. Stage 3 and 4 reasonings are the most common categories throughout adolescence and young adulthood. In contrast, few people supply Stages 5 and 6 responses at any point during development (Bee, 1992; Colby et al., 1983).

Does the research support Kohlberg's theory of moral development? In general, people move forward from one stage to the next in the sequence he suggested; however, some exceptions have been noted in the sequence (Gilligan et al., 1990; Kohlberg & Ryncarz, 1990; Walker et al., 1984). Furthermore, the theory is generally supported by cross-cultural research in such populations as West German students, rural Guatemalan Indians, Buddhist monks in Tibet, Black Caribbean boys in Honduras, and kibbutz residents in Israel (Boyes & Walker, 1988; Snarey, 1985).

Also, moral reasoning is related to other attitudes and behavior. For instance, people in the higher levels of moral development are more likely to be politically liberal and are more competent in dealing constructively with significant losses in their lives, such as the death of a family member (Emler et al., 1983; Lonky et al., 1984). From other research, we also know that parents are likely to promote the greatest increases in their children's moral development if they provide the stimulation of a more advanced stage of moral reasoning (Walker & Taylor, 1991)

One of the major controversies about Kohlberg's theory involves gender. Carol Gilligan's (1982) book, *In a Different Voice,* argues that Kohlberg's theory is too narrow. Specifically, Gilligan notes that Kohlberg was only concerned about justice, which she asserts is a traditionally masculine focus. Gilligan proposed that a comprehensive theory of moral development should also emphasize traditionally feminine

These individuals are protesting against nuclear weapons tests in Nevada. Many such protesters argue that their moral convictions would justify breaking the law in order to publicize these views.

concerns such as caring, compassion, and social relationships. Gilligan is correct that these factors are important in moral reasoning. However, we should emphasize that researchers usually find that women and men actually respond similarly on tests of moral reasoning (Colby & Kohlberg, 1987; Darley & Schultz, 1990; Greeno & Maccoby, 1986). Therefore, women and men do *not* live in different moral worlds, with men emphasizing justice and women emphasizing social relations. The psychological similarities between men and women are typically more noteworthy than the differences (Matlin, 1993a).

Would this male social worker be less likely than a female to emphasize caring and compassion when working with clients? Although theorists such as Gilligan propose gender differences in moral reasoning, most research shows gender similarities.

S E C T I O N   S U M M A R Y
COGNITIVE DEVELOPMENT

- In general, elderly people show little decline in sensory memory, straightforward short-term memory tasks, recognition memory, and long-term implicit memory; they are likely to perform relatively poorly on complex short-term memory tasks and long-term recall tasks (especially on stories and when the elderly person is low in verbal ability).

- On Piagetian tasks, many adult participants perform below the formal operational level, but some reach a more advanced stage, called the problem-finding stage.

- In general, fluid intelligence reaches a peak during the late teens and declines during adulthood; crystallized intelligence continues to grow throughout adulthood.

- Kohlberg proposed that moral reasoning develops through six stages; cross-cultural and other research generally supports his theory.

GENDER IN ADOLESCENCE AND ADULTHOOD

In Chapter 10 we examined children's beliefs about gender as well as three theories about the development of gender roles. Now let us discuss three activities that are critically important in adolescence and adulthood: work, love relationships, and parenting. As you will see, gender is relevant in all three areas.

Work

In Canada, 80% of the clerical workers are female, in contrast to 2% of those in construction trades (Mackie, 1991). Table 11.1 confirms that in the United States, certain occupations are almost exclusively male (e.g., carpenters and engineers), whereas others are almost exclusively female (e.g., nurses and secretaries). Gender clearly influences job choice.

TABLE 11.1 Percentage of Workers Who are Women in Selected Occupations

OCCUPATION	PERCENTAGE OF WORKERS WHO ARE WOMEN
Carpenters	2
Engineers	7
Lawyers	19
Physicians	20
Teachers (elementary, secondary)	73
Nurses	95
Secretaries	99

Source: U. S. Department of Labor, 1989

Gender also influences salaries. If we consider full-time workers in the United States, the average female salary is only about 65% of the average male salary (Blau & Winkler, 1989). Naturally, some of this pay discrepancy can be traced to the fact that male-dominated jobs pay more than female-dominated jobs. For example, mechanics are paid more than secretaries. However, pay discrepancies are found even within the same occupations. Consider a study of people who had received their bachelor's degree in engineering 11–15 years earlier and had worked full time since then. Females earned an average of $4,600 less each year than their male classmates (Jagacinski et al., 1987). Similar discrepancies have been reported for clerical workers and graduates of business administration programs (Dreher et al., 1989; Glenn & Feldberg, 1989).

Vocational Choice If you ask an adolescent boy what he wants to do for a living, he is likely to answer "a carpenter or a mechanic" or else "a lawyer or a doctor." He does not answer, "a nurse or a secretary," and he would never dream of responding, "I just want to be a husband and a father." As you might guess, males are more stereotyped in their career choices than females are (Betz & Fitzgerald, 1993). Young men are socialized to avoid feminine areas; they are not likely to choose work that usually carries a lower salary and fewer opportunities for promotion (Mackie, 1991).

In contrast, young women in the 1990s are increasingly likely to pursue some stereotypically masculine professions. For example, in 1992, 39% of American medical students were female, in contrast to only 10% in 1967 (Jonas & Etzel, 1988; Jonas et al., 1993). However, women are still seriously underrepresented in engineering and the sciences (Betz, 1992; Brush, 1991). Try Demonstration 11.3 to learn which factors tend to predict women's career choices. However, keep in mind the theme of individual differences. You may know a woman who plans to be a lawyer who has traditional ideas about gender roles and whose father is not supportive of her career plans.

DEMONSTRATION 11.3 Women's Career Choices

Think about the most ambitious female student from your high-school class—the one you thought was most likely to do well in a male-dominated career. Review the list of factors in the right-hand column, and place a + next to each item that describes this student in the column labeled "Most ambitious student." Then think of a female student from your high-school class who planned a more traditional, stereotypically female career. Review the list of factors once more, placing a + in the second column next to each item that describes this second student. When you have finished, count whether there are more + marks for the first student than for the second one.

MOST AMBITIOUS STUDENT	MORE TRADITIONAL STUDENT	FACTORS THAT ARE GENERALLY ASSOCIATED WITH A WOMAN CHOOSING A NONTRADITIONAL CAREER
_____	_____	High ability
_____	_____	Liberated gender-role values
_____	_____	High self-esteem
_____	_____	Highly educated parents
_____	_____	Female role models
_____	_____	Employed mother
_____	_____	Supportive father
_____	_____	Strong academic self-concept
_____	_____	Work experience as adolescent

Source: Based on Betz & Fitzgerald, 1987.

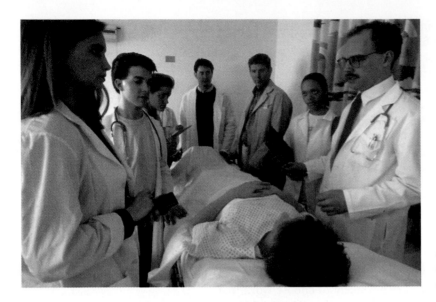

At present, 39% of U.S. medical students are women, so this group of medical students and residents is fairly typical.

Black adolescent females are more likely than White adolescent females to plan on working outside the home. In one study, 95% of Black high-school women had mothers who are employed (Malson, 1983). As one Black student said in an interview,

I'd never known a woman who stayed home with children . . . I did not know any housewives. That form of life was kind of alien. I did not even know that was possible. When I found out that people actually only stayed home and did nothing but raise children and clean house, I thought it was fascinating . . . I always assumed I'd work and have children. (Malson, 1983, p. 107).

Household Work Another, less visible kind of work is performed at home. Who makes the beds, prepares the meals, does the dishes, takes out the garbage, and picks up the socks? Most research shows that U.S. and Canadian women spend two to three times as many hours on housework as their husbands (Brayfreld, 1992; Douthitt, 1989; Gunter & Gunter, 1990). In one study, women did more housework than their husbands, even though both spouses had similar professional status. However, the women felt guilty that they were not being "wifely." As one woman said, "My sisters are very traditional, and my husband's family is super-traditional. They have wives who are not like me . . . subconsciously it bothers me" (Biernat & Wortman, 1991, p. 856). In other words, women may not be as strongly influenced as men are by gender roles in their career choices. However, stereotypical gender roles strongly dictate that women "should" do the housework—even if they work the same number of hours as their husbands.

In this section, we have seen that gender influences career choice, salaries, and the performance of housework. Gender also has important implications for romantic relationships.

Love Relationships

Adults typically believe that their work is important. However, they report that the most important events in their lives involve other people. For instance, Pleck (1985) found that 49% of men and 56% of women strongly agreed with the statement, "The most important things that happen to me involve my family." This section looks at intimate relationships, examining three common options for adults: marriage, gay relationship, and being single.

Marriage Currently, 63% of American adults and 66% of Canadian adults are married (U.S. Department of Commerce, 1987; Dumas, 1990). A meta-analysis has shown that both women and men are happier if they are married than if they are not (Wood et al., 1989). Surprisingly, however, a wife's marital satisfaction is not strongly correlated with her husband's marital satisfaction (Acitelli & Duck, 1987; Fitzpatrick, 1988; Whitbourne, 1986a).

People usually say that their marriages are happiest during the first months (Hatfield et al., 1984; Huston et al., 1986). Marital satisfaction is relatively low among couples with children living at home (Birchler, 1992; Hackel & Ruble, 1992). However, it often increases once children move away—an observation that students who are just leaving home may find somewhat worrisome. Older couples are likely to be strongly committed to the relationship, highly interdependent, and satisfied with their marriage (Sillars & Wilmot, 1989). Keep in mind, however, that these older couples represent a selected sample. Many who were not satisfied with the relationship have chosen to leave the marriage, and so the sample of older couples includes primarily those who are relatively happy.

According to some estimates, 40% of all people born in the 1970s who marry will end those marriages with a divorce. Data from both the United States and Canada suggest that the wife is usually the first one to mention divorce (Nett, 1993). This is consistent with other research showing that women are more likely than men to notice problems in a close relationship (Rubin et al., 1981). Divorce is a traumatic event for most couples, though divorced men tend to show more emotional and physical disturbances than divorced women (Price & McKenry, 1988).

Research has shown that both women and men are happier if they are married than if they are not.

What about the happily married couples? In a happy marriage, both wife and husband feel that their emotional needs are fulfilled, and each partner enriches the life of the other. Both understand and respect each other, and both are concerned for one another's happiness and welfare (Stinnett et al., 1984; Turner & Helms, 1989). Even though they may live in a society that emphasizes money, prestige, and power, their marriage is central in their lives (Sarnoff & Sarnoff, 1989).

Psychologists and sociologists have identified a number of factors that predict whether a marriage will remain stable or whether it will end in divorce (Balakrishnan et al., 1987; Birchler, 1992; Cate & Lloyd, 1992; Kurdek, 1991a, 1993). The factors that are related to stability include the following:

1. High level of education
2. Lack of financial problems
3. Both individuals at least in their 20s at the time of marriage
4. No premarital births
5. Long acquaintance prior to marriage
6. Having parents who were happily married.

In general, happy couples are also likely to be skilled in interpreting each other's emotions. Both consider their spouses to be their best friend. Furthermore, each is fairly high in stereotypically feminine traits such as being "understanding," "gentle," and "affectionate" (Antill, 1983; Bee, 1987; Whitbourne & Ebmeyer, 1990).

Interestingly, happily married couples even interpret their spouse's actions differently than unhappy couples. For example, suppose that Mary gives a gift to her husband, Jack. If Jack is satisfied with his marriage, he is likely to explain the gift by saying that Mary wanted to do something special for him. However, if Jack is dissatisfied with his marriage, he might say that she gave him the gift to justify spending some money on herself. Similarly, if Mary is satisfied with her marriage and Jack doesn't seem sexually interested, she might explain the disinterest by saying that he is experiencing pressure at work. If Mary is dissatisfied with her marriage, she may say that Jack doesn't love her. You can see how these explanation patterns can make an unhappy marriage less happy, while making a happy marriage even happier (Bradbury & Fincham, 1992; Fincham & Bradbury, 1990, 1992).

Gay Relationship A researcher visited the home of a lesbian in California to interview her for a project on lesbians and gay men. The researcher later wrote,

> She was very friendly, interested, talkative, and open. I felt like I was a friend whom she was inviting in to share part of her life. I liked her paintings, her roommate's photographs of the Bay Area, and the warm togetherness of their home. She and her roommate were obviously very much in love. Like most people who have a good, stable, five-year relationship, they seemed comfortable together, sort of part of one another, able to joke, obviously fulfilled in their relationship. They work together, have the same times off from work, do most of their leisure activities together. She is helping her roommate to learn to paint, while her roommate is teaching her about photography. They sent me home with a plateful of cookies, a good symbolic gesture of the kind of welcome and warmth I felt in their home. (Bell & Weinberg, 1978, p. 200)

A **gay person** is attracted to people of the same gender. In general, the terms *gay* and *lesbian* are preferred to the term *homosexual*, which focuses too narrowly on the sexuality of a relationship, rather than the broader psychological and emotional attachment that gay people feel for each other (Owens, 1993).

Research with gay people reveals that between 40% and 75% of lesbians and gay men are currently in a steady relationship (Peplau, 1988). These data clearly contradict the stereotype that gay people shun long-lasting relationships. Furthermore, surveys of lesbians, gay men, and heterosexuals have found no significant differences among the three groups on measures of satisfaction with the relationship (Kurdek, 1991b; Kurdek & Schmitt, 1986; Peplau et al., 1982).

Research also shows that gay people and heterosexuals are similar in their psychological adjustment (Gonsiorek & Weinrich, 1991; Hellwege et al., 1988; Herek, 1990; Kurdek, 1987; Obserstone & Sukoneck, 1976). Furthermore, children raised in gay households do not differ from children raised in heterosexual households on characteristics such as intelligence, general adjustment, development, moral judgments, and gender identity (Cramer, 1986; Patterson, 1992; Pennington, 1987).

Unfortunately, many gay people are victims of **homophobia,** which is an irrational, persistent fear and contempt for gay people (Kitzinger, 1987). The media tend to represent gay people in a negative fashion, and people may believe that gay people should not be hired for certain jobs (Gross, 1991; Mackie, 1991). Homophobia probably exists at your own college. For example, 55% of gay students at Rutgers University reported that they had been verbally abused on the campus, and 42% said they had been harassed by their roommates (Dodge, 1989).

Try to imagine how our culture's stereotypes about gay people would be reduced if we placed less emphasis on gender schemas. As we discussed in Chapter 10, gender is extremely important in our culture, and we encourage children to believe

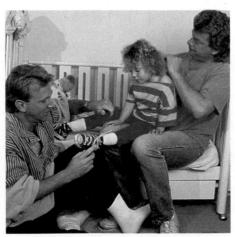

Researchers have found that lesbians and gay men have relationships that are as satisfying as heterosexual relationships.

that males are very different from females. If we placed less emphasis on gender, then we would not be so concerned that a gay person chooses to love someone of the same gender, rather than a person of the other gender.

Being Single In a study examining attitudes toward single people, Etaugh and Malstrom (1981) discovered that single people were perceived as being less sociable, attractive, and reliable in comparison with other people. Single people often discover that their married friends have strange biases. For instance, one of my single friends told me that a married acquaintance of hers believed that single people were not particularly concerned about saving money for the future. According to this stereotype, single people have only short-range goals and are incapable of planning for their old age.

The number of people who remain single has increased in recent years. For instance, among 25- to 29-year-olds in North America, 28% of females and 42% of males are single (Dumas, 1990; U.S. Department of Commerce, 1987).

Single people believe that being single has both advantages and disadvantages. Single women in one study frequently emphasized that they valued their independence (Simon, 1987). As one woman responded:

> Am I a "lone ranger," out on the range of life without companionship or help? Sometimes. In fact, often. But, just as often, I am sitting in the lap of family and friendship, drawing on the wisdom, and laughter, and camaraderie that sisters and buddies offer. It seems that I am both people. One of the reasons I never married, despite five reasonable offers, is that I thought it would be much harder in marriage to go back and forth between being that "lone ranger" and being close. (Simon, 1987, p. 37)

A common complaint raised by both single and divorced people is that they feel disadvantaged in settings where others expect everyone to be part of a couple. Some also mention loneliness, though single people are not as lonely as the stereotypes suggest (Barresi & Hunt, 1990; Cargan & Melko, 1985). In general, single people and married people are similar in their psychological adjustment (Gigy, 1980).

In this section we looked at three options for adults; marriage, gay relationships, and being single. Each of these options can bring loneliness and frustration, yet each can also bring warm relationships and the opportunity for personal growth. Now let us consider another social relationship that is important in the lives of most adults: being a parent.

Parenthood

A young father finds that he has become much more involved with fatherhood than he had ever anticipated:

> It's been a lot of fun to watch her grow. . . . I just didn't have any idea of what being a father was all about. . . . And, I'm really attached. I find myself thinking about her at work, rushing to the day care center to pick her up, just because every day she learns something new and you just want to see it and kind of share it with her. (Grossman, 1987, p. 89)

A mother of twin daughters comments on some of the many ways her children have affected her life:

> In many ways the children have brought us together. They have given us a joint aim in life. . . . It's worth going on and getting things better and working hard because of the pleasure we can get from the children and what we can do for them. It gives you a reason for doing it all. . . . (Boulton, 1983, p. 60)

For many women and men, parenthood represents a major life transition because they realize they are now responsible for the welfare of a new human being. For many years, psychologists concentrated their attention on mothers, ignoring men's reactions to fatherhood (Phares, 1992). More recent research is beginning to examine fathers (e.g., Bozette & Hanson, 1990; Hewlett, 1992). In general, the research shows that men and women are similar in their interest in becoming parents (Gerson, 1986).

Clear gender differences exist, however, in the amount of time that mothers and fathers spend with their children (Douthitt, 1989; Wilson et al., 1990). When the mother is not employed outside the home, fathers spend only one-fifth to one-quarter of the amount of time mothers spend in direct interaction with children. When the mother is employed, fathers usually increase their child-care responsibilities somewhat (Gottfried et al., 1988; Hoffman, 1989; Lamb, 1987). However, many mothers are disappointed that fathers are not more involved in child-care tasks (Hackel & Ruble, 1992).

Women and men also differ in the way they interact with their children. Most of mothers' interactions focus on caretaking, whereas fathers spend a greater percentage of their time in play. Lamb (1987) points out, though, that fathers and mothers are equally competent in taking care of newborns. Women are no better at "mothering" than men are at "fathering." However, mothers spend more time on the job, so they acquire more competence than fathers do. As the baby develops, fathers come to feel less confident about their parenting abilities, and they volunteer less often for caretaking. Thus, the differences between mothering and fathering increase as the babies grow up. Lamb assures us, though, that most fathers who become primary caretakers (for instance, when the mother dies) readily acquire the necessary skills. In short, when the opportunities arise, fathers can become skilled and sensitive in taking care of children.

SECTION SUMMARY

GENDER IN ADOLESCENCE AND ADULTHOOD

- Men and women typically pursue different kinds of careers, and they earn significantly different salaries—even in the same careers; males' career choices are more stereotyped than females' choices; women perform substantially more household chores, even when both spouses are employed.

- A meta-analysis has shown that married people are generally happier than unmarried people; marital happiness is relatively low during the years when children are in the home.

Researchers have discovered that fathers can be as skilled as mothers at taking care of infants.

- Researchers have identified a number of demographic and interpersonal factors related to marital happiness.
- Gay people tend to prefer steady relationships; they resemble heterosexuals in the quality of their relationships and their psychological adjustment; however, many gay people experience the effects of homophobia.
- Although stereotypes portray single people negatively, they are as well-adjusted as married people.
- Fathers and mothers have similar interests in becoming parents, though mothers usually gain more expertise by spending more time in child care.

PERSONALITY AND SOCIAL DEVELOPMENT

Think about the vastly different experiences that a group of 60-year-olds could have encountered in their six decades on earth. We need to emphasize the theme of individual differences when we examine personality and social development because these differences increase as people grow older. This increased variability during aging is called **individual fanning out;** this concept emphasizes that 60-year-olds are more different from one another than 10-year-olds (Hansson, 1989; Neugarten, 1982; Sherrod & Brim, 1986).

Let us begin this last section with a discussion of self-concept. Our next topic is the stability-change question, one of the three developmental issues introduced in Chapter 10. Then we consider interpersonal relationships, ethnicity during adolescence and adulthood, dealing with death, and an "In Depth" discussion of stereotypes about the elderly. Our final topic is successful aging.

Self-Concept

Chapter 10 introduced the term **self-concept,** or the schema of thoughts and feelings about oneself as an individual. We saw that toddlers can recognize themselves in a mirror and children develop feelings of competence. As you would suspect, adolescents and adults have a much more differentiated sense of who they are and how they have changed. For instance, a friend named Ann Hardy (1987) reflected on her life:

At the age of 69, I still don't feel "old," although chronologically, I'm not "young." I think one ages—given reasonable health—as one has been gradually aging in all the years before, very much depending on the quality of life one has built. My interests

According to the principle of individual fanning out, 60-year-olds differ more from each other than do 10-year-olds. These three elders include a participant in the U.S. National Senior Games, a turtle activist, and a violinist in a symphony orchestra.

haven't changed, except that we have the added joy of six grandchildren in our lives. Elderly people are as diverse as young people. Differences between them remain; previous likes and dislikes remain, for the most part. I am still me, "old" or not, though I feel that I have become more understanding, less judgmental, more open to new experiences, still trying to grow as a person.

Erikson's Psychosocial Approach Chapter 10 introduced Eric Erikson's (1950, 1968) theory that people confront a specific task during each of eight stages of development. Table 11.2 reviews the first four stages that describe childhood development and adds the four stages that are important in adolescence and adulthood.

Chapter 10 discussed Piaget's theory of cognitive development, and an earlier part of the current chapter briefly examined Kohlberg's theory of moral development. In Chapter 13, we will spend some time on Freud's theory of personality development. However, none of these developmental theories matches Erikson's theory with respect to its attention to older adulthood.

Throughout the life course, Erikson argues, individuals struggle with identity development. Erikson may have focused on identity because of the identity confusion he experienced in his own life (Green, 1989). Erikson was born in Germany, shortly after his Danish father abandoned his Jewish mother. Several years later, his mother married a Jewish doctor, and they both raised the young boy in the Jewish faith, under the name Erik Homburger. His Christian friends at school considered him to be Jewish, but his Jewish friends at the temple considered him to be Christian, because he looked very Scandinavian. During his adolescence, Erik's family pressured him to study medicine, yet he wanted to become an artist. Eventually, he pursued training in psychoanalysis with Anna Freud, daughter of Sigmund Freud, who was

TABLE 11.2 Erikson's Theory of Psychosocial Development, From Birth Through Old Age

STAGE	AGE	PSYCHOSOCIAL TASK	DESCRIPTION OF TASK
1	0–1	Trust versus mistrust	The infant whose needs are met by a caretaker develops a sense of trust in others.
2	1–3	Autonomy versus doubt	The toddler tries to learn independence and self-confidence.
3	3–6	Initiative versus guilt	The young child learns to initiate his or her own activities.
4	6–12	Competence versus inferiority	The child tries to develop skill in physical, cognitive, and social areas.
5	12–19	Identity versus role confusion	The adolescent tries out several roles and forms an integrated, single identity.
6	20–40	Intimacy versus isolation	The young adult tries to form close, permanent relationships and to make career commitments.
7	40–65	Generativity versus stagnation	The middle-aged person tries to contribute to the world through family relationships, work productivity, and creativity.
8	65 on	Integrity versus despair	The elderly person thinks back on life, experiencing satisfaction or disappointment.

Source: Erikson, 1950, 1968.

herself a prominent child psychoanalyst. He left Europe for the United States in 1933, changing his last name from Homburger to Erikson. It is clear that Erikson often confronted the question "Who am I?" especially during the first decades of his life.

As Table 11.2 shows, the major task for the adolescent in Stage 5 is to struggle with the question "Who am I, and where am I going?" In fact, it was Erikson who gave us a term popular in everyday English: *identity crisis*. Identity issues are particularly relevant for adolescents because of the major physical changes they experience in puberty and the cognitive changes that encourage abstract thought. In addition, they need to make decisions about occupations and education.

During Stage 6, the young adult develops an intimate relationship with another person. An individual who does not develop intimacy will be overwhelmed by a sense of isolation, according to Erikson. Young adults also struggle with career decisions.

In Stage 7, Erikson argues that a major task is child rearing, or attempting to influence the next generation. Generativity may also be expressed by helping other young people or by creative, productive work or volunteer activities that benefit others. Social responsibility is an important focus during this stage.

Erikson's Stage 8 requires looking back on life's accomplishments. For example, Anne Hardy (1987) reflected about her lifetime, which was devoted to working for racial equality and world peace:

> "This is the way it is" is something we can't settle for. We have to work toward being able to say, "That is the way it was, and we have helped to improve it." . . . A Fundamentalist relative asked me recently what I felt about eternity. I answered that for me eternity is being created daily in what I do, how I live vis-à-vis other human beings, what kind of values I gave and continue to give our children so that they in turn would have good values to pass on to their world and their children.

A person who can reminisce about a satisfying life achieves a sense of integrity, according to Erikson. In contrast, a person who has accomplished little develops a sense of despair.

Recent Research on Adult Identity Let us look at some of the more recent research on the question of adult identity. For example, Whitbourne (1986b) examined 94 adults between the ages of 24 and 61 in a book entitled *The Me I Know: A Study of Adult Identity*. In addition to questions about family identity, work identity, and age identity, she also explored people's life values. Demonstration 11.4 on the next page is a modification of this portion of the interview.

Whitbourne found that people considered their values to be a major part of their identity. Those whose identities were dominated by family roles described values that focused on doing things for others. Those whose identities were dominated by occupational accomplishments described values that focused on hard work and competence.

One of the most frequently mentioned values was honesty. In fact, 36 of the 94 respondents specifically mentioned this trait. For them, honesty meant not stealing, cheating, or lying. Some people also noted that they valued the ability to look at the world realistically and honestly. Still others emphasized honesty as a value to be transmitted to one's children or honesty in the workplace.

In addition to honesty, other frequently mentioned values were the Golden Rule, or doing unto others as you would have them do unto you, and trying to get along well with others, even when it required overlooking their faults. In summary, then, Whitbourne's study demonstrated that adult identity emphasizes a concern for the well-being of other people.

Other research illustrates that people in different cultures have different ideas about how one's identity is related to other people. Specifically, North American and many Western European cultures emphasize the importance of asserting yourself and appreciating how you are different from others (Markus & Kitayama, 1991). In these cultures, a person's identity would focus on the idea, "I am a unique individual." However, Asian, African, Latin-American, and many southern European

---

DEMONSTRATION 11.4 Important Values During Adulthood

Locate a friend or relative you would feel comfortable interviewing about personal issues. It would be ideal to locate someone at least 50 years old, but a younger person would be satisfactory. Tell this person that you will be conducting an informal interview about important values, and that he or she should feel free not to answer any questions that seem too personal. Each general question is followed by a probe, which you may find useful if your respondent requires clarification or hesitates about an answer.

1. Please describe for me your major values, the principles you try to live your life by.
   PROBE: What is important to you in the way you try to live your life?
2. How strongly do you feel about your values?

PROBE: How important to you is it that you follow these values?

3. How do your values affect the way you feel about yourself as a person?
   PROBE: Do you judge yourself by your values? How do you come out with respect to these values?
4. Do you think your values are changing?
   PROBE: Do you have any questions or doubts about your values?

If yes: 5a. How are they changing?
   PROBE: What is it about your values that is changing?

If no: 5b. Do you think your values are likely to change in the future?
   PROBE: Do you think you will ever have questions about your values in the future?

Source: Based on Whitbourne, 1986b, pp. 245–246.

---

cultures emphasize fitting in with others, paying attention to them, and living in interdependent relationships with them. In these cultures, a person's identity would focus on interconnectedness with others. The comparison between these two perspectives is illustrated by two popular sayings. In the United States, we say, "the squeaky wheel gets the grease." In contrast, a popular saying in Japan is "the nail that stands out gets pounded down" (Markus & Kitayama, 1991, p. 224).

The Stability-Change Question

In Chapter 10 we considered the stability-change question when we asked whether infants maintain their personal characteristics as they mature into children. Now we need to consider the same issue in adulthood. The prominent American psychologist, William James, wrote a century ago, "For most of us, by the age of 30, the character has set like plaster, and will never soften again" (James, 1892, p. 124). In other words, James clearly cast his vote for "stability" in the great stability-change debate.

You might vote for "change," however, if you had known Benjamin Carson as an angry high-school student and watched his transformation into a neurosurgeon. Ben Carson failed most of his math quizzes as a fifth-grader in inner-city Detroit. As a high-school student, Ben was known for his violent temper. He would attack anyone who offended him, using a bottle, brick, knife, or any other handy weapon. One day, in a rage, he thrust a knife at a boy. The boy happened to be wearing a large metal belt buckle, which broke the blade on Ben's knife. Ben instantly realized that he could have killed another person. He ran home, closed himself into the bathroom, and sat on the edge of the tub. He thought and prayed, and then emerged three hours later with his anger gone. The anger never returned, and Ben focused his attention on his school work, achieving an A average in the remainder of high school. He was accepted to Yale University for his undergraduate work and the University of Michigan for medical school. Ben Carson became a neurosurgeon and later achieved fame for his surgery in separating Siamese twins connected at the head (Woodford, 1989).

Personality Characteristics Does the research evidence support the stability view of William James or the change view suggested by life transformations such as Ben Carson's? Naturally, people who experience traumatic events are less likely to

Neurosurgeon Ben Carson visiting
Andrews University pre-med students.

show stability (Fiske & Chiriboga, 1990). Furthermore, a study is less likely to demonstrate stability if personality is first assessed when the individuals are teenagers, rather than young adults (Kogan, 1990).

Another factor that influences the results is the way that stability and change are measured (Bengston et al., 1985). For instance, when the studies are *correlational*, they tend to demonstrate that personality remains stable as people grow older. For example, people who are friendlier than average in high school tend to remain friendlier than average in old age; relatively unfriendly people tend to remain relatively unfriendly.

However, other studies measure the *average level* of a characteristic that a group of people possess; here, the results are inconsistent. That is, some personality characteristics stay at the same level as people age. For instance, a group of 30-year-olds will not systematically increase or decrease their anxiety level as they grow older. On the other hand, other personality characteristics show a systematic shift as people age. For instance, the average energy level of that group of 30-year-olds probably decreases systematically as people grow older.

Several years ago, my mother attended the 50th reunion of her high-school class in Great Falls, Montana, and her report of the event meshed well with the data on stability versus change. In general, she noted moderate stability in the extent to which people were extraverted or outgoing. The high-school senior who had been active in numerous school organizations was now, at 68, the extraverted master of ceremonies for the reunion, whereas the quieter people were still quiet. Of course, the correlation between high-school personality and adulthood personality was far from perfect. For instance, the woman who had graduated from a prestigious university, moved to California, and had traveled extensively, had become much more self-confident and outgoing. Another woman, initially similar in self-confidence, had attended the local college and now lived in a small town in Montana; her self-confidence had not changed. Still, consistent with the findings of Bengston and his coauthors, high-school extraversion seemed generally correlated with late-adulthood extraversion.

My mother also observed that a second personality characteristic *had* changed, when assessed in terms of average level. This characteristic was the willingness to share personal information and to laugh at oneself. As adolescents, they had been reluctant to talk about themselves and laugh at their foibles; as adults in their 60s, the average level of "sharing and laughing" had increased remarkably.

In short, the conclusions on the stability-change question are complex. Stability is more likely in correlational studies, whereas change and stability are equally likely in average-level studies; the outcome depends upon the characteristic being studied. We can find evidence for both stability and change across the life span (Kogan, 1990; Schlossberg, 1984; Whitbourne, 1986a).

Midlife Crises An important issue related to the stability-change question is the so-called *midlife crisis*. You have probably read in popular magazines that adults are supposed to experience some kind of major change in their lives in their early 40s. A typical article describes a happily married 39-year-old accountant who turns 40 and divorces his wife, abandons his children, and moves to Southern California with a woman barely older than his children.

Several psychologists have proposed theories focusing on a midlife crisis that involves substantial changes in a person's occupation, personal relationships, and values (e.g., Gould, 1978; Levinson et al., 1978; Vaillant, 1977). However, reviews of theories about midlife crises emphasize that the research does not support the concept (Chiriboga, 1989; Lieberman & Peskin, 1992; Tamir, 1989).

The concept of a midlife crisis is believable because each of us knows at least one person whose life changed drastically during middle age. Yes, some people do have midlife crises. Others have crises earlier or later. Many more never experience a major life upheaval; their lives have remained stable. We must conclude that individual differences are large with respect to midlife crises, and these major crises certainly are not universal.

Interpersonal Relationships

In Chapter 10 we considered the first major interpersonal relationship, attachment to parents. Now we pursue child-parent relationships during adolescence. In the previous section of this chapter, we examined a major interpersonal issue during adolescence and adulthood when we discussed love relationships. Another major interpersonal issue is friendship, our second topic.

Adolescent-Parent Relationships Perhaps you once read a teen novel that contained a passage like this:

> *All the scolding and criticism from her parents was simply too much for 15-year-old Meredith. Tears streaming down her pale cheeks, she tore into her bedroom, slamming the door behind her slender young legs. She hurled herself onto her bed, sobbing deeply into her lavender pillow. "I hate you, I hate you, I hate you!" she cried to her parents in a voice choked with emotion.*

Are the relationships between adolescents and their parents as stormy as the popular press suggests? Naturally, parent-child relationships change during puberty (Holmbeck & Hill, 1991; Paikoff & Brooks-Gunn, 1991; Vangelisti, 1992). After all, adolescents are preparing to lead independent lives. However, some research reports a *decline* in conflict during adolescence, rather than an increase (Galambos & Almeida, 1993). In addition, adolescents generally report feeling positive about their relationships with their parents (Galambos, 1992). Apparently, the generation gap is smaller than the myth suggests (Nielson, 1991). Once again, we see an important example of the difference between truth and reality.

Friendship Chapter 10 looked at friendship during childhood; we saw that these early friendships are based on concrete characteristics such as similar interests.

However, adolescents base their friendships not only on similar interests; the friend must also be dependable and caring and also someone with whom they can have good conversations about their problems and experiences (Berndt, 1992; Rawlins, 1992). In addition, the friend is typically similar in personality, attitudes, and values (Blieszner & Adams, 1992). These deeper friendships probably develop only after

Research shows that adolescents generally report feeling positive about their relationships with their parents.

People who have good interactions with their friends are likely to be more satisfied with their lives.

young people have lost most of their egocentrism—to use Piaget's term—and can appreciate the perspective of another person. Also, Erikson's approach suggests that identity crises associated with Stage 5 must be resolved in order to develop truly intimate friendships.

The nature of friendships may change as people progress through adulthood. A study of friendships between the ages of 18 and 75 showed that in old age, men placed more emphasis on concern and thoughtfulness toward their friends, in contrast to when they were younger. Older women showed more tolerance and less confrontation with their friends than when they were younger (Fox et al., 1985). Furthermore, life satisfaction seems to be correlated with interaction with friends (Aizenberg & Treas, 1985; Bee, 1987; Hochschild, 1973). As an elderly man concluded in one interview, "Without friends, you're like a book that nobody bothers to pick up . . . " (Fox et al., 1985, p. 500).

Ethnic Issues During Adolescence and Adulthood

One reason we need to examine ethnic groups is to dispel ethnic stereotypes. However, in dispelling these stereotypes, we must avoid another error—concluding that ethnic distinctions are irrelevant in the lives of adolescents and adults. That is, we must avoid stereotyping, yet simultaneously attend to the genuine distinctions between members of the White middle class and members of other ethnic groups (Nielsen, 1991; Sue, 1981). This section looks at two important areas: adolescent academic achievement and the status of the elderly.

Academic Achievement Table 11.3 shows the percentage of adults over the age of 24 in the United States who hold at least a bachelor's degree, as a function of ethnic group. As you can see, the percentages range from 9% for Native Americans and Hispanics to 37% for Asian Americans.

Black, Hispanic, and Native American adolescents are less likely than White adolescents to attend college, perhaps partly because the academic environment does not seem to be a nurturing one (Holden, 1991a). Furthermore, Black and Hispanic students are likely to have attended high schools that were essentially segregated, with more than half of the students from those two ethnic groups. These schools are less likely to be focused on attending college (Simons et al., 1991).

What are some of the factors that encourage academic success? Some students who achieve success credit the high schools they attended. For example, Burciaga

TABLE 11.3 Percentage of Adults over the Age of 24 with at Least a Bachelor's Degree, by Ethnic Group

ETHNIC GROUP	PERCENTAGE WITH BACHELOR'S DEGREE
Asian	37%
White	22%
Black	11%
Native American	9%
Hispanic	9%

Source: Kominski, 1993

(1993) attended a school in El Paso, Texas, in which 70% of the students are Mexican American, yet 100% of the graduates go to college. He credits the faculty for their enthusiasm, values, and motivation that encouraged every student to succeed. Similarly, Quevedo-García (1987) urges more schools to develop college-oriented programs for Hispanic students.

Obviously, parents are also responsible for encouraging academic success. For example, Soto (1988) interviewed the parents of high- and low-achieving Puerto Rican children. The successful students were more likely to have parents who had high aspirations for their child. These parents were also more aware of their child's educational progress and more likely to praise the child for his or her achievements.

Interviews with successful Black students also show that parents' encouragement was an important factor. Parents were often unable to provide much financial help because of low family income, but they had promoted values and study habits that encouraged their children's academic success (Lee, 1985). Furthermore, another study concluded that Black students whose parents encouraged them to develop racial pride and an appreciation of Black heritage tended to receive higher grades than students whose parents rarely mentioned racial issues (Bowman & Howard, 1985).

Another factor encouraging student success is called **bicultural efficacy,** which is a person's belief that he or she can live effectively within two different ethnic groups without compromising the sense of cultural identity (LaFromboise et al., 1993). For example, Native-American college students who were high in bicultural efficacy had higher grades, better study habits, and a stronger commitment to academic success.

When psychologists examine ethnic differences in achievement, they also need to explain why Asian students are generally so successful in school. In fact, Asian Americans are often stereotyped as the "ideal minority group." Many Asian students do excel in science and mathematics. For example, 42% of Asian high-school students take a course in trigonometry, in contrast to 21% of White students (Simons et al., 1991). However, we need to emphasize the large variability among the various Asian groups, as well as the variability within any single Asian group (Sue & Okazaki, 1990).

Researchers do not believe that Asian academic success can be traced to a genetic explanation (Sue & Okazaki, 1990). Instead, an important factor is probably that Asian families traditionally set high standards for academic achievement (Caplan et al., 1992). In one cross-cultural study, for example, Asian children performed better than U.S. children in almost every academic area. When the mothers were asked how satisfied they were with their children's performance, the U.S. mothers were much more satisfied than the Asian mothers (Lee, 1992). Another advantage for Asian students is that their peers also value achievement, so they can win admiration from their friends for doing well in school (Steinberg et al., 1992).

According to Teresa LaFromboise and her coauthors, students who are high in bicultural efficacy tend to excel academically. At Little Big Horn Tribal College in Montana, students from the Crow tribe are encouraged to learn about their Native-American heritage and also to master the academic subjects taught at other colleges.

Studies generally show that elderly Black people are more likely than elderly White people to receive social support from family members.

However, many Asian students complain that their families overemphasize success. This overemphasis on success is clearly stressful. Also, their families may discourage them from pursuing careers other than science and medicine. For example, a Chinese-American student recently told me that she passionately wanted to be a psychologist. Unfortunately, her parents said that they would be ashamed of her, because their friends' daughters wanted to become doctors, physicists, and biologists. Asian Americans also find that they may do well academically, but anti-Asian barriers keep them from participating in politics, sports, entertainment, and other influential or high-paying careers (Sue & Okazaki, 1990; Woo, 1989).

In summary, ethnicity is related to academic achievement. Important factors that contribute to these differences include schools, parents, a student's own bicultural efficacy, and the attitudes of peers.

The Status of Elders Elderly people of color experience some disadvantages and some advantages in comparison with elderly White people. For example, the **multiple-jeopardy hypothesis** predicts additional disadvantages for people who are Black and elderly; they experience both prejudice against Blacks and prejudice against elderly people. The multiple-jeopardy hypothesis is indeed supported by the research on income. Black elderly people are especially likely to live below the poverty line (Jackson, 1985; Minkler & Stone, 1985; Murray et al., 1989).

When we consider family support, however, Black elders seem to have the advantage over White elders. For example, elderly Blacks are more likely than elderly Whites to interact with and receive social support from their younger family members (George, 1988; Taylor & Chatters, 1991).

Ethnic background also has an important influence on living arrangements. For example, Lubben and Becerra (1987) examined data gathered on 952 elderly California residents from four different ethnic groups. Table 11.4 shows the percentage of each group who were living in the same home as their children (rather than with a spouse or alone). Consider, also, how elderly people who are not fluent in English may feel lonely and alienated if they live in a nursing home where the staff members cannot speak their language (Jette & Remien, 1988).

Although ethnicity may be related to financial status, family support, and living arrangements, it may have little impact on other aspects of growing old. For example, Harris and her coauthors (1989) found that Native-American, Hispanic, and White elderly people reported similar advantages and disadvantages to growing older. They valued the freedom and their family relations, and they regretted that their deteriorating health was creating problems and limitations. Now let us turn our attention to a topic that is relevant for elderly people from all ethnic backgrounds: awareness of dying.

TABLE 11.4 Percentage of Individuals 80 Years of Age and Older Who Are Living with Their Children, by Ethnic Group.

Total (Across all four ethnic groups)	ETHNIC GROUP			
	White	Black	Hispanic	Asian
22%	15%	24%	41%	56%

Source: Lubben & Becerra, 1987

Dealing with Death

Erik Erikson and his coauthors (1986) interviewed elderly people in preparing their book, *Vital Involvement in Old Age.* One respondent said, "You don't know whether you are going to be here tomorrow or not. Nobody does, of course, but when you are older your chances are more questionable." Many respondents did not hide their fear of death. One person said tremblingly, "On New Year's night, when they drop that ball, I am so glad I lived another year. I don't like to die at all! I am frightfully afraid of death!" (p. 65).

We mentioned earlier that Erikson's Stage 8 stressed looking back on one's life; this process is usually prompted by an awareness of death in the near future (Butler, 1963). This **life review** is a special kind of reminiscing about the past in which an older person recalls past experiences and tries to work through them to understand them more thoroughly (Sherman, 1991; Whitbourne, 1986a). In one study of people between the ages of 58 and 93, Romaniuk (1981) discovered that 56% of the participants had completed a life review and an additional 25% were currently in the process of life review. Only 19% indicated no concern with life review.

What are the thoughts and emotions of someone who is about to die? Some years ago, Elisabeth Kübler-Ross (1969) proposed that people who are terminally ill pass through a series of five distinct stages. The first stage of her theory is *denial;* the second, *anger;* the third, *bargaining* (for instance, promising to lead a better life if given more time before dying); the fourth *depression;* and the fifth, peaceful *acceptance* of death.

Kübler-Ross's pioneering work was useful because it urged physicians and other professionals to pay more attention to the emotional needs of dying patients and their families (Rainey, 1988). However, the research has been criticized for being based too heavily on personal impressions, rather than more concrete data. People do not seem to express these five emotions in any consistent pattern. In fact, depression seems to be the only emotion that is consistently present in people who are dying (Bee, 1992; Schneidman, 1980). In the words of one researcher,

> *I find no evidence . . . to support specific stages of dying. Rather, dying patients demonstrate a wide variety of emotions that ebb and flow throughout our entire life as we face conflicts and crises. (Pattison, 1978, p. 141)*

Fortunately, the death-education movement has grown stronger in recent years. For example, many textbooks and other resources offer both information and practical advice (e.g., Buckman, 1992; DeSpelder & Strickland, 1987; Kastenbaum, 1992).

Also, health professionals and others who work with people who are dying are acknowledging that the traditional hospital setting is not a supportive, compassionate place. A relatively new development is **hospice care,** in which death is viewed as normal, the family is involved in caring for the dying person, and medical care fo-

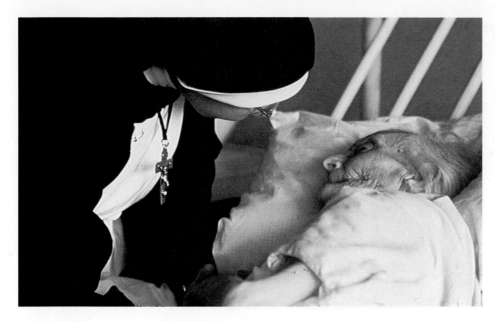

Hospice workers help dying people and their families.

cuses on relieving pain rather than keeping a person alive at all costs (Bee, 1992). Hospice programs can be based in the hospital or in people's homes. However, their primary goal is to allow people with terminal illnesses to die with dignity.

IN DEPTH: Attitudes Toward the Elderly

This chapter has probably encouraged you to think about your beliefs and opinions about elderly people. Our "In Depth" section explores the media's treatment of the elderly as well as the responses of laypeople and professionals. An important concept throughout this section is **ageism,** which is a bias against aging and elderly people. This bias can include myths, negative attitudes, stereotypes, and outright discrimination (Schaie, 1993; Whitbourne & Hulicka, 1990). According to ageist stereotypes, elderly people are more likely than young adults to be ill, sexually inactive, ugly, mentally ill, useless, depressed, and low in intelligence (Palmore, 1990; Spacapan & Oskamp, 1989). In each case, reality does not match the common stereotypes—a theme we have noted repeatedly throughout this book.

How the Elderly Are Treated in the Media A student in my introductory psychology course showed me an advertisement for a skin cream, "It's never too late. Then again, it's never too early, either." If we take this ad seriously, we should hand out samples when children sign up for nursery school. Ads make people feel guilty about aging skin and graying hair. Women are told to do something about their sagging bustline, and men are urged to buy expensive products to keep from becoming bald.

The Gray Panthers, a political action group concerned about treatment of the elderly, complain that the media show the elderly with blank or expressionless faces (Davis & Davis, 1985). Older adults object to the narrow range of images, and they would like to see elderly people who seem intelligent and well educated (Kaiser & Chandler, 1988).

The elderly are clearly underrepresented in television programs. For example, women over the age of 60 constitute 9% of the U. S. population, but only 3% of the characters on television (Holtzman & Akiyama, 1985; Passuth & Cook, 1985).

The next time you stop by a store that carries greeting cards, check out the birthday cards for adults. The card on the right in Figure 11.2 represents a large group of cards that show aging in a very negative light (Demos & Jache, 1981; Huyck & Duchon, 1986; Palmore, 1990). Even the fairly positive card on the left contains the negative phrase "over the hill." You might also want to inspect the cartoons in magazines and newspapers. One analysis showed that the elderly were frequently depicted as useless, outdated, and isolated (Sheppard, 1981).

In short, elderly people are often missing in the media. When they do appear, they are often portrayed negatively.

Figure 11.2

Examples of two birthday cards that focus on aging.

Reactions to the Elderly We need to emphasize that ageism, like many psychological concepts, is extremely complex. For example, not everyone is negative about the elderly—they may even be positive. Consider a study of Black and White children who were between the ages of 5 and 13. These children responded as positively to old adults as to young adults (Mitchell et al., 1985).

In general, however, people tend to be negative about the elderly. For example, Mary Kite and her colleagues (1991) asked college students and elderly community residents to rate a person who was described as either 35 years old or 65 years old and either a man or a woman. A typical item might ask participants to rate an individual on the characteristic "participates in activities outside the home," using a scale on which 0 represented extremely unlikely and 100 represented extremely likely.

Figure 11.3 shows how the participants rated the target individuals on the characteristic of sociability. As you can see, both young and old participants tended to believe that the young target was likely to be more sociable. You can see that the young participants were especially likely to be more positive about the young target.

However, elderly people were not uniformly devalued. They were likely to be judged as grouchy, critical, miserly, and hard of hearing. Still, they were also viewed as likable, experienced, and intelligent. In general, older women and older men were judged similarly; the exceptions were that older women were more likely to be seen as wrinkled and also active in their communities.

Kite and Johnson (1988) performed a meta-analysis of previous research that also demonstrated a significant negative bias against the elderly. However, the judgments varied with the characteristic that was being evaluated. For example, elderly people are judged to be fairly pleasant, but not very competent. Also, younger adults are more positive about specific elderly people than they are about elderly people in general. Other research has demonstrated, as you might expect, that people who have had frequent pleasant interactions with elderly people are more likely to report that elderly people are friendly, optimistic, and self-reliant (Knox et al., 1986).

We have discussed attitudes toward the elderly in some detail because they illustrate one of our themes. A simplistic view of ageism would suggest that everyone is guilty of stereotyping and discrimination toward all elderly people. However, reality is more complicated. To predict with any accuracy whether a person holds ageist views, we would need to know how old that person is, whether he or she is familiar with elderly people, and what attributes of the elderly are being judged.

We have been examining how laypeople react to the elderly. What are the attitudes of people who are responsible for the health and welfare of these elderly people? Research in this

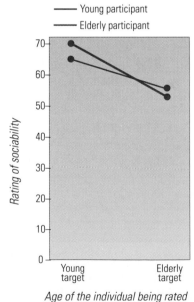

Age of the individual being rated

Figure 11.3

Ratings of a young (35-year-old) target and an elderly (65-year-old) target on a 100-point scale of sociability, as a function of age of the participants. (Based on Kite et al., 1991)

area shows that members of the U.S. Congress believe that elderly people are socially isolated and unreliable employees (Lubomudrov, 1987). Furthermore, physicians are less likely to give complete answers and explanations to elderly people (Greene et al., 1987). Also, psychologists believe that elderly people are less likely than young people to recover from depression (Ray et al., 1987).

One of the most dangerous stereotypes about the elderly is that they are helpless and must depend upon other people. A study of the staff members in nursing homes showed that those who held the greatest number of stereotypes about the elderly were the most likely to encourage them to be dependent (Kahana & Kiyak, 1984). Obviously, stereotypes about the elderly stand in the way of older adults who want to lead satisfying, productive lives. Let us now examine some components of successful aging.

Successful Aging

On the surface, elderly people might seem to have many reasons to be unhappy. We noted that physical, perceptual, and cognitive changes can occur during normal aging. Poor health, limited income, the loss of friends, and fear of death could all contribute to pessimism in old age. Patronizing and ageist treatment might make elderly people feel even less competent.

Impressively, however, age seems to have little effect on people's sense of well-being or happiness. For instance, a review of 15 studies showed that elderly people were—if anything—slightly higher in self-esteem than younger people (Bengtson et al., 1985). In general, age explains only a small amount of the variability in people's well-being (e.g., Krause, 1991; Stacey & Gatz, 1991). Figure 11.4 shows data collected by Costa and his colleagues (1987). They studied nearly 5,000 people on two occasions, nine years apart. Each line therefore represents a longitudinal study across this nine-year time span. However, the study also used the cross-sectional method, because four different age groups were represented throughout the study. As you can see, people in all age categories are reasonably similar in their life satisfaction.

Consistent with our theme of individual differences, elderly people vary tremendously in their life satisfaction. Psychologists and other researchers have tried to identify the factors related to successful aging. Of course, this topic is challenging because success is highly subjective; individuals and cultural groups differ in their ideas about success (Day, 1991). Obviously, good physical health is one important component. Social support from relatives and friends is also crucial (Day, 1991).

Another important factor is a sense of control or self-determination. You may recall the research by Rodin and Langer (1977) discussed in Chapter 2. Residents in a nursing home who were encouraged to take responsibility for themselves were rated as happier, more sociable, and more independent. Furthermore, they lived longer than people in the other group, who had been treated in the standard fashion—which encouraged dependence. Following that landmark research, people who work with

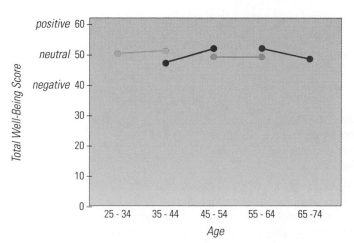

Figure 11.4

Ratings of life satisfaction, as a function of the age of respondent. (Note: Each respondent was interviewed on two occasions, nine years apart; the two dots at the end of each line represent the same individuals. However, each of the four lines represents a different group.) (Source: Costa et al., 1987)

the elderly have tried to design residences that allow elderly people more control over their environment (Lawton, 1990). Counselors and institutions are also beginning to promote choice and a sense of responsibility among the elderly people they serve (Schulz et al., 1991; Waters & Goodman, 1990).

Some of the more recent work is innovative. For example, research has often demonstrated that elderly people benefit from the assistance they receive from other people. However, Krause and his colleagues (1992) have also shown that elderly people benefit from the assistance they *give* to other people. By volunteering their services and offering support to others, elderly people develop greater feelings of personal control and higher levels of satisfaction with their lives.

According to research by Krause and his coauthors, elderly people show an increased sense of control when they help other people.

SECTION SUMMARY

PERSONALITY AND SOCIAL DEVELOPMENT

- Erikson's theory of identity development proposes that adolescents and adults struggle with identity, intimacy, generativity, and integrity.

- More recent research on identity emphasizes that honesty is a critical component of identity and that cultures have different perspectives on identity.

- Studies on adult development show both stability and change in personality; however, researchers do not find evidence for a universal midlife crisis.

- In general, adolescents and their parents have reasonably positive interactions; adolescent friendships are based on similarity, caring, and conversation; during later adulthood, people treat their friends with more concern and tolerance.

- Factors related to ethnicity and academic achievement include the nature of the schools, parents, bicultural efficacy, and peer reaction.

- Elderly Black people experience greater disadvantages in terms of income, but greater advantages in terms of family support; Chinese and Mexican elderly are especially likely to live with their children.

- People who are dying do not consistently experience the five stages popularized by Kübler-Ross.

- Elderly people are often missing from the media, and they are frequently represented negatively.

- People are often negative about the elderly, although important exceptions occur. Politicians, physicians, and psychologists may show ageist tendencies.

- Age has little effect on people's sense of well-being; factors related to successful aging include physical health, social support, and a sense of control.

REVIEW QUESTIONS

1. The theme of individual differences appears many times in this chapter. Try to recall as many examples of this theme as possible, including physical changes at puberty, perceptual changes in aging, moral development, and personality and social development.

2. Elderly people experience some deficits during the aging process, but in other respects, the elderly are similar to younger adults. Discuss this statement with respect to reaction time, perception, memory, and performance on other cognitive tasks.

3. This chapter frequently discusses myths and stereotypes, in which the popular belief does not match reality. Discuss the popular misconceptions—as well as the research—about the following topics: adolescent-parent relationships, midlife crisis, gay people, single people, the elderly, death and dying, and any other topics you can recall.

4. Imagine that you are going to be tutoring a 13-year-old student. Based on what you have read in this chapter, what might you expect about his or her physical development, moral development, career choices, identity development, and interpersonal relationships?

5. Gender is both relevant and irrelevant in the lives of adolescents and adults. Discuss gender comparisons in reactions to puberty, life expectancy, moral judgments, work, love relationships, and parenting.

6. Describe Erikson's last four stages of psychosocial development. Gather information from the sections on work, love relationships, and death and dying to provide more details on the central tasks in each of these four stages.

7. Ethnicity sometimes influences psychological development, but at other times it has little effect. Discuss this statement with respect to adolescent achievement and the status of the elderly.

8. Try to imagine yourself and several good friends (who are approximately your age) when you are 20 years older than now. What would correlational studies on this group of people probably reveal about the stability-change issue? How about studies that assess average level of a personality characteristic? What would you predict from the principle of individual fanning out?

9. What is ageism, and how is it revealed in the media? Discuss how laypeople and professionals demonstrate ageism. Finally, describe how ageism can affect the quality and duration of people's lives.

10. We noted how researchers can reach the wrong conclusion if their study includes confounding variables. Explain how a study on life happiness across the life span might reach an incorrect conclusion if it failed to control several confounding variables. Begin by listing several possible confounding variables.

NEW TERMS

puberty
menarche
dysmenorrhea
premenstrual syndrome (PMS)
ejaculation
menopause
male climacteric
confounding variable
implicit memory
meta-analysis
formal operational period
problem-finding stage
fluid intelligence

crystallized intelligence
preconventional morality
conventional morality
postconventional morality
gay person
homophobia
individual fanning out
self-concept
bicultural efficacy
multiple-jeopardy hypothesis
life review
hospice care
ageism

RECOMMENDED READINGS

Bee, H. L. (1992). *The journey of adulthood* (2nd ed.). New York: Macmillan. Bee's book about adulthood and aging has an engaging writing style and is particularly strong in its coverage of social relationships.

Birren, J. E., & Schaie, K. W. (Eds.). (1990). *Handbook of the psychology of aging* (3rd ed.). San Diego: Academic Press. This comprehensive handbook includes 28 chapters on various aspects of aging, such as theory, perception, memory, creativity, ethnic issues, and ethical problems in research on the elderly.

Nielsen, L. (1991). *Adolescence: A contemporary view* (2nd ed.). Fort Worth: Harcourt Brace Jovanovich. This mid-level textbook on adolescent development covers topics such as physical development, adolescent identity, gender, ethnic factors, and adolescents and their families.

Palmore, E. B. (1990). *Ageism negative and positive*. New York: Springer. If the "In Depth" section of Chapter 11 intrigued you, consult this book for information on the causes of ageism, ageism in institutions, and reducing ageism.

Van Hasselt, V. B., & Hersen, M. (Eds.). (1992). *Handbook of social development: A lifespan perspective*. New York: Plenum. About half of this book focuses on adolescence, adulthood, and old age. Some of the topics include adolescent family interaction, marriage, work, masculine gender roles, and widowhood.

CHAPTER 12
MOTIVATION AND EMOTION

Ashrita Furman, who manages a health food store in Queens, New York, is listed 11 times in the *Guinness Book of World Records*. For example, he set the record for continuous juggling, keeping three balls in the air for 6 hours, 7 minutes, and 4 seconds. He also has set the record for underwater pogo-stick bouncing; he made 3,647 jumps in 3 hours, 40 minutes—in the Amazon River. He also holds the records for long-distance walking with a full milk bottle balanced on his head (70 miles, without a drop spilled) and for continuous somersaulting (12.2 miles).

What motivates Ashrita Furman when many others who manage health food stores would be content to spend their days selling tofu and alfalfa sprouts? The activities are not physically enjoyable. Somersaulting, for instance, made him feel totally dizzy and nauseated. Instead, Ashrita is motivated by the challenge itself. As he commented, "What thrills me is to do something when I'm not even sure it's physically possible" ("Talk of the Town," 1989, p. 26).

Motivation, the first of two topics in this chapter, focuses on *why* people behave in certain ways. Why did you eat a second slice of chocolate fudge cake, when you felt completely full before the first slice? Why does sexual motivation increase for some people when their necks are stroked? And why is Ashrita Furman currently negotiating with the officials in Paris to pogo-stick up the Eiffel Tower? We can define **motivation** as the process of activating behavior, sustaining it, and directing it toward a particular goal.

The second part of this chapter examines emotion. **Emotion** is a subjective experience or feeling that is accompanied by changes in physiological reactions and behavior. Notice, then, that emotion is a complex topic because it involves three components: cognitive, physiological, and behavioral.

Consider how these three components of emotion might operate in a typical emotional situation. You have just received a phone call saying that a close friend has been in an automobile accident. He is in the intensive care unit at the hospital, in critical condition. Your subjective experiences include intense fear and concern, mingled with anxiety and surprise. Physiological reactions include an increase in heart rate and sweating. Behaviorally, your jaw drops, and your eyes widen.

The topics of motivation and emotion are intertwined in a complex fashion. Specifically, emotions are generally responsible for our motivated behavior. For example, your positive emotional reaction to a sexually attractive person motivates you to seek out this individual. Furthermore, while you are pursuing a motivated behavior, you have an emotional reaction. For example, people who are engaging in sexual behavior may experience a mixture of pleasure and guilt. Or consider achievement motivation. When the members of a basketball team are striving for the winning point in the final seconds of the last game of the tournament, they are likely to feel emotions such as anticipation, anger, fear, and joy.

We are often motivated by emotional reactions, even when we know they are irrational. Consider a study by Rozin and his coauthors (1986). College students watched an experimenter open a container of sugar and pour it into two identical bottles. The students were then instructed to take two labels, one marked *sugar* and one marked *sodium cyanide*, and apply one to each bottle, making their own choice. The students later avoided eating the sugar in the bottle marked with the poisonous

Ashrita Furman is listed 11 times in the Guinness Book of World Records. *Among his records is one for long-distance walking with a full milk bottle balanced on his head.*

label, even though they knew the contents could not be poisonous. A strong emotional reaction—perhaps a blend of fear and disgust—had motivated them to choose the other bottle.

Let us begin by considering the topic of motivation. In the second part of the chapter, we will explore emotion.

MOTIVATION

We humans frequently search for motives. The scandal newspaper at the supermarket asks why the wealthy hotel-chain owner cheated on her income tax, or why the New Jersey mother sold her infant twins to buy a sports car for her new boyfriend. On a more literary level, consider the questions your English professor might raise in examining a Shakespearean play. Why did Iago want Othello to believe that his wife, Desdemona, had been unfaithful? Why did Richard III murder the young princes, who were the rightful heirs to the throne?

Human behavior is activated by a variety of motives. Some motives are largely biological, emphasizing bodily needs such as hunger, thirst, and excretion. Others are primarily social motives, such as the needs for achievement, affiliation, and nurturance. We will cover several motives in other chapters. For example, the sleep motive was discussed in Chapter 5, and nurturance was examined in the parenthood section of Chapter 11. Chapter 17 considers affiliation and love, and Chapter 18 discusses aggression.

This chapter explores three representative human motives: hunger, sexuality, and achievement motivation. We begin with the most biological of these topics—hunger—and progress to the most social of the three—achievement motivation. However, we note that even hunger is influenced by social and cognitive factors; clearly, this most basic bodily need is influenced by more complex variables than simple nutritive value.

Hunger and Eating

The Roman Emperor Vitellius, not known for his vegetarian habits, was particularly fond of a stew consisting of flamingo tongues and peacock brains. People in modern-day China savor delicacies such as snake soup, wafer-thin slices of bear paw, and rat kebabs (Liu, 1991). Humans have no simple, universal rules that separate the delightful from the disgusting.

We begin by looking at the biological basis of hunger and eating, and then we consider some external influences in the environment. Our last two topics are obesity and eating disorders.

Biological Factors Regulating Eating Several internal factors trigger hunger and eating. For example, contractions of the empty stomach produce the subjective experience of hunger. However, sensations from the stomach cannot be completely responsible; as the early research demonstrated, people reported that they were hungry even when their stomachs had been removed for medical reasons (Wangensteen & Carlson, 1931). The explanation must be more complex, also involving regulation by both the brain and body chemistry.

In Chapter 3, you learned the hypothalamus is a portion of the brain that regulates eating and other motivated behaviors. The hypothalamus is responsible for **homeostasis**, or maintaining a constant, ideal internal environment (Logue, 1991). The hypothalamus regulates homeostasis for body temperature, liquid intake, and—most important for our current topic—food intake. As we will see, two parts of the hypothalamus work together to help maintain the right balance between eating too little and eating too much.

Lateral hypothalamus

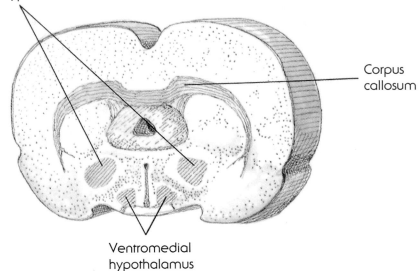

Corpus callosum

Ventromedial hypothalamus

Figure 12.1

The lateral hypothalamus (LH) and the ventromedial hypothalamus (VMH) in the rat's brain (this picture represents the view you would have if the front half of the rat's brain had been cut away).

Figure 12.1 shows the hypothalamus of a rat, the animal used for much of the research on hunger. The hypothalamus consists of several regions that function differently. Let us look at the early research that presented a neat, straightforward explanation for how the hypothalamus regulates eating. Then we consider more recent research showing that eating, like other psychological processes, is far from simple.

The early research suggested that the **lateral hypothalamus** (or **LH,** located at the side of the hypothalamus) functioned as the "start eating" center. That is, mild electrical stimulation of this region in rats caused them to start eating. Furthermore, when the LH was destroyed in other rats, they refused to eat. In contrast, it seemed that the **ventromedial hypothalamus** (or **VMH,** located toward the center of the hypothalamus) functioned as the "stop eating" center. That is, stimulation of this region caused rats to stop eating. Furthermore, as Figure 12.2 shows, when the VMH was destroyed, rats overate wildly until they doubled or tripled their normal weight. Summarizing these studies, one theorist proposed that the LH was the brain's hunger center and the VMH was its fullness or "satiety" center (Stellar, 1954).

However, the true story is more complex than the original theory. For instance, although rats with a destroyed LH refused to eat initially, they could be persuaded to eat eventually if they were first tube-fed and then offered delicacies such as moistened chocolate chip cookies. The rats did not regain their normal weight. However, the research demonstrated that rats can start eating even though they lack a lateral hypothalamus (Teitelbaum & Epstein, 1962).

Furthermore, although rats with a destroyed VMH initially ate huge quantities of food, after about three weeks they ate more normally (Logue, 1991; Weingarten, 1982). In other words, the more current research shows that rats can stop eating even though they lack a ventromedial hypothalamus.

In short, we can conclude that structures involved with the hypothalamus help regulate hunger and eating in order to maintain homeostasis. However, these structures do not operate in a simple on-off fashion (Keesey & Powley, 1986; Logue, 1991).

Body chemistry is another biological factor that regulates hunger and eating. For example, the level of glucose is important. **Glucose** is a simple sugar nutrient that provides energy. In general, when the level of glucose in your bloodstream is low, you feel hungry. When the glucose level is high, you feel full. The blood glucose level appears to be monitored by **glucostats,** neurons that are sensitive to glucose levels. Researchers are not certain where the glucostats are located, but the hypothalamus probably receives their messages about glucose levels.

Figure 12.2

Destruction of the ventromedial hypothalamus in the animal at the top caused it to eat much more. It now weighs about three times as much as the control animal shown at the bottom of the photo.

A second important body chemical, called **cholecystokinin** or **CCK,** is released from the small intestine during eating. This substance also seems to signal the organism to stop eating (e.g., Dourish et al., 1989). However, researchers disagree about the mechanisms for CCK; it may influence receptors in the stomach, or it may travel to the brain (Kalat, 1992).

Still another important body chemical is **insulin,** which is a hormone secreted by the pancreas. Insulin plays an important role in converting blood glucose into stored fat. As you may know, diabetics lack insulin; they must receive insulin injections so that they can use glucose as a source of energy. Insulin therefore influences hunger *indirectly*, by decreasing glucose levels. (See Figure 12.3.)

However, researchers have determined that insulin also influences hunger *directly*. In experiments, participants' blood glucose was maintained at a constant level while insulin injections artificially raised the insulin level (Rodin, 1985). People with elevated insulin levels were likely to report feeling hungry; they typically ate more food than those with a normal insulin level. Later, we will see how insulin rises when people think about food.

External Factors Regulating Eating Although hunger and eating can be influenced by physiological factors, our eating habits are also determined by other factors. Obviously, the taste of a food influences how much we eat. However, we also learn food preferences in our culture (Booth, 1991; Zellner, 1991). For example, my parents recall a Mexican geologist who tried to convince them to try a special delicacy of his region, a worm that lived exclusively in the maguey plant. They politely declined. One day they were eating particularly tasty tacos at his home. As my mother took another bite of her taco, a plump deep-fried worm fell to her plate. A moment earlier, the taco had tasted delicious, but once she realized that it contained a culturally forbidden food, she could not contemplate taking another bite.

Our culture determines not only what we eat, but when we eat. Americans tend to eat their evening meal about 6 p.m., whereas residents of Madrid are likely to begin at 10 p.m. Certainly, the stomach, hypothalamus, glucose, CCK, and insulin do not operate differently in Spain! Instead, learning is an important external factor. Another important external factor is the social situation in which we eat. For example, we typically eat more food in the company of others than when we are alone (Zajonc, 1965).

Obesity In the United States, 24% of men and 27% of women are considered to be obese. **Obesity** means that a person is 20% or more above the desirable weight (Kuczmarski, 1992). We saw that the factors influencing eating are complex, involving both internal and external forces. Similarly, the causes of obesity are complex, involving much more than simple overeating (Brownell & Wadden, 1992). Consider a study in which researchers carefully monitored all the food that two 260-pound women consumed. The researchers concluded that these women were maintaining stable body weights on only 1,000 calories per day, the caloric equivalent of just three peanut butter sandwiches (Wooley et al., 1979). When overweight people claim that they really do not eat excessive amounts, they may indeed be telling the truth.

If food intake cannot fully explain obesity, what can? Several important factors include genetic makeup and metabolism, set point, and an exaggerated insulin response to the sights and smells of food.

Genetic predisposition makes some people more likely than others to become obese (Brownell & Wadden, 1992; Grilo & Pogue-Geille, 1991). For instance, Stunkard and his colleagues (1990) studied identical twins who had been reared in different homes—and therefore ate different food. Still, the twins' body weights were highly correlated with each other ($r = +.72$). Furthermore, Bouchard and his colleagues (1990) found that when identical twins were given extra food for a 12-week period, their weight gains were significantly correlated ($r = +.55$). For example, one twin pair gained 12 and 13 pounds, whereas another twin pair gained 6 and 7 pounds eating the same diet. One inherited factor seems to be **metabolism,** or the energy

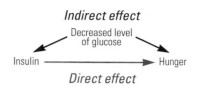

Indirect effect

Decreased level of glucose

Insulin ⟶ Hunger

Direct effect

Figure 12.3
The indirect and direct influence of insulin on hunger.

required to maintain the body; people with slow metabolism gain more weight (Brownell & Wadden, 1992).

A second major explanation for obesity involves the notion called **set point,** a mechanism that seems to keep people at roughly the same weight throughout their adult lives. You probably know some people who try valiantly to lose weight, and with heroic efforts they lose 15 pounds. However, they gain it back several months later, even though they have been eating sensibly ever since the initial weight loss. Sadly, 95% of people who lose weight on a diet will return to their pre-diet weight within five years (Martin et al., 1991).

One of the factors that determines an individual's set point is the number of **fat cells,** which are cells that store fat. Fat cells may shrink in size when an overweight person diets, but their number remains constant. Thus, conscientious dieters may decrease the size of their fat cells, but those cells sit around, waiting for an opportunity to swell up again (Brownell & Wadden, 1992; Sjostrom, 1980). Some researchers propose that the shriveled fat cells send hunger messages to the dieter's brain. As a consequence, dieters are likely to feel that they are continually hungry. To make the situation even worse, when overweight people begin a diet their metabolism often slows down, maintaining body functions by using up fewer calories. Therefore, it is harder to lose weight—and easier to gain it back.

Thus, overweight people may face a losing battle with genetics, set point, fat cells, and metabolism. Some overweight people have an additional handicap because they are particularly sensitive to external cues about eating. Demonstration 12.1 shows some of the characteristics of people who are externals, who eat because of the sight and smell of food, as well as other external cues about eating—rather than internal states of hunger. In a series of studies, Judith Rodin (1981, 1985) tested people who varied in their responsiveness to external food cues. These people went for 18 hours without food and then came to Rodin's laboratory at lunchtime. While blood samples were being drawn, researchers brought in a steak and placed it nearby. The steak was still grilling and crackling in the frying pan, providing a rich source of sights, sounds, and smells to remind these hungry people about food.

As expected from earlier research, thoughts about food produced a rise in insulin level in these hungry participants. Rodin discovered that people who had high scores for responsiveness to external food cues were likely to have especially large insulin responses when exposed to the grilling steak. Furthermore, you know from Fig-

People who are very responsive to external food cues are likely to have larger insulin responses when exposed to a grilling steak.

DEMONSTRATION 12.1   Sensitivity to External Cues About Eating

Answer each of the following questions either "yes" or "no."

_____ 1. If you are at a party, and you are standing near a conspicuous bowl of potato chips, do you begin munching them even though you are not really hungry?

_____ 2. Does an advertisement for food on television send you to the kitchen or other sources of snacks?

_____ 3. When you are in a shopping mall and the unmistakable aroma of chocolate chip cookies assails your senses, do you buy a cookie, even though you have just eaten?

_____ 4. In your home, are you tempted to eat a snack that is in plain view, though you would be safe if it were stored in the refrigerator?

_____ 5. When your watch indicates it is lunchtime, do you automatically go to lunch, even though you had a late breakfast and really are not hungry?

_____ 6. Does the sight of your favorite food make you very hungry and eager to begin eating?

Now count up the number of "yes" responses. In general, people with a large number of "yes" responses are especially sensitive to external eating cues.

TABLE 12.1 Strategies that May Encourage Weight Loss

1. Substitute low-calorie foods for high-calorie foods (e.g., melon for dessert rather than brownies); especially avoid foods that are high in fat.

2. Take moderately small portions, and avoid sitting near additional sources of the food.

3. Become aware of situations that encourage you to overeat (e.g., eat-all-you-want buffet restaurants), and arrange to avoid them.

4. Prior to a problem situation that you cannot avoid, plan a coping strategy (e.g., mentally rehearse how you will select only one cookie from a tray, rather than a handful).

5. If you do slip from time to time, do not condemn yourself and abandon your willpower.

6. Set a modest goal for yourself and reward yourself (but not with food!) if you meet that goal.

7. Exercise to use up more calories; exercise also tends to increase your metabolic rate, which will make it easier to keep the weight off.

ure 12.3 that insulin tends to increase the sensation of hunger, so the people sensitive to external food cues were especially likely to feel hungry. A person with a genetic predisposition toward obesity, who has a slow metabolism, a high set point, and a large number of fat cells already has difficulty losing weight. If this person also has the bad fortune to be responsive to external food cues, he or she will also feel hungrier than most people when tempted by inviting food cues.

Because obesity is not limited to a single cause, we should not expect a single cure. Table 12.1 lists some hints that may encourage weight loss.

Eating Disorders A young woman remarked, "When I say I overeat, it may not be what you think. I feel I'm gorging myself when I eat more than one cracker with peanut butter" (Bruch, 1978, p. 3). To save calories, she even avoided licking postage stamps. This woman has an eating disorder called **anorexia nervosa,** which is characterized by an irrational pursuit of thinness and concern about gaining weight (Sholevar, 1987). Anorexics feel fat, even when they look emaciated. The American Psychiatric Association (1994) specifies that a person can be classified as anorexic if body weight is 15% less than specified on standard weight charts and if no known physical illness accounts for the low weight.

About 95% of people with anorexia nervosa are females, and the most common age for this disorder is 12 to 18 years (American Psychiatric Association, 1994; Hsu, 1990; Polivy & Thomsen, 1988). However, clinicians need to be aware that men and older people can also become anorexic, even though young women are the most common victims.

Anorexics tend to be high achievers who are overly perfectionistic; they are also likely to be depressed and high in anxiety (Bruch, 1988; Hsu, 1990; Sholevar, 1987). How can we interpret this relationship? Like many correlations, we cannot clearly define which is the cause and which is the effect (Chapter 2). For instance, does a depressed person develop anorexia? Alternatively, do anorexics become depressed because of their physiological, starved condition?

Anorexia nervosa is a life-threatening disorder, and 2% to 8% of anorexics die from it (Kreipe et al., 1989). In anorexia, a person is more concerned about thinness than about maintaining a healthy body. As one father told me about his anorexic daughter, "She'd rather be dead than fat."

Bulimia nervosa (pronounced "boo-*lih*-mee-ah") is characterized by binge eating, or episodes in which people consume huge amounts of food. Bulimics also engage in some form of purging, such as vomiting or using laxatives (American Psychiatric Association, 1994). Bulimics may eat up to 50,000 calories at a time. They gobble the food quickly, often with little enjoyment of its taste. Like anorexics, bulimics are obsessed about food, eating, and body weight (Russell, 1990; Schlundt & Johnson, 1990).

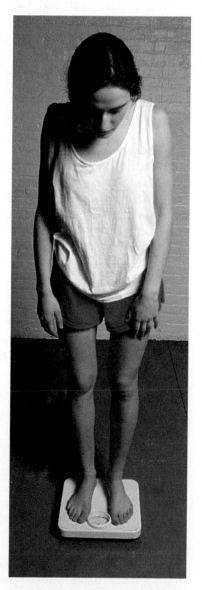

A person with anorexia nervosa has an irrational pursuit of thinness. For example, this young woman probably believes that she is overweight.

For some time, researchers have noticed a correlation between bingeing and dieting. That is, the same people who binge frequently are also likely to place themselves on strict diets when they are not bingeing. Most researchers assumed that bingeing *caused* dieting. However, Polivy and Herman (1985) argue that dieting causes bingeing. In other words, the clear majority of bulimics began restrictive diets *before* they began to binge.

Why should dieters develop bingeing habits? Polivy and Herman (1985) believe that cognitive factors are more important than physiological explanations. Specifically, when dieters temporarily eat too much, they then abandon restraint and begin to eat lustily. In a laboratory study, both dieters and nondieters were required to drink either two high-calorie milkshakes or none at all. Afterward, they were presented with several different kinds of ice cream, and they were encouraged to eat all they wanted.

As Figure 12.4 shows, the dieters actually ate more ice cream after drinking two milkshakes than when they had no milkshake "preload." It is as if the dieters told themselves, "Oh well, those two milkshakes ruined my diet for today . . . I might as well enjoy the ice cream!" This pattern of eating lustily after a high-calorie preload is called **counter-regulation.** In contrast, nondieters show normal regulation: They eat more with no preload than after a large preload.

How can dieters avoid becoming bingers? If they slip temporarily, they should not condemn themselves and abandon their sensible eating habits. More helpful still, our society should place less emphasis on slimness and attractiveness; our culture has strong biases against obese individuals (Rand & MacGregor, 1990; 1991). These biases are especially strong when we make judgments about women. (As you may recall, Chapter 2 showed that even preschoolers think that attractiveness is more important for females than for males.) This glorification of thin women—in fashion magazines, movies, and other media—is one factor in our culture that encourages women to starve themselves (Gordon, 1990; Rodin, 1992). In the long run, people would be healthier if they were a few pounds overweight, rather than beginning a severely restrictive diet that will encourage binge eating.

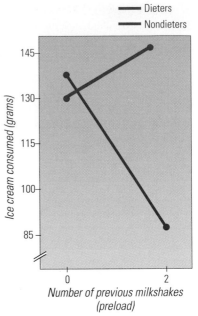

Figure 12.4

Consumption of ice cream as a function of number of previous milkshakes and body-weight category. (Based on Hibscher & Herman, 1977)

Sexuality

Ideas and decisions about sexuality are an important component of many students' daily lives. For example, when students were asked to write about an important current conflict in their lives, one young woman wrote about a controversy that had dominated her relationship with her boyfriend for the last four years:

> *The major issue which has always caused conflict in our relationship is sex. He wants to, I don't; but it's not that simple. . . . I just don't feel I am ready, there are things I want to do for myself first, before I get really deeply involved, and, never one to gamble, I don't want to chance anything. Besides, if something went wrong and if, for example, I got pregnant, I would be the one who was stuck. I have other reasons, though not so easily explained; it's a matter of self-esteem. I was raised in a very traditional environment, and I have my own dreams of how things will be. I want to wait until I am married. I know most people don't agree, they believe it is silly and prudish; but it is part of my moral code, something which I feel very strongly about, and something which is part of the many interwoven, inexplicable things which make up my identity.*

To discuss the topic of sexuality, we need to consider not only people's moral codes, but also topics as diverse as hormone levels and sexual passion. We begin with a discussion of the biological aspects of sexuality, and next discuss external and cognitive factors that influence sexuality. We then study the sexual response cycle and sexually transmitted diseases. In the last section, we consider sexual behavior, including some factors that must be considered whenever a person—such as the young woman quoted above—is making a decision about a sexual relationship.

Sex Hormones In most mammals other than humans, the level of the female hormone estrogen peaks at ovulation. The elevated hormone level makes the female animal sexually receptive (or "in heat"). In contrast, the male hormone level remains relatively constant, and male sexual behavior normally depends more on the presence of a sexually receptive female than on variations in hormone level (Feder, 1984).

In human females and males, hormones are critically important during puberty, as we saw in the last chapter; they are responsible for developing structures that are essential in sexual reproduction, as well as changes in adolescents' bodies. However, hormones are less important in regulating the pattern of sexual behavior. For example, sexual desire and sexual behavior are not significantly higher at the time of ovulation (Harvey, 1987; Wade & Cirese, 1991). Similarly, the day-to-day variation in the level of testosterone in men is generally unrelated to their sexual activity (Byrne, 1982). Hormones are clearly important in humans. However, sexual arousal depends more on external and cognitive cues than on hormone levels.

External and Cognitive Factors Touch is one of the most powerful sources of sexual arousal. A caress, a passionate kiss, or stroking the inside of the thigh . . . people vary in the kind of touch and the location of touch that they find most sexually stimulating.

Humans can also be effectively aroused by visual stimuli, either by the sight of a nude person or by erotic pictures. Research has demonstrated that men and women are similarly aroused when they see slides and movies showing foreplay and intercourse (Hyde, 1990; Schmidt & Sigusch, 1970). However, we need to be concerned about some potential problems with viewing erotic material. For instance, Weaver and his colleagues (1984) found that men who had viewed a video of attractive nude females in provocative poses were likely to rate their girlfriends as less physically attractive. Furthermore, Malamuth and Check (1985) found that men who frequently read sexually explicit magazines were more likely to believe that women enjoy forced sex—a rape myth that is clearly false. (Incidentally, these results are correlational; part of the results may be due to personality differences *before* reading the pornographic magazines.)

Touch and visual stimuli can be sexually arousing. However, human imagination and fantasy can create sexual excitement even without the aid of external stimuli. A saying captures the importance of cognitive factors: "The brain is our most important erogenous zone." As further evidence, researchers estimate that the majority of cases of sexual dysfunction are psychological, lending additional support to the notion that our thoughts play a critical role in sexual arousal and behavior (Hyde, 1990).

The Sexual Response Cycle Current models of the stages of sexual response emphasize cognitive factors. For example, a model proposed by Zilbergeld and Ellison (1980) stresses that sexual interest or desire precedes four more physiological stages of the sexual response cycle that include excitement, plateau, orgasm, and resolution (Masters & Johnson, 1966).

During the **excitement phase,** both women and men become sexually excited. (As we just discussed, a variety of stimuli can produce sexual excitement.) Breathing, heart rate, and muscle tension increase. Blood rushes into the genital region, causing erection in a man's penis and swelling in a woman's clitoris, which is the small, very sensitive organ located in front of the vagina.

In the **plateau phase,** the breathing, heart rate, and muscle tension increase even further. In the man, the penis reaches full erection, and fluid may appear at the tip of the penis. This fluid, however, may contain enough sperm to produce pregnancy. In the woman, the lower one-third of the vaginal wall becomes engorged with blood, and the clitoris becomes extremely sensitive.

In the **orgasmic phase,** muscles in the pelvic region and the genitals contract rhythmically, producing a pleasurable feeling of sexual release. In addition, the man ejaculates, expelling a milky fluid rich in sperm.

Touch is an extremely powerful source of sexual arousal.

During the final, or **resolution phase,** breathing, heart rate, and muscle tension return to normal. The genitals also gradually return to the size they were prior to excitement.

As you can see from this overview, men and women have somewhat similar sexual responses. This physiological similarity was highlighted in the classic research of Masters and Johnson (1966). In addition, men and women have similar psychological reactions to orgasm. Look at Demonstration 12.2 and try to guess whether a man or a woman wrote each description. In one study, people's guesses were no better than chance (Vance & Wagner, 1977). In short, women and men share more similarities than differences—even in the area of sexuality.

Sexually Transmitted Diseases An important source of worry and concern in the 1990s is the threat of sexually transmitted diseases (STDs). Two common ones that have been familiar for several decades are **gonorrhea** (a bacterial disease that infects the genital membranes) and **genital herpes** (a virus that causes bumps and sores in the genital area). **Syphilis** (which produces crater-shaped lesions and can cause blindness and sterility) is becoming increasingly common. For example, the incidence of syphilis increased by 200% in New York State between 1985 and 1990 (Aral & Holmes, 1991; Imperato, 1991).

However, the most dangerous sexually transmitted disease is **AIDS** or **Acquired Immunodeficiency Syndrome,** a disease that destroys the body's natural immunity. Once the immune system has been destroyed, diseases such as pneumonia and cancer can take over, leading eventually to death. Roughly 230,000 U.S. residents had died of AIDS by the end of 1993 (Surgeon General's Report, 1993). Chapter 19 (Health

---

DEMONSTRATION 12.2 Psychological Reactions to Orgasm

Each of these descriptions of an orgasm was written by a sexually experienced woman or man. Based on your ideas about gender, try to guess who wrote each passage. Place a W or an M in front of each description. The answers appear at the end of the chapter.

_____ 1. A sudden feeling of lightheadedness followed by an intense feeling of relief and elation. A rush. Intense muscular spasms of the whole body. Sense of euphoria followed by deep peace and relaxation.

_____ 2. To me an orgasmic experience is the most satisfying *pleasure* that I have experienced in relation to any other type of satisfaction or pleasure that I've had which were nonsexually oriented.

_____ 3. It is like turning a water faucet on. You notice the oncoming flow but it can be turned on or off when desired. You feel the valves open and close and the fluid flow. An orgasm makes your head and body tingle.

_____ 4. A build-up of tension which starts to pulsate very fast, and there is a sudden release from the tension and desire to sleep.

_____ 5. It is a pleasant, tension-relieving muscular contraction. It relieves physical tension and mental anticipation.

_____ 6. A release of a very high level of tension, but ordinarily tension is unpleasant whereas the tension before orgasm is far from unpleasant.

_____ 7. An orgasm is a great release of tension with spasmodic reaction at the peak. This is exactly how it feels to me.

_____ 8. A building of tension, sometimes, and frustration until the climax. A *tightening* inside, palpitating rhythm, explosion, and warmth and peace.

Source: From Vance & Wagner, 1977, pp. 207–210.

Psychology) considers AIDS in more detail. As we will see in that chapter, both heterosexual and gay people place their lives at risk by practicing unsafe sex.

Sexual Behavior Our earlier discussion of the sexual response cycle emphasized swelling genitals, heavy breathing, and beating hearts. But sexuality is much more complex than the physiological processes might imply, as we see when we shift our attention to this area.

A colleague recalled her graduate school professor saying that anything capable of a great deal of good is also capable of a great deal of harm (Smith, 1990). This statement clearly applies to sexuality. Under ideal circumstances, a sexual relationship can provide intense pleasure and feelings of intimacy. However—as described by the young woman at the beginning of this section—it can also lead to loss of self-esteem and worry.

Heterosexual individuals have an important responsibility; they must make thoughtful and informed decisions about pregnancy. Figure 12.5 shows the pregnancy rates for teenage women in five countries. As you can see, the rate in the United States for 1985 was roughly double the rate in Canada and Sweden (Jones, 1985). Currently in the United States, one out of ten teenage females becomes pregnant each year (National Center for Health Statistics, 1993). Each pregnant teenager faces a personal struggle, whether she chooses to have an abortion, to give up the child for adoption, or to spend the next 20 years raising the child.

Studies have demonstrated that teenagers are amazingly uninformed about important aspects of sexuality (Morrison, 1985). For instance, some believe that they cannot get pregnant the first time they have intercourse. Moreover, even well-informed teenagers (and adults, too) may make an important cognitive error: They believe that the statistics about pregnancy rates without the use of contraceptives apply to *other* people, not to themselves (Morrison, 1985). As Hayes (1987) concludes, numerous factors contribute to the incidence of unplanned pregnancy.

We have noted some of the negative aspects of sexuality. We need to discuss one other unpleasant topic relevant to some relationships—coercive sexual interactions. **Sexual coercion** involves forcing someone to have sex against her (or his) will (Allgeier, 1987).

The most extreme example of sexual coercion is **rape,** which is sexual intercourse that is forcibly committed, without consent (Hilberman, 1978). Rape can be committed by a stranger, but data show that people who have been raped are likely to know those who raped them (Katz & Mazur, 1979; Matlin, 1993a). Unfortunately,

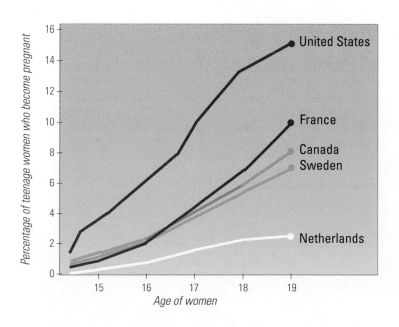

Figure 12.5

The rate of teenage pregnancies in the United States is substantially greater than the rate in other comparable countries.

(Source: Jones, 1985)

most cases of acquaintance rape go unreported (Koss et al., 1988). Consider the case of a young woman who had four previous dates with a male student at her college. On the fifth date, after fairly intensive sex play, he forced her to have sex, despite her objections. In a survey of college women, 28% reported a sexual experience that met the legal definition of rape (Koss et al., 1987). Rape and other forms of sexual assault are more common than most people believe. For example, in a recent survey of 12,300 Canadian women over the age of 18, 39% said that someone had either forced or attempted to force them into sexual activity by using threats or physical force ("Violence Against Women Survey," 1993).

Whereas rape involves physical violence or threatened violence, other kinds of sexual coercion involve different threats, such as "Sleeping with me is the best way to get that promotion." This is an extreme example of **sexual harassment,** or an unwelcome sexual advance, request for sexual favors, or other verbal or physical conduct of a sexual nature (Equal Employment Opportunity Commission, 1980). Table 12.2 lists some examples of rape and sexual harassment.

In coercive relationships, one person has more power than another. In contrast, **consensual sexual interactions** are defined as participation in sexual relationships "by fully informed adults who freely choose to engage in mutual sexual stimulation" (Allgeier, 1987, p. 11). When two mature people respect each other (and when neither feels guilty about the relationship), sexual interactions can offer uniquely positive pleasures. Most of you reading this book will be making—and have made—decisions about sexuality, and no book can make the decision for you. Any decision in the 1990s must take into account the possibilities of both pregnancy and life-threatening disease. However, as Allgeier (1987, p. 11) writes, "Humans are blessed with a potential capacity for experiencing intense intimacy and connection, not to mention exquisite sensations, in the context of their sexual interactions with one another."

Sexual harassment is a problem in the workplace and in academic settings. This woman probably feels that the man is standing too close to her. However, if he is her boss, she may feel she should not complain.

TABLE 12.2 Examples of Rape and Sexual Harassment

RAPE

- A college sophomore attends a party, where she meets an attractive male who also seems to be a student. After dancing together for about 15 minutes, he suggests that they go outside to cool off. Once outside, he throws her down, knocks her out, and rapes her.

- A 67-year-old woman answers her door to find a man who says he is from a delivery company. He begins beating her head with a wrench, rapes her, and steals her TV and jewelry.

- A 13-year-old girl leaves her home in the early evening to go to the corner store. A stranger grabs her, forces her to the ground, and rapes her.

SEXUAL HARASSMENT

- A woman takes a summer job in a restaurant. Her boss has been patting her and making suggestive comments for about a week, and then he suggests that they go to a motel after work that evening.

- A student at a community college is learning how to use a new machine. The instructor puts his hand on her inner thigh as he explains how to use the machine.

- A student at a university is taking a course required for her major. Last week she needed to talk to the course instructor about her paper, and he seemed too friendly, asking questions she thought were too personal. He asked her to come back today. This time, he says he would like to go to bed with her. She is repulsed by the idea, but she is afraid he may fail her in the course if she declines.

Note: Sexual coercion includes all cases of rape. However, Allgeier's (1987) definition of sexual coercion would exclude cases of sexual harassment that do not involve sexual intercourse, oral sex, or anal sex. Furthermore, males may be victims of rape or sexual harassment, although most victims are females.

Source: Examples based on Brownmiller, 1975; Burgess & Holmstrom, 1980; Dziech & Weiner; 1990.

Achievement Motivation

Neil Rudenstine's father worked as a prison guard, and his mother is still a waitress. Neither parent had much formal education, yet they instilled a love of learning in their children. Neil was the first person in the family to complete high school, but his academic career did not stop there. He went on to Princeton to receive a bachelor's degree, and then to Harvard for his PhD. In 1991, he became the 26th president of Harvard University (McMillen, 1991).

Rudenstine is clearly high in the **achievement motive,** which involves doing well relative to a standard of excellence and succeeding at a challenging task (Reeve, 1992). People who are achievers think about doing things well, even when there is no stimulus to excel (McClelland, 1985). Our discussion of the two other motives, hunger and sexuality, examined underlying physiological components. Researchers in achievement motivation have not developed physiological explanations; instead, cognitive components are critical.

In this section, we begin by examining individual differences in achievement motivation, followed by a discussion of gender comparisons in achievement motivation. We then consider how reward can sometimes decrease achievement-related behavior. Our final topic explores the relationship between achievement motivation and emotion.

Persistence is an important characteristic of people high in achievement motivation.

Individual Differences in Achievement Motivation In previous decades, achievement motivation was usually measured with an assessment instrument called the Thematic Apperception Test (TAT), which Chapter 14 will consider in detail. If you were to take the TAT, you would write a brief story about a series of ambiguous pictures. Your stories would be coded according to your emphasis on certain themes, such as your concern about achievement. In more recent research, achievement motivation is usually assessed by responses on questionnaires.

As you might expect, people who are high in achievement motivation are likely to be superior students, performing well on examinations (Atkinson & Raynor, 1974). They are also extremely persistent, even when they are working on a task that cannot actually be solved (French & Thomas, 1958; Reeve, 1992).

In addition, high achievers prefer being personally responsible for a project. When they are directly responsible, they feel satisfaction from a task well done. In contrast, they cannot be proud of a project where chance alone determines success (McClelland, 1985). Individuals with high achievement motivation also seek out situations where they can receive feedback on their performance (McClelland, 1985).

High achievers also prefer to work on more difficult tasks than low achievers. For example, Slade and Rush (1991) asked college students to work on a task that involved responding to dials on a simulated aircraft instrument panel. Each person could select one of five difficulty levels, and everyone continued for 13 blocks of four trials each. Based on test scores, the students had been previously classified as either high achievers or low achievers. As you can see from Figure 12.6, the two groups made similar choices for the first six blocks. However, the low achievers then became less ambitious, whereas the high achievers continued to select the more difficult tasks.

Now that you have learned some of the important characteristics of people who are high in achievement motivation, you can informally assess your own achievement motivation level by trying Demonstration 12.3.

Gender Comparisons in Motivation Related to Achievement In Chapter 11, we saw that women and men often pursue different careers, with relatively few women pursuing careers in fields such as engineering. As Kahn and Yoder (1989) explain, numerous psychologists have tried to explain women's absence in many areas in terms of personal "deficiencies" that inhibit their achievement.

In reality, however, men and women are similar in most characteristics related to achievement motivation. For example, men and women are similar in their achievement motive (Crew, 1982; Spence & Helmreich, 1983; Stewart & Chester, 1982).

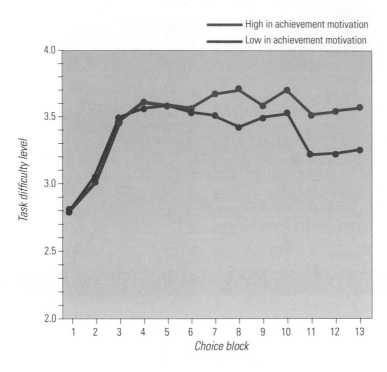

Figure 12.6

Average difficulty of task choices, according to level of achievement motivation.

(*Source:* Slade & Rush, 1991)

For many years, psychologists believed that women were more likely than men to be high in **fear of success,** or worrying that success in competitive achievement situations would lead to unpleasant consequences such as unpopularity (e.g., Horner, 1968, 1972). However, more recent research finds no major gender differences in fear of success (e.g., Heckhausen et al., 1985; Paludi, 1984). Instead, fear of success can limit achievement in both women and men who are trying to succeed in an area that is nontraditional for their gender.

DEMONSTRATION 12.3 Informal Assessment of Achievement Motivation

Naturally, a quick test cannot accurately measure any quality as complex as achievement motivation. However, answer each of the following questions honestly with a "yes" or "no."

_____ 1. Do you enjoy doing tasks well, even when no one tells you to do a good job?

_____ 2. Do you feel great satisfaction in mastering a difficult task that you were not sure could be done?

_____ 3. Is success especially pleasurable when you have competed against other people?

_____ 4. Are you a good student (for instance, were you in the top 10% of your high-school class)?

_____ 5. When you are working on a difficult task, do you persist even when you run into roadblocks?

_____ 6. Do you prefer a task for which you have personal responsibility, rather than one where chance plays an important role?

_____ 7. Do you like receiving feedback about how well you are doing when you are working on a project?

_____ 8. When given a choice of several tasks, would you pick one that is moderately challenging, rather than very easy or very difficult?

In general, people with a large number of "yes" answers tend to be high in achievement motivation, based on previous research (e.g., McClelland, 1985). Keep in mind, however, that overgeneralizations should not be made on the basis of a single, informal quiz.

Fear of success is as big an obstacle for a male trying to succeed in a feminine area as it is for a female trying to succeed in a masculine area.

One area in which gender differences sometimes emerge is in self-confidence. We know that women and men are similarly self-confident on tasks considered feminine, when the instructions do not emphasize competition, and when clear feedback is provided (Lenney, 1977; Matlin, 1993a). However, in other cases, men may be more self-confident than women. Furthermore, women's self-confidence appears to be more influenced by the comments of others, whereas men's self-confidence remains more stable (Roberts, 1991; Roberts & Nolen-Hoeksema, 1989).

Men and women may differ on some components of achievement motivation. However, the differences are not large enough to explain the striking differences in career choices—such as only 2% of carpenters and 7% of engineers being female (U.S. Department of Labor, 1989). Instead, the explanation is more likely to involve the kinds of gender stereotypes observed in young children (Chapter 10) and also in adults (Chapters 11 and 17).

The Paradoxical Effects of Reward on Achievement As a high-school junior, Roger volunteered after school in a facility for profoundly retarded children. He enjoyed helping people who could not accomplish much on their own, and he felt gratified when, after hours of training, a child finally mastered a task. The following summer, one staff member left suddenly and the facility was able to pay Roger for his work. However, when a permanent replacement was hired, Roger was told that the funds were no longer available to pay him, but he was welcome to work as a volunteer again. Roger politely declined; he was no longer interested in volunteering. Reward, in the form of a salary, had decreased Roger's original enthusiasm for his work.

The explanation of the paradoxical effect of reward involves **intrinsic motivation,** which is the desire to perform an activity for its own sake. People are likely to do something—and to do it well—when they find it inherently enjoyable (Deci & Ryan, 1990; Graef et al., 1983). In contrast, **extrinsic motivation** is the desire to perform an activity because of external rewards.

The problem is that extrinsic motivation can undermine intrinsic motivation. When people are intrinsically motivated to work on a task, and then they are offered an external reward—such as salary—intrinsic motivation often declines (Deci & Ryan, 1985). For instance, Roger's intrinsic motivation in working with the retarded children probably decreased once he began receiving a salary. Later when the external reward is no longer available (for instance, when Roger could no longer receive a salary), people no longer spontaneously work on the task. Without that extrinsic motivation, and with reduced intrinsic motivation, the task is no longer appealing. A simple operant conditioning approach (Chapter 6) suggests that reinforcement or reward should increase the probability of performing a task. An appreciation of human complexity, however, shows that reward can backfire.

A classic study by Deci (1971) illustrates how reward can decrease intrinsic motivation. In this experiment, students worked on an interesting puzzle called Soma for each of three sessions. During the first session, both the experimental and the control groups were introduced to the puzzle. Then the experimenter left the students alone for 8 minutes to see how long each group spent spontaneously playing with the puzzle. (Some current popular magazines were also available to read.) During the second session, the experimental manipulation was introduced: Students in the experimental group were told that they would receive $1 for every correct solution they produced with the Soma puzzle. The students in the control group received no payment. Theoretically, the external reward should decrease intrinsic motivation for the experimental group, but intrinsic motivation should remain high for the control group.

Everyone returned for a third session, for which neither group received pay. Figure 12.7 shows how students in the experimental group showed a substantial decline in the amount of time they spent spontaneously playing with the puzzle, relative to the control group and relative to their own previous time spent with the puzzle. As you can see, the people in the experimental group spent less time on the puzzle in Session 3 than in Session 1. In contrast, the people in the control group actually spent more time in Session 3 than in Session 1. Reward seemed to decrease intrinsic interest in the puzzle for those in the experimental group.

More recent research has identified a variety of other factors that can decrease intrinsic motivation—aside from payment for appropriate performance. Specifically, intrinsic motivation is likely to decrease when other people set deadlines, impose goals, and watch or evaluate performance (Deci & Ryan, 1990).

However, some rewards can—fortunately—increase intrinsic motivation (Deci & Ryan, 1985, 1987). If someone tries to use a *controlling* reward, for instance by offering a concrete reward such as money, intrinsic motivation is likely to decline. In contrast, if he or she uses an *informational* reward, by offering positive feedback that informs you about performance, intrinsic motivation is likely to rise. In other words, teachers are likely to enhance the intrinsic motivation of their students by congratulating them ("Superb essay, John—good organization of the three major themes"). In contrast, giving the top student a $5 award may actually decrease that student's enthusiasm in achievement for its own sake.

How Achievement Motivation Produces Emotions At the beginning of the chapter, we noted that emotions can sometimes stimulate motivation, and motivations can also produce emotions. Bernard Weiner (1985a, 1989) specifically focuses on the second issue, arguing that achievement motivation can lead both directly and indirectly to emotions. For example, if you do well on an examination, your direct reaction is positive emotions (e.g., "I am happy"). In addition, however, you make an **attribution,** or causal explanation for your success or failure. If you explain your success on an examination by saying that the high score is due to your ability, you will indirectly experience a second emotion—confidence—in addition to happiness. In contrast, if you explain your success in terms of luck, the second emotion is likely to be surprise.

Notice how the research on achievement motivation has evolved. The early research identified individual differences and situations that encouraged achievement. The studies by Deci and his colleagues shifted the emphasis to cognitive interpretations and intrinsic motivation. Finally, Weiner's work emphasizes cognitive interpretations of achievement and also notes that these interpretations have important emotional consequences.

General Theories of Motivation

We have explored three different kinds of motivation: hunger, sexuality, and achievement. We have seen that hunger and sexuality involve some biological factors, but cognitive and social factors are crucial in all three areas. Let us now consider several theoretical approaches to all motivated behavior, not limiting ourselves to the three topics we have discussed. Why do we act? What energizes our behavior, sustains it, and directs it toward a certain goal? Earlier in the century, theorists argued that motivation could be explained by **instincts,** which are inborn, internal forces that make organisms behave in predictable ways (e.g., McDougall, 1908). In this chapter, we consider four more current approaches to motivation. In Chapter 13, we will examine a fifth important approach—Maslow's hierarchy of needs—in connection with Maslow's humanistic theory of personality.

Drive Theories In the first half of this century, two very different kinds of psychologists argued that motivation could be explained by the concept of **drive,** which is the psychological energy from unmet needs that propels the organism to action (Weiner, 1991). Sigmund Freud, with his psychoanalytic approach to personality and psychological disorders, argued that we humans are motivated by two important drives, sex and aggression. Clark Hull, who conducted laboratory research with rats, maintained that humans and other animals are motivated by four drives—hunger, thirst, sex, and the avoidance of pain. As Deci and Ryan (1985) point out, it is intriguing that two such different traditions converged on such similar approaches. Both argued that internal forces push us to act and to reduce these drives.

Although drive theory may explain many aspects of thirst and hunger motivation, it does not provide all the answers. For example, how would it explain counter-regulation, in which dieters eat more after two milkshakes than after no preload? Neither Hull's nor Freud's approach answers why humans are curious. What kind of drive would explain why you peek through a hole at a construction site or why you have trouble handing your roommate a postcard without looking to see who sent it? Furthermore, neither approach explains achievement motivation—let alone subtleties such as the paradoxical effects of reward.

In short, drive theory has lost popularity during the second half of the century as cognitive approaches have become more prominent. Currently, most psychologists acknowledge that humans are conscious organisms who think, plan ahead, and figure out how to reach their goals (Geen, 1984).

Opponent-Process Theory Several years ago, a tightrope walker attracted some notoriety in New York City. On several occasions, he managed secretly to set up a tightrope between two buildings, high above the city streets. Crowds would gather to watch him teeter precariously and then land safely on the adjacent building . . .

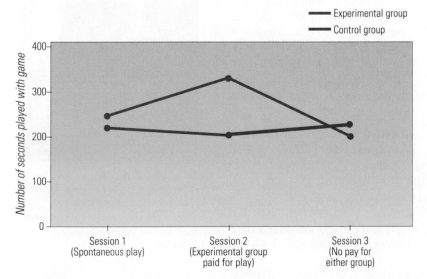

Figure 12.7

The amount of time spent playing with puzzle, as a function of presence or absence of external reward. (Based on Deci, 1971)

Opponent-process theory would argue that these skydivers' terror in risking their lives would trigger an extremely positive emotional response.

only to be led off in handcuffs by the New York City police. (As it turns out, tightrope walking between buildings is illegal.) What could possibly motivate such a bizarre activity? Sex, aggression, hunger, thirst? Not really. Avoidance of pain? Certainly not!

Richard Solomon (1980) proposes that the motivation for many behaviors can be explained by **opponent-process theory,** which argues that one emotional state will trigger an opposite emotional state that lasts long after the original emotion has disappeared. As Kimble (1990) points out, opponent-process theory is part of a general tendency for excitation and inhibition to balance each other in an organism, a tendency we saw earlier in the discussion of homeostasis and the hypothalamus.

Solomon's opponent-process theory has important applications, particularly in explaining the motivations of people who enjoy risky behavior. For example, the terror of teetering above New York City crosstown traffic triggers an ecstatically positive emotional response . . . an ecstasy that persists while our hero is marched off to jail. Indeed this ecstasy will motivate him to attempt other, similar escapades in the future. Opponent-process theory also proposes that this positive emotional response will grow stronger with each tightrope episode, providing additional motivation for engaging in this unusual activity.

Another interesting area that has been studied in humans is blood donation. As people prepare to give blood for the first time, anxiety produces a negative emotional reaction. This reaction triggers an opposite, positive emotional state as soon as they have donated blood (Piliavin et al., 1982). Each time they donate blood in the future, anxiety diminishes somewhat, and the positive response grows even stronger. As a consequence, the motivation to donate blood increases further.

Opponent-process theory explains why people learn to enjoy many events that are initially unpleasant. As Reeve (1992) explains, these include the enjoyment of riding on a terrifying roller coaster, eating a painfully hot chili pepper, and diving into near-freezing water.

Intrinsic Motivation In the section on achievement motivation, we discussed how some kinds of reward can decrease intrinsic motivation. However, in that discussion we did not really examine the nature of intrinsic motivation, which is the third theoretical approach to motivation to be discussed here. This approach provides additional evidence for the connection between motivation and emotion.

The concept of intrinsic motivation was originally proposed by Robert White (1959), who argued that many behaviors such as play and exploration do not need to be reinforced in order to be performed. White also argued that people—even young

Robert White—and others who believed that many human activities are intrinsically motivating—have argued that children feel pride in their accomplishments.

children—have an internal force that encourages them to be competent and effective. For instance, I recall one of my daughters, at age 1, playing with an old footstool that she had turned upside down. She would climb in and beam with pride at her accomplishment; then she would climb out, grinning once again about her sense of mastery. She did not look to her parents for approval. Competent interaction with her environment was its own reward (Deci & Ryan, 1985).

Researchers have discovered that enjoyment in life is correlated with experiencing daily activities as intrinsically motivating. As a math professor once remarked, "I love my work so much that every morning I leave my house and say, 'Just imagine getting paid for something that's so much fun!'" In one study, 107 working men and women rated the extent to which their work was intrinsically motivating, as well as their sense of well-being (Graef et al., 1983). The correlation between intrinsic motivation and happiness was +.28, which was statistically significant.

Try noticing how often you do activities because they are intrinsically motivating, rather than because they reduce some drive or accomplish some goal. Do you look out the window at an interesting sight? When pursuing a word in the dictionary, are you distracted into reading an irrelevant definition (even though you do not expect any reward from knowing the meaning of words such as *peplum,* or *centaury,* or *hendecagon*)? When you see a couple together in a restaurant, do you strain to hear their conversation because you are curious whether they are well acquainted or on their first date? This curiosity cannot be explained by drive or opponent-process theory. However, at least for some people, it is intrinsically motivating.

Incentive Theory We have explored three approaches to motivation that emphasize internal forces within the organism. A person or an animal is motivated to act because of a driving tension, an emotional state triggering an opposite emotional state, or some internal force that encourages competence and inquiry.

In contrast, **incentive theory** emphasizes how external goals motivate us to respond and to act. An incentive occurs before we actually do something, and it energizes us to do something—if the incentive is attractive—or *not* to do something—if the incentive is unattractive (Reeve, 1992). Incentive theory is consistent with the principles of operant conditioning discussed in Chapter 6.

Incentive theory explains some aspects of achievement motivation. A student is motivated by the incentive of good grades, an executive is motivated by the incentive of a raise, and a college instructor is motivated by the incentive of a promotion. Incentive theory argues that the probability of engaging in a particular activity depends both on the *expectation* of obtaining a particular goal and the *value* of that goal. For example, you are likely to study for a biology exam if you expect that studying will lead to a high grade and if that grade is valuable to you.

We have reviewed four general theoretical explanations for motivated behavior. In many areas of motivation, we can compare several theoretical approaches. We would rarely conclude that one approach is entirely correct and all others are entirely wrong. The complexity of human motivation suggests that the drive approach is limited. Opponent-process theory may have application for some puzzling kinds of behavior. However, most human motivation seems best explained by more subtle and all-encompassing approaches such as intrinsic motivation and incentive theory.

SECTION SUMMARY

MOTIVATION

- Motivation and emotion are intertwined; emotion leads to motivation, and motivated behavior produces emotion.

- Hunger is partially regulated by biological factors such as stomach contractions, hypothalamic activity, and levels of glucose, CCK, and insulin, but external factors such as culture and social setting are also important.

- Explanations for obesity include food intake, genetic predisposition and metabolism, set point, and insulin responses to external cues.

- Anorexia nervosa is a life-threatening pursuit of thinness; bulimia nervosa involves binge eating and purging and may be encouraged by dieting.

- In human sexuality, external and cognitive cues are more important determinants of arousal than hormones.

- In both women and men, the sexual response cycle includes several phases: sexual interest, excitement, plateau, orgasm, and resolution.

- Important topics concerned with sexual behavior include sexually transmitted diseases, the risk of pregnancy, and sexual coercion, as well as the sense of intimacy and connectedness that are part of consensual sexual interactions.

- People who are high in achievement motivation are likely to be good students who are persistent; they prefer tasks for which they can take personal responsibility and tasks that provide feedback and are challenging.

- Men and women are similar in their achievement motive and fear of success, but gender differences sometimes emerge in self-confidence.

- Intrinsic motivation may decrease when people receive controlling rewards and when others set deadlines, impose goals, and watch or evaluate performance.

- Achievement motivation produces emotions both directly and indirectly.

- Four current theoretical explanations for motivation include drive, opponent processes, intrinsic motivation, and incentive theory.

EMOTION

Imagine the ending of the opera *Rigoletto* drained of its emotions. Rigoletto is determined to kill the Duke of Mantua, who has seduced Rigoletto's precious daughter, Gilda. In the dark, the hired assassin stabs someone in man's attire. Rigoletto discovers that it is Gilda, instead of the Duke. In the emotion-drained version, he calmly pronounces, "Gosh, we should have checked more carefully." Or consider the soap opera "As the World Turns." Connor tells Cal that she's pregnant with his child, but Cal believes that the baby she's carrying is really Linc's. In the emotion-drained version, the two discuss the matter dispassionately and conclude that the father's identity doesn't really matter. Without emotions, our lives would be dominated by cold cognitions, filmed in black and white instead of passionate purple and vibrant turquoise.

As we noted at the beginning of the chapter, the emotions in our daily lives are rich, complicated experiences. These complicated experiences include cognitive, physiological, and behavioral reactions. For instance, try to recall the last time you experienced a particularly positive emotion. Can you reconstruct your cognitive, subjective experience? What were your physiological reactions—can you recall your heart beating faster? Did your behavioral reaction include a change in facial expression, and did you rush to share your good news with someone else?

We will begin the discussion of emotion by considering these three components of emotion—cognitive, physiological, and behavioral. You may recall the three different methods of measuring psychological responses, discussed in Chapter 2: self-report (a cognitive assessment), behavioral measures, and physiological measures. Our fourth topic is an "In Depth" examination of the effects of mood on cognitive processes. We end with a discussion of various theories of emotion.

Many remaining chapters in this textbook also discuss some aspect of emotion. For instance, Chapters 15 and 16 examine mood disorders and therapy for these disorders. Chapters 17 and 18 frequently discuss our emotional reactions to other people. Finally, Chapter 19 considers how stress influences health.

Cognitive Emotional Reactions

Psychologists can assess physiological reactions with equipment that measures breathing rate and blood pressure, and they can assess behavioral reactions in terms of facial expressions. But how do they measure people's *thoughts* about their emotions? Psychologists have not devised any perfectly objective measure that firmly establishes whether a person is experiencing joy, sorrow, or embarrassment. Similarly, psychologists interested in perception have not devised any perfectly objective way of assessing whether a person is experiencing the colors blue or red—yet perception researchers eagerly investigate color phenomena. Likewise, psychologists interested in emotion continue their work without clearly objective measures; most psychologists believe that people's self-reports are accurate reflections of their true feelings (Ortony et al., 1988; Scherer, 1986).

Psychologists frequently ask research participants to rate themselves on mood scales, using emotional terms such as *elated, angry,* and *fearful* (Mayer et al., 1991). You will see examples of research using rating scales in the "In Depth" section of this chapter, as well as in later chapters. These rating scales are also common in the assessment of **subjective well-being,** or a person's evaluation of his or her life (Diener & Diener, 1993).

In general, subjective well-being is not correlated with demographic variables such as age, gender, ethnic group, and education (Diener, 1984; Eysenck, 1990; Fujita et al., 1991; Myers, 1992). Also, people who have physical disabilities are not substantially less happy than other people (Diener & Diener, 1993; Eysenck, 1990).

Subjective well-being is somewhat correlated with income (Diener et al., 1993; Eysenck, 1990; Myers, 1992). For instance, people in relatively wealthy countries—such as Canada, Switzerland, and the United States—are significantly happier than people in relatively poor countries—such as Portugal and Greece. Within a particular country, income and happiness are correlated only up to a certain point. However, beyond the income necessary to buy the essentials, extra money does not buy extra happiness.

Other factors are more important than income in determining subjective well-being. These include such factors as having a warm, intimate love relationship and supportive friends, being healthy, and having a challenging, satisfying job (Myers, 1992). Interestingly, all of these important factors match our commonsense impressions; the factors that are *not* correlated with happiness are more surprising.

Research demonstrates that people with physical disabilities are similar to other people in their subjective well-being.

Cognitive judgments are important not only in evaluating an emotional reaction. On many occasions, they are also crucial in determining our emotional experiences. For example, George Mandler (1984, 1990) writes that emotions are related to schemas. As Chapter 7 noted, a **schema** is a generalized idea about objects, people, and events. For example, you have a schema for the events involved in buying a ticket to a concert. Mandler points out that we experience emotion when something prevents us from completing that schema. For example, imagine your emotional reaction in this situation. You decide to buy a ticket to a concert. You arrive at 11 A.M., and the line is moving forward at a regular pace. All the events match your schema until at 12:00 noon—when you are now first in line—the ticket-seller closes the window and smugly adjusts a sign saying, OFFICE CLOSED UNTIL 1 P.M. Disruption of the "ticket-buying schema" produces the emotional response of anger.

According to these cognitive explanations, we experience emotions when our goals are interrupted and also when they are achieved (Oatley, 1992; Oatley & Johnson-Laird, 1987). In addition, we appraise the significance of these events and try to figure out how they will affect our well-being (Lazarus, 1991a). We will note later in this chapter that we often do not need to use elaborate thought processes in order to experience emotion; however, they sometimes play an important role.

Physiological Emotional Reactions

In Chapter 3 we discussed the **autonomic division** of the nervous system, which helps control the glands, blood vessels, and internal organs. The autonomic nervous system has two components that respond in different ways to emotional experiences. In a frightening situation, the sympathetic system prepares your body for action. Your heart beats faster, your pupils widen, and you sweat and blush. The sympathetic nervous system directs the release of the substances epinephrine and norepinephrine. When the danger has passed, the parasympathetic nervous system restores your body to its normal state. It slows your heartbeat, constricts your pupils, and inhibits the further release of epinephrine and norepinephrine.

In Chapter 3, we also noted that the limbic system plays a central role in emotional experiences. (See Figure 3.15.) Recent research by LeDoux (1987, 1989) points to the amygdala as a key part of the limbic system. The amygdala receives information from the cortex, but also from brain regions that are involved in more primitive information processing, such as the thalamus (Derryberry & Tucker, 1992). This "early warning" from the thalamus allows you to respond to the first signs of danger, even before your cortex can analyze the information more completely. For example, if you are walking late at night and suddenly see a shape moving behind you, the amygdala responds to this early warning. At a more leisurely speed, the cortex can analyze whether the shape is dangerous or friendly.

Recent neuroscience research also demonstrates that the two hemispheres of the brain respond differently to positive and negative emotions (Davidson et al., 1990; Fox, 1991). For example, when 10-month-olds smile with delight as their mothers approach, their EEGs show greater activity in the left hemisphere. In contrast, when 10-month-olds act distressed if a stranger approaches, the right hemisphere is more active. Thus, even infants show a pattern of hemispheric specialization, a pattern that persists into adulthood—as we saw in Chapter 3.

We have seen that the autonomic nervous system and structures in the brain are responsible for processing emotions. Let us now consider several physiological measures of emotion and then discuss a practical application: Are lie detection tests useful?

Physiological Measures People who study the biological components of emotion usually collect certain measures of activity in the autonomic nervous system. These measures may include heart rate, finger temperature, skin conductance (which measures skin perspiration), pulse, breathing rate, and muscular tension (Levenson et al., 1992). In general, heart rate is the most accurate in discriminating

If you were walking in a dark area and saw this shape, your amygdala would immediately respond, even before the cortex could analyze whether the shape is dangerous.

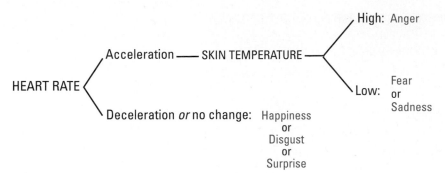

Figure 12.8

A "decision tree" for discriminating emotions, based on research by Ekman and his coauthors (1983).

among emotions, whereas muscle tension is the worst. However, even the best measures are far from consistent (Zajonc & McIntosh, 1992). A particular emotion—such as fear—is not systematically associated with specific increases and decreases in the measures.

Research indicates that autonomic nervous system activity can distinguish among several emotions, but not all of them. For instance, Ekman and his colleagues (1983) asked professional actors to move specific muscles in their faces in order to produce facial expressions that were consistent with six different emotions: happy, disgusted, surprised, angry, afraid, and sad. Measurements of heart rate and finger temperature allowed the researchers to distinguish three different subgroups of emotions, as shown in Figure 12.8.

Notice that anger is the only emotion associated with accelerated heart rate and high skin temperature. However, both fear and sadness are associated with accelerated heart rate and low skin temperature (Levenson, 1992; Zajonc & McIntosh, 1992). You may *feel* different when you are afraid than when you are sad, but your autonomic nervous system responds about the same. Furthermore, three very different emotions—happiness, disgust, and surprise—are all associated with lower heart rates. Physiological measures provide some indexes of emotional response. However, they cannot adequately discriminate among several emotions that are subjectively very different.

The Controversial "Lie Detector Test" Roger Coleman was a convicted murderer who vigorously protested that he was innocent. In 1992, on the morning he was scheduled to be executed, he was given one final lie detector test. When he failed that test, he was executed (Steinbrook, 1992).

A lie detector test, or—more properly—a **polygraph examination,** simultaneously measures several autonomic changes such as blood pressure, pulse, breathing patterns, and skin conductance. These measures are taken while a person is asked a structured series of questions. The examiner notes the pattern of arousal and decides on the basis of these data whether the person being tested is innocent or guilty (Saxe et al., 1985). Note that the polygraph does not really detect lies, but rather emotional arousal.

An ideal test for truthfulness requires a perfect correspondence between reality and the examiner's conclusion. That is, an innocent person should show minimal arousal of the autonomic nervous system, and an official who examines the polygraph should conclude that he or she is indeed innocent. A guilty person should show strong arousal, and an examination of the polygraph should lead to the conclusion "guilty."

Unfortunately, research on the polygraph exam shows that the results do not correspond perfectly with reality. For example, people who can control their physiological reactions can lie successfully and "beat" the test. Other people with overly reactive autonomic nervous systems may be telling the truth, yet the examiner would conclude "guilty." We can wonder whether Roger Coleman may have been telling the truth—and was understandably nervous about taking the polygraph test to decide whether he would live or die. The problem is that these polygraph tests are simply too unreliable to be trusted.

Facial expressions of happiness, disgust, and surprise produce similar heart rate in the person experiencing the emotions. However, the subjective experiences of these three emotions are vastly different from each other.

TABLE 12.3 Accuracy of Polygraph Judgments

	POLYGRAPH INTERPRETER CONCLUDES	
THE TRUTH	**Person Is a Thief**	**Person Is Innocent**
Person Is a Thief	76%	24%
Person Is Innocent	37%	63%

Note: Data represent the averages for six experienced interpreters.
Source: Kleinmuntz & Szucko, 1984.

Consider a representative study by Kleinmuntz and Szucko (1984). The participants in this research were 50 confessed thieves and 50 innocent people who had been suspected of theft, but had later been cleared when the real thieves had confessed. Six people, employed by a polygraph company, were asked to interpret the polygraphs. Table 12.3 shows the results. As you can see, 37% of the innocent people were falsely identified as thieves and 24% of the thieves falsely declared innocent.

Dozens of factors can affect the accuracy of the polygraph test. Obviously, the experience and training of the polygraph examiner is crucial (Steinbrook, 1992). Also, when the people being tested believe that the polygraph is accurate, the results are indeed reasonably accurate. However, the results are highly inaccurate for people who believe that the polygraph is inaccurate (Saxe, 1991).

Chapter 1 noted that applied psychologists emphasize the practical application of psychological knowledge. The investigation of polygraph testing is an example of how applied psychologists can influence public policy. The studies demonstrated that autonomic measures typically showed an unacceptably low correspondence with the innocence of the person being examined (Carroll, 1988; Gudjonsson, 1988). As a result, most state and federal courts exclude or restrict the use of polygraph results. Also, most private employers are prohibited from using polygraphs to test their employees (Steinbrook, 1992). Fortunately, most of you will not need to worry about being unjustly accused of a crime you did not commit—based on a test that is often inaccurate.

Behavioral Emotional Reactions

So far, we have discussed the cognitive and physiological components of emotion. Now we shift to the last component, behavioral reactions, focusing on the most common measure—facial expression. These facial expressions are an important component of nonverbal communication, a topic we also discussed in Chapter 9. Here, however, we emphasize how facial expressions can convey emotions.

Before reading further, try Demonstration 12.4 to test your accuracy in interpreting emotional expression. In general, people are fairly accurate in matching photos with their appropriate emotional labels (Ekman, 1973). For example, in a classic study, happiness was correctly identified by 97% of the respondents, and surprise was identified by 95%. However, only 67% accurately identified anger. Notice, then, that some facial expressions can be misinterpreted, just as some physiological responses might be confused with each other, and just as some polygraph tests might confuse the innocent and the guilty.

Are Facial Expressions Universal? Do people from different cultures express various emotions in a similar way, or do they differ? The answer seems to be that cultures are both similar and different (Mesquita & Frijda, 1992). In general, our immediate, involuntary facial expressions seem to be highly similar across cultures. However, when we must control our facial expressions—for example, in public settings—we tend to display the facial expression prescribed by our specific culture (Argyle, 1988; Ekman, 1984).

DEMONSTRATION 12.4 Identifying Behavioral Emotional Reactions

Examine the photos and match each one with one of the following six emotions: (1) fear, (2) happiness, (3) anger, (4) disgust, (5) surprise, (6) sadness. The answers appear at the end of the chapter.

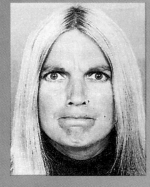 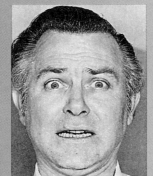 

  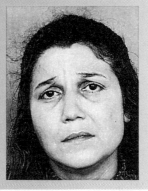

These culture-specific prescriptions about who can show which emotion—and in what circumstance—are called **display rules** (Ekman, 1993). We often work on our emotions and facial expressions, trying to make them more consistent with cultural expectations (Hochschild, 1990). Consider the display rule in our culture that males should not cry. One man recalls an early experience in suppressing an emotional expression:

> I was in the sixth grade at the time my grandfather died. I remember being called to the office of the school where my mother was on the phone. . . . She told me what had happened and all I said was, "Oh." I went back to class and a friend asked me what happened and I said, "Nothing." I remember wanting very much just to cry and tell everyone what had happened. But a boy doesn't cry in the sixth grade for fear of being called a sissy. So I just went along as if nothing had happened while deep down inside I was very sad and full of tears. (Hochschild, 1983, p. 67)

Let us consider some empirical evidence, first for the universality of facial expressions, and then for culture-specific display rules.

Paul Ekman (1973) tested people in Brazil, Chile, Argentina, and Japan, using photographs similar to those in Demonstration 12.4. In each country, people were asked to identify the name of the emotion displayed in the photos. Across all four cultures, the average accuracy was 85% for all six emotions. Similar results were obtained in other research with cultures as diverse as New Guinea, Turkey, and Estonia (Ekman et al., 1987; Ekman & Friesen, 1971).

What about the evidence for display rules? In a representative study, Ekman and Friesen (1969) contrasted the immediate and the delayed emotional responses of Americans and Japanese. Each participant in the study watched an extremely

In our culture, display rules demand that men conceal their sorrow. The man in front is clearly struggling to cover his sadness by trying to look brave.

unpleasant film about sinus surgery. Each person was seated alone in the room, and the facial expressions were secretly videotaped. The videotapes of the immediate facial expressions were highly similar for people in the two cultures; both groups showed disgust. Later, each person was interviewed about the film. In these delayed responses, the Americans continued to show negative expressions, but the Japanese produced happy faces. An important Japanese display rule is that one should not display negative emotions when an authority is present (Ekman, 1984).

This study and related research suggest that we react to a situation with a facial expression that is reasonably uniform in many cultures. Moments later, however, we assume the facial expression we have learned in our culture: An American boy conceals his sadness with a neutral countenance, and a Japanese man smiles to conceal his disgust.

Accuracy in Decoding Emotions As you might imagine, people vary tremendously in their ability to decode emotions. Even within one culture, sensitivity to nonverbal cues ranges widely. Think about someone you know who can sense your sadness when you are barely aware of it yourself. Another acquaintance may spend several hours with you, unaware that you are depressed. This ability to decode emotions can be measured with tests such as the Profile of Nonverbal Sensitivity (PONS). This test asks people to identify what is happening in 220 very brief filmed scenes, using nonverbal cues about the face, body, and tone of voice (Rosenthal et al., 1979).

Research using tests like the PONS shows that the ability to decode nonverbal cues increases systematically between childhood and adulthood, reaching a maximum between the ages of about 20 and 30 (Hall et al., 1978).

Females tend to be somewhat better than males at decoding nonverbal expressions. Gender differences seem to be largest in judging facial expression, somewhat smaller in judging body posture, and smallest in judging voice cues (Brody & Hall, 1994; Hall, 1984). These gender differences are found as early as elementary school and have also been observed in other cultures. Psychologists have not discovered a complete explanation for these differences, but one likely possibility is that females are encouraged to pay more attention to nonverbal behavior and that they have greater practice in trying to decipher emotions (Hall, 1984). Keep in mind, though, that gender differences in decoding ability are widespread, but not inevitable. In other words, you probably know women and men who defy the general trend. For example, can you think of a male friend who is better than most female friends at deciphering people's moods?

How accurate are we in decoding *false* facial expressions? In general, we are not very skilled at determining which people are experiencing real pain and which ones are "faking" a pained expression (Poole & Craig, 1992). We also are not especially skilled at detecting which smiles are genuine and which are false—though we could be more accurate if we paid attention to the muscles surrounding the eyes (Ekman, 1985; Ekman et al., 1990). Figure 12.9 shows both a genuine and a false smile.

Are experts better than the rest of us in detecting false facial expressions? Ekman and O'Sullivan (1991) asked people in various law-enforcement agencies—as well as other employed adults and college students—to judge whether people shown on a videotape were lying or telling the truth. The only group that was more accurate than chance were members of the U.S. Secret Service—possibly because their work requires them to pay attention to the nonverbal behavior of people who might harm the individuals they are guarding. Everyone else guessed at just a chance level, whether they were members of the Central Intelligence Agency or the Federal Bureau of Investigation, whether they were police or judges, or whether they were simply "regular" people like the rest of us. In short, then, people are reasonably competent in identifying the appropriate emotion for genuine facial expressions, even for people from another culture. However, they apparently are not attuned to the subtleties that differentiate between a genuine facial expression and a false one.

Cross-cultural research suggests that people in different parts of the world should be reasonably accurate in identifying this emotional reaction as happiness.

Genuine smile

False smile

Figure 12.9
Notice that in both a genuine and a false smile, the mouth expressions are similar. However, in the genuine smile, the skin is gathered slightly under the eye.

We have examined the cognitive, physiological, and behavioral components of emotions. However, these emotional reactions can have important consequences; for example, they can influence the way you perform a variety of cognitive tasks.

IN DEPTH: The Influence of Positive Emotions on Cognitive Processes

Imagine this scenario. You are on your way to an exam in an English course, and you are wondering what the major essay question will be. You have read short stories by five authors, and your professor typically asks you to find similar themes in your readings. (For instance, on the last exam, you were instructed to discuss how several authors treated the theme of good versus evil.) You are just about to enter the building when you spot a $10 bill half-buried in the leaves. No one else is in sight who could have lost the money, so you put the bill in your pocket. Delighted with this modest but unexpected windfall, you sit down to take your exam. Will that positive experience influence your performance on the test?

Alice M. Isen of Cornell University has conducted a wide range of studies on the influence of positive emotions on cognitive processes. She and her colleagues have found that a relatively minor manipulation of the independent variable (emotional state) has an important influence on an impressive variety of dependent variables (performance on many cognitive tasks). Isen has found that she did not need to spend $10 to make a research participant happy. A free sample notepad, a dime in the coin return of a public telephone—and even a list of 10 happy words— were each sufficient.

Isen's research makes an interesting topic for an "In Depth" section because it illustrates an investigator's search for generalizability. Her work has demonstrated that the influence of emotions is not limited to just one kind of cognitive task. Instead, emotions can affect many cognitive processes, which you read about in Chapters 7, 8, and 9. These include memory, problem solving, and word use.

Memory Isen, Daubman, and Gorgoglione (1987) wanted to discover whether positive emotions could enhance memory. In their research, students watched either an entertaining cartoon film (positive emotions) or a neutrally rated film about statistics (neutral emotions). Later, they heard a 30-word list that included 10 critical words subtly related to the American Revolution (such as *stars, stripes, colony,* and *doodle*). The results showed that people in the positive-emotions condition remembered a significantly larger number of these critical words. A likely explanation is that positive emotions encourage people to see subtle relationships among the words (Isen, 1990). Furthermore, as you know from Chapter 7, people recall more material if the list of words is well organized and interrelated.

Problem Solving Chapter 8 examined problem solving and creativity, which are also influenced by positive affect. In fact, turn back to Duncker's candle problem, illustrated in Demonstration 8.5 (p. 257). Isen, Daubman, and Nowicki (1987) found that people who had viewed a comedy film produced a larger number of useful solutions than people who had viewed a neutral film. Positive mood seems to increase the number of ways in which objects can be seen in relationship with one another.

As Demonstration 8.6 (p. 258) showed, the Remote Associates Test is one measure of creativity. This test requires people to see how words such as *food, catcher,* and *hot* are related to one another (in this case, they are all related to the word *dog*). People in the positive-emotions condition received an average score of 5 on the Remote Associates Test, in contrast to an average score of only 3 for people in the neutral-emotions control group. Once again, happy people are more likely to appreciate subtle relationships.

Word Use Chapter 9 introduced the concept of a **prototype,** or a best example of a concept. For instance, the concept *vehicle* includes some excellent prototype examples such as *car* and *truck,* as well as some nonprototype examples such as *raft, sled,* and *camel.* At least to North Americans, a camel is a highly unusual means of transportation!

Isen and Daubman (1984) wondered if positive mood might encourage people to broaden their categories and perceive items as being related when the relationship was fairly subtle. First, they encouraged positive emotions by showing people a comedy film, giving them a free candy bar, or serving refreshments. Similar participants in a control group either saw a neutral

According to the research of Alice M. Isen and her colleagues, the positive mood of these students should encourage them to detect subtle relationships when they work on cognitive tasks.

film or received no candy or refreshments. Then everyone rated a list of words, judging the extent to which each word was a good example of the category. Relative to the control group, people in the positive-emotions groups were much more generous with their ratings. If you are in a good mood, a camel is a reasonably fine vehicle, a yam is a good example of a vegetable, and a wristwatch is an excellent example of clothing.

In another study, Isen and her colleagues (1985) tested another component of word use and conceptual organization. Specifically, they hypothesized that people in a good mood would be more likely to think of unusual word associations, rather than straightforward ones.

To test this hypothesis, they distributed booklets containing 20 English words. Participants were instructed to supply a word association to each item, saying the first word that came to mind. The first 10 words on the list were positive for one-third of the participants, neutral for one-third, and negative for one-third. Thus, the independent variable was manipulated via the emotional tone of these first 10 words. The remaining 10 words on each list were identical, and all were neutral in tone. The unusualness of people's responses to these last 10 words constituted the dependent variable in this study.

Isen and her coauthors consulted some word-association norms to determine whether a participant's response was common or unusual. Figure 12.10 shows the results. As you can see, people supplied a greater number of unusual associations when their first 10 words in the task had been positive than when those words had been either neutral or negative. For example, when the stimulus word was *carpet,* a person in the positive-emotions group might supply an unusual response such as *plush* or *texture,* whereas people in the other two groups might merely say *rug.*

Thus, this study demonstrates that positive mood increases people's ability to detect subtle or unusual relationships. This research suggests, incidentally, that the positive emotions you experience when you find a $10 bill would encourage you to appreciate subtle relationships among short stories on an English examination.

Possible Explanations Isen and her colleagues have uncovered a large number of cognitive tasks influenced by positive mood. Even preschool children play more creatively and solve problems more effectively when they are in a good mood (Isen, 1990). But *why* do positive emotions influence cognitive organization, so that ideas seem more related than they would with neutral emotions? Unfortunately, we do not have a single, simple answer; the answer is undoubtedly complicated (Isen, 1990; Moore & Isen, 1990).

One possibility is that a positive mood produces a larger number of divergent ideas, creating a richer cognitive context when people try to remember, solve a problem, or think about language. Positive mood may possibly influence motivation, encouraging people to set more ambitious goals for themselves (Isen, 1987). Furthermore, positive mood could increase people's self-confidence, making mental processes more flexible (Izard, 1989). Factors such as these may work together to encourage people to process information in a more integrated fashion when they feel delighted with the world.

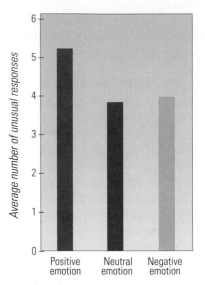

Figure 12.10

The number of unusual responses supplied on a word-association test, as a function of emotional condition. (Based on Isen et al., 1985)

General Theories of Emotion

So far, we have explored the cognitive, physiological, and behavioral aspects of emotion, as well as the influence of positive emotions on cognition. With this background, we can now consider an important question: How are emotional reactions produced? Suppose you are watching a science fiction movie, and—when you least expect it—the 17-legged alien leaps out of the refrigerator to attack our hero. You experience terror. But exactly what forces produce that subjective experience of terror? Like many questions in psychology, it is not obvious that there *is* a problem until you start to think about it. Perhaps the major issue in developing an explanation of emotional experience is the relative importance of physiological and cognitive forces. Is your terror produced by (1) your pounding heart, the knot in your digestive tract, and the physiological side effects of your terrified facial expression, or (2) your cognitive processes that assess the situation and choose the label "terror"?

We begin by considering the James-Lange theory, which emphasizes a physiological explanation; we also note some criticisms of this approach, as well as a more current variant. Then we discuss the Schachter-Singer theory, which emphasizes the importance of cognitive labels. Finally, we consider Izard's more complex theory, which argues that cognitive processes are important in some emotional reactions but unnecessary in other emotional reactions.

The James-Lange Theory William James, the first major American psychologist, explained emotional experiences using a theory that seemed unlikely when he proposed it in 1890. This explanation still seems to contradict most people's common sense. The commonsense explanation of emotions probably runs something like this: When you see the 17-legged alien, you experience terror, and this terror sets off physiological reactions (such as a knot in the stomach or an increase in blood pressure).

James (1890) argued, however, that the commonsense explanation places events in the wrong order. If he were watching the science fiction movie with you, he would claim that the perception of an emotion-arousing event (say, a 17-legged alien) directly produces physiological reactions. These physiological reactions send a message to the brain, producing the emotional experience of terror. As James wrote in his famous psychology textbook,

> *Common sense says, we lose our fortune, are sorry and weep; we meet a bear, are frightened and run; we are insulted by a rival, are angry and strike. . . . The more rational statement is that we feel sorry because we cry, angry because we strike, afraid because we tremble, and not that we cry, strike, or tremble, because we are sorry, angry, or fearful as the case may be. (p. 13)*

James argued that each emotion is signaled by a specific physiological pattern. He particularly emphasized physiological reactions in the abdominal organs (such as a tense feeling, or "knot in the stomach"). In 1887, a Danish psychologist named Carl Lange (pronounced "*Lang*-eh") suggested a similar theory, but he emphasized physiological reactions in the circulatory system (such as an increase in blood pressure). The **James-Lange theory** therefore proposes that physiological changes are the source of emotional feelings (Figure 12.11).

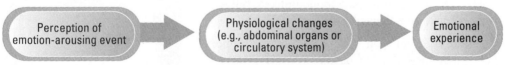

Figure 12.11
The James-Lange theory of emotion.

The Cannon-Bard Theory Several decades later, a physiologist named Walter Cannon (1927) wrote an article that criticized the James-Lange approach. Cannon argued that physiological changes are too slow to be the sources of emotional feeling. Furthermore, if emotional reactions are produced by physiological sensations, then each emotion should be linked with a unique combination of physiological changes. Cannon pointed out contradictory evidence, consistent with our discussion of this topic in the section on physiological measures.

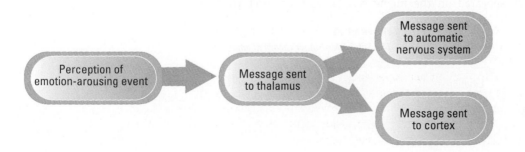

Figure 12.12
The Cannon-Bard theory of emotion.

Cannon and his colleague L. L. Bard proposed their own theory as a substitute for the James-Lange theory (Bard, 1928; Cannon, 1927). According to the **Cannon-Bard theory,** an important mediator in emotional experience is the thalamus, a part of the brain that receives messages from the sensory receptors. The thalamus, in turn, sends separate messages to the autonomic nervous system and to the cortex. As Figure 12.12 shows, you do not have to wait for your stomach to churn before your cortex knows that you are terrified. Instead, both events occur at the same time. For several decades the Cannon-Bard theory was more popular than the James-Lange approach.

The Facial Feedback Hypothesis Some recent research, however, provides support for the earlier James-Lange approach, though the new approach emphasizes feedback from facial expression, rather than from the abdominal organs and circulatory system. According to the **facial feedback hypothesis,** changes in your facial expression can *cause* changes in your emotional state (Laird, 1984; Zajonc et al., 1989). Thus, your terrified expression when the alien jumps out of the refrigerator encourages you to experience terror.

In a representative study, Strack and his coauthors (1988) asked participants to hold a pen in either their mouth or their teeth. At this point, you may be wondering about the sanity of these researchers. However, if you try holding a pen in your lips (without touching your teeth), you will find that your facial expression is much more grumpy than if you hold a pen in your teeth (without touching your lips). Notice, then, that people adopted nonsmiling or smiling facial expressions without ever hearing any emotional labels like "smile." With the pen still in position, the participants rated a series of cartoons on a scale that ranged from *not at all funny* to *very funny.* Impressively, the people wearing smiles judged the cartoons to be significantly funnier than did the unsmiling people!

In general, the research on facial feedback shows that facial expression has a modest effect on emotional experiences (Matsumoto, 1987). It would be unreasonable to claim that facial feedback is the main factor in all subjective emotions. However, researchers have demonstrated a possible mechanism for this effect: Frowning facial expressions actually restrict the flow of cooled air to the hypothalamus and other regions in the brain, producing an unpleasant emotional experience (Zajonc & McIntosh, 1992; Zajonc et al., 1989). This explanation may sound unlikely, but when a photographer tells you to say *cheese,* your mood may actually improve!

The Schachter-Singer Theory So far, you have heard about thumping hearts, knotted stomachs, and chilled brains—a variety of ways in which physiological reactions might mediate emotional experiences. It was not until the early 1960s that theorists described how cognitive interpretations might be relevant in forming our emotional experiences. Stanley Schachter and Jerome Singer (1962) proposed that these higher mental processes help us label whether we are experiencing joy or terror.

According to the **Schachter-Singer theory,** an emotion-arousing event causes physiological arousal, and you examine the external environment to help you interpret that event. For example, if your heart is pounding, you try to figure out *why.* If a 17-legged alien has suddenly appeared on the movie screen, you interpret your

Strack and his coauthors (1988) would predict that this young woman should rate the comic pages as being funnier when her lips are in the configuration on the bottom rather than the one on the top.

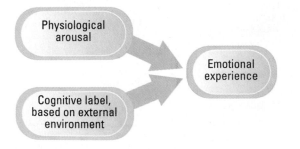

Figure 12.13
The Schachter-Singer theory of emotion.

arousal as terror. If a very attractive person has just sat down next to you and is gazing into your eyes, you interpret this arousal very differently! As Figure 12.13 shows, the combination of physiological arousal and a cognitive label produces an emotional experience.

To test their two-factor theory, Schachter and Singer (1962) gave epinephrine injections to college men. As you may recall, epinephrine increases arousal. Imagine that you were a participant in this study, and you had been told that epinephrine causes an increase in heart rate and breathing rate. Now the researchers lead you to another room, where another person (in reality an accomplice of the researchers) is acting strangely. This fellow seems extremely happy, playing basketball with a wad of paper, playing with a hula hoop, and flying paper airplanes. As you watch this very happy person, your heart rate and breathing rate begin to increase. What emotion would you feel? Schachter and Singer found that the participants in this condition felt no major change in their emotions. After all, they could attribute their arousal to the drug. The accomplice's joyfulness did not "rub off." Similarly, participants showed no major change in their emotions in another condition where people—informed about the effects of epinephrine—stayed in a room with a hostile person who complained about the insulting questionnaire he was completing and eventually stamped out of the room.

Now imagine that you were a participant in this study, except you have been told that the injection would cause no effects. Now you find yourself sitting in a room with a person who is either extremely happy (in one condition) or extremely hostile (in another condition). Your heart is pounding, and you are breathing rapidly. How can this be happening? You search around for a cognitive label, some emotional explanation for your reaction. If you are sitting with a basketball-playing optimist, it must be because you are happy. If you are sitting with a complaining pessimist, it must be because you are angry.

Schachter and Singer's complicated experiment—which included many more conditions than described here—did not turn out exactly as their theory had predicted. Furthermore, other research, which included additional precautions, failed to support the Schachter-Singer theory (Marshall & Zimbardo, 1979; Maslach, 1979; Reisenzein, 1983). Thirty years after the original research, theorists are not convinced that physiological arousal is essential for an emotional experience. Furthermore, many believe that people can have emotional experiences without any contribution from cognitive labels or higher mental processes. One such theorist is Carroll Izard, whose approach to emotions concludes this section.

Izard's Theory Carroll Izard (pronounced "Ih-zahrd") has proposed the richest and most complex approach to emotional experiences. **Izard's theory** suggests that two different kinds of emotion pathways are responsible for our feelings (Izard, 1989, 1991). Cognition is not necessary for the first kind of emotional experience, but it is for the second kind.

Imagine that it is late at night, your bedroom is dark, and you have emerged from bed for a drink of water. Suddenly you stub your toe, and you are instantly angry. The sensation of pain leads *immediately* to anger. You do not need to evaluate the stimuli in the environment, and you do not need to speculate about who could have left the object in your path. In this example, cognition is not necessary.

One source of evidence that cognition is not essential in all emotions comes from studies with 2-month-old infants. When these infants received their immunizations, Izard and his colleagues (1983) observed that the pain from the shot produced an angry reaction. Other researchers have also observed a clearly angry facial expression in 4-month-olds when their arms are restrained (Stenberg & Campos, 1990).

A cognitive explanation is not appropriate for these young infants, who cannot yet interpret or categorize the emotion-arousing events. Izard (1989) proposes that evolution has developed inborn nervous-system pathways for processing certain emotions very efficiently. He notes that these inborn pathways have not been studied

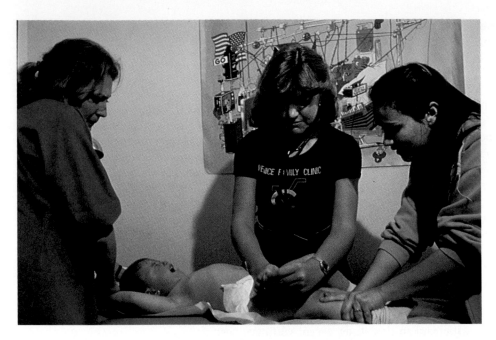

This baby is illustrating the first kind of emotional reaction in Izard's theory. The mother—looking on—is illustrating the second kind, which requires cognitive processes.

as extensively as the pathways involved in learning emotional responses. However, the important brain structures in this pathway are the thalamus and the amygdala, as we noted in our earlier discussion on page 392. The cortex plays no role in the inborn nervous-system pathway.

Robert Zajonc (pronounced "*Zye*-unce") also argues that cognition is not essential for all emotional processing. Zajonc (1980; 1984) summarizes research to support his position. In one study, various geometric shapes were presented for an extremely brief exposure—only 1 millisecond. Previous research had established that people prefer stimuli they have seen before, rather than unfamiliar stimuli. In this study, participants preferred the geometric shapes they had previously seen—even when they could not recognize them as being familiar. That is, they liked a stimulus (an emotional reaction) without remembering that it was familiar (a cognitive reaction). We do not always need to think, ponder, and weigh the pros and cons before we claim to like something!

However, cognition is clearly involved in other emotional reactions. Suppose that someone bumps into you on the sidewalk, and your immediate emotional response to the pain is anger. Then you notice that the person has a broken leg and is on crutches. Your anger is likely to be replaced by another emotional response—perhaps pity. This more complex emotion cannot be generated by primitive brain structures such as the thalamus or the amygdala. The cortex is required to note that the crutches and cast identify this person as having a broken leg. The cortex is also required to acknowledge that the accident was not intentional. As Izard (1989) notes, this second kind of emotional reaction requires "numerous cognitive processes, including comparison, matching, appraisal, categorization, imagery, memory, and anticipation" (p. 48). Figure 12.14 illustrates the two pathways for emotional reactions, as proposed in Izard's theory.

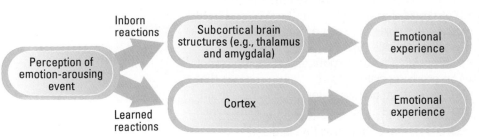

Figure 12.14

Izard's theory of emotion, which proposes two separate routes for the production of emotional experiences.

Let us briefly review the role of cognition in each theory of emotion. In the James-Lange theory, cognitions are not critical in determining the emotional experience; instead, physiological changes are important. Similarly, cognitions are not critical mediators in the Cannon-Bard theory or the facial feedback hypothesis; again, physiology is important. In the Schachter-Singer theory, however, cognitions are essential in interpreting physiological arousal ("Why is my heart pounding? It must be because I'm terrified by the sudden appearance of the 17-legged alien.") Finally, in Izard's theory, cognitions are important in one kind of emotional reaction; however, they are not involved in the more basic emotional reactions demonstrated in infants and in some immediate reactions in adulthood. Some variant of Izard's theory will probably be most useful in explaining the variety and richness of human emotions.

SECTION SUMMARY

EMOTION

● Cognitive emotional reactions are often assessed with rating scales; subjective well-being is not correlated with age, gender, ethnic group, education, or disability status; it is somewhat correlated with income, but more strongly correlated with social relationships and having a pleasurable job; the interruption and satisfaction of schemas leads to emotional reactions.

● The limbic system is involved in processing emotions; the two hemispheres of the brain respond differently to emotions; each emotion is not uniquely linked to a specific combination of physiological reactions; similarly, the polygraph examination is not very reliable in separating the innocent from the guilty.

● Immediate, involuntary facial expressions seem to be similar across cultures, but display rules vary from culture to culture; age and gender differences are often found in decoding emotions; in general, people are not accurate in decoding false facial expressions.

● Isen's work suggests that people in a happy mood are better able to appreciate subtle relationships, which facilitates memory, problem solving, and word use.

● Five theories of emotion are the James-Lange theory, the Cannon-Bard theory, the facial feedback hypothesis, the Schachter-Singer theory, and Izard's theory.

REVIEW QUESTIONS

1. Define the terms *motivation* and *emotion* and point out how these two concepts are intertwined. Then think of an episode in your life that involved both motivation and emotion. What kind of motivation was involved? Describe the three components of your emotional reaction (cognitive, physiological, and behavioral).

2. Imagine that it is 6:30 p.m., half an hour past your normal dinnertime. You are standing in front of a closed bakery shop, admiring the desserts while you wait for a friend to pick you up for dinner. Identify the various factors contributing to the sensation that you are hungry.

3. Many parts of the motivation section contrasted external and internal factors and their roles in determining motivation. Discuss the importance of both external and internal factors in determining hunger level, obesity, sexual interactions, and achievement motivation.

4. Individual differences are important in many aspects of motivation. Discuss individual differences in body weight, coercive versus consensual sexual interactions, and achievement motivation.

5. Now discuss two important group variables, culture and gender. Note the areas in which these variables are important as well as areas in which they are usually irrelevant. Be sure to include examples from both motivation and emotion.

6. A major portion of the section on emotions emphasized the cognitive, physiological, and behavioral components of emotions. What are the advantages and disadvantages of each index of emotion? Which do you think provides the best index of your own emotions?

7. Suppose that a friend is puzzled about why polygraph examinations are no longer legal in many situations. Describe these tests, their results, and the reasons they are not widely used in the 1990s. Based on this chapter, do you think jurors should decide a person's guilt on the basis of his or her facial expression?

8. The section on cross-cultural aspects of facial expression discussed immediate and delayed facial responses. Which theory of emotions best explains these two kinds of responses?

9. This chapter discussed the influence of positive affect on cognitive processes. Describe some of the higher mental processes influenced by emotion, and speculate about some tasks you perform that could be influenced by emotions. Finally, think of several practical applications for Isen's work.

10. This chapter examined four explanations for motivation and five for emotion. Describe each theoretical approach, indicating which theory or theories best explain a wide variety of motivations and emotions.

N E W   T E R M S

motivation
emotion
homeostasis
lateral hypothalamus (LH)
ventromedial hypothalamus (VMH)
glucose
glucostats
cholecystokinin (CCK)
insulin
obesity
metabolism
set point
fat cells
anorexia nervosa
bulimia nervosa
counter-regulation
excitement phase
plateau phase
orgasmic phase
resolution phase
gonorrhea
genital herpes
syphilis
Acquired Immunodeficiency Syndrome (AIDS)

sexual coercion
rape
sexual harassment
consensual sexual interactions
achievement motive
fear of success
intrinsic motivation
extrinsic motivation
attribution
instincts
drive
opponent-process theory
incentive theory
subjective well-being
schema
autonomic division
polygraph examination
display rules
prototype
James-Lange theory
Cannon-Bard theory
facial feedback hypothesis
Schachter-Singer theory
Izard's theory

A N S W E R S   T O   D E M O N S T R A T I O N S

DEMONSTRATION 12.2   1. W; 2. M; 3. W; 4. W; 5. M; 6. M; 7. M; 8. W.
DEMONSTRATION 12.4   1. anger; 2. fear; 3. disgust; 4. surprise; 5. happiness; 6. sadness.

RECOMMENDED READINGS

Hyde, J. S. (1990). *Understanding human sexuality* (4th ed.). New York: McGraw-Hill. Janet Hyde, who is well known for her work in the psychology of women, wrote this comprehensive textbook, which includes chapters on sexual preference, sexual dysfunctions, and physiological and behavioral aspects of sexuality.

Psychological Science (1992), Volume 3, Number 1. Most of this special issue is devoted to research and theories on emotion; the articles will give you some insights on important current issues.

Reeve, J. (1992). *Understanding motivation and emotion.* Fort Worth, TX: Harcourt Brace Jovanovich. This mid-level textbook covers all the topics in Chapter 12 and also personality and social aspects of motivation.

Rodin, J. (1992). *Body traps.* New York: Morrow. Judith Rodin is a well-known researcher in the areas of eating, body image, and health. This interesting book identifies various traps that plague North Americans with respect to body image and fitness.

Stein, N. L., Leventhal, B., & Trabasso, T. (Eds.). (1990). *Psychological and biological approaches to emotion.* Hillsdale, NJ: Erlbaum. This edited volume includes a chapter by Isen, summarizing her research, as well as chapters on cognitive, physiological, developmental, and abnormal aspects of emotion.

CHAPTER 13

PERSONALITY

THE PSYCHODYNAMIC APPROACH

The Structure of Personality
Freud's Methods
Defense Mechanisms
Stages of Psychosexual Development
Other Psychodynamic Theorists
Evaluation of the Psychodynamic Approach

THE HUMANISTIC APPROACH

Roger's Person-Centered Approach
Maslow's Hierarchy of Needs
Evaluation of the Humanistic Approach

THE TRAIT APPROACH

Allport's Trait Theory
Eysenck's Biosocial Theory
The Five-Factor Model
The Person-Situation Debate
The Biological Basis of Individual Differences
Evaluation of the Trait Approach

THE SOCIAL COGNITIVE APPROACH

Origins of the Social Cognitive Approach: Personal
    Construct Theory and Behaviorism
Observational Learning
Reciprocal Influences
Self-Efficacy
In Depth: The Social Cognitive Approach to Self-Concepts
Evaluation of the Social Cognitive Approach

Y ou may know someone like Susan. Her half of the dormitory room is spotless. Her desk is immaculate, adorned only by a carefully dusted lamp. The pencils, pens, and markers in the drawer are neatly arranged. Her dresser holds only one photograph, in a pale blue frame that matches her bedspread. Susan's clothes are neatly folded in the dresser drawers and precisely arranged in categories in her closet. You suspect she even polishes her wastebasket. Neatness seems be a crucial component of Susan's personality.

Personality is a pattern of characteristic feelings, thoughts, and behaviors that persists across time and situations; personality is "the underlying causes within the person of individual behavior and experience" (Cloninger, 1993, p. 2; Phares, 1988). For instance, Susan has probably always been neat and tidy; neatness persists across time. She is likely to keep the work area neat in her work-study job at the library, and her bedroom at home is certainly immaculate as well; neatness persists across situations. Furthermore, Susan's neatness distinguishes her from her roommate, whose idea of a neat room demands only a narrow path through her rumpled clothes on the floor; a clean desk means that you can fit one textbook in among the dirty coffee cups.

In this chapter, we will consider how four different theories explain personality processes:

1. The **psychodynamic approach,** which originated with Sigmund Freud, emphasizes childhood experiences and unconscious motivations and conflicts. A psychodynamic theorist, for instance, might trace Susan's neatness to her early toilet-training experiences.

2. The **humanistic approach** stresses that humans have enormous potential for personal growth. A humanistic theorist would be concerned about whether Susan's excessive neatness prevents her from being spontaneous, and whether it limits the development of her true potential.

3. The **trait approach** proposes that human personality is a combination of specific stable, internal personality characteristics, such as shyness or aggressiveness. A trait theorist would not focus on the factors that encouraged Susan to be so neat. Instead, he or she would try to determine whether Susan's neatness does persist across time and different situations, and whether neatness is related to other traits, such as promptness.

4. The **social cognitive approach** emphasizes observational learning and the central importance of cognitive factors. A psychologist who favored this approach might speculate that Susan observed and imitated her mother's emphasis on cleanliness. Furthermore, Susan's self-concept encouraged her toward even more fastidious behavior. Research in this area might focus on the relationship between neatness and feelings of personal competence.

Students in my introductory psychology class often wonder why psychologists bother with personality theories. A theory is important, however, because it provides a general framework for understanding how personality operates and for explaining why people behave in certain ways. In addition, each of the four approaches that we discuss identifies critical questions that should be answered. Research therefore advances in a more orderly and systematic fashion (Mendelsohn, 1993).

Furthermore, the personality approach we adopt has an important influence on our view of human nature (Rychlak, 1981a). Suppose that a person endorses only the psychodynamic view, which argues that humans are not rational, but governed by unconscious wishes. He or she would approach the judicial system differently than one who prefers the social cognitive view, which suggests that people commit crimes because they have observed antisocial models. Also, a supporter of the psychodynamic tradition would probably conclude that wars and other forms of interpersonal violence are inevitable. Firm supporters of the social cognitive or humanistic theories would disagree.

Finally, we will see in Chapter 15 that the various theories of personality provide different explanations for the origin of psychological disorders. These theories also make different recommendations about the treatment of these disorders, as we will see in Chapter 16.

In this chapter, we compare the four theoretical approaches on the following dimensions:

1. What is the source of data? Are the data obtained from an expert analyst, from an objective test, or from self-reports? Are the observations based on people in therapy, or from more general populations?

2. What does the approach propose as the cause of behavior? Is the cause internal or external to the person?

3. How comprehensive is the approach? Does it attempt to explain almost all behavior, or does it focus on isolated characteristics and behavior patterns?

4. What is the approach's outlook on human nature? Is it positive, neutral, or negative?

Before beginning, however, we need to discuss two precautions. First, these four perspectives do not need to be mutually exclusive. To some extent, the approaches focus on different aspects of human personality, so they are not in conflict. It would be a mistake to think that one approach must be correct, and all others must be wrong. Most psychologists favor one approach but admire some components of at least one other approach (Mischel, 1993). Second, human personality is so complex that it cannot be captured adequately even by four different perspectives (Phares, 1988). In fact, each approach provides just a partial view of individuals. Theorists from each of the four perspectives have been accumulating information about personality for several decades. Still, we need additional decades—and perhaps even new perspectives—to describe human personality adequately.

THE PSYCHODYNAMIC APPROACH

The psychodynamic approach emphasizes three central ideas: (1) childhood experiences determine adult personality; (2) unconscious mental processes influence everyday behavior; and (3) unconscious conflict underlies most human behavior. Sigmund Freud was the founder of the psychoanalytic approach. This narrower term, the **psychoanalytic approach,** refers specifically to Freud's original theory, developed about a century ago. More recent psychodynamic theorists place more emphasis on social roles and less emphasis on sexual forces, in contrast to Freud (Westen, 1990). In this section, we will begin with Freud's psychoanalytic approach and end by mentioning several of the newer psychodynamic theories.

Sigmund Freud was born in 1856 and grew up in a Jewish family in Vienna, Austria. He was trained in medicine, with specific interests in neurology and psychological problems. In his 30s, Freud began a brief collaboration with Joseph Breuer, a prominent Viennese physician. Together they developed a method in which people relieved various psychological symptoms by talking about them. The two men had a falling-out several years later, and Freud won acclaim on his own. Freud, in turn, inspired other influential scholars; we consider several of them later in this section.

We should stress that Freud's theories were controversial for the end of the nineteenth century. The Victorian era was known for its straitlaced attitudes toward sexuality. In fact, Freud's own wife, Martha, thought that her husband's psychoanalytic theories were "a form of pornography" (Gay, 1988, p. 61) because of the emphasis on sexual forces. At that time, too, psychologists favored the views of Wilhelm Wundt, the founder of scientific psychology, which emphasized conscious experience. In contrast, Freud focused on the unconscious. Freud's (1900/1953) groundbreaking book, *The Interpretation of Dreams,* was not well received. It sold only 351 copies in the first six years following publication (Gay, 1988). Given this opposition, we should be especially impressed that Freud's approach eventually became the most widely known of all personality theories.

Approximately a century after Freud proposed his theories, we must still acknowledge his influence. The important concepts of childhood experiences and unconscious motivation originated with Freud. His theory has been called "The single most sweeping contribution to the field of personality" (Phares, 1988, p. 75). As another current theorist described the scope of Freud's ideas, "Freud is now the standard against which other personality theories must be judged" (Rychlak, 1981a, pp. 14–15).

Even if many psychologists in the 1990s have abandoned Freud, his ideas still influence many other areas of life. Phrases such as "Freudian slip" and "unconscious" are part of our daily vocabulary. For example, my own examination of high-school health textbooks suggests that they have been influenced more by Freud than by any other theorist discussed in this chapter. In these books, terms such as "reaction formation" and "repression" are presented as if they were documented facts, rather than theoretical notions.

People in the humanities are particularly enchanted with psychoanalytic approaches. In fact, some writers have pointed out that psychoanalytic concepts "thrive in humanities departments in proportion to their decline in psychiatry departments" (Raymond, 1991, p. A5). Consider a review of the movie *The Stepfather.* Writing about the movie's teenage daughter, the reviewer comments on

> . . . the elements of desire which fuel the pre-Oedipal and post-Oedipal stages—most particularly masochism, which is associated with pre-Oedipal desires for union with the mother, and sadism, which is linked to post-Oedipal desires for dominance and control. (Erens, 1987–1988, p. 54)

In fact, film journals contain more references to Freudian theory than do current mainstream psychology journals.

Freud's personal history provides evidence that childhood experiences are critical. His father once remarked, after 7-year-old Sigmund had acted foolishly, "The boy will come to nothing" (Freud, 1900/1953, p. 216). Freud spent his lifetime demonstrating that his father's early prediction was incorrect.

We begin this overview of the psychodynamic approach by considering Freud's basic theories on the structure of personality. We then discuss his methods, his views on defense mechanisms, and the stages of psychosexual development. We end with a discussion of several other psychodynamic theories and an evaluation of psychodynamic theory.

Sigmund Freud strolling in the mountains with his daughter Anna Freud (who also became a psychoanalyst).

The Structure of Personality

Freud envisioned three basic components to human personality: the id, the ego, and the superego (Freud, 1933/1964). Humans are born with an **id,** which is immature and illogical. The id consists of the basic drives, such as eating and sexual activity; it provides the energy (or **libido**) for all human behavior. Freud also maintained that the id lacks moral judgment; it cannot distinguish between good and evil. The id is unconscious, without contacts to the external world.

The **ego,** in contrast, develops because of the need to deal with the outside world. Freud proposes that the ego begins to function about the age of 6 months, to serve as a mediator between the id and reality. At this age, infants can start to take past experiences into account. The ego operates according to the **reality principle;** for example, infants can delay their impulses until the situation seems appropriate.

So far, we have an irrational id, governed by pleasure, and a cooler, calmer ego, governed by reality. Freud's third personality component is the **superego,** which includes individual personal conscience, ideals, and values. The superego acquires its principles from society, via the parents. Because Victorian society in Freud's era was often stifling and discouraged sexual expression, Freud thought the superego suppressed the sexual impulses.

In Freud's theory, then, the ego acts as a supervisor. It must negotiate a compromise between the id's drives and the superego's rules about moral behavior. Finally, the ego must continually assess reality, delaying action when appropriate.

A description in one textbook may help you remember this trio:

> *Imagine a sex-starved hedonist [the id], a black-frock-coated Puritan minister [the superego], and a totally humorless computer scientist [the ego] chained together and turned loose in the world, and you have a good approximation of what Freud was trying to show us about the personality.*
>
> *Because they are chained together, the id, ego and superego cannot decide to go their separate ways. They have no alternative but to adjust to one another. And the result, for better or for worse, is the adult human personality. (Geiwitz & Moursund, 1979, p. 27)*

Freudian theory would say that this child's superego prevents her from taking a forbidden cookie, which her id is urging her to consume.

These three structures are critically important in Freudian theory because personality and behavior are created by the constant conflict and interplay among the id, the ego, and the superego (Domjan, 1993).

Let us discuss how the id, ego, and superego are related to a person's level of awareness. Freud compared the human mind to an iceberg. As in Figure 13.1, only a small part of the iceberg rises above the surface of the water. This portion is the **conscious,** which includes everything you are aware of at a particular moment. As Chapter 5 noted on states of consciousness, our conscious experiences refer to our sensory awareness of the environment and of ourselves. At this moment, for instance, thoughts in your conscious may include the definition for the conscious, a sketch of an iceberg, and the thought that you need to buy toothpaste tomorrow. As you can see in Figure 13.1, only the ego and the superego are included in the conscious. (Note, however, that parts of both the ego and superego are *not* in the conscious.)

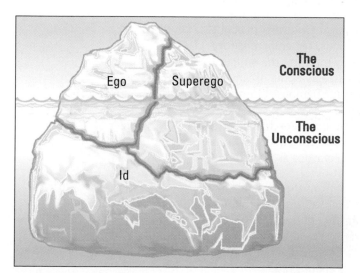

Figure 13.1

Freud's model of the conscious and the unconscious, similar to an iceberg. As you can see, the ego and the superego can be in the conscious or the unconscious, but the id is entirely unconscious.

Some additional material that is not in awareness at a particular time can be retrieved with a little effort; this material is called the **preconscious.** An example of the preconscious would be the names of your high-school mathematics teachers. The nature of material in the preconscious is not different from the material in the conscious; thoughts move fairly easily from one state to the other (Cloninger, 1993).

Freud was especially interested in the **unconscious,** which holds thoughts and desires that are far below the level of a person's awareness. Notice that most of the iceberg lies below the surface of the water. Similarly, Freud argues that most psychic processes are not conscious; they are hidden from the outside world. Your unconscious may hold a particularly traumatic childhood memory, for example. (As we will discuss shortly, a mechanism called *repression* is supposed to be responsible for pushing unacceptable thoughts back into the unconscious, rather than letting them emerge into awareness.) Although a traumatic memory will not reach consciousness during normal daily activities, Freud proposed that it may influence your behavior without your being aware of it. Notice in Figure 13.1 that the id is totally unconscious, and parts of the ego and superego are also unconscious.

Freud's Methods

As a physician, Freud studied people with serious psychological disorders. In traditional psychoanalysis, the patient is seen several times a week, and analysis may last for two or three years. The patient may lie on a couch, with the analyst sitting in a chair near the patient's head. (You have probably seen the setup in cartoons.) Modern analysts are likely to seat the patient in a chair, however. In all cases, the client is encouraged to relax.

A major psychoanalytic technique is **free association,** in which patients are encouraged to say anything that occurs to them, no matter how silly or irrelevant it may seem to their conscious judgment (Rychlak, 1981b). An analyst may stimulate recall with an open-ended question such as "What is on your mind today?" However, free associations do not need to be rational or tied to the present time. For example, a woman in therapy may suddenly have an image of a perfume bottle. Perhaps this image brings forth a recollection from childhood, such as a fight with a brother near her mother's bureau. Freud felt that free association was one tool that allowed access to the unconscious.

As we noted in the discussion of dreams in Chapter 5, Freud believed that the unconscious reveals itself in dreams via symbols. A second Freudian method was therefore dream analysis. As we saw in the discussion about the unconscious, people have desires or fears that cannot be expressed consciously. Freud argued that the ego relaxes its control when we sleep, so the unconscious is more obvious in dreams than when we are awake. However, people try to disguise their own wishes from themselves by constructing symbols. For instance, an individual may report a dream about riding on a bull in an amusement-park carousel. This conscious, remembered story line of a dream is called its **manifest content.** The analyst may interpret the bull as a symbol of the person's father. The underlying, unconscious aspects of the dream (as interpreted by the analyst) are called the **latent content.** Now try Demonstration 13.1 to see whether you can decode the latent content of a fairy tale.

A third Freudian method is the interpretation of reactions. For instance, a modern-day analyst worked with a 2-year-old girl who was concerned about broken crayons (Chehrazi, 1986). This analyst interpreted the broken crayons as a symbol of the girl's wish for a penis.

A fourth Freudian method is the interpretation of slips-of-the-tongue. The chapter on language discussed a cognitive interpretation of these slips-of-the tongue. Freud believed, however, that these slips reveal unconscious thoughts. For instance, suppose that a psychology professor, who is not an admirer of Freud, says, "Let me insult a comment about Freud" rather than "Let me *insert* a comment about Freud." The slip would presumably reveal the professor's true feelings about Freud.

DEMONSTRATION 13.1 Decoding a Fairy Tale

Psychoanalyst Bruno Bettelheim argues that children's fairy tales are filled with hidden messages, and children can translate the manifest content into the appropriate latent content at an unconscious level. Read the following summary of part of the fairy tale "Sleeping Beauty" and search for the latent-content items; place the corresponding number next to the relevant passage in the summary. To make the task more challenging, I listed four items irrelevant to the story.

Sleeping Beauty

A 15-year-old princess climbs a circular staircase, unlocks the door, and enters the forbidden little room. Inside, an old woman sits spinning cloth. Seeing the cylinder-shaped spindle, the young princess asks the old woman about the object that jumps in such an unusual fashion. She touches the spindle, her finger bleeds, and she falls into a deep sleep. After sleeping for 100 years, she is awakened by a kiss from the handsome prince. They are later married.

Possible Latent-Content Items

1. a brutal father figure
2. a penis
3. bowel movements
4. female genitals
5. sucking (oral needs)
6. menstruation
7. attachment to mother
8. sexual intercourse

Also, what is the implied message of this fairy tale? Check the end of the chapter for the answers to this demonstration.

Source: Based on Bettelheim, 1977; McAdams, 1990

Psychologists trained in experimental research techniques often feel uncomfortable about Freudian methods, which seem so subjective and difficult to verify. For example, how do we know that the little girl with the broken crayons is not simply worried about broken crayons rather than a missing penis? More generally, it is difficult to establish experimentally that any symbol represents a particular personality problem.

Defense Mechanisms

The conflict among the id, the ego, and the superego is central in Freudian theory. Freud proposes that the ego tries to resolve this conflict. Often, it resolves the conflict via **defense mechanisms,** which are mental activities that prevent dangerous thoughts or wishes from becoming directly effective. These defense mechanisms allow the energy associated with these dangerous ideas to be channeled into other thoughts and behaviors ("Psychodynamic Therapy: Part II, 1991).

Table 13.1 shows seven of the major defense mechanisms, which Sigmund Freud developed in collaboration with his daughter, Anna. As you carefully read the definition for each new term, try to think about how the underlying energy is channeled into a particular defense mechanism, and notice how reality is distorted. People are not consciously aware of why they are engaging in these defense mechanisms (Weiss, 1990). For example, the employee who is showing projection may not know why he or she believes the other employees look suspicious.

Freud proposed, incidentally, that defense mechanisms can produce some positive outcomes. For instance, he argued that the great Italian artist Leonardo da Vinci painted madonnas as a sublimated symbol of his mother (Freud, 1930/1963). Leonardo had been separated from his mother at a young age, and he longed to be reunited with her.

Freud's pessimism about human nature is often revealed in the defense mechanisms, however. For instance, why are you so extraordinarily helpful to your neighbor? According to Freud, your helpfulness may be caused by a reaction formation against the aggressiveness you truly feel toward the neighbor (Wallach & Wallach, 1983). You shovel snow from his sidewalk every winter morning—not because you want to help him. Instead, you unconsciously want to harm him.

TABLE 13.1 Freudian Defense Mechanisms

DEFENSE MECHANISM	DEFINITION	EXAMPLE
Repression	Pushing back unacceptable thoughts into the unconscious.	A rape victim cannot recall the details of the attack.
Regression	Acting in ways characteristic of earlier life stages.	A young adult, anxious on a trip to his parents' home, sits in the corner reading comic books, as he often did in grade school.
Reaction formation	Replacing an anxiety-producing feeling with its exact opposite, typically going overboard.	A man who is anxious about his interest in gay men begins dating women several times a week
Rationalization	Creating false but believable excuses to justify inappropriate behavior.	A student cheats on an exam, explaining that cheating is legitimate on an unfair examination.
Sublimation	Redirecting forbidden impulses toward a socially desirable goal.	A soldier, who enjoyed his tour in Vietnam, becomes a policeman in a dangerous urban neighborhood.
Displacement	Redirecting emotional feelings (e.g., anger) to a substitute target.	A husband, angry at the way his boss treated him, screams at his wife.
Projection	Attributing your own unacceptable feelings to another person.	An employee at a store, tempted to steal some merchandise, suspects that other employees are stealing.

Sources: D. S. Holmes, 1984b; Monte, 1987

Note: If you would like a mnemonic to help you recall these basic seven defense mechanisms, remember that the first four all begin with the letter *R* (they are actually listed in reverse alphabetical order), and the first letters of the other three (*S, D,* and *P*) can be remembered via the phrase "Study Diligently, Please." Also, these seven defense mechanisms are all considered to be "new terms" in this textbook.

Stages of Psychosexual Development

Freud's analysis of his patients convinced him that psychological disorders have their origin in childhood. As a result, much of adult personality can be explained by examining important early events.

Freud argued that the libido is centered at different body parts—or **erogenous zones**—as the individual matures. Pleasant stimulation of these zones reduces the tension that the person experiences. The first erogenous zone is the mouth, followed at later ages by the anus, and finally the genitals.

Furthermore, Freud proposed that children experience conflicts between urges in these erogenous zones and the rules of society. Society requires infants to learn to drink from a cup, rather than to suck. Society demands that toddlers be toilet trained, and it specifies that children should not masturbate. If a conflict in a particular erogenous zone is not successfully resolved—because the individual is either overindulged or underindulged—he or she may experience a fixation. A **fixation** means that a person is rigidly locked in conflict about that erogenous zone. Table 13.2 lists the five stages of psychosexual development. Let us explore them further.

Freud proposed that Leonardo da Vinci painted Madonnas as a form of sublimation.

An Overview of the Five Stages During the **oral stage,** the mouth experiences the most tension. The id tries to reduce this tension by encouraging the child to suck on nipples, thumbs, and pacifiers. A person fixated in the oral stage might be overly demanding or sarcastic—that is, sharp-tongued (Fenichel, 1945).

In the **anal stage,** the erogenous zone shifts to the anal region. Freud proposed that toddlers experience satisfaction when their anal region is stimulated, for instance by retaining or eliminating feces. Toilet training begins at this stage, and parents begin to insist that the child eliminate feces in the toilet. Conflict arises between the child's id and the new restrictions imposed by society. According to Freud's

Freud argued that humans first experience tension in the mouth area, during the oral stage.

TABLE 13.2   Freud's Five Stages of Psychosexual Development

AGE	STAGE	DESCRIPTION
0–18 months	Oral stage	Stimulation of the mouth produces pleasure; the baby enjoys sucking, chewing, biting.
18–36 months	Anal stage	Stimulation of the anal region produces pleasure; the toddler experiences conflict over toilet training.
3–6 years	Phallic stage	Self-stimulation of the genitals produces pleasure; the child struggles with negative feelings about the same-gender parent.
6–puberty	Latency	Sexual feelings are repressed; the child avoids members of the other gender.
Puberty onward	Genital stage	Adolescent or adult has mature sexual feelings and experiences pleasure from sexual relationships with others.

theory, unsuccessful resolution of this conflict produces fixation at the anal stage. A person may become "anal retentive," too orderly or overly concerned about punctuality—perhaps like Susan, the student described at the beginning of the chapter. On the other hand, a person can become "anal expulsive," or messy and perpetually late.

During the **phallic stage,** the erogenous zone shifts to the sex organs, and the child presumably finds pleasure in masturbation, or self-stimulation of the genitals. Freud proposed that boys in the phallic stage experience an Oedipus complex (pronounced "*Ed*-ih-pus"). In the ancient Greek tragedy *Oedipus Rex,* King Oedipus unknowingly kills his father and marries his mother. Similarly, in psychoanalysis, an **Oedipus complex** is a conflict in which a boy's sexual impulses are directed toward his mother, and he views his father as a rival. The young boy is afraid that his father may punish him for his desires by castrating him, or, cutting off his penis. A boy who develops normally will reduce this fear by identifying with his father, internalizing his father's values, and developing a strong superego.

Freud's explanation of the phallic stage in little girls was not as completely developed (Phares, 1988). However, Freud maintained that little girls experience the Electra complex, named after the Greek legend of Electra, who helped to kill her own mother. A young girl notices that she lacks a penis (experiencing penis envy) and decides that her mother was responsible for castrating her. She therefore develops hostile feelings for her mother while her love of her father grows.

How do children resolve these complexes? Freud proposed that children use a defense mechanism—specifically repression—to push back these unacceptable thoughts. Unsuccessful resolution of the phallic stage, however, can cause a person to be either overly proud or overly timid (Fenichel, 1945). We should note that children frequently *do* masturbate during preschool years; however, we do not have evidence that Freud's explanation for masturbation is correct.

During the **latency stage,** children's sexual feelings remain in the repressed state in which they were left at the end of the phallic stage. Children are presumably ashamed and disgusted about sexual issues, and so they tend to avoid members of the other gender.

Freud's final stage of psychosexual development is the **genital stage;** during puberty, sexual urges reappear and the genitals once again become an erogenous zone. Freud argued that genital pleasure in the earlier phallic stage comes from self-stimulation. In contrast, genital pleasure during the genital stage arises from sexual relationships with others.

Freud would explain the gender segregation in this classroom as a manifestation of the latency stage, in which children avoid members of the other gender.

Freudian Theory and Women In the last two decades, people who support the equality of women and men have argued that Freudian theory misrepresents women (e.g., Lerman, 1986a). Freud's writing often refers to female inferiority, which he traces primarily to women's lack of a penis. Freud argued that when young girls notice that they are missing a penis, they "feel themselves heavily handicapped . . . and envy the boy's possession of it" (Freud, 1925/1976, p. 327).

Freud believed that girls cannot experience an Electra conflict that is as intense as boys' Oedipal conflict, because they lack a large, obvious genital organ. Because the conflict is milder, girls identify less strongly with their mothers. As a consequence, their superegos never develop fully. Freud writes, "for women the level of what is ethically normal is different from what it is in men. . . . they show less sense of justice than men" (Freud, 1925/1976, p. 258).

We should note that psychological research has not produced evidence for females' penis envy (Fisher & Greenberg, 1977; Lerman, 1986a). In fact, most young girls are unconcerned about genital differences. Some, indeed, are relieved that they lack this anatomical structure. Consider, for instance, the little girl who took a bath with a young male cousin and observed the genital differences in silence. Later, she said softly to her mother, "Isn't it a blessing he doesn't have it on his face?" (Tavris & Offir, 1977, p. 155). Furthermore, as noted in Chapter 11, men and women do not differ significantly in their moral development. It is important to remember, however, that Freud was writing in a time when women were considered inferior, so his ideas reflect his own culture and historical context.

Other Psychodynamic Theorists

Freud has influenced our thinking about personality both directly through his own writing and indirectly through the ideas of his followers. We will discuss three of these theorists—Carl Jung, Alfred Adler, and Karen Horney—as well as the more recent object relations theory. You are already familiar with the best known of the theorists influenced by Freud—Erik Erikson; we discussed his eight stages of psychosocial development in Chapters 10 and 11. In general, you can see that these psychodynamic theorists place more emphasis on social roles and less emphasis on sexual factors, in contrast to Sigmund Freud.

Jung The Swiss analyst Carl Jung (pronounced "yoong") developed an early interest in Sigmund Freud's theory of dreams. However, Jung later believed that Freud overemphasized sexuality, so Jung's theories developed in a different direction (Jung, 1917/1953).

Jung's theory retained Freud's emphasis on the unconscious, but Jung argued that the unconscious contains two layers. The first layer, or **personal unconscious,** stores material that has been forgotten or repressed. Jung's personal unconscious is therefore comparable to Freud's notions about the unconscious.

However, Jung also proposed a second, deeper layer called the collective unconscious. Jung's **collective unconscious** stores memory fragments from our ancestral past. Jung's theory proposes, then, that all humans share the same collective unconscious. Jung argued that the collective unconscious can explain archetypes (pronounced "*are*-kih-tipes"). An **archetype** is a classic image or symbol that is found in a wide variety of cultures and religions. For instance, Figure 13.2 shows two mandalas, or figures with a circular design—each from a different country. The concepts of a collective unconscious and archetypes have been greeted more enthusiastically by artists and anthropologists than by psychologists.

Perhaps Jung's most important contribution to psychology was the idea that people could be categorized as either introverts or extraverts. An **introvert** tends to be shy and withdrawn, more oriented toward his or her own internal experience. In contrast, an **extravert** tends to be outgoing, more oriented toward other people and events. Jung's approach was an early forerunner of the trait approach, which we will examine in the third section of this chapter.

Adler Like Jung, Alfred Adler believed that Freud had overemphasized the importance of sexuality in his theory. Instead, Adler's theory emphasized people's striving toward power or superiority. Adler proposed that children feel physically weak and helpless in a world ruled by adults. When parents are either overprotective or neglectful, these feelings of inferiority can develop into an inferiority complex (Adler, 1924). People generally try to compensate in order to overcome these feelings of inferiority. They want to improve themselves and overcome difficulties.

Horney Karen Horney (pronounced "*Horn*-eye") challenged Freud's theory of penis envy and proposed that women are more likely to envy men's status in society than their genitals (Horney, 1926/1967). Like Adler, Horney proposed that young children feel relatively helpless and threatened. Children develop several strategies to cope with the anxiety generated by this helplessness (Enns, 1989; Horney, 1945). Specifically, they can move *toward* other people, showing affection or dependency. They can also move *against* other people, displaying aggression or hostility. Finally, they can move *away from* other people, protecting themselves by withdrawing from relationships. Horney proposed that normal people balance the three strategies. Psychological disorders develop, however, when one strategy dominates personality.

Object-Relations Approach We have summarized the ideas of three theorists who were strongly influenced by Freud. A more recent development is the **object-relations approach,** which focuses on the nature and development of ideas about the self in relationship to other people (Westen, 1991). This approach minimizes Freud's notions of drives and emphasizes the developing relationship between the self and objects—that is, significant persons ("Psychodynamic Therapy: Part II," 1991). The child's perception of this relationship during the first two years of life will have a significant impact on his or her later life (e.g., Fairbairn, 1952; Klein, 1948).

A prominent object-relations theorist is Nancy Chodorow (1978, 1989). She argues that boys and girls both identify with their mother initially. Infant girls grow up with a feeling of similarity to their mother, which develops into interdependence, or a connection with others in general. Infant boys, in contrast, must learn that they are different from their mother in order to develop a male identity. As a consequence, the two genders face different potential problems in their relationships; females may not develop sufficient independence, and males may not develop close attachments (Gilligan, 1982).

Figure 13.2

These mandalas were painted by artists from two different cultures. The one on the left is a Navajo sand painting, and the one on the right was created by an artist in Tibet. Jung argued that they are similar because we all share the same collective unconscious.

According to Horney, the young boy on the right is moving toward other people, rather than against them or away from them.

TABLE 13.3 A Summary of the Psychodynamic Approach

	PSYCHODYNAMIC APPROACH
Source of data	Obtained by expert analyst from people in therapy.
Cause of behavior	Internal conflict, unconscious forces, childhood experiences.
Comprehensiveness of theory	Very comprehensive.
Outlook on humans	Negative.

Evaluation of the Psychodynamic Approach

We have outlined Freud's theory and then briefly noted the contributions of four more recent theories. Let us now evaluate the psychodynamic approach, as represented by the prototype theorist, Sigmund Freud. Table 13.3 summarizes four important characteristics of psychodynamic theory.

What can we conclude about Freud's psychodynamic approach, roughly a century after it was formulated? By current standards, this theory has several major problems:

1. *It is difficult to test.* Psychodynamic theory emphasizes the unconscious, yet the unconscious rarely expresses itself directly. Therefore, it is difficult to measure. Furthermore, consider the following problem: Suppose that an analyst suspects that a man is pessimistic. Any pessimistic feelings expressed in therapy will be taken as evidence of pessimism. However, any optimistic feelings will also be taken as evidence of pessimism, because these feelings could be a reaction formation against the original pessimism. Some aspects of psychodynamic theory cannot be disproven, because the theory could predict both a particular characteristic and its opposite (Phares, 1988).

2. *When it is tested, the studies are often inadequate.* The psychodynamic approach is criticized for improper methodology. For instance, the observers may be biased, interpreting ambiguous observations so that they are consistent with a particular theory. How do we know that the little girl's concern over broken crayons (mentioned on page 412) represents penis envy, when we can find more obvious explanations? Furthermore, Freud's theory was based on a nonrepresentative sample from a different era. We cannot generalize from a small sample of troubled, well-to-do Viennese people—studied many decades ago—to a variety of cultures at the end of the twentieth century. Some psychodynamic theorists have conducted more rigorous research in recent years on topics such as the unconscious (e.g., Shulman, 1990; Silverman, 1983; Silverman & Weinberger, 1985). However, other theorists argue that we still have no clear-cut research evidence of basic Freudian concepts such as repression (e.g., Holmes, 1990).

3. *Freud's theory is biased against women.* As we noted earlier, Freud maintained that women have inferior moral judgment, a gender bias that is not supported by research. He also proposed that women are **masochistic** (pronounced "mass-uh-*kiss*-tick"), deriving pleasure from being mistreated. This view does a disservice to women, and it encourages people to think—incorrectly—that women enjoy being battered or raped (Caplan, 1984).

4. *It is too pessimistic about human nature.* Freudian theory proposes that we are helpful because of a reaction formation against our aggressive feelings. We do not help simply because we want to be moral or good (Wallach & Wallach, 1983). Furthermore, we act ethically because we fear punishment from our superegos, according to Freud. However, we learned in Chapter 10 that even very young children are

helpful toward others—before their superegos could be well developed. As Wallach and Wallach point out, humans *are* basically concerned about others; Freud's explanation was unnecessarily indirect and negative.

We have noted several problems with Freud's psychodynamic theory. Still, we need to remember that we cannot blame Freud for being unable to predict how humans and their society would behave a century after he developed his theories.

Most important, we must praise Freud for encouraging psychology to explore human motivations and emotions, rather than focusing only on thoughts and intellectual reactions. Freud's concept of the unconscious is clearly valuable to many modern psychologists (e.g., Jacoby et al., 1992; Loftus & Klinger, 1992). Freud also contributed useful concepts such as anxiety and defense mechanisms. Furthermore, Freud's theory is the most fully developed and comprehensive approach we consider in this chapter. He tried to explain an enormous range of human behaviors. Finally, we have to admire Freud's brilliance and persistence in developing a theory so different from the trends of his own era.

SECTION SUMMARY
THE PSYCHODYNAMIC APPROACH

- The psychodynamic approach stresses childhood experiences and unconscious motivations and conflicts; Freud's psychoanalytic theory (one kind of psychodynamic approach) was radically controversial when it was first presented, but it has had a strong impact on both psychology and other disciplines.

- Freud proposed three components of personality: the id, ego, and superego; the ego and the superego can be represented in the conscious, preconscious, or unconscious, whereas the id is totally unconscious.

- Freud's methods include free association, and the interpretation of dreams, reactions, and slips-of-the-tongue.

- Psychodynamic defense mechanisms include repression, regression, reaction formation, rationalization, sublimation, displacement, and projection.

- Freud argued that the erogenous zone shifts throughout development during five stages called oral, anal, phallic, latency, and genital.

- Other psychodynamic theorists and theories include Jung (collective unconscious and introvert/extravert categories), Adler (the inferiority complex), Horney (challenging penis envy; proposed movement toward, against, or away from others), Erikson (discussed in Chapters 10 and 11), and object-relations theory (the self in relationship to other people).

- Criticisms of psychodynamic theory include the difficulty of testing it, inadequate research, its bias against women, and its extreme pessimism. Positive features include its emphasis on emotions, some useful theoretical concepts, and its comprehensiveness.

THE HUMANISTIC APPROACH

The psychodynamic perspective paints a dismal portrait of human nature. In contrast, the humanistic approach optimistically argues that people have enormous potential for personal growth. Humanistic psychologists also propose that each of us has unique subjective experiences. Even your closest friend cannot fully understand what it is like to be *you*.

The humanistic approach gained prominence in the early 1960s when Carl Rogers (1961) and Abraham Maslow (1962) published important books. Many psychologists were dissatisfied with the two theories dominant at that time. On the one hand, the psychodynamic approach proposed that human kindness and caring often has its origins in evil impulses. On the other hand, the behaviorist approach—which we discussed in Chapter 6—focused on animal research. How could experiments with rats and pigeons inform us about higher human goals, such as the search for truth and beauty? (We should note that the social cognitive approach had not yet been proposed, and the humanistic theorists did not consider the trait approach to be a full-fledged personality theory.)

Rogers, Maslow, and others developed the humanistic approach as an alternative to the psychodynamic and behaviorist approaches, and so it is sometimes called *third force psychology*. This section examines the ideas of the two most prominent humanistic theorists, Rogers and Maslow, and ends with an evaluation of the humanistic approach.

Rogers's Person-Centered Approach

Carl Rogers (1902–1987) was born in Illinois and began his professional career working with troubled children, though he later extended his therapy to adults. In his clinical work, he used the term *clients,* because he felt that the standard term *patients* implied that these people were ill. Chapter 16 examines Rogers's approach to behavior disorders, called client-centered therapy. This approach requires the therapist to try to see the world from each client's point of view rather than from the therapist's own framework.

As we will see, the behaviorist approach emphasizes external stimuli. In contrast, Carl Rogers emphasizes that each of us interprets the same set of stimuli differently. As Rogers (1980) wrote, our different perceived realities means that there are as many different "real worlds" as there are people in this world.

Self-Actualization Carl Rogers used the term **self-actualization** to capture the natural, inborn tendency for humans to fulfill their true potential (Frick, 1989; Rogers, 1963, 1980). He marveled that this actualizing tendency could persist, even in the most hostile environments. Rogers draws a parallel with an observation from his own childhood:

> *I remember that in my boyhood, the bin in which we stored our winter's supply of potatoes was in the basement, several feet below a small window. The conditions were unfavorable, but the potatoes would begin to sprout—pale white sprouts, so unlike the healthy green shoots they sent up when planted in the soil in the spring. But these sad, spindly sprouts would grow 2 to 3 feet in length as they reached toward the distant light of the window. These sprouts were, in their bizarre, futile growth, a sort of desperate expression of the directional tendency I have been describing. They would never become plants, never mature, never fulfill their real potential. But under the most adverse circumstances, they were striving to become. Life would not give up, even if it could not flourish. (Rogers, 1980, p. 118)*

Rogers often thought of those potato sprouts when interacting with people in the back wards of large hospitals. The lives of these clients had been terribly warped. Despite unfavorable conditions, Rogers believed that these people were still striving toward growth. Rogers emphasized that this active self-development tendency provided the underlying basis of the person-centered approach.

Personality Development Carl Rogers did not propose any stages of development, as do the theories of Sigmund Freud or Erik Erikson. He did not believe that people passed through any well-specified series of changes. Instead, he thought that personality development depended upon the way a person is evaluated by others (Phares, 1988).

Rogers proposed that even young children need positive regard, to be highly esteemed by other people. Children also develop a need for positive *self*-regard, to be esteemed by oneself as well as others. A mature, independent person must have positive self-regard.

Rogers argued that people strive toward growth, even in less-than-favorable surroundings.

From his work with clients who had psychological disorders, Rogers found that self-actualizing tendencies were frequently stifled by restricting self-concepts. Specifically, these clients had learned that they had to act in ways that distorted their "true selves" in order to win positive regard from others.

Rogers proposed that most children experience **conditional positive regard;** parents and other important people withhold their love and approval if children fail to conform to their elders' standards. For instance, parents might award positive regard to their son only in certain conditions—for example, only if he makes the football team. However, they may withhold positive regard if he fails to achieve in athletics or if he succeeds in other areas, such as music or the debate club.

In contrast, Rogers believed that everyone should be given **unconditional positive regard,** or total, genuine love without any strings attached (Rogers, 1959). Once again, however, the person-centered approach emphasizes the individual's perception of reality. A mother may believe that she is giving unconditional positive regard.

Rogers believed that children need unconditional positive regard.

However, the child may perceive this to be *conditional* positive regard, and this is the reality that matters to the child (Ross, 1987). In short, children need to feel that the important people in their lives accept them for who they are.

The research partly supports Rogers's ideas. As you may recall from Chapter 10, Diana Baumrind's (1971, 1975) work on parenting styles indicated that parents do make a difference. Authoritarian parents, who demand unquestioning obedience from their children, do tend to produce unhappy, ineffective offspring; these children who clearly lack unconditional positive regard are not likely to experience self-actualization. However, permissive parents, who make few demands and allow children to make their own decisions, often produce immature offspring with little self-control. Baumrind found that the most successful parenting style was used by authoritative parents, who were loving but upheld clear-cut standards. Thus, it seems that unconditional positive regard—without clear-cut standards—does not encourage self-actualization. Children need to know that some parental rules will be upheld.

Maslow's Hierarchy of Needs

Abraham Maslow (1908–1970) was born in Brooklyn, New York. As a young psychologist, he was initially attracted to behaviorism. However, when his first child was born, Maslow realized that behaviorism could not account for the miracle of an infant's experience (Frick, 1989; Phares, 1988).

Maslow is probably best known for his theoretical exploration of self-actualization, the important tendency to realize our own potential. Maslow theorized that our human motives are arranged in a hierarchy, with the most basic needs at the bottom and the more highly developed needs (esteem needs and—finally—self-actualization needs) at the top (Maslow, 1970).

Figure 13.3 shows **Maslow's hierarchy of needs,** in which each lower need must be satisfied before the next level of need can be addressed. For instance, people whose homes have just been destroyed by a flood will primarily be concerned with physiological and safety needs, rather than the more lofty goal of self-actualization. Let us examine the five levels in Maslow's hierarchy, beginning with the most basic level.

1. *Physiological needs:* We need food, water, sleep, and sex. Notice that these needs are also those that motivate lower animals.

2. *Safety needs:* These include the needs for security, protection, and the avoidance of pain.

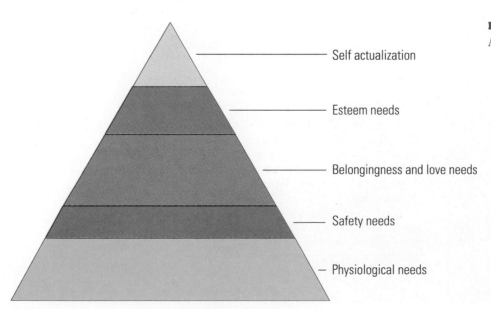

Self actualization

Esteem needs

Belongingness and love needs

Safety needs

Physiological needs

Figure 13.3
Maslow's hierarchy of needs.

3. *Belongingness and love needs:* These needs include affiliation with other people, affection, and feeling loved; sexual relationships as an expression of affection can also be included in this category.

4. *Esteem needs:* We also need to respect ourselves and to win the esteem of others. Otherwise, we feel discouraged and inferior, and Maslow proposes that we will not strive for the highest level in the hierarchy.

5. *Self-actualization needs:* A person who has satisfied all the lower needs can seek self-actualization, attempting to reach her or his full potential.

Pioneer social worker Jane Addams was one of the people Maslow identified as a self-actualizer.

Maslow became particularly intrigued with this highest level, self-actualization, in attempting to understand two of his favorite teachers, anthropologist Ruth Benedict and Gestalt psychologist Max Wertheimer (Maslow, 1971). He saw that they shared many underlying qualities. Later, he began to select other prominent people from both historical and modern times. These were healthy, well-adjusted people who had used their full potential. The list included social worker Jane Addams, presidents Thomas Jefferson and Abraham Lincoln, first lady and social activist Eleanor Roosevelt, and physicist Albert Einstein. Demonstration 13.2 encourages you to think about some of the characteristics of self-actualized people.

Evaluation of the Humanistic Approach

Table 13.4 summarizes four important characteristics of the humanistic approach, contrasting it with the psychodynamic approach. The data in the humanistic approach are from the self-reports from nonclinical populations in the case of Maslow and people in therapy in the case of Rogers (DeCarvalho, 1991). Behavior is motivated by self-concepts and the tendency to self-actualize. The theory is reasonably comprehensive, though not as far-reaching as the psychodynamic approach. Finally, compared with the psychodynamic approach, humanistic psychology proposes a blissfully positive interpretation of human nature.

The humanistic approach can be criticized for several reasons:

1. *It relies on subjective experience.* The humanistic approach emphasizes that reality lies in a person's own interpretation of the world. Some people have only a

---

DEMONSTRATION 13.2 Qualities of a Self-Actualized Person

Think about someone you know who seems to be a self-actualized person, who has lived up to his or her full potential. (Ideally, this is someone you know personally, so you are more familiar with this person's qualities.) Now read each of the characteristics listed below and decide whether they apply to the person you know. Place an X in front of each one that does describe this person.

_____ An acceptance of himself or herself

_____ An acceptance of other people

_____ Involvement in some cause outside of himself or herself

_____ Very spontaneous in both actions and emotions

_____ Focused on problems and solutions rather than himself or herself

_____ Resists pressures to conform

_____ Superior creativity

_____ Fresh appreciation of other people, rather than stereotyped reactions

_____ Strongly developed set of values

How many of these characteristics apply to your target person? If any did *not* apply, do you think that this person would be even more self-actualized if she or he possessed these qualities?

In addition, you might try evaluating several famous people on these dimensions. How would you rate Mother Theresa, various politicians, and some major entertainers?

Source: Based on Maslow, 1968, 1971.

TABLE 13.4 A Comparison of the Humanistic Approach with the Psychodynamic Approach

	PSYCHODYNAMIC APPROACH	HUMANISTIC APPROACH
Source of data	Obtained from expert analyst from people in therapy.	Obtained from self-reports from the general population and people in therapy.
Cause of behavior	Internal conflict, unconscious forces, childhood experiences.	Self-concepts, self-actualizing tendencies.
Comprehensiveness of theory	Very comprehensive.	Fairly comprehensive.
Outlook on humans	Negative	Positive.

limited ability to express themselves, so their self-reports probably do not reflect their experiences (Phares, 1988). We are therefore left with partly inadequate data.

2. *The studies are often inadequate.* Both Rogers and Maslow tended to study only a selected sample of the entire population. Specifically, they worked with people who were more intelligent and verbal than average. Humanistic principles may not be applicable to other groups. Furthermore, as Maslow (1971) himself admits, his work on self-actualizing people does not really qualify as *research.* An important criticism of this work, for example, is that his choice of self-actualized people is rather arbitrary. These individuals may have fulfilled their potential in some respects, but not others. Abraham Lincoln had periods of severe depression, for instance, and Eleanor Roosevelt's family relationships were less than ideal. Thus, much of the so-called support for the humanistic approach is too subjective. Even humanistic psychologists point out that important aspects of life, such as the meaningfulness of experience, cannot be adequately studied by traditional research techniques (Rogers, 1985).

3. *It is too selfish.* The characteristics listed in Demonstration 13.2 include "Involvement in some cause outside of himself or herself" as one of Maslow's qualities of a self-actualized person. However, altruism is not included in Maslow's hierarchy, and it is not central in other discussions of self-actualization. As Wallach and Wallach (1983, 1990) point out, the humanistic theorists emphasize self-liberation. However, when people focus on their own personal goals, they often ignore their responsibilities toward others. Our globe is plagued with hundreds of problems. Should issues such as acid rain, homelessness, social justice, and world peace be placed on the back burner while we all concentrate on self-actualization?

4. *It is too optimistic.* As Rogers's colleague and friend Rollo May (1986) observes, many humanistic theorists are overly optimistic. If you glance at today's newspaper, you will probably find little evidence that people are inherently good, striving toward self-actualization. Incidents of suicide, murder, battering, child abuse, and rape have all increased in recent decades. As soon as one global conflict is resolved, another one arises. Rollo May agrees with Rogers that many people perform heroic and prosocial deeds. As he said, following a list of human atrocities, "I am not arguing that we human beings are only evil. I am arguing that we are bundles of both evil and good potentialities" (May, 1986, p. 17). May's more neutral view of humans seems much more consistent with reality.

Despite these criticisms, humanistic psychology must be praised for its substantial strengths. For instance, the humanistic approach focuses on the present and the future, whereas the psychodynamic perspective makes us "captives of the past" (Phares, 1988, p. 217). The humanistic approach also deserves credit for pointing out that we humans do not share identical interpretations of reality. Furthermore, this approach offers an integrated view of humans. Each of us is a whole person, rather than a collection of isolated characteristics.

Finally, humanistic psychologists have been impressively influential. Humanistic principles are being applied in therapy, education, communication, business, and child rearing (Whitson & Olczak, 1991). A visit to any bookstore illustrates the impact of the humanistic approach: Dozens of self-help books promise a golden path to self-actualization. Although the names Rogers and Maslow may not be as well known as Freud, the humanistic approach has clearly shaped many aspects of popular psychology.

S E C T I O N   S U M M A R Y

THE HUMANISTIC APPROACH

- The humanistic approach emphasizes the potential for personal growth.

- Carl Rogers's person-centered approach emphasizes that people have different perceived realities and that they strive toward self-actualization; everyone should be given unconditional positive regard.

- Abraham Maslow's hierarchy proposes that needs must be fulfilled in a specified order, from physiological, safety, and love, to esteem and self-actualization; Maslow also proposed several characteristics descriptive of self-actualized people.

- The humanistic approach can be criticized for relying on subjective experience, as well as the inadequacy of the research, its basic selfishness, and its excessive optimism. Its strengths include its focus on the present and future, its emphasis on different realities, its integrated view of humans, and its influence on popular psychology.

THE TRAIT APPROACH

Of the four personality approaches described in this chapter, the trait approach places the most emphasis on our theme of individual differences. As the introduction to this chapter stressed, the trait approach proposes that personality is a combination of specific stable, internal personality characteristics called traits. Thus, a **trait** is a consistent tendency to have certain kinds of beliefs, desires, behaviors, and so forth (Wakefield, 1989).

The trait approach is not necessarily concerned with the way these individual differences arise. No trait theory explains *why* Susan should be neat, Sam should be stingy, and Paulette should be habitually late. Instead, the trait approach attempts to describe *how* people differ from each other. People who favor the trait approach tend to ask questions such as: Do people differ significantly on a particular trait? Does this trait remain stable across time, so that a person who is neat at age 5 will also be neat at age 55? Does this trait remain stable across situations, so that a person who is late to work will also be late to social events? Can we condense all traits down to just a small number of trait clusters?

Incidentally, you have already been exposed to some of the research by trait theorists in the developmental chapters, in connection with the stability-change issue, when we noted that traits remain somewhat stable across time. An infant's characteristics tend to be related to his or her characteristics during childhood. Furthermore, a young adult's characteristics tend to remain somewhat stable through later adulthood.

In this section, we first examine two psychologists who developed the trait approach: Gordon Allport and Hans Eysenck. Then we discuss an approach called the five-factor model of personality, followed by a controversial topic in personality: the person-situation debate. Our next topic involves biological research on personality. We conclude this section with an evaluation of the trait approach.

Allport's Trait Theory

Gordon Allport (1897–1967) began his undergraduate years at Harvard University with C's and D's on his examinations (Allport, 1967). It is hard to imagine how someone who began so unpromisingly and ended so prominently could have formulated a theory that focused on stability rather than change. A lucky meeting with Sigmund Freud helps to explain the change. After graduation, Allport decided to teach at a college in Turkey. After two years there and in Europe, he visited his brother, who was living in Vienna, Austria, on the way back to the United States. Allport arranged to pay a visit to Freud. (What would have happened if Allport's brother had been living in Salzburg or London instead of Vienna?) Freud invited him into his inner office. Allport wrote about their interaction,

> He did not speak to me but sat in expectant silence, for me to state my mission. I was not prepared for silence and had to think fast to find a suitable conversational gambit. I told him of an episode on the tram car on my way to his office. A small boy about four years of age had displayed a conspicuous dirt phobia. He kept saying to his mother, "I don't want to sit there . . . don't let that dirty man sit beside me." To him everything was schmutzig [dirty]. His mother was a well-starched Hausfrau [housewife], so dominant and purposive looking that I thought the cause and effect apparent.
>
> When I finished my story Freud fixed his kindly therapeutic eyes upon me and said, "And was that little boy you?" Flabbergasted and feeling a bit guilty, I contrived to change the subject. While Freud's misunderstanding of my motivation was amusing, it also started a deep train of thought. (Allport, 1967, p. 8)

This encounter convinced Allport that the psychodynamic approach plunged too deeply into symbols—rather than manifest content—producing misinterpretations (Elms, 1993). Allport resolved to focus on conscious motives rather than unconscious ones. In addition to his important trait theory, he wrote a classic textbook on personality (Allport, 1937; Craik et al., 1993). Before reading about Allport's theory, however, try Demonstration 13.3.

One of Allport's first research activities was to examine an unabridged dictionary, recording every term that could describe a person (Allport & Odbert, 1936). He located a total of 18,000! After eliminating many that seemed to describe temporary rather than enduring characteristics (e.g., *elated, shamefaced*), he still had a list of more than 3,000 traitlike words—clearly too many to study systematically.

Eventually, Allport (1937, 1961) decided to organize this overwhelming task by proposing three levels of traits:

1. A **cardinal trait** is one that dominates and shapes a person's behavior. For my daughter Beth, for instance, a single-minded interest in infants and children has shaped her life. At the age of 21 months, she showered affection and tiny gifts on her newborn sister. At 8 years of age, she volunteered as an unpaid parents' helper. As a college student, she studied early childhood education and

---

DEMONSTRATION 13.3 Listing Traits

Take a blank sheet of paper. In 5 minutes, list as many trait words as you can. Remember that a trait is a stable tendency (in other words, a characteristic that will last for years), and it describes a person's beliefs, desires, behaviors, and other personality characteristics. After your 5 minutes are finished, try to group together characteristics that seem rather similar, so that you end up with between 4 and 6 clusters of related characteristics. We will discuss this topic in connection with the so-called Big Five approach.

For this young woman, an intense interest in infants and children constitutes a cardinal trait.

started a Head-Start program for preschoolers in Nicaragua. She is now passionately anticipating running her own day-care center. Perhaps you know someone who is obsessed with becoming wealthy, or another person whose life focus is religion. Allport proposed that these cardinal traits are rare, however. Most of us lack a single theme in our lives.

2. A **central trait** is a general characteristic, found to some degree in every person. These basic building blocks shape much of our behavior, though they are not as overwhelmingly influential as cardinal traits. Some central traits could be honesty (which Chapter 11 noted was a dominant theme in adult personality), extraversion, and cheerfulness.

3. A **secondary trait** is a characteristic seen only in certain situations. These must be included to provide a complete picture of human complexity. For instance, some typical secondary traits might include "uncomfortable in large crowds" and "likes to drive sports cars."

Allport argued that a person's pattern of traits determined his or her behavior. No two people are completely identical, and as a result no two people respond completely identically to the same environmental situation. As Allport said, "The same fire that melts the butter hardens the egg" (Allport, 1937, p. 102).

Eysenck's Biosocial Theory

Hans Eysenck (pronounced "*Eye*-senk") was born in Germany in 1916 but left during Hitler's regime, eventually settling in London. Eysenck proposed that three major dimensions account for most of human behavior (Eysenck, 1953, 1975, 1992):

1. Introversion versus extraversion is a dimension fairly similar to Jung's categorization of people as either introverts or extraverts. However, Eysenck notes that few perfect introverts or extraverts exist. Instead, a person can be placed anywhere between these two extremes.

2. Stability versus instability refers to a person's general moodiness. A stable person is calm, even-tempered, and reliable. A person who is unstable is moody, touchy, and restless. Again, however, a person can be placed at any point along the stability-instability continuum.

3. Psychoticism can indicate a psychological disorder in extreme cases, but Eysenck proposes that it is a personality characteristic that can be applied in varying degrees to everyone. A person who is high in psychoticism is cold, solitary, and insensitive, showing no loyalty or concern for others.

More than the other theorists discussed so far, Eysenck has examined the biological basis of his three personality dimensions. For example, he reported that introverts and extraverts differ in their level of arousal in a specific structure of the brain, the reticular formation (Eysenck, 1970). In general, introverts have higher levels of arousal internally, so they tend to avoid external stimulation. In contrast, extraverts tend to have lower levels of arousal internally, so they tend to seek out external stimulation. On a social occasion, an introvert would back away, whereas an extravert would move into the center of the group.

The Five-Factor Model

How many basic trait dimensions do we need to capture all the rich complexity of the human personality? Some researchers propose as many as 16 basic traits, whereas others—such as Eysenck—suggest only 2 or 3 (Mischel, 1993). In other words, all the variety and subtlety contained in Allport and Odbert's (1936) list of more than 3,000 trait words (or your own shorter list of words from Demonstration 13.3) can be distilled into just a handful of different traits.

The most widely accepted solution to the search for trait clusters is called the five-factor model (Costa & McCrae, 1992a; Dingman, 1990; McCrae & Costa, 1990). The **five-factor model,** also called the **Big Five traits,** proposes that the most important clusters of traits include extraversion, agreeableness, conscientiousness, emotional stability, and openness to experience. Researchers have found evidence for this five-factor model in cross-cultural studies with people in Canada, Finland, Poland, and Germany (Paunonen et al., 1992) and in China (Costa & McCrae, 1992a).

Costa and McCrae have also developed a personality test, similar to the assessment tools we will discuss in Chapter 14. The **NEO Personality Inventory** received its name from the original three factors included in the test (neuroticism—another name for emotional stability, extraversion, and openness to experience); new items have also been added to measure agreeableness and conscientiousness (Costa & McCrae, 1992b). Demonstration 13.4 is an informal version of the five-factor model.

As Goldberg (1993) points out, the five-factor model has never claimed that these five dimensions capture all aspects of personality. Instead, "they seek to provide a scientifically compelling framework in which to organize the myriad individual differences that characterize humankind" (p. 27).

The Person-Situation Debate

A major ongoing controversy in studies examining the trait approach can be called **the person-situation debate.** Here are the two extreme positions in this debate:

1. *Person:* Each person possesses stable, internal traits that cause him or her to act consistently in a variety of situations.

2. *Situation:* Each person does not possess stable, internal traits. Instead, his or her behavior depends upon the specific characteristics of each situation.

People who support trait theory tend to cluster toward the *person* position. In contrast, behaviorists in the tradition of B. F. Skinner believe that environmental stimuli are far more important. If we can specify the external stimuli in a situation, we can predict how anyone would respond, without needing to discuss any internal characteristics. People who cluster toward the *situation* position might even suggest that we eliminate the personality chapter of introductory textbooks: There is no such thing as personality, only situations. Let us examine this controversy.

This demonstration allows you to assess yourself informally on each of the Big Five Traits. Use the basic 7-point rating scale shown below, each time supplying a number in the blank space to indicate where you belong on a given scale (e.g., sociable-retiring). After you have rated yourself on each of the three scales that comprise a dimension, calculate an average (e.g., for extraversion). Which end of each dimension seems most characteristic of your personality? Please keep in mind, however, that any informal demonstration such as this is not intended to provide an accurate diagnosis.

1	2	3	4	5	6	7

1. **Extraversion**   (Average rating =   )

_____ Sociable   Retiring

_____ Fun-loving   Sober

_____ Affectionate   Reserved

2. **Agreeableness**   (Average rating =   )

_____ Softhearted   Ruthless

_____ Trusting   Suspicious

_____ Helpful   Uncooperative

3. **Conscientious**   (Average rating =   )

_____ Well organized   Disorganized

_____ Careful   Careless

_____ Self-disciplined   Weak-willed

4. **Emotional Stability**   (Average rating =   )

_____ Calm   Worrying

_____ Secure   Insecure

_____ Self-satisfied   Self-pitying

5. **Openness to Experience** (Average rating =   )

_____ Imaginative   Down-to-earth

_____ Preference for variety   Preference for routine

_____ Independent   Conformity

Source: Based on McCrea & Costa, 1986.

Note: "Emotional stability" is also called "neuroticism"

Mischel's Position For many decades, personality psychologists had supported the person position, particularly because it matches our common sense about personality. Of course people are consistent! Julie is consistently unconcerned about others, whereas Pete is always compassionate. A strong challenge to this position was presented by Walter Mischel (pronounced "Mih-*shell*"), who came from a learning-theory tradition.

Mischel (1968) examined dozens of previous studies and discovered that the behaviors that are supposed to reflect the same internal trait are only weakly correlated with each other. For example, students' tendency to arrive on time for one event is correlated only +.19 with their tendency to arrive on time for another event (Dudycha, 1936). This very weak correlation does not support the person position.

But why do we persist in believing that personality characteristics are consistent across situations? Mischel (1968) proposed that traits are mostly in the minds of the beholder. If I think that some of my friends are characteristically punctual and others are characteristically late (and, incidentally, I *do* believe this), the apparent consistency is caused by my own cognitive biases. One of these biases is the primacy effect: We tend to maintain our first impression of someone even if he or she acts very differently on later occasions. Perhaps because my friend Suzanne arrived late and flustered to the dinner party where I first met her, I have failed to notice that she has been reasonably prompt since then.

Another source of bias is that we usually see a person in only a limited set of situations. Perhaps a young man in your high school seemed very friendly to you, but you saw him only in situations where he felt comfortable. On a college interview (where you did not see him), he may have been timid and withdrawn. Mischel (1979) argues that each of us does show some slight consistency from one situation to another, but the people who know us tend to exaggerate that consistency.

Factors Related to Consistency Bem and Allen (1974) suggested that some people may indeed behave highly consistently, whereas others behave inconsistently—perhaps friendly on some occasions and unfriendly on other occasions. Bem and Allen's data supported this hypothesis. However, more recent research has not (Borkenau, 1993). In other words—if I can say this without overwhelming you—the research has not been consistent about whether there are systematic individual differences in people's consistency!

Other researchers have demonstrated that people show more consistency if we measure the average behavior across several events, rather than just a single event (Epstein, 1983; Epstein & O'Brien, 1985). This makes sense. You might be late to class one day, but early four other days. Your *average* punctuality for classes is likely to be correlated with your *average* punctuality for other events. In addition, the correlations are higher if we measure general characteristics—such as "behaves in a cheerful manner"—rather than specific behaviors—such as "number of smiles" (Funder & Colvin, 1991).

Furthermore, traits are more easily expressed in some situations than others (Buss, 1989; Kenrick & Funder, 1988; Wiggins & Pincus, 1992). For instance, some situations constrain our behavior, so the traits cannot be easily expressed. At a funeral, the friendly people will not act much different from the unfriendly people. However, at a picnic, individual differences will be strong. Cross-situational consistency will be higher if we look only at *unconstrained* situations. Furthermore, consistency will be higher if the situation is familiar, if people receive no instructions about how they should act, and if they are observed for a long time, rather than a brief period.

Cross-situational consistency is higher in an unconstrained situation like a picnic, where the situation has less formal structure and individual differences can reveal themselves.

Conclusions About the Person-Situation Debate As Kenrick and Funder (1988) conclude in their review of the person-situation debate, "As with most controversies, the truth finally appears to lie not in the vivid black or white of either extreme, but somewhere in the less striking gray area" (p. 31). Behavior is probably not as consistent across situations as our intuitions suggest; systematic biases encourage us to believe in traits. However, some consistency really does exist. Furthermore, in some situations, for some people, some traits, and some methods of measuring those traits, the consistency can be reasonably high. Obviously, our theme of complexity fits the data on personality consistency!

In Chapter 10, we saw that we could not answer which factor is more important, nature or nurture. Both are important. Similarly, we cannot answer which factor is the better predictor of behavior, person or situation. Again, both are important. To predict how a person will behave, we need some measure of his or her internal traits, but we must also understand the characteristics of the external situation.

The Biological Basis of Individual Differences

The trait theory argues that if we want to understand personality, we must examine the characteristics that people bring to the situation. For many psychologists, the next logical step is to examine the biological bases of those characteristics (Brody, 1988). We should note, however, that some prominent psychologists believe that it is premature to rely too heavily on biological explanations in constructing personality theories (e.g. Costa & McCrae, 1992a, Magnusson & Törestad, 1993).

The most active biological research focuses on the genetic basis of personality. You may recall that Chapter 3 discussed how genetic researchers have conducted twin studies on personality, as well as in other areas such as cognitive abilities and psychological disorders.

The popular press has widely publicized the research on identical twins who have been reared apart (e.g., Bouchard et al., 1990; Lykken et al., 1992). After all, it's fascinating to read about a pair of twins who are both habitual gigglers—even though they were reared in different households and neither adoptive family was known for its sense of humor. Or consider the pair of twins reared in separate homes who behaved identically at the beach; both entered the water backwards and avoided water levels above their knees. Some critics suggest that the high degree of similarities between the twin pairs is partly due to a nonrandom sample (Adler, 1991). Furthermore, we must remember from the discussion in Chapter 8 that many unusual-looking outcomes can occur by chance alone.

The research on twins reared together and apart often calculates **heritability,** or an estimate of how much of the variation in some characteristic can be traced to differences in heredity, as opposed to differences in environment.[*] Heritabilities typically range between .39 and .58 for different personality traits such as aggressiveness and reactions to stress (Tellegen et al., 1988).

Researchers are more likely to conduct studies that compare the personalities of identical and fraternal twins. For example, Zuckerman (1991) reviews nine of these studies that examine three personality traits: sociability, emotionality, and impulsiveness. The correlations for pairs of identical twins range between +.41 and +.61; for pairs of fraternal twins, they range between +.01 and +.28. Zuckerman argues that the correlations are much higher for identical twins because they are more genetically similar to each other.

For many years, psychologists argued that children in a family are similar because of nurture; for example, friendly parents teach their children to be outgoing and friendly. However, Zuckerman (1991) reports that family environmental influ-

---

Heritability is calculated as a proportion, specifically, the proportion of the total variation that is due to heredity. This number can range between 0 (no heredity component) and 1.00 (all variation is due to heredity). In contrast, the correlation coefficients discussed in the next paragraph show the direction and strength of a relationship between two variables.

ences cannot be strong, because the personalities of two adopted (unrelated) children reared in the same home are correlated only +.07. In fact, Zuckerman concludes that only one-third of personality similarities between parents and their biological children can be traced to environmental factors; the other two-thirds comes from the parents' genes.

The biological approach, with its emphasis on genetics, is one of the major new developments in personality research during the 1990s (Chaplin, 1990). However, we are a long way from understanding the specific genetic maps of personality, though we suspect that each trait is influenced by many genes, rather than just one (Zuckerman, 1991). In short, biological factors may be able to account for a substantial portion of individual differences in personality traits.

Evaluation of the Trait Approach

Table 13.5 summarizes four important characteristics of the trait approach, contrasting it with the other two approaches discussed so far. As you can see, it is very different from the psychodynamic approach. Although it is similar to the humanistic approach in the way data are gathered, the two approaches differ considerably on the other three characteristics. The trait approach can be criticized for several reasons:

1. *It is not an integrated theory.* In fact, it may be more realistic to call the trait approach a research technique rather than a theory. The approach produces a wealth of information about people's characteristics, but no comprehensive view of humanity. It does not deal with unconscious forces, and (with the exception of biological research) it does not attempt to explain *why* people have certain traits to varying degrees.

2. *It underestimates the role of situations.* Taken to its extreme, trait theory predicts that people act consistently, even in different situations. As we saw in the research, however, people are far from predictable. A person may be friendly in one circumstance but withdrawn in another.

We cannot be too critical, however, because the trait approach never aspired to be comprehensive and integrated, and its goal is to look for trait consistency, independent of the situation. To its credit, it has provided abundant information about internal characteristics, such as the stability of traits. Furthermore, this approach has contributed to the measurement of personality, a topic we will examine more thoroughly in Chapter 14.

According to recent research on the biological approach to personality, genetics is more important than environment in explaining why these family members are similar in their personality traits.

TABLE 13.5	A Comparison of the Trait Approach with the Psychodynamic and Humanistic Approaches		
	PSYCHODYNAMIC APPROACH	**HUMANISTIC APPROACH**	**TRAIT APPROACH**
Source of data	Obtained from expert analyst from people in therapy.	Obtained from self-reports from the general population and people in therapy.	Obtained from observation of behavior and questionnaire responses from the general population as well as people in therapy.
Cause of behavior	Internal conflict, unconscious forces, childhood experiences.	Self-concepts, self-actualizing tendencies.	Stable, internal characteristics; some emphasize genetic basis.
Comprehensiveness of theory	Very comprehensive.	Fairly comprehensive.	Not very comprehensive.
Outlook on humans	Negative.	Positive.	Neutral.

THE TRAIT APPROACH

- Allport proposed three levels of traits: cardinal, central, and secondary; the combination of these traits determines a person's behavior.

- Eysenck proposed that three major dimensions account for most of human behavior: introversion-extraversion; stability-instability; and psychoticism.

- The five-factor model is the most widely accepted categorization of trait dimensions; these traits are extraversion, agreeableness, conscientiousness, emotional stability, and openness to experience.

- The resolution to the person-situation debate seems to be that people have traits that are somewhat consistent across situations, though our cognitive biases enhance this apparent consistency; cross-situational consistency is higher in unconstrained situations without instructions and when the observation period is long; consistency is also higher for some people, some traits, and some methods.

- Research suggests a sizable genetic component for many personality traits, based on data from identical twins reared apart, comparisons between identical and fraternal twins, and studies of adopted children.

THE SOCIAL COGNITIVE APPROACH

We began this chapter by exploring the psychodynamic approach, in which people are ruled by their sexual organs and other forces of unconscious conflict. Then we considered the humanistic approach, in which people are ruled by more noble motives, such as the striving for self-actualization. Our third topic was the trait approach, in which people are ruled by stable internal characteristics; some trait theorists would emphasize genetic components.

In contrast especially to the psychodynamic and the humanistic perspectives, the social cognitive approach makes humans seem much more levelheaded and less passionate. In fact, some personality theorists have pointed out that you can read volume after volume about the social cognitive approach without ever learning that humans have genitals! The social cognitive approach focuses on the way people observe, evaluate, regulate, and think. We may not always make the correct decision, but we are usually rational. Furthermore, we are ruled mostly by conscious forces and by relatively recent experiences.

We begin by investigating the origins of this social cognitive approach in George Kelly's personal construct theory and behaviorism. Then we review the basic concepts of observational learning. Our next topic is reciprocal influences, the concept that environmental factors, personal factors, and behaviors all interact to form a person's personality. Next we consider self-efficacy, or people's sense that they are competent and effective. Then the "In Depth" section focuses on the dynamic self-concept. We conclude with an evaluation of the social cognitive approach.

Origins of the Social Cognitive Approach: Personal Construct Theory and Behaviorism

The social cognitive approach to personality is becoming increasingly popular in the 1990s (McAdams, 1994). Its origins can be traced to two very different sources, George Kelly's personal construct theory and B. F. Skinner's behaviorism.

Personal Construct Theory George Kelly (1905–1967) is difficult to categorize; some books discuss him in connection with the humanistic approach (e.g., McAdams, 1990) and some classify him with the social cognitive approach (e.g., Cloninger, 1993; Messer & Warren, 1990). It's ironic that Kelly's approach resists easy classification, because his theory focuses on people's attempts to classify components of their world.

Specifically, we classify people, objects, and events in our world by developing **personal constructs,** or characteristic ways of interpreting how some things are alike and some differ from each other (Kelly, 1955). For example, I typically classify my friends in terms of the personal construct "altruistic/selfish." Sue's altruism is obvious in her work with the Algonquin Indians in Canada, and Bob's altruism is apparent in his concern for the well-being of gay teenagers. But Sam's dedication to his sports cars seem more selfish, as does Pat's concern with interior decoration. In fact, all these people share many similar characteristics (such as intelligence and friendliness), but I often divide the people in my world primarily according to this altruistic/selfish construct. Kelly stresses that people differ markedly in the personal constructs they choose to emphasize. As you can see, Kelly combines the humanistic emphasis on different interpretations of reality with the cognitive emphasis on thinking, classification, and concept formation.

Kelly's personal construct theory is an important component of the social cognitive approach. However, Kelly also contributed to the approach by inspiring one of his students, Walter Mischel, whose important challenge to trait theory was considered in the last section. One of Mischel's contributions to the social cognitive approach is the concept of interactionism. According to **interactionism,** we need to examine both internal personality characteristics (traits) and external environmental factors (situations) in order to understand personality.

The Behaviorist Approach   The social cognitive approach was also influenced by a second, very different explanation of personality, behaviorism. As discussed in Chapter 1, **behaviorism** is an approach to psychology that stresses the study of observable behavior instead of unobservable mental processes. Behaviorists were most influential in the development of learning theory, primarily the operant conditioning we examined in Chapter 6. In operant conditioning, reinforcement and punishment are the major determinants of behavior. You do your physics homework, and you are reinforced by good grades on exams, so you continue to do homework in the future. A girl burps at the dinner table, she receives chilling glances and negative comments from family members (punishment), and so she stops making these noises.

The behaviorist who had the strongest influence on personality theory was B. F. Skinner. Skinner worked primarily with pigeons and rats rather than people. Skinner rejected general theories, preferring to focus instead on research results (Phares, 1988). It is ironic, then, that a person who worked with nonhumans—and did not like theoretical approaches—had such an important impact on human personality theory.

Skinner emphasized that we do not need to talk about the human mind or internal characteristics when we discuss people's personal traits. For instance, if a young man is friendly and outgoing, his behavior can be explained in terms of past and present reinforcement and punishment—that is, strictly external factors. Skinner believed that we achieve nothing by discussing this man's "extraversion trait." To understand the essence of humans, Skinner and other behaviorists proposed that we need to examine only genetic factors and the stimuli, reinforcements, and punishments in the environment, not any enduring personal characteristics (Skinner, 1974).

Albert Bandura is one of the major theorists who found Skinner's approach inadequate (Grusec, 1992). Bandura (1986) argues that people learn much more by observational learning than by the trial-and-error learning involved in operant conditioning. Furthermore, Bandura emphasizes that people think about and interpret events. Unlike Skinner, Bandura stresses that the human mind makes an important contribution to personality. Bandura (1986) decided to call his approach social cognitive theory, because it emphasizes the contribution of social factors (e.g., observational learning) and thought (e.g., beliefs about competence) in explaining personality and behavior.

If you were to meet these students and become acquainted with them, what personal constructs would you use to classify them?

Skinner would propose that we can understand this politician's outgoing behavior by identifying genetic and environmental factors, without discussing internal characteristics.

Observational Learning

Observational learning, a major factor in the social cognitive approach, was discussed together with classical conditioning and operant conditioning (Chapter 6). In **observational learning,** new behaviors are learned by watching and imitating the behavior of others. For instance, a freshman arrives at college and observes other students, who serve as models. Specifically, he learns that it is appropriate to smile (but not too broadly) at the people nearby in the registration line. It is also appropriate to ask other students where they are from and what their major is. The freshman then imitates this behavior. (Incidentally, note that observational learning is more flexible than operant conditioning in explaining these more complex social interactions.)

You may also remember that observational learning does not require us to learn only from live models who are in the same room. We can also learn from symbolic models on television, in movies, and in books. (I know a teenager who became Holden Caulfield for a weekend, after reading *Catcher in the Rye*.) Social cognitive theorists emphasize that we acquire many of our typical ways of responding—our personality characteristics—via observational learning (Bandura, 1986, 1989). However, other more complex cognitive factors also play crucial roles in the development of personality.

Reciprocal Influences

My daughter Sally is outgoing and adventurous. At age 16, she went by herself to Mexico to perfect her Spanish, and she lived with a Mexican family. Sally made dozens of friends, including members of a local band. On her last evening there, her Mexican family and friends arranged a surprise farewell party, and the band played backup while she sang solo on her favorite Latin American song, "Doce Rosas." I picture myself at 16 and marvel at the difference in our personalities. I was not so outgoing, I could never have gone alone to a foreign country, and the option of singing solo in Spanish would have been only slightly less horrifying than walking barefoot on hot coals.

Bandura (1986) has proposed an explanation for the way initial individual differences become even stronger through reciprocal influences. According to the principle of **reciprocal influences,** three factors—personal/cognitive, behavior, and environmental—all influence one another (Figure 13.4). As a consequence, initial tendencies can become even stronger. For example, a person who is outgoing and friendly, who expects that she will be successful in interpersonal interactions (personal/cognitive), will be likely to introduce herself to strangers and react positively to them (behavior). Furthermore, someone who is outgoing and friendly is likely to seek out social situations rather than sitting in her room (environment). The environment, in turn, promotes even more friendly behavior, more self-confidence, and an even greater expectation for success in interpersonal interactions. In contrast, a shy, withdrawn person will dread interpersonal interactions, avoid strangers, and stay away from social situations. This behavior and the lack of exposure to new environments will encourage the person to become even more withdrawn and to expect future interactions to be unsuccessful.

Skinner's theory proposes that the environment shapes the human. In contrast, Bandura argues that behavior involves more complex processes; indeed, personality, behavior, and environment shape each other in a reciprocal fashion. This more complex approach is necessary to explain the impressive complexity of humans.

Bandura (1982a, 1989) adds another concept to social cognitive theory to account for even more complexity. He suggests that the three critical factors can be profoundly altered by chance encounters with people, objects, and events. Consider the case of Endesha Ida Mae Holland, the playwright whose autobiographical play, *From the Mississippi Delta,* opened off-Broadway in 1991. She grew up in Greenwood, Mississippi, dropped out of school in the ninth grade, and became a prostitute during her mid-teens. In 1963, she followed a man down the street, sensing that the

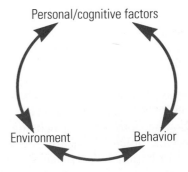

Figure 13.4
The principle of reciprocal influences.

stranger would pay well for the night's work. As it happened, the stranger was a civil-rights worker, going to his office at the Student Nonviolent Coordinating Committee. The committee needed local residents to help, so Endesha signed up. During her two years working in civil rights, one trip took her to Minneapolis, where she casually mentioned she would like to attend college there. The students answered, "If you ever want to go to school, come on back here and we'll help you." She returned to Mississippi, received her high-school diploma, and called her Minnesota friends.

After several years at the University of Minnesota, she found herself four credits shy of her bachelor's degree. She signed up for a drama course, but by accidentally transposing two numbers, ended up in an advanced playwriting seminar. Her future was determined at that point, and she later received a PhD. Resolving never to let her degrees go to her head, she then wrote her prize-winning play (Lederman, 1991). Endesha Holland's life was truly transformed by two chance encounters, one with the civil-rights worker and the other with the "wrong" drama course. Try Demonstration 13.5 to help you appreciate the importance of chance encounters.

Self-Efficacy

Let us examine the personal/cognitive part of Bandura's theory, because this component is most central to personality. Bandura (1982b, 1986) believes that the most important personal/cognitive characteristic is self-efficacy. **Self-efficacy** is the feeling people have that they are competent and effective, and that their behavior can influence what happens to them. It is not particularly critical that a person can, in fact, succeed on a particular task. Instead, it is much more important that a person *thinks* he or she can succeed (Bandura, 1992; Cantor & Kihlstrom, 1987). Thus, Bandura emphasizes people's thoughts and expectations, rather than their actual behavior. (Note that the behaviorists would have emphasized actual behavior, rather than thoughts and expectations.) If you are trying to decide whether to try a new dance step in public, the relevant factor is whether you *think* you are a good dancer, not whether you *are* a good dancer!

Research confirms that people with a strong sense of self-efficacy do indeed manage their lives more successfully. In general, these people tend to be more persistent and more successful in school. They also tend to be less depressed and anxious (Maddux & Stanley, 1986). People who are confident in their abilities typically approach new challenges with optimism, and they set high goals for themselves (Bandura & Jourden, 1991).

When people with high self-efficacy are initially unsuccessful, they try a new approach and work harder. Bandura points out that Van Gogh sold only one painting during his lifetime; early in Picasso's career, an unimpressed art dealer would not let him bring his pictures inside, out of the rain (cited in Evans, 1989). Still, both painters persisted. In contrast, a person with low self-efficacy would give up when faced with overwhelming rejection. Incidentally, self-efficacy is clearly related to achievement motivation, discussed in Chapter 12.

Endesha Ida Mae Holland, author of From the Mississippi Delta. *Dr. Holland says about her prize-winning play, "I decided that I would always tell how I got here, about the barriers I've had to face." Clearly, her life reveals the importance of chance encounters—a component of the social cognitive approach.*

DEMONSTRATION 13.5 Chance Encounters

Ask the following questions to three or more students:

1. How did you hear about the college you now attend?
2. What made you decide to apply to this college?
3. What factors encouraged you to actually attend this college?
4. (If the student has declared a major) How did you decide to pursue your current major? Was it an accident, or did you always know this was your goal?
5. (If the student is in a love relationship) How did you happen to meet your loved-one? Did chance play any role in your meeting?

In each case, try to determine whether chance encounters had any influence on each friend's life.

Vincent van Gogh, the nineteenth-century Dutch painter, is now well known for his colorful landscapes. However, he sold only one painting during his lifetime—an example of persistence arising from a sense of self-efficacy.

Bandura (1986, 1992) points out that self-efficacy is possible because humans can analyze their varied experiences and think about their own thought processes. In Chapters 7 and 10 we discussed the concept of metamemory, or your knowledge and awareness about your own memory. However, you can also contemplate numerous other personal attributes, in addition to your own memory. Consider how often you have evaluated your attributes such as athletic ability, academic ability, friendliness, and optimism. When you were reading the description of self-efficacy, you probably evaluated your own self-efficacy. We humans evaluate our skills and then use that information in regulating our future behavior (Bandura, 1991). The thoughts we have about ourselves are the focus of the next section, an "In Depth" examination of the self-concept.

IN DEPTH: The Social Cognitive Approach to Self-Concepts

We have discussed the notion of *self* in several previous chapters. The memory chapter mentioned the self-reference effect; we remember material better if we process it in terms of our own experience. (For instance, you will remember the term *reciprocal influences* better if you think how that concept applies to your own personality.) In the chapter on infancy and childhood, we discussed self-concept in connection with children recognizing themselves in the mirror, as well as Erik Erikson's theory on the development of self-concept. In the chapter on adolescence and adulthood, we again examined Erikson's theory and also noted the values that adults consider to be important components of the self-concept. Chapter 15 will examine the disrupted sense of self that accompanies several kinds of psychological disorders. In psychology in the 1990s, research on the self is pervasive!

This "In Depth" section focuses primarily on the work of Hazel Markus and her coauthors at the University of Michigan. They argue that the self-concept does not merely *reflect* ongoing behavior, so that your actions shape your thoughts about yourself. Instead, as noted in the discussion of reciprocal influences, the self-concept also *regulates* behavior; your thoughts about yourself influence how you behave. Markus and her colleague Elissa Wurf (1987) use the term **dynamic self-concept** to capture this idea that the self-concept is active and influential. Two important ideas relevant to the dynamic self-concept are the working self-concept and the idea of possible selves.

Working Self-Concept Early researchers in the area of self-concept tended to view the self-concept as unified and unchanging—a single lumplike structure that remained absolutely stable. Now we realize that a person's self-concept is complex; it contains many different dimensions (Markus & Wurf, 1987). Furthermore, at any given moment, some identities that are part of the complete self-concept will be inaccessible.

The **working self-concept** is the self-concept at a particular moment, consisting of all accessible self-knowledge. This working self-concept may shift 5 minutes from now. Thus, a young man who believes that he is attractive and sophisticated may shift his working self-concept (at least temporarily) when he looks in the mirror and discovers a conspicuous strand of spinach decorating his front teeth. At a particular moment, your working self-concept may include the knowledge that you are a good conversationalist (perhaps you are encouraging a shy friend, drawing him into a discussion). The knowledge that you are not skilled at sports may not be part of your working self-concept at this moment.

The working self-concept resembles the availability heuristic, discussed in connection with decision making in Chapter 8. When we make a decision, we base that decision on information that comes readily to mind, perhaps information from the recent past. In evaluating ourselves and in making decisions, we attend to information in our consciousness. Notice that the social cognitive approach emphasizes consciousness in contrast to Freud's emphasis on the preconscious or the unconscious.

According to Markus and Wurf (1987), the working self-concept shows both stability and change. (You may recall that in the two chapters on human development, we also concluded that personal characteristics show both stability and change.) For example, your working self-concept may stay reasonably stable with respect to your thoughts about your social skills. However, your working self-concept may be more changeable when you evaluate your academic competence; it might shift dramatically, depending on the most recent grade you received.

Research by Markus and Kunda (1986) demonstrates both stability and change in self-concept. In this research, people rated a series of cartoons and other items. Then they were shown information about how other participants presumably rated these stimuli. Sometimes these ratings were similar to their own, making them feel very similar to the other participants in the study. Other people received "ratings from other participants" that were very discrepant from their own ratings, making them feel very different. After performing this rating task, the participants were asked to make some judgments about themselves. They saw a series of adjectives—for example, *normal, independent,* and *average.* They were asked to indicate whether each adjective applied to themselves by pressing either a "me" or a "not me" button.

Let's first consider the words that people in the two conditions chose as applying to themselves. Their choices were not influenced by whether they had been in the "similar" or "different" condition. In other words, if a person thinks that she is *normal* and *independent,* she will still apply those words to herself, even after a session in which she was made to look either very similar to others or conspicuously unique.

Now let's consider a more subtle measure, response latency; this dependent variable *was* influenced by the independent variable. Figure 13.5 shows how long the participants took to press the button for the words that focused on similarity to other people (for example, *average* and *normal*). Imagine that you are a participant in the "same" condition, and the rating task had emphasized that you were just like everyone else. You might be anxious to re-establish your uniqueness. As a result, you might pause before admitting that any word like *average* could possibly apply to yourself. Furthermore, you would quickly reject other words (perhaps *ordinary*) by quickly pressing the "not me" button.

How would you react if you had been in the "different" condition? You might feel *too* unusual and be anxious to re-establish that you are normal—rather than weird. You would be likely

This ballplayer's self-concept probably includes thoughts about his athletic ability. If he were to strike out, however, his working self-concept could shift dramatically, though probably briefly.

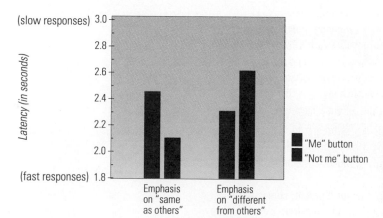

Figure 13.5

Latency of responding for words focusing on similarity, as a function of whether similarity or difference had been emphasized earlier in the session.

to decide fairly quickly that some of these similarity words (perhaps *normal*) apply to yourself. Furthermore, you might take a long time to admit that other words (perhaps *standard*) really do not apply to your personality.

So, is our self-concept stable or changeable? We must answer, "Both." The actual words we use to describe ourselves may remain stable. However, our social experiences can often change our self-concepts (Markus & Cross, 1990). For instance, in this study, the social experiences influence the speed with which people applied various traits to themselves. This study illustrates why researchers should include more than one dependent variable. If Markus and Kunda had measured just word types or just response latencies, their results would not have captured the rich complexity of self-concepts.

Possible Selves The **possible self** is the part of your self-concept that represents what you could become, what you would like to become, and what you are afraid of becoming (Ruvolo & Markus, 1992). Try Demonstration 13.6 to explore your own possible selves.

A number of personality theorists incorporate concepts similar to the possible-selves idea. For instance, humanistic psychologists emphasize that the goals we are seeking are as important as our current situations. In her more recent research, Markus and her colleagues have developed more fully the concept of possible selves. For example, your own "possible selves" may motivate and direct your behavior, allowing you to imagine yourself striving toward a goal (Cross & Markus, 1991). If you plan to become a physician, for example, that possible self can inspire you to work harder in your organic chemistry course.

In Chapter 7, you learned about the power of imagery as a mnemonic, and in Chapter 8, you learned that imagery can help you re-create elaborate scenes in your head. Imagery about the future can also lead you to revise your ideas about possible selves. Specifically, people who imagined themselves reaching success because of their own hard work were quick to reject any negative possible selves. They also worked persistently on an unpleasant task. Consistent with Bandura's ideas about reciprocal influences, our ideas about ourselves can motivate relevant behaviors.

Evaluation of the Social Cognitive Approach

Table 13.6 summarizes four important characteristics of the social cognitive approach, contrasting it with the other three approaches. As you can see, it differs most from the psychodynamic approach, but it is somewhat similar to the trait approach.

The social cognitive approach can be criticized for two major reasons.

1. *It is not comprehensive.* At present, the social cognitive approach is relatively narrow in scope. It does emphasize the importance of our thoughts about our own competence and how these thoughts organize our behavior. Still, the social cognitive approach has not yet integrated unconscious forces into the theory. Similarly, it underemphasizes emotions and sexual urges. Also, it has not examined in detail how personality develops from childhood to adulthood.

DEMONSTRATION 13.6 Possible Selves

Most people think about the future, including what things are in store for us and the kinds of people we might become. Sometimes we think about what we probably will be like, other times about what we hope to become, and still other times about what we are afraid of becoming.

On a sheet of paper, list all the hoped-for possible selves that you currently imagine for yourself. Then make a second column, listing all the feared possible selves that you currently imagine might be relevant.

Finally, describe how these possible selves actually influence your own behavior.

Source: Based on Cross & Markus, 1991, p. 235

TABLE 13.6   Contrasting the Four Approaches to Personality

	PSYCHODYNAMIC APPROACH	HUMANISTIC APPROACH	TRAIT APPROACH	SOCIAL COGNITIVE APPROACH
Source of data	Obtained from expert analyst from people in therapy.	Obtained from self-reports from the general population and people in therapy.	Obtained from observation of behavior and questionnaire responses from the general population as well as people in therapy.	Obtained from experiments, observation of behavior, and questionnaire responses from the general population.
Cause of behavior	Internal conflict, unconscious forces, childhood experiences.	Self concepts, self-actualizing tendencies.	Stable, internal characteristics; some emphasize genetic basis.	Reciprocal influence of personal/cognitive, behavior, and environment.
Comprehensiveness of theory	Very comprehensive.	Fairly comprehensive.	Not very comprehensive.	Not very comprehensive.
Outlook on humans	Negative.	Positive.	Neutral.	Neutral.

2. *It is not an integrated theory.* At present, the social cognitive approach consists of a collection of isolated ideas. We have observational learning, reciprocal influences, and self-efficacy from Bandura. Markus has developed the self-concept, and other theorists are actively researching other components. However, a loose collection of ideas does not constitute a satisfying, cohesive theory. We do not know how these concepts relate to each other. For example, how do observational learning and possible selves influence each other?

The problems with the social cognitive approach certainly will not doom it to failure. Researchers are likely to tackle these two problems in the near future, and they may find some satisfying solutions.

A major advantage of the social cognitive approach is that it is testable, partly because the theories are specific rather than general. Hypotheses can be proposed, data can be gathered, and the hypotheses can be accepted or rejected. In contrast, recall that the psychodynamic approach was frequently too general to be tested. Furthermore, that theory often proposed that a person would show either one characteristic or its exact opposite—a situation that makes testing impossible.

A second major advantage is that the social cognitive approach fits in successfully with the research on other aspects of human experience, specifically the wealth of knowledge that psychologists have gathered on human cognitive processes. Much of this information has been summarized in the chapters on sensation and perception, learning, memory, cognition, language, and child and adult development. The same brain that collects information to make a decision or produce a sentence also manages to form a working self-concept. Of the four approaches to personality considered in this chapter, the social cognitive approach is most compatible with other ongoing research on humans.

SECTION SUMMARY

THE SOCIAL COGNITIVE APPROACH

- The origins of the social cognitive approach can be traced to George Kelly's personal construct theory and also to behaviorism.
- Observational learning explains how we acquire some personality characteristics.
- According to the concept of reciprocal influences, personal/cognitive factors, behavior, and environment all influence one another.

- People high in self-efficacy are persistent and set high goals for themselves.
- The working self-concept shows both stability and change in different social situations; concepts of possible selves help guide our behavior.
- Criticisms of the social cognitive approach include that it is neither comprehensive nor well integrated. Positive features include its testability and its compatibility with other research on human cognitive process.

R E V I E W   Q U E S T I O N S

1. Imagine that a high-school student you know has asked you to describe the chapter you have most recently read in your psychology textbook. Define the word *personality* and summarize each of the four approaches.

2. Try to reproduce the information in Table 13.6 from memory. Label the columns with the names of the four approaches (psychodynamic, humanistic, trait, and social cognitive). Label the rows with the four dimensions we considered (source of the data, cause of behavior, comprehensiveness, and outlook on humans). Then compare your table with Table 13.6 on page 441.

3. Describe Freud's stages of normal human development. Now compare the following theorists with respect to their explanations about the origins of abnormal behavior: Freud, Adler, Horney, Rogers, Eysenck, Skinner, and Bandura.

4. Imagine that you are a talk-show host. The two invited guests today—miraculously—are Sigmund Freud and Carl Rogers. How might each respond to your questions: (a) Are wars inevitable? (b) Why do people sometimes perform heroic, altruistic acts? (c) What should people strive for in life?

5. Try to imagine a situation in which a person is blocked at the first level of Maslow's hierarchy. Then imagine blocking situations for the second, third, and fourth levels. Where would you locate yourself today in this hierarchy?

6. What is the person-situation debate? Think about a particularly noticeable trait of a close friend. Does this trait seem to persist across situations? What cognitive biases encourage you to believe in its persistence? How would trait theorists respond to someone who proposed that this particular trait would show little stability across situations?

7. Explain the concept of reciprocal influences. Can you identify some way in which this concept could be applied to your own life? How does the concept of possible selves apply to this diagram?

8. Which of the theories in this chapter deals with the self? Describe how the self is envisioned in those theories, elaborating in particular on Markus's research. How is the research by Markus and Kunda, illustrated in Figure 13.5 in the "In Depth" section, relevant to the person-situation debate?

9. How do the four approaches compare with respect to the emphasis on internal forces versus external stimuli? Also include behaviorism in this comparison.

10. Which of the four approaches to personality do you find most appealing? If you had to design your own comprehensive theory, what features of the other three approaches would you incorporate? Can you list any aspects of personality that you believe have not been addressed by any of these approaches?

N E W   T E R M S

personality
psychodynamic approach
humanistic approach
trait approach
social cognitive approach
psychoanalytic approach
id

latency stage
genital stage
personal unconscious
collective unconscious
archetype
introvert
extravert

libido
ego
reality principle
superego
conscious
preconscious
unconscious
free association
manifest content
latent content
defense mechanisms
repression
regression
reaction formation
rationalization
sublimation
displacement
projection
erogenous zones
fixation
oral stage
anal stage
phallic stage
Oedipus complex

object-relations approach
masochistic
self-actualization
conditional positive regard
unconditional positive regard
Maslow's hierarchy of needs
trait
cardinal trait
central trait
secondary trait
five-factor model
Big Five traits
NEO Personality Inventory
the person-situation debate
heritability
personal constructs
interactionism
behaviorism
observational learning
reciprocal influences
self-efficacy
dynamic self-concept
working self-concept
possible self

RECOMMENDED READINGS

Cloninger, S. C. (1993). *Theories of personality: Understanding persons.* Englewood Cliffs, NJ: Prentice Hall. This mid-level textbook examines each of the major personality theorists, using a clear and well-organized writing style; an interesting additional feature is that each chapter considers how that particular perspective might explain the personalities of two current or historical individuals (e.g., Maya Angelou and Albert Einstein).

McAdams, D. P. (1994) *The person: An introduction to personality psychology* (2nd ed.). Fort Worth: Harcourt Brace & Co. This is one of the more challenging personality textbooks, and it integrates research with theory. The author also relates the subject to literature and the arts.

Pervin, L. A. (Ed.). (1990). *Handbook of personality theory and research.* New York: Guilford. I would recommend this handbook for any college library; it includes chapters by well-known personality researchers on the psychodynamic approach, the Big Five traits, the person-situation debate, biological aspects of personality, and the self-concept.

Wallach, M. A., & Wallach, L. (1983). *Psychology's sanction for selfishness.* San Francisco: Freeman. I really enjoyed reading this book! It reviews the personality theories—with an emphasis on theories of Freud, Freud's followers, and the humanistic approaches. The book points out how all these major theories encourage us to focus on our own needs and desires, rather than the welfare of others.

Wiggins, J. S., & Pincus, A. L. (1992). Personality: Structure and assessment. *Annual Review of Psychology, 43,* 473–504. This chapter reviews recent research in personality, with an emphasis on the trait theory.

Zuckerman, M. (1991). *Psychobiology of personality.* New York: Cambridge University Press. If you are intrigued by the new research on the genetic basis of personality, I would recommend this book. It also examines neuropsychological correlates of personality.

ANSWERS TO THE DEMONSTRATION

DEMONSTRATION 13.1 Climbing the staircase and unlocking the door symbolizes sexual intercourse (No. 8); the small locked room represents the female genitals (No. 4); the spindle is a symbol for a penis (No. 2); and pricking the finger indicates menstruation (No. 6). As far as I know, the other four items on the list are not symbolized in this fairy tale! Incidentally, Bettelheim tells us about the implied message for anxious little girls hearing this story: "Don't worry and don't try to hurry things—when the time is ripe, the impossible problem will be solved, as if all by itself" (p. 233). (We can only speculate whether females who wait for a kiss from a handsome prince are likely to thrive in the 1990s.)

CHAPTER 14
ASSESSING INTELLIGENCE AND PERSONALITY

You have been tested since the moment you were born. When you were just a few minutes old, the person who delivered you calculated an Apgar score, a number between 0 and 10 that assesses a newborn's general health. Some months later, a pediatrician probably assessed your motor and cognitive development with a screening test. Several years after that, you may have been tested when you were about to start kindergarten.

The testing intensified once you entered school. At regular intervals, you took standardized intelligence and achievement tests (in addition to the normal quizzes and tests on class material). In high school, you probably spent many hours preparing for and taking PSATs, the SATs, or the ACTs. Then you probably spent your first hours at college taking tests in writing, foreign language, or mathematics. As your senior year approaches, many of you will sign up for the GREs, LSATs, GMATs, or MCATs if you plan on graduate school or professional degrees in law, business, or medicine. And some of you will be tested on your cognitive ability or personality when you apply for a job.

Tests are vitally important in shaping our lives, yet the average high-school student learns more about trigonometry than about the nature of psychological tests. A **psychological test** is an objective, standardized measure of a sample of behavior. Just as a lab technician makes observations on a small sample of a person's blood, a psychologist collects a small sample of a person's behavior (Anastasi, 1988). For instance, psychologists might test a child's arithmetic skills, a pilot's spatial ability, or an employee's honesty.

This chapter examines how we measure the individual differences that are the focus of Theme 2. We could measure a wide variety of human attributes such as motor skills, job aptitudes, social skills, and achievement motivation. In this chapter, we will focus on individual differences in two specific areas, cognitive skills (introduced in Chapters 7, 8, and 9) and personality (Chapter 13). As you will see, psychological testing is challenging because we cannot simply peel back a person's scalp and watch all these exciting psychological processes in action (Kail & Pellegrino, 1985). And we cannot simply peek into people's ears to assess their level of verbal ability or their extraversion. Instead, we must study mental processes by looking at a person's responses on standardized tests.

CONSTRUCTING AND EVALUATING TESTS

You have probably seen informal quizzes in newspapers and popular magazines. In several minutes, you can presumably test yourself and find out whether you are a wallflower or the life of a party, a Pollyanna or a pessimist. If you believe the claims of the articles, these quizzes can also assess whether you are a good roommate, a feminist, or a worrywart.

On the surface, these tests look reasonable. For instance, a quiz in *Seventeen* magazine is entitled "Are You a Worrywart?" (Weston, 1985). One question asks,

Right after you pop a letter into the mailbox, you
a. Go on your merry way.
b. Check to make sure it went down.
c. Panic! "Did I stamp it? Was it addressed right?" (p. 48)

Readers assign themselves 1 point for answer *a,* 2 points for *b,* and 3 points for *c,* and they score themselves on each of 11 questions. The key at the bottom of the quiz claims that people with total scores between 26 and 33 points tend to be cautious worrywarts, those between 19 and 25 are well-adjusted people who worry the right amount, and those between 11 and 18 points are too laid-back and apathetic.

Magazine quizzes like the worrywart test differ from the formal tests devised by psychologists in the way they are constructed and evaluated. A proper psychological test has three important properties:

1. *Standardization.* A psychological test is pretested with a large, representative sample of people so that we know, for example, the respondents' average score. (In contrast, the author of the worrywart test probably did not conduct pretesting; the three categories of scores are probably based on a good hunch, rather than formal testing.)

2. *Reliability.* A psychological test must provide a test taker with roughly the same score each time the test is taken. (In contrast, we do not know whether your score on the worrywart test would be the same tomorrow or much higher or lower.)

3. *Validity.* A psychological test should measure what it is supposed to measure, not some other characteristic. (In contrast, the worrywart test might measure the test taker's desire to appear well adjusted; true worrywarts may be reluctant to choose option *c* because it sounds too bizarre—even though *c* is their true response. The worrywart test would not be valid if it measures "desire to appear well adjusted" rather than worrywart tendencies.)

In this section, we examine standardization, reliability, and validity—the three characteristics of a psychological test. This discussion should convince you that a high-quality psychological test cannot be constructed casually.

Standardization

Suppose that during the freshman orientation at your college you take a test of writing ability, and you receive a score of 29. By itself, your score is meaningless. You cannot tell whether it is high, average, or low. To make this score meaningful, you would need to compare it with a norm or standard.

The test would first need to be administered to a large group of people, who all take the test in situations as uniform as possible—a process called **standardization.** The scores would be meaningless if one group had the instructions read to them, had no time limit, and had the opportunity to ask questions, whereas another group read the instructions to themselves, had only 45 minutes to complete the test, and had no opportunity to ask questions. Thus, the first step in standardizing a test requires the systematic administration of the test under uniform conditions.

A second important step in the standardization of a psychological test involves the determination of **norms,** or established standards of performance on the test. An individual's score on the test becomes meaningful by comparing the score with those standards. For instance, suppose that on the writing ability test on which you received a raw score of 29, the average student received a 20. That information about the norms is useful, because you now know your score was better than average. However, you would also need some normative information about variability. If most people received a score within 3 points of 20—so that the variability on the test was small—your score of 29 would be spectacular. However, if most people received a score within 10 points of 20—so that the variability was large—your score of 29 is still good, but not truly outstanding. The norms include information about both the average score and the variability of the scores (or, using the statistical terms discussed in Chapter 2 and the Appendix, the *mean* and the *standard deviation*).

We also need to emphasize another point about standardization: The population you are testing must be comparable to the population on which the test norms are based. For example, a test that is carefully normed on school-aged children living

When a test is standardized, it must be administered under uniform conditions.

in Los Angeles may not be useful in a small midwestern town, where the ethnic background, mastery of English, and school curriculum may be very different (Cohen et al., 1992).

Reliability

Reliability refers to the consistency of a person's scores. This consistency is established by reexamining the test takers with the same test on two different occasions, or by some other method of measuring the stability of the scores (Anastasi, 1988).

Every test involves some measurement error. Even objective measurements can show variation. If you weigh yourself now and one hour from now, your two weights probably will not be identical. However—if the scale is reliable—your weight will be reasonably consistent.

Unfortunately, psychological tests are not as reliable as bathroom scales, because psychological characteristics are more difficult to measure than physical characteristics. Still, reliability is one of the three qualities of a high-quality psychological test.

Three major methods can be used to measure the reliability of a test:

1. In **test-retest reliability,** the same identical test is administered on two occasions, usually one day to several weeks apart. The test-retest reliability is high if each person's score is similar on the two tests.

2. In **split-half reliability,** everybody takes just one test, but the items are split into two halves (often the even-numbered versus the odd-numbered questions). The split-half reliability is high if each person's score is similar on the two halves.

3. In **alternate-form reliability,** two alternate forms of the test are administered, usually one day to several weeks apart. The alternate-form reliability is high if each person's score is similar on the two tests.

Suppose, for example, that you are developing a test of basic arithmetic skills, and you want to examine its alternate-form reliability. You might give second-graders one version of the test on Tuesday and another version on Wednesday. Imagine that you selected six of the children and recorded their scores on the two versions of the test. Figure 14.1a shows high consistency in their scores; if other children showed similar consistency, this test would be high in reliability. In contrast, Figure 14.1b shows low consistency between the two administrations; if other children showed similar changes in their test scores, this test would be low in reliability.

For all three kinds of reliability, the researcher calculates a correlation coefficient, or r. As noted in Chapter 2, a correlation coefficient tells us whether a person's score on one measure is related to his or her score on another measure. A test is reliable if a person who receives a high score on the first measure also receives a high score on the second measure, and if medium- and low-scorers also show this same consistency, as in Figure 14.1a.

An r of 1.00 indicates a perfect correlation, or absolute consistency in the two scores. Psychological tests do not achieve r's of 1.00, because the tests are not perfect and because human behavior is too complex to be absolutely consistent. On the other hand, an r close to .00 indicates absolutely no relationship between the two scores. You might receive a very high score on the first measure and a very low score on the second measure, whereas a friend might receive a moderately low score on the first measure and a moderately high score on the second measure. Other people who take the test also show no particular pattern in their scores when there is a zero correlation (as in Figure 14.1b).

Psychologists are extremely satisfied if the reliability is greater than about .85. Many tests have lower reliability. Figure 14.2 shows a test whose alternate-form reliability was calculated to be .72 (moderately high). The tally mark in the top right cor-

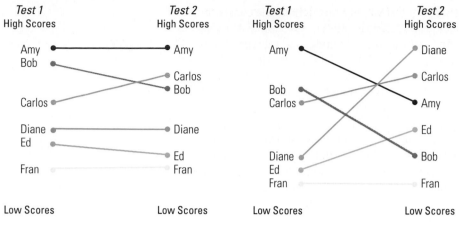

Test 1 High Scores — Test 2 High Scores / Low Scores — Low Scores

a. High Alternative Form Reliability

b. Low Alternative Form Reliability

Figure 14.1

Hypothetical scores on alternate forms of a test of arithmetic ability, illustrating high and low reliability.

ner represents a person whose score on Form 1 was between 70 and 74, and whose score on Form 2 was between 75 and 79. Although this person's score remained fairly consistent (as did the scores of many others), notice the exceptions. For example, one person received a good score (between 45 and 49) on Form 1 and a poor score (between 20 and 24) on Form 2. Overall, however, the scores show moderate consistency across the two tests.

Validity

Validity refers to a test's accuracy in measuring what it is supposed to measure. For instance, if a test is a valid measure of intelligence, people's scores on that test should be strongly correlated with their grades in school.

Consider this real-life example of a potentially invalid test. On June 20, 1989, the answer key to the year-end New York State Regents Examination in chemistry was stolen, and the answers were published in a newspaper, the New York *Post*. The criminal and ethical aspects of this theft are extremely important, but high schools throughout the state also faced a major practical problem: Should they actually give students the Regents Exam? Most high schools near New York City decided not to administer the test. If they had given the test, it would have been invalid. The test would have measured students' ability to locate and buy the New York *Post*, rather than their knowledge of chemistry. The test would not have measured what it is supposed to measure.

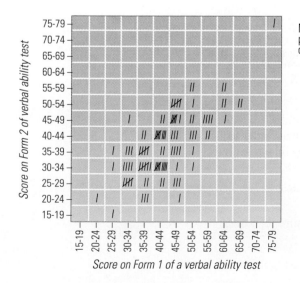

Note: Each tally mark represents one person, who obtained scores on each of two measures.

Figure 14.2

Illustration of an alternate-form reliability of .72 (Based on Anastasi, 1988; Anastasi & Drake, 1954)

Researchers need to consider the issue of test validity throughout the construction and evaluation of a psychological test (Anastasi, 1986). Psychologists have devised various validation procedures. An ideal validation includes several types of evidence about a test's validity (American Psychological Association, American Educational Research Association, & National Council on Measurement in Education, 1985). This chapter considers two approaches, content validity and criterion-related validity.

Content Validity Several years ago, I spoke with an irate student who complained that her final examination in a course contained an essay question on material that had not been included in either the class lectures or the textbook. She had spoken to her professor, who replied that indeed this topic had not been covered; however, he thought that it was something every psychology undergraduate ought to know.

This particular test had been low in **content validity,** or a test's ability to cover the complete range of material that it is supposed to cover. (I am assuming you agree with me that a test should not cover material never mentioned in a course!) A test should not cover too much, and it also should not cover too little. Suppose that your psychology professor announces that your final examination will be comprehensive. However, when you take the exam, you discover that it includes no questions on learning, memory, or thinking. This exam would lack content validity.

Criterion-Related Validity When psychologists use the term **criterion-related validity,** they are referring to a test's ability to predict a person's performance on a second measure—that is, an independent criterion. For example, suppose that researchers want to assess criterion-related validity for a test of intelligence. They could measure whether scores on that test are correlated with the number of years of education that each person achieves (Anastasi, 1988).

What other criteria would you consider important if you were developing a new intelligence test? One potential criterion is grades in school; we know that current intelligence tests predict students' grades in school with considerable accuracy (Richardson, 1991). But perhaps you want to predict something more ambitious, such as success in life. Psychologists have difficulty deciding upon the operational definition for "success in life"—should it be income, prestige of the profession, or . . . ? (You fill in the blank.) At present, theorists disagree about whether the current intelligence tests are correlated with any important measures of success in life (e.g., Barrett & Depinet, 1991; McClelland, 1973; Ree & Earles, 1992; Sternberg, 1990b). As you can imagine, criterion-related validity is useful only if the test makers select a compelling criterion.

S E C T I O N S U M M A R Y

CONSTRUCTING AND EVALUATING TESTS

- A psychological test is an objective, standardized measure of a sample of behavior; a good test must be standardized, reliable, and valid.

- Standardization requires norms gathered on a group of people tested under uniform conditions; the group being tested should resemble the group on whom the norms are based.

- Reliability, or consistency, can be measured in terms of test-retest reliability, split-half reliability, and alternate-form reliability.

- Validity, or a test's ability to measure what it is supposed to measure, can be assessed in terms of content validity and criterion-related validity.

DEMONSTRATION 14.1 Defining Intelligence

1. In one or two sentences, define the word *intelligence*.
2. Now, instead of a definition, think of the important characteristics of an ideally intelligent person. What kind of qualities would this intelligent person

have? Make a list of 10 characteristics that you think would be most descriptive of a highly intelligent person. Then check Table 14.1 for a list of characteristics that experts considered to be very important.

DEVELOPING INTELLIGENCE TESTS

Before you read further, try Demonstration 14.1. If you have difficulty defining the term *intelligence,* you are in good company; even the experts do not agree. In this book, we define **intelligence** as the ability to master the information and skills needed to succeed within a particular culture (Locurto, 1991). Intelligence therefore includes a wide range of cognitive skills, including perception, learning, memory, problem solving, and reasoning (Scarr, 1984).

Although experts have difficulty agreeing on a definition of intelligence, they agree quite well about the characteristics of an ideally intelligent person. Table 14.1 (p. 452) shows some of the characteristics that experts think are important. As you can see, some of these characteristics focus on verbal intelligence, whereas others stress problem-solving ability. Interestingly, however, the experts also judge some less academic, more practical characteristics to be important (Sternberg et al., 1981). Furthermore, when Sternberg and his colleagues asked nonexperts about the characteristics of an intelligent person, the nonexperts provided answers that were highly similar to those provided by the experts. Let us now turn our attention to the tests that have been used to measure human intelligence.

The History of Intelligence Testing

As far as we know, the first formal intelligence tests were administered in China as early as 2200 B.C. The testing apparently went on for days, and test takers occasionally died because of the intense strain (Cohen et al., 1992).

In the English-speaking world, the first major contributor to intelligence testing was Sir Francis Galton, also known for the statistical procedure he developed. Galton collected measurements on more than 9,000 men and women at the 1884 International Health Exhibition in London. These measures included head size, visual acuity, and reaction time—none of which would be included on a modern intelligence test (Fancher, 1985). Galton's most important contribution to psychology was not his specific measurement techniques, but the *idea* that individual differences in intelligence could be assessed.

The first forerunner of modern intelligence tests was constructed by the French psychologist Alfred Binet (pronounced "Bin-*nay*"). Binet had been appointed to design a test to identify slower learners in the Paris school system, so that they could receive special instruction. The test developed by Binet and his colleagues in 1911 geared the difficulty of the questions to the age of the child. For example, a 6-year-old might be asked to describe the difference between morning and evening and to count 13 pennies. Thus, Binet's test items were much more congruent with our current notions of intelligence than were Galton's more physiological measures.

Interestingly, Binet's intelligence scales were greeted with even more enthusiasm in the United States than in Binet's own country (Aiken, 1987). For example, Lewis Terman, working at Stanford University, constructed the Stanford-Binet

TABLE 14.1 Representative Characteristics of an Ideally Intelligent Person, as Judged by Experts in the Field of Intelligence

VERBAL INTELLIGENCE

Displays a good vocabulary
Reads with high comprehension
Displays curiosity

PROBLEM-SOLVING ABILITY

Able to apply knowledge to problems at hand
Makes good decisions
Poses problems in an optimal way

PRACTICAL INTELLIGENCE

Sizes up situations well
Determines how to achieve goals
Displays awareness of world around him or her

Source: Sternberg et al., 1981.

Intelligence Scale, which we will discuss shortly. When the United States entered World War I in 1917, the military needed a test that could efficiently classify its 1.5 million recruits. Accordingly, army psychologists revised some existing tests so that they could be administered in large groups (Samelson, 1987). So began the North American enchantment with intelligence testing and intelligence scores.

This brief history illustrates the saying, "Necessity is the mother of invention." The exploration of intelligence was certainly hastened by the need to construct tests that could sort large numbers of individuals for schools and for the military. Unfortunately, however, the tests were often technically crude, because more effort was spent administering these tests than refining them (Anastasi, 1988).

Current Tests of Intelligence

Let us now consider three of the most popular tests of intellectual skills, the Stanford-Binet test, the Wechsler scales, and the Scholastic Aptitude Test (SAT). The first two tests are administered individually by trained professionals, whereas (as many of you can testify) the SAT is a group test.

Tests of intelligence differ not only in the method of administration, but also with respect to whether they are supposed to measure achievement or aptitude. An **achievement test** is designed to measure current skills, usually based on previous learning in a subject area (Angoff, 1988; Kaplan & Saccuzzo, 1993). For example, you may have taken a standardized test in mathematics, American history, or a foreign language. Achievement tests therefore measure knowledge in a fairly specific area.

In contrast, an **aptitude test** is supposed to predict future success on the basis of current performance. These tests draw their material from a broader range of human experience, including information gained outside the classroom. Whereas an achievement test focuses backward, on material already learned, an aptitude test focuses forward, on a person's ability to learn something in the future. However, as you can imagine, the borderline between achievement and aptitude is not clear-cut. For example, the vocabulary and other verbal skills you have *achieved* will certainly influence the score you receive on an aptitude test. However, let us set aside this controversy and examine several tests that are designed to measure aptitude.

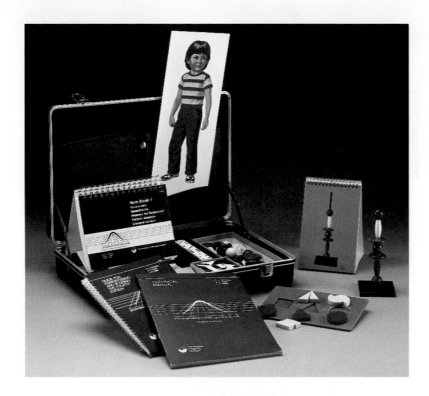

Figure 14.3

Test material used in the Stanford-Binet Intelligence Scale (4th ed.).

The Stanford-Binet Intelligence Scale As noted earlier, this test is derived from Alfred Binet's tests. Lewis Terman, working at Stanford University, found that the norms developed in Paris did not apply well to California children. Terman's revised version is called the Stanford-Binet Intelligence Scale. Like all major tests, the Stanford-Binet has been revised many times.

The material used in the current edition of the Stanford-Binet is illustrated in Figure 14.3. As you can see, it contains wooden shapes to be assembled in an order that matches a picture, blocks to be inserted in a form board, and a photograph of a unisex, multiethnic child, which young children use for pointing to specified body parts. The test also includes other tasks, such as arithmetic, vocabulary, and memory for sentences (Thorndike et al., 1986).

Originally, the term *intelligence quotient* was truly an arithmetical quotient, based on the child's mental age (derived from the raw score on the test) divided by the child's chronological age. The result was then multiplied by 100 to eliminate an awkward decimal point:

$$\text{Intelligence Quotient (IQ)} = \frac{\text{Mental Age}}{\text{Chronological Age}} \times 100$$

However, this method created problems. For example, it does not make sense for adults, whose mental-age test scores remain stable even though their chronological age is increasing. An intelligence quotient is no longer really a quotient. Instead, an **intelligence quotient, or IQ,** is currently calculated by consulting norms that assign a score of 100 to a person whose performance is exactly average for a particular age group; higher and lower IQs are assigned on the basis of where a person's score falls in comparison to the average.

Most IQ tests are designed so that the standard deviation of the distribution is established as 15 points. Thus an IQ of 115 means that a person scored exactly one standard deviation above the mean (100 + 15). As you can see from Figure 14.4, 34.1% (or about one-third) of IQ scores fall between 100 and 115. Similarly, 34.1% fall between 85 and 100. Notice that IQs higher than 145 or lower than 55 are very rare.

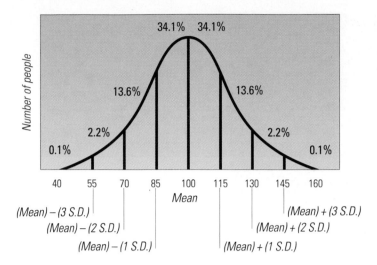

Figure 14.4

A normal, bell-shaped curve, showing the distribution of IQ scores for a very large sample of people. The percentage falling within each IQ range is listed above each segment of the curve.

The Wechsler Scales David Wechsler (pronounced "*Wex*-ler") was born in Romania and emigrated to the United States at the age of 6. As a young adult, he volunteered to help the Army in scoring its intelligence tests during World War I (Fancher, 1985). With this background, Wechsler decided to construct his own scales. His first task was to design an intelligence test specifically aimed at adults, because the previous tests were modifications of ones designed for children. At present, each of three Wechsler tests is specialized for a particular age range (see Table 14.2).

The Wechsler scales—like the Stanford-Binet—include both verbal and nonverbal (or performance) questions. Here are some typical items:

1. What does the word *unobtrusive* mean?
2. After you have heard this list of numbers, repeat them in order: 4, 7, 2, 9, 5, 1, 8, 3.
3. Arrange these five pictures in order, so that they tell a story.
4. Assemble these cutouts so that they make a familiar object.

As with all standardized tests, the reliability and the validity of the Wechsler scales have been examined extensively. The reliabilities generally range from about .88 to .98, which is excellent. Validity studies of the Wechsler scales do not produce such impressive data, though they are adequate. For example, criterion-related validity research has shown that people in white-collar jobs receive higher scores on the verbal portion than on the performance portion; in contrast, skilled workers receive higher scores on the performance portion (Anastasi, 1988). This makes sense, because the first group should be skilled with words and the second group should be skilled with spatial relationships. Furthermore, IQ scores are correlated approximately .70 with achievement in elementary school (Rattan & Rattan, 1987).

This child is taking the WISC-III.

TABLE 14.2	The Wechsler Scales	
ABBREVIATION	**NAME**	**INTENDED AGE RANGE**
WPPSI-R	Wechsler Preschool and Primary Scale of Intelligence — Revised	4–6
WISC-III	Wechsler Intelligence Scale for Children— Third Edition	6–16
WAIS-R	Wechsler Adult Intelligence Scale—Revised	adults

The Scholastic Aptitude Test So far, we have looked at tests that are administered individually. In contrast, the Scholastic Aptitude Test (SAT) is a group test; it is designed to measure aptitude for college work. Try Demonstration 14.2 to familiarize yourself with this test, in case you did not take it, or to refresh your memory, in case you did.

The SAT yields separate measures of verbal and mathematical abilities. Its name suggests that it is an aptitude test, yet you can see from Question 3 that it requires some knowledge of geometry. Thus, the SAT really measures past achievements and formal education, as well as aptitude for future work (Linn, 1982; Messick, 1980).

The SAT was revised in the spring of 1994 to emphasize more sophisticated thinking. This new version includes an essay section and a mathematics section in which students must supply the answers, rather than select the answer in a multiple-choice format. However, an important problem remains on the reading comprehension portion; students can guess the correct answer with reasonable accuracy, even without reading the appropriate passages (Katz et al., 1990). Thus, this portion of the test has a validity problem in that it is measuring something other than what it is supposed to measure.

DEMONSTRATION 14.2 The Scholastic Aptitude Test

Answer each of the questions below; they are sample items from the mathematical and verbal portions of the SAT. The answers appear at the end of the chapter.

1. There are 45 students in a certain physics class. If two-thirds of the students are boys, and one-half of the boys are blue-eyed, how many blue-eyed boys are in the class?
   (A) 15   (B) 30   (C) 34
   (D) 38   (E) 43

2. To which of the following is $\dfrac{a}{b} - \dfrac{a}{c}$ equal?

   (A) $\dfrac{a}{b-c}$ (B) $\dfrac{1}{b-c}$

   (C) $\dfrac{1}{bc}$ (D) $\dfrac{ab-ac}{bc}$

   (E) $\dfrac{ac-ab}{bc}$

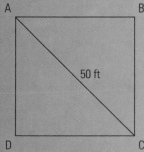

3. In the above figure, the distance from A to C in the square field $ABCD$ is 50 feet. What is the area, in square feet, of field $ABCD$?
   (A) $25\sqrt{2}$ (B) 625   (C) 1,250
   (D) 2,500   (E) 5,000

4. Choose the word or phrase that is most nearly *opposite* in meaning to the word in capital letters.
   LENIENCY:
   (A) wealth   (B) severity
   (C) status   (D) brevity
   (E) defense

5. Choose the word that *best* fits the meaning of the sentence as a whole. To many thoughtful people, the tremendous coverage of sporting events by television stations presents a _____: the instrument which has made us a sports-conscious nation is also the instrument which may destroy amateur and professional athletics in this country.
   (A) nuance   (B) hyperbole
   (C) handicap   (D) paradox
   (E) digression

6. Select the lettered pair that *best* expresses a relationship similar to that expressed in the original pair.
   COMPOSER: SYMPHONY:
   (A) playwright: rehearsal
   (B) actor: comedy
   (C) conductor: orchestra
   (D) director: movie
   (E) poet: sonnet

Consumer groups—as well as thousands of students—often ask whether the SATs are truly useful. Can they predict college success? It is true that high-school grade point averages (GPAs) are more accurate in predicting college grades. The correlation between high-school and college grades is typically about .48. In contrast, the correlation between SAT scores and college grades is about .42, which is less impressive. The value of the SAT scores comes when the data from high-school GPA and SAT are combined; together, they are correlated .55 with college grades (Kaplan, 1982; Willingham, 1990). Notice, however, that even this combination does a far-from-perfect job in predicting college success. Suppose that you were a college director of admissions. What other information would you gather and what additional tests would you construct, so that you could predict students' college grades with greater criterion-related validity?

However, we need to discuss a problem called *restricted range*. This problem prevents the correlation between *any* test scores (including SATs) and college grades from being impressively high. A **restricted range** means that you are only considering a narrow set of all possible scores when you are calculating the correlation. In the case of SAT scores, the sample of scores is restricted because not everyone who takes the SAT actually attends college. When we eliminate many of the lower scores, ending up with a more select sample, the correlation drops closer to zero.

To appreciate the concept of restricted range more completely, look at Figure 14.5, which shows the SAT scores of 21 hypothetical students and the grade point average they received in college. Let us also imagine that 11 additional students took the SAT but did not attend college because of lack of academic ability. However, their grade point averages were estimated, on data from other students. First look at *all* the scores in Figure 14.5, and you'll notice a reasonably strong correlation. Then cover up the lower scores (indicated in light green) and notice that the data remaining come closer to a zero correlation. When people apply to graduate school, the range becomes even more restricted; correlations between Graduate Record Examination (GRE) scores and academic success are even lower. In short, the criterion-related validity of SAT scores would be higher if the restricted-range problem did not exist.

The Two Extremes of Intelligence

Turn back to Figure 14.4 and notice the scores on the extreme left and the extreme right of the distribution, because we now direct our attention to retarded and gifted individuals.

Mental Retardation The essential features of **mental retardation** are (1) intellectual functioning that is significantly below average, (2) difficulty functioning in everyday settings, and (3) onset prior to age 18 (Grossman, 1983). An IQ below 70 is

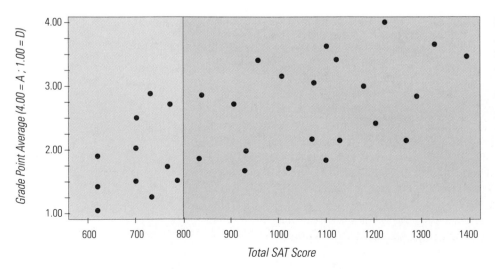

Figure 14.5

Hypothetical graph, showing relationship between total SAT scores and grades (or predicted grades). Note that the correlation is lower if we look only at a restricted range. [These scores are not *based on any actual data; please do not use this figure to estimate your G. P. A.!]*

TABLE 14.3 Categories of Mental Retardation

LEVEL OF RETARDATION	IQ RANGE	NUMBER OF AMERICANS	DESCRIPTION
Mild mental retardation	55–69	4,200,000	May complete sixth grade academic work; in supportive setting, may hold a job.
Moderate mental retardation	40–54	1,200,000	May complete second-grade academic work; may hold a job in a sheltered workshop.
Severe mental retardation	25–39	400,000	May learn to talk; often needs help even for simple tasks.
Profound	below 25	200,000	Little or no speech; requires constant help and supervision.

Sources: American Psychiatric Association, 1994; Grossman, 1983; Zigler & Hodapp, 1991.

considered to be significantly below average. However, the examiner must also consider an individual's adaptive functioning and social competence before making a diagnosis of mental retardation. Children who receive low scores on standardized intelligence tests may not be classified as mentally retarded if they can feed themselves, dress themselves, and show fairly normal motor skills (Grossman, 1983; Sternberg, 1990b). Table 14.3 shows the four general categories of mental retardation.

According to one estimate, 350 known causes of mental retardation have been identified (Spitz, 1986). The causes traditionally have been divided into two general categories, organic and cultural-familial. Between 25% and 50% of retarded individuals are categorized as having **organic retardation,** traceable to genetic disorders such as Down syndrome or to physical damage to the brain (Zigler & Hodapp, 1991). This brain damage can often be traced to an infectious disease, Fetal Alcohol Syndrome, or medical complications from a premature delivery.

Between 50% and 75% of mentally retarded people have **cultural-familial retardation;** their disorder has no clear organic cause. They may be retarded because they received fewer genes for high intelligence from their parents, because they grew up in an economically impoverished situation, or a combination of these two factors (Zigler & Hodapp, 1991).

In North America, mentally retarded people lived at home until the mid-1800s, when institutions were established. Residents of these institutions often lived in crowded conditions during that era, with little personal attention and no educational programs. In recent decades, however, real progress has been made in establishing smaller, more personalized group homes in the community, where retarded individuals are encouraged to live as independently as possible.

Let us now consider the cognitive components of retardation. Suppose that we want to compare a mentally retarded child with a younger, nonretarded child, who received the same raw score on a standard IQ test. How will the two children compare on cognitive tasks? On the Piaget-type tasks discussed in Chapter 10 (for example, conservation), the two will probably perform similarly (Zigler & Balla, 1982). However, on information-processing tasks such as memory (Chapter 7) and concept formation, the nonretarded child will frequently perform better (Weiss et al., 1986). It is not clear why retarded individuals have particular difficulty with some cognitive tasks but not others. However, retardation is clearly a complicated condition; it cannot be traced to a single, general cause that produces equal deficits on all tasks (Weiss et al., 1986).

Many retarded adults can live successfully in group homes, helping to prepare meals, and often holding jobs.

Retarded individuals also seem to have difficulty with metacognition. In earlier chapters, we discussed metamemory, which is your knowledge about your own memory. A more general term, **metacognition,** refers to your knowledge about your cognitive processes. Retarded individuals typically cannot describe or discuss their thought processes. They also have difficulty with a related aspect of metacognition, planning and monitoring their cognitive processes. Nonretarded people can plan how to solve a problem, and they check to see how they are progressing. In general, retarded individuals lack these metacognitive skills (Campione et al., 1982). As a result, they have trouble with long-range projects.

Giftedness No firm cutoff separates the gifted from other people. We could apply the term *gifted* to people in the top 5% of intelligence, or the top 1%, or even the top 0.1%. However, many school districts with special programs for **the gifted** often select those with IQs over 130, roughly the top 2% (Davis & Rimm, 1989; Horowitz & O'Brien, 1986).

We saw that retardation was not defined just in terms of IQ; the definition also included difficulty in normal functioning. Similarly, many theorists and educators emphasize that giftedness involves more than simply a high IQ score. Some argue, for instance, that the term *gifted* should be applied to people with exceptional creativity, leadership skills, or artistic abilities. Others propose that people are gifted only if they meet all three of the following criteria: (1) above-average ability, (2) creativity, and (3) focused motivation for completing a project (Mönks & Van Boxtel, 1985; Renzulli, 1986).

Gifted children are typically as well adjusted emotionally as children of average intelligence; if anything, they show somewhat better adjustment (Schneider, 1987). They also tend to be less confined by traditional gender stereotypes (Lubinski & Humphreys, 1990). However, gifted individuals may tend to be perfectionists or overly sensitive to criticism (Freeman, 1985). Furthermore, if gifted children become frustrated and disillusioned with school, they may develop a pattern of low achievement (Mills, 1992).

We mentioned that retarded individuals have difficulty with metacognition. As you might guess, gifted people tend to be exceptional with respect to metacognition. They are particularly skilled at planning, organizing, and transferring strategies from one task to another (Jackson & Butterfield, 1986). This understanding of their own

Gifted individuals are particularly exceptional in the kind of planning and organizing required for original projects.

thought processes and ability to monitor progress are especially useful during adulthood. In life outside of a school setting, success often depends on initiating and pursuing an original idea, rather than simply doing a task that has been assigned.

Broader Conceptions of Intelligence

So far we have examined the traditional tests of intelligence, as well as the categories of retardation and giftedness, based primarily on those traditional test scores. However, two cognitive psychologists have focused on broader definitions of intelligence that consider skills in artistic and interpersonal areas.

This gymnast would excel in Gardner's category of bodily-kinesthetic thinking.

Gardner's Theory of Multiple Intelligences Howard Gardner argues that the traditional IQ tests assess only the standard academic kinds of intelligence. **Gardner's theory of multiple intelligences** proposes seven different components of intelligence. This theory includes three standard areas: (1) language ability, (2) logical-mathematical thinking, and (3) spatial thinking. It also includes four other distinct abilities: (4) musical thinking, (5) bodily kinesthetic thinking, (6) interpersonal thinking, and (7) intrapersonal thinking (Gardner, 1983, 1988).

We are accustomed to individual differences in the first three areas. However, think of people you know who shine in the other four skills—perhaps someone who improvises on the piano (music) or a person who excels in sports (kinesthetic). Someone skilled in *inter*personal thinking has an unusual understanding of other people, whereas someone skilled in *intra*personal thinking has a highly accurate understanding of himself or herself.

Gardner's ideas about multiple intelligences have aroused considerable interest, and they have encouraged us to expand our ideas about the constituents of intelligence (e.g., Kantrowitz, 1993). However, critics wonder if the last four skills really should be classified as components of intelligence. Also, the various abilities may not be as independent as Gardner suggested. For instance, logical-mathematical thinking and spatial thinking tend to be highly correlated (Sternberg, 1985).

Sternberg's Triarchic Theory of Intelligence Robert Sternberg and Richard Wagner (1993) also argue that the traditional intelligence tests are too narrow in their emphasis on academic intelligence, rather than more practical, real-world kinds of intelligence. **Sternberg's triarchic theory of intelligence** specifies three important parts of intelligence: (1) componential intelligence, (2) experiential intelligence, and (3) contextual intelligence. People can excel in one, two, or all three kinds of intelligence.

Componential intelligence corresponds most closely with traditional notions of intelligence. This includes the metacognitive skills we discussed earlier that help you plan and devise strategies. This kind of intelligence also includes the kinds of skills you use in solving an intellectual problem and getting the work done—for example, doing the research for a term paper and actually writing the paper.

Experiential intelligence, as the name implies, is focused on how people perform on tasks with which they have either no previous experience or great experience. For instance, you may have a friend with average grades, who was able to figure out what to do when she lost her passport in Madrid; she seems to thrive in new, unfamiliar settings. A person who is high in experiential intelligence also figures out how to perform familiar tasks more automatically. He or she quickly learns to drive, leaving extra cognitive capacity for other more interesting activities, such as listening to music or talking. In short, experiential intelligence focuses on our performance on both familiar and unfamiliar tasks.

In Sternberg's triarchic theory, the third major kind of intelligence is **contextual intelligence,** or intelligence in everyday life—that is, street smarts. More formally, contextual intelligence requires adapting to, selecting, and shaping one's real-world context or environment. Part of contextual intelligence is called practical intelligence, or knowing the pathway to success in your culture or occupation. The other part of contextual intelligence is social intelligence, or the ability to understand others and interact successfully with them. You certainly know people who are high in other kinds of intelligence, yet they are socially inept. For instance, they ask too many questions in class, appearing to be completely unaware that neither the professor nor the other students are charmed.

What is the future of theories such as Gardner's and Sternberg's? Clearly, they have excited interest from both professionals and the public. However, sustained interest in these broader theories may depend upon developing tests of the alternative kinds of intelligence that are standardized, reliable, and valid.

According to Sternberg's triarchic theory, there are three kinds of intelligence. These include (a) componential intelligence, which is involved in writing a paper; (b) experiential intelligence, which contributes to doing well in an unfamiliar setting—as in the case of this exchange student in Japan; and (c) contextual intelligence, such as comforting a troubled friend.

DEVELOPING INTELLIGENCE TESTS

- Both experts and nonexperts believe that an intelligent person is one who is high in verbal skills, problem-solving ability, and practical intelligence.

- Galton pioneered the early testing of intelligence, but Binet's tests assessed attributes closer to our current notions of intelligence.

- The Stanford-Binet Intelligence Scale and the three Wechsler scales must be administered individually before converting the scores to IQ scores; the Scholastic Aptitude Test is a group test that is somewhat useful in predicting college success, but correlations are lowered by the restricted-range problem.

- Two general categories of retardation are organic and cultural-familial retardation; metacognition is a cognitive skill that is particularly difficult for retarded individuals. In contrast, gifted people excel at metacognition.

- Howard Gardner's theory of multiple intelligence proposes that intelligence consists of verbal ability, logical-mathematical thinking, spatial thinking, musical thinking, bodily kinesthetic thinking, interpersonal thinking, and intrapersonal thinking.

- Sternberg's triarchic theory of intelligence proposes three important aspects of intelligence: componential intelligence, experiential intelligence, and contextual intelligence.

CONTROVERSIAL TOPICS IN INTELLIGENCE TESTING

Intelligence testing is one of the more controversial areas in psychology; we will examine five important controversies in this section. Two of these controversies were introduced in the developmental chapters—the nature-nurture question and the stability-change question. Both are also important when we consider intelligence. A third important question is whether intelligence can primarily be captured by one general factor, or whether it consists of a number of specific factors. However, the final two topics have received the most attention from the popular media. They are controversial because of their implications for people who are often the victims of stereotypes and discrimination. These topics are ethnic-group comparisons in intelligence and gender comparisons in intelligence.

The Nature-Nurture Question

We first raised the nature-nurture question in Chapter 3 in connection with genetics. Then we examined the issue more thoroughly in Chapter 10 when we looked at the development of children's abilities. Let's examine the research on the nature-nurture question with respect to intelligence.

Much of the research on the nature-nurture question has been conducted on twins (e.g., Bouchard et al., 1990). Identical twins not only look the same, but they also share exactly the same genetic makeup. Studies by Bouchard and McGue (1981) have demonstrated that the correlations between the IQ scores for identical twins average .86 when they are reared in the same household; that correlation is remarkably high. When identical twins are reared in separate households (for instance because they were adopted by different families), the correlations average .72. These data tell us two things:

1. Nature is important, because the correlation remains very high, even when the twins have different nurturing experiences.

2. Nurture is important, because the correlation is higher when the twins are raised in the same environment than when raised in different environments.

In addition, consider fraternal twins, whose genetic overlap is 50%—the same as for any two siblings. When fraternal twins are reared together, the correlations between their IQ scores average .60. This correlation is substantially lower than the .86 correlation for identical twins (whose genetic overlap is 100%). These data, then, provide additional evidence that nature is important.

A central concept in the nature-nurture controversy is called heritability. This concept focuses on the variability among all IQ scores, which is impressively large. Specifically, **heritability** estimates how much of the variability found in scores is due to heredity (or nature) and how much is due to environment (or nurture). For instance, you might read the results of a study of urban American high-school students that reports a heritability index of .60 on the Stanford-Binet IQ test. This means that 60% of all the variability in these students' scores can be traced to hereditary factors, whereas 40% can be traced to environmental factors (Anastasi, 1988). At present, most research produces heritability indexes between .50 and .70 (Carroll, 1992; Locurto, 1991; Loehlin et al., 1988; Plomin & Rende, 1991). In other words, when explaining individual differences in intelligence, some studies give equal weight to nature and nurture, whereas others give somewhat more weight to nature. These estimates are supported by adoption studies, in which the IQs of adopted children are more strongly correlated with the IQs of their biological parents than with characteristics of their adoptive homes (Turkheimer, 1991).

If the heritability indexes typically range from .50 and .70, then that means that the proportion of variability due to environment ranges between .30 and .50. However, psychologists now acknowledge that these environmental factors are subtle, related to the concept of nonshared environmental experiences we discussed in Chapter 10. As Locurto (1991) explains, infants differ soon after birth in their temperament. As infants grow older, adults treat them according to these personal characteristics. A highly active child might be urged toward athletic activities; a contemplative child might be encouraged to look at books and play with toys that promote creative manipulation. As Locurto writes,

> In short, each baby's own characteristics—her temperament and other genotypic characteristics related to personality and intelligence—determine, to a large extent, how she will be reacted to and what types of environments she experiences. The end result is that each sibling experiences environments that match their abilities and dispositions. (p. 145)

Locurto's explanation is appealing, and it seems to explain many differences among siblings raised in the same family. To me, a logical step would be to examine how Bandura's (1986) model of reciprocal influences might explain why one boy becomes the class genius and his younger brother becomes the class clown. (See Figure 13.4 on page 436.)

The Stability-Change Question

Try to recall the names of the smartest people in your fourth-grade class. Do you suppose that they are still exceptional? Would the slowest learners still be considered slow? In other words, does intelligence remain stable across the life span? You may recall that we discussed the stability-change question with respect to personality in childhood (Chapter 10) and adulthood (Chapter 11). Now we apply the same question to intelligence.

In general, intelligence test scores remain fairly stable. For instance, intelligence tests administered at age 13 were correlated .78 with test scores at age 18 (Härnqvist, 1968). Even more impressive, a measure of intelligence gathered on infants at 6 months of age is correlated about .50 with IQ scores at the age of 3 years (Fagan, 1992). This might not strike you as particularly exciting until you begin to wonder how anyone could measure IQ on a 6-month-old. After all, a 6-month-old can barely sit up, and certainly could not respond to a single item on the WPPSI-R men-

To some extent, children's own characteristics determine which interests they pursue in their environment. Some of the variability in IQ scores can be explained because children create different environments for themselves.

tioned in Table 14.2. However, Fagan has devised a measure of intelligence that involves a preference for looking at novel items, rather than familiar ones. Children who enjoy the cognitive challenge of new sights are able to process information quickly and efficiently. These same children are likely to receive higher scores when they are old enough to talk and can be tested on standardized vocabulary tests (Fagan, 1992). Obviously, it will be even more interesting to see whether scores on these infant intelligence tests are correlated with intelligence scores during later childhood and adulthood.

Naturally, a particular individual's IQ score can change dramatically if his or her environment is sharply altered (for instance by enrollment in a good remedial program). However, the data on IQ tests generally favor stability rather than change.

Suppose that you decide to pursue graduate study, and you take the Graduate Record Examination (GRE). As you might guess, the stability-change question is relevant if you want to predict your score on the GRE. A study of about 23,000 students who took the SAT and then took the GRE General Test 4 or 5 years later showed that the correlations between the two scores were .86 for both the verbal and the mathematical sections (Angoff & Johnson, 1988). These data imply that your GRE scores will probably be fairly similar to your SAT scores. In short, scores on these college-testing exams tend to show the same stability as scores on IQ tests.

Lenny Ng received a perfect 800 on the math SAT exam . . . when he was 10 years old. He received straight A's throughout high school, and he is now enrolled at Harvard. The data on stability in intelligence would lead us to predict an extremely high math score if he were to take the math GREs when he completes college.

The General-Specific Question

One major theoretical argument dominated the early history of intelligence testing, and it still persists today: Does intelligence consist of a single core factor or many separate, unrelated abilities? Think about several people you consider to be extremely intelligent. Are they all intelligent in the same way, or do they have different strengths? Is one person highly verbal, another a whiz at math, and another skilled at fixing mechanical things?

The general-specific question was addressed by Charles Spearman (1904, 1923), who developed a statistical technique. This technique, called **factor analysis,** examines the correlations among many variables in order to identify closely related clusters of abilities that seem to be measuring the same, underlying factor. Spearman concluded that a single, general mental ability, which he called the **g factor,** underlies all the varying kinds of intelligence. Spearman did acknowledge that individuals may excel in certain areas—such as language, mathematics, or mechanical aptitude. Still, he argued that a person who was exceptional in one area was also likely to be strong in other areas.

Other psychologists disagreed. They proposed that a person might have outstanding verbal ability, for example, yet receive dismal scores on tests of memory and spatial ability. How many kinds of special abilities could we have? Some argued that intelligence could be divided into as few as seven factors (Thurstone, 1955). Others argued for as many as 180 extremely specific factors (Guilford, 1988).

In general, most contemporary psychologists would be reluctant to say that a single factor, *g,* could adequately capture all the diverse skills that comprise human intelligence (e.g., Horn, 1989). We already saw that Howard Gardner's theory of multiple intelligences identified seven factors, and Robert Sternberg's triarchic theory proposed three factors, each of which could be subdivided into at least two more specific factors. Thus, the trend is toward a model in which a person's intelligence can be traced to a small number of factors, perhaps fewer than 10. However, most psychologists interested in intelligence would be reluctant to match Guilford's estimate of 180 separate kinds of intellectual ability.

Ethnic-Group Comparisons in Intelligence

Researchers have discovered that Mexican, Puerto Rican, and other Hispanic children score 10 to 12 points below Anglo children on standardized IQ tests (Dunn, 1987). Furthermore, Black children consistently score about 15 points lower than

White children on a variety of IQ tests (Brody, 1992; Mackenzie, 1984). As we discuss these ethnic group comparisons in IQ scores, we need to keep reminding ourselves about an important part of Theme 2: The differences within any group of humans are larger than the differences between groups. For example, that 15-point difference between Blacks and Whites translates to a difference of 1 standard deviation. This number is dwarfed by the fact that the variability *within* any group is about 10 standard deviations (Brody, 1992). Let us first briefly examine the Hispanic-Anglo comparison and then discuss in somewhat greater detail the more extensive research on the Black-White comparison.

Comparing the Test Scores of Hispanics and Anglos You can probably guess some of the reasons that Hispanic students score somewhat lower than Anglo students. First of all, the Hispanic students may not be perfectly bilingual, an obvious disadvantage on a test that relies heavily on the English language (Costantino, 1992; Geisinger, 1992). As you know from Chapter 9, children who are completely bilingual often score higher on cognitive tests than their monolingual classmates. Couldn't we simply translate the tests into Spanish and measure children's intelligence in their first language? Unfortunately, research on translations of standardized tests such as the Wechsler Intelligence Scale shows that the translated versions are lower in reliability, though the reasons for this finding are not clear (Marín & Marín, 1991). As a result, we cannot be confident about the accuracy of these translated tests.

A further problem with the research that discovered the 10- to 12-point difference is that it did not control for socioeconomic class (Mercer, 1988; Willig, 1988). Socioeconomic class is correlated about .30 with IQ, so this is an important confounding variable. In most cases, too, the schools that Anglo students and Hispanic students attend are not comparable. When schools are successful in motivating and teaching Hispanic students, their achievement motivation and test scores can be outstanding (Jarboe, 1990). (See Figure 14.6.)

Comparing the Test Scores of Blacks and Whites The research on Black-White IQ differences has had an extremely turbulent history. In the late 1960s, educational psychologist Arthur Jensen wrote an article for the prestigious *Harvard Educational Review*. His article on IQ was supposed to have been followed by commentaries from other experts. However, the commentaries were postponed to a later issue of the journal because of deadlines (Fancher, 1985). Thus, Jensen's article had a stronger impact than originally intended.

Jensen's (1969) article concluded that programs designed to improve the intelligence of culturally deprived children actually had little benefit. However, the most controversial part of the article was Jensen's argument that the Black-White intelligence difference could be due to genetic differences. Unfortunately, the popular media tended to exaggerate and oversimplify Jensen's arguments, with articles bearing titles such as "Born Dumb." Blacks and liberal Whites were particularly sensitive to racial issues in the late 1960s, so you can imagine the reaction to these claims (Snyderman & Rothman, 1988).

We cannot summarize all the arguments that have been presented both for and against a genetic interpretation of ethnic differences in IQ. Brody (1992) comments upon some of the environmental factors that contribute to the difference:

> *Black and white Americans are reared in quasisegregated environments frequently having relatively little social contact with each other. There are different cultural exposures in music and the arts and language. Experiences of discrimination and racism are encountered at one time or another or even constantly by black Americans and not by white Americans. We have little or no scientific data that quantifies the effects of living in a quasiseparate environment on the development in IQ in black individuals. Nevertheless, the possibility exists that the cumulative effects of experiences that occur frequently to black individuals and virtually never to white individuals may account for some or all of the black-white IQ gap. (p. 303)*

Figure 14.6
At El Paso's Cathedral High School, Mexican-American students learn that academic subjects should be valued, and successful older students can serve as role models.

As we move toward somewhat greater opportunities for Blacks in North America, the gap on some educational tests has been decreasing (Angoff, 1988; Jones, 1983). However, as we noted in Chapter 10, half of Black children still live below the poverty line, in contrast to one-quarter of White children. Black children are still more likely to have been born prematurely or to have experienced birth complications—both factors related to lower IQs (Storfer, 1990).

Even though we cannot draw conclusions about the explanation for the 15-point IQ gap, let us consider some relevant research that tends to favor an environmental explanation for this gap. In general, research on Black children reared in White homes shows that their IQ scores are virtually identical to the scores for White children reared in White homes (Brody, 1992). Consider a similar study by Scarr and Weinberg (1976). They examined Black children adopted by White families in the Minneapolis, Minnesota, region. They found that the average IQ of these adopted children was 106, in contrast to an average IQ of 90 for Black children reared in their own homes in that region. Children raised in upper-middle-class homes, where educational goals are emphasized, tend to have above-average IQs—whether their skin color is black or white. Environment does make a difference. We should note, too, that this study still underestimates the potential influence of the environment, because the adopted children undoubtedly experienced racism in the world outside their adoptive families.

Many people have argued that IQ tests are aimed at White middle-class vocabulary and culture, so they are biased against other ethnic groups (e.g., Scarr, 1984). In general, though, the research does not find strong evidence for test bias (e.g., Bianchini, 1976; Kaplan, 1985; Oakland & Parmelee, 1985). However, other test-related factors may be important. For example, White children receive the same test scores, whether the examiner is familiar to them or unfamiliar. In contrast, Black and Hispanic children perform about 11 points better when they know the examiner (Fuchs & Fuchs, 1989).

Similarly, in another study, children were motivated to perform well by receiving a toy for good performance on an IQ test; children in a control group received no reward. White middle-class children performed similarly in the two conditions, but Black inner-city children received IQ scores that averaged 13 points higher in the reward condition (Johnson et al., 1984). Perhaps children in more privileged subcultures have been taught to try their hardest on an intelligence test; they are already highly motivated. Children from other ethnic groups may not receive these motivating instructions from their parents, so their scores can be influenced by other motivational factors, such as examiner familiarity and the possibility of a reward.

In summary, psychologists still have no clear-cut explanation for the ethnic-group differences in IQ scores. However, genetic explanations seem less likely than differences in language, environment, and motivation (Brody, 1992).* We also need to re-emphasize a point we made earlier; the differences between ethnic groups are much smaller than the differences within any single ethnic group.

IN DEPTH: Gender Comparisons in Intelligence

Take a moment to think about what you have heard and read about gender differences in mathematics, language, and other intellectual skills. Recently, I was sitting in the dentist's chair, my mouth open wide and assorted contraptions protruding at various angles. On the other side of a partition, I heard another patient—presumably unburdened by dental equipment—saying to the hygienist, "But it's a well-known fact that girls learn to talk sooner than boys." Had I not been

* Some readers may wonder why psychologists argue for a strong genetic basis for the IQ differences among various individuals, but for a strong environmental basis for IQ differences among various ethnic groups. The answer is that genetic differences help create IQ variability within each group. However, the genetic material for Anglos is not superior to the genetic material for other ethnic groups; instead, environmental factors account for Hispanic-Anglo and White-Black IQ discrepancies.

concerned about my dubious credibility in these circumstances, I would have jumped up from the chair and raced in to say, "No, actually, a meta-analysis done in 1988 shows that there is no real gender difference!"

The research on gender comparisons in intelligence is extremely complex, consistent with Theme 3 (Linn, 1986). However, consistent with Theme 2, we can conclude that for all of these skills, the differences *within* either gender are much larger than the differences *between* the two genders.

This boy and girl are probably similar in their ability to solve problems. Here they are trying to design a weight-bearing structure of balsa wood for a school competition.

We will focus our attention on three areas in which modest gender differences are sometimes reported. However, let us first consider areas in which there are *no* consistent gender differences.

First of all, reviews of the research conclude that females and males do not differ consistently in tests of total ability, such as IQ (Maccoby & Jacklin, 1974; McGuinness, 1985; Singleton, 1987). One reason for this similarity is that the items on intelligence tests are usually balanced carefully, so that gender differences rarely appear. In general, too, most kinds of learning and memory tasks do not show gender differences. Males and females are equally competent when they form concepts, perform reasoning tasks, and solve problems. They are also similar in creativity (Kesler et al., 1976; Hargreaves, 1977; Maccoby & Jacklin, 1974). Keep these many similarities in mind as we explore gender comparisons in verbal, spatial, and mathematic abilities. As you will see, the research in all these areas makes frequent use of the technique called **meta-analysis,** the systematic statistical method for synthesizing the results from numerous studies on a given topic.

Verbal Ability Some of the research conducted in the 1970s concluded that females were slightly more skilled than males on some verbal tasks (summarized in Matlin, 1993a). However, a meta-analysis conducted by Janet Hyde and Marcia Lynn in 1988—involving a total of 1,418,899 people—showed that gender differences in verbal ability no longer exist. Incidentally, females used to score somewhat better than males on the verbal portion of the SAT, so the company that constructs the SAT replaced questions from the humanities and the arts with questions emphasizing science and business. By 1986, males began scoring about 11 points higher than females; the company has not tried to rebalance the test to restore gender equity (Rosser, 1989).

One verbal area that seemed to show persistent gender difference was reading disabilities. A **reading disability** refers to poor reading skills that are not accounted for by the level of general intelligence. Typical surveys showed that boys were 4 to 6 times as likely as girls to be referred to reading clinics for reading disability (Finucci & Childs, 1981). However, Shaywitz and her coauthors (1990) devised an objective method of assessing reading disabilities. The ratio dropped from 4 boys to every 1 girl (based on teachers' assessments) to 1.1 boy for every 1 girl. In short, males and females are essentially similar in all areas of verbal ability.

Spatial Ability Try Demonstration 14.3 before reading further. When we examine gender comparisons in spatial ability, the results are more complicated. Part of the problem is that spatial ability is not unitary; instead, it has three separate components (Linn & Petersen, 1986).

One kind of ability involves spatial visualization, perhaps locating a particular object that is hidden in a larger design (Demonstration 14.3A). Meta-analyses reveal no gender differences on spatial visualization tasks (Feingold, 1988a; Linn & Petersen, 1986).

Spatial perception tasks require participants to identify a horizontal or vertical location. You may recognize Demonstration 14.3B from Chapter 10. Meta-analyses show that males receive somewhat higher scores than females on tasks like the water-level test (Linn & Petersen, 1986).

The third category of spatial tasks involves mental rotation, as you can see in Demonstration 14.3C. Gender differences on mental-rotation problems are larger than for any other cognitive task. However, in a typical study, the rotation task that produces the largest gender differences still accounts for only 16% of the variability in all scores (Sanders et al., 1982). Furthermore, Favreau (1993) points out that significant gender differences often arise from studies in which most males and females receive similar scores. For example, look at Figure 14.7, which Favreau derived from earlier research by Kail and his colleagues (1979). As you can see, most males and females received scores between 2 and 8. The statistically significant gender difference can be almost entirely traced to a few females with very slow rotation speeds.

DEMONSTRATION 14.3 Examples of Tests of Spatial Ability

Try these three kinds of tests of spatial ability.

a. EMBEDDED-FIGURE-TEST. Study the figure on the left in each pair. Then cover it up and try to find where it is hidden in each figure on the right. The left-hand figure may need to be shifted in order to locate it in the right-hand figure.

1.   2.   3.

b. WATER-LEVEL TEST. Examine the glass of water on the left. Now imagine that it is slightly tilted, as on the right. Draw in a line to indicate the location of the water level.

c. MENTAL-ROTATION TEST. If you mentally rotate the figure on the left, which of the five figures on the right would you obtain?

1.   a.   b.   c.   d.   e.

2.   a.   b.   c.   d.   e.

Mathematical Ability Of all the topics discussed in this section, mathematics has attracted the most widespread attention. Most of my students are surprised to learn that the only area in which males perform consistently better than females is on the math section of the SAT, where males' scores average 46 points higher than females' scores (Bridgeman & Wendler, 1991; Rosser, 1989). The most widely publicized SAT gender differences are actually based on the scores of intellectually talented seventh- and eighth-grade students, even though the test was not designed to test their aptitude (Benbow, 1988; Linn & Hyde, 1989).

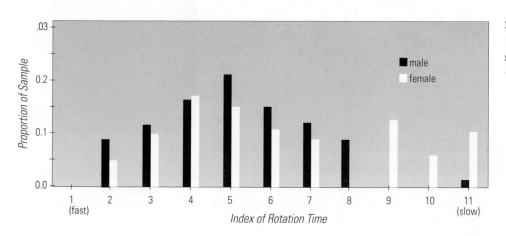

Figure 14.7

Time required to mentally rotate a geometric figure (based on Favreau, 1993, Kail et al., 1979)

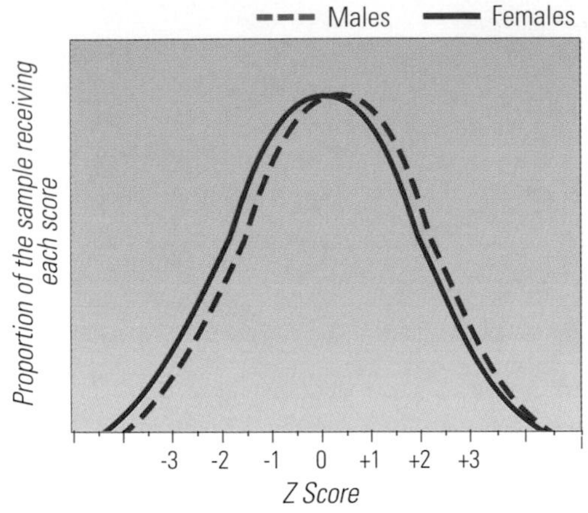

Figure 14.8

Performance of females and males on all mathematics tests except for the SAT, showing an effect size (d) of 0.15

Should we be concerned about the gender differences for high-school students' SAT scores? A number of researchers say that we should be alarmed (e.g., Bridgeman & Wendler, 1991; Chipman, 1994; Linn, 1992). Specifically, the math SAT *underpredicts* how well females will do in their college math courses. For example, if Jane and Bob receive identical scores in college math courses, we can go back to their records and check their math SATs. Bob's SAT is likely to have been about 35 points higher than Jane's. To be equitable, then, some educators argue that colleges should add about 35 points to females' math SAT scores.

Ironically, the math SAT—the one math test that counts the most in people's lives—is the only test on which gender differences are prominent; on most standardized math tests, males and females receive similar scores. The most dramatic illustration of this similarity comes from a meta-analysis conducted by Hyde and her coauthors (1990) on all math tests except the SAT; this analysis represented the testing of more than 3 million people. Figure 14.8 shows that the scores of males are only minimally better than the scores of females.

So far we have seen that females receive lower scores than males on the math SATs and similar scores on other standardized math tests. However, females fairly consistently receive higher grades in mathematics courses (Brooks, 1987; Kimball, 1989; Smith & Walker, 1988).

Explaining the Results Numerous theories have been developed to explain gender differences. As the years pass and more research accumulates, I find myself increasingly wondering if we have any cognitive gender differences substantial enough to require explaining. Perhaps the only ones are spatial perception, mental rotation, and the kind of math problems that comprise the math SAT exam. However, none of these differences is very large or very consistent. For that reason, explanations involving biological factors such as lateralization, hormones, or genetics (e.g., Halpern, 1992) do not seem particularly compelling.

Some social explanations have research support. For example, people who have participated more often in spatial activities, such as video games, score higher on tests of spatial ability; as you might expect, males are more likely than females to have experience with spatial activities (Law et al., 1993; Subrahmanyam & Greenfield, in press). Furthermore, males tend to take more courses in mathematics than females do, which may well contribute to the gender differences (Eccles, 1989). Also, parents' gender stereotypes about math abilities may indirectly influence their children's performance (Jacobs, 1991). Complex gender differences in attitudes and self-confidence could also contribute to differences in test scores (Matlin, 1993a; Mura, 1987). The gender differences have been changing significantly within just the last few decades (e.g., Feingold, 1988a); it will be interesting to see what the meta-analyses reveal in the twenty-first century! 🔍

Some of the gender differences in spatial ability can be traced to the fact that males have more experience with video games, which are highly spatial.

S E C T I O N   S U M M A R Y

CONTROVERSIAL TOPICS IN INTELLIGENCE TESTING

● Both nature and nurture are important determinants of intelligence; current research suggests that heritability ranges between .50 and .70; to some extent, a child's own characteristics determine whether he or she will pursue intellectual interests.

- Measures of intelligence—IQ, SAT/GRE, and even assessments of infant intelligence—show impressive stability over time.

- Some psychologists, such as Spearman, propose that a single mental ability (*g*) underlies intelligence, whereas others suggest as many as 180 separate factors; most favor fewer than 10 separate factors.

- The discrepancy between Hispanic and Anglo IQ scores can probably be traced to problems in English fluency, social class, and the quality of schools.

- The discrepancy between Black and White IQ scores can probably be traced to environmental and motivational factors; ethnic-group differences in IQ are much smaller than the differences within any ethnic group.

- Gender similarities are found in general intelligence, learning and memory, concept formation, reasoning, problem solving, creativity, verbal ability, some spatial tasks, and most mathematics tests; males excel on spatial perception and mental rotation tasks, as well as math SATs, whereas females excel in math grades.

ASSESSING PERSONALITY

So far, we have focused on intelligence tests, which are essential when educators want to assess cognitive abilities and skills. The other major category of psychology tests assesses individual differences in personality. Psychologists frequently use these personality tests to conduct research on specific psychological traits, such as extraversion-introversion (Wiggins & Pincus, 1992). They may also use personality tests to counsel people about everyday issues, such as career choice, and to aid the government and businesses in selecting employees. In this section, however, we will emphasize how psychologists use personality tests to aid in the clinical diagnosis of psychological disorders. This discussion will prepare you for the next two chapters, which examine psychological disorders and their treatment.

Chapters 13, 15, and 16 emphasize different theoretical approaches to personality and psychological disorders. As you might imagine, a psychologist's theoretical approach has a major influence on the kind of psychological test he or she favors. Someone who admires Skinner's behavioral approach to personality would be unlikely to ask people to free-associate to an inkblot. And a supporter of Freud's psychoanalytic approach probably would not conduct a behavioral assessment.

Look at the inkblot to the right, which is similar to those on the Rorschach Inkblot Test. Try to describe what the picture looks like and what it could be. Write down your answer. (You do not need to use complete sentences.)

When you have finished your description, go back over it and explain how you arrived at each part of that description. It is important to keep in mind, however, that this is not a true Rorschach Test, and that these tests cannot be interpreted adequately without expert training.

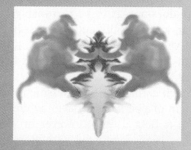

Let us consider three major categories of personality tests: projective tests, self-report inventories, and behavioral assessment. Before reading further, however, turn back to page 469 and try Demonstration 14.4.

Projective Tests

When psychologists administer **projective tests,** they ask people to respond to a standard set of stimuli that are vague and ambiguous. These stimuli presumably evoke a person's feelings, needs, and personality characteristics because people are *projecting* their psychological reactions onto the test stimuli. Projective tests have become somewhat less popular in recent years because of problems such as complex scoring systems and questionable validity (Groth-Marnat, 1990). However, the two most common projective tests are the Rorschach Inkblot Test and the Thematic Apperception Test.

The Rorschach Inkblot Test As an adolescent, Hermann Rorschach won the nickname "Klex," which is German for *inkblot* (Allison et al., 1988). The name was appropriate, because Rorschach developed his early interest in inkblots into a projective test that is the second most frequently used personality test (Lubin et al., 1984). (The most popular personality test, the MMPI, will be discussed shortly.) In the **Rorschach Inkblot Test,** people respond to a series of ambiguous inkblots, and the responses are analyzed according to characteristics such as recurring themes, number of responses, the region of the inkblot that attracts attention, and whether the nature of the response is common or unusual (Groth-Marnat, 1990).

The Rorschach consists of 10 inkblots, some colored and some black and white. During the first, or free-association phase, the examiner asks the individual to examine an inkblot and describe it. The examiner records the description word for word. During the second phase, the examiner asks the test taker to describe how he or she arrived at each response (Aiken, 1989). The Rorschach is designed to be administered and interpreted by rigorously trained professionals (Exner, 1991).

Be sure to try Demonstration 14.4, if you have not already done so. Consider how one person responded to one card in the Rorschach Test, a black-and-white design similar to the inkblot you saw in this demonstration. During the free-association phase, Mrs. T. reported that she saw "two elephants, two itty-bitty elephants . . . fighting over a roach—cockroach—in the middle. . . ." (Allison et al., 1988, p. 203). During the second phase, she elaborated on the elephants, "they both got their—their snozzoolas—[half laughs] or their trunks or whatever you call them wrapped around the cockroach" (p. 203).

The therapists' interpretation of this response focused on Mrs. T.'s defense mechanisms, which attempted to shrink a huge attacking creature into something small and playful. The interpretation also noted her phallic emphasis, because she focused on the elephants' trunks, yet blocked momentarily on the specific name for this penislike body part. As you can see, the Rorschach provides psychodynamically inclined professionals with a test rich with symbolic possibilities.

Some researchers argue that the Rorschach has reasonably high reliability and validity (Parker et al., 1988). The reliability does appear to be reasonably high, because it averages .83 (Parker, 1983). However, validity is difficult to assess because no single, universal scoring system has been developed. In general, though, the validity measures range between .40 and .50 (Groth-Marnat, 1990), correlations that many psychologists consider to be weak (Sundberg, 1990; Walsh & Betz, 1990).

An important advantage of the Rorschach is that it is an assessment technique that allows a tester to observe a broad segment of a person's behavior while he or she is providing reactions to the inkblot (Walsh & Betz, 1990). However, an important disadvantage is that very little research has been conducted with Rorschach responses provided by people of color. For example, only nine studies were conducted on Hispanic populations between 1949 and 1992 (Velásquez & Callahan, 1992). Psy-

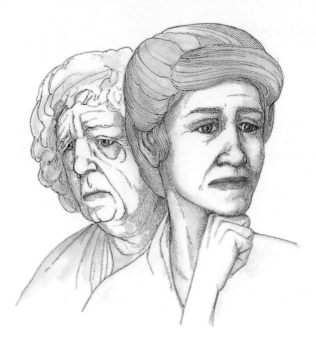

Figure 14.9

An item similar to those that appear on the Thematic Apperception Test.

chologists should therefore be especially cautious in using the Rorschach Test to make diagnoses on populations that are not Anglo.

The Thematic Apperception Test The second most popular projective test is called the **Thematic Apperception Test, or TAT.** The TAT consists of a series of ambiguous scenes, which the test taker is invited to describe, telling what is happening now, what happened in the past, and what will occur in the future. The TAT was first published by Christina Morgan and Henry Murray in 1935, and many different forms of the TAT are now in use.

Figure 14.9 shows a picture similar to those on the TAT. In responding to a picture like this, one woman wrote,

> *This is a woman who has been quite troubled by memories of a mother she was resentful toward. She has feelings of sorrow for the way she treated her mother; her memories of her mother plague her. These feelings seem to be increasing as she grows older and sees her children treating her the same way she treated her mother. She tries to convey this feeling to her own children, but does not succeed in changing their attitudes. She is living her past in the present, because the feeling of sorrow and guilt is reinforced by the way her children are treating her. (Aiken, 1989, p. 364)*

The TAT was designed to bring forth unconscious tendencies that a person may be unwilling or unable to reveal, such as difficulties with one's parents. In general, the pictures depict interpersonal relationships. Though the pictures look somewhat unusual, they are more realistic than the abstract shapes in the Rorschach. The test taker presumably projects his or her needs, concerns, and traits onto one or more of the characters in the scene. As you may recall, we discussed the use of the TAT in Chapter 12, in connection with achievement motivation.

As with the Rorschach Test, the person administering the test must be professionally trained, asking questions that encourage further clarification without being threatening or suggestive. Training is also necessary for interpreting the results. The examiner cannot simply flip through a test manual to discover the meaning of every sentence uttered by the test taker. The results are often interpreted within a psychodynamic framework, as with Rorschach. For instance, when a person omits reference to a gun shown in a TAT picture, the examiner may conclude that he or she tends to repress aggressive impulses. A tendency to introduce figures not shown on the cards may reveal the defense mechanism of projection (Phares, 1988).

Research on the TAT shows that it is sensitive to current motivational and emotional conditions. For instance, people who have been deprived of sleep do tend to tell stories about sleepy people, and people who have experienced recent failure tell stories about unsuccessful story characters (Anastasi, 1988). However, critics are skeptical about whether the test can measure more enduring personality traits (Anastasi, 1988; Mischel, 1986).

Unfortunately, reliability measures obtained on the TAT are low, with a median of about .30 for test-retest reliability (Kaplan & Saccuzzo, 1993). Many psychologists also question this test's validity (e.g., Groth-Marnat, 1990; Kaplan & Saccuzzo, 1993). Like the Rorschach, the TAT has been studied mostly with White populations; for example, only three studies conducted between 1949 and 1992 examined Hispanic test takers (Velásquez & Callahan, 1992).

Evaluation of Projective Tests One major advantage of projective tests is that their purpose is disguised: Test takers are seldom aware how their responses will be interpreted (Anastasi, 1988). In contrast, an objective self-report test often has one answer that looks socially acceptable, and test takers may be reluctant to select the other answer—even if it is more truthful. For instance, a suicidal person may be hesitant to say yes to the question, "Sometimes I think I may kill myself." However, he or she may mention death spontaneously on a projective test.

A second, related advantage proposed by psychodynamically inclined psychologists is that test takers can relax their defense mechanisms (such as repression or sublimation) when taking a projective test. This relaxation presumably allows the release of unconscious material (Groth-Marnat, 1990).

An important disadvantage of projective tests is that they are not as standardized as objective tests. Several alternative scoring systems may be used, and the accuracy also depends upon the examiner's professional skill.

Another disadvantage is that the test taker may misunderstand the task, resulting in invalid assessment. For instance, a friend of mine, knowing I was a psychologist, described how he had aced a psychological test. (From his description, it was the TAT.) He thought that he would be awarded a high score for finding a common thread interwoven through all the scenes. Because the first card showed a violin, he painstakingly forced each story to revolve around violins and music. His answers may have revealed creativity or persistence, but I doubt that they really revealed his unconscious personality traits.

Self-Report Tests

When you were reading about the projective tests, with their carefully ambiguous stimuli and their elaborate symbolic interpretations, did you find yourself muttering, "Wouldn't it be simpler just to *ask* people how they feel?" This is the approach of **self-report tests,** which are instruments that instruct people to answer questions about their behaviors, beliefs, and feelings. Let us look at the MMPI and then evaluate the general status of self-report tests.

The Minnesota Multiphasic Personality Inventory The most widely used personality test is the **Minnesota Multiphasic Personality Inventory (MMPI),** an objective personality test that asks a large number of true-false questions in order to assess personality traits.

In the late 1930s, a psychologist named Starke Hathaway and a psychiatrist named J. R. McKinley began to develop a set of personality scales to be used in diagnosing psychological disorders. They insisted that their test, which ultimately became the MMPI, should be based on research, rather than on unscientific intuitions. They collected about 1,000 questions from their clinical experience, other tests, and textbooks. These items covered a wide range of topics, such as psychological problems, physical symptoms, and attitudes (Butcher & Finn, 1983).

During the next phase of test development, the MMPI was administered to more than 1,500 unhospitalized people, including students and hospital visitors. The MMPI was also administered to more than 800 carefully selected psychiatric patients, representing the major clinical subgroups such as depression and schizophrenia. An item was selected for a particular scale of the MMPI only if the two groups—the normal group and the group with psychological disorders—showed significantly different response patterns. For instance, people with a particular psychological disorder were much more likely than people in the control group to say "true" to the item, "Someone has been trying to poison me." In contrast, an item was rejected if the two groups answered it the same way (for instance, if 61% of one group and 60% of the other group said "true"). It is important to realize that the *content* of the item is irrelevant; the critical point is whether the item discriminates between the normal group and the group with a psychological disorder.

In 1989, a revised form of the MMPI was published. This new MMPI-2 is based on a larger sample of test takers, with members of different ethnic groups represented in the same ratio as in the general population. The revised version also reworded test items that included gender-biased language, and it eliminated items that had outdated content or assumed that the test taker was Christian (Graham, 1990). However, some psychologists complain that 45% of the sample were college graduates, in contrast to only 17% in the general population. Many are also not convinced that the MMPI-2 is a substantial improvement over the "classic" MMPI (Adler, 1989, 1990).

The items on the new MMPI-2 are grouped into 15 clinical scales and 5 validity scales, making a total of 567 test questions. Table 14.4 shows some examples of scales, the characteristics they are supposed to assess, and some hypothetical test items. Notice, for example, that the "lie scale" helps assess one aspect of validity; anyone who says "yes" to the item "I smile at everyone I meet" cannot be telling the truth!

The reliability of the MMPI and MMPI-2 is considered to be reasonably high for a personality test. The test-retest reliability measures generally range between .75 and .85 (Graham, 1990; Kaplan & Saccuzzo, 1993).

Numerous studies were conducted to establish the validity of the MMPI, and several hundred have already been done on the MMPI-2. For example, 882 normal married couples took the MMPI-2, and each person's responses on that test were compared with his or her spouse's evaluation of the person on these same items; the

TABLE 14.4		Some Examples of Scales from the Minnesota Multiphasic Personality Inventory	
Name of Scale	Kind of Scale	Description	Hypothetical TEST ITEM (answer indicating the disorder is in parentheses)
Depression Scale	Clinical	Derived from patients who show extreme pessimism and feelings of hopelessness.	"I usually feel that life is interesting and worthwhile." *(False)*
Psychopathic Deviate Scale	Clinical	Derived from patients who show extreme disregard for social customs and who show aggressiveness	"My activities and interests are often criticized by others." *(True)*
Paranoia Scale	Clinical	Derived from patients who show abnormal suspiciousness or delusions.	"There are evil people trying to influence my mind." *(True)*
Lie Scale	Validity	Measures overly good self-image.	"I smile at everyone I meet.." *(True)*

Minnesota Multiphasic Personality Inventory - 2. Copyright © by the Regents of the University of Minnesota 1942, 1943, (renewed 1970), 1989. Reproduced by permission of the publisher.

pattern of correlations was high enough to suggest reasonable validity (Butcher et al., 1990). Furthermore, the responses of psychiatric patients were generally related to ratings of overt behavior that had been supplied by professionals (Graham, 1990).

A reasonable amount of research on the MMPI has been conducted with Hispanic and Black individuals, but little has been done with Asians or Native Americans (Greene, 1987; Velásquez & Callahan, 1992). Psychologists are encouraging researchers to conduct additional studies, keeping in mind the variety of different cultures within each ethnic group (Dana, 1988; Greene, 1987; Puente, 1990).

Even if some psychologists are not delighted with the MMPI-2, this instrument is clearly an important tool for clinical assessment. As Walsh and Betz (1990) conclude, "There is little question that the Minnesota Multiphasic Personality Inventory . . . is the most useful psychological test available in clinical and counseling settings for assessing the degree and nature of emotional upset" (p. 117).

Evaluation of Self-Report Tests A major advantage of self-report tests, such as the MMPI-2, is that they can be easily administered, even in large groups. They also can be objectively scored in a standardized fashion; the results do not depend upon the training or personal interpretations of the examiner. They also allow more complete, precise assessments than could be provided by casual observation.

However, one of the advantages also produces an important disadvantage. Because tests such as the MMPI are so easy to administer, they may be used inappropriately. A second disadvantage, particularly applicable to the MMPI, is often the length of the test. For example, after answering the first 500 questions on the MMPI, would you really answer the remaining 67 questions honestly and carefully? A third disadvantage was mentioned in the discussion of the advantages of projective tests: Test takers can often guess the socially appropriate answer on a self-report test. The MMPI includes the "lie scale" to assess this tendency to supply socially desirable responses, but most self-report tests do not. We discuss other aspects of self-report tests in the remaining chapters of this textbook. First, however, we need to discuss the third and last method of assessing personality.

Behavioral Assessment

The projective technique assumes that people will project their personality characteristics onto ambiguous stimuli, and the self-report technique asks people to answer questions about certain specific aspects of their personality. In contrast, **behavioral assessment** attempts to measure personality by objectively recording people's observable behavior, as well as events that happened beforehand and afterwards. This technique can help to identify problem behaviors; it can also help in the selection and evaluation of treatment (Groth-Marnat, 1990).

As the name implies, behavioral assessment is especially favored by behaviorists. After all, behaviorists emphasize people's behavior; they have no use for projective tests, and they do not trust the accuracy of the self-report technique. Behaviorists focus on what people *do*. They pay attention to the environmental conditions because they believe that these external situations are much more important than any enduring personal characteristics.

One of the most common methods of behavioral assessment is naturalistic observation (Haynes, 1990). As discussed in Chapter 2, **naturalistic observation** is the systematic recording of behavior in the natural environment, typically by trained observers. These observers first need to define the categories of behavior that they will record. For example, researchers who are examining a child's aggressive tendencies would need to write down their precise definitions of the categories they plan to observe (such as hitting, shoving, and verbal aggression).

Behavioral assessment can also include observations in clinic settings, as well as people's reports of their own behavior. For example, a person with an eating disorder might report the number of times she or he engaged in binge eating. Obviously, these self-assessments may have problems with both reliability and validity (Haynes, 1990).

Psychologists can conduct behavioral assessments of children in their normal everyday environment—for example, in a day-care center.

Psychologists frequently combine several techniques in trying to obtain a comprehensive view of an individual's personality. For instance, they could administer a TAT and an MMPI, but also record the person's behavior while taking the tests. We will discuss further applications of these personality assessment techniques in the chapters on psychological disorders and social psychology.

SECTION SUMMARY

ASSESSING PERSONALITY

- Projective tests require people to respond to ambiguous stimuli; the two most common projective tests are the Rorschach Inkblot Test and the Thematic Apperception Test. The advantages of these tests include a disguised purpose and the presumed ability to tap the unconscious; disadvantages include lack of standardization and potential reliability and validity problems.

- The most common self-report test is the Minnesota Multiphasic Personality Inventory (now the MMPI-2), currently the most popular personality test. The major advantages of self-report tests are that they are easily administered and they are standardized; disadvantages include the frequency of misuse, their length, and their tendency to elicit socially appropriate answers.

- Behavioral assessment can be conducted with naturalistic observation, as well as observation in other environments and observations provided by the individuals themselves.

REVIEW QUESTIONS

1. Imagine that you are designing a test to assess the personality dimension of optimism-pessimism. Define the terms *standardization, reliability,* and *validity,* and then describe how you could standardize the test and establish its reliability and validity. (Mention three measures of reliability and two of validity.)

2. Suppose that you are taking a test as part of a job application. Why would you want to know whether the test is standardized, reliable, and valid?

3. Trace the origins of the current intelligence tests, both in other countries and in North America. How are these tests relevant in the categorization of mentally retarded individuals and the gifted?

4. How is metacognition relevant in mental retardation, giftedness, and Sternberg's theory of intelligence? Speculate why metacognition should be centrally important in intelligence. (You may want to review Chapter 10 on the development of metamemory.)

5. What are the issues in the nature-nurture and stability-change questions? What is the general conclusion on these two issues with respect to intelligence?

6. One ongoing controversy in intelligence testing has focused on the number of different kinds of intelligence. Discuss this topic with respect to general mental ability (*g*) versus the proposal that intelligence consists of many different abilities. Also note Gardner's and Sternberg's contributions to this controversy.

7. Suppose you are part of a team designing a test for giftedness that will decide which children should be enrolled in gifted programs and which children should remain in regular programs. Describe three specific ways of measuring the test's reliability and two specific ways of assessing its validity. Based on the discussion of subtle environmental factors that influence intelligence, why would you recommend a gifted program that focuses on children's individual interests?

8. Probably the two most controversial topics in the field of intelligence concern ethnic-group differences and gender differences in intelligence. Summarize the

data on both issues, making sure that you acknowledge the complexity of the findings. Then describe some environmental factors that contribute to these differences.

9. List and describe the three major categories of personality tests. Which kind of personality theorist would most strongly support each of these three kinds of tests? Why?

10. Imagine that you are designing a personality test to assess some characteristic of your choice. Describe this characteristic and discuss how you could assess it using each of the three kinds of personality tests examined in this chapter. What would be the advantages and disadvantages of each kind of test?

N E W   T E R M S

psychological test
standardization
norms
reliability
test-retest reliability
split-half reliability
alternate-form reliability
validity
content validity
criterion-related validity
intelligence
achievement test
aptitude test
intelligence quotient (IQ)
restricted range
mental retardation
organic retardation
cultural-familial retardation
metacognition

the gifted
Gardner's theory of multiple intelligences
Sternberg's triarchic theory of intelligence
componential intelligence
experiential intelligence
contextual intelligence
heritability
factor analysis
g factor
meta-analysis
reading disability
projective tests
Rorschach Inkblot Test
Thematic Apperception Test (TAT)
self-report tests
Minnesota Multiphasic Personality
    Inventory (MMPI)
behavioral assessment
naturalistic observation

A N S W E R S   T O   D E M O N S T R A T I O N

DEMONSTRATION 14.2   1. A; 2. E; 3. C; 4. B; 5. D; 6. E.

DEMONSTRATION 14.3   A1. Orient the pattern as if it were a tilted capital M, with the left portion along the top of the white triangle. A2. This pattern fits along the right sides of the two black triangles on the left. A3. Rotate this figure about 100° to the right, so that it forms a Z, with the top line coinciding with the top line of the top white triangle. B. The line should be horizontal, not tilted. C1. c; C2. d.

R E C O M M E N D E D   R E A D I N G S

Brody, N. (1992). *Intelligence* (2nd ed.). San Diego: Academic Press. I would recommend this book for an in-depth discussion of important issues in theories of intelligence and the measurement of intelligence. Brody also includes a well-written section on group differences in intelligence, the nature-nurture issue, and social intelligence.

Geisinger, K. F. (Ed.). (1992). *Psychological testing of Hispanics.* Washington, DC: American Psychological Association. This book should serve as a model for the kind of systematic, thoughtful analysis that should be written when examining issues about ethnic groups. Topics include legal issues, biases, the design of tests, testing in industry, and testing for educational purposes.

Groth-Marnat, G. (1990). *Handbook of psychological assessment* (2nd ed.). New York: Wiley. This handbook is an extremely useful resource for college libraries, with chapters on topics such as the Wechsler scales, the Rorschach, the TAT, and behavioral assessment.

Kaplan, R. M., & Saccuzzo, D. P. (1993). *Psychological testing: Principles, applications, and issues* (3rd ed.). Pacific Grove, CA: Brooks/Cole. This mid-level textbook includes information about the basic principles of assessment, as well as intelligence and personality tests; some other interesting topics include career tests, measures of anxiety and stress, and legal aspects of testing.

Walsh, W. B., & Betz, N. E. (1990). *Tests and assessment* (2nd ed.). Englewood Cliffs, NJ: Prentice Hall. This clearly written textbook provides a good summary of test construction and the assessment of personality, cognitive ability, and career interests. Another interesting topic is the assessment of environment (e.g., the quality of a college's environment).

CHAPTER 15
PSYCHOLOGICAL DISORDERS

An executive in his early 30s came for treatment because he was plagued by the notion that he had placed, or was about to place, tacks in the coffee cups of coworkers. He would attempt to check the contents of their cups using paper towels to strain the contents. When no foreign objects were discovered, he would contemplate calling the police to turn himself in, thinking that the victim had already swallowed the tack. On one occasion, he wrote his immediate superior an anonymous note advising against drinking the coffee. (Climko & Sweeney, 1989, p. 169)

I hadn't washed my hair for three weeks. I hadn't slept for seven nights. My mother told me I must have slept, it was impossible not to sleep in all that time, but if I slept, it was with my eyes wide open. . . . The reason I hadn't washed my clothes or my hair was because it seemed so silly. I saw the days of the year stretching ahead like a series of bright, white boxes, and separating one box from another was sleep, like a black shade. Only for me, the long perspective of shades that set off one box from the next had suddenly snapped up, and I could see day after day glaring ahead of me like a white, broad, infinitely desolate avenue. It seemed silly to wash one day when I would only have to wash again the next. It made me tired just to think of it. (Plath, 1971, pp. 142–143)

Rich, who was 26 years old, was removed from an airplane by the airport police when he created a disturbance. When he was brought to the hospital, he claimed he was Jesus Christ and that he could move mountains. His speech was largely incoherent. For instance, he wanted to leave the city "because things happen here I don't approve of. I approve of other things and I don't approve of the other things. And believe me it's worse for them in the end." He also complained that the Devil wanted to kill him and that his food contained "ground-up corpses." (Adapted from Carson & Butcher, 1992)

Everyone reading this textbook has occasionally worried needlessly about a friend's safety. Everyone has at least occasionally felt depressed. And everyone has uttered a garbled sentence or two. However, these three individuals have psychological problems that markedly interfere with their normal functioning. Let us begin by discussing some general problems in defining, diagnosing, and explaining mental disorders, and then we will consider some specific psychological problems.

BACKGROUND ON PSYCHOLOGICAL DISORDERS

Defining Psychological Disorders

No clear-cut boundary divides psychologically well-adjusted people from those with disorders. In fact, every criterion we propose is somewhat arbitrary and likely to produce some exceptions (Davison & Neale, 1990). However, psychologists often specify that **psychological disorders** involve behavior that is (1) distressing, (2) dysfunctional, and (3) different from the social norms. Let us look more closely at these three components.

1. *Distressing.* Psychological disorders generally cause personal distress and suffering. If you have an anxiety disorder or if you experience severe depression, your normal functioning is clearly impaired (Wakefield, 1992). However, an important exception is a problem called antisocial personality disorder; people with this disorder are typically aggressive and deceitful, but they typically feel no guilt or personal distress.

2. *Dysfunctional.* **Dysfunctional** means that a mental mechanism fails to perform a natural function (Wakefield, 1992). For example, we should be able to cope with normal stress, but a person with an anxiety disorder feels tense, even under low-stress conditions. Again, however, this criterion does not always hold true. Consider a transvestite, a person who wears clothing normally associated with the other gender. Transvestic fetishism is listed as a disorder, yet many transvestites seem to lead very functional lives (Davison & Neale, 1990).

3. *Different from the Social Norm.* Most people are depressed for some time after a love relationship has ended. However, a college student who remains depressed for two years would violate the social norm. Similarly, a person who hears voices would deviate from the social norm. But once again the criterion is not absolute. A person who robs banks does differ from the social norm, yet he or she would not be considered to have a psychological disorder. Incidentally, we should emphasize that a behavior considered to be normal in one culture may be considered abnormal in another, as Figure 15.1 illustrates.

Figure 15.1

In Rajasthan, India, this woman's jewelry would look normal, though it would be considered abnormal in most communities in North America.

In short, the task of trying to define a psychological disorder points out the complexity we have emphasized in Theme 3. Criteria for psychological disorders (e.g., distressing, dysfunctional, and different from the social norm) are generally helpful in separating abnormal from normal. However, psychologists cannot construct firm criteria that are both necessary and sufficient in defining a psychological disorder.

If you follow the accounts of court trials, you are likely to hear the phrase, "not guilty by reason of insanity." Psychologists and psychiatrists do not use the terms *sanity* or *insanity* when they discuss psychological disorders. However, the **insanity defense** refers to the legal argument that in certain situations an individual should not be held legally responsible for criminal actions if he or she has a psychological disorder (Halgin & Whitbourne, 1993). When lawyers try to use the insanity defense, they attempt to argue that their clients cannot distinguish between right and wrong and/or that they are too mentally unstable to be responsible for their crimes. If this argument is successful, the court typically orders treatment in a mental institution. Notice, then, that the legal definition of mental disorders focuses on a person's incompetence—the "dysfunctional" part of the definition for psychological disorders.

Diagnosing Psychological Disorders

We have noted the difficulty of defining a psychological disorder; diagnosing a psychological disorder is similarly challenging. Typically, a mental health professional first conducts a **diagnostic interview,** which includes questions about the client's social relationships, psychological functioning, family background, and any previous psychological disorders. The client's responses convey useful information, and the session also provides the interviewer with an impression of the individual's general appearance, mood, and cognitive functioning. The interviewer may also administer a psychological test such as the Minnesota Multiphasic Personality Inventory (MMPI), discussed in the previous chapter.

The most frequently used resource for classifying psychological disorders is the **Diagnostic and Statistical Manual of Mental Disorders,** or **DSM.** The first edition was published in 1952, and the most recent edition, called the DSM-IV (or fourth edition) was published in 1994.

Each edition describes the specific criteria that must be met before a particular diagnosis can be assigned. However, the list of disorders and the criteria change over time to reflect recent research and current beliefs. For example, earlier editions of the DSM considered homosexuality to be a disorder. However, mental professionals now acknowledge that being gay or lesbian does not imply that someone has a psychological problem (Widiger & Trull, 1991).

Some professionals object to any diagnostic instrument that tries to specify who is normal and who is not. Consider a well-known study that added to the controversy. Dr. David Rosenhan, a psychologist, asked several other professionals to join him in testing the validity of psychiatric diagnoses. Each person was instructed to arrive at a mental hospital, complaining of just one symptom. In particular, they were to report that they had heard voices during the last three weeks that said "empty," "hollow," and "thud." Otherwise, they acted normal and provided accurate information to the hospital staff. Rosenhan (1973) found that all the pseudopatients were admitted to the mental hospital with a diagnosis of schizophrenia—a very serious disorder. They were kept in the hospital an average of 19 days. Furthermore, the hospital staff interpreted the pseudopatients' *normal* behavior as being abnormal. For instance, when Rosenhan took notes, note taking was considered a symptom of schizophrenia.

Rosenhan's study illustrated that psychiatric personnel have difficulty judging who is really disturbed and who is really normal. The study also demonstrated the effects of psychiatric labeling. Once an individual receives a label indicating a psychological disorder, all subsequent behavior is interpreted in terms of that label. In Chapter 17, we will see additional examples of how stereotypes can influence people's interpretations of behavior.

As you can imagine, Rosenhan's study provoked debate. Some felt that his results suggested that psychiatric diagnosis was invalid. Others pointed out that the staff at psychiatric hospitals would have been inhumane to turn away anyone who complained about hearing voices (Spitzer, 1975). However, the study did demonstrate that the mental health system has a bias toward an immediate diagnosis of "disordered" rather than "normal." The study may have inspired many psychologists and other mental health professionals to be more cautious in their diagnoses.

Chapter 14 considered the issue of reliability in psychological assessment. An ideal diagnostic system should produce reliable diagnoses, so that two professionals would provide the same diagnosis for an individual. In general, the reliability of the *Diagnostic and Statistical Manual* has been moderately strong, though not close to the ideal reliability of 1.00 (Eysenck et al., 1983).

Explaining Psychological Disorders

In this chapter, we examine the general categories of psychological disorders listed in Table 15.1, as well as the explanations for these disorders. These explanations fall into five categories, though clinicians often argue that any given disorder may have more than one explanation.

1. The *biological approach* explains disorders in terms of brain structure, neurotransmitters, hormones, genetic factors, and other biological factors. We have seen in previous chapters that psychological characteristics such as intelligence have a significant genetic component, and this chapter investigates the genetic basis for many psychological disorders. Some disorders are also associated with abnormal brain structures or inappropriate levels of neurotransmitters.

2. The *psychodynamic approach* argues that psychological disorders arise from two sources: childhood problems that determine adult personality, and unconscious conflict. For example, suppose that a man feels unresolved anger toward his mother because he believes she rejected him during childhood. If the man's wife dies,

TABLE 15.1 Psychological Disorders Discussed in Chapter 15	

A. DISORDERS BASED ON ANXIETY
1. Anxiety disorders
  a. Generalized anxiety disorders
  b. Panic disorders and agoraphobia
  c. Phobic disorders
  d. Obsessive-compulsive disorders
  e. Posttraumatic stress disorder
2. Somatoform disorders
  a. Conversion disorder
  b. Hypochondriasis
3. Dissociative disorders
  a. Dissociative amnesia
  b. Dissociative fugue
  c. Dissociative identity disorder
    (Multiple personality disorder)
	B. MOOD DISORDERS
	1. Major depression
	2. Bipolar disorder
	C. SCHIZOPHRENIC DISORDERS
	D. PERSONALITY DISORDERS
	1. Obsessive-compulsive personality disorder
	2. Schizoid personality disorder
	3. Borderline personality disorder
	4. Antisocial personality disorder

this emotional experience may trigger emotions associated with the childhood experiences. Psychodynamic theorists believe that depression represents anger turned inward against oneself. Also, psychological disorders may arise from unconscious processes such as (1) difficulty in repressing sexual and aggressive impulses, and (2) the exaggerated use of defense mechanisms.

3. The *behaviorist approach* looks outward to stimuli and reinforcers in the environment, rather than inward to forces within the individual. Thus, psychological disorders can be explained by a person's learning history. For instance, behaviorists propose that anxiety occurs when a person encounters a stimulus that was previously associated with stressful consequences. Furthermore, behaviorists suggest that depression is caused by a general decrease in reinforcement (Salinger, 1988).

4. The *social cognitive approach* emphasizes observational learning, which helps us understand how people can acquire some irrational fears by watching other people's actions. For example, a child can acquire a fear of spiders by observing a parent's fearful behavior. Additional psychological disorders are caused when people interpret situations inappropriately. For example, a student may conclude that one low score on an exam indicates general incompetence in all academic endeavors. The social cognitive approach also points out that psychological disorders are related to people's feelings that they are not effective, competent individuals.

5. The *sociocultural approach* emphasizes how social and cultural factors influence mental health. For instance, we will note that schizophrenia is more common in lower social classes. People living in poverty—with inadequate food, poor housing, and the constant threat of crime—experience more stress than people in higher income brackets (Kessler et al., 1985). The sociocultural approach also emphasizes that women are more likely than men to experience discrimination and low status. Similarly, people of color are more likely than White people to experience this kind of biased treatment. As a consequence, psychological disorders are more common in the groups that experience more stress. For instance, we will see that disorders such as phobias and depression occur significantly more often among women than among men. In short, the sociocultural perspective encourages us to look outside the individual to find the source of psychological disorders. This perspective suggests that the real causes are poverty and society's discrimination against certain groups of people (Mirowsky & Ross, 1989).

The sociocultural approach emphasizes that people living in poverty experience more stress, which leads to psychological disorders.

S E C T I O N   S U M M A R Y
BACKGROUND ON PSYCHOLOGICAL DISORDERS

- Psychological disorders involve behavior that is distressing, dysfunctional, and different from social norms.

- The insanity defense is used when lawyers argue that their clients cannot distinguish between right and wrong and/or they are too mentally unstable to be responsible for their crimes.

- A clinician's diagnosis is typically based on the criteria in the Diagnostic and Statistical Manual (e.g., DSM-IV); critics of the diagnostic process object to clinicians' tendency to provide an immediate diagnosis based on inadequate information; however, the DSM has fairly strong reliability.

- Theories about psychological disorders include the biological approach, the psychodynamic approach, the behaviorist approach, the social cognitive approach, and the sociocultural approach.

DISORDERS BASED ON ANXIETY

In this section, we consider many different disorders that are related to anxiety. People who experience these disorders usually report being unhappy, and their behavior is dysfunctional. However, these people typically live in the community, rather than in a hospital setting. According to estimates, this group of anxiety-related disorders affects between 8% and 15% of adults in the United States at some point in their lives (National Institute of Mental Health, 1985; Regier et al., 1988). In other words, millions of people are anxious, unhappy, afraid, and functioning at a level substantially below their potential.

We begin by discussing the most common of these disorders, known simply as anxiety disorders. Then we look briefly at two less-common categories, the somatoform disorders and the dissociative disorders.

Anxiety Disorders

Most of us feel anxious from time to time. You may feel anxious when facing a test for which you are unprepared, when you are about to go on stage for your first solo musical performance, and when you are worried about the outcome of a friend's surgery. However, when anxiety persists—without any clear explanation—and when that anxiety causes intense suffering, these problems are called **anxiety disorders.** Let us consider five of these disorders: generalized anxiety disorders, panic disorders and agoraphobia, phobic disorders, obsessive-compulsive disorders, and posttraumatic stress disorders.

Generalized Anxiety Disorders **Generalized anxiety disorders** are characterized by continuous, long-lasting uneasiness and tension. People with this disorder cannot identify a special cause of their anxiety (hence the word *generalized*). They also have physical symptoms such as nausea, dizziness, and muscle tension. A diagnosis of generalized anxiety disorder requires that a person report excessive anxiety about two or more life circumstances (for example, schoolwork and finances) for at least six months (American Psychiatric Association, 1994; Barlow, 1988).

Generalized anxiety disorders clearly disrupt normal thought processes. For instance, 86% of people with these disorders reported difficulty concentrating, and 55% said they were unable to recall important things (Beck et al., 1985). As you can imagine, a person with generalized anxiety disorder would have trouble studying well for an exam, performing competently at work, or enjoying a conversation with friends.

Panic Disorders and Agoraphobia Imagine how you might respond to the following experience:

> *The feeling was overwhelming. Ray could never remember being so frightened. He had been washing up before bed when it happened. Suddenly, out of the blue, his body was engulfed by a feeling of dread and impending doom . . . .*
>
> *He wanted to scream. He wanted to run and get help. He wanted to hide. But he could not focus his mind to cope with the onslaught of terror. His heart raced and seemed to want to jump out of his chest. He was short of breath and felt as if he was smothering.*
>
> *He tried to walk but was weak and unsteady on his feet. When he finally got to the bed, he lay there huddled and trembling, sure that he was dying or having a heart attack. He would later learn that he had had his first panic attack. (Zal, 1989)*

Agoraphobics become extremely anxious in places from which it is difficult to escape, such as this crowded subway car.

Panic disorders are marked by recurrent panic attacks of overwhelming anxiety that occur suddenly and unexpectedly. Each attack typically lasts only 20 minutes, but at the time, it seems as if the attack will never end (Baker, 1989; Rachman, 1988). Whereas generalized anxiety disorders are continuous, panic disorders involve specific panic attacks that occur without warning. Someone in the midst of a panic attack may feel smothering sensations, severe chest pains, and a fear of dying. In fact, it can often be mistaken for a heart attack.

After several severe panic attacks, people often become very concerned about when their next panic attack will occur. If they are worried that they will be unable to escape to a safe place when the attack occurs, the condition can sometimes lead to agoraphobia (Antony et al., 1992; Katon, 1990).

Agoraphobia is the fear of being in situations or public places where escape would be difficult. People with agoraphobia are afraid of situations such as traveling on a bus, being in a crowd, and leaving their home. About 75% of identified agoraphobics are female. However, this percentage probably underestimates the number of agoraphobic males, who are more likely to deny their fearfulness (Gournay, 1989a; McNally, 1990). Clearly, agoraphobia is disabling. For example, an agoraphobic student has difficulty sitting in a large lecture hall, and some people still remain fearful, even in their own homes, accompanied by close relatives (Fodor, 1982; Wardman, 1985). We noted, incidentally, that agoraphobia is often preceded by panic attacks; however, many agoraphobics have no previous history of panic attacks.

Phobic Disorders A **phobic disorder** is an excessive fear of a specific object, activity, or situation. This fear is out of proportion to the true danger, and it cannot be eliminated by rational thought. People with phobias realize that their fears are unreasonable. They avoid the feared object or situation, even if it means restricting their daily activities and missing pleasurable events (Öhman & Soares, 1993; Marks, 1987).

Many phobias involve a specific fear about one kind of object or animal. Common phobias include fears of snakes, insects, spiders, and mice (King et al., 1988). Perhaps 75% to 95% of identified phobics are female (Fodor, 1982; Turns, 1989), but again male gender roles may prevent many boys and men from reporting their fears. Phobias often begin in childhood, and they may lead to a lifetime of planning, in order to avoid the feared object. For example, one woman had a butterfly phobia, which led her to avoid trips to the countryside (Fodor, 1982).

People who have a **social phobia** are excessively afraid of social situations, where they are afraid they will do something embarrassing. A telephone survey revealed that 21% of the general public reported a fear of public speaking; thus, many individuals are reluctant to speak in front of an audience (Cirigliano & Lynn, 1992). However, a person with a social phobia is even reluctant to speak in front of others when the situation is nonthreatening. Males and females are equally likely to suffer from social phobias (Fodor, 1982). Notice that the phobias discussed in this section

Common phobias involve fear of snakes, insects, spiders, and mice.

can disrupt one's life. However, these phobias are not as disabling as agoraphobia, where the victim may be unable to leave home.

Obsessive-Compulsive Disorders Obsessive thoughts and compulsive actions are part of everyday life for many of us. We check a third time to make certain that an airplane ticket is safe in a pocket. We refuse to eat with a fork that has dropped on a recently cleaned floor, even though contamination is highly unlikely. The diagnosis of obsessive-compulsive disorder is made only when these obsessive thoughts become frequent and intense, or when the compulsive rituals begin to interfere with a person's functioning (Baer & Jenike, 1986).

Obsessive-compulsive disorders are disabling conditions that involve recurrent, time-consuming obsessions and/or compulsions (American Psychiatric Association, 1994; Turner et al., 1985). **Obsessions** are persistent, unwanted thoughts that are unreasonable. Typical obsessions include inappropriate worry over germs or illness (for example, worry about becoming infected by shaking someone's hand) and excessive concerns about others (for example, concern about being responsible for someone's injury, as in the quotation at the beginning of this chapter).

Obsessions focus on persistent *thoughts,* whereas **compulsions** focus on persistent *actions.* That is, compulsions are repetitive behaviors performed according to certain rules. Obsessive thoughts are often linked with compulsive actions. For example, the executive's persistent thoughts about tacks in coffee cups led him to strain his colleagues' coffee with paper towels. People with compulsions usually realize that their compulsive behavior is unreasonable. Common compulsions include hand washing, counting, and checking the location of an object. Between 30% and 40% of people with obsessive-compulsive disorders report that the problems began during childhood. However, preschool children commonly develop harmless rituals that soon disappear; parents should be concerned only when rituals persist and interfere with normal functioning (Neziroglu & Yaryura-Tobias, 1991).

Posttraumatic Stress Disorder An article in the *Harvard Mental Health Letter* describes a Vietnam veteran who sought help for his problems 10 years after his combat duty. During his year in Vietnam, his best friend was killed while he stood a few feet away. He himself had killed a young Vietcong boy by hitting him with a rifle butt. He reports that he still has nightmares about Vietnam and that he still jumps at the sound of a backfiring automobile. In moments of anger, he strikes his wife, and he often carries a gun. In addition, he says he is constantly bored, depressed, and alienated ("Post-traumatic Stress," 1991).

As the name implies, **posttraumatic stress disorder (PTSD)** is a pattern of disordered reactions following a traumatic event. These reactions may include anxiety, irritability, inability to concentrate, and emotional numbness. People with PTSD say that they often have flashbacks to the traumatic events (Eth et al., 1989).

Researchers in the United States have focused on three major kinds of traumas that can lead to PTSD. The Vietnam War underscored the fact that people in combat may experience traumas, even if they are not physically wounded; 2.8 million Americans served in Southeast Asia during that war (King & King, 1991). Individuals who have been raped or battered may also experience posttraumatic stress disorder (Herman, 1992). Furthermore, children and adults who have experienced natural and human-made disasters can develop PTSD. These can include events such as nuclear accidents, earthquakes, and floods (Davidson & Baum, 1990; Nolen-Hoeksema & Morrow, 1991; Rubonis & Bickman, 1991).

Many people who experience PTSD require counseling or therapy, whereas others apparently recover without professional assistance. Recovery takes time and is clearly facilitated by supportive friends and family (Solomon et al., 1988).

Table 15.2 summarizes the five major kinds of anxiety disorders we have discussed so far. Now we consider two other kinds of problems related to anxiety, the somatoform disorders and the dissociative disorders.

Many veterans of the Vietnam War have experienced posttraumatic stress disorder. Reminders of that war, such as the Vietnam Memorial, may trigger flashback memories.

TABLE 15.2 The Anxiety Disorders

NAME	DESCRIPTION
a. Generalized anxiety disorders	Continuous, long-lasting uneasiness and tension
b. Panic disorders and agoraphobia	Recurrent attacks of overwhelming anxiety (panic disorder) which often lead to a fear of being in public places (agoraphobia)
c. Phobic disorders	Excessive fear of a specific object, activity, or situation
d. Obsessive-compulsive disorders	Persistent, unwanted, unreasonable thoughts (obsessions) and repetitive behaviors performed according to rules (compulsions)
e. Posttraumatic stress disorder	Disorders following a traumatic event; the disorders may include anxiety, irritability, inability to concentrate, and emotional numbness.

Somatoform Disorders

The **somatoform disorders** are anxiety-based problems in which the individual complains about physical illnesses and symptoms, yet no organic explanation can be detected. Notice that the distinctive feature of these somatoform disorders is a concern about one's body. The physical symptoms in the somatoform disorders are not intentionally produced; a person with this disorder cannot consciously control which symptoms he or she will experience (American Psychiatric Association, 1994; Barsky, 1989). Let us look at two kinds of somatoform disorders: conversion disorder and hypochondriasis.

Conversion Disorders **Conversion disorders** are characterized by a loss in physical functioning of some body part—with no medical explanation for the condition. Conversion disorders are usually triggered by some traumatic event. A person suddenly becomes blind or deaf, or may report complete loss of feeling in one hand. For example, many female Cambodian refugees who had been forced to watch brutal executions lost most of their vision several days later. Symbolically, they refused to see the terror surrounding them (Rozée & Van Boemel, 1989). In the general population, however, conversion disorders are relatively rare (Barsky, 1989).

Hypochondriasis The disorder known as **hypochondriasis** involves persistent, excessive anxiety about having a serious disease—one that could even be deadly. Hypochondriasis (pronounced "high-poe-konn-*dry*-us-sis") typically involves numerous physical complaints. Hypochondriacs continually visit their physicians, whose reassurances are seldom satisfying.

As you might imagine, people who have had previous experience with disease are particularly likely to become hypochondriacs, as are people whose family members have had illnesses (Barsky, 1989). A man who has had a previous heart attack or a woman whose sister died from breast cancer are alert for even minor physical symptoms. These people *should* be concerned about early indicators of illness. However, hypochondriacs are so excessively worried and preoccupied with illness that their anxiety interferes with normal living.

Dissociative Disorders

The dissociative disorders resemble the somatoform disorders because both are reactions to extreme stress. However, the somatoform disorders involve physical symptoms. In contrast, dissociative disorders involve psychological symptoms. Specifically, the **dissociative disorders** actually split off (or dissociate) a person's identity, memory, or consciousness. Ordinary people have a sense of who they are. They remember their life events, and they are conscious of their attributes and surroundings. In contrast, people who have dissociative disorders suddenly lose their

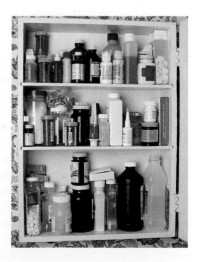

The medicine cabinet of a hypochondriac, who takes many medications for imagined disorders.

memory or change their identity. It is important to stress that dissociative disorders are relatively rare, even though the soap operas and tabloid newspapers are overpopulated with cases of amnesia and multiple personality (Nemiah, 1989).

Dissociative Amnesia In 1980, a Florida park ranger discovered a woman who was close to death; she was incoherent and covered with animal and insect bites. This woman, who was dubbed "Jane Doe," could remember neither her name nor her past. An older couple in Illinois was convinced that Jane Doe was their daughter who had left for Florida several years earlier. However, the young woman never recalled her past (Carson & Butcher, 1992).

Dissociative amnesia involves the forgetting of past experiences following a stressful event. We all have less than perfect memories, as Chapter 7 emphasized. However, dissociative amnesia is characterized by extensive memory loss. The amnesia may be limited to a specific time period surrounding a traumatic episode, or a person may forget his or her entire life history.

Dissociative Fugue The word *fugue* (pronounced "fewg") is derived from the Latin word for *flight*. The critical features of a **dissociative fugue** include (1) sudden, unplanned travel away from a familiar location, (2) assuming a new identity, and (3) inability to recall one's earlier identity (Nemiah, 1989). Occasionally, a victim of a fugue takes on an entirely new life and a more outgoing personality, with the disorder lasting several years. More often, a fugue is less dramatic, involving briefer travel and an incomplete new identity.

Dissociative fugues typically follow severe stress, such as a natural disaster or a serious quarrel with a family member. When people recover from a fugue, they typically recall none of the events that occurred during the fugue period.

Dissociative Identity Disorder The critical feature of amnesia is forgetting, and the critical features of fugue are travel and a new identity replacing the old identity. In contrast, **dissociative identity disorder** occurs when a person has two or more distinct, well-developed personalities (American Psychiatric Association, 1994). Incidentally, you may be more familiar with the name used in previous editions of the DSM, **multiple personality disorder.** An individual with this disorder may shift from one personality to the other as often as every few minutes . . . or as rarely as every few years. Typically, the personalities are dramatically different from each other. Dissociative identity disorder therefore involves a distinctive unawareness of one's other personalities.

Consider the case of Paula, a college student who received A's on the first two exams in a college course but failed to appear for the third exam (Oltmanns et al., 1991). Paula's instructor suggested that she speak with a psychologist after Paula had written an essay about a long-term abusive and incestuous relationship with her father. The psychologist learned that Paula had developed a second personality, named Sherry, when she was in high school, in response to her father's sexual abuse. The psychologist had initially thought that Paula was faking a dramatic set of symptoms to win the sympathy of her family. He later accepted the diagnosis of multiple personalities, however, because Paula was not familiar with the characteristics of this disorder. Paula seemed to experience a genuine disruption of consciousness when her father became abusive; the studious Paula would "leave" the situation, and irresponsible Sherry would be left to deal with him.

The dissociative identity disorder is extremely intriguing, but we do not know how often it occurs. In the last decade, the estimated incidence has been increasing in the United States, often in connection with physical or sexual abuse during childhood (Nemiah, 1989; Ross, 1989). However, the phenomenon has not been reported nearly as often by mental health professionals in other countries such as Great Britain, New Zealand, and Czechoslovakia, which suggests that the diagnosis or incidence of multiple personalities may be partly a cultural phenomenon (Aldridge-Morris, 1989). To review the varieties of somatoform disorders and dissociative disorders, read through Table 15.3.

This woman, who came to be known as "Jane Doe," suffered from severe dissociative amnesia.

TABLE 15.3 The Somatoform Disorders and Dissociative Disorders

NAME	DESCRIPTION
1. Somatoform Disorders	Physical illness without an organic explanation
a. Conversion disorder	Loss in physical functioning of a body part
b. Hypochondriasis	Persistent anxiety about having a serious disease
2. Dissociative Disorders	Splitting off of a person's identity, memory, or consciousness
a. Dissociative amnesia	Forgetting of past experiences
b. Dissociative fugue	Sudden travel and adoption of a new identity
c. Dissociative identity disorder (Multiple personality disorder)	Two or more distinct, well-developed personalities

Explaining Disorders Based on Anxiety

We have considered a variety of psychological disorders, each connected with anxiety. Some disorders, such as a specific phobia, may have little impact on an individual's life. Others, such as agoraphobia and dissociative identity disorder, cause major disruptions in interpersonal relationships, work performance, and ability to enjoy life. How does anxiety arise, and why does it produce the particular symptoms we have outlined? We now discuss how several explanations introduced at the beginning of the chapter account for one or more of the anxiety-based disorders.

The Biological Approach One intriguing biological explanation for phobias is known as **biological preparedness**; humans have an inborn predisposition—established through evolution—to fear certain objects and situations more than others (McNally, 1987; Seligman, 1971). For instance, people are likely to develop phobias about cats, dogs, and spiders, all of which are potentially more harmful than petunias, robins, and ladybugs (Kent, 1991).

Furthermore, the concept of **autonomic lability** suggests that there are large individual differences in the tendency for the autonomic nervous system to be easily aroused (Davison & Neale, 1990). Individuals who are easily aroused are more likely to develop phobias and other anxiety disorders.

Some of the disorders based on anxiety could have a genetic component. For example, people with panic disorder, agoraphobia, or obsessive-compulsive disorder are more likely than people in a control group to have a close relative with an anxiety disorder (Crowe, 1991; Macdonald et al., 1991). One factor that may be inherited is the autonomic lability we have just discussed. However, we need to be cautious about accepting this research uncritically. A young woman may have inherited the disposition toward agoraphobia from her mother, but she also had an opportunity to watch her mother's fearful behavior; observational learning could account for the daughter's modeling of her mother's agoraphobia (Davison & Neale, 1990).

The Psychodynamic Approach Sigmund Freud suggested that anxiety can be caused by a variety of events, such as separation from mother or a fear of castration (removal of the genitals). Anxiety may therefore be a signal of unconscious fantasies about dangerous situations (Freud, 1909; Taylor & Arnow, 1988). This anxiety stimulates a variety of defense mechanisms. As discussed in Chapter 13, psychodynamic theorists believe that these defense mechanisms may be helpful. However, psychological disorders result from overusing them. For example, psychodynamic theorists would suggest that people develop phobias as a defense mechanism, to protect themselves from repressed conflicts that are too painful to confront (Davison & Neale, 1990).

The Behaviorist and Social Cognitive Approaches Behaviorists explain phobias in terms of classical conditioning, and this kind of learning may account for the acquisition of some phobias (e.g., Öhman & Soares, 1993). However, most people

This young man is experiencing a panic attack. Theorists explain this disorder in terms of the biological, psychodynamic, behaviorist, social cognitive, and sociocultural approaches.

with phobias cannot recall a traumatic conditioning event to account for their fears (Barlow, 1988; Mineka, 1986; Taylor & Arnow, 1988). Instead, most theorists who favor a learning approach now favor observational learning, rather than classical conditioning. For example, children learn to be afraid of dentists by modeling their parents' anxious behavior in the dentist's office (Bandura, 1986). Furthermore, the children of hypochondriacs model their parents' excessive concern with body ailments (Carson & Butcher, 1992; Kellner, 1985). Disorders are therefore produced by observing inappropriate models (Merluzzi et al., 1986).

Another social cognitive explanation is called **attentional bias;** people with phobias focus their attention on feared aspects of the environment (Kent, 1991; Mineka & Sutton, 1992). When a woman with a cat phobia walks through a neighborhood, she will spot cats sitting everywhere . . . cats that would be missed by someone with no cat phobia. Interestingly, as the phobia decreases during therapy, she is likely to remark, "This neighborhood doesn't seem to have as many cats as it did before" (Kent, 1991). This attentional bias in phobics explains why an initial weak phobia grows stronger.

The Sociocultural Approach We noted earlier that the majority of people with simple phobias and agoraphobia are female. The reason for this finding is not clear, but gender stereotypes seem to encourage women to be passive and dependent. Agoraphobic women, for example, typically have not lived on their own. Women are socialized to be dependent on other people, and agoraphobics receive a stronger dose of this message (Fodor, 1982; Padawer & Goldfried, 1984). In contrast, a somewhat fearful young boy would be discouraged from developing these fears into phobias.

Combining the Approaches We have no compelling research evidence for the psychodynamic explanation of anxiety-based disorders. However, the other approaches help us construct a general explanation. Biological preparedness makes all humans somewhat predisposed toward certain anxieties. Autonomic lability and other inherited factors make some individuals especially anxious. Some phobias may be learned through classical conditioning, and others through observational learning. Gender roles encourage these fears in females and discourage them in males. Finally, attentional bias explains how a weak fear can become exaggerated.

SECTION SUMMARY
DISORDERS BASED ON ANXIETY

- Generalized anxiety disorders involve continuous uneasiness and tension, typically accompanied by disrupted thought processes.

- Panic disorders entail recurrent but separate attacks of overwhelming anxiety, which may lead to agoraphobia—a fear of being unable to escape to a safe place when in an unpleasant situation.

- Phobic disorders involve an excessive fear of a specific object, activity, or situation; social phobias involve an excessive fear of social situations.

- Obsessive-compulsive disorders are also related to anxiety, and are marked by persistent, unwanted thoughts (obsessions) and repetitive behaviors based on those obsessions (compulsions).

- Posttraumatic stress disorder may follow a traumatic event; it includes reactions such as anxiety and emotional numbness.

- The somatoform disorders include conversion disorders (loss of physical functioning in a body part) and hypochondriasis (persistent anxiety about a serious disease).

- The dissociative disorders involve a splitting off of one's identity; they include dissociative amnesia (forgetting one's past), dissociative fugue (fleeing a familiar location and assuming a new identity), and dissociative identity disorder (also known as multiple personality disorder, developing two or more distinct personalities).

● An explanation of disorders related to anxiety probably involves a combination of biological, behaviorist, social cognitive, and sociocultural approaches.

MOOD DISORDERS

From time to time, you have probably felt dissatisfied and discouraged. Most people have occasional periods in which they feel pessimistic, sad, and isolated from other people. In most cases, these discouraged moods improve. However, a substantial number of North Americans experience a major mood disorder at some point in their lives.

The primary characteristic of **mood disorders** is persistent, extreme disturbances of mood or emotional state. The more common kind of mood disorder is called **major depression;** it is characterized by frequent episodes of intense hopelessness and lowered self-esteem. The less common mood disorder, called **bipolar disorder,** is characterized by some depressive episodes and some manic episodes. **Mania** is an abnormally positive, overexcited state, accompanied by high self-esteem.

Let us begin by discussing the general characteristics of major depression, followed by an "In Depth" examination of the cognitive characteristics of major depression. Then we consider why women are more likely than men to develop depression. After an overview of bipolar disorders, we discuss several theoretical approaches to the explanation of mood disorders.

The General Characteristics of Major Depression

Depression is clearly the most common psychological disorder; 75% of people admitted to psychiatric hospitals have a diagnosis of depression (Gotlib & Hammen, 1992). Furthermore, between 8% and 18% of the general population will experience a major depressive episode at least once in their lives (Gotlib, 1992). Table 15.4 shows nine criteria for a major depressive episode; a diagnosis of major depression requires evidence of at least five of these criteria.

People who are depressed are likely to report physical problems, such as indigestion, headaches, backaches, and general pain. Loss of sexual interest is also common (Hamilton, 1989; Lombardi, 1990). As you can imagine, these physical problems would naturally make a person even more depressed. Let us focus, however, on the

---

TABLE 15.4 Criteria for Major Depressive Episode, as Listed in the DSM-IV

At least five of these nine symptoms must be present during a two-week period:

1. depressed mood
2. reduced interest in almost all activities
3. significant weight gain or weight loss, without dieting
4. insomnia or too much sleep
5. too much or too little motor activity
6. fatigue or loss of energy
7. feelings of worthlessness or guilt
8. reduced ability to concentrate or think
9. recurrent thoughts of death

Source: Based on American Psychiatric Association, 1994

psychological components of depression. We will consider emotional and behavioral components in this section, and then the following section will focus on cognitive components in more detail.

Emotions Depressed people describe themselves as feeling apathetic, discouraged, and hopeless. When some people develop a severe depressive episode, their customary sadness and withdrawal become more exaggerated. Others, in contrast, plunge rapidly into a prolonged episode of tearfulness, dejection, and longing for better times in the past (Gold, 1990; Oltmanns et al., 1991). People who are depressed can easily visualize sad events, whereas nondepressed people have difficulty doing so (Pietromonaco & Markus, 1985).

Demonstration 15.1 includes items similar to six questions on the Beck Depression Inventory, a scale that is often used to assess depression. Sadness is so pervasive in depressed people that thoughts about negative emotions emerge automatically in their daily life. In a representative study, depressed psychiatric patients were likely to report that they often had negative thoughts such as "I'm no good," "My future is bleak," and "My life is a mess" (Eaves & Rush, 1984).

Behavior In addition to physical and emotional changes, severely depressed people also show behavioral changes. For instance, their speed of performance decreases. They are less able to do daily chores, let alone more challenging tasks in the workplace (Williams et al., 1988).

Social behavior is also different for severely depressed people, in comparison to nondepressed people. Depressed people make fewer contacts with people in their social networks (Gotlib, 1992). Depressed people are more worried about taking risks, so they are more likely than nondepressed people to avoid social interactions that might be somewhat risky (Pietromonaco & Rook, 1987). This tendency can lead to further isolation from other people.

DEMONSTRATION 15.1 **Assessing Depression**

Think about how you have felt during the last *week*, including today. Carefully inspect each set of statements and circle the number in front of the item that most accurately describes your feelings.

A. 1. I have not felt sad during the past week.
   2. I have felt occasional sadness.
   3. I have felt sad most of the time.
   4. I have felt so sad that it's unbearable.

B. 1. I have never cried during the past week.
   2. I have cried once or twice during the past week.
   3. I have cried often during the past week.
   4. I used to cry often, but now I am so sad I'm beyond crying.

C. 1. Life is about as satisfying as it has been in the past.
   2. I don't enjoy life as much as I used to.
   3. It's hard to find satisfaction with life now.
   4. Everything about my life is dissatisfying.

D. 1. People are just as interesting as they have always been.
   2. People aren't as interesting as they used to be.
   3. Most people aren't interesting to me.
   4. I've lost my interest in other people.

E. 1. I am just as efficient as I've always been.
   2. It's hard to be as efficient as I've been in the past.
   3. I really have to push myself to get things done.
   4. Somehow I can't accomplish anything these days.

G. 1. I am fairly happy with myself.
   2. I feel neutral about myself.
   3. I am disappointed in myself.
   4. I hate myself.

To score your answers, add up all the points. *It is important to stress that this is not a standardized test of depression, and no 6-item test can assess depression accurately.* However, people who are depressed would be likely to receive higher scores on this informal assessment.

Because depressed people are more worried about risks, they tend to avoid social interactions.

Furthermore, when depressed people do actually interact with other people, their behavior and conversational patterns may produce negative reactions and rejection. Researchers do not know exactly what behaviors lead to these rejections. Perhaps depressed people disclose more negative information about themselves, and they may be less sympathetic listeners. In any event, people who have been talking with a depressed stranger end up feeling more depressed themselves, in contrast to people who have been talking with a nondepressed stranger (Coyne et al., 1987; Jacobson & Anderson, 1982). As you might imagine, students who have a depressed roommate are likely to be somewhat depressed by the end of the semester, in contrast to those with a nondepressed roommate (Burchill & Stiles, 1988).

However, the most alarming behavioral problem of serious depression is suicide attempts. Suicide is relevant to our discussion of depression because researchers estimate that 50% to 85% of people with suicidal inclinations show signs of depression (Berman & Jobes, 1991; Boyer & Guthrie, 1985). Before you read further, try to answer the questions in Demonstration 15.2.

DEMONSTRATION 15.2   Myths and Realities About Suicide

Decide whether each of the following questions is true or false. Then turn the page to see the answers in Table 15.5.

_____ 1. People who actually talk about suicide are not likely to commit suicide.

_____ 2. People who attempt suicide are likely to have a high family incidence of suicide attempts.

_____ 3. Men are more likely than women to attempt suicide.

_____ 4. Men are more likely than women to actually kill themselves by suicide.

_____ 5. Suicidal people typically give many warnings about suicidal intentions.

_____ 6. Suicidal people are fully intent on dying.

_____ 7. A person who has attempted suicide is not likely to attempt suicide again.

_____ 8. When a person has been severely depressed and the depression begins to lift, the danger of suicide decreases substantially.

_____ 9. Suicide is found just as often among the poor as among the rich.

_____ 10. Unemployed people are more likely to commit suicide.

According to the statistics, about 200,000 U.S. residents attempt suicide each year, resulting in about 15,000 deaths (Hirschfeld & Davidson, 1988). The suicide rate in Canada is even higher than in the United States (Leenaars & Domino, 1993; Leenaars & Lester, 1992). Even these chilling statistics probably underestimate the incidence of suicide, because many people disguise their suicides to look like accidents. Sadly, the reported incidence of suicide has been increasing steadily. For example, between 1960 and 1987, there was a 186% increase in suicides for people between the ages of 15 and 24 (Berman & Jobes, 1991). In other words, the 1987 suicide rate was almost *three times* the rate in 1960. (Of course, it is possible that the methods of reporting suicide may have shifted somewhat since 1960 and could account for a portion of the difference.)

Some ethnic-group differences also have been reported. Specifically, the suicide rate is significantly higher among most Native American populations than among Whites, though statistics vary widely among the different Native American tribes. Furthermore, the suicide rate for Blacks is somewhat lower than the national average (Berman & Jobes, 1991; Howard-Pitney et al., 1992). Thus, the data on Native American populations support the sociocultural approach, but the data on Blacks contradict this approach.

This year, some of you reading this book will have a friend or family member who begins to talk about suicide. What should you do? Unfortunately, no simple formula can prevent suicide, but here is some general advice (Berman & Jobes, 1991; Colt, 1991; Schneidman, 1980):

1. *Take the suicide threat seriously.* As noted in Table 15.5, people usually do give warnings about suicidal thoughts.

2. *Provide caring support.* Show genuine support and empathy for a suicidal person. Even if you know the person only slightly, provide empathy and understanding.

3. *Try to clarify the central problem.* As we will discuss shortly, depressed people have cognitive difficulties. If you can help isolate the critical problem, the situation may not seem so overwhelming.

4. *If you think someone is suicidal, ask direct questions.* Asking "Are you thinking about killing yourself?" when a friend is extremely depressed will not "put the

---

TABLE 15.5 Myths and Realities About Suicide: The Answers to Demonstration 15.2

1. *False.* About 80% of people who actually commit suicide have discussed their suicidal intentions with someone.
2. *True.* A high family incidence of suicide is found among people who attempt suicide as well as among those who actually kill themselves.
3. *False.* Between three and ten times as many women as men attempt suicide.
4. *True.* About five times as many men as women actually kill themselves by suicide.
5. *True.* Research indicates that suicidal people give many clues and warnings about their suicidal intentions.
6. *False.* Most suicidal people are undecided about living or dying. They gamble with death, leaving it to others to save them.
7. *False.* About half of those who attempt suicide will try it again.
8. *False.* Suicides are most likely to occur within about three months of an improvement, when depressed people have the energy to put their suicide plan into effect.
9. *True.* Suicide is found at roughly the same rate in all social classes.
10. *True.* Unemployment, financial distress, and other recent life-style changes increase the risk of suicide.

Sources: Berman & Jobes, 1991; Boyer & Guthrie, 1985; Garrison, 1989; Schneidman, 1980.

idea" into the depressed person's mind. Furthermore, if the answer is yes, ask if he or she has made any specific plans. This sounds like a gruesome question, but someone who has a specific plan is more likely to attempt suicide.

5. *Suggest alternative actions.* Offer other solutions to the central problem. However, do not adopt a falsely cheerful "everything will just work out" attitude, and do not suggest "just try to snap out of it."

6. *Encourage consulting a professional.* Even if you have talked someone out of a suicide attempt, the problem still needs further attention. Help the person find a counselor or other professional; offer to go along, if it would be helpful.

7. *The worst thing you can do is nothing.* Take action and show concern; ignoring the problem is not a helpful solution.

IN DEPTH: The Cognitive Characteristics of Major Depression

In the list of criteria for major depression (Table 15.4 on page 491), we listed "reduced ability to concentrate or think." People who are depressed often complain about poor memory (Yager, 1989). Research confirms that depressed people are likely to have difficulty on memory tasks, especially if they are severely depressed (Johnson & Magaro, 1987; Wright & Salmon, 1990). As you can imagine, depressed people might easily become even more depressed if they have difficulty paying attention, thinking, and remembering.

In the last 15 years, researchers have identified another kind of cognitive difference between depressed and nondepressed people. Specifically, the two groups differ in the way they process pleasant and unpleasant information (Gotlib & Hammen, 1992). Let us consider three specific areas in which these cognitive biases occur: (1) negative evaluations; (2) negative attributional patterns; and (3) negatively biased recall.

Negative Evaluations According to social cognitive theory, depressed individuals have negative self-schemas. In Chapter 7, we saw that a **schema** is a generalized idea about objects, people, and events that are encountered frequently. A **self-schema** is therefore a generalized idea about yourself, one that is based on your past reactions and experiences (Segal, 1988).

Research by Michael Gara and his colleagues (1993) demonstrates that depressed people have negative self-schemas, and also negative schemas about other people. The 31 depressed people in this study all met the DSM criteria for depression and had experienced an average of 3.6 depressive episodes. The 27 control-group people were all volunteers from the community who were comparable in age and gender. Both groups of people were asked to list at least five attributes for themselves, their mother, their father, four other significant people in their lives, and three less significant people. They then rated each of the attributes describing each of the 10 individuals they had listed.

The relative number of positive and negative descriptions was calculated from the ratings. Figure 15.2 shows these data, for people's descriptions of themselves and their descriptions of others. In contrast to people in the depressed group, the people in the control group had more positive self-descriptions as well as fewer negative self-descriptions. Furthermore, the two groups' judgments about other people virtually matched their judgments about themselves. In short, when depressed people make judgments, these self-schemas and schemas about other people are relatively negative.

Depressed people also make negative evaluations about their future. For example, Susan Andersen and her colleagues (1992) studied college students who were nondepressed, mildly depressed, or depressed. (These classifications were based on students' scores on the Beck Depression Inventory, which is similar to Demonstration 15.1.) These researchers asked the students to judge whether certain events would happen to them in the future. Some of these events were positive and some were negative, and they ranged in probability from very likely (e.g., "listen to music," "catch a cold") to very unlikely ("win a Nobel prize," "be struck by lightning").

Figure 15.3 shows the students' responses. As you can see, depressed people expect relatively few happy events in the future, in contrast to mildly depressed and nondepressed people. In other words, depressed people have negative future-event schemas.

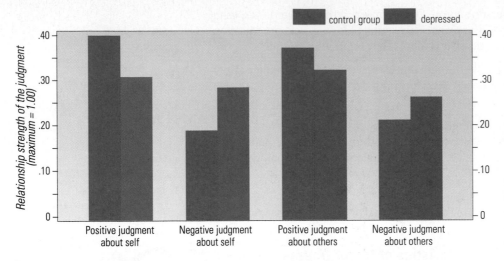

Figure 15.2

Positive and negative judgments about oneself and others, for control-group and depressed people (based on Gara et al., 1993).

Furthermore, depressed people seem to make these pessimistic judgments automatically, without a great deal of thought. Andersen and her colleagues increased the workload in working memory by asking people to remember a six-digit number while they were making judgments about the future. Nondepressed and mildly depressed people took longer to make the judgments when they also had to remember the number; depressed people made the judgments rapidly. In other words, a depressed person can keep a number like 285394 in memory and quickly make judgments such as "Yes, I am likely to get a fatal disease" and "No, I am not likely to achieve my life goals." These negative future-event schemas come to mind quickly and automatically, with little apparent cognitive effort.

Negative Attributional Patterns We have seen that depressed people have negative schemas about themselves, other people, and their future. They also tend to provide negative explanations for the events in their lives.

Imagine for a moment that you have received a low score on an important test. Try to think about the explanations you would provide for that poor performance. How would you explain it? Psychologists use the term **attribution** to describe the explanations we create about the reasons for our own behavior and the behavior of other people.

In general, depressed people provide *internal* explanations for unpleasant events; they blame themselves, rather than the external circumstances. They are also likely to provide *stable* explanations, blaming a permanent characteristic, rather than one that is simply temporary. Finally, they are likely to provide *global* explanations, blaming a general tendency that applies to a variety of skills and behaviors rather than a very specific one. If a seriously depressed woman receives a low score on a biology test, for example, she might be likely to say, "This just shows

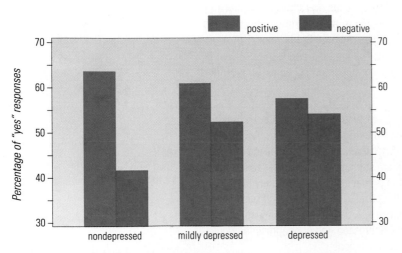

Figure 15.3

Percentage of "yes" responses for positive and negative events in the future, based on level of depression (Andersen et al., 1992).

A depressed person tends to explain an unpleasant event in terms of internal, stable, and global factors. For example, this unemployed man may believe he cannot get a job because he is not competent in any line of work and never will be.

how stupid I am—I'm never going to make it through college." In other words, she blames her supposed lack of ability (internal). She presumes her stupidity is long-lasting (stable). And she assumes her stupidity applies to all subjects, not just biology (global). In summary, depressed people typically explain their poor performance as internal, stable, and global.

Nondepressed people tend to show a different pattern. They blame failure on *external* factors ("That room was too noisy"). Their attributions are also likely to involve *unstable* causes ("I didn't get enough sleep the night before that test"). And attributions apply only to *specific* areas ("I may not be great at understanding biology, but I'm doing well in all my other courses").

Many researchers have investigated these intriguing attributional patterns. In 1986, Sweeney and his colleagues managed to locate 104 studies involving about 15,000 participants. They conducted a meta-analysis, which confirmed that depressed people do tend to use an internal, stable, global attributional style to explain negative events; nondepressed people, in contrast, use an external, unstable, specific attributional style. More recent studies typically confirm

---

DEMONSTRATION 15.3 Factors in a Male-Female Romantic Relationship

If you are a female in a romantic relationship with a male, answer the following questions from your point of view. If you are a male in a romantic relationship with a female, try to answer the questions from the female's point of view. Other students may wish to apply this demonstration to a particular male-female relationship with which they are familiar.

Answer each question *yes* or *no*. The answers appear at the end of the chapter.

1. He talks over his problems with me.
2. He is always trying to change me.
3. He respects my opinion.
4. He acts as though I am in the way.
5. He won't take no for an answer when he wants something.
6. He gives me as much freedom as I want.
7. He is always thinking of things that would please me.
8. He argues back no matter what I say.
9. He encourages me to follow my own interests.
10. He makes fun of me.
11. He wants to have the last word on how we spend our time.
12. He lets me make up my own mind.
13. He has a good time with me.
14. He wants to control everything I do.
15. He is happy to go along with my decisions.
16. He says I'm a big problem.

Source: Based on Schaefer & Burnett, 1987.

that conclusion, but occasionally researchers do find discrepancies (Gotlib & Hammen, 1992; Metalsky et al., 1993). It's too early to explain why the results are sometimes inconsistent regarding attributions for unpleasant events.

Negatively Biased Recall A third source of negative bias in the thought processes of depressed people can be found in their patterns of recall. Here the results are consistent: Depressed people recall much more negative material than positive material (Gara et al., 1993; Gotlib, 1992; Haaga et al., 1991; Mineka & Sutton, 1992). For example, depressed people are more likely than nondepressed people to remember negative information about themselves. Depressed people are also *less* likely to remember a wide variety of positive information, such as praise from a supervisor, pleasant themes in stories, and happy events.

The concept of availability explains why this biased recall has important implications for depressed people. As Chapter 8 explained, we use the **availability heuristic** whenever we estimate frequency or probability in terms of how easy it is to think of examples of something. Imagine that it's evening, and a depressed person is reviewing the day's events; many more negative than positive events come to mind. The depressed person will base his or her overall evaluation on the relative availability of those negative events: "Yes, another lousy day . . . " (Mineka & Sutton, 1992).

Notice the pervasiveness of the negative thinking: (1) Depressed people have negative self-schemas as well as negative schemas about other people and the future; (2) Depressed people tend to have negative patterns for explaining unhappy events; (3) Depressed people recall unpleasant information more accurately than pleasant information. Obviously, these cognitive biases can intensify the depression of individuals who are already discouraged.

Gender and Depression

According to surveys, women are two to three times as likely as men to show signs of depression (McGrath, 1991; Mollica, 1989; Zigler & Glick, 1986). These gender differences are true for both Whites and Blacks in the United States and Canada, as well as in most other developed countries (Husaini et al., 1991; Statistics Canada, 1992; Stoppard, 1989; Jenkins et al., 1991).

Factors Related to Depression in Women Some characteristics tend to be associated with depression in women. For instance, depression is somewhat more common among divorced women, married women with several young children, women who do not work outside the home, and women who have not had an advanced education (Hammen, 1982; Hock & DeMeis, 1990; Jack, 1987a). However, personal and social factors are typically more helpful in predicting depression. Before you read further, try Demonstration 15.3 on page 497. Research relevant to this demonstration was conducted by Schaefer and Burnett (1987). This study showed that women were significantly more likely to be depressed if their husbands were hostile, detached, or overly controlling. In contrast, those with supportive, encouraging husbands were unlikely to be depressed.

Why Are Women More Depressed? Biologically based explanations do not offer satisfactory support for the gender differences in depression rates (Nolen-Hoeksema, 1987, 1990). The gender differences also cannot be traced to therapist bias (Nolen-Hoeksema, 1990; Scarf, 1979). A controversial possibility is that men are more likely to abuse alcohol or engage in antisocial behavior, both of which could mask depression. Some theorists support this possibility, but others reject it (e.g., Mollica, 1989; Pyke & Toukmanian, 1989; Stoppard, 1989; Strickland, 1992); at present, we cannot draw conclusions about this potential explanation. However, here are some other explanations that have received support:

1. *Women are less likely to find gratification in their lives* (Gove, 1980; Strickland, 1992). That is, women are depressed because of unpleasant realities such as rape and battering (Strickland, 1992). They are also depressed because low-paying

jobs and housework provide little reward. People tend to be more impressed by someone with a large income than someone who is skilled in taking care of others (Barnett et al., 1992; Jack, 1987b; Zigler & Glick, 1986).

2. *Women are more likely to derive their identity from another person.* Women are more likely to derive their sense of self from being "the wife of John Garcia" or "the mother of Pat and Chris." In contrast, John Garcia is likely to have an identity based on his own accomplishments, perhaps "the vice-president of First National Bank." Research has demonstrated that women tend to be depressed if they derive their identity from other people, rather than having their own, independent sense of self (Jack, 1991; Warren & McEachren, 1983, 1985).

3. *Women are more likely to worry about their depression, whereas men are more likely to distract themselves.* When depressed, women report that they are more likely to think and talk about their feelings. These activities tend to focus attention on the depression, making women even more depressed. In contrast, men are more likely to report that they do something physical or avoid thinking about the depression (Nolen-Hoeksema, 1987, 1990; Nolen-Hoeksema et al., 1993). People who continually ignore their emotions may develop psychological problems other than depression. However, a strategy often recommended for both women and men is to distract yourself temporarily from a depressed mood until you can think more clearly about the problem.

In this section we have looked at the characteristics of depressed people. Depressed people believe they are unworthy, or as one woman described her feelings, a piece of litter that was being blown along the sidewalk and being kicked aside (Scarf, 1979). In contrast, people with a diagnosis of bipolar disorder may feel as if they are litter today, but next week their self-esteem is so high that they consider themselves among the most important individuals in the universe.

Bipolar Disorder

For a person with a bipolar disorder, ordinary human experiences become magnified to larger-than-life proportions (Goodwin & Jamison, 1990). Sadness and fatigue are exaggerated, but so are joy and energy. The name *bipolar* suggests two poles. Like the two poles of the earth, depression and mania represent opposite ends of the human emotional spectrum. You are already familiar with the description of depression from the previous sections; now let us consider the manic episodes that people with bipolar disorder also experience.

Consider a track coach named George who was in the midst of a manic episode when he was admitted to the hospital. George declared that he was the coach of the U.S. Olympic track team, and he offered to hold tryouts for the other patients in the hospital. He rapidly paced the halls of the ward and flew into a rage at the slightest irritation. When a staff member blocked his entrance to the nursing station, George threatened to report her to the president of the Olympic committee. He had not slept for three days (Oltmanns et al., 1991).

Less than 1% of the population will experience bipolar disorder, in contrast to between 8% and 18% for major depression (Altman et al., 1989; Goodwin & Jamison, 1990). Also unlike depression, bipolar disorder affects roughly the same number of men and women (Mollica, 1989). Some of the important characteristics of the manic phase of a bipolar disorder include inflated self-esteem and increased talkativeness, with the feeling that one's thoughts are racing. During a manic experience, a person may become deeply involved in pleasurable activities that will produce painful consequences at a later time. For example, such people often spend money wildly and make foolish business investments (American Psychiatric Association, 1994).

During a manic episode, people feel on top of the world. As one person describes the experience, "When you're high, it's tremendous. The ideas and feelings

Women are likely to work at low-paying jobs and are therefore more likely to develop depression, according to one explanation for women's relatively high depression rate.

are fast and frequent like shooting stars and you follow them until you find better and brighter ones . . . . Feelings of ease, intensity, power, well-being, financial omnipotence and euphoria now pervade one's marrow. But, somewhere, this changes. The fast ideas are far too fast and there are far too many; overwhelming confusion replaces clarity" (Goodwin & Jamison, 1990, pp. 17–18).

Some people with bipolar disorders have such grandiose schemes during a manic episode that they may withdraw their life savings to undertake a project that is bound to fail. Others, however, are more fortunate: Their mania may be expressed as artistic creativity. For instance, Handel composed the *Messiah* in just 24 days of a manic episode. Others who may have been manic-depressives include composer Hector Berlioz, playwright Eugene O'Neill, and authors Virginia Woolf and Ernest Hemingway (Leo, 1984).

We know that people in the midst of a manic episode have grandiose self-esteem and excessive optimism. However, we do not have many details about cognitive processes during mania. Several interesting studies have shown that memory is impaired during mania. Also, intriguingly, manic patients are more likely than control-group people to show overinclusive thinking . . . they link items together that are only remotely related (Johnson & Magaro, 1987). You may recall Isen's research demonstrating that people in a happy mood were better able to appreciate subtle relationships between items (Chapter 12). These two observations may well be connected with each other.

However, the mania cannot last forever. The bubble bursts, and mood returns to normal—or it may crash into a depression. The painful consequences of some of the wild behavior may even intensify the depression.

What causes mood disorders, both major depression and bipolar disorder? Why do people develop these disabling disorders that influence so many psychological processes?

Georg Friedrich Handel was probably a manic-depressive, according to recent analyses.

Explaining Mood Disorders

Researchers have been extremely active in developing explanations for mood disorders. Researchers who favor the biological approach have examined both depression and bipolar disorder, whereas those who prefer psychological explanations have focused most of their attention on depression (Halgin & Whitbourne, 1993).

The Biological Approach Genetic factors clearly influence a person's chances of developing a mood disorder; both depression and bipolar disorder have a significant inherited component (Gershon et al., 1989; Gotlib & Hammen, 1992; Winokur, 1991). For example, when one member of an identical-twin pair has a diagnosis of major depression, the other member stands a 65% chance of also exhibiting depression. For fraternal twins (who are less genetically similar), the rate drops to 15% (Nurnberger & Gershon, 1982). People with bipolar disorder are also highly likely to have relatives with some kind of mood disorder—either bipolar disorder or depression (Goodwin & Jamison, 1990).

You may be wondering exactly what factors are inherited. Researchers are reasonably convinced that the relevant factor involves the balance in the neurotransmitter system. As Chapter 3 described, **neurotransmitters** are the chemical substances stored in the ends of axons, which allow electrical messages to be transmitted to nearby neurons. Unfortunately, researchers are not certain exactly which neurotransmitters are relevant and how their effects combine. For some time, they have known that two neurotransmitters, serotonin and norepinephrine, are related to mood disorders (Golden & Janowsky, 1990). These neurotransmitters are found in the limbic system and the hypothalamus; both structures are involved in regulating emotions (Figure 3.15). At one point, depression seemed to be related to a deficiency in one or both neurotransmitters; manic episodes seemed to be related to an excess in one or both substances.

However, our complexity theme would lead you to suspect that this explanation is too simple . . . and it is. For instance, some drugs relieve depression but have no effect on serotonin or norepinephrine levels (Carlson, 1991). A further complication is that there may well be several different kinds of biologically based depression, even though the symptoms may look similar. The serotonin/norepinephrine explanation may account for some kinds, but not others (Golden & Janowsky, 1990). In summary, the data inform us that biological factors are important in the mood disorders, but we do not have clear details on how the neurotransmitters operate.

The Psychodynamic Approach As you will recall, psychodynamic theorists emphasize that psychological disorders can be traced to childhood problems and unconscious conflict. Freud argued that depression is related to feelings of loss. If a man's wife dies, this emotional experience may trigger emotions connected with his childhood. A woman may become angry toward a parent who died; she turns her anger inward and develops depression. Many therapists who endorse Freud's original views therefore suggest that people can relieve their depression by "getting their anger out" (Mendelson, 1990).

However, many psychodynamic theorists have broadened their perspectives of depression. For example, depression may not be traceable to particular traumatic incidents, such as death, but rather to the quality of the mother-child interactions during early childhood (Klein, 1940). According to other psychodynamic theorists, shame is a critical factor in depression; when you have done a "bad thing," you are ashamed about your "bad self" and feel worthless (Tangney et al., 1992). In brief, depression is caused by emotional reactions toward death, by never having experienced a warm relationship, by shame, and by other sources of conflict.

Psychodynamic theorists believe that depression can be traced to some kind of loss, such as a death or a more figurative kind of loss, as well as other conflict-arousing experiences.

The Behaviorist Approach Peter Lewinsohn (1974) argues that learning theory can explain depression. The death or departure of a loved one produces a reduction in rewards; we do not need complex explanations based on hidden conflict. Poor interpersonal skills may also prevent someone from developing warm social relationships; you'll recall from the section on social behavior that this explanation probably is accurate. However, in recent years, behaviorists have not been as active as cognitive theorists in developing explanations of depression (Rehm, 1990).

The Social Cognitive Approach A variety of different social cognitive theories have been offered. They all share one important underlying idea: Depression can be traced to maladaptive cognitive reactions to life events. In other words, depressed people interpret reality differently from nondepressed people, and this cognitive style is related to depression.

Aaron Beck proposed a social cognitive theory suggesting that some people have negative schemas about themselves and life events (Beck, 1976; Segal, 1988). We saw evidence for this and other negative biases in the "In Depth" section. The basic premise is that most people have a tendency to view the world through rose-colored glasses. However, depressed people view the world through mud-colored glasses. Taylor (1989) provides a vivid example of a woman who had told her therapist she felt very depressed after seeing a movie. The movie had been extremely sad, and she could relate it to her own life. The therapist advised her to select a happier movie next time. So the woman selected an upbeat movie. On the following visit, she reported to the therapist that the movie left her very depressed. After all, the happy movie showed her how delightful life could be, and the contrast with her own miserable life had made her more depressed than ever!

According to Beck's view, depressed people exaggerate their problems, ignore the positive events, and misinterpret innocent statements. In short, their beliefs are self-defeating (Beck, 1982). Beck would argue that negative self-schemas cause depression.

Other social cognitive theorists place more emphasis on the attributional styles we discussed earlier. They argue that people who are depressed explain their poor performance in terms of internal, stable, and global attribution patterns: "It's my fault, I'll always be that way, and I'm incompetent at everything!" Depressed people may also believe that horrible consequences are likely to result from a relatively minor event. When a stressful life event does occur, this person experiences hopeless depression (Abramson et al., 1989; Alloy, 1988; Peterson & Seligman, 1985). To the depressed, things are disastrous, and life will never improve.

These two cognitive theories are actually compatible, and they can be combined with the earlier information about biased recall to explain how some people can endure numerous personal tragedies and still maintain an underlying optimism. For others, relatively minor stress leaves them helpless and depressed. Individual differences in cognitive styles may help explain why some people are hopeful and others are depressed.

Many aspects of the social cognitive approach have received support. However, most evidence suggests that this pessimism is a *result* of depression, not a *cause* (Haaga et al., 1991). It certainly can help us understand, however, why a person who has experienced stressful life experiences may decline from being merely discouraged into a deep depression.

The Sociocultural Approach The sociocultural perspective suggests that we look to social pressures—rather than the individual—for explanations of depression. As we saw, women are two to three times more likely than men to develop depression. The sociocultural approach emphasizes that women's low status and more limited rewards encourage depression.

Life is clearly more stressful for certain groups in the United States. They experience more of the "environmental stresses that are responsible for the higher rates of emotional disturbance among the poor, the powerless, the disenfranchised, and the exploited" (Albee, 1983, p. 1043). People who are economically poor do indeed have higher rates of depression (Mollica, 1989). Refugees and immigrants are also more likely to be depressed (Jenkins et al., 1991).

Blacks also have a higher rate of depressive symptoms than the national average, even after correcting for differences in social class (Brown, 1990; Redmond, 1988). Basically, people who lack a sense of control over important factors in their lives are at greater risk for depression (Albee, 1992; Mirowsky & Ross, 1989).

Our culture's values in the 1990s also encourage depression. Martin Seligman, well known for his work on cognitive aspects of depression, has analyzed data from large-scale studies on this disorder. He reports that depression is about 20 times more likely for those born after 1950 than for those born before 1910 (Seligman, 1989). This increasing rate of depression has been confirmed in research examining depression rates in the United States, Canada, New Zealand, Sweden, Italy, and Korea (Cross-National Collaborative Group, 1992; Klerman & Weissman, 1989).

Seligman (1989) attributes this increased depression to our current emphasis on the self. In previous eras, people felt strong commitments to their country, their religion, or their family—all institutions larger than the self. Seligman speculates that many people are currently committed only to buying material possessions and advancing themselves. As a result, they have difficulty finding meaning in life. Depression can result from this sense of meaninglessness. Seligman offers a clear prescription for depression in the 1990s: We should be less concerned with ourselves and more concerned about other people and the common good.

Combining the Approaches How do all the pieces fit together in explaining depression? Let's consider a general explanation that combines the approaches. Keep in mind, however, that some factors in this model may not be relevant to everyone. For example, some individuals may not have any biological disposition toward depression, but depression is induced by overwhelming life stress.

Figure 15.4 shows how life stress—often increased by sociocultural factors—combines with potential biological factors to produce a depressed mood. This depressed mood produces the four consequences we have discussed: (1) physical health

Seligman argues that people concerned about the welfare of others are less likely to develop depression. In this photo, volunteers are painting a home to help low-income residents.

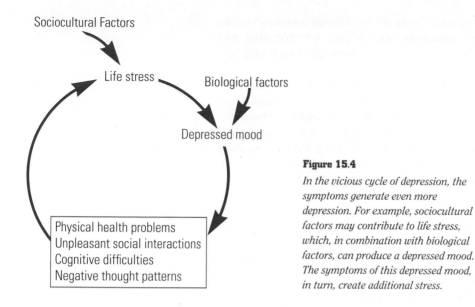

Figure 15.4

In the vicious cycle of depression, the symptoms generate even more depression. For example, sociocultural factors may contribute to life stress, which, in combination with biological factors, can produce a depressed mood. The symptoms of this depressed mood, in turn, create additional stress.

problems; (2) unpleasant social interactions; (3) cognitive difficulties; and (4) negative thought patterns. These factors make life even more stressful, which increases depression still further. After all, it is stressful to feel sick, to have other people reject you, to have cognitive problems, and to have negative views about yourself and your life. A vicious cycle begins, in which depression grows steadily worse. As we see in the next chapter, however, this vicious cycle can be interrupted, and depression can be treated successfully.

SECTION SUMMARY
MOOD DISORDERS

- The characteristics of major depression include physical problems; apathy and negative emotions; unpleasant social interactions; hopelessness; contemplation of suicide; decreased thinking skills; negative evaluations of self, other people, and the future; negative attributional patterns; and negatively biased recall.

- Women are two to three times as likely as men to become depressed; some possible explanations include low gratification, derived identity, and worrying about depression.

- People with bipolar disorders experience both depressive and manic episodes; during manic episodes, they exhibit inflated self-esteem, talkativeness, racing thoughts, and overinvolvement in potentially harmful activities.

- The explanation for mood disorders is undoubtedly complex; the vicious cycle of depression includes stressful events (often sociocultural in origin) that frequently combine with biological factors to produce a depressed mood. The depressed mood produces physical health problems, unpleasant social interactions, cognitive difficulties, and negative thought patterns; these four factors, in turn, create more stress.

SCHIZOPHRENIC DISORDERS

A young woman, hospitalized with a diagnosis of schizophrenia at the age of 19, recalled that she first began to hallucinate at the age of 9. In the classroom, she would "see" a troop of elves jumping merrily from desk to desk and then tweaking the teacher's nose. At other times, her desk seemed to behave like a hungry animal, reaching out to bite her dress (Asarnow & Goldstein, 1986).

In the previous section, we focused on depression and bipolar disorder, which primarily involve disordered *emotions*. **Schizophrenia,** in contrast, primarily involves severely disordered *thoughts,* though perceptual, emotional, social, and behavioral processes may also be disturbed.

Schizophrenia is a term originally introduced by a Swiss psychiatrist (Bleuler, 1911/1950). The name comes from the Greek words for "split mind." Unfortunately, some people assume that schizophrenia really means "split personality." However, dissociative identity disorder (multiple personality) is an unrelated problem, based on anxiety. In schizophrenia, the mind is split in a different sense, because schizophrenics experience a splitting or disorganization of normal thought processes. In some cases, this disorganization is so extensive that individuals lose their contact with reality.

Schizophrenia is much less common than mood disorders. Roughly 1% of the U.S. and Canadian populations develops schizophrenia at some point during their lifetimes (Gottesman, 1991). However, it is such a serious disorder that people admitted to psychiatric hospitals may remain there for some time. As a result, schizophrenia accounts for the greatest number of residents—at any one time—in public psychiatric hospitals (Kay, 1991). Men and women are equally likely to develop schizophrenia, though for some unexplained reason, men usually develop it at an earlier age (Karno & Norquist, 1989; Lewine, 1991).

Specific symptoms of schizophrenia vary from person to person. In fact, no single feature is present in every schizophrenic person (Torrey, 1988a). People with schizophrenia differ so vastly from one another that some researchers have suggested that there are really several disorders, not just one (Gottesman, 1991; Kay, 1991).

What are some of the symptoms that make schizophrenia so disabling? What is its pattern of development? Finally, how can we explain this disorder that so profoundly alters an individual's attention, thinking, emotions, social interactions, and behavior?

The Characteristics of Schizophrenic Disorders

As you review these symptoms, you should remember that schizophrenics differ dramatically, just as psychologically healthy people show wide individual differences (Theme 2).

Attention Problems As you learned in Chapter 5, normal people can pay selective attention to one message, screening out the stream of other distracting thoughts and perceptual stimuli. For instance, as you read this sentence, you can ignore a conversation out in the hallway, the visual clutter that surrounds you, and hundreds of other stimuli that could divert you from your goal of completing the sentence. However, schizophrenics are more easily distracted (Mirsky & Duncan, 1986).

Let's look at some of the research evidence on attention in schizophrenics. Turn back to Demonstration 5.1 (page 137) to refresh your memory about the Stroop effect as a test of selective attention. Cohen and Servan-Schreiber (1992) reviewed three studies that contrasted schizophrenics and control-group people on the Stroop test. In all three cases, schizophrenics were significantly more distracted than people in the control group when a color name was printed in a conflicting color (e.g., the word *blue* printed in the color *red*). Other research by Holzman and Matthysse (1990) shows that the majority of schizophrenics have difficulty tracking and following objects with their eyes. Still other studies by Posner and his colleagues (1988) demonstrate that schizophrenics have more difficulty shifting their visual attention to objects located in the right portion of their visual field, as opposed to their left visual field. Control-group people did not show this asymmetric response pattern. Therefore, on three different kinds of tasks, schizophrenics show abnormal attention patterns.

An individual with schizophrenia would have difficulty tracking this taxi as it moves from right to left in this busy street scene.

Disorganized Thinking   Just as schizophrenics have trouble focusing their vision on a single object, they also have trouble focusing their thinking. You can appreciate this disorganized thinking by considering the speech pattern of schizophrenics. Before you read further, try Demonstration 15.4.

Notice how Sylvia Frumkin leaps from doctors to makeup to Ringo Starr to family members to Hobbits . . . in just a single paragraph. In many cases, the connection between two thoughts seems weak (for instance, between the second and third sentences), and sometimes it seems nonexistent (for instance between the third and

---

DEMONSTRATION 15.4   Characteristics of Schizophrenic Language

Read the following passage, a recording of a monologue that a schizophrenic woman named Sylvia Frumkin addressed to another woman at a psychiatric center (Sheehan, 1982, p. 72).

I'm a doctor, you know. I don't have a diploma, but I'm a doctor. I'm glad to be a mental patient, because it taught me how to be humble. I use Cover Girl creamy natural makeup. Oral Roberts has been here to visit me. My sister's name is Joyce Frumkin, and I like her. . . . I'm only five foot four and I'm the tallest one in my family. This place is where *Mad* magazine is published. The Nixons make Noxon metal polish. When I was a little girl, I used to sit and tell stories to myself. When I was older, I turned off the sound on the TV set and made up dialogue to go with the shows I watched. The people in Creedmoor are Hobbits. I dictated the Hobbit stories to Tolkien, and he took them all down. I'm the Hobbit. Ask John Denver. He told me I was. I'm the only person who ever got Ringo Starr angry. All the trouble started when my father decided to move from Brooklyn to Queens when I was seven. . . .

Next, read through this passage again, with a pen in hand. Count the number of times there is an abrupt break between two sentences, with no apparent link between them.

Now locate a letter from a relative or friend (or else ask someone to quickly write a page about what has happened recently in his or her life). Again, count the number of times an abrupt break occurs between two sentences. Notice that in Ms. Frumkin's monologue, abrupt breaks are more common than linked sentences. In contrast, your letter probably contains more linked sentences.

fourth sentences). Schizophrenics like Sylvia Frumkin do not seem to show any concern that a listener might see no relationship among those ideas. We should note, incidentally, that some language that seems disordered to a listener might actually be connected in a meaningful fashion for the schizophrenic (Domjan, 1993).

Some schizophrenic speech shows more interest in the sound of language than its meaning. Sylvia's reference to Nixon and Noxon is one example. Consider how another schizophrenic individual responded when a psychologist asked about the color of a test item: "Looks like clay. Sounds like gray. Take you for a roll in the hay. Hay day. Mayday" (Chaika, 1985, p. 31). Another feature commonly found in schizophrenic speech is a **neologism** or invented word (Wróbel, 1990). For example, one schizophrenic individual invented the word *prestigitis,* as used in his sentence, "People die, and all the microbes talk over there, and prestigitis you know is sending you from here to another world" (Davison & Neale, 1990, p. 380).

Schizophrenics also show decreased skills in other cognitive areas. In one study, for example, 16 individuals with schizophrenia were compared with their identical twins who did not have schizophrenia (Goldberg et al., 1990). The schizophrenics scored significantly lower on tests of memory, conceptual ability, attention, and verbal fluency.

Hallucinations Schizophrenics often experience **hallucinations,** or strong mental images that seem like they truly occurred. The most common hallucinations are auditory, such as voices coming from outside one's head. The voices may speak directly to the person, or the voices may comment on the person's behavior. Less often, the hallucinations are visual, as in the elves in the girl's report at the beginning of

This painting created by a schizophrenic individual conveys the emotional torment and altered perceptions that are part of this disorder. He painted it while gazing at his own face in a mirror.

this section. Smells, tastes, and skin-sense hallucinations also may occur.

We have noted before that the distinction between so-called normal behavior and psychological disorders can be blurry. A colleague of mine provided a good example. She is a clinical psychologist, and one of her responsibilities is to test the graduates of a theological seminary, to determine whether they are psychologically healthy and suitable for the ministry. What should she conclude if a man who is a minister-to-be says that he hears God talking to him? Is this normal, or is it a sign of schizophrenia (Krauthamer, 1989)?

One proposal is that hallucinations result from a failure in metacognitive skills. Specifically, schizophrenics may have trouble discriminating between experiences that really happened and those they they created in their imaginations (Bentall, 1990). Interestingly, research shows that schizophrenics have more difficulty than normal people in discriminating words they actually said out loud from words they merely *thought* about saying out loud (Harvey, 1985).

Delusions A **delusion** is a false belief that a person firmly holds, despite any objective evidence. For example, Sylvia Frumkin claimed she was a doctor one moment and a Hobbit the next. Some delusions are more long-lasting; a person with one or more persistent, bizarre delusions is called a **paranoid schizophrenic.** For example, Baur (1991) describes a Mr. Clauson, who was extremely concerned that he would be bombarded by plums. He was frequently seen energetically hurrying down the halls of the psychiatric hospital, with wads of cotton protruding from his ears to prevent green plums from entering his ears and growing there.

Emotional Disturbances Schizophrenics often show **flat affect,** or little sign of either positive or negative emotion. In flat affect, the voice is a monotone, and the face has no expression. Some schizophrenics may also show inappropriate emotion. As a college student, for instance, I accompanied some people from a local psychiatric hospital to a performance of *The Sound of Music.* One man, diagnosed as a schizophrenic, began to laugh out loud at one of the saddest parts of the play, when Maria decides she must leave the family to return to the abbey. Some schizophrenics show inconsistent moods. A person wearing a bland expression may suddenly erupt in a burst of anger. These dramatic shifts in mood may be partly traceable to disordered thought processes.

Social Problems Schizophrenics usually have trouble with interpersonal relationships (American Psychiatric Association, 1994). Sometimes they are socially withdrawn, as if in their own isolated world. Other schizophrenics may cling to their acquaintances, unaware that too much closeness makes people feel uncomfortable. In general, people with schizophrenia have little experience in the kinds of everyday social skills that normal people take for granted.

Behavioral Disturbances Schizophrenics typically show motor disturbances (Crider, 1991). One individual may make facial grimaces, and another may repeat a purposeless gesture. Others may have difficulty coordinating their motor movements or maintaining an appropriate posture (Manschreck, 1989). Still others may stand rigidly for prolonged periods. A person whose most prominent symptom is unusual body movements is called a **catatonic schizophrenic.**

The Course of Schizophrenia

Schizophrenia typically develops during adolescence or early adulthood, though an onset during childhood or old age is also possible (American Psychiatric Association, 1994; Asarnow & Goldstein, 1986). Intriguingly, when trained viewers look at home movies of people who became schizophrenic as adults, they can often spot characteristic attributes—such as lack of eye contact and physical clumsiness—during the first five years of life (Walker & Lewine, 1990). A casual observer seldom notices anything atypical.

A schizophrenic may make unusual body movements or adopt abnormal body postures.

The disorder becomes obvious when a clear deterioration occurs. This decline may include social withdrawal, peculiar behavior, or unusual language disturbances. Friends and relatives begin to comment that the individual no longer seems to be the same person as before. Major symptoms that may develop later include incoherent speech, delusions, and hallucinations.

Most schizophrenics do not return to a perfectly normal state. The prognosis is best, though, for people who are relatively well-adjusted during the most severe period of the disorder (Carpenter & Strauss, 1991). A decade ago, researchers thought that people were more likely to recover if they had primarily positive symptoms; more recent research shows that the two conditions do not differ in the outcome of their disorder (Kay, 1991).

Although schizophrenics are not likely to recover completely, some can still lead productive lives that include stable employment and satisfying social relationships. Consider, for example, Dr. Frederick Frese, who is a psychologist working with the Ohio Department of Mental Health. After graduating from college, Frese became a Marine Corps officer. However, he found it extremely stressful to work around atomic weapons. He began to believe that some of his fellow Marines were being controlled through posthypnotic suggestion by the Chinese. After release from the Marines, he recovered long enough to graduate from business schools and work successfully with a major company. This work was interrupted by a second acute episode in which he reported the experience of turning into a monkey, a reptile, a worm, and finally a single atom at the center of an atom bomb. During a 10-year period, he was hospitalized nine times.

In the past 13 years, however, Frese has not been rehospitalized. He earned a PhD in psychology and has worked as a psychologist and administrator, primarily helping other schizophrenic individuals. Until several years ago, Frese's colleagues were not aware of his personal experience with schizophrenia. However, he realized he could help remove the stigma about mental illness by telling people that he is a schizophrenic. He now delivers lectures around the United States, encouraging both professionals and nonprofessionals to be less judgmental about people with serious mental illness (Frese, 1991). In addition, he offers a hopeful message to people with psychological disorders, "It was not and is not easy . . . . But if I can do it so can you" (Frese, 1989, p. 5).

Dr. Frederick Frese, who works with schizophrenic people at the Western Reserve Psychiatric Habilitation Center in Ohio.

Explaining Schizophrenic Disorders

Finding an explanation for schizophrenia is challenging. After all, we need a mechanism to explain a wide variety of disorders in attention, thinking, emotions, social interactions, and behavior—as well as hallucinations and delusions. Let us first consider several biological explanations before turning to psychological and sociocultural factors.

Biological Approaches Three major areas in which biological factors could operate are in the genetic transmission of schizophrenia, brain abnormalities, and neurotransmitter abnormalities.

The accumulated research evidence strongly supports a genetic contribution to the development of schizophrenic disorders (Gottesman, 1991; Holzman & Matthysse, 1990; Lyons et al., 1991). For example, suppose that Sheila is a schizophrenic. If she has an identical twin, that twin stands about a 48% chance of being schizophrenic. If she has a fraternal twin, that twin stands about a 17% chance of having schizophrenia (Gottesman, 1991). Remember that the incidence of schizophrenia in the general population is only 1%.

However, you might argue that the responsible factor might be some environmental stress, shared by both siblings. For these reasons, adoption studies are helpful. Several adoption studies suggest that genetics plays a significant role (Gottesman, 1991). For example, a study in Finland identified 184 children who had been born to schizophrenic mothers and given up for adoption (Tienari et al., 1987). So far, 7% of these children have developed schizophrenia. The researchers also selected a control group of children, also given up for adoption, who were born to normal mothers. These children were matched on a case-by-case basis on relevant variables, including the fact that they were adopted. So far, only 1.5% of these children have developed schizophrenia.

For comparison's sake, the genetic component of schizophrenia is larger than the genetic component of several common medical problems, such as diabetes, ulcers, and heart disease (Loehlin et al., 1988). Perhaps the most famous example of the genetic component of schizophrenia is the Genain quadruplets (see Figure 15.5).

Genetics is clearly important in the development of schizophrenia. However, it cannot be the complete story. After all, the Finnish study showed that only a fraction of the children of the schizophrenic mothers developed schizophrenia. Furthermore, other research on the genetics of schizophrenia shows that only about 10% of schizophrenics have a schizophrenic parent (Gottesman, 1991).

Figure 15.5

The Genain quadruplets, four sisters with schizophrenia, in a picture taken at their 51st birthday party. The chances of all four being diagnosed as schizophrenic is about 1 in 2,000,000, so a genetic explanation seems likely. (We should note, however, that environmental factors could also have contributed to the development of their disorder.)

In reviewing the research on brain structure and schizophrenia, Heinrichs (1993) remarks, ". . . the human brain is a difficult organ to observe directly. Encased and obscured by a boney mantle, indispensable but inaccessible, it does not yield up secrets readily" (pp. 224–225). Early researchers had suspected that something might be abnormal about the brain structure of schizophrenics, but systematic research was not possible until the development of brain imaging techniques (as discussed in Chapter 3). Now, researchers have used CT scans, PET scans, and MRIs to discover some intriguing findings. For example, PET scans can trace chemical activity in various parts of the living brain, telling us which areas are most metabolically active. Figure 15.6a shows a PET scan of a normal volunteer on a task requiring attention, perhaps watching for a faint light to appear. Red and yellow indicate high activity levels, and you can see that the frontal cortex of this normal person is highly active. Notice, however, that the PET scan of a person with schizophrenia (Figure 15.6b) shows minimal activity in the frontal cortex (Gershon & Rieder, 1992). These data are consistent with our earlier data that schizophrenics have difficulty on attention tasks.

Research on brain structure has revealed a second interesting finding: Many schizophrenics have enlarged ventricles, which are the cavities that contain cerebrospinal fluid. If parts of a schizophrenic's brain are filled with fluid, then the brain tissue must be decreased. The problem is that only 25% to 50% of schizophrenics show these structural abnormalities (Frith, 1992; Heinrichs, 1993). A professor of mine once said, "When you look at a number, ask yourself two questions: Why is it so large? and Why is it so small?" (Martin, 1967). The percentage is as *high* as 25% to 50%, which suggests that brain structure is indeed related to schizophrenia. However, the percentage is as *low* as 25% to 50%, which suggests that you can have schizophrenia with relatively normal brain structure.

Now let us turn our attention to a third potential biological mechanism for schizophrenia—the neurotransmitters. Whereas serotonin and norepinephrine are involved in mood disorders, the neurotransmitter dopamine plays a role in schizophrenia. According to the **dopamine hypothesis,** schizophrenia is caused by too much dopamine at critical synapses in the brain. As usual, some evidence is persuasive. For example, the most effective drugs used to treat schizophrenia are ones that block the dopamine receptors (Gottesman, 1991). Also, drugs that make schizophrenia worse—such as amphetamine and cocaine—are ones that increase dopamine levels (Gray et al., 1991). But, as you now might expect, the mechanism is not that simple. For instance, if the drugs that treat the symptoms of schizophrenia operate simply by blocking the receptors, then why does it take weeks—rather than minutes—for the improvements to occur (Pinel, 1993)? Researchers realize that dopamine levels cannot yet explain the results completely, but no better hypothesis about neurotransmitters has been proposed.

In short, biological explanations provide some enticing hints, and the factors of genetics, brain structure, and neurotransmitters are undoubtedly important. However, we do not yet have a satisfying, complete explanation of the biology of schizophrenia.

Psychological Approaches In general, the standard psychological explanations have not been fully developed to account for the specific disorders found in schizophrenia. Although some theorists have tried to explain schizophrenia in psychodynamic, behaviorist, and social cognitive frameworks, other more specific explanations are more widely accepted.

One very prominent psychological explanation is the family dynamics approach. According to the **family dynamics approach,** the risk of schizophrenia is greater in families with (1) communication problems or (2) high expressed emotion. In general, researchers have discovered that schizophrenics are somewhat more likely than normal people to grow up in homes where communication is fragmented or muddled (Goldstein, 1984). Children cannot understand what the other family

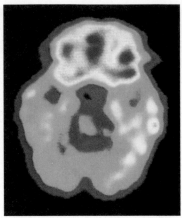

a. normal

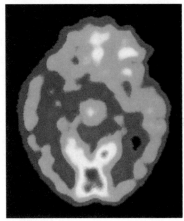

b. schizophrenic

Figure 15.6

PET scans made while participants were performing an attention task. (Red and yellow regions indicate high activity; blue and purple areas indicate low activity.)

members are saying, so they create their own private world that encourages schizophrenic thinking. Incidentally, Doane and her colleagues (1989) studied two groups of parents who had schizophrenic children. One group was Anglo and the other was English-speaking Mexican American. Mothers and fathers in the Anglo group received communication-deviance scores that were similar to the scores of their counterparts in the Mexican-American group. Thus, this concept of faulty communication patterns may not be limited to Anglo Americans.

The family dynamics approach also proposes that a high level of expressed emotion can make schizophrenia more likely if a person is predisposed to this disorder. High **expressed emotion** means that a family member is highly critical of another family member. For example, one mother told her son that he was "not any benefit to himself or any benefit to society or any benefit to the family situation" (Leff & Vaughan, 1985, p. 41). As you can imagine, remarks like this are not likely to raise a child's self-esteem! Research on the families of schizophrenics shows that expressed emotion may not *cause* a schizophrenic episode. However, research with both Anglo and Mexican-American families does demonstrate that expressed emotion is related to relapse rate. That is, people who were in recovery were more likely to have another episode of schizophrenia if their families were high in expressed emotion (Hooley, 1988; Karno et al., 1987).

However, if you are thinking critically as you read about the family dynamics approach, you may have spotted another potential explanation. Maybe the family dynamics do not *cause* a relapse in schizophrenic symptoms. Instead, communication problems and high expressed emotion may be the *result* of trying to communicate with a schizophrenic who is close to a relapse . . . which is clearly a challenging task for even the most admirable parents.

According to the family dynamics approach, this father's high level of expressed emotion would make schizophrenia more likely if this child were biologically predisposed to the disorder.

The Sociocultural Approach Our earlier discussion of sociocultural approaches to depression focused on gender. In contrast, the sociocultural approach to schizophrenia focuses on social class. Specifically, schizophrenia is reported more often in lower social classes (Karno & Norquist, 1989). Being poor presents long-term stress: You may not have enough money to pay the rent, and the landlord may threaten to sell the building anyway. Also, people who are economically poor often find that their lives are controlled by other people (e.g., unreasonable bosses or unsympathetic people in a welfare office). As a result, they may not have the opportunity to take charge of their lives and effectively cope with stress.

Another possible explanation for the correlation between social class and schizophrenia is called *downward mobility.* That is, people with severe psychiatric disorders like schizophrenia are unlikely to hold high-paying jobs. As a result, they are more likely to drift downward into low-income groups. According to most current theorists, social class is both a cause and an effect of schizophrenia (Karno & Norquist, 1989; Zigler & Glick, 1986). Consistent with patterns we have seen throughout this book, the interpretation of correlations usually involves complex explanations.

Combining the Approaches Any explanation of schizophrenia must somehow combine biological, psychological, and sociocultural explanations. After all, many people have a genetic predisposition toward schizophrenia, but they turn out normal. Many other people grow up in dysfunctional or impoverished families, but they also turn out normal.

At present, the most likely explanation seems to involve some variation of the diathesis-stress model. According to the **diathesis-stress model,** people are born with a biological predisposition (that is, a *diathesis*) that makes them more likely to develop a particular disorder such as schizophrenia (Halgin & Whitbourne, 1993). When individuals with that biological predisposition are faced with extreme stresses such as family problems or sociocultural factors, they are likely to develop schizophrenia (Gottesman, 1991).

SCHIZOPHRENIC DISORDERS

- Schizophrenic disorders include a wide variety of symptoms that vary from person to person; these disorders include attention problems, disorganized thinking, hallucinations, emotional disturbances, social problems, and behavioral disturbances.

- Schizophrenia usually develops during adolescence and early adulthood; full recovery from schizophrenia is not common, but some schizophrenics lead productive lives nonetheless.

- Biological explanations for schizophrenia include the genetic transmission of schizophrenia, brain-structure abnormalities, and the dopamine hypothesis.

- One very widely accepted psychological approach to schizophrenia is the family dynamics explanation, involving communication problems and high expressed emotion; the sociocultural approach emphasizes that factors such as lower social class can contribute to schizophrenia.

- The diathesis-stress model argues that a biological predisposition toward schizophrenia combines with psychological and sociocultural stresses to make schizophrenia more likely.

PERSONALITY DISORDERS

In Chapter 13, we saw that personality traits are relatively stable ways in which individuals differ from one another. When these traits become inflexible and maladaptive, they are called **personality disorders.** We began the present chapter by considering disorders arising from anxiety, and then we looked at disorders involving primarily mood or thought. Now we turn our attention to disorders involving personality problems. People with personality disorders typically share these four problems (Perry & Vaillant, 1989):

1. A disability at work and in social relationships;
2. Frequent interpersonal conflicts;
3. An ability to cause distress to other people;
4. An inflexible response to stress.

Let us begin by considering the variety of personality disorders, and then we will look at one personality disorder in more detail.

The Variety of Personality Disorders

The current edition of the *Diagnostic and Statistical Manual of Mental Disorders* lists numerous personality disorders. As Trull (1992) points out, these diagnostic categories clearly came from very different schools of thought. As a result, the end product looks like a patchwork quilt with overlapping categories and no strong underlying theme.

A further problem is that many of the personality disorders sound like some of the psychological problems we have already discussed. For example, the name obsessive-compulsive personality disorder sounds nearly the same as the obsessive-compulsive disorder we considered in the section on anxiety problems. Range (1993) suggests that it is helpful to stress the term *personality* when we encounter a name of a personality disorder. In this case, **obsessive-compulsive personality disorder** is characterized by a personality that overemphasizes details, conscientiousness, and perfectionism (Perry & Vaillant, 1989). Each of those characteristics is admirable . . . to a degree. But this perfectionism can become such an overemphasized part of the individual's personality that he or she cannot complete a project or make a decision.

People with obsessive-compulsive personality disorder overemphasize details so much that they have great difficulty trying to make decisions about relatively minor issues, such as which sweater to wear.

For example, I know a young man who spent close to 10 minutes standing in front of an array of desserts, trying to decide which one to purchase. His friends were not amused.

A different disorder, **schizoid personality disorder,** is marked by emotional coolness, a lack of close friends, and a preference for being alone (American Psychiatric Association, 1994). People with this disorder can function much better than people with schizophrenia, which involves much more severe thought disorders (Perry & Vaillant, 1989).

In the past decade, one of the most extensively researched personality disorders has been borderline personality disorder (Halgin & Whitbourne, 1993). **Borderline personality disorder** involves unstable interpersonal relationships, unstable self-image, unstable mood, and impulsiveness. The name of this disorder is not very enlightening; what *border* are we discussing? The name was created about 40 years ago to describe people who are at the borderline between serious disorders such as schizophrenia and the less disabling disorders (Goldstein, 1990). People with borderline personality disorder can think more clearly than people with schizophrenia and they are more socially skilled. Still, they are often manipulative in their relationships with friends and relatives (Meissner, 1988).

Antisocial Personality Disorder

Of all the personality disorders, antisocial personality disorder seems to have attracted the most attention. As the name implies, **antisocial personality disorder** is marked by a variety of antisocial behaviors, including lying, violence, and other actions that show little concern for the welfare of others. The diagnosis is given only if an individual is at least 18 years of age and showed similar behavior problems prior to the age of 15 (American Psychiatric Association, 1994).

Consider the case of Howard, an American soldier who met and married an Englishwoman. When he was discharged from the Army, he headed back to the United States—on the day his wife gave birth to their first child. She managed to trace him to New York, and he swore that he would be trustworthy from that day on. The following week, he left for Florida without telling her. When explaining his actions to another person, he said that he had simply forgotten . . . he had other things to do (Doren, 1987).

According to estimates, about 3% of American males have this disorder, in contrast to less than 1% of American females (Perry & Vaillant, 1989). Thus, the gender ratio for antisocial personality disorder is the reverse of the gender ratio for depression. (It is worth noting that males are also more likely to develop substance abuse problems, including alcoholism; these problems were considered in Chapter 5.)

Let us consider some of the more common characteristics of antisocial personality disorder:

1. *Aggressiveness.* People with antisocial personality disorder often become involved in physical fights. Spouse abuse and child beating are also common.

2. *Lying and deception.* Antisocial personalities often begin lying during childhood. Some may develop elaborate deceptions. For example, a man named Stephen had been teaching at a small college in Wisconsin, where he had received excellent evaluations from his students. However, school officials later discovered that he had faked his college transcripts and letters of recommendation in order to apply for the position. He apparently had no academic training (Doren, 1987).

3. *Lack of guilt.* Antisocial personalities typically do not feel guilty about their immoral behavior or the harm it does to other people. As a consequence, they are unlikely to seek therapy. They fail to acknowledge any problem (Iacono, 1988).

4. *Low tolerance for frustration.* Most antisocial personalities want pleasures now, without frustrating delays (Millon, 1981). This interest in immediate pleasures

Ted Bundy was attractive and charming, yet he murdered many women, apparently without experiencing guilt. His characteristics are consistent with those of the antisocial personality.

may partially explain the observation that antisocial personalities tend to have high rates of alcoholism (Lewis et al., 1985).

5. *Exploitation of others.* People with antisocial personality disorder are likely to exploit other people. They are often likable, outgoing, and charming. As in the case of Howard, who was mentioned earlier, they often appear sincere when they apologize for wrongdoing. However, they typically continue to exploit the person to whom they have just apologized.

The best publicized examples of antisocial personality disorder are those who come into conflict with the law. However, clinicians who work with this disorder argue that only a minority actually break the law. As Millon (1981) points out, our competitive society tends to admire aggressive, clever, charming people who may bend the law, although they do not actually break it. The typical antisocial personality is probably more likely to be a successful businessperson than a mass murderer.

Explaining Antisocial Personality Disorder

Some biological explanations have been proposed for antisocial personality disorder. For instance, research suggests that the disorder has a hereditary component (Davison & Neale, 1990; Doren, 1987; Newman et al., 1985). Some speculate that the disorder may be caused by faulty functioning of the limbic system (see Figure 3.15). However, research on the biological underpinnings of antisocial personality disorder is not as extensive as for depression or schizophrenia.

Psychological explanations have also not been fully developed. Psychodynamic theorists propose that the disorder can be traced to rejecting parents. The child does not acquire the parents' moral values and therefore does not develop conscientious behavior.

Behaviorists argue that antisocial behavior develops when parents do not reinforce children's positive, socially admirable behavior. Those who endorse a social cognitive explanation maintain that children become antisocial when they lack appropriate adult models or when their models act aggressively (Millon, 1981).

Clinicians agree that this disorder is difficult to explain and also difficult to treat. For instance, one antisocial individual joked with his therapist about the possibility of the death penalty after he committed a series of crimes that included first-degree murder. With defiance in his voice, he stated, "They can do what they want with me, but they'll never break me. I'll never surrender to the system" (Doren, 1987, p. 246). Individuals with disorders related to anxiety, those with mood disorders, and schizophrenics appear to be tormented by their psychological problems. In contrast, individuals with antisocial personality disorder believe that the rest of the world has a problem, but that they do not.

Throughout this chapter, we have examined psychological disorders in which humans become anxious, depressed, disorganized, and inflexible. However, Lyn Abramson and her coauthors (1989) present an interesting suggestion: Perhaps the real mystery is *not* why some individuals develop depression and other disabling psychological problems. Instead, the mystery may be that so many people continue to remain competent and caring in a world where natural disasters and our fellow humans present so many obstacles to a fulfilling life.

SECTION SUMMARY

PERSONALITY DISORDERS

● Personality disorders are personality traits that have become inflexible and maladaptive; the various personality disorders do not seem especially similar to one another.

- Obsessive-compulsive personality disorder involves overemphasis on details, conscientiousness, and perfectionism; people with schizoid personality disorder are emotionally cold and lack friends; borderline personality disorder is characterized by unstable interpersonal relationships, self-image, and mood, as well as impulsiveness.

- Common characteristics of the antisocial personality include aggressiveness, lying, lack of guilt, low tolerance for frustration, and exploitation of others; both biological and psychological explanations for this disorder have been offered, but none has been fully developed.

R E V I E W   Q U E S T I O N S

1. We discussed the fact that no clear-cut boundary separates people with psychological disorders from those considered normal. Select an example of an anxiety disorder, a somatoform disorder, and a mood disorder and provide an illustration of normal behavior that might be considered somewhat similar to each disorder.

2. Suppose that a neighbor believes that her adolescent child has a psychological disorder. How is a clinician likely to make a diagnosis? What are some possible problems that can occur when psychological problems are diagnosed?

3. Make a diagram to indicate the classifications within the anxiety disorders, somatoform disorders, and dissociative disorders. Describe each disorder and try to explain why each of these would affect a person's daily life—though not as seriously as schizophrenia would.

4. What is the difference between major depression and bipolar disorders? How would each of these disorders disrupt a person's cognitive, emotional, and interpersonal behavior?

5. We noted that women and men differ in the likelihood that they will develop phobias, major depression, and antisocial personality disorder. Review the explanations for the greater likelihood of women developing the first two disorders (adding any ideas of your own) and then speculate about reasons for men's greater likelihood of developing antisocial problems.

6. We noted that schizophrenics experience intense disorganization. Describe how the thought processes, emotional experiences, and social interactions of schizophrenics reveal this disorganization.

7. In discussing disorders based on anxieties, mood disorders, and schizophrenia, we examined a number of cognitive problems that people with these disorders may experience. (For example, attention problems were discussed for all three, though the nature of these problems varied). Discuss as many of these as you can recall, using the terminology from earlier chapters in the book whenever possible.

8. What is the biological approach to psychological disorders? How is this approach used to explain the disorders based on anxiety? Describe three major components of this approach, and provide examples of each of these for depression and schizophrenia.

9. Describe the sociocultural approach to psychological disorders. If you supported a sociocultural explanation for these disorders, would you suggest therapy for a person who had a disorder, or would you favor another solution?

10. Describe some major characteristics of a person with antisocial personality disorder. Contrast that person with someone who has been diagnosed as having major depression.

NEW TERMS

psychological disorders
dysfunctional
insanity defense
diagnostic interview
Diagnostic and Statistical Manual of Mental
    Disorders (DSM)
anxiety disorders
generalized anxiety disorders
panic disorders
agoraphobia
phobic disorders
social phobia
obsessive-compulsive disorders
obsessions
compulsions
posttraumatic stress disorder (PTSD)
somatoform disorders
conversion disorders
hypochondriasis
dissociative disorders
dissociative amnesia
dissociative fugue
dissociative identity disorder
multiple personality disorder
biological preparedness
autonomic lability

attentional bias
mood disorders
major depression
bipolar disorder
mania
schema
self-schema
attribution
availability heuristic
neurotransmitters
schizophrenia
neologism
hallucinations
delusion
paranoid schizophrenic
flat affect
catatonic schizophrenic
dopamine hypothesis
family dynamics approach
expressed emotion
diathesis-stress model
personality disorders
obsessive-compulsive personality disorder
schizoid personality disorder
borderline personality disorder
antisocial personality disorder

ANSWERS TO DEMONSTRATIONS

DEMONSTRATION 15.3 Begin with a score of zero, and add one point for a *yes* answer to each of the following items: 2, 4, 5, 8, 10, 11, 14, and 16. Then subtract one point for a *yes* answer to each of the following items: 1, 3, 6, 7, 9, 12, 13, and 15.

In general, scores above zero indicate a relationship that is likely to encourage depression in women, whereas scores below zero indicate a relationship that is less likely to encourage depression.

RECOMMENDED READINGS

American Psychiatric Association. (1994). *Diagnostic and statistical manual of mental disorders* (4th ed.). Washington, DC: American Psychiatric Association. This new edition, the DSM-IV, is clear and well organized, providing descriptions and criteria for each disorder, as well as information on its incidence and course of development.

Gotlib, I. H., & Hammen, C. L. (1992). *Psychological aspects of depression: Toward a cognitive-interpersonal integration.* Chichester, England: Wiley. This book provides a good summary of the symptoms of depression as well as theoretical explanations, with primary emphasis on social cognitive approaches.

Gottesman, I. I. (1991). *Schizophrenia genesis: The origins of madness.* New York: Freeman. Gottesman, an active researcher in the field of schizophrenia, has written an ideal book for nonprofessionals interested in schizophrenia. Throughout the book, he includes first-person accounts written by people with schizophrenia.

Halgin, R. P., & Whitbourne, S. K. (1993). *Abnormal psychology: The human experience of psychological disorders.* Fort Worth: Harcourt Brace Jovanovich. This undergraduate textbook begins and ends each chapter with an engaging case study. It is clearly written and well organized, with a good blend of research and description.

Kaplan, H. J., & Sadock, B. J. (Eds.). (1989). *Comprehensive textbook of psychiatry/V,* Vols. 1 & 2 (5th ed.). Baltimore, MD: Williams & Wilkins. You will not be likely to pick up one of these two volumes for casual reading! However, if you have access to this psychiatry textbook in a library, it can serve as a valuable detailed resource.

Ruiz, D. S. (Ed.). (1990). *Handbook of mental health and mental disorder among Black Americans.* New York: Greenwood Press. This book examines a wide variety of topics related to mental health issues and Black Americans. Topics include statistics on the incidence of psychological disorders, potential biases in treatment, violence, social policy, and—a refreshing topic—positive mental health.

CHAPTER 16

TREATING PSYCHOLOGICAL DISORDERS

According to estimates, roughly one in five North Americans is currently struggling with a psychological disorder (Backer & Richardson, 1989). In Chapter 15, we considered the nature of these disorders; now we will examine a variety of treatment approaches.

Consider, for example, the case of Mr. W., a Cambodian refugee who had visited the hospital emergency room in Seattle on several occasions when he experienced symptoms that suggested a heart attack. The medical tests were all negative, but the consulting psychiatrist encouraged Mr. W. to describe his earlier experiences during the political upheavals in Cambodia. At one point, his father and a sister had died from starvation. Later on, Mr. W. and his brother escaped by walking more than 200 miles to Thailand, where they spent three impoverished years before emigrating to the United States. He had not been able to contact his family members who had remained in Southeast Asia, and he still had frequent nightmares about the years of starvation.

Mr. W. was diagnosed as having both panic disorder and posttraumatic stress disorder. He received medication for his anxiety, as well as psychodynamic psychotherapy, where he was encouraged to talk and write about his earlier experiences. He eventually discontinued the medication and has been symptom free for three years (Katon, 1991).

Although Mr. W.'s past experiences were unusually horrifying, the nature of his treatment was fairly standard. As we will see, many psychological disorders are treated with a combination of drug treatment and one or more psychotherapy approaches. We first examine the major approaches to psychotherapy and then consider two kinds of biological treatment—drug therapy and electroconvulsive therapy. The last part of the chapter raises important issues such as the evaluation of therapy, conducting therapy with diverse groups of clients, and the community mental health movement.

PSYCHOTHERAPY APPROACHES

At present, professionals offer more than 250 different kinds of psychotherapy, representing such diversity that it is difficult to find a general definition applicable to all methods (Corsini, 1989; Parloff, 1987). However, one description that captures the critical elements is that **psychotherapy** is a special collaborative relationship in which one person tries to help another in coping with a personal problem (Schacht & Strupp, 1991).

Therapy can be provided by individuals from many different backgrounds, as Table 16.1 shows. Furthermore, these professionals represent many different theoretical orientations. We will focus on the following four approaches:

1. *Psychodynamic therapy,* which emphasizes emotions and argues that psychological disorders arise from childhood problems and unconscious conflict.

2. *Humanistic therapy,* which also focuses on emotions but argues that psychological disorders are created when an individual's full development has been blocked.

3. *Behavior therapy,* which emphasizes behaviors and proposes that psychological disorders can be traced to inappropriate learning.

4. *Cognitive therapy,* which emphasizes thought processes, tracing psychological disorders to maladaptive thinking.

We need to emphasize, though, that few therapists in the 1990s would confine themselves to the techniques of just one approach. For example, the boundary between behavior therapy and cognitive therapy is now especially blurred. In fact, many who are attracted to both behavioral and cognitive approaches call themselves **cognitive-behavior therapists.** The term **eclectic approach** applies to therapists who select what seems best from a variety of theoretical approaches (Norcross, 1987).

Despite some flexibility, therapists usually prefer a treatment that is consistent with their theory of personality and their beliefs about the origins of psychological problems. For instance, if we consider the diversity of approaches covered throughout the entire chapter, the professionals who trace problems to inappropriate learning will favor behaviorist therapy. In contrast, people will favor a biological treatment—such as medication—if they believe that disorders are caused by neurotransmitter imbalances. Finally, those who support a sociocultural explanation—that poverty and discrimination cause psychological problems—will favor a more global, community psychology approach, to be discussed at the end of this chapter.

Let us now consider the major psychotherapy approaches. Later, after discussing biological treatment, we will evaluate the relative effectiveness of various methods of treating psychological disorders.

Psychodynamic Approaches

Psychoanalysis is a therapy based on the psychoanalytic theory of Sigmund Freud; it attempts to resolve problems by examining childhood experiences and making people aware of the conflicts buried in their unconscious. Therapy truly focuses on unconscious conflicts, rather than outward problems. Therefore, the key to psychoanalysis is to use a variety of methods to uncover these buried conflicts. Conscious insight releases the energy previously wasted on the conflict, allowing the person to have a more satisfying life. Let us first examine the classic psychoanalytic

TABLE 16.1 Major Professionals Involved in Psychotherapy

TYPE	DESCRIPTION
Clinical and counseling psychologists	Psychologists with PhD degrees (with more emphasis on research) or PsyD degrees (with more emphasis on applied work). All have been trained to treat psychological disorders.
Psychiatrists	Physicians with MD degrees who specialize in treating psychological disorders. They can prescribe medication.
Psychoanalysts	Usually psychiatrists (though sometimes psychologists) who have received training in the psychoanalytic techniques emphasized by Sigmund Freud and his followers.
Clinical social workers	People who have earned an MSW (Master of Social Work), which usually requires 2 years of study after a bachelor's degree.
Other therapists	People from a wide variety of backgrounds, including pastoral counselors (typically with a religious connection) and psychiatric nurses (with either an RN or a master's degree).

concepts. Then we will consider some more recent developments in the psychodynamic approach, which is the broader discipline derived from the psychoanalytic tradition that places more emphasis on social relationships.

Psychoanalytic Concepts Classical psychoanalysis requires many years of therapy, with several sessions each week, to allow in-depth probing of the unconscious. A basic goal of therapy, according to Freud, is to help individuals weaken their repressions, which will allow them to confront this repressed material (Weiss, 1990). An individual undergoing psychoanalysis would relax on a couch, such as the one shown in Figure 16.1. Freud developed the method of **free association,** in which clients relax and express their thoughts freely and without censorship. Freud encouraged spontaneity of expression; clients should express any ideas that came to mind, no matter how trivial, silly, or embarrassing they might seem (Nye, 1992).

A second method Freud developed is **dream analysis,** in which the therapist interprets the hidden meaning of the patient's dream. Freud argued that the conscious, remembered aspect of a dream (its **manifest content**) was a distorted version of unconscious sexual or aggressive conflicts (its **latent content**). The analyst's task is to decode the symbols in the manifest content so that the latent content could be revealed to the patient. Freud proposed that both free association and dream analysis could be used to circumvent defense mechanisms such as repression. (As you will recall from earlier chapters, people presumably develop defense mechanisms to protect themselves from conflict.)

Three other psychoanalytic concepts describe important processes that usually occur during psychoanalysis. These are transference, resistance, and insight.

In **transference,** the client transfers a variety of positive and negative reactions associated with parents and other childhood authority figures, directing these feelings toward the therapist. These feelings may include anger, seductiveness, appeals for sympathy, and jealousy of other patients ("Psychodynamic therapy: Part III," 1991). The therapist encourages transference, so that the client can reveal childhood feelings toward important adults. For example, a 50-year-old male business executive had been in therapy for a year. Here is a transcript of his interchange with the male therapist:

Patient: *I really don't feel like talking today.*

Analyst: *(Remains silent for several minutes, then) Perhaps you'd like to talk about why you don't feel like talking.*

Patient: *There you go again, making demands on me, insisting I do what I just don't feel up to doing. (Pause) Do I always have to talk here, when I don't feel like it? (Voice becomes angry and petulant) Can't you just get off my back? You don't really give a damn how I feel, do you?*

Analyst: *I wonder why you feel I don't care.*

Patient: *Because you're always pressuring me to do what I feel I can't do. (Davison & Neale, 1990, p. 518)*

This client had been plagued by his feelings of weakness and incompetence, despite his professional success. The analyst had begun to suspect that these feelings originated with the client's childhood experiences with his extremely critical father, who never seemed satisfied with his son's accomplishments. The analyst reasoned from the client's tone of voice and overreaction that the patient had transferred the anger from the father to the analyst. The episode provided a key for the client to reevaluate his childhood fears of expressing anger toward his father.

A second process that frequently occurs during psychoanalysis is **resistance,** which consists of all the conscious and unconscious forces that work against the treatment process. It is stressful to recall unpleasant memories that had previously

Figure 16.1

Freud's consulting room in Vienna. Clients were encouraged to relax on this couch and supply free associations. Freud reasoned that repressions would be likely to weaken under these conditions.

been unconscious, and this stress provokes resistance. Examples of resistance include refusing to discuss an important topic or protesting that the therapist's interpretation is incorrect. The therapist notes any examples of resistance during therapy, because they provide clues about conflict-laden issues and the activation of defense mechanisms.

A third concept is also important in classical psychoanalysis. The term **insight** refers to the client's awareness of the unconscious conflicts that cause his or her psychological problems. Insight grows gradually during the course of psychoanalysis as the therapist pieces together evidence from free association, dream analysis, transference, and resistance.

Current Psychodynamic Approaches We have looked at the major psychoanalytic concepts developed by Sigmund Freud about a century ago. In the 1990s, however, few therapists follow Freud's principles completely. The term **psychodynamic therapy** refers to a variety of approaches descended from Freudian theories; they focus on childhood problems and unconscious conflict but emphasize social interactions more than Freud did. They may still use some of the familiar terms, such as *transference*. However, they are likely to differ from one another in terms of their views about human nature, the nature of psychological disorders, and the kinds of activities that promote psychological change (Goldfried et al., 1990; Schacht & Strupp, 1991).

Unlike Freud's patients in leisurely turn-of-the-century Vienna, few people seeking therapy today have the time or the financial resources to spend one hour each day in therapy for several years. Many therapists in the Freudian tradition offer brief psychodynamic therapy. Although the specific characteristics may differ from one therapist to the next, the general attributes of **brief psychodynamic therapy** include the following (Flegenheimer, 1989; Hirschfeld & Shea, 1989):

1. Therapy is likely to consist of 20 to 40 weekly sessions, rather than several years of daily sessions;

2. The therapist and the client select a specific, central issue that requires resolution, rather than Freud's intentionally broad-ranging scope.

3. The individual's current social problems are emphasized, rather than his or her early childhood experiences.

4. Not everyone is a suitable candidate for brief psychodynamic therapy. People with severe personality disorders may be too hostile toward the therapist; well-motivated, intelligent people are ideal clients.

Let us briefly consider one of the most popular brief psychodynamic therapies. An important theorist involved in developing interpersonal psychotherapy was an American named Harry Stack Sullivan (1892–1949). Sullivan focused on children's early interactions with their mother as well as their continuing efforts to establish friendships with peers. Sullivan proposed that our self-concepts are created by the way other people react to us (Butler & Strupp, 1991; Sullivan, 1953). If an individual's interpersonal relationships have been traumatic, he or she may hold distorted views about current relationships with friends and relatives. **Interpersonal psychotherapy** focuses on improving the quality of a person's current interactions with other people. It has been especially useful in treating people who are depressed, but not depressed enough to be hospitalized (Weissman & Klerman, 1990).

Psychodynamic approaches no longer dominate psychotherapy as they did several decades ago. Many professionals object to components of Freud's theory or its subjective nature. As we discussed in Chapter 13, psychodynamic concepts are often difficult to test empirically. Still, Freudian ideas have had widespread influence on many contemporary therapists (Arlow, 1989).

In brief psychodynamic therapy, the therapist and the client agree upon a central issue that can be resolved relatively quickly; ideal candidates are bright and intelligent, interacting in a friendly fashion with the therapist.

Humanistic Approaches

As we discussed in the personality chapter, the humanistic approach stresses that humans have tremendous potential for personal growth and self-actualization. However, people can run into roadblocks. For example, parents may withhold their love and approval unless a young person conforms to their standards (conditional positive regard). The goals of **humanistic therapy** are to remove the blocks to personal growth and to help people appreciate their true selves. In general, humanistic therapy is typically used with less serious psychological disorders. Let us consider the two most prominent humanistic psychotherapies: Carl Rogers's approach and Gestalt therapy.

Rogers's Person-Centered Therapy Several years ago, a survey asked 800 clinical and counseling psychologists to list the psychotherapists they believed to be most influential. Carl Rogers was ranked first, followed by cognitive therapist Albert Ellis in the second position and Sigmund Freud in the third (Warga, 1988).

As its name suggests, **person-centered therapy** attempts to focus on the person's own point of view, instead of the therapist's interpretations. In fact, it is the client's responsibility to become sensitive to his or her inner experiences (Nye, 1992). Therapists are not supposed to lead the client. Instead, therapists act as companions, to help them "ride the wave" through feelings of hopelessness and emerge with greater understanding on the other side (Rice & Greenberg, 1991; Rogers, 1986).

Rogers (1986) proposes three conditions that are particularly likely to encourage growth in person-centered therapy:

1. **Congruence,** also known as genuineness; the therapist expresses what he or she genuinely feels, rather than maintaining a formal "I'm the expert" attitude;

2. **Unconditional positive regard,** or a positive, nonjudgmental attitude toward the client;

3. **Empathic understanding,** or the therapist's accurate feelings about the client's emotions.

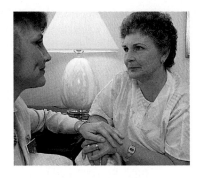

In Rogers's person-centered therapy, the client is central in discovering the answers; the therapist acts as a companion.

These conditions allow the therapist to enter the client's world, creating an atmosphere in which the client can move in advantageous directions (Gelso & Fretz, 1992). In fact, an important goal of therapy is not merely to solve current problems, but also to promote psychological growth.

An important tool in person-centered therapy is **active listening,** in which the therapist attempts to understand both the content and the emotion of a client's statement. The therapist then uses **reflection,** or summarizing content and emotion, communicating this summary back to the client. Rogers believes that it is valuable to offer a symbolic mirror that reflects the client's own views. Although active listening originated in person-centered therapy, it is now standard in most other therapeutic approaches. Now try Demonstration 16.1, which features an example of person-centered therapy.

Gestalt Therapy Another important humanistic approach is called Gestalt therapy (pronounced "Geh-*shtalt*"). This approach is usually traced to Fritz Perls (1893–1970). Perls spent his early years in Germany, where he became familiar with the Gestalt research on perception and cognitive processes, which we discussed in Chapters 1 and 4. The Gestalt approach to perception, for example, argues that we perceive objects as well-organized, whole structures, rather than separated, isolated parts. Gestalt therapy is somewhat similar because it emphasizes that—in healthy humans—the parts are also integrated into a whole being. However, the relationship between the classic Gestalt psychologists (who did not emphasize emotions or therapy) and current Gestalt therapists is not very strong (Sherrill, 1986).

The goal of **Gestalt therapy** is for clients to become aware of what they are doing and how they can change themselves, while also learning to accept and value themselves (Yontef & Simkin, 1989). Gestalt therapy emphasizes getting in touch

DEMONSTRATION 16.1   Person-Centered Therapy

In the following interview, Carl Rogers interacts with a 28-year-old client named Jim, who had been hospitalized for 19 months with the diagnosis of schizophrenia. Read through the interview once to understand the general method. Then read through again, noting the technique of reflection. During this second reading, pay particular attention to the following: (1) Rogers's congruence (his genuineness, rather than pompous formality); (2) unconditional positive regard; and (3) empathic understanding.

Client: I just ain't no good to nobody, never was, and never will be.

Therapist: Feeling that now, hm? That you're just no good to yourself, no good to anybody. Never will be any good to anybody. Just that you're completely worthless, huh?—Those really are lousy feelings. Just feel that you're no good at all, hm?. . .

Client: I'm gonna take off.

Therapist: You're going to take off? Really run away from here? Is that what you mean? Must be some—what's the—what's the background of that? Can you tell me? Or I guess what I mean more accurately is I know you don't like the place but it must be that something special came up or something?

Client: I just want to run away and die. . . . All day yesterday and all morning I wished I were dead. I even prayed last night that I could die.

Therapist: I think I caught all of that, that—for a couple of days now you've even prayed for that. One way this strikes me is that to live is such an awful thing to you, you just wish you could die, and not live.

[During the following interchange, the two explore Jim's statement about wanting to die, or at least leave the hospital.]

Client: I might go today. Where, I don't know, but I don't care.

Therapist: Just feel that your mind is made up and that you're going to leave. You're just—just going to leave, hm?

Client: (Muttering in discouraged tone) That's why I want to go, 'cause I don't care what happens.

Therapist: Huh?

Client: That's why I want to go, cause I don't care what happens.

Therapist: M-hm, m-hm. That's why you want to go, because you really don't care about yourself. You just don't care what happens. And I guess I'd just like to say—I care about you. And I care what happens. . . . (Jim bursts into tears and unintelligible sobs.)

Source: (Based on Rogers, 1987, pp. 202–205)

with one's feelings at this very moment. It places more emphasis on feelings than on thoughts, and more emphasis on the present than on the past. In addition, it encourages clients to take responsibility for their own feelings, rather than searching for the historical basis of these reactions. Although person-centered therapy and Gestalt therapy have somewhat different emphases, they both focus on helping people discover their genuine emotions.

Behaviorist Approaches

Behavior therapy uses the principles of learning theory to encourage appropriate behavior and eliminate undesirable behavior. In other words, behavior therapists apply techniques based on the principles of classical and operant conditioning that we discussed in Chapter 6. An important feature of behavior therapy is that the therapist and the client explicitly specify the treatment goals in terms of observable behavior. (In contrast, therapists who favor the classical psychoanalytic or the humanistic approaches would be reluctant to list specific goals.) Let us consider systematic desensitization, which is based on classical conditioning, as well as some behavior modification techniques.

Systematic Desensitization The goal of **systematic desensitization** is to reduce fear or anxiety by gradually exposing the client to increasingly anxiety-provoking versions of the feared stimulus, while he or she is relaxed. The purpose of systematic desensitization is to extinguish learned fearful reactions. During the first phase, the therapist and client work together to construct a **fear hierarchy,** with the least anxiety-provoking items at the beginning and the most terrifying items at the end. For example, a student with a phobia about fire might place at the beginning of the list, "looking at an unlit candle." The item at the end of the list might be "lighting a candle with a match" (Halgin & Whitbourne, 1993).

The client is then given systematic relaxation training, learning to relax all muscles while imagining being in a serene, beautiful place. The reasoning behind this technique is that anxiety is not compatible with relaxation.

After the client has learned to relax, the therapist presents the item at the beginning of the fear hierarchy. If the client feels anxious, the therapist immediately encourages the relaxing imagery. Gradually, they work their way through the hierarchy. Therapy sometimes involves imagining the feared stimulus. Other times, therapy uses **in vivo treatment,** (pronounced "in *vee*-voe"), in which clients interact with the actual feared object. For example, in vivo treatment of a snake phobia might involve a final goal of actually handling a live snake. In general, the research demonstrates that in vivo treatment is more effective than treatment in which clients simply imagine the feared stimulus (Emmelkamp et al., 1992; Harris et al., 1991).

As you might imagine, systematic desensitization is especially useful in treating anxiety-based disorders. The technique has been used successfully with both adults and children, in treating problems such as simple phobias, social phobia, agoraphobia, obsessive-compulsive disorder, and posttraumatic stress disorder (Bowers, 1991; Gournay, 1989b; Zinbarg et al., 1992).

Behavior Modification As you may recall from Chapter 6, **behavior modification** is the systematic use of techniques from learning theory to change human behavior. When therapists use the phrase, they usually imply the use of operant conditioning, rather than classical conditioning (Eysenck, 1991). In other words, appropriate behavior is shaped through the use of rewards and punishment. Consider an example in which an entire ward in a mental hospital adopted a token economy, with tokens awarded for good behavior. Ayllon and Azrin (1968) rewarded the residents for activities such as combing their hair and doing work on the ward. These token re-

Systematic desensitization is used to help people overcome their phobia about flying in an airplane. Training is especially effective when it involves contact with the feared object. This program includes a step in which clients experience a plane flight.

wards could later be exchanged for special activities, such as listening to records and watching movies. Grooming and performing chores both increased so dramatically that other institutions soon adopted token economies. These token economies have also been used successfully to treat behavior problems of children in classroom settings, delinquent adolescents, and adults with psychological disorders who live at home (Lazarus & Fay, 1984).

A second operant conditioning technique uses behavioral contracts and record-keeping to change unwanted behaviors. The client works together with the therapist to devise a contract, which describes specific goals that are desirable for the client. Behavioral contracts must involve goals that the client considers important, or they will not be successful. During treatment, the client keeps a careful record of the relevant behavior. Consider, for example, how this method can be used to reduce bulimic episodes, in which a client consumes large quantities of food. For instance, a therapist asked a bulimic college student named Andrea to keep a systematic record of her bingeing and vomiting episodes (Kuehnel & Liberman, 1986). She also kept notes about when each episode occurred, in an effort to identify situations that triggered the problem behaviors.

One instrumental conditioning technique is record keeping. This therapist is instructing her client about how to keep systematic records on certain targeted behaviors.

Andrea and the therapist worked out a set of short-term goals. For example, within the first month, she should reduce the vomiting episodes from the current level of six times a week to two times a week. They also established long-term goals, specifying the complete elimination of vomiting and the reduction of bingeing to once a month. By the end of the therapy sessions, six months later, Andrea had eliminated the problem behaviors. A similar program, using behavioral techniques with 14 bulimics, demonstrated a better recovery rate than in a control group that had no goal setting or record keeping (Kirkley et al., 1985).

Behaviorists stress that clients should pay attention to *when* the problem behavior occurs, because this information provides hints for therapy. For instance, one man who wanted to quit smoking noticed that he was likely to smoke in social settings—while having coffee with friends or when talking on the phone. The behavioral program he worked out allowed him to smoke only in the bathroom (hardly a social setting!). Smoking was no longer pleasurable, and he quit smoking after one month. A follow-up one year later revealed that he was still not smoking (Martin & Pear, 1983).

If you are intrigued by behaviorist techniques, you may wish to turn back to Demonstration 6.3 on page 193. This demonstration showed how behavior modification methods can increase or decrease certain behaviors. Keep in mind, however, that behavior therapists have completed extensive training. Do not plan a major transformation on your own, or you may be disappointed.

A more controversial behavioral method is **aversion therapy,** in which inappropriate behavior is followed by punishment. As you can imagine, many professionals oppose using any form of punishment with clients, because of the ethical problems of delivering painful stimuli and because—as we saw in Chapter 6—punishment is generally less effective than reinforcement (Sandler & Steele, 1991). Sherman (1990) describes a situation in which aversion therapy may be justifiable. A severely retarded woman had a habitual behavior of slamming her arm into the side of her head, using such force that both her arm and head were bloody. Baseline records showed that she hit herself as often as 423 times in a 16-minute period.

After all other behavioral techniques had failed, the therapist devised an effective program that involved a quick slap to her thigh whenever she beat her head. (Interestingly, the pain from the slap was much milder than the pain she had given to herself.) Sherman stresses, however, that she was simultaneously rewarded with hugs, small bites of food, and praise for periods in which she did *not* hit her head. This combination of behaviorist techniques effectively decreased the frequency of self-abuse. Obviously, aversion therapy is usually only a last resort—and then only if appropriate behavior is rewarded.

Let us summarize the behaviorist approaches by comparing them with the extremely different psychodynamic approaches. Psychodynamic therapists believe that people are driven by hidden conflicts of which they are unaware. In contrast, behaviorists emphasize that people can be objective and rational, able to identify their problems (Messer, 1986). Psychodynamic therapists believe that therapy should address the underlying, unconscious dynamics, not the symptom. However, behaviorists target the symptom itself by eliminating inappropriate behaviors and promoting appropriate behaviors; if you successfully change the behavior, you have eliminated the problem (Eysenck, 1991). Finally, psychodynamic therapists concentrate on the past history that could have produced the problem, whereas behaviorists concentrate on the present, observable behavior.

Cognitive Approaches

The behaviorist approaches we have discussed emphasize observable behaviors and well-defined problems. In contrast, the cognitive approaches emphasize people's *thoughts.* **Cognitive therapy** proposes that people are plagued by psychological disorders because their thinking is inappropriate or maladaptive; recovery requires a restructuring of the client's thoughts. Furthermore, a change in the client's thoughts will produce a change in his or her behavior (Dobson & Block, 1988).

In the 1990s, cognitive therapy has become one of the most prominent and most widely used approaches to psychological disorders (Haaga & Davison, 1991; Persons, 1989). It has been a standard therapy for depression for some time (Beck, 1991). However, cognitive therapy is now also used in treating anxiety-based disorders such as panic attacks and hypochondriasis (Adler, 1991; Warwick & Salkovskis, 1989), schizophrenia (Brenner et al., 1989), and personality disorders (Beck & Freeman, 1990). As you might imagine, its emphasis on thought processes makes it less suitable for young children, but it is effective for children who are old enough to think abstractly (Durlak et al., 1991).

You are likely to see several variations of the name *cognitive therapy.* For instance, those who favor Albert Bandura's personality theory may refer to *social cognitive therapy.* Those who borrow some of the behaviorist techniques and combine them with cognitive therapy may use the name *cognitive-behavior therapy.* The distinction between the names *cognitive therapy* and *cognitive-behavior therapy* is actually fairly blurred (Brewin, 1988; "Treatment of Mood Disorders," 1988).

In this section, we will discuss three major cognitive approaches: Albert Ellis's Rational-Emotive Theory, Aaron Beck's cognitive therapy, and Donald Meichenbaum's stress-inoculation training. Although the details of these techniques differ, all three emphasize **cognitive restructuring,** an approach that focuses on changing one's maladaptive thought patterns (Golden & Dryden, 1987).

Ellis's Rational-Emotive Therapy This cognitive approach was founded in 1955 by Albert Ellis, a clinical psychologist practicing in New York City. Ellis originally tried a psychodynamic approach, but he felt that this technique was not particularly effective or scientifically based (Wiener, 1988). He became increasingly convinced that people's emotions depend upon the way they structure their thoughts. Ellis's approach emphasizes that irrational thoughts cause psychological disorders. Here are several of the unreasonable beliefs he frequently noticed among his clients (Ellis & Harper, 1975):

1. I must have love and approval from the people I care about—at *all* times.
2. I must be thoroughly competent and achieving.
3. When I am frustrated or rejected, it is a major catastrophe.
4. Because something influenced my life in the past, it must continue to dominate my life.

DEMONSTRATION 16.2 Disputing Irrational Beliefs

Take a few minutes to identify a personal belief that you suspect may be irrational. Often, these irrational beliefs are based on the idea that you must be perfect or must satisfy everyone. Here are some examples:

"I must win the approval of everyone in my sorority."

"I must meet my parents' expectations at all times."

"I should receive an A in each of my courses this semester."

Now complete the following questions (based on Ellis, 1979).

1. What irrational belief do you want to dispute and give up? (Describe this belief in some detail.)
2. Can you rationally support this belief?
3. What evidence do you have that this belief is true?
4. What evidence do you have that the belief is false?
5. What are the worst possible things that could actually happen to you if you do not achieve the goal specified in Item 1?
6. What good things could happen or could you make happen if you never achieve the goal specified in Item 1?

Does this technique help you think more flexibly about this particular belief?

Ellis points out that people create problems for themselves when they go beyond the data at hand and overgeneralize (Dryden & Ellis, 1987). For instance, a man who observes a group of people laughing may infer (without any rational evidence) that they are laughing at him. He may draw other irrational conclusions such as, "They think I am stupid" and "I am an incompetent, rotten person."

Basically, **Rational-Emotive Therapy** (or **RET**) encourages people to examine their beliefs carefully and rationally, to make positive statements about themselves, and to solve problems effectively. Ellis first works with his clients to detect irrational beliefs. These beliefs are likely to contain words such as "should," "must," and "always." Ellis then urges clients to debate their irrational beliefs. Demonstration 16.2 encourages you to debate yourself about an irrational belief that you might have.

Consider how Ellis (1986) used the technique of debating irrational beliefs to help a woman named Jane, who was overly anxious about social interactions. She was extremely shy and felt very incompetent about talking with men. Ellis encouraged Jane to debate several unreasonable beliefs, such as, "Where is it written that I *have* to be interesting and clever?" and "When I don't speak well and impress people, how does that make me a stupid, inadequate person?" (p. 281).

Jane was also encouraged to construct some positive statements to repeat to herself several times a day, such as "I *can* speak up to others, even when I feel uncomfortable doing so" and "I'm an intelligent person." Finally, Ellis worked with her on strategies for solving practical problems, such as how to meet appropriate men and how to handle job interviews. Notice, then, that Rational-Emotive Therapy can emphasize behaviors as well as cognitions. It encourages people to develop practical skills and changes in behavior, not simply a new way of thinking about the world (Brewin, 1989; Moses, 1989). Furthermore, Ellis urges clients to continue developing their ability to think rationally when they encounter new stresses in the future (Huber & Baruth, 1989).

Beck's Cognitive Therapy In Chapter 15, our discussion of the social cognitive approach to depression noted Aaron Beck's proposal that depressed people have negative schemas about themselves and life events. **Beck's cognitive therapy** attempts to correct these systematic errors in reasoning, known as cognitive distortions. Some of the reasoning errors that this therapy addresses includes the following (Beck, 1991; Weishaar & Beck, 1987):

1. Drawing a conclusion based on a detail taken out of context, and ignoring other relevant information;

2. Overgeneralization, or drawing a general rule from one or just a few isolated incidents and applying the conclusion broadly to unrelated situations;

3. Mental filtering, or dwelling on a negative detail while ignoring the positive side;

4. "All-or-nothing" thinking, so that experiences must be categorized as either completely good or completely bad, rather than somewhere in between the two extremes.

5. Automatic thoughts, or negative ideas that emerge quickly and spontaneously. (As we saw in the "In Depth" section in Chapter 15, depressed people make very rapid, pessimistic judgments about their futures.)

In many respects, Albert Ellis's and Aaron Beck's approaches have similar goals, so it is easy to confuse them. But Ellis targets a fixed number of specific irrational beliefs, whereas Beck identifies a more general tendency to develop a negative self-schema, so that the client's entire attitude is consistently pessimistic. The specific methods of the two therapists also differ, with Ellis more likely to instruct and lecture, and Beck more likely to encourage clients to discover and test their irrational beliefs on their own.

Consider how Beck's cognitive therapy helped one young man who was planning to postpone his dream of going to college. He argued that people would consider him stupid if he did not appear completely confident and sure of himself (Weishaar & Beck, 1987). The therapist urged him to design an experiment to test his beliefs. At college registration, he asked several students for directions, for information regarding schedules, and for help with a confusing computerized list. Following the experiment, he reported that every one of the students had been friendly, and they were often as confused as he. In fact, by gathering information with his questions, he was also able to help other lost students. The experiment helped him develop a positive attitude toward college and toward his own abilities. He also learned that his original view of reality was quite different from what actually occurred.

Many studies have demonstrated that cognitive therapy techniques are successful in helping people with severe depression as well as less serious mood disorders treated in college counseling centers (Beck, 1991; Dobson, 1989; Hogg & Deffenbacher, 1988; Hollon et al., 1987). For example, a meta-analysis combined the results of 69 studies on the effectiveness of self-statement modification. The technique of **self-statement modification** encourages people to replace negative statements about themselves with more positive statements. The average person who used this technique was better adjusted after therapy than 77% of people in a control group (Dush et al., 1983). Thus, self-statement modification does not help everyone, but it is reasonably effective.

Meichenbaum's Stress Inoculation Training Donald Meichenbaum (1985) agrees with Ellis and Beck that clients should use cognitive restructuring, but his technique is more focused on eliminating future stress, rather than reinterpreting past failures. Specifically, **stress inoculation training** helps people to prepare for difficult or unpleasant situations by anticipating problems and practicing methods of controlling stress. Clients are taught relaxation techniques and problem-solving methods. Then they develop some helpful statements that can guide them through a crisis. For example, a young woman might devise a series of statements she can say to herself when she gives a presentation in front of her speech communications class: "It's natural to feel tense"; "Worrying is only going to make me more nervous"; and "Take a deep breath." Notice, then, that these cognitive statements can be used to guide and shape behavior.

Suppose that a student is reluctant to attempt college registration because he or she believes that others will interpret questions as a sign of stupidity. Cognitive therapy would suggest that the student test the validity of these beliefs in an actual registration situation.

TABLE 16.2 The Four Major Approaches to Treating Psychological Disorders

	THERAPY APPROACH			
	Psychodynamic	**Humanistic**	**Behaviorist**	**Cognitive**
1. Psychological component emphasized	Emotions	Emotions	Behaviors	Thoughts
2. Source of the problem	Childhood problems and unconscious conflicts	Blocking of full development	Inappropriate learning	Maladaptive thinking
3. Focus of therapy	Bring the conflict to consciousness	Discover true emotions and goals	Identify and correct specific undesirable behaviors	Restructure maladaptive thinking
4. Techniques of therapy	Psychoanalysis, using free association and dream analysis	Conversations, largely guided by client	Systematic desensitization and behavior modification	Client conducts self-statement modification, stress-inoculation

Note: For simplicity's sake, the psychodynamic approach is represented by Freud's classic psychoanalytic treatment.

To summarize, the cognitive therapies propose that psychological disorders are caused by maladaptive thinking, not by unconscious conflicts (psychodynamic theory), or blocking of full development (humanistic therapy), or inappropriate conditioning (behaviorist approaches). Cognitive therapy focuses on current or future problems and uses a variety of techniques to encourage clients to think more logically. Table 16.2 summarizes the four major therapies we have discussed, and it will help you clarify the similarities and differences. We will compare the effectiveness of these methods in a later section.

Other Psychotherapies

Even when we consider the numerous variations of the four major approaches to psychotherapy, the total is only a portion of the hundreds of different kinds of psychotherapy currently available. The diversity of these other approaches is impressive. In some, the therapist says and does nothing. In others, people are symbolically reborn. Still other approaches treat clients as children, or encourage them to scream or to meditate quietly (Corsini, 1989). Two general approaches that can be used with the methods we have discussed and also encompass many of the other psychotherapies are group therapy and family therapy.

Group Therapy In **group therapy,** the therapist works with an interacting group of seven or eight people who have something in common. The therapist usually does not actively direct the conversation, but lets it unfold naturally. The group is encouraged to use its own resources and to develop a sense of belonging and common goals (Meissner, 1988; Woody et al.; 1989). Although many of these groups are mostly inspired by the humanistic or psychodynamic approaches, they may also use some behaviorist or cognitive techniques (Long, 1988; Tuttman, 1992).

One of the major advantages of group therapy is that it encourages people to realize that others have similar problems—they are not alone. Consider how group therapy can help gay men struggling in a society that is biased against gay people (Dworkin & Gutiérrez, 1992; Schwartz & Hartstein, 1986). In group therapy, the men would not need to hide their sexual orientation. They can rapidly identify with the group, yet they can appreciate the diversity of gay relationships. Together, they can deal with the fact that they may have internalized some of society's biases, feeling somewhat guilty and apologetic, rather than proud of their identity. They can share

Group therapy is helpful for people who share similar problems.

strategies about dealing with mutual problems, such as relationships with family members or coming out (telling others that they are gay). Group therapy can also be helpful for widows or widowers, people with disabling diseases, alcoholics, and people whose relatives have problems.

Family Therapy As the name implies, **family therapy** considers the entire family—not just one family member—to be the client. According to the family therapy approach, families show recurring patterns of interactions, and many problems involve disturbed relationships among several family members—rather than just a single person (Goldenberg & Goldenberg, 1991; Hazelrigg et al., 1987). Furthermore, the family's dysfunction may reveal itself in the symptoms of one or more family members. Generally, therapy includes all members of the nuclear family—even younger children. The approach and goals of family therapy resemble those of group therapy, except that the family is a preformed group whose members have interacted for many years before coming to therapy (Meissner, 1988).

Consider the case of the Chapin family, who sought family therapy when their 16-year-old son was suspended from school (Taylor, 1986). The therapist met with the parents and their four children to sort out problems. These problems involved not only the one son, but also the husband's resentment about the wife's new job, the wife's overprotectiveness, and the troubled interactions among the children. By the time the Chapins ended their therapy sessions, they were not problem free, but they had resolved the crises and had figured out how to handle future difficulties.

S E C T I O N   S U M M A R Y
PSYCHOTHERAPY APPROACHES

- Sigmund Freud's psychoanalytic technique used free association and dream analysis to help people examine childhood experiences and make them aware of unconscious conflicts; other psychoanalytic concepts include transference, resistance, and insight.

- Current psychodynamic therapy is more likely than classical psychoanalytic techniques to emphasize social interactions; brief psychodynamic therapy is shorter and more focused; interpersonal psychotherapy is a brief psychodynamic therapy that focuses on current interactions with other people.

- Humanistic approaches stress that people have tremendous potential for growth and self-actualization; therapy involves removing the blocks to personal growth.

- In Carl Rogers's person-centered therapy, the therapist encourages growth by showing congruence, unconditional positive regard, empathic understanding, active listening, and reflection. Gestalt therapy emphasizes clients' getting in touch with their current feelings.

- Behaviorist approaches try to eliminate undesirable behavior by using the principles of learning, such as systematic desensitization and behavior modification techniques.

- The cognitive approaches argue that psychological disorders can be corrected by restructuring the client's maladaptive thoughts.

- Albert Ellis's Rational-Emotive Therapy encourages people to examine their beliefs rationally, to make positive statements about themselves, and to solve problems effectively. Aaron Beck's cognitive therapy encourages people to discover that their pessimistic self-schemas are not logical or realistic. Donald Meichenbaum's stress inoculation training helps people anticipate problems and practice methods of controlling stress.

- Other approaches to therapy, which also can be combined with the previous methods, include group therapy and family therapy.

BIOLOGICAL TREATMENTS

We have discussed several psychotherapy approaches to psychological disorders. People recall their dreams, figure out how to eliminate roadblocks, learn new behavior patterns, or devise alternative ways of viewing their lives. In all these approaches, however, therapists focus attention on emotions, behaviors, and thoughts. In contrast, biological treatments emphasize the physiology of the central nervous system. These biological approaches therefore focus on neurotransmitters, rather than theories of personality. The two most important biological approaches in the 1990s are drug therapies and electroconvulsive therapy.

Drug Therapies

During the early 1950s, a French surgeon was looking for a medication to calm his patients prior to anesthesia. He eventually tried chlorpromazine, a sedating antihistamine similar to remedies for the common cold. Chlorpromazine proved to be such an effective sedative that researchers eventually decided to give it to hospitalized people with psychological disorders (Delay & Deniker, 1952; McKim, 1991). The success of this drug in calming schizophrenics inspired researchers to investigate other drugs that could relieve psychological disorders. By the mid-1950s, several hundred thousand hospitalized people received drug treatment. They could now function well enough to leave the straitjackets and padded cells of mental hospitals and return to more normal lives in their communities.

As the name suggests, **drug therapies** involve treating psychological disorders with medication. In this chapter we will examine how drugs can be used to treat four important disorders that were discussed in Chapter 15: anxiety disorders, depression, bipolar disorder, and schizophrenia.

Treating Anxiety More people receive medication for anxiety than for any other psychological disorder (Schatzberg & Cole, 1991). **Antianxiety drugs** reduce tension and create drowsiness by depressing activity in the central nervous system. Some representative antianxiety drugs include Valium and Librium. Unfortunately, physicians sometimes prescribe these drugs too freely, when people might be better served by a therapist who could help determine the source of the anxiety rather than merely treating the symptoms (Hughes & Pierattini, 1992). In addition, these antianxiety drugs frequently produce side effects such as fatigue, memory disturbances, and poor balance. Another problem is that some highly anxious people—for instance, people with panic disorder—are reluctant to take any medications in the first place (Telch, 1988). Furthermore, people who stop taking these drugs often report withdrawal symptoms such as irritability, depression, and insomnia (Gitlin, 1990).

Some of the disorders related to anxiety are actually more successfully treated by antidepressant drugs, which we will consider in the next section. For example, antidepressants have been helpful in panic disorder and agoraphobia, generalized anxiety, obsessive-compulsive disorders, and posttraumatic stress disorder (Neziroglu & Yaryura-Tobias, 1991; Noyes, 1991; Walker & Ashcroft, 1989). As we will see, however, antidepressants also have some harmful side effects. In many cases, though, either antianxiety drugs or antidepressants may be useful for the short-term treatment of anxiety, fear, and tension, especially in combination with psychotherapy (Baldessarini & Cole, 1988).

Treating Depression A variety of **antidepressant drugs** can help make a person's mood more positive. For many years, the two major classes of antidepressants were the MAO inhibitors and the tricyclics. These two kinds of medications worked by different mechanisms, but both ultimately bolstered the action of two relevant neurotransmitters, serotonin and norepinephrine. Each is reasonably effective in relieving the symptoms of depression (Greenberg et al., 1992). However, each also needs to be prescribed with caution. For example, a person taking MAO inhibitors needs to avoid certain kinds of food, or blood-pressure disorders might arise (Hughes & Pierattini, 1992). Furthermore, overdoses of the tricyclic drugs can be lethal, so that people with suicidal tendencies should be given only a limited quantity at one time (Potter et al., 1991).

In 1988, a new drug was introduced called Prozac or fluoxetine; approximately 8 million people now take this antidepressant (Gutheil, 1991; Kramer, 1993). Prozac prevents serotonin from being reabsorbed, thereby raising the level of available serotonin. Many people greeted Prozac as the new "miracle drug," especially because it seemed to have less troublesome side-effects. However, several studies have shown that Prozac and other new antidepressants do not seem to be any more effective than the more established antidepressants (Greenberg et al., 1992; Potter et al., 1991).

Antidepressants cannot help everyone who suffers from depression. They are most effective for people who are severely depressed, who have had previous depressive episodes, and whose family history suggests a genetic component. In the future, researchers may be able to identify several distinct kinds of depression, some not responsive to medication and some responsive to different classes of antidepressants. However, no methods can currently predict who will be most likely to respond to drug therapy (Andreasen, 1984; Potter et al., 1991). A further problem is that the drugs work slowly, often requiring two to six weeks for a person to respond (Holden, 1991b).

Despite their drawbacks, antidepressants can be extremely effective when combined with psychotherapy in helping many people function more normally. For example, Joan Nobiling is an advocate for people with psychological disorders; she herself suffers from depression. After she gave a presentation at my college, I asked her to provide a summary of how she felt medication had helped her:

Medication is a must for me. I find it impossible, no matter how much assistance I receive from family, friends, my psychiatrist, or my self-help method, to function without first having my chemical imbalance "balanced." That's what medications, in my case an MAO inhibitor and Trilafon, an anti-psychotic drug, do for me. Then I'm able to use all of my supports, and I am able to enjoy living.

It's like someone who's drowning. They have to be able to get their head up from under the water to breathe. Then they can resume swimming. (Nobiling, 1991)

Joan Nobiling, an advocate for people who have psychological disorders, feels that medication is an essential part of her treatment.

Treating Bipolar Disorders The most effective treatment for bipolar disorders is lithium. If you have taken a chemistry course, you may recall an element in the upper left-hand corner of the periodic table called *lithium*—hardly a substance you would expect to find in a psychology course! Nevertheless, **lithium** is very useful in treating bipolar disorders. As Goodwin and Jamison (1990) conclude in their respected book on bipolar disorders, "To be sure, even the combination of drugs and psychotherapy cannot yield a completely satisfactory outcome for every patient. But the treatment approaches now available do allow most manic-depressive patients to lead relatively normal lives . . . " (p. 597).

Like sodium, its chemical relative, lithium is present in the human body. Therapeutic doses of lithium seem to affect all major neurotransmitters, but no comprehensive explanation has been developed to explain exactly *how* lithium works (Gitlin, 1990; Lazarus, 1986). Lithium is typically first administered in a hospital, so that the level of the drug in the bloodstream can be carefully monitored; an overdose can be toxic, and too little medication is ineffective (Gitlin, 1990). In straightforward cases, a frantically manic person—like the man described in Chapter 15 who was devising grandiose plans for Olympic tryouts—can return to normal in several days. Unfortunately, however, people who are experiencing a manic episode may resist taking any medication because they do not wish to diminish their energy and productivity.

Treating Schizophrenia At the beginning of this section on drug therapies, we noted the accidental discovery that chlorpromazine dramatically aided schizophrenia. Chlorpromazine is one of the **antipsychotic drugs,** which reduce symptoms of schizophrenia such as agitation, confusion, delusions, and hallucinations. This drug and other antipsychotics are especially helpful in decreasing symptoms such as hallucinations and agitated motor movements. They typically have little effect on symptoms such as flat affect and impoverished speech (Hughes & Pierattini, 1992).

Most antipsychotics operate by binding onto the receptors associated with the neurotransmitter dopamine. As a result, dopamine cannot reach the receptors; a reduction in dopamine diminishes many schizophrenic symptoms.

Numerous other antipsychotics have been developed since chlorpromazine. In general, the challenge is to find a medication for which the **target effects** (or improvement of the major symptoms of a disorder) outweigh the **side effects** (undesirable medical or psychological problems). For example, antipsychotics often make people drowsy and less alert (Whitaker, 1992). Between 10% and 40% of people who take the standard antipsychotics develop a condition called tardive dyskinesia (Gitlin, 1990; Herz et al., 1989). **Tardive dyskinesia** is characterized by involuntary body movements and abnormal gait in walking. Unfortunately, this disorder is typically irreversible. To avoid tardive dyskinesia and other harmful side effects, some researchers recommend using the antipsychotic drugs only when a relapse is occurring (Herz et al., 1989).

Another hopeful alternative is a new antipsychotic called clozapine. Clozapine seems to reduce schizophrenic symptoms, with minimal side effects. However, white blood cells must be monitored, because clozapine inhibits the production of white blood cells in about 2% of the population. Mysteriously, clozapine does not seem to operate by blocking dopamine—still more evidence about the complexity of neurotransmitters in psychological disorders (Hughes & Pierattini, 1992).

When antipsychotic medications are effective, they can have extremely specific target effects. Consider Miss R., a young woman with schizophrenia. Her hallucinations included hearing voices saying the letter A. Just as Hester Prynne was forced to wear the letter A (for adultery) in Hawthorne's *The Scarlet Letter,* Miss R. believed that voices haunted her with the letter A to remind her about her own previous sexual activities. With antipsychotic medication, Miss R. reported a 75% reduction in the frequency of hearing the letter A, as well as a reduction in other symptoms such as delusions (Janowsky, 1986).

Conclusions About Drug Therapies Without a doubt, drug therapies are an important component of treating many psychological disorders in the 1990s. In many cases, they can make seriously disturbed clients more receptive to therapy. However, every medication has some side effects. Also, in keeping with the theme of individual differences, medication seems to help some people without improving others. Obviously, any drug treatment should be monitored frequently and carefully, noting any side effects as well as any lack of target effects. Furthermore, psychologists would strongly argue that any disorder serious enough to be treated medically requires psychotherapy as well.

Electroconvulsive Therapy

Let us now turn our attention to a very different kind of biological treatment— one that may initially sound barbaric. In **electroconvulsive therapy (ECT)**, a person receives a series of electric shocks that produce convulsions, which often relieve the symptoms of severe depression where other treatments have failed. ECT should not be considered for mild or moderate depression, but it can be useful when a person is overwhelmingly preoccupied with suicide or has delusions as well as severe depression (Gitlin, 1990; Potter et al., 1991).

A person scheduled for ECT is given a sedative and a muscle relaxant to reduce body movements during therapy. Then an electric current, about 100 volts in intensity, is passed through one or both hemispheres of the brain (see Figure 16.2). Treatment is repeated periodically for several weeks. We need to dispel some common misunderstandings: (1) The modern ECT method is *not* painful, though it may be slightly uncomfortable. (2) The convulsion, rather than the shock, produces the helpful effects. (3) A person who receives ECT awakes with no recall of the experience, and is typically less depressed. (4) The clear majority who have had ECT are positive about the effectiveness of ECT and would be willing to have it again if necessary (Abrams, 1988).

A meta-analysis of all the English-language publications on ECT has shown that this treatment is substantially more effective than either antidepressants or control-group treatments (Janicak et al., 1985). As a panel organized by the National Institutes of Health concluded, "Not a single controlled study has shown another

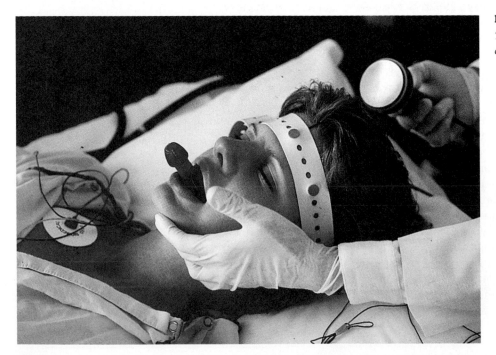

Figure 16.2

This woman is about to receive electroconvulsive therapy (ECT).

form of treatment to be superior to ECT in the short-term management of severe depressions" (Holden, 1985, p. 1511). Although some authors stress the substantial individual differences in the success of ECT, others agree with the positive assessments of its effectiveness (Endler, 1982; Sackeim et al, 1993; Scott 1989).

When treatment is supervised appropriately, physical problems are minimal. However, one important side effect is memory loss. ECT does cause temporary confusion; a typical person will not be able to recall his or her age until about half an hour after treatment (Daniel et al., 1987). People may also have some difficulty learning new material for about two months after the last ECT treatment (Gitlin, 1990). However, some would argue that modest and temporary memory problems are a relatively minor problem compared to the danger of suicide.

Table 16.3 summarizes the major biological treatments, that is, the four kinds of drug therapy and electroconvulsive therapy. Note that every one of these treatments carries a potential risk. In some cases, the risks may outweigh the benefits. However, in the case of severe disorders, the biological approaches can form the cornerstone of successful treatment. In many cases, they can eliminate symptoms of psychological disorders, making individuals more receptive to psychotherapy. Foreshadowing a point to be emphasized later in the chapter, though, it is important to note this point: If people had easy access to services that helped prevent psychological disorders or helped avoid a relapse, many drug prescriptions and ECT treatments would probably not be necessary.

TABLE 16.3 Summary of the Biological Treatments

KIND OF TREATMENT	PSYCHOLOGICAL DISORDER FOR WHICH TREATMENT IS INTENDED	TYPICAL BRAND NAMES	SIDE EFFECTS
I. Drug Treatments			
A. Antianxiety drugs	Anxiety disorders	Valium, Librium, Miltown, Equanil	Potential addiction, reduced effectiveness
B. Antidepressant drugs	Severe depression (Occasionally, anxiety)	MAO inhibitors: Nardil, Parnate, Marplan	Dry mouth, blood pressure disorders if some yeast products are eaten
		Tricyclics: Tofranil, Elavil	Weight gain, dry mouth, danger of suicide from overdose
		Prozac	Headache, upset stomach, nervousness
C. Lithium	Bipolar disorders	Eskalith, Lithobid, Lithonate	Digestive problems; drowsiness and motor problems if dosage is too high
D. Antipsychotics	Schizophrenia	Thorazine (chlorpromazine), Mellaril, Stelazine	Potential tardive dyskinesia, drowsiness, reduced alertness
		Clozapine	Inhibits white blood cell production in 2% of population
II. Electroconvulsive therapy (ECT)	Severe depression (with suicidal tendencies or delusions)	—	Temporary disorientation, potential loss of some memory

Source: Gitlin, 1990

S E C T I O N   S U M M A R Y
BIOLOGICAL TREATMENTS

- Antianxiety drugs reduce tension and depress activity in the central nervous system; however, they are often overprescribed.

- Antidepressants—such as MAO inhibitors, the tricyclics, and Prozac—can be useful for relieving severe depression for some individuals.

- Lithium can help people with bipolar disorders.

- The traditional antipsychotic drugs reduce some symptoms of schizophrenia; a new drug called clozapine may reduce many schizophrenic symptoms.

- Electroconvulsive therapy is useful for some severely depressed people; the most important drawback is potential memory loss.

ISSUES IN TREATING PSYCHOLOGICAL DISORDERS

So far we have emphasized a variety of psychological and biological approaches in treating psychological problems. We noted earlier, however, that many therapists prefer an eclectic approach, selecting the appropriate treatment from a variety of theoretical approaches. Furthermore, many therapists now favor drug therapy in combination with psychotherapy for people whose psychological disorders are severe (Gitlin, 1990).

Our discussion has occasionally noted that a particular therapy has been successful in treating a certain disorder. Now, however, we will focus more specifically on the question of evaluating psychotherapy. We will also discuss therapy and gender, as well as therapy with members of different ethnic groups. The chapter concludes with a discussion of community mental health.

IN DEPTH: Evaluating Therapeutic Approaches

Suppose that a friend seems deeply depressed. Should you recommend therapy? So far, you have read about a variety of approaches in which people explore hidden conflicts, remove roadblocks to self-actualization, learn new behavior patterns, and restructure their thoughts. Let us begin by examining whether psychotherapy is generally helpful, and then we will compare the effectiveness of various therapeutic approaches. In the final section, we will emphasize the similarities among the therapies.

Does Psychotherapy Work? As Chapter 2 emphasized, researchers often have difficulty measuring hidden psychological processes. If we want to discover whether psychotherapy works, we cannot look inside someone's ear at a dial labeled *Current Mental Health* and see whether the dial moves upward after therapy. How can we accurately measure a psychological process?

One such method of measurement mentioned in Chapter 2 is the self-report. Several dozen researchers have asked people to indicate their satisfaction with psychotherapy. In the typical study, about 75% said they were satisfied (Lebow, 1982). However, you can probably anticipate problems with this approach. For instance, the most depressed or anxious people may not have completed a questionnaire. Also, respondents may give socially desirable responses, rather than honest ones. Both of these factors would make the responses more optimistic than in reality.

Another problem is that these self-report studies seldom include a control group of people who did not participate in therapy. Some of the respondents could have shown **spontaneous remission,** that is, recovery without any therapy. Researchers can learn more from a study that compares people who have had psychotherapy and similar people who were assigned to a no-treatment control group. Furthermore, mental health should be measured either by objective tests, like those discussed in Chapter 14, or by a trained clinician who does not know whether a person is in the "therapy" or the "no-treatment" condition. These controlled experiments on the effectiveness of psychotherapy are labeled **outcome research.**

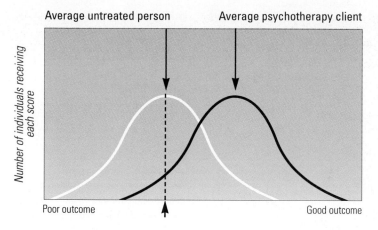

Average untreated person Average psychotherapy client

Adjustment of the person, after no treatment or psychotherapy

Figure 16.3

A comparison of the average psychotherapy client with the average untreated person. Note that most psychotherapy clients (80%) have an outcome that is more positive than the average untreated person (which is indicated by the arrow).

The first major analysis of outcome research was conducted by Hans Eysenck (1952), whose trait approach to personality was discussed in Chapter 13. Eysenck's surprising conclusion was that psychotherapy was not any more effective than no treatment at all. If other psychologists had agreed with Eysenck, they would have packed up their bags and switched professions . . . and you would not be reading this chapter more than 40 years later! Many critics challenged Eysenck's techniques and conclusions, inspiring more systematic research (Strupp, 1986).

The next landmark in outcome research occurred when Mary Lee Smith and her colleagues applied the meta-analysis technique to summarize the large number of studies that had been conducted (Smith & Glass, 1977; Smith, Glass, & Miller, 1980). In the 1980 study, for instance, they located 475 studies that compared a therapy group with an untreated control condition. On 88% of the comparisons, the therapy groups demonstrated greater improvement than the control groups.

Smith and her colleagues also analyzed the *amount* of improvement demonstrated in the studies. Figure 16.3 shows the distribution of scores for untreated people. As you can see, the distribution for psychotherapy clients is substantially more positive. For instance, the arrow indicates the score received by the average untreated person. (In this distribution, 50% receive a higher score than average, and 50% receive lower than average.) Of the psychotherapy clients, 80% received a score that was more positive than the score of the average untreated person. Psychotherapy does not benefit everyone, a conclusion that must be stressed. However, it is reasonably effective.

Which Psychotherapy Works Best? We saw the difficulty of testing whether psychotherapy is effective. An even trickier question is to ask which psychotherapy works best. In this section, we consider answers provided by meta-analysis and a large-scale study.

In their first meta-analysis, Smith and Glass (1977) compared several major psychotherapy approaches. Figure 16.4 shows their results, in terms of percentile scores in relationship to the no-treatment control group. If we set the average score for the control group at the 50th percentile, then the average score for the therapy groups ranged between the 60th and the 82nd percentile.

In general, many meta-analytic studies have shown that the behavioral and cognitive approaches are slightly but significantly more helpful than the psychodynamic and humanistic therapies (Dobson, 1989; Lambert et al., 1986; Shapiro & Shapiro, 1982). We need to stress, however, that the differences are small. Furthermore, a meta-analysis by Robinson and her colleagues (1990) controlled for another factor. Specifically, some researchers whose studies were included in the meta-analysis clearly favored one therapeutic approach over another. For example, a group of researchers from a behavioral tradition might compare behavioral therapy with psychodynamic therapy in treating depression. When Robinson and her coauthors took these initial preferences into account, no psychotherapy approach was superior to any other approach in treating depression. Also, this study showed that psychotherapy was comparable to drug therapy in its effectiveness, and both approaches worked better than no treatment at all.

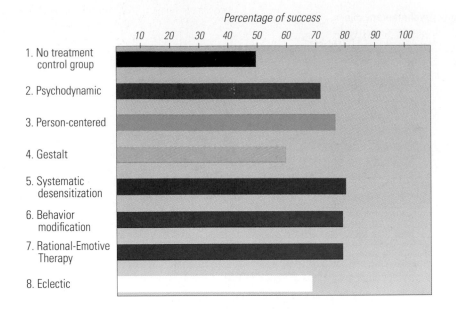

Percentage of success

1. No treatment control group
2. Psychodynamic
3. Person-centered
4. Gestalt
5. Systematic desensitization
6. Behavior modification
7. Rational-Emotive Therapy
8. Eclectic

Figure 16.4

The effectiveness of various kinds of psychotherapy, relative to no-treatment control (based on Smith & Glass, 1977). Note: *Therapeutic approaches are listed in the order discussed in this chapter. The success of each approach is listed relative to the average for the control group.*

Irene Elkin and her colleagues (1985, 1989) used a different approach to the question of which therapeutic approach works best. Their project focuses exclusively on depression, so that we do not need to be concerned that some therapies might be at a disadvantage because they are used with more serious disorders—a possible confounding variable in the Smith and Glass (1977) meta-analysis. Elkin's project compares three treatments: Beck's cognitive therapy (focusing on restructuring disordered thoughts), interpersonal psychotherapy (focusing on improving interpersonal relations and emotions), and a common antidepressant medication called imipramine. In addition, they included a pill-placebo condition. A **placebo** (pronounced "pluh-*see*-bow") is an inactive substance given to a control group instead of a medication. The clients may show some spontaneous remission in this condition and may also show improvement because they interact with a supportive, encouraging psychiatrist.

This study differed from previous, more limited studies because it employed 28 experienced therapists—each carefully trained in a therapeutic method—treating clients at three different locations in the United States. A total of 240 patients were randomly assigned to one of the four conditions, providing a well-controlled experiment.

After 16 weeks of treatment, each client was evaluated on several different tests by a clinical psychologist who was not aware of the client's treatment condition. Let us consider data that analyzed what percentage of people in each group could be considered "recovered" because they received low scores on a standardized depression scale. Elkin and her colleagues (1989) first analyzed the group of individuals who were initially only mildly or moderately depressed; surprisingly, the four treatment groups did not differ significantly from one another in their recovery rate. Follow-up research conducted over the next 18 months showed that the recovery rates remained similar for the four groups (Shea et al., 1992).

All this research on comparative therapy has inspired two other questions: (1) Are some people especially responsive to certain therapies? and (2) Do the therapies share underlying similarities?

Client-Treatment Interactions For some time, educators have acknowledged that some children learn better with one teaching approach, whereas others learn better with an alternative method (Snow, 1977). In the 1990s, psychotherapists are proposing a similar pattern called **client-treatment interaction;** perhaps some clients respond well to Therapy A, whereas other clients respond well to Therapy B (Shoham-Salomon & Hannah, 1991). As Smith and Sechrest (1991) argue, the research on therapy has shown that the various therapy methods produce similar success rates. However, perhaps all therapies would be more successful if therapists and clients worked together more closely to match each client with an appropriate therapy.

Perhaps Chris, who likes to examine his thoughts about relationships, would do best with interpersonal psychotherapy. In contrast, Pat might prefer to examine new cognitive interpretations of events; she might find cognitive therapy most helpful.

Clearly, the idea of client-treatment interactions matches our two themes about individual differences and the complexity of human psychological processes. At present, however, it is still in the hypothetical stages. Perhaps we can look forward to large-scale studies about the effectiveness of matching each client with a therapy approach that is most appropriate for each person's unique characteristics.

Underlying Similarities in Therapies This section has focused on differences among the therapies. However, we should also emphasize the similarities. All therapies offer support, reassurance, suggestions, and attention from the therapist. In all therapies, self-fulfilling prophecies may operate because clients anticipate that they *should* recover. Furthermore, all therapies share a common goal of reducing anxieties and improving the client's behavior, functioning, and self-efficacy—even though their specific routes to competent functioning may differ (Lambert et al., 1986; Strupp, 1986). Ideally, the therapist and the client form a **working alliance** in which the therapist's skills join together with the client's observational insights to facilitate the counseling process (Gelso & Fretz, 1992).

In addition, an active ingredient in all therapies is the personality of the therapist. Effective therapists of all persuasions are people who are warm, genuine, and caring. Therapists who encourage trust and develop empathy with their clients are more likely to provide successful therapy, no matter which approach they favor (Kokotovic & Tracey, 1990).

Therapy and Gender

Before you read further, try Demonstration 16.3, which focuses on gender. Gender issues are often relevant in therapy because therapists may encourage traditional gender roles in both women and men. For example, a woman who is depressed because of her low status at work and in her family will encounter further problems if her therapist conveys an attitude that suggests, "I'm the one who knows everything, and you are relatively powerless." In contrast, therapy will be helpful if her therapist can treat her as an active participant who has definite strengths (Lerner, 1989; Watson & Williams, 1992).

DEMONSTRATION 16.3 Beliefs about Gender

Read the following statements and place a check mark in front of each statement that you believe is correct. This demonstration is discussed later in the chapter.

_____ 1. If a man and a woman are doing equally well at the same job, they should receive equal pay.

_____ 2. If a man and a woman are doing equally well at the same job and they have been employed an equal number of years, they both should have the same chance of being promoted.

_____ 3. If a man and a woman perform equally well on a college examination, they should receive the same grade.

_____ 4. If a man and a woman perform equally well throughout college and are equivalent on all important measures, they

should both have the same chance of receiving admission to graduate school.

_____ 5. If a man and a woman perform equally well throughout college and are equivalent on all important measures, they should both have the same chance of being offered a prestigious job.

_____ 6. A man and a woman who are equally well qualified for political office should have an equal chance of being elected.

_____ 7. If a husband and a wife both spend the same number of hours on the job, they should spend the same number of hours on chores around the home.

_____ 8. A man has no right to physically abuse his wife, because she is not his "property."

Some potential biases against women in therapy include encouraging traditionally feminine gender roles and having low expectations for women clients (American Psychological Association, 1975; Hansen & Reekie, 1990). Another problem occurs when therapists have sexual relationships with their clients—obviously unethical conduct (Canadian Psychological Association, 1992; Pope, 1990).

Clearly, therapists should not harm the very people they are hired to help. Furthermore, both men and women deserve to be treated in an unbiased fashion.

In recent years, an increasing number of therapists have adopted a feminist approach to therapy. A **feminist** is a woman or man whose beliefs, values, and attitudes reflect a high regard for women as human beings (Hunter College Women's Studies Collective, 1983; Lerman, 1986b). Check over your own answers to Demonstration 16.3. If you have checked a large number of these items, you are a feminist. Notice that the definition emphasizes that men can be feminists, if they respect women and men equally.

A **feminist approach to therapy** argues that men and women should be valued equally, that women's inferior status in society often causes psychological problems, and that gender-stereotyped behavior harms both women and men (Betz & Fitzgerald, 1993; Matlin, 1993a). Feminist therapists argue that the therapist and client should be reasonably equal in power (Howard, 1986). Group therapy is often used to emphasize clients' potential for change (Kravetz, 1987).

Feminist therapy can be combined with other approaches. For example, Luepnitz (1988) describes how traditional family therapy often blames women for the family's psychological disorders. Luepnitz feels that the answer is *not* to start blaming men for children's problems but to help the entire family function more effectively. For example, a therapist can emphasize his or her own respect for a mother during family therapy, thus encouraging the entire family to develop greater appreciation for her contributions.

More recently, therapists have begun to focus on male gender roles, pointing out how the socialization of boys and young men creates later difficulties in intimate relationships, as well as psychological problems related to exaggerated gender roles (Betz & Fitzgerald, 1993; Osherson, 1987, 1992). In his presidential address to the American Psychiatric Association, Alan Stone declared, "There can be no new psychology of women that does not require a new psychology of men" (Stone, 1984, p. 14). Feminist therapists encourage us to create new therapy techniques to help both men and women become more fully human.

Therapy and Ethnic Group

At present in the United States, 11% of the population is Black, 9% Hispanic, 3% Asian, and 1% Native American (U.S. Bureau of the Census, 1992). In Canada, one in six residents was born outside the country (Beiser, 1990). As a consequence, North American clinicians need to be sensitive to different values and beliefs when they provide mental health services (Comas-Díaz & Griffith, 1988).

In general, Whites are more likely than other ethnic groups to use mental health services—even college counseling centers (Atkinson, 1987; Trimble & LaFromboise, 1985; Cheung, 1991). Some of the reasons for this underutilization by people of color include: (1) lack of awareness that mental health clinics exist; (2) shame in talking about personal problems to someone who is not a family member; (3) distrust of therapists, especially White therapists; (4) language barriers; (5) economic barriers; (6) reluctance to recognize that help is necessary; and (7) culturally based preference for nontherapy interventions such as prayer and rituals (Bernheim, 1990; Ho, 1987; Myers et al., 1991; Sue & Sue, 1985).

In most cases, a member of an ethnic group is not able to see a therapist from his or her own background. For example, the American Psychological Association includes about 65,000 PhD psychologists; of these, only 76 are Native Americans (DeAngelis, 1993). Even if a majority of those 76 were clinicians, they could not serve the Native American population of about 1.5 million people (LaFromboise, 1988). Most Native Americans who need psychological help will therefore see someone from a different ethnic background.

As we noted, language can be another barrier. For example, not many mental health professionals are fluent in Spanish, yet half of the Hispanic adult population speaks little or no English (Lorenzo, 1989). To help make the situation more vivid if your own first language is English, try imagining what it would be like to describe psychological problems to someone who speaks only Spanish. You may know enough Spanish to ask about the weather, but could you describe to a Hispanic therapist how and why you feel depressed? Could you precisely capture the subtleties of anxiety, let alone the terrors of schizophrenia?

Bias Against Some Ethnic Groups Although some research indicates that therapists are not biased in their approach to people of color, several studies suggest that we need to be concerned (Atkinson, 1985; Gong-Guy et al., 1991; López, 1989; Sue & Sue, 1990). Consider, for example, an experiment in which white psychiatrists were asked to look at a three-page summary of an interview with a 25-year-old male client with marital and work problems (Geller, 1988). This summary discussed his childhood, his anxiety symptoms, and his present social interactions. In addition, each psychiatrist received one of three additional descriptions (assigned at random): (1) the man was White, with an IQ of 120; (2) the man was Black, with an IQ of 120; and (3) the man was White, with an IQ of 85.

One of the most interesting findings was the psychiatrists' evaluation of the patient's ability to do the work required in psychotherapy. Those who judged the Black, 120-IQ man felt him to be significantly less verbal, competent, introspective, and knowledgeable about psychology, in comparison to those who judged *either* White man, even the one with a reported IQ of only 85. In other words, skin color influenced their judgments about intellectual capacity more than the measured intelligence scores. The psychiatrists were also more likely to recommend drug treatment for the Black man than for either of the White men. It is possible that this bias is at least partially responsible for the fact that Black people are much more likely than White people to be involuntarily committed to a mental institution (Lindsey & Paul, 1989).

Sometimes the assessment process is biased, though the therapist may not intend to be biased. For instance, Mexican-American clients were judged to have more emotional and thought disorders when they were interviewed in English than in Spanish (Martinez, 1986). Also, Puerto Ricans who took the Thematic Apperception Test (TAT) in English were judged to have more serious problems than they really had (Suarez, 1983). As you may recall from Chapter 14, the TAT requires people to tell a story about a picture. Pauses and inappropriate word usage are interpreted as evidence of psychological problems on this test—clearly a bias against those not fluent in English.

Traditional psychological tests, including projective assessments, have often been criticized for showing bias in assessing Hispanics and other people of color. Costantino and his colleagues (1988, 1991) have developed TEMAS (in English, the initials stand for Tell-Me-A-Story; in Spanish, the word means *themes*). TEMAS is a test that is similar to the TAT; it is a multicultural thematic apperception test for use with Hispanic, Black, and White children and adolescents. TEMAS presents a number of improvements over the traditional thematic apperception tests. For example, the pictures are in color and they show familiar situations. Also, the test requires the examiner to speak Spanish with Spanish-dominant examinees. Extensive normative and validity data make this test especially useful.

Therapy with People of Color We noted many reasons why people of color may avoid seeking help. Furthermore, those who do seek help are likely to search for

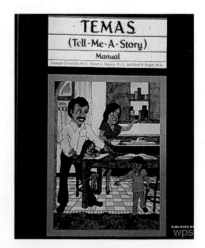

The cover of the TEMAS manual, published by Western Psychological Services. This picture shows a daughter doing her homework and a father telling his son to do his homework. TEMAS, like the TAT, is designed to test factors such as achievement motivation and interpersonal relationships.

any evidence of anxiety, rejection, or bias in the therapist (Baker, 1988). Clients who think the therapist is not supportive are not likely to return for another session. In general, the research shows that Blacks are more likely than Whites to report negative experiences with mental health professionals; comparable data are not available for other ethnic groups (Gary, 1987).

White therapists need to be flexible and eagerly committed to learning more about the culture of their clients from other ethnic groups. Here are some important general strategies that mental health professionals should keep in mind (Allodi, 1990; Boyd-Franklin, 1989; Comas-Díaz, 1989; Hunt, 1989; Sue & Sue, 1990; Trimble & LaFromboise, 1985):

1. Search the client's history for strengths that can promote the counseling process;

2. Encourage the client to be active in identifying and learning skills associated with positive growth;

3. Show empathy, caring, and an appreciation of human potential;

4. Be aware of any biased beliefs or feelings that might interfere with the counseling relationship;

5. Learn about the history, experiences, and cultural values of the client's ethnic group, but be aware of the diversity within any particular group; let the client teach you about his or her background;

6. Develop interventions that respect the client's cultural values; be aware that some therapy methods may be more successful than others; for example, McKinley (1987) reports a high success-rate for group therapy with Hispanic clients;

7. Be aware that refugees from some countries are likely to have experienced torture, which is associated with high levels of anxiety and depression;

8. Learn about appropriate patterns for nonverbal communication with clients from different ethnic groups; for example, Hispanics are more accustomed than Anglos to shaking hands as a greeting, as well as other forms of touching.

Techniques sensitive to culture are currently being developed to *prevent* psychological disorders, not just to treat them. For example, ongoing research with Puerto Rican children in New York City features *cuentos,* or Puerto Rican folktales (Costantino et al., 1986; Malgady et al., 1990). A panel of Puerto Rican psychologists and parents selected 40 stories with main characters from Puerto Rican folklore.

Dr. Giuseppe Costantino and Migdalia Coubertier discuss a cuento *with Puerto Rican mothers and their children, with a videotape of the* cuento *in the background.*

This photo illustrates the cuento *of Rosita who, feeling unloved by her mother and stepfather, decides to run away from home. As a runaway, she is exploited by unscrupulous circus owners. During one of her circus performances, she is happily reunited with her mother, who had been looking for her.*

These stories were then adapted, using an urban setting and secondary characters from different ethnic groups so that the stories would resemble the children's current experiences. The themes of the stories address issues such as compliance with parents' requests, control of anxiety, and the advantages of waiting for a reward. Therapists and mothers read the *cuentos* to the children, who ranged in age from kindergarten to third grade and had been previously identified as being at risk for psychological problems. The group met weekly for 20 weeks, each time discussing the stories after reading them together.

Figure 16.5 shows the scores on a measure of anxiety, taken one year after the therapy had ended. As you can see, the children in the *cuento* condition were substantially lower in anxiety than children in a treatment group that involved art and play therapy or those in a no-treatment control group. The method has also been adapted successfully with fourth- through sixth-graders, who constructed stories based on pictures of Hispanic characters in urban, family, and school settings (Costantino et al., 1993). Furthermore, Puerto Rican adolescents have responded favorably to stories based on male and female heroic role models from Puerto Rican history (Malgady et al., 1990). In short, this research provides a model of culture-sensitive therapy that could be adapted for use with other ethnic groups.

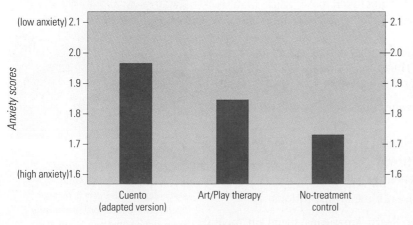

Figure 16.5

Anxiety scores for Puerto Rican children, measured one year after treatment (based on Costantino et al., 1986). Note: High scores indicate lower anxiety and better adjustment.

The Community Mental Health Approach

George Albee, a psychologist affiliated with the University of Vermont, describes his impressions when a cab driver took him to a psychiatric hospital in Brooklyn, New York, where Albee was scheduled to give a lecture:

> We drove through long stretches of Bedford-Stuyvesant, which looked a lot like a post-World War II bombed-out city. Buildings were boarded up, or scorched from fires; able-bodied men were passing around bottles in brown paper bags, teenagers who should have been in school were rapping on our cab windows and asking for quarters, teenage prostitutes shared the littered sidewalks with teenage mothers and teenage muggers. In short, we saw the pathology that characterizes this urban monument to an economic system which encourages discrimination, prejudice, involuntary unemployment, and that results in every form of social pathology. (Albee, 1987, p. 37)

Albee had arrived early, so he waited outside for an hour and was astonished to see a series of chauffeur-driven limousines pull up to the hospital entrance. A well-dressed woman emerged from each limousine. Obviously puzzled, Albee questioned one of the chauffeurs. The fellow responded, "Psychoanalysis . . . every day we bring our employers here for their hour-long psychoanalytic session." Albee suddenly realized that he was witnessing a prototype of the problems of the mental health system in the United States.

The irony is that millions of people with psychological problems will never come into contact with a therapist. At the beginning of the chapter we noted that roughly one in five North Americans is currently struggling with a psychological disorder. Many therapists, however, offer only one-on-one treatment, though some therapy does occur in small groups.

The **community psychology approach** to psychological disorders emphasizes that our current mental health policy is inadequate because it emphasizes hospitalization or one-on-one therapy sessions. Instead, the community psychology approach focuses on the prevention of psychological disorders as well as treatment in community mental health centers. Let us first consider the issue of preventing psychological disorders. Then we will discuss the implications of deinstitutionalization, as well as other options in the community.

Preventing Disorders As we saw in Chapter 15, the **sociocultural approach** to psychological disorders emphasizes that social and cultural factors are largely responsible for these disorders. As Albee argues, if we want to reduce the incidence of mental illness, we must attack the crucial social problems, such as poverty, prejudice, unemployment, and so forth (cited in Freiberg, 1991). In other words, we should change society to eliminate discrimination on the basis of gender, ethnic group, and other social categories—hardly an easy task! Notice that this approach—holding society accountable for problems—is very different and much more radical than tracing psychological disorders to an individual person's biological makeup or past experiences.

Some of the prevention techniques that community psychologists recommend include the following (Albee & Gullotta, 1986; The Commission on the Prevention of Mental-Emotional Disabilities, 1987a; Mirowsky & Ross, 1989):

1. Education, to help groups alter their behavior, learn problem-solving skills, and prepare for changes in their lives;
2. Health care, especially good prenatal nutritional and medical monitoring to reduce the danger of brain damage in newborns;
3. Promotion of feelings of competency, to enhance self-esteem;
4. Community organization, to try to improve our major institutions.

Only a small portion of the money that North Americans spend on mental health is funneled into prevention. As a result, most projects are small scale, though

According to the sociocultural approach, the way to address psychological disorders is through health care, education, community organization, and promotion of self-esteem.

the results are often encouraging. A typical project is the *cuento* approach with high-risk Puerto Rican children, described earlier. Another program offered a 10-week training program to women on welfare; the sessions emphasized life-coping skills and stress management. After training, the women were better at problem solving. They were also more likely to take charge of their lives, and they were less depressed (The Commission on the Prevention of Mental-Emotional Disabilities, 1987b). Perhaps by the late 1990s, public policy may be more likely to emphasize the prevention of psychological disorders.

Problems with Deinstitutionalization In the 1960s, the mental health system in the United States adopted a program of **deinstitutionalization,** or discharging people from mental hospitals into the community. In theory, this policy could be useful because it could return people to the supportive environment of family and friends. Deinstitutionalization could also encourage independence and coping abilities—certainly an admirable goal. In practice, however, the policy has not worked. For instance, many people who would have been in a psychiatric hospital are now cared for in general hospitals that do not have psychiatric units. In fact, more than 60% of all people admitted to hospitals because of psychological disorders are treated in short-term general hospitals (Kiesler, 1991). These hospitals are expensive and not particularly effective in treating psychological problems.

A major dilemma is that many people with long-term problems have nowhere to go when they are released from a hospital. Ideally, people could turn to support systems in the community, yet the hospitals that release them frequently have no plans for follow-up (Torrey, 1988b). According to one estimate, about 250,000 people with schizophrenia and bipolar disorder are now living in public shelters, in jails, and on the street, in contrast to only about 60,000 in state mental hospitals (Torrey, 1991).

As Levine and Rog (1990) emphasize, the homeless mentally ill population is probably the most disabled group of people in the United States. Because they do not have an established residence, they are usually excluded from programs designed to offer long-term services to people with psychological disorders. Several researchers estimate that between 28% and 37% of the homeless population experiences mental illness (Dennis et al., 1991). The stress and instability of homelessness ensure that even relatively problem-free people would develop psychological disorders. Some plans have been proposed by the National Institute of Mental Health, targeting homeless individuals with schizophrenia, major mood disorders, and other severe psychological disorders ("The Severely Mentally Ill," 1992), but the status of these proposals is currently uncertain.

According to studies, a large number of homeless people have psychological disorders.

The goal of deinstitutionalization was to provide care for the chronically mentally ill in the community and to help integrate them into the mainstream. Unfortunately, these efforts have failed (Bernheim & Lehman, 1985). The solution is not simply to put these people back into hospitals, but the current policy is certainly far from ideal.

Other Options in the Community The community psychology approach argues that the problem of mental illness is too complicated to be remedied by any single program. Instead, a systematic approach requires a variety of different organizations and services. These include community mental health centers, intermediate care facilities, hotlines, assistance for family members, and organizations for people with long-term mental illnesses.

Ideally, mental health centers should be available in the community to offer emergency services and education about preventing psychological disorders. They should also offer well-planned outpatient services, so that people could live at home and receive therapy and rehabilitation at the center. The centers could provide systematic aftercare for people who have been released from a hospital.

Intermediate care facilities should also be available. For instance, in a **halfway house,** people who have recently been discharged from a hospital live together with trained staff in a home and learn the skills necessary to live independently. Research on halfway-house programs show that they are effective in preventing psychiatric relapses, and they are also economical (Coursey et al., 1990).

Many communities sponsor a **crisis hotline,** a phone number to call for immediate counseling and comfort. These services are used not only by people who have already been hospitalized for a psychological disorder, but also by others who are experiencing a crisis—such as rape victims, drug abusers, victims of domestic violence, and people considering suicide. Hotline volunteers provide counseling and information about services available in the community.

The families of the mentally ill are another community resource. The majority of discharged mental patients return to live with their families. However, until recently, families were not counseled; instead, family members were frequently told by psychologists and psychiatrists that they were to blame for the problems in the first place (Lefley, 1989). Consider the stress a family faces when a family member with a serious psychological disorder lives at home. This person's symptoms may include bizarre speech, self-destructive ideas and behavior, social withdrawal, and lack of motivation. The family must figure out how to find services, how to cope with family conflicts, what to tell friends and neighbors, and how to reduce their own guilty feelings (Bernheim, 1989; Youngstrom, 1991).

These families also live with constant fears. As one parent commented,

> *There are no mental vacations. Even when you are physically away from the ill person, you are thinking about her, "Is she all right? Should I call to check? Did she remember to shut off the stove after cooking dinner? Did she wander out in the middle of the night?" (Bernheim et al., 1982, p. 76)*

Clearly, families deserve **family consultation,** or supportive family counseling to relieve their own anxieties and help make them more effective in providing for their disabled family member. These intervention programs have been shown to be successful for serious disorders such as schizophrenia (Smith, 1992).

Many families become involved in an organization called the National Alliance for the Mentally Ill (NAMI), a group that also welcomes people with psychological disorders as well as other interested people in the community. Members receive support, comfort, and helpful strategies from other families in similar situations (Backer & Richardson, 1989).

A final community resource is the people themselves—those living with psychological disorders. An excellent example of a community resource is Operation Friendship, in Rochester, New York. Operation Friendship is a psychosocial club run by community members who have psychological disorders. As stated in their brochure:

> *Our goal is to make OPERATION FRIENDSHIP a part of this community where our being present is not based on what is wrong with us, but rather on what we can do to be helpful, to contribute, a place where people believe in our potential to do a better job . . . where opportunities we need come together in one place. (Operation Friendship, 1989)*

Members of a community psychosocial group called Operation Friendship work together to do outreach with their membership.

Operation Friendship acknowledges that an important part of therapy is **empowerment,** or developing a sense of self-worth and control over one's own life (Rose & Black, 1985). People help themselves and each other with a variety of services and programs that include meals, trips, courses, self-esteem groups, and assistance in applying for jobs. As one member says, "You can experience something negative on the outside—like not getting the job you applied for—and you can recover like that . . . because you can come here and get support and acceptance, instantly" (Jacobson, 1987, p. 4C).

In summary, a comprehensive program for treating psychological disorders should involve some form of psychotherapy, either in groups or individually, appropriate drug therapy for more serious problems, and a variety of services available in the community. These community services should encourage families and individuals to develop a sense of empowerment and competence.

SECTION SUMMARY

ISSUES IN TREATING PSYCHOLOGICAL DISORDERS

- Research on psychotherapy shows that clients are generally satisfied; several meta-analyses confirm that psychotherapy clients are typically better adjusted after therapy, compared to controls.

- Meta-analyses comparing the different psychotherapy approaches show somewhat more positive outcomes for behavioral and cognitive approaches; a large-scale study by Elkin and her colleagues reported that treatment conditions were equally effective.

- According to the client-treatment interaction approach, some clients respond well to one kind of therapy, whereas others respond well to a different kind; however, all successful therapies share the characteristic of having a warm, caring therapist.

- The feminist approach to therapy argues that men and women should be valued equally and that the therapist and client should have more nearly equal power in therapy sessions; recently, some therapists have begun to address potentially harmful aspects of the male gender role.

- Whites are more likely than other ethnic groups to use mental health services, and some research (but not all) shows bias against people of color; therapists working with people of color should be alert to their own biases and be sensitive to cultural differences.

- The community mental health approach emphasizes the prevention of disorders, adequate follow-up for people discharged from hospitals, community mental health centers, halfway houses, crisis hotlines, family consultation, and community organizations for the mentally ill that encourage empowerment.

1. In one sentence each, describe how the following approaches explain the origin of psychological disorders: psychological (psychodynamic, humanistic, behaviorist, and cognitive), biological, and sociocultural.

2. In one sentence each, describe the therapeutic approach that corresponds to each of the theoretical approaches in the previous question.

3. In describing a feature shared by all psychotherapy approaches, Corsini (1989, p. 5) said, "All psychotherapies are intended to change people: to make them think differently (cognition), to make them feel differently (affection), and to make them act differently (behavior). Psychotherapy is learning." Using this description, point out how the four psychotherapy approaches each emphasize different components of that description.

4. Focusing on the classical psychoanalytic approach, describe two techniques that encourage the expression of the unconscious, as well as two other important processes that may occur during analysis. Also, describe how brief psychodynamic therapy differs from classical psychoanalysis. Finally, what are the features of interpersonal psychotherapy?

5. Suppose that a behaviorist was treating the young man who was afraid to go to college (described in connection with Beck's cognitive therapy). How would a behaviorist use systematic desensitization and behavior modification techniques to encourage him to register for classes?

6. Suppose that a therapist finds the cognitive and humanistic approaches most appealing. Describe how the approaches of Albert Ellis, Aaron Beck, and Carl Rogers could be integrated in treating someone who suffers from depression.

7. Your textbook described three cognitive approaches to psychotherapy. Describe each, pointing out their similarities and differences. How could you use each of these three approaches to help address a personal problem you wish could be corrected?

8. Considering the biological treatments for psychological disorders, list the treatment(s) that can be used for each of the following problems: (a) severe depression, (b) bipolar disorder, (c) schizophrenia, and (d) anxiety.

9. Suppose that a relative of yours is considering psychotherapy but wonders whether it would be worth the time and money. Based on the "In Depth" section, what would you reply, and what would you suggest about the specific therapeutic approaches to be used?

10. The chapter ends by considering the community approach to mental health. In an ideal society, how would your own community provide services to help prevent psychological disorders and meet the needs of people with psychological problems?

N E W   T E R M S

psychotherapy
cognitive-behavior therapists
eclectic approach
psychoanalysis
free association
dream analysis
manifest content
latent content
transference
resistance
insight
psychodynamic therapy
brief psychodynamic therapy
interpersonal psychotherapy
humanistic therapy
person-centered therapy
congruence
unconditional positive regard
empathic understanding
active listening
reflection
Gestalt therapy
behavior therapy
systematic desensitization
fear hierarchy
in vivo treatment
behavior modification
aversion therapy
cognitive therapy
cognitive restructuring

Rational-Emotive Therapy (RET)
Beck's cognitive therapy
self-statement modification
stress inoculation training
group therapy
family therapy
drug therapies
antianxiety drugs
antidepressant drugs
lithium
antipsychotic drugs
target effects
side effects
tardive dyskinesia
electroconvulsive therapy (ECT)
spontaneous remission
outcome research
placebo
client-treatment interaction
working alliance
feminist
feminist approach to therapy
community psychology approach
sociocultural approach
deinstitutionalization
halfway house
crisis hotline
family consultation
empowerment

R E C O M M E N D E D   R E A D I N G S

Gitlin, M. J. (1990). *The psychotherapist's guide to psychopharmacology.* New York: Free Press. Michael Gitlin is a psychiatrist who has written a clear guide to drug therapy and electroconvulsive therapy. I have recommended this book to friends who want to know about medications prescribed for psychological disorders.

Kanfer, F. H., & Goldstein, A. P. (Eds.). (1991). *Helping people change: A textbook of methods* (4th ed.). New York: Pergamon. This book contains 11 chapters on various therapy approaches; all are written by experts in the field. Topics include cognitive-behavior modification, group methods, aversion methods, and fear-reduction methods.

Saltzman, N., & Norcross, J. C. (Eds.). (1990). *Therapy wars: Contention and convergence in differing clinical approaches.* San Francisco: Jossey-Bass. Despite its confrontational title, *Therapy Wars* is unique. In each chapter, a case study of a person with a psychological disorder is presented, and then several therapists from differing approaches discuss how they would treat that individual.

Sue, D. W., & Sue, D. (1990). *Counseling the culturally different: Theory and practice* (2nd ed.). New York: Wiley. Several books are now available in which therapy for a particular ethnic group is described. These authors discuss some important general issues about therapy with people of color, and then they include a separate chapter on counseling each of four major ethnic groups.

Walker, C. E. (Ed.). (1991). *Clinical psychology: Historical and research foundations.* New York: Plenum. This book contains 19 chapters addressing different critical issues in clinical psychology. Some examples include the history of clinical psychology, psychological disorders in the elderly, and psychodynamic therapy.

CHAPTER 17
SOCIAL COGNITION

magine yourself glancing up from your textbook at the end of this sentence and discovering that all other human beings had suddenly vanished. How would your life be transformed without social relationships and activities? We humans are basically sociable creatures who organize many aspects of our lives in terms of our interactions with other people (Fiske, 1992). As a result, a life spent in solitude would seem grossly distorted and frighteningly bleak. In the next two chapters, we examine the topic of **social psychology,** which focuses on the way that other people influence our thoughts, feelings, and behaviors.

This first chapter on social psychology examines **social cognition,** or how we think about other people and ourselves. For example, when I began to prepare this chapter, I was waiting for a woman who teaches at another university to return my phone call. In previous years, I had spoken with several other individuals from this same university, and my consistent impression was that these professors were far too impressed with their own self-importance. I anticipated a similarly chilly interaction with this woman, especially because her recent book had been so highly praised. When she actually called, she was surprisingly warm and enthusiastic. My social cognitive processes worked at full speed to reconcile my expectations with reality. You've probably had many similar experiences when people are more likable—or more loathsome—than you had expected.

In this chapter, we consider attitudes, person perception, stereotypes, and interpersonal attraction. Chapter 18 examines social influence, or how other people have an impact on group interactions, social pressure, conflict, and altruism. We must stress, however, that the topics in the two chapters are closely interrelated. For instance, if we have stereotypes about members of a group (Chapter 17), we are more likely to develop conflicts with them and less likely to show altruism (Chapter 18).

When you read about social cognition in the present chapter, remember that the human mind struggling to understand social relationships is the same human mind we examined in the earlier chapters on cognition. Throughout those chapters, we emphasized that humans are typically efficient and accurate in perceiving, remembering, and thinking; most errors are actually "smart," sensible errors. We also discussed how people perceive objects, remember stories, and think about problems.

The same rules generally hold true when people perceive, remember, and think about other people. We are surrounded by a complex social world, so rich with human interactions that we cannot achieve perfect accuracy in understanding that world. We approach the social world with the same kinds of heuristics we use for stimuli that are not social. These **heuristics,** or rules-of-thumb, are similar to the cognitive shortcuts discussed in earlier chapters—especially when our capacity is strained (Fiske, 1993a). Still, taking everything into account, we are admirably accurate and efficient. As two social psychologists concluded, "Human perception and cognition are functional and adaptive systems" (Higgins & Bargh, 1987, p. 387).

ATTITUDE AND ATTITUDE CHANGE

An **attitude** is a psychological tendency that is expressed by an evaluation of something (Eagly & Chaiken, 1993). Your attitude toward something can be positive, neutral, or negative. For example, you might have a positive attitude toward a city's new program for homeless people, a neutral attitude toward the governor of your state, and a negative attitude toward television violence. Some researchers emphasize that these attitudes are represented in terms of structures in memory (e.g., Judd et al., 1991). As a consequence, all the rules of memory you learned in Chapter 7—such as the importance of schemas and the likelihood of forgetting—also apply to your attitudes.

Social psychologists frequently debate three long-standing issues concerning attitudes and attitude change: (1) What is the relationship between attitudes and behavior? (2) What happens when a person's attitudes are inconsistent with each other, as in the case of cognitive dissonance? and (3) What persuasion techniques produce the greatest change in attitudes?

How Attitudes Influence Behavior

About 60 years ago, a psychologist named Richard LaPiere (1934) traveled around the United States with a Chinese couple, eating in restaurants and staying overnight in hotels. Prejudice against Asians was fairly common during that era. However, only one out of 250 establishments refused to serve the couple in their 10,000 miles of travel. Later, LaPiere wrote to these same establishments and asked whether the owners would provide restaurant and hotel services to Asian people. Over 90% responded that they would not. From this study, we might conclude that negative attitudes had little influence on actual negative behavior.

Of course, you can probably think of several reasons why the study was flawed. For instance, the people who actually served the Chinese couple may not have been the same ones who answered LaPiere's letter. Furthermore, when the couple actually appeared at Joe's Sandwich Shoppe, the fact that they were Chinese may not have been as salient as other characteristics, such as the fact that they were apparently very pleasant people (Greenwald, 1989).

Still, the more recent research has confirmed that attitudes often have less influence on behavior than we might expect. Try Demonstration 17.1 before you read further. In a representative study, Fiske and her coauthors (1983) examined the relationship between people's attitudes about nuclear war and their actual behavior.

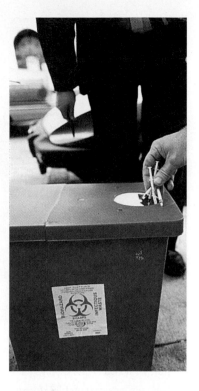

An attitude is a psychological tendency that is expressed by an evaluation of something. For example, what is your attitude toward the needle-exchange program, in which drug addicts can exchange their used needles for clean ones, thereby reducing the spread of AIDS?

DEMONSTRATION 17.1 **The Relationship Between Attitudes and Behavior**

1. Think of an issue on which your attitudes are either strongly positive or strongly negative. Issue 1 can concern politics, the environment, an international issue, or something concerned with public policy.

2. Think of a second issue on which your attitudes are as close to neutral as possible. Issue 2 should concern one of the topics listed above.

3. Now answer each of the following questions about your behavior regarding both Issue 1 and Issue 2 during the past three years:

	Issue 1	Issue 2
a. How many letters to the editor (e.g., of a newspaper) have you written?	_____	_____
b. How many local or national organizations do you belong to that are concerned with this issue?	_____	_____
c. How many letters to Congress have you written?	_____	_____
d. How many petitions have you signed on this issue?	_____	_____

4. Add up the numbers you listed for Issue 1 and then for Issue 2. If your total for Issue 1 is much higher than the total for Issue 2, then your attitudes do strongly influence your behavior. Otherwise, the two factors are not really related.

Source for questions in Item 3: Fiske et al., 1983

If the stimulus situation is ideal, a person with a strong attitude about an issue often shows behavior that is consistent with that attitude.

Suppose that attitudes do really have a strong influence on behavior. Then we would expect that people who have passionate attitudes about nuclear weapons issues (either pro or con) would *do* something significant, such as writing letters or signing petitions. However, the correlation between intensity of attitudes and nuclear-issue behavior was only +.18, a relationship that is barely statistically significant.

Research in other areas confirms that the relationship between attitudes and behavior is typically not very strong. For example, people who have strong attitudes on environmental issues do not necessarily engage in behaviors that are relevant to the environment, such as lowering their thermostat setting in the winter (Stern, 1992). Check your own responses to Demonstration 17.1 to see whether your behaviors are consistent with your attitudes.

The complexity of human behavior predicts, however, that we would find a less-than-perfect relationship between attitudes and behavior. Can you think of some possible explanations for the low correlations, based on Demonstration 17.1?

One factor that reduces the strength of the correlation is that the stimulus situation may be less than ideal (Kleinke, 1984; Stern, 1992). For instance, maybe you would be happy to sign a petition concerning an important issue, but you have never been in the same room with a relevant petition. Another important factor is **subjective norms,** or your beliefs about what other people think you ought to do (Ajzen, 1991). If you believe that your friends would raise their eyebrows if you signed a petition, then you may pass by a perfect stimulus situation, such as a petition in the lobby of your college's student union. Yet another important factor is knowledge; people who know more about certain issues are more likely to show behavior that is consistent with their attitudes (Davidson et al., 1985). Perhaps you feel you would like to write a letter to a newspaper, but you do not feel sufficiently well informed.

Figure 17.1 illustrates how these three other important factors can influence the relationship between attitudes and behavior. As we have seen, attitudes have some influence on behavior. However, that influence may be weak if the situation is not ideal, if subjective norms oppose the behavior, and if knowledge is minimal.

Cognitive Dissonance

We have examined inconsistencies between attitudes and behaviors; now let us consider what happens when someone holds two inconsistent attitudes. For example, I know a young woman who had decided during high school that she would not apply to any colleges outside of her native New York state. However, the college that offered

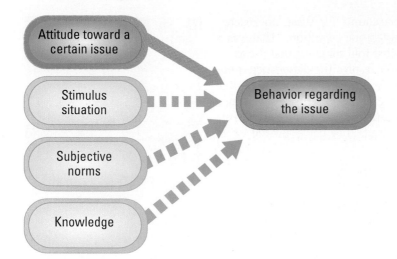

Figure 17.1

The relationship between an attitude toward a certain issue and behavior is also influenced by other factors.

the best program in her major turned out to be located in Boston—a city obviously outside New York's boundaries. In September, she found herself driving in the family car to attend school in Boston; her behavior and current attitude clearly did not match her original attitude.

According to Leon Festinger's classic theory of **cognitive dissonance,** a discrepancy between two inconsistent cognitions produces psychological distress; people will be motivated to reduce this dissonance (discrepancy) by changing one of the cognitions (Festinger, 1957). This Boston-bound college student, for example, began to praise Boston's restaurants, sights, and shopping—feeling sorry for her high-school classmates who had remained in New York.

The Original Research One of the first studies on cognitive dissonance, conducted by Festinger and Carlsmith (1959), has been called the most important experiment in social psychology (Aronson, 1991a). In this study, college students were instructed to perform an extremely boring task—turning pegs one quarter of a turn and then turning them back again. They continued for a full hour, undoubtedly producing the attitude, "That was a boring experiment." Then participants performed one of three additional tasks. Students in the control group simply waited for a short period. Students in a second condition were offered $20 to persuade another person that the experiment had been exciting and interesting. Students in the third condition were offered only $1 for the same persuasion efforts. At the end of the experiment, all the students were asked about their attitudes toward the dull task.

Who liked the peg-turning task the best? Reinforcement theory would suggest that people who had received the most reinforcement would be most positive about the task. Specifically, the $20 people should have liked it better than those in the other two groups. However, Festinger and Carlsmith found exactly the opposite: The $1 participants liked it better than those in the other two groups. (See Figure 17.2).

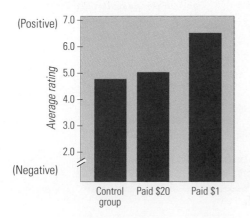

Figure 17.2

Attitudes toward a boring task, as a function of condition. (Based on Festinger & Carlsmith, 1959)

Let us see how cognitive dissonance theory accounts for these unexpected results. Participants are faced with a mismatch between one cognition, "That was a boring experiment," and another cognition, "I have just told someone that it was an exciting experiment." Now the $20 participants could resolve the dissonance quite readily because they had a reason for saying that the experiment was exciting. After all, they had been paid $20 for a few minutes' work. The $1 participants could not use this justification, so they were forced to modify their attitude toward the experiment, making it more positive and consistent with the message they had conveyed when persuading the other individual.

More Recent Research Cognitive dissonance theory has generated more than 1,000 research articles and dozens of controversies (Cooper & Fazio, 1984; Tesser & Shaffer, 1990). Researchers have discovered, for instance, that people are indeed physiologically aroused when they experience cognitive dissonance (Croyle & Cooper, 1983). They have also learned that attitudes do not change if you are allowed to express your true emotions in a written essay prior to the measurement of attitudes (Pyszczynski et al., 1993).

In a field as ripe with research as cognitive dissonance, someone is certain to propose a different explanation for the results. Daryl Bem's (1972) theory provides one of the most widely accepted alternatives. Bem's **self-perception theory** proposes that we are not driven by some need within ourselves to be consistent. Instead, we come to know our attitudes by noticing our own observable behaviors. For instance, when Sarah asks John whether he likes movies, he may not have previously evaluated his attitude. Instead, he infers his attitude from his actions, noting that he has seen four movies in the last two weeks. He answers that he loves movies.

Do we adjust our attitudes so that they are consistent with each other (dissonance theory), or do we observe our behaviors to know about our attitudes (self-perception theory)? A resolution to the controversy is that the two approaches are actually complementary; they operate in different circumstances. When we behave in a way that clearly contradicts a strongly held attitude, we feel tense and aroused, and we feel forced to change either our interpretation of that behavior or else that strongly held attitude—thus supporting dissonance theory. However, when we behave in a way that *slightly* contradicts an attitude, or when we have not yet formed an attitude, we feel neither tension nor arousal, and self-perception theory operates (Fazio et al., 1977; Tesser & Shaffer, 1990). Figure 17.3 summarizes the resolution of the dissonance theory/self-perception theory debate.

Persuasion

We have seen how people respond to an inconsistency in their attitudes. Now let us see how persuasion can be used to change people's attitudes. At the beginning of this chapter, we mentioned that the principles governing normal cognitions about nonsocial stimuli also operate in social contexts. This generalization is especially clear in the area of persuasion, where we often employ the kind of heuristics discussed in earlier chapters.

This woman smoking a cigarette holds two dissonant cognitions, "I am smoking a cigarette" and "Cigarettes cause cancer and other harmful diseases." How would you guess she resolves this cognitive dissonance?

Figure 17.3

Summary of when dissonance theory and self-perception theory operate.

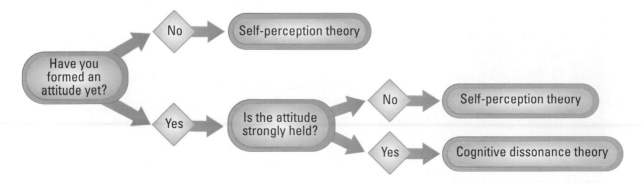

In the 1990s, our world is overloaded with information. If you carefully weighed the pros and cons of every decision, you would find yourself at 4 p.m. still trying to decide what to have for breakfast. As we saw in Chapter 8, we typically do not identify and analyze every relevant piece of information whenever we make a choice. Instead, we usually pick out just a few reliable features on which to base our decisions.

A theory proposed by Petty and Cacioppo (1986a, 1986b) predicts when we will carefully consider the issues in a persuasive argument and when we will use decision-making shortcuts. Their **elaboration likelihood model** argues that when you are involved in an issue and when you have the ability to analyze a message, you consider it carefully and perform *elaboration;* that is, you relate the message to other ideas and issues. However, when you are not involved or when you are not able to analyze a message, you are not as sensitive to the quality of the message's argument; that is, you are more likely to use decision-making heuristics, or rules-of-thumb.

Think about your own responses to persuasion. Does the elaboration likelihood model explain the way you process the messages that are designed to persuade you? I know that when I hear something regarding an issue I care about deeply, that message captures my attention completely. For instance, several dozen of my friends and relatives have traveled to Central America. When I see an article on Central America in a magazine, I read every word carefully and relate it to my previous knowledge. However, I am less informed and involved with Eastern Europe. If I read an article about an Eastern European country, I am less likely to process it analytically and more likely to judge its merits by certain rules-of-thumb. (For instance, does the author seem to be a trustworthy expert?) In the interest of "cognitive economy," I take some shortcuts to help my decision making (DeBono & Harnish, 1988; Eagly & Chaiken, 1993).

As you might imagine, the research on persuasion has numerous applications in areas such as environmental education, advertising, health psychology, and politics (Eagly, 1992; Zimbardo & Leippe, 1991). In fact, consider one rather worrisome application of the elaboration likelihood model in politics (Milburn, 1991). As you have probably heard, U.S. voters in the 1990s are less interested in politics than they used to be. As a result, during an election, they will be less likely to analyze the quality of a politician's argument and more likely to rely on cognitive shortcuts.

What are the heuristics that people use when someone is trying to persuade them, and they are not sufficiently involved with the issue to analyze the argument carefully? Researchers have discovered dozens of characteristics that affect persuasiveness (O'Keefe, 1990); we will consider five that are especially relevant to heuristics and the elaboration likelihood model. The first three heuristics concern the person who is trying to do the persuading, and the last two concern the situation.

Expertise of the Persuader When an authority speaks, we listen, and we are likely to change our attitude. Words from an expert make us stop searching for additional information, so they represent a heuristic, or shortcut for decision making. Characteristics such as education, occupation, and experience can establish a person's expertise (O'Keefe, 1990). For example, an undergraduate student I know recently applied to a psychology graduate program. I called a senior faculty member in that department, asking which faculty members would be best to work with. Her response—that Dr. X was very supportive, whereas Dr. Y was rarely available—was much more persuasive than if it had come from a physics professor.

Social psychology research confirms that expertise is a critical factor in persuasion (DeBono & Harnish, 1988; Zimbardo & Leippe, 1991). A classic study on expertise demonstrated that people were more persuaded by an article about a cure for the common cold when they thought it had appeared in the prestigious *New England Journal of Medicine,* rather than the popular family magazine *Life* (Hovland & Weiss, 1951).

People are more readily persuaded to change their attitudes when the persuader is an expert. In 1988, Surgeon General C. Everett Koop announced that cigarettes and other tobacco products are addicting, and many Americans were convinced by his message.

Trustworthiness of the Persuader An expert is persuasive, but a trustworthy person may be even more convincing (McGinnies & Ward, 1980; O'Keefe, 1990). A trustworthy person is someone who has nothing personal to gain from changing your attitude. For instance, some female faculty members at my college tried for several years to persuade the biology department to change the name of its introductory course from "Biology of Man" to an unbiased name such as "Human Biology." Our efforts were stunningly unsuccessful. Then a male professor in the psychology department who is a strong feminist made the same argument, and the name was changed immediately. He was more persuasive, apparently because members of the biology department believed he had nothing personal to gain in a pro-women effort.

Try noticing how people try to influence you by establishing their trustworthiness. For example, a waiter at a restaurant will gain your trust for the evening (as well as a larger tip) by suggesting a less expensive dish than you had ordered. You might think that the waiter is simply being honest and helpful, but this is actually a standard technique for establishing trustworthiness (Cialdini, 1986).

Attractiveness of the Persuader The "In Depth" section of Chapter 2 emphasized that attractive people have many advantages over less attractive people. It may not be fair, but attractive people are also more effective persuaders (Garramone et al., 1990; O'Keefe, 1990; Pallak, 1983). The next time you see an advertisement that looks persuasive, try asking yourself whether you would respond differently if the models were less physically appealing.

Advertisers use physically appealing models to make their message more convincing. Do we ever see models who look like "real people" in fashion ads?

CANALI

We have seen that several characteristics of the persuader cause us to take shortcuts when we are not especially involved in an issue. We tend to be more easily convinced to change our attitudes when the persuader is an expert who is trustworthy and attractive. In the interest of cognitive economy, we may not bother to scrutinize what these persuaders actually say. Instead, we use these three heuristics to assess the credibility of the persuader. We also use two heuristics involving the situation: audience response and frequency.

Audience Response Consider how you might react to an ad for a politician who is addressing a group of cheering supporters. In fact, audience response can be an important heuristic, according to a study by Axsom and his colleagues (1987). These researchers found that people who were highly involved in a controversy were not influenced by the enthusiasm of the audience on a tape recording of a speech. However, people who had low involvement were influenced by the audience. When the tape included many apparently spontaneous bursts of clapping and cheers of approval, the participants were persuaded. They were not persuaded when the audience response consisted of only a few tentative hand claps.

Frequency The final persuasion heuristic is the simplest of all: To convince people, simply repeat the message over and over (Zimbardo & Leippe, 1991). The classic research in this area was conducted by Robert Zajonc (pronounced *"Zye-unce"*). Zajonc (1968) showed participants some nonsense words—such as *CIVADRA* and *KADIRGA*—one at a time, at frequencies ranging from 0 to 25 exposures. Later, the participants rated the various nonsense words. Figure 17.4 shows the clear-cut results. According to Zajonc's **mere exposure effect,** we often prefer items (objects, ideas, and people) with which we have had repeated contact. Try Demonstration 17.2 at this point, before you read further.

Does the mere exposure effect account for any of your own preferences? For example, do you vote for the candidate whose name and face you have seen most often? Do you buy the brand of paper towels your parents had in their home? When we do not care deeply enough about an issue to investigate it completely, we often use a simple heuristic: Prefer whatever is most familiar.

The mere exposure effect has been demonstrated for a wide variety of stimuli presented in many different circumstances. Furthermore, a meta-analysis conducted on 20 years of research concluded that the mere exposure effect "is a robust, reliable phenomenon" (Bornstein, 1989, p. 278). Naturally, we eventually become bored if a simple stimulus is repeated often enough (Bornstein et al., 1990). You certainly can think of several ads that you've seen *too* often! Also, people who are especially prone to boredom may show little or none of the mere exposure effect (Bornstein et al., 1990).

Incidentally, some researchers have been concerned that the mere exposure effect might be partially explained by **demand characteristics,** those clues that participants discover about the experiment, suggesting how they are supposed to respond. A clever study by Mita and his coauthors (1977) minimized demand characteristics, so that the participants were not aware that frequency had been manipulated. Specifically, people in this experiment saw either a photo of themselves (printed the way people see themselves in a mirror) or the same photo reversed (the way other people see them). The participants preferred the mirror-image version—the one with which

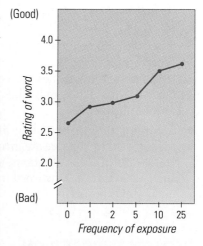

Figure 17.4

People rate nonsense words more positively if they have seen them frequently. (Zajonc, 1968)

The study by Mita and his coauthors (1977) predicts that you'd prefer the left-hand photo of Dan Rather, because it's oriented the way you usually see him. However, he should prefer the photo on the right, the version he sees in the mirror each morning.

they were most familiar. Their close friends, however, preferred the reversed version—the image they had seen most often. Did your own response on Demonstration 17.2 confirm the mere exposure effect?

Summary of Persuasion Factors We have looked at five factors that can influence whether you will be persuaded to change your attitudes. Keep in mind, however, that the three characteristics of persuaders and the two characteristics of the situation will not have much impact if you care strongly about an issue or if you choose to examine the issue carefully. For example, suppose that you are strongly opposed to nuclear power. You are not likely to change your attitude, no matter how expert, trustworthy, or attractive the people appear to be in pronuclear advertisements, no matter how enthusiastic the response of an audience might be, and no matter how often you see the ads. However, if the issue does not seem very important or if you are too hassled to study the situation carefully, you are likely to use these five heuristics in making the decision.

SECTION SUMMARY

ATTITUDE AND ATTITUDE CHANGE

- Our behavior often does not match our attitudes; the correlation is likely to be weak if the situation is not ideal, if subjective norms oppose the behavior, and if we are not well informed on the issue.

- When we hold two contradictory attitudes, we feel aroused, and we change one of those attitudes, consistent with cognitive dissonance theory. However, as self-perception theory argues, we assess our attitude by observing our behavior when our behavior differs only slightly from the attitude or when we have not yet formed an attitude.

- According to the elaboration likelihood model of persuasion, we consider messages carefully when we are involved in an issue and possess the necessary analytical ability. In other situations, we take cognitive shortcuts and rely on heuristics, such as expertise, trustworthiness, attractiveness, audience response, and frequency of exposure.

PERSON PERCEPTION

Recently, I received a phone call from a friend who lives in another city. She was considering leaving her husband because he had taken money from their joint bank account, without her knowledge, for some shady business deal that failed. I was astonished. I had only met Bill a few times, but he had seemed caring, intelligent, and considerate. He had changed his infant daughter's diapers, fed her, and played with her enthusiastically—an ideal father! He clearly seemed to love and respect his wife. All this background did not mesh with the new information. And *why* would he do such a thing? I knew that his work was not going well; was it the lure of quick financial gain?

Person perception is the area within social cognition that examines both impression formation and attribution. **Impression formation** involves integrating various pieces of information about a person. In Bill's case, for instance, I tried to integrate traits such as *caring, intelligent,* and *considerate* with *deceitful.* **Attribution** involves the explanations we create about the reasons for the behavior of other people, as well as for our own behavior. In struggling for possible reasons for Bill's behavior, I focused on attribution. Let us first discuss impression formation and then consider the related topic of attribution.

Impression Formation

Imagine that you have just met a student named Cindy. The impression you form of Cindy is likely to be shaped by factors we have discussed in other chapters, such as her attractiveness (Chapter 2). This impression also depends heavily upon what Cindy says and how she says it (McCann & Higgins, 1990). As Chapter 9 emphasized, we engage in a "dance" with our conversational partners that is governed by pragmatic rules. We combine this wealth of visual and auditory information to form an impression—which may not be accurate. Unfortunately, we often face serious consequences if these impressions are not correct (Cook, 1988). Consider what might happen if John thinks that a potential roommate seems pleasant, but he turns out to be extremely inconsiderate. Susan might ask for a letter of recommendation from a professor who turns out to dislike her. Diana and Tony decide to get married, yet neither really assessed the other accurately. This section explores three common reasons why people make errors in person perception.

Once again, psychologists interested in social cognition emphasize the similarities between our reactions to people and our reactions to nonsocial objects. For example, bottom-up and top-down processing work together in impression formation, in the same kind of coordinated fashion we use when we perceive objects (Fiske, 1992). Furthermore, we must take mental shortcuts when we form impressions—just as we take mental shortcuts when we are deciding whether to change our

---

DEMONSTRATION 17.3   The Primacy Effect

Read the following paragraphs about Jim:

1. Jim left the house to get some stationery. He walked out into the sun-filled street with two of his friends. Jim entered the stationery store and talked with an acquaintance while he waited for the clerk to catch his eye. On his way out, he stopped to chat with a school friend. While walking toward school, he met the young woman to whom he had been introduced the night before, and they talked for a short while.

2. After school, Jim left the classroom alone and started on his long walk home. Coming down the street toward him, he saw the young woman he had met on the previous evening. Jim crossed the street and entered a candy store, where he noticed a few familiar faces. Jim waited quietly until the counterman took his order. He sat down at a side table to finish his drink, and then went home.

Now describe Jim, noting especially whether he seemed to be friendly or shy.

Then, try to clear your head of your current impression of Jim, and read the two paragraphs about Jim in the reverse order, beginning with paragraph 2 and ending with paragraph 1. Does your impression of Jim seem different now?

What is your first impression of each of these students? If you are like most people, you quickly formed an impression. However, how is it possible for you to create any clear impressions, given so little information about these individuals?

attitudes. Let us consider how impression formation is influenced by these mental shortcuts in the form of schemas, as well as two other factors, the primacy effect and the negativity effect.

Schemas and Impression Formation In the memory chapter, we introduced a useful concept called schemas. A **schema** is a generalized idea about a frequently encountered object, event, or person. The memory chapter emphasized objects and events; now we focus on the person schema.

A **person schema** consists of selected bits of information about a person, organized into a coherent picture. For instance, your schema for a student you met yesterday might be, "She's the cheerleader type, with blond fluffy hair, a phony smile, expensive clothes, guys hanging around her . . . a definite airhead." You may have formed this schema after a 30-second conversation. Furthermore, you knit all the diverse pieces of information into a well-organized schema that oversimplifies what you really saw during that conversation (Zebrowitz, 1990). Once again, we find that social cognition involves mental shortcuts.

A schema is not always accurate. For example, the blond student may be a physics major planning on graduate school, or she might be a talented artist, rather than an airhead. However, your schema will probably be influenced by both the primacy effect and the negativity bias.

The Primacy Effect Before you read further, try Demonstration 17.3, which illustrates the primacy effect. Did Jim strike you differently when you read the paragraphs in the reverse order? The **primacy effect** is the tendency for early information to be considered more important than later information. Basically, we create a knowledge structure on the basis of this early information, and this knowledge structure guides us as we "fill in the blanks" (Bierhoff, 1989). The primacy effect explains why first impressions are so important—as in Demonstration 17.3.

The section on decision making in Chapter 8 (thinking) introduced a similar effect. When we need to make an estimate, we often use the anchoring and adjustment heuristic. That is, we make an initial guess that serves as an anchor, and then we make additional adjustments, based on other available information. The anchoring and adjustment heuristic is less than ideal, however, because we often weigh the first guess too heavily, and we fail to make large enough adjustments when we acquire additional information. Similarly, when you first read the paragraphs in Demonstration

17.3, you formed a first impression based on Jim's many interactions with friends in Paragraph 1, and you probably did not substantially adjust that first impression when the information in Paragraph 2 actually suggested shy, introverted behavior.

Demonstration 17.3 is based on a study by Luchins (1957). People who read Paragraph 1 before Paragraph 2 judged Jim to be friendly and outgoing, whereas those who read the paragraphs in the reverse order judged him to be shy and withdrawn. No doubt the primacy effect operated in judging people you have met in college, too.

Notice that the primacy effect is further evidence that we tend to simplify our social world. By relying too heavily on our first impressions, we do not pay close attention to later information and we tend to oversimplify. However, the problem is that oversimplification can lead to errors in impression formation.

How often do we make these impression-formation errors in everyday life? Social psychologists tend to conclude that people are reasonably accurate (Fiske, 1993a; Funder, 1987). For example, Berry (1991) asked students to rate a series of people with respect to their power and warmth, based on either a photograph of the person's face or a recording of the person's voice. These first impressions were significantly correlated with the ratings these people actually gave themselves. For example, if people rated Phil as being both strong and warm, based on either a photo or a tape recording, it was likely that Phil also rated himself as being both strong and warm.

However, even if we are reasonably accurate in our initial impressions, we should try to improve our accuracy. Specifically, when we try to assess people, we should ask whether we are placing too much emphasis on those first impressions. We can minimize the impact of the primacy effect by paying equal attention to more recent information.

Let us now consider an important by-product of the primacy effect, called the self-fulfilling prophecy. Consider this example, which I vividly recall from my seventh-grade experience at summer camp. On the first day of camp, a girl named Jan immediately impressed all of us with her sense of humor, her athletic ability, and her friendliness. We all tried to sit at Jan's table at mealtime, and she led the singing around the campfire. We elected her to represent us at the camp council during the second week of camp, and she remained our leader for the entire session. In September, I met another student from Jan's school and eagerly asked how Jan was doing. The student looked puzzled at my enthusiasm and asked, "Oh, you mean Jan, the fat girl?" At camp our first impression of Jan had been extremely positive, and we continued to have high expectations for her; she then lived up to those high expectations. Students at her school apparently had a different first impression, so she "became" a different person.

A **self-fulfilling prophecy** operates in situations where your expectations about someone lead him or her to act in ways that confirm your original expectation (Jussim, 1986). In Chapter 2, we saw that participants in an experiment tended to fulfill the experimenter's expectations (Rosenthal, 1973). We also saw in the "In Depth" section of that chapter, on physical attractiveness, that women tended to become more socially skilled on the telephone if the men who were their conversational partners had been led to believe that they were physically attractive (Snyder et al., 1977).

The research on the self-fulfilling prophecy shows that our expectations can indeed influence another person's behavior (Jussim, 1990). The effects are statistically significant, though they are not very strong. For example, a study of sixth-grade math teachers showed that their expectations did influence students' math performance (Jussim & Eccles, 1992). Furthermore, when children in elementary school were told that they would each be working with a child with a behavior problem (hyperactivity), they acted in a less friendly fashion with the supposedly hyperactive children. These supposedly hyperactive children, in turn, did not enjoy the social interactions, and they believed they had done poorly on a task (Harris et al., 1992). In short, one person's expectations can have an impact on another person's responses.

The Negativity Bias The beginning of this section on person perception mentioned Bill, my friend's husband who is caring, intelligent, considerate . . . and deceitful. An effect called the **negativity bias** predicts that impression formation is more strongly influenced by a person's negative traits than by his or her positive traits.

For some time, researchers have known that people give more weight to negative characteristics (Fiske, 1992). For instance, suppose that you were asked to rate various people on a scale where +10 was likable and −10 was dislikable. You might rate a person described as *kind* by assigning a +7. You might rate someone described as *dishonest* by assigning a −7. How about someone described as *kind and dishonest?* A simple average would yield a rating of zero. However, studies have systematically demonstrated that the negativity bias operates, and people typically supply a rating of about −3 for *kind and dishonest* (Anderson, 1981). Similarly, my present rating of Bill is more influenced by his deceit than by his positive qualities.

According to a current explanation (Skowronski & Carlston, 1987, 1989), when we judge whether people are morally good or bad, we expect good people to be *consistently* good. In contrast, we expect bad people to be sometimes bad and sometimes good. A person who steals a car (a dishonest act) may have filed an accurate tax form with the IRS (an honest act). A positive quality (such as *kind*) can be characteristic of either good or bad people, so it is not very helpful in our "diagnosis" of a person. In contrast, a negative quality (such as *dishonest*) is characteristic of only bad people; it *is* helpful in the diagnosis. Consequently, we are more influenced by negative traits than by positive traits.

In summary, when we form impressions of other people, our schemas may oversimplify the situation. Furthermore, these schemas are shaped more by initial information than by later information (primacy effect), and they are shaped more by negative information than by positive information (negativity bias).

Attribution

Suppose you read that a famous billionaire has left his wife for a much younger woman. Don't you want to know *why?* Suppose that your best friend suddenly snubs you. Do you search for a rationale? A common human characteristic is to look for attributions, which we defined earlier as the explanations for people's behavior. We do not *always* search for attributions for everyone's behavior, however. It would be too time consuming, and it is not exactly a high-paying job. Nonetheless, we are likely to make attributions when we are not preoccupied with other tasks (Higgins & Bargh, 1987; Weiner, 1985b).

This section focuses primarily on our attributions for the behavior of other people. However, we also make attributions for our own behavior, as we attempt to explain why we received a high grade on a paper, why we were grumpy toward a friend, and why we made a particular mistake. You may recall that we discussed these self-attributions in connection with achievement motivation in Chapter 12 and in connection with cognitive characteristics of major depression in Chapter 15.

In general, when we are searching for attributions for another person's behavior, we make one of two general kinds of attributions (Brehm & Kassin, 1993; Weary et al., 1989). A **person attribution** indicates that we believe that an internal trait—located within the person—was responsible for the behavior. These person attributions may involve a person's ability, motivation, attitude, or emotions. In contrast, a **situation attribution** indicates we believe that the specific situation—a force located outside the person—was responsible for the behavior. These situation attributions may involve the physical, social, or societal explanations for why an event occurred.

For example, suppose that you see a homeless man. What attribution would you make for his poverty? If you favor a *person attribution,* you believe that he lacks the motivation to get a proper job. If you favor a *situation attribution,* you blame the economic situation and other external circumstances. Interestingly, Wagstaff (1983)

How would you explain this person's homelessness? Would you trace his situation to an internal problem, or to a society that does not take care of its members?

found that politically conservative people tend to supply person attributions for poverty, whereas politically liberal people favor situation attributions.

The research on attributions has been an extremely active component of social cognition (e.g., Bierhoff, 1989; Hewstone, 1989; Alicke, 1991). We will consider two consistent biases in the way people make attributions, called the fundamental attribution error and the actor-observer bias.

The Fundamental Attribution Error We are typically surprised when people we know act inconsistently. We do not expect a self-confident friend to stammer and stumble when called on in class. Basically, we assume that a self-confident person should remain confident in all situations. In Chapter 4 we discussed perceptual constancies, or our tendencies to see an object as staying the same, despite changes in the way we view the object. Thus, a textbook seems to remain rectangular, even when we view it from an angle. Similarly, we expect constancy in humans; a friend should remain self-confident, even when we view this friend in a new setting (Swann, 1984).

However, the complexity of humans suggests that they will *not* remain constant, but will instead change in response to different situations (unlike a textbook). Unfortunately, though, we humans often have biased attributions. When we try to explain the behavior of other people, we tend to overemphasize the internal, or person attribution. The **fundamental attribution error** refers to the tendency to overestimate the role of internal, personal causes and underestimate the role of external, situational causes. This attribution error is called *fundamental* because it is so widespread and basic that it seems to be a fundamental characteristic of social cognition—at least in research in North America. Another name for this phenomenon is the *correspondence bias*.

Sharon Brehm and Saul Kassin (1993) provide an interesting example of the fundamental attribution error. Perhaps you recall the widely publicized arrest of Pee Wee Herman in 1991. Television viewers knew him as a clean-cut, goofy, sexless character in a children's TV show. The fundamental attribution error led everyone to believe that these characteristics would persist in his normal, off-screen personality. Then the real Pee Wee Herman, Paul Reubens, was arrested for indecent exposure in an X-rated movie theater. The general public was amazed that someone so clean-cut would be capable of this kind of activity!

 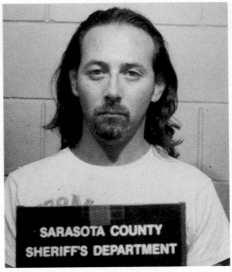

According to Brehm and Kassin (1993), many people demonstrated the fundamental attribution error when they were surprised that the actor who played the sexless Pee Wee Herman (left) would be arrested for indecent exposure in an X-rated movie theater; Paul Reubens is shown at the Sheriff's Department (right). The public believed that the TV character's personal characteristics would remain stable in all situations, even in the actor's personal life.

Let us consider a representative study illustrating the fundamental attribution error. Gilbert and Jones (1986) set up an intentionally artificial situation that demonstrated how people refuse to attribute a person's behavior to external forces. Imagine that you are a participant in this study. When you report to the psychology lab, you are told that you will be reading a series of 14 questions to John in the other room. Furthermore, you will instruct John precisely about how he will respond to your questions. For instance, when you ask John, "What do you think of the legalization of marijuana?" the experimenter has told you that you must say to him, "Press the green button to indicate a liberal response." Furthermore, the experimenter has made it clear to you that John has been given a set of liberal responses which he must supply. John has absolutely no opportunity to express his own personal opinion on the issues.

John answers a total of 14 questions—always supplying the answer you have specifically given him. Then the experimenter tells you to rate John on a 15-point scale, with a rating of 1 being most liberal and a rating of 15 being most conservative. Wouldn't you imagine that you might say something like, "I can't possibly rate John, because I don't know what he *really* thinks?" Actually, Gilbert and Jones found no such hesitation. Using this 15-point scale, participants gave a rating of 7.2 to the partners who had been supplied with the liberal responses. Other participants, who had given their partners a set of conservative responses, gave these partners a rating of 9.7. This difference was clearly statistically significant. Even though the partners were obviously constrained by the situation, the participants thought these partners really believed the statements they had been forced to make.

Edward Jones (1990) argues that the fundamental attribution error is simply another variation of that familiar heuristic, anchoring and adjustment. Basically, when we want to explain someone's behavior, we first establish an anchor by saying that the explanation is totally personal, a part of the person's internal character. Then we make some adjustments, pointing out how the situation is somewhat responsible. However, as we saw in Chapter 8, those adjustments are never large enough. We are strongly governed by our top-down processes, which insist that people's personalities are responsible for their actions. As a consequence, we fail to pay enough attention to the bottom-up information about the stimulus situation.

Other research by Gilbert and his coauthors (1988) offers further support to the view that the person attribution acts as the anchor, and adjustments are made for the situation. In this research, half of the participants were given an additional memory task to occupy part of their attention while they made judgments about attributions. These participants were significantly more likely than control-group participants to

DEMONSTRATION 17.4   The Actor-Observer Bias

For each of the following characteristics, rate yourself by checking the item in Column A, the item in Column B, or the final option, "Depends on the situation." Put the letter *M* (for *Myself*) in the appropriate column.

COLUMN A	COLUMN B	DEPENDS ON THE SITUATION
1. _____ Serious	_____ Easygoing	_____
2. _____ Energetic	_____ Relaxed	_____
3. _____ Realistic	_____ Idealistic	_____
4. _____ Quiet	_____ Talkative	_____
5. _____ Cautious	_____ Bold	_____
6. _____ Uninhibited	_____ Self-controlled	_____
7. _____ Happy-go-lucky	_____ Conscientious	_____
8. _____ Future-oriented	_____ Present-oriented	_____
9. _____ Tough-minded	_____ Sensitive	_____
10. _____ Calm	_____ Intense	_____
11. _____ Lenient	_____ Firm	_____
12. _____ Reserved	_____ Emotionally expressive	_____

Now think about a friend—someone you know reasonably well, but not your best friend. With this person in mind, go through those 12 items once more, this time placing the letter *F* (for *Friend*) in Column A, Column B, or "Depends on the situation."

use person attributions, rather than situation attributions. These results suggest that we are especially likely to make the fundamental attribution error if we are busy or preoccupied (Jones, 1990). We simply do not have the time or the energy to make the appropriate adjustments based on the situation.

The Actor-Observer Bias   Before you read further, try Demonstration 17.4, which asks you to make judgments about yourself and a friend.

We saw that the fundamental attribution error leads us to attribute the behavior of other people to internal causes. However, we do not show this same attribution pattern for our own behavior. The **actor-observer bias** is the tendency to attribute our own behavior to external, situational causes, whereas we attribute the behavior of others to internal, personal causes. That is, we provide different interpretations, depending upon whether we are the actor or someone observing another person. Notice, then, that the actor-observer bias emphasizes that we make the fundamental attribution error in judging others, but not in judging ourselves.

Now check over your responses to Demonstration 17.4. Count up the number of "depends on the situation" responses you supplied for yourself, in contrast to your friend. The actor-observer effect predicts that you will select many "depends on the situation" responses for yourself, because you believe that your behavior can be attributed to situational causes. In contrast, you envision your friend to have much greater constancy and to be governed by stable, internal traits. Indeed, research similar to this demonstration has supported the actor-observer bias (Nisbett et al., 1973; Ross & Nisbett, 1991).

One likely explanation for the actor-observer bias is that people see themselves as having many different facets to their personality. They believe that they have the capacity to respond differently to different situations because they have so many varied traits—for example, being either serious or easygoing as the situation demands (Sande et al., 1988).

The actor-observer bias is especially noticeable when something bad happens. We tend to manufacture excuses for our own behavior. After all, we would rather blame this bad event on external factors beyond our control, instead of admitting to some personal problem. For example, one study examined newspaper advice columns, specifically, "Ann Landers" and "Dear Abby." When people described their problems, they tended to blame their own misdeeds on external, situational factors. In contrast, they blamed the misdeeds of other people on internal, personal factors (Schoeneman & Rubanowitz, 1985).

An unfortunate consequence of the actor-observer effect is that we tend to blame the victim in making judgments about other people. Consider the case of Mrs. W., a married middle-aged woman who was raped by a stranger. She resisted to the best of her ability and received a knife wound and a concussion. Despite convincing evidence that there had been a genuine rape, everyone blamed her, including the police, the hospital staff, and even her own husband. For instance, a psychiatrist who saw her bleeding and battered when she was admitted to the hospital asked, "Haven't you really been rushing toward this very thing all your life?" (Russell, 1975).

The actor-observer bias suggests that we should be more forgiving of other people. When a friend does something you consider wrong, ask yourself how you might explain this action if you were in his or her shoes. Could external forces account for the behavior? When something tragic happens to other people, do not automatically begin searching for internal personality flaws that can allow you to conclude, "They got what they deserved."

Throughout this section on person perception, we have noted that people oversimplify their social worlds and make judgments that reflect certain systematic biases. As we have emphasized in earlier chapters, people are often governed by top-down processing. Our concepts, expectations, and prior knowledge help us achieve reasonably accurate person perception—though they can lead us astray. Of course, humans also use bottom-up processing, attending to information in the environment (Higgins & Bargh, 1987). We *can* pay attention to what we actually see and hear about other people. As a consequence, we are reasonably effective in judging others. However, we can increase our effectiveness by being aware of oversimplification and biases—and by correcting for these tendencies.

SECTION SUMMARY

PERSON PERCEPTION

- Impression formation, which is one component of person perception, often involves a person schema, in which we organize information about a person into a coherent picture.

- Two biases in impression formation include the primacy effect (with its by-product, self-fulfilling prophecy) and the negativity bias.

- Attribution, which is the second component of person perception, involves the explanations about the reasons for people's behavior.

- Two biases in attribution include the fundamental attribution error and the actor-observer bias.

STEREOTYPES, PREJUDICE, AND DISCRIMINATION

A student in a wheelchair confides that several grammar-school classmates had been instructed by their parents not to play with her because she was different. A Black college administrator arrives at her office to find that someone has written "Nigger Die" on the walls, desk, and chair. An outstanding woman accountant is denied partnership in her firm, on the grounds that she is not feminine enough; she is told that she needs a course at charm school and should wear makeup and jewelry. A lesbian

In 1993, a Black college administrator at the University of Colorado found that her office was vandalized with racist graffiti.

What kind of stereotypes do you have about these Asian-American students?

woman discovers that someone has thrown a brick—attached to a dead rat—through the window of her home.

In this chapter we consider three interconnected concepts related to these examples. A **stereotype** is a structured set of beliefs about the way a group of people think and act (Ashmore & DelBoca, 1979; Hamilton et al., 1992). Stereotypes are similar to the person schemas we discussed in the previous section. However, person schemas apply to individual people, whereas stereotypes apply to groups. Both person schemas and stereotypes involve overactive top-down processing and failure to pay attention to stimulus information. Stereotypes are often negative, though they can be positive. For example, a Mexican-American professor told me that people often expect him to play the guitar, consistent with their stereotypes about his ethnic group. Similarly, a Black student revealed that people expect him to be a "natural athlete."

Whereas stereotypes emphasize beliefs and cognitive reactions, prejudices emphasize attitudes and evaluative reactions. **Prejudice** is a negative attitude toward a group of people (Duckitt, 1992a). Interestingly, a person who is prejudiced against one "low-status" group is also likely to be prejudiced against other "low-status" groups. Specifically, a study of college students showed that prejudices against Blacks, women, the elderly, and gay people were significantly interrelated (Bierly, 1985).

A third related term, **discrimination,** involves action against a person or a group of people. Thus, stereotyped beliefs and prejudiced attitudes often reveal themselves in discriminatory behavior. For example, you may know someone who believes that Black people are lazy (a stereotype), has a negative attitude toward them (prejudice), and would refuse to hire Black people for a job (discrimination).

We have noted some of these biases in earlier chapters. For instance, Chapter 2 addressed biases based on a person's appearance, and Chapter 11 examined biases against both gay people and the elderly. Biases about gender and ethnic group have been discussed in many chapters. Stereotypes, prejudice, and discrimination also may focus on religion, social class, and people with disabilities. (Can you think of other categories?)

We begin this section by looking at two of the most common biases, which have also been the most extensively researched: racism and sexism. Next is an "In Depth" discussion of the cognitive basis of stereotypes, followed by a summary about stereotypes and self-fulfilling prophecies. We end this section with some ideas about overcoming stereotypes and other biases.

Racism

Racism is bias against certain racial or ethnic groups; this bias can be revealed in stereotypes, prejudice, or discrimination. Psychologists and sociologists did not begin examining racism until the 1920s (Duckitt, 1992b; Reid, 1992). This neglect is especially surprising when we consider the long history of racial bias in the United States. (See Figures 17.5 and 17.6.) In the United States, Blacks have consistently experienced the greatest prejudice compared to other ethnic groups (Sears, 1988).

In recent years, the old-fashioned, obvious forms of bigotry may be less prevalent (Smith, 1990). For example, Blacks are no longer required to use a different drinking fountain. Still, we find abundant evidence of racism in many facets of everyday life. At the personal level, Tatum (1992) reports that the White students in her course on the Psychology of Racism frequently comment that their parents had not allowed Black friends to visit their homes. Also, the National Institute Against Prejudice and Violence has reported hundreds of incidents of campus violence in recent years (Reid, 1992). In 1993, for example, an all-White fraternity at Rider College in New Jersey held a "Dress Like a Nigger Night" ("In Brief," 1993). In Toronto, someone hurled a bomb into a club popular with South Asian teens (Hayes, 1992).

Racism is also obvious at the national level. For example, the federal government is much harsher when companies violate the pollution laws in predominantly White areas. The average fine was $334,000 in communities where most residents are White, but only $55,000 in communities where most residents are people of color ("Coming Clean," 1992).

Still, some White people in the 1990s feel that Blacks are making inappropriate demands for change, a bias called **symbolic racism** (Reid, 1988; Weigel & Howes, 1985). Try Demonstration 17.5, which contains items similar to those included on tests of symbolic racism (Sears, 1988). Many researchers argue, however, that symbolic racism may not really be very different from the standard, "old-fashioned" racism that has characterized North American race relation for centuries (Eagly & Chaiken, 1993; Sniderman & Tetlock, 1986; Weigel & Howes, 1985).

An experiment by Frey and Gaertner (1986) examined contemporary racism. White college women were randomly assigned to a condition in which they were led

Figure 17.5

As recently as the 1960s, Black people faced discrimination in public places. These segregated drinking fountains were located in the county courthouse in Albany, Georgia.

Figure 17.6

During World War II, the U.S. government forced 120,000 Japanese Americans into concentration camps, without any legal trial (Nagata & Crosby, 1991). This discrimination can be partly traced to racism. In this photo, a man bids farewell to his brother.

DEMONSTRATION 17.5 Symbolic Racism

Answer true or false to each of the following items, based on your true beliefs about Black people. (Please note that this test is appropriate for Blacks as well as Whites, because Black people can be racist—just as women can be sexist.)

_____ 1. Blacks are getting too demanding in their push for equal rights.

_____ 2. Blacks should not push themselves where they are not wanted.

_____ 3. It is easy to understand the anger of Black people in America.

_____ 4. Over the past few years, the government and news media have shown more respect to Blacks than they deserve.

_____ 5. Over the past few years, Blacks have received more economically than they deserve.

_____ 6. Blacks who receive money from welfare programs really do need the help.

_____ 7. Black people miss out on jobs and promotions because of racial discrimination.

_____ 8. The civil rights people have not pushed fast enough.

Check your answers on page 589.

to believe that they would be working with a female partner who was either Black or White. This partner was working on a task that was described as either easy or difficult, and during the work session, she requested help on the task. How often did the student help? When the task was difficult—so the request for help appeared justified—the White students helped Black and White partners almost equally. However, when the task was easy—so the partner did not seem to be trying hard enough—the White students helped White partners more than twice as often as Black partners. (See Figure 17.7.) In other words, they did not go out of their way to help Black partners unless the need seemed truly legitimate. When it was more acceptable to say "No," these students showed clear discrimination against Black partners.

A component of modern racism is the belief that Blacks already have equality with Whites and they no longer experience racism. Andrew Hacker (1992) is a White political science professor whose book, *Two Nations: Black and White, Separate, Hostile, Unequal,* demonstrates that inequalities still exist. One illustration of these inequalities comes from an exercise that Hacker tries with the White students in his classes. He asks them to imagine that an official pays them a visit to announce that a mistake has been made: They were supposed to have been born Black. In fact, tonight they will become Black, both in skin color and in facial features. However, his organization regrets the error they made and is prepared to compensate them. What is a proper amount of money, assuming that they will live 50 years longer?

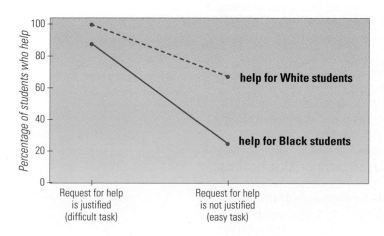

Figure 17.7

When a request for help is justified, White students help Black students almost as much as they help other White students. When a request for help is not justified, White students help Black students much less. (Based on Frey & Gaertner, 1986)

Hacker found that his White students typically asked for $50 million or $1 million for every year they would live as a Black person. Does this surprise you? As the White students explained, they would require this much money to protect themselves from the discriminations and dangers that Black people face.

Sexism

Sexism is bias toward people on the basis of their gender. A person is sexist who believes that women cannot be competent lawyers. A person is also sexist who believes that men cannot be competent nursery school teachers. Institutions—as well as individuals—can be sexist. Like racism, this bias can be revealed in stereotypes, prejudice, and discrimination.

Consider the case of sex discrimination that accountant Ann Hopkins brought to court (Fiske, 1993b; Fiske et al., 1991). Hopkins was working at a prestigious accounting firm, Price Waterhouse. She was being considered for promotion to partner, the only woman out of 88 candidates that year. (In the entire firm, only 7 out of 662 partners were women.) She had brought in business worth $25 million, at the top of the 88 candidates. However, the company did not promote her. The firm claimed that she lacked interpersonal skills, and they branded her "macho." A sympathetic coworker suggested that she would improve her chances if she would "walk more femininely, talk more femininely, dress more femininely, wear makeup, have her hair styled, and wear jewelry" (Fiske, 1989, p. 12).

Ann Hopkins, the highly competent accountant who was turned down for partner status because of sex discrimination.

Ann Hopkins's lawsuit became the first Supreme Court case to use psychology research to document sex discrimination; psychologist Susan Fiske and her colleagues provided the documentation from research on gender stereotypes. The court eventually ruled that Price Waterhouse had been guilty of sex discrimination because they had treated a woman with an assertive personality in a different manner from a man with an assertive personality. In 1991, Ann Hopkins was promoted to partner and was also awarded a financial settlement for back pay.

Ellen Berscheid (1992), a prominent social psychologist, discusses how far the field of psychology has come in recent decades. Several decades ago, women faculty members were rare, and research on gender was scarce. In the 1990s, women are active researchers, and hundreds of studies on gender and sex discrimination could be used to support the case of Ann Hopkins (Fiske et al., 1993).

When we think about the topics of stereotypes, prejudice, and discrimination, we typically consider the damage done to women. However, we should point out that men also can be victims of sexism. For instance, consider a study by Glick and his colleagues (1988), who asked managers and business professionals to look at some résumés and judge which people they would consider competent enough to actually interview for a job. When the personal characteristics of the job applicant were neutral (rather than stereotypically feminine or masculine), these managers were 27% more likely to interview a male, rather than a female, for a sales management job. For a dental receptionist job, in contrast, a job applicant with neutral characteristics was 59% more likely to be recommended for an interview if the applicant was female, rather than male. Even in the current era, people are more willing to hire a man for a "man's job" and to hire a woman for a "woman's job."

Furthermore, gender stereotypes still thrive as we approach the 21st century. Although some progress has been made, a glance through current magazines will convince you that the media still believe that men should look serious, businesslike, and macho, whereas women should look home-loving, sexy, and submissive (Itzin, 1986; Matlin, 1993a).

People are very accurate in identifying the characteristics that are stereotypical of women and men. Try Demonstration 17.6 to test your accuracy in guessing these stereotypes.

However, the problem with stereotypes is that they are often inaccurate. For example, Martin (1987) asked female and male college students to judge whether certain characteristics described themselves. They were also asked to judge whether

---

DEMONSTRATION 17.6 Stereotypes About Women and Men

In this demonstration, you must guess what most college students think about women and men. Put a W in front of those characteristics you think students associate with women more than men, and an M in front of those associated with men more than women. The answers appear at the end of the chapter.

_____ 1. forceful

_____ 2. affectionate

_____ 3. adventurous

_____ 4. aggressive

_____ 5. emotional

_____ 6. gentle

_____ 7. self-confident

_____ 8. rude

_____ 9. submissive

_____ 10. independent

_____ 11. ambitious

_____ 12. appreciative

_____ 13. active

_____ 14. dominant

_____ 15. sensitive

_____ 16. nagging

_____ 17. inventive

_____ 18. sentimental

---

these same characteristics described male students and female students at their university. If stereotypes are accurate, the students' judgments about male and female students should match their judgments about themselves. However, Martin found that males and females responded quite similarly to each other when judging their own characteristics, but they believed that "typical males" and "typical females" were quite different from each other. For instance, males and females rated themselves similar in independence and hostility, yet they thought that "typical males" were much more independent and hostile than "typical females." Also, they rated themselves similar in "helpfulness" and gentleness," yet they thought that "typical females" were much more helpful and gentle than "typical males."

Typically, we find that gender differences are smaller than our stereotypes depict them to be (Deaux & Major, 1987; Matlin, 1993a). Unger has called this phenomenon "the illusion of sex differences." She writes, "Men and women are especially alike in their beliefs about their own differences" (Unger, 1979, p. 1086). As in the case of schemas, our stereotypes reveal that we rely too heavily on top-down processing, specifically our beliefs that women and men are different from each other. As a consequence, we do not pay enough attention to bottom-up processing (i.e., actual behavior). If we looked more closely at the actual behavior of women and men, we could appreciate our similarities. The following "In Depth" section examines how our cognitive processes encourage us to form and maintain stereotypes.

IN DEPTH: The Cognitive Basis of Stereotypes

For many years, psychologists emphasized the motivational aspects of stereotypes (Deaux, 1985). For example, according to the **scapegoat theory,** people who are frustrated and unhappy about something will choose a relatively powerless group of people to take the blame for a situation that is not their fault (Aronson, 1988).

In recent years, however, psychologists have increasingly endorsed the **cognitive approach to stereotypes,** which argues that most stereotypes are produced by normal human thought processes (Hamilton et al., 1993). One cognitive process that is characteristic of most humans is the tendency to divide the people we meet into categories such as females versus males, Blacks versus Whites, and gay people versus heterosexual people (Hamilton, 1979; Hamilton et al., 1990). We also categorize on the basis of religion, age, socioeconomic class, and other social attributes. This basic categorization process is a necessary component of stereotyping. We could not have stereotypes of women and men, for example, unless we first made a distinction between them.

Stereotypes help us simplify and organize the world by creating categories in a habitual, automatic fashion. One of the primary ways we categorize people is on the basis of gender. Furthermore, we automatically categorize most aspects of human experience into the "male" and

According to the cognitive approach to stereotypes, you would tend to categorize the people in this picture according to characteristics such as gender and race.

"female" compartments (Bem, 1993). For example, we categorize clothes, leisure activities, personal characteristics, occupations, and abilities. We accomplish this gender categorization with very little thought. In fact, after you finish your reading today, try *not* to pay attention to the gender of the first person you meet. It is very difficult to suppress this tendency to split the world in half, using gender as the great divide.

Once we have a stereotype in place, the stereotype often guides the way we cognitively process information. Specifically, it can guide the way we perceive people, remember them, and evaluate them. In general, stereotypes have the same impact on our cognitive processes, whether these stereotypes focus on gender, race, sexual preference, or any of the dozens of other stereotypes we hold. In all cases, too, the effect of these biases is to maintain the status quo, encouraging us to create our own exaggerated versions of reality (Jussim, 1991). Let us now consider how stereotypes influence person perception, memory, and evaluation.

Stereotypes and Person Perception Cognitive psychologists propose that humans are so bombarded with stimuli that we pay attention to some information and ignore other information. We saw earlier that we use a person schema when we perceive one individual person (for example, a caring, intelligent, considerate husband). Similarly, a stereotype encourages us to pay attention to certain behaviors when we perceive people from a certain group.

For example, John Darley and Paget Gross (1983) conducted an experiment in which one group of participants was led to believe that a 9-year-old White girl came from a high socioeconomic background, and another similar group was led to believe that she came from a low socioeconomic background. Two other groups also received these differing background stories and then watched a videotape of a girl taking an academic test. Both of these groups actually watched the same videotaped performance, though their expectations were certainly different. All participants were asked to judge the girl's ability level by indicating the grade level appropriate for her performance on tests of liberal arts, reading, and mathematics.

Figure 17.8 shows the estimates for the mathematics test. (The other two tests showed similar results.) Notice that when the participants had not witnessed any videotaped performance, social class had little influence on their judgment. When they had watched her performance, however, social class had an important impact. Participants believed that she was working at the fourth-grade level if they thought she was upper class, but at the third-grade level if they thought she was lower class. The expectations had encouraged people to perceive her behavior very differently in the two conditions. For example, if she were to scratch her head, those who thought she was upper class might have perceived this gesture as a sign of thoughtful contemplation. In contrast, those who thought she was lower class might have perceived this same

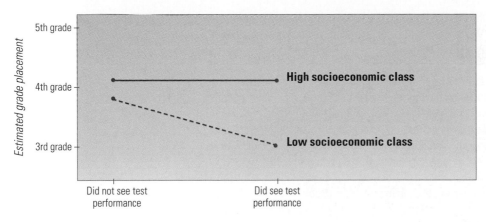

Figure 17.8

Average grade placement for mathematics-test performance, as a function of the participants' beliefs about the child's social class and whether or not they witnessed her performance on the test. (Darley & Gross, 1983)

gesture as a sign that she felt stumped by a question. This selective perception encouraged those who had seen the videotapes to have very different evaluations of the young girl. As David Hamilton (1981) commented about the powerful influence of expectations on perception, "I wouldn't have seen it if I hadn't believed it" (p. 137).

Another way that stereotypes influence person perception is that they encourage us to perceive all members of another group as being similar to one another, a phenomenon known as **outgroup homogeneity.** We perceive members of our own group as diverse and heterogeneous, but people in that other group? "They are all the same!"

In a recent talk, Black poet Maya Angelou provided a perfect example of outgroup homogeneity. She was describing her close friendship with a White woman. One time this White woman was discussing a Black woman they had both met some years earlier. Maya Angelou could not recall who this woman was, so she asked, "What color was she?" The White friend replied, "But I told you she was Black." Ms. Angelou responded, "Yes, but what color of Black?" To a White person, everybody we compartmentalize as Black is Black, and we fail to appreciate the richness of skin colors between pale tan and rich black. Similarly, to a person of color, all White people may look highly similar.

Psychologists have uncovered evidence of outgroup homogeneity for many different stereotypes (Linville et al., 1986; Quattrone, 1986). For example, White people tend to think that Black people are homogeneous (Linville & Jones, 1980). Young people think that old people are "all the same," whereas old people think that young people are "all the same" (Brewer & Lui, 1984; Linville, 1982). Furthermore, students at two rival universities perceived the students at the other university as being highly homogeneous (Quattrone & Jones, 1980). And you will not be surprised to learn that engineering students think business students are highly similar, whereas business students think that engineering students are highly similar (Judd et al., 1991). In fact, can you think of any way of splitting humans into categories for which the group to which you belong seems *more* homogeneous than the outgroup? Apparently, we are willing to believe that members of our own group display the kind of individual differences that represent one theme of this textbook, but we deny this same diversity to people in other groups (Judd & Park, 1988).

Stereotypes and Memory   We have seen that stereotypes can influence perception; they can also influence memory. Specifically, our stereotypes tend to bias memory so that we remember attributes consistent with those stereotypes (Fiske & Taylor, 1991). Consider Cohen's (1981) study of people's stereotypes about occupations. People in this study watched a videotape of a woman having a birthday dinner with her husband. If they had been told that the woman was a waitress, people remembered that she was drinking beer during part of the video and that she owned a television. Other people watching the same video were told that the woman worked as a librarian. These people remembered that she wore glasses and that she owned records. In general, then, when we are uncertain about something in memory, we tend to "fill in the blanks" in a fashion consistent with our stereotypes (Halpern, 1985).

Throughout this chapter, we have stressed that the cognitive processes operate the same way, whether we think about people or about objects and events. Cohen's results are highly similar to the results of the study by Brewer and Treyens (1981), discussed in the memory chapter. As

According to Cohen's (1981) research on stereotypes about occupations, people who had been told that this woman is a librarian would be likely to remember that she was wearing glasses.

Demonstration 7.4 illustrated, people who thought they had been in a professor's office tended to recall seeing books, even though none were actually present. We tend to reconstruct memories that are compatible with our stereotypes and schemas.

Children also show enhanced memory for material that is consistent with gender stereotypes. For example, Meehan and Janik (1990) presented photos of people engaged in stereotypical, neutral, and nonstereotypical behavior. Although each kind of photo was shown equally often, the children estimated that they had seen the stereotypical photos more often.

However, you may be wondering whether there are exceptions. For example, you have probably had the experience of recalling an event precisely because it was the *opposite* of a stereotype! Consistent with our theme about human complexity, research shows that we sometimes recall counter-stereotypical information more accurately. Social psychologists are beginning to discover which factors are important in determining whether people are more likely to remember stereotypical or counter-stereotypical information. Here are several important factors (Fiske & Taylor, 1991; Hamilton et al., 1990; Stangor & Ruble, 1989):

1. When people have *well-developed* stereotypes and expectations, they are more likely to remember stereotypical information; with *weak* stereotypes, they may remember counter-stereotypical information.

2. When people are instructed to *remember* material, they are more likely to remember stereotypical information; when instructed to *form an impression,* they may remember counter-stereotypical information.

3. When people are making a *complex* judgment, they are more likely to remember stereotypical information; when making *simple* judgments, they may recall counter-stereotypical information.

In short, we must know some details about the individuals and the task before we can predict whether they will be more likely to recall consistent or inconsistent information. However, a related conclusion is more straightforward: Recall is lowest for material that is *unrelated* to the stereotype. Thus, if you are asked to remember information about a man named Pete, you may recall that he loves to play baseball (stereotypical for a male) and that his favorite subject is English poetry (counter-stereotypical for a male). You will probably forget that he lives in a brown house (irrelevant to the male stereotype).

Stereotype and Evaluation Two factors operate when people evaluate individuals from different social groups. First, they generally downgrade people who belong to a group that is considered to have low status in a culture. For example, they tend to associate positive words with Whites and negative words with Blacks (Dovidio et al., 1986). Also, when students worked together in pairs, they were more likely to react in a negative fashion for female partners than for male partners (Lott, 1987). Specifically, both males and females made negative statements about female partners and tended to move away from them. However, people are not consistently biased against all members of a low-status group. For example, they may not respond negatively to all women. Instead, they may downgrade only women who are aggressive (Fiske & Taylor, 1991; Swim et al., 1989).

A second factor also operates during evaluation, especially when both groups are equal in status. Specifically, we tend to show **ingroup favoritism,** evaluating members of our own group more favorably than members of another group. For example, in fifth grade, my teacher divided us at random into two teams for a math contest. I can vividly recall how attractive, intelligent, and nice most of my team members were, compared to the people in the other group.

In a representative study, Jennifer Crocker and her colleagues (1987) randomly assigned participants to either Group A or Group B by asking them to select a letter (A or B) from a box. The participants then rearranged themselves to sit at either Table A or Table B, and they were instructed not to talk to each other during the study. After several other tasks, all participants rated the members of both groups. The results showed that they rated members of their own group much more favorably. Other research has confirmed this ingroup favoritism (Fiske & Taylor, 1991; Schaller, 1992).

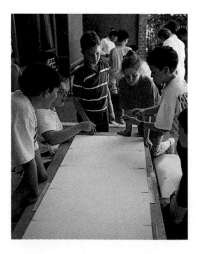

According to the principle of ingroup favoritism, the children in the group at the front of the photo should like their own group members better than the children in other groups—even if they were assigned to the groups entirely at random.

Notice, then, that we humans have become accustomed to categorizing other humans. Even when we cannot categorize on the basis of obvious characteristics such as race, gender, social class, or occupation, we still seek ways to subdivide people. We may even use categories as clearly arbitrary as letters of the alphabet randomly drawn from a box. Once we have established these categories, we frequently use stereotypes to simplify and bias our perceptions, memories, and evaluations of other members of our species. These biased cognitive activities, in turn, serve to maintain and strengthen our stereotypes.

Stereotypes and Self-Fulfilling Prophecies

The earlier section on impression formation showed that self-fulfilling prophecies can influence behavior. Individuals often live up to the schemas and expectations that other people have created. Self-fulfilling prophecies also operate in the case of stereotypes; people live up to the schemas and expectancies that other people have created for the group to which they belong. The effects of stereotypes are not confined to the cerebral cortex of the onlooker. Instead, they can guide the behavior of the person who has been stereotyped (Fiske & Taylor, 1991).

According to the research on self-fulfilling prophecies, this woman may begin acting in a more stereotypically feminine way if her boss has traditional views about women.

Consider a study in which White interviewers interacted with either White or Black people. With Black candidates, the interviewers were less friendly and personal. The interviewers also sat farther away and leaned away from the candidate; in addition, they ended the interview sooner and spoke less smoothly (Word et al., 1974). In a second study, Word and his colleagues (1974) trained interviewers to imitate either the impersonal interview style used with Black people or the friendly interview style used with White people. Then these interviewers used either the impersonal style or the friendly style with a new set of White students. Those students who had been treated in the impersonal style performed less well. If White interviewers judge Black candidates as less competent than White candidates, part of the blame may lie in the interviewers' own influence on the candidates.

Self-fulfilling prophecies also operate for gender (Deaux & Major, 1987). For instance, women tend to act in a stereotypically feminine fashion when they interact with someone who seems to have traditional views about women (von Baeyer et al., 1981). It seems likely, too, that men might act in a more stereotypically masculine way when others expect them to be macho, rather than gentle and compassionate.

We must emphasize, however, that people are not always at the mercy of their stereotypes (Fiske, 1993a). For example, stereotypes are less likely to operate when we have extensive stimulus information, so that bottom-up processing is easier (Lott, 1985; Swim et al., 1989; Wright, 1988). Also, self-fulfilling prophecies do not always influence our behavior. We are not simply marionettes, with other people pulling our strings. Our own self-concepts are usually stronger determinants of behavior than are the expectancies of other people (Swann & Ely, 1984). Still, we should be concerned about any instances when self-fulfilling prophecies keep people from fulfilling their true potential.

Reducing Biases

We have examined how stereotypes, prejudice, and discrimination can harm people. Now let us consider some ways of overcoming these biases.

Any serious attempt to overcome unequal treatment will require major changes in the structure of society and institutions. For example, suppose that a company sincerely wants to incorporate more people of color into managerial positions. The plan will not be effective if just one Hispanic person is hired or promoted. This employee's "solo status" is likely to encourage even more discrimination and racial tension. Furthermore, if just one Hispanic person is hired and he or she fails to confirm the stereotypes, people may say, "Well, Guillermo's not like all the other Hispanic people." In fact, researchers have discovered that a minority group must constitute roughly 20% of a group for discrimination to drop substantially (Pettigrew & Martin, 1987). Let us look at some other methods for reducing biases.

Contact Under Positive Circumstances We saw in the section on attitudes that mere familiarity with a stimulus often encourages more positive attitudes. Several decades ago, people concerned with social justice thought that desegregation might work because White people would have more opportunities to become familiar with other ethnic groups. However, simple contact will not help unless the circumstances are ideal (Rothbart & John, 1985; Smith, 1990). For example, desegregation often failed to change attitudes because Blacks and Whites usually did not have equal status when they interacted in newly desegregated schools and public places (Aronson, 1987, 1988). In rare cases where equal status was ensured—as in public housing—interracial cooperation was much more likely (Deutsch & Collins, 1951).

Elliot Aronson devised a creative method of encouraging contact under positive circumstances. Specifically, he set up a situation in an ethnically diverse fifth-grade classroom, ensuring that children could be similar in status (Aronson, 1991b; Aronson et al., 1978). Prior to the study, Aronson and his colleagues had visited a newly desegregated school in Austin, Texas, and noticed that one or two students (invariably Anglos) seemed to have all the answers. In contrast, the Mexican-American and Black students were either incorrect or silent.

Aronson and his colleagues designed a **jigsaw classroom,** in which all the children must work together to ensure good grades—just as all the pieces must fit together in a jigsaw puzzle in order to complete the picture. For example, the researchers constructed a five-paragraph biography of Eleanor Roosevelt. One paragraph was then handed to each member of a five-person learning group. Each child learned only one piece of the puzzle, and the children had to learn from each other in order to master the complete biography.

Consider a representative example of a five-member group that included Carlos, a Mexican-American boy whose second language was English. Initially, the other children were impatient with Carlos's halting English. However, a classroom assistant announced that the other students would need to know information about Carlos's segment to succeed on the exam. The children soon realized that they could learn more from Carlos by paying attention to him and asking him skillful questions. After a couple of weeks, they concluded that Carlos was much smarter than they had originally thought. The Anglo students began to like him, and he began to like school more (Aronson, 1987). Research in the United States, Canada, Japan, and Israel has documented that children and also college students can develop more positive attitudes toward individuals in other groups when equal status is encouraged via a jigsaw classroom or some other kind of cooperative learning situation (Aronson, 1991b; Desforges et al., 1991).

Overcoming Mindlessness Another technique for reducing biases requires us to use some method to overcome mindlessness. In the "In Depth" section, we saw that humans have a strong tendency to categorize people into social groups. When we are trapped by our categories, we show mindlessness and fail to pay attention to the true qualities of the people we meet (Langer, 1989a). Some degree of categorization is probably inevitable, but we should encourage people to question their automatic categories.

For example, in Chapter 18, we will see that other people can force us to perform cruel actions. However, other people can also encourage us to become more noble. Blanchard and his colleagues (1991) interviewed a series of college students on the subject of racism as each one walked between classes. In some conditions, the interviewer also stopped a second person at the same time. As it happened, this second person was actually a member of the research team, who offered an opinion that strongly condemned racism. Those students who had heard another person oppose racism gave significantly stronger opinions against racism, compared to students who did not hear another person's views. When we hear strong opinions from another person, we reconsider our own thoughts and often modify them.

Patricia Devine and her colleagues have shown that our emotional reactions can also force us to rethink our stereotypes. As a consequence, we can learn to inhibit the mindless, spontaneous influence of these stereotypes (Devine & Monteith, 1993; Devine et al., 1991; Monteith et al., 1993). Their work suggests that people who see themselves as being nonprejudiced will feel guilty and self-critical when they realize that they are responding in a stereotypical way. They react to these emotions by inhibiting their stereotypical responses. For example, suppose you see yourself as an individual who is not racist. You notice three Black adults on a street corner in the afternoon, and you respond with the mindless stereotype, "Why don't they get a job?" However, the moment that stereotype comes to mind, you scold yourself, "I can't believe I actually thought that! I'm sounding like a racist." The guilt and the self-criticism you experience will play an important role in keeping you from automatically producing such stereotypes in the future.

We have seen that one person's opinion can influence the opinion of another person and that guilt and criticism can inhibit stereotypes. Let's combine that information to suggest a third method of overcoming mindlessness: We can express disapproval at racial slurs, jokes that are sexist, and remarks that reveal hurtful biases. I once asked students in my psychology of women class to write anonymous descriptions about how their behavior had changed since they had taken the course. One student wrote that the previous week, one of his fraternity brothers had made a joke about rape. He said that it had been difficult, but he responded that rape was not a joking matter. Althea Smith (1990) runs antiprejudice training programs, and she writes on this subject:

> I start the training by pointing out that not everyone needs to get arrested or demonstrate to reduce injustice or send his or her child to an inner-city segregated school to fight racism. However, all people can combat racism in small ways by encouraging their children to play, socialize, and get along with culturally diverse people; they can refuse to laugh at racist jokes; or they can voice disapproval at racial slurs. (p. 189)

If you are concerned about reducing some of your own stereotypes, try talking to someone from another social group. Focus on identifying the characteristics you have in common, rather than the categories that separate you. Denise Burden-Patmon (1989) is a professor of English who provides a useful example. She found herself standing in a downtown Boston train car, next to a young Black male whose dress and mannerisms suggested "problem youth." Most well-educated people would focus upon the boundary that separated themselves from this young man.

However, Burden-Patmon took another approach that allowed her to overcome mindlessness. She turned to him and asked how he was feeling that day. He was initially shocked, but a wonderful conversation soon developed. She learned that he had abused drugs and had been in jail, but he responded warmly when he learned that she taught English. He revealed that he had written some poetry while in jail, and even began to recite some of it on the train! A mutual appreciation of poetry allowed both of them to conquer an unnecessary category boundary.

Students can reduce their own stereotypes by focusing on interests they have in common, rather than the categories that separate them.

S E C T I O N   S U M M A R Y

STEREOTYPES, PREJUDICE, AND DISCRIMINATION

● A stereotype is a structured set of beliefs, prejudice is a negative attitude, and discrimination involves action; these biases can be based on race, gender, appearance, sexual preference, religion, social class, disability status, and other social categories.

- Racism is still present at the individual level as well as the national level; an example of contemporary racism is the refusal to help Black people unless their need is obvious.

- Sexism may harm men as well as women; gender differences are typically smaller than stereotypes suggest.

- The tendency to divide people into social groups serves as the basis for stereotypes, which then guide the way we perceive people, remember them, and evaluate them.

- Stereotypes encourage self-fulfilling prophecies.

- Ideas for reducing biases include increasing the number of members from another social group, encouraging equal status for members of different groups, and various methods of overcoming mindlessness.

CLOSE RELATIONSHIPS

This chapter on social cognition has examined how we think about other people and ourselves. For example, the first section investigated our attitudes and how they can be influenced by other people. The section on person perception focused on the impressions we form of other people, as well as the attributions we make for their behavior. In the third section, we emphasized the negative aspects of social cognition when we examined systematic biases against groups of people.

We will end this chapter by considering close relationships, the positive aspect of social cognition. Chapters 10 and 11 examined friendships among children and adults, and Chapter 11 discussed love relationships. Now we will focus on the social psychological aspects of these relationships.

Take a moment to think about the phrase, "close relationship." Who is the person with whom you have the closest, deepest, most intimate, and most involved relationship? When Berscheid and her colleagues (1989) asked this question of 250 undergraduates at the University of Minnesota, they supplied the responses shown in Figure 17.9. Furthermore, male and female students provided similar answers. Let us look at the two most common kinds of close relationships, friendship and romantic relationships. As you read about these two kinds of relationships, however, think about the way both are influenced by the social processes we have discussed in the earlier sections of this chapter. For instance, cognitive dissonance may encourage us to like someone more (or less) than we did originally. Impression formation is a crucial factor during the initial phases of both friendship and love (Wood, 1993). For example, can you recall your first impressions of the person with whom you have the closest relationship? Stereotypes, prejudice, and discrimination may keep us from forming close relationships with individuals who come from different social categories. Let us now focus on the important determinants of both friendship and love.

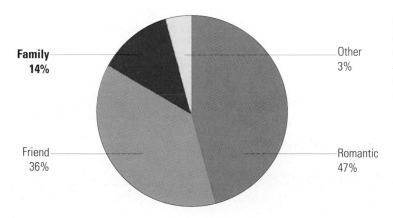

Figure 17.9

Percentage of undergraduate students nominating each relationship type. Note: The "other" category includes interactions such as work relationships. (Berscheid et al., 1989)

Family
14%

Other
3%

Friend
36%

Romantic
47%

Friendship

When we hear the word *friendship,* many people think of long, intimate talks in which deep secrets may be revealed. However, the research on actual friendships shows that most friends meet briefly in public places for superficial chats (Duck & Miell, 1986). But what factors determine which people we choose to be our friends? Among the most important are similarity, proximity, and attractiveness.

Similarity Think about your closest friends; why did those friendships develop? You and your friends probably share similar backgrounds, interests, and personal characteristics. In general, research confirms the importance of similarity (Duck, 1991; Kalbfleisch, 1993).

Our initial impressions of people are certainly influenced by their perceived similarity. For example, Gonzales and her colleagues (1983) asked people to complete surveys assessing their own attitudes and social behavior. Each person's answers were then used to construct a bogus set of responses, which indicated either 0%, 50%, or 100% agreement with his or her own responses. About two weeks later, each participant received a bogus completed survey, with the explanation that it had been completed by another student. They were asked to rate their personal feelings toward this student, on a scale with a maximum positive score of 14. The participants gave a rating of 12.0 to people whose responses showed 100% agreement, compared to a 9.0 for 50% agreement, and a 6.4 for 0% agreement. When it comes to first impressions of potential friends, opposites certainly do *not* attract!

One interesting explanation of the similarity effect is a two-step model of interpersonal attraction. This model proposes that we first screen out the people very different from ourselves and then seek out very similar people (Byrne et al., 1986; Rosenbaum, 1986). Look at Figure 17.10 and figure out whether it seems to account for your own friendship patterns. For instance, think about several people you have met this year. Were some so very different that you soon avoided them? Then, from the group of others, did you later find yourself developing friendships with people similar to yourself?

Proximity Do your closest friends live near you, or did you meet them because they sit near you in class? Do you have trouble maintaining a friendship with someone you rarely see anymore? As you learned in the discussion of the mere exposure effect, we like something (or someone) better if we see it more often.

In a classic study of friendship patterns, Festinger and his colleagues (1950) interviewed women who lived in the married students' housing at the Massachusetts Institute of Technology. Couples had been assigned apartments at random, rather than on the basis of prior friendships. When the women were asked to list their three closest friends, about two-thirds of the friends lived in the same building. Roughly half lived on the same floor, and next-door neighbors were especially popular.

Attractiveness We have seen the powerful effects of attractiveness throughout this book, most recently in the section on persuasion. As you might expect, we also tend to like attractive people. In fact, the literal meaning of the word *attractive* suggests that other people are attracted to these physically appealing people.

Figure 17.10

The two-step model of attraction.

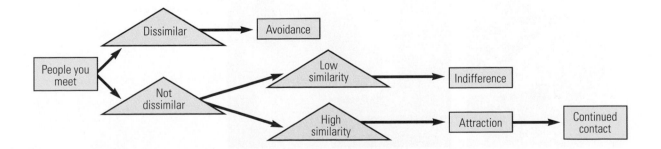

Are your same-gender friends roughly similar to you in attractiveness? In other words, are you *matched* for physical appearance? Feingold (1988b) performed a meta-analysis of a number of studies and discovered that men tended to be similar to their friends in physical attractiveness. However, women showed no matching tendencies. The explanation for these findings is not clear. Can you think of one?

We have seen that similarity, proximity, and attractiveness have an impact on friendship patterns. Now let us turn our attention to that more intense form of interpersonal attraction: love.

Love

In his book *De l'amour,* Stendhal writes, "When you are to see the woman you love in the evening, the expectation of such great happiness makes all the moments that separate you from it unbearable" (Stendhal, 1927, p. 63). In the film, *Out in Suburbia,* a middle-aged lesbian woman says about the woman she loves, "I really realized that I had fallen in love and that all the loving feelings I had ever felt . . . I was feeling, and they were *so* intensified, and it was wonderful . . . it still is!"

This section on love relationships addresses three important issues: What variables predict love relationships? What is the psychological nature of love? Finally, what are the characteristics of long-term love relationships?

Factors Related to Love Relationships Many of the factors that are important in friendships are also important in love relationships. Consider similarity, for instance. Dating and married couples tend to be similar in age, race, social class, religion, education, intelligence, and number of siblings. Couples are also similar in their personalities, attitudes, and their tendency to reveal personal information about themselves (Brehm, 1992; Buss, 1985; Hendrick & Hendrick, 1983; Hendrick et al., 1988).

Interestingly, people prefer those who share the same opinion of themselves (Swann et al., 1992). Specifically, people with positive self-concepts are more committed to spouses who think highly of them, compared with those whose spouses think poorly of them. This finding is not surprising. However, people with negative self-concepts are more committed to spouses who think poorly of them, compared with those whose spouses think highly of them! As you can imagine, this second tendency can be destructive for a person with low self-esteem.

Proximity is also an important factor: We tend to fall in love with people who live nearby and whom we see often (Brehm, 1992). As one psychologist writes, "Conceptions of romantic love aside, the 'one and only' typically lives within driving distance: It is naturally easier to become intimate with someone who is close-by" (Buss, 1985, p. 48).

We tend to fall in love with people whose attractiveness matches our own.

TABLE 17.1 Characteristics That Males and Females Rate as Important for Sexual Relationships and Meaningful Relationships

	MALES JUDGING FEMALES	FEMALES JUDGING MALES
SEXUAL RELATIONSHIP	Build/figure	Attractiveness
	Sexuality	Sexuality
	Attractiveness	Warmth
	Facial features	Personality
	Buttocks	Tenderness
MEANINGFUL RELATIONSHIP	Honesty	Honesty
	Personality	Fidelity
	Fidelity	Personality
	Sensitivity	Warmth
	Warmth	Kindness

Source: Nevid, 1984.

Naturally, attractiveness is also important (Brehm, 1992; Hatfield & Sprecher, 1986). We tend to fall in love with physically appealing people. However, that tendency is modified by a second trend: We also tend to fall in love with people whose attractiveness matches our own. In romantic couples, the attractiveness of the partners is moderately correlated (Feingold, 1988b).

However, attractiveness matters more for sexual relationships than for more permanent partnerships. Nevid (1984) asked students at a large Eastern university to rate on a 5-point scale the degree to which they judged a characteristic to be important. The students provided ratings for both a "purely sexual relationship" and a meaningful, long-term relationship. Table 17.1 shows the five most important characteristics for males judging females and for females judging males. As you will note, both men and women emphasize somewhat different characteristics for a sexual relationship.

Notice, however, that men and women are nearly identical in their judgments for meaningful relationships. Both want honesty, personality, fidelity, warmth, and sensitivity or kindness from a partner. These characteristics resemble the 10 ideal

DEMONSTRATION 17.7 The Importance of Various Features of Love

Think about your ideas regarding love. Then read each characteristic listed here and rate how *central* each one is to the nature of love. If a term is an extremely poor feature of love, rate it 1. If a term is an extremely good feature of love, rate it 8. Assign intermediate numbers to features that are somewhere between poor and good. When you are done, check the end of the chapter to see how Fehr's students rated these items.

_____ 1. Respect
_____ 2. Sacrifice
_____ 3. Dependency
_____ 4. Trust
_____ 5. Energy
_____ 6. Patience
_____ 7. Caring
_____ 8. Security
_____ 9. Protectiveness
_____ 10. Uncertainty
_____ 11. Friendship
_____ 12. Contentment
_____ 13. Honesty
_____ 14. Scary
_____ 15. Laughing

Source: Based on Fehr, 1988

qualities identified in a study on couples in a noncollege population: good companion, considerate, honest, affectionate, dependable, intelligent, kind, understanding, interesting to talk to, and loyal (Buss & Barnes, 1986).

As you may have noticed, none of these lists for long-term relationships mentions attractiveness. However, perhaps you can anticipate a problem. A bias against unattractive people operates when we first meet someone. We may reject someone who does not meet our standards of attractiveness. So we do not ever have the opportunity to know or develop a long-term relationship with a person who is a good companion, considerate, honest, and otherwise admirable—but not especially attractive.

The Nature of Love Be sure to try Demonstration 17.7 before you read further in this section. This demonstration is based on research by Beverley Fehr (1988), who asked students in Western Canada to rate how central a variety of characteristics is to their concept of love. Compare your own answers with those of Fehr's students; do you agree about which ones are central and which are largely irrelevant?

Fehr found that the items with the highest ratings were trust, caring, honesty, friendship, and respect. Similar findings were reported by students and patrons at a shopping mall in Eastern Canada (Button & Collier, 1991; Fehr, 1993). Also, a study in California found that men and women did not differ in their ratings of the central attributes; gays and heterosexuals also did not differ (Rousar & Aron, 1990). If you glance back at the important personal factors in long-term relationships, shown in Table 17.1, you'll note that the two lists are conceptually similar.

In fact, other research shows that people seem to have a prototype of love (Fehr, 1993; Fehr & Russell, 1991). As you may recall from Chapter 9, a **prototype** is the best example of a concept. For example, a prototypical vehicle is a car or a truck, rather than a wheelbarrow or an elevator. Our prototype of love is an ideal that is characterized by friendship, caring, and affection. A kind of love that involves infatuation, lust, or dependency does not match our general concept of love.

A variety of theorists have tried to categorize different kinds of love. For example, Robert Sternberg developed a three-part theory of intelligence, which we considered in Chapter 14. Similarly, he proposed a three-part theory of love, the **triangular theory of love,** which consists of three components: intimacy, passion, and decision/commitment (Sternberg, 1986b, 1988). **Intimacy** is the close, connected feeling of warmth in love relationships. Some important aspects of intimacy include valuing the loved one as part of your life, having high regard for this person, and wanting to promote this person's welfare. **Passion** includes the drives that lead to physical attraction, romance, and sexual relationships. It often creates intense physiological arousal, obsessive thoughts about the loved one, and jealousy when thinking about this person falling in love with another (Hatfield, 1988). The **decision/commitment** component consists of two aspects, the decision that you love someone and the commitment to maintain that love.

As Figure 17.11 shows, these three components form a triangle. A person may experience one, two, or all three components of love. Located in the center of the triangle is complete love, which combines all three kinds of love. Although Sternberg's theory has received considerable attention (Hendrick & Hendrick, 1992), we will need to see whether it is supported by future research.

Just as Sternberg's theory reminds us of Chapter 14, a theory proposed by Shaver and his colleagues reminds us of Chapter 10. You may recall that Chapter 10 examined **attachment,** the close emotional bond of affection between an infant and his or her caregivers. Shaver and his coauthors have proposed three categories of adult love-relationship styles, with names that resemble terms used by developmental psychologists (Hazan & Shaver, 1987; Shaver et al., 1988):

1. **Secure attachment style** means that you feel comfortable getting close to others and depending upon them.

2. **Avoidant attachment style** means that you feel somewhat uncomfortable getting close to others and trusting them completely.

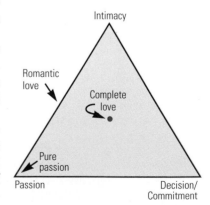

Figure 17.11

Sternberg's triangular theory of love, with its three components located at the three corners. Note that the figure also includes three examples.

3. Anxious/ambivalent attachment style means that you want to get closer to others than they would like; your intensity sometimes scares people away.

As Hendrick and Hendrick (1992) point out in their book *Romantic Love,* the research on love relationships is too new to be confined to a single theory. In fact, we may need an approach that includes the prototype theory to describe how we think about an ideal love relationship, the triangular theory to illustrate which emotional components are strongest, and the attachment theory to demonstrate how our styles of approaching a romantic partner may differ.

Long-Lasting Love Relationship Earlier in the chapter, we examined the kinds of first impressions we have for strangers. We conclude the chapter by looking at the kinds of loving partnerships that last for decades.

In Chapter 11, we discussed the high rate of divorce in North America. Even those marriages that hold together may not be blissful. For instance, married couples tend to use more negative comments toward each other than toward strangers, whereas they direct more positive comments toward strangers than toward each other (Birchler et al., 1975; Byrne & Murnen, 1988). Can you think of any reasons why strangers receive a higher ratio of pleasant messages than spouses do? In the learning chapter, we saw that reinforcement and praise are more effective in changing behavior than are punishment and negative comments. Unfortunately, we humans often fail to apply this rule when we interact with people we love.

What are the characteristics of happy couples, who remain deeply in love for many years? Researchers have identified a number of important characteristics (Branden, 1988; Brehm, 1992; Lauer & Lauer, 1985):

1. They tend to express love verbally, and they express their admiration and appreciation for each other.

2. Their partner is their best friend.

3. They regard their relationship as a long-term, important commitment.

4. They show physical affection for each other and agree about their sex life (though sexuality is typically not the most important aspect of their partnership).

5. They offer each other an emotional support system.

A happy long-term partnership is one that stresses intimacy, commitment, and—in many cases—passion. Couples in love with each other after many decades truly enjoy each other's company. These sentiments are best summarized by a woman who wrote,

I feel that liking a person in marriage is as important as loving that person. Friends enjoy each other's company. We spend an unusually large amount of time together. We work at the same institution, offices just a few feet apart. But we still have things to do and to say to each other on a positive note after being together through the day. (Lauer & Lauer, 1985, p. 24)

According to researchers, couples who have long-lasting relationships tend to express love and affection and enjoy a close friendship.

S E C T I O N   S U M M A R Y
CLOSE RELATIONSHIPS

- The most important determinants of friendship include similarity, proximity, and—to a more limited extent—attractiveness.

- Love relationships are also influenced by similarity, proximity, and attractiveness—though attractiveness is more important for purely sexual relationships than for permanent partnerships.

- Fehr suggests that we have a prototype for love relationships; characteristics such as trust, caring, honesty, friendship, and respect are important features of this prototype.

- Sternberg's triangular theory of love is based on three components: intimacy, passion, and decision/commitment.

- Shaver and his colleagues argue that people differ in their styles of attachment to their romantic partners; their attachment style may be secure, avoidant, or anxious/ambivalent.

- Long-lasting love relationships are based on expressing love and admiration, as well as friendship, commitment, affection, and support.

REVIEW QUESTIONS

1. Discuss the relationship between attitudes and behavior. Are they as closely related as you would have guessed before reading the chapter? Think of three topics from your own life concerned with attitudes and behavior, and see whether the correspondence between attitudes and behavior depends upon the four factors discussed in Figure 17.1.

2. In what way do dissonance theory and self-perception theory make different predictions about conflicting cognitions? Review Figure 17.3, and describe an incident from your experience to illustrate each theory.

3. Many parts of this chapter emphasize that we humans are overwhelmed by information, so we use shortcuts, schemas, and heuristics to simplify our social worlds. How is this theme relevant in persuasion, person perception, and stereotypes?

4. What factors influence (a) the likelihood that someone will persuade you, (b) your friendship with another person, and (c) your tendency to love another person? Point out any similarities among these lists.

5. Why is the primacy effect important in connection with the concepts of the person schema and self-fulfilling prophecy? Describe similar effects in connection with stereotypes.

6. Discuss the fundamental attribution error and the actor-observer bias. Why might both of these errors lead us to evaluate other people more negatively than we evaluate ourselves?

7. You have probably stereotyped another person on the basis of race, gender, or some other characteristic. Discuss how that stereotyping was promoted by our tendency to categorize. Next, describe how your stereotype influenced your perceptions, memory, and evaluations. Finally, note how these biases could be systematically reduced.

8. The section on the nature of love relationships examined the prototype view, the triangular theory, and the attachment approach. Briefly describe each of these three theories. Then, think of recent movies, television shows, or books with which you are familiar. Which love relationship portrayed in these media is the closest to the prototypical ideal of love? Name a media couple who is strong on each of Sternberg's three components. Finally, name a person to represent each of the attachment styles in the theory proposed by Shaver and his colleagues.

9. This chapter emphasized heuristics and schemas, which characterize top-down processing. Discuss how bottom-up processing also can be important as far as (a) the elaboration likelihood model, (b) person-perception accuracy, (c) our ability to overcome stereotypes, and (d) the factors that influence our close relationships.

10. Many students take a psychology course to help them get along with other people. What practical advice have you learned in this chapter about (a) attitudes, (b) person perception, (c) stereotypes, prejudice, and discrimination, and (d) interpersonal attraction?

NEW TERMS

social psychology
social cognition
heuristics
attitude
subjective norms
cognitive dissonance
self-perception theory
elaboration likelihood model
mere exposure effect
demand characteristics
person perception
impression formation
attribution
schema
person schema
primacy effect
self-fulfilling prophecy
negativity bias
person attribution
situation attribution
fundamental attribution error

actor-observer bias
stereotype
prejudice
discrimination
racism
symbolic racism
sexism
scapegoat theory
cognitive approach to stereotypes
outgroup homogeneity
ingroup favoritism
jigsaw classroom
prototype
triangular theory of love
intimacy
passion
decision/commitment
attachment
secure attachment style
avoidant attachment style
anxious/ambivalent attachment style

ANSWERS TO DEMONSTRATIONS

DEMONSTRATION 17.5. Symbolic racism is revealed by true answers to items 1, 2, 4, and 5, and by false answers to items 3, 6, 7, and 8.

DEMONSTRATION 17.6. Studies by Cowan and Stewart (1977) and Williams and Bennett (1975) have shown that people tend to respond W to numbers 2, 5, 6, 9, 12, 15, 16, and 18; they tend to respond M to numbers 1, 3, 4, 7, 8, 10, 11, 13, 14, and 17.

DEMONSTRATION 17.7. Research by Fehr (1988) shows that students supplied the following average ratings:

1. Respect, 7.0
2. Sacrifice, 5.4
3. Dependency, 2.8
4. Trust, 7.5
5. Energy, 4.3
6. Patience, 6.0
7. Caring, 7.3
8. Security, 5.0
9. Protectiveness, 5.1
10. Uncertainty, 2.9
11. Friendship, 7.1
12. Contentment, 5.8
13. Honesty, 7.2
14. Scary, 2.3
15. Laughing, 5.5

RECOMMENDED READINGS

Aron, A., & Aron, E. N. (1989). *The heart of social psychology: A backstage view of a passionate science.* Lexington, MA: D. C. Heath. This book examines some of the prominent studies in social psychology, as well as interviews with prominent researchers; it looks at topics such as why psychologists enjoy doing research and how they develop theories.

Brehm, S. S., & Kassin, S. M. (1993). *Social psychology* (2nd ed.). Boston: Houghton Mifflin. I really enjoyed reading this superb textbook, which offers a clearly written overview of the field, with strong coverage of the recent research; the authors also have a refreshing sense of humor.

Duck, S. (1991). *Understanding relationships.* New York: Guilford. This brief book provides a summary of the research on close relationships, as well as some practical advice for personal relationships.

Fiske, S. T., & Taylor, S. E. (1991). *Social cognition* (2nd ed.). New York: McGraw-Hill. This textbook specifically focuses on cognitive aspects of social psychology, including attributions, schemas, person memory, attitudes, and stereotypes.

Matlin, M. W. (1993a). *The psychology of women* (2nd ed.). Fort Worth, TX: Harcourt Brace Jovanovich. My textbook takes a life-span approach to women's lives, from infancy through old age. Stereotypes about gender are discussed throughout the book.

Oskamp, S. (1991). *Attitudes and opinions* (2nd ed.). Englewood Cliffs, NJ: Prentice-Hall. This well-organized undergraduate textbook examines such topics as the structure and measurement of attitudes, public opinion polling, and political attitudes.

CHAPTER 18
SOCIAL INFLUENCE

On January 28, 1986, the space shuttle *Challenger* exploded shortly after it was launched. Six astronauts and schoolteacher Christa McAuliffe were killed instantly. Later investigations revealed that engineers had warned NASA administrators about the defective O-rings, which had been responsible for the tragedy. One engineer had pleaded with a NASA administrator, "I sure wouldn't want to be the person that had to stand in front of a board of inquiry to explain why I launched." However, both NASA and the general public were swept up in the excitement about sending the first civilian into space. The NASA administrators decided to launch the shuttle—with tragic results.

On March 16, 1968, U.S. soldiers massacred about 400 unarmed women, children, and elderly men in the Vietnamese village of My Lai. One soldier, Varnado Simpson, personally killed 25 people. He reported that the crucial moment came after he had killed a young woman and her baby:

> *My mind just went. The training came to me and I just started killing. Old men, women, and children, water buffaloes, everything. We were told to leave nothing standing. We did what we were told, regardless of whether they were civilians. . . . You didn't have to look for people to kill, they were just there. I cut their throats, cut off their hands, cut out their tongue, their hair, scalped them. I did it. A lot of people were doing it and I just followed. I just lost all sense of direction. (Cited in Bilton & Sim, 1992, p. 130)*

In 1939, Germany invaded Poland. A 16-year-old Catholic girl named Stefania became deeply concerned about her Jewish friends, and she risked her life bringing food to them in the ghetto area of Warsaw. Eventually, she even built a false ceiling in her small apartment. This space served as a hiding place for 13 Jews for a period of 2½ years. During a particularly traumatic seven-month period, the Germans ordered Stefania to house several German soldiers and nurses in the apartment, yet they never learned about the 13 people in the attic (Fogelman & Wiener, 1985).

In this chapter, we will explore how people influence each other. We will see that members of a close-knit group can encourage each other to make irrational decisions, as in the *Challenger* incident; we often act differently in a group than when we are alone. Social pressure can encourage conformity, compliance, and obedience, as in the Massacre in My Lai, Vietnam. Social forces can encourage conflict and aggression on some occasions and astonishing altruism and kindness on other occasions. We can become the soldier in My Lai or young Stefania in Warsaw.

Chapter 17 emphasizes social cognition, or our thoughts about other people. The current chapter emphasized how social situations influence our actions. We consider four topics: (1) group processes; (2) yielding to social pressure; (3) aggression, conflict, and conflict resolution; and (4) altruism. Notice, then, that the first two sections examine the nature of group interactions, whereas the last two explore how interactions among people can be either negative (aggressive) or positive (altruistic).

GROUP PROCESSES

According to social psychologists, a **group** is defined as two or more people who influence one another through social interactions (Baron et al., 1993). Think about a group to which you belong—maybe a social organization, an athletic team, or a group of students who often study together. In your interactions, the members of the group depend upon one another and they also influence one another. Several processes are likely to occur within your group. In this section, we will discuss how people adopt social roles, and how the presence of another person influences performance through either social facilitation or social loafing. We will also explore two aspects of group decision making: how decision making becomes more polarized in a group and how a group can make unwise decisions in an effort to preserve the group harmony.

Social Roles

As we will emphasize throughout this chapter, a group can influence its members in many different ways. One of the most powerful functions of a group is to create roles for its members. A **role** is the shared expectation about how someone in a group ought to behave (Levine & Moreland, 1990). Think about a group you know, such as your high-school graduating class. Certain roles were defined for the class officers, for example. Once elected, these class officers probably began to act more self-important and self-confident. Another role found in most groups is "the newcomer." The established old-timers expect the newcomers to be anxious, passive, conforming, and dependent. Furthermore, the old-timers are more likely to accept newcomers who assume this role (Moreland & Levine, 1989). Still other roles are defined by organizations and by families. For example, think about the different roles that a parent and a child play in your own family.

One of the most clearly defined sets of roles exists in the prison system. Established policies and unwritten traditions both specify that guards have all the power, and the prisoners must obey. Philip Zimbardo and his colleagues demonstrated the power of these roles when they arranged to have college students play the parts of guards and prisoners in a simulated prison study (Haney et al., 1973; Zimbardo et al., 1973). College men volunteered to participate in this study and—by the flip of a coin—were assigned to either the guard or the prisoner role. The guards were given uniforms, billy clubs, and whistles. They were also told to enforce certain prison rules. In contrast, the prisoners were "arrested" at their homes, "booked" at an actual police station, and driven to "jail"—a prisonlike setup in the Stanford University psychology department basement.

Try to imagine how you would behave if you were assigned the role of either guard or prisoner. In Chapter 17, we discussed a study in which people were assigned to either Group A or Group B. Two distinctive groups emerged after a few minutes of sitting at different tables—without any specifically assigned roles (Crocker et al., 1987). What happens when the roles are more clearly defined?

Within a short time, the guards began to act "guardlike." Some tried to be tough but fair, holding strictly to the prison rules. But about a third of them became cruel and abusive. One guard, for instance, placed a prisoner in a small closet overnight for "solitary confinement." They shouted commands, took pleasure when imposing arbitrary rules, and treated the prisoners like animals.

The prisoners and guards readily assumed their roles in Zimbardo's simulated prison experiment.

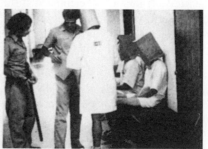

In contrast, the prisoners quickly became depressed, apathetic, and helpless—or else rebellious and angry. In fact, the situation grew so intolerable that the study had to be abandoned after only six days. The line between roles and reality had become too blurry, and it would have been unethical to continue the experiment.*

The Zimbardo prison study illustrated that we can take our roles very seriously. Like the self-fulfilling prophecy discussed in Chapter 17, we live up to the expectations of other people, and the roles help specify those expectations.

We have seen that a group can encourage its members to act out specified roles. As we will see in the next two sections, a group can also influence its members' productivity through two processes known as social facilitation and social loafing.

Social Facilitation

Suppose that you need to accomplish a truly mindless task, such as washing dishes or raking leaves. Would you finish faster if someone else is nearby or if you are alone? Now suppose that you are working on a difficult assignment, such as writing an essay about an incomprehensible poem or solving a set of challenging math problems. Would you rather be alone in the room or have someone else present?

The early research with both humans and other animals showed that the presence of others sometimes helps performance and sometimes hurts it. An intriguing solution to this contradiction was proposed in 1965 by Robert Zajonc (pronounced "*Zeye*-unce"). Zajonc suggested that we are aroused and energized when another person is nearby. That person does not need to talk, work, or do anything special; mere presence is all that is required.

Zajonc (1965) proposed that when we are aroused, we are more likely to produce a dominant response—one that is readily available. Consider what happens when people are asked to give word associations, for instance to the word *house*. When they work on this task by themselves, they tend to produce somewhat unusual associations, such as *hill* or *mansion*. However, when they work with someone else present in the room, they are more likely to produce common or dominant responses, such as *home* (Matlin & Zajonc, 1968).

So how does this tendency to produce a dominant response help us to predict whether people perform better alone or in a group? Zajonc (1965) proposed that on an easy task, the dominant response is a correct response, so we will perform better and faster in the presence of another person. However, on a difficult task, the dominant response is an error, so we will perform worse and more slowly in the presence of another person. (See Figure 18.1.) **Social facilitation** is the name of this tendency to do better on easy tasks and worse on difficult tasks when another person is present. Incidentally, you'll notice that this name is only half correct, because *facilitation* occurs only on easy tasks.

Close to 300 studies on the social facilitation effect have now been performed, and the presence of another person has been shown to have an important influence on performance (Geen, 1991). However, social facilitation has a greater impact on performance *speed* than on performance *accuracy* (Bond & Titus, 1983). Thus, we can conclude that you will wash dishes and rake leaves more quickly with another person nearby. In contrast, the presence of another person will slow your performance on more difficult tasks, such as writing essays or solving math problems. Social facilitation has a more modest influence on *accuracy,* however. With another person present, you perform only slightly more accurately on easy tasks and slightly less accurately on difficult tasks.

---

* *You may wonder whether it was ethical to conduct the experiment in the first place. To help prevent long-term harm to the participants in the prison study, Zimbardo provided extensive debriefing after the study was completed. The participants' responses on subsequent questionnaires indicated that their recovery had been satisfactory (Zimbardo et al., 1972). The research provided valuable information that even encouraged prison reform; still, we need to be concerned that some participants may have experienced psychological harm.*

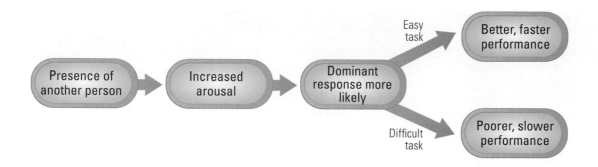

Figure 18.1
Zajonc's explanation of social facilitation.

In the past decade, some psychologists have questioned whether arousal is the critical factor in social facilitation (Baron et al., 1993; Hogg & Abrams, 1988). For example, Sanna and Shotland (1990) suggest that the important factor is not arousal but the expected evaluation from the other individual. Specifically, if you expect to perform well and you anticipate a positive evaluation from a nearby person, your performance will be better than when you work alone. In contrast, if you expect poor performance and a negative evaluation from a nearby person, your performance will be worse than when you work alone. At present, we do not have enough information to conclude whether social facilitation operates simply because of arousal or because we expect to be evaluated (Brehm & Kassin, 1993).

Social Loafing

In social facilitation research, one person works on a task with another person nearby. In social loafing research, everyone works together on the same task. These group tasks may include committees, sports teams, musical groups, and courtroom juries (Williams & Karau, 1991). According to the principle of **social loafing,** each individual works less hard in a group than if he or she worked independently. The social loafing effect has been observed for many different kinds of activities, such as swimming, listing thoughts, judging the quality of written material, and solving maze problems (Geen, 1991).

You can probably think of many examples of social loafing from your own experience. However, social loafing does not always occur. For example, the effect disappears and people work diligently when the task is interesting or relevant to their lives (Geen, 1991). People are also less likely to engage in social loafing if they know that someone can identify and evaluate what they have done (Baron et al., 1993). After all, it's worth working hard if your efforts will be noticed, even if you are part of a group.

Group Polarization

Several years ago, the members of a group at my college called Students for Peace decided to support a nationwide Fast for El Salvador, and 32 of them signed a pledge to go without eating for one to three days. This was a position that was more extreme than most of them would have taken individually. At about the same time, the College Republicans passed a resolution to petition the student council to stop funding the Students for Peace organization. This, too, was a position that was more extreme than most of them would have taken individually.

Demonstration 18.1 shows an example from a study about group polarization. In **group polarization,** group members take a more extreme position on a particular issue after discussing it than they would have taken without discussion. Thus, the average position of the Students for Peace became more liberal, whereas the average position of the College Republicans became more conservative. Notice, then, that *group polarization* means that the whole group adopts a more extreme position after discussion. It does not mean that the attitudes *within* each group become more polarized, with group members more likely to disagree with each other following discussion. Group polarization is especially likely when a group is highly cohesive.

Members of a group are likely to show social loafing; each will work less hard than if he or she were working independently.

DEMONSTRATION 18.1 An Item From the Choice Dilemma Questionnaire

Answer this dilemma without discussing it with anyone else.

Mr. J., an American prisoner of war in World War II, has the choice of possible escape with the risk of execution if apprehended, or of continuing to endure the severe privations of the camp.

Imagine that you are advising Mr. J. Here are several probabilities or odds that his escape would succeed. Please check the *lowest* probability of success that you would consider acceptable for an escape to be attempted.

_____ Place a check here if you think Mr. J. should not try to escape, no matter what the probabilities.

_____ The chances are 9 in 10 that the escape would succeed.

_____ The chances are 7 in 10 that the escape would succeed.

_____ The chances are 5 in 10 that the escape would succeed.

_____ The chances are 3 in 10 that the escape would succeed.

_____ The chances are 1 in 10 that the escape would succeed.

Notice whether your response was safe or risky. Wallach and Kogan (1959) found that after discussion with other group members, people tended to shift toward more extreme, risky selections.

Source: Wallach & Kogan, 1959.

Consider what happened when Myers and Bishop (1970) gathered together groups of relatively prejudiced high-school students to discuss racial issues. As Figure 18.2 shows, these students grew even more prejudiced after discussion. In contrast, groups of students who were relatively unprejudiced became even less prejudiced after discussion. Notice, then, that discussion caused each group to adopt a more extreme or polarized position than it had taken initially.

Think about some practical applications of the group polarization effect. For example, prior to the presidential election of 1992, politicians at the Republican National Convention became more conservative in comparison to their initial position. In contrast, the politicians at the Democratic National Convention became more liberal. Group polarization also occurs in juries discussing legal cases and on faculty committees discussing tenure decisions. Also, terrorists tend to plot more risky actions when they discuss plans in a group (Brehm & Kassin, 1993; McCauley & Segal, 1987; Wellman, 1993).

Several explanations have been suggested for group polarization (Brehm & Kassin, 1993). One recent theory is related to the tendency to categorize, which we discussed in Chapter 17. According to the social categorization explanation of group polarization, people's opinions are influenced primarily by persuasive arguments

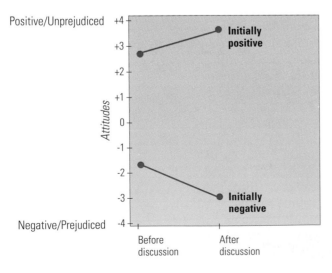

Figure 18.2

After discussion with group members, people who initially had positive attitudes toward Black people became even more positive (i.e., less prejudiced), and people who initially had negative attitudes toward Black people became even more negative (i.e., more prejudiced). (Myers & Bishop, 1970)

from ingroup members, the group to which they belong; they tend to ignore arguments from outgroup members. As a consequence, discussion will tend to polarize each group, driving it further away from a neutral position (Turner & Oakes, 1989).

Groupthink

We have seen that a group can cause its members to make more extreme decisions than they would have prior to discussion. In addition, a group can cause its members to make unwise decisions. For example, in the early 1970s, community leaders in my rural county began meeting to create a regional health center. These people knew each other socially, and they soon became a tightly knit, cohesive group, dedicated to the goal of helping their community. As the project became more elaborate and more expensive, several physicians and other outsiders tried to warn them to plan a more modest building. However, they decided to construct an elegant, large health center. Several years later, the center went bankrupt.

The health center decision, like the *Challenger* fiasco described at the beginning of the chapter, is an example of groupthink. In **groupthink,** the harmony of a group becomes more important than wise decision making. The group members work hard to maintain a positive view of the group's functioning (Turner et al., 1992), and they stop thinking critically.

In the decision-making section of Chapter 8, we saw that we often use heuristics—such as availability, representativeness, and anchoring and adjustment—in making decisions. Overwhelmed by the variety of information we should consider in making a decision, we allow our decisions to be guided by a small number of rules-of-thumb. However, when people make decisions in groups, they must consider group processes as well as cognitive information relevant to the decision. When a group is tightly knit and harmonious, the members seem to adopt an unspoken heuristic, "Preserve group harmony by going along uncritically with whatever consensus seems to be emerging" (Janis, 1989, p. 57).

Psychologist Irving Janis (1982, 1989) had examined several historic fiascos in which a government leader and his advisors were more concerned about group harmony than wise decisions. Some of these unwise decisions included the British decision to try to appease Hitler in 1938, President Truman's decision to escalate the Korean War in 1950, President Kennedy's decision to invade Cuba in 1961, and President Johnson's decision to intensify the Vietnam War. In the case of Johnson and his advisors, for example, the group ignored abundant evidence that escalation of the war

Kennedy and his advisors were influenced by groupthink in 1961 when they decided to invade Cuba. In later major decisions, Kennedy took precautions to minimize groupthink.

would not defeat the North Vietnamese and would in fact bring disapproval from many U.S. citizens.

Some of the symptoms of groupthink include the following (Baron et al., 1993; Janis, 1982, 1989):

1. The illusion of invulnerability, in which group members believe that everything will work out because this group is special and morally superior;

2. Self-censorship, in which group members keep any doubts to themselves;

3. The illusion of unanimity, in which people believe that the group opinion is unanimous and unified—partly because of self-censorship;

4. Direct pressure on dissenters, often suggesting that they are upsetting the group's harmony.

You are probably familiar with a situation in which groupthink operated. Did these four factors help push that group toward an inappropriate decision? Research on groupthink generally shows that these factors are important in real-life situations (Tetlock et al., 1992). However, groupthink is more difficult to demonstrate in a laboratory setting (Baron et al., 1993; Turner et al., 1992).

How can we prevent groupthink? Janis (1982, 1989) makes several proposals to encourage critical thinking:

1. Arrange to spend a block of time surveying any troublesome warning signs;

2. Recommend that group members discuss the issue with people outside the group who seem to support other positions;

3. Encourage two group members to play devil's advocate, arguing as persuasively as possible for another solution to the problem;

4. Hold a second-chance meeting after reaching the initial decision, to discuss any remaining doubts.

In 1962, President Kennedy was faced with a second crisis about Cuba. U.S. spy planes over Cuba had reported that Soviet nuclear weapons appeared to be aimed at the United States, though the Soviet foreign minister assured us that his country had no such plans. Ultimately, Kennedy resolved the Cuban missile crisis by avoiding groupthink. Specifically, Kennedy decided not to attend all sessions in which the crisis was discussed, so other group members were not obliged to follow the leader. He also encouraged each group member to play devil's advocate, challenging any statements that seemed unwise. Furthermore, new advisors were brought in to question the group's policies and to make new suggestions. Kennedy's awareness of group processes, combined with efforts to reduce groupthink, may have prevented a nuclear war (Suedfeld & Tetlock, 1992a).

SECTION SUMMARY

GROUP PROCESSES

- People adopt certain roles in a group situation; for example, in Zimbardo's simulated prison study, college men randomly assigned to the role of guard or prisoner soon began to act according to these roles.

- According to Zajonc's explanation of social facilitation, the presence of others encourages people to perform better on easy tasks but worse on difficult tasks; expected evaluation from the other individual may also be important.

- In social loafing, each person works less hard in a group than if he or she worked independently.

- In group polarization, group members take more extreme positions after discussing an issue than they would have taken without discussion.

- In tightly knit groups, members emphasize harmony rather than wise decision making; several precautions can encourage more critical thinking, thereby avoiding groupthink.

Conformity   Compliance   Obedience

Figure 18.3

The continuum of social influence, with the least pressure for conformity and the most pressure for obedience (After Brehm & Kassin, 1993)

YIELDING TO SOCIAL PRESSURE

A student named Jim recalls a time he yielded to social pressure during the autumn before his 10th birthday. It seems that a new boy, Wally, had moved to the neighborhood and several other boys had decided to play a trick on the newcomer. To join the club, they said, Wally had to be buried under leaves. Reluctantly, Jim joined the other boys in heaping leaves upon Wally, who was eager to be initiated into the club—a club that Jim knew did not exist. The boys announced that they would return after 10 minutes to welcome Wally to the club. Of course, they planned never to return, but instead watched from a living room window as Wally emerged from the leaves half an hour later—damp, dirty, and disappointed. Jim wishes he could rewind the video and—resisting the lure of conformity—could say, "Don't do it, Wally!"

Social pressure certainly operated in some of the scenarios we discussed in the first section of this chapter. For instance, social pressure may have compelled some of the gentler guards in the prison study to act more dictatorial. Social pressure may also have encouraged moderate group members toward group polarization and some reluctant members of tightly knit groups to join in groupthink. Now we need to focus more specifically on the nature of social pressure as we examine conformity, compliance, and obedience. We can view these three kinds of social influence along a continuum, with minimum social pressure in the case of conformity and maximum social pressure in the case of obedience. (See Figure 18.3.) Keep in mind, however, that social pressure can be used to encourage positive social behavior, as well as negative social behavior. For example, the children in Jim's neighborhood could have pressured Jim to go trick-or-treating for UNICEF or to help them look for a neighbor's lost cat.

Conformity

Conformity can be defined as a change in beliefs or behaviors in response to group pressure when the group does not directly request this change (Zimbardo & Leippe, 1991). Let's begin by considering the classic study by Asch on conformity, and then we will examine several factors that influence conformity. Finally, we will see how conformity has implications for environmental psychology.

The Asch Conformity Experiments Solomon Asch (1952, 1955), a pioneering social psychologist, demonstrated that college students often conform with a group, even when this group adopts a position that is clearly incorrect. Imagine that you are a participant in one of Asch's studies. You arrive in the laboratory and learn that you will be looking at a vertical line and deciding which of three other lines matches its length. (See Figure 18.4.) The experimenter asks you and several other

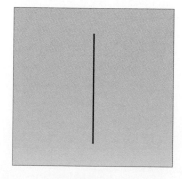
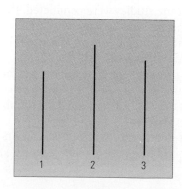

Figure 18.4

In Asch's (1955) classic study, participants were asked which of the three lines on the right matched the line on the left.

The students in this group show a high degree of conformity in the clothes they wear. Do students at your college tend to conform with respect to their clothing?

students to announce your judgments aloud, according to your seating position. The study begins uneventfully, and you begin to wonder about the point of the study. The five people to your right and the one person to your left all supply the same judgments you give.

On the third trial, however, something strange happens. The first five people have all given the wrong answer, supplying a comparison line that is clearly shorter than the line on the left. Have you entered "The Twilight Zone"? As you may have guessed from this description, all the other participants in Asch's study are confederates who have been hired by the experimenter to supply the wrong answer. In fact, you are the only genuine subject in this study, and the experimenter wants to measure your tendency to show conformity. We should note, incidentally, that the dependent measure is the subject's outward response; he or she may privately maintain a different opinion.

When Asch tested 50 subjects, he found that they conformed on 37% of the trials. Consistent with one of the themes of this book, however, Asch noted tremendous individual differences. Of the 50 participants, 14 conformed more than half the time, but 13 never once went along with the group.

Factors Influencing Conformity Asch's conformity study is easily one of the most famous in American social psychology. However, we must make an observation that is rarely included in textbooks: In at least two studies, researchers found almost no evidence of conformity. Specifically, Perrin and Spencer (1981) obtained conformity only once in 396 trials, using British subjects. Lalancette and Standing (1990) found no instances of conformity, using 40 Canadian subjects. Except for the nationality of the participants and the year in which the studies were conducted, the research methods were highly similar. As Lalancette and Standing remarked, " . . . the evidence suggests that it is an unstable phenomenon. Conformity is not universal, but appears momentarily in certain groups, at particular times" (p. 10).

Because conformity varies so much from one group to the next, we need to be especially cautious in drawing comparisons. For example, if we want to compare two conditions, then we must be sure that the subjects in these conditions are highly similar in order to avoid an important confounding variable.

One factor that influences the magnitude of conformity is group size (Zimbardo & Leippe, 1991). For example, Asch (1955) found that the subjects conformed

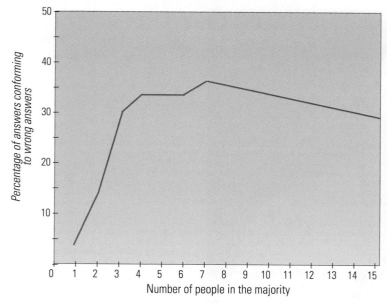

Figure 18.5

The percentage of answers that conform to the wrong answers supplied by the majority depends upon the number of people in that majority. (Asch, 1955)

less than 5% of the time when only one person provided the wrong answer. However, as Figure 18.5 shows, conformity rose rapidly as two, three, and four confederates supplied the wrong answer. As you can see, though, conformity did not rise as the number of confederates increases beyond four. When you have a chance, try Demonstration 18.2, which is a modification of a study by Milgram and his colleagues (1969) about the relationship between group size and conformity.

How does gender influence conformity? The U.S. legal system had a long history of believing that women would conform to a group's viewpoint, rather than maintain their own views. Specifically, women were given the right to vote in 1920, but they did not win the right to serve on federal juries until 1957 (Forsyth, 1990). Many—but not all—studies in this area show some gender differences in conformity (Becker, 1986; Eagly & Carli, 1981). However, Eagly and Carli calculated that only 1% of all the variation in influenceability can be accounted for by gender. As these authors conclude, "A sex difference as small as this may have few implications for social interaction" (p. 11). When a difference is this small, you are likely to know many conforming men and nonconforming women.

Another factor that influences conformity is the presence of a person who consistently expresses a dissenting or minority viewpoint[*] (Mugny & Pérez, 1991). For example, Nemeth and Chiles (1988) demonstrated that people were much less likely to show conformity in judging the color of a slide if they had been exposed to an individual who refused to conform in an earlier task. Nemeth and her colleagues suggest

[*] *"Minority viewpoint" refers to one or more people who take an unpopular stand; it does not refer to racial or ethnic group.*

DEMONSTRATION 18.2   The Influence of Group Size on Conformity

Persuade four other people to join you for a brief demonstration. Assemble your group near a classroom building or dormitory at least two stories high. One of you should stare persistently at a window on the top floor while the others stand some distance away. Note what percentage of the passersby look upward. Several minutes later, repeat the study with two people staring at the same window, and then—after appropriate intervals—repeat it with three and then four. (You remain behind to record the data.) Milgram and his coauthors (1969) found that conformity among passersby increased from 40% when one person looked up, to nearly 80% with five people looking up at the same window.

Mohandas Gandhi is an example of the power of minority influence. His opposition to British rule in India caused other Indians to question the status quo and ultimately achieve Indian independence.

that a persistent minority viewpoint forces us to think more carefully about issues in the future. Earlier, we saw that Janis proposed several precautions that would encourage group members to think critically, rather than to succumb mindlessly to groupthink. Similarly, the presence of a minority viewpoint seems to encourage us to think more critically before yielding to the dominant opinion (Nemeth, 1986; Nemeth & Staw, 1989).

Conformity and Environmental Psychology We mentioned earlier that group pressure can sometimes influence people to behave in a more noble fashion. Some examples of the positive aspects of conformity can be found in **environmental psychology,** the applied area of psychology that studies interactions between people and their environment (Bell et al., 1990). We considered some aspects of environmental psychology in Chapter 17; for example, we saw that violations of pollution laws lead to larger fines in communities with predominantly White residents, rather than people of color.

Elliot Aronson (1988) addressed another popular topic in environmental psychology: How can we convince people not to waste natural resources? In particular, people in California are urged to conserve water, but their conservation efforts usually fall short of ideal. For instance, Aronson noted that a sign in the men's shower room at the University of California at Santa Cruz urged students to save water by turning off the water while soaping up. However, a systematic observation showed that only 6% of the students conformed to the request. Aronson then asked several male students to act as models by turning off the shower while soaping up. Conformity—in terms of other students conforming to the models and obeying the sign—zoomed up to 67%.

Other research shows that people are less likely to litter when someone else avoids littering or when a clean environment suggests that other people have been resisting the temptation to litter (Cialdini et al., 1990). Another potential application of conformity involves recycling. The average U.S. resident generates about four pounds of solid waste every day, including almost two pounds of paper that could be recycled (Nickerson, 1992). On some college campuses, prominent labels on barrels urge students to separate their garbage into containers for paper, glass, aluminum, and plastic. The social pressures encourage students to conform by recycling their garbage appropriately.

On a college campus where recycling is emphasized, the social pressures encourage students to conform and divide their trash.

We have been discussing conformity, the most subtle of the group-influence forces. Notice that conformity operates through group pressure toward uniformity; no one *tells* you that you must choose Line 1, for instance. In this section, we have seen that different groups show different levels of conformity, that conformity is more likely as group size increases, and that some gender differences have occasionally been observed. We also noted that people are less likely to conform when a minority viewpoint consistently disagrees with the majority position. Finally, we discussed how the pressure to conform could be used to address environmental concerns.

Compliance

Psychologist Robert Cialdini knows about compliance from firsthand experience. He writes:

> *All my life I've been a patsy. For as long as I can recall, I've been an easy mark for the pitches of peddlers, fund-raisers, and operators of one sort or another. True, only some of these people have had dishonorable motives. The others—representatives of charitable agencies, for instance—have had the best of intentions. No matter. With personally disquieting frequency, I have always found myself in possession of unwanted magazine subscriptions or tickets to the sanitation workers' ball. (Cialdini, 1993, p. xiii)*

Compliance means going along with a stated request from someone who does not have the specific authority to make you obey. Compliance can be contrasted with two related concepts we have already discussed. *Persuasion,* considered in Chapter 17, usually refers to attitudes, whereas *compliance* refers to behavior. *Conformity,* which we just finished discussing, relies upon more subtle group pressures, rather than a stated request.

Compliance can be used to encourage appropriate social behavior. Consider an example related to environmental psychology: A 20-minute television program was created for a specific community in Virginia, showing them how to reduce their air-conditioning bills. After seeing the film, the residents reduced their energy use by 10% (Aronson & Gonzales, 1990). Two of the most effective compliance techniques are called the foot-in-the-door technique and the door-in-the-face technique.

The Foot-in-the-Door Technique Has a friend ever asked you for a small favor—perhaps to borrow your class notes—and then you later discovered yourself performing a much larger favor? If so, your friend has mastered the **foot-in-the-door technique,** a two-step compliance method; in which an influencer achieves compliance with a small request before making a larger request. People who have first said yes to the small favor are more likely to say yes to the larger favor, in contrast to those who were asked only about the larger favor. For example, fund-raisers often find that if they can convince someone to donate $50, they can count on this individual to donate an even more generous sum at a later date (Wellman, 1993).

Consider a study by Freedman and Fraser (1966). These researchers made telephone calls to 36 phone numbers, selected at random from a telephone directory. The people who answered the phone were asked whether they would answer a short survey as part of a consumer research project, and then the researcher asked eight simple questions such as "What brand of soap do you use in your kitchen sink?" A control group of 36 people were not contacted at this point, so they had no opportunity to perform a small favor. Three days after the experimental group had performed the small favor, people in both groups were contacted about performing a large favor. They were asked to allow five or six men from the consumer research project to spend two hours going through their homes, classifying all household products. Of those who had first complied with the small favor, 53% agreed to the large favor. However, of those who were asked only about the large favor, only 22% agreed.

If this resident allows the salesperson to "put her foot in the door," he may find that a small request will soon become a major purchase.

Notice that the name *foot-in-the-door* is appropriate; once the foot is in the door, you soon find yourself inviting the entire salesperson inside, and you are vulnerable to larger requests. In a book on political psychology, Fischer and Johnson (1986) point out how politicians use this technique:

> The "foot in the door" strategy of initially funding public programs on a low-level basis is an instance of this strategy. The fact that we have already spent hundreds of millions of dollars on the MX, a weapon of dubious military utility, is an advantage to those who favor the MX because they can use this fact to argue against "throwing away" the sunk costs that were paid for by taxpayers' hard-earned dollars. (p. 59)

The Door-in-the-Face Technique In the comic strip "Calvin and Hobbes," little Calvin asks, "Mom, can I set fire to my mattress?" She replies, "No, Calvin." He then asks, "Can I ride my tricycle on the roof?" "No, Calvin," she again replies. And then Calvin asks the real question, "Then can I have a cookie?" At his tender age, Calvin has already learned the **door-in-the-face technique,** a two-step compliance technique in which an influencer achieves compliance by first making a request that is so large that it is certain to be denied, and then making a smaller, more reasonable request. (See Table 18.1.)

To test the door-in-the-face technique, Cialdini and his colleagues (1975) asked one sample of college students for a very large favor—to spend two hours each week

TABLE 18.1 Two Compliance Techniques

	COMPLIANCE TECHNIQUE	
	Foot-in-the-Door	**Door-in-the-Face**
Order of requests	Small, then large	Large, then small
Research example	"Answer the following eight questions"	"Work weekly with juvenile delinquents"
	then	*then*
	"Let research team into your home"	"Work one day with juvenile delinquents"

as a counselor to juvenile delinquents, for a minimum of two years. As you might imagine, everybody refused. So then they asked the students if they would be willing to chaperone a group of juvenile delinquents on a day-long trip to the zoo. An impressive 50% said that they would. In contrast, when the researchers asked a similar sample of students for this relatively small favor, without first asking about the large favor, only 17% said yes.

In the section on groupthink, I mentioned a community health center that ultimately went bankrupt. Actually, I was impressed that the fund-raisers had been able to collect as much money as they did. The secret, as it happened, was the door-in-the-face technique. The fund-raisers had learned from community leaders about each family's occupations, and they used this information to calculate an outlandishly high donation request. For example, if a family had an estimated income of $35,000, they would say, "We have calculated that a family with your income should contribute about $2,000 over a three-year period." This family probably would not donate $2,000, but they might actually contribute $500. Without the initial door-in-the-face interaction, however, this family probably would have given only $100.

Notice, incidentally, that the door-in-the-face technique resembles the anchoring-and-adjustment heuristic discussed in Chapter 8. People rely heavily on the initial anchor—in this case $2,000—and they make fairly modest downward adjustments. Now try Demonstration 18.3 before you read further.

Obedience

So far, we have considered only relatively mild social pressure. A student selects a matching line that is clearly too short, consistent with the majority judgment (conformity), or a community member agrees to let a research team into her home (compliance). The third kind of social pressure is stronger. In **obedience,** an authority specifically commands us to change our behavior. Let us first consider the Milgram obedience studies. Then we will look at some historical examples of obedience. This section ends with some conclusions about obedience.

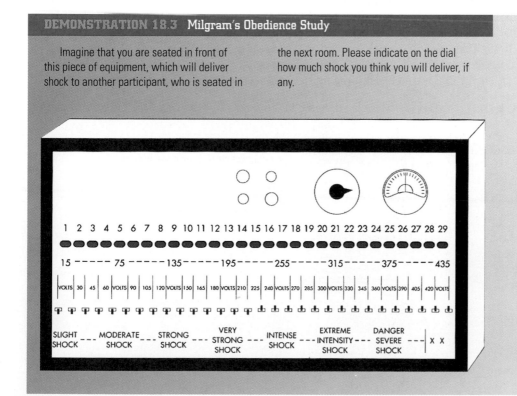

DEMONSTRATION 18.3 Milgram's Obedience Study

Imagine that you are seated in front of this piece of equipment, which will deliver shock to another participant, who is seated in the next room. Please indicate on the dial how much shock you think you will deliver, if any.

Milgram's Obedience Studies Stanley Milgram's research on obedience is clearly among the most famous studies in psychology (Blass, 1992). Try to imagine yourself participating in one of these classic studies (Milgram, 1963, 1974). After seeing an ad in the local paper, you report to Yale University's psychology department for a study on memory and learning. You meet the experimenter as well as another participant, a pleasant middle-aged man. The two of you draw lots, and you are assigned the role of the teacher; the other participant will be the learner. You are seated in front of an electric-shock generator, as shown in Demonstration 18.3, and he is strapped into a chair where he will receive electric shock. You are instructed to press a switch and deliver shock whenever he makes a mistake on the learning task. Furthermore, you are told to increase the intensity of shock after each error.

When Milgram described the study to psychologists and psychiatrists, most thought that people would refuse to deliver more than a mere 150-volt shock. Does this match your own predictions for Demonstration 18.3? Contrast these predictions with the results. In the proximity condition, the teacher sat in the same room as the learner, who cried out in response to the more painful shocks. In the voice-feedback condition, the teacher could hear the learner crying out in the same fashion from an adjacent room. As Figure 18.6 shows, obedience was highest in the remote condition, where the learner was presumably sitting in an adjacent room and did not cry out. The majority in this condition delivered the full 450 volts of electric shock.

We need to stress that the "learners" in Milgram's research were really confederates, and they received no actual shock. At the end of the study, the "teachers" were debriefed and assured that the "learners" had felt no pain. However, many psychologists have objected to this study, arguing that the study was unethical. After all, the participants were deceived, and they also experienced mental torment (Baumrind, 1964; Blass, 1992; Collier et al., 1991). Still, Milgram (1964) argued that the studies were worthwhile because they provided valuable insights into the way we humans obey authority. Let us consider several real-life examples of obedience before we draw some conclusions.

Historical Examples of Obedience Milgram's experiments are powerful because they show us that ordinary people can perform an action that seriously violates their conscience (Mixon, 1989). Their behavior reminded everyone of the German citizens who had systematically slaughtered millions of innocent people between the years of 1933 and 1945. These good citizens obeyed the commands of Nazi authorities. They built gas chambers and guarded death camps, producing daily quotas of corpses with the same efficiency that would be admired in the manufacturing of appliances (Milgram, 1974).

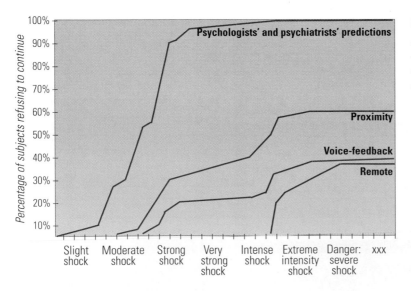

Figure 18.6

Percentage of participants who refused to continue the Milgram experiment, as a function of shock level and the task condition. (Based on Milgram, 1974)

Blind obedience is not confined to Europe. After all, it was American soldiers who slaughtered the Vietnamese civilians at My Lai, as we noted at the beginning of the chapter. More recent examples include the Iran-Contra incident (Kelman & Hamilton, 1989) and the Jonestown massacre. In the case of Jonestown, Guyana, Reverend Jim Jones led a group of nearly 1,000 of his religious followers as they committed mass suicide by drinking a beverage laced with cyanide.

In many cases, the power of the authority can be terrifying. In Nazi Europe, people were killed for defying authority. In Vietnam, soldiers who ignored an order in battle were sometimes executed on the spot (Bilton & Sim, 1992). And followers of Jim Jones had been mutilated and murdered for failing to obey orders (Osherow, 1988). However, people often obey an authority, even when the threat is minimal. Kelman and Hamilton (1989) dedicate their book *Crimes of Obedience* to Martin Luther King, Jr., who urged people to consult their conscience before blindly obeying an immoral authority:

> . . . *an individual who breaks a law that conscience tells him is unjust, and willingly accepts the penalty by staying in jail to arouse the conscience of the community over its injustice, is in reality expressing the very highest respect for law. (M. L. King, Jr., 1963, cited in Kelman & Hamilton, 1989, p. vii)*

Dr. Martin Luther King, Jr., urged people to consult their conscience, rather than obey an immoral command. In this photo, Dr. King is one of the leaders in the 1966 civil-rights march in Selma, Alabama.

Conclusions About Obedience The Milgram research carried clear implications for real-life events, but it also contributed to psychological theory. In Chapter 13, we pointed out that some psychologists emphasize the importance of the situation, rather than internal traits. In the case of the Milgram studies, people are more likely to obey if they are high in a trait involving a submissive attitude toward authority (Blass, 1991). However, the power of the situation is even stronger; in a compelling situation, ordinary citizens seem to obey an authority unquestioningly.

Why did people obey the experimenter in the Milgram studies? One reason we obey is simple embarrassment. We would feel awkward saying, "No, I refuse." Another reason is based on an earlier discussion; our role as subordinates encourages us to obey both military leaders and experimenters, even when we are wrongfully hurting other people. A third reason is that authorities typically use the foot-in-the-door technique. For instance, the experimenter in the Milgram studies began by specifying mild shock. Gradually, the situation became more serious, but by then, the participants were entrapped (Ross, 1988).

A final reason we obey is that we are sometimes guilty of mindlessness, or failure to think through all the consequences of obedience (Langer, 1989a). We continue on, delivering the shock without critical analysis. Whenever we find ourselves confronted by an illegal or inhumane command, we need to evaluate the situation critically and determine whether we can resist an immoral authority.

SECTION SUMMARY

YIELDING TO SOCIAL PRESSURE

- In the Asch conformity experiments, people often conformed to the majority position, even when it was incorrect; conformity depends to a great extent on the nature and size of the group; gender has little influence on conformity, but a minority viewpoint can be important.

- Two effective compliance methods are the foot-in-the-door technique (small request followed by large) and the door-in-the-face technique (large request followed by small).

- In Milgram's obedience studies, participants usually obeyed the experimenters' commands, but obedience depended upon the task conditions; obedience is encouraged by embarrassment, social roles, the foot-in-the-door technique, and mindlessness.

AGGRESSION, CONFLICT, AND CONFLICT RESOLUTION

In September 1990, Brian Watkins and his family were vacationing in New York City. As these tourists from Utah were waiting at a Manhattan subway station, a gang of teenagers punched Brian's mother, Karen, and knocked her down. When Brian came to his mother's rescue, one gang member stabbed a 4-inch knife into Brian's chest. He died an hour later. Unfortunately, as Figure 18.7 shows, the homicide rate among adolescent males in the United States is more than four times higher than the rate in Canada, Great Britain, and other developed nations.

In November 1989, about 30 men dressed in military uniforms in El Salvador tortured and killed six priests. One of the priests, Ignacio Martín-Baró, was the chairperson of the psychology department at Central American University. Ironically, Martín-Baró was a social psychologist who conducted research on the influence of war on children and on the psychological effects of torture (Marín, 1991).

In addition to the startling, newsworthy acts of aggression we hear about in the media, we also encounter more ordinary aggression and conflict in our daily lives. A fight breaks out during a hockey game. A friend reveals that her boyfriend beat her up last night. Your roommate refuses to turn the radio down when you are trying to study. We can easily compile a long list of everyday aggressions.

This section begins with several explanations of aggression, and then we will discuss whether gender is related to aggression. Our other two topics are conflict development and conflict resolution.

Explaining Aggression

Before you read further, clarify your own beliefs about aggression by trying Demonstration 18.4. **Aggression** can be defined as a deliberate attempt to injure or destroy someone, either physically or psychologically (Berkowitz, 1990). Let us consider several explanations for aggression, beginning with one approach that has little support from the psychological research.

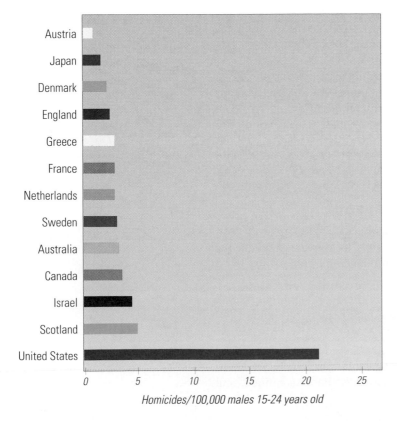

Figure 18.7

The homicide rate among males ages 15–24 in developed nations for 1986 and 1987. (Based on Prothrow-Stith, 1992)

Homicides/100,000 males 15-24 years old

DEMONSTRATION 18.4 Beliefs About Aggression

Answer each of the following questions with a T (true) or an F (false). The answers appear at the end of the chapter.

_____ 1. Aggression is caused by a simple inborn drive.

_____ 2. Humans are the only animals that often kill members of their own species.

_____ 3. Humans are instinctively aggressive.

_____ 4. Research has demonstrated that men are consistently more aggressive than women.

_____ 5. The aggressive instinct can be controlled by participating in substitute activities, such as watching football games and violent movies.

_____ 6. If children are allowed to play aggressively, they will get it out of their system and be better adjusted in the long run.

_____ 7. Extreme acts of violence, such as child and spouse abuse, are typically committed by people with psychological disorders.

_____ 8. War is an expression of our aggression instinct.

Source: Based on Aronson, 1988; Goldstein, 1989; Groebel & Hinde, 1989a.

Is There an Aggression Instinct? Nobel prizewinner Konrad Lorenz argued that all animals—including humans—have a "fighting instinct" (Lorenz, 1974). In other words, we are born with a predisposition toward violence; we do not need to learn to be violent. Lorenz also rejected the possibility that aggression is mainly a response to something in the environment (Berkowitz, 1990).

However, the majority of psychologists do not favor this instinctive position (e.g., Lore & Schultz, 1993). In one of the most impressive rejections of the instinct approach, 20 scientists from 12 countries gathered in 1986 in Seville, Spain. They drafted the **Seville Statement,** which asserts that it is scientifically incorrect to say that humans have an inborn tendency to be aggressive or that evolution has favored aggressive members of our species. The document, which has been endorsed by organizations such as the American Psychological Association and the American Anthropological Association, includes the following passage.

> *The fact that warfare has changed so rapidly over time indicates that it is a product of culture. Its biological connection is primarily through language, which makes possible the coordination of groups, the transmission of technology, and the use of tools. War is biologically possible, but it is not inevitable, as evidenced by its variation in occurrence and nature over time and space. There are cultures which have not engaged in war for centuries, and there are cultures which have engaged in war frequently at some times and not at others. (Adams, 1990, pp. 1167–1168)*

The Seville Statement has now been circulated and endorsed in many countries throughout the world (Adams, 1989, 1993).

Biological Explanations The instinct approach argues that all humans share an inevitable tendency to be aggressive; that position has little support. In contrast, the biological approach argues that biological factors, such as genetics and brain abnormalities, contribute to individual differences in aggression; this position is supported by the research. For example, twin studies and adoption studies provide evidence of a genetic component for criminal behavior (DiLalla & Gottesman, 1991). Furthermore, autopsies performed on violent criminals occasionally show some kind of brain damage, such as a brain tumor. Other research suggests that some violent individuals show a decrease in aggression after a brain tumor has been removed (Berkowitz, 1990; Geen, 1990).

Observational Learning In Chapter 6 we discussed experimental, quasi-experimental, and correlational research on television violence. These studies show that many children become more aggressive after they observe violent programs. However, some children manage to remain gentle and considerate, despite the horrors they have seen on the family TV set. A child who observes violence is not condemned to a life of crime, although aggression is indeed more likely.

Let us consider a related question. What happens when adults view violent pornography? Surveys of pornographic violence emphasize that sexual aggressors are typically portrayed in a positive fashion, and they are seldom punished for their actions (Check & Malamuth, 1986; Palys, 1986). We should not be surprised to learn, then, that both college and noncollege men who have been exposed to pornography are more likely than other men to believe the myth that women enjoy rape (Check, 1984; Malamuth & Check, 1985). Furthermore, men who have seen a movie containing sexually violent episodes are more likely than men in a control group to approve of wife battering (Malamuth, 1987; Malamuth & Check, 1981). Also, men who have seen a sexually violent movie are less likely to sympathize with a rape victim when they serve as jury members in a reenacted rape trial.[*] That is, they are more likely to believe that a victim's injury was not very severe, and they are more likely to consider her a worthless person (Donnerstein & Linz, 1984).

According to reviews of the literature, violent pornography also increases rape fantasies, decreases support for women's rights, and increases tolerance for rapists (Intons-Peterson & Roskos-Ewoldsen, 1989). In general, however, researchers point out that violent pornography is more likely than nonviolent pornography to have these effects (Zillmann, 1992). As a review of the literature concludes,

> . . . some forms of pornography, under some conditions, promote certain antisocial attitudes and behavior. Specifically, we should be most concerned about the detrimental effects of exposure to violent images in pornography and elsewhere, particularly material that portrays the myth that women enjoy or in some way benefit from rape, torture, or other forms of sexual violence. (Donnerstein et al., 1987, p. 171)

The Influence of Frustration Observational learning explains how people might learn certain aggressive acts. However, it does not clarify what motivates them to perform these aggressive acts. According to the **frustration-aggression hypothesis,** external events are important; people are most likely to act aggressively when they are frustrated because their goals have been blocked (Berkowitz, 1990; Dollard et al., 1939).

The original theorists argued that frustration inevitably produced aggression. However, we now know that the *interpretation* of frustration is important. For example, an aggressive reaction is more probable if the frustration can be traced to an identifiable source, such as a rival (Groebel & Hinde, 1989a). Aggression is also more probable when the frustration arouses negative emotions (Berkowitz, 1989). Try to recall a time when you were recently frustrated. Were you more likely to react aggressively if you could identify the villain and if you were seething with anger?

Aggression and Gender

According to the stereotype, men are eager to fight and insult, whereas women are much less aggressive. Research on gender differences in aggression shows that

Men who have seen sexually violent movies are more likely to believe the myth that women enjoy rape and that rape victims are not seriously hurt by the rape incident.

---

[*] *Many students wonder about the ethics of presenting sexually violent material to people who then become less sympathetic to victims of rape. Clearly, researchers must provide appropriate debriefing about the reality of rape. In several experiments, research participants see a film or read a story that includes a rape scene. Participants who are then debriefed about the true horror of rape are less accepting of rape myths than control-group participants (Intons-Peterson et al., 1989; Malamuth & Check, 1984). Obviously, the debriefing statement must be carefully worded and persuasively delivered.*

women and men are more similar than most people believe. For example, one survey of the literature showed significant gender differences in only about one-third of the research studies (Eagly, 1987).

Gender differences tend to be larger in studies of children, rather than adults (Hyde, 1986). Gender differences are also larger when aggression is measured in terms of physical injury or pain, rather than psychological harm (Eagly & Steffen, 1986). For example, typical research shows that men are more likely than women to deliver electric shock to somebody, but men and women are equally likely to deliver insults.

The explanation for the occasional gender differences is not clear. The media certainly portray a greater number of violent males than violent females. Gender differences in physical strength may be another contributing factor. Also, women are more likely than men to feel guilty about aggression; these feelings may inhibit aggressive actions (Frodi et al., 1977).

The data show an additional important pattern. Gender differences are relatively small when we examine interactions with strangers. However, research throughout North America documents a high incidence of domestic violence; men are much more likely than women to injure their spouses severely (Eagly, 1987; Herman, 1989; Morval, 1992). For example, in one of my classes, a young woman vividly described how her ex-husband tracked her down in her new apartment and hurled her through the bedroom wall. A recent Canadian study reported that 45% of women over the age of 18 had experienced violence from husbands, boyfriends, or other men they knew ("The Violence Against Women Survey," 1993).

However, remember that men and women are similarly aggressive in many situations; biological forces do *not* guarantee that men must be aggressive. Ironically, people who accept the myth that men are inevitably more violent may believe—erroneously—that men are biologically incapable of controlling their tempers.

The Growth of Conflict

Conflict, which is closely related to aggression, is an interpersonal process that occurs when the actions of one party interfere with the actions of another party (Kelley, 1986). Conflict can occur between two people (you and a classmate, for instance), between two groups (for example, between ethnic groups, as in the former Yugoslavia), or between two nations (a glance at any newspaper provides numerous examples). Obviously, the dynamics change somewhat when we consider nations, rather than individuals, but many of the same elements can be found in all conflicts.

Conflict analysts point out that participants in a conflict can take three different approaches to a conflict. In a **lose-lose approach,** both parties will suffer a net loss. War is often an example of a lose-lose approach. Between World War II and 1989, for example, there were 127 wars and about 22,000,000 deaths related to war (Nelson, 1991; Sivard, 1989). Even the winner in a war usually loses more in terms of human suffering than any positive outcome the war was supposed to accomplish.

Most competitive sports are examples of a **win-lose approach,** in which one player's win is balanced by the other player's loss. Most competitive situations in business also involve a win-lose approach.

However, in a **win-win approach,** both parties gain by cooperating. Here, there are only winners, and no losers. A good example of a win-win approach to conflict occurred several years ago in Southern California. Two neighborhoods located next to each other had experienced increasing violence at their mutual boundary. The conflict was heightened because one neighborhood had mostly Mexican-American residents, whereas the other neighborhood had mostly gay male residents. Fortunately, some of the residents decided to do something about the violence and planned a street fair for everyone. The fair became an annual event, and the project, known as Sunset Junction Neighborhood Alliance, provided many opportunities for members of the two groups to plan and work together, rather than in conflict (Rebecca, 1983). Clearly, a win-win approach favors successful conflict resolution, whereas conflict escalation is more likely with either a lose-lose or a win-lose approach (Deutsch & Shichman, 1986; Heitler, 1990).

We tend to think that conflict is inevitably wrong and unproductive. However, some nonaggressive conflict can be helpful, assuming that people enter the conflict with a win-win approach. For instance, groupthink occurs because the group members want to avoid conflict at all cost. Also, conflict often nourishes social change. What would happen if civil rights reformers were routinely stifled? Would we have wheelchair access to public places if people with disabilities systematically kept their needs quiet? Conflict can also be a creative force that benefits both sides (Pettit et al., 1985). A conflict between the sales and production divisions of a company may be resolved by designing a better product, or one that can be manufactured at a lower cost.

Let us consider several factors that tend to fuel a conflict and encourage the parties to adopt either a lose-lose or a win-lose approach. These factors include issues proliferation, stereotypes, and enemy images.

Some conflict can be productive. For example, people with disabilities probably would never have won wheelchair access to public transportation in some areas if they had kept quiet about their needs. Here, in Austin, Texas, a man boards a bus that is equipped with a hydraulic lift.

Issues Proliferation Often, a conflict starts small, but then each party adds additional grievances, which were not part of the original problem (DeMott, 1987). The tendency for parties in a conflict to increase the number of controversial topics is called **issues proliferation.** Two roommates in conflict over an insulting remark may suddenly start dragging in each other's annoying habits and other long-forgotten injustices. Whenever you hear yourself saying, "And another thing . . ." in the midst of a conflict, you know you are engaging in issues proliferation. You will be more likely to resolve the conflict if it remains more narrowly focused.

Stereotypes In Chapter 17, we saw how stereotypes can distort reality. A similar stereotypical distortion occurs in conflict; we simplify an extremely complex situation into categories such as "good guys" versus "bad guys" (Rubin, 1991a; Smith, 1992).

Stereotypes also lead us to make attributional errors (Rubin, 1991a). For example, when the Soviets invaded Afghanistan during the 1980s, U.S. politicians attributed this action to a stable, internal characteristic of Soviet policymakers—their presumed tendency to take over other countries. The United States invested billions of dollars in additional military resources as a result of this perceived threat. However, another highly likely interpretation is that the Soviet Union was simply trying to keep its government from collapsing, and the action was prompted by a specific external situation (Pruitt & Rubin, 1986).

The truth is that the actions of other people are often ambiguous. In conflict situations, however, we tend to supply evil motivations to our rivals. Someone who has been quarreling with you for months does you a favor, and you find yourself asking, "I wonder what she wants from me?" If you find yourself in this situation, try several more charitable attributions!

Enemy Images According to a concept called **enemy images,** we see ourselves as good and peace-loving, whereas our enemies are evil, aggressive, and warlike. These enemies, however, also have an image of us. Whereas they see *themselves* as good and peace-loving, they see *us* as evil, aggressive, and warlike (Moyer, 1985). Reality is usually ambiguous; we all have our peace-loving and aggressive sides.

One of the first to notice the intriguing symmetry of enemy images was Urie Bronfenbrenner (1961), who pointed out that Russians and Americans both thought that the other country's government could not be trusted. This mistrust persisted into the 1980s. For example, many U.S. citizens mistakenly believed that the Soviets—rather than the Americans—first invented the atomic bomb (Silverstein, 1989). Enemy images can be found in different forms during the 1990s. For example, many North Americans had negative images of Iraqis during the Gulf War; Iraq residents also had negative images of Americans (White, 1991). Furthermore, a survey of newspapers in 1992 showed that the Croats and the Serbs had exaggerated enemy images

The two enemy images from previous eras in the United States: the Germans in World War I (left) and the Japanese in World War II (right). (Keen, 1986)

of each other during the early days of the conflict in the former Yugoslav republic ("Enemy Images," 1992).

Enemy images help escalate conflict because they encourage us to think of our adversaries as evil, rather than humans who share the same kinds of strengths and weaknesses we ourselves have. Consider the rival team at a sports event; do enemy images encourage you to see them as immoral and evil?

Successful conflict resolution is more likely if we avoid issues proliferation, stereotyping, and enemy images. Let us consider some other approaches to conflict resolution at both the interpersonal and the international level.

Interpersonal Conflict Resolution

Try Demonstration 18.5 to prepare for our discussion about resolving interpersonal conflicts. If you are serious about resolving a conflict, you may want to read one of the recent books on the subject (e.g., Cahn, 1992; Heitler, 1990; Weeks, 1992).

Successful problem solving in a conflict situation depends upon finding **perceived common ground,** or an alternative that satisfies the wishes of both parties (Pruitt & Rubin, 1986). Several conditions contribute to this perceived common ground:

1. The perception that the other person is ready to solve the problem. (Note that enemy images tend to discourage this viewpoint.)

2. Trust, or the perception that the other person is concerned about your welfare.

3. Contact and communication, in which both parties have equal status. (Recall from Chapter 17 that discrimination is likely when one person has more status than the other.)

Before you begin to resolve a conflict, consider whether any conflict actually exists! As you might guess from our discussion of social psychology, many conflicts are illusory; the two participants in the conflict may actually want the same goals (Carnevale & Pruitt, 1992). Also, keep in mind some pointers from previous chapters. In Chapter 8, you learned about creative problem solving; conflicts can often be resolved by figuring out innovative methods of expanding the number of options or the

DEMONSTRATION 18.5 Interpersonal Conflict

Take a moment to think about a recent conflict you have had with a friend or a romantic partner. This conflict can either be resolved, or it can be ongoing. How concerned are you about your own welfare in this conflict? To what extent are you concerned about the other person's welfare? Now examine the figure below. This diagram is called a *dual-concern model,* because it points out that our choices depend upon the relative concern we have about our own welfare and the welfare of another person (Carnevale & Pruitt, 1992; Pruitt & Rubin, 1986). Where would you place your own conflict on this diagram? If you selected "inaction," are you satisfied with the decision to do nothing? If you categorized the conflict as "yielding," decide whether you are satisfied not to have your own preferences satisfied. (In fact, that solution may be ideal.) If the conflict falls in the "contending region," ask yourself whether you have considered the position of the other individual. Finally, if you categorized the conflict as "problem solving," this section provides the perfect opportunity to begin to resolve this conflict!

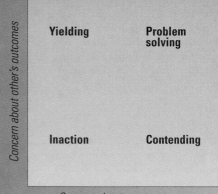

quantity of resources (Rubin, 1991b). In Chapter 12, you learned that thought processes are more flexible when people's emotions are positive. Find a pleasant setting for your conversation, and maintain an optimistic outlook.

One of the most useful skills in creative problem solving is effective listening. Focus on what the other person is saying, rather than on the response you plan to make. Try discovering what is *right* in the speaker's statements, not what is wrong. Imagine how the situation feels from his or her perspective (DeMott, 1987; Heitler, 1990).

Your goal in conflict resolution should be to identify an integrative solution that meets both parties' hopes. If that approach is not successful, work to identify the issues that have the highest priority, discarding the less important ones. Another possibility is that many colleges and universities now have Dispute Settlement Centers, in which a mediator can help you resolve troublesome conflicts. Even more promising is a new program to teach conflict management in schools, beginning in elementary classrooms. Through the Community Board Program, for example, selected children wear "Conflict Manager" T-shirts. They help resolve conflicts that arise on the playground or at lunch (Amsler, 1991). These programs have not yet been thoroughly studied, but the early feedback suggests that they have been successful in reducing the incidence of school violence (Deutsch, 1993).

International Peacemaking

Researchers argue that conflicts between individuals, groups, communities, and nations all share certain basic similarities, and the same conflict-resolution principles can be used in many superficially different disputes. The topic of international peacemaking has a surprisingly long history. In fact, William James tried to involve the American Psychological Association in peace research in 1910 (Kimmel & VandenBos, 1992).

In the Community Board Program, a conflict manager tries to resolve a conflict that has arisen on the playground.

As I write this chapter in late 1993, the United States is not currently involved in an arms race, but the stockpile of nuclear weapons is frightening; we may be involved in another conflict by the time you read this book. A major problem with these large-scale international conflicts is that high levels of tension can produce cognitive rigidity, and the political leaders may have trouble devising new alternatives and options (Carnevale & Pruitt, 1992; Deutsch, 1983).

One barrier that has important implications for international conflict resolution is called reactive devaluation (Ross, 1992; Ross & Stillinger, 1991). According to the concept of **reactive devaluation,** the mere act of offering a particular concession makes that offer less attractive to the recipient. Our enemy images force us to devalue anything proposed by "the enemy"—even an idea that would benefit everyone! For example, in 1986, California residents were asked to evaluate a proposal for nuclear disarmament that called for 50% reduction of long-range "strategic" weapons, followed by further reductions during the next 15 years. When residents were told that the proposal had been made by a U.S. leader, 90% approved; when they were told it had been made by a Soviet leader, only 44% approved. (Incidentally, beware of reactive devaluation in your own interpersonal conflicts, as well!)

One technique of conflict resolution that is especially useful in international peacemaking is called GRIT. **GRIT, or Graduated and Reciprocated Initiatives in Tension Reduction,** consists of a series of steps in which one party announces a step it will take to reduce tension, the party actually takes the step, and then the party states its expectations for some kind of reciprocation. If the other party reciprocates, the first party then starts another round of these initiatives (Deutsch & Shichman, 1986; Fisher, 1990; Osgood, 1962). Once the process begins, each side becomes increasingly committed to conflict resolution (Rubin, 1991b).

An advantage of GRIT is that one small gesture of conciliation creates a more positive atmosphere that can encourage trust. One of the best international applications of GRIT occurred in 1963, when President Kennedy decided to try to de-escalate conflict with the Soviet Union. It was only a few months after the Cuban missile crisis (discussed in connection with groupthink). Kennedy announced that the United States would stop all nuclear tests in the atmosphere in an effort to reduce tension, and it would not resume testing unless some other nation did. The Soviet Union responded by announcing that it would halt production of its strategic bombers. Several other reciprocal gestures continued throughout the next few months, with one of the most important accomplishments being a permanent ban on open-air testing of nuclear weapons (DeMott, 1987).

In the 1990s, the United States has so many nuclear weapons that they represent roughly 200,000 times the force of the nuclear bomb that destroyed Hiroshima in World War II.

Unfortunately, this period of reduced international tension ended when the United States became involved in Vietnam, introducing a new source of tension. However, the successful de-escalation is one example of the value of GRIT in both international and small-scale conflict (Lindskold, 1978, 1985).

SECTION SUMMARY

AGGRESSION, CONFLICT, AND CONFLICT RESOLUTION

- Aggression is not based on an "aggression instinct"; biological factors are related to individual differences in aggression; observational learning and frustration both contribute to aggression.

- About one-third of studies show males to be more aggressive than females; the differences are larger with children than with adults, and with physical rather than verbal aggression; however, domestic violence is an important issue throughout North America.

- Conflict escalates with a lose-lose or a win-lose approach; it also increases when the parties in a conflict employ issues proliferation, stereotypes, and enemy images.

- Interpersonal conflict resolution is facilitated by finding perceived common ground, determining whether the conflict may be illusory, creative problem solving, optimism, and effective listening; conflict resolution is now included in programs at both the college level and in earlier school years.

- International peacemaking is often hampered by reactive devaluation; strategies such as GRIT (Graduated and Reciprocated Initiatives in Tension Reduction) are essential in avoiding devastating wars.

ALTRUISM

Suzie Valadez, 66 years old, works about 14 hours every day. Early in the morning, she prepares hundreds of sandwiches and then drives across the border from her home in El Paso into Ciudad Juarez. Her destination is a garbage dump, where she will distribute the sandwiches, clothing, and medical supplies to the people who live there. She herself had dropped out of school after the 10th grade and has experienced many personal tragedies, but she passionately enjoys helping other people (Colby & Damon, 1992).

In 1944, a young Swedish diplomat named Raoul Wallenberg was sent into Budapest, Hungary, with the instructions to save as many Jews as possible from the Gestapo. Wallenberg was an imaginative young man whose heroes were Charlie Chaplin and the Marx Brothers. Wallenberg decided to issue Swedish protective passports to thousands of Jews. In a typical act of creative heroism, he climbed on top of a train carrying Jews to the death camps. He then ran along the roof, dropping fake Swedish passports through the air vents. Finally, he ordered the train to stop and release all the "Swedish citizens." Raoul Wallenberg eventually saved more than 100,000 women, men, and children through creative but exceptionally risky actions ("Wallenberg," 1990).

Suzie Valadez and Raoul Wallenberg both exemplify **altruism,** or acts of concern for other people, without any hope of reward (Grusec, 1991b). We will begin by examining the factors that influence altruism and then consider the relationship between altruism and gender. The third topic is the bystander effect, a situation in which people avoid altruism. Finally, an "In-Depth" section examines a question that makes altruism especially mysterious: How can we explain altruism, especially because people often act so admirably when they have no prospect of reward?

Suzie Valadez, who brings food, clothes, and medical supplies to people who live on the fringes of a garbage dump in Ciudad Juarez, Mexico.

Factors Affecting Altruism

Throughout the two chapters on social psychology, we have emphasized the importance of the social situation. Situational factors are also influential when we consider altruism. For example, you are more likely to be altruistic when you have seen another person serving as a model for altruistic behavior. For instance, you are more likely to donate blood if you have just seen someone else volunteer (Rushton & Campbell, 1977). Altruism is also more likely in a rural or suburban area than in a city (Kohn, 1990; Steblay, 1987).

Altruism also depends upon special circumstances. For example, you are more likely to help if you are not in a rush, hurrying off to other pressing duties (Darley & Batson, 1973). You are also more likely to help when you are in a good mood (Dovidio, 1984; Salovey et al., 1991). Isen's research, discussed in Chapter 12, indicated that people in a good mood perform better on a variety of tasks. Happy people also seem to be more likely to consider positive, altruistic activities (Isen & Simonds, 1978).

These four determinants of altruism depend upon the situation and changeable circumstances. However, researchers have also discovered systematic individual differences in altruism (e.g., Carlo et al., 1991; Eisenberg, 1993). These enduring tendencies persist across time, emphasizing once again our theme of individual differences. Try Demonstration 18.6 to test your own altruistic tendencies.

An interesting study on individual differences in altruism was conducted by Samuel and Pearl Oliner (1988). They interviewed more than 700 people who had

Raoul Wallenberg, the young Swedish diplomat who was responsible for saving more than 100,000 Jews during World War II.

DEMONSTRATION 18.6 Testing Altruism

This test is a shortened version of the self-report altruism scale, devised by Rushton and his colleagues (1981). In each case, indicate how often you have performed each action.

	Never 0	Once 1	More than once 2	Often 3	Very often 4
1. I have given directions to a stranger.					
2. I have given money to a stranger who needed it (or asked me for it).					
3. I have done volunteer work for charity.					
4. I have given money to a charity.					
5. I have helped carry a stranger's belongings (books, parcels, etc.).					
6. I have delayed an elevator and held the door open for a stranger.					
7. I have pointed out a clerk's error (in a bank, at the supermarket) in undercharging me for an item.					
8. I have helped a classmate whom I did not know that well with a homework assignment when my knowledge was greater than his or hers.					
9. I have helped an acquaintance to move households.					
10. I have offered my seat on a bus or train to a stranger who was standing.					

When you have completed the items, calculate your score by adding together the numbers at the top that correspond to your answers. The maximum score on this version of the altruism scale would be 40 points.

rescued Jews in Nazi Europe during World War II. These were people like Stefania, described at the beginning of the chapter, who risked their own lives to help others—even total strangers. The Oliners found that the characteristic that most distinguished these rescuers from those who had not been rescuers was that they reported a strong sense of empathy and feeling of attachment to other people, including people they did not know.

The Oliners found that altruistic people were likely to come from families who used reasoning to teach children why some behaviors were inappropriate. As children, they were often encouraged to think about the consequences of their actions for other people, a technique that seems likely to encourage compassion. The parents themselves served as models of altruistic behavior. Children were also encouraged to ignore social class, race, and religion in choosing their friends. As a consequence, these same children grew into adults who could appreciate the similarities that bind all humans to each other. They were less likely to emphasize the kinds of boundaries that separate "us" from "them." In the previous chapter, we saw how discrimination could be reduced by overcoming boundaries. The Oliners' study emphasizes how the ability to overcome boundaries can also produce empathy and altruism toward all humankind.

Anne Colby and William Damon (1992) identified other personal characteristics of altruistic individuals in their book, *Some Do Care: Contemporary Lives of Moral Commitment*. Suzie Valadez, who helps the families in Ciudad Juarez, is just one of the 23 inspiringly altruistic people they interviewed in depth. These people were similar in their disregard for risks and their strong sense of values and goals. Even in the most dismal circumstances, they remained positive. Many were inspired by their religious beliefs, though they came from all religious backgrounds. All of them continually discovered new strategies for increasing their helpfulness to other people.

Altruism and Gender

Try to create a mental picture of someone being altruistic and helpful to another person. Is this altruistic person male or female? In general, men and women are similar in their altruism. In a representative study, for example, Mills and her colleagues (1989) asked visitors to a Toronto science museum to read three stories. In each story, they could choose either an altruistic or a selfish response. The results showed that both women and men chose the altruistic option 75% of the time.

Eagly (1987) has proposed that men are supposed to be altruistic and heroic in situations involving strangers, whereas women are supposed to place the needs of other people—especially family members—before their own. However, social psychologists rarely study how people help family members and friends. Instead, most of the research investigates the kind of helpfulness at which men are supposed to excel.

In a meta-analysis by Eagly and Crowley (1986), the overall results showed that males were slightly more helpful than females in their interactions with strangers. However, the gender differences were very inconsistent across studies. In general, men were more helpful than women in the presence of an audience, but the genders were similar when no one else was present. Furthermore, men were more helpful when the task was a dangerous one for women, such as picking up a hitchhiker. In contrast, men and women were similar on safe tasks, such as answering a stranger who asked "Excuse me, could you tell me what time it is?" In most helping situations, then, men and women are more similar than different. This theme has been repeated throughout the textbook, and the current chapter has provided evidence of gender similarities in conformity, aggression, and altruism.

The Bystander Effect

So far, we have considered a number of factors related to altruism. Now we turn to a situation in which people often *fail* to help, even when they know someone is in danger. This apparent apathy is called the **bystander effect,** a phenomenon in which the presence of other people inhibits helpfulness.

This bystander puzzle was first brought to public attention in 1964. Catherine ("Kitty") Genovese was walking toward her apartment building at 3:20 in the morning. A man stabbed her, and she screamed, "Oh, my God, he stabbed me! Please help me! Please help me!" The man left briefly, then returned to attack her a second time. She shouted, "I'm dying! I'm dying." He drove away this time, but was soon back. This last time, he stabbed her again and then raped her (Dowd, 1984; Shear, 1989).

The murder of Catherine Genovese was certainly sadistic, but it was not the sadism that concerned both psychologists and the general public. Instead, the puzzle was that 38 neighbors heard or saw at least part of the crime—18 witnessed all three attacks—and *none* summoned the police until more than half an hour after the initial attack.

After hearing about the remarkable apathy of these bystanders, Bibb Latané and John Darley (1970) decided to study this phenomenon in the laboratory. Each participant in their study was led into a small room, where he or she was instructed to discuss personal problems through an intercom system, presumably with one, two, or five other people in nearby rooms. After an uneventful beginning, one of the other people mentioned that he had a seizure disorder. Soon afterwards, he began to stutter badly and then cry out that he was having a seizure. Latané and Darley observed how many participants rushed out to help the young man.

They discovered that 100% of the participants who thought they were in a two-person group rushed out to try to get help. However, when people thought they were in a six-person group, only 62% left their room at some point. Those who left also took significantly longer to do so than in the two-person group. When people think they are part of a larger group, no individual feels responsible for helping, an effect called **diffusion of responsibility.** The term makes sense, because people seem to believe that the responsibility for altruism has been diffused across a large number of people. You can see the similarity between this effect and the social loafing we discussed earlier.

After 10 years of research on the bystander effect, Latané and Nida (1981) examined dozens of studies that had been conducted in a variety of laboratory and real-life settings. They concluded that when other people are nearby and do not communicate with each other, individuals are significantly less likely to be helpful. We can therefore add group size to the list of variables that influence altruism.

According to the bystander effect, a person is less likely to help someone in need if other people are around.

IN DEPTH: Explaining Altruism

According to Jencks (1990), one of the classic puzzles about social theory is why humans should perform actions that help society. *Why* should Suzy Valadez spend the majority of her waking hours passing out sandwiches at a garbage dump? *Why* did Raoul Wallenberg repeatedly risk his life to save thousands of Jews during World War II?

This "In Depth" section focuses on the research of a psychologist named C. Daniel Batson. His research provides an excellent example of a systematic series of studies designed to test a specific hypothesis: Will people help others, even when there is no possibility of personal benefit? Batson agrees that altruism can sometimes be selfishly motivated (Batson, 1987, 1990, 1991). However, it can sometimes be entirely altruistic and not the least bit selfish.

Batson proposes that we often help other people because we experience **empathy,** or an emotional reaction that involves a subjective grasp of another person's feelings or experiences (Brothers, 1989). Thus, you may feel empathy for someone who has cancer. According to Batson's **empathy-arousal hypothesis,** empathy has the power to motivate altruism. From previous research, we know that people are more likely to perform altruistic actions when they experience empathy (e.g., Eisenberg & Miller, 1987). This makes sense; we are more eager to help people if we experience some of the same emotions they are feeling.

As we mentioned, altruism can sometimes be selfishly motivated. We may help other people for two major selfish reasons: (1) We want to *avoid* the personal pain of seeing someone

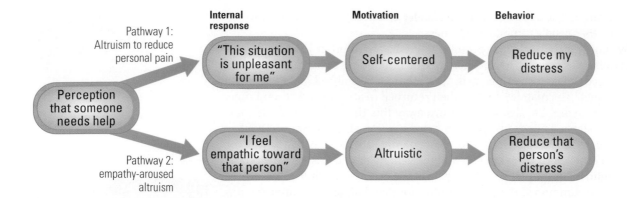

Figure 18.8
Two pathways for altruism. (Based on Batson, 1987)

suffer or the guilt of not helping someone in distress; and (2) We want to share vicariously the *joy* the victim feels when his or her life improves. Notice, then, that these reasons represent two somewhat different kinds of selfishness; the first avoids personal pain and the second seeks out personal pleasure. Batson's primary contribution to the research on altruism is that he has demonstrated that people can be altruistic when their empathy is aroused, even when neither of those selfish reasons can operate. Let us consider the research comparing the empathy-arousal hypothesis with each of these two more selfish hypotheses.

Empathy-Arousal vs. Avoiding Personal Pain As we noted, Batson agrees that we sometimes help other people to avoid experiencing pain and guilt. However, he emphasizes that we often help other people even when those selfish motives are missing—as long as we experience empathy. Figure 18.8 shows these two pathways.

Let us consider a representative study that demonstrates altruism, even when that altruism does not involve the avoidance of personal pain. Imagine that you are participating in a study conducted by Batson. You have been told that you will be paired with another student, named Elaine, and she will be receiving electric shocks while she performs a task. Your job is to observe. On closed-circuit TV you hear Elaine tell how she was thrown from a horse onto an electric fence, as a child, and these shocks remind her of that trauma. The experimenter then asks you whether you would be willing to trade places. Batson and his colleagues (1981) led half of the participants to believe that their own interests and values were very similar to Elaine's (high-empathy condition) by showing them Elaine's responses to a questionnaire. Her responses were constructed to match their own previous responses quite closely. The other half of the participants were shown a questionnaire in which Elaine's responses were very different from their own (low-empathy condition). A second variable in this study was difficulty of escape. In the easy-escape condition, people were told they could leave after viewing two trials in which Elaine suffered. In the difficult-escape condition, people could either watch Elaine suffer for 10 trials, or switch places.

Figure 18.9 shows the results. Notice that when empathy is low and participants can easily escape, these participants leave the experiment; few are altruistic. However, when empathy is low and escape is difficult, people often volunteer to trade places with Elaine. Apparently, these people want to reduce the unpleasant feeling of watching someone else's pain, consistent with Pathway 1 in Figure 18.8.

Now turn your attention to the two conditions in which empathy is high, and people are encouraged to feel genuine compassion for Elaine. Consistent with Batson's hypothesis, when empathy is aroused, people are highly likely to be altruistic. Their tendency to help is roughly similar, whether they could easily escape or whether escape is difficult. If altruism only involves the avoidance of personal pain, then people in the easy-escape, high-empathy condition would have rushed to leave the experiment. Instead, about 90% of them volunteered to trade places with Elaine. As Batson (1990, 1991) argues, we humans do have the capacity to improve others' welfare for their sake, and not simply for our own selfish reasons.

Empathy Arousal vs. Vicarious Joy Another possible explanation for human altruism relies on a different form of selfishness. Maybe when we feel empathy with other people,

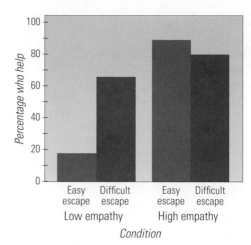

Figure 18.9

Percentage of people who help a needy person, as a function of the level of empathy and how difficult it would be for them to escape watching a victim's pain. (Based on Batson et al., 1981)

we help them because we hope to share their joy vicariously when their situation improves (Smith et al., 1989). This motivation sounds somewhat more noble than the "avoiding personal pain" rationale. However, we still help other people for our own emotional goals.

Indeed, we often do help others because we imagine ourselves feeling joyous when their lives improve. However, Batson and his colleagues tested whether people can be altruistic, even when they will never learn whether the victim's situation improves. In a representative study, Batson and his coworkers (1991) asked students to listen to a tape recording, presumably to be broadcast on a local radio station. The recording described Katie, a senior at their university whose parents had been killed in an automobile crash. She needed to raise money to support her two younger siblings, or else she would be forced to place them up for adoption. Empathy was aroused by encouraging the participants to imagine the emotions Katie is now feeling. After listening to the recording, students were asked whether they would be willing to help Katie address envelopes to potential donors.

The critical question in this study is whether the participants would still help, even if they know it would not be possible to learn how their efforts had actually helped Katie. After all, these individuals know they cannot experience the vicarious joy when Katie tells them that the donors were generous. The results showed that 83% of the participants in the no-feedback condition volunteered to help Katie. This percentage was actually higher than the 58% volunteer rate in a feedback condition, where participants were told they would hear about the outcome of their altruism.

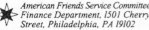
According to Batson's empathy-arousal hypothesis, people will want to donate to the organization described in this ad because their empathy has been aroused. Batson and his colleagues argue that people will be altruistic, even when their generosity will not help them avoid personal pain and even when they cannot experience vicarious joy.

Conclusions About Altruism In summary, the research has shown that we can be altruistic for a variety of reasons. We can be altruistic because we want to avoid personal pain and guilt. We can also be altruistic because we want to experience vicarious joy. However, we can also be altruistic when neither of those more selfish rationales is relevant; here, we help other people because we feel a bond with them, our empathy is aroused, and we want to improve their lives.

SECTION SUMMARY

ALTRUISM

- Factors that encourage altruism include watching an altruistic model, a rural or suburban setting, no time pressure, and a good mood; altruistic people are also likely to have had families who encouraged compassion and emphasized overcoming boundaries between people; altruistic people also have strong values, goals, and optimism.

- Men are more likely than women to help strangers when an audience is present or when the task is especially dangerous for women; in other situations, men and women are equally helpful.

- According to the bystander effect, we are less likely to help when other people are present, through diffusion of responsibility.

- We sometimes help others because we want to avoid personal pain or guilt and because we want to experience vicarious joy. However, Batson's empathy-arousal hypothesis argues that we can be altruistic because we feel an empathic bond with others, which encourages us to help them.

REVIEW QUESTIONS

1. This chapter examined many ways in which being in a group can influence a person's performance. Discuss this issue, being sure to discuss social roles, social facilitation, social loafing, group polarization, groupthink, conformity, and the bystander effect.

2. Some of the material in this chapter is related to the discussion of social cognition in the previous chapter. Discuss how social cognition effects—such as self-fulfilling prophecy and the cognitive basis of stereotyping—are related to social roles, stereotyping in conflict situations, enemy images, and any other topics you believe to be relevant.

3. From your own experience in group settings, try to recall examples of group polarization, groupthink, and conformity. Can you think of an occasion when a minority viewpoint kept others from complying with a majority viewpoint?

4. We noted that conformity, compliance, and obedience can be placed along a continuum showing increasing social pressure. Discuss how these social pressures are relevant in each case, and then show how each of these three kinds of social pressure could be used by someone to encourage altruistic behavior.

5. Discuss the possible explanations for both aggression and altruism, trying to point out parallels when possible.

6. We discussed gender at four places throughout this chapter: conformity, aggression, pornography, and altruism. Summarize the conclusions in these four areas.

7. Using an example of a conflict you recently faced, outline how you could help increase the perceived common ground. What other steps could you take to resolve that conflict? Finally, how would knowledge about reactive devaluation and GRIT help you as you begin resolving this conflict?

8. The section on international peacemaking emphasized the GRIT model. However, much of the material in the section on interpersonal conflict resolution is also relevant for international peacemaking. Imagine that you are advising the leaders of two countries that are currently in conflict. What kinds of advice would be relevant for them?

9. Based on what you know about altruism, describe all the factors that increase the likelihood of altruism. In other words, if you were in a situation where you needed help, describe the characteristics of the setting and the helper that would increase the chances of altruism.

10. Many of the principles in this chapter have implications for working with children. Imagine that you are teaching a grade of your choice, between kindergarten and high school. Turn back to the chapter outline and point out how almost every topic could help you understand children's current behavior or encourage them to be better human beings.

N E W   T E R M S

group
role
social facilitation
social loafing
group polarization
groupthink
conformity
environmental psychology
compliance
foot-in-the-door technique
door-in-the-face technique
obedience
aggression
Seville Statement
frustration-aggression hypothesis

conflict
lose-lose approach
win-lose approach
win-win approach
issues proliferation
enemy images
perceived common ground
reactive devaluation
GRIT (Graduated and Reciprocated Initiatives in Tension Reduction)
altruism
bystander effect
diffusion of responsibility
empathy
empathy-arousal hypothesis

A N S W E R S   T O   D E M O N S T R A T I O N S

DEMONSTRATION 18.4 1. F; 2. T; 3. F; 4. F; 5. F; 6. F; 7. F; 8. F.

R E C O M M E N D E D   R E A D I N G S

Cialdini, R. B. (1993). *Influence: Science and practice* (3rd ed.). New York: HarperCollins. Cialdini has written a fascinating book, filled with numerous examples and good reviews of the literature on group influence.

Colby, A., & Damon, W. (1992). *Some do care: Contemporary lives of moral commitment.* New York: Free Press. I strongly recommend this book! The portraits of altruistic individuals are superb, and the book includes thoughtful analyses of the moral basis of behavior.

Geen, R. G. (1990). *Human aggression.* Pacific Grove, CA: Brooks/Cole. This brief textbook provides a good overview of factors related to aggression, the role of the media, and individual differences in aggression.

Rubin, J. Z., Pruitt, D. G., & Kim, S. H. (1994). Social conflict: Escalation, stalemate, and settlement (2nd ed.). New York: McGraw-Hill. This textbook contains clear descriptions of the origin, escalation, and resolution of conflicts.

Suedfeld, P., & Tetlock, P. E. (Eds.). (1992). *Psychology and social policy.* New York: Hemisphere. Many principles from social psychology carry important applications for social policy; this book contains relevant chapters addressing issues such as political decision making, nuclear war, pornography, media aggression, and policy on firearms.

CHAPTER 19

HEALTH PSYCHOLOGY

Cindy is a college student who is feeling extremely stressed this semester. Her parents were divorced last summer, and her father will not pay for college. Cindy is currently working two jobs, in addition to attending college full time. One month ago, Cindy's mother was hospitalized for major depression, so Cindy had to miss a chemistry exam and drive four hours to consult with the psychiatrist. On the way back, her car broke down.

Linda and her husband had been married for only five months. The newlyweds often told each other they were so happy they had met because the AIDS threat was so scary. Linda's husband had suffered from chronic fatigue and other worrisome symptoms, but he was not tested for AIDS until the day before he died. In fact, he tested positive . . . as did Linda, when she was tested several days later. She has now been a widow for seven years. When she dates a man she likes, she must struggle with telling him about her HIV status early in the relationship (Seligmann, 1992).

A friend of mine has a PhD is psychology. He's a well-liked professor and an excellent administrator. And he was—until about a year ago—a smoker. He tells me that quitting smoking was the hardest thing he's ever done, far harder than writing his PhD dissertation. He explained, "I'm convinced that smoking is an addiction. It is not subject to rational thought processes. Sometimes you stand back and observe, in amazement, how irrational your behavior is—just to have a cigarette!"

A student struggling with stress, a woman living with AIDS, and a man fighting the urge to smoke are all relevant to health psychology, an important area of applied psychology. As Chapter 1 noted, **applied psychology** emphasizes practical applications of psychological research. **Health psychology** is the scientific study of behaviors related to health improvement, disease prevention, and recovery from disease (Brannon & Feist, 1992).

Health psychology is gaining attention in the 1990s as we realize that many fatal diseases have a psychological component. When people died a century ago in North America, the most common causes were infectious diseases, such as pneumonia and tuberculosis. In contrast, the current leading reasons for death are heart disease, cancer, lung diseases, and other problems that can be partly traced to emotional and behavioral factors such as stress, cigarette smoking, and improper diet (Brannon & Feist, 1992).

A chapter on health psychology provides an appropriate conclusion to an introductory psychology textbook, because so many diverse research areas can be applied to this topic (Goldstein & Krasner, 1987). In particular, this chapter will emphasize the applications of research on emotions, personality, and social psychology. For example, the section on stress and coping shows that stressful emotional experiences are often linked with serious illnesses; emotions can even alter the immune system that protects your body from infectious diseases. The second section of this chapter emphasizes individual differences in health. This section targets three personality characteristics that are correlated with health; it also examines how ethnicity, social class, and gender are related to health. The last two sections explore two health issues that are especially crucial at the end of the twentieth century: AIDS and cigarette smoking. These two topics may initially seem to have little in common. However, in both cases, risky behavior can be life-threatening. In both cases, too, social psychologists are working together with educators and health psychologists to develop persuasive techniques to help people change their attitudes and their behavior.

People differ in their reactions to the same event. This couple is enjoying the celebration, but other couples might perceive their wedding day as stressful.

STRESS AND COPING

Stress involves the arousal of your mind and body in response to demands placed upon yourself (Schafer, 1992). Keep in mind, however, that people vary tremendously in their reactions to the same event—consistent with a theme of this book. For example, you have probably attended a wedding where the bride and groom looked panic-stricken. At another wedding, the couple seemed relaxed and joyful; they did not seem to perceive the situation as being stressful. People use their cognitive processes to interpret and evaluate whether situations are stressful (Lazarus, 1991b; Lazarus & Folkman, 1984).

Let us begin our discussion of stress by considering a model for the way stress operates. Then we will look at several sources of stress, the effects of stress, and methods of coping with stress.

Selye's General Adaptation Syndrome

A model developed by Hans Selye is one of the most influential approaches to the study of stress (Taylor, 1991). Selye (1956) called his model of stress the **general adaptation syndrome,** or **GAS;** it consists of three stages of response to a stressful situation. As Figure 19.1 shows, the unpleasant situation that produces the stress is called the **stressor.** The general adaptation syndrome includes three phases:

1. In the **alarm phase,** the individual prepares for action. As discussed in previous chapters, the sympathetic division of the nervous system becomes activated in response to stress. The goal is to regain **homeostasis,** which is the state of internal balance or stability.

2. In the **resistance phase,** your body tries to cope with the stressor by releasing stress hormones. For example, research with 9-month-old infants shows that the stress of separation from mother leads to a significant elevation of the hormone cortisol (Gunnar & Brodersen, 1992). In addition, measures such as

Figure 19.1

Hans Selye's general adaptation syndrome (GAS) model of response to stress.

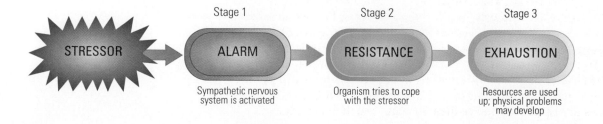

Stage 1 — **ALARM** — Sympathetic nervous system is activated

Stage 2 — **RESISTANCE** — Organism tries to cope with the stressor

Stage 3 — **EXHAUSTION** — Resources are used up; physical problems may develop

STRESSOR

blood pressure, heart rate, respiration, and body temperature all increase. Toward the end of the resistance phase, the activity of the sympathetic system declines and the activity of the parasympathetic system increases.

3. The **exhaustion phase** occurs if the stressor persists. The activity of the sympathetic system declines further still, and now the parasympathetic system is dominant. When the individual uses up the available resources, he or she is likely to develop physical problems and illness. Selye's model therefore helps us explain how stressful events in the environment can influence the development of diseases (Krantz et al., 1985).

Sources of Stress

If you were to list all the sources of stress that you, your family, and your friends have faced, that list could be partitioned into three major categories: catastrophes, important life events, and daily hassles.

Catastrophes A catastrophe is a large-scale disaster that affects numerous people and causes extensive damage. Catastrophes include major earthquakes, hurricanes, floods, nuclear accidents, and widespread war. In 1980, for example, residents of Washington State experienced a catastrophe when the volcano Mount Saint Helens erupted, spewing thick layers of ash on the town of Othello, about 150 miles away. This stressor clearly influenced physical health. Emergency room visits increased by 21%, and stress-related illnesses tripled. Furthermore, the death rate increased by 19%, compared to the same period in the previous year (Adams & Adams, 1984). In terms of Selye's model, many people had moved beyond the resistance phase of Stage 2, and physical health problems developed in the exhaustion phase of Stage 3. A review of the literature demonstrated that health problems increased in 14 of the 15 catastrophes that were studied (Hovanitz, 1993).

Important Life Events A second category of stressors is major life events. Try Demonstration 19.1 before you read further. This demonstration is based on a scale developed by Yeaworth and her colleagues (1980) for use with students. This scale corresponds to a similar instrument called the Social Readjustment Rating

---

DEMONSTRATION 19.1 **The Life Change Event Scale**

The following items are part of a scale developed by Yeaworth and her coauthors (1980) for use with students; this scale assesses stress from major life changes. If you add up the total number of points for all these stressful events that have occurred within the last year, individuals with higher total scores would be more likely to develop physical illnesses. However, please note that this list does not include all items on the scale, so your informal assessment of life-change events may not be strongly correlated with health.

EVENT	VALUE
Parents getting divorced or separated	86
Family member (other than yourself) having trouble with alcohol	79
Parent or relative in your family (other than yourself) getting very sick	74
Breaking up with a close girlfriend or boyfriend	74
Parent losing a job	69
Starting a new school	57
Moving to a new home	51
Starting a job	34
Brother or sister getting married	26

Scale (Holmes & Rahe, 1967), which was developed for older adults. On both scales, the minimum score for any event is 0 and the maximum score is 100.

Many studies have shown that people with high total scores on the Social Readjustment Rating Scale are likely to develop physical illnesses such as tuberculosis, diabetes, arthritis, heart disease, and multiple sclerosis (Holmes & Masuda, 1974; Hovanitz, 1993; Krantz et al., 1985). One explanation for this correlation may be that stressful life events *cause* physical illness. However, you learned in Chapter 2 to be skeptical about drawing cause-and-effect conclusions in correlational studies. An alternate possibility is that physical illness causes stressful life events. For instance, frequent absences from work may create trouble with the supervisor. In addition, both the stressful life events and illness scales are often measured by self-report, which may show systematic biases, as well as systematic memory errors (Schroeder & Costa, 1984); the correlation may therefore be traceable to a third factor.

In general, the more carefully controlled studies on the Social Readjustment Rating Scale tend to show correlations between life events and physical illness that range between .20 and .35. In other words, these stressful life events are moderately related to illness (Maddi et al., 1987). Incidentally, we would not expect these two factors to be strongly correlated because individuals respond in different ways to the same presumably stressful event. For example, one person might be devastated when parents announce a divorce, whereas another might experience relief and express the belief that a divorce was a wise decision, given the circumstances (Elliot, 1991).

Two special categories of life stressors have inspired additional research. Specifically, people who are responsible for taking care of family members with serious illnesses are likely to develop illnesses themselves (Biegel et al., 1991; Chiriboga et al., 1990). For example, if you know a woman who is taking care of her husband who has Alzheimer's disease or is recovering from heart disease, a stroke, or cancer, this individual is likely to develop a stress-related disease herself.

A second category of life stressors is perhaps more surprising. For some people, a *positive* life event can produce negative health consequences. Brown and McGill (1989) found that people with low self-esteem were likely to show an increase in number of illnesses when a positive life event happened to them. The authors suggest that a positive event—such as a new love interest—disrupts their sense of identity, and this disruption is stressful. We saw in Chapter 17 that people who have low opinions of themselves prefer spouses who also evaluate them negatively. For people low in self-esteem, consistency may be preferable to good news!

Daily Hassles Think for a moment about the days when you feel most stressed. A student I know described a miserable day that included an unreasonable biology test, a car that refused to start, getting stuck in a friend's snowy driveway, and rushing from school to rehearse for a play. A Hassles Scale developed by Kohn and his colleagues (1990) showed that college students' hassles tended to cluster into five categories: academic difficulties, time pressure, alienation from academics, romantic problems, and assorted social problems. This hassles scale was correlated with health problems in both college students and older adults (Kohn et al., 1991; Kohn & Macdonald, 1992). In fact, some research shows that the accumulation of daily hassles is a better predictor of future illness than a scale that only counts the major life events (DeLongis et al., 1982; Eckenrode, 1984; Lazarus, 1984).

We have been discussing how catastrophes, major life events, and minor daily hassles create stresses that encourage physical illness. Two cautions are necessary, however. First, individual differences in the way people interpret and handle stress may be even more important than these environmental events (Depue & Monroe, 1986); we will address these individual differences later in this chapter. Second, the relationship between stress and illness is moderately strong, but the correlation is far from perfect. Please do not assume that you need to search for a stressor that is responsible for every cold or every heart attack!

In some cases, such as this high-school play, performance actually improves under mild stress.

The Effects of Stress

Mild stress can sometimes improve your performance in an athletic event or in a theatrical performance. However, severe stress can impair your thinking and disrupt your emotions. Stress also produces physiological responses. Your car skids across a patch of ice, and your body automatically prepares itself for an emergency. The sympathetic system secretes adrenaline, which increases your heart rate and dilates the pupils in your eyes. Your saliva production decreases and your mucus membranes dry up, producing wider air passages to your lungs—and a noticeably drier mouth. You are also likely to perspire heavily, a response that cools your energized body.

In addition to these immediate physiological effects, long-term stress can also suppress the immune system (Ader & Cohen, 1993). The **immune system** protects the body against infection, allergies, bacteria, viruses, cancer, and other dangers (Taylor, 1991). **Lymphocytes** are part of the immune system; they are the white blood cells that defend the body against viruses and other harmful agents. Research in both the laboratory and in naturalistic settings has shown that stress can reduce the number of lymphocytes. For example, studies have demonstrated that lymphocyte production is decreased after the death of a spouse (Schleifer et al., 1983).

Additional research has shown that stress also influences other aspects of the immune system. For instance, students in dental school had lower levels of antibodies during exam time than during vacations (Jemmott et al., 1983; Jemmott & Locke, 1984). When the immune system is weakened, diseases are more likely to develop.

Coping with Stress

Coping refers to the thoughts and behaviors we use to handle stress or anticipated stress. Studies on methods of coping with stress emphasize wide individual differences (Rodin & Salovey, 1989). This theme about variability was emphasized for me recently. Two of my friends became widows after their husbands died of cancer. One woman asked her husband's friends to conduct the memorial service, because she knew it would be too stressful for her to speak. Another friend organized the service herself, greeting all who attended with warmth and strength. As she buried the urn with his ashes in her backyard, she smiled and said, "Well, I'm burying Sam here for now, but if I move, I'll just dig him up and bury him again." Both women had been equally close to their husbands, but they responded in very different ways to the stressful event.

How do people cope with stress? Arthur Stone and John Neale (1984) gave a questionnaire on coping strategies to 60 married couples. Table 19.1 shows their responses. Notice that direct action is the most common response, but several other coping strategies are also popular.

Methods of coping with stress can be divided into two major categories: problem-focused coping and emotion-focused coping (Coyne & Downey, 1991; Lazarus, 1993; Lazarus & Folkman, 1984). **Problem-focused coping** includes taking direct action to solve problems as well as changing your thoughts. These two strategies focus on altering the problem that is creating the stress. In contrast, **emotion-focused coping** is directed at regulating emotional response to the problem. Let us consider these two categories.

Problem-Focused Coping   We saw in Stone and Neale's (1984) study that direct action is a popular coping response. In a stressful situation, you try to define the problem, generate several possible solutions, and determine the costs and benefits of each alternative. You then select among these alternatives and move forward. We have discussed this kind of approach in the problem-solving section of Chapter 8 as well as in the conflict-resolution section of Chapter 18. Research shows that people who tend to use this strategy are likely to experience lower levels of stress. Also, no consistent gender differences have been observed in the tendency to use direct action as a coping strategy (D'Zurilla & Sheedy, 1991; Lazarus, 1993).

A second kind of problem-focused coping can be directed inward. You can reduce stress by cognitive adjustments such as shifting your level of aspiration. For example, a student whose grades seem inadequate for medical school may decide to pursue a less challenging health-related career. These internal coping strategies are called **cognitive reappraisals** (Lazarus & Folkman, 1984).

We are more likely to use these two kinds of problem-focused strategies when we believe that conditions and interpretations can actually be changed. When we believe that nothing can be done about a stressful situation, we are likely to try emotion-focused forms of coping.

Emotion-Focused Coping   This second category of coping strategies consists of denial, seeking social support, and miscellaneous stress-reduction approaches.

A good example of denial was described by a former student who told me that she had spent her high-school years believing that her family was perfect. Years later, she realized that she had been using denial to avoid thinking about her father's alcoholism. When reality is simply too unpleasant, we may deny that the problem exists. **Denial** is the refusal to recognize the reality of threatening external events (Taylor, 1991).

TABLE 19.1   Coping Strategies Used by Adults and the Frequency of Their Use

COPING STRATEGY	FREQUENCY OF USE (%)
1. Doing something to solve the problem (direct action)	46%
2. Accepting the problem	30%
3. Diverting attention away from the problem	26%
4. Expressing emotion	25%
5. Trying to see the problem in a different light	24%
6. Doing something relaxing	17%
7. Seeking social support	14%
8. Seeking religious comfort	6%
9. Miscellaneous other strategies	7%

Source: Based on Stone & Neale, 1984

Short-term denial can sometimes be adaptive. These victims of the January 1994 earthquake in Los Angeles could have developed psychological disorders if they did not show some denial in the hours following this disaster.

Some denial may be adaptive immediately after an event because it prevents us from being overwhelmed with panic. Denial allows us to process new information in tolerable doses. For instance, the survivors of Hiroshima's atomic bombing would probably have developed severe psychological disorders if they had not used denial to avoid thinking about widespread death and destruction (Lifton, 1967). However, high levels of denial more than a year after the trauma may be harmful (Janoff-Bulman & Timko, 1987; Suls & Fletcher, 1985). At this point, the traumatized individual should be dealing with problems realistically.

Seeking Social Support We saw in Table 19.1 that some people cope with stress by seeking support from other people. Our family and friends can provide emotional reassurance, boost our self-esteem, and express their caring concern. Companions and confidants can enhance both our emotional and physical well-being (Connidis & Davies, 1990, 1992).

Several large-scale studies confirm that social support is related to health status (Brannon & Feist, 1992). People are less likely to die at an early age if they have a large number of high-quality social relationships (e.g., House et al., 1988). Social support also appears to help people cope with a variety of stress-related illnesses (Compas, 1987; DeLongis et al., 1988; Hobfoll, 1988). However, Taylor and Dakof (1987) point out that we should be cautious in interpreting these data because most of the research is correlational or else it includes potential confounding variables. For example, several studies show that cancer patients with high social support are likely to have better recovery rates. Unless the study is carefully conducted, an alternative explanation might be that a person with severe symptoms tends to drive away people who might provide social support.

In general, however, the research suggests that social support actually causes modest improvements in health (Cohen, 1991; Kennedy et al., 1990). Social support serves as a buffer that allows people to perceive threatening events as being less stressful. Also, social support enhances general self-esteem and well-being.

Some research suggests that people who discuss their traumatic experiences with others may actually improve the functioning of their immune system (Pennebaker, 1990). For example, Pennebaker and his coauthors (1988) asked healthy undergraduates to write about either superficial topics (control group) or traumatic experiences (experimental group) during four brief daily sessions. Measurement of the immune system showed that lymphocytes were more responsive in those students who had discussed their traumatic experiences. Furthermore, the experimental group also showed a drop in the number of visits to the health center, relative to the control group.

However, we should mention an unsuccessful attempt to replicate these findings. Greenberg and Stone (1992) reported that students who had written about their problems were no more healthy than students in a control group. The two groups were similar in their physical symptoms and the frequency of their visits to the student health center during the following two months. In summary, disclosing your emotions—either in writing or to a confidant—may sometimes lead to improved health. However, the research does not show a strong, consistent effect.

Other Coping Strategies Authorities on stress reduction often recommend exercise (Rice, 1992; Schafer, 1992). Exercise seems to promote both psychological and physical changes that reduce stress. In addition, people often report that their muscles feel less tense and they feel more tranquil after they have finished exercising (Brown, 1991; Dubbert, 1992; Everly, 1989).

Another stress-management strategy involves relaxation (Rice, 1992; Schafer, 1992). Several factors encourage effective relaxation: a quiet setting; a mental device that focuses your attention, such as a word to be repeated; a comfortable position; and a passive attitude that calmly redirects attention toward relaxation if your mind wanders toward stressful topics.

Maybe you have read claims from celebrities who have cured assorted stress-related illnesses by laughing their way to health. In fact, laughter does have a modest influence in buffering or reducing stress (Hall & Goldstein, 1986; Lefcourt & Davidson-Katz, 1990a; Nezu et al., 1988). However, be skeptical about any claim that seems simplistic. Like other psychological processes, stress reduction is too complex to be accomplished by a single technique.

SECTION SUMMARY
STRESS AND COPING

- Selye's general adaptation syndrome (GAS) model of stress includes three stages of response: alarm, resistance, and exhaustion.

- Stress-related illnesses are somewhat correlated with three measures of stress: catastrophes, important life events, and minor daily hassles.

- Stress can impair behavior and thinking, disrupt emotions, alter physiological functions, and suppress the immune system.

- Problem-focused coping includes problem solving and cognitive adjustment; emotion-focused coping includes denial and seeking support from others.

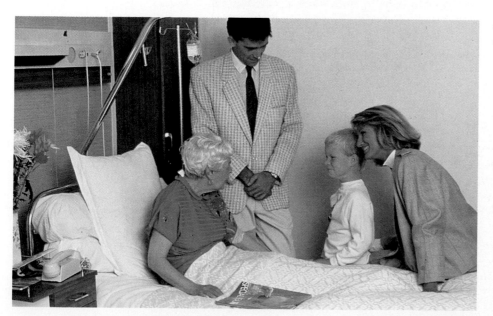

Social support helps people cope with stress-related illnesses.

PSYCHOSOCIAL FACTORS RELATED TO HEALTH AND ILLNESS

When we considered sources of stress in the previous section, we examined forces in the environment that are related to stress and illness. The eruption of a volcano, the death of a family member, and countless daily hassles all predict health problems. However, we need also to consider individual differences in the way people respond to those external forces. These more internal factors may be just as important as the forces in the environment. We first consider three personality characteristics and then discuss two social categories: ethnicity/social class and gender.

Type A Behavior Pattern and Hostility

People with a **Type A behavior pattern** exhibit personality characteristics such as ambitiousness, aggressiveness, competitiveness, and impatience. People with Type A behaviors speak rapidly and work quickly. They are also likely to respond to hassles with irritation and hostility (Rosenman, 1990).

In contrast, people with **Type B behavior pattern** rarely experience time urgency; they are seldom impatient or hostile. For example, I know a woman with Type B characteristics who discovered three weeks after the switch to daylight savings time that her watch had been an hour off. She was simply unconcerned about time.

About 20 years ago, researchers were convinced that people with Type A characteristics were more likely than those with Type B characteristics to develop heart disease (e.g., Friedman & Rosenman, 1974). However, the current conclusions are more cautious. For example, researchers now acknowledge that paper-and-pencil tests of Type A behavior pattern are not very effective in predicting heart disease. A structured interview is generally more accurate. The structured interview allows the interviewer to record speech patterns, gestures, and facial expressions. The combination of the test responses plus the nonverbal behaviors is more strongly correlated with heart disease (Booth-Kewley & Friedman, 1987; Matthews, 1988; Thoresen & Low, 1990). Now try Demonstration 19.2 before you read further.

Furthermore, some researchers argue that only certain aspects of the Type A behavior pattern are likely to lead to heart disease (Dembroski et al., 1989; Rhodewalt & Smith, 1990). Specifically, time urgency and ambitiousness may be fairly innocent. Instead, heart problems may be more closely related to the hostility and anger com-

---

DEMONSTRATION 19.2   Assessing Hostility

The following items are similar to those items from the MMPI which Barefoot and his colleagues (1983) used to assess hostility. In front of each item, write T if the statement is true about you and F if the statement is false. Check your responses against the key at the end of the chapter.

_____ 1. When someone does something wrong, I feel obligated to do something wrong in return.

_____ 2. Many times I've been in the position of taking orders from someone less competent than myself.

_____ 3. Most people are so incompetent that they need a lot of argument to help them see the truth.

_____ 4. My relatives tend to think highly of me.

_____ 5. People usually understand my way of doing things.

_____ 6. It seems perfectly fair to take advantage of people if the opportunity is just sitting there.

_____ 7. I make friends with people because they are likely to be useful to me.

_____ 8. I often find that people let me down.

_____ 9. Even when people are rude to me, I try to be gentle in return.

_____ 10. I usually try to cover up my poor opinion of a person so that he or she never knows how I feel.

The most dangerous component of the Type A behavior pattern may actually be hostility.

ponents, which only some Type A people have. Demonstration 19.2 provides an informal assessment of your own hostility tendencies. Naturally, no informal 10-item test can provide a good assessment of a characteristic as complex as hostility. Still, a high score on this demonstration may encourage you to rethink the way you deal with other people—for the sake of your own health and also the well-being of others.

In a representative study on hostility and heart disease, 255 medical students completed the Minnesota Multiphasic Personality Inventory (MMPI), the popular test discussed in Chapter 14. The scores on this test were significantly related to the incidence of coronary heart disease 25 years later (Barefoot et al., 1983). Those with high hostility scores were five times as likely as those with low hostility scores to develop heart disease.

Not every study shows a significant relationship between hostility and heart disease, though the majority do (Rhodewalt & Smith, 1990; Thoresen & Powell, 1992). Consider why hostility might be an important factor. Hostile people probably tend to expect the worst from others, an expectation that provokes unfriendliness from them. A vicious cycle begins, producing stress and conflict. In addition, hostile people may be more physiologically aroused than others, creating additional stress for the endocrine and immune systems (Smith & Pope, 1990; Williams et al., 1985).

The picture is not yet clear enough to tell us whether looking at your watch and setting ambitious goals for yourself are activities that will predispose you to heart disease (Thoresen & Powell, 1992). However, people who scream at their secretaries and who seem eternally angry may be more likely to develop heart problems.

Type A behavior pattern and its related characteristic, hostility, are the personality attributes that have received the most attention. However, two other personality characteristics are becoming increasingly prominent—psychological control and explanatory style. Let us first consider psychological control and then examine explanatory style in more detail.

Psychological Control

A student described a disturbing experience she had while working in a nursing home. She had befriended a woman living in the nursing home who had been a psychiatrist. The student was interested in the psychiatrist's remarks about Freudian theory as well as her comments about how the nurses' treatment of other residents was likely to make those people feel helpless. The student then left for two months; on returning, she sought out the psychiatrist. Astonishingly, the psychiatrist no longer recognized the student, and she no longer talked. The elderly woman looked transformed. She was no longer well dressed and carefully groomed. Now her clothing was improperly buttoned and her hair was disheveled. The nursing home records showed no evidence of a stroke or other organic reason for her decline. Naturally, some purely medical condition could still be involved, but another possibility involves psychological control.

In Chapters 2 and 11, we discussed how nursing homes can take away people's sense of psychological control. A lowered sense of control seems to produce a decline in physical health. In those chapters, we discussed a study in which residents of a nursing home were encouraged to establish a sense of control by making decisions about their activities. These individuals with control were happier and lived longer than those with standard nursing-home care (Rodin & Langer, 1977).

Psychological control is important when we consider illness at any age, not just illness for residents of nursing homes. When people develop a serious illness, they feel powerless and vulnerable. If they feel they can do something to influence their future health, they feel more powerful (Helgeson, 1992). Health psychologists have examined how psychological control can influence cognitive processes, motivation, and emotion (Lefcourt & Davidson-Katz, 1990b; Rodin et al., 1990; Steptoe & Appels, 1989). In general, research shows that people high in psychological control take better care of themselves. That is, they read articles about healthful habits, they ask questions when they visit their physicians, and they follow the advice these physicians give them. A possible disadvantage to psychological control is that decision

Research indicates that people who are high in psychological control are more likely to follow the advice of a physician, for example, getting regular exercise after a stroke.

DEMONSTRATION 19.3 Measuring Explanatory Style

Try to vividly imagine yourself in each of the two following situations. If the situation really did happen to you, what do you feel would have caused it? Please select the major cause if this event happened to you. Read each situation, write one cause in the blank, and answer three questions about the cause.

1. Suppose that you meet a friend who acts hostilely toward you.

   Cause _____

   (a) Is this cause due to something about you or something about the other person or the circumstances? (Circle the appropriate number on the rating scale.)

   | 1 | 2 | 3 | 4 | 5 | 6 | 7 |

   other person/   me
   circumstances

   (b) In the future will this cause again be present?

   | 1 | 2 | 3 | 4 | 5 | 6 | 7 |

   no   yes

   (c) Is the cause something that just influences this situation, or does it also influence other areas of your life?

   | 1 | 2 | 3 | 4 | 5 | 6 | 7 |

   this situation   many areas

2. Suppose you do a project that is highly praised.

   Cause _____

   (a) Is this cause due to something about you or something about the other person or the circumstances?

   | 1 | 2 | 3 | 4 | 5 | 6 | 7 |

   other person/   me
   circumstances

   (b) In the future will this cause again be present?

   | 1 | 2 | 3 | 4 | 5 | 6 | 7 |

   no   yes

   (c) Is the cause something that just influences this situation, or does it also influence other areas of your life?

   | 1 | 2 | 3 | 4 | 5 | 6 | 7 |

   this situation   many areas

Source: Based on Peterson et al., 1982

TABLE 19.2	The Explanatory Style of Optimists and Pessimists	
	PESSIMISTS	**OPTIMISTS**
Unhappy events	Internal, stable, global	External, unstable, specific
Happy events	External, unstable, specific	Internal, stable, global

making can be stressful (Kukde & Neufeld, 1992). However, the generally positive effects of control have convinced many health-care providers to involve patients in making decisions about their treatment.

IN DEPTH: Explanatory Style

A third personality characteristic related to health involves the explanations we supply for the events in our lives (Burns & Seligman, 1990). This research is especially important because it shows some interesting applications of research using the correlational method. Before reading further, try Demonstration 19.3.

The questions in this demonstration are a modified version of the **Attributional Style Questionnaire (ASQ),** which measures people's explanations for the causes of good and bad events. As discussed in Chapters 12 and 15, people differ from one another in their explanatory style. When they contemplate bad events—such as the first episode in Demonstration 19.3— some people use a pessimistic explanatory style. An unhappy event has an internal cause ("It's my fault"); a stable cause ("It will always be this way"); and a global cause ("It's this way in many different situations"). In contrast, people with an optimistic explanatory style explain an unhappy event in terms of an external cause ("It's his fault"), an unstable cause ("It won't happen tomorrow"), and a specific cause ("It's just limited to this area"). When explaining *happy* events, however, a pessimistic explanatory style attributes these events to external, unstable, and specific causes. In contrast, an optimistic explanatory style attributes happy events to internal, stable, and global causes. (See Table 19.2.)

We focus once again on explanatory style because it is related not only to achievement and depression, but also to illness patterns. We will examine several studies, including one on contemporary college students, one on baseball players, and a longitudinal one on people who were college students in the 1940s.

Contemporary College Students and Illness Patterns Christopher Peterson and Martin Seligman (1987) asked college students to complete a version of the ASQ that was similar to Demonstration 19.3, except that it contained 24 bad events. (With 24 items, the test-retest reliabilities for each of the three dimensions are reasonably high, with r's between .70 and .85.) Each participant also listed all the illnesses he or she had experienced during the previous month. One month later, they again completed the illness measure. One year later, they reported the number of visits they had made to a physician for diagnosis or treatment of an illness.

How was explanatory style related to illness? The first component—whether the explanation was internal or external—was not associated with later illness. However, a score derived by adding stability and globality together was predictive. That is, people with an optimistic explanatory style (with bad events attributed to unstable, specific causes) reported fewer illnesses and fewer visits to a physician.

If you have developed the proper skepticism, you might criticize this study. After all, it is possible that people who are frequently sick develop a negative explanatory style. Also, people who are depressed might tend to over-report illnesses, and we know from Chapter 15 that depressed people have negative explanatory styles. However, Peterson and Seligman (1987) addressed these concerns by statistically subtracting for number of illnesses reported at the first session and for depression level assessed at the first session. Explanatory style was still significantly correlated with illness reports one month later ($r = .22$) and doctor visits one year later ($r = .23$). Note, however, that the correlations are statistically significant but moderately low.

Baseball Hall of Fame Members One problem with the ASQ assessment technique is that the participant must be alive in order to take this test. Peterson and Seligman wanted to conduct a study on members of the Baseball Hall of Fame. However, they faced a major problem: Almost all of their potential participants were dead. Therefore, they created a new assessment technique called the content analysis of verbatim explanation (or CAVE) technique. The CAVE technique analyzes documents such as letters or diary entries. In the case of baseball players, it analyzes their quotations in the sports pages. Participants, therefore, do not need to be alive to participate in a study, but they do need to leave their words behind when they die.

Peterson and Seligman (1987) selected 94 members of the Baseball Hall of Fame who were active players between 1900 and 1950. Then they combed the sports pages of major newspapers during baseball seasons from 1900 to 1950, searching for quotes that included a causal explanation for a good or a bad event. Independent judges, who were unaware of details about the study, then rated the quotes for internality, stability, and globality. In addition, these researchers recorded the age at which the baseball player had died (or his age at the time of the study).

Impressively, players who supplied internal, stable, and global explanations for bad events lived shorter lives ($r = .26$). Explanations for good events produced an even stronger correlation—which led Peterson and Seligman to wish they had included good events in their college-student study. That is, players who supplied external, unstable, and specific explanations for good events lived shorter lives ($r = .45$). Two members of the Hall of Fame who had very different explanatory styles are shown in Figure 19.2.

Longitudinal Study of Illness Patterns Christopher Peterson, Martin Seligman, and George Vaillant (1988) used the CAVE technique to assess participants in a study of students who had attended Harvard University during the 1940s. Participants in this study included only the healthiest and the most academically successful students. Peterson and his colleagues focused on the responses that these men gave to open-ended questionnaires completed in 1946, which asked about difficult wartime experiences. In particular, they searched for descriptions of bad events that were accompanied by a causal explanation. Once more, judges rated each cause according to its internality, stability, and globality. Fortunately, each man's physician had also provided a health rating at five-year intervals.

Peterson and his colleagues added the internal, stable, and global subscales together to create a single explanatory-style score. Then they calculated correlations between these scores

 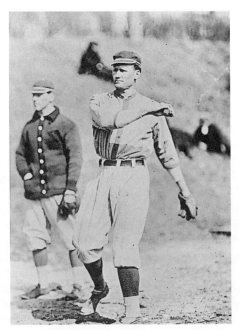

Figure 19.2

Explanatory style and longevity.

(left) Zack Wheat had a highly optimistic (internal, stable, global) pattern for explaining his success. *He remarked, "I'm a better hitter than I used to be because my strength has improved and my experience has improved." He died at the age of 83.*

(right) Walter Johnson had a highly pessimistic (internal, stable, global) pattern for explaining his failure *late in his career. He remarked, "I can't depend on myself to pitch well. I'm growing old. I have had my day." He died at the age of 59.*

TABLE 19.3 Correlations Between Negative Explanatory Style and Poor Physical Health

AGE	CORRELATION (r)
30	.04
35	.03
40	.13
45	.37
50	.18
55	.22
60	.25

Source: Based on Peterson et al., 1988.

and the measures of physical health, after first statistically subtracting for each man's initial physical and mental health. Table 19.3 shows the correlation between negative explanatory style and poor physical health, at ages 30 to 60. Clearly, explanatory style is not related to health when the men were younger; nearly all the men were healthy then. However, by the age of 45, health becomes more variable and psychological factors begin to play an important role.

Why Does Explanatory Style Influence Health? Several alternative pathways could account for the relationship between explanatory style and illness (Burns & Seligman, 1990; Peterson & Seligman, 1987; Peterson et al., 1988).

1. A pessimistic explanatory style may influence the immune system, similar to the way stress operates.

2. People with pessimistic explanatory styles may become passive when faced with disease; they may avoid seeking medical advice or avoid following it.

3. People with pessimistic explanatory styles may neglect their health and not obtain adequate sleep, nutrition, or exercise.

4. People with pessimistic explanatory styles may be poor problem solvers; they do not tackle a problem that could become a crisis.

Explanatory style is also related to other characteristics such as psychological control and overall optimistic mood, a variable that is also correlated with reduced stress and better health (Scheier & Carver, 1987; Scheier et al., 1986; Snyder et al., 1990). Furthermore, people with optimistic explanatory styles are probably lower in hostility, another variable related to health. Research by Robbins and her colleagues (1991) shows that many of these desirable characteristics are correlated with each other and they are related to various measures of physical health. Clearly, researchers need to sort out the critical underlying personality characteristics that are most strongly associated with good health. The next step will be to see whether individuals at risk for health problems can be trained to become stronger in the relevant characteristics. Then long-range health outcomes can be assessed, providing an experimental test of the relationship between personality and good health. Let us now turn our attention toward two social factors that influence health: ethnicity/social class and gender.

Ethnicity and Social Class

Ethnicity and social class are relevant to health psychology because members of some racial and ethnic groups are more susceptible to certain physical illnesses. For instance, in the United States, Blacks are more likely than Whites to die of cancer. Blacks and Hispanics also have a higher incidence of AIDS (Phillip, 1993; Rodin & Salovey, 1989).

One of the most striking health differences among ethnic groups in the United States is that Blacks are about twice as likely as Whites to have hypertension (high blood pressure). By some estimates, Blacks are between 6 and 15 times more likely than Whites to die of diseases related to hypertension (Gentry, 1985; Savage et al., 1987; Thompson, 1980). Possible explanations for the differences include genetic makeup, diet, and access to medication. Blacks are also about 50% more likely than Whites to have a chronic illness or other disability (Clark & Maddox, 1992).

Many studies on racial and ethnic differences are confounded by socioeconomic class. In the United States, economically disadvantaged people do not have the same access to health care that the upper classes enjoy (Brislin, 1993; Rodin & Salovey, 1989). People from lower social classes are less likely to have a personal physician and more likely to receive treatment in clinics. Health care is lower in quality when you see a different physician on each visit. In addition, clinics are not likely to encourage a sense of control or optimistic explanatory style.

Social class has a clear-cut impact on death rates. For example, an adult with an income of less than $9,000 per year is roughly five times as likely to die in any given year as someone with an income greater than $25,000 per year (Pappas et al., 1993). Social class and other factors related to health make life in an inner-city area especially hazardous. For example, McCord and Freeman (1990) found that Black men in Harlem were less likely to reach the age of 65 than men living in Bangladesh.

Ethnic background has an additional influence on health care: We must also consider the interactions between immigrants and North American physicians, who need to be sensitive to other health-care practices. For example, 10,000 members of the Hmong tribe in Laos have settled in Minnesota. The Hmong often prefer to seek care from shamans, ritual healers from the Southeast Asian tradition. Physicians can learn to coordinate their medical care with traditional healing methods. For example, a child with an ear infection might therefore take an antimicrobial medicine prescribed by an American doctor, as well as an herbal mixture recommended by the shaman. Similarly, Mexican-Americans may combine medicine from an American doctor with herbs purchased at a *botanica* (Mayers, 1989). Herbal medicines may indeed have healing properties. In addition, cultural beliefs should be respected (unless the practice is known to be harmful). As we have seen, psychological factors can influence the immune system and other health processes.

Health care for immigrants may be more effective when people seek traditional healing customs in addition to standard U.S. medical care. In this photo, a man purchases items from a botanica, *an herbal stall in Mexican culture, which sells herbs, potions, and roots intended to help the users improve their health.*

Gender

Currently, the average woman in North America has a life expectancy of 78 years, in contrast to 71 for men. Women's relative longevity is found in every ethnic group. For instance, Black women have a life expectancy of 74 years, in contrast to 65 for Black men (Strickland, 1988). Women and men are at risk for different diseases. For example, women are much more likely to develop breast cancer. In contrast, men are more likely to develop cancer in the respiratory and digestive systems. Men are roughly twice as likely as women to develop heart disease (Cleary, 1987; Travis, 1988).

One factor that may benefit women's health is that they are more likely than men to rate good health as being highly important and more likely to visit a physician (Rodin & Salovey, 1989; Verbrugge, 1985). However, physicians are less likely to diagnose and treat heart disease in a woman, unless the problem is severe (Holloway & Yam, 1992).

Another factor that may contribute to gender differences in longevity is employment patterns. Men are more likely to have hazardous jobs, such as construction work or police work. Men are also more likely to be involved in motor vehicle accidents and to consume alcohol and other drugs (Taylor, 1991). In summary, consistent with Theme 3, no single factor accounts for the gender differences in health. The explanation involves a variety of factors, such as health habits, employment patterns, and risky behaviors.

PSYCHOSOCIAL FACTORS RELATED TO HEALTH AND ILLNESS

- When assessed in a structured interview, Type A behavior pattern predicts heart disease; hostility may be the most important component of Type A behavior.

- Psychological control is also related to health; people high in control typically want to influence their future health.

- College students with an optimistic explanatory style have fewer illnesses; studies of baseball players and men who attended college during the 1940s also show that those with an optimistic style have greater longevity.

- Ethnic differences are found in the incidence of some diseases; some of these differences can be traced to social class, which is clearly related to health status.

- Women live longer than men, a gender difference that may be traceable to health habits, employment, and less risky behavior.

ACQUIRED IMMUNODEFICIENCY SYNDROME (AIDS)

We began this chapter with a discussion of stress, which contributes to many health problems. We then considered how health is associated with three personality characteristics, as well as ethnic/social class factors and gender. In the last two sections of the chapter, we discuss two health hazards that are critically important in the 1990s: AIDS and smoking.

To a large extent, we have no control over the way we die. The evening news shows the horrifying wreck of a car hit head-on by a drunk driver; the innocent victim had no way of avoiding death. But the irony of AIDS and smoking is that we can control whether we have unsafe sex or share needles with someone who might have AIDS. We also have the potential to avoid smoking. Nonetheless, thousands of people court suicide every day by engaging in risky behavior. Health psychologists are challenged to find methods to help people change their high-risk activities. Let us begin with a discussion of AIDS and then consider smoking in the final section.

Acquired immunodeficiency syndrome, or **AIDS,** is a viral disease that is spread by infected blood, semen, or vaginal secretions. The Surgeon General's Office estimated that roughly 230,000 U.S. residents would die of AIDS by the end of 1993 ("Surgeon General's Report," 1993). By October of that year, Canadian deaths from AIDS had reached 5,801 (Division of HIV/AIDS Epidemiology, 1993). Worldwide, an estimated 13,000,000 are infected with the AIDS virus, with the rate reaching 25% of the population in some urban areas of Africa (Kelly & Murphy, 1992; Mann et al., 1992).

AIDS is an important topic in health psychology because the disease is spread primarily by high-risk behavior. At present, no medicine can prevent or cure AIDS. Therefore, the primary method of halting AIDS is through education and changes in behavior (Chang et al., 1990). Our overview of AIDS begins with some background information and then discusses psychological aspects of AIDS and AIDS prevention.

Medical Aspects of AIDS

AIDS is triggered by a virus called **human immunodeficiency virus (HIV),** which has the potential to destroy part of the immune system. In particular, HIV invades white blood cells called T-helper lymphocytes. Inside these lymphocytes, the HIV replicates itself. As it replicates, it destroys these lymphocytes—the very lymphocytes that help fight diseases in people who are infected with HIV. When a lymphocyte is destroyed, many HIV viruses are released, and each can infect a new lymphocyte.

As a consequence, the immune system is substantially weakened (Baum & Temoshok, 1990; Klimas et al., 1991).

People infected with HIV may have no symptoms and may not realize that they are infected. The average incubation period between the initial HIV infection and the diagnosis of AIDS is estimated to be about 10 years ("Preventing risk behaviors," 1992). Unfortunately, even during this inactive period, a person can pass the disease on to other people.

Some of the early signs of AIDS include unexplained weight loss, night sweats, frequent diarrhea, fatigue, unexplained fevers, persistent infections, and swollen lymph glands. Later, the individual usually develops severe cancers or infections. A common kind of cancer in people with AIDS is Kaposi's sarcoma, a cancer that harms the cells inside certain small blood vessels. This blood-vessel damage may occur internally, or it may be visible just under the skin, where it produces blue or purple discolorations. In addition, people with AIDS frequently develop an infectious disease called *Pneumocystis carinii* pneumonia, a disease that is particularly deadly for people whose immune system no longer works properly (Hall, 1988). Tragically, once the AIDS diagnosis is established, life expectancy is roughly one to two years (Anderson & May, 1992; Ickovics & Rodin, 1992).

Transmission of AIDS

As the poster in Figure 19.3 illustrates, anyone can get AIDS who engages in risky behavior with an infected person. Unfortunately, it is usually impossible to tell whether a person is infected. Therefore, any contact with blood, semen, or vaginal secretions is potentially dangerous unless you are certain that these secretions could not possibly be infected with the AIDS virus.

People who currently face the greatest risk of developing AIDS are those in the following categories:

1. Intravenous (IV) drug users, currently the most common category of reported risk (Rango & Rampolla, 1990).
2. Gay and bisexual males who have had anal intercourse without condom protection. (We should note, incidentally, that lesbian women are at low risk for contracting AIDS via sexual activity.)
3. Women who have had heterosexual contact with infected men. Between 1987 and 1991, the number of AIDS cases among women in the United States increased by more than 1000% (Ickovics & Rodin, 1992).
4. Men who have had heterosexual contact with infected women.
5. Babies born to infected women (Stuber, 1991). In the United States, 4,906 cases of pediatric AIDS had been reported by September, 1993 (HIV/AIDS Surveillance Report, 1993).

In the first part of this chapter, we saw how people could acquire a disease through years of accumulated stressful experiences, and these diseases were not necessarily fatal. In the case of AIDS, a single act—lasting only minutes—can lead to a disease. Tragically, unless a cure is discovered between the time I write these words and the time you read them, that disease is fatal.

Psychological Symptoms in AIDS

HIV can have several direct effects on the central nervous system, When lymphocytes have been infected with HIV, they secrete substances that change the levels of certain brain chemicals. Furthermore, proteins in the HIV itself can change the functioning of the pituitary and adrenal glands. HIV may also alter the functioning of dopamine, an important neurotransmitter. Not surprisingly, then, people with AIDS often report cognitive problems, such as difficulty remembering and paying attention (Adler, 1989; Hall, 1988).

AIDS does not discriminate.

Anyone can get AIDS from sexual contact or sharing needles with an infected person. **Call 1-800-541-AIDS**
But we know how to prevent AIDS. Learn how to protect yourself.

New York State Health Department

Other psychological consequences include pain, reduced energy level, and altered body image—each of which can clearly influence a person's self-image. Unfortunately, people with AIDS are often blamed for their own disease. You have probably heard about people who have been fired and denied housing, facing discrimination because they had AIDS. For instance, in Florida, three young brothers tested positive for HIV, and their family's home was burned down (Robinson, 1987). Combined with the knowledge that death is almost inevitable, these stressors are likely to exceed the coping ability of most people (Herek & Glunt, 1988; Namir et al., 1987). Understandably, research on people with AIDS shows that they are more likely than control populations to report anxiety, depression, and anger (Hays et al., 1990a; Kelly & St. Lawrence, 1988).

Some people respond to a diagnosis of AIDS with denial. In fact, Taylor and her colleagues (1992) reported the astonishing finding that men who knew they had tested positive for HIV were significantly more optimistic about not developing AIDS than men who knew they had tested negative. Those who deny that they have AIDS are not likely to take precautions against infecting other people. As a consequence, the disease is spread even further.

What is the most effective way to cope with the terror of having AIDS? In general, people who use active coping strategies—rather than denial—are likely to have the highest self-esteem and the least depression (Namir et al., 1987). Some of these active strategies include talking to people, increasing physical exercise, and becoming involved in AIDS-related political activities. We discussed the importance of social support earlier in the chapter. This feeling of connectedness and concern is also vitally important when people are trying to cope with AIDS (Celentano & Sonnega, 1991; Hays et al., 1990b).

AIDS-Prevention Programs

At present, we have no vaccine against AIDS and no cure for the disease. Health psychologists who focus on AIDS therefore face a variety of challenges. They must deal with the psychological needs of people with AIDS and address the problem of biases and stereotypes about people with AIDS. In addition, they often attend to the psychological needs of family members, partners, and those who take care of individuals with AIDS.

Another priority for health psychologists is designing programs to educate people about AIDS and to help prevent AIDS. An underlying problem in many programs is one we raised in Chapter 17: Attitudes are often unrelated to behavior. People know that the consequences of high-risk behavior can be deadly, and they certainly have negative *attitudes* about acquiring AIDS. However, their *behavior* may still be risky.

Figure 19.3
This advertisement stresses that no population is immune to AIDS.

According to research, people with AIDS who take an active approach to life are likely to be relatively well adjusted. Volunteering at an AIDS office such as this one might promote psychological adjustment.

Education has persuaded an impressive number of people to avoid AIDS risks. Still, the success rate is far from satisfactory. AIDS prevention requires further reduction in high-risk sexual behavior and IV drug abuse.

High-Risk Sexual Behavior Many people simply fail to realize that they are engaging in risky sexual behavior. For example, in one survey of university students, 75% said that they faced a lower-than-average risk of contracting AIDS, compared to their peers; 20% said they had an average risk, and only 5% said they had an above-average risk (Moore & Rosenthal, 1991). Unless this sample was biased, we would expect 50% to rate themselves as average or above-average. A good number of students are probably trying to fool themselves about the risk of AIDS.

According to the research, only a small percent of sexually active people regularly use a condom (Campbell et al., 1992). For example, a study of Canadian college and university students showed that only 25% of the men and 16% of the women reported consistently using a condom during intercourse (MacDonald et al., 1990). Alarmingly, the women with the largest number of sexual partners are *less* likely to use condoms regularly than those who had just one partner (Campbell et al., 1992; MacDonald et al., 1990). Surveys of heterosexuals in the United States show that only 10% to 17% regularly use condoms (Adler, 1993; "Update," 1993).

Students may believe that they are not vulnerable, but unfortunately, the data suggest they are. Estimates based on samples from 19 U.S. universities report that for every 10,000 students, 50 men and 2 women will test positive for HIV (Gayle et al., 1990). Many students may be HIV positive and not know it. Others may be HIV positive and not share this information with potential sexual partners. For example, in one study of sexually active California students, 20% of the men and 4% of the women said that they would lie about their HIV status in order to have sex (Cochran & Mays, 1990).

At present, gay men in North America face greater risks of contracting AIDS than do heterosexuals. Research shows that older gay men have reduced the incidence of risky sexual behavior. However, gay men under the age of 25 are highly likely to take unwise risks (Gelman, 1993; Hays et al., 1990c).

How can people be persuaded to take AIDS more seriously? As you might expect, no single approach can be effective when the issue is so complex. A national survey found that 87% of responding school districts had curricula dealing with AIDS. Almost all of these educational programs covered the risks of intercourse in spreading AIDS. Most also emphasized that abstinence is the best way to prevent AIDS (Ruder et al., 1990). However, these programs cannot reach those who have already dropped out of school. The high-school dropout rate is 41% for Hispanics, 25% for Blacks, and 16% for Whites (Amaro, 1988). Clearly, people should be reached through community groups and the media, as well as school programs (Levine et al., 1993). We need to be more creative in persuading sexually active men and women to convert their *knowledge* about AIDS risks into less risky *behavior*.

High-Risk IV Drug Abuse We have known for decades that IV drug abuse is highly risky. However, those risks increased when AIDS began to spread. Now an injection of a mind-altering drug can also include an injection of the HIV virus.

Many IV users report that they have changed their behaviors to reduce the risk of AIDS (Des Jarlais & Friedman, 1988). For example, in one study, 46% of IV drug users said that they shared needles in 1984, in contrast to only 14% in 1990 (Harris et al., 1990). However, the participants in this study were extremely promiscuous, and they seldom used condoms during intercourse. As a consequence, AIDS-infected drug abusers are likely to spread the disease to their sexual partners.

Most drug abusers are unlikely to think extensively about future plans, including the risks of developing AIDS. Unfortunately, people who do not think about the future are not likely to worry about health issues and change their high-risk behavior. Some programs have been developed to educate IV drug users about the dangers of contaminated needles (Fullilove et al., 1989; Levine et al., 1993). At present, how-

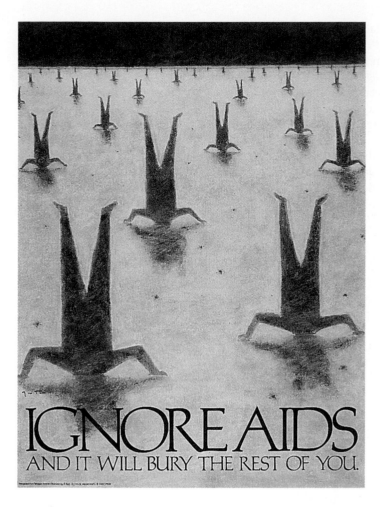

IGNORE AIDS
AND IT WILL BURY THE REST OF YOU.

Media campaigns have produced effective ads like this one, encouraging AIDS prevention.

ever, the prospect for changing the health habits of IV drug abusers appears dismal unless they can be encouraged to think more carefully about their futures.

SECTION SUMMARY

ACQUIRED IMMUNODEFICIENCY SYNDROME (AIDS)

- AIDS is triggered by HIV, which destroys part of the immune system; the symptoms include weight loss, fatigue, swollen lymph glands, cancer, and pneumonia.
- People with the highest risk of AIDS include IV drug users and people who engage in unprotected intercourse with an infected person, whether they are gay, bisexual, or heterosexual.
- AIDS can directly affect the central nervous system; other psychological effects include pain, altered self-image, and an increase in anxiety, depression, and anger.
- High-risk sexual behavior and dangerous IV drug practices have decreased somewhat, and most schools offer AIDS-education programs; nevertheless, numerous people still engage in risky behaviors.

SMOKING

Cigarette smoking is the major preventable cause of death in the United States (Jones, 1991). Health psychologists are interested in the smoking issue, especially because they need to explain why a habit so clearly dangerous as smoking should be so difficult to overcome.

At present, about 25% of adults in the United States smoke (Krogh, 1991). As recently as 1989, men were more likely than women to smoke (Pierce et al., 1989). However, the smoking rate is decreasing faster for men than for women. A survey in Canada showed that males and females between the ages of 15 and 24 are equally likely to smoke (Eliany, 1992). In the United States, teenage girls are *more* likely to smoke than teenage boys (Russell & Epstein, 1988). According to one estimate, by the year 2000, North America will probably have more female than male smokers (Pierce et al., 1989).

It is difficult to draw conclusions about ethnic differences in smoking rates. Some studies show that Whites are more likely to smoke than other ethnic groups, but other studies show they have lower smoking rates (deMoor et al., 1989; Escobedo et al., 1989; Fiore et al., 1989; Maddahian et al., 1988). However, one of the highest smoking rates can be found among male immigrants from Southeast Asia; between 57% and 72% of them are reported to be smokers (Chen, 1992).

Educational status is probably the factor with the greatest impact on smoking (Jones, 1991). Notice in Figure 19.4 that college graduates are much less likely to smoke than those with less education (Pierce et al., 1989). One likely explanation for these effects is that college-educated people are more oriented toward future plans, so they are less likely to engage in an activity that will harm their future health (Schelling, 1989).

Let us begin by noting some health consequences of smoking. Then we will consider the success of efforts to stop smoking, as well as some smoking-prevention programs.

Health Consequences of Smoking

According to recent estimates, about 400,000 deaths each year can be traced to tobacco (Cowley, 1992). As some have pointed out with irony, the tobacco industry is the only business that regularly kills its best customers. Another way of looking at the data is that a 25-year-old male who smokes one pack each day shortens his life by an average of five years. If he smokes two packs each day, he shortens his life by an average of 8 years (Fielding, 1985a).

Here are some of the health hazards that produce illness and early death in smokers:

1. *Lung cancer.* Every year, about 90,000 people in the United States die from lung cancer caused by smoking (Sarafino, 1990). The average male smoker is 22 times as likely to die from lung cancer as a nonsmoker. Furthermore, lung cancer is quickly replacing breast cancer as the leading cause of cancer deaths in American women (Fielding, 1985a; Toufexis, 1989).

2. *Other lung diseases.* Cigarette smokers are also much more likely to develop diseases, such as emphysema, that harm the lung tissue and make breathing more difficult.

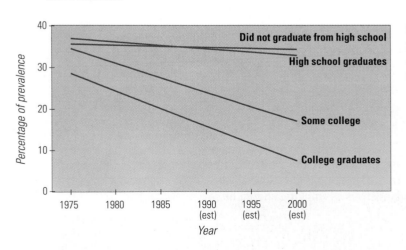

Figure 19.4

The prevalence of smoking as a function of educational status between 1975 and the year 2000. (Pierce et al., 1989)

3. *Other cancers.* Smokers also develop cancers in regions of the body other than the lung. Smokers are more likely to develop cancer of the larynx, the mouth, the esophagus, the digestive system, the bladder, the pancreas, the kidney, and—in women—the cervix (Fielding, 1985a; Schilit & Gomberg, 1991).

4. *Heart disease.* Cigarette smoking causes about 225,000 heart-disease deaths each year in the United States (Fielding, 1985a). However, people who have not smoked in 10 years run a risk of heart disease that is no greater than for non-smokers.

5. *Strokes.* Smoking also increases the chance of dying from a stroke. About 26,500 U.S. smokers die from strokes each year (Toufexis, 1989).

6. *Accidents.* Smokers are more likely than nonsmokers to be involved in automobile accidents, perhaps because smoking impairs performance on complex information-processing tasks (Spilich et al., 1992).

Fires started by cigarettes also claim many lives each year, and Chapter 10 emphasized that pregnant women who smoke are likely to harm their unborn children. Furthermore, about 3,000 lung-cancer deaths each year can be traced to second-hand smoke (Cowley, 1992). Because cigarettes cause so much harm to both smokers and their families, it is no surprise that many smokers want to stop. Let us now consider efforts to stop smoking.

Trying to Stop Smoking

About 90% of all smokers say that they would like to quit (Imperato & Mitchell, 1986). Why is quitting so difficult? Researchers now believe that the nicotine in tobacco is actually addicting (Miller, 1991; Surgeon General, 1988). Nicotine alters mood and acts as a reinforcer for using tobacco. Nicotine causes a physical dependence, similar to drugs such as heroin and cocaine that were discussed in Chapter 5.

People who try to stop smoking experience genuine tobacco withdrawal symptoms, including anxiety, hunger, irritability, restlessness, and weight gain (Hughes, 1992). In fact, nicotine is clearly more addicting than alcohol. For example, researchers in one study questioned people who had sought treatment for alcohol dependence and who were also trying to stop smoking (Kozlowski et al., 1989). These individuals were asked whether it was harder to stop smoking or to stop drinking; 80% responded that quitting smoking was more difficult.

An increasing number of businesses and public places have no-smoking policies.

External forces also make it difficult to stop smoking. Breaking the habit is more difficult if your friends, other students, or the people at work smoke. With increasing numbers of colleges, public places, and worksites adopting no-smoking policies, however, the environment may be more encouraging for those who want to stop smoking (Biener et al., 1989).

Another external barrier to giving up cigarettes is the tobacco industry, which currently spends $3.6 billion each year on advertising and promoting cigarettes. As you probably have heard, their ads are well known to young children; 6-year-olds are as familiar with "Joe Camel" as with Mickey Mouse ("Tobacco Industry," 1993). Advertisements show glamorous people, surrounded by friends, enjoying life to the fullest. The advertising companies are clearly aware of the factors we discussed in Chapter 17, which persuade potential buyers.

About 1,500,000 Americans stop smoking each year (Lichtenstein & Glasgow, 1992). The smoker who finally gives up cigarettes averages six previous unsuccessful attempts to quit (Silvis & Perry, 1987). One group of people who are particularly likely to quit smoking are those who have recently suffered a heart attack (Jeffery, 1989; Weinstein, 1989). Perhaps the decision-making heuristic of availability works for these people (Chapter 8). A vivid example of a recent life-threatening trauma comes readily to mind when they are tempted to smoke.

Health psychologists point out that physicians should take the opportunity during routine physical exams to advise smokers about the health risks of smoking. They should also give their patients appropriate literature and ask for their concrete plans for giving up cigarettes (Raw, 1986). Chapter 17 discussed how the expertise and trustworthiness of the persuader are both important factors in persuasion, so physicians should have the potential to persuade. They could be especially influential if they heighten their patients' cognitive dissonance, so that the patients appreciate the discrepancy between their beliefs that smoking is harmful and their actions of continuing to smoke.

About 90% of smokers quit on their own (Lichtenstein & Glasgow, 1992). However, a variety of smoking-cessation programs are available (Fielding, 1985b; Lichtenstein & Glasgow, 1992). They often use behavioral or cognitive-behavioral techniques. One approach uses contracts that require the smoker to deposit money with the program's staff member, to be returned only if the smoker successfully gives up cigarettes. Most programs require smokers to keep records of their smoking so that they can become more aware of the situations where smoking is most likely. We discussed some of these applications of operant conditioning in Chapter 16.

An increasing number of business organizations are sponsoring smoking-cessation programs for their employees (Grunberg, 1991). An important advantage of these groups is that they create peer pressure (Chapter 18), which encourages people not to smoke. In one program, for instance, both the company and employees collected reward money that was distributed to those who stopped smoking. At the six-month follow-up, close to 90% of the participants had successfully stopped smoking (Stachnik & Stoffelmayr, 1983).

The most effective way to overcoming smoking is one that attempts more than one approach (Kottke et al., 1988; Lichtenstein & Glasgow, 1992). This program might include using transdermal patches—small "nicotine patches" worn directly on the skin. Well-controlled studies show that they increase the success rate significantly (Tonnesen et al., 1991). Psychological components of an antismoking campaign should include specific recommendations from physicians, enrollment in a smoking-cessation program, and antismoking messages from the media.

Smoking-Prevention Programs

Even the most successful approaches are not particularly effective in helping people stop smoking. Instead, most health psychologists encourage the development of programs to prevent people from starting an addiction to cigarettes. These efforts

The American Cancer Society has developed effective no-smoking ads aimed at teenagers.

also need to focus on young children, because most users acquire the habit in their early teens. Furthermore, people who do not become regular smokers during the teen years are not likely to begin smoking later in life (Silvis & Perry, 1987).

Any program directed at preventing smoking should stress that only a minority of teenagers and adults smoke. In one study, a group of eighth graders estimated that 53% of their peers smoked, when in reality "only" 23% did so. These students may inaccurately perceive peer pressure to smoke, but they need to know that the majority is on their side (Leventhal et al., 1987).

Richard Evans and his colleagues (1981, 1984, 1988) developed a smoking-prevention program based on some of the principles we have discussed in this textbook. They created a series of films in which teenagers served as narrators as well as actors. In these simulated scenes, they were being urged by friends to try smoking. The films were supplemented with other cognitive-behavioral techniques, as well as color posters with captions such as "YOU can resist social pressures to smoke." The researchers used the quasi-experimental method, assigning junior high schools to either the experimental or the control group. One year later, the smoking rate in the experimental group was one-half the rate of the control group. A similar program found that these psychosocial techniques were successful with students in predominantly Hispanic schools in New York City (Botvin et al., 1989).

Perhaps even more important than these isolated programs would be a more broad-based approach that trains young people to take their lives and their health more seriously. A primary advantage of these programs may be that they encourage adolescents to become more aware of future plans. As we noted at the beginning of this section, people who think about the future are more concerned about staying healthy and avoiding activities that would jeopardize their longevity.

SECTION SUMMARY

SMOKING

- Cigarette smoking is lower among college-educated people; gender differences are now minimal, and ethnic-group differences are inconsistent.

- Health consequences of smoking include lung cancer, other lung diseases, other cancers, coronary heart disease, strokes, and accidents.

- Smoking is difficult to stop, especially because nicotine is addicting; helpful tactics include physicians' advice, programs that include cognitive-behavioral techniques, and groups that create peer pressure to not smoke.

- Smoking-prevention programs should be aimed at young people, providing films that show teenagers resisting temptation, and encouraging them to become more future-oriented.

R E V I E W   Q U E S T I O N S

1. This question helps you review parts of the entire text. Make a list of the 18 previous chapter titles. Then skim this Health Psychology chapter, jotting down notes next to each chapter title whenever you see a relevant application.

2. Try to recall a recent time when you experienced stress. Relate that experience to Selye's general adaptation syndrome model. Which of the three major categories of sources of stress seems most relevant to that situation? How did stress influence your behavior, cognitive processes, emotions, and physiological activities? What coping strategies did you use?

3. The section on stress describes how stress affects the immune system. What does AIDS do to the immune system and how might the coping responses of people living with AIDS have some influence on the course of their disease?

4. Suppose that a middle-aged relative tells you that he has read that people who are always "on the go" and time conscious are more likely to die of heart attacks. How would you explain the current findings on this topic?

5. The section on psychological control emphasized that control may actually influence longevity. Think about an elderly person you know, and list some of the ways in which this person could achieve greater personal control over life events. Describe some of the theories about how control actually might influence longevity.

6. In Demonstration 19.3, you rated your explanatory style. Relate your own style to Seligman's findings, and note how you explain both positive and negative events. Which of the explanations for Seligman's results do you find the most compelling?

7. How are gender and ethnicity/social class relevant in (a) patterns of coping with stress, (b) health and illness, (c) likelihood of getting AIDS, and (d) smoking? A talk by Schelling (1989) noted that a good way to remember which groups have shown the greatest decrease in smoking is "Those people who wear neckties to work." What did he mean?

8. Imagine that you have been appointed to coordinate a state education committee on teaching health issues to junior-high students. What techniques would you use to encourage health-conscious life-styles? What kind of media approaches would you use to supplement the school program?

9. In both the section on AIDS and the section on smoking, we discussed how people persist in high-risk behaviors, even though they know that these activities are dangerous. How are the topics of AIDS and smoking related, and how are they different?

10. In the sections on AIDS and smoking, we frequently referred to an individual's thoughts about the future. Note how this concept is relevant to those two topics, and point out how it could be applied to helping people make long-range plans for dealing with stress.

N E W   T E R M S

applied psychology
health psychology
stress
general adaptation syndrome (GAS)
stressor
alarm phase
homeostasis
resistance phase
exhaustion phase
immune system
lymphocytes

coping
problem-focused coping
emotion-focused coping
cognitive reappraisals
denial
Type A behavior pattern
Type B behavior pattern
Attributional Style Questionnaire (ASQ)
Acquired immunodeficiency syndrome
  (AIDS)
human immunodeficiency virus (HIV)

A N S W E R S   T O   D E M O N S T R A T I O N S

DEMONSTRATION 19.2   Give yourself 1 point for every T response you provided for these items: 1, 2, 3, 6, 7, and 8. Give yourself an additional point for every F response you provided for these items: 4, 5, 9, and 10. In general, those with higher scores tend to be higher in hostility than those with low scores.

R E C O M M E N D E D   R E A D I N G S

Brannon, L., & Feist, J. (1992). *Health psychology: An introduction to behavior and health* (2nd ed.). Belmont, CA: Wadsworth. This textbook is extremely well organized, clear, and comprehensive.

Krogh, D. (1991). *Smoking: The artificial passion.* New York: Freeman. Krogh's book outlines the history of smoking and provides a readable account of the attraction and the dangers of smoking.

Rathus, S. A., & Boughn, S. (1993). *AIDS: What every student needs to know.* Fort Worth, TX: Harcourt Brace Jovanovich. This book uses some excellent teaching techniques to convey the facts about AIDS. It also includes some exercises showing students how to be more assertive in encouraging their sexual partners to practice safer sex.

Snyder, C. R., & Forsyth, D. R. (Eds.). (1990). *Handbook of social and clinical psychology: The health perspective.* New York: Pergamon. This superb resource book includes many relevant chapters on health psychology, including humor and health, gender and health, Type A behavior pattern, explanatory style, and psychological control.

Taylor, S. E. (1991). *Health psychology* (2nd ed.). New York: McGraw-Hill. Shelley Taylor discusses each of the topics included in this chapter and also examines additional issues such as alcoholism, how the health system treats patients, and the management of chronic illnesses.

APPENDIX

STATISTICAL PROCEDURES AND CALCULATIONS

The research methods chapter (Chapter 2) gave you an overview of how statistics is used in psychology. You learned about descriptive statistics—specifically central tendency and variability—as well as inferential statistics. That information provided an essential background for the research discussed throughout the textbook.

For many of you, this course in introductory psychology will be your only exposure to statistical methods. Therefore, you may want to know some more details about statistical procedures and calculations. Consider several examples of situations where statistics might be useful for you.

1. You may pursue a career in business, and your boss has asked you to construct a frequency distribution to show the number of sick-days reported by the 75 company employees during 1993.

2. You may teach grade school, and you want to know how to interpret the percentile scores that are listed for your students on their last standardized mathematics test.

3. You may become a physician. Perhaps you are concerned about a woman with bulimia nervosa. Her weight is about average for her height, but you are concerned that her weight during the daily weigh-ins is too variable. You want to calculate the standard deviation for these weights.

Let's consider how each of these issues can be addressed by considering frequency distributions, percentiles, and standard deviations. This information also provides a brief preview of these topics for those of you who will take a statistics course in the future. (Most psychology majors are required to take a statistics course; it is also a frequent requirement for students majoring in sociology, political science, mathematics, economics, education, and biology.)

FREQUENCY DISTRIBUTIONS AND HISTOGRAMS

A **frequency distribution** is a summary of data that shows how often each score occurs. To construct a frequency distribution, divide the entire range of scores into equal intervals. Then tally the number of scores that fall in each interval.

Suppose, for example, that you have been instructed to construct a frequency distribution and a histogram illustrating the number of employee sick-days. Your first step is to construct a table like Table A.1.

A frequency distribution allows you to summarize a large amount of data into one well-organized table. However, you may want to convert these data into a figure that provides a more visual representation. You might, therefore, decide to construct a **histogram,** which is a graphic representation of a frequency distribution. As you can see, the height of each bar represents how often each score occurs. Figure A.1 is a histogram of the data in Table A.1. Many people feel that they can appreciate the general trend in data more quickly by looking at a histogram than by consulting a less visual frequency distribution, presented in table form.

TABLE A.1	Frequency Distribution of the Number of Sick-Days Reported by 75 Employees for 1993
INTERVAL	**NUMBER OF EMPLOYEES IN EACH INTERVAL**
0–1	23
2–3	10
4–5	6
6–7	9
8–9	7
10–11	8
12–13	6
14–15	3
16–17	2
18+	1

PERCENTILES

You have probably noticed the terms *percentile score* or *percentile rank* if you took a standardized test such as the Scholastic Aptitude Test (SAT) when you were applying for college. For example, if you took the SAT in November of 1993, a score of 600 on the verbal portion was listed as the 92nd percentile. A **percentile score** indicates the percentage of people who received scores below your own score. In this case, if you received a percentile score of 92, it would mean that 92% of the people who took the test received a score lower than you did. A percentile score is useful because it allows you to understand where your score falls relative to other scores.

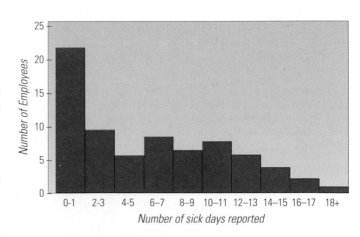

Figure A.1

A histogram of the frequency distribution in Table A.1, illustrating the number of sick-days reported by 75 employees for 1993.

Percentile scores are especially important in education. Suppose that you are a fourth-grade teacher who is trying to figure out why one of your students, Gordon, is doing poorly in mathematics. You consult Gordon's records and discover that his raw score on the mathematics portion of a standardized test from last year is 27. A raw score, by itself, is meaningless. You have no hint about whether a 27 is low, medium, or high.

Most standardized tests therefore list a percentile score next to the raw score. Suppose that Gordon's percentile score is 73. You would then know that Gordon scored higher than 73% of students; his performance on that test was clearly above average. You would conclude that Gordon seems to have the skill to perform the work. You might suspect a motivational problem or a specific learning disability associated with a particular kind of mathematical skill.

Note, incidentally, that a student cannot obtain a percentile score of 100. That score would mean the student scored higher than 100% of students, including himself or herself—a logical impossibility! Instead, an extremely high raw score is often assigned a percentile score of 99+. For example, in November 1993, a verbal SAT score of 750 to 800 was assigned a percentile score of 99+. Also, note that a percentile score of 50 means that a student has received a score that is at the median of the distribution. As discussed in Chapter 2, the **median** is the score that falls precisely in the middle of a distribution of scores. Figure A.2 illustrates several percentile scores.

STANDARD DEVIATIONS

As we discussed in Chapter 2, a **standard deviation** is a measure of **variability,** or the extent to which scores differ from one another. Variability can easily be measured in terms of **range,** or the difference between the highest and lowest scores in a distribution. However, the range takes into account only *two* scores. Psychologists are much more likely to measure variability in terms of the standard deviation, which uses *all* scores in calculating the "spread-outedness" of these scores. The standard deviation is based on the distance of each score from the mean. Turn back to Figure 2.10 to contrast one distribution, whose standard deviation is 5.7, with a second distribution, whose standard deviation is only 2.2.

Let us imagine that you are a physician who is monitoring a woman with bulimia nervosa. You are particularly concerned

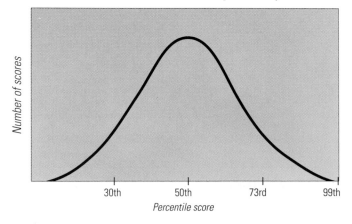

Figure A.2

Examples of percentile scores. (Note: 30th percentile means that 30% of the test takers received scores lower than this particular score.)

about the fact that her weight seems to vary too much from one day to the next—which suggests that she may be bingeing on some days and restricting her intake on other days. Suppose that she reports to your office on six consecutive days and you record her weight each time:

123   125   122   125   130   125

To calculate the standard deviation, you will use this formula, expressed in words instead of symbols:

$$\text{Standard deviation} = \sqrt{\frac{\text{Sum of (deviations)}^2}{\text{Number of scores}}}$$

Let's go through the procedure, step by step.

1. Calculate the mean of these scores.

123
125
122
125
130
125
750

    $6)\overline{750}$ $\quad$ $\dfrac{125}{}$ $\quad$ Mean (symbolized $\overline{X}$) = 125

2. Subtract the mean from each of your scores. Check your accuracy; the sum of these new deviation scores should equal zero.

Score	Mean		Deviation score
123	− 125	=	−2
125	− 125	=	0
122	− 125	=	−3
125	− 125	=	0
130	− 125	=	+5
125	− 125	=	0
			0 ✓

3. Take each of these deviation scores, square it, and add together these squared deviation scores.

Deviation score	Squared Deviation score	
−2	$(-2)^2$	= 4
0	$(0)^2$	= 0
−3	$(-3)^2$	= 9
0	$(0)^2$	= 0
+5	$(+5)^2$	= 25
0	$(0)^2$	= 0

    Sum of the squared deviation scores $\qquad$ 38

4. Divide the sum of the deviation scores by the number of observations you made.

    $6)\overline{38}$ $\quad \dfrac{6.3}{}$

5. Take the square root of the number you calculated in step 4.

    $\sqrt{6.3} = 2.5$

    Notice that large standard deviations indicate greater variability in the scores. Suppose, for example, that you were to calculate a standard deviation of 2.5 for a bulimic woman's weight measurements, prior to the beginning of therapy. Suppose that the standard deviation of her weight measurements, taken after several months of therapy, was 1.1. You could therefore conclude that her newer set of weight measurements was less variable. (However, you would actually need to conduct a statistical test on your data to determine whether that decrease had been statistically significant.)

The term *standard deviation* is conceptually more difficult than a term such as *mean* or *range*. It is easy to see how both *mean* and *range* are related to the actual scores in the distribution. In contrast, it is difficult to look at the weight scores listed earlier and appreciate how the standard deviation of 2.5 relates to those scores. One helpful point that makes the standard deviation seem more concrete is this: When you have a large number of scores in a typical distribution, 68% of the scores lie within one standard deviation of each side of the mean. That is, roughly one-third of all scores lie between the mean and a point one standard deviation *above* the mean. Furthermore, roughly one-third of all scores lie between the mean and a point one standard deviation *below* the mean. The remaining one-third of all scores lie outside these boundaries (specifically, one-sixth above the boundary and one-sixth below the boundary). Figure A.3 shows this general principle. (Note, incidentally, that in the case of the hypothetical bulimic woman, one-third of her weight scores lie outside of the interval 125 ± 2.5.)

Let us also relate standard deviations to IQ scores, because most of you are familiar with the kind of scores that are typical on intelligence tests. On many IQ tests, the size of the standard deviation is 15. This means that about 68% of IQ scores should lie within one standard deviation of each side of the mean. If the mean is 100, then 68% of people should receive scores between 85 and 115. Figure A.4 notes, also, that 95% of all scores lie within two standard deviations of each side of the mean, or between IQ scores of 70 and 130.

Finally, I should stress that most psychologists use computers to calculate the majority of statistical measures. When you need to calculate the standard deviation for six scores, as we did earlier, you can easily figure out a standard deviation by hand. However, the process quickly becomes cumbersome as you increase the number of scores. With the aid of a statistical package

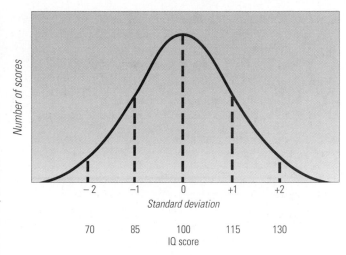

Figure A.4

The distribution of scores on an IQ test showing scores one and two standard deviations away from the mean. (Note: Roughly two-thirds— 68%—of IQ scores lie within one standard deviation of the mean; 95% of IQ scores lie within two standard deviations of the mean.)

for the computer, psychologists simply enter all the scores in a distribution. The printout supplies a variety of useful information, such as the mean, median, frequency distribution, histogram, and standard deviation.

N E W   T E R M S

frequency distribution	standard deviation
histogram	variability
percentile score	range

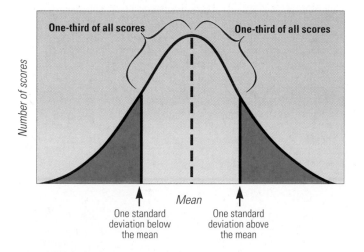

Figure A.3

A distribution of scores, showing the mean and points one standard deviation above and below the mean.

A guide has been provided for words whose pronunciation may be ambiguous; the accented syllable is indicated by italics.

Accommodation Piaget's concept proposing that humans change their thought structures to fit the stimuli they encounter.

Acetylcholine (ACh) In the nervous system, a neurotransmitter found in synapses in the brain, where it is important in such functions as arousal, attention, memory, aggression, sexuality, and thirst. ACh can also be found at the junction between neurons and muscle fibers, where it acts as an excitatory neurotransmitter, causing muscle fibers to contract.

Achievement motive Motivation involving doing well relative to a standard of excellence and succeeding at a challenging task.

Achievement test Test designed to measure current skills, usually based on previous learning in a subject area.

Acquired immunodeficiency syndrome (AIDS) Sexually transmitted viral disease—spread by infected blood, semen, or vaginal secretions—that destroys the body's natural immunity to diseases. Once the immune system has been destroyed, diseases such as pneumonia and cancer can take over, leading eventually to death.

Acquisition In general, the process of learning a new response. In classical conditioning, acquisition involves producing a conditioned response to a conditioned stimulus. Pertaining to memory, acquisition is the first stage of remembering in which we perceive the item and record its important features.

Action potential Brief change in the electrical charge of an axon.

Activation-synthesis hypothesis In the neurocognitive model of the function of dreams, a core concept which proposes that the hindbrain sends a haphazard pattern of signals to the cerebral cortex (activation), and then the cerebral cortex tries to make sense out of all these random signals (synthesis).

Active listening In person-centered therapy, technique by which the therapist attempts to understand both the content and the emotion of a client's statement.

Active touch Touch perception in which we actively explore and touch objects.

Actor-observer bias Tendency to attribute our own behavior to external, situational causes, whereas we attribute others' behavior to internal, personal causes.

Acuity Ability to see precise details.

Adaptation Phenomenon in which the perceived intensity of a repeated stimulus decreases over time. For example, touch adaptation guarantees that we stop noticing touch after a few minutes of mild constant pressure.

Additive bilingualism Situation in which an individual acquires proficiency in a second language with no loss in the first language. Both languages are respected and considered prestigious.

Adoption studies Studies to determine whether adopted children are more like their biological parents (who contribute genes) or their adoptive parents (who contribute a home environment).

Adrenal glands Two structures on top of the kidneys that produce several dozen kinds of hormones, including sex hormones, epinephrine, and hormones that regulate the concentration of minerals in the body and the concentration of sugar in the blood.

Age regression During hypnosis, a hypnotized person is given suggestions to re-experience an event that occurred at an earlier age and to act like and feel like a person of that particular age.

Ageism Bias against aging and elderly people. This bias can include myths, negative attitudes, stereotypes, and outright discrimination.

Aggression A deliberate attempt to injure or destroy someone, either physically or psychologically.

Agoraphobia Type of anxiety disorder involving fear of being in situations or public places where escape would be difficult.

AIDS *See* Acquired immunodeficiency syndrome.

Alarm phase First phase of the general adaptation syndrome (response to stress), during which the individual prepares for action.

Algorithm In problem solving, a method that always produces a solution to a problem sooner or later.

Alignment heuristic Rule-of-thumb stating that figures will be remembered as being more lined up than they really are.

Alpha waves During relaxation states, brain waves occurring at the frequency of 8 to 12 per second.

Alternate-form reliability Method for measuring the reliability of a test in which two alternate forms of the test are administered, usually 1 day to several weeks apart. The alternate-form reliability is high if each person's score is similar on the two tests.

Altruism Action that benefits another person, including comforting, helping, sharing, rescuing, and cooperating. Acts of concern for other people, without any hope of reward. Also known as prosocial behavior.

Alzheimer's disease Disorder that involves a severe decline in emotions and thinking skills, gradually growing worse over time.

Amnesia Loss of memory.

Amplitude In vision, the height of the light wave; amplitude is related to the brightness of a visual stimulus. In audition, the size of the change in pressure created by the sound wave; amplitude is related to the loudness of the auditory stimulus.

Anal stage One of the stages of psychosexual development, during which the erogenous zone shifts to the anal region. Freud proposed that toddlers experience satisfaction when their anal region is stimulated, for instance by retaining or eliminating feces.

Analog code Mental representation that closely resembles the physical object. Mental images may be stored in analog codes.

Analogy approach In problem solving, a strategy in which persons use a solution to an earlier problem to help solve a new one.

Anchoring and adjustment heuristic Strategy for making an estimate in which people begin by guessing a first approximation (an anchor) and then make adjustments to that number on the basis of additional information. Typically, people rely too heavily on the anchor, and their adjustments are too small.

Androgen hormones Hormones that produce changes in males during early prenatal development, guiding the development of the male reproductive system.

Anorexia nervosa Eating disorder that is characterized by an irrational pursuit of thinness and concern about gaining weight. Anorexics feel fat, even when they look emaciated. The American Psychiatric

Association specifies that a person can be classified as anorexic if body weight is 15% less than specified on standard weight charts and if no known physical illness accounts for the low weight.

Anterograde amnesia An impaired ability to form long-term memory for new information.

Antianxiety drugs Drugs designed to reduce tension and create drowsiness by depressing activity in the central nervous system. Examples include Valium and Librium.

Antidepressant drugs Drugs designed to help make a person's mood more positive. Examples include the MAO inhibitors, the tricyclics, and Prozac.

Antipsychotic drugs Drugs that reduce the symptoms of schizophrenia such as agitation, confusion, delusions, and hallucinations.

Antisocial personality disorder Type of personality disorder characterized by a variety of antisocial behaviors, including lying, violence, and other actions that show little concern for the welfare of others. The diagnosis is given only if an individual is at least 18 years of age and showed similar behavior problems prior to the age of 15.

Anxiety disorders Anxiety that persists—without any clear explanation—and that causes intense suffering. Five types of anxiety disorders are generalized anxiety disorders, panic disorders and agoraphobia, phobic disorders, obsessive-compulsive disorders, and posttraumatic stress disorders.

Anxious/ambivalent attachment style Adult love-relationship style in which the individual wants to get closer to others than they would like; the individual's intensity sometimes scares people away.

Anxious avoidant attachment Type of attachment in which a baby enjoys exploration; after separation, the baby actively avoids the caretaker.

Anxious resistant attachment Type of attachment in which a baby displays a mixture of seeking and resisting contact with the caregiver.

Aphasia Language difficulty; one of the possible disabilities resulting from a stroke.

Applied psychologists Psychologists whose focus is on changing both actions and thoughts.

Applied psychology Area of psychology emphasizing practical applications of psychological research.

Aptitude test Test designed to predict future success on the basis of current performance. Aptitude tests draw their material

from a broad range of human experience, including information gained outside the classroom.

Archetype (*are*-kih-tipe) According to Jung, a classic image or symbol that is found in a wide variety of cultures and religions.

Assimilation Piaget's concept proposing that humans use and modify stimuli they encounter in terms of their current thought structure.

Attachment Close emotional bond of affection between an infant and his or her caregivers.

Attention Concentration of mental activity.

Attentional bias A social-cognitive explanation for phobias which proposes that people with phobias focus their attention on feared aspects of the environment.

Attitude Psychological tendency that is expressed by an evaluation of something.

Attribution In person perception, the explanation we create about the reasons for our own behavior and the behavior of other people. Attributions often involve causal explanations for success or failure.

Attributional Style Questionnaire (ASQ) Questionnaire that measures people's explanations for the causes of good and bad events.

Auditory canal Tube running inward from the outer ear, through which sound enters.

Auditory cortex Portion of the cortex primarily located in a deep groove on each side of the surface of the brain. The auditory cortex codes both simple and complex auditory stimuli.

Auditory nerve Bundle of neurons that carries information from the inner ear toward higher levels of auditory processing.

Authoritarian parents Parenting style in which parents demand unquestioning obedience from their children, punish children forcefully when children do not meet their standards, and are less likely to be affectionate with their children.

Authoritative parents Effective parenting style in which parents are affectionate but provide control when necessary. Parents respect each child's individuality, they are loving, and they allow children to express their own points of view. However, they have clear-cut standards, which they uphold in a consistent fashion.

Autobiographical memory Memory for events from a person's own life.

Automatic processing Placing material into memory with no direct effort.

Autonomic division In the nervous system, the division that helps control the glands, blood vessels, the intestines, the heart, and

other internal organs. The autonomic nervous system usually works automatically, unlike the somatic division.

Autonomic lability Concept suggesting that there are large individual differences in the tendency for the autonomic nervous system to be easily aroused. Individuals who are easily aroused are more likely to develop phobias and other anxiety disorders.

Availability heuristic Rule-of-thumb used when people estimate frequency or probability in terms of how easy it is to think of examples of something.

Aversion therapy Behaviorist approach in which inappropriate behavior is followed by punishment, and appropriate behavior is rewarded.

Avoidant attachment style Adult love-relationship style in which the individual feels somewhat uncomfortable getting close to others and trusting them completely.

Axon In the nervous system, the long fiber that carries information away from the cell body toward other neurons.

Balanced-placebo design Research design consisting of four groups of participants, half of whom expect that they will be doing something (e.g., drinking alcohol) and half of whom do not. Furthermore, half of the participants actually do receive something (e.g., alcohol) and half receive a placebo. This research design is used to sort out the effects of the variable itself (e.g., alcohol), as opposed to the effects of people's expectations about how they *should* behave.

Base rate How often the item occurs in the population.

Baseline measure In behavior modification, the response rate before beginning the behavior modification program.

Basilar membrane Membrane on the base of the organ of Corti in the inner ear, which contains hair cells (the receptors for hearing).

Beck's cognitive therapy Therapy that attempts to correct systematic errors in reasoning known as cognitive distortions.

Behavior modification The systematic use of techniques from learning theory to change human behavior.

Behavior therapy Psychotherapy that uses the principles of learning theory (classical and operant conditioning) to encourage appropriate behavior and eliminate undesirable behavior. An important feature of behavior therapy is that the therapist and the client explicitly specify the treatment goals in terms of observable behavior.

Behavioral assessment The measurement of personality by objectively recording people's observable behavior, as well as events that happened beforehand and afterwards.

Behavioral measures In a research study, measurement that objectively records people's observable behavior.

Behaviorism Approach to psychology that stresses the study of observable behavior instead of hidden mental processes.

Beta waves During waking states, rapid brain waves at the frequency of at least 14 per second.

Biased sample In a research study, a sample in which some members of the population are more likely to be chosen than others.

Bicultural efficacy A person's belief that he or she can live effectively within two different ethnic groups without compromising the sense of cultural identity.

Big Five traits In personality research, the five most important clusters of personality traits, including extraversion, agreeableness, conscientiousness, emotional stability, and openness to experience.

Bilingual A person who uses two languages that differ in speech sounds, vocabulary, and syntax.

Binge drinking Alcohol consumption of five or more drinks in a row at least once in the past two weeks.

Binocular In depth perception, factors requiring two eyes that can provide information about distance.

Binocular disparity In vision, source of distance information provided by two eyes that present slightly different views of the world. The difference between the two retinal images of an object is known as binocular disparity.

Binocular vision Characteristic of the human visual system based on both eyes working together and having partially overlapping fields of view.

Biological approach Approach to psychology, also called neuroscience approach, that proposes that each behavior, emotion, and thought is caused by a physical event in the brain or other part of the nervous system.

Biological motion In motion perception, the pattern of movement exhibited by people and other living things.

Biological preparedness Built-in bias ensuring that some relationships between stimuli and responses will be learned more readily than others. A biological explanation for phobias which proposes that hu-

mans have an inborn predisposition—established through evolution—to fear certain objects and situations more than others.

Biological psychologists Psychologists, also called physiological psychologists, who examine how genetic factors, the brain, the nervous system, and other biological factors influence behavior.

Biology Scientific discipline that examines the structure and function of living things.

Bipolar cells In the eye, cells that receive the electrical message converted from light by the rods and cones; the bipolar cells then pass this electrical message on to the ganglion cells.

Bipolar disorder Mood disorder in which there are some depressive episodes and some manic episodes.

Blind spot In the eye, the location where the optic nerve leaves the retina. Neither rods nor cones inhabit the blind spot, so a person cannot see anything that reaches this part of the retina.

Blood-brain barrier Mechanism that keeps many chemicals from entering the brain. Alcohol, however, can cross the blood-brain barrier, causing damage to the brain.

Borderline personality disorder Type of personality disorder characterized by unstable interpersonal relationships, unstable self-image, unstable mood, and impulsiveness.

Bottom-up processing In perception, processing that depends on the information from the senses at the bottom (or most basic) level of perception, with sensory information flowing from this low level upward to the higher, more cognitive levels.

Brief psychodynamic therapy Psychodynamic therapy with the following general attributes: (1) therapy is likely to consist of 20 to 40 weekly sessions; (2) the therapist and client select a specific, central issue that requires resolution; and (3) the individual's current social problems are emphasized.

Brightness The quality of a visual stimulus, which is determined by the height or amplitude of a light wave; psychological reaction corresponding to the intensity of light waves.

Bulimia nervosa (boo-*lih*-mee-ah) Eating disorder characterized by binge eating, or episodes in which people consume huge amounts of food. Bulimics also engage in some form of purging, such as vomiting or using laxatives.

Bystander effect Apparent apathy and inaction in the face of crisis, where the presence of other people inhibits helpfulness.

Cannon-Bard theory Early theory of emotion in which the thalamus is an important mediator in emotional experience; this theory was proposed in place of the James-Lange theory, which emphasized the importance of physiological change.

Cardinal trait In Allport's theory, personality trait that dominates and shapes behavior.

Case study Research method that is an in-depth description and analysis of a single person. The data typically include an interview, observation, and test scores; most often, the individual selected for a case study is highly unusual.

Catatonic schizophrenic Person whose most prominent schizophrenic symptom is unusual body movements such as facial grimaces, repetition of purposeless gestures, difficulty in coordinating motor movements or maintaining an appropriate posture, or standing rigidly for prolonged periods.

Cell body In the nervous system, the area of the neuron that contains the cell nucleus, as well as other structures that help the cell function properly.

Central executive In Alan Baddeley's model of working memory, the component that integrates information from the phonological loop and the visuospatial sketch pad, as well as material retrieved from long-term memory. The central executive also plays a major role in planning and controlling behavior.

Central nervous system Portion of the nervous system that includes the spinal cord and brain.

Central tendency Statistical measure of the most typical, characteristic score (mean, median, or mode).

Central trait In Allport's theory, a general characteristic, found to some degree in every person, such as honesty, extraversion, or cheerfulness.

Cephalocaudal principle Principle of motor development stating that parts of the body near the head (*cephalo* in Greek) develop before the parts near the feet (*caudal* literally means *tail* in Greek).

Cerebellum A structure located at the lower rear of the brain, playing an important role in learning, in maintaining posture, and in controlling motor movements.

Cerebral cortex Outer surface of the two cerebral hemispheres of the brain; it processes all perceptions and complex thoughts.

Cholecystokinin (CCK) Body chemical, released from the small intestine during eating, which seems to signal the organism to stop eating.

Chromatic adaptation   Visual phenomenon in which prolonged exposure to yellow produces blue and prolonged exposure to green produces red.

Chromosomes   Structures carrying genetic information in virtually every cell of the body. In humans, the genes are located on 23 pairs of chromosomes.

Chunk   Basic unit in short-term memory.

Circadian rhythm   Daily cycle lasting approximately 24 hours, with each cycle including both a sleeping and a waking period.

Classical conditioning   Conditioning in which people learn that certain environmental stimuli can predict certain events.

Client-treatment interaction   Model proposing that some clients respond well to Therapy A, whereas other clients respond well to Therapy B. Perhaps all therapies would be more successful if each client could be matched with an appropriate therapy.

Clinical psychologists   Psychologists who assess and treat people with psychological disorders. On the basis of an interview and psychological tests, clinical psychologists provide a diagnosis of the problem followed by either individual or group psychotherapy.

Cochlea   Bony, fluid-filled coil in the ear that contains the auditory receptors.

Cognition   Mental activities involving the acquisition, storage, retrieval, and use of knowledge.

Cognition-first view   View that language depends upon achievements in cognitive development.

Cognitive approach   Approach that focuses on unobservable mental processes such as perceiving, remembering, thinking, and understanding.

Cognitive approach to stereotypes   Approach stating that most stereotypes are products of normal human thought processes, such as categorization.

Cognitive-behavior therapists   Psychotherapists who combine both cognitive and behaviorist techniques to target inappropriate thoughts as well as inappropriate behaviors.

Cognitive-developmental theory   Theory of gender development stating that children's own thought processes are primarily responsible for the development of gender typing.

Cognitive dissonance   A discrepancy between two inconsistent cognitions produces psychological distress; people will be motivated to reduce this dissonance by changing one of the cognitions.

Cognitive map   Internal representation of the way our spatial environment is arranged.

Cognitive modeling   In educational psychology, the technique in which a teacher performs actions while verbalizing reasons for those actions. The teacher models not only correct procedures, but also how to cope with errors.

Cognitive reappraisals   Problem-focused coping strategies that attempt to reduce stress by internal cognitive adjustments, such as shifting one's level of aspiration.

Cognitive restructuring   Therapeutic approach that emphasizes changing one's inappropriate thought patterns.

Cognitive therapy   Psychotherapy that proposes that people are plagued by psychological disorders because their thinking is inappropriate or maladaptive; recovery requires a restructuring of the client's thoughts. Furthermore, a change in the client's thoughts will produce a change in his or her behavior.

Collective unconscious   According to Jung, the second, deeper layer of the unconscious that stores memory fragments from our ancestral past. All humans share the same collective unconscious.

Color constancy   Phenomenon by which an object's perceived hue tends to stay the same, despite changes in the wavelength of the reflected light.

Color deficiency   Difficulty in discriminating between different colors. Although relatively rare in females, about 5% of males have a color deficiency.

Community psychology approach   Approach to psychotherapy that emphasizes the prevention of psychological disorders, as well as treatment in community mental health centers.

Compliance   Going along with a stated request from someone who does not have the specific authority to make you obey.

Componential intelligence   According to Sternberg, the type of intelligence that corresponds most closely with traditional notions of intelligence. This includes metacognitive skills that help a person plan and devise strategies, and the kinds of skills that are used in solving intellectual problems and in getting the work done.

Compulsions   Repetitive behaviors performed according to certain rules, often linked with obsessive thoughts. People with compulsions usually realize that their compulsive behavior is unreasonable. Common compulsions include hand washing, counting, and checking the location of an object.

Computed tomography (CT scan)   Imaging technique that passes X-ray beams through the head from a variety of angles, plotting a two-dimensional picture that resembles a horizontal "slice" through the brain. Then the patient's head is moved either up or down, and a second picture is plotted. Eventually, an entire series of computer-generated pictures is assembled.

Computer-assisted instruction (CAI)   Instructional technique in which students learn at their own rate, using computers that are programmed to deliver individualized instruction. Information is presented in small chunks, and students master a relatively easy chunk before proceeding to a somewhat more difficult topic. Students answer questions and receive immediate feedback about whether each response is correct.

Computer simulation   Writing a computer program that will perform the task using the same strategies that a human would, such as in research on problem solving.

Concrete operational period   One of Piaget's four periods of human development, during which children acquire important mental operations, that is, methods of manipulating information mentally.

Conditional positive regard   According to Carl Rogers, the situation in which positive regard is given only in certain conditions; moreover, parents and other important people withhold their love and approval if the child fails to conform to their own standards.

Conditioned response   In classical conditioning, the response that is elicited by the conditioned stimulus.

Conditioned stimulus   In classical conditioning, the stimulus that is predictive of the unconditioned stimulus.

Conduction deafness   Type of deafness involving problems in either the outer or the middle ear. These disabilities always involve a problem with the mechanical aspects of the auditory system, so that sound cannot be conducted appropriately from the eardrum to the receptors.

Cones   Photoreceptors used for color vision under well-lit conditions.

Confabulation   Major problem with "hypnotically refreshed" memory, in which hypnotized subjects may simply make up an item in memory to replace one that they cannot retrieve.

Conflict   Interpersonal process that occurs when the actions of one party interfere with the actions of another party.

Conformity Change in beliefs or behaviors in response to group pressure when the group does not directly request this change.

Confounding variable In an experiment, any variable—other than the independent variable—that is not equivalent in all conditions.

Congruence In person-centered therapy, the therapist expresses what he or she genuinely feels, rather than maintaining a formal "I'm the expert" attitude; also known as genuineness.

Conjunction fallacy Mistake in decision making in which people judge the probability of the conjunction (two events occurring together) to be greater than the probability of one single event.

Connectionist approach Pertaining to memory, the model that proposes that the activation of one cue leads to the activation of other, related concepts. Also known as parallel distributed processing approach or the PDP approach. In the activation-synthesis model of the function of dreams, the approach that proposes that the activation of one cue leads to the activation of other, related concepts.

Conscious In psychoanalytic theory, the conscious includes everything you are aware of at a particular moment. Our conscious experiences refer to our sensory awareness of the environment and of ourselves.

Consciousness Awareness of the environment and of ourselves, both external and internal stimuli.

Consensual sexual interactions Participation in sexual relationships by fully informed adults who freely choose to engage in mutual sexual stimulation.

Conservation According to Piaget, the mental operation by which children realize that a given quantity stays the same, no matter how its shape or physical arrangement may change.

Constancy Tendency to perceive objects as having constant characteristics (such as size and shape), despite changes in the information about them that reaches the eyes.

Constituent Group of words that seem to belong together as a unit. Typically, a constituent contains more than one word but less than an entire sentence.

Content validity In testing, a test's ability to cover the complete range of material that it is supposed to cover.

Contextual intelligence According to Sternberg, a type of everyday intelligence—that is, street smarts. Contextual intelligence requires adapting to, selecting, and shaping one's real-world context or environment.

Continuity-stages question Is development a gradual process, with adults simply having a greater *quantity* of some particular skill? Alternatively, do children and adults differ in the *quality* of their psychological processes? Although many skills show continuity throughout development, there is evidence for stages in several areas of development.

Continuous reinforcement schedule In operant conditioning, situations in which the subject is reinforced on every correct trial.

Contralateral arrangement Crossover arrangement of the two hemispheres of the brain in which the right side of the cortex is more strongly connected with the left side of the body and the left side of the cortex is more strongly connected with the right side of the body.

Control condition In an experiment, the group that is left unchanged; in contrast to the experimental condition, they receive no special treatment.

Control of processing Situation in which a person pays attention to some aspect of language that is fairly subtle and typically ignored.

Conventional morality Morality in which decisions are based on internalized standards derived from interactions with others.

Conversion disorders Psychological disorders characterized by a loss in physical functioning of some body part—with no medical explanation for the condition. Conversion disorders are usually triggered by some traumatic event.

Coping Thoughts and behaviors we use to handle stress or anticipated stress.

Cornea In the eye, the clear membrane just in front of the iris, with a curved surface that helps to bend light rays when they enter the eye.

Corpus callosum Bridge between the two hemispheres of the brain; a thick bundle of about 800,000 axons that permits communication between the two hemispheres.

Correlation coefficient In correlational research, a number (symbolized as *r*) that indicates the direction and the strength of a relationship between two variables. The correlation coefficient can range between -1.00 and $+1.00$.

Correlational research Research in which psychologists try to determine whether two variables or measures are related. In correlational research, behavior can be observed in real-life settings, with neither random assignment to groups nor the manipulation of independent variables.

Cortisol Hormone that is related to stress.

Counseling psychologists Psychologists who assess and treat people with less severe psychological problems than those treated by clinical psychologists. Some provide marriage or career counseling; others work in college mental health clinics.

Counter-regulation For dieters, the pattern of eating lustily after a high-calorie preload.

Creativity Ability to produce unusual, high-quality solutions when solving problems.

Crisis hotline Community service that provides a phone number to call for immediate counseling and comfort. Hotline volunteers provide counseling and information about services available in the community. These services are used not only by people who have already been hospitalized for a psychological disorder, but also by others who are experiencing a crisis—such as rape victims, drug abusers, victims of domestic violence, and people considering suicide.

Criterion Willingness to say, "I detect the stimulus," when it is not clear whether the stimulus has been presented.

Criterion-related validity In testing, a test's ability to predict a person's performance on a second measure—that is, an independent criterion.

Critical thinking Thinking that involves deciding what to believe and how to act after carefully evaluating the evidence and the reasoning in a situation.

Cross-sectional method Research method used by developmental psychologists in which researchers test individuals of different ages at the same time.

Crystallized intelligence Mental ability that involves specific acquired skills such as verbal ability. Crystallized intelligence continues to grow throughout adulthood.

Cultural-familial retardation Mental retardation with no clear organic cause. Individuals may be retarded because they received fewer genes for high intelligence from their parents, because they grew up in an economically impoverished situation, or a combination of these two factors.

Dark adaptation Increase in sensitivity that occurs as the eyes remain in the dark.

Debriefing In a research study, telling the participants afterward about the purpose of the study, the nature of the anticipated results, and any deceptions used.

Decay Theory stating that each item in memory decays spontaneously as time passes.

Decision/commitment Component of Sternberg's triangular theory of love, which consists of two aspects, the decision that you love someone and the commitment to maintain that love.

Decision frame In decision making, the situation in which people are influenced by the wording of a question while downplaying the importance of other relevant information.

Decision making Cognitive task that requires making a choice about the likelihood of uncertain events. It can occur in situations when people make predictions about the future, select among two or more alternatives, and make estimates about frequency when only scanty evidence is available.

Deep structure Pertaining to sentence structure, the underlying, more abstract representation of the sentence.

Default assignment In the connectionist approach to memory, the process by which a person fills in missing information about an item, based on information about similar items.

Defense mechanisms Mental activities that prevent dangerous thoughts or wishes from becoming directly effective. These defense mechanisms allow the energy associated with these dangerous ideas to be channeled into other thoughts and behaviors.

Deinstitutionalization Program adopted by the mental health system to discharge people from mental hospitals into the community. In theory, this policy could be useful because it could return people to the supportive environment of family and friends and encourage independence and coping abilities. In practice, the policy has created problems.

Delusion False belief that a person firmly holds, despite any objective evidence.

Demand characteristics In a research study, the clues discovered by the participants about the purpose of the study, including rumors they hear about the study, the description supplied when they signed up to participate, the activities of the researchers, and the laboratory setting itself.

Demographic information Characteristics often used to classify people, such as gender, age, marital status, race, education, income, and so forth.

Dendrites In the nervous system, slender, branched fibers that carry neural impulses in the direction of the cell body in a neuron.

Denial Refusal to recognize the reality of threatening external events.

Dependence Condition in which continued use of a psychoactive drug is necessary to prevent withdrawal symptoms. Dependence involves: (1) avoiding the negative symptoms of withdrawal, and (2) experiencing the positive, reinforcing qualities associated with the drug. Dependence may be psychological, as well as physical.

Dependent variable In an experiment, the variable that concerns the responses the participants make; it is a measure of their behavior.

Depressants Psychoactive drugs that depress central nervous system functioning. These substances reduce pain and tension, and slow down thinking and actions. Depressants include tranquilizers, barbiturates, opiates, and alcohol.

Depth of processing The method used to mentally process stimuli; deep processing makes material more memorable than shallow processing.

Descriptive statistics Statistics that provide some measure of central tendency ("What is the typical score?") and variability ("Are the other scores clustered closely around the typical score, or are they more spread out?").

Detection In detection studies, psychologists provide low-intensity stimuli and record whether people report them. Two major approaches to detection are the classical psychophysics approach and the signal detection theory approach.

Detection threshold In the classical psychophysics approach, the smallest amount of energy required for the observer to report the stimulus on half (50%) of the trials.

Development Changes in physical, cognitive, and social abilities that occur throughout the life span.

Developmental psychologists Psychologists who examine how humans mature and change throughout the life span.

Diagnostic and Statistical Manual of Mental Disorders (DSM) Manual for classifying psychological disorders, containing descriptions of the major categories of disorders, as well as a description of specific criteria that must be met before a diagnosis can be assigned. The fourth edition is scheduled for publication in 1994.

Diagnostic interview Interview conducted by a mental health professional that includes questions about the client's social relationships, psychological functioning, family background, and any previous psychological disorders. The client's responses convey useful information, and the session also provides the interviewer with an impression of the individual's general appearance, mood, and cognitive functioning. The interviewer may also administer a psychological test.

Diathesis-stress model Model stating that neither predisposition (diathesis) nor a stressful life event is sufficient by itself to produce a psychological disorder; instead, a disorder arises from the combination of both factors.

Dichotic listening technique (die-*kot*-ick) Task in which people wear earphones that present two different simultaneous messages, one to each ear. Listeners are instructed to repeat a message presented to one ear while ignoring a different message presented to the other ear.

Diffusion of responsibility Situation in which, when people think they are part of a larger group, no individual feels responsible for helping.

Discrimination In psychophysics, the smallest amount that a stimulus must be changed to be perceived as just noticeably different.

Discrimination In social psychology, discrimination involves action against a person or a group of people.

Discriminative stimulus In operant learning, a stimulus signaling that a response will be reinforced.

Disorders of Excessive Sleepiness (DOES) Disorder in which people sleep too much during the day after a full night's sleep.

Disorders of Initiating and Maintaining Sleep (DIMS) Formal term for insomnia, or difficulty in falling asleep and/or remaining asleep.

Displacement Defense mechanism that involves redirecting emotional feelings (e.g., anger) to a substitute target.

Display rules Culture-specific prescriptions about who can show which emotion—and in what circumstance. For instance, a display rule in our culture says that males should not cry.

Dissociative amnesia Psychological disorder involving the forgetting of past experiences following a stressful event. Dissociative amnesia is characterized by extensive memory loss. The amnesia may be limited to a specific time period surrounding a traumatic episode, or a person may forget his or her entire life history.

Dissociative disorders Psychological disorder involving the splitting off (or dissociating) of a person's identity, memory, or consciousness.

Dissociative fugue (fewg) Psychological disorder with the following features: (1) sudden, unplanned travel away from a familiar location, (2) assuming a new identity, and (3) inability to recall one's earlier identity.

Dissociative identity disorder Psychological disorder that occurs when a person has two or more distinct, well-developed personalities. Typically the personalities are dramatically different from each other, and there is a distinct unawareness of the other personalities. Previously known as multiple personality disorder.

Distinctive features In visual perception, characteristics of letters and other stimuli such as straight versus curved lines.

Divided attention Situation in which people try to distribute their attention among two or more competing tasks.

Door-in-the-face technique Two-step compliance technique in which an influencer achieves compliance by first making a request that is so large it is certain to be denied, and then making a smaller, more reasonable request.

Dopamine In the nervous system, an inhibitory neurotransmitter for muscle fibers.

Dopamine hypothesis Hypothesis that schizophrenia is caused by too much dopamine at critical synapses in the brain.

Down syndrome Genetic abnormality involving an extra chromosome added to the 21st pair of chromosomes. Individuals with Down syndrome are typically retarded and have smaller brain size. When interacting with other people, they are often friendly and cheerful.

Dream analysis Psychoanalytic technique in which the therapist interprets the hidden meaning of the client's dream. Freud argued that the conscious, remembered aspect of a dream (its manifest content) was a distorted version of unconscious sexual or aggressive conflicts (its latent content).

Drive In motivation, the psychological energy from unmet needs that propels the organism to action.

Drug therapies Treatment of psychological disorders with medication.

Dual-encoding model A model of reading that proposes that a word's meaning can be reached through either of two routes. Common words are recognized directly from the printed symbols. Difficult or unfamiliar words are first translated from the ink marks on the page to a sound code, and then the word's meaning is located.

Dynamic self-concept View that the self-concept is active and influential, capable of change.

Dysfunctional Failure of a mental mechanism to perform a natural function.

Dysmenorrhea Pain during menstruation.

Eardrum Thin membrane that vibrates in sequence with the sound waves.

Echoic memory Auditory sensory memory, which is so fragile that it usually fades within 2 seconds.

Eclectic approach Approach to psychotherapy that selects what seems best from a variety of theoretical perspectives.

Ecological validity A principle stating that results obtained in research should be generalizable to real-life settings.

Effortful processing Deliberate attempt to place something in memory.

Ego In psychoanalytic theory, the component of the personality that deals with the outside world. The ego serves as a mediator between the id and reality.

Egocentrism According to Piaget, the phenomenon of a child seeing the world from only one point of view—his or her own.

Ejaculation Release of semen.

Elaboration likelihood model Model arguing that when people are involved in an issue and when they have the ability to analyze a message, they consider it carefully and perform elaboration; that is, they relate the message to other ideas and issues. However, when people are not involved or are not able to analyze a message, they will not be as sensitive to the quality of the message's argument; that is, they are more likely to use decision-making heuristics.

Electrical stimulation Method for mapping brain function in which the researcher places a small electrode in a specific location of the brain and delivers a weak electrical current to identify the functions of the brain tissue in that region.

Electroconvulsive therapy (ECT) During this treatment, a person receives a series of electric shocks that produce convulsions, which often relieve the symptoms of severe depression where other treatments have failed.

Electroencephalography (EEG) Technique in which electrodes are placed on the scalp, and the electrical message from the thousands of neurons beneath the electrodes are then recorded on graph paper. The EEG is helpful in diagnosing brain disease and also provides useful information about brain activity when people are sleeping.

Emblem A gesture that is clearly understood by most members of a culture. Each emblem can be translated into a verbal phrase.

Embryo The developing human during the first 2 months of prenatal development after conception.

Emotion Subjective experience or feeling that is accompanied by changes in physiological reactions and behavior.

Emotion-focused coping Method of coping with stress that is directed at regulating emotional responses to the problem.

Empathic understanding In person-centered therapy, the therapist's accurate feelings about the client's emotions.

Empathy Emotional reaction that involves a subjective grasp of another person's feelings or experiences.

Empathy-arousal hypothesis Hypothesis stating that empathy has the power to motivate altruism.

Empirical evidence Scientific evidence obtained by careful observation or experimentation.

Empowerment Development of a sense of self-worth and control over one's own life.

Encoding Pertaining to memory, the first stage of remembering, in which we transform sensory stimuli into a form that can be placed in memory.

Encoding specificity principle Principle stating that recall is better if the retrieval context is like the encoding context.

Endocrine system Collection of glands that release their chemicals (hormones) into the bloodstream.

Endorphins In the nervous system, chemicals that occur naturally in the brain and that, when released, decrease a person's sensitivity to pain.

Enemy images Tendency for us to see ourselves as good and peace-loving, whereas our enemies are evil, aggressive, and warlike. These enemies, however, see themselves as good and peace-loving, whereas they see us as evil, aggressive, and warlike.

Environmental psychology The applied area of psychology that studies interactions between people and their environment.

Epinephrine Hormone manufactured by the adrenal glands; epinephrine makes the heart pound vigorously due to fright.

Erogenous zones In psychoanalytic theory, parts of the body in which humans feel tension; pleasant stimulation of these zones reduces the tension that the person experiences. The first erogenous zone is the mouth, followed at later ages by the anus, and finally the genitals.

Excitatory potential In the nervous system, the vesicles release a neurotransmitter that excites the postsynaptic neuron, which—as a consequence—is more likely to produce an action potential.

Excitement phase Phase of the sexual response cycle during which both men and women become sexually excited. Breathing, heart rate, and muscle tension increase. Blood rushes into the genital region, causing erection in a man's penis and swelling in a woman's clitoris.

Exhaustion phase Third phase of the general adaptation syndrome (response to stress) that occurs if the stressor persists. When the individual uses up the available resources, he or she is likely to develop physical problems and illnesses.

Expanding retrieval practice A technique for remembering a relatively small number of items. Each time a person practices retrieving the names, he or she increases the delay period between practices.

Experiential intelligence According to Sternberg, the type of intelligence that focuses on how people perform on tasks with which they have either no previous experience or great experience.

Experiment Research design in which researchers systematically manipulate a variable under controlled conditions and observe how the participants respond. If the behavior changes when only the manipulated behavior is changed, then the researchers can conclude that they have discovered a cause-and-effect relationship.

Experimental condition In an experiment, the group that is changed in some way. A particular variable is present in the experimental condition that is absent in the control condition.

Experimental method Research method in which researchers manipulate the independent variable to determine its effects on the dependent variable, that is, the behavior of the participants in the experiment.

Experimental psychologists Psychologists who conduct research on topics such as perception, learning, cognition (which includes memory, thinking, and language), motivation, and emotion.

Experimenter bias Researchers' biases and expectations that can influence the results of a study.

Explicit memory The conscious recollection of a person's previous experiences.

Expressed emotion High expressed emotion means that a family member shows highly critical or overinvolved attitudes toward another family member.

Extinction In classical conditioning, the gradual disappearance of a conditioned response that happens when a conditioned stimulus is repeatedly presented without the unconditioned stimulus.

Extravert Individual who tends to be outgoing and more oriented toward other people and events than does an introvert.

Extrinsic motivation Desire to perform an activity because of external rewards.

Facial feedback hypothesis Theory of emotion stating that changes in facial expression can cause changes in a person's emotional state.

Factor analysis Statistical technique that examines the correlations among many variables in order to identify closely related clusters of abilities that seem to be measuring the same, underlying factor.

Family consultation Supportive family counseling for families of the mentally ill to relieve their own anxieties and help make them more effective in providing for their disabled family member.

Family dynamics approach Explanation for schizophrenia which proposes that the risk of schizophrenia is greater in families with (1) communication problems or (2) high expressed emotion.

Family therapy Psychotherapy that considers the entire family—not just one family member—to be the client. According to the family therapy approach, families show recurring patterns of interactions, and many problems involve disturbed relationships among several family members rather than just a single person.

Fat cells Cells that store fat. Fat cells may shrink in size when an overweight person diets, but the number remains constant. Shriveled fat cells may send hunger messages to the brain, causing dieters to feel that they are continually hungry.

Fear hierarchy In systematic desensitization, a hierarchy with the least anxiety-provoking items at the beginning and the most terrifying items at the end.

Fear of success Worry that success in competitive achievement situations will lead to unpleasant consequences such as unpopularity.

Feature detectors Cells in the visual cortex that respond to very specific features (e.g., a horizontal line) located in a more complex stimulus.

Feminist A woman or man whose beliefs, values, and attitudes reflect a high regard for women as human beings.

Feminist approach to therapy Approach to psychotherapy emphasizing that men and women should be valued equally, that women's inferior status in society often causes psychological problems, and that gender-stereotyped behavior harms both women and men. Feminist therapists argue that the therapist and client should be reasonably equal in power.

Fetal alcohol syndrome Condition of children born to women who drank alcohol heavily during pregnancy. These children have characteristic facial features, including widely spaced eyes and flattened nose, and are likely to be mentally retarded.

Fetal period The developing human from 2 months after conception until the baby is born about 7 months later.

Figure-ground relationship In shape perception, when two areas share a common boundary, the figure is the distinct shape with clearly defined edges. The ground is the part that forms the background in the scene.

Filled pause An interruption in the flow of speech.

First language The bilingual speaker's native language.

Five-factor model In personality research, the five most important clusters of personality traits, including extraversion, agreeableness, conscientiousness, emotional stability, and openness to experience. Also known as the Big Five traits.

Fixation In psychoanalytic theory, becoming rigidly locked in conflict about a particular erogenous zone.

Fixed-interval schedule In operant learning, situations in which reinforcement is given for the first correct response made after the specified period of time has passed.

Fixed-ratio schedule In operant learning, situations in which reinforcement is given after a fixed number of responses have been made.

Flashbulb memory Phenomenon whereby people often have very vivid memories of a situation in which they first learned of a surprising and emotionally arousing event.

Flat affect Little sign of either positive or negative emotion, often characteristic of schizophrenics. In flat affect, the voice is a monotone, and the face has no expression.

Flavor Experience of taste, smell, touch, pressure, and pain associated with substances in the mouth.

Fluid intelligence   Ability to solve new problems. Fluid intelligence reaches a peak in the late teens and then declines slowly but steadily throughout adulthood.

Focused attention   Complicated kind of search that requires processing objects one at a time and focusing attention to identify each object.

Foot-in-the-door technique   Two-step compliance technique in which an influencer achieves compliance with a small request before making a larger request. People who have said "yes" to a small favor are more likely to say "yes" to the larger favor, in contrast to those who were only asked about the larger favor.

Forebrain   The largest part of the brain in humans, consisting of the following structures: cerebral cortex, thalamus, hypothalamus, pituitary gland, and limbic system.

Formal operational period   One of Piaget's four stages of human development, in which teenagers and adults can think scientifically and systematically, solve problems without the help of concrete representation, contemplate complex ideas, and think flexibly about a variety of problems.

Fovea   (*foe*-vee-uh) In the eye, the tiny region of the retina in which vision is the most precise.

Fraternal twins   Twins who came from two separate eggs and are thus no more genetically similar than two siblings.

Free association   As an implicit memory test, people are instructed to supply the first word that comes to mind in response to a stimulus word. Implicit memory is demonstrated if a person supplies a word from a list of items that had been exposed earlier.

Free association   Psychoanalytic technique in which clients relax and express their thoughts and emotions freely and without censorship.

Free-running   Natural tendency for humans to adopt a 25-hour cycle when deprived of zeitgebers.

Frequency   Number of cycles a sound wave completes in one second.

Frequency theory   Theory of auditory processing proposing that the entire basilar membrane vibrates at a frequency that matches the frequency of a tone.

Frontal lobe   Part of the cerebral cortex that includes the motor cortex, which controls voluntary movement for different parts of the body. The frontal lobe also includes the prefrontal cortex, which is responsible for complex cognitive tasks.

Frustration-aggression hypothesis   Hypothesis stating that people are most likely to act aggressively when they are frustrated because their goals have been blocked. External events are important in the motivation for aggressive acts.

Functional fixedness   Barrier to problem solving in which the function assigned to an object tends to remain fixed or stable.

Functionalism   Approach to psychology proposing that psychological processes are adaptive; they allow humans to survive and to adapt successfully to their surroundings.

Fundamental attribution error   Tendency to overestimate the role of internal, personal causes and underestimate the role of external, situational causes in explaining the behavior of other people.

g factor   According to Spearman, a single, general mental ability, underlying all the varying kinds of intelligence.

Ganglion cells   In the eye, cells that collect synaptic messages from the bipolar cells and send this information (in the form of action potentials) out of the eye, in the direction of the brain.

Gardner's theory of multiple intelligences   Theory that proposes seven different components of intelligence: (1) language ability, (2) logical-mathematical thinking, (3) spatial thinking, (4) musical thinking, (5) bodily kinesthetic thinking, (6) interpersonal thinking, and (7) intrapersonal thinking.

Gate-control theory   Theory proposing that people experience pain only if pain messages pass through a gate in the spinal cord on their route to the brain. When the gate is open, people experience pain. However, the brain can send messages to the spinal cord, indicating that the gate should be closed, thereby blocking pain messages from reaching the brain. As a consequence, people feel no pain.

Gay person   One who is attracted to people of the same gender. In general, the terms *gay* and *lesbian* are preferred to *homosexual* because the word *homosexual* focuses too narrowly on the sexuality of a relationship, rather than the broader psychological and emotional attachments that gay people feel for each other.

Gender constancy   Concept that a person's gender stays the same in spite of changes in outward physical appearance.

Gender roles   Set of expectations about appropriate activities for females and males.

Gender-schema theory   Theory proposing that children use gender as an important schema to structure and guide their view of the world.

General adaptation syndrome (GAS)   Model of stress, developed by Hans Selye, consisting of three stages of response to stressful situations: (1) the alarm phase, (2) the resistance phase, and (3) the exhaustion phase.

General Problem Solver (GPS)   Computer program, the basic strategy of which is means-ends analysis.

Generalized anxiety disorders   Disorders characterized by continuous, long-lasting uneasiness and tension. People with this disorder cannot identify a specific cause of their anxiety. They also have physical symptoms such as nausea, dizziness, and muscle tension.

Generic masculine   Use of masculine pronouns and nouns to refer to all human beings—both males and females—instead of males alone.

Genes   Basic units of genetics. In humans, the genes are located on 23 pairs of chromosomes in virtually every cell of the body.

Genital herpes   Viral sexually transmitted disease that causes bumps and sores in the genital area.

Genital stage   Final stage of psychosexual development in which, during puberty, sexual urges reappear and the genitals once again become an erogenous zone. Freud argued that genital pleasure during the genital stage arises from sexual relationships with others.

Geons   In recognition-by-components theory, the simple three-dimensional shapes that are the components of more complex patterns.

Gestalt approach   (geh-*shtahlt*) Approach to perception that emphasizes that humans perceive objects as well-organized, whole structures rather than as separated, isolated parts.

Gestalt therapy   (Geh-*shtalt*) Psychotherapy, the goal of which is for clients to become aware of what they are doing and how they can change themselves, while also learning to accept and value themselves. It emphasizes getting in touch with one's feelings at this very moment. It places more emphasis on feelings than on thoughts, and more emphasis on the present than on the past. In addition, it encourages clients to take responsibility for their own feelings, rather than searching for the historical basis of these reactions.

Gestures Hand movements that accompany speech.

Gifted Based on the definition of school districts with special programs for the gifted, individuals with IQs over 130, roughly the top 2%. In addition, some argue that giftedness includes exceptional creativity, leadership skills, or artistic abilities. Others propose that people are gifted only if they meet all of three criteria: (1) above-average ability, (2) creativity, and (3) focused motivation for completing a project.

Glucose Simple sugar nutrient that provides energy.

Glucostats Neurons that are sensitive to glucose levels.

Gonads Sex glands, including the testes in males and the ovaries in females. The gonads produce a variety of hormones that are crucial in sexual development and reproduction.

Gonorrhea Bacterial sexually transmitted disease that infects the genital membranes.

Graceful degradation In the connectionist approach to memory, the brain's ability to provide partial memory.

Graded structure In the prototype approach to meaning, the assumption that all members of a category are *not* created equal. Instead, a category has a graded structure, in which the most representative or prototypical members have priority and the category's nonprototypical members have lower status.

GRIT (Graduated and Reciprocated Initiatives in Tension Reduction) Conflict resolution technique, especially useful in international peacemaking, that consists of a series of steps in which one party announces a step it will take to reduce tension, the party actually takes the step, and then the party states its expectations for some kind of reciprocation. If the other party reciprocates, the first party then starts another round of these initiatives.

Group Two or more people who influence one another through social interactions.

Group polarization Phenomenon in which group members take a more extreme position on a particular issue after discussing it than they would have taken without discussion.

Group therapy Psychotherapy conducted with an interacting group of 7 or 8 people who have something in common. The therapist usually does not actively direct the conversation, but lets it unfold naturally. The group is encouraged to use its own resources and to develop a sense of belonging and common goals.

Groupthink Situation in which the harmony of a group becomes more important than wise decision making. The group members work hard to maintain a positive view of the group's functioning, and they stop thinking critically.

Habituation Situation whereby a stimulus is presented many times until the individual stops responding to it.

Hair cells In the ear, the receptors for hearing, which are embedded in a part of the cochlea called the basilar membrane.

Halfway house Intermediate care facility in which people who have recently been discharged from a hospital live together with trained staff in a home and learn the skills necessary to live independently.

Hallucinations Strong mental images that seem as if they truly occurred in the absence of physical stimuli. The most common hallucinations are auditory, such as voices coming from outside one's head, but they may also include visions, smells, tastes, and skin-sense hallucinations.

Hallucinogens Chemical substances that alter people's perceptions of reality and may cause vivid hallucinations. Hallucinogens include several synthetic drugs, such as LSD and PCP, as well as substances extracted from plants, such as marijuana.

Health psychology Scientific study of behaviors related to health improvement, disease prevention, and recovery from disease.

Heritability In the nature-nurture question, the extent to which the variation in some characteristic can be traced to differences in heredity as opposed to differences in environment. The heritability index can vary between zero (little of the variation can be traced to heredity) and 1.0 (almost all of the variation can be traced to heredity).

Heuristics Rules-of-thumb that are generally accurate.

Hidden-observer phenomenon Hypnotic phenomenon in which a hypnotized person seems to have two separate selves. One part is apparently hypnotized and the other part is more rational.

Hierarchy System in which items are arranged in a series of classes, from the most general to the most specific.

Hindbrain Structure located in the bottom portion of the brain and consisting of the medulla, pons, cerebellum, and reticular formation.

Histogram Graph in which the data are arranged so that they show the frequency of each score.

Homeostasis The maintenance of a constant, ideal internal environment; state of internal balance or stability. The hypothalamus regulates homeostasis for body temperature, liquid intake, and food intake.

Homophobia Irrational, persistent fear and contempt for gay people.

Hormones Chemicals released by the endocrine system. Hormones circulate through all parts of the bloodstream, yet they influence only specific target organs.

Hospice care The goal of hospice care is to allow people with terminal illnesses to die with dignity. In hospices, death is viewed as normal, the family is involved in caring for the dying person, and medical care focuses on relieving pain rather than keeping a person alive at all costs. Hospice programs can be based in the hospital or in people's homes.

Hue Color of a visual stimulus, determined in part by the wavelength of light.

Human immunodeficiency virus (HIV) Virus with the potential to destroy part of the immune system through invasion of white blood cells called T-helper lymphocytes.

Humanistic approach Approach stressing that humans have enormous potential for personal growth. They have the ability to care deeply for other people and to establish meaningful, productive lives for themselves.

Humanistic therapy Psychotherapy designed to remove the blocks to personal growth and to help people appreciate their true selves. Examples include Carl Rogers's person-centered therapy and Gestalt therapy.

Hypnosis Social interaction in which one person (the subject) responds to suggestions offered by another person (the hypnotist); these responses may focus on perception, memory, and action.

Hypochondriasis (high-poe-konn-*dry*-ussis) Psychological disorder involving persistent, excessive anxiety about having a serious disease—one that could even be deadly. Hypochondriasis typically involves numerous physical complaints.

Hypothalamus That part of the brain lying just below the thalamus and controlling the autonomic nervous system. Several distinct clusters of neurons regulate different kinds of motivated behavior such as eating, drinking, sexual behavior, aggression, and activity level.

Hypothesis Tentative set of beliefs about the

nature of the world, a statement about what is expected to happen if certain conditions are true. A hypothesis tells what relationship a researcher expects to find between an independent variable and a dependent variable.

Hypothetico-deductive reasoning Process of thinking up possible solutions to a problem and then creating a systematic plan for selecting a correct solution.

Iconic memory (eye-*conn*-ick) Visual sensory memory, which is so fragile that it usually fades before we can recall all of it.

Id In psychoanalytic theory, the component of personality that consists of the basic drives, such as eating and sexual activity, providing the energy (or libido) for all human behavior. The id lacks moral judgment and it is unconscious.

Identical twins Twins who came from a single fertilized egg and are genetically identical.

Illusion An incorrect perception that does not correspond to the actual physical stimulus. Illusions lead us to make errors in the orientation of lines, in the lengths of lines, and in the perception of contours.

Illusory contour A figure in which we see edges even though they are not physically present.

Illustrator Nonverbal action that accompanies speech and quite literally provides an illustration.

Immune system System that protects the body against infection, allergies, bacteria, viruses, cancer, and other dangers.

Implicit memory Memory that involves performing a task, that is, actually doing something.

Impression formation Integration of various pieces of information about a person.

In vivo treatment (in *vee*-voe) In systematic desensitization, a technique in which clients interact with the actual feared object.

Incentive theory Motivation theory that emphasizes how external goals motivate people to respond and to act. An incentive occurs before people actually do something, and it energizes them to do something—if the incentive is attractive—or *not* to do something—if the incentive is unattractive.

Independent variable In an experiment, the variable that the experimenters manipulate.

In-depth interview Research method that requires the interviewer to gather answers

to open-ended questions, often over a period of many hours or days.

Individual fanning out Increased variability during aging; the fact that individual differences increase as people grow older. For example, 60-year-olds are more different from one another than 10-year-olds are.

Industrial/organizational psychologists Psychologists who focus on human behavior in business and industry. Some help organizations hire and train employees, others study the work setting, and others measure consumer attitudes.

Infancy Period that extends from birth through the first 12-18 months of life.

Inferential statistics Statistics used when researchers want to draw conclusions about their data based on evidence. Inferential statistics provide a formal procedure for using data to test for statistical significance.

Ingroup favoritism Tendency, influenced by stereotypes, to evaluate members of our own group more favorably than members of another group.

Inhibited children Children who are fearful of strangers and unfamiliar objects or events.

Inhibitory potential In the nervous system, the vesicles release a neurotransmitter that inhibits the postsynaptic neuron which, as a consequence, is less likely to produce an action potential.

Insanity defense The legal argument that in certain situations an individual should not be held legally responsible for criminal actions if he or she has a psychological disorder.

Insight In psychoanalysis, the client's awareness of the unconscious conflicts causing his or her psychological problems. Insight grows gradually during the course of psychoanalysis as the therapist pieces together evidence from free association, dream analysis, transference, and resistance.

Insomnia Difficulty in falling asleep and/or remaining asleep.

Instinctive drift principle Principle indicating that when an animal is engaged in operant conditioning, its behavior will drift in the direction of instinctive behaviors related to the task it is learning.

Instincts Inborn, internal forces that make organisms behave in predictable ways.

Instrumental conditioning Type of conditioning that involves learning to make a response because it produces a reinforcing effect and learning not to make a response because it produces a punishing effect. Also known as operant conditioning.

Insulin Hormone secreted by the pancreas that plays an important role in converting blood glucose into stored fat.

Intelligence Ability to master the information and skills needed to succeed within a particular culture. Intelligence therefore includes a wide range of cognitive skills, such as perception, learning, memory, problem solving, and reasoning.

Intelligence quotient (IQ) Performance on intelligence tests can be scored and transformed into an intelligence quotient, which is currently computed by assigning a score of 100 to a person whose performance is average for a particular age group. Higher and lower IQ scores are then based on where a person's score falls in comparison to the average.

Interactionism In the social cognitive approach, the need to examine both internal personality characteristics (traits) and external environmental factors (situations) in order to understand personality.

Interference Theory stating that forgetting occurs because other items get in the way of the information a person wants to remember.

Interpersonal psychotherapy Psychodynamic therapy that focuses on improving the quality of a person's current interactions with other people. A person with traumatic interpersonal relationships as a child may hold distorted views about current relationships with friends and relatives.

Intimacy The close, connected feeling of warmth in love relationships. Important aspects of intimacy include valuing the loved one as part of your life, having high regard for this person, and wanting to promote this person's welfare.

Intrinsic motivation Desire to perform an activity for its own sake. People are likely to do something—and to do it well—when they find it inherently enjoyable.

Intrinsic punishment Internalized sense of dissatisfaction for poor performance.

Intrinsic reinforcement Internalized sense of satisfaction at performing well.

Introspection Observation of one's own conscious psychological reactions.

Introvert Individual who tends to be shy and withdrawn, more oriented toward his or her own internal experience than an extravert.

Iris In the eye, just behind the cornea, a ring of muscles that contracts and dilates to change the amount of light that enters the eye. The color of the iris can range from pale blue to dark brown.

Issues proliferation   Tendency for parties in a conflict to increase the number of controversial topics, thus increasing the areas of conflict.

Izard's theory   (Ih-zahrd) Theory of emotion suggesting that two different kinds of emotion pathways are responsible for our feelings. Cognition is not necessary for the first kind of emotional experience, but it is for the second kind.

James-Lange theory   Theory of emotion proposing that physiological changes are the source of emotional feelings.

Jet lag   Disturbances in body rhythm caused by lengthy journeys involving time zone changes.

Jigsaw classroom   Method of encouraging equal status in an interracial classroom in which all children must work together to ensure good grades.

Just-noticeable difference (jnd)   Smallest change needed in physical stimulus in order for the observer to notice the change.

Key-word method   In memory improvement, method using visual imagery to link a key word with another word.

Latency stage   One of the stages of psychosexual development during which children's sexual feelings remain in the repressed state in which they were left at the end of the phallic stage. According to Freud, children are presumably ashamed and disgusted about sexual issues, and so they tend to avoid members of the other gender.

Latent content   Underlying, unconscious aspects of a dream.

Lateral hypothalamus (LH)   The "start eating" center of the brain, located at the side of the hypothalamus.

Lateralization   Brain hemispheric specialization (with the left hemisphere being more competent on language tasks and the right hemisphere being more competent on spatial tasks). Although the two brain hemispheres have somewhat different functions, these differences should not be exaggerated.

Law of closure   In shape perception, the law stating that a figure with a gap will be perceived as a closed, intact figure.

Law of effect   In operant conditioning, responses resulting in rewarding consequences are learned, whereas responses with punishing consequences are weakened and not learned.

Law of good continuation   In shape perception, the law stating that people tend to perceive smooth, continuous lines, rather than discontinuous fragments.

Law of proximity   In shape perception, the law stating that objects near each other tend to be perceived as a unit.

Law of similarity   In shape perception, the law stating that objects similar to each other tend to be seen as a unit.

Learning   Relatively permanent change in behavior or knowledge due to experience.

Lens   In the eye, the structure directly behind the iris and the pupil that changes shape to focus on objects that are nearby or far away. The lens helps bend the light rays so that they gather in focus at the back of the eye, at a point on or near the retina.

Lesion   A wound or disruption of the brain. Lesions can be produced in laboratory animals to confirm some suspicions about the functions of brain structure.

Libido   Energy for all human behavior provided by the id.

Life review   Special kind of reminiscing about the past in which an older person recalls past experiences and tries to work through them to understand them more thoroughly.

Lightness constancy   Phenomenon in which an object's perceived lightness stays the same, in spite of changes in the amount of light falling on it.

Linearization problem   Dilemma involving speech production, in which people may have a general thought they want to express, or a mental image that needs to be conveyed verbally. These ideas need to be translated into a statement that is linear, with one word following after another in a line.

Linguistic determinism   Hypothesis stating that the structure of language influences the structure of thought. Also known as the Whorfian hypothesis.

Lithium   Chemical that is useful in treating bipolar disorder.

Localization   The ability to determine the direction from which a sound is coming.

Long-term memory (LTM)   A relatively permanent kind of memory, which has an enormous capacity. LTM stores memories that are decades old, as well as memories that arrived a few minutes ago.

Long-term potentiation   In memory research, the phenomenon in which brief electrical stimulation to neurons in the brain (of anesthetized animals) produces an increase in synaptic transmission that lasts for weeks afterwards.

Longitudinal method   Research method used by developmental psychologists in which researchers select one group of individuals who are the same age and then retest them periodically as they grow older.

Lose-lose approach   Approach to conflict in which both parties will suffer a net loss. War is an example of the lose-lose approach.

Loudness   Psychological reaction that corresponds to the physical characteristic of amplitude; loudness is measured in decibels (dB).

Lucid dreaming   Type of dreaming in which dreamers know they are dreaming and have the sense that they are conscious. Consciousness seems divided into a dreaming component and a more detached observational component. Lucid dreamers can modify the content of their dreams more readily than other people.

Lymphocytes   White blood cells, part of the immune system, that defend the body against viruses and other harmful agents.

Magnetic resonance imaging (MRI)   Imaging technique used to provide a picture of the living human brain by passing a strong (but harmless) magnetic field through a patient's head. The MRI scanner picks up radiation from hydrogen molecules, providing a picture of a "slice" of the human brain.

Major depression   Mood disorder characterized by frequent episodes of intense hopelessness and lowered self-esteem.

Male climacteric   (klie-mack-terr-ick) Physical change experienced by men during middle age that includes decreased fertility and decreased frequency of orgasm.

Mania   Mood disorder characterized by an abnormally positive, over-excited state, accompanied by high self-esteem.

Manifest content   The conscious, remembered story line of a dream.

Maslow's hierarchy of needs   Theory stating that human motives are arranged in a hierarchy, with the most basic needs (physiological, safety, belongingness and love) at the bottom and the more highly developed needs (esteem and self-actualization) at the top. Each lower need must be satisfied before the next level of need can be addressed.

Masochistic   (mass-uh-kiss-tick) Deriving pleasure from being mistreated.

Matrix   Chart that represents all possible

combinations. In problem solving, a matrix is an excellent way to keep track of items, particularly when the problem is complex.

Mean   In statistics, a measure of central tendency that is the simple average of all scores, obtained by adding all the scores together and dividing by the number of scores.

Meaning-making   Children's active attempts to make sense out of their world and their experiences. They try to construct general principles based on these experiences.

Means-ends analysis   In problem solving, the problem solver divides the problem into a number of subproblems, or smaller problems. Each of these subproblems is solved by assessing the difference between the original situation and the goal, and then reducing that difference.

Median   In statistics, a measure of central tendency that is the score which falls precisely in the middle of a distribution of scores. To calculate a median, arrange the scores in order from lowest to highest and identify the score in the middle, with half the scores above and half the scores below.

Meditation   Techniques for focusing attention and avoiding rambling or worried thoughts. Some meditation techniques focus on body movement; others emphasize that the meditator should be motionless and passive. Other common techniques focus attention on a specific repeated sound or on an external object.

Medulla   That part of the brain found just above the spinal cord and important in several basic functions, such as controlling breathing and heart rate.

Memory   Storing of information over time, involving encoding, storage, and retrieval.

Menarche   (*men*-are-kee) The first menstrual period.

Menopause   Time when menstrual periods have stopped for at least a year.

Mental imagery   Mental representations of things that are not physically present. Unlike a perceptual image, a mental image is not produced by stimulating the sensory receptors.

Mental retardation   Features include (1) intellectual functioning that is significantly below average, (2) difficulty functioning in everyday settings, and (3) onset prior to age 18.

Mental set   Barrier to problem solving in which problem solvers keep using the same solution they have used in previous problems, even though there may be eas-

ier ways of approaching the problem.

Mere exposure effect   Tendency to prefer items (objects, ideas, and people) with which we have had repeated contact.

Meta-analysis   Systematic, statistical method for synthesizing the results from numerous studies on a given topic, yielding a single number that indicates whether a particular factor has an overall effect on behavior.

Metabolism   Energy required to maintain the body; people with slow metabolism gain more weight.

Metacognition   Knowledge and awareness about a person's own thought processes.

Metacomprehension   Thoughts about a person's own reading comprehension.

Metalinguistics   Knowledge about the form and structure of language.

Metamemory   Knowledge and awareness of a person's own memory.

Method of loci   In memory improvement, method that instructs people to associate items to be learned with a series of physical locations.

Midbrain   The part of the brain that continues upward from the pons portion of the hindbrain. All the signals that pass between the spinal cord and the forebrain—as well as visual information—must pass through this structure.

Mindlessness   Barrier to problem solving in which a person uses information too rigidly, without becoming aware of the potentially novel characteristics of the current situation.

Minnesota Multiphasic Personality Inventory (MMPI)   Objective personality test that asks a large number of true-false questions in order to assess personality traits.

Mnemonics   Use of a strategy to help memory.

Mode   In statistics, a measure of central tendency that is the score which occurs most often in a group of scores. The mode can be established by inspecting the data and noting which number appears most frequently.

Modeling   Learning new behaviors by watching and imitating the behavior of others (models). Also known as observational learning and social learning.

Monocular   In depth perception, factors seen with one eye that can provide information about distance.

Mood disorders   Psychological disorders characterized by persistent, extreme disturbances of mood or emotional state. Examples include major depression, bipolar disorder, and mania.

Morpheme   Smallest language unit that has meaning.

Motherese   Language spoken to children by adults; it has simple vocabulary, emphasis on important words, well-formed short sentences, long pauses, slow rate of speech, and high voice pitch.

Motivated forgetting   Phenomenon by which people forget unpleasant memories.

Motivation   Process of activating behavior, sustaining it, and directing it toward a particular goal. Motivation moves us to act and accomplish.

Multilingual   A person who uses three or more languages.

Multiple-jeopardy hypothesis   Hypothesis predicting additional disadvantages for people who are Black and elderly; they experience both prejudice against Blacks and prejudice against elderly people.

Multiple personality disorder   Psychological disorder that occurs when a person has two or more distinct, well-developed personalities. Typically the personalities are dramatically different from each other, and there is a distinct unawareness of the other personalities. Currently known as dissociative identity disorder.

Multiple sclerosis (MS)   Disease that destroys the myelin sheath, causing numbness, weakness, visual disturbances, and motor problems.

Myelin sheath   Insulating material (part fat and part protein) that coats the larger axons in the nervous system.

Narcolepsy   Disorder in which people have uncontrollable bouts of disabling sleep during the day, even though they may sleep 12 hours each night.

Naturalistic observation   Research method involving systematic observing and recording of behavior in a natural setting, typically by trained observers. Researchers often use naturalistic observation as a first step in a research project to identify variables that would be worthwhile studying with one of the other research techniques.

Nature   In the nature-nurture question, nature refers to differences between people determined by the genes they inherited from their biological parents.

Nature-nurture question   Can development be primarily explained by nature or by genetics? Alternatively, is development primarily determined by nurture, that is, by learning and experience? The appropriate answer is that development is determined by both nature and nurture.

Negative correlation   In correlational research, the situation in which people who receive a high score on Variable 1 receive a *low* score on Variable 2; people with a low score on Variable 1 receive a *high* score on Variable 2. A strong negative correlation coefficient will be close to −1.00.

Negative hallucinations   Hypnotic phenomenon in which subjects can be encouraged *not* to see objects that are present.

Negative reinforcement   In operant conditioning, something negative that is taken away or avoided after the correct response has been made.

Negativity bias   Effect predicting that impression formation is more strongly influenced by a person's negative traits than by his or her positive traits.

NEO Personality Inventory   Personality test developed by Costa and McCrae that measures neuroticism, extraversion, and openness to experience, as well as agreeableness and conscientiousness.

Neodissociation theory   Theory of hypnosis, proposed by Ernest Hilgard, stressing that hypnosis produces a dissociation or division in consciousness, so that behaviors, thoughts, and feelings operate independently, as if there are two separate channels.

Neologism   Invented word; a feature commonly found in schizophrenic speech.

Neonatal period   First 4 weeks after birth.

Nerve deafness   Type of deafness involving problems in the inner ear, specifically in the cochlea or auditory nerve.

Nerves   Bundles of axons from neurons in the peripheral nervous system. Nerves carry communication between the peripheral nervous system and the central nervous system.

Network model   Theory of meaning proposing that concepts are organized in memory in a netlike pattern, with many interconnections. The meaning of a particular concept, such as *apple,* depends on the concepts to which it is connected.

Neurocognitive model   Model of the function of dreams, developed by J. Allan Hobson and John Antrobus and based on neurophysiology and cognitive psychology. A core concept is the activation-synthesis hypothesis, which proposes that the hindbrain sends a haphazard pattern of signals to the cerebral cortex (activation), and then the cerebral cortex tries to make sense out of all these random signals (synthesis).

Neuromodulators   In the nervous system, chemical substances acting at the synapse to modify the effects of neurotransmitters, either increasing or decreasing neuronal activity. Neuromodulators are also likely to spread beyond the synapse and influence more distant neurons.

Neuron   In the nervous system, a specialized cell that processes, stores, and transmits information throughout the body.

Neuroscience approach   Approach to psychology, also called biological approach, that proposes that each behavior, emotion, and thought is caused by a physical event in the brain or other part of the nervous system.

Neurotransmitters   In the nervous system, chemical substances stored in the ends of axons, which allow electrical messages to be transmitted to nearby neurons.

Nictitating-membrane reflex   In rabbits, the response of an unusual inner eyelid that slides over a rabbit's eye to protect it when a puff of air is presented.

Nightmare   Dream that occurs during REM sleep, in which a series of events produces anxiety.

90°-angle heuristic   Rule-of-thumb in which people tend to represent and remember angles in a mental map as being closer to 90° than they really are.

Nonshared environmental experiences   Differences between siblings due to the fact that parents treat each child differently, siblings create different environments for each other, and each child has different experiences outside the family.

Nonverbal communication   All human communications that do not involve words, including tone of voice, hand movements, posture, rate of speaking, and facial expression.

Norms   In testing, established standards of performance on the test. An individual's score on the test becomes meaningful by comparing the score with those standards.

Nurture   In the nature-nurture question, nurture refers to differences between people determined by the way they were reared; that is, by their environment.

Obedience   Social pressure in which an authority specifically commands us to change our behavior.

Obesity   Condition in which a person is 20% or more above the desirable weight.

Object permanence   The knowledge that an object exists even if it is temporarily out of sight.

Object-relations approach   Psychodynamic approach that focuses on the nature and development of ideas about the self in relation to other people. This approach minimizes Freud's notions of drives and emphasizes the developing relationship between the self and objects—that is, significant persons.

Observational learning   Learning of new behaviors by watching and imitating the behavior of others. Also known as modeling and social learning.

Obsessions   Persistent, unwanted thoughts that are unreasonable. Typical obsessions include inappropriate worry over germs or illness and excessive concerns about other people.

Obsessive-compulsive disorder   Disabling conditions that involve recurrent, time-consuming obsessions and/or compulsions.

Obsessive-compulsive personality disorder   Type of personality disorder characterized by a personality that overemphasizes details, conscientiousness, and perfectionism.

Occipital lobe   (ox-*sip*-ih-tul) That part of the cerebral cortex at the back of the head. An important part of this region of the brain is the visual cortex.

Oedipus complex   (*Ed*-ih-pus) In psychoanalysis, a conflict in which a boy's sexual impulses are directed toward his mother, and he views his father as a rival. The young boy is afraid that his father may punish him for his desires by castrating him. A boy who develops normally will reduce this fear by identifying with his father, internalizing his father's values, and developing a strong superego.

Operant conditioning   Type of conditioning that involves learning to make a response because it produces a reinforcing effect and learning not to make a response because it produces a punishing effect. Also known as instrumental conditioning.

Operational definition   In a research study, a precise definition that specifies exactly what operations will be performed and how the concept is to be measured.

Opiates   Class of depressants that includes drugs such as morphine and heroin. These psychoactive drugs suppress pain at the level of the spinal cord and within the brain, as well as creating a blissful feeling and a decrease in anxiety.

Opponent-process theory   In color perception, a theory describing the mechanisms of ganglion cells and other cells closer to the cortex; specifically, these cells respond by increasing their activity when one color is present and decreasing their activity when another color is present.

Opponent-process theory   In motivation, a theory arguing that one emotional state will trigger an opposite emotional state that lasts long after the original emotion has disappeared.

Optic chiasm   (*kye*-as-em) Location at which the two optic nerves come together.

Optic nerve   In the eye, the collection of ganglion-cell axons that travel out of the eye and onward to higher levels of visual processing.

Oral stage   One of the stages of psychosexual development during which the mouth experiences the most tension. According to Freud, the id tries to reduce this tension by encouraging the child to suck on nipples, thumbs, and pacifiers.

Organic retardation   Mental retardation caused by a genetic disorder (such as Down syndrome) or to physical damage to the brain caused by an infectious disease, Fetal Alcohol Syndrome, or medical complications from a premature delivery.

Orgasmic phase   Phase in the sexual response cycle during which the muscles in the pelvic region and the genitals contract rhythmically, producing a pleasurable feeling of sexual release. In addition, the man ejaculates, expelling a milky fluid rich in sperm.

Outcome research   Controlled experiments on the effectiveness of psychotherapy.

Outgroup homogeneity   Perception influenced by stereotypes that all members of another group are similar, whereas members of one's own group are perceived as diverse and heterogeneous.

Outshining hypothesis   When applied to memory, the hypothesis that context can trigger memory when better memory cues are absent; however, context can be completely outshone when other, better cues are present.

Overextension   Use of a word to refer to other objects in addition to the appropriate word.

Panic disorders   Type of anxiety disorder marked by recurrent panic attacks of overwhelming anxiety that occur suddenly and unexpectedly. Each attack typically lasts only 20 minutes, but at the time, it seems as if the attack will never end. Someone in the midst of a panic attack may feel smothering sensations, severe chest pains, and a fear of dying.

Paralanguage   The use of vocal cues other than the words themselves, such as voice tone, pitch, pauses, and inflection of the voice.

Parallel distributed processing approach (PDP approach)   Pertaining to long-term memory, the model that proposes that the activation of one cue leads to the activation of other, related concepts. Also known as the connectionist approach.

Parallel search   Searching long-term memory by handling all the characteristics at the same time.

Paranoid schizophrenic   Person with one or more persistent, bizarre delusions.

Parasympathetic system   Part of the autonomic nervous system that tends to slow down body functions and conserves energy.

Parietal lobe   (puh-*rye*-ih-tull) Part of the cerebral cortex, upward and forward from the occipital lobe. The parietal lobe registers information about body movement, the location of body parts, and touch. At the front of the parietal lobe is the somatosensory cortex, the part of the brain that handles the skin senses.

Parkinson's disease   Disease traced to a deficit in dopamine production, with symptoms such as tremors of the hands, altered body posture, and difficulty walking, caused by a deterioration in the neurons in the part of the brain that releases dopamine.

Partial reinforcement schedule   In operant conditioning, situations in which the subject is reinforced only part of the time. Also known as intermittent reinforcement.

Partial-report technique   Method for estimating the true capacity of iconic memory that requires participants to report only a specified portion of the display.

Passion   Drives that lead to physical attraction, romance, and sexual relationships. It often creates intense physiological arousal, obsessive thoughts about the loved one, and jealousy when thinking about this person falling in love with another.

Passive touch   Touch perception in which an object is placed on the skin of a passive person.

Perceived common ground   In a conflict situation, the likelihood of finding an alternative that satisfies both parties' wishes.

Perception   Interpretation of basic sensations; perception involves organization and meaning.

Perceptual span   Region seen when the eye pauses after a saccadic movement.

Peripheral nervous system   Everything in the nervous system except the brain and spinal cord. The peripheral nervous system transmits messages from the sensory receptors to the central nervous system, and back out from the central nervous system to the muscles and glands.

Permastore   A relatively permanent, very long-term form of memory.

Permissive parenting   Parenting style in which parents make few demands on their children, allowing them to make their own decisions. Children from permissive families tend to be immature; they have little self-control, and they explore less than children from authoritarian and authoritative families.

Person attribution   Type of attribution indicating that we believe that an internal trait—located within the person—was responsible for the behavior, in contrast to situation attribution.

Person-centered therapy   Psychotherapy developed by Carl Rogers that attempts to focus on the person's own point of view, instead of the therapist's interpretations. Rogers proposed three conditions that are likely to encourage growth in person-centered therapy: congruence, unconditional positive regard, and empathic understanding.

Person perception   Area within social cognition that examines both impression formation (integrating various pieces of information about a person) and attribution (the explanations we create about the reasons for our own behavior and the behavior of others).

Person schema   Generalized idea about a person that consists of selected bits of information about the person, organized into a coherent picture.

Person-situation debate   Controversy with the following positions: The *person* position states that each person possesses stable, internal traits that cause him or her to act consistently in a variety of situations. The *situation* position states that each person does not possess stable, internal traits; instead, his or her behavior depends upon the specific characteristics of each situation.

Personal constructs   In the social cognitive approach, characteristic ways of interpreting how some things are alike and some differ from each other.

Personal unconscious   According to Jung, the first layer of the unconscious that stores material which has been forgotten or repressed.

Personality   Pattern of characteristic feelings, thoughts, and behaviors that persists across time and situations; personality is "the underlying causes within the person of individual behavior and experience."

Personality disorders Psychological disorders in which personality traits become inflexible and maladaptive. People with personality disorders typically share these problems: (1) a disability at work and in social relationships, (2) frequent interpersonal conflicts, (3) an ability to cause distress to other people, and (4) an inflexible response to stress.

Personality psychologists Psychologists who investigate how people are influenced by relatively stable inner factors.

Phallic stage One of the stages of psychosexual development during which the erogenous zone shifts to the sex organs, and the child presumably finds pleasure in masturbation, or self-stimulation of the genitals. Freud proposed that boys in the phallic stage experience an Oedipus complex and girls an Electra complex.

Phantom limb pain Phenomenon reported by about 70% of people who have had an arm or a leg amputated; they continue to report pain in the missing limb, even though pain receptors cannot be stimulated.

Phobic disorder Type of anxiety disorder involving excessive fear of a specific object, activity, or situation. This fear is out of proportion to the true danger, and it cannot be eliminated by rational thought.

Phoneme Basic unit of speech, such as the sounds *th, a,* and *t* in the word *that.*

Phoneme restoration Situation in which people think that they hear a phoneme, even though the correct sound vibrations never reach their ears.

Phonological loop In Alan Baddeley's model of working memory, the component that stores a limited number of sounds. Memories in the phonological loop decay within 2 seconds unless the material is rehearsed.

Physiological measures In a research study, measurements that are objective recordings of physiological states such as heart rate, breathing rate, perspiration, and brain activity.

Pitch Psychological reaction that corresponds to the frequency of a tone.

Pituitary gland Hormone-producing gland attached by a stalk to the bottom part of the hypothalamus and regulated by the hypothalamus. The pituitary gland manufactures its own hormones (such as growth hormone) and also regulates the other hormonal glands in the body.

Place theory Theory of auditory processing proposing that each frequency of vibration causes a particular place on the basilar membrane to vibrate.

Placebo (pluh-*see*-bow) Inactive substance given to a control group instead of a medication. In drug therapy, clients may show some spontaneous remission in this condition and may also show improvement because they interact with a supportive, encouraging psychiatrist.

Plasticity When one region of the brain is damaged, another region may eventually take over some of the functions originally performed by the damaged portion. Furthermore, a person who has experienced brain damage can sometimes learn to make better use of skills that were impaired but not completely destroyed.

Plateau phase Phase of sexual response cycle during which breathing, heart rate, and muscle tension increase further. In the man, the penis reaches a full erection, and fluid may appear at the tip. In the woman, the lower one third of the vaginal wall becomes engorged with blood, and the clitoris becomes extremely sensitive.

Polygraph examination Lie detector test that simultaneously measures several autonomic changes such as blood pressure, pulse, breathing patterns, and skin conductance. These measures are taken while a person is asked a structured series of questions. The examiner notes the pattern of arousal and decides on the basis of these data whether the person being tested is innocent or guilty.

Pons Bulging structure in the brain, located above the medulla. Functions as a bridge, connecting the lower brain regions with the higher brain regions. The pons is important in muscle control, such as facial expression and skillful use of fingers.

Positive correlation In correlational research, the situation in which people who receive a high score on Variable 1 are likely to receive a high score on Variable 2; people who receive a low score on Variable 1 are likely to receive a low score on Variable 2. A strong positive correlation coefficient will be close to +1.00.

Positive hallucinations Hypnotic phenomenon in which subjects can be encouraged to perceive objects that are not present.

Positive reinforcement In operant conditioning, something positive that is added to the situation after the correct response has been made.

Positron emission tomography (PET scan) Imaging technique that provides a picture of the living brain by tracing the chemical activity of various parts of the living brain.

A radioactive chemical is injected into blood vessels that carry the chemical to the brain, and the active cells in the brain temporarily accumulate the chemical. A machine then passes X-ray beams through the head.

Possible self That part of the self-concept that represents what a person could become, what he or she would like to become, and what he or she is afraid of becoming.

Postconventional morality Morality in which decisions are based on one's own abstract principles about right and wrong.

Posthypnotic amnesia During hypnosis, instructions given to the subject by the hypnotist that the subject will not recall anything about the hypnosis session after leaving the hypnotic state.

Posthypnotic suggestion During hypnosis, instructions given to the subject by the hypnotist that are to be carried out after the subject returns to the conscious waking state.

Posttraumatic stress disorder (PTSD) Pattern of disordered reactions following a traumatic event. These reactions may include anxiety, irritability, inability to concentrate, and emotional numbness, as well as flashbacks to the traumatic events.

Practical significance In a research study, results having some important, practical implications for the real world.

Pragmatics Social aspects of language involving how people use language to communicate and to accomplish their social goals. Pragmatics includes listeners' background knowledge, conversational interactions, and politeness.

Preattentive processing In attention, the automatic registration of the features in a display of objects.

Preconscious In psychoanalytic theory, the preconscious holds material just slightly below the surface of awareness; this material can be easily retrieved.

Preconventional morality Morality in which decisions are based on rules made by other people.

Prefrontal cortex Part of the cerebral cortex responsible for complex cognitive tasks, such as making plans, forming concepts, and inhibiting inappropriate actions.

Prejudice Negative attitude toward a group of people.

Premenstrual syndrome (PMS) Variety of symptoms that may occur during the week preceding menstruation, including headache, painful breasts, and a variety of psychological reactions such as depression, anxiety, and irritability.

Prenatal period   Prebirth development.

Preoperational period   One of Piaget's four major periods of human development, during which language develops. The child can now represent thought by using symbols and words, rather than simple physical actions.

Primacy effect   Tendency for early information to be considered more important than later information.

Primary reinforcer   Reinforcer that can satisfy a basic biological need, most likely food or water.

Proactive interference   Phenomenon by which old memories work in a forward direction to interfere with new memories.

Problem-finding stage   Stage of cognitive development in which people can think creatively, solve complex problems that are not clear-cut, and ask intriguing new questions.

Problem-focused coping   Method of coping with stress that includes taking direct action to solve problems as well as changing one's thoughts.

Problem solving   Mental activity used when persons want to achieve a certain goal and this goal is not readily available.

Projection   Defense mechanism that involves attributing your own unacceptable feelings to another person.

Projective tests   Psychological tests that ask people to respond to a standard set of stimuli that are vague and ambiguous. These stimuli presumably evoke a person's feelings, needs, and personality characteristics. The two most common projective tests are the Rorschach Inkblot Test and the Thematic Apperception Test (TAT).

Propositional viewpoint   View of mental images that people store information in terms of abstract descriptions. These descriptions can then be used to generate a mental image.

Prosocial behavior   Action that benefits another person, including comforting, helping, sharing, rescuing, and cooperating. Also known as altruism.

Prototype   Pertaining to concepts, the best example of a concept. People establish meaning by placing items in categories.

Prototype approach   Pertaining to meaning, theory proposing that people decide whether an item belongs to a category by comparing that item with a prototype.

Proximodistal principle   Principle of motor development stating that the parts near the center of the infant's body develop before the more distant parts.

Psychiatrists   Professionals who receive training in medicine, rather than psychology, with an orientation toward treating certain disorders with medication.

Psychoactive drugs   Chemical substances that influence the brain, altering consciousness and producing psychological changes. Psychoactive drugs usually work via the neurotransmitters.

Psychoanalysis   Therapy technique based on the psychoanalytic theory of Sigmund Freud; it attempts to resolve problems by examining childhood experiences and making people aware of the conflicts buried in their unconscious.

Psychoanalytic approach   Psychodynamic approach that refers specifically to Sigmund Freud's original theory.

Psychodynamic approach   Approach that emphasizes childhood experience as determinant of adult personality, unconscious mental processes as influence on everyday behavior, and conflict as an underlying cause of most human behavior.

Psychodynamic therapy   Variety of approaches descended from Freudian theories; they focus on childhood problems and unconscious conflict but emphasize social interactions more than Freud did.

Psychological disorders   Disorders involving behavior that is (1) distressing, (2) dysfunctional, and (3) different from the social norms.

Psychological test   Objective, standardized measure of a sample of behavior.

Psychology   Scientific study of behavior and mental processes.

Psychophysics   Area of psychology that examines the relationship between physical stimuli (such as sights or sounds) and our psychological reactions to those stimuli.

Psychotherapy   Treatment of psychological disorders through a special collaborative relationship in which one person tries to help another in coping with a personal problem.

Puberty   Period of development in which a young person becomes physically capable of sexual reproduction.

Punishment   In operant conditioning, something negative that is added or something positive that is taken away following an inappropriate response. Punishment tends to decrease the probability of the response that it follows; however, it does not automatically increase the frequency of the appropriate behavior.

Pupil   In the eye, the opening in the center of the iris.

Pursuit movement   Eye movement used for tracking a moving object.

Quasi-experiment   Research study resembling an experiment but lacking random assignment of participants to groups. Instead, researchers locate a situation in which groups already exist that differ substantially from each other.

Racism   Bias against certain racial or ethnic groups; this bias can be revealed in stereotypes, prejudice, or discrimination.

Random assignment   In an experiment, the process by which people are assigned to experimental groups using a system—such as a coin toss—ensuring that everybody has an equal chance of being assigned to any one group. If the number of participants is sufficiently large, then random assignment usually guarantees that the various groups will be reasonably similar with respect to important characteristics.

Random sample   In a research study, a sample in which every member of the population has an equal chance of being selected. When a sample is random, it is more likely to be a representative sample, in which the characteristics of the sample are similar to the characteristics of the population.

Range   In statistics, a measure of variability that is the difference between the highest and the lowest scores.

Rape   Sexual intercourse that is forcibly committed, without consent.

Rational-Emotive Therapy (RET)   Cognitive therapy, developed by Albert Ellis, that encourages people to examine their beliefs carefully and rationally, to make positive statements about themselves, and to solve problems effectively.

Rationalization   Defense mechanism that involves creating false but believable excuses to justify inappropriate behavior.

Reaction formation   Defense mechanism that involves replacing an anxiety-producing feeling with its exact opposite, typically going overboard.

Reactive devaluation   Barrier to international conflict resolution in which the mere act of offering a particular concession makes that offer less attractive to the recipient.

Reading disability   Poor reading skills that are not accounted for by the level of general intelligence.

Reality principle   In psychoanalytic theory, the delay by infants of their impulses until the situation seems appropriate.

Recall   Measure of explicit memory that asks a person to reproduce items that had been learned earlier.

Receptor cells   In the eye, retinal cells that respond to light; the two kinds are cones and rods.

Reciprocal influences   Principle stating that initial individual differences become even stronger because three factors—personal/cognitive, behavior, and environment—all influence each other.

Recognition   Measure of explicit memory that asks a person to identify which items on a list had been learned earlier.

Recognition-by-components theory   Theory stating that more complex patterns are recognized in terms of their parts, or components. The underlying assumption is that an object can be represented as an arrangement of simple three-dimensional shapes (geons).

Reflection   In person-centered therapy, the technique by which the therapist summarizes the content and emotion of a client's statements, communicating this summary back to the client.

Regression   Defense mechanism that involves acting in ways characteristic of earlier life stages.

Rehearsal   In memory, the repetition of items to be remembered.

Reliability   In testing, the consistency of a person's scores. This consistency is established by reexamining the test takers with the same test on two different occasions, or by some other method of measuring the stability of the scores.

REM sleep   Rapid eye movement sleep, associated with dreaming, during which the EEG shows long sections in which the rapid brain waves resemble the waves in Stage 1 sleep.

Replications   Studies in which a phenomenon is tested several times, often under different conditions.

Representative sample   In a research study, a sample in which the characteristics of the sample are similar to the characteristics of the population.

Representativeness heuristic   Rule-of-thumb used when people decide whether the sample they are judging matches the appropriate prototype. For example, tossing a coin five times and getting five heads would violate the representativeness heuristic.

Repression   Defense mechanism that involves pushing back unpleasant memories and unacceptable thoughts into the unconscious.

Resistance   In psychoanalysis, the process consisting of all the conscious and unconscious forces that work against the treatment process. It is stressful to recall unpleasant memories that had previously been unconscious, and this stress provokes resistance.

Resistance phase   Second phase of the general adaptation syndrome (response to stress) during which the body tries to cope with the stressor by releasing stress hormones. In addition, measures such as blood pressure, heart rate, respiration, and body temperature all increase.

Resolution phase   Final phase of the sexual response cycle during which breathing, heart rate, and muscle tension return to normal. Genitals also gradually return to the size they were prior to excitement.

Restricted range   In testing, the situation in which only a narrow set of all possible scores are considered in calculating the correlation between the test and another condition, such as college grades.

Reticular formation   That part of the brain running up from the hindbrain through to the midbrain with axons reaching upward into the cerebral cortex at the top of the brain. Important in attention and in sleep, as well as simple learning tasks.

Retina   In the eye, the structure that absorbs light rays and converts them into patterns of action potentials that can be transmitted to the brain by the neurons; this process is called transduction.

Retinotopic arrangement   Correspondence between the pattern of information on the retina (the sensory receptors inside the eye) and the pattern of information on part of the visual cortex.

Retrieval   Pertaining to memory, the third stage of remembering in which we successfully locate the item and use it.

Retrieval failure   Theory specifying that memory failures occur when the proper retrieval cues are not available.

Retroactive interference   Phenomenon by which new memories work in a backward direction to interfere with old memories.

Rods   Photoreceptors used for the perception of blacks, grays, and whites. When the lighting is poor, rods function better than cones.

Role   Shared expectation about how someone in a group ought to behave.

Rooting reflex   Reflex pertaining to touch whereby, if a person touches a baby's cheek on one side of the mouth, the baby's head will turn in the direction of the touch.

Rorschach Inkblot Test   Projective test in which people respond to a series of ambiguous inkblots, and the responses are analyzed according to characteristics such as recurring themes, number of responses, the region of the inkblot that attracts attention, and whether the nature of the response is common or unusual.

Rotation heuristic   Rule-of-thumb stating that figures which are slightly tilted will be remembered as being either more vertical or more horizontal than they really are.

Saccadic movement   (suh-*kaad*-dick) Rapid, jumpy movement of the eye from one location to the next, necessary to bring the fovea into position over the object we want to see clearly. Saccadic movements are used in reading.

Sample   Individuals selected because they are representative of the population to be studied, with the intention of discovering something about the population from which the sample was drawn.

Scapegoat theory   Theory stating that people who are frustrated and unhappy about something will choose a relatively powerless group to take the blame for a situation that is not its fault.

Schachter-Singer theory   Theory of emotion stating that an emotion-arousing event causes physiological arousal; people examine the external environment to help interpret that event.

Schema   (*skee*-muh) In observational learning, a generalized idea that captures the important components, but not every exact detail. Pertaining to memory and person perception, a generalized idea about objects, people, and events that are encountered frequently.

Schizoid personality disorder   Type of personality disorder characterized by emotional coolness, a lack of close friends, and a preference for being alone.

Schizophrenia   Psychological disorder that involves severely disordered thoughts, though perceptual, emotional, social, and behavioral processes may also be disturbed. Schizophrenics experience disorganized thought processes. In some cases, this disorganization is so extensive that individuals lose contact with reality.

Scientific method   Basis for psychology research, consisting of four basic steps: (1) identification of the research problem; (2) design and conducting of a study, including gathering appropriate data; (3) examination of the data; (4) communication of the results.

Second language The bilingual speaker's non-native language.

Secondary reinforcer Reinforcer that does not satisfy a basic biological need but acquires its rewarding power by association with another established reinforcer.

Secondary trait In Allport's theory, a characteristic seen only in certain situations, such as "uncomfortable in large crowds" and "likes to drive sports cars."

Secure attachment Positive attachment experience in which an infant tends to use the caretaker as a secure base for exploration. A baby may wander away from the caregiver for a while to explore the surroundings, returning frequently; after separation from a caregiver, the baby actively seeks interaction.

Secure attachment style Adult love-relationship style in which the individual feels comfortable getting close to others and depending on them.

Selective attention Focusing attention on one of several simultaneous messages, ignoring everything else.

Self-actualization In Carl Rogers's person-centered approach, the natural, inborn tendency for humans to fulfill their true potential.

Self-concept Schema of thoughts and feelings about oneself as an individual.

Self-efficacy Feeling that people have that they are competent and effective.

Self-fulfilling prophecy Situation in which your expectations about someone lead him or her to act in ways that confirm your original expectation.

Self-perception theory Theory in social psychology proposing that humans are not driven by some need within themselves to be consistent. Instead, we come to know our attitudes by noticing our own observable behaviors.

Self-reference effect In memory, the deepest, most effective way of processing stimuli, which is in terms of our own experience.

Self-report Research method for assessing psychological processes in which participants report their own thoughts, emotions, behaviors, or intentions. Self-reports are commonly measured with a rating scale.

Self-report tests Psychological tests that instruct people to answer questions about their behaviors, beliefs, and feelings. An example is the Minnesota Multiphasic Personality Inventory (MMPI).

Self-schema A generalized idea about oneself, one that is based on past reactions and experiences.

Self-statement modification Therapeutic technique in which people are encouraged to replace negative statements about themselves with more positive statements.

Sensation Immediate, basic experiences generated by simple stimuli.

Sensitivity In psychophysics, the ability to detect a weak stimulus.

Sensorimotor period One of Piaget's four major periods of human development, in which the infant's major cognitive tasks include sensory activities (such as seeing and hearing) and motor activities (such as kicking, sucking, and reaching).

Sensory memory Storage system that records information from the senses with reasonable accuracy as the information first enters the memory. The capacity of sensory memory is relatively large, but each item fades extremely quickly—in less than 2 seconds.

Serial search Searching long-term memory by handling the characteristics one at a time.

Set point Mechanism that seems to keep people at roughly the same weight throughout their adult lives.

Seville Statement A document, drafted by scientists from 12 countries, stating that it is scientifically incorrect to say that humans have an inborn tendency to be aggressive or that evolution has favored aggressive members of our species.

Sex chromosomes One of 23 pairs of chromosomes that determines whether someone is male or female. Females have a pair of sex chromosomes called X chromosomes (XX); males have one sex chromosome called X and one called Y (XY).

Sexism Bias toward people on the basis of their gender, which can be revealed in stereotypes, prejudice, and discrimination.

Sexual coercion Forcing someone to have sex against her (or his) will. The most extreme example of sexual coercion is rape.

Sexual harassment Unwelcome sexual advance, request for sexual favors, or other verbal or physical conduct of a sexual nature.

Shape constancy Phenomenon in which an object's perceived shape stays the same, despite changes in its orientation toward the viewer.

Shaping In operant conditioning, the systematic reinforcement of gradual improvements toward the desired behavior.

Shift schedules Work schedules in which

people must work during the normal sleeping hours. As a consequence, these workers sleep fewer hours, and they wake up more often during sleep.

Short-term memory (STM) Memory that contains only the small amount of material we are currently using. Memories in STM are reasonably fragile; they can be lost from memory within about 30 seconds unless they are somehow repeated or rehearsed. Also known as working memory.

Sibling deidentification Process during late childhood whereby children often deliberately try *not* to be like their siblings.

Side effects Undesirable medical or psychological problems due to the use of medication.

Signal detection theory In contrast to the classical psychophysics approach, signal detection theory assesses both the observer's sensitivity (or ability to detect a weak stimulus) and the observer's criterion (or willingness to say, "I detect the stimulus," when it is not clear whether the stimulus has been presented). Expectations and prior knowledge influence the probability of the observer's recognition.

Single-cell recording technique Method for obtaining precise recordings of brain activity by inserting a microelectrode next to (or even into) a single neuron.

Situation attribution Type of attribution indicating that we believe that the specific situation—a force located outside the person—was responsible for the behavior. Situation attributions may involve the physical, social, or societal explanations for why an event occurred.

Size constancy Phenomenon in which an object's perceived size stays the same, even though the distance changes between the viewer and the object.

Sleep State during which the body is less active and people are less responsive to the environment; however, the neurons in the brain are active.

Sleep apnea Disorder involving frequent lapses of breathing during sleep. A person with sleep apnea may experience interrupted breathing more than 300 times each night. Each time, the individual wakes up briefly and then begins to breathe normally again.

Slip of the tongue Error in which sounds are rearranged between two or more different words.

Social cognition How we think about other people and ourselves.

Social cognitive approach Approach to personality that emphasizes observational learning and the central importance of cognitive factors.

Social facilitation Tendency to do better on easy tasks and worse on difficult tasks when another person is present.

Social learning Learning new behaviors by watching and imitating the behavior of others in a social situation. Also known as observational learning and modeling.

Social-learning theory With respect to gender development, the theory explaining that girls learn to act "feminine" and boys learn to act "masculine" through two major mechanisms: (1) they receive rewards and punishments for their own behavior; and (2) they watch and imitate the behavior of others.

Social loafing Phenomenon in which each individual works less hard in a group than if he or she worked independently.

Social phobia Type of phobic disorder in which people are excessively afraid of social situations, because they are afraid they will do something embarrassing.

Social psychology Approach to psychology focusing on the way that other people influence our thoughts, feelings, and behaviors.

Social role theory Theory of hypnosis, first proposed by William James and later developed by Theodore Barber, stressing that the hypnotized person simply acts out a social role consistent with the social situation.

Sociocultural approach Approach that proposes that human behavior and mental processes are strongly influenced by social context, which includes factors such as culture, ethnic group, and gender. Pertaining to psychological disorders, an approach emphasizing that social and cultural factors (poverty, prejudice, unemployment, and so forth) are largely responsible for these disorders.

Sociology Scientific discipline that examines how groups and institutions function in society.

Somatic division In the nervous system, sensory neurons that transmit sensory information into the central nervous system, as well as motor neurons that carry motor commands out of the central nervous system to the muscles.

Somatoform disorders Anxiety-based problems in which the individual complains about physical illnesses and symptoms, yet no organic explanation can be detected. The distinctive feature of these disorders is a concern about one's body.

Sound Perception of successive air pressure changes.

Sound waves Tiny disturbances in air pressure that cause sound.

Spacing effect A rule about practice in which persons will recall more material if they distribute their practice throughout several study sessions. In contrast, persons will remember less material if they mass their learning into a single, uninterrupted session.

Spinal cord Column of neurons that runs from the base of the brain, down the center of the back, and is protected by a series of bones; one of the components of the central nervous system.

Split-half reliability Method for measuring the reliability of a test in which everybody takes just one test, but the items are split into two halves (often the even-numbered versus the odd-numbered questions). The split-half reliability is high if each person's score is similar on the two halves.

Spontaneous recovery In classical conditioning, the reappearance of the conditioned response after previous extinction.

Spontaneous remission Recovery from a psychological disorder, without any therapy.

Stability-change question Do people maintain their personal characteristics as they mature from infants into adults (stability)? Alternatively, do these characteristics shift (change)? The stability-change question asks whether the individuals in a group maintain the same relative ranks on a particular characteristic as they grow older. There is some stability as infants mature into children.

Stage 1 sleep Stage of light sleep during which the EEG records small, irregular brain waves. A person can be readily awakened from Stage 1 sleep.

Stage 2 sleep Stage of sleep during which the EEG shows very rapid bursts of activity known as sleep spindles.

Stage 3 sleep Stage of sleep during which the EEG begins to show a few delta waves. Breathing slows substantially, and muscles are completely relaxed.

Stage 4 sleep Stage of deep sleep during which the EEG shows almost exclusively delta waves.

Standard deviation Measure of variability; the extent to which scores differ from each other and deviate from the mean.

Standardization In testing, the process of determining norms on a group of people who have taken a test under uniform conditions.

Statistical significance In inferential statistics, the situation in which the findings are likely to be due to a real difference between two groups, rather than due to chance alone.

Stereotype Structured set of beliefs about the way a group of people thinks and acts. Similar to person schemas, except that a schema applies to an individual person and a stereotype applies to a group.

Sternberg's triarchic theory of intelligence Theory that specifies three important parts of intelligence: (1) componential intelligence, (2) experiential intelligence, and (3) contextual intelligence.

Stimulants Chemicals that increase central nervous system functioning by increasing the release of neurotransmitters such as dopamine in the cortex and the reticular activating system. Stimulants include caffeine, nicotine, the amphetamines, and cocaine.

Stimulus discrimination Process whereby organisms learn to differentiate between similar stimuli.

Stimulus generalization In classical conditioning, the tendency for similar stimuli other than the original conditioned stimulus to produce the conditioned response.

Storage Pertaining to memory, the second stage of remembering, in which we hold the information in memory for later use.

Stress Arousal of mind and body in response to demands placed upon a person.

Stress-induced analgesia Phenomenon in which psychological stress triggers the release of endorphins, making painful stimuli seem less intense.

Stress inoculation training Therapeutic technique that helps people to prepare for difficult or unpleasant situations by anticipating problems and practicing methods of controlling stress (relaxation techniques, problem-solving methods, and developing helpful statements that can guide them through a crisis).

Stressor Unpleasant situation that produces stress.

Stroke Disorder in which a blood clot or some other obstruction reduces blood flow to a region of the brain.

Stroop effect Phenomenon in which people take much longer to say the color of a stimulus when it is used to print an inappropriate color name, rather than appearing as a simple solid color.

Structuralism Approach to psychology that involves the examination of the structure of the mind and the organization of the basic elements of sensations, feelings, and images.

Subjective norms Our beliefs about what other people think we ought to do.

Subjective well-being   Person's evaluation of his or her life.

Sublimation   Defense mechanism that involves redirecting forbidden impulses toward a socially desirable goal.

Subtractive bilingualism   Situation in which an individual acquires proficiency in a second language and the new language replaces the first language.

Superego   In psychoanalytic theory, the component of the personality that includes individual personal conscience, ideals, and values. The superego acquires its principles from society, via the parents.

Surface structure   Pertaining to sentence structure, the structure that is represented by the words which are actually spoken or written.

Survey method   Research method in which researchers select a large group of people and ask them questions about their behaviors or thoughts. Typically, the researchers also collect demographic information about the characteristics often used to classify people, such as gender, age, marital status, race, education, and income.

Symbolic racism   Racial bias reflecting the feeling among some Whites that Blacks are making inappropriate demands for change.

Sympathetic system   Part of the autonomic nervous system that prepares the body for action through the secretion of epinephrine.

Synapse   In the nervous system, the location at which the axon of one neuron connects with the dendrite of a neighboring neuron.

Syntax   In grammar, the organizational rules for determining word order, sentence organization, and relationships among words.

Syphilis   Sexually transmitted disease that produces crater-shaped lesions and can cause blindness and sterility.

Systematic desensitization   Behaviorist approach to reducing fear or anxiety by substituting a response that is incompatible with anxiety (i.e., relaxation).

Tardive dyskinesis   Condition caused by side effects from using antipsychotic drugs, characterized by involuntary body movements and abnormal gait in walking. This disorder is typically irreversible.

Target effects   Improvement of the major symptoms of a disorder through the use of medication.

Taste   Perceptions created when a substance makes contact with the special receptors in the mouth.

Taste aversion   Development of an intense dislike for a food through classical conditioning.

Telegraphic speech   Characteristic of children's early sentences that includes nouns and verbs but leaves out the extra words such as prepositions and articles that only serve grammatical functions.

Temperament   Individual differences in behavior that are present early in life and show stability as the individual matures.

Temporal lobes   Part of the cerebral cortex that is located on the sides of the head. The temporal lobes contain the auditory cortex, which processes information about sounds, speech, and music. Parts of the temporal lobes are also important in processing complex visual stimuli.

Terminal buttons   In the nervous system, the knobs located at the far end of the axon.

Test-retest reliability   Method of measuring the reliability of a test in which the identical test is administered on two occasions, usually 1 day to several weeks apart. The test-retest reliability is high if each person's score is similar on the two tests.

Thalamus   Plays an important role in perception; nearly all the information from the senses is processed by the thalamus on its route from the sensory receptors to the cerebral cortex and is organized and transformed there.

Thematic Apperception Test (TAT)   Projective test that consists of a series of ambiguous scenes, which the test taker is invited to describe, telling what is happening now, what happened in the past, and what will occur in the future.

Theory of misapplied constancy   Theory of illusions proposing that observers interpret certain cues in an illusion as cues for maintaining size constancy.

Thinking   Manipulation of mental representations to reach a conclusion. Includes mental imagery, problem solving, and decision making.

Thought suppression   Intentional, conscious removal of a thought from consciousness.

Thyroid gland   Gland that regulates the body's metabolism through production of a hormone.

Timbre   (*tam*-burr) Sound quality of a tone.

Tip-of-the-nose phenomenon   Ability to recognize that an odor is familiar, combined with the inability to identify its name.

Tip-of-the-tongue experience   People's sensation of being confident that they know the word for which they are searching, yet cannot recall it.

Token economy   Tool in behavior modification in which good behavior is quickly reinforced by a symbol or token; the tokens can then be accumulated and exchanged for a reinforcer.

Tolerance   Condition in which frequent use of a psychoactive drug produces the ability to withstand higher doses than could be tolerated earlier.

Top-down processing   In perception, processing that emphasizes the importance of the observers' concepts, expectations, and prior knowledge—the kinds of information stored at the top (or highest level) of perception.

Total time hypothesis   Principle stating that the amount a person learns depends on the total amount of time he or she practices.

Trait   Consistent tendency to have certain kinds of beliefs, desires, behaviors, and so forth.

Trait approach   Approach to personality proposing that human personality is a combination of specific stable, internal personality characteristics, such as shyness or aggressiveness.

Transduction   In vision, the process by which the retina absorbs light rays and converts them into patterns of action potentials that can be transmitted to the brain by the neurons.

Transference   In psychoanalysis, the process by which the client transfers a variety of positive and negative reactions associated with parents and other childhood authority figures, directing these feelings toward the therapist.

Triangular theory of love   Theory by Robert Sternberg stating that love consists of three components: intimacy, passion, and decision/commitment.

Trichromatic theory   Theory of color vision that point out that the retina contains three kinds of cones, each sensitive to light from a different portion of the spectrum.

Twin studies   Research that compares identical and fraternal twins.

Type A behavior pattern   Personality type with such characteristics as ambitiousness, aggressiveness, competitiveness, and impatience. People with Type A behaviors speak rapidly and work quickly; they are also likely to respond to hassles with irritation and hostility.

Type B behavior pattern   Personality type of people who rarely experience time urgency; they are seldom impatient or hostile.

Unconditional positive regard   According to Carl Rogers, total, genuine love without special conditions or strings attached. In person-centered therapy, therapist's positive, nonjudgmental attitude toward the client.

Unconditioned response   In classical conditioning, an unlearned response to a stimulus.

Unconditioned stimulus   In classical conditioning, the stimulus that elicits an unlearned response.

Unconscious   In psychoanalytic theory, psychic processes—thoughts and desires—that are far below the level of conscious awareness.

Uninhibited children   Children who approach strangers and unfamiliar objects or events without hesitation.

Validity   In testing, a test's accuracy in measuring what it is supposed to measure.

Variability   In statistics, the measures that indicate the extent to which the scores are spread out, that is, how much the scores differ from one another. The standard deviation and range are measures of variability.

Variable-interval schedule   In operant learning, situations in which reinforcement is given for the first response made after a varying period of time has passed.

Variable-ratio schedule   In operant learning, situations in which reinforcement is given after a varying number of responses have been made.

Ventromedial hypothalamus (VMH)   The "stop eating" center of the brain, located toward the center of the hypothalamus.

Vicarious punishment   In observational learning, punishment of the learner that occurs when the model receives punishment.

Vicarious reinforcement   In observational learning, reinforcement of the learner that occurs when the model receives reinforcement.

Visual acuity   Ability to see precise details in a scene.

Visual agnosia   (ag-*know*-zhia) Disorder in which a person has normal basic visual abilities and no evidence of a general disorder such as Alzheimer's disease; however, he or she cannot recognize objects by sight.

Visual cortex   Outer part of the brain that is concerned with vision, located at the back of the brain just above the neck.

Visuospatial sketch pad   In Alan Baddeley's model of working memory, the component that stores visual and spatial information, operating like a pad of paper used to work on a geometry problem.

Wavelength   Distance between two peaks of light, which travels in waves. This distance is measured in nanometers (nm). Wavelength is a characteristic of light that helps to determine the hue or color of a visual stimulus.

Weber's law   (*Vay*-bur) According to Weber's law, a weak or small stimulus does not require much change before a person notices that the stimulus has changed; a strong or large stimulus requires a proportionately greater change before a person notices that it has changed.

Well-controlled study   Experiment in which researchers use precautions such as random assignment to reduce confounding variables. With a well-controlled study, researchers can feel more confident about drawing cause-and-effect conclusions.

Whorfian hypothesis   Hypothesis stating that the structure of language influences the structure of thought. Also known as linguistic determinism.

Win-lose approach   Approach to conflict in which one player's win is balanced by the other player's loss. Most competitive situations in business involve a win-lose situation.

Win-win approach   Approach to conflict in which both parties gain by cooperating. A win-win approach favors successful conflict resolution.

Withdrawal symptoms   Undesirable effects of discontinued use of a psychoactive drug. These symptoms vary, depending upon the psychoactive drug, but may include nausea, vomiting, abdominal cramps, and muscle spasms.

Working alliance   In psychotherapy, the therapist and the client form a working alliance in which the therapist's skills join together with the client's observational insights to facilitate the counseling process.

Working memory   Short-term memory is sometimes called working memory because it handles the material we are currently working with, rather than items not attended to in sensory memory or items stored in long-term memory.

Working self-concept   Self-concept at a particular moment, consisting of all accessible self-knowledge.

Zeitgebers   (*tsite*-gay-burs) Clues that help people adopt a 24-hour cycle, such as clocks and watches, the position of the sun, outdoor temperature, and mealtimes.

Zero correlation   In correlational research, a correlation that indicates no substantial relationship between the two variables.

Aboud, F. (1988). *Children and prejudice.* Oxford, England: Basil Blackwell.

Abraham, W. C., Corballis, M., & White, K. G. (1991). Introduction. In W. C. Abraham, M. Corballis, & K. G. White (Eds.), *Memory mechanisms: A tribute to G. V. Goddard* (pp. xv–xxii). Hillsdale, NJ: Erlbaum.

Abrams, R. (1988). *Electroconvulsive therapy.* New York: Oxford University Press.

Abramson, L. Y., Metalsky, G. I., & Alloy, L. B. (1989). Hopelessness-depression: A theory-based subtype of depression. *Psychological Review, 9,* 358–372.

Acitelli, L. K., & Duck, S. (1987). Postscript: Intimacy as the proverbial elephant. In D. Perlman & S. Duck (Eds.), *Intimate relationships* (pp. 297–308). Beverly Hills, CA: Sage.

Ackerman, D. (1990). *A natural history of the senses.* New York: Random House.

Adams, D. (1989). The Seville Statement on violence and why it is important. *Journal of Humanistic Psychology, 29,* 328–337.

Adams, D. (1990). The Seville Statement on Violence. *American Psychologist, 45,* 1167–1168.

Adams, D. (1993, April). Update. *The Seville Statement on Violence Newsletter,* pp. 1–2.

Adams, P. R., & Adams, G. R. (1984). Mount Saint Helens's ashfall: Evidence for a disaster stress reaction. *American Psychologist, 39,* 252–260.

Ader, R., & Cohen, N. (1993). Psychoneuroimmunology: Conditioning and stress. *Annual Review of Psychology, 44,* 53–85.

Adlaf, E. M., & Smart, R. G. (1991). Drug use among adolescent students in Canada and Ontario: The past, present and future. *The Journal of Drug Issues, 21,* 59–72.

Adler, A. (1924). *The practice and theory of individual psychology.* New York: Harcourt, Brace.

Adler, T. (1989, February). Two new AIDS drugs may improve cognition. *APA Monitor,* p. 8.

Adler, T. (1989, November). Revision brings test 'to the 21st century.' *APA Monitor,* pp. 1, 6.

Adler, T. (1990, April). Does the 'new' MMPI beat the 'classic'? *APA Monitor,* pp. 18–19.

Adler, T. (1991, January). Seeing double? Controversial twins study is widely reported, debated. *The APA Monitor,* pp. 1, 8.

Adler, T. (1991, July). Memory researcher wins Troland Award. *APA Monitor* (7), p. 12.

Adler, T. (1991, November). Therapy may best treat panic disorder. *APA Monitor,* p. 10.

Adler, T. (1993, March). Condom use not routine for at-risk heterosexuals. *APA Monitor,* p. 40.

Aggleton, J. P. (Ed.). (1992). *The amygdala: Neurobiological aspects of emotion, memory, and mental dysfunction.* New York: Wiley.

Agnati, L. F., Bjelke, B., & Fuxe, K. (1992, July–August). Volume transmission in the brain. *American Scientist, 80,* 362–373.

Aiken, L. R. (1987). *Assessment of intellectual functioning.* Boston: Allyn and Bacon.

Aiken, L. R. (1989). *Assessment of personality.* Boston: Allyn & Bacon.

Ainsworth, M. D. S. (1979). Infant-mother attachment. *American Psychologist, 34,* 932–937.

Ainsworth, M. D. S. (1989). Attachments beyond infancy. *American Psychologist, 44,* 709–716.

Ainsworth, M. D. S. (1990). Epilogue. In M. T. Green-berg, D. Cicchetti, & E. M. Cummings (Eds.), *Attachment in the preschool years: Theory, research, and intervention* (pp. 463–487). Chicago: University of Chicago Press.

Aizenberg, R., & Treas. J. (1985). The family in late life: Psychosocial and demographic considerations. In J. E. Birren & K. W. Schaie (Eds.), *Handbook of the psychology of aging* (2nd ed., pp. 169–189). New York: Van Nostrand Reinhold.

Ajzen, I. (1991). The theory of planned behavior. *Organizational Behavior and Human Decision Processes, 50,* 179–211.

Albee, G. W. (1982). Preventing psychopathology and promoting human potential. *American Psychologist, 1982,* 1043–1050.

Albee, G. W. (1987). Powerlessness, politics, and prevention. The community mental health approach. In F. Hurrelmann, F. X. Kaufmann, & F. Lösel (Eds.), *Social intervention: Potential and constraints* (pp. 37–52). Berlin: Walter de Gruyter.

Albee, G. W. (1992). Genes don't hurt people: People hurt people [Review of *Social causes of psychological distress*]. *Contemporary Psychology, 37,* 16–17.

Albee, G. W., & Gullotta, T. P. (1986). Facts and fallacies about primary prevention. *Journal of Primary Prevention, 6,* 207–218.

Aldridge-Morris, R. (1989). *Multiple personality: An exercise in deception.* Hove, England: Erlbaum.

Alicke, M. D. (1991). The broad scope of attribution [Review of *Causal attribution: From cognitive processes to collective beliefs*]. *Contemporary Psychology, 36,* 979–980.

Allen, M. (1983). Models of hemispheric specialization. *Psychological Bulletin, 93,* 73–104.

Allgeier, E. R. (1987). Coercive versus consensual sexual interactions. In V. P. Makosky (Ed.), *The G. Stanley Hall Lecture Series* (Vol. 7, pp. 7–63). Washington, DC: American Psychological Association.

Allison, J., Blatt, S. J., & Zimet, C. N. (1988). *The Interpretation of psychological tests.* Washington, DC: Hemisphere.

Allodi, F. (1990). Refugees as victims of torture and trauma. In W. H. Holtzman & T. H. Bornemann (Eds.), *Mental health of immigrants and refugees* (pp. 245–252). Austin, TX: University of Texas Press.

Alloy, L. B. (Ed.). (1988). *Cognitive processes in depression.* New York: Guilford.

Allport, A. (1989). Visual attention. In M. Posner (Ed.), *Foundations of cognitive science* (pp. 631–682). Cambridge, MA: MIT Press.

Allport, G. W. (1937). *Personality: A psychological interpretation.* New York: Henry Holt.

Allport, G. W. (1961). *Pattern and growth in personality.* New York: Holt, Rinehart and Winston.

Allport, G. W. (1967). Gordon W. Allport. In E. G. Boring & G. Lindzey (Eds.), *A history of psychology in autobiography* (Vol. V). New York: Appleton-Century-Crofts.

Allport, G. W., & Odbert, H. S. (1936). Trait-names: A psycho-lexical study. *Psychological Monographs, 47,* (Whole No. 211).

Almagor, U. (1990). Some thoughts on common scents. *Journal for the Theory of Social Behavior, 20,* 181–195.

Altman, E. G., Janicak, P. G., & Davis, J. M. (1989). Mania: Clinical manifestations and assessment. In J. G. Howells (Ed.), *Modern perspectives in the psychiatry of the affective disorders* (pp. 292–302). New York: Brunner/Mazel.

Alvarez, C. (1987). El hilo que nos une: Becoming a Puerto Rican woman. In R. Benmayor, A. Juarbe, C. Alvarez, & B. Vázquez (Eds.), *Stories to live by: Continuity and change in three generations of Puerto Rican women* (pp. 24–42). New York: Centro de Estudios Puertorriqueños (Hunter College).

Amabile, T. M. (1983). *The social psychology of creativity.* New York: Springer-Verlag.

Amaro, H. (1988). Considerations for prevention of HIV infection among Hispanic women. *Psychology of Women Quarterly, 12,* 429–443.

American Academy of Pediatrics. (1991). Marijuana: A continuing concern for pediatricians. *Pediatrics, 88,* 1070–1072.

American Psychiatric Association. (1987). *Diagnostic and statistical manual of mental disorders* (Third Edition-Revised). Washington, DC: Author.

American Psychiatric Association. (1994). *Diagnostic and statistical manual of mental disorders* (4th ed.). Washington, DC: Author.

American Psychological Association. (1973). *Ethical principles in the conduct of research with human participants.* Washington, DC: Author.

American Psychological Association. (1975). Report of the task force on sex bias and sex-role stereotyping in psychotherapeutic practice. *American Psychologist, 30,* 1169–1175.

American Psychological Association. (1982). *Ethical principles in the conduct of research with human participants.* Washington DC: Author.

American Psychological Association, (1983), *Publication manual of the American Psychological Association* (3rd ed.). Washington, DC: Author.

American Psychological Association. (1990). Ethical principles of psychologists. *American Psychologist, 45,* 390–395.

American Psychological Association. (1992). Ethical principles of psychologists and code of conduct. *American Psychologist, 47,* 1597–1611.

American Psychological Association, American Educational Research Association, & National Council on Measurement in Education. (1985). *Standards for educational testing.* Washington, DC: American Psychological Association.

Amsler, T. (1991, Fall–Winter). The fourth "R": School conflict resolution comes of age. *Peace Reporter,* p. 7.

Anand, P. G., & Ross, S. M. (1987). Using computer-assisted instruction to personalize arithmetic materials for elementary school children. *Journal of Educational Psychology, 79,* 72–78.

Anastasi, A. (1986). Evolving concepts of test validation. *Annual Review of Psychology, 37,* 1–15.

Anastasi, A. (1988). *Psychological testing* (6th ed.). New York: Macmillan.

Anastasi, A., & Drake, J. (1954). An empirical comparison of certain techniques for estimating the reliability of speeded tests. *Education and Psychological Measurement, 14,* 529–540.

Anch, A. M., Browman, C. P., Mitler, M. M., & Walsh,

J. K. (1988). *Sleep: A scientific perspective.* Englewood Cliffs, NJ: Prentice Hall.

Andersen, S. M., Spielman, L. A., & Bargh, J. A. (1992). Future-event schemas and certainty about the future: Automaticity in depressives' future-event predictions. *Journal of Personality and Social Psychology, 63,* 711–723.

Anderson, J. R. (1987). Skill acquisition: Compilation of weak-method problem solutions. *Psychological Review, 94,* 192–210.

Anderson, J. R. (1993). Problem solving and learning. *American Psychologist, 48,* 35–44.

Anderson, J. R., & Reder, L. (1979). An elaborative processing explanation of depth of processing. In L. S. Cermak & F. I. M. Craik (Eds.), *Levels of processing in human memory.* Hillsdale, NJ: Erlbaum.

Anderson, N. H. (1981). *Foundation of information integration theory.* New York: Academic Press.

Anderson, R. (1992). *The aftermath of stroke: The experience of patients and their families.* Cambridge, Great Britain: Cambridge University Press.

Anderson, R. M., & May, R. M. (1992, May). Understanding the AIDS pandemic. *Scientific American,* pp. 58–66.

Andreasen, N. C. (1984). *The broken brain: The biological revolution in psychiatry.* New York: Harper & Row.

Andreasen, N. C. (1989). Nuclear magnetic resonance imaging. In N. C. Andreasen (Ed.), *Brain imaging: Applications in psychiatry* (pp. 67–121). Washington, DC: American Psychiatric Press.

Angoff, W. H. (1988). The nature-nurture debate, aptitudes, and group differences. *American Psychologist, 43,* 713–720.

Angoff, W. H., & Johnson, E. G. (1988). *A study of the differential impact of curriculum on aptitude test scores.* Princeton, NJ: Educational Testing.

Anschutz, L., Camp, C. J., Markley, R. P., & Kramer, J. J. (1985). Maintenance and generalization of mnemonics for grocery shopping by older adults. *Experimental Aging Research, 11,* 157–160.

Antill, J. K. (1983). Sex role complementarity versus similarity in married couples. *Journal of Personality and Social Psychology, 45,* 145–155.

Antony, M. M., Brown, T. A., & Barlow, D. H. (1992). Current perspectives on panic and panic disorder. *Current Directions in Psychological Science, 1,* 79–82.

Antrobus, J. (1987). Cortical hemisphere asymmetry and sleep mentation. *Psychological Review, 94,* 359–368.

Antrobus, J. (1990). The neurocognition of sleep mentation: Rapid eye movements, visual imagery, and dreaming. In R. R. Bootzin, J. F. Kihlstrom, & D. L. Schacter (Eds.), *Sleep and cognition* (pp. 1–24). Washington, DC: American Psychological Association.

Antrobus, J. (1991). Dreaming: Cognitive processes during cortical activation and high afferent thresholds. *Psychological Review, 98,* 96–121.

Appelle, S. (1991). Haptic perception of form: Activity and stimulus attributes. In M. A. Heller & W. Schiff (Eds.), *The psychology of touch* (pp. 169–188). Hillsdale, NJ: Erlbaum.

Aral, S. O., & Holmes, K. K. (1991, February). Sexually transmitted diseases in the AIDS era. *Scientific American, 264,* 62–69.

Argyle, M. (1988). *Bodily communication* (2nd ed.). London: Methuen.

Arlin, P. (1989). Problem solving and problem finding in young artists and scientists. In M. L. Commons, J. D. Sinnott, F. A. Richards, & C. Armon (Eds.), *Adult development* (Vol. 1, pp. 197–216). New York: Praeger.

Arlow, J. A. (1989). Psychoanalysis. In R. J. Corsini & D. Wedding (Eds.), *Current psychotherapies* (4th ed., pp. 19–62). Itasca, IL: Peacock.

Aron, A., & Aron, E. N. (1989). *The heart of social psychology: A backstage view of a passionate science.* Lexington, MA: D. C. Heath.

Aronson, E. (1987). Teaching students what they think they already know about prejudice and desegregation. In V. P. Makosky (Ed.), *The G. Stanley Hall Lecture Series* (Vol 7, pp. 69–84). Washington, DC: American Psychological Association.

Aronson, E. (1988). *The social animal* (5th ed.). New York: Freeman.

Aronson, E. (1991a). Leon Festinger and the art of audacity. *Psychological Science, 2,* 213–217.

Aronson, E. (1991b). How to change behavior. In R. C. Curtis & G. Stricker (Eds.), *How people change: Inside and outside therapy* (pp. 101–112). New York: Plenum.

Aronson, E., & Gonzales, M. H. (1990). Alternative social influence processes applied to energy conservation. In J. Edwards, R. S. Tindale, L. Heath, & E. J. Posavac (Eds.), *Social influence processes and prevention* (pp. 301–325). New York: Plenum.

Aronson, E., Stephan, W., Sikes, J., Blaney, N., & Snapp, M. (1978). *The jigsaw classroom.* Beverly Hills, CA: Sage.

Asarnow, J. R., & Goldstein, M. J. (1986). Schizophrenia during adolescence and early adulthood: A developmental perspective on risk research. *Annual Psychology Review, 6,* 211–235.

Asch, S. E. (1952). *Social psychology.* Englewood Cliffs, NJ: Prentice-Hall.

Asch, S. E. (1955). Opinions and social pressures. *Scientific American, 193*(5), 31–35.

Ashmore, R. D., & DelBoca, F. K. (1979). Sex stereotypes and implicit personality theory: Toward a cognitive-social psychological conceptualization. *Sex Roles, 5,* 219–248.

Aslin, R. N. (1988, April). *Visual perception in human infants: The eyes have it.* Paper presented at the convention of the Eastern Psychological Association, Buffalo, NY.

Aslin, R. N., & Smith, L. B. (1988). Perceptual development. *Annual Review of Psychology, 39,* 435–473.

Asso, D. (1983). *The real menstrual cycle.* Chichester, England: Wiley.

Association for Women in Psychology Ad Hoc Committee on Sexist Language. (1975, November). Help stamp out sexism: Change the language! *APA Monitor,* p. 16.

Atkinson, D. R. (1985). Research on cross-cultural counseling and psychotherapy: A review and update of reviews. In P. Pedersen (Ed.), *Handbook of cross-cultural counseling and therapy* (pp. 191–197). Westport, CT: Greenwood.

Atkinson, D. R. (1987). Counseling Blacks: A review of relevant research. *Journal of College Student Personnel, 28,* 552–558.

Atkinson, J. W., & Raynor, J. O. (Eds.). (1974). *Motivation and achievement.* Washington, DC: Winston.

Atkinson, R. C., & Shiffrin, R. M. (1968). Human memory: A proposed system and its control processes. In K. W. Spence & J. T. Spence (Eds.), *The psychology of learning and motivation: Advances in research and theory* (Vol. 2). New York: Academic Press.

Axelrod, S. (1983). Introduction. In S. Axelrod & J. Apsche (Eds.), *The effects of punishment on human behavior* (pp. 1–11). New York: Plenum.

Axsom, D., Yates, S., & Chaiken, S. (1987). Audience response as a heuristic cue in persuasion. *Journal of Personality and Social Psychology, 53,* 30–40.

Ayllon, T., & Azrin, N. H. (1968). *The token economy: A motivational system for therapy and rehabilitation.* New York: Appleton-Century-Crofts.

Baars, B. J. (1986). *The cognitive revolution in psychology.* New York: Guilford.

Babkoff, H., Caspy, T., Mikulincer, M., & Sing, H. C. (1991). Monotonic and rhythmic influences: A challenge for sleep deprivation research. *Psychological Bulletin, 109,* 411–428.

Backer, T. E., & Richardson, D. (1989). Building bridges: Psychologists and families of the mentally ill. *American Psychologist, 44,* 546–550.

Baddeley, A. D. (1982). *Your memory: A user's guide.* New York: Macmillan.

Baddeley, A. D. (1986). *Working memory.* Oxford: Oxford University Press.

Baddeley, A. D. (1988). Cognitive psychology and human memory. *Trends in Neurosciences, 11,* 176–181.

Baddeley, A. D. (1990). *Human memory: Theory and practice.* Boston: Allyn and Bacon.

Baddeley, A. D. (1992). Working memory. *Science, 255,* 556–559.

Baddeley, A. D., & Hitch, G. J. (1974). Working memory. In G. Bower (Ed.), *Recent advances in learning and memory* (Vol. 8, pp. 47–90). New York: Academic Press.

Badets, J. (1993, Summer). Canada's immigrants: Recent trends. *Canadian Social Trends,* pp. 8–11.

Baer, L., & Jenike, M. A. (1986). Introduction. In M. A. Jenike, L. Baer, & W. E. Minichiello (Eds.), *Obsessive-compulsive disorders* (pp. 1–9). Littleton, MA: PSG Publishing.

Bahrick, H. P. (1984). Semantic memory content in permastore: Fifty years of memory for Spanish learned in school. *Journal of Experimental Psychology: General, 113,* 1–35.

Bahrick, H. P., & Hall, L. K. (1991). Lifetime maintenance of high school mathematics content. *Journal of Experimental Psychology: General, 120,* 20–33.

Baillargeon, R. (1986). Representing the existence and the location of hidden objects: Object permanence in 6- and 8-month-old infants. *Cognition, 23,* 21–41.

Baillargeon, R. (1991). Reasoning about the height and location of a hidden object in 4.5- and 6.5-month-old infants. *Cognition, 38,* 13–42.

Baillargeon, R. (1992). The object concept revisited. In C. E. Cranrud (Ed.), *Visual perception and cognition in infancy, Carnegie-Mellon Symposia on Cognition* (Vol. 23). Hillsdale, NJ: Erlbaum.

Baillargeon, R., & DeVos, J. (1991). Object permanence in young infants: Further evidence. *Child Development, 62,* 1227–1246.

Baillargeon, R., Spelke, E. S., & Wasserman, S. (1985). Object permanence in five-month-olds. *Cognition, 20,* 191–208.

Baker, E. L. (1987). The state of the art of clinical hypnosis. *International Journal of Clinical and Experimental Hypnosis, 35,* 203–214.

Baker, F. M. (1988). Afro-Americans. In L. Comas-Días & E. Griffith (Eds.), *Clinical guidelines in cross-cultural mental health* (pp. 151–181). New

Academic Press.

York: Wiley.

Baker, R. (1989). Synthesis. In R. Baker (Ed.), *Panic disorder: Theory, research and therapy* (pp. 325–344). Chichester, England: Wiley.

Balakrishnan, T. R., Rao, K. V., Lapierre-Adamcyk, E., & Kroti, K. J. (1987). A hazard model analysis of the covariates of marriage dissolution in Canada. *Demography, 24,* 395–406.

Baldessarini, R. J., & Cole, J. O. (1988). Chemotherapy. In A. M. Nicholi, Jr. (Ed.), *The new Harvard guide to psychiatry* (pp. 481–533). Cambridge, MA: Harvard University Press.

Bales, J. (1988, December). Vincennes: Findings could have helped avert tragedy, scientists tell Hill panel. *APA Monitor,* pp. 10–11.

Balota, D. A., Pollatsek, A., & Rayner, K. (1985). The interaction of contextual constraints and parafoveal visual information in reading. *Cognitive Psychology, 17,* 364–390.

Baltes, P. B. (1973). Prototypical paradigms and questions in life-span research on development and aging. *The Gerontologist, 113,* 458–467.

Baltes, P. B., & Kliegl, R. (1989). On the dynamics between growth and decline in the aging of intelligence and memory. In K. Poeck (Ed.), *Proceedings of the XIIIth World Congress of Neurology.* Heidelberg: Springer.

Balthazard, C. G., & Woody, E. Z. (1985). The "stuff" of hypnotic performance: A review of psychometric approaches. *Psychological Bulletin, 98,* 283–296.

Banaji, M. R., & Crowder, R. G. (1989). The bankruptcy of everyday memory. *American Psychologist, 44,* 1185–1193.

Bandura, A. (1963, October 22). What TV violence can do to your child. *Look,* pp. 46–52.

Bandura, A. (1982a). The psychology of chance encounters and life paths. *American Psychologist, 37,* 747–755.

Bandura, A. (1982b). Self-efficacy mechanism in human agency. *American Psychologist, 37,* 122–147.

Bandura, A. (1986). *Social foundations of thought and action: A social cognitive theory.* Englewood Cliffs, NJ: Prentice-Hall.

Bandura, A. (1989). Social cognitive theory. *Annals of Child Development, 6,* 1–60.

Bandura, A. (1991). Social cognitive theory of self-regulation. *Organizational Behavior and Human Decision Processes, 50,* 248–287.

Bandura, A. (1992). Self-efficacy: Thought control of action. In R. Schwarzer (Ed.), *Self-efficacy: Thought control of action* (pp. 3–38). Washington, DC: Hemisphere.

Bandura, A., & Jourden, F. J. (1991). Self-regulatory mechanisms governing the impact of social comparison on complex decision making. *Journal of Personality and Social Psychology, 60,* 941–951.

Bandura, A., Ross, D., & Ross, S. A. (1961). Transmission of aggression through imitation of aggressive models. *Journal of Abnormal and Social Psychology, 63,* 575–582.

Bandura, A., Ross, D., & Ross, S. A. (1963). Imitation of film-mediated aggressive models. *Journal of Abnormal and Social Psychology, 66,* 311–318.

Banks, W. P., & Krajicek, D. (1991). Perception. *Annual Review of Psychology, 42,* 305–331.

Barber, T. X. (1979). Suggested ("hypnotic") behavior: The trance paradigm versus an alternative paradigm. In E. Fromm & R. E. Shor (Eds.), *Hypnosis: Developments in research and new perspectives* (pp. 217–274). Chicago: Aldine.

Barber, T. X. (1986). Realities of stage hypnosis. In B.

Zilbergeld, M. G. Edelstien, & D. L. Araoz (Eds.), *Hypnosis: Questions and answers* (pp. 22–27). New York: Norton.

Barclay, C. R. (1986). Schematization of autobiographical memory. In D. C. Rubin (Ed.), *Autobiographical memory* (pp. 82–99). New York: Cambridge University Press.

Barcus, F. E. (1983). *Images of life on children's television.* New York: Praeger.

Bard, P. A. (1928). A diencephalic mechanism for the expression of rage with special reference to the sympathetic nervous system. *American Journal of Physiology, 84,* 490–515.

Barefoot, J. C., Dahlstrom, W. G., & Williams, R. B., Jr. (1983). Hostility, CHD incidence, and total mortality: A 25-year follow-up study of 255 physicians. *Psychosomatic Medicine, 45,* 59–63.

Barinaga, M. (1991a). How the nose knows: Olfactory receptor cloned. *Science, 252,* 209–210.

Barinaga, M. (1991b). How long is the human lifespan? *Science, 254,* 936–938.

Barlow, D. H. (1988). *Anxiety and its disorders.* New York: Guilford.

Barnett, R. C., Marshall, N. L., & Singer, J. D. (1992). Job experiences over time, multiple roles, and women's mental health: A longitudinal study. *Journal of Personality and Social Psychology, 62,* 634–644.

Baron, J. (1988). *Thinking and deciding.* New York: Cambridge University Press.

Baron, J. (1991). Some thinking is irrational. *Behavioral and Brain Sciences, 14,* 486–487.

Baron, R. S., Kerr, N. L., & Miller, N. (1993). *Group process, group decision, group action.* Pacific Grove, CA: Brooks/Cole.

Barrera, M., & Maurer, D. (1981). Recognition of mother's photographed face by the three-month-old infant. *Child Development, 52,* 714–716.

Barresi, C. M., & Hunt, K. (1990). The unmarried elderly. In T. H. Brubaker (Ed.), *Family relationships in later life* (2nd ed., pp. 169–192). Newbury Park, CA: Sage.

Barrett, G. V., & Depinet, R. L. (1991). A reconsideration of testing for competence rather than for intelligence. *American Psychologist, 46,* 1012–1024.

Barsalou, L. W. (1987). The instability of graded structure: Implications for the nature of concepts. In U. Neisser (Ed.), *Concepts and conceptual development: Ecological and intellectual factors in categorization.* New York: Cambridge University Press.

Barsky, A. J. (1989). Somatoform disorders. In H. I. Kaplan and B. J. Sadock (Eds.), *Comprehensive textbook of psychiatry/V* (5th ed., Vol. 1, pp. 1009–1027). Baltimore, MD: Williams & Wilkins.

Bartoshuk, L. M. (1971). The chemical senses: I. Taste. In J. W. Kling & L. A. Riggs (Eds.), *Woodworth & Schlosberg's experimental psychology* (3rd ed.). New York: Holt, Rinehart and Winston.

Bartoshuk, L. M. (1991a). Taste, smell, and pleasure. In R. C. Bolles (Ed.), *The hedonics of taste* (pp. 15–28). Hillsdale, NJ: Erlbaum.

Bartoshuk, L. M. (1991b). Sensory factors in eating behavior. *Bulletin of the Psychonomic Society, 29,* 250–255.

Basher, S. K. (1991). Personal communication.

Bates, E., Thal, D., & Janowsky, J. S. (1993). Early language development and its neural correlates. In I. Rapin & S. Segalowitz (Eds.), *Handbook of neuropsychology* (Vol. 6). Amsterdam: Elsevier.

Bates, J. E. (1989). Concepts and measures of temperament. In G. A. Kohnstamm, J. E. Bates, & M.

K. Rothbart (Eds.), *Temperament in childhood* (pp. 3–26). Chichester, England: Wiley.

Batson, C. D. (1987). Prosocial motivation: Is it ever truly altruistic? *Advances in Experimental Social Psychology, 20,* 65–122.

Batson, C. D. (1990). How social an animal? The human capacity for caring. *American Psychologist, 45,* 336–346.

Batson, C. D. (1991). *The altruism question: Toward a social-psychological answer.* Hillsdale, NJ: Erlbaum.

Batson, C. D., Batson, J. G., Slingsby, J. K., Harrell, K. L., Peekna, H. M., & Todd, R. M. (1991). Empathic joy and the empathy-altruism hypothesis. *Journal of Personality and Social Psychology, 61,* 413–426.

Batson, C. D., Duncan, B. D., Ackerman, P., Buckley, T., & Birch, K. (1981). Is empathic emotion a source of altruistic motivation? *Journal of Personality and Social Psychology, 40,* 290–302.

Baum, A., & Temoshok, L. (1990). Psychosocial aspects of acquired immunodeficiency syndrome (AIDS). In L. Temoshok & A. Baum (Eds.), *Psychosocial perspectives on AIDS* (pp. 1–16). Hillsdale, NJ: Erlbaum.

Baumeister, R. F. (1991). *Escaping the self.* New York: Basic Books.

Baumrind, D. (1964). Some thoughts on ethics of research: After reading Milgram's "Behavioral study of obedience." *American Psychologist, 19,* 421–423.

Baumrind, D. (1971). Current patterns of parental authority. *Developmental Psychology Monographs, 4* (1, Pt. 2).

Baumrind, D. (1975). Early socialization and adolescent competence. In S. E. Dragestin & G. H. Elder (Eds.), *Adolescence in the life cycle.* New York: Wiley.

Baur, S. (1991). *The dinosaur man: Tales of madness and enchantment from the back ward.* New York: HarperCollins.

Baydar, N., & Brooks-Gunn, J. (1991). Effects of maternal employment and child-care arrangements on preschoolers' cognitive and behavioral outcomes: Evidence from the children of the national longitudinal survey of youth. *Developmental Psychology, 27,* 932–945.

Beach, F. (1989). Personal communication.

Beatty, W. W., Butters, N., & Janowsky, D. S. (1986). Patterns of memory failure after scopolamine treatment: Implications for cholinergic hypotheses of dementia. *Behavioral and Neural Biology, 45,* 196–211.

Bebko, J. M., Burke, L., Craven, J., & Sarlo, N. (1992). The importance of motor activity in sensorimotor development: A perspective from children with physical handicaps. *Human Development, 35,* 226–240.

Beck, A. T. (1976). *Cognitive therapy and the emotional disorders.* New York: International Universities Press.

Beck, A. T. (1982). *Depression: Clinical, experimental, and theoretical aspects.* New York: Harper & Row.

Beck, A. T. (1991). Cognitive therapy: A 30-year retrospective. *American Psychologist, 46,* 368–375.

Beck, A. T., Emery, G., & Greenberg, R. L. (1985). *Anxiety disorders and phobias: A cognitive perspective.* New York: Basic Books.

Beck, A. T., & Freeman, A. (Eds.). (1990). *Cognitive therapy of personality disorders.* New York: Guilford.

Becker, B. J. (1986). Influence again: An examination

of reviews and studies of gender differences in social influence. In J. S. Hyde & M. C. Linn (Eds,), *The psychology of gender: Advances through meta-analysis* (pp. 178–209). Baltimore: Johns Hopkins University Press.

Bédard, J., & Chi, M. T. H. (1992). Expertise. *Current Directions in Psychological Science, 1,* 135–139.

Bee, H. L. (1987). *The journey of adulthood.* New York: Macmillan.

Bee, H. L. (1992). *The Journey of adulthood* (2nd ed.). New York: Macmillan.

Begg, I., & White, P. (1985). Encoding specificity in interpersonal communication. *Canadian Journal of Psychology, 39,* 70–87.

Beilin, H. (1992). Piaget's enduring contribution to developmental psychology. *Developmental Psychology, 28,* 191–204.

Beiser, M. (1990). Mental health of refugees in resettlement countries. In W. H. Holtzman & T. H. Bornemann (Eds.), *Mental health of immigrants and refugees* (pp. 51–65). Austin, TX: University of Texas Press.

Belenky, M. F., Clinchy, B. M., Goldberger, N. R., & Tarule, J. M. (1986). *Women's ways of knowing: The development of self, voice, and mind.* New York: Basic Books.

Bell, A. P., & Weinberg, M. S. (1978). *Homosexualities.* New York: Simon and Schuster.

Bell, J. (1991). *Evaluating psychological information: Sharpening your critical thinking skills.* Boston: Allyn & Bacon.

Bell, P. A., Fisher, J. D., Baum, A., & Greene, T. C. (1990). *Environmental psychology* (3rd ed.). Fort Worth: Holt, Rinehart and Winston.

Bell, R. (1980). *Changing bodies, changing lives.* New York: Random House.

Bellack, A. S., Hersen, M., & Kazdin, A. E. (Eds.). (1990). *International handbook of behavior modification and therapy* (2nd ed.). New York: Plenum Press.

Belsky, J. (1990). *The psychology of aging: Theory, research, and interventions* (2nd ed.). Pacific Grove, CA: Brooks/Cole.

Bem, D. J. (1972). Self-perception theory. *Advances in Experimental Social Psychology, 6,* 1–62.

Bem, D. J., & Allen, A. (1974). On predicting some of the people some of the time: The search for cross-situational consistency in behavior. *Psychological Review, 81,* 506–520.

Bem, S. L. (1981). Gender schema theory: A cognitive account of sex typing. *Psychological Review, 88,* 354–364.

Bem, S. L. (1985). Androgyny and gender schema theory: A conceptual and empirical integration. In T. B. Sonderegger (Ed.), *Nebraska Symposium on Motivation, 1984: Psychology and gender* (pp. 179–226). Lincoln, NE: University of Nebraska Press.

Bem, S. L. (1989). Genital knowledge and gender constancy in preschool children. *Child Development, 60,* 649–662.

Bem, S. L. (1993). *The lenses of gender: Transforming the debate on sexual inequality.* New Haven: Yale University Press.

Benbow, C. P. (1988). Sex differences in mathematical reasoning ability in intellectually talented preadolescents: Their nature, effects, and possible causes. *Behavioral and Brain Sciences, 11,* 169–232.

Bengston, V. L., Reedy, M. N., & Gordon, C. (1985). Aging and self-conceptions: Personality processes and social contexts. In J. E. Birren & K. W. Schaie (Eds.), *Handbook of the psychology of aging* (pp.

544–593). New York: Van Nostrand Reinhold.

Benjamin, L. T., Jr., Durkin, M., Link, M., Vestal, M., & Acord, J. (1992). Wundt's American doctoral students. *American Psychologist, 47,* 123–131.

Benmayor, R. (1987). "For every story there is another story which stands before it." In R. Benmayor, A. Juarbe, C. Alvarez, & B. Vázquez (Eds.), *Stories to live by: Continuity and change in three generations of Puerto Rican women* (pp. 1–13). New York: Centro de Estudios Puertorriqueños (Hunter College).

Bentall, R. P. (1990). The illusion of reality: A review and integration of psychological research on hallucinations. *Psychological Bulletin, 107,* 82–95.

Berck, J. (1992). *No place to be: Voices of homeless children.* Boston: Houghton Mifflin.

Berger, T. W., Rinaldi, P. C., Weisz, D. J., & Thompson, R. F. (1983). Single-unit analysis of different hippocampal cell types during classical conditioning of rabbit nictitating membrane response. *Journal of Neurophysiology, 50,* 1197–1219.

Berger, T. W., & Thompson, R. F. (1982). Hippocampal cellular plasticity during extinction of classically conditioned nictitating membrane behavior. *Behavioral Brain Research, 4,* 63–76.

Berk, L. E. (1991). *Child development* (2nd ed.). Boston: Allyn and Bacon.

Berkowitz, L. (1984). Some effects of thoughts on anti- and prosocial influences of media events: A cognitive-neoassociation analysis. *Psychological Bulletin, 95,* 410–427.

Berkowitz, L. (1989). Frustration-aggression hypothesis: Examination and reformulation. *Psychological Bulletin, 106,* 59–73.

Berkowitz, L. (1990). Biological roots: Are humans inherently violent? In B. Glad (Ed.), *Psychological dimensions of war* (pp. 24–40). Newbury Park, CA: Sage.

Berman, A. L., & Jobes, D. A. (1991). *Adolescent suicide assessment and intervention.* Washington, DC: American Psychological Association.

Berndt, T. J. (1989). Obtaining support from friends during childhood and adolescence. In D. Belle (Ed.), *Children's social networks and social supports* (pp. 308–331). New York: Wiley.

Berndt, T. J. (1992). Friendship and friends' influence in adolescence. *Current Directions in Psychological Science, 1,* 156–159.

Bernheim, K. F. (1989). Psychologists and families of the severely mentally ill: The role of family consultation. *American Psychologist, 44,* 561–564.

Bernheim, K. F. (1990). Personal communication.

Bernheim, K. F., & Lehman, A. F. (1985). *Working with families of the mentally ill.* New York: Norton.

Bernheim, K. F., Lewine, R. R. J., & Beale, C. T. (1982). *The caring family: Living with chronic mental illness.* New York: Random House.

Bernstein, I. L. (1978). Learned taste aversions in children receiving chemotherapy. *Science, 200,* 1302–1303.

Bernstein, I. L., & Meachum, C. L. (1990). Food aversion learning: Its impact on appetite. In E. D. Capaldi & T. L. Powley (Eds.), *Taste, experience, and feeding* (pp. 170–178). Washington, DC: American Psychological Association.

Berry, D. S. (1991). Accuracy in social perception: Contributions of facial and vocal information. *Journal of Personality and Social Psychology, 61,* 298–307.

Berscheid, E. (1992). A glance back at a quarter century of social psychology. *Journal of Personality and Social Psychology, 63,* 525–533.

Berscheid, E., Snyder, M., & Omoto, A. M. (1989). Issues in studying close relationships: Conceptualizing and measuring closeness. In C. Hendrick (Ed.), *Close relationships* (pp. 63–91). Newbury Park, CA: Sage.

Besharov, D. J. (1990). *Recognizing child abuse: A guide for the concerned.* New York: Free Press.

Bettelheim, B. (1977). *The uses of enchantment: The meaning and importance of fairy tales.* New York: Vintage Books.

Betz, N. E. (1992). Career counseling for women in the sciences and engineering. In W. B. Walsh & S. H. Osipow (Eds.), *Career counseling for women.* Hillsdale, NJ: Erlbaum.

Betz, N. E., & Fitzgerald, L. F. (1987). *The career psychology of women.* New York: Academic Press.

Betz, N. E., & Fitzgerald, L. F. (1993). Individuality and diversity: Theory and research in counseling psychology. *Annual Review of Psychology, 44,* 343–381.

Bialystok, E. (1988). Levels of bilingualism and levels of linguistic awareness. *Developmental Psychology, 24,* 560–567.

Bialystok, E. (1991). Metalinguistic dimensions of bilingual language proficiency. In E. Bialystok (Ed.), *Language processing in bilingual children* (pp. 113–140). Cambridge, England: Cambridge University Press.

Bialystok, E. (1992). Selective attention in cognitive processing: The bilingual edge. In R. J. Harris (Ed.), *Cognitive processing in bilinguals* (pp. 501–513). Amsterdam: Elsevier.

Bianchini, J. C. (1976, May). *Achievement tests and differentiated norms.* Paper presented at the U.S. Office of Education Invitational Conference on Achievement Testing of Disadvantaged and Minority Students for Educational Program Evaluation, Reston, VA.

Biederman, I. (1987). Recognition-by-components: A theory of human image understanding. *Psychological Review, 94,* 115–147.

Biederman, I. (1990). Higher-level vision. In E. N. Osherson, S. M. Kosslyn, & J. M. Hollerbach (Eds.), *An invitation to cognitive science* (Vol 2, pp. 41–72). Cambridge, MA: MIT Press.

Biederman, I., Hilton, H. J., & Hummel, J. E. (1991). Pattern goodness and pattern recognition. In G. R. Lockhead & J. R. Pomerantz (Eds.), *The perception of structure* (pp. 73–95). Washington, DC: American Psychological Association.

Biegel, D. E., Sales, E., & Schulz, R. (1991). *Family caregiving in chronic illness.* Newbury Park, CA: Sage.

Biener, L., Abrams, D. B., Emmons, K., & Follick, M. J. (1989). Evaluating worksite smoking policies: Methodologic issues. *New York State Journal of Medicine, 89,* 5–10.

Bierhoff, H. (1989). *Person perception and attribution.* Marburg, Germany: Springer-Verlag.

Bierly, M. M. (1985). Prejudice toward contemporary out-groups as a generalized attitude. *Journal of Applied Social Psychology, 15,* 189–199.

Biernat, M., & Wortman, C. B. (1991). Sharing of home responsibilities between professionally employed women and their husbands. *Journal of Personality and Social Psychology, 60,* 844–860.

Bilton, M., & Sim, K. (1992). *Four hours in My Lai.* New York: Penguin.

Bilyk, S. (1992). Personal communication.

Birchler, G. R. (1992). Marriage. In V. B. Van Hasselt & M. Hersen (Eds.), *Handbook of social development: A lifespan perspective* (pp. 397–419). New York: Plenum.

Birchler, G. R., Weiss, R. L., & Vincent, J. P. (1975). Multimethod analysis of social reinforcement exchange between maritally distressed and nondistressed spouse and stranger dyads. *Journal of Personality and Social Psychology, 31,* 349–360.

Birren, J. E., Cunningham, W. R., & Yamamoto, K. (1983). Psychology of adult development and aging. *Annual Review of Psychology, 34,* 543–575.

Birren, J. E., & Schaie, K. W. (Eds.). (1990). *Handbook of the psychology of aging* (3rd ed.). San Diego: Academic Press.

Bjork, R. A. (1988). Retrieval practice and the maintenance of knowledge. In M. M. Gruneberg, P. Morris, & R. Sykes (Eds.), *Practical aspects of memory* (Vol. 2, pp. 396–401). London: Academic Press.

Bjork, R. A., & Richardson-Klavehn, A. (1987). On the puzzling relationship between environmental context and human memory. In C. Izawa (Ed.), *Current issues in cognitive processes* (pp. 313–344). Hillsdale, NJ: Erlbaum.

Blackburn, C. (1988, April). Matters of taste. *Piedmont Airlines,* pp. 24–27.

Blanchard, F. A., Lilly, T., & Vaughn, L. A. (1991). Reducing the expression of racial prejudice. *Psychological Science, 2,* 101–105.

Blass, T. (1991). Understanding behavior in the Milgram obedience experiment: The role of personality, situations, and their interactions. *Journal of Personality and Social Psychology, 60,* 398–413.

Blass, T. (1992). The social psychology of Stanley Milgram. *Advances in Experimental Social Psychology, 25,* 277–329.

Blau, F. D., & Winkler, A. E. (1989). Women in the labor force: An overview. In J. Freeman (Ed.), *Women: A feminist perspective* (4th ed., pp. 265–286). Mountain View, CA: Mayfield.

Bleuler, E. (1911/1950). *Dementia praecox or the group of schizophrenias.* New York: International Universities.

Blieszner, R., & Adams, R. G. (1992). *Adult friendship.* Newbury Park, CA: Sage.

Bliss, T. V. P., & Lømo, T. (1973). Long-lasting potentiation of synaptic transmission in the dentate area of the anaesthetized rabbit following stimulation of the perforant path. *Journal of Physiology, 232,* 331–356.

Blum, J. E. (1991). *Alcohol and the addictive brain: New hope for alcoholics from biogenetic research.* New York: The Free Press.

Blum, J. S., Chow, K. L., & Pribram, K. H. (1950). A behavioral analysis of the organization of the parieto-temporo-preoccipital cortex. *Journal of Comparative Neurology, 93,* 53–100.

Blumenthal, A. L. (1975). A reappraisal of Wilhelm Wundt. *American Psychologist, 30,* 1081–1088.

Bock, J. K. (1987). Co-ordinating words and syntax in speech plans. In A. W. Ellis (Ed.), *Progress in the psychology of language* (Vol. 3, pp. 337–390). London: Erlbaum.

Bodenhausen, G. V. (1990). Stereotypes as judgmental heuristics: Evidence of circadian variations in discrimination. *Psychological Science, 5,* 319–322.

Bohannon, J. N., III. (1993). Theoretical approaches to language acquisition. In J. B. Gleason (Ed.), *The development of language* (pp. 239–297). New York: Macmillan.

Bonaiuto, P., Giannini, A. M., & Bonaiuto, M. (1991). Visual illusory productions with or without amodal completion. *Perception, 20,* 243–257.

Bond, C. F., Jr., & Titus, L. J. (1983). Social facilitation: A meta-analysis of 241 studies. *Psychological Bulletin, 94,* 265–292.

Boneau, C. A. (1992). Observations on psychology's past and future. *American Psychologist, 47,* 1586–1596.

Booth, D. A. (1991). Learned ingestive motivation and the pleasures of the palate. In R. C. Bolles (Ed.), *The hedonics of taste* (pp. 29–58). Hillsdale, NJ: Erlbaum.

Booth-Kewley, S., & Friedman, H. S. (1987). Psychological predictors of heart disease: A quantitative review. *Psychological Bulletin, 101,* 343–362.

Borkenau, P. (1993). To predict some of the people more of the time: Individual traits and the prediction of behavior. In K. H. Craik, R. Hogan, & R. N. Wolfe (Eds.), *Fifty years of personality psychology* (pp. 237–247). New York: Plenum.

Bornstein, M. H. (1989). Stability in early mental development: From attention and information processing in infancy to language and cognition in childhood. In M. H. Bornstein & N. A. Krasnegor (Eds.), *Stability and continuity in mental development: Behavioral and biological perspectives* (pp. 147–170). Hillsdale, NJ: Erlbaum.

Bornstein, M. H., Tal, J., Rahn, C., Galperín, C. Z., Pêcheux, M-G., Lamour, M., Toda, S., Azuma, H., Ogino, M., & Tamis-Lemonda, C. S. (1992). Functional analysis of the contents of material speech to infants of 5 and 13 months in four cultures: Argentina, France, Japan, and the United States. *Developmental Psychology, 28,* 593–603.

Bornstein, R. F. (1989). Exposure and affect: Overview and meta-analysis of research, 1968–1987. *Psychological Bulletin, 106,* 265–289.

Bornstein, R. F., Kale, A. R., & Cornell, K. R. (1990). Boredom as a limiting condition on the mere exposure effect. *Journal of Personality and Social Psychology, 58,* 791–800.

Botman, H. I., & Crovitz, H. F. (1989/1990). Dream reports and autobiographical memory. *Imagination, Cognition and Personality, 9,* 213–224.

Botvin, G. J., Dusenbury, L., Baker, E., James-Ortiz, S., & Kerner, J. (1989). A skills training approach to smoking prevention among Hispanic youth. *Journal of Behavioral Medicine, 12,* 279–296.

Bouchard, C., Tremblay, A., Després, J., Nadeau, A., Lupien, P. J., Thériault, G., Dussault, J., Moorjani, S., Pinault, S., & Fournier, G. (1990). The response to long-term overfeeding in identical twins. *New England Journal of Medicine, 322,* 1477–1487.

Bouchard, T. J., Jr., Lykken, D. T., McGue, M., Segal, N. L., & Tellegen, A. (1990). Sources of human psychological differences: The Minnesota Study of Twins Reared Apart. *Science, 250,* 223–228.

Bouchard, T. J., Jr., & McGue, M. (1981). Familial studies of intelligence: A review. *Science, 212,* 1055–1059.

Boulton, M. G. (1983). *On being a mother.* London: Tavistock.

Bower, G. H. (1970). Analysis of a mnemonic device. *American Scientist, 58,* 496–510.

Bower, G. H., Clark, M. C., Lesgold, A. M., & Winzenz, D. (1969). Hierarchical retrieval schemes in recall of categorized word lists. *Journal of Verbal Learning and Verbal Behavior, 8,* 323–343.

Bower, G. H., & Winzenz, G. (1970). Comparison of associative learning strategies. *Psychonomic Science, 20,* 119–120.

Bower, T. G. R. (1989). *The rational infant: Learning in infancy.* New York: Freeman.

Bowers, K. S. (1976). *Hypnosis for the seriously curi-

ous.* Monterey, CA: Brooks/Cole.

Bowers, K. S. (1984). Hypnosis. In N. E. Endler & J. M. Hunt (Eds.), *Personality and the behavioral disorders* (2nd ed., Vol. 1, pp. 439–475). New York: Wiley.

Bowers, W. A. (1991). Psychosocial treatment for simple phobia, obsessive-compulsive disorder, posttraumatic stress disorder, and social phobia. In W. Coryell & G. Winokur (Eds.), *The clinical management of anxiety disorders* (pp. 28–40). New York: Oxford University Press.

Bowman, P. J., & Howard, C. (1985). Race-related socialization, motivation, and academic achievement: A study of black youths in three-generation families. *Journal of the American Academy of Child Psychiatry, 24,* 134–141.

Boyd-Franklin, N. (1989). *Black families in therapy.* New York: Guilford.

Boyer, J. L., & Guthrie, L. (1985). Assessment and treatment of the suicidal patient. In E. E. Beckham & W. R. Leber (Eds.), *Handbook of depression* (pp. 606–633). Homewood, IL: Dorsey.

Boyes, M. C., & Walker, L. J. (1988). Implications of cultural diversity for the universality claims of Kohnberg's theory of moral reasoning. *Human Development, 31,* 44–59.

Boykin, A. W. (1986). The triple quandary and the schooling of Afro-American children. In U. Neisser (Ed.), *The school achievement of minority children* (pp. 57–92). Hillsdale, NJ: Erlbaum.

Boykin, A. W., & Toms, F. D. (1985). *Black child socialization: A conceptual framework.* In H. P. McAdoo & J. L. McAdoo (Eds.), *Black children* (pp. 33–51). Beverly HIlls, CA: Sage.

Boynton, R. M. (1988). Color vision. *Annual Review of Psychology, 39,* 69–100.

Bozette, F. W., & Hanson, S. M. H. (Eds.). (1990). *Fatherhood and families in cultural context.* New York: Springer.

Bradbury, T. N., & Fincham, F. D. (1992). Attributions and behavior in marital interaction. *Journal of Personality and Social Psychology, 63,* 613–628.

Bradshaw, J. L. (1989). *Hemispheric specialization and psychological function.* Chichester, England: Wiley.

Brady, J. (1982, November). Perfume. *Signature,* pp. 77–89.

Branden, N. (1988). A vision of romantic love. In R. J. Sternberg & M. L. Barnes (Eds.), *The psychology of love* (pp. 218–231). New Haven, CT: Yale University Press.

Brandimonte, M. A., Hitch, G. J., & Bishop, D. V. M. (1992). Influence of short-term memory codes on visual image processing: Evidence from image transformation tasks. *Journal of Experimental Psychology: Learning, Memory, and Cognition, 18,* 157–165.

Brannon, L., & Feist, J. (1992). *Health psychology: An introduction to behavior and health* (2nd ed.). Belmont, CA: Wadsworth.

Bransford, J. D., & Franks, J. J. (1971). Abstraction of linguistic ideas. *Cognitive Psychology, 2,* 331–350.

Brayfield, A. A. (1992). Employment resources and housework in Canada. *Journal of Marriage and the Family, 54,* 19–30.

Brehm, S. S. (1992). *Intimate relationships* (2nd ed.). New York: McGraw-Hill.

Brehm, S. S., & Kassin, S. M. (1993). *Social psychology* (2nd ed.). Boston: Houghton Mifflin.

Breland, K., & Breland, M. (1961). The misbehavior of organisms. *American Psychologist, 16,* 681–684.

Brenner, H. D., Böker, W., Hodel, B., & Wyss, H. (1989). Cognitive treatment of basic pervasive dysfunctions in schizophrenia. In S. C. Schulz & C. A. Tamminga (Eds.), *Schizophrenia: Scientific progress* (pp. 358–371). New York: Oxford.

Bretherton, I. (1985). Attachment theory: Retrospect and prospect. *Monographs of the Society for Research in Child Development, 50*(1), 3–35.

Bretherton, I. (1992). Attachment and bonding. In V. B. Van Hasselt & M. Hersen (Eds.), *Handbook of social development: A lifespan perspective* (pp. 133–155). New York: Plenum.

Brewer, M. B., & Lui, L. (1984). Categorization of the elderly by the elderly: Effects of perceiver's category membership. *Personality and Social Psychology Bulletin, 10*, 585–595.

Brewer, W. F. (1992). The theoretical and empirical status of the flashbulb memory hypothesis. In E. Winograd & U. Neisser (Eds.), *Affect and accuracy in recall: Studies of "flashbulb" memories* (pp. 274–305). New York: Cambridge University Press.

Brewer, W. F., & Treyens, J. C. (1981). Role of schemata in memory for places. *Cognitive Psychology, 13*, 207–230.

Brewin, C. R. (1988). *Cognitive foundations of clinical psychology*. Hove, England: Lawrence Erlbaum.

Brewin, C. R. (1989). Cognitive change processes in psychotherapy. *Psychological Review, 96*, 379–394.

Bridgeman, B. (1988). *The biology of behavior and mind*. New York: Wiley.

Bridgeman, B., & Wendler, C. (1991). Gender differences in predictors of college mathematics performance and in college mathematics course grades. *Journal of Educational Psychology, 83*, 275–289.

Briere, J., & Lanktree, C. (1983). Sex-role related effects of sex bias in language. *Sex Roles, 9*, 625–632.

Brislin, R. (1993). *Understanding culture's influence on behavior*. Fort Worth: Harcourt Brace Jovanovich.

Broberg, D. J., & Bernstein, I. L. (1987). Candy as a scapegoat in the prevention of food aversions in children receiving chemotherapy. *Cancer, 60*, 2344–2347.

Broca, P. (1861). Remarques sur le siège de la faculté du langage articulé, suivies d'une observation d'aphémie (perte de la parole). *Bulletin de la Societe Anatomique (Paris), 36*, 330–357.

Brody, L. R., & Hall, J. A. (1994). Gender and emotion. In M. Lewis & J. Haviland (Eds.), *Guilford handbook of emotions*. New York: Guilford.

Brody, N. (1988). *Personality: In search of individuality*. San Diego: Academic Press.

Brody, N. (1992). *Intelligence* (2nd ed.). San Diego, CA: Academic Press.

Bromley, D. B. (1986). *The case-study method in psychology and related disciplines*. Chichester, England: Wiley.

Bronfenbrenner, U. (1961). The mirror image in Soviet-American relations: A social psychologist's report. *Journal of Social Issues, 17*, 45–56.

Bronstein, P. A., & Quina, K. (1988). Perspectives on gender balance and cultural diversity in the teaching of psychology. In P. A. Bronstein & K. Quina (Eds.), *Teaching a psychology of people: Resource for gender and sociocultural awareness* (pp. 3–11). Washington, DC: American Psychological Association.

Brooke, O. G., Anderson, H. R., Bland, J. M., Peacock, J. L., & Stewart, C. M. (1989). Effects on birth weight of smoking, alcohol, caffeine, socioeconomic factors, and psychosocial stress. *British Medical Journal, 298*, 795–801.

Brooks, C. I. (1987). Superiority of women in statistics achievement. *Teaching of Psychology, 14*, 45.

Brooks-Gunn, J., & Reiter, E. O. (1990). The role of pubertal processes. In S. Shirley Feldman & G. R. Elliott (Eds.), *At the threshold: The developing adolescent* (pp. 16–53). Cambridge, MA: Harvard University Press.

Brothers, L. (1989, November). Empathy: Therapeutic and biological views. *The Harvard Medical School Mental Health Letter, 6*(5), 4–6.

Brown, A. S. (1991). A review of the tip-of-the-tongue experience. *Psychological Bulletin, 109*, 204–223.

Brown, D. R. (1990). Depression among Blacks: An epidemiological perspective. In D. S. Ruiz & J. P. Comer (Eds.), *Handbook of mental health and mental disorder among Black Americans* (pp. 71–93). New York: Greenwood Press.

Brown, G. G., & Bornstein, R. A. (1991). Anatomic imaging methods for neurobehavioral studies. In R. A. Bornstein & G. G. Brown (Eds.), *Neurobehavioral aspects of cerebrovascular disease* (pp. 83–108). New York: Oxford University Press.

Brown, J. A. (1958). Some tests of the decay theory of immediate memory. *Quarterly Journal of Experimental Psychology, 10*, 12–21.

Brown, J. D. (1991). Staying fit and staying well: Physical fitness as a moderator of life stress. *Journal of Personality and Social Psychology, 60*, 555–561.

Brown, J. D., & McGill, K. L. (1989). The cost of good fortune: When positive life events produce negative health consequences. *Journal of Personality and Social Psychology, 57*, 1103–1110.

Brown, P. (1991). *The hypnotic brain: Hypnotherapy and social communication*. New Haven: Yale University Press.

Brown, P., & Levinson, S. C. (1987). *Politeness: Some universals of language usage*. Cambridge, England: Cambridge University Press.

Brown, R. (1988). More than P's and Q's [Review of *Politeness: Some universals of language usage*]. *Contemporary Psychology, 33*, 749–750.

Brown, R., Cazden, C., & Bellugi-Klima, U. (1968). The child's grammar from 1 to 3. In J. P. Hill (Ed.), *Minnesota Symposium on Child Development* (Vol. 2, pp. 28–73). Minneapolis: University of Minnesota Press.

Brown, R., & Kulik, J. (1977). Flashbulb memories. *Cognition, 5*, 73–99.

Brown, R., & Lenneberg, E. H. (1954). A study in language and cognition. *Journal of Abnormal and Social Psychology, 49*, 454–462.

Brown, R., & McNeill, D. (1966). The "tip of the tongue" phenomenon. *Journal of Verbal Learning and Verbal Behavior, 5*, 325–377.

Brownell, K. D., & Wadden, T. A. (1992). Etiology and treatment of obesity: Understanding a serious, prevalent, and refractory disorder. *Journal of Consulting and Clinical Psychology, 60*, 505–517.

Brownmiller, S. (1975). *Against our will: Men, women, and rape*. New York: Bantam.

Bruce, D. (1985). The how and why of ecological memory. *Journal of Experimental Psychology: General, 114*, 78–90.

Bruch, H. (1978). *The gold cage: The enigma of anorexia nervosa*. Cambridge, MA: Harvard University Press.

Bruch, H. (1988). *Conversations with anorexics*. New York: Basic Books.

Brugge, J. F., & Reale, R. A. (1985). Auditory cortex. In A. Peters & E. G. Jones (Eds.), *Cerebral cortex* (Vol. 4, pp. 229–271). New York: Plenum.

Brush, S. G. (1991). Women in science and engineering. *American Scientist, 79*, 404–419.

Bryden, M. P., & Steenhuis, R. E. (1991). Issues in the assessment of handedness. In F. L. Kitterle (Ed.), *Cerebral laterality: Theory and research* (pp. 35–51). Hillsdale, NJ: Erlbaum.

Buchholz, D. (1988). Sleep disorders. *Treatment Trends, 3*, 1–9.

Buck, L., & Axel, R. (1991). A novel multigene family may encode odorant receptors: A molecular basis for odor recognition. *Cell, 65*, 175–187.

Buckley, K. W. (1989). *Mechanical man: John Broadus Watson and the beginnings of behaviorism*. New York: Guilford.

Buckman, R. (1992). *"I don't know what to say" . . . How to help and support someone who is dying*. New York: Vintage.

Burchill, S. A. L., & Stiles, W. B. (1988). Interactions of depressed college students with their roommates: Not necessarily negative. *Journal of Personality and Social Psychology, 55*, 410–419.

Burciaga, J. A. (1993). *Drink cultura: Chicanismo*. Santa Barbara, CA: Capra Press.

Burden-Patmon, D. (1989, December). Stand and deliver: Achieving against the odds. *Wheelock Bulletin*, pp. 2, 15.

Burgess, A. W., & Holmstrom, L. L. (1980). Rape typology and the coping behavior of rape victims. In S. L. McCombie (Ed.), *The rape crisis intervention handbook* (pp. 27–40). New York: Plenum.

Burgoon, J. K. (1985). Nonverbal signals. In M. L. Knapp & G. R. Miller (Eds.), *Handbook of interpersonal communication* (pp. 344–390). Beverly Hills, CA: Sage.

Burgoon, M. (1990). Language and social influence. In H. Giles & W. P. Robinson (Eds.), *Handbook of language and social psychology* (pp. 51–72). Chichester, England: Wiley.

Burns, M. O., & Seligman, M. E. P. (1990). Explanatory style, helplessness, and depression. In C. R. Snyder & D. R. Forsyth (Eds.), *Handbook of social and clinical psychology: The health perspective* (pp. 267–284). New York: Pergamon.

Bushman, B. J., & Cooper, H. M. (1990). Effects of alcohol on human aggression: An integrative research review. *Psychological Bulletin, 107*, 341–354.

Bushnell, I. W. R. (1982). Discrimination of faces by young infants. *Journal of Experimental Psychology, 33*, 298–308.

Buss, A. H. (1989). Personality as traits. *American Psychologist, 44*, 1378–1388.

Buss, D. M. (1985, January–February). Human mate selection. *American Scientist*, 47–51.

Buss, D. M., & Barnes, M. (1986). Preferences in human mate selection. *Journal of Personality and Social Psychology, 50*, 559–570.

Butcher, J. N., & Finn, S. (1983). Objective personality assessment in clinical settings. In M. Hersen, A. Kazdin, & A. S. Bellack (Eds.), *The clinical psychology handbook* (pp. 329–344). New York: Pergamon.

Butcher, J. N., Graham, J. R., Williams, C. L., & Ben-Porath, Y. S. (1990). *Development and use of the MMPI-2 content scales*. Minneapolis: University of Minnesota Press.

Butler, R. N. (1963). The life review: An interpretation of reminiscence in the aged. *Psychiatry, 26,* 65–76.

Butler, S. F., & Strupp, H. H. (1991). The role of affect in time-limited dynamic psychotherapy. In J. D. Safran & L. S. Greenberg (Eds.), *Emotion, psychotherapy, and change* (pp. 83–112). New York: Guilford.

Button, C. M., & Collier, D. R. (1991, June). *A comparison of people's concepts of love and romantic love.* Paper presented at the Canadian Psychological Association Conference, Calgary, Alberta.

Byrne, D. (1982). Predicting human sexual behavior. In A. G. Kraut (Ed.), *The G. Stanley Hall Lecture Series* (Vol 2). Washington, D. C.: American Psychological Association.

Byrne, D., Clore, G. I., & Smeaton, G. (1986). The attraction hypothesis: Do similar attitudes affect anything? *Journal of Personality and Social Psychology, 51,* 1167–1170.

Byrne, D., & Murnen, S. K. (1988). Maintaining loving relationships. In R. J. Sternberg & M. L. Barnes (Eds.), *The psychology of love* (pp. 293–310). New Haven, CT: Yale University Press.

Cahn, D. D. (1992). *Conflict in intimate relationships.* New York: Guilford.

Cain, W. S. (1988). Olfaction. In R. C. Atkinson, R. J. Herrnstein, G. Lindzey, & R. D. Luce (Eds.), *Stevens' handbook of experimental psychology* (2nd ed., Vol. 1, pp. 409–459). New York: Wiley.

Camp, C. J., & McKitrick, L. A. (1992). Memory interventions in Alzheimer's-type dementia populations: Methodological and theoretical issues. In R. I. West & J. D. Sinnot (Eds.), *Everyday memory and aging: Current research and methodology* (pp. 155–172). New York: Springer.

Campaign 2000. (1992). *Countdown 92: Campaign 2000 child poverty indicator report.* Ottawa, Ontario: Author.

Campbell, S. M., Peplau, L. A., & DeBro, S. C. (1992). Women, men, and condoms: Attitudes and experiences of heterosexual college students. *Psychology of Women Quarterly, 16,* 273–288.

Campione, J. C., Brown, A. L., & Ferrara, R. A. (1982). Mental retardation and intelligence. In R. J. Sternberg (Ed.), *Handbook of human intelligence* (pp. 392–490). New York: Cambridge University Press.

Campos, J. J., Langer, A., & Krowitz, A. (1970). Cardiac responses on the visual cliff in prelocomotor human infants. *Science, 170,* 196–197.

Canadian Psychological Association (1991). *Canadian code of ethics for psychologists.* Old Chelsea, Québec: Author.

Canadian Psychological Association. (1992). *Companion manual to the Canadian code of ethics for psychologists, 1991.* Old Chelsea, Québec: Author.

Cannon, L. W., Higginbotham, E., & Leung, M. L. A. (1988). Race and class bias in qualitative research on women. *Gender & Society, 2,* 449–462.

Cannon, W. B. (1927). The James-Lange theory of emotion: A critical examination and an alternative theory. *American Journal of Psychology, 39,* 106–124.

Cantor, N., & Kihlstrom, J. F. (1987). *Personality and social intelligence.* Englewood Cliffs, NJ: Prentice-Hall.

Caplan, N., Choy, M. H., & Whitmore, J. K. (1992, February). Indochinese refugee families and academic achievement. *Scientific American,* pp. 36–42.

Caplan, P. J. (1984). The myth of women's masochism. *American Psychologist, 39,* 130–139.

Cappella, J. N. (1985). The management of conversations. In M. L. Knapp & G. R. Miller (Eds.), *Handbook of interpersonal communication* (pp. 393–438). Beverly Hills, CA: Sage.

Caramazza, A., Yenni-Komshian, G., Zurif, E., & Carbone, E. (1973). The acquisition of a new phonological contrast: The case of stop consonants in French-English bilinguals. *Journal of the Acoustical Society of America, 54,* 421–428.

Cargan, L., & Melko, M. (1985). Being single on Noah's ark. In L. Cargan (Ed.), *Marriage and family: Coping with change.* Belmont, CA: Wadsworth.

Carlo, G., Eisenberg, N., Troyer, D., Switzer, G., & Speer, A. L. (1991). The altruistic personality: In what contexts is it apparent? *Journal of Personality and Social Psychology, 61,* 450–458.

Carlson, N. R. (1991). *Physiology of behavior* (4th ed.). Boston: Allyn & Bacon.

Carnevale, P. J., & Pruitt, D. G. (1992). Negotiation and mediation. *Annual Review of Psychology, 43,* 531–582.

Carney, J. (1989, January 16). Can a driver be too old? *Time,* p. 28.

Caron, R. F., Caron, A. J., & Myers, R. S. (1982). Abstraction of invariant face expressions in infancy. *Child Development, 53,* 1008–1015.

Carp, F. M. (1989). Maximizing data quality in community studies of older people. In M. P. Lawton & A. R. Herzog (Eds.), *Special research methods for gerontology* (pp. 93–122). Amityville, NY: Baywood.

Carpenter, W. T., Jr., & Strauss, J. S. (1991). The prediction of outcome in schizophrenia IV: Eleven-year follow-up of the Washington IPSS cohort. *Journal of Nervous and Mental Disease, 179,* 517–525.

Carroll, D. (1988). How accurate is polygraph lie detection? In A. Gale (Ed.), *The polygraph test* (pp. 19–28). London: Sage.

Carroll, J. B. (1992). Cognitive abilities: The state of the art. *Psychological Science, 3,* 266–270.

Carson, R. C., & Butcher, J. N. (1992). *Abnormal psychology and modern life* (9th ed.). New York: HarperCollins.

Carver, R. P. (1990). *Reading rate: A review of research and theory.* San Diego: Academic Press.

Case, R. (1987). The structure and process of intellectual development. *International Journal of Psychology, 22,* 571–607.

Caspi, A., & Moffit, T. E. (1991). Individual differences are accentuated during periods of social change: The sample case of girls at puberty. *Journal of Personality and Social Psychology, 61,* 157–168.

Cassell, E. J. (1990). Introduction: The nature of suffering and the goals of medicine. In T. W. Miller (Ed.), *Chronic pain* (Vol. 1, pp. xix–xxxv). Madison, CT: International Universities Press.

Cassell, J., & McNeill, D. (1991). Gesture and the poetics of prose. *Poetics Today, 12,* 375–403.

Cate, R. M., & Lloyd, S. A. (1992). *Courtship.* Newbury Park, CA: Sage.

Celentano, D. D., & Sonnega, A. B. (1991). Coping processes and strategies and personal resources among persons with HIV-spectrum disease. In P. I. Ahmed (Ed.), *Living and dying with AIDS* (pp. 105–121). New York: Plenum.

Centerwall, B. S. (1992). Television and violence: The scale of the problem and where to go from here. *JAMA, 267,* 3059–3063.

Cernoch, J. M., & Porter, R. H. (1985). Recognition of maternal axillary odors by infants. *Child Development, 56,* 1593–1598.

Cervone, D. (1989). Effects of envisioning future activities on self-efficacy judgments and motivation: An availability heuristic interpretation. *Cognitive Therapy and Research, 13,* 247–261.

Chaika, E. (1985, August). Crazy talk. *Psychology Today, 19,* 30–35.

Chance, P. (1988). *Learning and behavior* (2nd ed.). Belmont, CA: Wadsworth.

Chang, H. H., Murphy, D., Diferdinando, G. T., & Morse, D. L. (1990). Assessment of AIDS knowledge in selected New York State sexually transmitted disease clinics. *New York State Journal of Medicine, 90,* 126–128.

Chaplin, W. F. (1990). Personality: Beyond the Big Five and biology [Review of *Personality: Evolutionary heritage and human distinctiveness*]. *Contemporary Psychology, 35,* 940–941.

Chapman, M. (1988). *Constructive evolution: Origins and development of Piaget's thought.* New York: Cambridge University Press.

Chase, M. H., & Morales, F. R. (1990). The atonia and myoconia of active (REM) sleep. *Annual Review of Psychology, 41,* 557–584.

Chastain, G. (1986). Word-to-letter inhibition: Word-inferiority and other interference effects. *Memory & Cognition, 14,* 361–368.

Check, J. V. P. (1984). *The effects of violent and nonviolent pornography.* Ottawa, Ontario: Canadian Department of Justice.

Check, J.V. P., & Malamuth, N. M. (1986). Pornography and social aggression: A social learning theory analysis. In M. L. McLaughlin (Ed.), *Communication Yearbook* (Vol. 9, pp. 181–213). Beverly Hills, CA: Sage.

Chehrazi, S. (1986). Female psychology. *Journal of the American Psychoanalytic Association, 34,* 111–162.

Chen, M. S. (1992). *Healthy Asian Americans—Pacific Islanders: Model or myth?* Paper presented at the annual convention of the American Psychological Association, Washington, DC.

Cherry, E. C. (1953). Some experiments on the recognition of speech with one and with two ears. *Journal of Acoustical Society of America, 25,* 975–979.

Cheung, F. K. (1991). The use of mental health services by ethnic minorities. In H. F. Myers, P. Wohlford, L. P. Guzman, & R. J. Echemenda (Eds.), *Ethnic minority perspectives on clinical training and services in psychology* (pp. 23–31). Washington, DC: American Psychological Association.

Chi, M. T. H., Bassok, M., Lewis, M. W., Reimann, P., & Glaser, R. (1989). Self-explanations: How students study and use examples in learning to solve problems. *Cognitive Science, 13,* 145–182.

Children's Defense Fund. (1988). *A vision for America's future.* Washington, DC: Author.

Children's Defense Fund. (1992). *The state of America's children 1992.* Washington, DC: Author.

Chipman, S. (1994). Gender and school learning: Mathematics. In T. Husen & T. H. Pastelthwaite (Eds.), *International encyclopedia of education.* London: Pergamon Press.

Chiriboga, D. A. (1989). Mental health at the midpoint: Crisis, challenge, or relief? In S. Hunter & M. Sundel (Eds.), *Midlife myths: Issues, findings, and practice implications* (pp. 116–144). Newbury Park: Sage.

Chiriboga, D. A., Weiler, P. G., & Nielsen, K. (1990).

The stress of caregivers. In D. E. Biegel & A. Blum (Eds.), *Aging and caregiving: Theory, research, and policy* (pp. 121–138). Newbury Park, CA: Sage.

Chodorow, N. J. (1978). *The reproduction of mothering.* Berkeley: The University of California Press.

Chodorow, N. J. (1989). *Feminism and psychoanalytic theory.* New Haven, CT: Yale University Press.

Chomsky, N. (1957). *Syntactic structures.* The Hague: Mouton Publishers.

Chomsky, N. (1965). *Aspects of the theory of syntax.* Cambridge, MA: MIT Press.

Chomsky, N. (1988). *Language and problems of knowledge: The Managua Lectures.* Cambridge, MA: MIT Press.

Chrisler, J. C., & Levy, K. B. (1989, March). *The media construct a menstrual monster: A content analysis of PMS articles in the popular press.* Paper presented at the meeting of the Association for Women in Psychology, Newport, RI.

Christensen, L. B. (1991). *Experimental methodology* (5th ed.). Boston: Allyn and Bacon.

Christianson, S.-A. (1989). Flashbulb memories: Special, but not so special. *Memory & Cognition, 17,* 435–443.

Churchland, P. M., & Churchland, P. S. (1990, January). Could a machine think? *Scientific American,* pp. 32–37.

Churchland, P. S., & Sejnowski, T. J. (1992). *The computational brain.* Cambridge, MA: MIT Press.

Cialdini, R. (1986). Interpersonal influence: Being ethical and effective. In S. Oskamp & S. Spacapan (Eds.), *Interpersonal processes* (pp. 148–165). Newbury Park, CA: Sage.

Cialdini, R. B., Reno, R. R., & Kallgren, C. A. (1990). A focus theory of normative conduct: Recycling the concept of norms to reduce littering in public places. *Journal of Personality and Social Psychology, 58,* 1015–1026.

Cialdini, R. B. (1993). *Influence: Science and practice.* (3rd ed.). New York: HarperCollins.

Cialdini, R. B., Vincent, J. E., Lewis, S. K., Catalan, J., Wheeler, D., & Darby, B. L. (1975). Reciprocal concessions procedure for inducing compliance: The door-in-the-face technique. *Journal of Personality and Social Psychology, 31,* 206–215

Cirigliano, M. D., & Lynn, L. A. (1992, April 30). Diagnosis and treatment of stage fright. *Hospital Practice,* pp. 58–62.

Clark, D. O., & Maddox, G. L. (1992). Racial and social correlates of age-related changes in functioning. *Journal of Gerontology: Social Sciences, 47,* S222–S232.

Clark, E. V. (1991). Acquisitional principles in lexical development. In S. A. Gelman & J. P. Byrnes (Eds.), *Perspectives on language and thought: Interrelations in development* (pp. 31–71). New York: Cambridge University Press.

Clark, H. H. (1985). Language use and language users. In G. Lindzey & E. Aronson (Eds.), *Handbook of social psychology* (2nd ed., Vol. 2, pp. 179–231). New York: Random House.

Clark, H. H. (1991). Words, the world, and their possibilities. In G. R. Lockhead & J. R. Pomerantz (Eds.), *The perception of structure* (pp. 263–277). Washington, DC: American Psychological Association.

Clark, H. H., & Brennan, S. E. (1991). Grounding in communication. In L. R. Resnick, J. M. Levine, & S. D. Teasley (Eds.), *Perspectives on socially shared cognition* (pp. 127–149). Washington, DC: American Psychological Association.

Clark, H. H., & Clark, E. V. (1977). *Psychology and language: An introduction to psycholinguistics.* New York: Harcourt Brace Jovanovich.

Clark, H. H., & Wilkes-Gibbs, D. (1986). Referring as a collaborative process. *Cognition, 22,* 1–39.

Clark, R. E., & Salomon, G. (1986). Media in teaching. In M. C. Wittrock (Ed.), *Handbook of research on teaching* (3rd ed., pp. 464–478). New York: Macmillan.

Clarke-Stewart, K. A. (1989). Infant day care: Maligned or malignant. *American Psychologist, 44,* 266–273.

Clarke-Stewart, K. A. (1991). A home is not a school: The effects of child care on children's development. *Journal of Social Issues, 47,* 105–123.

Cleary, P. D. (1987). Gender differences in stress-related disorders. In R. C. Barnet, L. Biener, & G. K. Baruch (Eds.), *Gender and stress* (pp. 39–72). New York: Free Press.

Clement, J. (1991). Nonformal reasoning in experts and in science students: The use of analogies, extreme cases, and physical intuition. In J. Voss, D. Perkins, & J. Siegel (Eds.), *Informal reasoning and education.* Hillsdale, NJ: Erlbaum.

Climko, R. P., & Sweeney, D. R. (1989). Obsessional states. In J. G. Howells (Ed.), *Modern perspectives in the psychiatry of the neuroses* (pp. 168–186). New York: Brunner/Mazel.

Cloninger, S. C. (1993). *Theories of personality: Understanding persons.* Englewood Cliffs, NJ: Prentice-Hall.

Cochran, S. D., & Mays, V. M. (1990). Sex, lies, and HIV. *New England Journal of Medicine, 322,* 774–775.

Cockburn, J., & Smith, P. T. (1991). The relative influence of intelligence and age on everyday memory. *Journal of Gerontology: Psychological Sciences, 46,* P31–P36.

Coen, C. W. (1985). Introduction. In C. W. Coen (Ed.), *Functions of the brain* (pp. ix–xiv). Oxford: Clarendon.

Cohen, C. E. (1981). Person categories and social perception: Testing some boundaries of the processing effects of prior knowledge. *Journal of Personality and Social Psychology, 40,* 441–452.

Cohen, G. (1989). *Memory in the real world.* London: Erlbaum.

Cohen, G., Eysenck, M. W., & LeVoi, M. E. (1986). *Memory: A cognitive approach.* Milton Keynes, England: Open University Press.

Cohen, J. D., & Servan-Schreiber, D. (1992). Context, cortex, and dopamine: A connectionist approach to behavior and biology in schizophrenia. *Psychological Review, 99,* 45–77.

Cohen, R. J., Swerdlik, M. E., & Smith, D. K. (1992). *Psychological testing and assessment: An introduction to tests and measurement* (2nd ed.). Mountain View, CA: Mayfield.

Cohen, S. (1991). Social supports and physical health: symptoms, health behaviors, and infectious disease. In E. Mark Cummings, A. L. Greene, & K. H. Karraker (Eds.), *Life-span developmental psychology: Perspectives on stress and coping* (pp. 213–234). Hillsdale, NJ: Erlbaum.

Coile, D. C., & Miller, N. E. (1984). How radical animal activists try to mislead humane people. *American Psychologist, 39,* 700–701.

Colby, A., & Damon, W. (1992). *Some do care: Contemporary lives of moral commitment.* New York: Free Press.

Colby, A., & Kohlberg, L. (1987). *The measurement of moral judgment: Vol. I. Theoretical foundations and research validation.* Cambridge, England: Cambridge University Press.

Colby, A., Kohlberg, L., Gibbs, J., & Lieberman, M. (1983). A longitudinal study of moral judgment. *Monographs of the Society for Child Development* (Serial No. 201).

Cole, R. A., & Jakimik, J. (1980). A model of speech perception. *Psychological Review, 81,* 348–374.

Coleman, R. M. (1986). *Wide awake at 3:00 A.M.* New York: Freeman.

Collier, G., Minton, H. L., & Reynolds, G. (1991). *Currents of thought in American social psychology.* New York: Oxford University Press.

Collins, A. M., & Loftus, E. F. (1975). A spreading-activation theory of semantic memory. *Psychological Review, 82,* 407–428.

Collins, P. H. (1987, Fall). The meaning of motherhood in Black culture and Black mother/daughter relationships. *Sage, 4,* 3–9.

Collins, W. A., & Gunnar, M. R. (1990). Social and personality development. *Annual Review of Psychology, 41,* 387–416.

Colt, G. H. (1991). *The enigma of suicide.* New York: Summit.

Colwill, R. M., & Rescorla, R. A. (1990). Evidence for the hierarchical structure of instrumental learning. *Animal Learning & Behavior, 18,* 71–82.

Comas-Díaz, L. (1989). Culturally relevant issues and treatment implications for Hispanics. In D. R. Koslow & E. P. Salet (Eds.), *Crossing cultures in mental health* (pp. 31–48). Washington, DC: SIETAR International.

Comas-Díaz, L., & Griffith, E. (1988). Introduction: On culture and psychotherapeutic care. In L. Comas-Díaz & E. Griffith (Eds.), *Clinical guidelines in cross-cultural mental health* (pp. 1–32). New York: Wiley.

Coming clean. (1992, September 21). *Newsweek,* p. 6.

The Commission on the Prevention of Mental-Emotional Disabilities. (1987a). A framework for prevention. *The Journal of Primary Prevention, 7,* 199–203.

The Commission on the Prevention of Mental-Emotional Disabilities. (1987b). Adulthood. *The Journal of Primary Prevention, 7,* 215–218.

Committee on the Use of Animals in Research (1991). *Science, medicine, and animals.* Washington, DC: National Academy Press.

Compas, B. E. (1987). Coping with stress during childhood and adolescence. *Psychological Bulletin, 101,* 393–403.

Comstock, G., & Paik, H. (1991). *Television and the American child.* San Diego: Academic Press.

Condry, J. (1989). *The psychology of television.* Hillsdale, NJ: Erlbaum.

Condry, J.C., & Condry, S. (1976). Sex differences: A study of the eye of the beholder. *Child Development, 47,* 812–819.

Connidis, I. A., & Davies, L. (1990). Confidants and companions in later life: The place of family and friends. *Journal of Gerontology: Social Sciences, 45,* S141–S149.

Connidis, I. A., & Davies, L. (1992). Confidants and companions: Choices in later life. *Journal of Gerontology: Social Sciences, 47,* S115–S122.

Cook, M., (1988). Person perception. In G. M. Breakwell, H. Foot, & R. Gilmour (Eds.), *Doing social psychology* (pp. 185–201). Cambridge, England: Cambridge University Press.

Cook, M., Mineka, S., Wolkenstein, B., & Laitsch, K. (1985). Observational conditioning of snake fears in unrelated rhesus monkeys. *Journal of Abnormal Psychology, 95,* 195–207.

Cooper, J., & Fazio, R. H. (1984). A new look at dissonance theory. *Advances in Experimental Social Psychology, 17,* 229–266.

Cooper, L. A., & Shepard, R. N. (1984). Turning something over in the mind. *Scientific American, 251*(6), 106–114.

Cooper, W. E., Tye-Murray, N., & Eady, S. J. (1985). Acoustical cues to the reconstruction of missing words in speech perception. *Perception & Psychophysics, 38,* 30–40.

Corballis, M. C. (1983). *Human laterality.* New York: Academic Press.

Corballis, M. C. (1988). Recognition of disoriented shapes. *Psychological Review, 95,* 115–123.

Coren, S. (1981). The interaction between eye movements and visual illusions. In D. F. Fisher, R. A. Monty, & J. W. Senders (Eds.), *Eye movements: Cognition and visual perception.* Hillsdale, NJ: Erlbaum.

Coren, S., & Girgus, J. S. (1978). *Seeing is deceiving: The psychology of visual illusions.* Hillsdale, NJ: Erlbaum.

Coren, S., & Porac, C. (1983). Subjective contours and apparent depth: A direct test. *Perception & Psychophysics, 33,* 197–200.

Coren, S., & Porac, C. (1987). Individual differences in visual-geometric illusions: Predictions from measures of spatial cognitive abilities. *Perception & Psychophysics, 41,* 211–219.

Coren, S., Ward, L. M., & Enns, J. T. (1994). *Sensation and perception* (4th ed.). Fort Worth, TX: Harcourt Brace & Company.

Corsini, R. J. (1989). Introduction. In R. J. Corsini & D. Wedding (Eds.), *Current psychotherapies* (4th ed., pp. 1–16). Itasca, Il: Peacock.

Costa, P. T., Jr., & McCrae, R. R. (1992a). Four ways five factors are basic. *Personality and Individual Differences, 13,* 653–665.

Costa, P. T., Jr., & McCrae, R. R. (1992b). Normal personality assessment in clinical practice: The NEO Personality Inventory. *Psychological Assessment, 4,* 5–13.

Costa, P. T., Jr., Zonderman, A. B., McCrae, R. R., Cornoni-Huntley, J., Locke, B. Z., & Barbano, H. E. (1987). Longitudinal analyses of psychological well-being in a national sample: Stability of mean levels. *Journal of Gerontology, 42,* 50–55.

Costantino, G. (1992). Overcoming bias in educational assessment of Hispanic students. In K. F. Geisinger (Ed.), *Psychological testing of Hispanics* (pp. 89–97). Washington, DC: American Psychological Association.

Costantino, G., Malgady, R. G., Casullo, M. M., & Castillo, A. (1991). Cross-cultural standardization of TEMAS in three Hispanic subcultures. *Hispanic Journal of Behavioral Sciences, 13,* 48–62.

Costantino, G., Malgady, R. G., & Rogler, L. H. (1986). Cuento therapy: A culturally sensitive modality for Puerto Rican children. *Journal of Consulting and Clinical Psychology, 54,* 639–645.

Costantino, G., Malgady, R. G., & Rogler, L. H. (1993). Storytelling Through Pictures: Culturally sensitive psychotherapy for Hispanic children and adolescents. *Journal of Clinical Child Psychology, 23,* 13–20.

Costantino, G., Malgady, R. G., Rogler, L. H., & Tsui, E. C. (1988). Discriminant analysis of clinical outpatients and public school children by TEMAS: A Thematic Apperception Test for Hispanics and Blacks. *Journal of Personality Assessment, 52,* 670–678.

Cotman, C. W., & Lynch, G. S. (1990). The neurobiology of learning and memory. In P. D. Eimas &

A. M. Galaburda (Eds.), *Neurobiology of cognition* (pp. 201–241). Cambridge, MA: MIT Press.

Cotton, R. (1990). Is there still too much extrapolation from data on middle-aged white men? *JAMA, 263,* 1049–1055.

Coursey, R. D., Ward-Alexander, L., & Katz, B. (1990). Cost-effectiveness of providing insurance benefits for posthospital psychiatric halfway house stays. *American Psychologist, 45,* 1118–1126.

Cowan, G., & Hoffman, C. D. (1986). Gender stereotyping in young children: Evidence to support a concept-learning approach. *Sex Roles, 14,* 11–224.

Cowan, M. L., & Stewart, B. J. (1977). A methodological study of sex stereotypes. *Sex Roles, 3,* 205–216.

Cowan, N. (1984). On short and long auditory stores. *Psychological Bulletin, 96,* 341–370.

Cowan, N. (1988). Evolving conceptions of memory storage, selective attention, and their mutual constraints within the human information-processing system. *Psychological Bulletin, 104,* 163–191.

Cowley, G. (1991, August 19). Sweet dreams or nightmare? *Newsweek,* pp. 44–51.

Cowley, G. (1992, June 29). Poison at home and at work. *Newsweek,* p. 55.

Cowley, G., Kahn, J., & Downey, V. (1992, May 18). Live longer with vitamin C. *Newsweek,* p. 60.

Cox, M. J., Owen, M. T., Henderson, V. K., & Margand, N. A. (1992). Prediction of infant-father and infant-mother attachment. *Developmental Psychology, 28,* 474–483.

Coyne, J. C., & Downey, G. (1991). Social factors and psychopathology: Stress, social support, and coping processes. *Annual Review of Psychology, 42,* 401–425.

Coyne, J. C., Kahn, J., & Gotlib, I. H. (1987). Depression. In T. Jacob (Ed.), *Family interaction and psychopathology* (pp. 509–533). New York: Plenum.

Craik, F. I. M (1977). Depth of processing in recall and recognition. In S. Dornic (Ed.), *Attention and performance* (Vol. 6). Hillsdale, NJ: Erlbaum.

Craik, F. I. M. (1990). Changes in memory with normal aging: A functional view. In R. J. Wurtman (Ed.), *Advances in Neurology, Vol. 51: Alzheimer's Disease* (pp. 201–205). New York: Raven Press.

Craik, F. I. M. (1992). Memory changes in normal aging. In R. Kostavic, S. Knezevic, H. Wisniewski, & G. Spilich (Eds.), *Neurodevelopment, aging and cognition.* Boston: Birkhauser.

Craik, F. I. M., Byrd, M., & Swanson, J. M. (1987). Patterns of memory loss in three elderly samples. *Psychology and Aging, 2,* 79–86.

Craik, F. I. M., & Lockhart, R. S. (1972). Levels of processing: A framework for memory research. *Journal of Verbal Learning and Verbal Behavior, 11,* 671–684.

Craik, F. I. M., & Lockhart, R. S. (1986). CHARM is not enough: Comments on Eich's model of cued recall. *Psychological Review, 93,* 360–364.

Craik, K. H., Hogan, R., & Wolfe, R. N. (Eds.). (1993). *Fifty years of personality psychology.* New York: Plenum.

Cramer, D. (1986). Gay parents and their children: A review of research and practical implications. *Journal of Counseling and Development, 64,* 504–507.

Crandall, C. S. (1984). The overcitation of examples of poor performance: Fad, fashion, or fun? *American Psychologist, 39,* 1499.

Crew, J. C. (1982). An assessment of needs among black business majors. *Psychology, 19,* 18–22.

Crider, A. (1991). Motor disturbances in schizophrenia. *Behavioral and Brain Sciences, 14,* 22–23.

Crocker, J., Thompson, L. L., McGraw, K. M., & Ingerman, C. (1987). Downward comparison, prejudice, and evaluation of others: Effects of self-esteem and threat. *Journal of Personality and Social Psychology, 52,* 907–916.

Crook, C. (1987). Taste and olfaction. In P. Salapatek & L. Cohen (Eds.), *Handbook of infant perception* (Vol. 1, pp. 237–264). Orlando, FL: Academic.

Cross, S., & Markus, H. (1991). Possible selves across the life span. *Human Development, 34,* 230–255.

Cross-National Collaborative Group. (1992). The changing rate of major depression: Cross-national comparisons. *JAMA, 268,* 3098–3105.

Crovitz, H. F., & Daniel, W. F. (1984). Measurements of everyday memory: Toward the prevention of forgetting. *Bulletin of the Psychonomic Society, 22,* 413–414.

Crowder, R. G. (1982). Decay of auditory memory in vowel discrimination. *Journal of Experimental Psychology: Learning, Memory, and Cognition, 8,* 153–162.

Crowder, R. G., & Wagner, R. K. (1992). *The psychology of reading: An introduction* (2nd ed.). New York: Oxford University Press.

Crowe, R. R. (1991). Genetic studies of anxiety disorders. In M. T. Tsuang, K. S. Kendler, & M. J. Lyons (Eds.), *Genetic issues in psychosocial epidemiology* (pp. 175–190). New Brunswick, NJ: Rutgers University Press.

Croyle, R. T., & Cooper, J. (1983). Dissonance arousal: Physiological evidence. *Journal of Personality and Social Psychology, 45,* 782–791.

Curtiss, S. (1977). *Genie: A psycholinguistic study of a modern-day "wild child."* New York: Academic.

Culter, A. (1987). Speaking for listening. In A. Allport, D. MacKay, W. Prinz, & E. Scheerer (Eds.), *Language perception and production* (pp. 24–40). London: Academic Press.

Cutting, J. E. (1983). Perceiving and recovering structure from events. In SIGGRAPH/SIGART Interdisciplinary Workshop (Ed.), *Motion: Representation and perception.* New York: Association for Computing Machinery.

Czeisler, C. A., Johnson, M. P., Duffy, J. F., Brown, E. N., Ronda, J. M., & Kronauer, R. E. (1990). Exposure to bright light and darkness to treat physiological maladaptation to night work. *New England Journal of Medicine, 322,* 1253–1260.

Czeisler, C. A., Kronauer, R. E., Allan, J. S., Duffy, J. F., Jewett, M. E., Brown, E. N., & Ronda, J. M. (1989). Bright light induction of strong (Type O) resetting of the human circadian pacemaker. *Science, 244,* 1328–1333.

Dana, R. H. (1988). Culturally diverse groups and MMPI interpretation. *Professional Psychology: Research & Practice, 19,* 490–495.

Daniel, W. F., Crovitz, H. F., & Weiner, R. D. (1987). Neuropsychological aspects of disorientation. *Cortex, 23,* 169–187.

Dannemiller, J. L., & Stephens, B. R. (1988). A critical test of infant pattern preference models. *Child Development, 59,* 210–216.

Danziger, K. (1990). *Constructing the subject: Historical origins of psychological research.* Cambridge, England: Cambridge University Press.

Darley, J. M., & Batson, C. D. (1973). From Jerusalem to Jericho: A study of situational and dispositional variables in helping behavior. *Journal of*

Personality and Social Psychology, 27, 269–275.

Darley, J. M., & Gross, P. H. (1983). A hypothesis-confirming bias in labeling effects. *Journal of Personality and Social Psychology, 44,* 20–33.

Darley, J. M., & Shultz, T. R. (1990). Moral judgments: Their content and acquisition. *Annual Review of Psychology, 41,* 525–556.

Dartnall, H. J. A., Bowmaker, J. J., & Mollon, J. D. (1983). Microspectrophotometry of human photoreceptors. In J. D. Mollon & L. T. Sharpe (Eds.), *Color vision* (pp. 69–80). London: Academic.

Darwin, C. J., Turvey, M. T., & Crowder, R. G. (1972). An auditory analogue of the Sperling partial report procedure: Evidence for brief auditory storage. *Cognitive Psychology, 3,* 255–267.

Datan, N., Rodeheaver, D. & Hughes, F. (1987). Adult development and aging. *Annual Review of Psychology, 38,* 153–180.

Davidoff, J. (1991). *Cognition through color.* Cambridge, MA: MIT Press.

Davidson, A. R., Yantis, S., Norwood, M., & Montano, D. E. (1985). Amount of information about the attitude object and attitude-behavior consistency. *Journal of Personality and Social Psychology, 49,* 1184–1198.

Davidson, L. M., & Baum, A. (1990). Posttraumatic stress in children following natural and human-made trauma. In M. Lewis & S. M. Miller (Eds.), *Handbook of developmental psychopathology* (pp. 251–259). New York: Plenum.

Davidson, R. J., Ekman, P., Saron, C. D., Senulis, J. A., & Friesen, W. V. (1990). Approach-withdrawal and cerebral asymmetry: Emotional expression and brain physiology I. *Journal of Personality and Social Psychology, 58,* 330–341.

Davis, G. A., & Rimm, S. B. (1989). *Education of the gifted and talented* (2nd ed.). Englewood Cliffs, NJ: Prentice-Hall.

Davis, K. L., Thal, L. J., Gamzu, E. R., Davis, C. S., Woolson, R. F., Gracon, S. I., Drachman, D. A., Schneider, L. S., Whitehouse, P. J., Hoover, T. M., Morris, J. C., Kawas, C. H., Knopman, D. S., Earl, N. L., Kumar, V., Doody, R. S., and the Tacrine Collaborative Study Group. (1992). A double-blind, placebo-controlled multicenter study of tacrine for Alzheimer's disease. *The New England Journal of Medicine, 327,* 1253–1259.

Davis, P., & Schwartz, G. (1987). Repression and the inaccessibility of affective memories. *Journal of Personality and Social Psychology, 52,* 155–162.

Davis, P. W., & Solomon, E. P. (1986). *The world of biology* (3rd ed.). Philadelphia: Saunders.

Davis, R. H., & Davis, J. A. (1985). *TV's image of the elderly.* Lexington, MA: Lexington Books.

Davison, G. C., & Neale, J. M. (1990). *Abnormal psychology* (5th ed.). New York: Wiley.

Dawes, R. M. (1988). *Rational choice in an uncertain world.* San Diego: Harcourt Brace Jovanovich.

Day, A. T. (1991). *Remarkable survivors: Insights into successful aging among women.* Washington, DC: Urban Institute Press.

Day, R. H. (1987). Visual size constancy in infancy. In B. E. McKenzie & R. H. Day (Eds.), *Perceptual development in early infancy* (pp. 67–91). London: Erlbaum.

DeAngelis, T. (1993, March). Law helps American Indians enter field. *APA Monitor,* pp. 26–27.

Deaux, K. (1985). Sex and gender. *Annual Review of Psychology, 36,* 49–81.

Deaux, K., & Major, B. (1987). Putting gender into context: An interactive model of gender-related behavior. *Psychological Review, 94,* 369–389.

Deaux, K., & Wrightsman, L. S. (1988). *Social psy-*

chology (5th ed.). Pacific Grove, CA: Brooks/Cole.

De Blesser, R. (1988). Localisation of aphasia: Science or fiction. In G. Denes, C. Semenza, & P. Bisiacchi (Eds.). *Perspectives on cognitive neuropsychology* (pp. 161–185). Hove, England: Erlbaum.

DeBono, K. G., & Harnish, R. J. (1988). Source expertise, source attractiveness, and the processing of persuasive information: A functional approach. *Journal of Personality and Social Psychology, 55,* 541–546.

DeCarvalho, R. J. (1991). *The founders of humanistic psychology.* New York: Praeger.

DeCasper, A. J., & Spence, M. J. (1986). Prenatal maternal speech influences newborns' perception of speech sounds. *Infant Behavior and Development, 9,* 133–150.

Deci, E. L. (1971). Effects of externally mediated rewards on intrinsic motivation. *Journal of Personality and Social Psychology, 18,* 105–115.

Deci, E. L., & Ryan, R. M. (1985). *Intrinsic motivation and self-determination in human behavior.* New York: Plenum.

Deci, E. L., & Ryan, R. M. (1987). The support of autonomy and the control of behavior. *Journal of Personality and Social Psychology, 53,* 1024–1037.

Deci, E. L., & Ryan, R. M. (1990). A motivational approach to self: Integration in personality. *Nebraska Symposium on Motivation, 38,* 237–288.

DeFries, J. C., Plomin, R., & LaBuda, M. C. (1987). Genetic stability of cognitive development from childhood to adulthood. *Developmental Psychology, 23,* 4–12.

de Groot, A. (1966). Perception and memory versus thought: Some old ideas and recent findings. In B. Kleinmuntz (Ed.), *Problem solving.* New York: Wiley.

DeHart, G. (1990). Personal communication.

Deikman, A. J. (1966). Deautomatization and the mystic experience. *Psychiatry, 29,* 324–338.

Delay, J., & Deniker, P. (1952). *Trente huit-cas de psychoses traitees par la cure prolongee et continue de 4560 RP.* Paris: Masson et Cie.

DelGiudice, G. T. (1986). The relationship between sibling jealousy and presence at a sibling's birth. *Birth, 13,* 250–254.

Dell, G. S. (1986). A spreading-activation theory of retrieval in sentence production. *Psychological Review, 93,* 283–321.

Dell, G. S. (1988). The retrieval of phonological forms in production: Tests of predictions from a connectionist model. *Journal of Memory and Language, 27,* 124–142.

Dell, G. S., & Brown, P. M. (1991). Mechanisms for listener-adaptation in language production: Limiting the role of the "model of the listener." In D. J. Napoli & J. A. Kegl (Eds.), *Bridges between psychology and linguistics: A Swarthmore Festschrift for Lila Gleitman* (pp. 105–129). Hillsdale, NJ: Erlbaum.

DeLongis, A., Coyne, J. C., Dakof, G., Folkman, S., & Lazarus, R. S. (1982). Relationship of daily hassles, uplifts, and major life events to health status. *Health Psychology, 1,* 119–136.

DeLongis, A., Folkman, S., & Lazarus, R. S. (1988). The impact of daily stress on health and mood: Psychological and social resources as mediators. *Journal of Personality and Social Psychology, 54,* 486–495.

Dember, W. N. (1990). William James on sensation and perception. *Psychological Science, 1,* 163–166.

Dembroski, T. M., Macdougall, J. M., Costa, P. T., &

Grandits, G. A. (1989). Components of hostility as predictors of sudden death and myocardial infarction in the Multiple Risk Factor Intervention Trial. *Psychosomatic Medicine, 51,* 514–522.

Dement, W. C. (1986). Normal sleep, disturbed sleep, transient and persistent insomnia. *Acta Psychiatrica Scandinavica, 74,* 41–46.

deMoor, C., Elder, J. P., Young, R. L., Wildey, M. B., & Molgaard, C. A. (1989). Generic tobacco use among four ethnic groups in a school age population. *Journal of Drug Education, 19,* 257–270.

Demos, V., & Jache, A. (1981). When you care enough: An analysis of attitudes toward aging in humorous birthday cards. *Gerontologist, 21,* 209–215.

DeMott, D. W. (1987). *Peacebuilding: A textbook* (2nd ed.). Geneseo, NY: High Falls Publications.

Dempster, F. N. (1981). Memory span: Sources of individual and developmental differences. *Psychological Bulletin, 89,* 63–100.

Dempster, F. N. (1988). The spacing effect: A case study in the failure to apply the results of psychological research. *American Psychologist, 43,* 627–634.

Denmark, F., Russo, N. F., Frieze, I. H., & Sechzer, J. A. (1988). Guidelines for avoiding sexism in psychological research: A report of the Ad Hoc Committee on Nonsexist Research. *American Psychologist, 43,* 582–585.

Dennett, D. (1991). *Consciousness explained.* Boston: Little Brown.

Dennis, D. L., Buckner, J. C., Lipton, F. R., & Levine, I. S. (1991). A decade of research and services for homeless mentally ill persons: Where do we stand? *American Psychologist, 46,* 1129–1138.

Depue, R. A., & Monroe, S. M. (1986). Conceptualization and measurement of human disorder in life stress research: The problem of chronic disturbance. *Psychological Bulletin, 99,* 36–51.

DeRenzi, E. (1986). Current issues in prosopagnosia. In H. D. Ellis, M. A. Jeeves, F. Newcombe, & A. Young (Eds.), *Aspects of face processing.* Dordrecht: Martinus Nijhoff.

Derryberry, D., & Tucker, D. M. (1992). Neural mechanisms of emotion. *Journal of Consulting and Clinical Psychology, 60,* 329–338.

Desforges, D. M., Lord, C. G., Ramsey, S. L., Mason, J. A., Van Leeuwen, M. D., West, S. C., & Lepper, M. R. (1991). Effects of structured cooperative contact on changing negative attitudes toward stigmatized social groups. *Journal of Personality and Social Psychology, 60,* 531–544.

Desimone, R., Albright, T. D. Gross, C. G., & Bruce, C. (1984). Stimulus selective properties of inferior temporal neurons in the macaque. *Journal of Neuroscience, 4,* 2051–2062.

Des Jarlais, D. C., & Friedman, S. R. (1988). The psychology of preventing AIDS among intravenous drug users: A social learning conceptualization. *American Psychologist, 43,* 865–870.

Desor, J. A., & Beauchamp, G. K. (1974). The human capacity to transmit olfactory information. *Perception & Psychophysics, 16,* 551–556.

Desor, J. A., Maller, O., & Greene, L. S. (1977). Preference for sweet in humans: Infants, children and adults. In J. M. Weiffenbach (Ed.), *Taste and development: The genesis of sweet preference.* Bethesda, MD: U.S. Department of Health, Education and Welfare.

DeSpelder, L. A., & Strickland, A. L. (1987). *The last dance: Encountering death and dying* (2nd ed.). Palo Alto, CA: Mayfield.

Deutsch, D. (1992, August). Paradoxes of musical

pitch. *Scientific American, 267*, 88–95.

Deutsch, M. (1983). The prevention of World War III: A psychological perspective. *Political Psychology, 4*, 3–31.

Deutsch, M. (1993). Educating for a peaceful world. *American Psychologist, 48*, 510–517.

Deutsch, M., & Collins, M. E. (1951). *Interracial housing: A psychological evaluation of a social experiment.* Minneapolis: University of Minnesota Press.

Deutsch, M., & Shichman, S. (1986). Conflict: A social psychological perspective. In M. Hermann (Ed.), *Political psychology* (pp. 219–250). San Francisco: Jossey-Bass.

de Villiers, J. G., & de Villiers, P. A. (1985). The acquisition of English. In D. I. Slobin (Ed.), *The crosslinguistic study of language acquisition* (Vol. 1, pp. 27–139). Hillsdale, NJ: Erlbaum.

Devine, P. G., & Monteith, M. J. (1993). The role of discrepancy associated affect in prejudice reduction. In D. M. Mackie & D. L. Hamilton (Eds.), *Affect, cognition, and stereotyping: Interactive processes in intergroup perception.* Orlando, FL: Academic Press.

Devine, P. G., Monteith, M. J., Zuwerink, J. R., & Elliot, A. J. (1991). Prejudice with and without compunction. *Journal of Personality and Social Psychology, 60*, 817–830.

Dey, E. L., Astin, A. W., Korn, W. S., & Riggs, E. R. (1992). *The American freshman: National norms for Fall 1992.* Los Angeles: Higher Education Research Institute, UCLA.

Diamond, J. B. (1991). Inner strength: Being African and American. In D. Schoem (Ed.), *Inside separate worlds: Life stories of young Blacks, Jews, and Latinos* (pp. 181–202). Ann Arbor: University of Michigan Press.

Diaz, R. M. (1985). Bilingual cognitive development: Addressing three gaps in current research. *Child Development, 56*, 1376–1388.

Diener, E. (1984). Subjective well-being. *Psychological Bulletin, 95*, 542–575.

Diener, E., & Diener, C. (1993). *Most people in the United States are happy and satisfied.* Unpublished manuscript.

Diener, E., Sandvik, E., Seidlits, L., & Diener, M. (1993). The relationship between income and subjective well-being: Relative or absolute? *Social Indicators Research, 28*, 195–223.

DiLalla, L. F., & Gottesman, I. I. (1991). Biological and genetic contributions to violence—Widom's untold tale. *Psychological Bulletin, 109*, 125–129.

Dillman, D. A. (1991). The design and administration of mail surveys. *Annual Review of Sociology, 17*, 225–249.

Dingman, J. M. (1990). Personality structure: Emergence of the five-factor model. *Annual Review of Psychology, 41*, 417–440.

Dion, K. K. (1986). Stereotyping based on physical attractiveness: Issues and conceptual perspectives. In C. P. Herman, M. P. Zanna, & E. T. Higgins (Eds.), *Physical appearance, stigma, and social behavior: The Ontario Symposium* (Vol. 3, pp. 7–21). Hillsdale, NJ: Erlbaum.

Dittmann, A. T. (1987). The role of body movement in communication. In A. W. Siegman & S. Feldstein (Eds.), *Nonverbal behavior and communication* (2nd ed., pp. 37–64). Hillsdale, NJ: Erlbaum.

Division of HIV/AIDS Epidemiology. (1993, October). Quarterly Surveillance Update: AIDS in Canada. Ottawa, Canada: Author.

Doane, J. A., Kiklowitz, D. J., Oranchak, E., Apondaca,

R. F., Karno, M., Strachan, A. M., & Jenkins, J. H. (1989). Parental communication deviance and schizophrenia: A cross-cultural comparison of Mexican- and Anglo-Americans. *Journal of Abnormal Psychology, 98*, 487–490.

Dobson, K. S. (1989). A meta-analysis of the efficacy of cognitive therapy for depression. *Journal of Consulting and Clinical Psychology, 57*, 414–419.

Dobson, K. S., & Block, L. (1988). Historical and philosophical bases of the cognitive-behavioral therapies. In K. S. Dobson (Ed.), *Handbook of cognitive-behavioral therapies* (pp. 3–38). New York: Guilford.

Dodge, S. (1989, December 13). Rutgers panel outlines ways to fight homophobia. *The Chronicle of Higher Education*, p. A51.

Dodge, S. (1992, April 15). Colleges are trying ways to enhance academic advising. *The Chronicle of Higher Education*, pp. A41–A42.

Doescher, S. M., & Sugawara, A. I. (1990). Sex role flexibility and prosocial behavior among preschool children. *Sex Roles, 22*, 111–123.

Dollard, J., Doob, L. W., Miller, N. E., Mowrer, O. H., & Sears, R. R. (1939). *Frustration and aggression.* New Haven, CT: Yale University Press.

Domjan, M. (1987). Animal learning comes of age. *American Psychologist, 42*, 556–564.

Domjan, M. (1989). Personal communication.

Domjan, M. (1993). *The principles of learning and behavior* (3rd ed.). Pacific Grove, CA: Books/Cole.

Domjan, M., & Burkhard, B. (1986). *The principles of learning and behavior* (2nd edition). Pacific Grove, CA: Brooks/Cole.

Domjan, W. (1993). Personal communication.

Donnerstein, E., & Linz, D. (1984, January). Sexual violence in the media: A warning. *Psychology Today*, pp. 14–15.

Donnerstein, E., Linz, D., & Penrod, S. (1987). *The question of pornography.* New York: Free Press.

Doren, D. M. (1987). *Understanding and treating the psychopath.* New York: Wiley.

Dourish, C. T., Rycroft, W., & Iversen, S. D. (1989). Postponement of satiety by blockade of brain cholecystokinin (CCK-B) receptors. *Science, 245*, 1509–1511.

Douthitt, R. A. (1989). The division of labor within the home: Have gender roles changed? *Sex Roles, 20*, 693–704.

Dovidio, J. F. (1984). Helping behavior and altruism: An empirical and conceptual overview. In L. Berkowitz (Ed.), *Advances in experimental social psychology, 17*, 362–427.

Dovidio, J. F., Evans, N., & Tyler, R. B. (1986). Racial stereotypes: The contents of their cognitive representations. *Journal of Experimental Social Psychology, 22*, 22–37.

Dowd, M. (1984, March 12). Twenty years after the murder of Kitty Genovese, the question remains: Why? *New York Times*, pp. B1, B4.

Dreher, G. F., Dougherty, T. W., & Whitely, W. (1989). Influence tactics and salary attainment: A gender-specific analysis. *Sex Roles, 20*, 535–550.

Dryden, W., & Ellis, A. (1987). Rational-Emotive Therapy (RET). In W. Dryden & W. L. Golden (Eds.), *Cognitive-behavioural approaches to psychotherapy* (pp. 129–168). Cambridge, England: Hemisphere.

Dubbert, P. M. (1992). Exercise in behavioral medicine. *Journal of Consulting and Clinical Psychology, 60*, 613–618.

Duck, S. (1991). *Understanding relationships.* New York: Guilford.

Duck, S., & Miell, D. (1986). Charting the development of personal relationships. In R. Gilmour & S. Duck (Eds.), *The emerging field of personal relationships* (pp. 133–143). Hillsdale, NJ: Erlbaum.

Duckitt, J. (1992a). *The social psychology of prejudice.* New York: Praeger.

Duckitt, J. (1992b). Psychology and prejudice: A historical analysis and integrative framework. *American Psychologist, 47*, 1182–1193.

Dudycha, G. J. (1936). An objective study of punctuality in relation to personality and achievement. *Archives of Psychology, 204*, 1–319.

Dumas, J. (1990). *Report on the demographic situation in Canada 1990.* Ottawa: Statistics Canada.

Duncan, S., Jr., & Fiske, D. W. (1977). *Face-to-face interaction.* Hillsdale, NJ: Erlbaum.

Duncker, K. (1945). On problem solving. *Psychological Monographs, 58* (Whole No. 270).

Dunham, P., & Dunham, F. (1992). Lexical development during middle infancy: A mutually driven infant-caregiver process. *Developmental Psychology, 28*, 414–420.

Dunn, J. F. (1988). *The beginnings of social understanding.* Cambridge, MA: Harvard University Press.

Dunn, J. F. (1991). Sibling influences. In M. Lewis & S. Feinman (Eds.), *Social influences and socialization in infancy* (pp. 97–109). New York: Plenum.

Dunn, J. F., & Plomin, R. (1990). *Separate lives: Why siblings are so different.* New York: Basic Books.

Dunn, J. F., & Shatz, M. (1989). Becoming a conversationalist despite (or because of) having an older sibling. *Child Development, 60*, 399–410.

Dunn, L. M. (1987). *Bilingual Hispanic children on the U.S. mainland: A review of research on their cognitive, linguistic, and scholastic development.* Circle Pines, MN: American Guidance Service.

Durlak, J. A., Fuhrman, T., & Lampman, C. (1991). Effectiveness of cognitive-behavior therapy for maladapting children: A meta-analysis. *Psychological Bulletin, 110*, 204–214.

Dusek, D. E., & Girdano, D. A. (1987). *Drugs: A factual account* (4th ed.). New York: Random House.

Dush, D. M., Hirt, M. L., & Schroeder, H. (1983). Self-statement modification with adults: A meta-analysis. *Psychological Bulletin, 94*, 408–422.

Dworkin, S. H., & Gutiérrez, F. J. (Eds.). (1992). *Counseling gay men and lesbians: Journey to the end of the rainbow.* Alexandria, VA: American Association for Counseling and Development.

Dwyan, J., & Bowers, K. (1983). The use of hypnosis to enhance recall. *Science, 222*, 184–185.

Dziech, B. W., & Weiner, L. (1990). *The lecherous professor: Sexual harassment on campus* (2nd ed.). Urbana, IL: University of Illinois Press.

D'Zurilla, T. J., & Sheedy, C. F. (1991). Relation between social problem-solving ability and subsequent level of psychological stress in college students. *Journal of Personality and Social Psychology, 61*, 841–846.

Eagly, A. H. (1987). *Sex differences in social behavior: A social-role interpretation.* Hillsdale, NJ: Erlbaum.

Eagly, A. H. (1992). Uneven progress: Social psychology and the study of attitudes. *Journal of Personality and Social Psychology, 63*, 693–710.

Eagly, A. H., Ashmore, R. D., Makhijani, M. G., & Longo, L. C. (1991). What is beautiful is good, but . . . : A meta-analytic review of research on the physical attractiveness stereotype. *Psychological Bulletin, 110,* 109–128.

Eagly, A. H., & Carli, L. L. (1981). Sex of researchers and sex-typed communications as determinants of sex differences in influenceability: A meta-analysis of social influence studies. *Psychological Bulletin, 90,* 1–20.

Eagly, A. H., & Chaiken, S. (1993). *The psychology of attitudes.* Fort Worth, TX: Harcourt Brace Jovanovich.

Eagly, A. H. & Crowley, M. (1986). Gender and helping behavior: A meta-analytic review of the social psychological literature. *Psychological Bulletin, 100,* 283–308.

Eagly, A. H., & Steffen, V. J. (1986). Gender and aggressive behavior: A meta-analytic review of the social psychological literature. *Psychological Bulletin, 100,* 309–330.

Eaton, W. O., & Saudino, K. J. (1992). Prenatal activity level as a temperament dimension? Individual differences and developmental functions in fetal movement. *Infant Behavior and Development, 15,* 57–70.

Eaves, G., & Rush, A. J. (1984). Cognitive patterns in symptomatic and remitted unipolar depression. *Journal of Abnormal Psychology, 93,* 31–40.

Ebbinghaus, H. (1885). *Über das Gedachtnis.* Leipzig: Duncker & Humblot.

Eccles, J. S. (1989). Bringing young women to math and science. In M. Crawford & M. Gentry (Eds.), *Gender and thought* (pp. 36–58). New York: Springer-Verlag.

Eckenrode, J. (1984). Impact of chronic and acute stressors on daily reports of mood. *Journal of Personality and Social Psychology, 46,* 907–918.

Edelman, M. W. (1993). *The measure of our success: A letter to my children and yours.* New York: HarperCollins.

Eich, E. (1985). Context, memory, and integrated item/context imagery. *Journal of Experimental Psychology: Learning, Memory, and Cognition, 11,* 764–770.

Eimas, P. D., Siqueland, E. R., Jusczyk, R., & Vigorito, J. (1971). Speech perception in infants. *Science, 171,* 303–306.

Eisenberg, N. (1993). Does true altruism exist? [Review of *The altruism question: Toward a social-psychological answer*]. *Contemporary Psychology, 38,* 350–351.

Eisenberg, N., & Lennon, R. (1983). Sex differences in empathy and related capacities. *Psychological Bulletin, 94,* 100–131.

Eisenberg, N., & Miller, P. A. (1987). The relation of empathy in prosocial and related behaviors. *Psychological Bulletin, 101,* 91–119.

Eisenberg, N., & Mussen, P. H. (1989). *The roots of prosocial behavior in children.* New York: Cambridge University Press.

Ekman, P. (1973). Cross-cultural studies of facial expression. In P. Ekman (Ed.), *Darwin and facial expression* (pp. 169–222). New York: Academic.

Ekman, P. (1976, Summer). Nonverbal communication/Movements with precise meaning. *Journal of Communication, 26,* 13–26.

Ekman, P. (1984). Expression and the nature of emotion. In K. R. Scherer & P. Ekman (Eds.), *Approaches to emotion* (pp. 319–343). Hillsdale, NJ: Erlbaum.

Ekman, P. (1985). *Telling lies: Clues to deceit in the marketplace, politics, and marriage.* New York: Norton.

Ekman, P. (1993). Facial expression and emotion.

American Psychologist, 48, 384–392.

Ekman, P., Davidson, R. J., & Friesen, W. V. (1990). The Duchenne smile: Emotional expression and brain physiology, II. *Journal of Personality and Social Psychology, 58,* 342–353.

Ekman, P., & Friesen, W. V. (1969). The repertoire of nonverbal behavior: Categories, origins, usage, and coding. *Semiotica, 1,* 49–98.

Ekman, P., & Friesen, W. V. (1971). Constants across cultures in the face and emotion. *Journal of Personality and Social Psychology, 17,* 124–129.

Ekman, P., Friesen, W. V., O'Sullivan, M., Chan, A., Diacoyanni-Tarlatzis, I., Heider, K., Krause, R., LeCompte, W. A., Pitcairn, T., Ricci-Bitti, P. E., Scherer, K., Tomita, M., & Tzavaras, A. (1987). Universals and cultural differences in the judgments of facial expressions of emotion. *Journal of Personality and Social Psychology, 53,* 712–717.

Ekman, P., Levenson, R. W., & Friesen, W. V. (1983). Autonomic nervous system activity distinguishes among emotions. *Science, 221,* 1208–1210.

Ekman, P., & O'Sullivan, M. (1991). Who can catch a liar? *American Psychologist, 46,* 913–920.

Eliany, M. (1992, Autumn). Alcohol and drug consumption among Canadian Youth. *Canadian Social Trends,* pp. 10–13.

Eliany, M., Wortley, S., & Adlaf, E. (1992). *Alcohol and other drug use by Canadian Youth.* Toronto: Minister of Supply and Services Canada.

Elkin, I., Parloff, M. B., Hadley, S. W., & Autry, J. H. (1985). NIMH Treatment of Depression Research Program: Background and research plan. *Archives of General Psychiatry, 42,* 305–316.

Elkin, I., Shea, T., Watkins, J. T., Imber, S. D., Sotsky, S. M., Collins, J. F., Glass, D. R., Pilkonis, P. A., Leber, W. R., Docherty, J. P., Fiester, S. J., & Parloff, M. B. (1989). National Institute of Mental Health Treatment of Depression Collaborative Research Program: General effectiveness of treatments. *Archives of General Psychiatry, 46,* 971–982.

Elkind, D. (1981). *The hurried child: Growing up too fast too soon.* Reading, MA: Addison-Wesley.

Elkind, D. (1987). *Miseducation: Preschoolers at risk.* New York: Knopf.

Elliott, L. B. (1991). *The effects of divorce on the college population.* Paper presented at SUNY Geneseo.

Ellis, A. (1979). The practice of rational-emotive therapy. In A. Ellis & J. M. Whiteley (Eds.), *Theoretical and empirical foundations of rational-emotive therapy.* Monterey, CA: Brooks/Cole.

Ellis, A. (1986). Rational-emotive therapy. In I. L. Kutash & A. Wolf (Eds.), *Psychotherapist's casebook* (pp. 277–287). San Francisco: Jossey-Bass.

Ellis, A., & Harper, R. A. (1975). *A new guide to rational living.* North Hollywood, CA: Wilshire.

Ellis, H. C. (1987). Recent developments in human memory. In V. P. Makosky (Ed.), *G. Stanley Hall Lecture Series* (Vol. 7, pp. 161–206). Washington, DC: American Psychological Association.

Elms, A. C. (1993). Allport's *Personality* and Allport's personality. In K. H. Craik, R. Hogan, & R. N. Wolfe (Eds.), *Fifty years of personality psychology* (pp. 39–55). New York: Plenum.

Emler, N., Renwick, S., & Malone, B. (1983). The relationship between moral reasoning and political orientation. *Journal of Personality and Social Psychology, 45,* 1073–1080.

Emmelkamp, P. M. G., Bouman, T. K., & Scholing, A. (1992). *Anxiety disorders: A practitioner's guide.* Chichester, England: Wiley.

Empson, J. (1989). *Sleep and dreaming.* London: Faber and Faber.

Endler, N. S. (1982). *Holiday of darkness: A psychologist's personal journey out of his depression.* New York: Wiley.

Enemy images in Croatia and Serbia documented. (1992, Fall). *Psychologists for Social Responsibility Newsletter, 11*(3), p. 4.

Engen, T. (1987). Remembering odors and their names. *American Scientist, 75,* 497–503.

Engen, T. (1991). *Odor sensation and memory.* Westport, CT: Praeger.

Englander-Golden, P., Sonleitner, F. J., Whitmore, M. R., & Corbley, G. J. M. (1986). Social and menstrual cycles: Methodological and substantive findings. In V. L. Olesen & N. F. Woods (Eds.), *Culture, society and menstruation* (pp. 77–96). Washington, DC: Hemisphere.

Engle, R. W., Fidler, D. S., & Reynolds, L. H. (1981). Does echoic memory develop? *Journal of Experimental Child Psychology, 32,* 459–473.

Enns, C. Z. (1989). Toward teaching inclusive personality theories. *Teaching of Psychology, 16,* 111–117.

Epstein, R. (1991). Skinner, creativity, and the problem of spontaneous behavior. *Psychological Science, 2,* 362–370.

Epstein, S. (1983). Aggregation and beyond: Some basic issues on the prediction of behavior. *Journal of Personality, 51,* 360–392.

Epstein, S., & O'Brien, E. J. (1985). The person-situation debate in historical and current perspective. *Psychological Bulletin, 98,* 513–537.

Equal Employment Opportunity Commission. (1980). Guidelines on Discrimination Because of Sex. *Federal Register, 45,* 74676–74677.

Erens, P. B. (1987–1988). The stepfather. *Film Quarterly, 41*(2), 48–54.

Erickson, D. (1991, April). Love and terror: Is a chemical messenger key to treating Alzheimer's? *Scientific American, 264,* 148–150.

Erikson, E. H. (1950). *Childhood and society.* New York: Norton.

Erikson, E. H. (1968). *Identity: Youth and crisis.* New York: Norton.

Erikson, E. H., Erikson, J. M., & Kivnick, H. Q. (1986). *Vital involvement in old age.* New York: Norton.

Eron, L. D., & Huesmann, L. R. (1987). Television as a source of maltreatment of children. *School Psychology Review, 16,* 195–202.

Escobedo, L. G., Remington, P. L., & Anda, R. F. (1989). Long-term age-specific prevalence of cigarette smoking among Hispanics in the United States. *Journal of Psychoactive Drugs, 21,* 307–318.

Estes, W. K. (1991). Cognitive architectures from the standpoint of an experimental psychologist. *Annual Review of Psychology, 42,* 1–28.

Etaugh, C., & Malstrom, J. (1981). The effect of marital status on person perception. *Journal of Marriage and the Family, 43,* 801–805.

Eth, S., Randolph, E. T., & Brown, J. A. (1989). Post-traumatic stress disorder. In J. G. Howells (Ed.), *Modern perspectives in the psychiatry of the neuroses* (pp. 210–234). New York: Brunner/Mazel.

Evans, D. A., Funkenstein, H., Albert, M. S., Scherr, P. A., Cook, N. R., Chown, M. J., Herbert, L. E., Hennekens, C. H., & Taylor, J. O. (1989). Prevalence of Alzheimer's disease in a community population of older persons higher than previously reported. *JAMA, 262,* 2551–2556.

Evans, E. F. (1982). Basic physics and psychophysics of sound. In H. B. Barlow & J. D. Mollon (Eds.), *The senses* (pp. 239–250). Cambridge, England: Cambridge University Press.

Evans, R. B. (1990). William James and his *Principles.* In M. G. Johnson & T. B. Henley (Eds.), *Reflections on The Principles of Psychology: William James after a century* (pp. 11–31). Hillsdale, NJ: Erlbaum.

Evans, R. I. (1989). *Albert Bandura: The man and his ideas—A dialogue.* New York: Praeger.

Evans, R. I., Dratt, L. M., Raines, B. E., & Rosenberg, S. S. (1988). Social influences on smoking initiation: Importance of distinguishing descriptive versus mediating process variables. *Journal of Applied Social Psychology, 18,* 925–943.

Evans, R. I., Rozelle, R. M., Maxwell, S. E., Raines, B. E., Dill, C. A., Guthrie, T. J., Henderson, A. H., & Hill, P. C. (1981). Social modeling films to deter smoking in adolescents: Results of a three-year field investigation. *Journal of Applied Psychology, 66,* 399–414.

Evans, R. I., Smith, C. K., & Raines, B. E. (1984). Deterring cigarette smoking in adolescents: A psychosocial-behavioral analysis of an intervention strategy. In A. Baum, S. E. Taylor, & J. E. Singer (Eds.), *Handbook of psychology and health* (Vol. 4, pp. 301–318). Hillsdale, NJ: Erlbaum.

Everly, G. S., Jr. (1989). *A clinical guide to the treatment of the human stress response.* New York: Plenum.

Ewin, D. M. (1986). Hypnosis and pain management. In B. Zillbergelt, M. G. Edelstien, & D. L. Araoz (Eds.), *Hypnosis: Questions and answers* (pp. 282–288). New York: Norton.

Exner, J. E., Jr. (1991). *The Rorschach: A comprehensive system, Vol. 2: Interpretation* (2nd ed.). New York: Wiley.

Eysenck, H. J. (1952). The effects of psychotherapy: An evaluation. *Journal of Consulting Psychology, 16,* 319–324.

Eysenck, H. J. (1953). *The structure of human personality.* New York: Wiley.

Eysenck, H. J. (1970). *Readings in extraversion-introversion: Bearings on basic psychological processes* (Vol. 3). New York: Wiley.

Eysenck, H. J. (1975). *The inequality of man.* San Diego, CA: EDITS.

Eysenck, H. J. (1991). Behavioral psychotherapy. In C. E. Walker (Ed.), *Clinical psychology: Historical and research foundations* (pp. 417–442). New York: Plenum.

Eysenck, H. J. (1992). Four ways five factors are *not* basic. *Personality and Individual Differences, 13,* 667–673.

Eysenck, H. J., Wakefield, J. A., & Friedman, A. F. (1983). Diagnosis and clinical assessment: The DSM-III. *Annual Review of Psychology, 34,* 167–193.

Eysenck, M. W. (1990). *Happiness: Facts and myths.* Hillsdale, NJ: Erlbaum.

Eysenck, M. W. (1991). Creativity. In M. W. Eysenck (Ed.), *The Blackwell dictionary of cognitive psychology* (pp. 86–87). Oxford, England: Basil Blackwell.

Faden, R. R., Beauchamp, T. L., & King, N. M. P. (1986). *A history and theory of informed consent.* New York: Oxford University Press.

Fagan, J. F., III. (1992). Intelligence: A theoretical viewpoint. *Current Directions in Psychological Science, 1,* 82–86.

Fagot, B. I., & Leinbach, M. D. (1993). Gender-role development in young children: From discrimination to labeling. *Developmental Review, 13,* 205–224.

Fagot, B. I., Leinbach, M. D., & O'Boyle, C. (1992). Gender labeling, gender stereotyping, and parenting behaviors. *Developmental Psychology, 28,* 225–230.

Fairbairn, W. R. D. (1952). *Psychoanalytic studies of the personality.* London: Routledge & Kegan Paul.

Fancher, R. E. (1985). *The intelligence men: Makers of the IQ controversy.* New York: Norton.

Fantz, R. E. (1961). The origin of form perception. *Scientific American, 204*(5), 66–72.

Farah, M. J. (1988). Is visual imagery really visual? Overlooked evidence from neuropsychology. *Psychological Review, 95,* 307–317.

Farah, M. J. (1989). The neural basis of mental imagery. *Trends in Neuroscience, 12,* 395–399.

Farah, M. J. (1990). *Visual agnosia: Disorders of object recognition and what they tell us about normal vision.* Cambridge, MA: MIT Press.

Farah, M. J., McMullen, P. A., & Meyer, M. M. (1991). Can recognition of living things be selectively impaired? *Neuropsychologia, 29,* 185–193.

Farthing, G. W. (1992). *The psychology of consciousness.* Englewood Cliffs, NJ: Prentice-Hall.

Favreau, O. E. (1993). Do the Ns justify the means? Null hypothesis testing applied to sex and other differences. *Canadian Psychology/Psychologie canadienne, 34,* 64–78.

Fazio, R. H. Zanna, M. P., & Cooper, J. (1977). Dissonance and self-perception: An integrative view of each theory's proper domain of application. *Journal of Experimental Social Psychology, 13,* 464–479.

Feder, H. H. (1984). Hormones and sexual behavior. *Annual Review of Psychology, 35,* 165–200.

Feeney, D. M. (1987). Human rights and animal welfare. *American Psychologist, 42,* 593–599.

Fehr, B. (1988). Prototype analysis of the concepts of love and commitment. *Journal of Personality and Social Psychology, 55,* 557–579.

Fehr, B. (1993). How do I love thee . . . ? Let me consult my prototype. In S. Duck (Ed.), *Individuals in relationships.* Newbury Park, CA: Sage.

Fehr, B., & Russell, J. A. (1991). The concept of love viewed from a prototype perspective. *Journal of Personality and Social Psychology, 60,* 425–438.

Feingold, A. (1988a). Cognitive gender differences are disappearing. *American Psychologist, 43,* 95–103.

Feingold, A. (1988b). Matching for attractiveness in romantic partners and same-sex friends: A meta-analysis and theoretical critique. *Psychological Bulletin, 104,* 226–235.

Feldman, S. (1992, Spring). Children in crisis. *American Educator,* pp. 8–17, 46.

Fenichel, O. (1945). *The psychoanalytic theory of neurosis.* New York: Norton.

Fenson, L., Dale, P., Reznick, S., Thal, D., Bates, E., Hartung, J., Pethick, S., & Reilly, J. (1991). *The MacArthur Communicative Development Inventories: Technical manual.* San Diego: San Diego State University.

Fernald, A. (1991). Prosody in speech to children: Prelinguistic and linguistic functions. *Annals of Child Development, 8,* 43–80.

Fernald, A., & Mazzie, C. (1991). Prosody and focus in speech to infants and adults. *Developmental Psychology, 27,* 209–221.

Fernandez, E., & Turk, D. C. (1989). The utility of cognitive coping strategies for altering pain perception: A meta-analysis. *Pain, 38,* 123–135.

Fernandez, E., & Turk, D. C. (1992). Sensory and affective components of pain: Separation and synthesis. *Psychological Bulletin, 112,* 205–217.

Festinger, L. (1957). *A theory of cognitive dissonance.* Stanford, CA: Stanford University Press.

Festinger, L., & Carlsmith, J. M. (1959). Cognitive consequences of forced compliance. *Journal of Abnormal and Social Psychology, 58,* 203–210.

Festinger, L., Schachter, S., & Back, K. (1950). *Social pressures in informal groups: A study of human factors in housing.* New York: Harper.

Fetal alcohol syndrome. (1990, November). *The Harvard Mental Health Letter, 7*(5), 1–4.

Field, T. (1994). Quality infant daycare and grade school behavior and performance. *Child Development,* in press.

Fielding, J. (1985a). Smoking: Health effects and control, Part I. *New England Journal of Medicine, 313,* 491–498.

Fielding, J. (1985b). Smoking: Health effects and control, Part II. *New England Journal of Medicine, 313,* 555–561.

Fincham, F. D., & Bradbury, T. N. (1990). *The psychology of marriage: Basic issues and applications.* New York: Guilford.

Fincham, F. D., & Bradbury, T. N. (1992). Assessing attributions in marriage: The relationship attribution measure. *Journal of Personality and Social Psychology, 62,* 457–468.

Fine, M., & Gordon, S. M. (1989). Feminist transformations of/despite psychology. In M. Crawford & M. Gentry (Eds.), *Gender and thought* (pp. 146–174). New York: Springer-Verlag.

Finke, R. A. (1989). *Principles of mental imagery.* Cambridge, MA: MIT Press.

Finkelstein, N. W., & Haskins, R. (1983). Kindergarten children prefer same-color peers. *Child Development, 54,* 502–508.

Finn, K. L. (1991, Fall). Uncovering a hidden problem. *University of Michigan Medical Center Advance,* pp. 2–12.

Finucci, J. M., & Childs, B. (1981). Are there really more dyslexic boys than girls? In A Ansara, N. Geschwind, A. Galaburda, M. Albert, & N. Gartrell (Eds.), *Sex differences in dyslexia* (pp. 1–9). Towson, MD: Orton Dyslexia Society.

Fiore, M. C., Novotny, T. E., Pierce, J. P., Hatziandreu, E. J., Patel, K. M., & Davis, R. M. (1989). Trends in cigarette smoking in the United States: The changing influence of gender and race. *JAMA, 261,* 49–55.

Fischer, G. W., & Johnson, E. J. (1986). Behavioral decision theory and political decision making. In R. R. Lau & D. O. Sears (Eds.), *Political cognition* (pp. 55–65). Hillsdale, NJ: Erlbaum.

Fischman, M. W., & Foltin, R. W. (1991). Cocaine and the amphetamines. In I. B. Glass (Ed.), *The international handbook of addiction behaviour* (pp. 85–89). London: Routledge.

Fisher, R. J. (1990). *The social psychology of intergroup and international conflict resolution.* New York: Springer-Verlag.

Fisher, R. P., & Craik, F. I. M. (1977). Interaction between encoding and retrieval operations in cued recall. *Journal of Experimental Psychology: Human Learning and Memory, 3,* 701–711.

Fisher, S., & Greenberg, R. P. (1977). *The scientific credibility of Freud's theories and therapy.* New York: Basic Books.

Fisher, S., Raskin, A., Uhlenhuth, E. H. (1987). *Cocaine: Clinical and biobehavioral aspects.* New York: Oxford University Press.

Fishkin, J. (1992, July 1). Point of view: A voice for 'We the people' in the electoral process. *Chronicle of Higher Education*, p. A40.

Fiske, A. P. (1992). The four elementary forms of sociality: Framework for a unified theory of social relations. *Psychological Review, 99,* 689–723.

Fiske, M., & Chiriboga, D. A. (1990). *Change and continuity in adult life*. San Francisco: Jossey-Bass.

Fiske, S. T. (1989). *Interdependence and stereotyping: From the laboratory to the Supreme Court (and back)*. Paper presented at American Psychological Association, New Orleans.

Fiske, S. T. (1992). Thinking is for doing: Portraits of social cognition from Daguerreotype to laserphoto. *Journal of Personality and Social Psychology, 63,* 877–889.

Fiske, S. T. (1993a). Social cognition and social perception. *Annual Review of Psychology, 44,* 155–194.

Fiske, S. T. (1993b). Controlling other people: The impact of power on stereotyping. *American Psychologist, 48,* 621–628.

Fiske, S. T., Bersoff, D. N., Borgida, E., Deaux, K., & Heilman, M. E. (1991). Social science research on trial: Use of sex stereotyping research in *Price Waterhouse v. Hopkins. American Psychologist, 46,* 1049–1060.

Fiske, S. T., Bersoff, D. N., Borgida, E., Deaux, K., & Heilman, M. E. (1993). Accuracy and objectivity on behalf of the APA. *American Psychologist, 48,* 55–56.

Fiske, S. T., Pratto, F., & Pavelchak, M. A. (1983). Citizens' images of nuclear war: Content and consequences. *Journal of Social Issues, 39,* 41–65.

Fiske, S. T., & Taylor, S. E. (1991). *Social cognition* (2nd ed.). New York: McGraw-Hill.

Fitzpatrick, M. A. (1988). *Between husbands & wives: Communication in marriage*. Beverly Hills, CA: Sage.

Flaherty, C. F. (1985). *Animal learning and cognition*. New York: Knopf.

Flavell, J. H. (1985). *Cognitive development* (2nd. ed.). Englewood Cliffs, NJ: Prentice-Hall.

Flavell, J. H. (1992). Cognitive development: Past, present, and future. *Developmental Psychology, 28,* 998–1005.

Flavell, J. H., Beach, D. R., & Chinsky, J. M. (1966). Spontaneous verbal rehearsal in a memory task as a function of age. *Child Development, 37,* 283–299.

Flegenheimer, W. V. (1989). Brief psychotherapy. In J. G. Howells (Ed.), *Modern perspectives in the psychiatry of the neuroses* (pp. 286–302). New York: Brunner/Mazel.

Flores d'Arcais, G. B. (1988). Language perception. In F. J. Newmeyer (Ed.), *Linguistics: The Cambridge survey* (Vol. 3, pp. 97–123). Cambridge, England: Cambridge University Press.

Fodor, I. G. (1982). Gender and phobia. In I. Al-Issa (Ed.), *Gender and psychopathology* (pp. 179–197). New York: Academic.

Fogel, A. (1984). *Infancy: Infant in family and society*. St. Paul: West.

Fogelman, E., Wiener, V. L. (1985, August). The few, the brave, the noble. *Psychology Today*, pp. 60–65.

Foley, J. M. (1980). Binocular distance perception. *Psychological Review, 87,* 411–434.

Foley, J. M. (1985). Binocular distance perception: Egocentric distance tasks. *Journal of Experimental Psychology: Human Perception and Performance, 11,* 132–149.

Forsyth, D. R. (1990). *Group dynamics* (2nd ed.). Pacific Grove, CA: Brooks/Cole.

Foss, D. J. (1988). Experimental psycholinguistics. *Annual Review of Psychology, 39,* 301–348.

Foulkes, D. (1962). Dream reports from different stages of sleep. *Journal of Abnormal and Social Psychology, 65,* 14–25.

Foulkes, D. (1990). Reflective consciousness and dreaming [Review of *Conscious mind, sleeping brain: Perspectives on lucid dreaming*]. *Contemporary Psychology, 35,* 120–121.

Fouts, D. H. (1987, Winter). Signing interactions between mother and infant chimpanzees. *Friends of Washoe, 6,* 4–8.

Fouts, R. S., Fouts, D. H., & Van Cantfort, T. E. (1989). The infant Loulis learns signs from cross-fostered chimpanzees. In R. A. Gardner, B. T. Gardner, & T. E. Van Cantfort (Eds.), *Teaching sign language to chimpanzees* (pp. 280–292). Albany: State University of New York Press.

Fox, L. H., Tobin, D., & Brody, L. (1979). Sex-role socialization and achievement in mathematics. In M. A. Wittig & A. C. Petersen (Eds.), *Sex-related differences in cognitive functioning* (pp. 303–332). New York: Academic.

Fox, M., Gibbs, M., & Auerback, D. (1985). Age and gender dimensions of friendship. *Psychology of Women Quarterly, 9,* 489–501.

Fox, N. A. (1991). If it's not left, it's right: Electroencephalograph asymmetry and the development of emotion. *American Psychologist, 46,* 863–872.

Fox, N., & Fein, G. G. (Eds.). (1990). *Infant day care: The current debate*. Norwood, NJ: Ablex.

Frankenburg, W. K., & Dodds, J. B. (1967). The Denver Developmental Screening Test. *Journal of Pediatrics, 71,* 181–191.

Franklin, N., & Tversky, B. (1990). Searching imagined environments. *Journal of Experimental Psychology: General, 119,* 63–76.

Frederickson, P. A. (1987). The relevance of sleep disorders medicine to psychiatric practice. *Psychiatric Annals, 17,* 91–100.

Freedman, J. L. (1986). Television violence and aggression: A rejoinder. *Psychological Bulletin, 100,* 372–378.

Freedman, J. L., & Fraser, S. C. (1966). Compliance without pressure: The foot-in-the-door technique. *Journal of Personality and Social Psychology, 4,* 195–203.

Freedman, R. (1986). *Beauty bound*. Lexington, MA: D. C. Heath.

Freeman, J. (1985). Emotional aspects of giftedness. In J. Freeman (Ed.), *The psychology of gifted children* (pp. 247–264). Chichester, England: Wiley.

Freiberg, P. (1991, January). The guru of prevention calls for social change. *APA Monitor*, pp. 28–29.

Freiberg, P. (1991, April). More high school seniors say 'no.' *APA Monitor*, pp. 28–29.

French, E. G., & Thomas, F. H. (1958). The relationship of achievement motivation to problem-solving effectiveness. *Journal of Abnormal and Social Psychology, 56,* 45–48.

Frese, F. J., III. (1989). *A psychologist/consumer's view of mental health services*. Paper presented at the Fifth National Mental Health Consumer/Expatient Conference, Columbia, SC.

Frese, F. J., III. (1991). *Schizophrenia: Surviving in the world of normals*. Beachwood, Ohio: Wellness Reproductions.

Freud, S. (1900/1953). *The interpretation of dreams*. London: Hogarth.

Freud, S. (1909). Analysis of a phobia in a five-year-old boy. *In standard edition of the complete psychological works of Sigmund Freud*. London: Hogarth Press.

Freud, S. (1925/1976). *Some physical consequences of the anatomical distinction between the sexes*. In J. Strachey (Ed., Trans.), *The complete psychological works: Standard edition* (Vol. 19). New York: Norton.

Freud, S. (1930/1963). In J. Strachey (Ed., Trans.), *Civilization and its discontents*. New York: Norton.

Freud, S. (1933/1964). New introductory lectures on psychoanalysis. In J. Strachey (Ed.), *The standard edition of the complete psychological works of Sigmund Freud* (Vol. 23). London: Hogarth.

Frey, D. L., & Gaertner, S. I. (1986). Helping and the avoidance of inappropriate interracial behavior: A strategy that perpetuates a nonprejudiced self image. *Journal of Personality and Social Psychology, 50,* 1083–1090.

Frey, K. S., & Ruble, D. N. (1992). Gender constancy and the "cost" of sex-typed behavior: A test of the conflict hypothesis. *Developmental Psychology, 28,* 714–721.

Frick, R. W. (1988). Issues of representation and limited capacity in the auditory short-term store. *British Journal of Psychology, 79,* 213–240.

Frick, W. B. (1989). *Humanistic psychology*. Bristol, IN: Wyndham Hall Press.

Friedman, H., & Goldman-Rakic, P. S. (1988). Activation of the hippocampus by working memory: A 2-deoxyglucose study of behaving rhesus monkeys. *Journal of Neuroscience, 7,* 4693–4706.

Friedman, L., Bliwise, D. L., Yesavage, J. A., & Salom, S. R. (1991)., A preliminary study comparing sleep restriction and relaxation treatments for insomnia in older adults. *Journal of Gerontology, 46,* P1–P8.

Friedman, M., & Rosenman, R. (1974). *Type A behavior pattern and your heart*. New York: Knopf.

Friedrich-Cofer, L., & Huston, A. C. (1986). Television violence and aggression: The debate continues. *Psychological Bulletin, 100,* 364–371.

Frith, C. D. (1992). *The cognitive neuropsychology of schizophrenia*. Hove, England: Erlbaum.

Frodi, A., Macauley, J., & Thome, P. R. (1977). Are women always less aggressive than men? A review of the experimental literature. *Psychological Bulletin, 84,* 634–660.

Fuchs, D., & Fuchs, L. S. (1989). Effects of examiner familiarity on Black, Caucasian, and Hispanic children: A meta-analysis. *Exceptional Children, 55,* 303–308.

Fujita, F., Diener, E., & Sandvik, E. (1991). Gender differences in negative affect and well-being: The case for emotional intensity. *Journal of Personality and Social Psychology, 61,* 427–434.

Fulginiti, V. A. (1992). Editorial: Violence and children in the United States. *American Journal of Diseases of Children, 146,* 671–672.

Fullilove, M., Fullilove, R., III, Morales, E. (1989). Psychoeducation: A tool for AIDS prevention in minority communities. *Journal of Psychotherapy and the Family, 6,* 143–160.

Funder, D. C. (1987). Errors and mistakes: Evaluating the accuracy of social judgment. *Psychological Bulletin, 101,* 75–90.

Funder, D. C., & Colvin, C. R. (1991). Explorations in behavioral consistency: Properties of persons, situations, and behaviors. *Journal of Personality and Social Psychology, 60,* 773–794.

Furman, W., & Buhrmester, D. (1992). Age and sex differences in perceptions of networks of personal relationships. *Child Development, 63,* 103–115.

Furstenberg, F. F., & Cherlin, A. J. (1991). *Divided families: What happens to children when parents part.* Cambridge, MA: Harvard University Press.

Gabrieli, J. D. E., Cohen, N. L., & Corkin, S. (1988). The impaired learning of semantic knowledge following bilateral medial temporal-lobe resection. *Brain and Cognition, 7,* 157–177.

Gackenbach, J., & LaBerge, S. (Eds.). (1988). *Conscious mind, sleeping brain: Perspectives on lucid dreaming.* New York: Plenum.

Gaffan, D., & Harrison S. (1987). Amygdalectomy and disconnection in visual learning for auditory secondary reinforcement by monkeys. *Journal of Neuroscience, 7,* 2285–2292.

Galambos, N. L. (1992). Parent-child relations. *Current Directions in Psychological Science, 1,* 146–149.

Galambos, N. L., & Almeida, D. M. (1994). Does parent-adolescent conflict increase in early adolescence? *Journal of Marriage and the Family,* in press.

Galambos, S. J., & Goldin-Meadow, S. (1990). The effects of learning two languages on levels of metalinguistic awareness. *Cognition, 34,* 1–56.

Galambos, S. J., & Hakuta, K. (1988). Subject-specific and task-specific characteristics of metalinguistic awareness in bilingual children. *Applied Psycholinguistics, 9,* 141–162.

Galanter, E. (1962). Contemporary psychophysics. In R. Brown, E. Galanter, E. H. Hess, & G. Mandler (Eds.), *New directions in psychology.* New York: Holt, Rinehart and Winston.

Gallistel, C. R. (1990). The *organization of learning.* Cambridge, MA: MIT Press.

Galvin, R. M. (1982, August). Control of dreams may be possible for a resolute few. *Smithsonian Magazine,* pp. 110–117.

Gannon, L., Luchetta, T., Rhodes, K., Pardie, L., & Segrist, D. (1992). Sex bias in psychological research: Progress or complacency. *American Psychologist, 47,* 389–396.

Gara, M. A., Woolfolk, R. L., Cohen, B. D., Goldston, R. B., Allen, L. A., & Novalany, J. (1993). Perception of self and other in major depression. *Journal of Abnormal Psychology, 102,* 93–100.

Garbarino, J., & Kostelny, K. (1992). Cultural diversity and identity formation. In J. Garbarino (Ed.), *Children and families in the social environment* (pp. 179–199). New York: Walter de Gruyter.

Garcia, J. (1984). Evolution of learning mechanisms. In B. L. Hammond (Ed.), *Psychology and learning.* Washington, DC: American Psychological Association.

Garcia, J., & Koelling, R. (1966). Relation of cue to consequence in avoidance learning. *Psychonomic Science, 4,* 123–124.

Garcia, J., McGowan, G. K., & Green, K. F. (1972). Biological constraints on conditioning. In A. H. Black & W. F. Prokasy (Eds.), *Classical conditioning II: Current research and theory.* New York: Appleton-Century-Crofts.

Gardner, B. T., & Gardner, R. A. (1975). Evidence for sentence constituents in the early utterances of child and chimpanzee. *Journal of Experimental Psychology: General, 104,* 244–267.

Gardner, H. (1983). *Frames of mind: The theory of multiple intelligences.* New York: Basic.

Gardner, H. (1985). *The mind's new science: A history of the cognitive revolution.* New York: Basic Books.

Gardner, H. (1988, August). *Scientific psychology: Should we bury it or praise it?* Paper presented at the annual meeting of the American Psychological Association, Atlanta, GA.

Gardner, H. (1988, Summer). Multiple intelligences in today's schools. *Human Intelligence Newsletter, 9*(2), 1–2.

Gardner, R. A., & Gardner, B. T. (1988). Feedforward versus feedbackward: An ethological alternative to the law of effect. *Behavioral and Brain Sciences, 11,* 429–448.

Gardner, R. A., & Gardner, B. T. (1989). Cross-fostered chimpanzees: I. Testing vocabulary. In P. G. Heltne & L. A. Marquardt (Eds.), *Understanding chimpanzees* (pp. 220–241). Cambridge, MA: Harvard University Press.

Gardner, R. A., Gardner, B. T., & Van Cantfort, T. E. (Eds.). (1989). *Teaching sign language to chimpanzees.* Albany, NY: State University of New York Press.

Gardner, R. C., & Lambert, W. E. (1959). Motivational variables in second-language acquisition. *Canadian Journal of Psychology, 13,* 266–272.

Garnham, A. (1985). *Psycholinguistics: Central topics.* London: Methuen.

Garramone, G. M., Steele, M. E., Pinkelton, B. (1990). The role of cognitive schemata in determining candidate characteristic effects. In F. Biocca (Ed.), *Television and political advertising* (Vol. 1, pp. 311–328). Hillsdale, NJ: Erlbaum.

Garrison, C. Z. (1989). The study of suicidal behavior in the schools. In I. S. Lann, E. K. Mościcki, E. K. Maris, & R. Maris (Eds.), *Strategies for studying suicide and suicidal behavior* (pp. 120–130). New York: Guilford.

Garvey, C. (1984). *Children's talk.* Cambridge, MA: Harvard University Press.

Gary, L. (1987). Attitudes of Black adults toward community mental health centers. *Hospital and Community Psychiatry, 38,* 1100–1105.

Gay, P. (1988). *Freud: A life for our time.* New York: Norton.

Gayle, H. D., Keeling, R. P., Garcia-Tunon, M., Kilbourne, B. W., Narkunas, J. P., Ingram, F. R., Rogers, M. F., & Curran, J. W. (1990). Prevalence of the human immunodeficiency virus among university students. *New England Journal of Medicine, 323,* 1538–1541.

Gazzaniga, M. S. (1983). Right hemisphere language following brain bisection. *American Psychologist, 38,* 525–537.

Gazzaniga, M. S. (1986). Introduction. In G. Lynch (Ed.), *Synapses, circuits, and the beginnings of memory* (pp. vii–x). Cambridge, MA: Bradford.

Gazzaniga, M. S., & LeDoux, J. E. (1978). *The integrated mind.* New York: Plenum.

Geen, R. G. (1984). Human motivation: New perspectives on old problems. In A. M. Rogers & C. J. Scheirer (Eds.), *The G. Stanley Hall Lecture Series* (Vol. 4, pp. 5–57). Washington, DC: American Psychological Association.

Geen, R. G. (1990). *Human aggression.* Pacific Grove, CA: Brooks/Cole.

Geen, R. G. (1991). Social motivation. *Annual Review of Psychology, 42,* 377–399.

Geiselman, R. E., Fisher, R. P., MacKinnon, D. P., & Holland, H. L. (1985). Eyewitness memory enhancement in the police interview: Cognitive retrieval mnemonics versus hypnosis. *Journal of Applied Psychology, 70,* 401–412.

Geisinger, K. F. (Ed.). (1992). *Psychological testing of Hispanics.* Washington, DC: American Psychological Association.

Geiwitz, J., & Moursund, J. (1979). *Approaches to personality: An introduction to people.* Monterey, CA: Brooks/Cole.

Geller, J. D. (1988). Racial bias in the evaluation of patients for psychotherapy. In L. Comas-Díaz & E. Griffith (Eds.), *Clinical guidelines in cross-cultural mental health* (pp. 112–134). New York: Wiley.

Gelman, D. (1993, January 11). The young and the reckless. *Newsweek,* pp. 60–61.

Gelman, R. (1969). Conservation acquisition: A problem of learning to attend to relevant attributes. *Journal of Experimental Child Psychology, 7,* 67–87.

Gelman, R. (1983). Recent trends in cognitive development. In C. J. Scheirer & A. M. Rogers (Eds.), *The G. Stanley Hall Lecture Series* (Vol. 3, pp. 141–175).

Gelso, C. J., & Fretz, B. R. (1992). *Counseling psychology.* Fort Worth, TX: Harcourt Brace Jovanovich.

Genesee, F., Tucker, R., & Lambert, W. E. (1975). Communication skills of bilingual children. *Child Development, 46,* 1010–1014.

Gentry, W. D. (1985). Relationship of anger-coping styles and blood pressure among Black Americans. In M. Chesney & R. H. Rosenman (Eds.), *Anger and hostility in cardiovascular and behavioral disorders* (pp. 139–147). Washington, DC: Hemisphere.

George, L. K. (1988). Social participation in later life: Black-white differences. In J. S. Jackson (Ed.), *The black American elderly: Research on physical and psychosocial health* (pp. 99–126. New York: Springer.

Gerbner, G., Gross, L., Signorielli, N., & Morgan, M. (1986). *Television's mean world: Violence Profile No. 14–15.* Philadelphia, PA: University of Pennsylvania, Annenberg School of Communications.

Gergen, M. M. (1988, September). Building a feminist methodology. *Contemporary Social Psychology, 13*(2), 47–53.

Gershon, E. S., Berrettini, W. H., Nurnberger, J. I., Jr., & Goldin, L. R. (1989). Genetic studies of affective illness. In J. J. Mann (Ed.), *Models of depressive disorders* (pp. 109–142). New York: Plenum.

Gershon, E. S., & Rieder, R. O. (1992, September). Major disorders of mind and brain. *Scientific American,* pp. 127–133.

Gerson, M. J. (1986). The prospect of parenthood for women and men. *Psychology of Women Quarterly, 10,* 49–62.

Gescheider, G. A. (1985). *Psychophysics: Method and theory.* Hillsdale, NJ: Erlbaum.

Gettys, C. F., Mehle, T., & Fisher, S. (1986). Plausibility assessments in hypothesis generation. *Organizational Behavior and Human Decision Processes, 37,* 14–33.

Gibbons, B. (1992, February). Alcohol, the legal drug. *National Geographic,* pp. 2–35.

Gibbs, N. R. (1988, June 27). The sweet smell of success? *Time Magazine,* p. 54.

Gibson, E. J. (1969). *Principles of perceptual learning and development.* Englewood Cliffs, NJ: Prentice-Hall.

Gibson, E. J. (1988). Exploratory behavior in the development of perceiving, acting, and the acquiring of knowledge. *Annual Review of Psychology, 39,* 1–41.

Gibson, E. J., & Walk, R. D. (1960). The "visual cliff." *Scientific American, 202*(4), 64–71.

Gibson, J. J. (1959). Perception as a function of stimulation. In S. Koch (Ed.), *Psychology: A study of a science* (Vol. 1, pp. 456–501). New York: McGraw-Hill.

Gibson, J. J. (1962). Observations on active touch. *Psychological Review, 69,* 477–491.

Gibson, J. J. (1979). *The ecological approach to visual perception.* Boston: Houghton Mifflin.

Gigy, L. L. (1980). Self-concept of single women. *Psychology of Women Quarterly, 5,* 321–340.

Gilbert, D. T., & Jones, E. E. (1986). Perceiver-induced constraint: Interpretations of self-generated reality. *Journal of Personality and Social Psychology, 50,* 269–280.

Gilbert, D. T., Pelham, B. W., & Krull, D. S. (1988). On cognitive busyness: When person perceivers meet persons perceived. *Journal of Personality and Social Psychology, 54,* 733–740.

Gilbert, M. J. (1989). Alcohol use among Latino adolescents: What we know and what we need to know. In B. Segel (Ed.), *Perspectives on adolescent drug use* (pp. 35–53). New York: The Haworth Press.

Gilhooly, K. J. (1982). *Thinking: Directed, undirected, and creative.* London: Academic Press.

Gillam, B. (1980). Geometric illusions. *Scientific American, 242,* 102–111.

Gilligan, C. (1982). *In a different voice.* Cambridge, MA: Harvard University Press.

Gilligan, C., Murphy, J. M., & Tappan, M. B. (1990). Moral development beyond adolescence. In C. N. Alexander & E. J. Langer (Eds.), *Higher stages of human development* (pp. 208–225). New York: Oxford University.

Gilovich, T. (1991). *How we know what isn't so: The fallibility of human reason in everyday life.* New York: Free Press.

Ginsburg, H. P., & Koslowski, B. (1976). Cognitive development. *Annual Review of Psychology, 27,* 29–61.

Ginsburg, H. P., & Opper, S. (1988). *Piaget's theory of intellectual development* (3rd ed.). Englewood Cliffs, NJ: Prentice-Hall.

Gitlin, M. J. (1990). *The psychotherapist's guide to psychopharmacology.* New York: Free Press.

Glaser, R., & Chi, M. T. H. (1988). Overview. In M. T. H. Chi, R. Glaser, & M. J. Farr (Eds.). *The nature of expertise* (pp. xv–xxxvi). Hillsdale, NJ: Erlbaum.

Glass, I. B. (Ed.). (1991). *The international handbook of addiction behaviour.* London: Tavistock/Routledge.

Glees, P. (1988). *The human brain.* Cambridge, England: Cambridge University Press.

Glenberg, A. M., Sanocki, T., Epstein, W., & Morris, C. (1987). Enhancing calibration of comprehension. *Journal of Experimental Psychology: General, 116,* 119–136.

Glenn, E. N., & Feldberg, R. L. (1989). Clerical work: The female occupation. In J. Freeman (Ed.), *Women: A feminist perspective* (4th ed., pp. 287–311). Mountain View, CA: Mayfield.

Glick, P., Zion, C., & Nelson, C. (1988). What mediates sex discrimination in hiring decisions. *Journal of Personality and Social Psychology, 55,* 178–186.

Glickstein, M. (1988, September). The discovery of the visual cortex. *Scientific American, 259,* 118–127.

Gogel, W. C. (1977). The metric of visual space. In W. Epstein (Ed.), *Stability and constancy in visual perception: Mechanisms and processes.* New York: Wiley.

Gold, J. R. (1990). Levels of depression. In B. B. Wolman & G. Stricker (Eds.), *Depressive disorders:*

Facts, theories and treatment methods (pp. 203–228). New York: Wiley.

Goldberg, L. R. (1993). The structure of phenotypic personality traits. *American Psychologist, 48,* 26–34.

Goldberg, M. E., & Bruce, C. J. (1986). The role of the arcuate frontal eye fields in the generation of saccadic eye movements. In H. J. Freund, U. Buttner, B. Cohen, & J. Noth (Eds.), *Progress in brain research,* (Vol. 64, pp. 143–174). Amsterdam: Elsevier.

Goldberg, S. (1993). Early attachment: A passing fancy of a long term affair? *Canadian Psychology/Psychologie canadienne, 34,* 307–314.

Goldberg, T. E., Ragland, J. D., Torrey, E. F., Gold, J. M., Bigelow, L. B., & Weinberger, D. R. (1990). Neuropsychological assessment of monozygotic twins discordant for schizophrenia. *Archives of General Psychiatry, 47,* 1066–1072.

Golden, R. N., & Janowsky, D. S. (1990). Biological theories of depression. In B. B. Wolman & G. Stricker (Eds.), *Depressive disorders: Facts, theories, and treatment methods* (pp. 3–21). New York: Wiley.

Golden, W. L., & Dryden, W. (1987). Cognitive-behavioural therapies: Commonalities, divergences and future developments. In W. Dryden & W. L. Golden (Eds.), *Cognitive-behavioural approaches to psychotherapy* (pp. 356–378). Cambridge, England: Hemisphere.

Goldenberg, G., Podreka, I., Steiner, M., Suess, E., Deecke, L., & Willmes, K. (1988). Pattern of regional cerebral blood flow related to visual and motor imagery: In M. Denis, J. Engelkamp, & J. T. E. Richardson (Eds.), *Cognitive and neuropsychological approaches to mental imagery* (pp. 363–373). Dordrecht, The Netherlands: Martinus Nijhoff.

Goldenberg, I., & Goldenberg, H. (1991). *Family therapy: An overview* (3rd ed.). Pacific Grove, CA: Brooks/Cole.

Goldfried, M. R., Greenberg, L. S., & Marmar, C. (1990). Individual psychotherapy: Process and outcome. *Annual Review of Psychology, 41,* 659–688.

Goldman, M. S., Brown, S. A., Christiansen, B. A., & Smith, G. T. (1991). Alcoholism and memory: Broadening the scope of alcohol-expectancy research. *Psychological Bulletin, 110,* 137–146.

Goldman-Rakic, P. S. (1988). Topography of cognition: Parallel distributed networks in primate association cortex. *Annual Review of Neuroscience, 11,* 137–156.

Goldman-Rakic, P. S. (1990). Cortical localization of working memory. In J. M. McGaugh, N. M. Weinberger, & G. Lynch (Eds.), *Brain organization and memory: Cells, systems, and circuits* (pp. 285–298). New York: Oxford University Press.

Goldsmith, H. H. (1993). Nature-nurture issues in behavior-genetic context: Overcoming barriers to communication. In R. Plomin & G. E. McClearn (Eds.), *Nature, nurture, and psychology.* Washington, DC: American Psychological Association.

Goldsmith, H. H., & Rieser-Danner, L. A. (1990). Assessing early temperament. In C. R. Reynolds & R. W. Kamphaus (Eds.), *Handbook of psychological and educational assessment of children: Personality, behavior, and context* (pp. 245–278). New York: Guilford.

Goldstein, A. (1976). Opioid peptides endorphins in pituitary and brain. *Science, 193,* 1081–1086.

Goldstein, A. P., & Krasner, L. (1987). *Modern applied psychology.* New York: Pergamon.

Goldstein, E. B. (1989). *Sensation and perception* (3rd ed.). Belmont, CA: Wadsworth.

Goldstein, E. G. (1990). *Borderline disorders: Clinical models and techniques.* New York: Guilford.

Goldstein, J. H. (1989). Beliefs about human aggression. In J. Groebel & R. A. Hinde (Eds.), *Aggression and war: The biological and social bases* (pp. 10–24). Cambridge, England: Cambridge University Press.

Goldstein, M. (1984). *Family factors that antedate the onset of schizophrenia and related disorders: The results of a fifteen-year prospective longitudinal study.* Paper presented at the Regional Symposium of the World Psychiatric Association Meeting, Helsinki, Finland.

Golub, S. (1992). *Periods: From menarche to menopause.* Newbury Park, CA: Sage.

Gong-Guy, E., Cravens, R. B., & Patterson, T. E. (1991). Clinical issues in mental health service delivery to refugees. *American Psychologist, 46,* 642–648.

Gonsiorek, J. C., & Weinrich, J. D. (Eds.). (1991). *Homosexuality: Research implications for public policy.* Newbury Park, CA: Sage.

Gonzales, H. M., Davis, J. M., Loney, G. L., Lokens, C. K., & Junghans, C. M. (1983). Interactional approach to interpersonal attraction. *Journal of Personality and Social Psychology, 44,* 1192–1197.

Goodall, J. (1990). *Through a window: My thirty years with the chimpanzees of Gombe.* Boston: Houghton Mifflin.

Goodwin, C. J. (1991). Misportraying Pavlov's apparatus. *American Journal of Psychology, 104,* 135–141.

Goodwin, F. K., & Jamison, K. R. (1990). *Manic-depressive illness.* New York: Oxford University Press.

Gordon, R. A. (1990). *Anorexia and bulimia: Anatomy of a social epidemic.* Cambridge, MA: Blackwell.

Gotlib, I. H. (1992). Interpersonal and cognitive aspects of depression. *Current Directions in Psychological Science, 1,* 149–154.

Gotlib, I. H., & Hammen, C. L. (1992). *Psychological aspects of depression: Toward a cognitive-interpersonal integration.* Chichester, England: Wiley.

Gottesman, I. I. (1991). *Schizophrenia genesis: The origins of madness.* New York: Freeman.

Gottfried, A. E., Gottfried, A. W., & Bathurst, K. (1988). Maternal employment and children's development. In A. E. Gottfried & A. W. Gottfried (Eds.), *Maternal employment and children's development* (pp. 11–58). New York: Plenum Press.

Gould, J. L., & Marler, P. (1987). Learning by instinct. *Scientific American, 256*(1), 74–85.

Gould, R. L. (1978). *Transformations: Growth and change in adult life.* New York: Simon & Schuster.

Gournay, K. (1989a). Introduction: The nature of agoraphobia and contemporary issues. In K. G. Gournay (Ed.), *Agoraphobia: Current perspectives on theory and treatment* (pp. 5–22). London: Routledge.

Gournay, K. (1989b). The behavioural (exposure) treatment of agoraphobia: A review and an outcome study. In K. Gournay (Ed.), *Agoraphobia: Current perspectives on theory and treatment* (pp. 23–59). London: Routledge.

Gove, W. R. (1980). Mental illness and psychiatric treatment among women. *Psychology of Women Quarterly, 4,* 345–362.

Graef, R., Csikszentmihalyi, M., & Gianinno, S. M. (1983). Measuring intrinsic motivation in everyday life. *Leisure Studies, 2,* 155–168.

Grafman, J. (1989). Plans, actions, and mental sets: Managerial knowledge units in the frontal lobes. In E. Perecman (Ed.), *Integrating theory and practice in clinical neuropsychology* (pp. 93–138). Hillsdale, NJ: Erlbaum.

Graham, J. R. (1990). *MMPI-2: Assessing personality and psychopathology.* New York: Oxford University Press.

Gray, E., & Cosgrove, J. (1985). Ethnocentric perception of childrearing practices in protective services. *Child Abuse and Neglect, 9,* 389–396.

Gray, J. A., Feldon, J., Rawlins, J. N. P., Hemsley, D. R., & Smith, A. D. (1991). The neuropsychology of schizophrenia. *Behavioral and Brain Sciences, 14,* 1–84.

Green, B. F., & Hall, J. A. (1984). Quantitative methods for literature reviews. *Annual Review of Psychology, 35,* 37–53.

Green, D. G., & Powers, M. K. (1982). Mechanisms of light adaptation in rat ratina. *Vision Research 22,* 209–216.

Green, M. (1989). *Theories of human development: A comparative approach.* Englewood Cliffs, NJ: Prentice-Hall.

Greenberg, B. S. (1975). British children and television violence. *Public Opinion Quarterly, 39,* 521–547.

Greenberg, M. A., & Stone, A. A. (1992). Emotional disclosure about traumas and its relation to health: Effects of previous disclosure and trauma severity. *Journal of Personality and Social Psychology, 63,* 75–84.

Greenberg, R. P., Bornstein, R. F., Greenberg, M. D., & Fisher, S. (1992). A meta-analysis of antidepressant outcome under "blinder" conditions. *Journal of Consulting and Clinical Psychology, 60,* 664–669.

Greene, F. (1985). Form light, form bright . . . . *Neuropsychology Foundation Monographs, 1,* 2–11.

Greene, M. G., Hoffman, S., Charon, R., & Adelman, R. (1987). Psychosocial concerns in the medical encounter: A comparison of the interactions of doctors with their old and young patients. *The Gerontologist, 27,* 164–168.

Greene, R. L. (1987). Ethnicity and MMPI performance: A review. *Journal of Consulting and Clinical Psychology, 55,* 497–512.

Greenfield, P. M., & Childs, C. P. (1991). Developmental continuity in biolcultural context. In R. Cohen & A. W. Siegel (Eds.), *Context and development* (pp. 135–599). Hillsdale, NJ: Erlbaum.

Greenfield, P. M., & Savage-Rumbaugh, E. S. (1990). Grammatical combination in *Pan paniscus:* Processes of learning and invention in the evolution and development of language. In S. T. Parker & K. R. Gibson (Eds.), *"Language" and intelligence in monkeys and apes* (pp. 540–578). New York: Cambridge University Press.

Greenfield, P. M., & Savage-Rumbaugh, E. S. (1991). Imitation, grammatical development, and the invention of protogrammar by an ape. In N. A. Krasnegor, D. M. Rumbaugh, R. L. Schiefelbusch, & M. Studdert-Kennedy (Eds.), *Biological and behavioral determinants of language development* (pp. 235–258). Hillsdale, NJ: Erlbaum.

Greeno, C. G., & Maccoby, E. E. (1986). How different is the "different voice"? *Signs, 11,* 310–316.

Greeno, J. G. (1977). Process of understanding in problem solving. In J. J. Castellan, Jr., D. B. Pisoni, & G. R. Potts (Eds.), *Cognitive theory* (Vol. 2, pp. 43–84). Hillsdale, NJ: Erlbaum.

Greenough, W. T. (1991). The animal rights assertions: A researcher's perspective. *Psychological Science Agenda, 4*(3), 10–12.

Greenough, W. T. (1992). Animal rights replies distort(ed) and misinform(ed). *Psychological Science, 3,* 142.

Greenwald, A. G. (1989). Why are attitudes important? In A. R. Pratkanis, S. J. Breckler, & A. G. Greenwald (Eds.), *Attitude structure and function* (pp. 1–10). Hillsdale, NJ: Erlbaum.

Greenwald, A. G., Spangenberg, E. R., Pratkanis, A. R., & Eskenazi, J. (1991). Double-blind tests of subliminal self-help audiotapes. *Psychological Science, 2,* 119–122.

Gregory, R. L. (1987). *The Oxford companion to the mind.* New York: Oxford University Press.

Griffin, D. R. (1991, November). Essay: Animal thinking. *Scientific American, 265*(5), p. 144.

Grilo, C. M., & Pogue-Geile, M. F. (1991). The nature of environmental influences on weight and obesity: A behavioral genetic analysis. *Psychological Bulletin, 110,* 520–537.

Groebel, J., & Hinde, R. A. (1989a). A multi-level approach to the problems of aggression and war. In J. Groebel & R. A. Hinde (Eds.), *Aggression and war: Their biological and social bases* (pp. 223–229). Cambridge, England: Cambridge University Press.

Groninger, L. D. (1971). Mnemonic imagery and forgetting. *Psychonomic Science, 23,* 161–163.

Gross, L. (1991). Out of the mainstream: Sexual minorities and the mass media. *Journal of Homosexuality, 21,* 19–46.

Grossman, F. K. (1987). Separate and together: Men's autonomy and affiliation in the transition to parenthood. In P. W. Berman & F. A. Pedersen (Eds.), *Men's transitions to parenthood: Longitudinal studies of early family experience* (pp. 89–112). Hillsdale, NJ: Erlbaum.

Grossman, H. J. (1983). *Manual on terminology and classification in mental retardation.* Washington, DC: American Association on Mental Deficiency.

Groth-Marnat, G., (1990). *Handbook of psychological assessment* (2nd ed.). New York: Wiley.

Growdon, J. H. (1992). Treatment for Alzheimer's disease? *The New England Journal of Medicine, 327,* 1306–1308.

Grunberg, N. E. (1991). Cigarette smoking at work: data, issues, and models. In S. M. Weiss, J. E. Fielding, & A. Baum (Eds.), *Health at work* (pp. 75–98). Hillsdale, NJ: Erlbaum.

Grusec, J. E. (1991a). Socializing concern for others in the home. *Developmental Psychology, 27,* 338–342.

Grusec, J. E. (1991b). The socialization of altruism. In M. S. Clark (Ed.), *Prosocial behavior* (pp. 9–33). Newbury Park, CA: Sage.

Grusec, J. E. (1992). Social learning theory and developmental psychology: The legacies of Robert Sears and Albert Bandura. *Developmental Psychology, 28,* 776–786.

Gudjonsson, G. H. (1988). How to defeat the polygraph tests. In A. Gale (Ed.), *The polygraph test* (pp. 126–136). London: Sage.

Guilford, J. P. (1988). Some changes in the structure-of-intellect model. *Educational and Psychological Measurement, 48,* 1–4.

Gulick. W. L., Gescheider, G. A., & Frisina, R. D. (1989). *Hearing: Physiological acoustics, neural coding, and psychoacoustics.* New York: Oxford University Press.

Gunnar, M. R., & Brodersen, L. (1992). Infant stress reactions to brief maternal separations in human and nonhuman primates. In T. M. Field, P. N. McCabe, & N. Schneiderman (Eds.), *Stress and coping in infancy and childhood* (pp. 1–18). Hillsdale, NJ: Erlbaum.

Gunnar, M. R., Larson, M. C., Hertsgaard, L., Harris, M. L., & Brodersen, L. (1992). The stressfulness of separation among nine-month-old infants: Effects of social context variables and infant temperament. *Child Development, 63,* 290–303.

Gunnar, M. R., Mangelsdorf, S., Larson, M., & Hertsgaard, L. (1989). Attachment, temperament, and adrenocortical activity in infancy: A study of psychoendocrine regulation. *Developmental Psychology, 25,* 355–363.

Gunter, B. (1986). *Television and sex role stereotyping.* London: John Libbey.

Gunter, N. C., & Gunter, B. G. (1990). Domestic division of labor among working couples: Does androgyny make a difference? *Psychology of Women Quarterly, 14,* 355–370.

Gutheil, T. G. (1991, September). Risks and benefits of Prozac. *Harvard Mental Health Letter,* p. 8.

Gutherie, R. V. (1976). *Even the rat was white: A historical view of psychology.* New York: Harper & Row.

Haaga D. A. F., & Davison, G. C. (1991). *Helping people change: A textbook of methods* (4th ed., pp. 248–304). New York: Pergamon.

Haaga, D. A. F., Dyck, M. J., & Ernst, D. (1991). Empirical status of cognitive theory of depression. *Psychological Bulletin, 110,* 215–236.

Haaland, K. Y. (1992). Introduction to the special section on the emotional concomitants of brain damage. *Journal of Consulting and Clinical Psychology, 60,* 327–328.

Haber, R. N. (1985). Perception: A one-hundred year perspective. In S. Koch & D. E. Leary (Eds.), *A century of psychology as science* (pp. 250–281). New York: McGraw-Hill.

Hackel, L. S., & Ruble, D. N. (1992). Changes in the marital relationship after the first baby is born: Predicting the impact of expectancy disconfirmation. *Journal of Personality and Social Psychology, 62,* 944–957.

Hacker, A. (1992). *Two nations: Black and white, separate, hostile, unequal.* New York: Charles Scribner's Sons.

Haensly, P. A., & Reynolds, C. R. (1989). Creativity and intelligence. In J. A. Glover, R. R. Ronning, & C. R. Reynolds (Eds.), *Handbook of creativity* (pp. 135–145). New York: Plenum.

Hagen, M. A. (1985). James J. Gibson's ecological approach to visual perception. In S. Koch & D. E. Leary (Eds.), *A century of psychology as science* (pp. 231–249). New York: McGraw-Hill.

Haier, R. J., Siegel, B. V., Jr., MacLachlan, A., Soderling, E., Lottenberg, S., & Buchsbaum, M. S. (1992). Regional glucose metabolic changes after learning a complex visuospatial/motor task: A positron emission tomographic study. *Brain Research, 570,* 134–143.

Hale, S., Lima, S. D., & Myerson, J. (1991). General cognitive slowing in the nonlexical domain: An experimental validation. *Psychology and Aging, 6,* 512–521.

Halgin, R. P., & Whitbourne, S. K. (1993). *Abnormal psychology: The human experience of psychological disorders.* Fort Worth: Harcourt Brace Jovanovich.

Hall, J. A. (1984). *Nonverbal sex differences: Commu-*

nication accuracy and expressive style. Baltimore: Johns Hopkins University Press.

Hall, J. A., Rosenthal, R., Archer, D., DiMatteo, M. R., & Rogers, P. L. (1978, May). Decoding wordless messages. *Human Nature,* pp. 68–75.

Hall, N., R., & Goldstein, A. L. (1986, March/April). Thinking well: The chemical links between emotions and health. *The Sciences,* pp. 34–40.

Hall, N. R. S. (1988). The virology of AIDS. *American Psychologist, 43,* 907–913.

Hall, S. S. (1991, March–April). Journey out of time. *In Health,* pp. 71–79.

Hall, W. G., & Oppenheim, R. W. (1987). Development. *Annual Review of Psychology, 38,* 91–128.

Halpern, D. F. (1985). The influence of sex-role stereotypes on prose recall. *Sex Roles, 12,* 363–375.

Halpern, D. F. (1987). Analogies as a critical thinking skill. In D. E. Berger, K. Pezdek, & W. P. Banks (Eds.), *Applications of cognitive psychology: Problem solving, education, and computing* (pp. 75–86). Hillsdale, NJ: Erlbaum.

Halpern, D. F. (1989). *Thought and knowledge: An introduction to critical thinking* (2nd ed.). Hillsdale, NJ: Erlbaum.

Halpern, D. F. (1992). *Sex differences in cognitive abilities* (2nd ed.). Hillsdale, NJ: Erlbaum.

Halpern, D. F., Salzman, B., Harrison, W., & Widaman, K. (1983). The multiple determination of illusory contours: 2. An empirical investigation. *Perception, 12,* 293–303.

Halpin, J. A., Puff, C. R., Mason, H. F., & Marston, S. P. (1984). Self-reference and incidental recall by children. *Bulletin of the Psychonomic Society, 22,* 87–89.

Hamers, J. F., & Blanc, M. H. A. (1989). *Bilinguality and bilingualism.* Cambridge, England: Cambridge University Press.

Hamilton, D. L. (1979). A cognitive-attributional analysis of stereotyping. In L. Berkowitz (Ed.), *Advances in experimental social psychology* (Vol. 12, pp. 53–84). New York: Academic.

Hamilton, D. L. (1981). Illusory correlation as a basis for stereotyping. In D. L. Hamilton (Ed.), *Cognitive processes in stereotyping and intergroup behavior* (pp. 115–144). Hillsdale, NJ: Erlbaum.

Hamilton, D. L., Gibbons, P. A., Stroessner, S. J., & Sherman, J. W. (1992). Stereotypes and language use. In G. R. Semin & K. Fiedler (Eds.), *Language, interaction and social cognition* (pp. 102–128). London: Sage.

Hamilton, D. L., Sherman, S. J., & Ruvolo, C. M. (1990). Stereotype-based expectancies: Effects on information processing and social behavior. *Journal of Social Issues, 46,* 35–60.

Hamilton, D. L., Stroessner, S. J., & Mackie, D. M. (1993). The influence of affect on stereotyping: The case of illusory correlations. In D. M. Mackie & D. L. Hamilton (Eds.), *Affect, cognition, and stereotyping: Interactive processes in group perception* (pp. 39–61). San Diego: Academic Press.

Hamilton, M. (1989). Mood disorders: Clinical features. In H. I. Kaplan & B. J. Sadock (Eds.), *Comprehensive textbook of psychiatry/V* (5th ed., Vol. 1, pp. 892–913). Baltimore: Williams & Wilkins.

Hammen, C. L. (1982). Gender and depression. In I. Al-Issa (Ed.), *Gender and psychopathology* (pp. 133–152). New York: Academic Press.

Haney, C., Banks, C., & Zimbardo, P. (1973). Interpersonal dynamics in a simulated prison. *International Journal of Criminology and Penology, 1,* 69–97.

Hannay, H. J. (1986). Some issues and concerns in neuropsychological research: An introduction. In H. J. Hannay (Ed.), *Experimental techniques in human neuropsychology* (pp. 3–14). New York: Oxford University Press.

Hansen, F. J., & Reekie, L. J. (1990). Sex differences in clinical judgments of male and female therapists. *Sex Roles, 23,* 51–64.

Hansson, R. O. (1989). Old age: Testing the parameters of social psychological assumptions. In S. Spacapan & S. Oskamp (Eds.), *The social psychology of aging* (pp. 25–51). Newbury Park: Sage.

Hardy, A. (1987). *Personal communication.*

Hardy, J. A., & Higgins, G. A. (1992). Alzheimer's disease: The amyloid cascade hypothesis. *Science, 256,* 184–185.

Hardyck, C. (1991). Shadow and substance: Attentional irrelevancies and perceptual constraints in hemispheric processing of language stimuli. In F. L. Kitterle (Ed.), *Cerebral laterality: Theory and research* (pp. 133–153). Hillsdale, NJ: Erlbaum.

Hargreaves, D. J. (1977). Sex roles in divergent thinking. *British Journal of Educational Psychology, 47,* 25–32.

Härnqvist, K. (1968). Relative changes in intelligence from 13 to 18. *Scandinavian Journal of Psychology, 9,* 50–82.

Harris, B. (1979). Whatever happened to little Albert? *American Psychologist, 34,* 151–160.

Harris, G., Begg, I., & Upfold, D. (1980). On the role of the speaker's expectations in interpersonal communication. *Journal of Verbal Learning and Verbal Behavior, 19,* 597–607.

Harris, J. E. (1980). Memory aids people use: Two interview studies. *Memory & Cognition, 8,* 31–38.

Harris, M. B., Begay, C., & Page, P. (1989). Activities, family relationships and feelings about aging in a multicultural elderly sample. *International Journal of Aging and Human Development, 29,* 103–117.

Harris, M. J., Milich, R., Corbitt, E. M., Hoover, D. W., & Brady, M. (1992). Self-fulfilling effects of stigmatizing information on children's social interactions. *Journal of Personality and Social Psychology, 63,* 41–50.

Harris, R. E., Langrod, J., Hebert, J. R., Lowinson, J., Zang, E., & Wynder, E. L. (1990). Changes in AIDS risk behavior among intravenous drug abusers in New York City. *New York State Journal of Medicine, 90,* 123–126.

Harris, R. J., Sardarpoor-Bascom, F., & Meyer, T. (1989). The role of cultural knowledge in distorting recall for stories. *Bulletin of the Psychonomic Society, 27,* 9–10.

Harris, S. L., Alessandri, M., & Nathan, A. M. (1991). Behavior therapy with children. In M. Hersen, A. E. Kazdin, & A. Bellack (Eds.), *The clinical psychology handbook* (2nd ed., pp. 567–579). New York: Pergamon.

Hartman, B. J. (1982). An exploratory study of the effects of disco music on the auditory and vestibular systems. *Journal of Auditory Research, 22,* 271–274.

Hartup, W. W. (1983). Peer relations. In P. H. Mussen (Ed.), *Handbook of child psychology* (Vol. 4, pp. 103–196). New York: Wiley.

Harvey, P. D. (1985). Reality monitoring in mania and schizophrenia. *Journal of Nervous and Mental Disorders, 173,* 67–73.

Harvey, S. M. (1987). Female sexual behavior: Fluctuations during the menstrual cycle. *Journal of Psychosomatic Research, 31,* 101–110.

Harwood, R. L. (1992). The influence of culturally derived values on Anglo and Puerto Rican mothers' perceptions of attachment behavior. *Child Development, 63,* 822–839.

Harwood, R. L., & Miller, J. G. (1991). Perceptions of attachment behavior: A comparison of Anglo and Puerto Rican Mothers. *Merrill-Palmer Quarterly, 37,* 583–599.

Hasher, L., & Zacks, R. T. (1979). Automatic and effortful processes in memory. *Journal of Experimental Psychology: General, 108,* 356–388.

Hasher, L., & Zacks, R. T. (1984). Automatic processing of fundamental information: The case of frequency of occurrence. *American Psychologist, 39,* 1372–1388.

Haskins, R. (1985). Public aggression among children with varying day care experiences. *Child Development, 56,* 689–703.

Hatfield, E. (1988). Passionate and companionate love. In R. J. Sternberg & M. L. Barnes (Eds.), *The psychology of love* (pp. 191–217). New Haven, CT: Yale University Press.

Hatfield, E., & Sprecher, S. (1986). *Mirror, mirror . . . The importance of looks in everyday life.* Albany: State University of New York Press.

Hatfield, E., Traupmann, J., & Sprecher, S. (1984). Older women's perceptions of their intimate relationships. *Journal of Social and Clinical Psychology, 2,* 108–124.

Haugeland, J. (1985). *Artificial intelligence: The very idea.* Cambridge, MA: MIT Press.

Hayes, C. (1951). *The ape in our house.* New York: Harper & Row.

Hayes, C. D. (Ed.). (1987). *Risking the future* (Vol. 1). Washington, D. C.: National Academy Press.

Hayes, D. (1992, October). The dances, the firebomb, and the clash of cultures. *Toronto Life,* pp. 39–43, 119–124.

Hayes, J. R. (1989). Cognitive processes in creativity. In J. A. Glover, R. R. Ronning, & C. R. Reynolds (Eds.), *Handbook of creativity* (pp. 135–145). New York: Plenum.

Haynes, S. N. (1990). Behavioral assessment of adults. In G. Goldstein & M. Hersen (Eds.), *Handbook of psychological assessment* (2nd ed. pp. 423–463). New York: Pergamon.

Hays, R. B., Catania, J. A., McKusick, L., & Coates, T. J. (1990a). Help-seeking for AIDS-related concerns: A comparison of gay men with various HIV diagnoses. *American Journal of Community Psychology, 18,* 743–755.

Hays, R. B., Chauncey, S., & Tobey, L. A. (1990b). The social support networks of gay men with AIDS. *Journal of Community Psychology, 18,* 374–385.

Hays, R. B., Kegeles, S. M., & Coates, T. J. (1990c). High HIV risk-taking among young gay men. *AIDS, 4,* 901–907.

Hazan, C., & Shaver, P. (1987). Romantic love conceptualized as an attachment process. *Journal of Personality and Social Psychology, 52,* 511–524.

Hazelrigg, M. D., Cooper, H. M., & Borduin, C. M. (1987). Evaluating the effectiveness of family therapies: An integrative review and analysis. *Psychological Bulletin, 101,* 428–442.

Hearnshaw, L. S. (1987). *The shaping of modern psychology,* London: Routledge & Kegan Paul.

Heath, L., Kruttschnitt, C., & Ward D. (1986). Television and violent criminal behavior: Beyond the Bobo doll. *Victims and Violence, 1,* 177–190.

Heckhausen, H., Schmalt, H. D., & Schneider, K. (1985). *Achievement motivation in perspective.* Orlando, FL: Academic Press.

Heider, E. R. (1972). Universals in color naming and memory. *Journal of Experimental Psychology,*

93, 10–20.

Heilman, K. M., & Valenstein, E. (1985). Introduction. In K. M. Heilman & E. Valenstein (Eds.), *Clinical neuropsychology* (2nd Ed., pp. 3–16). New York: Oxford University Press.

Heinrichs, R. W. (1993). Schizophrenia and the brain. *American Psychologist, 48,* 221–233.

Heitler, S. M. (1990). *From conflict to resolution.* New York: Norton.

Helgeson, V. S. (1992). Moderators of the relation between perceived control and adjustment to chronic illness. *Journal of Personality and Social Psychology, 63,* 656–666.

Heller, M.A. (1984). Active and passive touch: The influence of exploration time on form recognition. *Journal of General Psychology, 110,* 243–249.

Heller, M. A. (1991). Introduction. In M. A. Heller & W. Schiff (Eds.), *The psychology of touch* (pp. 1–19). Hillsdale, NJ: Erlbaum.

Heller, M. A., & Schiff, W. (1991a). Conclusions: The future of touch. In M. A. Heller & W. Schiff (Eds.), *The psychology of touch* (pp. 327–337). Hillsdale, NJ: Erlbaum.

Heller, M. A., & Schiff, W. (Eds.), (1991b). *The psychology of touch.* Hillsdale, NJ: Erlbaum.

Hellige, J. B. (1991). Cerebral laterality and metacontrol. In F. L. Kitterle (Ed.), *Cerebral laterality: Theory and research* (pp. 117–132). Hillsdale, NJ: Erlbaum.

Hellwege, D. R., Perry, K., & Dobson, J. (1988). Perceptual differences in gender ideals among heterosexual and homosexual males and females. *Sex Roles, 19,* 734–746.

Hendin, H., Haas, A. P., Singer, P., Ellner, M., & Ulman, R. (1987). *Living high.* New York: Human Sciences.

Hendrick, C., & Hendrick, S. S. (1983). *Liking, loving and relating.* Pacific Grove, CA: Brooks/Cole.

Hendrick, S. S., & Hendrick, C. (1992). *Romantic love.* Newbury Park, CA: Sage.

Hendrick, S. S., Hendrick, C., & Adler, N. L. (1988). Romantic relationships: Love, satisfaction, and staying together. *Journal of Personality and Social Psychology, 54,* 980–988.

Henker, F. O. (1981). Male climacteric. In J. G. Howells (Ed.), *Modern perspectives in the psychiatry of middle age.* New York: Brunner/Mazel.

Henley, N. M. (1989). Molehill or mountain? What we know and don't know about sex bias in language. In M. Crawford & M. Gentry (Eds.), *Gender and thought: Psychological perspectives* (pp. 59–78). New York: Springer-Verlag.

Hennessey, B. A., & Amabile, T. M. (1984, April). *The effect of reward and task label on children's verbal creativity.* Paper presented at the meeting of the Eastern Psychological Association, Baltimore, MD.

Herek, G. M. (1990). Gay people and government security clearances: A social science perspective. *American Psychologist, 45,* 1035–1042.

Herek, G. M., & Glunt, E. K. (1988). An epidemic of stigma: Public reactions to AIDS. *American Psychologist, 43,* 886–891.

Hergenhahn, B. R. (1988). *An introduction to theories of learning* (3rd ed.). Englewood Cliffs, NJ: Prentice-Hall.

Herman, J. L. (1989, April). Wife-beating. *Harvard Medical School Mental Health Letter, 5,* 4–6.

Herman, J. L. (1992). *Trauma and recovery.* New York: Basic Books.

Herrmann, D. J. (1991). *Super memory.* Emmaus, PA: Rodale Press.

Herrnstein, R. J. (1984). Objects, categories, and discriminative stimuli. In H. L. Roitblat, T. G. Bever, & H. S. Terrace (Eds.), *Animal cognition* (pp. 233–261). Hillsdale, NJ: Erlbaum.

Herrnstein, R. J., Loveland, D. H., & Cable, D. (1976). Natural concepts in pigeons. *Journal of Experimental Psychology: Animal Behavior Processes, 2,* 285–302.

Herz, M. I., Glazer, W., Mirza, M., Mostert, M., Hafez, H., Smith, P., Trigoboff, E., Miles, D., Simon, J., & Finn, J. (1989). Intermittent medication in schizophrenia: A preliminary report. In S. C. Schulz & C. A. Tamminga (Eds.), *Schizophrenia: Scientific progress* (pp. 333–340). New York: Oxford University Press.

Hess, B., Markson, E. W., & Stein, P. J. (1988). Racial and ethnic minorities: An overview. In P. S. Rothenberg (Ed.), *Racism and sexism* (pp. 88–98). New York: St. Martin's Press.

Heston, L. L., & White, J. A. (1991). *The vanishing mind: A practical guide to Alzheimer's Disease and other dimentias.* New York: Freeman.

Hetherington, E. M., & Parke, R. D. (1986). *Child psychology* (3rd ed.). New York: McGraw-Hill.

Hewlett, B. S. (Ed.). (1992). *Father-child relations: Cultural and biosocial contexts.* New York: Aldine de Gruyter.

Hewstone, M. (1989). *Causal attribution: From cognitive processes to collective beliefs.* Oxford, England: Basil Blackwell.

Hibscher, J. A., & Herman, C. P. (1977). Obesity, dieting and the expression of "obese" characteristics. *Journal of Comparative and Physiological Psychology, 91,* 374–380.

Hicks, R. A., & Guista, M. (1982). The energy levels of habitual long and short sleepers. *Bulletin of the Psychonomic Society, 19,* 131–132.

Hicks, R. A., Mistry, R., Lucero, K., Marical, C., & Pellegrini, R. J. (1990). Self-reported sleep durations of college students: Normative data for 1978–79 and 1988–89. *Perceptual and Motor Skills, 70,* 370.

Higgins, E. T., & Bargh, J. A. (1987). Social cognition and social perception. *Annual Review of Psychology, 38,* 369–425.

Hilberman, E. (1978). The impact of rape. In M. T. Notman & C. C. Nadelson (Eds.), *The woman patient* (Vol. 1, pp. 303–322). New York: Plenum.

Hilgard, E. R. (1986). *Divided consciousness: Multiple controls in human thought and action* (Expanded edition). New York: Wiley.

Hilgard, E. R. (1987). *Psychology in America: A historical survey.* San Diego: Harcourt Brace Jovanovich.

Hilgard, E. R. (1991). Suggestibility and suggestions as related to hypnosis. In J. F. Schumaker (Ed.), *Human suggestibility: Advances in theory, research, and application* (pp. 37–58). New York: Routledge, Chapman and Hall.

Hilgard, E. R., Leary, D. E., & McGuire, G. R. (1991). History of psychology: A survey and critical assessment. *Annual Review of Psychology, 42,* 79–107.

Hilgard, E. R., Morgan, A. H. & Macdonald, H. (1975). Pain and dissociation in the cold pressor test: A study of hypnotic analgesia with "hidden reports" through automatic key-pressing and automatic talking. *Journal of Abnormal Psychology, 84,* 280–289.

Hill, R. D., Evankovich, K. D., Sheikh, J. I., & Yesavage, J. A. (1987). Imagery mnemonic training in a patient with primary degenerative dementia. *Psychology and Aging, 2,* 204–205.

Hinson, R. E., Poulos, C. X., Thomas, W., & Cappell, H. (1986). Pavlovian conditioning and addictive behavior: Relapse to oral self-adminstration of morphine. *Behavioral Neuroscience, 100,* 368–375.

Hirschfeld, R. M. A., & Davidson, L. (1988). Risk factors for suicide. In A. J. Frances & R. E. Hales (Eds.), *Review of psychiatry* (Vol. 7). Washington, DC: American Psychiatric Press.

Hirschfeld, R. M. A., & Shea, M. T. (1989). Mood disorders: psychosocial treatments. In H. I. Kaplan & B. J. Sadock (Eds.), *Comprehensive textbook of psychiatry/V* (5th ed., Vol. 1, pp. 933–944). Baltimore, MD: Williams & Wilkins.

Hirsh-Pasek, K., & Golinkoff, R. M. (1991). Language comprehension: A new look at some old themes. In N. A. Krasnegor, D. M. Rumbaugh, R. L. Schiefelbusch, & M. Studdert-Kennedy (Eds.), *Biological and behavioral determinants of language development* (pp. 301–320). Hillsdale, NJ: Erlbaum.

Hirst, W. (1986). The psychology of attention. In J. E. LeDoux & W. Hirst (Eds.), *Mind and brain* (pp. 105–141). Cambridge, England: Cambridge University Press.

HIV/AIDS Surveillance Report (1993, October). Atlanta, GA: Center for Disease Control and Prevention.

Ho, M. K. (1987). *Family therapy with ethnic minorities.* Newbury Park, CA: Sage.

Hobfoll, S. E. (1988). *The ecology of stress.* New York: Hemisphere.

Hobson, J. A. (1988). *The dreaming brain.* New York: Basic.

Hobson, J. A. (1990). Activation, input source, and modulation: A neurocognitive model of the state of the brain-mind. In R. R. Bootzin, J. F. Kihlstrom, & D. L. Schacter (Eds.), *Sleep and cognition* (pp. 25–40). Washington, DC: American Psychological Association.

Hobson, J. A., & McCarley, R. W. (1977). The brain as a dream state generator: An activation-synthesis hypothesis of the dream process. *American Journal of Psychiatry, 134,* 1335–1348.

Hoch, C., & Reynolds, C. (1986). Sleep disturbances and what to do about them. *Geriatric Nursing, 7,* 24–27.

Hochberg, J. (1988). Visual perception. In R. C. Atkinson, R. J. Herrnstein, G. Lindzey, & R. D. Luce (Eds.), *Stevens' handbook of experimental psychology* (2nd ed., pp. 195–276). New York: Wiley.

Hochschild, A.R. (1973). *The unexpected community.* Englewood Cliffs, NJ: Prentice-Hall.

Hochschild, A. R. (1983). *The managed heart.* Berkeley: University of California Press.

Hochschild, A. R. (1990). Ideology and emotion management: A perspective and path for future research. In T. D. Kemper (Ed.), *Research agendas in the sociology of emotions* (pp. 117–142). Albany: State University of New York Press.

Hock, E., & DeMeis, D. K. (1990). Depression in mothers of infants: The role of maternal employment. *Developmental Psychology, 26,* 285–291.

Hofferth, S. L., & Phillips, D. A. (1991a). Child care policy research. *Journal of Social Issues, 47,* 1–13.

Hofferth, S. L., & Phillips, D. A. (Eds.). (1991b). Child care policy research [Special issue]. *Journal of Social Issues, 47(2).*

Hoffman, L. W. (1989). Effects of maternal employment in the two-parent family. *American Psychologist, 44,* 283–292.

Hogarth, R. (1987). *Judgment and choice* (2nd ed.).

Chichester, England: Wiley.

Hogg, J A., & Deffenbacher, J. L. (1988). A comparison of cognitive and interpersonal-process group therapies in the treatment of depression among college students. *Journal of Counseling Psychology, 35,* 304–310.

Hogg, M. A., & Abrams, D. (1988). *Social identifications: A social psychology of intergroup relations and group processes.* London: Routledge.

Holcomb, H. H., Links, J., Smith, C., & Wong, D. (1989). Positron emission tomography: Measuring the metabolic and neurochemical characteristics of the living human nervous system. In N. C. Andreasen (Ed.), *Brain imaging: Applications in psychiatry* (pp. 235–370). Washington, DC: American Psychiatric Press.

Holden, C. (1985). A guarded endorsement for shock therapy. *Science, 228,* 1510–1511.

Holden, C. (1991a). Minorities need more nurture. *Science, 254,* 796.

Holden, C. (1991b). Depression: The news isn't depressing. *Science, 254,* 1450–1452.

Hollingworth, L. S. (1914). Functional periodicity: An experimental study of mental and motor abilities of women during menstruation. *Teachers College, Columbia University. Contributions to Education, No. 69,* pp. v–14, 86–101.

Hollon, S. D., DeRubeis, R. J., & Evans, M. D. (1987). Causal mediation of change in treatment for depression: Discriminating between nonspecificity and noncausality. *Psychological Bulletin, 102,* 139–149.

Holloway, M. (1991, March). Trends in pharmacology: R$_X$ for addiction. *Scientific American, 264*(3), 95–103.

Holloway, M., & Yam, P. (1992, March): Reflecting differences. *Scientific American,* pp. 13–18.

Holmbeck, G. N., & Hill, J. P. (1991). Conflictive engagement, positive affect, and menarche in families with seventh-grade girls. *Child Development, 62,* 1030–1048.

Holmes, D. S. (1984a). Meditation and somatic arousal reduction: A review of the experimental evidence. *American Psychologist, 39,* 1–10.

Holmes, D. S. (1984b). Defense mechanisms. In R. Corsini (Ed.). *Encyclopedia of psychology* (Vol. 1, pp. 347–350). New York: Wiley.

Holmes, D. S. (1987). The influence of meditation versus rest on physiological arousal: A second examination. In M. A. West (Ed.), *The psychology of meditation* (pp. 81–103). New York: Oxford University Press.

Holmes, D. S. (1990). The evidence for repression: An examination of sixty years of research. In J. L. Singer (Ed.), *Repression and dissociation: Implications for personality theory, psychopathology, and health* (pp. 85–102). Chicago: The University of Chicago Press.

Holmes, T. H., & Masuda, M. (1974). Life change and illness susceptibility. In B. S. Dohrenwend & B. P. Dohrenwend (Eds.), *Stressful life events: Their nature and effects* (pp. 45–72.). New York: Wiley.

Holmes, T. H., & Rahe, R. H. (1967). The social readjustment rating scale. *Journal of Psychosomatic Research, 11,* 213–218.

Holtzman, J. M., & Akiyama, H. (1985). *What children see: The aged on television in Japan and the United States, 25,* 62–68.

Holzman, P. S., & Matthysse, S. (1990). The genetics of schizophrenia: A review. *Psychological Science,* 279–286.

Honer, W. G., Geiwirtz, G., & Turey, M. (1987, August 22). Psychosis and violence in cocaine smokers.

The Lancet, 8556, 451.

Hood, D. C., & Finkelstein, M. A. (1986). Sensitivity to light. In K. R. Boff, L. Kaufman, & M. P. Thomas (Eds.), *Handbook of perception and human performance* (pp. 5-1—5-66). New York: Wiley.

Hooley, J. M. (1988, October). How do family attitudes affect relapse in schizophrenia? *Harvard Medical School Mental Health Letter,* p. 8.

Hoosain, R. (1991). *Psycholinguistic implications for linguistic relativity: A case study of Chinese.* Hillsdale, NJ: Erlbaum.

Hopson, D. P., & Hopson, D. S. (1990). *Different and wonderful: Raising Black children in a race-conscious society.* New York: Prentice-Hall.

Horn, J. L. (1989). Cognitive diversity: A framework of learning. In P. L. Ackerman, R. J. Sternberg, & R. Glaser (Eds.), *Learning and individual differences: Advances in theory and research* (pp. 61–116). New York: Freeman.

Horn, J. L., & Cattell, R. B. (1967). Age differences in fluid and crystallized intelligence. *Acta psychologica, 26,* 107–129.

Horner, M. S. (1968). *Sex differences in achievement motivation and performance in competitive and non-competitive situations.* Unpublished doctoral dissertation, University of Michigan.

Horner, M. S. (1972). Toward an understanding of achievement-related conflicts in women. *Journal of Social Issues, 28,* 157–175.

Horney, K. (1926/1967). The flight from womanhood. In H. Kelman (Ed.), *Feminine psychology* (pp. 54–70). New York: Norton.

Horney, K. (1945). *Our inner conflicts.* New York: Norton.

Horowitz, F. D., & O'Brien, M. (1986). Gifted and talented children: State of knowledge and directions for research. *American Psychologist, 41,* 1147–1152.

Horowitz, F. D., & O'Brien, M. (1989). In the interest of the nation: A reflective essay on the state of our knowledge and the challenges before us. *American Psychologist, 44,* 441–445.

Hostetler, A. J. (1988, April). Exploring the 'gatekeeper' of memory. *APA Monitor, 19,* 3.

House, J. S., Landis, K. R., & Umberson, D. (1988). Social relationships and health. *Science, 241,* 540–545.

Houston, J. P. (1991). *Fundamentals of learning and memory* (4th ed.). Fort Worth, TX: Harcourt Brace Jovanovich.

Hovanitz, C. A. (1993). Physical health risks associated with aftermath of disaster: Basic paths of influence and their implications for preventative intervention. *Journal of Social Behavior and Personality, 8,* 213–254.

Hoving, K. L., Spencer, T., Robb, K., & Schulte, D. (1978). Developmental changes in visual information processing. In P. A. Ornstein (Ed.), *Memory development in children* (pp. 21–68). Hillsdale, NJ: Erlbaum.

Hovland, C. I., & Weiss, W. (1951). The influence of source credibility on communication effectiveness. *Public Opinion Quarterly, 15,* 635–650.

How often do abused children become child abusers? (1991, July). *The Harvard Mental Health Letter,* p. 8.

Howard, D. (1986). Dynamics of feminist therapy. In D. Howard (Ed.), *The dynamics of feminist therapy* (pp. 1–4). New York: Haworth Press.

Howard-Pitney, B., LaFromboise, T. D., Basil, M., September, B., & Johnson, M. (1992). Psychological and social indicators of suicide ideation and sui-

cide attempts in Zuni adolescents. *Journal of Counsulting and Clinical Psychology, 60.* 473–476.

Howe, M. L., Brainerd, C. J., & Reyna, V. F. (Eds.). (1992). *Development of long-term retention.* New York: Springer-Verlag.

Howe, M. L., Kelland, A., Bryant-Brown, L., & Clark, S. L. (1992a). Measuring the development of children's amnesia and hypermnesia. In M. L. Howe, C. J. Brainerd, & V. F. Reyna (Eds.), *Development of long-term retention* (pp. 56–102). New York: Springer-Verlag.

Howe, M. L., O'Sullivan, J. T., & Marche, T. A. (1992b). Toward a theory of the development of long-term retention. In M. L. Howe, C. J. Brainerd, & V. F. Reyna (Eds.), *Development of long-term retention* (pp. 245–255) New York: Springer-Verlag.

Howes, C., & Olenick, M. (1986). Family and child care influences on toddlers' compliance. *Child Development, 57,* 202–216.

Howes, C., Phillips, D. A., & Whitebook, M. (1992). Thresholds of quality: Implications for the social development of children in center-based child care. *Child Development, 63,* 449–460.

Hsu, F.-H., Anantharaman, R., Campbell, M., & Nowatzyk, A. (1990, October). A grandmaster chess machine. *Scientific American,* pp. 44–50.

Hsu, L. K. G. (1990). *Eating disorders.* New York: Guilford.

Hubbell, S. (1988, May 16). Annals of husbandry: The sweet bees. *New Yorker,* pp. 75–94.

Hubel, D. H. (1979, September). The brain. *Scientific American, 242.* 38–47.

Hubel, D. H., & Wiesel, T. N. (1965). Receptive fields of single neurons in two nonstriate visual areas (18 and 19) of the cat. *Journal of Neurophysiology, 28,* 229–289.

Hubel, D. H., & Wiesel, T. N. (1979). Brain mechanisms and vision. *Scientific American, 241*(3), 150–162.

Huber, C. H., & Baruth, L. G. (1989). *Rational-emotive family therapy: A system perspective.* New York: Springer.

Huber, V. L., Neale, M. A., & Northcraft, G. B. (1987). Decision bias and personnel selection strategies. *Organizational Behavior and Human Decision Processes, 40,* 136–147.

Hudspeth, A. J. (1989). How the ear's works work. *Nature, 341,* 397–404.

Huesmann, L. R. (1986). Psychological processes promoting the relation between exposure to media violence and aggressive behavior by the viewer. *Journal of Social Issues, 42,* 125–139.

Huesmann, L. R., & Eron, L. D. (Eds.). (1986). *Television and the aggressive child: A cross-national comparison.* Hillsdale, NJ: Erlbaum.

Huesmann, L. R., Eron, L. D., Klein, R., Brice, P., & Fischer, P. (1983). Mitigating the imitation of aggressive behaviors by changing children's attitudes about media violence. *Journal of Personality and Social Psychology, 44,* 899–910.

Hughes, J. R. (1992). Tobacco withdrawal in self-quitters. *Journal of Consulting and Clinical Psychology, 60,* 689–697.

Hughes, J. R., & Pierattini, R. A. (1992). An introduction to pharmacotherapy for mental disorders. In J. Grabowski & G. R. VandenBos (Eds.), *Psychopharmacology: Basic mechanisms and applied interventions* (pp. 97–125). Washington, DC: American Psychological Association.

Hulicka, I. M. (1982). Memory functioning in late adulthood. In F. I. M. Craik & S. Trehub (Eds.),

Aging and cognitive processes (pp. 331–351). New York: Plenum.

Hull, J. G., & Bond, C. F. (1986). Social and behavioral consequences of alcohol consumption and expectancy: A meta-analysis. *Psychological Bulletin, 99,* 347–360.

Hunt, D. J. (1989). Issues in working with Southeast Asian refugees. In D. R. Koslow & E. P. Salett (Eds.), *Crossing cultures in mental health* (pp. 49–63). Washington, DC: SIETAR International.

Hunt, E., & Agnoli, F. (1991). The Whorfian hypothesis: A cognitive psychology perspective. *Psychological Review, 98,* 377–389.

Hunter College Women's Studies Collective (1983). *Women's realities, women's choices.* New York: Oxford University Press.

Hurvich, L. M. (1981). *Color vision.* Sunderland, MA: Sinauer.

Husaini, B. A., Moore, S. T., Castor, R. S., Neser, W., Whitten-Stovall, R., Linn, J. G., & Griffin, D. (1991). Social density, stressors, and depression: Gender differences among the Black elderly. *Journal of Gerontology: Psychological Sciences, 46,* P236–P242.

Huston, T. L., McHale, S. M., & Crouter, A. C. (1986). When the honeymoon's over: Changes in the marriage relationship over the first year. In R. Gilmour & S. Duck (Eds.), *The emerging field of personal relationships* (pp. 109–132). Hillsdale, NJ: Erlbaum.

Huttenlocher, J., & Goodman, J. (1987). The time to identify spoken words. In A. Allport, D. MacKay, W. Prinz, & E. Scheerer (Eds.), *Language perception and production* (pp. 431–444). London: Academic Press.

Huyck, M. H., & Duchon, J. (1986). Over the miles: coping, communicating, and commiserating through age-theme greeting cards. In L. Nahemow, K. A. McCluskey-Fawcett, & P. E. McGhee (Eds.), *Humor and aging* (pp. 139–159). Orlando, FL: Academic.

Hyde, J. S. (1986). Gender differences in aggression. In J. S. Hyde & M. C. Linn (Eds.), *The psychology of gender: Advances through meta-analysis* (pp. 51–66). Baltimore: Johns Hopkins University Press.

Hyde, J. S. (1986). Introduction: Meta-analysis and the psychology of gender. In J. S. Hyde & M. C. Linn (Eds.), *The psychology of gender: Advances through meta-analysis* (pp. 1–13). Baltimore: Johns Hopkins University Press.

Hyde, J. S. (1990). *Understanding human sexuality* (4th ed.). New York: McGraw-Hill.

Hyde, J. S., Fennema, E., & Lamon, S. J. (1990). Gender differences in mathematics performance: A meta-analysis. *Psychological Bulletin, 107,* 139–155.

Hyde, J. S., & Linn, M. C. (1988). Gender differences in verbal ability: A meta-analysis. *Psychological Bulletin, 104,* 53–69.

Hypnosis. (1991, April). *The Harvard Mental Health Letter,* pp. 1–4.

Iacono, W. G. (1988). Psychotherapy for psychopaths? [Review of *Understanding and treating the psychopath*]. *Contemporary Psychology, 33,* 116–117.

Ianazzi, C. (1992). *Personal communication.*

Ickovics, J. R., & Rodin, J. (1992). Women and AIDS in the United States: Epidemiology, natural history, and mediating mechanisms. *Health Psychology, 11,* 1–16.

Imperato, P. J. (1991). The current syphilis epidemic in New York State. *New York State Journal of Medicine, 91,* 521.

Imperato, P. J., & Mitchell, G. (1986). Cigarette smoking: A "chosen" risk. *New York State Journal of Medicine, 86,* 485–489.

In brief. (1993, February 3). *The Chronicle of Higher Education,* p. A4.

Innis, N. K. (1992). Animal psychology in America as revealed in APA presidential addresses. *Journal of Experimental Psychology: Animal Behavior Processes, 18,* 3–11.

Intons-Peterson, M. J. (1988). *Children's concepts of gender.* Norwood, NJ: Ablex.

Intons-Peterson, M. J. (1993). Imagery and classification. In A. Collins, S. Gathercole, M. Conway, & P. Morris (Eds.), *Theories of memory.* Hillsdale, NJ: Erlbaum.

Intons-Peterson, M. J., & Fournier, J. (1986). External and internal memory aids: When and how often do we use them? *Journal of Experimental Psychology: General, 115,* 267–280.

Intons-Peterson, M. J., & Reddel, M. (1984). What do people ask about a neonate? *Developmental Psychology, 20,* 358–359.

Intons-Peterson, M. J., & Roskos-Ewoldsen, B. (1989). Mitigating the effects of violent pornography. In S. Gubar & J. Hoff (Eds.), *For adult users only: The dilemma of violent pornography* (pp. 218–239). Bloomington, IN: Indiana University Press.

Intons-Peterson, M. J., Roskos-Ewoldsen, B., Thomas, L., Shirley, M., & Blut, D. (1989). Will educational materials reduce negative effects of exposure to sexual violence? *Journal of Social and Clinical Psychology, 8,* 256–275.

Intons-Peterson, M. J., Russell, W., & Dressel, S. (1992). The role of pitch in auditory imagery. *Journal of Experimental Psychology: Human Perception and Performance, 18,* 233–240.

Iosub, S., Bamji, M., Stone, R. K., Gromisch, D. S., & Wasserman, E. (1987). More on human immune deficiency virus embryopathy. *Pediatrics, 80,* 512–516.

Irwin, D. E., & Yeomans, J. M. (1986). Sensory registration and informational persistence. *Journal of Experimental Psychology: Learning, Memory, and Cognition, 10,* 699–715.

Irwin, D. E., Zacks, J. L., & Brown, J. S. (1990). Visual memory and the perception of a stable visual environment. *Perception & Psychophysics, 47,* 35–46.

Isabella, R. A. (1993). Origins of attachment: Maternal interactive behavior across the first year. *Child Development, 64,* 605–621.

Isen, A. M. (1987). Positive affect, cognitive processes, and social behavior. *Advances in Experimental Social Psychology, 20,* 203–253.

Isen, A. M. (1990). The influence of positive and negative affect on cognitive organization: Some implications for development. In N. L. Stein, B. Leventhal, & T. Trabasso (Eds.), *Psychological and biological approaches to emotion* (pp. 75–94). Hillsdale, NJ: Erlbaum.

Isen, A. M., & Daubman, K. A. (1984). The influence of affect on categorization. *Journal of Personality and Social Psychology, 47,* 1206–1217.

Isen, A. M., Daubman, K. A., & Gorgoglione, J. M. (1987). The influence of positive affect on cognitive organization: Implications for education. In R. E. Snow & M. J. Farr (Eds.), *Aptitude, learning, and instruction* (Vol. 3, pp. 143–164). Hillsdale, NJ: Erlbaum.

Isen, A. M., Daubman, K. A., & Nowicki, G. P. (1987). *Journal of Personality and Social Psychology, 52,* 1122–1131.

Isen, A. M., Johnson, M. M. S., Mertz, E., & Robinson, G. F. (1985). The influence of positive affect on the unusualness of word associations. *Journal of Personality and Social Psychology, 48,* 1413–1426.

Isen, A. M., & Simonds, S. F. (1978). The effect of feeling good on a helping task that is incompatible with good mood. *Social Psychology, 41,* 346–349.

Itzin, C. (1986). Media images of women: The social construction of ageism and sexism. In S. Wilkinson (Ed.), *Feminist social psychology* (pp. 119–134). Milton Keynes, England: Open University Press.

Ivry, R. B. (1992). An alternative to associative learning theories. [Review of *The organization of learning.*] *Contemporary Psychology, 37,* 209–210.

Izard, C. E. (1989). The structure and functions of emotions: Implications for cognition, motivation, and personality. In I. S. Cohen (Ed.), *The G. Stanley Hall Lecture Series* (Vol. 9, pp. 37–73). Washington, DC: American Psychological Association.

Izard, C. E. (1991). *The psychology of emotions.* New York: Plenum.

Izard, C. E., Hembree, E. A., Dougherty, L. M., & Spizzirri, C. C. (1983). Changes in facial expressions of 2- and 19-month-old infants following acute pain. *Developmental Psychology, 19,* 418–426.

Jack, D. C. (1987a). Silencing the self: The power of social imperatives in female depression. In R. Formanek & A. Gurian (Eds.), *Women and depression: A lifespan perspective* (pp. 161–181). New York: Springer.

Jack, D. C. (1987b). Self-in-relation theory. In R. Formanek & A. Gurian (Eds.), *Women and depression: A lifespan perspective* (pp. 41–45). New York: Springer.

Jack, D. C. (1988). *Combining the strengths of qualitative with quantitative research methods.* Paper presented at the American Psychological Association, Atlanta, Georgia.

Jack, D. C. (1991). *Silencing the self: Women and depression.* Cambridge, MA: Harvard University Press.

Jacklin, C. N. (1989). Female and male: Issues of gender. *American Psychologist, 44,* 127–133.

Jackson, J. J. (1985). Race, national origin, ethnicity, and aging. In R. Binstock & E. Shanas (Eds.), *Handbook of aging and the social sciences* (pp. 264–303). New York: Van Nostrand Reinhold.

Jackson, N. E., & Butterfield, E. C. (1986). A conception of giftedness designed to promote research. In R. J. Sternberg & J. E. Davidson (Eds.), *Conceptions of giftedness* (pp. 151–181). New York: Cambridge University Press.

Jacobs, J. E. (1991). Influence of gender stereotypes on parent and child mathematics attitudes. *Journal of Educational Psychology, 83,* 518–527.

Jacobs, S. (1985). Language. In M. L. Knapp & G. R. Miller (Eds.), *Handbook of interpersonal communication* (pp. 313–343). Beverly Hills, CA: Sage.

Jacobson, N. S., & Anderson, E. A. (1982). Interpersonal skill and depression in college students: An analysis of the timing of self-disclosures. *Behavior Therapy, 13,* 271–282.

Jacobson, S. W. (1987, September 1). Between two

worlds. *Rochester Times-Union*, pp. 1C, 4C.

Jacoby, L. L., Lindsay, D. S., & Toth, J. P. (1992). Unconscious influences revealed: Attention, awareness, and control. *American Psychologist, 47,* 802–809.

Jaffe, J. H. (1991). Opiates. In I. B. Glass (Ed.), *The international handbook of addiction behaviour* (pp. 64–68). London: Tavistock/Routledge.

Jagacinski, C. M., LeBold, W. K., & Linden, K. W. (1987). The relative career advancement of men and women engineers in the United States. *Work and Stress, 1,* 235–247.

James, W. (1890). *The principles of psychology.* New York: Henry Holt.

James, W. (1892). *Psychology: The briefer course.* New York: Henry Holt.

Jameson, D., & Hurvich, L. M. (1989). Essay concerning color constancy. *Annual Review of Psychology, 40,* 1–22.

Janicak, P. G., Davis, J. M., Gibbons, R. D., Eriksen, S., Chang, S., & Gallagher, P. (1985). Efficacy of ECT: A meta-analysis. *American Journal of Psychiatry, 142,* 297–302.

Janis, I. L. (1982). *Groupthink: Psychological studies of policy decisions and fiascoes.* Boston: Houghton Mifflin.

Janis, I. L. (1989). *Crucial decisions: Leadership in policymaking and crisis management.* New York: Free Press.

Janoff-Bulman, R., & Timko, C. (1987). Coping with traumatic life events: The role of denial in light of people's assumptive worlds. In C. R. Snyder & C. E. Ford (Eds.), *Coping with negative life events* (pp. 135–159). New York: Plenum.

Janowsky, D. S. (1986). Psychopharmacologic therapy. In I. L. Kutash & A. Wolf (Eds.), *Psychotherapist's casebook* (pp. 312–331). San Francisco: Jossey-Bass.

Jarboe, J. (1990, May). The way out. *Texas Monthly,* pp. 102–104, 146–154.

Jeffery, R. W. (1989). Risk behaviors and health: Contrasting individual and population perspectives. *American Psychologist, 44,* 1194–1202.

Jemmott, J. B., Borysenko, M., McClelland, D. C., Chapman, R., Meyer, D., & Benson, H. (1983). Academic stress, power motivation, and decrease in salivary secretory immunoglobulin: A secretion rate. *Lancet, 1,* 1400–1402.

Jemmott, J. B., & Locke, S. E. (1984). Psychosocial factors, immunologic mediation, and human susceptibility to infectious diseases: How much do we know? *Psychological Bulletin, 95,* 52–77.

Jencks, C. (1990). Varieties of altruism. In J. J. Mansbridge (Ed.), *Beyond self-interest,* (pp. 53–67). Chicago: University of Chicago Press.

Jenkins, J. H., Kleinman, A., & Good, B. J. (1991). Cross-cultural studies of depression. In J. Becker & A. Kleinman (Eds.), *Psychosocial aspects of depression* (pp. 67–99). Hillsdale, NJ: Erlbaum.

Jenkins, J. J. (1974). Remember that old theory of memory? Well, forget it. *American Psychologist, 29,* 785–795.

Jensen, A. R. (1969). How much can we boost IQ and scholastic achievement? *Harvard Educational Review, 39,* 1–123.

Jespersen, O. (1922). *Language.* London: George Allen and Unwin.

Jette, C. C. B., & Remien, R. (1988). Hispanic geriatric residents in a long-term care setting. *Journal of Applied Gerontology, 7,* 350–366.

Jewett, M. E., Kronauer, R. E., & Czeisler, C. A. (1991). Light-induced suppression of endogenous circadian amplitude in humans. *Nature,*

350, 59–62.

Joanette, Y., & Brownell, H. H. (1990). Introduction. In Y. Joanette & H. H. Brownell (Eds.), *Discourse ability and brain damage: Theoretical and empirical perspectives* (pp. xiii–xvi). New York: Springer-Verlag.

Johansson, G. (1975). Visual motion perception. *Scientific American, 232,* 76–88.

Johansson, G. (1985). About visual event perception. In W. H. Warren, Jr., & R. W. Shaw (Eds.), *Persistence and change: Proceedings of the First International Conference on Event Perception* (pp. 29–54). Hillsdale, NJ: Erlbaum.

Johansson, G., von Hofsten, C., & Jansson, G. (1980). Event perception. *Annual Review of Psychology, 31,* 27–63.

Johnson, B. A. (1991). Cannabis. In I. B. Glass (Ed.), *The international handbook of addiction behaviour* (pp. 69–76). London: Tavistock/Routledge.

Johnson, C. M., Bradley-Johnson, S., McCarthy, R., & Jamie, M. (1984). Token reinforcement during WISC-R administration. *Applied Research on Mental Retardation, 5,* 43–52.

Johnson, G. (1991). *In the palaces of memory: How we build the worlds inside our heads.* New York: Knopf.

Johnson, J. R. (1985). Cognitive prerequisites: The evidence from children learning English. In D. I. Slobin (Ed.), *The crosslinguistic study of language acquisition: Volume 2. Theoretical issues* (pp. 961–1004). Hillsdale, NJ: Erlbaum.

Johnson, M. H., & Magaro, P. A. (1987). Effects of mood and severity on memory processes in depression and mania. *Psychological Bulletin, 101,* 28–40.

Johnson-Laird, P. N. (1988). *The computer and the mind: An introduction to cognitive science.* Cambridge, MA: Harvard University Press.

Johnston, L. D., O'Malley, P. M., & Bachman, J. G. (1991). *Drug use among American high school seniors, college students and young adults, 1975–1990.* Rockville, MD: National Institute on Drug Abuse.

Johnston, W. A., & Dark, V. J. (1986). Selective attention. *Annual Review of Psychology, 37,* 43–75.

Jonas, H. S., Etzel, S. I., & Barzansky, B. (1993). Educational programs in US medical schools. *JAMA,* 1061–1068.

Jonas, H. S., & Etzel, S. I. (1988). Graduate medical education. *Journal of the American Medical Association, 260,* 1063–1071.

Jones, E. E. (1990). *Interpersonal perception.* New York: Freeman.

Jones, E. F. (1985). Teenage pregnancy in developed countries: Determinants and policy implications. *Family Planning Perspectives, 17,* 53–64.

Jones, L. V. (1983, November). *White-black achievement differences: The narrowing gap.* Invited address presented at the meeting of the Federation of Behavioral, Psychological, and Cognitive Sciences. Washington, DC.

Jones, R. T. (1991). Tobacco. In D. A. Ciraulo & R. I. Shader (Eds.), *Clinical manual of chemical dependence* (pp. 321–343). Washington, DC: American Psychiatric Press.

Jordan, N. (1989, June). Spare the rod, spare the child. *Psychology Today,* p. 16.

Josephson, W. L. (1987). Television violence and children's aggression: Testing the priming, social script, and disinhibition predictions. *Journal of Personality and Social Psychology, 53,* 882–890.

Joy, L. A., Kimball, M. M., & Zabrack, M. L. (1986). Television and children's aggressive behavior. In

T. M. Williams (Ed.), *The impact of television: A natural experiment in three communities* (pp. 303–360). Orlando, FL: Academic.

Judd, C. M., Drake, R. A., Downing, J. W., & Krosnick, J. A. (1991). Some dynamic properties of attitude structures: Context-induced response facilitation and polarization. *Journal of Personality and Social Psychology, 60,* 193–202.

Judd, C. M., & Park, B. (1988). Out-group homogeneity: Judgments of variability at the individual and group levels. *Journal of Personality and Social Psychology, 54,* 778–788.

Judd, C. M., Ryan, C. S., & Park, B. (1991). Accuracy in the judgment of in-group and out-group variability. *Journal of Personality and Social Psychology, 61,* 366–379.

Jung, C. G. (1917/1953). On the psychology of the unconscious. In H. Read., M. Fordham, & G. Adler (Eds.), *Collected works of C. G. Jung* (Vol. 7). Princeton, NJ: Princeton University Press.

Jusczyk, P. W. (1986). Speech perception. In K. R. Boff, L. Kaufman, & J. P. Thomas (Eds.), *Handbook of perception and human performance* (pp. 27.1–27.5). Hillsdale, NJ: Erlbaum.

Jussim, L. (1986). Self-fulfilling prophecies: A theoretical and integrative review. *Psychological Review, 93,* 429–445.

Jussim, L. (1990). Social reality and social problems: The role of expectancies. *Journal of Social Issues, 46,* 9–34.

Jussim, L. (1991). Social perception and social reality: A reflection-construction model. *Psychological Review, 98,* 54–73.

Jussim, L., & Eccles, J. S. (1992). Teacher expectations II: Construction and reflection of student achievement. *Journal of Personality and Social Psychology, 63,* 947–961.

Just, M. A., & Carpenter, P. A. (1985). Cognitive coordinate systems: Accounts of mental rotation and individual differences in spatial ability. *Psychological Review, 92,* 137–172.

Kagan, J. (1992). Yesterday's premises, tomorrow's promises. *Developmental Psychology, 28,* 990–997.

Kagan, J., Reznick, J. S., & Snidman, N. (1988). Biological bases of childhood shyness. *Science, 240,* 167–171.

Kagan, J., & Snidman, N. (1991). Temperamental factors in human development. *American Psychologist, 46,* 856–862.

Kahana, E., & Kiyak, H. (1984). Attitudes and behavior of staff in facilities for the aged. *Research on Aging, 6,* 395–416.

Kahn, A. S., & Yoder, J. D. (1989). The psychology of women and conservatism. *Psychology of Women Quarterly, 13,* 417–432.

Kahneman, D., & Tversky, A. (1972). Subjective probability: A judgment of representativeness. *Cognitive Psychology, 3,* 430–454.

Kahneman, D., & Tversky, A. (1973). On the psychology of prediction. *Psychological Review, 80,* 237–251.

Kahneman, D., & Tversky, A. (1984). Choices, values, and frames. *American Psychologist, 39,* 341–350.

Kail, R. V., Jr. (1992). Processing speed, speech rate, and memory. *Developmental Psychology, 28,* 899–904.

Kail, R. V., Jr. (1984). *The development of memory in children* (2nd ed.). New York: Freeman.

Kail, R. V., Jr., Carter, P., & Pellegrino, J. (1979). The locus of sex differences in spatial ability. *Perception & Psychophysics, 26,* 182–186.

Kail, R. V., Jr. & Pellegrino, J. W. (1985). *Human in-*

telligence: Perspectives and prospects. New York: Freeman.

Kaiser, S. B., & Chandler, J. L. (1988). Audience responses to appearance codes: Old-age imagery in the media. *The Gerontologist, 28,* 692-699.

Kalat, J. W. (1988). *Biological psychology* (3rd ed.). Belmont, CA: Wadsworth.

Kalat, J. W. (1992). *Biological psychology* (4th ed.). Belmont, CA: Wadsworth.

Kalbfleisch, P. J. (1993). Looking for a friend and a lover: Perspectives on evolving interpersonal relationships. In P. J. Kalbfleisch (Ed.), *Interpersonal communication: Evolving interpersonal relationships* (pp. 3–10). Hillsdale, NJ: Erlbaum.

Kanfer, F. H., & Goldstein, A. P. (Eds.). (1991). *Helping people change: A textbook of methods* (4th ed.). New York: Pergamon.

Kanizsa, G. (1976). Subjective contours. *Scientific American, 234*(4), 48–52.

Kantrowitz, B. (1993, June 28). He's the next best thing: A student of genius. *Newsweek,* pp. 47–48.

Kaplan, H. J., & Sadock, B. J. (Eds.). (1989). *Comprehensive Textbook of psychiatry/V, Vols. 1 & 2* (5th ed.). Baltimore, MD: Williams & Wilkins.

Kaplan, R. M. (1982). Nader's raid on the testing industry: Is it in the best interest of the consumer? *American Psychologist, 37,* 15–23.

Kaplan, R. M. (1985). The controversy related to the use of psychological tests. In B. B. Wolman (Ed.), *Handbook of intelligence* (pp. 465–504). New York: Wiley.

Kaplan, R. M., & Saccuzzo, D. P. (1993). *Psychological testing: Principles, applications, and issues* (3rd ed.). Pacific Grove, CA: Brooks/Cole.

Karno, M., Jenkins, J. H., Selva, A., Santana, F., Telles, C., Lopez, S., & Mintz, J. (1987). Expressed emotion and schizophrenic outcome among Mexican-American families. *Journal of Nervous and Mental Disease, 175,* 143–151.

Karno, M., & Norquist, G. S. (1989). Schizophrenia: Epidemiology. In H. I. Kaplan & B. J. Sadock (Eds.), *Comprehensive textbook of psychiatry/V* (5th ed., Vol. 1, pp. 699–705). Baltimore: Williams & Wilkins.

Kastenbaum, R. (1992). *The psychology of death* (2nd ed.). New York: Springer.

Katon, W. J., (1990). *Panic disorder in the medical setting.* Washington, DC: American Psychiatric Press.

Katz, P. A., & Boswell, S. (1986). Flexibility and traditionality in children's gender roles. *Genetic, Social, and General Psychology Monographs, 112,* 103–147.

Katz, S., Lautenschlager, G. J., Blackburn, A. B., & Harris, F. H. (1990). Answering reading comprehension items without passages on the SAT. *Psychological Science, 1,* 122–127.

Katz, S., & Mazur, M. A. (1979). *Understanding the rape victim.* New York: Wiley.

Katzman, R. (1986). Alzheimer's disease. *New England Journal of Medicine, 314,* 964–973.

Kay, P., & Kempton, W. (1984). What is the Sapir-Whorf hypothesis? *American Anthropologist, 86,* 65–79.

Kay, S. R. (1991). *Positive and negative syndromes in schizophrenia: Assessment and research.* New York: Brunner/Mazel.

Keen, S. (1986). *Faces of the enemy: Reflections of the hostile imagination.* San Francisco: Harper & Row.

Keesey, R. E., & Powley, T. L. (1986). The regulation of body weight. *Annual Review of Psychology, 37,* 109–133.

Keith, T. Z., Reimers, T. M., Fehrmann, P. G., Pottebaum, S. M., Aubrey, L. W. (1986). Parental involvement, homework, and TV time: Direct and indirect effects on high school achievement. *Journal of Educational Psychology, 78,* 373–380.

Keith-Spiegel, P., & Koocher, G. P. (1985). *Ethics in psychology.* Hillsdale, NJ: Erlbaum.

Kelley, H. H. (1986). Toward a taxonomy of interpersonal conflict processes. In S. Oskamp & S. Spacapan (Eds.), *Interpersonal processes* (pp. 122–147). Newbury Park, CA: Sage.

Kellner, R. (1985). Functional somatic symptoms and hypochondriasis: A survey of empirical studies. *Archives of General Psychiatry, 42,* 821–833.

Kelly, G. A. (1955). *The psychology of personal constructs.* New York: Norton.

Kelly, J. A., & Murphy, D. A. (1992). Psychological interventions with AIDS and HIV: Prevention and treatment. *Journal of Consulting and Clinical Psychology, 60,* 576–585.

Kelly, J. A., & St. Lawrence, J. S. (1988). *The AIDS health crisis.* New York: Plenum.

Kelly, M. H., Bock, J. K., & Keil, F. C. (1986). Prototypicality in a linguistic context: Effects on sentence structure. *Journal of Memory and Language, 25,* 59–74.

Kelly, M. H., & Rubin, D. C. (1988). Natural rhythmic patterns in English verse: Evidence from child counting-out rhymes. *Journal of Memory and Language, 27,* 718–740.

Kelman, H. C., & Hamilton, V. L. (1989). *Crimes of obedience: Toward a social psychology of authority and responsibility.* New Haven: Yale University Press.

Kennedy, S., Kiecolt-Glaser, J. K., & Glasser, R. (1990). Social support, stress, and the immune system. In B. R. Sarason, I. G. Sarason, & G. R. Pierce (Eds.), *Social support: An interactional view* (pp. 253–266). New York: Wiley.

Kenrick, D. T., & Funder, D. C. (1988). Profiting from controversy: Lessons from the person-situation debate. *American Psychologist, 43,* 23–34.

Kent, D. (1990, May). A conversation with Claude Steele. *APS Observer,* pp. 11–17.

Kent, G. (1991). Anxiety. In W. Dryden & R. Rentoul (Eds.), *Adult clinical problems: A cognitive-behavioural approach* (pp. 27–55). London: Routledge.

Keren, G. (1987). Facing uncertainty in the game of bridge: A calibration study. *Organizational Behavior and Human Decision Processes, 39,* 98–114.

Kesler, M. S., Denny, N. W., & Whitely, S. E. (1976). Factors influencing problem solving in middle-aged and elderly adults. *Human Development, 19,* 310–320.

Kessler, R. C., Price, R. H., & Wortman, C. B. (1985). Social factors in psychopathology: Stress, social support and coping processes. *Annual Review of Psychology, 36,* 531–572.

Kiang, N. Y., & Peake, W. T. (1988). Physics and physiology of hearing. In R. C. Atkinson, R. J. Herrnstein, G. Lindzey, & R. D. Luce (Eds.), *Stevens' handbook of experimental psychology* (2nd ed., Vol. I, pp. 277–326). New York: Wiley.

Kidder, L. H., & Judd, C. M. (1986). *Research methods in social relations* (5th ed.). New York: Holt, Rinehart and Winston.

Kiesler, C. A. (1991). Changes in general hospital psychiatric care, 1980–1985. *American Psychologist, 46,* 416–421.

Kihlstrom, J. F. (1985). Hypnosis. *Annual Review of Psychology, 36,* 385–418.

Kihlstrom, J. F. (1987). The cognitive unconscious. *Science, 327,* 1445–1452.

Kihlstrom, J. F., & McConkey, K. M. (1990). William James and hypnosis: A centennial reflection. *Psychological Sciences, 1,* 174–177.

Kihlstrom, J. F., Schacter, D. L., Cork, R. C., Hurt, C. A., & Behr, S. E. (1990). Implicit and explicit memory following surgical anesthesia. *Psychological Science, 1,* 303–306.

Killackey, H. P. (1990). The neocortex and memory storage. In J. L. McGaugh, N. M. Weinberger, & G. Lynch (Eds.), *Brain organization and memory: Cells, systems, and circuits* (pp. 265–270). New York: Oxford University Press.

Kimball, J. P. (1973). Seven principles of surface structure parsing in natural language. *Cognition, 2,* 15–47.

Kimball, M. M. (1989). A new perspective on women's math achievement. *Psychological Bulletin, 105,* 198–214.

Kimble, D. P. (1988). *Biological psychology.* New York: Holt, Rinehart and Winston.

Kimble, D. P. (1992). *Biological psychology* (2nd ed.). Fort Worth, TX: Harcourt Brace Jovanovich.

Kimble, G. A. (1990). Mother nature's bag of tricks is small. *Psychological Science, 1,* 36–41.

Kimble, G. A. (1992). *A modest proposal for a minor revolution in the language of psychology.* Paper presented at the convention of the American Psychological Society.

Kimmel, P. R., & VandenBos, G. R. (1992). *Peace: Abstracts of the psychological and behavioral literature, 1967–1990.* Washington, DC: American Psychological Association.

King, D. W., & King, L. A. (1991). Validity issues in research on Vietnam veteran adjustment. *Psychological Bulletin, 109,* 107–124.

King, N. J., Hamilton, D. I., & Ollendick, T. H. (1988). *Children's phobias: A behavioural perspective.* Chichester, England: Wiley.

Kirkley, B. G., Schneider, J. A., Agras, W. S., & Bachman, J. A. (1985). Comparison of two group treatments for bulimia. *Journal of Consulting and Clinical Psychology, 53,* 43–48,

Kite, M. E., Deaux, K., & Miele, M. (1991). Stereotypes of young and old: Does age outweigh gender? *Psychology and Aging, 6,* 19–27.

Kite, M. E., & Johnson, B. T. (1988). Attitudes toward older and younger adults: A meta-analysis. *Psychology and aging, 3,* 233–244.

Kitzinger, C. (1987). *The social construction of lesbianism.* London: Sage.

Klatzky, R. L. (1992). Image, not mind [Review of *Principles of mental imagery*]. *Contemporary Psychology, 37,* 1263–1264.

Klatzky, R. L., Lederman, S. J., & Matula, D. E. (1991). Imagined haptic exploration in judgments of object properties. *Journal of Experimental Psychology: Learning, Memory, and Cognition, 17,* 314–322.

Klein, M. (1940). Mourning and its relation to manic-depressive states. In *Contributions to psychoanalysis, 1921–1945* (pp. 282–310). London: Hogarth Press.

Klein, M. (1948). *Contributions to psycho-analysis, 1921–1945.* London: Hogarth Press.

Klein, S. B., & Kihlstrom, J. F. (1986). Elaboration, organization, and the self-reference effect in memory. *Journal of Experimental Psychology: General, 115,* 26–38.

Kleinke, C. L. (1984). Two models for conceptualizing the attitude-behavior relationship. *Human Relations, 37,* 333–350.

Robinson, J. (1987, September 12). Senators told of family's plight with AIDS. *Boston Globe*, p. 1.

Robinson, J. L., Kagan, J., Reznick, J. S., & Corley, R. (1992). The heritability of inhibited and uninhibited behavior: A twin study. *Developmental Psychology, 28*, 1030–1037.

Robinson, L. A., Berman, J. S., & Neimeyer, R. A. (1990). Psychotherapy for the treatment of depression: A comprehensive review of controlled outcome research. *Psychological Bulletin, 108*, 30–49.

Rock, I. (1983). *The logic of perception*. Cambridge, MA: MIT Press.

Rock, I. (1987). A problem-solving approach to illusory contours. In S. Petry & G. E. Meyer (Eds.), *The perception of illusory contours* (pp. 62–70). New York: Springer-Verlag.

Rodgers, J. E. (1982). The malleable memory of eyewitnesses. *Science Digest, 3*, 32–35.

Rodin, J. (1981). Current status of the internal-external hypothesis for obesity: What went wrong. *American Psychologist, 36*, 361–372.

Rodin, J. (1985). Insulin levels, hunger, and food intake: An example of feedback loops in body weight regulation. *Health Psychology, 4*, 1–24.

Rodin, J. (1992). *Body traps*. New York: Morrow.

Rodin, J., & Langer, E. J. (1977). Long-term effects of a control-relevant intervention with the institutionalized aged. *Journal of Personality and Social Psychology, 35*, 897–902.

Rodin, J., & Salovey, P. (1989). Health psychology. *Annual Review of Psychology, 40*, 533–579.

Rodin, J., Schooler, C., & Schaie, K. W. (Eds.). (1990). *Self-directedness: Causes and effects throughout the life course*. Hillsdale, NJ: Erlbaum.

Roediger, H. L. (1990). Implicit memory: Retention without remembering. *American Psychologist, 45*, 1043–1056.

Rogers, C. R. (1959). A theory of therapy, personality, and interpersonal relationships, as developed in the client-centered framework. In S. Koch (Ed.), *Psychology: A study of a science* (Vol. 3). New York: McGraw-Hill.

Rogers, C. R. (1961). *On becoming a person: A therapist's view of psychotherapy*. Boston: Houghton Mifflin.

Rogers, C. R. (1963). Actualizing tendency in relation to "motives" and to consciousness. In M. R. Jones (Ed.), *Nebraska symposium on motivation* (pp. 1–24). Lincoln, NE: University of Nebraska Press.

Rogers, C. R. (1980). *A way of being*. Boston: Houghton Mifflin.

Rogers, C. R. (1985). Toward a more human science of the person. *Journal of Humanistic Psychology, 25*, 7–24.

Rogers, C. R. (1986). Client-centered therapy. In I. L. Kutash & A. Wolf (Eds.), *Psychotherapist's casebook* (pp. 197–208). San Francisco: Jossey-Bass.

Rogers, C. R. (1987). A silent young man. In G. S. Belkin (Ed.), *Contemporary psychotherapies* (2nd ed., pp. 199–209). Monterey, CA: Brooks/Cole.

Rogers, T. B. (1983). Emotion, imagery, and verbal codes: A closer look at an increasingly complex interaction. In J. Yuille (Ed.), *Imagery, memory, and cognition* (pp. 285–305). Hillsdale, NJ: Erlbaum.

Rogers, T. B., Kuiper, N. A., & Kirker, W. S. (1977). Self-reference and the encoding of personal information. *Journal of Personality and Social Psychology, 35*, 677–688.

Roitblat, H. L. (1987). *Introduction to comparative cognition*. New York: Freeman.

Roitblat, H. L., & von Fersen, L. (1992). Comparative cognition: Representations and processes in learning and memory. *Annual Review of Psychology, 43*, 671–710.

Romaniuk, M. (1981). Reminiscence and the second half of life. *Experimental Aging Research, 7*, 315–336.

Rosch, E. H. (1973). Natural categories. *cognitive Psychology, 4*, 328–350.

Rosch, E. H. (1977). Human categorization. In N. Warren (Ed.), *Advances in cross-cultural psychology* (Vol. 1). London: Academic Press.

Rosch, E. H., & Mervis, C. B. (1975). Family resemblances: Studies in the internal structure of categories. *Cognitive Psychology, 7*, 573–605.

Rose, S. M., & Black, B. L. (1985). *Advocacy and empowerment: Mental health care in the community*. London: Routledge & Kegan Paul.

Rosekrans, M., & Hartup, W. (1967). Imitative influences of consistent and inconsistent response consequences to a model on aggressive behavior in children. *Journal of Personality and Social Psychology, 7*, 429–434.

Rosen, C. M. (1987, September). The eerie world of reunited twins. *Discover*, 36–46.

Rosenbaum, M. (1986). The repulsion hypothesis: On the nondevelopment of relationships. *Journal of Personality and Social Psychology, 51*, 1156–1166.

Rosenberg, S. (1993). Chomsky's theory of language: Some recent observations. *Psychological Science, 4*, 15–19.

Rosenhan, D. L. (1973). On being sane in insane places. *Science, 179*, 250–258.

Rosenman, R. H. (1990). Type A Behavior Pattern: A personal overview. *Journal of Social Behavior and Personality, 5*, 1–24.

Rosenthal, R. (1968, September). Self-fulfilling prophecy. *Psychology Today, 2*(4), pp. 44–51.

Rosenthal, R. (1973, September). The pygmalion effect lives. *Psychology Today, 7*(4), p. 56–63.

Rosenthal, R. (1976). *Experimenter effects in behavioral research* (Enlarged ed.). New York: Halstead Press.

Rosenthal, R., Hall, J. A., DeMatteo, M. R., Rogers, P. L., & Archer, D. (1979). *Sensitivity to nonverbal communication: The PONS test*. Baltimore: The Johns Hopkins University Press.

Ross, A. O. (1987). *Personality: The scientific study of complex human behavior*. New York: Holt, Rinehart and Winston.

Ross, C. A. (1989). *Multiple personality disorder: Diagnosis, clinical features and treatment*. New York: Wiley.

Ross, L. (1992, August). *Reactive devaluation and other barriers to dispute resolution*. Paper presented at the Annual Convention of the American Psychological Association, Washington, DC.

Ross, L., & Nisbett, R. E. (1991). *The person and the situation: Perspectives of social psychology*. New York: McGraw-Hill.

Ross, L., & Stillinger, C. (1991). Barriers to conflict resolution. *Negotiation Journal, 7*, 389–404.

Ross, L. D. (1988). Situationist perspectives on the obedience experiments. [Review of A. G. Miller's *The obedience experiments: A case study of controversy in social science*.] *Contemporary Psychology, 33*, 101–104.

Rosser, P. (1989). *The SAT gender gap*. Washington, DC: Center for Women Policy Studies.

Roşu, D., & Natanson, K. (1987, April). Out of the mouths of babes. *Michigan Today*, p. 5.

Rothbart, M., & John, O. P. (1985). Social categorization and behavioral episodes: A cognitive analysis of the effects of intergroup contact. *Journal of Social Issues, 41*, 81–104.

Rothbart, M. K., & Mauro, J. A. (1990). Questionnaire approaches to the study of infant temperament. In J. Colombo & J. Fagen (Eds.), *Individual differences in infancy: Reliability, stability, prediction* (pp. 411–429). Hillsdale, NJ: Erlbaum.

Rotton, J., & Kelly, I. W. (1985). Much ado about the full moon: A meta-analysis of lunar-lunacy research. *Psychological Bulletin, 97*, 286–306.

Rousar, E. E., III, & Aron, A. (1990, July). *Valuing, altruism, and the concept of love*. Paper presented at the Fifth International Conference on Personal Relationships, Oxford, England.

Rovee-Collier, C. K. (1987, April). *Infant memory*. Paper presented at the annual meeting of the Eastern Psychological Association, Crystal City, Virginia.

Rovee-Collier, C. K., Griesler, P. C., & Early, L. A. (1985). Contextual determinants of retrieval in three-month-old infants. *Learning and Motivation, 16*, 139–157.

Rovee-Collier, C. K., & Hayne, H. (1987). Reactivation of infant memory: Implications for cognitive development. *Advances in Child Development and Behavior, 20*, 185–238.

Rozée, P. D., & Van Boemel, G. (1989). The psychological effects of war trauma and abuse on older Cambodian refugee women. *Women & Therapy, 8*, 23–50.

Rozin, P., Millman, L., & Nemeroff, C. (1986). Operation of the laws of sympathetic magic in disgust and other domains. *Journal of Personality and Social Psychology, 50*, 703–712.

Rubin, D. C. (1992). Constraints on memory. In E. Winograd & U. Neisser (Eds.), *Affect and accuracy in recall* (pp. 265–273). New York: Cambridge University Press.

Rubin, D. C., & Kontis, T. C. (1983). A schema for common cents. *Memory & Cognition, 11*, 335–341.

Rubin, D. C., & Wallace, W. T. (1989). Rhyme and reason: Analyses of dual retrieval cues. *Journal of Experimental Psychology: Learning, Memory, and Cognition, 15*, 698–709.

Rubin, D. H., Krasilnikoff, P. A., Leventhal, J. M., Weile, B., & Berget, A. (1986, August 23). Effect of passive smoking on birth-weight. *Lancet, 8504*, pp. 415–417.

Rubin, E. (1915/1958). Synoplevede Figurer. Copenhagen: Cyldendalske. Abridged translation by M. Wertheimer: Figure and ground. In D. C. Beardsley & M. Wertheimer (Eds.), *Readings in perception*. Princeton, NJ: Van Nostrand.

Rubin, J. Z. (1991a). Psychological approach. In V. A. Kremenyuk (Ed.), *International negotiation: Analysis, approaches, issues* (pp. 216–228). San Francisco: Jossey-Bass.

Rubin, J. Z. (1991b). The timing of ripeness and the ripeness of timing. In L. Kriesberg & S. J. Thorson (Eds.), *Timing and the de-escalation of international conflicts*. Syracuse, NY: Syracuse University Press.

Rubin, Z., Peplau, L. A., & Hill, C.T. (1981). Loving and leaving: Sex differences in romantic attachments. *Sex Roles, 7*, 821–835.

Rubinstein, B. (1986, October 20). Making the private-school grade. *New York*, pp. 54–57.

Rubonis, A. V., & Bickman, L. (1991). Psychological impairment in the wake of disaster: The disaster-psychopathology relationship. *Psychological Bulletin, 109*, 384–399.

Kleinmuntz, B., & Szucko, J. J. (1984, March 29). A field study of the fallibility of polygraphic lie detection. *Nature, 308,* pp. 449–450.

Klerman, G. L., & Weissman, M. M. (1989). Increasing rates of depression. *JAMA, 261,* 2229–2235.

Klimas, N., Baron, G. C., & Fletcher, M. A. (1991). The immunology of HIV-1 infection. In P. M. McCabe, N. Schneiderman, T. M. Field, & J. S. Skyler (Eds.), *Stress, coping and disease* (pp. 193–209). Hillsdale, NJ: Erlbaum.

Kline, D. W., Kline, T. J. B., Fozard, J. L., Kosnik, W., Schieber, F., & Sekuler, R. (1992). Vision, aging, and driving: The problems of older drivers. *Journal of Gerontology: Psychological Sciences, 47.* P27–P34.

Kline, D. W., & Schieber, F. (1981). What are the age differences in visual sensory memory? *Journal of Gerontology, 36,* 86–89.

Knox, V. J., Gekoski, W. L., Johnson, E. A. (1986). Contact with and perceptions of the elderly. *The Gerontologist, 26,* 309–313.

Kogan, N. (1990). Personality and aging. In J. E. Birren & K. W. Schaie (Eds.), *Handbook of the psychology of aging* (3rd ed., pp. 330–346). San Diego: Academic Press.

Kohlberg, L. (1964). The development of moral character and moral ideology. In M. Hoffman & L. Hoffman (Eds.), *Review of child development research* (Vol. 1). New York: Russell Sage Foundation.

Kohlberg, L. (1966). A cognitive-developmental analysis of children's sex-role concepts and attitudes. In E. E. Maccoby (Ed.), *The development of sex differences* (pp. 82–173). Stanford, CA: Stanford University Press.

Kohlberg, L. (1969). Stage and sequence: The cognitive-developmental approach to socialization. In D. A. Goslin (Ed.), *Handbook of socialization theory and research.* Chicago, IL: Rand McNally.

Kohlberg, L. (1984). *Essays on moral development: Vol. 2, The psychology of moral development.* San Francisco: Freeman.

Kohlberg, L., & Ryncarz, R. A. (1990). Beyond justice reasoning: Moral development and consideration of a seventh stage. In C. N. Alexander & E. J. Langer (Eds.), *Higher stages of human development* (pp. 191–207). New York: Oxford University Press.

Kohlberg, L., & Ullian, D. Z. (1974). Stages in the development of psychosexual concepts and attitudes. In R. C. Friedman, R. M. Richart, & R. I. Van de Wiele (Eds.), *Sex differences in behavior* (pp. 209–222). New York: Wiley.

Kohn, A. (1988, April). You know what they say . . . *Psychology Today,* pp. 36–41.

Kohn, A. (1990). *The brighter side of human nature.* New York: Basic.

Kohn, P. M., Lafreniere, K., & Gurevich, M. (1990). The inventory of college students' recent life experiences: A decontaminated hassles scale for a special population. *Journal of Behavioral Medicine, 13,* 619–630.

Kohn, P. M., Lafreniere, K., & Gurevich, M. (1991). Hassles, health, and personality. *Journal of Personality and Social Psychology, 61,* 478–482.

Kohn, P. M., & Macdonald, J. E. (1992). Hassles, anxiety, and negative well-being. *Anxiety, Stress, and Coping, 5,* 151–163.

Kokotovic, A., & Tracey, T. (1990). Working alliance in the early phase of counseling. *Journal of Counseling Psychology, 37,* 16–21.

Kolb, B., & Whishaw, I. Q. (1985). *Fundamentals of human neuropsychology* (2nd ed.). New York: Freeman.

Kominski, R. (1993, September). *We the Americans: Our education.* Washington, DC: Bureau of the Census.

Koretz, J. F., & Handelman, G. H. (1988). How the human eye focuses. *Scientific American, 259*(1), 92–99.

Koss, M. P., Dinero, T. E., Siebel, C. A., & Cox, S. L. (1988). Stranger and acquaintance rape: Are there differences in the victim's experience? *Psychology of Women Quarterly, 12,* 1–24.

Koss, M. P., Gidycz, C. A., & Wisniewski, N. (1987). The scope of rape: Incidence and prevalence in a national sample of higher education students. *Journal of Consulting and Clinical Psychology, 55,* 162–170.

Kosslyn, S. M. (1975). Information representation in visual images. *Cognitive Psychology, 7,* 341–370.

Kosslyn, S. M. (1980). *Image and mind.* Cambridge, MA: Harvard University Press.

Kosslyn, S. M. (1988). Aspects of a cognitive neuroscience of mental imagery. *Science, 240,* 1621–1626.

Kosslyn, S. M., & Koenig, O. (1992). *Wet mind: The new cognitive neuroscience.* New York: Free Press.

Kosslyn, S. M., Seger, C., Pani, J. R., & Hillger, L. A. (1990). When is imagery used in everyday life? A diary study. *Journal of Mental Imagery, 14,* 131–152.

Kottke, T. E., Battista, R. N., DeFriese, G. H., & Brekke, M. L. (1988). Attributes of successful smoking cessation interventions in medical practice: A meta-analysis of 39 controlled trials. *JAMA, 259,* 2882–2889.

Koulack, D. (1991). *To catch a dream: Explorations of dreaming.* Albany: State University of New York Press.

Kozlowski, L. T., Wilkinson, A., Skinner, W., Kent, C., Franklin, T., & Pope, M. (1989). Comparing tobacco cigarette dependence with other drug dependencies. *JAMA, 261,* 898–901.

Kramer, P. D. (1993). *Listening to Prozac.* New York: Viking.

Krank, M. D. (1989). Pavlovian conditioning: Providing a bridge between cognition and biology. *Behavioral and Brain Sciences, 12,* 151.

Krantz, D. S., Grunberg, N. E., & Baum, A. (1985). Health psychology. *Annual Review of Psychology, 36,* 349–383.

Krause, N. (1991). Stressful events and life satisfaction among elderly men and women. *Journal of Gerontology: Social Sciences, 46,* S84–S92.

Krause, N., Herzog, A. R., & Baker, E. (1992). Providing support to others and well-being in later life. *Journal of Gerontology: Psychological Sciences, 47,* P300–P311.

Krauss, R. M., Morrel-Samuels, P., & Colasante, C. (1991). Do conversational hand gestures communicate? *Journal of Personality and Social Psychology, 61,* 743–754.

Krauthamer, C. (1989). Personal communication.

Kravetz, D. (1987). Benefits of consciousness-raising groups for women. In C. M. Brody (Ed.), *Women's therapy groups: Paradigms of feminist treatment* (pp. 55–66). New York: Springer.

Kreipe, R. E., Churchill, B. H., & Strauss, J. (1989). Long-term outcome of adolescents with anorexia nervosa. *American Journal of Diseases of Children, 143,* 1322–1327.

Kristiansen, C. M. (1983). Newspaper coverage of diseases and actual mortality statistics. *European Journals of Social Psychology, 13,* 193–194.

Krogh, D. (1991). *Smoking: the artificial passion.* New York: Freeman.

Krueger, L. E. (1992). The word-superiority effect and phonological recoding. *Memory & Cognition, 20,* 685–694.

Kryter, K. D. (1985). *The effects of noise on man* (2nd ed.). Orlando, FL: Academic.

Kübler-Ross, E. (1969). *On death and dying* (2nd ed.). New York: Macmillan.

Kuczmarski, R. J. (1992). Prevalence of overweight and weight gain in the United States. *American Journal of Clinical Nutrition, 55* (Supplement), 495S–502S.

Kuehnel, J. M., & Liberman, R. P. (1986). Behavior modification. In I. L. Kutash & A. Wolf (Eds.), *Psychotherapist's casebook* (pp. 240–262). San Francisco: Jossey-Bass.

Kuhl, P. K., Williams, K.A., Lacerda, F., Stevens, K. N., & Lindblom, B. (1992). Linguistic experience alters phonetic perception in infants by 6 months of age. *Science, 255,* 606–608

Kuhn, D. (1984). Cognitive development. In M. H. Bornstein & M. E. Lamb (Eds.), *Developmental psychology: An advanced textbook* (pp. 133–180). Hillsdale, NJ: Erlbaum.

Kuhn, D. (1992). Cognitive development. In M. H. Bornstein & M. E. Lamb (Eds.), *Developmental psychology: An advanced textbook* (3rd ed., pp. 211–272). Hillsdale, NJ: Erlbaum.

Kukde, M. P., & Neufeld, R. W. J. (1992). *Stress of control: Cognitive demands of exercising choice during active coping.* Paper presented at the annual meeting of the Canadian Psychological Association, Québec City.

Kurdek, L. A. (1987). Sex role self schema and psychological adjustment in coupled homosexual and heterosexual men and women. *Sex Roles, 17,* 549–562.

Kurdek, L. A. (1991a). Predictors of increases in marital distress in newlywed couples: A 3-year prospective longitudinal study. *Developmental Psychology, 27,* 627–636.

Kurdek, L. A. (1991b). Correlates of relationship satisfaction of cohabiting gay and lesbian couples: Integration of contextual, investment, and problem-solving models. *Journal of Personality and Social Psychology, 61,* 910–922.

Kurdek, L. A. (1993). Predicting marital dissolution: A 5-year prospective longitudinal study of newlywed couples. *Journal of Personality and Social Psychology, 64,* 221–242.

Kurdek, L. A., & Schmitt, J. P. (1986). Relationship quality of partners in heterosexual married, heterosexual cohabiting, and gay and lesbian relationships. *Journal Personality and Social Psychology, 51,* 711–720.

Kwentus, J., Schulz, S. C., Fairman, P., & Isrow, L. (1985). Sleep apnea: A review. *Psychosomatics, 26,* 713–724.

Kymissis, E., & Poulson, C. L. (1990). The history of imitation in learning theory: The language acquisition process. *Journal of the Experimental Analysis of Behavior, 54,* 113–127.

LaBerge, S. (1990). Lucid dreaming: Psychophysiological studies of consciousness during REM sleep. In R. R. Bootzin, J. F. Kihlstrom, & D. L. Schacter (Eds.), *Sleep and cognition* (pp. 109–126). Washington, DC: American Psychological Association.

Labouvie-Vief, G. (1992). A neo-Piagetian perspective on adult cognitive development. In R. J. Sternberg & C. A. Berg (Eds.), *Intellectual development* (pp. 197–228). Cambridge, England: Cambridge University Press.

LaFromboise, J., & Low, K. (1989). American Indian children and adolescents. In J. Gibbs & L. Huang (Eds.), *Children of color: Psychological interventions with minority youth.* San Francisco: Jossey-Bass.

LaFromboise, T. D. (1988). American Indian mental health policy. *American Psychologist, 43,* 388–397.

LaFromboise, T. D., Coleman, H. L. K., & Gerton, J. (1993). Psychological impact of biculturalism: Evidence and theory. *Psychological Bulletin, 114,* 395–412.

Laird, J. D. (1984). Facial response and emotion. *Journal of Personality and Social Psychology, 47,* 909–917.

Lalancette, M. & Standing, L. (1990). Asch fails again. *Social Behavior and Personality, 18,* 7–12.

Lamb, M. E. (1987). Introduction: The emergent American father. In M. E. Lamb (Ed.), *The father's role: Cross-cultural perspectives* (pp. 3–25). Hillsdale, NJ: Erlbaum.

Lambert, M. J., Shapiro, D. A., & Bergin, A. E. (1986). The effectiveness of psychotherapy. In S. L. Garfield & A. E. Bergin (Eds.), *Handbook of psychotherapy and behavior change* (pp. 157–211). New York: Wiley.

Lambert, W. E. (1990). Persistent issues in bilingualism. In B. Harley, P. Allen, J. Cummins, & M. Swain (Eds.), *The development of second language proficiency* (pp. 201–218). Cambridge, England: Cambridge University Press.

Lambert, W. E. (1992). Challenging established views on social issues. *American Psychologist, 47,* 533–542.

Lambert, W. E., Genesee, F., Holobow, N., & Chartrand, L. (1991). *Bilingual education for majority English-speaking children.* Montreal, Québec, Canada: McGill University, Psychology Department.

Lamborn, S. D., Mounts, N. S., Steinberg, L., & Dornbusch, S. M. (1991). Patterns of competence and adjustment among adolescents from authoritative, authoritarian, indulgent, and neglectful families. *Child Development, 62,* 1049–1065.

Lande, J. S., Scarr, S., & Gunzenhauser, N. (Eds.). (1989). *Caring for children: Challenge to America.* Hillsdale, NJ: Erlbaum.

Landers, S. (1988, March). Public interest. *APA Monitor, 19,* 22–23.

Lang, H. (1992). *Gender differences in actual health behavior and attitudes towards appropriate health behavior.* Unpublished manuscript, SUNY Geneseo.

Langer, E. J. (1989a). *Mindfulness.* Reading, MA: Addison-Wesley.

Langer, E. J. (1989b). Minding matters: The consequences of mindlessness-mindfulness. *Advances in Experimental Social Psychology, 22,* 137–173.

Langer, E. J., & Piper, A. I. (1987). The prevention of mindlessness. *Journal of Personality and Social Psychology, 53,* 280–287.

Langer, E. J., & Rodin, J. (1976). The effects of choice and enhanced personal responsibility for the aged: A field experiment in an institutional setting. *Journal of Personality and Social Psychology, 34,* 191–198.

Langlois, J. H., Ritter, J. M., Roggman, L. A., & Vaughn, L. S. (1991). Facial diversity and infant preferences for attractive faces. *Developmental Psychology, 27,* 79–84.

LaPiere, R. T. (1934). Attitudes vs. actions. *Social Forces, 13,* 230–237.

Lappin, J. S., & Preble, L. D. (1975). A demonstration of shape constancy. *Perception & Psychophysics, 25,* 180–184.

Larkin, J. H. (1985). Understanding, problem representations, and skill in physics. In S. F. Chipman, J. W. Segal, & R. Glaxer (Eds.), *Thinking and learning skills* (Vol. 2, pp. 141–159). Hillsdale, NJ: Erlbaum.

Larkin, J. H., & Simon, H. A. (1987). Why a diagram is (sometimes) worth ten thousand words. *Cognitive Science, 11,* 65–99.

Larson, J. H., Crane, D. R., & Smith, C. W. (1991). Morning and night couples: The effect of wake and sleep patterns on marital adjustment. *Journal of Marital and Family Therapy, 17,* 53–65.

Latané, B., & Darley, J. M. (1970). *The unresponsive bystander: Why doesn't he help?* New York: Appleton.

Latané, B., & Nida, S. (1981). Ten years of research on group size and helping. *Psychological Bulletin, 89,* 308–324.

Lattal, K. A. (Ed.). (1992). Reflections on B. F. Skinner and psychology [Special Issue]. *American Psychologist, 47,* (11).

Lauer, J. C., & Lauer, R. H. (1985, June). Marriages made to last. *Psychology Today,* pp. 22–26.

Lavie, P., & Hobson, J. A. (1986). Origin of dreams: Anticipation of modern theories in the philosophy and physiology of the eighteenth and nineteenth centuries. *Psychological Bulletin, 100,* 229–240.

Lavigne, V. D., & Finley, G. E. (1990). Memory in middle-aged adults. *Educational Gerontology, 16,* 447–461.

Lavond, D. G., Lincoln, J. S., McCormick, D. A., & Thompson, R. F. (1984). Effect of bilateral lesions of the dentate and interpositus nuclei on conditioning of heart-rate and nictitating membrane/eyelid response in the rabbit. *Brain Research, 305,* 323–330.

Law, D. J., Pellegrino, J. W., & Hunt, E. B. (1993). Comparing the tortoise and the hare: Gender differences and experience in dynamic spatial reasoning tasks. *Psychological Science, 4,* 35–40.

Lawless, H. T., & Engen, T. (1977). Associations to odors: Interference, memories, and verbal labeling. *Journal of Experimental Psychology: Human Learning and Memory, 3,* 52–59.

Lawton, M. P. (1990). Residential environment and self-directedness among older people. *American Psychologist, 45,* 638–640.

Lazarus, A. A., & Fay, A. (1984). Behavior therapy. In T. B. Karasu (Ed.), *The psychiatric therapies* (pp. 483–538). Washington, DC: American Psychiatric Association.

Lazarus, J. H. (1986). *Endocrine and metabolic effects on lithium.* New York: Plenum Press.

Lazarus, R. S. (1984). Puzzles in the study of daily hassles. *Journal of Behavioral Medicine, 7,* 375–389.

Lazarus, R. S. (1991a). Cognition and motivation in emotion. *American Psychologist, 46,* 352–367.

Lazarus, R. S. (1991b). *Emotion and adaptation.* New York: Oxford University Press.

Lazarus, R. S. (1993). From psychological stress to the emotions: A history of changing outlooks. *Annual Review of Psychology, 44,* 1–21.

Lazarus, R. S., & Folkham, S. (1984). *Stress, appraisal, and coping.* New York: Springer.

Lebow, J. (1982). Consumer satisfaction with mental health treatment. *Psychological Bulletin, 91,* 244–259.

Leccese, A. P. (1991). *Drugs and society: Behavioral medicines and abusable drugs.* Englewood Cliffs, NJ: Prentice-Hall.

Lederman, D. (1991, November 27). A prize-winning playwright seeks to inspire. *The Chronicle of Higher Education,* p. A5.

LeDoux, J. E. (1987). Emotion. In F. Plum (Ed.), *Handbook of physiology* (Vol. 5, pp. 419–459). Bethesda, MD: American Physiological Society.

LeDoux, J. E. (1989). Cognitive-emotional interactions in the brain. *Cognition and Emotion, 3,* 267–289.

Lee, C. (1985). Successful rural black adolescents. A psychosocial profile. *Adolescence, 77,* 131–141.

Lee, L. C. (1992). *The search for universals: Whatever happened to race and culture?* Paper presented at the convention of the American Psychological Association, Washington, DC.

Leenaars, A. A., & Domino, G. (1993). A comparison of community attitudes towards suicide in Windsor and Los Angeles. *Canadian Journal of Behavioural Science, 25,* 253–266.

Leenaars, A. A., & Lester, D. (1992). Comparison of rates and patterns of suicide in Canada and the United States, 1960-1988. *Death Studies, 16,* 417–430.

Lefcourt, H. M., & Davidson-Katz, K. (1990a). The role of humor and the self. In C. R. Snyder & D. R. Forsyth (Eds.), *Handbook of social and clinical psychology* (pp. 41–56). New York: Pergamon.

Lefcourt, H. M., & Davidson-Katz, K. (1990b). Locus of control and health. In C. R. Snyder & D. R. Forsyth (Eds.), *Handbook of social and clinical psychology: The health perspective* (pp. 247–266). New York: Pergamon.

Leff, J., & Vaughan, C. (1985). *Expressed emotion in families.* New York: Guilford.

Lefley, H. P. (1989). Family burden and family stigma in major mental illness. *American Psychologist, 44,* 556 560.

Leigh, B. C. (1989). In search of the seven dwarves: Issues of measurement and meaning in alcohol expectancy research. *Psychological Bulletin, 105,* 362–373.

Leinbach, M. D., & Fagot, B. I. (1991). Attractiveness in young children: Sex-differentiated reactions of adults. *Sex Roles, 25,* 269–284.

Lender, M. E., & Martin, J. K. (1982). *Drinking in America: A history.* New York: Free Press.

Lenney, E. (1977). Women's self-confidence in achievement settings. *Psychological Bulletin, 84,* 1–13.

Lennie, P. (1980). Parallel visual pathways: A review. *Vision Review, 20,* 561–594.

Leo, J. (1984, October 8). The ups and downs of creativity. *Time,* p. 76.

Leo, J. (1985, February 18). Salvaging victims of torture. *Time,* p. 86.

Lerman, H. G. (1986a). From Freud to feminist personality theory: Getting here from there. *Psychology of Women Quarterly, 10,* 1–18.

Lerman, H. G. (1986b). *A mote in Freud's eye: From psychoanalysis to the psychology of women.* New York: Springer.

Lerner, H. G. (1989). *Women in therapy.* New York: Harper & Row.

Lerner, J. V., & Galambos, N. L. (Eds.). (1991). *Employed mothers and their children.* New York: Garland.

Lesgold, A. (1988). Problem solving. In R. J. Sternberg & E. E. Smith (Eds.), *The psychology of human thought.* Cambridge, England: Cambridge University Press.

Levenson, R. W. (1992). Autonomic nervous system differences among emotions. *Psychological Science, 3,* 23–27.

Levenson, R. W., Ekman, P., Heider, K., & Friesen, W. V. (1992). Emotion and autonomic nervous system activity in the Minangkabau of West Sumatra. *Journal of Personality and Social Psychology, 62,* 972–988.

Leventhal, H., Glynn, K., & Fleming, R. (1987). Is the smoking decision an "informed choice"? Effects of smoking risk factors on smoking beliefs. *JAMA, 257,* 3373–3376.

Levine, I. S., & Rog, D. J. (1990). Mental health services for homeless mentally ill persons: Federal initiatives and current service trends. *American Psychologist, 45,* 963–968.

Levine, J. M., & Moreland, R. L. (1990). Progress in small group research. *Annual Review of Psychology, 41,* 585–634.

Levine, M., Toro, P. A., & Perkins, D. V. (1993). Social and community interventions. *Annual Review of Psychology, 44,* 525–558.

Levinson, D. J., Darrow, C. M., Klein, E. B., Levinson, M. H., & McKee, B. (1978). *The seasons of a man's life.* New York: Knopf.

Levy, J. (1983). Language, cognition, and the right hemisphere. *American Psychologist, 38,* 538–541.

Levy, J. (1985, May). Right brain, left brain: Fact and fiction. *Psychology Today, 19,* 38–44.

Lewine, R. R. J. (1991). Ontogenetic implications of sex differences in schizophrenia. In E. F. Walker (Ed.), *Schizophrenia: A life-course developmental perspective* (pp. 195–211). San Diego, CA: Academic Press.

Lewinsohn, P. H. (1974). A behavioral approach to depression. In R. J. Friedman & M. M. Katz (Eds.), *The psychology of depression: Contemporary theory and research.* Washington, DC: Winston-Wiley.

Lewis, C. E., Robins, L., & Rice, J. (1985). Association of alcoholism with antisocial personality in urban men. *Journal of Nervous and Mental Disorders, 173,* 166–174.

Lewis, E. R., Everhart, T. E., & Zeevi, Y. Y. (1969). Study of neural organization in Aplysia with the scanning electron microscope. *Science, 165,* 1140–1143.

Lewis, J. W., Terman, G. W., Shavit, Y., Nelson, L. R., & Liebeskind, J. C. (1984). Neural, neurochemical, and hormonal bases of stress-induced analgesia. In L. Kruger & J. C. Liebeskind (Eds.), *Neural mechanisms of pain* (pp. 277–288). New York: Raven.

Lewis, M., & Brooks, J. (1978). Self-knowledge in emotional development. In M. Lewis & L. Rosenblum (Eds.), *The development of affect* (pp. 205–226). New York: Plenum.

Liben, L. S., & Signorella, M. L. (Eds.). (1987). *Children's gender schemata.* San Francisco: Jossey-Bass.

Lichtenstein, E., & Glasgow, R. E. (1992). Smoking cessation: What have we learned over the past decade? *Journal of Consulting and Clinical Psychology, 60,* 518–527.

Lieberman, D. A. (1990). *Learning: Behavior and Cognition.* Belmont, CA: Wadsworth.

Lieberman, M. A., & Peskin, H. (1992). Adult life crises. In J. E. Birren, R. B. Sloane, & G. D. Cohen (Eds.), *Handbook of mental health and aging* (2nd ed., pp. 119–143). San Diego: Academic Press.

Liebert, R. M., & Sprafkin, J. (1988). *The early window* (3rd ed.). Elmsford, NY: Pergamon.

Lifton, R. J. (1967). *Death in life: Survivors of Hiroshima.* New York: Simon & Schuster.

Light, L. L., & Albertson, S. A. (1989). Direct and indirect tests of memory for category exemplars in young and older adults. *Psychology and Aging, 4,* 487–492.

Light, L. L., & Singh, A. (1987). Implicit and explicit memory in young and older adults. *Journal of Experimental Psychology: Learning, Memory, and Cognition, 13,* 531–541.

Lindsey, K. P., & Paul, G. L. (1989). Involuntary commitments to public mental institutions: Issues involving the overrepresentation of blacks and assessment of relevant functioning. *Psychological Bulletin, 106,* 171–183.

Lindskold, S. (1978). Trust development, the GRIT proposal, and the effects of conciliatory acts on conflict and cooperation. *Psychological Bulletin, 85,* 772–793.

Lindskold, S. (1985). GRIT: Reducing distrust through carefully introduced conciliation. In S. Worchel & W. G. Austin (Eds.), *Psychology of intergroup relations* (2nd ed., pp. 305–322). Chicago: Nelson-Hall.

Lindsley, J. R. (1975). Producing simple utterances: How far ahead do we plan? *Cognitive Psychology, 7,* 1–19.

Linn, M. C. (1986). Meta-analysis of studies of gender differences: Implications and future directions. In J. S. Hyde & M. C. Linn (Eds.), *The psychology of gender: Advances through meta-analysis* (pp. 210–231). Baltimore: Johns Hopkins University Press.

Linn, M. C. (1992). Gender differences in educational achievement. In Educational Testing Service (Ed.), *Sex equity in educational opportunity, achievement, and testing: Proceedings of the 1991 Invitational Conference of the Educational Testing Service.* Princeton, NJ: Educational Testing Service.

Linn, M. C., & Hyde, J. S. (1989, November). Gender, mathematics, and science. *Educational Researcher, 18,* pages 17–19, 22–27.

Linn, M. C., & Petersen, A. C. (1986). A meta-analysis of gender differences in spatial ability: Implications for mathematics and science achievement. In J. S. Hyde & M. C. Linn (Eds.), *The psychology of gender: Advances through meta-analysis* (pp. 67–101). Baltimore: Johns Hopkins University Press.

Linn, R. I. (1982). Admissions testing on trial. *American Psychologist, 37,* 279–291.

Linville, P. W. (1982). The complexity-extremity effect and age-based stereotyping. *Journal of Personality and Social Psychology, 42,* 193–211.

Linville, P. W., & Jones, E. E. (1980). Polarized appraisals of outgroup members. *Journal of Personality and Social Psychology, 38,* 689–703.

Linville, P. W., Salovey, P., & Fischer, G. W. (1986). Stereotyping and perceived distributions of social characteristics: An application to ingroup-outgroup perception. In J. F. Dovidio & S. L. Gaertner (Eds.), *Prejudice, discrimination, and racism* (pp. 165–208). New York: Academic.

Lipsitt, L. P., & VandenBos, G. R. (1992). Foreword. In M. Glantz & R. Pickens (Eds.), *Vulnerability to drug abuse* (pp. xv–xvi). Washington, DC: American Psychological Association.

Liu, M. (1991, July 29). Pass a snake, hold the rat. *Newsweek,* p. 35.

Liu, S. S. (1971). Differential conditioning and stimulus generalization of the rabbit's nictitating membrane response. *Journal of Comparative and Physiological Psychology, 77,* 136–142.

Livingstone, M. S. (1987). Art, illusion and the visual system. *Scientific American, 258*(1), 78–85.

Locurto, C. (1989). The dark side of hegemony. *Behavioral and Brain Sciences, 12,* 153–154.

Locurto, C. (1991). *Sense and nonsense about IQ: The case for uniqueness.* New York: Praeger.

Loehlin, J. C., Willerman, L., & Horn, J. M. (1988). Human behavior genetics. *Annual Review of Psychology, 39,* 101–133.

Loftus, E. F. (1991). The glitter of everyday memory . . . and the gold. *American Psychologist, 46,* 16–18.

Loftus, E. F. (1992). When a lie becomes memory's truth: Memory distortion after exposure to misinformation. *Current Directions in Psychological Science, 1,* 121–123.

Loftus, E. F., Donders, K., Hoffman, H. G., & Schooler, J. W. (1989). Creating new memories that are quickly accessed and confidently held. *Memory & Cognition, 17,* 607–616.

Loftus, E. F., Fienberg, S. E., & Tanur, J. M. (1985). Cognitive psychology meets the national survey. *American Psychologist, 40,* 175–180.

Loftus, E. F., & Hoffman, H. G. (1989). Misinformation and memory: The creation of new memories. *Journal of Experimental Psychology: General, 118,* 100–104.

Loftus, E. F., & Ketcham, K. (1991). *Witness for the defense.* New York: St. Martin's Press.

Loftus, E. F., & Klinger, M. R. (1992). Is the unconscious smart or dumb? *American Psychologist, 47,* 761–765.

Loftus, E. F., Miller, D. G., & Burns, H. J. (1978). Semantic integration of verbal information into a visual memory. *Journal of Experimental Psychology, 4,* 19–31.

Logue, A. W. (1991). *The psychology of eating and drinking: An introduction.* New York: Freeman.

Lombardi, K. L. (1990). Depressive states and somatic symptoms. In B. B. Wolman & G. Stricker (Eds.), *Depressive disorders: Facts, theories and treatment methods* (pp. 149–161). New York: Wiley.

Long, G. M. (1980). Iconic memory: A review and critique of the study of short-term visual storage. *Psychological Bulletin, 88,* 785–820.

Long, S. (1988). The six group therapies compared. In S. Long (Ed.), *Six group therapies* (pp. 327–338). New York: Plenum.

Lonky, E., Kaus, C. R., & Roodin, P. A. (1984). Life experience and mode of coping: Relations to moral judgment in adulthood. *Developmental Psychology, 20,* 1159–1167.

López, S. R. (1989). Patient variable biases in clinical judgment: Conceptual overview and methodological considerations. *Psychological Bulletin, 106,* 184–203.

Lore, R. K., & Schultz, L. A. (1993). Control of human aggression: A comparative perspective. *American Psychologist, 48,* 16–25.

Lorenz, K. (1974). *The eight deadly sins of civilized man.* New York: Harcourt Brace Jovanovich.

Lorenzo, G. (1989). Current issues in the assessment and treatment of ethnic minority populations. *Psychotherapy in Private Practice, 7,* 133–140.

Lott, B. (1985). The devaluation of women's competence. *Journal of Social Issues, 41,* 43–60.

Lott, B. (1987). Sexist discrimination as distancing behavior: I. A laboratory demonstration. *Psychology of Women Quarterly, 13,* 341–355.

Lovelace, E. A., & Coon, V. E. (1991). Aging and word finding: Reverse vocabulary and Cloze tests. *Bulletin of the Psychonomic Society, 29,* 33–35.

Lovelace, E. A., & Twohig, P. (1984). *Perceptions of memory function by older adults.* Paper presented at meeting of American Psychological Association, Toronto.

Lu, Z.-L., Williamson, S. J., & Kaufman, L. (1992). Behavioral lifetime of human auditory sensory memory predicted by physiological measures. *Science, 258,* 1668–1670.

Lubben, J. E., & Becerra, R. M. (1987). Social support among Black, Mexican, and Chinese elderly. In D. E. Gelfand & C. M. Barresi (Eds.), *Ethnic dimensions of aging* (pp. 130–144). New York: Springer.

Lubin, B., Larsen, R. M., & Matarazzo, J. D. (1984). Patterns of psychological test usage in the United States: 1935–1982. *American Psychologist, 39,* 451–454.

Lubinski, D., & Humphreys, L. G. (1990). A broadly based analysis of mathematical giftedness. *Intelligence, 14,* 327–355.

Lubomudrov, S. (1987). Congressional perceptions of the elderly: The use of stereotypes in the legislative process. *The Gerontologist, 27,* 77–81.

Luce, R. D., & Krumhansl, C. L. (1988). Measurement, scaling, and psychophysics. In R. C. Atkinson, R. J. Herrnstein, G. Lindzey, & R. D. Luce (Eds.), *Stevens' handbook of experimental psychology* (2nd ed., pp. 3–74). New York: Wiley.

Luchins, A. S. (1957). Primacy-recency in impression formation. In C. I. Hovland (Ed.), *The order of presentation in persuasion* (pp. 33–61). New Haven: Yale University Press.

Luepnitz, D. A. (1988). *The family interpreted: Feminist theory in clinical practice.* New York: Basic Books.

Lykken, D. T., McGue, M., Tellegen, A., & Bouchard, T. J., Jr. (1992). Emergenesis: Genetic traits that may not run in families. *American Psychologist, 47,* 1565–1577.

Lynn, S. J., Rhue, J. W., & Weekes, J. R. (1990). Hypnotic involuntariness: A social cognitive analysis. *Psychological Review, 97,* 169–184.

Lyons, M. L., Kendler, K. S., Provet, A. G., & Tsuang, M. T. (1991). The genetics of schizophrenia. In M. T. Tsuang, K. S. Kendler, & M. J. Lyons (Eds.), *Genetic issues in psychosocial epidemiology* (pp. 119–152). New Brunswick, NJ: Rutgers University Press.

Lyons, W. (1986). *The disappearance of introspection.* Cambridge, MA: MIT Press.

Lytton, H., & Romney, D. M. (1991). Parents' differential socialization of boys and girls: A meta-analysis. *Psychological Bulletin, 109,* 267–296.

Maccoby, E. E. (1984). Socialization and developmental change. *Child Development, 55,* 317–328.

Maccoby, E. E. (1986). Social groupings in childhood: Their relationship to prosocial and antisocial behavior in boys and girls. In D. Olweus, J. Block, & M. Radke-Yarrow (Eds.), *Development of antisocial and prosocial behavior* (pp. 263–284). Orlando, FL: Academic Press.

Maccoby, E. E. (1990a). *Gender differentiation: Explanatory viewpoints.* Paper presented at the convention of American Psychological Society, Dallas, TX.

Maccoby, E. E. (1990b). Gender and relationships: A developmental account. *American Psychologist, 45,* 513–520.

Maccoby, E. E. (1992). The role of parents in the so-

cialization of children: An historical overview. *Developmental Psychology, 28,* 1006–1017.

Maccoby, E. E., & Jacklin, C. N. (1974). *The psychology of sex differences.* Stanford, CA: Stanford University Press.

Macdonald, A. M., Murray, R. M., & Clifford, C. A. (1991). The contribution of heredity to obsessional disorder and personality: A review of family and twin study evidence. In M. T. Tsuang, K. S. Kendler, & M. J. Lyons (Eds.), *Genetic issues in psychosocial epidemiology* (pp. 191–212). New Brunswick, NJ: Rutgers University Press.

MacDonald, N. E., Wells, G. A., Fisher, W. A., Warren, W. K., King, M. A., Doherty, J. A., & Bowie, W. R. (1990). High-risk STD/HIV behavior among college students. *JAMA, 263,* 3155–3159.

MacGregor, J. N. (1987). Short-term memory capacity: Limitation or optimization? *Psychological Review, 94,* 107–108.

Mackenzie, B. (1984). Explaining race differences in IQ: The logic, the methodology, and the evidence. *American Psychologist, 39,* 1214–1233.

Mackie, M. (1991). *Gender relations in Canada: Further explorations.* Toronto: Butterworths.

Maclay, E. (1990). *The art of Bev Doolittle.* New York: Bantam Books.

MacLeod, C., & Campbell, L. (1992). Memory accessibility and probability judgments: An experimental evaluation of the availability heuristic. *Journal of Personality and Social Psychology, 63,* 890–902.

MacLeod, C. M. (1991). Half a century of research on the Stroop effect: An integrative review. *Psychological Bulletin, 109,* 163–203.

MacLeod, C. M., & Bassili, J. N. (1989). Are implicit and explicit tests differentially sensitive to item-specific vs. relational information? In S. Lewandowsky, J. C. Dunn, & K. Kirsner (Eds.), *Implicit memory: Theoretical issues* (pp. 159–172). Hillsdale, NJ: Erlbaum.

Maddahian, E., Newcomb, M. D., & Bentler, P. M. (1988). Adolescent drug use and intention to use drugs: Concurrent and longitudinal analyses of four ethnic groups. *Addictive Behaviors, 13,* 191–195.

Maddi, S. R., Barton, P. T., & Puccetti, M. C. (1987). Stressful events are indeed a factor in physical illness: Reply to Schroeder and Costa (1984). *Journal of Personality and Social Psychology, 52,* 833–843.

Maddux, J. E., & Stanley, M. A. (1986). Self-efficacy theory in contemporary psychology: An overview. *Journal of Social and Clinical Psychology, 4,* 249–255.

Magnusson, D., & Törestad, B. (1993). A holistic view of personality: A model revisited. *Annual Review of Psychology, 44,* 427–452.

Maki, R. H., & Berry, S. L. (1984). Metacomprehension of text material. *Journal of Experimental Psychology: Learning, Memory, and Cognition, 10,* 663–679.

Malamuth, N. M. (1987). Do sexually violent media indirectly contribute to antisocial behavior? In M. R. Roth (Ed.), *The psychology of women: Ongoing debates* (pp. 441–459). New Haven, CT: Yale University Press.

Malamuth, N. M., & Check, J. V. P. (1981). The effects of mass media exposure on acceptance of violence against women: A field experiment. *Journal of Research in Personality, 15,* 436–446.

Malamuth, N. M., & Check, J. V. P. (1984). Debriefing effectiveness following exposure to pornographic rape depictions. *The Journal of Sex Research, 20,*

1–13.

Malamuth, N. M., & Check, J. V. P. (1985). The effects of aggressive pornography on beliefs in rape myths: Individual differences. *Journal of Research in Personality, 19,* 299–320.

Malgady, R. G., Rogler, L. H., & Costantino, G. (1990). Culturally sensitive psychotherapy for Puerto Rican children and adolescents: A program of treatment outcome research. *Journal of Consulting and Clinical Psychology, 58,* 704–712.

Malson, M. R. (1983). Black women's sex roles: The social context for a new ideology. *Journal of Social Issues, 39,* 101–114.

Mandler, G. (1984). *Mind and body: Psychology of emotion and stress.* New York: Norton.

Mandler, G. (1990). A constructivist theory of emotion. In N. L. Stein, B. Leventhal, & T. Trabasso (Eds.), *Psychological and biological approaches to emotion* (pp. 21–43). Hillsdale, NJ: Erlbaum.

Mandler, J. M. (1988). How to build a baby: On the development of an accessible representational system. *Cognitive Development, 3,* 113–116.

Mandler, J. M. (1992a). The foundations of conceptual thought in infancy. *Cognitive Development, 7,* 273–285.

Mandler, J. M. (1992b). How to build a baby: II. Conceptual primitives. *Psychological Review, 99,* 587–604.

Mandler, J. M., & McDonough, L. (1993). Concept formation in infancy. *Cognitive Development, 8,* 291–318.

Manjarréz, C. A. (1991). *Mis palabras.* In D. Schoem (Ed.), *Inside separate worlds: Life stories of young Blacks, Jews, and Latinos* (pp. 50–63). Ann Arbor: University of Michigan Press.

Mann, J., Tarantola, D. J. M., & Netter, T. W. (Eds.). (1992). *AIDS in the world.* Cambridge, MA: Harvard University Press.

Manschreck, T. C. (1989). Motor and cognitive disturbances in schizophrenic disorders. In S. Charles Schulz & C. A. Tamminga (Eds.), *Schizophrenia: Scientific progress.* New York: Oxford University Press.

Mansfield, T. S., & Busse, T. V. (1981). *The psychology of creativity and discovery.* Chicago: Nelson Hall.

Marcus, R. F. (1986). Naturalistic observation of co-operation, helping, and sharing and their associations with empathy and affect. In C. Zahn-Waxler, E. M. Cummings, & R. Iannotti (Eds.), *Altruism and aggression* (pp. 256–279). Cambridge, England: Cambridge University Press.

Marín, G. (1991). Obituary: Ignacio Martín-Baró, S. J. (1942–1989). *American Psychologist, 46,* 532.

Marín, G., & Marín, B. V. (1991). *Research with Hispanic populations.* Newbury Park, CA: Sage.

Marks, I. M. (1987). *Fears, phobias, and rituals.* New York: Oxford University Press.

Markus, H. R., & Cross, S. (1990). The interpersonal self. In L. A. Pervin (Ed.), *Handbook of personality: Theory and research* (pp. 576–608). New York: Guilford.

Markus, H. R., & Kitayama, S. (1991). Culture and self: Implications for cognition, emotion, and motivation. *Psychological Review, 98,* 224–253.

Markus, H. R., & Kunda, Z. (1986). Stability and malleability of the self-concept. *Journal of Personality and Social Psychology, 51,* 858–866.

Markus, H. R., & Wurf, E. (1987). The dynamic self-concept: A social psychological perspective. *Annual Review of Psychology, 38,* 299–337.

Marlatt, G. A. (1992). Substance abuse: Implications of a biopsychosocial model for prevention, treatment, and relapse prevention. In J. Grabowski &

G. R. VandenBos (Eds.), *Psychopharmacology: Basic mechanisms and applied interventions* (pp. 131–162). Washington, DC: American Psychological Association.

Marshall, G. D., & Zimbardo, P. G. (1979). Affective consequences of inadequately explained physiological arousal. *Journal of Personality and Social Psychology, 37,* 970–988.

Martin, C. L. (1987). A ratio measure of sex stereotyping. *Journal of Personality and Social Psychology, 52,* 489–499.

Martin, C. L., & Little, J. K. (1990). The relation of gender understanding to children's sex-typed preferences and gender stereotypes. *Child Development, 61,* 1427–1439.

Martin, D. W. (1990). *Doing psychology experiments* (3rd ed.). Monterey, CA: Brooks/Cole.

Martin, E. (1967). Class lecture at University of Michigan.

Martin, E. (1987). *The woman in the body.* Boston: Beacon.

Martin, G., & Pear, J. (1983). *Behavior modification: What it is and how to use it.* Englewood Cliffs, NJ: Prentice-Hall.

Martin, G., & Pear, J. (1992). *Behavior modification: What it is and how to do it* (4th ed.). Englewood Cliffs, NJ: Prentice-Hall.

Martin, R. J., White, B. D., & Hulsey, M. G. (1991). The regulation of body weight. *American Scientist, 79,* 528–541.

Martinez, C. (1986). Hispanics: Psychiatric issues. In C. B. Wilkinson (Ed.), *Ethnic psychiatry* (pp. 61–88). New York: Plenum.

Martinez, J. L., Jr., & Mendoza, R. H. (Eds.). (1984). *Chicano psychology* (2nd ed.). New York: Academic Press.

Martinez-Arizala, A., & McCarty, G. E. (1987). Narcolepsy. *Military Medicine, 152,* 470–472.

Martyna, W. (1980). Beyond the "He/Man" approach: The case for nonsexist language. *Signs, 5,* 482–493.

Maslach, C. (1979). Negative emotional biasing of unexplained arousal. *Journal of Personality and Social Psychology, 37,* 953–969.

Maslow, A. H. (1962). *Toward a psychology of being.* Princeton, NJ: Van Nostrand.

Maslow, A. H. (1968). *Toward a psychology of being* (2nd ed.). Princeton, NJ: Van Nostrand.

Maslow, A. H. (1970). *Motivation and personality* (2nd ed.). New York: Harper & Row.

Maslow, A. H. (1971). *The farther reaches of human nature.* New York: Viking.

Massaro, D. W. (1987). *Speech perception by ear and eye.* Hillsdale, NJ: Lawrence Erlbaum.

Massaro, D. W. (1993). Information processing models: Microscopes of the mind. *Annual Review of Psychology, 44,* 383–425.

Masters, W. H., & Johnson, V. E. (1966). *Human sexual response.* Boston: Little, Brown.

Mastropieri, M. A., & Scruggs, T. E. (1991). *Teaching students ways to remember: Strategies for learning mnemonically.* Cambridge, MA: Brookline Books.

Matlin, M. W. (1985). Current issues in psycholinguistics. In T. M. Shlechter & M. P. Toglia (Eds.), *New directions in cognitive science* (pp. 217–241). Norwood, NJ: Ablex.

Matlin, M. W. (1993a). *The psychology of women* (2nd ed.). Fort Worth, TX: Harcourt Brace Jovanovich.

Matlin, M. W. (1993b). *Invited address: "But I thought I was going to ace that test!": Metacognition and the college student.* Paper presented at the annual meeting of the Southeastern Psychological Association, Atlanta, GA.

Matlin, M. W. (1994). *Cognition* (3rd ed.). Fort Worth, TX: Harcourt Brace & Company.

Matlin, M. W., & Foley, H. J. (1992). *Sensation and perception* (3rd ed.). Boston: Allyn & Bacon.

Matlin, M. W., & Stang, D. J. (1978). *The Pollyanna Principle: Selectivity in language, memory, and thought.* Cambridge, MA: Schenkman.

Matlin, M. W., & Zajonc, R. B. (1968). Social facilitation of word associations. *Journal of Personality and Social Psychology, 10,* 455–461.

Matson, J. L. (1990). *Handbook of behavior modification with the mentally retarded* (2nd ed.). New York: Plenum Press.

Matsumoto, D. (1987). The role of facial response in the experience of emotion: More methodological problems and a meta-analysis. *Journal of Personality and Social Psychology, 52,* 769–774.

Matthews, K. A. (1988). CHD and Type A behaviors: Update on and alternatives to the Booth-Kewley and Friedman quantitative review. *Psychological Bulletin, 104,* 373–380.

Matthews, K. A., Wing, R. R., Kuller, L. H., Meilah, E. N., & Kelsey, S. F. (1990). Influences of natural menopause on psychological characteristics and symptoms of middle-aged healthy women. *Journal of Consulting and Clinical Psychology, 58,* 345–351.

May, R. (1986). The problem of evil. In R. May, C. Rogers, & A. Maslow (Eds.), *Politics and innocence* (pp. 12–23). Dallas, TX: Saybrook.

Mayer, J. D., Salovey, P., Gomberg-Kaufman, S., & Blainey, K. (1991). A broader conception of mood experience. *Journal of Personality and Social Psychology, 60,* 100–111.

Mayer, R. E. (1982). The psychology of mathematical problem solving. In F. K. Lester & J. Garofalo (Eds.), *Mathematical problem solving: Issues in research* (pp. 1–13). Philadelphia, PA: The Franklin Institute.

Mayer, R. E. (1985). Implications of cognitive psychology for instruction in mathematical problem solving. In E. A. Silver (Ed.), *Teaching and learning mathematical problem solving* (pp. 123–138). Hillsdale, NJ: Erlbaum.

Mayer, R. E. (1988). *Teaching for thinking: Research on the teachability of thinking skills.* Paper presented at the Convention of the American Psychological Association, Atlanta, GA.

Mayer, R. E. (1991). Problem solving. In M. W. Eysenck (Ed.), *The Blackwell dictionary of cognitive psychology* (pp. 284–288). Oxford, England: Basil Blackwell.

Mayers, R. S. (1989). Use of folk medicine by elderly Mexican-American women. *Journal of Drug Issues, 19,* 283–295.

Mayes, L. C., Granger, R. H., Bornstein, M. H., & Zuckerman, B. (1992). The problem of prenatal cocaine exposure: A rush to judgment. *JAMA, 267,* 406–408.

Mazur, J. E. (1990). *Learning and behavior* (2nd ed.). Englewood Cliffs, NJ: Prentice-Hall.

McAdams, D. P. (1990). *The person: An introduction to personality psychology.* San Diego: Harcourt Brace Jovanovich.

McAdams, D. P. (1994). *The person: An introduction to personality psychology* (2nd ed.). Fort Worth: Harcourt Brace & Company.

McCann, C. D., & Higgins, E. T. (1990). Social cognition and communication. In H. Giles & W. P. Robinson (Eds.), *Handbook of language and social psychology* (pp. 13–32). Chichester, England: Wiley.

McCartney, K., & Phillips, D. (1988). Motherhood and child care. In B. Birns & D. H. Hay (Eds.), *The different faces of motherhood* (pp. 157–183). New York: Plenum.

McCauley, C. R., & Segal, M. E. (1987). Social psychology of terrorist groups. In C. Hendrick (Ed.), *Review of personality and social psychology: Group processes and intergroup relations* (Vol. 9, pp. 231–256). Beverly Hills, CA: Sage.

McClelland, D. C. (1973). Testing for competence rather than for "intelligence." *American Psychologist, 28,* 1–14.

McClelland, D. C. (1985). *Human motivation.* Glenview, IL: Scott, Foresman.

McClelland, J. L., (1981). Retrieving general and specific knowledge from stored knowledge of specifics. *Proceedings of the Third Annual Conference of the Cognitive Science Society,* 170–172.

McClelland, J. L., Rumelhart, D. E., & the PDP Research Group. (1986). *Parallel distributed processing* (Vol. 2). Cambridge, MA: MIT Press.

McCloskey, M., Wible, C. G., & Cohen, N. J. (1988). Is there a special flashbulb-memory mechanism? *Journal of Experimental Psychology: General, 117,* 171–181.

McConkie, G. W., & Zola, D. (1984). Eye movement control during reading. The effect of word units. In W. Prinz & A. F. Sanders (Eds.), *Cognition and motor processes* (pp. 63–74). Berlin: Springer-Verlag.

McCord, C., & Freeman, H. P. (1990). Excess mortality in Harlem. *The New England Journal of Medicine, 322,* 173–177.

McCormick, D. A., Clark, G. A., Lavond, D. G., & Thompson, R. F. (1982). Initial localization of the memory trace for a basic form of learning. *Proceedings of the National Academy of Science, 79,* 2731–2742.

McCrae, R. R., & Costa, P. T., Jr. (1986). Clinical assessment can benefit from recent advances in personality psychology. *American Psychologist, 41,* 1001–1003.

McCrae, R. R., & Costa, P. T., Jr. (1990). *Personality in adulthood.* New York: Guilford.

McDougall, W. (1908). *Social psychology.* New York: G. P. Putnam's Sons.

McFarlane, J., Martin, C. L., & Williams, T. M. (1988). Mood fluctuations: Women versus men and menstrual versus other cycles. *Psychology of Women Quarterly, 12,* 201–223.

McGaugh, J. L. (1989). Involvement of hormonal and neuromodulatory systems in the regulation of memory storage. *Annual Review of Neuroscience, 12,* 255–287.

McGaugh, J. L., & Gold, P. E. (1988). Hormonal modulation of memory. In R. B., Brush & S. Levine (Eds.), *Psychoendocrinology.* New York: Academic Press.

McGinnies, E., & Ward, C. D. (1980). Better liked than right: Trustworthiness and expertise as factors in credibility. *Personality and Social Psychology Bulletin, 6,* 467–472.

McGinty, D., & Szymusiak, R. (1988). Neuronal unit activity patterns in behaving animals: Brainstem and limbic system. *Annual Review of Psychology, 39,* 135–168.

McGrath, E. (1991, November). Women and depression: Report of the National Task Force. *Harvard Mental Health Letter,* pp. 4, 5.

McGuinness, D. M. (1985). Sensorimotor biases in cognitive development. In R. L. Hall (Ed.), *Male-*

female differences: A biocultural perspective (pp. 57–126). New York: Praeger.

McHugh, M. C., Koeske, R. D., & Frieze, I. H. (1986). Issues to consider in conducting nonsexist psychological research: A guide for researchers. *American Psychologist, 41,* 879–890.

McKelvie, S. J. (1992). Grappling with confusion: Experiences with the methods course. Paper presented at Canadian Psychological Association, Quebec City.

McKim, W. A. (1991). *Drugs and behavior: An introduction to behavioral pharmacology* (2nd ed.). Englewood Cliffs, NJ: Prentice-Hall.

McKinlay, J. B., McKinlay, S. M., & Brambilla, D. J. (1987). Health status and utilization behavior associated with menopause. *American Journal of Epidemiology, 125,* 110–121.

McKinley, V. (1987). Group therapy as a treatment modality of special value for Hispanic patients. *International Journal of Group Psychotherapy, 37,* 255–268.

McKitrick, L. A., Camp, C. J., & Black, F. W. (1992). Prospective memory intervention in Alzheimer's disease. *Journal of Gerontology: Psychological Sciences, 47,* P337–P343.

McLeod, J. M., Atkin, C. K., & Chaffee, S. H. (1972). Adolescents, parents and television use: Adolescent self-report measures from Maryland and Wisconsin samples. In G. A. Comstock & E. A. Rubinstein (Eds.), *Television and social behavior: Vol. III. Television and adolescent aggressiveness* (pp. 239–313). Washington, DC: U.S. Government Printing Office.

McMillen, L. (1991, April 3). For the Harvard presidency, an American success story. *Chronicle of Higher Education,* p. A3.

McNally, J. L. (1992, May). *Geneseo freshman class profiles 1975–1992: Based on American Council on Education student information form.* Unpublished report #93-2, SUNY Geneseo.

McNally, R. J. (1987). Preparedness and phobias: A review. *Psychological Bulletin, 101,* 283–303.

McNally, R. J. (1990). Psychological approaches to panic disorders: A review. *Psychological Bulletin, 108,* 403–419.

McNaughton, B. L., & Morris, R. G. M. (1987). Hippocampal synaptic enhancement and information storage within a distributed memory system. *Trends in Neurosciences, 10,* 408–415.

McNeil, B. J., Pauker, S. G., Sox, H. C., & Tversky, A. (1982). On the elicitation of preferences for alternative therapies. *New England Journal of Medicine, 306,* 1259–1262.

McNeill, D. (1985). So you think gestures are nonverbal? *Psychological Review, 92,* 350–371.

McTear, M. F. (1985). *Children's conversations.* Oxford, England: Basil Blackwell.

Meddis, R., Pearson, A., & Langford, G. (1973). An extreme case of healthy insomnia. *Electroencephalography and Clinical Neurophysiology, 35,* 213–214.

Meehan, A. M., & Janik, L. M. (1990). Illusory correlations and the maintenance of sex role stereotypes in children. *Sex Roles, 22,* 83–95.

Meichenbaum, D. (1985). *Stress inoculation training.* New York: Pergamon Press.

Meissner, W. W. (1988). The psychotherapies: Individual, family, and group. In A. M. Nicholi, Jr. (Ed.), *The new Harvard guide to psychiatry* (pp. 449–480). Cambridge, MA: Harvard University Press.

Meissner, W. W. (1988). *Treatment of patients in the borderline spectrum.* Northvale, NJ: Jason Aron-

son.

Melzack, R. (1986). Neurophysiological foundations of pain. In R. A. Sternbach (Ed.), *The psychology of pain* (pp. 1–24). New York: Raven Press.

Melzack, R. (1990). The tragedy of needless pain. *Scientific American, 262,* 27–33.

Melzack, R. (1992, April). Phantom limbs. *Scientific American, 266,* 120–126.

Melzack, R., & Wall, P. D. (1965). Pain mechanisms: A new theory. *Science, 150,* 971–979.

Mendlesohn, G. A. (1993). It's time to put theories of personality in their place, or, Allport and Stagner got it right, why can't we? In K. H. Craik, R. Hogan & R. N. Wolfe (Eds.), *Fifty years of personality psychology* (pp. 103–115). New York: Plenum.

Mendelson, M. (1990). Psychoanalytic views on depression. In B. B. Wolman & G. Stricker (Eds.), *Depressive disorders: Facts, theories, and treatment methods* (pp. 22–37). New York: Wiley.

Mendelson, W. B. (1987). *Human sleep: Research and clinical care.* New York: Plenum.

Mensink, G., & Raaijmakers, J. G. W. (1988). A model for interference and forgetting. *Psychological Review, 95,* 434–455.

Mercer, J. R. (1988). Ethnic differences in IQ scores: What do they mean? (A response to Lloyd Dunn). *Hispanic Journal of Behavioral Sciences, 10,* 199–218.

Merluzzi, T. V., Rudy, T. E., & Krejci, M. J. (1986). Social skill and anxiety: Information processing perspectives. In R. E. Ingram (Ed.), *Information processing approaches to clinical psychology* (pp. 109–129). Orlando, FL: Academic Press.

Mervis, C. B., Catlin, J., & Rosch, E. (1976). Relationships among goodness-of-example, category norms, and word frequency. *Bulletin of the Psychonomic Society, 7,* 283–284.

Mesquita, B., & Frijda, N. (1992). Cultural variations in emotions: A review. *Psychological Bulletin, 112,* 179–204.

Messer, S. B. (1986). Behavioral and psychoanalytic perspectives at therapeutic choice points. *American Psychologist, 41,* 1261–1272.

Messer, S. B., & Warren, S. (1990). Personality change and psychotherapy. In L. A. Pervin (Ed.), *Handbook of personality: Theory and research* (pp. 371–398). New York: Guilford.

Messick, S. (1980). *The effectiveness of coaching for the SAT: Review and reanalysis of research from the fifties to the FTC.* Princeton, NJ: Educational Testing Service.

Metalsky, G. I., Joiner, T. E., Jr., Hardin, T. S., & Abramson, L. Y. (1993). Depressive reactions to failure in a naturalistic setting: A test of the hopelessness and self-esteem theories of depression. *Journal of Abnormal Psychology, 102,* 101–109.

Meyer, G. E., & Petry, S. (1987). Top-down and bottom-up: The illusory contour as a microcosm of issues in perception. In S. Petry & G. E. Meyer (Eds.), *The perception of illusory contours* (pp. 3–26). New York: Springer-Verlag.

Michael, J. (1985). Fundamental research and behaviour modification. In C. F. Lowe, M. Richelle, D. E. Blackman, & C. M. Bradshaw (Eds.), *Behaviour analysis and contemporary psychology* (pp. 159–170). London: Erlbaum.

Middlebrooks, J. C., & Green, D. M. (1991). Sound localization by human listeners. *Annual Review of Psychology, 42,* 135–159.

Midkiff, E. E., & Bernstein, I. L. (1985). Targets of learned food aversions in humans. *Physiology &*

Behavior, 34, 839–841.

Mikulincer, M., Babkoff, H., Caspy, T., & Sing, H. (1989). The effects of 72 hours of sleep loss on psychological variables. *British Journal of Psychology, 80,* 145–162.

Milburn, M. A. (1991). *Persuasion and politics: The social psychology of public opinion.* Pacific Grove, CA: Brooks/Cole.

Milgram, S. (1963). Behavioral studies of obedience. *Journal of Abnormal and Social Psychology, 67,* 371–378.

Milgram, S. (1964). Issues in the study of obedience: A reply to Baumrind. *American Psychologist, 19,* 848–852.

Milgram, S. (1974). *Obedience to authority.* New York: Harper & Row.

Milgram, S., Bickman, L., & Berkowitz, L. (1969). Note on the drawing power of crowds of different size. *Journal of Personality and Social Psychology, 13,* 79–82.

Miller, E., Cradock-Watson, J. E., & Pollock, T. M. (1982, October 9). Consequences of confirmed maternal rubella at successive stages of pregnancy. *Lancet, 8302,* 781–784.

Miller, G. A. (1956). The magical number seven, plus or minus two: Some limits on our capacity for processing information. *Psychological Review, 63,* 81–97.

Miller, G. A. (1962). *Psychology: The science of mental life.* New York: Harper & Row.

Miller, G. A. (1981). *Language and speech.* San Francisco: W. H. Freeman.

Miller, G. A. (1990). The place of language in a scientific psychology. *Psychological Science, 1,* 7–14.

Miller, G. A. (1991). *The science of words.* New York: W. H. Freeman.

Miller, G. A., & Gildea, P. M. (1987). How children learn words. *Scientific American, 257,* 94–99.

Miller, L. (1989). On the neuropsychology of dreams. *Psychoanalytic Review, 76,* 375–401.

Miller, N. E. (1985). The value of behavioral research on animals. *American Psychologist, 40,* 423–40.

Miller, N. E. (1991). Commentary on Ulrich: Need to check truthfulness of statements by opponents of animal research. *Psychological Science, 2,* 422–423.

Miller, N. S. (1991). Nicotine addiction as a disease. In J. A. Cocores (Ed.), *The clinical management of nicotine dependence* (pp. 66–78). New York: Springer-Verlag.

Miller, R. J., Hennessy, R. T., & Leibowitz, H. W. (1973). The effect of hypnotic ablation of the background on the magnitude of the Ponzo perspective illusion. *International Journal of Clinical and Experimental Hypnosis, 21,* 180–191.

Millon, T. (1981). *Disorders of personality.* New York: Wiley.

Mills, C. J. (1992). Academically talented children: The case for early identification and nurturance. *Pediatrics, 89,* 156–157.

Mills, R. S. L., Pedersen, J., & Grusec, J. E. (1989). Sex differences in reasoning and emotion about altruism. *Sex Roles, 20,* 603–621.

Milner, B. R. (1970). Memory and medial temporal regions of the brain. In K. H. Pribram & D. E. Broadbent (Eds.), *Biology of memory* (pp. 29–50). Orlando, FL: Academic Press.

Milner, B. R., Corkin, S., & Teuber, H. L. (1968). Further analysis of the hippocampal amnesic syndrome: 14-year follow-up study of H.M. *Neuropsychologia, 6,* 215–234.

Milner, D. (1983). *Children & race.* Beverly Hills: Sage.

Mineka, S. (1986). The frightful complexity of the origins of fears. In J. B. Overmier & F. R. Brush (Eds.), *Affect, conditioning, and cognition: Essays on the determinants of behavior.* Hillsdale, NJ: Erlbaum.

Mineka, S., Davidson, M., Cook, M., & Keir, R. (1984). Observational conditioning of snake fear in rhesus monkeys. *Journal of Abnormal Psychology, 93,* 355–372.

Mineka, S., & Sutton, S. K. (1992). Cognitive biases and the emotional disorders. *Psychological Science, 3,* 65–69.

Minkler, M., & Stone, R. (1985). The feminization of poverty and older women. *Gerontologist, 25* 351–357.

Miringoff, M. L. (1992). *Index of social health: Monitoring the social well-being of the nation.* Tarrytown, NY: Fordham Institute for Innovation in Social Policy.

Mirowsky, J., & Ross, C. E. (1989). *Social causes of psychological distress.* New York: Aldine de Gruyter.

Mirsky, A. F., & Duncan, C. C. (1986). Etiology and expression of schizophrenia: Neurobiological and psychosocial factors. *Annual Review of Psychology, 37,* 291–319.

Mischel, W. (1966). A social-learning view of sex differences in behavior. In E. Maccoby (Ed.), *The development of sex differences* (pp. 56–81). Stanford: Stanford University Press.

Mischel, W. (1968). *Personality and assessment.* New York: Wiley.

Mischel, W. (1979). On the interface of cognition and personality: Beyond the person-situation debate. *American Psychologist, 34,* 740–754.

Mischel, W. (1986). *Introduction to personality: A new look* (4th ed.). New York: Holt, Rinehart and Winston.

Mischel, W. (1993). *Introduction to personality* (5th ed.). Fort Worth, TX: Harcourt Brace Jovanovich.

Miserandino, M. (1991). Memory and the seven dwarfs. *Teaching of Psychology, 18,* 169–171.

Mishkin, M. (1966). Visual mechanisms beyond the striate cortex. In R. Russel (Ed.), *Frontiers in physiological psychology* (pp. 93–119). New York: Academic Press.

Mishkin, M., & Appenzeller, T. (1987). The anatomy of memory. *Scientific American, 256(6),* 80–89.

Mishler, E. G. (1986). *Research interviewing.* Cambridge, MA: Harvard University Press.

Mistretta, C. M. (1981). Neurophysiological and anatomical aspects of taste development. In R. N. Aslin, J. R. Alberts, & M. P. Petersen (Eds.), *Development of perception* (Vol. 1, pp. 433–455). New York: Academic.

Mita, T. H., Dermer, M., & Knight, J. (1977). Reversed facial images and the mere-exposure hypothesis. *Journal of Personality and Social Psychology, 35,* 597–601.

Mitchell, J., Wilson, K., Revicki, D., & Parker, L. (1985). *The Gerontologist, 25,* 182–187.

Mixon, D. (1989). *Obedience and civilization: Authorized crime and the normality of evil.* London: Pluto Press.

Moar, I., & Bower, G. H. (1983). Inconsistency in spatial knowledge. *Memory & Cognition, 11,* 107–113.

Moely, B. E., Olson, F. A., Halwes, T. G., & Flavell, J. H. (1969). Production deficiency in young children's clustered recall. *Developmental Psychology, 1,* 26–34.

Mollica, R. F. (1989). Mood disorders: Epidemiology. In H. I. Kaplan & B. J. Sadock (Eds.), *Comprehensive textbook of psychiatry/V* (5th ed., Vol. 1, pp. 859–867). Baltimore: Williams & Wilkins.

Monk, T. H., Reynolds, C. F., III, Buysse, D. J., Hoch, C. C., Jarrett, D. B., Jennings, J. R., & Kupfer, D. J. (1991). Circadian characteristics of healthy 80-year-olds and their relationship to objectively recorded sleep. *Journal of Gerontology, 46,* M171–M175.

Mönks, F. J., & Van Boxtel, H. W. (1985). Gifted adolescents: A developmental perspective. In J. Freeman (Ed.), *The psychology of gifted children* (pp. 275–295). Chichester, England: Wiley.

Monte, C. F. (1987). *Beneath the mask: An introduction to theories of personality* (3rd ed.). New York: Holt, Rinehart and Winston.

Monteith, M. J., Devine, P. G., & Zuwerink, J. R. (1993). Self-directed versus other-directed affect as a consequence of prejudice-related discrepancies. *Journal of Personality and Social Psychology, 64,* 198–210.

Moorcroft, W. H. (1987). An overview of sleep. In J. Gackenback (Ed.), *Sleep and dreams* (pp. 3–29). New York: Garland.

Moorcroft, W. H. (1989). *Sleep, dreaming, and sleep disorders.* Lanham, MD: University Press of America.

Moore, B. S., & Isen, A. M. (1990). Affect and social behavior. In B. S. Moore & A. M. Isen (Eds.), *Affect and social behavior* (pp. 1–21). Cambridge, England: Cambridge University Press.

Moore, L. M., Nielsen, C. R., & Mistretta, C. M. (1982). Sucrose taste thresholds: Age-related differences. *Journal of Gerontology, 37,* 64–69.

Moore, S., & Rosenthal, D. (1991). Adolescent invulnerability and perceptions of AIDS risk. *Journal of Adolescent Research, 6,* 164–180.

Moore, T. E. (1991). *Subliminal auditory self-help tapes.* Paper presented at the annual convention of the American Psychological Association, San Francisco.

Moore, T. E. (1992a). Subliminal perception: Facts and fallacies. *Skeptical Inquirer, 16,* 273–281.

Moore, T. E. (1992b). *Subliminal self-help: Fact or artifact?* Paper presented at the annual convention of the American Psychological Association, Washington, DC.

Moreland, R. L., & Levine, J. M. (1989). Newcomers and oldtimers in small groups. In P. B. Paulus (Ed.), *Psychology of group influence* (2nd ed., pp. 143–186). Hillsdale, NJ: Erlbaum.

Morris, N., & Jones, D. M. (1990). Memory updating in working memory: The role of the central executive. *British Journal of Psychology, 81,* 111–121.

Morrison, D. M. (1985). Adolescent contraceptive behavior: A review. *Psychological Bulletin, 98,* 538–568.

Morton, J., & Johnson, M. (1991). The perception of facial structure in infancy. In G. R. Lockhead & J. R. Pomerantz (Eds.), *The perception of structure* (pp. 317–325). Washington, DC: American Psychological Association.

Morval, M. V. G. (1992). À propos de la violence familiale. *Canadian Psychology/Psychogie canadienne, 33,* 144–150.

Moses, S. (1989, October). Therapist touts a blend of techniques. *APA Monitor,* p. 25.

Moskowitz, B. A. (1978). The acquisition of language. *Scientific American, 239,* 92–108.

Moskowitz, H. R. (1978). Odors in the environment: Hedonics, perfumery, and odor abatement. In E. C. Carterette & M. P. Friedman (Eds.), *Handbook of perception* (Vol. 10). New York: Academic.

Moulton, J., Robinson, G. M., & Elias, C. (1978). Sex bias in language use: "Neutral pronouns that aren't." *American Psychologist, 33,* 1032–1036.

Moyer, R. S. (1985). *Teaching psychology courses about the nuclear arms race.* Paper presented at the Massachusetts Psychological Association.

Mugny, G., & Pérez, J. A. (1991). *The social psychology of minority influence.* Cambridge, England: Cambridge University Press.

Mumford, M. D., & Gustafson, S. B. (1988). Creativity syndrome: Integration, application, and innovation. *Psychological Bulletin, 103,* 27–43.

Mura, R. (1987). Sex-related differences in expectations of success in undergraduate mathematics. *Journal for Research in Mathematics Education, 18,* 15–24.

Murray, C. B., Khatib, S., & Jackson, M. (1989). Social indices and the Black elderly: A comparative life cycle approach to the study of double jeopardy. In R. L. Jones (Ed.), *Black adult development and aging* (pp. 167–187). Berkeley, CA: Cobb & Henry.

Mussen, P., & Eisenberg-Berg, N. (1977). *Roots of caring, sharing and helping: The development of prosocial behavior.* San Francisco: Freeman.

Myers, D. G. (1992). *The pursuit of happiness.* New York: Morrow.

Myers, D. G., & Bishop, G. D. (1970). Discussion effects on racial attitudes. *Science, 169,* 778–779.

Myers, H. F., Wohlford, P., Guzman, L. P., Echemendia, R. J. (Eds.). (1991). *Ethnic minority perspectives on clinical training and services in psychology.* Washington, DC: American Psychological Association.

Myers, N. A., & Perlmutter, M. (1978). Memory in the years from two to five. In P. A. Ornstein (Ed.), *Memory development in children* (pp. 191–218). Hillsdale, NJ: Erlbaum.

Myshko, D. (1991, Fall). The challenge of Alzheimer's disease. *Managed Care Insights, 2,* pp. 7–9, 12.

Nagata, D. K. (1989). Japanese American children and adolescents. In J. T. Gibbs & L. N. Huang (Eds.), *Children of color.* San Francisco: Jossey-Bass.

Nagata, D. K., & Crosby, F. (1991). Comparisons, justice, and the internment of Japanese-Americans. In J. Suls & T. A. Wills (Eds.), *Social comparison: Contemporary theory and research* (pp. 347–368). Hillsdale, NJ: Erlbaum.

Namir, S., Wolcott, D. L., Fawzy, F. I., & Alumbaugh, M. J. (1987). Coping with AIDS: Psychological and Health Implications. *Journal of Applied Social Psychology, 1987, 17,* 309–328.

Nash, M. (1987). What, if anything, is regressed about hypnotic age regression? A review of the empirical literature. *Psychological Bulletin, 102,* 42–52.

National Center for Health Statistics. (1993). *Healthy people 2000 Review, 1992.* Hyattsville, MD: Public Health Service.

National Institute of Mental Health (1985). *Mental health, United States, 1985.* Washington, DC: U.S. Government Printing Office.

National Institute on Deafness and Other Communication Disorders. (1989). *A report of the Task Force on the National Strategic Research Plan.* Washington, DC: Author.

Nebes, R. D. (1989). Semantic memory in Alzheimer's disease. *Psychological Bulletin, 106,* 377–394.

Nebes, R. D. (1992a). Cognitive dysfunction in Alzheimer's disease. In F. I. M. Craik & T. A. Salthouse (Eds.), *The handbook of aging and cogni-*

tion (pp. 373–445). Hillsdale, NJ: Erlbaum.

Nebes, R. D. (1992b). Semantic memory dysfunction in Alzheimer's disease: Disruption of semantic knowledge or information-processing limitation? In L. R. Squire & N. Butters (Eds.), *Neuropsychology of memory*, (2nd ed., pp. 233–240). New York: Guilford Press.

Nebes, R. D., & Brady, C. B. (1992). Generalized cognitive slowing and severity of dementia in Alzheimer's disease: Implications for the interpretation of response-time data. *Journal of Clinical and Experimental Neuropsychology, 14*, 317–326.

Nebes, R. D., Brady, C. B., & Reynolds, C. F., III. (1992). Cognitive slowing in Alzheimer's disease and geriatric depression. *Journal of Gerontology: Psychological Sciences, 47*, P331–P336.

Neisser, U. (1987). From direct perception to conceptual structure. In U. Neisser (Ed.), *Concepts and conceptual development* (pp. 11–24). New York: Cambridge University Press.

Neisser, U. (1989). Domains of memory. In P. R. Solomon, G. R. Goethals, C. M. Kelley, & B. R. Stephens (Eds.), *Memory: Interdisciplinary approaches* (pp. 67–83). New York: Springer-Verlag.

Neisser, U., & Becklen, R. (1975). Selective looking: Attending to visually specified events. *Cognitive Psychology, 7*, 480–494.

Neisser, U., & Harsch, N. (1992). Phantom flashbulbs: False recollections of hearing the news about *Challenger*. In E. Winograd & U. Neisser (Eds.), *Affect and accuracy in recall* (pp. 9–31). New York: Cambridge University Press.

Nelson, D. L. (1993). Implicit memory. In P. E. Morris & M. Gruneberg (Eds.), *Aspects of memory* (Vol. 2). London: Routledge.

Nelson, L. (1991). Psychological factors in war and peacemaking. *Contemporary Social Psychology, 15*, 172–178.

Nelson, T. O. (1992). *Consciousness and metacognition*. Paper presented at the convention of the American Psychological Association, Washington, DC.

Nelson, T. O., & Leonesio, R. J. (1988). Allocation of self-paced study time and the "labor-in-vain effect." *Journal of Experimental Psychology: Learning, Memory, and Cognition, 14*, 676–686.

Nemeth, C. J. (1986). Differential contributions of majority and minority influence. *Psychological Review, 93*, 23–32.

Nemeth, C. J., & Chiles, C. (1988). Modeling courage: The role of dissent in fostering independence. *European Journal of Social Psychology, 18*, 275–280.

Nemeth, C. J., & Staw, B. M. (1989). The tradeoffs of social control and innovation in groups and organizations. *Advances in Experimental Social Psychology, 22*, 175–210.

Nemiah, J. C. (1989). Dissociative disorders (hysterical neuroses, dissociative type). In H. I. Kaplan & B. J. Sadock (Eds.), *Comprehensive textbook of psychiatry/V* (5th ed., Vol. 1, pp. 1028–1044). Baltimore, MD: Williams & Wilkins.

Nett, E. M. (1993). *Canadian families: Past & present* (2nd ed.). Toronto: Butterworths.

Neugarten, B. L. (1982, August) *Successful aging*. Paper presented at the meeting of the American Psychological Association, Washington, DC.

Nevid, J. S. (1984). Sex differences in factors of romantic attraction. *Sex Roles, 11*, 401–411.

Newell, A. & Simon, H. A. (1972). *Human problem solving*. Englewood Cliffs: Prentice-Hall.

Newman, J. P., Widom, C. S., & Nathan, S. (1985).

Passive avoidance in syndromes of disinhibition: Psychopathy and extraversion. *Journal of Personality and Social Psychology, 48*, 1316–1327.

Neziroglu, F., & Yaryura-Tobias, J. A. (1991). *Over and over again: Understanding obsessive-compulsive disorder*. Lexington, MA: Lexington Books.

Nezu, A. M., Nezu, C. M., & Blissett, S. E. (1988). Sense of humor as a moderator of the relation between stressful events and psychological distress: A prospective analysis. *Journal of Personality and Social Psychology, 54*, 520–525.

Nickerson, R. S. (1990). William James on reasoning. *Psychological Science, 1*, 167–171.

Nickerson, R. S. (1992, August). *Psychology and environmental change*. Paper presented at the annual convention of the American Psychological Association, Washington, DC.

Nickerson, R. S., & Adams, M. J. (1979). Long-term memory for a common object. *Cognitive Psychology, 11*, 287–307.

Nickerson, R. S., Perkins, D. N., & Smith, E. E. (1985). *The teaching of thinking*. Hillsdale, NJ: Erlbaum.

Nieburg, P. , Marks, J. S., McLaren, N. M., & Remington, P. L. (1985). The fetal tobacco syndrome. *JAMA, 253*, 2998–2999.

Nielsen, L. (1991). *Adolescence: A contemporary view* (2nd ed.). Fort Worth, TX: Harcourt Brace Jovanovich.

Nielsen, L. L., & Sarason, I. G. (1981). Emotion, personality, and selective attention. *Journal of Personality and Social Psychology, 41*, 945–960.

Nisbett, R. E., Caputo, C., Legant, P., & Maracek, J. (1973). Behavior as seen by the actor and as seen by the observer. *Journal of Personality and Social Psychology, 27*, 154–164.

Nisbett, R. E., & Ross, L. (1980). *Human inference: Strategies and shortcomings of social judgment*. Englewood Cliffs, NJ: Prentice-Hall.

Nisbett, R. E., & Wilson, T. D. (1977). Telling more than we can know. Verbal reports on mental processes. *Psychological Review, 84*, 231–259.

Nobiling, J. (1991). Personal communication.

Nofsinger, R. E. (1991). *Everyday conversation*. Newbury Park, CA: Sage.

Nolen-Hoeksema, S. (1987). Sex differences in unipolar depression: Evidence and theory. *Psychological Bulletin, 101*, 259–282.

Nolen-Hoeksema, S. (1990). *Sex differences in depression*. Stanford, CA: Stanford University Press.

Nolen-Hoeksema, S., & Morrow, J. (1991). A prospective study of depression and posttraumatic stress symptoms after a natural disaster: The 1989 Loma Prieta earthquake. *Journal of Personality and Social Psychology, 61*, 115–121.

Nolen-Hoeksema, S., & Morrow, J., & Fredrickson, B. L. (1993). Response styles and the duration of episodes of depressed mood. *Journal of Abnormal Psychology, 102*, 20–28.

Norcross, J. C. (1987). Eclectic psychotherapy: An introduction and overview. In J. C. Norcross (Ed.), *Casebook and eclectic psychotherapy* (pp. 3–24). New York: Brunner/Mazel.

Novick, L. R. (1988). Analogical transfer, problem similarity, and expertise. *Journal of Experimental Psychology: Learning, Memory, and Cognition, 14*, 510–520.

Novick, L. R., & Coté, N. (1992). *The nature of expertise in anagram solution*. Proceedings of the Fourteenth Annual Conference of the Cognitive Science Society (pp. 450–455). Hillsdale, NJ: Erlbaum.

Noyes, R., Jr. (1991). Treatments of choice for anxiety disorders. In W. Coryell & Winokur (Eds.), *The clinical management of anxiety disorders* (pp. 140–153). New York: Oxford University Press.

Nurnberger, J. I., & Gershon, E. S. (1982). Genetics. In E. S. Paykel (Ed.), *Handbook of affective disorders*. New York: Guilford Press.

Nye, R. D. (1992). *Three psychologies: Perspectives from Freud, Skinner, and Rogers* (4th ed.). Pacific Grove, CA: Brooks/Cole.

Oakland, T., & Parmelee, R. (1985). Mental measurement of minority-group children. In B. B. Wolman (Ed.), *Handbook of intelligence* (pp. 699–736). New York: Wiley.

Oatley, K. (1992). *Best laid schemes: The psychology of emotions*. Cambridge: Cambridge University Press.

Oatley, K., & Johnson-Laird, P. N. (1987). Towards a cognitive theory of emotions. *Cognition and Emotion, 1*, 29–50.

Oberstone, H. K., & Sukoneck, H. (1976). Psychological adjustment and life style of single lesbians and single heterosexual women. *Psychology of Women Quarterly, 1*, 172–188.

O'Donnell, J. M. (1985). *The origins of behaviorism: American psychology, 1870–1920*. New York: New York University Press.

Oetting, E. R., Edwards, R. W., & Beauvais, F. (1989). Drugs and Native-American youth. In B. Segal (Ed.), *Perspectives on adolescent drug use* (pp. 1–34). New York: Haworth Press.

Office for Protection from Research Risks. (1986). *Public Health Service policy on humane care and use of laboratory animals*. Bethesda, MD: National Institutes of Health.

Ogden, J. A., & Corkin, S. (1991). Memories of H. M. In W. C. Abraham, M. Corballis, & K. G. White (Eds.), *Memory mechanisms: A tribute to G. V. Goddard* (pp. 195–215). Hillsdale, NJ: Erlbaum.

Öhman, A., & Soares, J. J. F. (1993). On the automatic nature of phobic fear: Conditioned electrodermal responses to masked fear-relevant stimuli. *Journal of Abnormal Psychology, 102*, 121–132.

Ohzawa, I., DeAngelis, G. C., & Freeman, R. D. (1990). Stereoscopic depth discrimination in the visual cortex: Neurons ideally suited as disparity detectors. *Science, 249*, 1037–1041.

O'Keefe, D. J. (1990). *Persuasion: Theory and research*. Newbury Park, CA: Sage.

Oldfield, S. R., & Parker, S. P. A. (1986). Acuity of sound localisation: A topography of auditory space: III. Monaural hearing conditions. *Perception, 15*, 67–81.

Oliner, S. P., & Oliner, P. M. (1988). *The altruistic personality*. New York: Free Press.

Oltmanns, T. F., Neale, J. M., & Davison, G. C. (1991). *Case studies in abnormal psychology* (3rd ed.). New York: Wiley.

Olzak, L. A., & Thomas, J. P. (1986). Seeing spatial patterns. In K. R. Boff, L. Kaufman, & J. P. Thomas (Eds.), *Handbook of perception and human performance* (pp. 7–1—7–56). New York: Wiley.

Operation Friendship. (1989, December). *Operation Friendship's friendly focus*. Rochester, New York: Author.

Orford, J. (1985). *Excessive appetites: A psychological view of addictions*. New York: Wiley.

Ormrod, J. E., Ormrod, R. K., Wagner, E. D., & McCallin, R. C. (1988). Reconceptualizing map learning. *American Journal of Psychology, 101*, 425–433.

Orne, M. T. (1951). The mechanisms of hypnotic age regression: An experimental study. *Journal of Abnormal Psychology, 46,* 213–225.

Orne, M. T. (1962). On the social psychology of the psychological experiment: With particular reference to demand characteristics and their implications. *American Psychologist, 17,* 776–783.

Orne, M. T. (1986). The validity of memories retrieved in hypnosis. In B. Zilbergeld, M. G. Edelstein, & D. L. Araoz (Eds.), *Hypnosis: Questions and answers* (pp. 45–46). New York: Norton.

Ornstein, R., & Thompson, R. F. (1984). *The amazing brain.* Boston: Houghton Mifflin.

Ortony, A., Clore, G. L., & Collins, A. (1988). *The cognitive structure of emotions.* Cambridge, England: Cambridge University Press.

Osgood, C. E. (1962). *An alternative to war or surrender.* Urbana: University of Illinois Press.

Osherow, N. (1988). Making sense of the nonsensical: An analysis of Jonestown. In E. Aronson (Ed.), *Readings about the social animal* (5th ed., pp. 68–86). New York: Freeman.

Osherson, S. (1987). *Finding our fathers: How a man's life is shaped by his relationship with his father.* New York: Fawcett.

Osherson, S. (1992). *Wrestling with love: How men struggle with intimacy with women, children, parents, and each other.* New York: Fawcett.

Oskamp, S. (1991). *Attitudes and opinions* (2nd ed.). Englewood Cliffs, NJ: Prentice-Hall.

Oswald, I. (1987a). Sleep. In R. L. Gregory (Ed.), *The Oxford companion to the mind* (pp. 718–719). New York: Oxford University Press.

Oswald, I. (1987b). Dreaming. In R. L. Gregory (Ed.), *The Oxford companion to the mind* (pp. 201–203). New York: Oxford University Press.

Owens, R. E., Jr. (1992). *Language development: An introduction* (3rd ed.). New York: Merrill.

Owens, R. E., Jr. (1993). Personal communication.

Padawer, W. J., & Goldfried, M. R. (1984). Anxiety-related disorders, fears, and phobias. In E. A. Blechman (Ed.), *Behavior modification with women* (pp. 341–372). New York: Guilford.

Padilla, A. M. (1988). Early psychological assessments of Mexican-American children. *Journal of the History of the Behavioral Sciences, 24,* 111–117.

Paikoff, R. L., & Brooks-Gunn, J. (1991). Do parent-child relationships change during puberty? *Psychological Bulletin, 110,* 47–66.

Paivio, A. (1978). Comparisons of mental clocks. *Journal of Experimental Psychology: Human Perception and Performance, 4,* 61–71.

Palca, J. (1991). Fetal brain signals time for birth. *Science, 253,* 1360.

Pallak, S. R. (1983). Salience of a communicator's physical attractiveness and persuasion: A heuristic versus systematic processing interpretation. *Social Cognition, 2,* 156–168.

Pallis, C. A. (1955). Impaired identification of faces and places with agnosia for colors. *Journal of Neurology, Neurosurgery and Psychiatry, 18,* 218–224.

Palmore, E. B. (1990). *Ageism negative and positive.* New York: Springer.

Paludi, M. A. (1984). Psychometric properties and underlying assumptions of four objective measures of fear of success. *Sex Roles, 10,* 765–781.

Palys, P. S. (1986). Testing the common wisdom: The social content of video pornography. *Canadian Psychology, 27,* 22–35.

Panksepp, J. (1986). The neurochemistry of behavior. *Annual Review of Psychology, 37,* 77–107.

Pappas, G., Queen, S., Hadden, W., & Fisher, G. (1993). The increasing disparity in mortality between socioeconomic groups in the United States, 1960 and 1986. *New England Journal of Medicine, 329,* 103–109.

Parker, K. C. H. (1983). A meta-analysis of the reliability and validity of the Rorschach. *Journal of Personality Assessment, 42,* 227–231.

Parker, K. C. H., Hanson, R. K. Hanson, & Hunsley, J. (1988). MMPI, Rorschach, and WAIS: A meta-analytic comparison of reliability, stability, and validity. *Psychological Bulletin, 103,* 367–373.

Parks, T. E. (1986). Illusory figures: A (mostly) atheoretical review. *Psychological Bulletin, 95,* 282–300.

Parloff, M. B. (1987, February). Psychotherapy: An import from Japan. *Psychology Today,* pp. 74–75.

Passuth, P. M., & Cook, F. L. (1985). Effects of television viewing on knowledge and attitudes about older adults: A critical reexamination. *The Gerontologist, 25,* 69–77.

Pastalan, L. A. (1982). Environmental design and adaptation to the visual environment of the elderly. In R. Sekuler, D. Kline, & K. Dismukes (Eds.), *Handbook of perception* (Vol. 4). New York: Academic Press.

Patterson, C. J. (1992). Children of lesbian and gay parents. *Child Development, 63,* 1025–1042.

Patterson, D. R., Everett, J. J., Burns, G. L., & Marvin, J. A. (1992). Hypnosis for the treatment of burn pain. *Journal of Consulting and Clinical Psychology, 60,* 713–717.

Patterson, M. L. (1983). *Nonverbal behavior: A functional perspective.* New York: Springer-Verlag.

Pattison, E. M. (1978). The living-dying process. In C. A. Garfield (Ed.), *Psychosocial care of the dying patient* (pp. 133–168). New York: McGraw-Hill.

Pauker, S. G., & Kopelman, R. I. (1992). Clinical problem-solving. *The New England Journal of Medicine, 326,* 40–43.

Paunonen, S. V., Jackson, D. N., Trzebinski, J., & Forsterling, F. (1992). Personality structure across cultures: A multimethod evaluation. *Journal of Personality and Social Psychology, 62,* 447–456.

Pavlov, I. P. (1927). *Conditioned reflexes.* London: Oxford University Press.

Payne, J. W. (1985). Psychology of risky decisions. In G. Wright (Ed.), *Behavioral decision making* (pp. 3–23). New York: Plenum.

Peal, E., & Lambert, W. E. (1962). The relation of bilingualism to intelligence. *Psychological Monographs, 546.*

Pearson, R. W., Ross, M., & Dawes, R. M. (1992). In J. M. Tanur (Ed.), *Questions about questions: Inquiries into the cognitive bases of surveys* (pp. 65–94). New York: Russell Sage Foundation.

Pelletier-Stiefel, J., Pepler, D., Crozier, K., Stanhope, L., Corter, C., & Abramovitch, R. (1986). Nurturance in the home: A longitudinal study of sibling interaction. In A. Fogel & G. F. Melson (Eds.), *Origins of nurturance* (pp. 3–24). Hillsdale, NJ: Erlbaum.

Pellizzer, G., & Georgopoulos, A. P. (1993). Mental rotation of the intended direction of movement. *Current Directions in Psychological Science, 2,* 12–17.

Penfield, W., & Rasmussen, T. (1950). *The cerebral cortex of man.* New York: Macmillan.

Pennebaker, J. W. (1990). *Opening up: The healing power of confiding in others.* New York: Morrow.

Pennebaker, J. W., Kiecolt-Glaser, J. K., & Glaser, R. (1988). Disclosure of traumas and immune function: Health implications for psychotherapy. *Journal of Consulting and Clinical Psychology, 56,* 239–245.

Pennington, S. B. (1987). Children of lesbian mothers. In F. W. Bozett (Ed.), *Gay and lesbian parents* (pp. 58–74). New York: Praeger.

Peplau, L. A. (1988, July). *Research on lesbian and gay relationships: A decade review.* Paper presented at the International Conference on Personal Relationships, University of British Columbia, Vancouver, Canada.

Peplau, L. A., Padesky, C., & Hamilton, M. (1982). Satisfaction in lesbian relationships. *Journal of Homosexuality, 8,* 23–35.

Perfetti, C. A. (1993). Component harmonies in reading [Review of *Reading and its development: Component skills approaches*]. *Contemporary Psychology, 38,* 136–137.

Perkins, D. N. (1981). *The mind's best work.* Cambridge, MA: Harvard University Press.

Pernanen, K. (1991). *Alcohol in human violence.* New York: Guilford.

Perrin, S., & Spencer, C. (1981). Independence or conformity in the Asch experiment as a reflection of cultural and situational factors. *British Journal of Social Psychology, 20,* 205–209.

Perry, J. C., & Vaillant, G. E. (1989). Personality disorders. In H. I. Kaplan & B. J. Sadock (Eds.), *Comprehensive textbook of psychiatry/V* (5th ed., Vol. 2, pp. 1352–13877). Baltimore, MD: Williams & Wilkins.

Perry, N. W., & Wrightsman, L. S. (1991). *The child witness: Legal issues and dilemmas.* Newbury Park, CA: Sage.

Persons, J. B. (1989). *Cognitive therapy in practice: A case formulation approach.* New York: Norton.

Pert, C. B., & Snyder, S. H. (1973). Opiate receptor: Demonstration in nervous tissue. *Science, 179,* 1011–1014.

Pervin, L. A. (Ed.). (1990). *Handbook of personality theory and research.* New York: Guilford.

Peterson, C., & Seligman, M. E. P. (1985). The learned helplessness model of depression: Current status of theory and research. In E. E. Beckham & W. R. Leber (Eds.), *Handbook of depression* (pp. 914–939). Homewood, IL: Dorsey.

Peterson, C., & Seligman, M. E. P. (1987). Explanatory style and illness. *Journal of Personality, 55,* 237–265.

Peterson, C., Seligman, M. E. P., & Vaillant, G. (1988). Pessimistic explanatory style is a risk factor for physical illness: A thirty-five-year longitudinal study. *Journal of Personality and Social Psychology, 55,* 23–27.

Peterson, C., Semmel, A., von Bayer, C., Abramson, L. Y., Metalsky, G. I., & Seligman, M. E. P. (1982). The Attributional Style Questionnaire. *Cognitive Therapy and Research, 6,* 287–299.

Peterson, G. C. (1980). Organic mental disorders associated with brain trauma. In H. I. Kaplan, A. M. Freedman, & B. J. Sadlock (Eds.), *Comprehensive textbook of psychiatry* (3rd ed., Vol. 3, pp. 1422–1437). Baltimore: Williams & Wilkins.

Peterson, L. R., & Peterson, M. (1959). Short-term retention of individual verbal items. *Journal of Experimental Psychology, 58,* 193–198.

Petitto, L. A., & Marentette, P. F. (1991). Babbling in the manual mode: Evidence for the ontogeny of language. *Science, 251,* 1493–1496.

Petry, S., & Meyer, G. E. (Eds.). (1987). *The percep-*

tion of illusory contours. New York: Springer-Verlag.

Pettigrew, T. F., & Martin, J. (1987). Shaping the organizational context for black American inclusion. *Journal of Social Issues, 43,* 41–78.

Pettit, R., Holtzman, R. E., & Wollman, N. (1985). Using conflict constructively. In N. Wollman (Ed.), *Working for peace* (pp. 111–119). San Luis Obispo, CA: Impact Publishers.

Petty, R. E., & Cacioppo, J. T. (1986a). The elaboration likelihood model of persuasion. *Advances in Experimental Social Psychology, 19,* 123–205.

Petty, R. E., & Cacioppo, J. T. (1986b). *Communication and persuasion.* New York: Springer-Verlag.

Phares, E. J. (1988). *Introduction to personality* (2nd ed.). Glenview, IL: Scott, Foresman.

Phares, V. (1992). Where's Poppa? The relative lack of attention to the role of fathers in child and adolescent psychopathology. *American Psychologist, 47,* 656–664.

Phillip, M. (1993, April 8). AIDS: Fighting a killer through education. *Black Issues in Higher Education,* pp. 22–23.

Phillips, D., McCartney, K., & Scarr, S. (1987). Child-care quality and children's social development. *Developmental Psychology, 23,* 537–543.

Phillips, D. P., & Brugge, J. F. (1985). Progress in neurophysiology of sound localization. *Annual Review of Psychology, 36,* 245–274.

Piaget, J. (1983). Piaget's theory. In P. H. Mussen (Ed.), *Handbook of child psychology* (4th ed., Vol. 1, pp. 103–128). New York: Wiley.

Pickles, J. O. (1988). *An introduction to the physiology of hearing* (2nd ed.). London: Academic Press.

Pierce, J. P., Fiore, M. C., Novotny, T. E., Hatziandreu, E. J., & Davis, R. M. (1989). Trends in cigarette smoking in the United States. *JAMA, 261,* 56–65.

Pietromonaco, P. R., & Markus, H. (1985). The nature of negative thoughts in depression. *Journal of Personality and Social Psychology, 48,* 799–807.

Pietromonaco, P. R., & Rook, K. S. (1987). Decision style in depression: The contribution of perceived risks versus benefits. *Journal of Personality and Social Psychology, 52,* 399–408.

Piliavin, J. A., Callero, P. L., & Evans, D. E. (1982). Addiction to altruism? Opponent-process theory and habitual blood donation. *Journal of Personality and Social Psychology, 43,* 1200–1213.

Pinel, J. P. J. (1993). *Biopsychology* (2nd ed.). Boston: Allyn & Bacon.

Pinker, S. (1985). Visual cognition: An introduction. In S. Pinker (Ed.), *Visual cognition* (pp. 1–63). Cambridge, MA: MIT Press.

Pinker, S., & Birdsong, D. (1979). Speakers' sensitivity to rules of frozen word order. *Journal of Verbal Learning and Verbal Behavior, 18,* 497–508.

Plath, S. (1971). *The bell jar.* New York: Harper & Row.

Plaut, D. C., & Farah, M. J. (1990). Visual object representation: Interpreting neurophysiological data within a computational framework. *Journal of Cognitive Neuroscience, 2,* 320–343.

Pleck, J. H. (1985). *Working wives/working husbands.* Beverly Hills, CA: Sage.

Plomin, R. (1990a). The role of inheritance in behavior. *Science, 248,* 183–188.

Plomin, R. (1990b). *Nature and nurture.* Pacific Grove, CA: Brooks/Cole.

Plomin, R., DeFries, J. C., & McClearn, G. E. (1990). *Behavioral genetics: A primer* (2nd ed.). New York: Freeman.

Plomin, R., & Neiderhiser, J. M. (1992). Genetics and

experience. *Current Directions in Psychological Science, 1,* 160–163.

Plomin, R., & Rende, R. (1991). Human behavioral genetics. *Annual Review of Psychology, 42,* 161–190.

Plous, S. (1991). An attitude survey of animal rights activists. *Psychological Science, 2,* 194–196.

Plous, S. (1993). *The psychology of judgment and decision making.* New York: McGraw-Hill.

Polivy, J., & Herman, C. P. (1985). Dieting and binging: A causal analysis. *American Psychologist, 40,* 193–201.

Polivy, J., & Thomsen, L. (1988). Dieting and other eating disorders. In E. A. Blechman & K. D. Brownell (Eds.), *Handbook of behavioral medicine for women* (pp. 345–355). New York: Pergamon.

Pollatsek, A., Bolozky, S., Well, A. D., & Rayner, K. (1981). Asymmetries in the perceptual span for Israeli readers. *Brain and Language, 14,* 174–180.

Poole, G. D., & Craig, K. D. (1992). Judgments of genuine, suppressed, and faked facial expressions of pain. *Journal of Personality and Social Psychology, 63,* 797–805.

Pope, K. S. (1990). Therapist-patient sexual involvement: A review of the research. *Clinical Psychology Review, 10,* 477–490.

Poretz, M., & Sinrod, B. (1989). *The first really important survey of American habits.* Los Angeles: Price Stern Sloan.

Porter, R. H., Cernoch, J. M., & McLaughlin, F. J. (1983). Maternal recognition of neonates through olfactory cues. *Physiology & Behavior, 30,* 151–154.

Porter, R. H., & Moore, J. D. (1981). Human kin recognition by olfactory cues. *Physiology & Behavior, 27,* 493–495.

Posner, M. I., Early, T. S., Reiman, E., Pardo, P. J., & Dhawan, M. (1988). Asymmetries in hemispheric control of attention in schizophrenia. *Archives of General Psychiatry, 45,* 814–821.

Post-traumatic stress: Part I. (1991, February). *The Harvard Mental Health Letter,* pp. 1–4.

Potter, W. Z., Rudorfer, M. V., & Manji, H. (1991). The pharmacologic treatment of depression. *New England Journal of Medicine, 325,* 633–641.

Potts, R., Huston, A. C., & Wright, J. C. (1986). The effects of television form and violent content on boys' attention and social behavior. *Journal of Experimental Child Psychology, 41,* 1–17.

Poulos, C. X., & Cappell, H. (1991). Homeostatic theory of drug tolerance: A general model of physiological adaptation. *Psychological Review, 98,* 390–408.

Poulton, E. C. (1989). *Bias in quantifying judgments.* Hillsdale, NJ: Erlbaum.

Powers, S., & López, R. L. (1985). Perceptual, motor and verbal skills of monolingual and bilingual Hispanic children: A discriminant analysis. *Perceptual and Motor Skills, 60,* 999–1002.

Press, G. A., Amaral, D. G., & Squire, L. R. (1989). Hippocampal abnormalities in amnesic patients revealed by high-resolution magnetic resonance imaging. *Nature, 341,* 54–57.

Pressley, M., & Ghatala, E. S. (1988). Delusions about performance on multiple-choice comprehension tests. *Reading Research Quarterly, 23,* 454–464.

Preventing risk behaviors among students. (1992, October). *HIV/AIDS Prevention Newsletter (Centers for Disease Control),* pp. 1–2.

Pribram, K. H. (1954). Toward a science of neuropsychology: Method and data. In R. A. Patton (Ed.),

Current trends in psychology and the behavioral science (pp. 115–152). Pittsburgh: University of Pittsburgh Press.

Price, S. J., & McKenry, P. C. (1988). *Divorce.* Beverly Hills: Sage.

Prideaux, G. D. (1985). *Psycholinguistics.* New York: Guilford Press.

Prigatano, G. P. (1992). Personality disturbances associated with traumatic brain injury. *Journal of Consulting and Clinical Psychology, 60,* 360–368.

Prothrow-Stith, D. (1992, June 15). Can physicians help curb adolescent violence? *Hospital Practice,* pp. 193–207.

Pruitt, D. G., & Rubin, J. Z. (1986). *Social conflict.* New York: Random House.

Pruitt, D. G., & Rubin, J. Z. (1994). *Social conflict* (2nd ed.). New York: McGraw-Hill.

Psychodynamic Therapy, Part II (1991, November). *Harvard Mental Health Letter,* pp. 1–4.

Psychodynamic Therapy: Part III. (1991, December). *The Harvard Mental Health Letter,* pp. 1–4.

Puente, A. E. (1990). Psychological assessment of minority group members. In G. Goldstein & M. Hersen (Eds.), *Handbook of psychological assessment* (2nd ed., pp. 505–520). New York: Pergamon.

Pugh, E. N., Jr. (1988). Vision: Physics and retinal physiology. In R. C. Atkinson, R. J. Herrnstein, G. Lindzey, & R. D. Luce (Eds.), *Stevens' handbook of experimental psychology* (2nd ed., Vol. 1, pp. 75–163). New York: Wiley.

Pyke, S. W., & Toukmanian, S. (1989). A fuzzy generalization. *Canadian Psychology/Psychologie Canadienne, 30,* 63–64.

Pylyshyn, Z. W. (1978). Imagery and artificial intelligence. In C. W. Savage (Ed.), *Perception and cognition issues in the foundations of psychology* (Minnesota Studies in the Philosophy of Science, Vol. 9, pp. 19–56). Minneapolis: University of Minnesota Press.

Pylyshyn, Z. W. (1984). *Computation and cognition.* Cambridge, MA: MIT Press.

Pyszczynski, T., Greenberg, J., Solomon, S., Sideris, J., & Stubing, M. J. (1993). Emotional expression and the reduction of motivated cognitive bias: Evidence from cognitive dissonance and distancing from victims' paradigms. *Journal of Personality and Social Psychology, 64,* 177–186.

Quattrone, G. A. (1986). On the perception of a group's variability. In S. Worchel & W. Austin (Eds.), *Psychology of intergroup relations* (Vol. 2, pp. 25–48). Chicago: Nelson-Hall.

Quattrone, G. A., & Jones, E. E. (1980). The perception of variability within ingroups and outgroups: Implications for the law of small numbers. *Journal of Personality and Social Psychology, 38,* 141–152.

Quevedo-García, E. L. (1987). Facilitating the development of Hispanic college students. *New Directions for Student Services, 38,* 49–63.

Rachman, S. (1988). Panics and their consequences: A review and prospect. In S. Rachman & J. D. Maser (Eds.), *Panic: Psychological perspectives* (pp. 259–303). Hillsdale, NJ: Erlbaum.

Rados, R., & Cartwright, R. D. (1982). Where do dreams come from? *Journal of Abnormal Psychology, 91,* 433–436.

Rafferty, Y., & Shinn, M. (1991). The impact of homelessness on children. *American Psychologist, 46,* 1170–1179.

Rainey, L. C. (1988). The experience of dying. In H. Wass, F. M. Berardo, & R. A. Neimeyer (Eds.), *Dying: Facing the facts* (2nd ed., pp. 137–157). Washington, DC: Hemisphere.

Ramachandran, V. S. (1987). Visual perception of surfaces: A biological theory. In S. Petry & G. E. Meyer (Eds.), *The perception of illusory contours* (pp. 93–108). New York: Springer-Verlag.

Ramachandran, V. S. (1992, May). Blind spots. *Scientific American, 266,* 86–91.

Ramachandran, V. S., & Gregory, R. L. (1991). Perceptual filling in of artificially induced scotomas in human vision. *Nature, 350,* 699–702.

Rand, C. S. W., & Macgregor, A. M. C. (1990). Morbidly obese patients' perceptions of social discrimination before and after surgery for obesity. *Southern Medical Journal, 83,* 1390–1395.

Rand, C. S. W., & Macgregor, A. M. C. (1991). Successful weight loss following obesity surgery and the perceived liability of morbid obesity. *International Journal of Obesity, 15,* 577–579.

Range, L. (1993). Personal communication.

Rango, N. A., & Rampolla, M. (1990). Expanding the focus of human immunodeficiency virus prevention in the 1990s. *New York State Journal of Medicine, 90,* 116–119.

Ransdell, S. E., & Fischler, I. (1987). Memory in a monolingual mode: When are bilinguals at a disadvantage? *Journal of Memory and Language, 26,* 392–405.

Rao, S. M., & Huber, S. J., & Bornstein, R. A. (1992). Emotional changes with multiple sclerosis and Parkinson's disease. *Journal of Consulting and Clinical Psychology, 60,* 369–378.

Raskin, P. A., & Israel, A. C. (1981). Sex-role imitation in children: Effects of sex of child, sex of model, and sex-role appropriateness of modeled behavior. *Sex Roles, 7,* 1067–1076.

Rathus, S. A., & Boughn, S. (1993). *AIDS: What every student needs to know.* Fort Worth, TX: Harcourt Brace Jovanovich.

Rattan, A. I., & Rattan, G. (1987). A historical perspective on the nature of intelligence. In R. S. Dean (Ed.), *Introduction to assessing human intelligence* (pp. 5–28). Springfield, IL: Thomas.

Raw, M. (1986). Smoking cessation strategies. In W. R. Miller & N. Heather (Eds.), *Treating addictive behaviors* (pp. 279–287). New York: Plenum.

Rawlins, W. K. (1992). *Friendship matters: Communication, dialectics, and the life course.* New York: Aldine De Gruyter.

Ray, D. C., McKinney, K. A., & Ford, C. V. (1987). Differences in psychologists' ratings of older and younger clients. *The Gerontologist, 27,* 82–86.

Raymond, C. (1991, May 29). Study of patient histories suggests Freud suppressed or distorted facts that contradicted his theories. *The Chronicle of Higher Education,* pp. A4–A5.

Rayner, K., & Pollatsek, A. (1987). Eye movements in reading: A tutorial review. In M. Coltheart (Ed.), *Attention and performance XII: The psychology of reading.* Hillsdale, NJ: Erlbaum.

Rebecca, M. (1983). Personal communication.

Rebok, G. W. (1987). *Life-span cognitive development.* New York: Holt, Rinehart and Winston.

Rebok, G. W., Brandt, J., & Folstein, M. (1990, April–June). Longitudinal cognitive decline in patients with Alzheimer's disease. *Journal of Geriatric Psychiatry and Neurology, 3,* 91–97.

Rediehs, M. H., Reis, J. S., & Creason, N. S. (1990). Sleep in old age: Focus on gender differences. *Sleep, 13,* 410–424.

Redmond, S. P. (1988). An analysis of the general well-being of Blacks and Whites: Results of a national study. *Journal of Sociology and Social Welfare, 15,* 57–71.

Ree, M. J., & Earles, J. A. (1992). Intelligence is the best predictor of job performance. *Current Directions in Psychological Science, 1,* 86–89.

Reed, S. K., Dempster, A., & Ettinger, M. (1985). Usefulness of analogous solutions for solving algebra word problems. *Journal of Experimental Psychology: Learning, Memory, and Cognition, 11,* 106–125.

Reeder, G. D., McCormick, C. B., & Esselman, E. D. (1987). Self-referent processing and recall of prose. *Journal of Educational Psychology, 79,* 243–248.

Reese, E. P. (1986). Learning about teaching from teaching about learning: Presenting behavioral analysis in an introductory survey course. In V. P. Makosky (Ed.), *The G. Stanley Hall Lecture Series* (Vol. 6, pp. 65–127). Washington, DC: American Psychological Association.

Reeve, J. (1992). *Understanding motivation and emotion.* Fort Worth, TX: Harcourt Brace Jovanovich.

Regenbogen, V. S. (1988). Personal communication.

Regier, D., Boyd, J., Burke, J., Rae, D., et al. (1988). One-month prevalence of mental disorders in the United States. *Archives of General Psychiatry, 45,* 977–986.

Register, P. A., & Kihlstrom, J. F. (1987). Hypnotic effects on hypermnesia. *International Journal of Clinical and Experimental Hypnosis, 35,* 155–169.

Rehm, L. P. (1990). Cognitive and behavioral theories. In B. B. Wolman & G. Stricker (Eds.), *Depressive disorders: Facts, theories, and treatment methods* (pp. 64–91). New York: Wiley.

Reicher, G. M. (1969). Perceptual recognition as a function of meaningfulness of stimulus materials. *Journal of Experimental Psychology, 81,* 275–280.

Reid, P. T. (1988). Racism and sexism: Comparisons and conflicts. In P. A. Katz & D. A. Taylor (Eds.), *Eliminating racism: Profiles in controversy* (pp. 203–221). New York: Plenum.

Reid, P. T. (1992, August). *I hear you knocking, but you can't come in: Barriers for ethnic minorities and women in psychology and society.* Paper presented at the annual convention of the American Psychological Association, Washington, DC.

Reisberg, D. (Ed.). (1992). *Auditory imagery.* Hillsdale, NJ: Erlbaum.

Reisenzein, R. (1983). The Schachter theory of emotion: Two decades later. *Psychological Bulletin, 94,* 239–264.

Reitman, J. S. (1974). Without surreptitious rehearsal, information in short-term memory decays. *Journal of Verbal Learning and Verbal Behavior, 13,* 365–377.

Renzulli, J. S. (1986). The three-ring conception of giftedness: A developmental model for creative productivity. In R. J. Sternberg & J. E. Davidson (Eds.), *Conceptions of giftedness* (pp. 53–92). New York: Cambridge University Press.

Rescorla, L., Hyson, M. C., & Hirsh-Pasek, K. (Eds.). (1991). *Academic instruction in early childhood: Challenge or pressure?* San Francisco: Jossey-Bass.

Rescorla, R. A. (1968). Probability of shock in the presence and absence of CS in fear conditioning. *Journal of Comparative and Physiological Psychology, 66,* 1–5.

Rescorla, R. A. (1987). A Pavlovian analysis of goal-directed behavior. *American Psychologist, 42,* 119–129.

Rescorla, R. A. (1988). Pavlovian conditioning: It's not what you think it is. *American Psychologist, 43,* 151–160.

Rescorla, R. A. (1991). Associative relations in instrumental learning: The Eighteenth Bartlett Memorial Lecture. *Quarterly Journal of Experimental Psychology, 43B,* 1–23.

Rescorla, R. A., & Holland, P. C. (1982). Behavioral studies of associative learning in animals. *Annual Review of Psychology, 33,* 265–308.

Resnick, S. M. (1992). Positron emission tomography in psychiatric illness. *Current Directions in Psychological Science, 1,* 92–98.

Revusky, S. H. (1971). The role of interference in association over a delay. In W. K. Honig & P. H. R. James (Eds.), *Animal memory* (pp. 155–213). New York: Academic Press.

Reynolds, A. G. (1991a). The cognitive consequences of bilingualism. In A. G. Reynolds (Ed.), *Bilingualism, multiculturalism, and second language learning: The McGill Conference in Honour of Wallace E. Lambert* (pp. 145–182). Hillsdale, NJ: Erlbaum.

Reynolds, A. G. (Ed.). (1991b). *Bilingualism, multiculturism, and second language learning: The McGill Conference in Honour of Wallace E. Lambert.* Hillsdale, NJ: Erlbaum.

Reynolds, C. F. (1986, Spring). Sleep problems. *Generations,* pp. 24–27.

Reznick, J. S., & Goldfield, B. A. (1992). Rapid change in lexical development in comprehension and production. *Developmental Psychology, 28,* 406–413.

Rhodewalt, F., & Smith, T. W. (1990). Current issues in Type A behavior, coronary proneness, and coronary heart disease. In C. R. Snyder & D. R. Forsyth (Eds.), *Handbook of social and clinical psychology: The health perspective* (pp. 197–220). New York: Pergamon.

Rice, L. N., & Greenberg, L. S. (1991). Two affective change events in client-centered therapy. In J. D. Safran & L. S. Greenberg (Eds.), *Emotion, Psychotherapy, and change* (pp. 197–226). New York: Guilford.

Rice, M. L. (1989). Children's language acquisition. *American Psychologist, 44,* 149–156.

Rice, P. L. (1992). *Stress and health* (2nd ed.). Pacific Grove, CA: Brooks/Cole.

Richardson, J. T. E., & Zucco, G. M. (1989). Cognition and olfaction: A review. *Psychological Bulletin, 105,* 352–360.

Richardson, K. (1991). *Understanding intelligence.* Buckingham, England: Open University Press.

Rieser, P. A., & Underwood, L. E. (1990). Disorders of growth and short stature: Medical overview. In C. S. Holmes (Ed.), *Psychoneuroendocrinology: Brain, behavior, and hormonal interactions* (pp. 10–16). New York: Springer-Verlag.

Rizzo, T. A. (1989). *Friendship development among children in school.* Norwood, NJ: Ablex.

Robbins, A. S., Spence, J. T., & Clark, H. (1991). Psychological determinants of health and performance: The tangled web of desirable and undesirable characteristics. *Journal of Personality and Social Psychology, 61,* 755–765.

Roberts, T. (1991). Gender and the influence of evaluations on self-assessments in achievement settings. *Psychological Bulletin, 109,* 297–308.

Roberts, T., & Nolen-Hoeksema, S. (1989). Sex differences in reactions to evaluative feedback. *Sex Roles, 21,* 725–747.

Ruder, A. M., Flam, R., Flatto, D., & Curran, A. S. (1990). AIDS education: Evaluation of school and worksite based presentations. *New York State Journal of Medicine, 90,* 129–133.

Ruiz, D. S. (Ed.). (1990). *Handbook of mental health and mental disorder among Black Americans.* New York: Greenwood Press.

Rumelhart, D. E., McClelland, J. L., & the PDP Research Group. (1986). *Parallel distributed processing* (Vol. 1). Cambridge, MA: MIT Press.

Runeson, S., & Frykholm, G. (1983). Kinematic specifications of dynamics as an informational basis for person-and-action perception: Expectation, gender-recognition, and deceptive intension. *Journal of Experimental Psychology: General, 112,* 585–615.

Rushton, J. P. , & Campbell, A. C. (1977). Modeling, vicarious reinforcement and extraversion on blood donating in adults: Immediate and long-term effects. *European Journal of Social Psychology, 7,* 297–306.

Rushton, J. P., Chrisjohn, R. D., & Fekken, G. C. (1981). The altruistic personality and the self-report altruism scale. *Personality and Individual Differences, 2,* 293–302.

Rushton, W. A. H. (1958). Kinetics of cone pigments measured objectively in the living human fovea. *Annals of the New York Academy of Science, 74,* 291–304.

Russell, D. (1975). *The politics of rape.* New York: Stein and Day.

Russell, G. F. M. (1990). The diagnostic status and clinical assessment of bulimia nervosa. In M. M. Fichter (Ed.), *Bulimia nervosa: Basic research, diagnosis and therapy* (pp. 17–36). Chichester, England: Wiley.

Russell, M. J. (1976). Human olfactory communication. *Nature, 260,* 520–522.

Russell, P. O., & Epstein, L. H. (1988). Smoking. In E. A. Blechman & K. D. Brownell (Eds.), *Handbook of behavioral medicine for women* (pp. 369–383). New York: Pergamon.

Russo, N. F. (1983). Psychology's foremothers: Their achievements in context. In A. N. O'Connell & N. F. Russo (Eds.), *Models of achievement* (pp. 9–24). New York: Columbia University Press.

Ruvolo, A. P., & Markus, H. R. (1992). Possible selves and performance: The power of self-relevant imagery. *Social Cognition, 10,* 95–124.

Ryan, R. M. (1984). An appropriate, original look at appropriate originality [Review of *The social psychology of creativity*]. *Contemporary Psychology, 29,* 533–535.

Rychlak, J. F. (1981a). *Instructor's manual to Introduction to personality and psychotherapy* (2nd ed.). Boston: Houghton Mifflin.

Rychlak, J. F. (1981b). *Introduction to personality and psychotherapy* (2nd ed.). Boston: Houghton Mifflin.

Ryerse, C. (1990). *Thursday's child: Child poverty in Canada.* Ottawa, Ontario: National Youth in Care Network.

Rymer, R. (1992a, April 13). A silent childhood-I. *The New Yorker,* pp. 41–81.

Rymer, R. (1992b, April 20). A silent childhood-II. *The New Yorker,* pp. 43–77.

Sackeim, H. A., Prudic, J., Devanand, D. P., Kiersky, J. E., Fitzsimons, L., Moody, B. J., McElhiney, M. C., Coleman, E. A., & Settembrino, J. M. (1993). Effects of stimulus intensity and electrode placement on the efficacy and cognitive effects of electroconvulsive therapy. *New England Journal of Medicine, 328,* 839–883.

Safire, W. (1979, May 27). "I led the pigeons to the flag." *The New York Times Magazine,* pp. 9–10.

Salamé, P., & Baddeley, A. (1982). Disruption of short-term memory by unattended speech: Implications for the structure of working memory. *Journal of Verbal Learning and Verbal Behavior, 21,* 150–164.

Salinger, K. (1988). The future of behavior analysis in psychopathology. *Behavior Analysis, 23,* 53–60.

Salovey, P., Mayer, J. D., & Rosenhan, D. L. (1991). Mood and helping: Mood as a motivator of helping and helping as a regulator of mood. In M. S. Clark (Ed.), *Prosocial behavior* (pp. 215–237). Newbury Park, CA: Sage.

Salthouse, T. A. (1987). Age, experience and compensation. In C. Schooler & K. W. Schaie (Eds.), *Cognitive functioning and social structure over the life course* (pp. 142–157). Norwood, NJ: Ablex.

Salthouse, T. A. (1991). *Theoretical perspectives on cognitive aging.* Hillsdale, NJ: Erlbaum.

Saltzman, N., & Norcross, J. C. (Eds.). (1990). *Therapy wars: Contention and convergence in differing clinical approaches.* San Francisco: Jossey-Bass.

Samelson, F. (1987). Was early mental testing (a) racist inspired, (b) objective science, (c) a technology for democracy, (d) the origin of multiple-choice exams, (e) none of the above? (Mark the RIGHT answer). In M. M. Sokal (Ed.), *Psychological testing and American society 1890–1930* (pp. 113–127). New Brunswick, NJ: Rutgers University Press.

Samuel, A. G., & Ressler, W. H. (1986). Attention within auditory word perception: Insights from the phonemic restoration illusion. *Journal of Experimental Psychology: Human Perception and Performance, 12,* 70–79.

Sande, G. N., Goethals, G. R., & Radloff, C. E. (1988). Perceiving one's own traits and others': The multifaceted self. *Journal of Personality and Social Psychology, 54,* 13–20.

Sanders, B., Soares, M. O., & D'Aquila, J. M. (1982). The sex difference on one test of spatial visualization: A nontrivial difference. *Child Development, 53,* 1106–1110.

Sandler, J., & Steele, H. V. (1991). Aversion methods. In F. H. Kanfer & A. P. Goldstein (Eds.), *Helping people change: A textbook of methods* (4th ed., pp. 202–247). New York: Pergamon.

Sanna, L. J., & Shotland, R. L. (1990). Valence of anticipated evaluation and social facilitation. *Journal of Experimental Social Psychology, 26,* 82–92.

Santrock, J. W., & Yussen, S. R. (1989). *Child development* (4th ed.). Dubuque, Iowa: Wm. C. Brown.

Sarafino, E. P. (1990). *Health psychology: Biopsychosocial interactions.* New York: Wiley.

Sarno, M. T. (1991). Management of aphasia. In R. A. Bornstein & G. G. Brown (Eds.), *Neurobehavioral aspects of cerebrovascular disease* (pp. 314–336). New York: Oxford University Press.

Sarnoff, I., & Sarnoff, S. (1989). *Love-centered marriage in a self-centered world.* New York: Hemisphere.

Savage, D. D., McGee, D. L., & Oster, G. (1987). Reduction of hypertension-associated heart disease among Black Americans: Past experience and new perspectives on targeting resources. *The Milbank Quarterly, 65,* 297–321.

Savage-Rumbaugh, E. S. (1986). *Ape language.* New York: Columbia University Press.

Savage-Rumbaugh, E. S. (1991a). Language learning in the bonobo: How and why they learn. In N. Krasnegor, D. M. Rumbaugh, M. Studert-Kennedy, & R. L. Schiefelbusch (Eds.), *Biological and behavioral determinants of language development* (pp. 209–229). Hillsdale, NJ: Erlbaum.

Savage-Rumbaugh, S. (1991b). Multi-tasking: The Pan-human rubicon. *Seminars in the Neurosciences, 3,* 417–422.

Savage-Rumbaugh, S., Sevcik, R. A., Brakke, K. E., Rumbaugh, D. M., & Greenfield, P. M. (1990). In C. Rovee-Collier & L. P. Lipsitt (Eds.), *Advances in infancy research* (Vol. 6, pp. 221–278). Norwood, NJ: Ablex.

Saxe, L. (1991). Lying: Thoughts of an applied social psychologist. *American Psychologist, 46,* 409–415.

Saxe, L., Dougherty, D., & Cross, T. (1985). The validity of polygraph testing: Scientific analysis and public controversy. *American Psychologist, 40,* 355–366.

Scarborough, E., & Furumoto, L. (1987). *Untold lives: The first generation of American women psychologists.* New York: Columbia University Press.

Scarf, M. (1979, November). The more sorrowful sex. *Psychology Today, 12.* 45–52, 89–90.

Scarr, S. (1984). Intelligence: What an introductory psychology student might want to know. In A. M. Rogers & C. J. Scheirer (Eds.), *The G. Stanley Hall Lecture Series* (Vol. 4, pp. 61–99). Washington, DC: American Psychological Association.

Scarr, S., & Eisenberg, M. (1993). Child care research: Issues, perspectives, and results. *Annual Review of Psychology, 44,* 613–644.

Scarr, S., & Weinberg, R. A. (1976). IQ test performance of black children adopted by white families. *American Psychologist, 31,* 726–739.

Schacht, T. E., & Strupp, H. H. (1991). Psychodynamic psychotherapy. In C. E. Walker (Ed.), *Clinical psychology: Historical and research foundations* (pp. 395–416). New York: Plenum Press.

Schachter, S., Christenfeld, N., Ravina, B., & Bilous, F. (1991). Speech disfluency and the structure of knowledge. *Journal of Personality and Social Psychology, 60,* 362–367.

Schachter, S., & Singer, J. E. (1962). Cognitive, social, and physiological determinants of emotional state. *Psychological Review, 69,* 379–399.

Schacter, D. L. (1992). Understanding implicit memory: A cognitive neuroscience approach. *American Psychologist, 47,* 559–569.

Schaefer, E. S., & Burnett, C. K. (1987). Stability and predictability of quality of women's marital relationships and demoralization. *Journal of Personality and Social Psychology, 53,* 1129–1136.

Schafer, W. (1992). *Stress management for wellness* (2nd ed.). Fort Worth, TX: Harcourt Brace Jovanovich.

Schaie, K. W. (1965). A general model for the study of developmental problems. *Psychological Bulletin, 64,* 92–107.

Schaie, K. W. (1993). Ageist language in psychological research. *American Psychologist, 48,* 48–51.

Schaller, M. (1992). In-group favoritism and statistical reasoning in social inference: Implications for formation and maintenance of group stereotypes. *Journal of Personality and Social Psychology, 63,* 61–74.

Schatzberg, A. F., & Cole, J. O. (1991). *Manual of clinical psychopharmacology* (2nd ed.). Washington, DC: American Psychiatric Press.

Scheibel, A. B. (1992). Structural changes in the

aging brain. In J. E. Birren, R. B. Sloane, & G. D. Cohen (Eds.), *Handbook of mental health and aging* (2nd ed., pp. 147–173). San Diego: Academic Press.

Scheier, M. F., & Carver, C. S. (1987). Dispositional optimism and physical well-being: The influence of generalized outcome expectancies on health. *Journal of Personality, 55,* 169–210.

Scheier, M. F., Weintraub, J. K., & Carver, C. S. (1986). Coping with stress: Divergent strategies of optimists and pessimists. *Journal of Personality and Social Psychology, 51,* 1257–1264.

Schelling, T. C. (1989, April). *Behavioral responses to risk: The case of cigarette smoking.* Paper presented at Eastern Psychological Association, Boston.

Scherer, K. R. (1986). Studying emotion empirically: Issues and a paradigm for research. In K. R. Scherer, H. G. Wallbott, & A. B. Summerfield (Eds.), *Experiencing emotion.* Cambridge, England: Cambridge University Press.

Schieber, F. (1992). Aging and the senses. In J. E. Birren, R. B. Sloane, & G. D. Cohen (Eds.), *Handbook of mental health and aging* (2nd ed., pp. 251–306). San Diego: Academic Press.

Schilit, R., & Gomberg, E. S. L. (1991). *Drugs and behavior: A sourcebook for the helping professions.* Newbury Park, CA: Sage.

Schleifer, S. J., Keller, S. E., Camerino, M., Thornton, J. C., & Stein, M. (1983). Suppression of lymphocyte stimulation following bereavement. *JAMA, 250,* 374–377.

Schlesinger, K. (1985). A brief introduction to a history of psychology. In G. A. Kimble & K. Schlesinger (Eds.), *Topics in the history of psychology* (Vol. 1, pp. 1–20). Hillsdale, NJ: Erlbaum.

Schlossberg, N. K. (1984). Exploring the adult years. In A. M. Rogers & C. James Scheirer (Eds.), *The G. Stanley Hall Lecture Series* (Vol. 4, pp. 105–154). Washington, DC: American Psychological Association.

Schlundt, D. G., & Johnson, W. G. (1990). *Eating disorders: Assessment and treatment.* Boston: Allyn and Bacon.

Schmajuk, N. A., & DiCarlo, J. J. (1991). A neural network approach to hippocampal function in classical conditioning. *Behavioral Neuroscience, 105,* 82–110.

Schmajuk, N. A., & DiCarlo, J. J. (1992). Stimulus configuration, classical conditioning, and hippocampal function. *Psychological Review, 99,* 268–305.

Schmidt, G., & Sigusch, V. (1970). Sex differences in response to psychosexual stimulation by films and slides. *Journal of Sex Research, 6,* 268–283.

Schnaitter, R. (1987). American practicality and America's psychology [Review of *The origins of behaviorism: American psychology, 1870–1920*]. *Contemporary Psychology, 32,* 736–737.

Schnapf, J. L., & Baylor, D. A. (1987). How photoreceptor cells respond to light. *Scientific American, 256*(4), 40–47.

Schneider, B. A., & Trehub, S. E. (1992). Sources of developmental change in auditory sensitivity. In L. A. Werner & E. W. Rubel (Eds.), *Developmental Psychoacoustics* (pp. 3–46). Washington, DC: American Psychological Association.

Schneider, B. H. (1987). *The gifted child in peer group perspective.* New York: Springer-Verlag.

Schneider, J. W., & Hacker, S. L. (1973). Sex role imagery and the use of the generic "man" in introductory texts: A case in the sociology of sociology. *American Sociologist, 8,* 12–18.

Schneider, W. (1984). Developmental trends in the metamemory-memory behavior relationship: An integrative review. In D. L. Forrest-Pressley & T. G. Waller (Eds.), *Cognition, metacognition, and communication.* New York: Academic Press.

Schneider, W. (1987). Connectionism: Is it a paradigm shift for psychology? *Behavior Research Methods, Instruments, & Computers, 19,* 73–83.

Schneidman, E. S. (1980). Suicide. In E. S. Schneidman (Ed.), *Death: Current perspectives* (2nd ed., pp. 416–434). Palo Alto, CA: Mayfield.

Schober, M. F., & Clark, H. H. (1989). Understanding by addressees and overhearers. *Cognitive Psychology, 21,* 211–232.

Schoeneman, T. J., & Rubanowitz, D. E. (1985). Attributions in the advice columns: Actors and observers, causes and reasons. *Personality and Social Psychology Bulletin. 11,* 315–325.

Schooler, C. (1987). Cognitive effects of complex environments during the life span: A review and theory. In C. Schooler & K. W. Schaie (Eds.), *Cognitive functioning and social structure over the life course* (pp. 24–49). Norwood, NJ: Ablex.

Schroeder, D. H., & Costa, P. T. (1984). Influence of life event stress on physical illness: Substantive effects or methodological flaws? *Journal of Personality and Social Psychology, 46,* 853–863.

Schultz, D. P., & Schultz, S. E. (1992). *A history of modern psychology* (5th ed.). Fort Worth, TX: Harcourt Brace Jovanovich.

Schulz, R., Heckhausen, J., & Locher, J. L. (1991). Adult development, control, and adaptive functioning. *Journal of Social Issues, 47,* 177–196.

Schunk, D. H. (1981). Modeling and attributional effects on children's achievement: A self-efficacy analysis. *Journal of Educational Psychology, 73,* 93–105.

Schunk, D. H. (1991). *Learning theories: An educational perspective.* New York: Macmillan.

Schwartz, B. (1984). *Psychology of learning and behavior* (2nd ed.). New York: Norton.

Schwartz, B. (1989). *Psychology of learning and behavior* (3rd ed.). New York: Norton.

Schwartz, B., & Reisberg, D. (1991). *Learning and memory.* New York: Norton.

Schwartz, R., & Hartstein, N. (1986). Group psychotherapy with gay men. In T. S. Stein & C. J. Cohen (Eds.), *Contemporary perspectives on psychotherapy with lesbians and gay men* (pp. 157–177). New York: Plenum.

Schwartz, S. H. (1971). Modes of representation and problem solving: Well evolved is half solved. *Journal of Experimental Psychology, 91,* 347–350.

Schwartz-Bickenbach, D., Schulte-Hobein, B., Abt, S., Plum, C., & Nau, H. (1987). Smoking and passive smoking during pregnancy and early infancy: Effects on birth weight, lactation period, and nicotine concentrations in mother's milk and infant's urine. *Toxicology Letters, 35,* 73–81.

Schwarz, N., Bless, H., Strack, F., Klumpp, G., Rittenauer-Schatka, H., & Simons, A. (1991). Ease of retrieval as information: Another look at the availability heuristic. *Journal of Personality and Social Psychology, 61,* 195–202.

Scott, A. I. F. (1989). Which depressed patients will respond to electroconvulsive therapy? The search for biological predictors of recovery. *British Journal of Psychology, 154,* 8–17.

Scott, S. (1973). *The relation of divergent thinking to bilingualism: Cause or effect?* Unpublished manuscript. Department of Psychology, McGill University.

Scoville, W. B., & Milner, B. (1957). Loss of recent memory after bilateral hippocampal lesions. *Journal of Neurology, Neurosurgery, and Psychiatry, 20,* 11–21.

Scruggs, T. E., Mastropieri, M. A., Jorgensen, C., & Monson, J. (1986). Effective mnemonic strategies for gifted learners. *Journal of the Education of the Gifted, 9,* 105–121.

Seabrook J. (1993, January 11). The flash of genius. *The New Yorker,* pp. 38–52.

Searleman, A. (1988). From swampland to prime real estate: The right hemisphere [Review of *Language, aphasia, and the right hemisphere*]. *Contemporary Psychology, 33,* 663–664.

Searleman, A., & Herrmann, D. J. (1994). *Memory from a broader perspective.* New York: McGraw-Hill.

Sears, D. O. (1988). Symbolic racism. In P. A. Katz & D. A. Taylor (Eds.), *Eliminating racism: Profiles in controversy* (pp. 53–84). New York: Plenum.

Segal, S. J., & Fusela, V. (1970). Influence of imaged pictures and sounds on detection of visual and auditory signals. *Journal of Experimental Psychology, 83,* 458–464.

Segal, Z. V. (1988). Appraisal of the self-schema construct in cognitive models of depression. *Psychological Bulletin, 103,* 147–162.

Seith, P. (1992). Personal communication.

Seligman, M. E. P. (1971). Preparedness and phobias. *Behavior Therapy, 2,* 307–320.

Seligman, M. E. P. (1989). Research in clinical psychology: Why is there so much depression today? In I. S. Cohen (Ed.), *The G. Stanley Hall Lecture Series* (Vol. 9, pp. 75–96). Washington, DC: American Psychological Association.

Seligman, J. (1992, October 5). The HIV dating game. *Newsweek,* pp. 56–57.

Selkoe, D. J. (1991, November). Amyloid protein and Alzheimer's disease. *Scientific American, 265,* 68–78.

Selye, H. (1956). *The stress of life.* New York: McGraw-Hill.

Serbin, L. A., & O'Leary, K. D. (1975, December). How nursery schools teach girls to shut up. *Psychology Today, 9,* 57–58, 102–103.

The severely mentally ill and the homeless mentally ill. (1992, July). *APS Observer,* pp. 15–16.

Sexton, M., & Hebel, R. (1984). A clinical trial of change in maternal smoking and its effect on birth weight. *Journal of the American Medical Association, 251,* 911–915.

Shaffer, D. R. (1989). *Developmental psychology* (2nd ed.). Pacific Grove, CA: Brooks/Cole.

Shaffer, L. H. (1975). Multiple attention in continuous verbal tasks. In P. M. Rabbitt & S. Dornic (Eds.), *Attention and performance* (Vol. 5). London: Academic.

Shapiro, C. M. (1982). Energy expenditure and restorative sleep. *Biological Psychology, 15,* 229–239.

Shapiro, D. A., & Shapiro, D. (1982). Meta-analysis of comparative therapy outcome research: A critical appraisal. *Behavior Psychotherapy, 10,* 4–25.

Shapiro, D. H. (1984). Overview: Clinical and physiological comparison of meditation with other self-control strategies. In D. H. Shapiro & R. N. Walsh (Eds.), *Meditation: Classic and contemporary perspectives* (pp. 5–11). New York: Aldine.

Shatz, M., & Gelman, R. (1973). The development of communication skills. Modifications in the speech of young children as a function of listener. *Monographs of the Society for Research in Child*

Development, 38 (2, Serial No. 152).

Shaughnessy, J. J., & Mand, J. L. (1982). How permanent are memories for real life events? *American Journal of Psychology, 95,* 51–65.

Shaughnessy, J. J., & Zechmeister, E. B. (1990). *Research methods in psychology* (2nd ed.). New York: McGraw-Hill.

Shaver, P. R., & Brennan, K.A. (1992). Attachment styles and the "Big Five" personality traits: Their connections with each other and with romantic relationship outcomes. *Personality and Social Psychology Bulletin, 18,* 536–545.

Shaver, P. R., Hazan, C., & Bradshaw, D. (1988). Love as attachment: The integration of three behavioral systems. In R. J. Sternberg & M. L. Barnes (Eds.), *The psychology of love* (pp. 68–99). New Haven, CT: Yale University Press.

Shaywitz, S. E., Shaywitz, B. A., Fletcher, J. M., & Escobar, M. D. (1990). Prevalence of reading disability in boys and girls. *JAMA, 264,* 998–1002.

Shea, M. T., Elkin, I., Imber, S. D., Sotsky, S. M., Watkins, J. T., Collins, J. F., Pilkonis, P. A., Keckham, E., Glass, D. R., Dolan, R. T., & Parloff, M. B. (1992). *Archives of General Psychiatry, 49,* 782–787.

Shear, M. (1989, March/April). Murder evokes rage. *New Directions for Women,* p. 6.

Sheehan, P. W. (1988). Memory distortion in hypnosis. *International Journal of Clinical and Experimental Hypnosis, 36,* 296–311.

Sheehan, S. (1982). *Is there no place on earth for me?* Boston: Houghton Mifflin.

Shepard, R. N. (1978). Externalization of mental images and the act of creation. In B. S. Randhawa & W. E. Coffman (Eds.), *Visual learning, thinking, and communication* (pp. 133–190). New York: Academic Press.

Shepard, R. N. (1990). *Mind sights.* New York: Freeman.

Shepard, R. N., & Chipman, S. (1970). Second-order isomorphism of internal representation: Shape of states. *Cognitive Psychology, 1,* 1–17.

Shepard, R. N., & Metzler, J. (1971). Mental rotation of three-dimensional objects. *Science, 171,* 701–703.

Sheppard, A. (1981). Responses to cartoons and attitudes toward aging. *Journal of Gerontology, 36,* 122–126.

Sherman, E. (1991). *Reminiscence and the self in old age.* New York: Springer.

Sherman, W. M. (1990). *Behavior modification.* New York: Harper & Row.

Sherrill, R. E. (1986). Gestalt therapy and Gestalt psychology. *The Gestalt Journal, 9,* 53–66.

Sherrod, L. R., & Brim, O. G., Jr. (1986). Epilogue: Retrospective and prospective views of life-course research on human development. In A. B. Sørensen, F. E. Weinert, & L. R. Sherrod (Eds), *Human development and the life course: Multidisciplinary perspectives* (pp. 557–580). Hillsdale, NJ: Erlbaum.

Shields, P. J., & Rovee-Collier, C. (1992). Long-term memory for context-specific category information at six months. *Child Development, 63,* 245–259.

Shirley, M. N. (1931). *The first two years.* Minneapolis: University of Minnesota Press.

Shoham-Salomon, V., & Hannah, M. T. (1991). Client-treatment interaction in the study of differential change processes. *Journal of Consulting and Clinical Psychology, 59,* 217–225.

Sholevar, G. P. (1987). Anorexia nervosa and bulimia. In H. L. Field & B. B. Domangue (Eds.), *Eating*

disorders throughout the life span (pp. 31–47). New York: Praeger.

Shulman, D. G. (1990). The investigation of psychoanalytic theory by means of the experimental method. *International Journal of Psycho-Analysis, 71,* 487–498.

Siegel, S. (1984). Pavlovian conditioning and heroin overdose: Reports by overdose victims. *Bulletin of the Psychonomic Society, 22,* 428–430.

Siegel, S. (1988). State dependent learning and morphine tolerance. *Behavioral Neuroscience, 102,* 228–232.

Sillars, A. L., & Wilmot, W. W. (1989). Marital communication across the life span. In J. F. Nussbaum (Ed.), *Life-span communication: Normative processes* (pp. 225–253). Hillsdale, NJ: Erlbaum.

Silverman, L. H. (1983). The subliminal psychodynamic activation method: Overview and comprehensive listing of studies. In J. Masling (Ed.), *Empirical studies of psychoanalytic theories* (Vol. 1, pp. 69–100). Hillsdale, NJ: Analytic Press.

Silverman, L. H., & Weinberger, J. (1985). Mommy and I are one: Implications for psychotherapy. *American Psychologist, 12,* 1296–1308.

Silverstein, B. (1989). Enemy images: The psychology of U. S. attitudes and cognitions regarding the Soviet Union. *American Psychologist, 44,* 903–913.

Silverstein, L. B. (1991). Transforming the debate about child care and maternal employment. *American Psychologist, 46,* 1025–1032.

Silvis, G. L., & Perry, C. L. (1987). Understanding and deterring tobacco use among adolescents. *Chemical Dependency, 34,* 363–379.

Simon, B. L. (1987). *Never married women.* Philadelphia, PA: Temple University Press.

Simon, H. A. (1992). What is an "explanation" of behavior. *Psychological Science, 3,* 150–161.

Simons, J. M., Finlay, B., & Yang, A. (1991). *The adolescent and young adult fact book.* Washington, DC: Children's Defense Fund.

Simonton, D. K. (1990). Creativity in the later years: Optimistic prospects for achievement. *The Gerontologist, 30,* 626–631.

Singer, J. L., & Singer, D. G. (1981). *Television, imagination, and aggression: A study of preschoolers.* Hillsdale, NJ: Erlbaum.

Singer, J. L., Singer, D. G., & Rapaczynski, W. (1984, Spring). Family patterns and television viewing as predictors of children's beliefs and aggression. *Journal of Communication, 34,* 73–89.

Singer, J. M., & Fagen, J. W. (1992). Negative affect, emotional expression, and forgetting in young infants. *Developmental Psychology, 28,* 48–57.

Singleton, C. H. (1987). Sex roles in cognition. In D. J. Hargreaves & A. M. Colley (Eds.), *The psychology of sex roles* (pp. 60–91). New York: Hemisphere.

Sivard, R. L. (1989). *World military and social expenditures, 1989.* Washington, DC: World Priorities.

Sjostrom, L. (1980). Fat cells and bodyweight. In A. J. Stunkard (Ed.), *Obesity.* Philadelphia: Saunders.

Skinner, B. F. (1938). *The behavior of organisms: An experimental analysis.* New York: Appleton-Century-Crofts.

Skinner, B. F. (1953). *Science and human behavior.* New York: Macmillan.

Skinner, B. F. (1957). *Verbal behavior.* Englewood Cliffs, NJ: Prentice-Hall.

Skinner, B. F. (1971). *Beyond freedom and dignity.* New York: Knopf.

Skinner, B. F. (1974). *About behaviorism.* New York:

Knopf.

Skinner, B. F. (1987). *Upon further reflection.* Englewood Cliffs, NJ: Prentice-Hall.

Skinner, B. F. (1988a, June). Skinner joins aversives debate. *APA Monitor, 19,* 22–23.

Skinner, B. F. (1988b, August). *The school of the future.* Paper presented at the meeting of the American Psychological Association, Atlanta, GA.

Skinner, B. F. (1990). Can psychology be a science of mind? *American Psychologist, 45,* 1206–1210.

Skowronski, J. J., & Carlston, D. E. (1987). Social judgment and social memory: The role of cue diagnosticity in negativity, positivity, and extremity biases. *Psychological Bulletin, 105,* 131–142.

Skowronski, J. R., & Carlston, D. E. (1989). Negativity and extremity biases in impression formation: A review of explanations. *Psychological Bulletin, 105,* 1–12.

Slade, L. A., & Rush, M. C. (1991). Achievement motivation and the dynamics of task difficulty choices. *Journal of Personality and Social Psychology, 60,* 165–172.

"Sleeping pills and anti-anxiety drugs." (1988, December). *The Harvard Medical School Mental Health Letter,* pp. 1–4.

Slobin, D. I. (1985). *The cross-linguistic study of language acquisition* (Vols. 1 & 2). Hillsdale, NJ: Erlbaum.

Slovic, P., Fischhoff, B., & Lichtenstein, S. (1982). Facts versus fears: Understanding perceived risk. In D. Kahneman, P. Slovic, & A. Tversky (Eds.), *Judgment under uncertainty: Heuristics and biases* (pp. 463–489). New York: Cambridge University Press.

Slovic, P., Kunreuther, H., & White, G. F. (1974). Decision processes, rationality and adjustment to natural hazards. In G. F. White (Ed.), *Natural hazards, local, national and global.* New York: Oxford University Press.

Small, M. Y. (1990). *Cognitive development.* San Diego, CA: Harcourt Brace Jovanovich.

Smart, R. G., & Adlaf, E. M. (1992). Recent studies of cocaine use and abuse in Canada. *Canadian Journal of Criminology, 34,* 1–13.

Smetana, J. G. (1986). Pre-school children's conceptions of sex-role transgressions. *Child Development, 57,* 862–871.

Smith, A. (1990). Social influence and antiprejudice training programs. In J. Edwards, R. S. Tindale, L. Heath, & E. J. Posavac (Eds.), *Social influence processes and prevention* (pp. 183–196). New York: Plenum.

Smith, B., & Sechrest, L. (1991). Treatment of aptitude × treatment interactions. *Journal of Consulting and Clinical Psychology, 59,* 233–244.

Smith, E. E. (1989). Concepts and induction. In M. I. Posner (Ed.), *Foundations of cognitive science* (pp. 501–526). Cambridge, MA: MIT Press.

Smith, G. J. (1985). Facial and full-length ratings of attractiveness related to the social interactions of young children. *Sex Roles, 12,* 287–293.

Smith, J. (1992). Family intervention: Service implications. In M. Birchwood & N. Tarrier (Eds.), *Innovations in the psychological management of schizophrenia: Assessment, treatment and services* (pp. 235–251). Chichester, England: Wiley.

Smith, K. D., Keating, J. P., & Stotland, E. (1989). Altruism revisited: The effect of denying feedback on a victim's status to empathic witnesses. *Journal of Personality and Social Psychology, 57,* 641–650.

Smith, M. B. (1992). Nationalism, ethnocentrism, and the new world order. *Journal of Humanistic*

Psychology, 32, 76–91.

Smith, M. C. (1983). Hypnotic memory enhancement of witnesses: Does it work? *Psychological Bulletin, 94,* 387–407.

Smith, M. L. (1988). Recall of spatial location by the amnesic patient H.M. *Brain and Cognition, 7,* 178–183.

Smith, M. L., & Glass, G. V. (1977). Meta-analysis of psychotherapy outcome studies. *American Psychologist, 32,* 752–760.

Smith, M. L., Glass, G. V., & Miller, T. I. (1980). *The benefits of psychotherapy.* Baltimore: Johns Hopkins University Press.

Smith, M. S. (1990). Personal communication.

Smith, R. (1988). Does the history of psychology have a subject? *History of the Human Sciences, 1,* 147–177.

Smith, S. E., & Walker, W. J. (1988). Sex differences on New York state regents examinations: Support for the differential course-taking hypothesis. *Journal of Research in Mathematics Education, 19,* 81–85.

Smith, S. M. (1988). Environmental context-dependent memory. In G. M. Davies & D. M. Thomson (Eds.), *Memory in context: Context in memory* (pp. 13–34). Chichester, England: Wiley.

Smith, S. M., Glenberg, A., & Bjork, R. A. (1978). Environmental context and human memory. *Memory & Cognition, 6,* 342–353.

Smith, T. W., & Pope, M. K. (1990). Cynical hostility as a health risk: Current status and future directions. *Journal of Social Behavior and Health, 5,* 77–88.

Snarey, J. R. (1985). Cross-cultural universality of social-moral development: A critical review of Kohlbergian research. *Psychological Bulletin, 97,* 202–232.

Sniderman, P. M., & Tetlock, P. E. (1986). Reflections on American racism. *Journal of Social Issues, 42,* 173–187.

Snodgrass, J. G., Levy-Berger, G., & Haydon, M. (1985). *Human experimental psychology.* New York: Oxford University Press.

Snow, C. E. (1993). Bilingualism and second language acquisition. In J. Berko Gleason & N. B. Ratner (Eds.), *Psycholinguistics.* Fort Worth, TX: Harcourt Brace Jovanovich.

Snow, C. W. (1989). *Infant development.* Englewood Cliffs, NJ: Prentice-Hall.

Snow, R. E. (1977). Individual differences and instructional theory. *Educational Researcher, 6,* 11–15.

Snyder, C. R., & Forsyth, D. R. (Eds.). (1990). *Handbook of social and clinical psychology: The health perspective.* New York: Pergamon.

Snyder, C. R., Irving, L. M., & Anderson, J. R. (1990). Hope and health. In C. R. Snyder & D. R. Forsyth (Eds.), *Handbook of social and clinical psychology: The health perspective* (pp. 285–305). New York: Pergamon.

Snyder, M., Tanke, E. D., & Berscheid, E. (1977). Social perception and interpersonal behavior: On the self-fulfilling nature of social stereotypes. *Journal of Personality and Social Psychology, 35,* 656–666.

Snyder, S. H. (1977). Opiate receptors and internal opiates. *Scientific American, 236,* 44–56.

Snyder, S. H. (1985, October). The molecular basis of communication between cells. *Scientific American, 253,* 132–141.

Snyder, T., & Gackenbach, J. (1988). In J. Gackenbach & S. LaBerge (Eds.), *Conscious mind, dreaming brain* (pp. 221–259). New York: Plenum Press.

Snyderman, M., & Rothman, S. (1988). *The IQ controversy, the media and public policy.* New Brunswick, NJ: Transaction.

Solomon, P. R., Vander Schaaf, E. R., Nobre, A. C., Weisz, D. J., & Thompson, R. F. (1983). Hippocampus and trace conditioning of the rabbit's nictitating membrane response. *Neuroscience Abstracts, 9,* 645.

Solomon, R. L. (1980). The opponent-process theory of acquired motivation. *American Psychologist, 35,* 691–712.

Solomon, Z., Mikulincer, M., & Avitzur, E. (1988). Coping, loss of control, social support, and combat-related posttraumatic stress disorder: A prospective study. *Journal of Personality and Social Psychology, 55,* 279–285.

Solso, R. L. (1991). *Cognitive psychology* (3rd ed.). Boston: Allyn & Bacon.

Sommer, B. (1983). How does menstruation affect cognitive competence and psychophysiological response? In S. Golub (Ed.), *Lifting the curse of menstruation* (pp. 53–90). New York: Haworth.

Soper, B., & Rosenthal, G. (1988). The number of neurons in the brain: How we report what we do not know. *Teaching of Psychology, 15,* 153–156.

Soto, L. D. (1988). The home environment of higher and lower achieving Puerto Rican children. *Hispanic Journal of Behavioral Sciences, 10,* 161–167.

Spacapan, S., & Oskamp, S. (1989). Introduction to the social psychology of aging. In S. Spacapan & S. Oskamp (Eds.), *The social psychology of aging* (pp. 9–24). Newbury Park, CA: Sage.

Spear, N. E., Miller, J. S., & Jagielo, J. A. (1990). Animal memory and learning. *Annual Review of Psychology, 41,* 169–211.

Spearman, C. (1904). "General intelligence" objectively determined and measured. *American Journal of Psychology, 15,* 201–293.

Spearman, C. (1923). *The nature of "intelligence" and the principles of cognition.* London: Macmillan.

Spelke, H. W., Hirst, W., & Neisser, U. (1976). Skills of divided attention. *Cognition, 4,* 215–230.

Spence, J. T., & Helmreich, R. L. (1983). Achievement-related motives and behaviors. In J. T. Spence (Ed.), *Achievement and achievement motives* (pp. 7–68). San Francisco: Freeman.

Sperling, G. (1960). The information available in brief visual presentations. *Psychological Monographs, 74,* 1–29.

Sperling, S. (1988). *Animal liberators: Researchers and morality.* Berkeley, CA: University of California Press.

Sperry, R. W. (1982). Some effects of disconnecting the cerebral hemispheres. *Science, 217,* 1223–1226.

Spiegel, D., Bierre, P., & Rootenberg, J. (1989). Hypnotic alteration of somatosensory perception. *American Journal of Psychiatry, 146,* 749–754.

Spielman, A., & Herrera, C. (1991). Sleep disorders. In S. J. Ellman & J. S. Antrobus (Eds.), *The mind in sleep: Psychology and psychophysiology* (2nd ed., pp. 25–80). New York: Wiley.

Spilich, G. J., June, L., & Renner, J. (1992). Cigarette smoking and cognitive performance. *British Journal of Addiction, 87,* 1313–1326.

Spitz, H. H. (1986). *The raising of intelligence.* Hillsdale, NJ: Erlbaum.

Spitzer, R. L. (1975). On pseudoscience in science, logic in remission, and psychiatric diagnosis: A critique of D. L. Rosenhan's "On being sane in insane places." *Journal of Abnormal Psychology, 84,* 442–452.

Sprafkin, J., Gadow, K. D., & Grayson, P. (1987). Effects of viewing aggressive cartoons on the behavior of learning disabled children. *Journal of Child Psychology and Psychiatry and Allied Disciplines, 28,* 387–398.

Springer, S. P., & Deutsch, G. (1989). *Left brain, right brain* (3rd ed.), New York: Freeman.

Squire, L. R. (1987). *Memory and brain.* New York: Oxford University Press.

Squire, L. R. (1992). Memory and the hippocampus: A synthesis from findings with rats, monkeys, and humans. *Psychological Review, 99,* 195–231.

Squire, L. R., Amaral, D. G., & Press, G. A. (1990). Magnetic resonance imaging of the hippocampal formation and mammillary nuclei distinguish medial temporal lobe and diencephalic amnesia. *The Journal of Neuroscience, 10,* 3106–3117

Squire, L. R., Knowlton, B., & Musen, G. (1993). The structure and organization of memory. *Annual Review of Psychology, 44,* 453–495.

Sroufe, L. A., Cooper, R. G., & DeHart, G. B. (1992). *Child development: Its nature and course.* New York: McGraw-Hill.

Stacey, C. A., & Gatz, M. (1991). Cross-sectional age differences and longitudinal change on the Bradburn Affect Balance Scale. *Journal of Gerontology: Psychological Sciences, 46,* P76–P78.

Stachnik, T. J., & Stoffelmayr, B. E. (1983). Worksite smoking cessation programs: A potential for national impact. *American Journal of Public Health, 73,* 1395–1396.

Staddon, J. E. R., & Simmelhag, V. L. (1971). The "superstition" experiment: A reexamination of its implications for the principles of adaptive behavior. *Psychological Review, 78,* 3–43.

Stangor, C., & Ruble, D. N. (1989). Strength of expectancies and memory for social information: What we remember depends on how much we know. *Journal of Experimental Social Psychology, 25,* 18–35.

Stanovich, K. (1992). *How to think straight about psychology* (3rd ed.). Glenview, IL: Scott Foresman.

Stasser, G., & Taylor, L. A. (1991). Speaking turns in face-to-face discussions. *Journal of Personality and Social Psychology, 60,* 675–684.

Statistics Canada. (1992). *Mental health statistics, 1989–90.* Ottawa: Author.

Steblay, N. M. (1987). Helping behavior in rural and urban environments: A meta-analysis. *Psychological Bulletin, 102,* 346–356.

Steele, C. M., & Josephs, R. A. (1990). Alcohol myopia: Its prized and dangerous effects. *American Psychologist, 45,* 921–933.

Stein, N. L., Leventhal, B., & Trabasso, T. (Eds.). (1990). *Physiological and biological approaches to emotion.* Hillsdale, NJ: Erlbaum.

Steinberg, L., Dornbusch, S. M., & Brown, B. B. (1992). Ethnic differences in adolescent achievement: An ecological perspective. *American Psychologist, 47,* 723–729.

Steinbrook, R. (1992). The polygraph test—a flawed diagnostic method. *The New England Journal of Medicine, 327,* 122–123.

Steinmetz, G. (1992, February). The preventable tragedy: Fetal alcohol syndrome. *National Geographic,* pp. 36–39.

Stellar, E. (1954). The physiology of motivation. *Psychological Review, 61,* 5–22.

Stenberg, C. R., & Campos, J. J. (1990). The development of anger expressions in infancy. In N. L. Stein, B. Leventhal, & T. Trabasso (Eds.), *Psycho-*

logical and biological approaches to emotion (pp. 247–282). Hillsdale, NJ: Erlbaum.

Stendhal (Beyle, M.) (1927). *On love.* New York: Honi & Liveright.

Stephan, C. W., & Langlois, J. H. (1984). Baby beautiful: Adult attributions of infant competence as a function of infant attractiveness. *Child Development, 55,* 576–585.

Steptoe, A., & Appels, A. (Eds.). (1989). *Stress, personal control and health.* Chichester, England: Wiley.

Stern, D. (1985). *The interpersonal world of the infant.* New York: Basic Books.

Stern, P. C. (1992). Psychological dimensions of global environmental change. *Annual Review of Psychology, 43,* 269–302.

Sternbach, R. A. (1968). *Pain: A psychophysiological analysis.* New York: Academic.

Sternbach, R. A. (1978). Psychological dimensions and perceptual analyses, including pathologies of pain. In E. C. Carterette & M. P. Friedman (Eds.), *Handbook of perception* (Vol. 6B). New York: Academic.

Sternberg, R. J. (1985). Human intelligence: The model is the message. *Science, 230,* 1111–1118.

Sternberg, R. J. (1986a). *Intelligence applied.* San Diego: Harcourt Brace Jovanovich.

Sternberg, R. J. (1986b). A triangular theory of love. *Psychological Review, 93,* 119–135.

Sternberg, R. J. (1988). Triangulating love. In R. J. Sternberg & M. L. Barnes (Eds.), *The psychology of love* (pp. 119–138). New Haven, CT: Yale University Press.

Sternberg, R. J. (1990a). Wisdom and its relations to intelligence and creativity. In R. J. Sternberg (Ed.), *Wisdom: Its nature, origins, and development* (pp. 142–159). New York: Cambridge University Press.

Sternberg, R. J. (1990b). *Metaphors of mind: Conceptions of the nature of intelligence.* Cambridge, England: Cambridge University Press.

Sternberg, R. J., Conway, B. E., Ketron, J. L., & Bernstein, M. (1981). People's conceptions of intelligence. *Journal of Personality and Social Psychology, 41,* 37–55.

Sternberg, R. J., & Lubart, T. I. (1991). An investment theory of creativity and its development. *Human Development, 34,* 1–31.

Sternberg, R. J., & Powell, J. S. (1983). Comprehending verbal comprehension. *American Psychologist, 38,* 878–893.

Sternberg, R. J., & Wagner, R. K. (1993). The *g*-ocentric view of intelligence and job performance is wrong. *Current Directions in Psychological Science, 2,* 1–4.

Stevens, J. C., & Cain, W. S. (1987). Old-age deficits in the sense of smell as gauged by thresholds, magnitude matching, and odor identification. *Psychology and Aging, 2,* 36–42.

Stewart, A. J., & Chester, N. L. (1982). Sex differences in human social motives: Achievement, affiliation, and power. In A. J. Stewart (Ed.), *Motivation and society* (pp. 172–218). San Francisco: Jossey-Bass.

Stine, E. L., Wingfield, A., & Poon, L. W. (1989). Speech comprehension and memory through adulthood: The roles of time and strategy. In L. W. Poon, D. C. Rubin, & B. A. Wilson (Eds.), *Everyday cognition in adulthood and later life* (pp. 195–221). New York: Cambridge University Press.

Stinnett, N., Walters, J., & Kaye, E. (1984). *Relationships in marriage and the family* (2nd ed.). New York: Macmillan.

Stokes, G. (1992). *On being old: The psychology of later life.* London: Falmer.

Stone, A. A. (1984). Presidential address: Conceptual ambiguity and morality in modern psychiatry. In P. P. Rieker & E. Carmen (Eds.), *The gender gap in psychotherapy* (pp. 5–14). New York: Plenum.

Stone, A. A., & Neale, J. M. (1984). New measures of daily coping: Development and preliminary results. *Journal of Personality and Social Psychology, 46,* 892–906.

Stoppard, J. M. (1989). An evaluation of the adequacy of cognitive/behavioural theories for understanding depression in women. *Canadian Psychology/Psychologie Canadienne, 30,* 39–47.

Storfer, M. D. (1990). *Intelligence and giftedness: The contributions of heredity and early environment.* San Francisco: Jossey-Bass.

Strack, F., Martin, L. L., & Stepper, S. (1988). Inhibiting and facilitating conditions of facial expressions: A non-obtrusive test of the facial feedback hypothesis. *Journal of Personality and Social Psychology, 54,* 768–777.

Strang, J., & Shapiro, H. (1991). Tripping the light fantastic: The phenomenon of the hallucinogens. In I. B. Glass (Ed.), *The international handbook of addiction behaviour* (pp. 77–84). London: Tavistock/Routledge.

Strasburger, V. C. (1991). Children, adolescents, and television. *Feelings and their medical significance, 33*(1), pp. 1–6.

Straus, M. A., & Gelles, R. J. (1980). *Behind closed doors: Violence in the American family.* New York: Anchor/Doubleday.

Streissguth, A. P., Martin, D. C., Barr, H. M., Sandman, B. M., Kirchner, G. L., & Darby, D. L. (1984). Intrauterine alcohol and nicotine exposure: Attention and reaction time in 4-year-old children. *Developmental Psychology, 20,* 533–541.

Strickland, B. R. (1988). Sex-related differences in health and illness. *Psychology of Women Quarterly, 12,* 381–399.

Strickland, B. R. (1992). Women and depression. *Current Directions in Psychological Science, 1,* 132–135.

Stroop, J. R. (1935). Studies of interference in serial verbal reactions. *Journal of Experimental Psychology, 18,* 643–662,

Strupp, H. H. (1986). Psychotherapy: Research, practice, and public policy (how to avoid dead ends). *American Psychologist, 41,* 120–130.

Stunkard, A. J., Harris, J. R., Pedersen, N. L., & McClearn, G. E. (1990). The body-mass index of twins who have been reared apart. *New England Journal of Medicine, 322,* 1483–1487.

Stuss, D. T. (1991). Self, awareness, and the frontal lobes: A neuropsychological perspective. In J. Strauss & G. R. Goethals (Eds.), *The self: Interdisciplinary approaches* (pp. 255–278). New York: Springer-Verlag.

Stuss, D. T., & Benson, D. F. (1984). Neuropsychological studies of the frontal lobe. *Psychological Bulletin, 95,* 3–28.

Stuss, D. T., Gow, C. A., & Hetherington, C. R. (1992). "No longer Gage": Frontal lobe dysfunction and emotional changes. *Journal of Consulting and Clinical Psychology, 60,* 349–359.

Suarez, M. G. (1983). *Implications of Spanish-English bilingualism on the TAT stories.* Unpublished dissertation, University of Connecticut.

Subrahmanyam, K., & Greenfield, P. M. (in press). Effect of video game practice on spatial skills in girls and boys. *Journal of Applied Developmental Psychology.*

Suddath, R. L., Christison, G. W., Torrey, E. F., Casanova, M. F., & Weinberger, D. R. (1990). Anatomical abnormalities in the brains of monozygotic twins discordant for schizophrenia. *The New England Journal of Medicine, 322,* 789–845.

Sue, D. W. (Ed.). (1981). *Counseling the culturally different.* New York: Wiley.

Sue, D. W., & Sue, D. (1985). Asian-Americans and Pacific Islanders. In P. Pedersen (Ed.), *Handbook of cross-cultural counseling and therapy* (pp. 141–155). Westport, CT: Greenwood Press.

Sue, D. W., & Sue, D. (1990). *Counseling the culturally different; Theory and practice* (2nd ed.). New York: Wiley.

Sue, S. (1992). *Asian American psychology: The untold story.* Paper presented at the convention of the American Psychological Association, Washington, DC.

Sue, S., & Okazaki, S. (1990). Asian-American educational achievements: A phenomenon in search of an explanation. *American Psychologist, 45,* 913–920.

Suedfeld, P., & Tetlock, P. E. (1992a). Psychological advice about political decision making: Heuristics, biases, and cognitive defects. In P. Suedfeld & P. E. Tetlock (Eds.), *Psychology and social policy* (pp. 51–70). New York: Hemisphere.

Suedfeld, P., & Tetlock, P. E. (Eds.). (1992b). *Psychology and social policy.* New York: Hemisphere.

Sullivan, H. S. (1953). *The interpersonal theory of psychiatry.* New York: Norton.

Sullivan-Bolyai, J., Hull, H. F., Wilson, C., & Corey, L. (1983). Neonatal herpes simplex virus infection in King County, Washington. *JAMA, 250,* 3059–3062.

Suls, J., & Fletcher, B. (1985). The relative efficacy of avoidant and nonavoidant coping strategies: A meta-analysis. *Health Psychology, 4,* 249–288.

Sulzer-Azaroff, B., & Mayer, G. R. (1991). *Behavior analysis for lasting change.* Fort Worth, TX: Harcourt Brace Jovanovich.

Sundberg, N. D. (1990). *Assessment of persons* (2nd ed.). Englewood Cliffs, NJ: Prentice-Hall.

Surgeon General. (1988). *The health consequences of smoking: Nicotine addiction.* Rockville, MD: U.S. Department of Health and Human Services.

Surgeon General's report to the American public on HIV infection and AIDS. (1993, October). Atlanta, GA: Center for Disease Control and Prevention.

Suzuki-Slakter, N. S.. (1988). Elaboration and metamemory during adolescence. *Contemporary Educational Psychology, 13,* 206–220.

Swann, W. B., Jr. (1984). Quest for accuracy in person perception: A matter of pragmatics. *Psychological Review, 91,* 457–477.

Swann, W. B., Jr., & Ely, R. J. (1984). A battle of wills: Self-verification versus behavioral confirmation. *Journal of Personality and Social Psychology, 46,* 1287–1302.

Swann, W. B., Jr., Hixon, J. G., & De La Ronde, C. (1992). Embracing the bitter "truth": Negative self-concepts and marital commitment. *Psychological Science, 3,* 118–121.

Swanson, H. L. (1987). The influence of verbal ability and metamemory on future recall. *British Journal of Educational Psychology, 57,* 179–190.

Sweeney, P. D., Anderson, K., & Bailey, S. (1986). Attributional style in depression: A meta-analytic review. *Journal of Personality and Social Psychology, 50,* 974–991.

Swim, J., Borgida, E., Maruyama, G., & Myers, D. G.

(1989). Joan McKay versus John McKay: Do gender stereotypes bias evaluations? *Psychological Bulletin, 105,* 409–429.

"Take a look at college drinking." (1992, April). *Office of Substance Abuse Prevention Bulletin,* p. 4.

Talbot, J. D., Marrett, S., Evans, A. C., Meyer, E., Bushnell, M. C., & Duncan, G. H. (1991). Multiple representations of pain in human cerebral cortex. *Science, 251.* 1355–1358.

Talk of the Town. (1989, February 27). *The New Yorker,* pp. 25–27.

Tamir, L. M. (1989). Modern myths about men at midlife: An assessment. In S. Hunter & M. Sundel (Eds.), *Midlife myths: Issues, findings, and practice implications* (pp. 157–179). Newbury Park, NJ: Sage.

Tangney, J. P., Wagner, P., & Gramzow, R. (1992). Proneness to shame, proneness to guilt, and psychopathology. *Journal of Abnormal Psychology, 101,* 469–478.

Tanzi, R. E., Gusella, J. F., Watkins, P. C., Bruns, G. A. P., St. George-Hyslop, P. H., Van Keuren, M. L., Patterson, D., Pagan, S., Kurnit, D. M., & Neve, R. L. (1987). Amyloid protein gene: cDNA, mRNA distribution, and genetic linkage near the Alzheimer's locus. *Science, 235,* 880–884.

Tardif, T. Z., & Sternberg, R. J. (1988). What do we know about creativity? In R. J. Sternberg (Ed.), *The nature of creativity* (pp. 429–440). Cambridge, England: Cambridge University Press.

Tartter, V. C. (1986). *Language processes.* New York: Holt, Rinehart and Winston.

Tatum, B. D. (1992). Talking about race. *Harvard Educational Review, 62,* 1–24.

Tauber, R. T. (1988). Overcoming misunderstanding about the concept of negative reinforcement. *Teaching of Psychology, 15,* 152–153.

Tavris, C., & Offir, C. (1977). *The longest war: Sex differences in perspective.* New York: Harcourt Brace Jovanovich.

Taylor, C. B., & Arnow, B. (1988). *The nature and treatment of anxiety disorders.* New York: Free Press.

Taylor, I., & Taylor, M. M. (1983). *The psychology of reading.* New York: Academic.

Taylor, I., & Taylor, M. M. (1990). *Psycholinguistics: Learning and using language.* Englewood Cliffs, NJ: Prentice-Hall.

Taylor, R. J., & Chatters, L. M. (1991). Extended family networks of older Black adults. *Journal of Gerontology: Social Sciences, 46,* S210–S217.

Taylor, S. E. (1986). *Health psychology.* New York: Random House.

Taylor, S. E. (1989). *Positive illusions.* New York: Basic Books.

Taylor, S. E. (1991). *Health psychology* (2nd ed.). New York: McGraw-Hill.

Taylor, S. E., & Brown, J. D. (1988). Illusion and well-being: A social psychological perspective on mental health. *Psychological Bulletin, 103,* 193–210.

Taylor, S. E., & Dakof, G. A. (1987). Social support and the cancer patient. In S. Spacapan & S. Oskamp (Eds.), *The social psychology of health* (pp. 95–116). Newbury Park, CA: Sage.

Taylor, S. E., Kemeny, M. E., Aspinwall, L. G., Schneider, S. G., Rodriguez, R., & Herbert, M. (1992). Optimism, coping, psychological distress, and high-risk sexual behavior among men at risk for acquired immunodeficiency syndrome (AIDS). *Journal of Personality and Social Psychology, 63,* 460–473.

Teghtsoonian, M. (1983). Olfaction: Perception's Cinderella. *Contemporary Psychology, 28,* 763–764.

Teitelbaum, P. H., & Epstein, A. N. (1962). The lateral hypothalmic syndrome: Recovery of feeding and drinking after lateral hypothalamic lesions. *Psychological Review, 69,* 74–90.

Telch, M. J. (1988). Combined pharmacological and psychological treatment for panic sufferers. In S. Rachman & J. D. Maser (Eds.), *Panic: Psychological perspectives* (pp. 167–187). Hillsdale, NJ: Erlbaum.

Tellegen, A., Lykken, D. T., Bouchard, T. J., Jr., Wilcox, K. J., Segal, N. L., & Rich, S. (1988). Personality similarity in twins reared apart and together. *Journal of Personality and Social Psychology, 54,* 1031–1039.

Terrace, H. S. (1979). *Nim: A chimpanzee who learned sign language.* New York: Knopf.

Terrace, H. S. (1981). A report to an Academy, 1980. In T. Sebeok & R. Rosenthal, (Eds.), *The clever Hans phenomenon: Communication with horses, whales, apes and people. Annals of the New York Academy of Sciences, 364,* 115–129.

Terrace, H. S., Petitto, L. A., Sanders, R. J., & Bever, T. G. (1979). Can an ape create a sentence? *Science, 206,* 891–902.

Tesser, A., & Shaffer, D. R. (1990). Attitudes and attitude change. *Annual Review of Psychology, 41,* 479–523.

Teti, D. M. (1992). Sibling interaction. In V. B. Van Hasselt & M. Hersen (Eds.), Handbook of social development: A lifespan perspective (pp. 201–226). New York: Plenum.

Teti, D. M., & Nakagawa, M. (1990). Assessing attachment in infancy: The Strange Situation and alternate systems. In E. D. Gibbs & D. M. Teti (Eds.), Interdisciplinary assessment of infants (pp. 191–214). Baltimore: Paul H. Brookes.

Teti, D. M., Nakagawa, M., Das, R., & Wirth, O. (1991). Security of attachment between preschoolers and their mothers: Relations among social interaction, parenting stress, and mothers' sorts of the attachment Q-Set. *Developmental Psychology, 27.* 440–447.

Tetlock, P. E., Peterson, R. S., McGuire, C., Chang, S., & Feld, P. (1992). Assessing political group dynamics: A test of the groupthink model. *Journal of Personality and Social Psychology, 63,* 403–425.

Thaler, R. (1980). Toward a positive theory of consumer choice. *Journal of Economic Behavior and Organization, 1,* 39–60.

Thelen, E. (1992). Development as a dynamic system. *Current Directions in Psychological Science, 1,* 189–192.

Thomas, J. C. (1974). An analysis of behavior in the Hobbits-Orcs program. *Cognitive Psychology, 6,* 257–269.

Thomas, J. C. (1989). Problem solving by human-machine interaction. In K. J. Gilhooly (Ed.), *Human and machine problem solving* (pp. 317–362). New York: Plenum.

Thompson, E., Palacios, A., & Varela, F. J. (1992). Ways of coloring: Comparative color vision as a case study for cognitive science *Behavioral and Brain Sciences, 15,* 1–74.

Thompson, G. E. (1980, May). Hypertension: Implications of comparisons among blacks and whites. *Urban Health,* pp. 31–33.

Thompson, R. F. (1985). *The brain: An introduction to neuroscience.* New York: Freeman.

Thompson, R. F., & Donegan, N. H. (1986). The search for the engram. In J. L. Martinez & R. P. Kesner (Eds.), *Learning and memory: A biologi-*

cal view (pp. 3–52). San Diego: Academic Press.

Thompson, S. K. (1975). Gender labels and early sex-role development. *Child Development, 46,* 339–347.

Thompson, T. L., Filley, C. M., Mitchell, W. D., Culig, K. M., LoVerde, M., & Byyny, R. L. (1990). Lack of efficacy of Hydergine in patients with Alzheimer's disease. *New England Journal of Medicine, 323,* 445–448.

Thomson, J. R., & Chapman, R. S. (1977). Who is "Daddy" revisited: The status of two-year-olds' overextended words in use and comprehension. *Journal of Child Language, 4,* 359–375.

Thoresen, C. E., & Low, K. G. (1990). Women and the Type A behavior pattern: Review and commentary. *Journal of Social Behavior and Personality, 5,* 117–133.

Thoresen, C. E., & Powell, L. H. (1992). Type A behavior pattern: New perspectives on theory, assessment, and intervention. *Journal of Consulting and Clinical Psychology, 60.* 595–604.

Thorndike, E. L. (1898). Animal intelligence; An experimental study of the associative processes in animals. *Psychological Monographs, 2* (Whole no. 8).

Thorndike, E. L. (1913). *Educational psychology.* New York: Teachers College Press.

Thorndike, R. L., Hagen, E. P., & Sattler, J. M. (1986). *The Stanford-Binet Intelligence Scale: Fourth Edition, Guide for administering and scoring.* Chicago: Riverside.

Thurstone, L. L. (1955). *The differential growth of mental abilities* (Psychometric Laboratory Rep. No. 14). Chapel Hill: University of North Carolina Press.

Tienari, P., Sorri, A., Lahti, I., Naarla, M., Wahlberg, K. E., Moring, J., Pahjola, J., & Wynne, L. C. (1987). Interaction of genetic and psychosocial factors in schizophrenia. *Schizophrenia Bulletin, 13,* 477–484.

Tobacco industry seeks new recruits. (1993, Spring). *American Educator,* p. 42.

Tonnesen, P., Norregaard, J., Simonsen, K., & Sawe, U. (1991). A double-blind trial of a 16-hour transdermal nicotine patch in smoking cessation. *New England Journal of Medicine, 325,* 311–315.

Torrey, E. F. (1988a). *Surviving schizophrenia.* New York: Harper & Row.

Torrey, E. F. (1988b). *Nowhere to go: The tragic odyssey of the homeless mentally ill.* New York: Harper & Row.

Torrey, E. F. (1991, March). Care of the mentally ill. *The Harvard Mental Health Letter, 7,* p. 8.

Toufexis, A. (1989, January 23). A not-so-happy anniversary. *Time,* p. 54.

Travis, C. B. (1988). *Women and health psychology.* Hillsdale, NJ: Erlbaum.

Treatment of mood disorders—Part III. (1988, November). *The Harvard Medical School Mental Health Letter,* pp. 1–4.

Trehub, A. (1991). *The cognitive brain.* Cambridge, MA: MIT Press.

Treisman, A. M. (1991). Search, similarity, and integration of features between and within dimensions. *Journal of Experimental Psychology: Human Perception and Performance, 17,* 652–676.

Treisman, A. M. (1986, November). Features and objects in visual processing. *Scientific American, 255*(5), 114B–125.

Treisman, A. M., & Gelade, G. (1980). A feature-integration theory of attention. *Cognitive Psychology, 12,* 97–136.

Trepanier, M. L., & Romatowski, J. A. (1985). Attributes and roles assigned to characters in children's writing: Sex differences and sex-role perceptions. *Sex Roles, 13,* 263–272.

Trevarthen, C. (1987). Split-brain and the mind. In R. L. Gregory (Ed.), *The Oxford companion to the mind* (pp. 740–746). New York: Oxford University Press.

Trimble, J. E., & LaFromboise, T. (1985). American Indians and the counseling process: Culture, adaptation, and style. In P. Pedersen (Ed.), *Handbook of cross-cultural counseling and therapy* (pp. 127–140). Westport, CT: Greenwood.

True, R. H. (1990). Psychotherapeutic issues with Asian American women. *Sex Roles, 22,* 477–486.

Trull, T. J. (1992). Personality disorder diagnoses: How valid are they? [Review of *Personality disorders: New perspectives on diagnostic validity*]. *Contemporary Psychology, 37,* 231–232.

Tsai, M., & Uemura, A. (1988). Asian Americans: The struggles, the conflicts, and the successes. In P. A. Bronstein & K. Quina (Eds.), *Teaching a psychology of people* (pp. 125–133). Washington, DC: American Psychological Association.

Tucker, D. M., & Williamson, P. A. (1984). Asymmetric neural control systems in human self-regulation. *Psychological Review, 91,* 185–215.

Tulving, E. (1983). *Elements of episodic memory.* New York: Oxford University Press.

Turkheimer, E. (1991). Individual and group differences in adoption studies of IQ. *Psychological Bulletin, 110,* 392–405.

Turkkan, J. S. (1989a). Classical conditioning: The new hegemony. *Behavioral and Brain Sciences, 12,* 121–179.

Turkkan, J. S. (1989b). Classical conditioning beyond the reflex: An uneasy rebirth. *Behavioral and Brain Sciences, 12,* 161–179.

Turner, J. C., & Oakes, P. J. (1989). Self-categorization theory and social influence. In P. B. Paulus (Ed.), *Psychology of group influence* (2nd ed., pp. 233–275). Hillsdale, NJ: Erlbaum.

Turner, J. S., & Helms, D. B. (1989). *Contemporary adulthood* (4th ed.). New York: Holt, Rinehart and Winston.

Turner, M. E., Pratkanis, A. R., Probasco, P., & Leve, C. (1992). Threat, cohesion, and group effectiveness: Testing a social identity maintenance perspective on groupthink. *Journal of Personality and Social Psychology, 63,* 781–796.

Turner, S. M., Beidel, D. C., & Nathan, R. S. (1985). Biological factors in obsessive-compulsive disorders. *Psychological Bulletin, 97,* 430–450.

Turns, D. M. (1989). Epidemiology of the neuroses. In J. G. Howells (Ed.), *Modern perspectives in the psychiatry of the neuroses* (pp. 1–22). New York: Brunner/Mazel.

Tuttman, S. (1992). A group therapist examines psychodynamic factors in alienation and detachment. In J. S. Rutan (Ed.), *Psychotherapy for the 1990s* (pp. 191–209). New York: Guilford.

Tversky, A., & Kahneman, D. (1973). Availability: A heuristic for judging frequency and probability. *Cognitive Psychology, 5,* 207–232.

Tversky, A., & Kahneman, D. (1974). Judgments under uncertainty: Heuristics and biases. *Science, 185,* 1124–1131.

Tversky, A., & Kahneman, D. (1982). Judgment under uncertainty: Heuristics and biases. In D. Kahneman, P. Slovic, & A. Tversky (Eds.), *Judgment under uncertainty: Heuristics and biases* (pp. 3–20). New York: Cambridge University Press.

Tversky, A., & Kahneman, D. (1983). Extensional versus intuitive reasoning: The conjunction fallacy in probability judgment. *Psychological Review, 90,* 293–315.

Tversky, B. (1981). Distortions in memory for maps. *Cognitive Psychology, 13,* 407–433.

Tversky, B. (1990). Distortions in memory for visual displays. In S. R. Ellis, M. Kaisin, & A. Grunewald (Eds.), *Spatial instruments and spatial displays.* Hillsdale, NJ: Erlbaum.

Ullman, S. (1983). The measurement of visual motion. *Trends in NeuroSciences, 6,* 177–179.

Unger, R. K. (1979). Toward a redefinition of sex and gender. *American Psychologist, 34,* 1085–1094.

Update: Acquired immunodeficiency syndrome—United States, 1992. (1993). *JAMA, 270,* pp. 930–932.

U.S. Bureau of the Census. (1992). *Statistical abstract of the United States 1992.* Washington, DC: U.S. Government Printing Office.

U.S. Congress, Office of Technology Assessment (1987). *Losing a million minds: Confronting the tragedy of Alzheimer's disease and other dementias.* Washington, DC: U.S. Government Printing Office.

U.S. Department of Commerce. (1987, March). Marital status and living arrangements. *Current Population Reports,* Series P-20, No. 423.

U.S. Department of Education (1992). *Digest of educational statistics 1992.* Washington, DC: U.S. Government Printing Office.

U.S. Department of Labor. (1989). *Handbook of labor statistics.* Washington, DC: U.S. Government Printing Office.

Vaillant, G. E. (1977). *Adaptation to life.* Boston: Little Brown.

Vance, E. B., & Wagner, N. N. (1977). Written descriptions of orgasm: A study of sex differences. In D. Byrne & L. A. Byrne (Eds.), *Exploring human sexuality* (pp. 201–212). New York: Thomas Y. Crowell.

van der Heijden, A. H. C. (1981). *Short-term visual information forgetting.* London: Routledge & Kegan Paul.

Vandell, D. L., & Ramanan, J. (1992). Effects of early and recent maternal employment on children from low-income families. *Child Development, 63,* 938–949.

Van Essen, D. C., Anderson, C. H., & Felleman, D. J. (1992). Information processing in the primate visual system: An integrated systems perspective. *Science, 255,* 419–422.

Vangelisti, A. L. (1992). Older adolescents' perceptions of communication problems with their parents. *Journal of Adolescent Research, 7,* 382–402.

Van Hasselt, V. B., & Hersen, M. (Eds.). (1992). *Handbook of social development: A lifespan perspective.* New York: Plenum.

Van Hoesen, G. W., & Damasio, A. R. (1987). Neural correlates of cognitive impairment in Alzheimer's disease. In V. B. Mountcastle & F. E. Bloom (Eds.), *Handbook of physiology* (Vol. 5, pp. 871–898). Bethesda, MD: American Physiological Society.

Van Houten, R., & Doleys, D. M. (1983). Are social reprimands effective? In S. Axelrod & J. Apsche (Eds.), *The effects of punishment on human behavior* (pp. 45–70). New York: Academic Press.

Van Orden, G. C., Pennington, B. F., & Stone, G. O. (1990). Word identification in reading and the promise of subsymbolic psycholinguistics. *Psychological Review, 97,* 488–522.

Vasquez, M. J. T., & Barón, A., Jr. (1988). The psychology of the Chicano experience: A sample course structure. In P. A. Bronstein & K. Quina (Eds.), *Teaching a psychology of people* (pp. 147–155). Washington, DC: American Psychological Association.

Vaughan, D., Asbury, T., & Tabbara, K. F. (1989). *General Opthalmology* (12th ed.). East Norwalk, CT: Appleton & Lange.

Vaughan, E., & Seifert, M. (1992). Variability in the framing of risk issues. *Journal of Social Issues, 48,* 119–135.

Velásquez, R. J., & Callahan, W. J. (1992). Psychological testing of Hispanic Americans in clinical settings: Overview and issues. In K. F. Geisinger (Ed.), *Psychological testing of Hispanics* (pp. 253–265). Washington, DC: American Psychological Association.

Venn, J. (1986). Hypnosis and the Lamaze method: A reply to Wideman and Singer. *American Psychologist, 41,* 475–476.

Verbrugge, L. M. (1985). Gender and health: An update on hypotheses and evidence. *Journal of Health and Social Behavior, 26,* 156–182.

Violence Against Women Survey. (1993, November 18). *The Daily Statistics Canada,* pp. 1–10.

von Baeyer, C. L., Sherk, D. L., & Zanna, M. P. (1981). Impression management in the job interview: When the female applicant meets the male "chauvinist" interviewer. *Personality and Social Psychology Bulletin, 7,* 45–51.

Vorhees, C. V., & Mollnow, E. (1987). Behavioral teratogenesis: Long-term influences on behavior from early exposure to environmental agents. In J. D. Osofsky (Ed.), *Handbook of infant development* (2nd ed., pp. 913–971). New York: Wiley.

Wade, C., & Cirese, S. (1991). *Human sexuality* (2nd ed.). San Diego: Harcourt Brace Jovanovich.

Wade, N. J., & Swanston, M. (1991) *Visual perception: An introduction.* New York: Routledge, Chapman, and Hall.

Wagstaff, G. F. (1983). Attitudes to poverty, the Protestant ethic, and political affiliation: A preliminary investigation. *Social Behavior and Personality, 11,* 45–47.

Wakefield, J. C. (1989). Level of explanation in personality theory. In D. M. Buss & N. Cantor (Eds.), *Personality psychology: Recent trends and emerging directions* (pp. 333–346). New York: Springer-Verlag.

Wakefield, J. C. (1992). The concept of mental disorder: On the boundary between biological facts and social values. *American Psychologist, 47,* 373–388.

Walbaum, S. (1993). Personal communication.

Waldrop, M. M. (1988). Toward a unified theory of cognition. *Science, 241,* 296–298.

Walker, C. E. (Ed.). (1991). *Clinical psychology: Historical and research foundations.* New York: Plenum.

Walker, E., & Lewine, R. R. J. (1990). Prediction of adult-onset schizophrenia from childhood home movies of the patients. *American Journal of Psychiatry, 147,* 1052–1056.

Walker, L., & Ashcroft, G. (1989). Pharmacological approaches to the treatment of panic. In R. Baker (Ed.), *Panic disorder: Theory research and therapy,* (pp. 301–314). Chichester, England: Wiley.

Walker, L. J., de Vries, B., & Richard, S. L. (1984). The hierarchical nature of stages of moral development. *Developmental Psychology, 20,* 960–966.

Walker, L. J., & Taylor, J. H. (1991). Family interactions and the development of moral reasoning. *Child Development, 62,* 264–283.

Walker-Andrews, A. S. (1986). Intermodal perception of expressive behaviors: Relation of eye and voice? *Developmental Psychology, 22,* 373–377.

Wallace, B. C. (1991). *Crack cocaine: A practical treatment approach for the chemically dependent.* New York: Brunner/Mazel.

Wallach, H., & Slaughter, V. (1988). The role of memory in perceiving subjective contours. *Perception & Psychophysics, 43,* 101–106.

Wallach, M. A., & Kogan, N. (1959). Sex differences and judgment processes. *Journal of Personality, 27,* 555–564.

Wallach, M. A., & Wallach, L. (1983). *Psychology's sanction for selfishness.* San Francisco: Freeman.

Wallach, M. A., & Wallach, L. (1990). *Rethinking goodness.* Albany: State University of New York Press.

Wallenberg. (1990, Autumn). *The Giraffe Gazette,* p. 6.

Wallis, C. (1984, July 11). Unlocking pain's secrets. *Time Magazine, 124,* 58–66.

Walsh, W. B., & Betz, N. E. (1990). *Tests and assessment* (2nd ed.). Englewood Cliffs, NJ: Prentice-Hall.

Wangensteen, O. H., & Carlson, A. J. (1931). Hunger sensation after total gastrectomy. *Proceedings of the Society for Experimental Biology, 28,* 545–547.

Ward, S. L., & Overton, W. F. (1990). Semantic familiarity, relevance, and the development of deductive reasoning. *Developmental Psychology, 26,* 488–493.

Wardman, W. (1985). The experience of agoraphobia. In J. C. Clarke & W. Wardman (Eds.), *Agoraphobia: A clinical and personal account* (pp. 29–43). Sydney, Australia: Pergamon.

Warga, C. (1988, September). You are what you think. *Psychology Today,* pp. 54–58.

Warr, P., & Parry, G. (1982). Paid employment and women's psychological well-being. *Psychological Bulletin, 91,* 498–516.

Warren, L. W., & McEachren, L. (1983). Psychosocial correlates of depressive symptomatology in adult women. *Journal of Abnormal Psychology, 92,* 151–160.

Warren, L. W., & McEachren, L. (1985). Derived identity and depressive symptomatology in women differing in marital and employment status. *Psychology of Women Quarterly, 9,* 133–144.

Warren, R. M. (1984). Perceptual restoration of obliterated sounds. *Psychological Bulletin, 96,* 371–383.

Warren, R. M., & Warren, R. P. (1970, December). Auditory illusions and confusions. *Scientific American, 223*(6), 30–36.

Warrington, E. K., & Weiskrantz, L. (1970). Amnesic syndrome: Consolidation or retrieval? *Nature, 228,* 629–630.

Warwick, D. P. (1975, February). Deceptive research: Social scientists ought to stop lying. *Psychology Today,* pp. 38–40, 105–106.

Warwick, H. M. C., & Salkovskis, P. M. (1989). Hypochondriasis. In J. Scott, J. M. G. Williams, & A. T. Beck (Eds.), *Cognitive therapy in clinical practice: An illustrative casebook* (pp. 78–102). London: Routledge.

Washton, A. M., & Gold, M. S. (1987). *Cocaine.* New York: Guilford.

Waters, E. B., & Goodman, J. (1990). *Empowering*

older adults: Practical strategies for counselors. San Francisco: Jossey-Bass.

Watson, G., & Williams, J. (1992). Feminist practice in therapy. In J. M. Ussher & P. Nicoloson (Eds.), *Gender issues in clinical psychology* (pp. 212–236). London: Routledge.

Watson, J. B. (1913). Psychology as the behaviorist views it. *Psychological Review, 20,* 158–177.

Watson, J. B., & Rayner, R. (1920). Conditioned emotional reactions. *Journal of Experimental Psychology, 3,* 1–14.

Weary, G., Stanley, M. A., & Harvey, J. H. (1989). *Attribution.* New York: Springer-Verlag.

Weaver, J. B., Masland, J. L., & Zillman, D. (1984). Effect of erotica on young men's aesthetic perception of their female sexual partners. *Perceptual and Motor Skills, 58,* 929–930.

Webb, W. B. (1982). Sleep and biological rhythms. In W. B. Webb (Ed.), *Biological rhythms, sleep, and performance* (pp. 87–110). New York: Wiley.

Webb, W. B. (1988). An objective behavioral model of sleep. *Sleep, 11,* 488–496.

Webbink, P. (1986). *The power of the eyes.* New York: Springer Publishing.

Wechsler, H., & Isaac, N. (1992). 'Binge' drinkers at Massachusetts colleges. *JAMA, 267,* 2929–2931.

Weeks, D. (1992). *The eight essential steps to conflict resolution.* Los Angeles: Jeremy P. Tarcher.

Wegner, D. M. (1992). You can't always think what you want: Problems in the suppression of unwanted thoughts. *Advances in Experimental Social Psychology, 25,* 193–225.

Wegner, D. M., Schneider, D. J., Carter, S., III, & White, L. (1987). Paradoxical effects of thought suppression. *Journal of Personality and Social Psychology, 53,* 5–13.

Weick, K. E. (1985). Systematic observational methods. In G. Lindzey & E. Aronson (Eds.), *Handbook of social psychology* (Vol. 1, pp. 567–634). New York: Random House.

Weigel, R. H., & Howes, P. W. (1985). Conceptions of racial prejudice: Symbolic racism reconsidered. *Journal of Social Issues, 41,* 117–138.

Weiner, B. (1985a). An attributional theory of achievement motivation and emotion. *Psychological Review, 92,* 548–573.

Weiner, B. (1985b). "Spontaneous" causal thinking. *Psychological Bulletin, 97,* 74–84.

Weiner, B. (1989). *Human motivation.* Hillsdale, NJ: Erlbaum.

Weiner, B. (1991). Metaphors in motivation and attribution. *American Psychologist,* 921–930.

Weingarten, H. P. (1982). Diet palability modulates sham feeding in VMH-lesioned and normal rats: Implications for finickiness and evaluation of sham-feeding data. *Journal of Comparative and Physiological Psychology, 96,* 223–233.

Weinstein, L. N., Schwartz, D. G., & Arkin, A. M. (1991). Qualitative aspects of sleep mentation. In S. J. Ellman & J. S. Antrobus (Eds.), *The mind in sleep: Psychology and psychophysiology* (2nd ed., pp. 172–213). New York: Wiley.

Weinstein, N. D. (1989). Effects of personal experience on self-protective behavior. *Psychological Bulletin, 105,* 31–50.

Weinstein, S. (1968). Intensive and extensive aspects of tactile sensitivity as a function of body part, sex, and laterality. In D. R. Kenshalo (Ed.), *The skin senses.* Springfield, IL: Thomas.

Weisberg, R. W. (1993). *Creativity: Beyond the myth of genius* (2nd ed.). New York: Freeman.

Weisberg, R. W., & Suls, J. M. (1973). An information-processing model of Duncker's candle problem.

Cognitive Psychology, 4, 255–276.

Weishaar, M. E., & Beck, A. T. (1987). Cognitive therapy. In W. Dryden & W. L. Golden (Eds.), *Cognitive-behavioural approaches to psychotherapy* (pp. 61–91). Cambridge, England: Hemisphere.

Weiss, B., Weisz, J. R., & Bromfield, R. (1986). Performance of retarded and nonretarded persons on information-processing tasks: Further tests of the similar structure hypothesis. *Psychological Bulletin, 100,* 157–175.

Weiss, J. (1990, March). Unconscious mental functioning. *Scientific American,* pp. 103–109.

Weissman, M. M., & Klerman, G. L. (1990). Interpersonal psychotherapy for depression. In B. B. Wolman & G. Stricker (Eds.), *Depressive disorders: Facts, theories and treatment methods* (pp. 379–395). New York: Wiley.

Weitzman, M., & Adair, R. (1988). Divorce and children. *The Pediatric Clinics of North America, 35,* 1313–1323.

Wellman, H. M. (1985). A child's theory of mind: The development of conceptions of cognition. In S. R. Yussen (Ed.), *The growth of reflection in children* (pp. 169–203). New York: Academic Press.

Wellman, P. J. (1993). Personal communication.

Werker, J. F., & Tees, R. C. (1984). Cross-language speech perception: Evidence for perceptual reorganization during the first year of life. *Infant Behavior and Development, 7,* 49–63.

Wessells, M. G. (1982). *Cognitive psychology.* New York: Harper & Row.

West, M. A. (1987). Traditional and psychological perspectives on meditation. In M. A. West (Ed.), *The psychology of meditaiton* (pp. 5–22). New York: Oxford University Press.

Westen, D. (1990). Psychoanalytic approaches to personality. In L. A. Pervin (Ed.), *Handbook of personality* (pp. 21–65). New York: Guilford.

Westen, D. (1991). Social cognition and object relations. *Psychological Bulletin, 109,* 429–455.

Wester, W. C. (1986). The relationship between hypnosis and other activities such as sleep. In B. Zilbergeld, M. G. Edlelstien, & D. L. Araoz (Eds.), *Hypnosis: Questions and answers* (pp. 5–8). New York: Norton.

Westheimer, G. (1988). Vision: Space and movement. In R. C. Atkinson, R. J. Herrnstein, G. Lindzey, & R. D. Luce (Eds.), *Stevens' handbook of experimental psychology* (2nd ed., Vol. I, pp. 165–193). New York: Wiley.

Weston, C. (1985, November). Pop quiz: Are you a worrywart? *Seventeen,* p. 48.

Wheeler, D. L. (1991, April 24). New genetic tools allow researchers to accelerate pace of building detailed maps of human chromosomes. *Chronicle of Higher Education,* pp. A4–A6.

Wheeler, D. L. (1992, November 11). Ambitious computer project would link myriad pieces of information on the brain. *Chronicle of Higher Education,* pp. A8, A9, A11.

Whitaker, L. C. (1992). *Schizophrenic disorders: Sense and nonsense in conceptualization, assessment, and treatment.* New York: Plenum.

Whitbourne, S. K. (1985). *The aging body: Physiological changes and psychological consequences.* New York: Springer-Verlag.

Whitbourne, S. K. (1986a). *Adult development* (2nd. ed.). New York: Praeger.

Whitbourne, S. K. (1986b). *The me I know: A study of adult identity.* New York: Springer-Verlag.

Whitbourne, S. K. (1992). Sexuality in the aging male. In L. Glasse & J. Hendricks (Eds.), *Gender & aging* (pp. 45–57). Amityville, NY: Baywood.

Whitbourne, S. K., & Ebmeyer, J. B. (1990). *Identity and intimacy in marriage.* New York: Springer-Verlag.

Whitbourne, S. K., & Hulicka, I. M. (1990). Ageism in undergraduate psychology texts. *American Psychologist, 45,* 1127–1136.

White, N. M., & Milner, P. M. (1992). The psychobiology of reinforcers. *Annual Review of Psychology, 43,* 443–471.

White, R. K. (1991). Enemy images in the United Nations-Iraq and East-West conflicts. In R. W. Rieber (Ed.), *The psychology of war and peace: The image of the enemy* (pp. 59–70). New York: Plenum Press.

White, R. W. (1959). Motivation reconsidered: The concept of competence. *Psychological Review, 66,* 297–333.

Whitebook, M., Howes, C., Phillips, D., & Pemberton, C. (1989, November). *Young Children,* pp. 41–45.

Whitehead, W., III, & Kuhn, W. F. (1990). Chronic pain: An overview. In T. W. Miller (Ed.), *Chronic pain* (Vol. 1, pp. 5–48). Madison, CT: International Universities Press.

Whitman, T. L., Hantula, D. A., & Spence, B. H. (1990). Current issues in behavior modification with mentally retarded persons. In J. L. Matson (Ed.), *Handbook of behavior modification with the mentally retarded* (2nd ed., pp. 9–50). New York: Plenum Press.

Whitson, E. R., & Olczak, P. V. (1991). Criticisms and polemics surrounding the self-actualization construct: An evaluation. *Journal of Social Behavior and Personality, 6,* 75–95.

Whorf, B. L. (1956). Science and linguistics. In J. B. Carroll (Ed.), *Language, thought, and reality: Selected writings of Benjamin Lee Whorf.* Cambridge, MA: MIT Press.

Wickelgren, W. A. (1965). Acoustic similarity and intrusion errors in short-term memory. *Journal of Experimental Psychology, 70,* 102–108.

Wickens, D. D., Dalezman, R. E., & Eggemeier, F. T. (1976). Multiple encoding of word attributes in memory. *Memory & Cognition, 4,* 307–310.

Widiger, T. A., & Trull, T. J. (1991). Diagnosis and clinical assessment. *Annual Review of Psychology, 42,* 109–133.

Widner, H., Tetrud, J., Rehncrona, S., Snow, B., Brundin, P., Gustavii, B., Björklund, A., Lindvall, O., & Langston, J. W. (1992). Bilateral fetal mesencephalic grafting in two patients with parkinsonism induced by 1-methyl-4-phenyl-1, 2, 3, 6-tetrahydropyridine (MPTP). *The New England Journal of Medicine, 327,* 1556–1563.

Widom, C. S. (1989). Does violence beget violence? A critical examination of the literature. *Psychological Bulletin, 106,* 3–28.

Wiener, D. (1988). *Albert Ellis: Passionate skeptic.* New York: Praeger.

Wiertelak, E. P., Maier, S. F., & Watkins, L. R. (1992). Cholecystokinin antianalgesia: Safety cues abolish morphine analgesia. *Science, 256,* 830–833.

Wiggins, J. S., & Pincus, A. L. (1992). Personality: Structure and assessment. *Annual Review of Psychology, 43,* 473–504.

Wilkes-Gibbs, D., & Clark, H. H. (1992). Coordinating beliefs in conversation. *Journal of Memory and Language, 31,* 183–194.

Williams, J. E., & Bennett, S. M. (1975). The definition of sex stereotypes via the adjective check list. *Sex Roles, 1,* 327–337.

Williams, J. M. G., Watts, F. N., MacLeod, C., & Mathews, A. (1988). *Cognitive psychology and emotional disorders.* Chichester, England: Wiley.

Williams, K. D., & Karau, S. J. (1991). Social loafing and social compensation: The effects of expectations of co-worker performance. *Journal of Personality and Social Psychology, 61,* 570–581.

Williams, R. B., Jr., Barefoot, J. C., & Shekelle, R. B. (1985). The health consequences of hostility. In M. A. Chesney & R. H. Rosenman (Eds.), *Anger and hostility in cardiovascular and behavioral disorders* (pp. 173–185). Washington, DC: Hemisphere.

Williams, R. J., & Karacan, I. (1985). Recent developments in the diagnosis and treatment of sleep disorders. *Hospital and Community Psychiatry, 36,* 951–957.

Willig, A. C. (1988). A case of blaming the victim: The Dunn monograph on bilingual Hispanic children on the U.S. mainland. *Hispanic Journal of Behavioral Science, 10,* 219–236.

Willingham, W. W. (1990). Introduction: Interpreting predictive validity. In W. W. Willingham, C. Lewis, R. Morgan, & L. Ramist (Eds.), *Predicting college grades: An analysis of institutional trends over two decades* (pp. 3–21). Princeton, NJ: Educational Testing.

Wilson, M. N. (1986). The black extended family: An analytical consideration. *Developmental Psychology, 22,* 246–258.

Wilson, M. N., Tolson, T. F. J., Hinton, I. D., & Kiernan, M. (1990). Flexibility and sharing of childcare duties in Black families. *Sex Roles, 22,* 409–425.

Winckelgren, I. (1992). How the brain 'sees' borders where there are none. *Science, 256,* 1520–1521.

Winograd, E., & Neisser, U. (Eds.). (1992). *Affect and accuracy in recall: Studies of "flashbulb" memories.* New York: Cambridge University Press.

Winokur, G. (1991). Epidemiology and genetics of depression and mania. In M. T. Tsuang, K. S. Kendler, & M. J. Lyons (Eds.), *Genetic issues in psychosocial epidemiology* (pp. 153–174). New Brunswick, NJ: Rutgers University Press.

Wise, P. H., & Meyers, A. (1988). Poverty and child health. *The Pediatric Clinics of North America, 35,* 1169–1186.

Wise, R. A. (1988). The neurobiology of craving: Implications for the understanding and treatment of addiction. *Journal of Abnormal Psychology, 97,* 118–132.

Wolf, N. (1991). *The beauty myth: How images of beauty are used against women.* New York: William Morrow.

Woo, D. (1989). The gap between striving and achieving: The case of Asian American women. In Asian Women United of California (Eds.), *Making waves: An anthology of writings by and about Asian American women* (pp. 185–194). Boston: Beacon Press.

Wood, G. (1984). Research methodology: A decision-making perspective. In A. M. Rogers & C. J. Scheirer (Eds.), *The G. Stanley Hall Lecture Series* (Vol. 4, pp. 191–217). Washington, DC: American Psychological Association.

Wood, R. (1993). Deceptive schemata: Initial impressions of others. In P. J. Kalbfleisch (Ed.), *Interpersonal communication: Evolving interpersonal relationships* (pp. 69–86). Hillsdale, NJ: Erlbaum.

Wood, W., Rhodes, N., & Whelan, M. (1989). Sex differences in positive well-being: A consideration of emotional style and marital status. *Psychological Bulletin, 106,* 249–264.

Wood, W., Wong, F. Y., & Chachere, J. G. (1991). Effects of media violence on viewers' aggression in unconstrained social interaction. *Psychological Bulletin, 109,* 371–383.

Woodford, J. (1989, February). The transformation of Benjamin Carson. *Michigan Today,* pp. 6–7.

Woods, P. J. (1987). *Is psychology the major for you? Planning for your undergraduate years.* Washington, DC: American Psychological Association.

Woody, R. H., Hansen, J. C., & Rossberg, R. H. (1989). *Counseling psychology: Strategies and services.* Pacific Grove, CA: Brooks/Cole.

Wooley, S., Wooly, O. W., & Dyrenforth, S. (1979). Theoretical, practical, and social issues in behavioral treatments of obesity. *Journal of Applied Behavior Analysis, 12,* 3–25.

Word, C. H., Zanna, M. P., & Cooper, J. (1974). The nonverbal mediation of self-fulfilling prophecies in intersocial interaction. *Journal of Experimental Social Psychology, 10,* 109–120.

Wright, B. A. (1988). Attitudes and the fundamental negative bias: Conditions and corrections. In H. E. Yuker (Ed.), *Attitudes toward persons with disabilities* (pp. 3–21). New York: Springer.

Wright, J. H., & Salmon, P. G. (1990). Learning and memory in depression. In C. D. McCann & N. S. Endler (Eds.), *Depression: New directions in theory, research, and practice* (pp. 211–236). Toronto: Wall & Thompson.

Wróbel, J. (1990). *Language and schizophrenia.* Amsterdam: John Benjamins.

Wundt, W. (1912/1973). *An introduction to psychology* (R. Pintner, Translator). London: George Allen. Reproduced by Arno Press, New York.

Wurtman, R. J. (1984). Alzheimer's disease. *Scientific American, 252,* 62–74.

Yager, J. (1989). Clinical manifestations of psychiatric disorder. In H. I. Kaplan & B. J. Sadock (Eds.), *Comprehensive textbook of psychiatryV* (5th ed., Vol. 1, pp. 553–582). Baltimore: Williams & Wilkins.

Yates, J. F. (1990). *Judgment and decision making.* Englewood Cliffs, NJ: Prentice-Hall.

Yeaworth, R. C., York, J., Hussey, M. A., Ingle, M. E., & Goodwin, T. (1980). The development of an adolescent life change event scale. *Adolescence, 15,* 91–98.

Yellott, J. I. (1981). Binocular depth inversion. *Scientific American, 245*(1), 148–159.

Yeni-Komshian, G. H. (1993). Speech perception. In J. B. Gleason & N. B. Ratner (Eds.), *Psycholinguistics* (pp. 89–131). Fort Worth, TX: Harcourt Brace Jovanovich.

Yerkes, R. M., & Morgulis, S. (1909). The method of Pawlow in animal psychology. *Psychological Bulletin, 6,* 257–273.

Yontef, G. M., & Simkin, J. S. (1989). Gestalt therapy. In R. J. Corsini & D. Wedding (Eds.), *Current psychotherapies* (4th ed., pp. 323–361). Itasca, Il.: Peacock.

Youngstrom, N. (1991, May). Clinicians should help families cope with mentally ill. *APA Monitor,* p. 6.

Youths learn alternatives to violence. (1992, September). *Children's Defense Fund Reports, 13,* pp. 1, 4.

Yu, B., Zhang, W., Jing, Q., Peng, R., Zhang, G., & Simon, H. A. (1985). STM capacity for Chinese and English language materials. *Memory & Cognition, 13,* 202–207.

Yussen, S. R., & Levy, V. M. (1975). Developmental changes in predicting one's own span of short-term memory. *Journal of Experimental Child Psychology, 19,* 502–508.

Zahn-Waxler, C., Cummings, E. M., & Iannotti, R. (1986). Altruism and aggression: Problems and progress in research. In C. Zahn-Waxler, E. M. Cummings, & Ronald Iannotti (Eds.), *Altruism and aggression* (pp. 1–15). Cambridge, England: Cambridge University Press.

Zahn-Waxler, C., Radke-Yarrow, M., Wagner, E., & Chapman, M. (1992a). Development of concern for others. *Developmental Psychology, 28,* 126–136.

Zahn-Waxler, C., Robinson, J. L., & Emde, R. (1992b). The development of empathy in twins. *Developmental Psychology, 28,* 1038–1047.

Zahn-Waxler, C., & Smith, K. D. (1992). The development of prosocial behavior. In V. B. Van Hasselt & M. Hersen (Eds.), *Handbook of social development: A lifespan perspective* (pp. 229–256). New York: Plenum.

Zajonc, R. B. (1965). Social facilitation. *Science, 149,* 269–275.

Zajonc, R. B. (1968). Attitudinal effects of mere exposure. *Journal of Personality and Social Psychology Monograph, 9,* 1–29, Pt. 2.

Zajonc, R. B. (1980). Feeling and thinking: Preferences need no inferences. *American Psychologist, 35,* 151–175.

Zajonc, R. B. (1984). On the primacy of affect. *American Psychologist, 39,* 117–123.

Zajonc, R. B., & McIntosh, D. N. (1992). Emotions research: Some promising questions and some questionable promises. *Psychological Sciences, 3,* 70–74.

Zajonc, R. B., Murphy, S. T., & Inglehart, M. (1989). Feeling and facial efference: Implications of the vascular theory of emotion. *Psychological Review, 96,* 395–416.

Zal, H. M. (1989). *Panic disorder: The great pretender.* New York: Plenum.

Zamansky, H. S., & Bartis, S. P. (1985). The dissociation of an experience: The hidden observer observed. *Journal of Abnormal Psychology, 94,* 243–248.

Zebrowitz, L. A. (1990). *Social perception.* Pacific Grove, CA: Brooks/Cole.

Zeki, S. (1992, September). The visual image in mind and brain. *Scientific American, 267,* 68–76.

Zelinski, E. M., & Gilewski, M. J. (1988). Memory for prose and aging: A meta-analysis. In M. L. Howe & C. J. Brainerd (Eds.), *Cognitive development in adulthood: Progress in cognitive development research* (pp. 133–158). New York: Springer-Verlag.

Zellner, D. A. (1991). How foods get to be liked: Some general mechanisms and some special cases. In R. C. Bolles (Ed.), *The hedonics of taste* (pp. 199–217). Hillsdale, NJ: Erlbaum.

Zhang, G., & Simon, H. A. (1985). STM capacity for Chinese words and idioms: Chunking and acoustical loop hypothesis. *Memory & Cognition, 13,* 193–210.

Zigler, E. F. (1987). Formal schooling for four-year-olds? No. *American Psychologist, 42,* 254–260.

Zigler, E. F., & Balla, D. A. (1982) *Mental retardation: The developmental-difference controversy.* Hillsdale, NJ: Erlbaum.

Zigler, E. F., & Glick, M. (1986). *A developmental approach to adult psychopathology.* New York: Wiley.

Zigler, E. F., & Hodapp, R. M. (1991). Behavioral functioning in individuals with mental retardation. *Annual Review of Psychology, 42,* 29–50.

Zilbergeld, B., & Ellison, C. R. (1980). Desire discrepancies and arousal problems in sex therapy. In S. R. Leiblum & L. A. Pervin (Eds.), *Principles and practice of sex therapy.* New York: Guilford Press.

Zillmann, D. (1992). Pornography research, social advocacy, and public policy. In P. Suedfeld & P. E. Tetlock (Eds.), *Psychology and social policy* (pp. 165–178). New York: Hemisphere.

Zimbardo, P. G., Haney, C., & Banks, W. C. (1973, April 8). A Pirandellian prison. *New York Times Magazine,* pp. 38–60.

Zimbardo, P. G., Haney, C., Banks, W. C., & Jaffe, D. (1972). *The psychology of imprisonment: Privation, power, and pathology.* Unpublished paper, Stanford University.

Zimbardo, P. G., & Leippe, M. R. (1991). *The psychology of attitude change and social influence.* New York: McGraw-Hill.

Zinbarg, R. E., Barlow, D. H., Brown, T. A., & Hertz, R. M. (1992). Cognitive-behavioral approaches to the nature and treatment of anxiety disorders. *Annual Review of Psychology, 43,* 235–267.

Zivin, J. A., & Choi, D. W. (1991, July). Stroke therapy. *Scientific American, 265,* 56–63.

Zuckerman, M. (1991). *Psychobiology of personality.* New York: Cambridge University Press.

Chapter 1   Chapter opening, © Harald Sund/The Image Bank; p. 3, © Dorothy Littell/Stock, Boston; p. 4 (top), © The Bettmann Archive; (bottom), © Archives of the History of American Psychology; p. 6 (top, left to right), © The Bettmann Archive; © Archives of the History of American Psychology; © Courtesy of Wellesley College Archives; © Dept. of Manuscripts and University Archives Cornell University Library; (bottom, left to right), © Archives of the History of American Psychology; © Archives of the History of American Psychology; © Culver Pictures; © Archives of the History of American Psychology; p. 7, © Yves de Braine/Black Star; p. 9 (top), © Chris Johnson/Stock, Boston; (bottom), ©Drew Appleby; p. 10 (top), © The Bettmann Archive; (bottom), Courtesy of the Carl Rogers Memorial Library; p. 11 (top), © William Carter; (bottom), © Yoav Levy/Phototake; p. 12 (top), © Joseph McNally; (bottom), © John P. Fox/Beaver College; p. 13 (both); © Robert V. Guthrie Collection; p. 15, © Robert E. Daemmrich/Tony Stone Images; p. 16, © Steve Sherman.

Chapter 2   Chapter opening, © Bart Connally/San Jose, CA; p. 22, © Joel Gordon 1989; p. 25, © Comstock; p. 28, © Comstock; p. 34, From *Genie: A Psycholinguistic Study of a Modern Day "Wild Child,"* by S. Curtiss. Academic Press, 1977; p. 35, © Rob Nelson/Black Star; p. 38, © Judy Allen-Newberry; p. 40, © David Frazier; p. 41, © Bob Daemmrich/Stock, Boston; p. 43, © Ron Pretzer/LUXE; p. 46 (top), © Custom Medical Stock Photography; (bottom), © Janeart, Ltd./The Image Bank; p. 47, © Louise Wadsworth; p. 53, © David Frazier.

Chapter 3   Chapter opening, © Dr. Dennis Kunkel/Phototake; p. 61, © Phototake; p. 62, © Dr. E.R. Lewis, University of California at Berkeley; p. 67 (top), © Dr. William Feindel/Montreal Neurological Institute; (bottom), © Charles Gupton/Stock, Boston; p. 68, © Courtesy of Drs. Michael E. Phelps and John C. Mazziotta, UCLA School of Medicine; p. 71, © Dan McCoy/Rainbow; p. 73, © Bonnie Kamin; p. 75, © 1991-Custom Medical Stock Photography; p. 79, © Innervisions; p. 81, © Ron Pretzer/LUXE; p. 82, © Will McIntyre/Science Source/Photo Researchers; p. 83 (top), © John Harding; (bottom), © 1991 Richard Falco/Black Star; p. 84, © Dr. Dennis Dickson, Albert Einstein College of Medicine/Peter Arnold, Inc.; p. 88 (top), © Dan McCoy/Rainbow; (bottom), © James Schnepf/Gamma Liaison; p. 89 (left), © Wide World Photos; (right), © Rhoda Sidney/PhotoEdit.

Chapter 4   Chapter opening, © Eric Meola/The Image Bank; p. 96, © L. West/FPG; p. 97, © Bill Gallery/Stock, Boston; p. 100, © Courtesy of Dr. E. R. Lewis, University of California at Berkeley; p. 104, © Tate Gallery/Art Resource; p. 106, © Elinore Matlin; p. 110, For more information on Bev Doolittle's limited edition fine art prints call 1-800-243-4246 in the U.S. or 1-800-263-4001 in Canada; p. 111 (top left), ©Drew Appleby; (others), © Ron Pretzer/LUXE; p. 113, © Sverker Runeson/Uppsala Universitet; p. 114 (top), Stanford University Photographic Services; (bottom), ©Ric Ergenbright; p. 115 (both), ©Ron Pretzer/LUXE; p. 121, © Dr. G. Bredberg/Science Photo Library/Photo Researchers, Inc.; p. 123, © Charles Blanket/Time Magazine; p. 124, © Jack Vartoogian; p. 126, © Bob Daemmrich/Stock, Boston; p. 127 (top), © Steve Leonard/Tony Stone Images; (bottom), Courtesy of the Original Great American Chocolate Chip Cookie Co., Inc.; p. 128, © Ron Pretzer/LUXE; p. 129, © A. K. Das.

Chapter 5   Chapter opening, ©John Garrett/Tony Stone Images; p. 135, © Tom Walker/Stock, Boston; p. 136, © Drew Appleby; p. 140, © Owen Franken/Stock, Boston; p. 141, © Joel Gordon 1992; p. 142, © Michel Heron/Woodfin Camp; p. 147, © Tony Freeman/PhotoEdit; p. 148 (left), © Bildarchiv Foto Marburg/Art Resource; (right), ©The Detroit Institute of Arts. Gift of Mr. and Mrs. Bert L. Smokler and Mr. and Mrs. Lawrence Fleischman; p. 149, © 1982 Pier Angelo Simone; p. 153, © Joel Gordon 1993; p. 157, © Kal Muller/Woodfin Camp; p. 160, © David Parker/Photo Researchers.

Chapter 6   Chapter opening, © Garry Gay/The Image Bank; p. 176 (top), © Gabe Palmer/The Stock Market; (bottom), © Steven Lunetta; p. 177

(top), © Matthew McVay/Stock, Boston; (bottom), © Catherine Karnow/Woodfin Camp; p. 179, Guy Connolly/US Department of Agriculture; p. 180, © David Frazier; p. 181, © Lawrence Migdale/Stock, Boston; p. 183, © Dr. Robert Epstein; p. 184, © Louise Wadsworth; p. 186, © John Coulbourn; p. 187, © Bill Swersey/Gamma-Liaison; p. 188, © David Austen/Stock, Boston; p. 189, © Louise Wadsworth; p. 191 (all at top of page), © Courtesy Dr. R. J. Herrnstein, Harvard University; (bottom), © Breck P. Kent/Animals, Animals; p. 192, © Cathlyn Melloan/Tony Stone Images; p. 193, © Charles Gupton/Stock, Boston; p. 196 (top), © Roy Morsch/The Stock Market; (bottom), © Jodi Buren; p. 199, © Robert Ginn/Unicorn.

Chapter 7   Chapter opening, © Manfred Mehlig/Tony Stone Images; p. 207, © Doug Mazzapica/Black Star; p. 208, © Ron Pretzer/LUXE; p. 209, ©Ron Pretzer/LUXE; p. 212, © Ron Pretzer/LUXE; p. 213, © Drew Appleby; p. 218, © Comstock; p. 219, © The Bettmann Archive; p. 221, © Academic Press; p. 224, © Photofest; p. 226 (top), © David Frazier; (bottom), ©Drew Appleby; p. 227, © Hank Morgan/Science Source/Photo Researchers; p. 230, © Louise Wadsworth; p. 233, © David Frazier; p. 234, (both), Courtesy of G. A. Press; p. 236, © Drew Appleby; p. 240, © Ron Pretzer/LUXE.

Chapter 8   Chapter opening, ©Romilly Lockyer/The Image Bank; p. 255, ©Alan Odie/PhotoEdit; p. 256, AP/Wide World Photos; p. 257, ©Ron Pretzer/LUXE; p. 258, ©P&G Bowater/The Image Bank; p. 260, © Joseph Nettis/Tony Stone Images; p. 263, Courtesy of the Scleroderma Research Foundation, 1-800-441-2873; p. 264, © Ron Pretzer/LUXE; p. 266 (top), © Ron Pretzer/LUXE; (bottom), © Reuters/Bettmann; p. 269, © Ron Pretzer/LUXE.

Chapter 9   Chapter opening, © Robert Llewellyn; p. 274, ©Elinore Matlin; p. 275 (top), © Calvin Larsen/Photo Researchers; (bottom), © Jim Corwin/Photo Researchers; p. 278, © Drew Appleby; p. 279, © Louise Wadsworth; p. 281, © R. Michael Stuckey, Comstock; p. 285, © David Woods/The Stock Market; p. 286 (top left), © Drew Appleby; (top right), © Myrleen Ferguson/PhotoEdit; (bottom), © Dr. R. Allen Gardner/University of Nevada at Reno; p. 287, GSU/Language Research Center; p. 289, © Hans Reinhard/OKAPIA 1989/Photo Researchers; p. 290 (both), © Ron Pretzer/LUXE; p. 292, © Dr. Arnold Matlin; p. 295, © Dr. Arnold Matlin.

Chapter 10   Chapter opening, © Kirkendall-Spring Photographers; p. 300, © Renate Hiller/Monkmeyer Press; p. 301 (top), © Francis Leroy, Biocosmos/Science Photo Library/Photo Researchers; (bottom), © Petit Format/Nestle/Science Source, Photo Researchers, Inc.; p. 303 (top three), © George Steinmetz; (bottom), By permission of the American Cancer Society; p. 306, © Elizabeth Robbins/Courtesy of Dr. Richard D. Walk; p. 307, © Barbara Filet/Tony Stone Images; p. 308, Professor Carolyn K. Rovee-Collier; p. 309, © Louise Wadsworth; p. 310, © W. Hille/Leo de Wys; p. 311 (all), © Louise Wadsworth; p. 314 (top), © Kenneth Garrett/FPG; (bottom), © Lee Kuhn/FPG; p. 315, © Quesada/Burke Photography, New York; p. 316 (top), © Myrleen Ferguson/PhotoEdit; (bottom), © Julie Houck/Stock Boston; p. 320, (left) © Michael A. Keller/The Stock Market; (right), © Joan Trasdale/The Stock Market; p. 321, © Bob Daemmrich/The Image Works; p. 322, (top) © Philip Jon Bailey/Stock, Boston; (bottom), © Dale Durfee/Tony Stone Images; p. 324, © Louise Wadsworth; p. 325, © Dan McCoy/Rainbow; p. 326, © Leo de Wys Inc./Bob Krist; p. 327, © Robert Brenner/PhotoEdit; p. 328, © Don Smetzer/Tony Stone Images; p. 330, © Louise Wadsworth; p. 332 (top to bottom), © David Young-Wolff/PhotoEdit, © Bob Daemmrich/The Image Works, ©Robert Foothorap/Black Star, © Renee Lynn/Photo Researchers, © Bob Daemmrich; p. 333, © John Chaisson/Gamma-Liaison; p. 334, © Tony Freeman/PhotoEdit; p. 335, © Tony Freeman/PhotoEdit.

Chapter 11   Chapter opening, © Larry Ulrich; p. 340, © David Young-Wolff/PhotoEdit; p. 342, (top) © Michael Newman/PhotoEdit; (bottom two), © Dr. Leon A. Pastalan/University of Michigan; p. 343, © Janeart